Financial Analysis, Planning & Forecasting
Theory and Application
Third Edition

Financial Analysis, Planning & Forecasting
Theory and Application

Third Edition

Cheng F Lee
Rutgers University, USA

John Lee
Center for PBBEF Research, USA

World Scientific

NEW JERSEY · LONDON · SINGAPORE · BEIJING · SHANGHAI · HONG KONG · TAIPEI · CHENNAI · TOKYO

Published by

World Scientific Publishing Co. Pte. Ltd.

5 Toh Tuck Link, Singapore 596224

USA office: 27 Warren Street, Suite 401-402, Hackensack, NJ 07601

UK office: 57 Shelton Street, Covent Garden, London WC2H 9HE

Library of Congress Cataloging-in-Publication Data
Names: Lee, John C., author. | Lee, Cheng F., author.
Title: Financial analysis, planning and forecasting : theory and application /
Alice C. Lee, John C. Lee, & Cheng F. Lee.
Other titles: Financial analysis, planning & forecasting
Description: 3rd edition. | New Jersey : World Scientific, [2016] |
Earlier edition published as: Financial analysis, planning and forecasting.
Identifiers: LCCN 2015031798 | ISBN 9789814723848 (alk. paper)
Subjects: LCSH: Business enterprises--Finance--Textbooks.
Classification: LCC HG4014 .L39 2016 | DDC 658.15--dc23
LC record available at http://lccn.loc.gov/2015031798

British Library Cataloguing-in-Publication Data
A catalogue record for this book is available from the British Library.

Desk Editors: Philly Lim/Dipasri Sardar

Typeset by Stallion Press
Email: enquiries@stallionpress.com

Printed in Singapore

Preface

Organization and Suggestions

We draw upon our years of teaching and research experience on the subject of financial analysis, planning and forecasting for this textbook. Overall, our goal is an introductory level book that reviews, discusses, and integrates both theoretical and practical corporate analysis and planning. Financial analysis, planning, and forecasting, are classified into five parts: (1) Information and Methodology for Financial Analysis; (2) Alternative Finance Theories and Cost of Capital; (3) Capital Budgeting and Leasing Decisions; (4) Corporate Policies and Their Interrelationships; (5) Financial Planning and Forecasting.

We focus on three principles to frame our discussion of the material: (1) to integrate theory with practice; (2) to strike a balance between the overview and detailed understanding; and (3) to demonstrate how basic quantitative training required by management schools can be used to improve the usefulness of accounting and financial information in management decisions.

Furthermore, the theory used and discussed in this book can be grouped into the following classical theoretical areas of corporate finance: (1) Pre-M&M Theory, (2) M&M Theory, (3) CAPM, and (4) Option Pricing Theory (OPT). The interrelationships among these theories are carefully analyzed. Meaningful real-world examples of using these theories are jointly discussed, step by step, with relevant data and methodology. Finally, alternative planning and forecasting models are used to show how the interdisciplinary approach can be used to make meaningful financial-management decisions.

Prerequisites to an understanding of this book include one term of accounting; one term of economics; one term of quantitative methods (or statistics); one term of financial management; and/or one term of computer programming. To assist the student in learning and integrating new concepts, we provide approximately 40% review of the prerequisite material and 60% new information related to financial management.

To further the learning process and application of the material, the book contains both problem sets and project approach assignments. Overall, there are 491 problem sets, which are given at the end of each of the 26 chapters. These questions are used to reinforce the microview of understanding financial management. In addition, five projects are suggested at the end of each part of the text. These projects make for a useful term assignment that extends the topic material into a more macroview of understanding financial analysis, planning, and forecasting.

Based on our personal teaching experiences at various universities, we find that this book can be used in a second undergraduate Financial Management course and a second MBA and Master in Quantitative Finance, as well as a financial analysis, planning and forecasting course.

In this second edition, we have extensively updated and expanded the topics of financial analysis, planning, and forecasting. The new chapters included in this new edition are as follows:

Chapter 7 Risk Estimation and Diversification.
Chapter 8 Risk and Return Trade-off Analysis.
Chapter 9 Options and Option Strategies.
Chapter 10 Option-Pricing Theory and Firm Valuation.
Chapter 18 Short-Term Financial Analysis and Planning.
Chapter 19 Credit Management.
Chapter 20 Cash, Marketable Securities, and Inventory Management.
Chapter 24 Time-Series: Analysis, Model, and Forecasting.

In this new edition, we add two new chapters, i.e., Chapter 6 Valuation of Bonds and Stocks and Chapter 21 Short-Term Financing. In addition, we combine original Chapters 18 and 19 to create Chapter 20 Credit, Cash, Marketable Securities, and Inventory Management. Furthermore, we update and revise most of the Chapters of this book. The Chapters with major revisions are Chapters 1–7, 10, 11, 16–18, 24, and 25.

Acknowledgments

The first and second editions of this book have been worked on and critically reviewed by numerous individuals, including colleagues and previous students. We especially benefited from the insightful corrections, discussions, and suggestions of Joe E. Finnerty, Odet Palmon, Jack C. Francis, and Russel H. Fogler. We are also indebted to the following individuals: Joseph D. Vinso, John Thatcher, Severin C. Carlson, William C. Hunter, Russel P. Boisjoly, Robert J. Moreland, Paul G. Fellow, Randy P. Beatty, Joan C. Junkus, Douglas Schaller, Perry A. Milanesi, Paul Newbold, Bob Cummings, Tom J. Frecka, Andrew H. Chen, James A. Gentry, Charles M. Linke, J. Kenton Zumwalt, Timothy J. Nantell, Annie H. Lin, Quentin C. Chu, Gerrard M. Nussbaum, Raj Agrawal, James S. Ang, Ren-Raw Chen, Sheng-Syan Chen, Thomas C. Chian, Chin-Chen Chien, Charles Corrado, Mao-Wei Hung, Ji-Chai Lin, Hun Y. Park, John Wald, K.C. John Wei, Chunchi Wu, Chau-Chen Yanb, Gili Yen, and Gillian Yeo.

For the first edition, we are indebted to the Finance Editor at Addison-Wesley, Bill Hamilton, who kept the project moving, and to the Addison-Wesley staff.

For the second edition, we appreciate the extensive help from Ms. Sandhya of World Scientific Publishing, our research assistants David Chen, Wei-Kang Shih and Shin-Ying Mai, and our secretary Ms. Miranda Mei-Lan Luo. Finally, we would like to thank the financial support from Wintek Corporation and the Polaris Financial Group that allowed us to write the second edition of this book.

In the third edition, we would especially like to thank our assistants Danielle Flanagan, Lauren Flanagan, Shivani A. Patel, and Yaqing Xiao for their invaluable help.

There are undoubtedly some errors in the finished product, both typographical and conceptual. I would like to invite readers to send suggestions, comments, criticisms, and corrections to the author Professor Cheng F. Lee at the Department of Finance and Economics, Rutgers University at 100 Rockafeller Road- Room 5188 Piscataway, NJ 08854.

Cheng F. Lee
John Lee

Contents

Chapter 1

Introduction

1.1. Introduction

In this chapter, we shall (i) discuss the fundamental concepts of financial analysis and planning, (ii) explain the basic objectives and philosophy of the book, and (iii) lay out the structure of the book.

First, the basic definition of financial management is used as a background for discussing financial analysis and planning. Secondly, the objectives and the philosophy of the book are given in order to specify its unique nature. Finally, the structure of the book is presented to show how these objectives and this philosophy are expanded on in the later chapters.

1.2. Financial Management: Analysis And Planning

1.2.1. *Basic Definitions*

Financial management is composed of three of the major policies of a firm: its investment, financing, and dividend policies. During periods of economic uncertainty and/or high inflation, financial management is important for three major reasons: increased investment risk, increased costs of equity and debt financing, and an increased shareholder preference for current rather than future income. Financial management is also important during periods of low inflation and certainty, but it takes on significant importance during periods of uncertainty and high inflation. To achieve sound financial management under such conditions, managers should be well acquainted with the theory and methodology, and with the application of financial analysis and planning to real-world situations.

There are two possible approaches in defining financial management. One approach is a descriptive one; the other is an analytical and operational one. In this book, we will take an analytical approach. Also, throughout the course of the book, we will use the terms *financial management and financial analysis and planning* interchangeable.

Of the three major areas of financial management, investment policy is perhaps the most important because it establishes the firm's total assets and their composition, thus determining how the financial community perceives the firm. Financing policy can affect the composition of the firm's optimal capital structure, or mix of sources of funds. That is, this policy determines how each investment should be financed to maintain the firm's current capital structure, or to move the firm towards a better capital mix. The dividend policy of a firm describes the proportion of current earnings to be paid to stockholders in the form of cash dividends. Dividend policy generally provides signals to security holders and builds expectation in the market. Two important considerations here are the firm's objective of *shareholder-wealth maximization* and the *investor*'s preferences for *current income.*

In order to provide proper financial management, the manager must fully understand how these three policies overlap and affect one another.

1.2.2. *Objectives of Financial Management*

The main objective of a firm is to maximize the wealth of its shareholders. Consequently, there are two basic objectives of financial management: to determine a firm's present market value and to delineate ways of improving its future market value. The investment, financing, and dividend policies discussed earlier determine the market value of the firm to its shareholders. From the analysis of these policies, a financial manager can go one step further to suggest desired investment, financing, and dividend policies that will improve the market value of the firm. To do this, it is necessary to have a working understanding of realistic financial theory as well as some practical operational experience.

1.2.3. *Planning Horizon Classification*

Financial management is generally described by the time horizon with which the manager is concerned: short-term or long-term.

Short-term planning and analysis covers periods of less than 1 year. Short-term management might be described more properly as working capital management, because it involves the determination of an optimal mixture of current assets and current liabilities. Working-capital management includes cash management, inventory management, accounts receivable management, and the like. Although at first glance short-term planning and analysis may seem of lesser importance, it can be quite difficult and important because of the volatility of capital markets during periods of high inflation.

Long-term financial management encompasses essentially all decision making that has an impact over a period of 1 year or more. This includes the determination of a firm's long-term investment, financing, and dividend policies. Although working-capital management is discussed intermittently, this book is primarily concerned with the long-term aspects of financial management. Four mathematical techniques, simultaneous equations, linear programming, goal programming, and the econometric method, are popular approaches to financial planning that we will investigate in detail.

1.3. Objectives and Philosophy of the Book

The motivation for writing this book derived from the belief that many texts available for use in upper-level undergraduate and graduate-level corporate finance courses seem to have either a theoretical or a practical approach. These two divergent approaches need to be integrated, and that is what we attempt to do in this book. We offer a solid integration of theory and practitioner-oriented procedures for attacking the various problems confronted in the current business environment.

With respect to the tools and methods of analysis we offer throughout the text, we urge the reader not to take them as sure-fire cures or perfect methods of analysis. Even the most reasonable approaches can be incorrectly applied or applied in the wrong situations. However, the well-trained manager can always make the necessary modifications to these theories and models to make them usable in actual business situations.

We also do not claim to cover all the topics in corporate finance, though we have covered those we believe to be most important. One purpose of this book is to offer a number of approaches to financial analysis and planning that have been generally accepted in practice and that show reasonable support from generally accepted financial theory.

Another objective is to relate how accounting information, economic data, finance theory and statistical, econometric, and operations research methods can be used to aid in financial analysis and planning. Computer facilities are helpful in performing the last category mentioned, but they are not critical for a satisfactory understanding of these areas. We believe each of these areas offers great promise in the preparation of better operating and financial planning for the firm, and each is discussed in turn.

Given that this is a text about corporate finance, it is only proper that we devote considerable effort to the derivation and explanation of that theory. We attempt to integrate theory with practice and critically evaluate it as well. By "critically evaluate" we mean that we devote an entire chapter to the challenges of the numerous irrelevance propositions relating to the dividend and financing decisions, as these challenges have vast implications for financial management.

We hope that this text can add a new approach to financial planning and analysis. Its interdisciplinary approach is a major thrust, integrating the various business disciplines, which the reader has learned in earlier courses, into a corporate finance book. Armed with this type of approach, the managers of the future can hopefully put some of it into action and learn what does and does not work in the business world.

While the student may not be able to master all the methodology and applications discussed in this book, he should be better able to develop an understanding of these topics, so that he will not feel that only the truly brilliant and learned can understand these concepts. This understanding should enable the manager to do a better job if he did not have such knowledge. It is our hope that the topics discussed in this text will have a "snowball effect," building upon each other to create a better understanding of financial management.

In the next section, we will discuss how we relate the objectives of the book to its structure. This book is divided into five parts, and we will discuss the interrelationships between these parts and the chapters contained in each part. This is done to show how these interrelationships can increase the reader's knowledge of financial management.

1.4. Structure of the Book

It is the belief of the authors that the teaching of financial analysis and planning is most effective if presented in a certain optimum sequence, which we will follow here.

The value of information cannot be understated in the task of financial analysis and planning. In fact, if no information were available, decision making could become almost impossible. Information is the base for financial decision making, but to make the available information useful, the analyst must know how to use it. For that reason, we believe it is appropriate to discuss how statistical and mathematical tools can be used to analyze the information.

To accomplish this goal, Part I, Information and Methodology for Financial Analysis, discusses how statistical methods, regression analysis techniques, and other related mathematical tools can be used to analyze accounting information.

In this part, readers will learn: (i) how statistical distributions, both normal and lognormal, can be used to analyze accounting information, (ii) how regression analysis, factor analysis, and discriminant analysis can make financial ratios more useful in financial planning and analysis, and (iii) how mathematics, statistical methods, and regression analysis techniques can be used in interest-rate determination and the use of these interest rates.

In Chapter 2, Accounting Information and Financial Management, statistical methods, regression analysis, and related econometric methodology are used in static and dynamic ratio analysis, and to do break-even analysis. Here important accounting information and basic quantitative methods are reviewed and generalized.

In Chapter 3, Factor Analysis and Discriminant Analysis: Theory and Methods, linear algebra, matrix algebra, and basic multivariate statistical distribution concepts are introduced. Detailed understanding of this chapter is not necessary for an overall understanding of this book.

Chapter 4, Applications of Factor Analysis and Discriminant Analysis in Financial Management, shows how factor analysis can be used to identify important financial ratios and how discriminant analysis can be used for: (i) credit analysis, (ii) bankruptcy prediction, and (iii) bond rating. In addition, methods for estimating default probability are also discussed in some detail.

Chapter 5, Interest Rate, Rate-of-Return, and Growth Rate, shows the arithmetic, algebraic, and statistical methods used in deterministic and stochastic interest-rate determination and analysis. The concept and effects of inflation on interest rates and equity rates-of-return are also discussed here.

In summary, Chapters 2 through 5 give the reader an important foundation in the information and methodology for performing sound financial analysis and planning.

Part II, Alternative Finance Theories and the Cost of Capital, discusses how finance theory can make financial planning and analysis more general and useful. Classical theory, the new classical theory, capital asset pricing theory, and option-pricing theory are the four theoretical bases used here. These four theories are interrelated, and therefore are presented together.

Chapter 6, Valuation of Bonds and Stocks, discusses the basic concepts and methods to evaluate stocks and bonds. Furthermore, the chapter explains risk, return, and market efficiency and exchange rates and investing overseas. The chapter ends with the Appendix, which addresses the relationship between exchange rates and interest rates.

Chapter 7, Valuation, Capital Structure, and Risk Premiums, discusses the classical and the new classical theories and other related issues. Chapter 8, 9, 10, and 11, Capital Asset Pricing Model (CAPM), Arbitrage Pricing Model, and Option-Pricing Model, shows the use of portfolio theory to derive new finance theories for financial management.

In the first seven chapters, some of the empirical results are obtained by using the information and methods discussed in Part I. Most of the important knowledge needed for practical financial analysis is reinforced by the action taken and learning-by-doing approach.

Part III, Capital Budgeting and Leasing Decisions, shows the use of the cost of capital and cash flow information in capital budgeting and leasing decisions.

Chapter 12, Alternative Cost of Capital Analysis and Estimation, shows the empirical uses of four theories in the determination of the cost of capital. Chapter 13, Capital Budgeting under Certainty, and Chapter 14, Capital Budgeting under Uncertainty, introduce a major area of financial decision making, that of capital budgeting. In these two chapters, information, theory, and methodologies from Parts I and II are used in making investment decisions. A linear programming technique is introduced in Chapter 10 in performing capital rationing analysis. Issues related to multiperiod capital budgeting and the impact of inflation are also discussed.

Chapter 15 is devoted to an extension of capital budgeting to the lease-buy decisions that a firm faces. Examples are used to illustrate the various methods that can be employed in making these decisions. This chapter also discusses the basic types of leasing arrangement that are available and their implications. In addition, finance theories discussed in Part II are used to show the accounting approach to leasing decisions can be different from an economic approach.

Part IV, Corporate Policies an Their Interrelationships, explores mergers, dividend policy, the interaction between investment, financing, and dividend policy, and the use of stochastic dominance in the capital structure analysis with risky debt.

Chapter 16, Mergers: Theory and Evidence, discusses problems related to firm mergers. Two different types of mergers available are defined and contrasted. The theory underlying mergers is observed from an economic and a finance viewpoint. The various accounting treatments of merged firms and detailed, are the effect of these treatments on earnings, earnings per share, and other financial ratios. Finally, empirical evidence concerning mergers is examined from a traditional and CAPM viewpoints.

In Chapter 17, Dividend Policy and Empirical Evidence, we discuss an area in financial management that has been the subject of much debate. Dividend Policy is first looked at in a theoretical framework. Modigliani and Miller's arguments concerning firm valuation and its relation to dividend payouts and changes in these payouts are discussed. Gordon and Lintner's high-dividend-high-valuation theory is explained and contrasted with the approach of Modigliani and Miller.

The information content of dividends is also examined in this chapter. In addition, the residual theory approach to dividends and its relation to investment financing are explained. The CAPM framework is applied to dividends, and various forms are discussed in detail. Finally, empirical evidence is shown.

Chapter 18, Interaction of Financing, Investment, and Dividend Policies, discusses the subject of the interrelation of the three major activities of financial management. Also, debt capacity and optimal capital structure are discussed in the context of these interrelationships. In the Appendix to Chapter 18, stochastic dominance and its applications to optimal capital structure analysis are briefly discussed. This method of analysis is applied to analyze the impacts of risky debt on optimal capital structure determination. This appendix is not required for the understanding of later chapters.

Part V discusses the issue of Short-term Financial Decision. Chapter 19 discusses short-term financial analysis and planning. Chapter 20 discusses credit, cash, marketable securities, and inventory management. Chapter 21, discusses short term financing. Finally, Chapter 22 discusses Elementary Applications of Programming Techniques in Working-Capital Management, introduces the use of linear and goal programming in working-capital management.

Part VI, Financial Planning and Forecasting, covers alternative methods to perform financial planning and forecasting.

Three alternative long-term financial planning and forecasting methods are discussed in Part VI. In Chapter 23, Long-Range Financial Planning — A Linear Programming Modeling Approach, we show how Carleton's model can be incorporated with information and theory to carry out, theoretically and empirically, financial planning and forecasting. Chapter 24, Simultaneous-Equation Models for Financial Planning, shows how simultaneous-equation models can be used in financial planning and forecasting. Johnson & Johnson is used in an empirical example of this technique. Chapter 25, discusses how to use time-series analysis to do analysis, model, and forecasting. Chapter 26, Econometric Approaches to Financial Planning and Forecasting, discusses how econometric specification and modeling techniques can be used to empirically analyze financial planning and forecasting decisions.

In summary, Parts I and II give the reader knowledge of the information, theories and methodologies needed for financial planning and analysis. Parts III, IV, V, and VI show how financial planning and analysis can be accomplished analytically and empirically.

Problem Set

1. Discuss the various elements and objectives of financial management, their importance, related concepts and interrelationships.
2. Briefly discuss the relationship between short-term financial management and long-term financial management.
3. Use a flowchart to discuss and evaluate the structure of this book.

References for Chapter 1

Anderson, TW (2003). *An Introduction to Multivariate Statistical Analysis*, 3rd ed. New York: John Wiley and Sons.

Beranek, W (1981). Research directions in finance. *Quarterly Journal of Economics and Business*, 21, 6–24.

Bodie, Z, A Kane, and A Marcus (2011). *Investments*, 9th ed. New York: McGraw-Hill Book Company.

Brealy, RA, SC Myers, and F Allen (2013). *Principles of Corporate Finance*, 11th ed. New York: McGraw-Hill Book Company.

Brigham, EF and PR Daves (2012). *Intermediate Financial Management*, 11th ed. Hinsdale, OH: South-Western College Pub.

Copeland, TE, JF Weston, and K Shastri (2004). *Financial Theory and Corporate Policy* 4th ed. Reading, Massachusetts: Addison-Wesley Publishing Company.

Fama, EF and MH Miller (1972). *Theory of Finance*. New York: Holt, Rinehart and Winston.

Jensen, MC and WH Meckling (1978). Can the corporation survive? *Financial Analysts Journal*, 31–37.

Johnston, J and J Dinardo (1996). Econometrics Methods 4th ed. New York: McGraw-Hill.

Lee, CF and JC Junkus (1983). Financial Analysis and Planning: An Overview. *Journal of Economics and Business*, 34, 257–283.
Lee, CF (1983). *Financial Analysis and Planning: Theory and Application, A Book of Readings.* Reading, Massachusetts: Addition-Wesley Publishing Company.
Lee, CF and AC Lee (2013). *Encyclopedia of Finance*, 2nd ed. New York, NY: Springer.
Lee, CF, JC Lee, and AC Lee (2013). *Statistics for Business and Financial Economics*, 3rd ed. New York, NY: Springer.
Mao, JCF (1969). *Quantitative Analysis of Financial Decisions.* New York: The Macmillian Company.
Penman, SH (2010). *Financial Statement Analysis and Security Valuation*, 5th ed. New York: McGraw-Hill/Irwin.
Pogue, GA and K Lull (1974). Corporate finance: An overview, *Sloan Management Review*, 15, 19–38.
Ross, S, RW Westerfield, and J Jaffe (2012). *Corporate Finance*, 10th ed. (Mcgraw-Hill/Irwin, New York, NY).
Van Horne, JC (2008). *Fundamentals of Financial Management* 13th ed. Englewood Cliffs, N.J.: Prentice Hall Inc.

Part I

Information and Methodology for Financial Analysis

Chapter 2

Accounting Information and Regression Analysis

2.1. Introduction

Accounting information, market information, and basic aggregated economic data are the basic inputs needed for financial analysis and planning; statistical methods, regression analysis, operation research programming techniques, and computer programming knowledge are important tools for achieving financial planning and forecasting. When performing financial analysis and planning, it is important to know how to use the appropriate tools in analyzing the relevant data.

The main purposes of this chapter are (i) to show how algebraic and statistical methods are used in cost–volume–profit (CVP) analysis and (ii) to demonstrate how regression methods can be used to analyze the dynamic adjustment process of financial ratios and obtain new insights into the use of financial ratios in financial analysis, planning, and forecasting. Recall that for financial management, the three major policies of the firm are investment, financing, and dividend policy. The basic concept of CVP analysis can be used in the areas of investment and financing, specifically for capital budget decision making and leverage analysis. Similarly, ratio analysis can be used to determine a firm's liquidity position, leverage position, the effectiveness of asset utilization, and profitability performance.

This chapter is organized as follows. Section 2.2 reviews four important financial statements: the balance sheet, the statement of earnings, the statement of equity, and the statement of cash flow. Section 2.3 discusses possible weaknesses of accounting information, and proposes possible methods to minimize these weaknesses. In Section 2.4, static ratio analysis is reviewed and dynamic financial ratio analysis is presented. Furthermore, both single-equation and simultaneous-equation approaches to dynamic financial analysis are explored. In Section 2.5, CVP analysis is extended from deterministic analysis to stochastic analysis. The concepts of statistical distributions are used to improve the robustness of CVP analysis. The relationship between accounting income and economic income is explored in Section 2.6. Finally, Section 2.7 summarizes the key concepts of the chapter. In addition, there are two appendixes to this chapter reviewing basic econometric methods. Appendix 2.A reviews basic concepts and methods of simple regression and multiple regressions, and Appendix 2.B discusses how to compile cash flow statement using the indirect method.

2.2. Financial Statements: A Brief Review

Corporate annual and quarterly reports generally contain four basic financial statements: balance sheet, statement of earnings, statement of retained earnings, and statement of changes in financial position. Using Johnson & Johnson (JNJ) annual consolidated financial statements as examples, we discuss the usefulness and problems associated with each of these statements in financial analysis and planning. Finally, the use of annual *versus* quarterly financial data is addressed.

2.2.1. *Balance Sheet*

The balance sheet describes a firm's financial position at one specific point in time. It is a static representation, such as a snapshot, of the firm's financial composition of assets and liabilities at one point in time. The balance sheet of JNJ, shown in Table 2.1, is broken down into two basic areas of classification — total assets (debit) and total liabilities and shareholders' equity (credit).

On the debit side, accounts are divided into six groups: current assets, marketable securities — non-current, property, plant and equipment (PP&E), intangible assets, deferred taxes on income, and other assets. Current assets represents short-term accounts, such as cash and cash equivalents, marketable securities and accounts receivable, inventories, deferred tax on income, and prepaid expense. It should be noted that deferred tax on income in this group is a current deferred tax and will be converted into income tax within 1 year.

Property encompasses all fixed or capital assets such as real estate, plant and equipment, special tools, and the allowance for depreciation and

Table 2.1. Consolidated balance sheets of Johnson & Johnson Corporation and consolidated subsidiaries (2007–2012) (Dollars in Millions).

Assets	2007	2008	2009	2010	2011	2012
Current Assets						
Cash and Cash Equivalent ($)	7,770	10,768	15,810	19,355	24,542	14,911
Marketable Securities	1,545	2,041	3,615	8,303	7,719	6,178
Account Receivable	9,444	9,719	9,646	9,774	10,581	11,309
Inventory	5,110	5,052	5,180	5,378	6,285	7,495
Deferred Taxes on Income	2,609	3,430	2,793	2,224	2,556	3,139
Prepaid Expenses and Other Receivable	3,467	3,367	2,497	2,273	2,633	3,084
Total Current Assets	**29,945**	**34,377**	**39,541**	**47,307**	**54,316**	**46,116**
	—	—	—	—	—	—
Marketable Securities — Non-current	2	—	—	—	—	—
PP&E, Net	14,185	14,365	14,759	14,553	14,739	16,097
Intangible Assets, Net	28,763	27,695	31,185	32,010	34,276	51,176
Deferred Taxes on Income	4,889	5,841	5,507	5,096	6,540	4,541
Other Assets	3,170	2,634	3,690	3,942	3,773	3,417
Total Assets	**80,954**	**84,912**	**94,682**	**102,908**	**113,644**	**121,347**
Liabilities and Shareholder's Equity	—	—	—	—	—	—
Current Liabilities	—	—	—	—	—	—
Loans and Notes Payable	2,463	3,732	6,318	7,617	6,658	4,676
Accounts Payable	6,909	7,503	5,541	5,623	5,725	5,831
Accrued Liabilities	6,412	5,531	5,796	4,100	4,608	7,299
Accrued Rebates, Returns, and Promotion	2,318	2,237	2,028	2,512	2,637	2,969
Accrued Salaries, Wages, and Commissions	1,512	1,432	1,606	2,642	2,329	2,423
Taxes on Income	223	417	442	578	854	1,064
Total Current Liabilities	**19,837**	**20,852**	**21,731**	**23,072**	**22,811**	**24,262**
Long-term Debt	7,074	8,120	8,223	9,156	12,969	11,489
Deferred Tax liability	1,493	1,432	1,424	1,447	1,800	3,136
Employee Related Obligations	5,402	7,791	6,769	6,087	8,353	9,082
Other Liabilities	3,829	4,206	5,947	6,567	10,631	8,552
Shareowners' Equity	—	—	—	—	—	—
Preferred Stock-without Par Value	—	—	—	—	—	—
Common Stock-Par Value $1.00	3,120	3,120	3,120	3,120	3,120	3,120

(Continued)

Table 2.1. (*Continued*)

Assets	2007	2008	2009	2010	2011	2012
Net Receivable from Employee Stock Plan	—	—	—	—	—	—
Accumulated Other Comprehensive Income	−693	−4,955	−3,058	−3,531	−5,632	−5,810
Retained Earnings	55,280	63,379	70,306	77,773	81,251	85,992
Less: Common Stock Held in Treasury	14,388	19,033	19,780	20,783	21,659	18,476
Total Shareowners' Equity	**43,319**	**42,511**	**50,588**	**56,579**	**57,080**	**64,826**
Total Liabilities and Shareholders' Equity	**80,954**	**84,912**	**94,682**	**102,908**	**113,644**	**121,347**

amortization. Intangible assets refer to the assets of research and development (R&D).

The credit side of the balance sheet in Table 2.1 is divided into current liabilities, long-term liabilities, and shareowner's equity. Under current liabilities, the following accounts are included: accounts, loans, and notes payable; accrued liabilities; accrued salaries and taxes on income. Long-term liabilities include various forms of long-term debt, deferred tax liability, employee-related obligations, and other liabilities. The stockholder's equity section of the balance sheet represents the net worth of the firm to its investors. For example, as of December 31, 2012, JNJ had $0 million preferred stock outstanding, $3,120 million in common stock outstanding, and $85,992 million retained earnings. Sometimes there are preferred stock and hybrid securities (e.g., convertible bond and convertible preferred stock) on the credit side of the balance sheet.

The balance sheet is useful because it depicts the firm's financing and investment policies. The use of comparative balance sheets, those that present several years' data, can be used to detect trends and possible future problems. JNJ has presented on its balance sheet information from six periods: December 31, 2007, December 31, 2008, December 31, 2009, December 31, 2010, December 31, 2011, and December 31, 2012. The balance sheet, however, is static and therefore should be analyzed with caution in financial analysis and planning.

2.2.2. *Statement of Earnings*

JNJ's statement of earnings is presented in Table 2.2 and describes the results of operations for a 12-month period ending December 31. The usual

Table 2.2. Consolidated statements of earnings of JNJ Corporation and subsidiaries (2007–2012) (dollars in millions).

(Dollars in Millions Except Per Share Figures)	2007	2008	2009	2010	2011	2012
Sales to Customers ($)	61,095	63,747	61,897	61,587	65,030	67,224
Cost of Products Sold	17,751	18,511	18,447	18,792	20,360	21,658
Gross Profit	43,344	45,236	43,450	42,795	44,670	45,566
Selling, Marketing and administrative expenses	20,451	21,490	19,801	19,424	20,969	20,869
Research Expense	7,680	7,577	6,986	6,844	7,548	7,665
Purchased in-process R&D	807	181	—	—	—	1,163
Interest Income	−452	−361	−90	−107	−91	−64
Interest Expense, net of portion capitalized	296	435	451	455	571	532
Other (income) expense, Net	1,279	−1,015	547	−768	2,743	1,626
	30,061	26,307	27,695	25,848	32,309	31,791
Earnings before Provision for Taxes on Income	13,283	16,929	15,755	16,947	12,361	13,775
Provision for Taxes on Income	2,707	3,980	3,489	3,613	2,689	3,261
Net Earnings	10,576	12,949	12,266	13,334	9,672	10,853
Basic Net Earnings per Share ($)	3.67	4.62	4.45	4.85	3.54	3.94
Diluted Net Earnings per Share ($)	3.63	4.57	4.40	4.78	3.49	3.86

income-statement periods are annual, quarterly, and monthly. Johnson has chosen the annual approach. Both the annual and quarterly reports are used for external as well as internal reporting. The monthly statement is used primarily for internal purposes, such as the estimation of sales and profit targets, judgment of controls on expenses, and monitoring progress toward longer-term targets. The statement of earnings is more dynamic than the balance sheet, because it reflects changes for the period. It provides an analyst with an overview of a firm's operations and profitability on a gross, operating, and net income basis. JNJ's income includes sales, interest income, and other net income/expenses. Costs and expenses for JNJ include the cost of goods sold (selling, marketing, and administrative expenses), depreciation, depletion, and amortization. The difference between income and cost and expenses results in the company's Net Earnings. A comparative statement of earnings is very useful in financial analysis and planning because it allows insight into the firm's operations, profitability, and financing decisions over time. For this reason JNJ presents the statement of earnings of six consecutive years: 2007, 2008, 2009, 2010, 2011, and 2012. Armed with this information, evaluating the firm's future is easier.

2.2.3. *Statement of Equity*

JNJ's statements of equity are shown in Table 2.3. These are the earnings that a firm retains for reinvestment rather than paying them out to shareholders in the form of dividends. The statement of equity is easily understood if it is viewed as a bridge between the balance sheet and the statement of earnings. The statement of equity presents a summary of those categories that have an impact on the level of retained earnings: the net earnings and the dividends declared for preferred and common stock. It also represents a summary of the firm's dividend policy and shows how net income is allocated to dividends and reinvestment. JNJ's equity is one source of funds for investment, and this internal source of funds is very important to the firm. The balance sheet, the statement of earnings, and the statement of equity allow us to analyze important firm decisions on the capital structure, cost of capital, capital budgeting, and dividend policy of that firm.

2.2.4. *Statement of Cash Flows*

Another extremely important part of the annual and quarterly report is the statement of cash flows. This statement is very helpful in evaluating a firm's use of its funds and in determining how these funds were raised. Statements of cash flow for JNJ are shown in Table 2.4. These statements of cash flow are composed of three sections: cash flows from operating activities, cash flows from investing activities, and cash flows from financing activities. The statement of cash flows, whether developed on a cash or working-capital basis, summarizes long-term transactions that affect the firm's cash position. For JNJ, the sources of cash are essentially provided by operations. Application of these funds includes dividends paid to stockholders and expenditures for PPE, etc. Therefore, this statement reveals some important aspects of the firm's investment, financing, and dividend policies; making it an important tool for financial planning and analysis.

The cash flow statement shows how the net increase or decrease in cash has been reflected in the changing composition of current assets and current liabilities. It highlights changes in short-term financial policies. It helps

Table 2.3. Consolidated statements of equity of JNJ Corporation and subsidiaries (2007–2012) (Dollars in Millions).

(Dollars in millions)	Total	Comprehensive Income	Retained Earnings	Accumulated Other Comprehensive Income	Common Stock Issued Amount	Treasury Stock Amount
Balance, December 30, 2007	**$43,319**		**55,280**	**(693)**	**3,120**	**(14,388)**
Net earnings	12,949	12,949	12,949	—	—	—
Cash dividends paid	(5,024)	—	(5,024)	—	—	—
Employee stock compensation and stock option plans	2,180	—	175	—	—	2,005
Conversion of subordinated debentures	—	—	(1)	—	—	1
Repurchase of common stock	(6,651)	—	—	—	—	(6,651)
Business combinations	—	—	—	—	—	—
Other comprehensive income, net of tax:	—	—	—	—	—	—
Currency translation adjustment	(2499)	(2499)	—	(,2499)	—	—
Unrealized gains/(losses) on securities	(59)	(59)	—	(59)	—	—
Pension liability adjustment	(1,870)	(1,870)	—	(1,870)	—	—
Gains on derivatives & hedges	166	166	—	166	—	—
Reclassification adjustment	—	(27)	—	—	—	—
Total comprehensive income	—	8,660	—	—	—	—
Note receivable from ESOP	—	—	—	—	—	—
Balance, December 28, 2008	**$42,511**	—	**63,379**	**(4,955)**	**3,120**	**19,033**

(Continued)

Table 2.3. (*Continued*)

(Dollars in millions)	Total	Comprehensive Income	Retained Earnings	Accumulated Other Comprehensive Income	Common Stock Issued Amount	Treasury Stock Amount
Net earnings	12,266	12,266	12,266	—	—	—
Cash dividends paid	(5,327)	—	(5,327)	—	—	—
Employee stock compensation and stock option plans	1,402	—	25	—	—	1,377
Conversion of subordinated debentures	2	—	(4)	—	—	6
Repurchase of common stock	(2,130)	—	—	—	—	(2,130)
Business combinations (Other)	(33)	—	(33)	—	—	—
Other comprehensive income, net of tax:	—	—	—	—	—	—
Currency translation adjustment	1,363	1,363	—	1,363	—	—
Unrealized gains/(losses) on securities	(55)	(55)	—	(55)	—	—
Pension Liability adjustment	565	565	—	565	—	—
Gains/(losses) on derivatives & hedges	24	24	—	24	—	—
Reclassification adjustment	—	(15)	—	—	—	—
Total comprehensive income	—	14,163	—	—	—	—
Note receivable from ESOP	—	—	—	—	—	—
Balance, January 3, 2010	**50,588**	—	**70,306**	**(3,058)**	**3,120**	**(19,780)**

(*Continued*)

Table 2.3. (*Continued*)

(Dollars in millions)	Total	Comprehensive Income	Retained Earnings	Accumulated Other Comprehensive Income	Common Stock Issued Amount	Treasury Stock Amount
Net earnings	13,334	13,334	13,334	—	—	—
Cash dividends paid	(5,804)	—	(5,804)	—	—	—
Employee stock compensation and stock option plans	1,730	—	(62)	—	—	1,792
Conversion of subordinated debentures	1	—	(1)	—	—	2
Repurchase of common stock	(2,797)	—	—	—	—	(2,797)
Other comprehensive income, net of tax:	—	—	—	—	—	—
Currency translation adjustment	(461)	(461)	—	(461)	—	—
Unrealized gains/(losses) on securities	54	54	—	54	—	—
Pension liability adjustment	(21)	(21)	—	(21)	—	—
Gains/(losses) on derivates & hedges	(45)	(45)	—	(45)	—	—
Reclassification adjustment	—	(9)	—	—	—	—
Total comprehensive income	—	12,861	—	—	—	—
Note receivable from ESOP	—	—	—	—	—	—
Balance, January 2, 2011	**$56,579**	—	**77,773**	**(3,531)**	**3,120**	**(20,783)**

(*Continued*)

Table 2.3. (*Continued*)

(Dollars in millions)	Total	Comprehensive Income	Retained Earnings	Accumulated Other Comprehensive Income	Common Stock Issued Amount	Treasury Stock Amount
Net earnings	9,672	9,672	9,672	—	—	—
Cash dividends paid	(6,156)	—	(6,156)	—	—	—
Employee stock compensation and stock option plans	1,760	—	111	—	—	1,649
Conversion of subordinated debentures	—	—	—	—	—	—
Repurchase of common stock	(2,525)	—	—	—	—	(2,525)
Other	(149)	—	(149)	—	—	—
Other comprehensive income, net of tax:	—	—	—	—	—	—
Currency translation adjustment	(557)	(557)	—	(557)	—	—
Unrealized gains on securities	424	424	—	424	—	—
Pension liability adjustment	(1,700)	(1,700)	—	(1,700)	—	—
Losses on derivatives & hedges	(268)	(268)	—	(268)	—	—
Reclassification adjustment	—	—	—	—	—	—
Total comprehensive income	—	7,571	—	—	—	—
Note receivable from ESOP	—	—	—	—	—	—
Balance, January 1, 2012	**$57,080**	—	**81,251**	**(5,632)**	**3,120**	**(21,659)**

(*Continued*)

Table 2.3. (*Continued*)

(Dollars in millions)	Total	Comprehensive Income	Retained Earnings	Accumulated Other Comprehensive Income	Common Stock Issued Amount	Treasury Stock Amount
Net earnings	10,853	10,853	10,853	—	—	—
Cash dividends paid	(6,614)	—	(6,614)	—	—	—
Employee stock compensation and stock option plans	3,269	—	19	—	—	3,250
Conversion of subordinated debentures	—	—	—	—	—	—
Repurchase of common stock	(12,919)	—	—	—	—	(12,919)
Other comprehensive income, net of tax:	—	—	—	—	—	—
Currency translation adjustment	1,230	1,230	—	1,230	—	—
Unrealized gains on securities	−253	−253	—	−253	—	—
Pension liability adjustment	−1,331	−1,331	—	−1,331	—	—
Gains on derivatives & hedges	176	176	—	176	—	—
Reclassification adjustment	—	—	—	—	—	—
Total comprehensive income	—	10,675	—	—	—	—
Note receivable from ESOP	—	—	—	—	—	—
Balance, December 30, 2012	**$64,826**	—	**85,992**	**(5,810)**	**3,120**	**(18,476)**

Table 2.4. Consolidated Statements of Cash Flow of JNJ Corporation and Subsidiaries (Dollars in Millions).

(Dollars in Millions)	2007	2008	2009	2010	2011	2012
Cash flows from operating activities						
Net earnings	10,576	12,949	12,266	13,334	9,672	10,514
Adjustments to reconcile net earnings to cash flows:	—	—	—	—	—	—
Depreciation and amortization of property and intangibles	2,777	2,832	2,774	2,939	3,158	3,666
Purchased in-process R&D	807	181	—	—	—	—
Deferred tax provision	−1,762	22	−436	356	−836	−39
Accounts receivable allowances	22	86	58	12	32	92
Changes in assets and liabilities, net of effects from acquisitions:	—	—	—	—	—	—
Increase in accounts receivable	−416	−736	453	−207	−915	−9
(Increase)/decrease in inventories	14	−101	95	−196	−715	−1
(Decrease)/increase in accounts payable and accrued liabilities	2,642	−272	−507	20	493	2,768
Decrease/(increase) in other current and non-current assets	−1,578	−1,600	1,209	−574	−1,625	−2,172
Increase in other current and non-current liabilities	564	984	31	87	4,413	−2,555
Net cash flows from operating activities	13,646	14,345	15,943	16,385	14,298	16,385
Cash flows from investing activities	—	—	—	—	—	—
Additions to PP&E	−2,942	−3,066	−2,365	−2,384	−2,893	−2,934
Proceeds from the disposal of assets	457	785	154	524	1,342	1,509
Acquisitions, net of cash acquired	−1,388	−1,214	−2,470	−1,296	−2,797	−4,486
Purchases of investments	−9,659	−3,668	−10,040	−15,788	−29,882	−13,434
Sales of investments	7,988	3,059	7,232	11,101	30,396	14,797
Other (primarily intangibles)	−368	−83	−109	−38	−778	38
Net cash used by investing activities	−5,912	−4,187	−7,598	−7,854	−4,612	−4,510

(*Continued*)

Table 2.4. (*Continued*)

(Dollars in Millions)	2007	2008	2009	2010	2011	2012
Cash flows from financing activities	—	—	—	—	—	—
Dividends to shareholders	−4,670	−5,024	−5,327	−5,804	−6,156	−6,614
Repurchase of common stock	−5,607	−6,651	−2,130	−2,797	−2,525	−12,919
Proceeds from short-term debt	19,626	8,430	9,484	7,874	9,729	3,268
Retirement of short-term debt	−21,691	−7,319	−6,791	−6,565	−11,200	−6,175
Proceeds from long-term debt	5,100	1,638	9	1,118	4,470	45
Retirement of long-term debt	−18	−24	−219	−32	−16	−804
Proceeds from the exercise of stock options	1,562	1,486	882	1,226	1,246	2,720
Other	—	—	—	—	—	−83
Net cash used by financing activities	−5,698	−7,464	−4,092	−4,980	−4,452	−20,562
Effect of exchange rate changes on cash and cash equivalents	275	−323	161	−6	−47	45
Increase/ (Decrease) in cash and cash equivalents	3,687	2,998	5,042	3,545	5,187	−9,631
Cash and cash equivalents, beginning of year	4,083	7,770	10,768	15,810	19,355	24,542
Cash and cash equivalents, end of year	7,770	10,768	15,810	19,355	24,542	14,911
Supplemental cash flow data	—	—	—	—	—	—
Cash paid during the year for:	—	—	—	—	—	—
Interest	314	525	533	491	576	616
Income taxes	4,099	4,068	2,368	2,442	2,970	2,507
Supplemental schedule of non-cash investing and financing activities	—	—	—	—	—	—
Treasury stock issued for employee compensation and stock option plans, net of cash proceeds	738	593	541	673	433	615
Conversion of debt	9	—	2	1	1	—
Acquisitions	—	—	—	—	—	—
Fair value of assets acquired	1,620	1,328	3,345	1,321	3,025	19,025
Fair value of liabilities assumed	−232	−114	−8,75	−52	−228	−1,204
Net cash paid for acquisitions	1,388	1,214	2,470	1,269	2,797	4,486

answer questions such as: Has the firm been building up its liquidity assets or is it becoming less liquid?

The statement of cash flow can be used to help resolve differences between finance and accounting theories. There is value for the analyst in viewing the statement of cash flow over time, especially in detecting trends that could lead to technical or legal bankruptcy in the future. Collectively, the balance sheet, the statement of retained earnings, the statement of equity, and the statement of cash flow present a fairly clear picture of the firm's historical and current position. The procedure for compiling Table 2.4 can be found in Appendix 2.B.

2.2.5. *Interrelationship among Four Financial Statements*

It should be noted that the balance sheet, statement of earnings, statement of equity, and statement of cash flow are interrelated. These relationships are briefly described as follows:

(1) Retained earnings calculated from the statement of equity for the current period should be used to replace the retained earnings item in the balance sheet of the previous period. Therefore, the statement of equity is regarded as a bridge between the balance sheet and the statement of earnings.
(2) We need the information from the balance sheet, the statement of earnings, and the statement of equity to compile the statement of cash flow.
(3) Cash and cash equivalent item can be found in the statement of cash flow. In other words, the statement of cash flow describes how the cash and cash equivalent changed during the period. It is known that the first item of the balance sheet is cash and cash equivalent.

2.2.6. *Annual versus Quarterly Financial Data*

Both annual and quarterly financial data are important to financial analysts; which one is the most important depends on the time horizon of the analysis. Depending upon pattern changes in the historical data, either annual or quarterly data could prove to be more useful. As Gentry and Lee discuss, understanding the implications of using quarterly data versus annual data is important for proper financial analysis and planning.

Quarterly data has three components: trend-cycle, seasonal, and irregular or random components. It contains important information about seasonal fluctuations that "reflects an intra-year pattern of variation which is repeated constantly or in evolving fashion from year to year."[1] Quarterly data has the disadvantage of having a large irregular, or random, component that introduces noise into analysis.

Annual data has both the trend-cycle component and the irregular component, but it does not have the seasonal component. The irregular component is much smaller in annual data than in quarterly data. While it may seem that annual data would be more useful for long-term financial planning and analysis, seasonal data reveals important permanent patterns that underlie the short-term series in financial analysis and planning. In other words, quarterly data can be used for intermediate-term financial planning to improve financial management.

Use of either quarterly or annual data has a consistent impact on the mean-square error of regression forecasting (see Appendix 2.A), which is composed of variance and bias. Changing from annual to quarterly data will generally reduce variance while increasing bias. Any difference in regression results, due to the use of different data, must be analyzed in light of the historical patterns of fluctuation in the original time-series data.

2.3. Critique of Accounting Information

2.3.1. *Criticism*

At first glance, accounting information seems to be heavily audited and regulated, automatically determining what numbers are presented. However, careful analysis makes it apparent that accountants work with a fairly broad framework of rules that increase the distance between accounting and financial valuation. This leeway in accounting rules also tends to make accounting information more random. In addition, Hong (1977) shows that the selection of "last in, first out" (LIFO) or "first in, last out" (FIFO) methods for tax and depreciation based upon historic cost generally introduces a bias in a firm's market-value determination. This combination of discrepancy, bias, and randomness means that accounting information does not represent the "true" information. As a result, both time-series and cross-sectional comparisons of accounting information are difficult to analyze.

A major problem with the use of accounting information rises due to errors made in classifying transactions into individual accounts. There are several types of classification errors.

[1] *Ibid.*

One classification error occurs when a bookkeeper enters an item into the wrong account. This is dealt with by modern auditing through the use of sampling techniques, where the auditor certifies that the probability of a material error, an error that would alter a manager's or investor's decision, is within an acceptable limit.

The difference between accountancy and finance theory is another case of classification error. An accountant defines income as the change in shareholder's wealth due to operations of the firm; this includes the use of accruals in wealth determination. The finance discipline defines a firm's income as cash income, or the difference between cash revenues and cash expenses (those payments made to generate current revenue). Due to the accruals used in accounting, accounting income is numerically different from cash income because of the difference in timing.

Another problem with accounting information derives from depreciation costs. There are various accepted ways to spread the cost of an asset over its useful life.[2] The choice of a depreciation method can cause a wide variation in net income.[3] A straight-line method will reduce income less than an accelerated method in the first years of depreciation. In the later years, accelerated depreciation will reduce income less than a straight-line method.

The use of historical costs for pricing an asset acquisition also causes problems in using accounting information. Such reliance on historical cost is particularly troublesome in times of high inflation, because historical cost values are no longer representative of the underlying values of the assets and liabilities of the firm. The accounting profession is attempting to deal with this problem through the use of supplementary disclosure of selected financial statement items, as required by Financial Accounting Standard

---

[2]Depreciation is a procedure that allocates the acquisition costs of the asset to subsequent periods of time on a systematic and rational basis. There are several widely used methods of allocating the acquisition costs: straight-line, declining balance, and sum-of-the-years digits.

[3]There is a limit on the ability of the firm to manipulate its financial statements by repeatedly changing accounting methods, for depreciation, inventory valuation, or any other of the numerous decisions permitted by generally accepted accounting principles (GAAP). The limitation on constant changes in accounting methods is provided by several sources. Accounting Principle Board 20 requires that any changes must be justified on the basis of fair representation and the change and the justification must be disclosed.

The American Institute of Certified Public Accountants, through the Auditing Standards Board, requires that the auditor certify that accounting principles have been consistently observed in the current period in relation to the preceding periods [AU 150.02].

Board 33, for large, publicly traded firms.[4] Accountants are also developing replacement cost and other inflation-adjusted accounting procedures.

2.3.2. *Methods for Improvement*

Three possible methods for improving the representativeness or accuracy of accounting information in financial analysis and planning is the use of alternative information, statistical tools, and finance and economic theories.

Use of Alternative Information

Of the many types of alternative information that is used to improve accounting data, the most practical and consistent type is market information. Stock prices and replacement costs can be used to adjust reported accounting earnings. According to the theory of efficient capital markets, the market price of a security represents the market's estimate of the value of that security. Furthermore, the market value (or the "intrinsic" value) of a common stock represents the firm's "true" earning potential perceived by investors. An example of the use of market information to complement accounting information is the use of the option-pricing model in capital budgeting under uncertainty in Chapter 10.

Statistical Adjustments Another method of improving accounting information is the use of statistical tools. By using a time-series decomposition technique suggested by Gentry and Lee (1983), quarterly earnings can be divided into three components: trend-cycle, seasonal, and irregular components. This decomposition procedure can be used to remove some undesirable noise associated with accounting numbers. Therefore, this statistically adjusted accounting earnings data can be used to improve its usefulness in determining a firm's intrinsic value.

For long-term financial planning and analysis, the trend-cycle component is the major source of information. The seasonal and irregular components introduce noise that clouds the analysis, and this noise can be removed. For short-term (or intermediate-term) planning and analysis, the seasonal component also produces valuable information. Thus, both trend-cycle and seasonal components should be used in working-capital management. Note that the source(s) of noise can also be eliminated by moving average or other statistical methods.

[4]Financial Accounting Standards Board Statement #33, Stamford CT, June 1974.

Application of Finance and Economic Theories The third method of improving accounting information is the use of finance and economic theories. For example, there is the Modigliani and Miller valuation theory, the capital-asset pricing theory, and the option-pricing theory, which will be discussed in Chapters 4, 9, and 17. By applying these theories, one can adjust accounting income to obtain a better picture of income measurement, i.e., finance income (cash flow). Also, the use of finance theory combined with market and other information gives an analyst another estimate of income measurement. In addition, the various earnings estimates can shed additional light on the firm's value determination. To do these kinds of empirical tests, Lee and Zumwalt (1981) use a multiple regression model to investigate the association between six alternative accounting profitability measures and the security rate-of-return determination. Their empirical results suggest that accounting profitability information is an important extra-market information component of asset pricing. In other words, it is shown that different accounting profitability measures should be used by security analysts and investors to determine the equity rates-of-return for different industries.

2.4. Static Ratio Analysis and its Extension

In order to make use of financial statements, an analyst needs some form of measurement for analysis. Frequently, ratios are used to relate one piece of financial data to another. The ratio puts the two pieces of data on an equivalent base, which increases the usefulness of the data. For example, net income as an absolute number is meaningless to compare across firms of different sizes. However, if one creates a net profitability ratio (NI/Sales), comparisons are easier to make. Analysis of a series of ratios will give us a clear picture of a firm's financial condition and performance.

Analysis of ratios can take one of two forms. First, the analyst can compare the ratios of one firm with those of similar firms or with industry averages at a specific point in time. This is a type of cross-sectional analysis technique, that may indicate the relative financial condition and performance of a firm. One must be careful, however, to analyze the ratios while keeping in mind the inherent differences between a firm's production functions and its operations. Also, the analyst should avoid using "rules of thumb" across industries because the composition of industries and individual firms varies considerably. Furthermore, inconsistency in a firm's accounting procedures can cause accounting data to show substantial differences between firms, which can hinder ratio comparability. This variation in accounting procedures can also lead to problems in determining the "target ratio" (to be discussed later).

The second method of ratio comparison involves the comparison of a firm's present ratio with their past and expected ratios. This form of time-series analysis will indicate whether the firm's financial condition has improved or deteriorated. Both types of ratio analysis can take one of the two following forms: static determination and its analysis, or dynamic adjustment and its analysis.

2.4.1. *Static Determination of Financial Ratios*

The static determination of financial ratios involves the calculation and analysis of ratios over a number of periods for one company, or the analysis of differences in ratios among individual firms in one industry. An analyst must be careful of extreme values in either direction, because of the interrelationships between ratios. For instance, a very high liquidity ratio is costly to maintain, causing profitability ratios to be lower than they need to be. Furthermore, ratios must be interpreted in relation to the raw data from which they are calculated, particularly for ratios that sum accounts in order to arrive at the necessary data for the calculation. Even though this analysis must be performed with extreme caution, it can yield important conclusions in the analysis for a particular company. Table 2.5 presents ratio data for the domestic pharmaceutical industry.

Short-term Solvency, or Liquidity Ratios

Liquidity ratios are calculated from information on the balance sheet; they measure the relative strength of a firm's financial position. Crudely interpreted, these are coverage ratios that indicate the firm's ability to meet short-term obligations. The current ratio (CR) (ratio 1 in Table 2.5) is the most popular of the liquidity ratios because it is easy to calculate and it has intuitive appeal. It is also the most broadly defined liquidity ratio, as it does not take into account the differences in relative liquidity among the individual components of current assets. A more specifically defined liquidity ratio is the quick or acid-test ratio (ratio 2), which excludes the least liquid portion of current assets, inventories. Cash ratio (ratio 3) is the ratio of the company's total cash and cash equivalents to its current liabilities. It is most often used as a measure of company liquidity. A strong cash ratio is

Table 2.5. Company ratios period 2011–2012.

Ratio Classification	Formula	JNJ 2011	JNJ 2012	Industry 2008	Industry 2009
Short-term Solvency, or Liquidity Ratios					
(1) CR	$\frac{\text{Current asset}}{\text{Current liabilities}}$	2.38	1.9	—	—
(2) Quick Ratio*	$\frac{\text{Cash+MS+receivables}}{\text{Current liabilities}}$	1.88	1.34	—	—
(3) Cash Ratio*	$\frac{\text{Cash+MS}}{\text{Current liabilities}}$	1.41	0.87	—	—
(4) Networking-capital to total asset	$\frac{\text{Net working-capital}}{\text{Total asset}}$	0.28	0.18	—	—
Long-term solvency, or Financial Leverage Ratios					
(5) Debt-to-Asset	$\frac{\text{Total debt}}{\text{Total asset}}$	0.48	0.45	—	—
(6) Debt-to-Equity	$\frac{\text{Total debt}}{\text{Total equity}}$	0.96	0.84	—	—
(7) Equity Multiplier	$\frac{\text{Total asset}}{\text{Total equity}}$	2.00	1.87	—	—
(8) Times Interest Paid	$\frac{\text{EBIT}}{\text{Interest expenses}}$	22.65	26.89	—	—
(9) Long-term Debt Ratio	$\frac{\text{Long-term debt}}{\text{Long-term debt+Total equity}}$	0.19	0.15	—	—
(10) Cash Coverage Ratio	$\frac{\text{EBIT+Depreciation}}{\text{Interest expenses}}$	28.18	33.78	—	—
Asset Management, or Turnover (Activity) Ratios					
(11) Day's Sales in Receivables (Average Collection Period)	$\frac{\text{Account receivable}}{\text{Sales/365}}$	59.39	61.40	—	—
(12) Receivable Turnover	$\frac{\text{Sales}}{\text{Accounts receivable}}$	6.15	5.94	—	—
(13) Day's Sales in Inventory	$\frac{\text{Inventory}}{\text{Cost of goods sold/365}}$	112.67	126.31	—	—
(14) Inventory-Turnover	$\frac{\text{Cost of goods sold}}{\text{Inventory}}$	3.24	2.89	—	—
(15) Fixed Asset Turnover	$\frac{\text{Sales}}{\text{Fixed assets}}$	1.33	1.00	—	—

(*Continued*)

Table 2.5. (*Continued*)

Ratio Classification	Formula	JNJ 2011	JNJ 2012	Industry 2008	Industry 2009
(16) Total Asset Turnover	$\frac{\text{Sales}}{\text{Total assets}}$	0.57	0.55	—	—
(17) Networking-Capital Turnover	$\frac{\text{Sales}}{\text{Net working-capital}}$	2.06	3.08	—	—
Profitability Ratios					
(18) Profit Margin	$\frac{\text{Net income}}{\text{Sales}}$	14.87%	16.14%	—	—
(19) ROA	$\frac{\text{Net income}}{\text{Total assets}}$	8.51%	8.94%	—	—
(20) ROE	$\frac{\text{Net Income}}{\text{Total equity}}$	16.94%	16.74%	—	—
Market Value Ratios					
(21) Price-earnings ratio	$\frac{\text{Market price per share}}{\text{Earnings per share}}$	18.53	17.63	—	—
(22) Market-to-book ratio	$\frac{\text{Market price per share}}{\text{Book value per share}}$	1.58	1.58	—	—
(23) Earnings yield	$\frac{\text{Earnings per share}}{\text{Market price per share}}$	5.40%	5.67%	—	—
(24) Dividend yield	$\frac{\text{Dividend per share}}{\text{Market price per share}}$	3.43%	3.45%	—	—
(25) PEG ratio**	$\frac{\text{Price-earnings ratio}}{\text{Earnings growth rate (\%)}}$	300.02	269.49	—	—
(26) Enterprise value-Earnings before interest, tax, depreciation and amortization (EBITDA) ratio***	$\frac{\text{Enterprise value}}{\text{EBITDA}}$	13.14	12.96	—	—

*MS is the marketable securities.

**For price-earnings-growth (PEG) ratio, the earnings growth rate is estimated by sustainable growth gate.

***Enterprise value = Total market value of equity + Book value of total liabilities — Cash, EBITDA is earnings before interest, taxes, depreciation, and amortization.

Total market value of equity = market price per share * shares outstanding (basic).

For the earnings per share, we used the basic net earnings per share in JNJ.

Since earnings statement only provide EBT, our Earnings before interest and tax (EBIT) = EBT + interest expense.

Book value per share = total asset/share outstanding (basic).

Price-earnings ratio = market price per share/ earnings per share (basic).

useful to creditors when deciding how much debt they're willing to extend to the asking party. (Investopedia.com)

The networking-capital to total asset ratio (ratio 4) is the NWC divided by the total assets of the company. A relatively low value might indicate relatively low levels of liquidity.

Long-term Solvency or Financial Leverage Ratios

If an analyst wishes to measure the extent of a firm's debt financing, a leverage ratio (LR) is the appropriate tool to use. This group of ratios reflects the financial risk posture of the firm. The two sources of data from which these ratios can be calculated are the balance sheet and the statement of earnings.

The balance-sheet LR measures the proportion of debt incorporated into the capital structure. The debt–equity ratio measures the proportion of debt that is matched by equity; thus this ratio reflects the composition of the capital structure. The debt–asset ratio (ratio 5), on the other hand, measures the proportion of debt-financed assets currently being used by the firm. Other commonly used LR include the equity multiplier ratio (7) and the time interest paid ratio (8).

Debt-to-equity (6) is a variation on the total debt ratio. It's total debt divided by total equity.

Long-term debt ratio (9) is long-term debt divided by the sum of long-term debt and total equity.

Cash coverage ratio (10) is defined as the sum of EBIT and depreciation divided by interest. The numerator is often abbreviated as EBITDA.

The income-statement LR measures the firm's ability to meet fixed obligations of one form or another. The time interest paid, which is earnings before interest and taxes over interest expense, measures the firm's ability to service the interest expense on its outstanding debt. A more broadly defined ratio of this type is the fixed-charge coverage ratio, which includes not only the interest expense but also all other expenses that the firm is obligated by contract to pay. (This ratio is not included in Table 2.5 because there is not enough information on fixed charges for these firms to calculate this ratio.)

Asset Management or Turnover (Activity) Ratios

This group of ratios measures how efficiently the firm is utilizing its assets. With activity ratios, one must be particularly careful about the interpretation of extreme results in either direction; very high values may indicate possible problems in the long term, and very low values may indicate a current problem of low sales or not taking a loss for obsolete assets. The reason that high activity may not be good in the long term is that the firm may not be able to adjust to an even higher level of activity and therefore may miss out on a market opportunity. Better analysis and planning can help a firm get around this problem.

The days-in-accounts-receivable or average collection-period ratio (11) indicates the firm's effectiveness in collecting its credit sales. The other activity ratios measure the firm's efficiency in generating sales with its current level of assets, appropriately termed turnover ratios. While there are many turnover ratios that can be calculated, there are three basic ones: inventory-turnover (14), fixed assets turnover (15), and total assets turnover (16). Each of these ratios measures a quite different aspect of the firm's efficiency in managing its assets.

Receivables turnover (12) is computed as credit sales divided by accounts receivable. In general, a higher accounts receivable turnover suggests more frequent payment of receivables by customers.

In general, analysts look for higher receivables turnover and shorter collection periods, *but this combination may imply that the firm's credit policy is too strict*, allowing only the lowest risk customers to buy on credit. Although this strategy could minimize credit losses, it may hurt overall sales, profits, and shareholder wealth.

Day's sales in inventory ratio (13) estimates how many days, on average, a product sits in the inventory before it is sold.

Net working-capital turnover (17) measures how much "work" we get out of our working-capital.

Profitability Ratios

This group of ratios indicates the profitability of the firm's operations. It is important to note here that these measures are based on past performance. Profitability ratios are generally the most volatile, because many of the variables affecting them are beyond the firm's control. There are three groups of profitability ratios; those measuring margins, those measuring returns, and those measuring the relationship of market values to book or accounting values.

Profit-margin ratios show the percentage of sales dollars that the firm was able to convert into profit. There are many such ratios that can be calculated to yield insightful results, namely: profit margin (18), ROA (19), and return on equity (ROE) (20).

Return ratios are generally calculated as a return on assets (ROA) or equity. The ROA ratio (19) measures the profitability of the firm's asset utilization. The ROE ratio (20) indicates the rate-of-return earned on the book value of owner's equity. Market-value analyses include (i) market-value/book-value ratio and (ii) price per share/earnings per share (P/E) ratio. These ratios and their applications will be discussed in Chapter 6.

Overall, all four different types of ratios (as indicated in Table 2.5) have different characteristics stemming from the firm itself and the industry as a whole. For example, the collection-period ratio (which is Accounts Receivable times 365 over Net Sales) is clearly the function of the billings, payment, and collection policies of the pharmaceutical industry. In addition, the fixed-asset turnover ratios for those firms are different, which might imply that different firms have different capacity utilization.

Market Value Ratios

A firm's profitability, risk, quality of management, and many other factors are reflected in its stock and security prices. Hence, market value ratios indicate the market's assessment of the value of the firm's securities.

The PE ratio (21) is simply the market price of the firm's common stock divided by its annual earnings per share. Sometimes called the *earnings multiple*, the PE ratio shows how much the investors are willing to pay for each dollar of the firm's earnings per share. Earnings per share comes from the income statement. Therefore, earnings per share is sensitive to the many factors that affect the construction of an income statement, such as the choice of GAAP to management decisions regarding the use of debt to finance assets. Although earnings per share cannot reflect the value of patents or assets, the quality of the firm's management, or its risk, and stock prices can reflect all of these factors. Comparing a firm's PE ratio to that of the stock market as a whole, or with the firm's competitors, indicates the market's perception of the true value of the company.

Market-to-book ratio (22) measures the market's valuation relative to balance sheet equity. The book value of equity is simply the difference between the book values of assets and liabilities appearing on the balance sheet. The price-to-book-value ratio is the market price per share divided by the book value of equity per share. A higher ratio suggests that investors are more optimistic about the market value of a firm's assets, its intangible assets, and the ability of its managers.

Earnings yield (23) is defined as earnings per share divided by market price per share and is used to measure return on investment. Dividend yield (24) is defined as dividend per share divided by market price per share, which is used to determine whether this company's stock is an income stock or a gross stock. A gross stock dividend yield is very small or even zero. For example, the stock from a utility industry dividend yield is very high. In addition, in the early stage of Microsoft and Apple computer they didn't even pay cash dividend, therefore their dividend yield was zero.

PEG ratio is defined as price-earnings ratio divided by earnings growth rate. The PEG ratio is used to determine a stock's value while taking the company's earnings growth into account, and is considered to provide a more complete picture than the PE ratio. While a high PE ratio may make a stock look like a good buy, factoring in the company's growth rate to get the stock's PEG ratio can tell a different story. The lower the PEG ratio, the more the stock may be undervalued given its earnings performance. The PEG ratio that indicates an over or underpriced stock varies by industry and by company type, though a broad rule of thumb is that a PEG ratio below one is desirable. Also, the accuracy of the PEG ratio depends on the inputs used. Using historical growth rates, for example, may provide an inaccurate PEG ratio if future growth rates are expected to deviate from historical growth rates. To distinguish between calculation methods using future growth and historical growth, the terms "forward PEG" and "trailing PEG" are sometimes used.

Enterprise value is an estimate of the market value of the company's operating assets, which means all the assets of the firm except cash. Since market values are usually unavailable, we use the right-hand side of the balance sheet and calculate the enterprise value as:

$$\text{Enterprise value} = \text{Total market value} + \text{Book value of all liabilities} - \text{Cash}.$$

Notice that the sum of the value of the market values of the stock and all liabilities equals the value of the firm's assets from the balance sheet identity. Enterprise value is often used to calculate the Enterprise value-EBITDA ratio (26):

$$\text{EBITDA ratio} = \frac{\text{Enterprise value}}{\text{EBITDA}}.$$

This ratio is similar to the PE ratio, but it relates the value of all the operating assets to a measure of the operating cash flow generated by those assets.

Estimation of the Target of a Ratio

An issue that must be addressed at this point is the determination of an appropriate proxy for the target of a ratio. For an analyst, this can be an insurmountable problem if the firm is extremely diversified, and if it does not have one or two major product lines in industries where industry averages are available. One possible solution is to determine the relative industry share of each division or major product line, then apply these percentages to the related industry averages. Lastly, derive one target ratio for the firm as a whole with which its ratio can be compared. One must be very careful in any such analysis, because the proxy may be extremely over- or underestimated. The analyst can also use Standard Industrial Classification (SIC) codes to properly define the industry of diversified firms. The analyst can then use 3- or 4-digit codes and compute their own weighted industry average.

Often an industry average is used as a proxy for the target ratio. This can lead to another problem, the inappropriate calculation of an industry average, even though the industry and companies are fairly well-defined. The issue here is the appropriate weighing scheme for combining the individual company ratios in order to arrive at one industry average. Individual ratios can be weighed according to equal weights, asset weights, or sales weights. The analyst must determine the extent to which firm size, as measured by asset base or market share, affects the relative level of a firm's ratios and the tendency for other firms in the industry to adjust toward the target level of this ratio. One way this can be done is to calculate the coefficients of variation for a number of ratios under each of the weighing schemes and to compare them to see which scheme consistently has the lowest coefficient variation. This would appear to be the most appropriate weighing scheme. Of course, one could also use a different weighing scheme for each ratio, but this would be very tedious if many ratios were to be analyzed. Note, that the median rather than the average or mean can be used to avoid needless complications with respect to extreme values that might distort the computation of averages. In the dynamic analysis that follows, the equal-weighted average is used throughout.

2.4.2. *Dynamic Analysis of Financial Ratios*

In basic finance and accounting courses, industry norms are generally used to determine whether the magnitude of a firm's financial ratios is acceptable. Taken separately, ratios are mere numbers. This can lead to some problems in making comparisons among and drawing conclusions from them. In addition, by making only static, one-ratio-to-another comparisons, we are not taking advantage of all the information they can provide. A more dynamic analysis can improve our ability to compare companies with one another and to forecast future ratios. Regressing CR against past ratios helps one analyze the dynamic nature and the adjustment process of a firm's financial ratio.

Single-Equation Dynamic Adjustment Process

1. Basic Model. Lev (1969) uses the concept of the partial-adjustment model to define a dynamic financial-ratio adjustment process as

$$Y_{j,t} = Y_{j,\,t-1} + \delta_j(Y^*_{j,t} - Y_{j,\,t-1}), \tag{2.1}$$

where $0 \leq \delta_j \leq 1$ and

$\delta_j = A$ partial adjustment coefficient;
$Y_{j,t}$ = Firm's jth financial ratio period t;
$Y_{j,\,t-1}$ = Firm's jth financial ratio period $t{-}1$; and
$Y^*_{j,i}$ = Firm's jth financial ratio target in period t.

This model is used in a wide variety of empirical applications of the dynamic properties of financial analysis and forecasting, such as investment, financing, and dividend decisions. The relationship postulates that at any time, t, only a fixed fraction of the desired adjustment is achieved in that period. Thus, the coefficient of adjustment, δ_j, reflects the fact that there are limitations to the periodic adjustment of ratios. Therefore, the coefficient of adjustment should be interpreted cautiously.

Lev (1969) suggests that differences across ratios in their speed of adjustment coefficient, δ_j, are a function of two conflicting types of costs: (1) the cost of adjustment and (2) the cost of being out of equilibrium. These two costs must be balanced for each ratio. Equation (2.1) implies that a firm's current financial ratio is equal to the last period's financial ratio plus an adjustment term. The adjustment factor depends upon two elements: the partial adjustment coefficient, δ_i, and the difference between $Y^*_{j,t}$ and $Y_{j,\,t-1}$. However, $Y^*_{j,t}$ is not an observable variable, so we must find some alternative proxy.

To resolve the problem associated with determining the target ratio ($Y^*_{j,t}$), Lev assumes that: (1) $Y^*_{j,t}$ is exactly equal to the industry average of the jth financial ratio in the previous period, denoted as $X_{j,\,t-1}$ and

(2) $Y^*_{j,t}$ is proportional to $X_{j,\,t-1}$, that is $CX_{j,\,t-1}$ where C is the related proportional constant. A generalized proxy of $Y^*_{j,t}$ can be defined as

$$Y^*_{j,t} = CX_{j,\,t-1} + \tau_{j,t}, \tag{2.2}$$

where $0 \leq C \leq 1$ and $\tau_{j,t}$ represents the proxy error. Proxy error is the error arising from the fact that the substitute, or proxy, ratio only partially approximates the desired target ratio. If $C = 1$ and $\tau_{j,t} = 0$, then $X_{j,\,t-1}$ is the perfect proxy for $Y^*_{j,t}$. We can then substitute $X_{j,\,t-1}$ for $Y^*_{j,t}$ in Eq. (2.1) and obtain:

$$Y_{j,t} - Y_{j,\,t-1} = \delta_j[X_{j,\,t-1} - Y_{j,\,t-1}]. \tag{2.3}$$

In order to estimate the partial adjustment coefficient, δ_j, a simple time-series regression can be run and used in the empirical study. The linear form of this regression is defined as

$$Z_{j,t} = A_j + B_j W_{j,\,t-1} + \varepsilon_{j,t}, \tag{2.4}$$

where

$$Z_{j,t} = Y_{j,t} - Y_{j,\,t-1};$$
$$W_{j,\,t-1} = X_{j,\,t-1} - Y_{j,\,t-1};$$
$$A_j \text{ and } B_j = \text{regression parameters}$$

and

$$\varepsilon_{j,t} = \text{the error term.}$$

2. Extensions of this model. Lev also suggests a log-linear form of this model in order to study the dynamic ratio-adjustment process:

$$Z\prime_{j,t} = A\prime_j + B\prime_j W\prime_{j,\,t-1} + \varepsilon\prime_{j,t}, \tag{2.5}$$

where

$$Z'_{j,t} = \log(Y_{j,t}) - \log(Y_{j,\,t-1}),$$
$$W'_{j,\,t-1} = \log(X_{j,\,t-1}) - \log(Y_{j,i-1})$$

and

$$\varepsilon'_{j,t} = \text{the error term.}$$

One of the possible advantages of the log-linear form of this model over the linear form is that the estimated B'_j represents the elasticity of change, while the estimated B_j does not. The argument is based upon the fact that

$$B'_j = \frac{\partial \log\left(\dfrac{Y_{j,t}}{Y_{j,t-1}}\right)}{\partial \log\left(\dfrac{X_{j,t-1}}{Y_{j,t-1}}\right)} = \frac{\%\text{ change in }\left[\dfrac{\mathrm{Y_{j,t}}}{Y_{j,t-1}}\right]}{\%\text{ change in }\left[\dfrac{\mathrm{X_{j,t-1}}}{Y_{j,t-1}}\right]}. \tag{2.6}$$

This model can be generalized by assuming that the optimal ratio level attained by the firm is last period's industry ratio average times an adjustment factor, as follows:

$$Y^*_{j,t} = CX_{j,t-1}. \tag{2.7}$$

The adjustment coefficient, C, indicates that firms tend to maintain a fixed deviation from the industry mean in their adjustment process. Furthermore, the analysis of the coefficient and the partial adjustment coefficient (δ_j) should be very helpful in demonstrating the dynamic nature of a firm's financial structure, its financial ratios, and their adjustment toward the industry mean.

As for predicting future ratios, Lev finds that the model's predictive powers can be enhanced substantially through the following extension to multiple regression:

$$Y_{j,t} = \hat{A} + \hat{B}_1 X_{j,t-1} + \hat{B}_2 Y_{j,t-1} + \varepsilon_{j,t}. \tag{2.8}$$

This model is found to be substantially more accurate in the prediction of future ratios, while the model detailed in Eq. (2.4) is better at estimating the partial adjustment coefficient, B_j. With this model, analysts can forecast future possibilities. Furthermore, once the future ratios are estimated, one can work backward and determine the estimated levels of individual accounts, which facilitates planning ahead to meet unpleasant future economic situations.

3. Empirical Data. Annual financial ratio data for JNJ and the industry as a whole will be used to show how Eqs. (2.4) and (2.5) perform in empirical financial ratio analysis. The sample period from 1992 to 2004 for JNJ in terms of Eq. (2.5) has been empirically estimated. The estimated B'_j and A'_j and the information needed to estimate these two regression parameters are

Table 2.6. Dynamic Adjustment Ratio Regression Results.

Variable	CR	LR
Mean Z	0.0075	−0.03083
Mean W	−0.14583	0.361666667
Var(Z)	0.013039	0.006099
Cov(Z,W)	0.074	0.009
B_j\`	0.810*	0.259
t-statistics	[3.53]	[1.06]
A_j\`	0.032	−0.042

*Partial adjustment coefficient significant at 95% level.

Table 2.7. Ratio Correlation Coefficient Matrix.

	CR	AT	GPM	LR
CR	1.0			
AT	−0.443841	1.0		
GPM	0.363273	0.381393	1.0	
LR	−0.51175	0.21961	−0.05028	1.0

listed in Table 2.6. Based upon the procedure discussed in Appendix 2.A, the estimated mean Z, mean W, Var (W), and COV (Z, W) can be used to estimate B'_j and A'_j Estimates of Table 2.6 indicate the partial adjustment coefficients associated with both CR and LR for JNJ.

The accounting general ledger items used in calculating ratios are interrelated. A ratio is merely calculated by using at least two such items. Hence, important financial ratios of a firm may be interrelated. The correlation coefficient matrix among CR, asset turnover (AT), gross profit margin (GPM), and LR for JNJ is presented in Table 2.7 to show the interrelationship. Fisher's z-statistics imply that the sample correlation coefficients between CR and GPM, CR and LR, AT and LR, and GPM and LR are statistically significant at the 95% level. Based upon approximations of Fisher's z-statistics, the sample correlation coefficients (as indicated in Table 2.7) can be statistically tested.[5]

As shown in Table 2.7, the LR is fairly negatively correlated with CR (−0.51175) and GPM (−0.05028) but positively correlated with the activity ratio (AT, 0.21961). Also, GPM is somewhat positively correlated with the CR (0.363273). Thus, it can show that these ratios are interrelated. This tells us that we must use a system of ratios in simple analysis, or use simultaneous equations in a statistical analysis.

[5] $z-$ statistics $= 1/2 \log[(1+\rho)/(1-\rho)]$, where ρ is the simple correlation coefficient.

2.4.3. *Statistical Distribution of Financial Ratios*

Normal and log-normal distributions are two of the most popular statistical distributions used in accounting and financial analysis. The density function of a normal distribution is

$$F[X] = \frac{1}{\sigma\sqrt{2\pi}} e^{-(X-\mu)^2/2\sigma^2} (-\infty < \mathrm{X} < +\infty), \tag{2.10}$$

where μ and σ^2 are the population mean and variance, respectively, and e and π are given constants; that is, $\pi = 3.14159$ and $e = 2.71828$.

Normal distributions with different means and variances are graphed in Figs. 2.1 and 2.2. In these two figures, $F(X)$ represents the frequency of the variable X. The variance of Fig. 2.1 is larger than the variance of Fig. 2.2.

If a variable is normally distributed, the information that fully describes the distribution is the mean and the variance. The relative skewness of normal distribution is 0, and the kurtosis of a normal distribution is equal to 3.

There is a direct relationship between the normal distribution and the log-normal distribution. If Y is log-normally distributed, then $X = \log Y$ is normally distributed. Following this definition, the mean and the variance of Y can be defined as

$$\mu_Y = \exp\left(\mu_x + \frac{1}{2}\sigma_x^2\right), \tag{2.11a}$$

$$\sigma_Y^2 = \exp(2\mu_x + \sigma_x^2)(\exp(\sigma_x^2) - 1), \tag{2.11b}$$

where exp represents an exponential with base e.

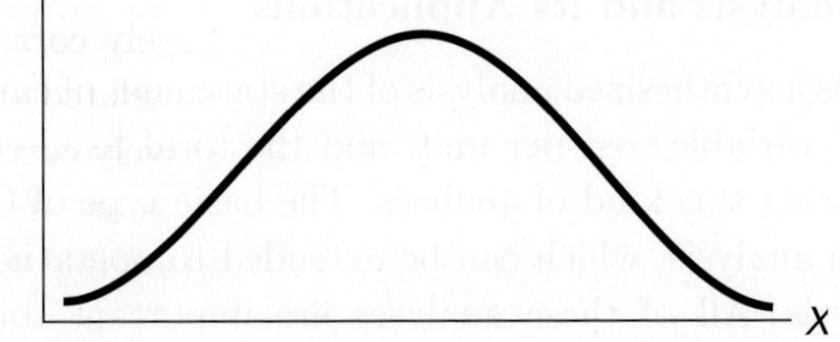

Fig. 2.1. Normal distribution with large variance.

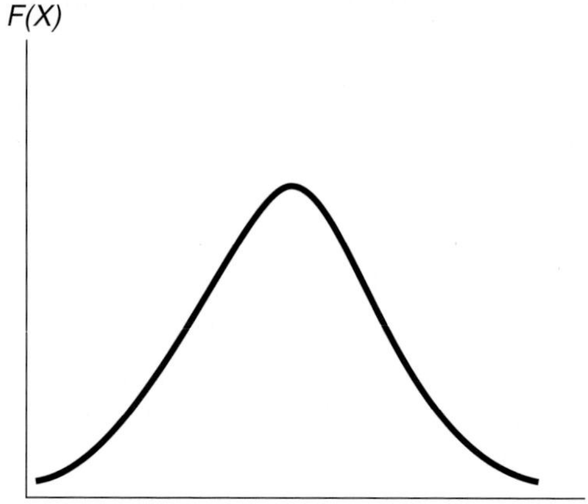

Fig. 2.2. Normal distribution with small variance.

Deakin (1976) finds that the cross-sectional distribution of financial ratios is log-normally distributed instead of normally distributed. Upon analyzing the raw data, he finds that within the pharmaceutical industry, only the debt–asset ratio is normally distributed; this occurs in 15 out of the 19 years of his dataset. All other ratios are log-normally distributed. However, after taking the log transformation, the CR becomes normally distributed in 12 out of the 19 years; while the normality of the debt-asset ratio drops from 15 to only 6 of the 19 years.

Generally, it seems that financial ratios are not normally distributed and that log transformation does help normalize the data in some, but not all, cases. The reason we need a normal distribution for analyzing ratios is in testing the significance of a difference, such as between the behavior of firm and industry figures for the same ratio. It is necessary for the analyst to look at data with and without transformations, in order to determine which set of data fits the normal distribution more closely.

2.5. CVP Analysis and its Applications

CVP analysis is a synthesized analysis of the statement of earnings. Volume, price per unit, variable cost per unit, and the total fixed cost are the key variables for doing this kind of analysis. The basic type of CVP analysis is the break-even analysis, which can be extended to operating and financial leverage analysis. All of these analyses are important tools of financial analysis and control. Technically, ratio-variable inputs are required for performing these analyses. Conceptually, CVP and its derived relationships are designed to analyze the statement of earnings in terms of an aggregated ratio indicator. Hence, CVP analysis can be regarded as one kind of financial ratio analysis.

2.5.1. *Deterministic Analysis*

Deterministic break-even analysis is an important concept in basic microeconomics, accounting, finance, and marketing courses. Mathematically, the operating profit (EBIT) can be defined as

$$\text{Operating Profit} = \text{EBIT} = Q(P - V) - F, \tag{2.12}$$

where

Q = Quantity of goods sold;
P = Price per unit sold;
V = Variable cost per unit sold;
F = Total amount of fixed costs; and
$P - V$ = Contribution margin.

If operating profit is equal to zero, Eq. (2.12) implies that $Q(P-V)-F = 0$ or that $Q(P - V) = F$, that is

$$Q^* = \frac{F}{(P - V)}. \tag{2.13}$$

Equation (2.13) represents the break-even quantity, or that quantity of sales at which fixed costs are just covered. There are two kinds of break-even analysis, linear and non-linear. The two forms are shown graphically in Figs. 2.3 and 2.4.

There are very important economic interpretations of these alternative break-even analyses. Linear representation of the total revenue curve implies that the firm operates within a perfect output or product market. The linear total cost curve implies that the input market is linear or perfect and the return (economies) to scale is constant. If these conditions do not hold, linear break-even analysis becomes either unrealistic or only an approximation of the real situation facing the firm.

In the real world, returns (economies) to scale can either be constant, increasing, or decreasing. A non-linear representation of the variable cost and total revenue curves is a more accurate representation of the real break-even level of sales using this form of analysis.

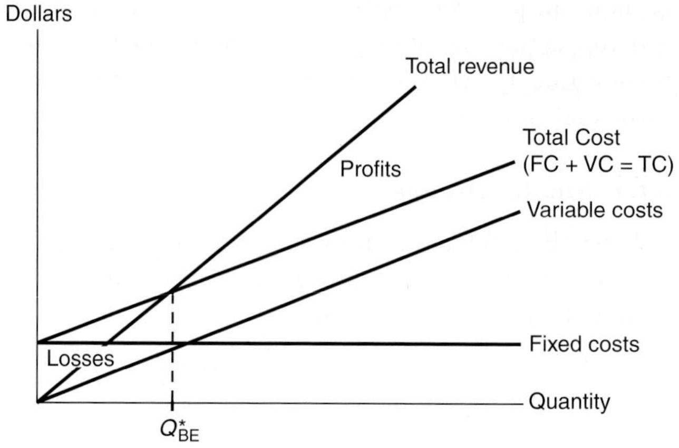

Fig. 2.3. Linear break-even analysis.

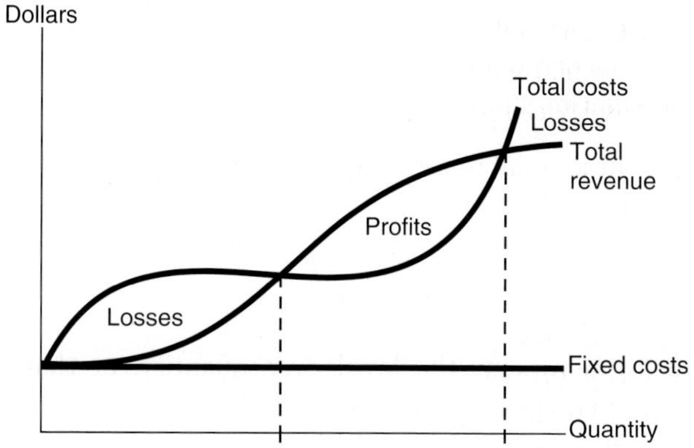

Fig. 2.4. Non-linear break-even analysis.

Break-even analysis can be used in three separate but related ways in financial management. That is: (i) to analyze a program of modernization and automation, (ii) to study the effects of a general expansion in the level of operations, and (iii) in new-product decision. These operating leverage decisions can be defined more precisely in terms of the way a given change in volume affects profits. For this purpose, we use the definition of degree of operating leverage (DOL) represented as Eq. (2.14):

$$\text{DOL} = \frac{\%\text{ Change in profits}}{\%\text{ Change in sales}} = \frac{Q(P-V)}{Q(P-V)-F} = 1 + \frac{\text{Fixed Costs}}{\text{Profits}}. \tag{2.14}$$

The first equality in Eq. (2.14) is the basic definition of DOL. The second equality is obtained by substituting the definition of profits and sales from Eq. (2.12) (see Appendix 6.B for derivation). The third equality implies that the DOL increases with a firm's exposure to fixed costs (see Appendix 6.B for derivation).

Based upon the definition of linear break-even quantity, defined in Eq. (2.13), the DOL can be rewritten as

$$DOL = \frac{1}{[1 - (Q^*/Q)]}. \tag{2.15}$$

There are two important implications of this formulation: (1) if $Q > Q^*$, then DOL > 0, and the change in profits is in the same direction as the change in sales; and (2) if $Q < Q^*$, then DOL < 0 and the change in losses is in the opposite direction from the change in sales (i.e., if sales increase, losses will decrease). Both Eqs. (2.14) and (2.15) can be used to calculate the DOL at any level of output, Q. If company XYZ's break-even quantity Q^* is 50,000 units, then DOL at 100,000 production units is 2. This implies that 1% change of XYZ's sales will generate a 2% change in its profit.

2.5.2. *Stochastic Analysis*

In reality, net profit is a random variable because the quantity used in the analysis should be the quantity sold, which is unknown and random, rather than the quantity produced which is internally determined. This is the simplest form of stochastic CVP analysis; for there is only one stochastic variable and no need to be concerned about independence among variables. The distribution of sales is shown graphically in Fig. 2.5.

A slightly more complicated form of stochastic CVP analysis is obtained when it is assumed that both the quantity of good sold (Q) and the contribution margin ($P - V$) are stochastic variables and are independently distributed. The independence assumption is reasonable because the second stochastic variable is defined as the contribution margin, rather than the three separate random variables Q, P, and V. In this situation, quantity and price are probably not independent, because both distributions are determined by imperfections in the product market. Furthermore, these three variables are generally highly negatively correlated, while the normality of their distributions is questionable (needs further empirical testing). Under the contribution margin approach, one variable that is subtracted from

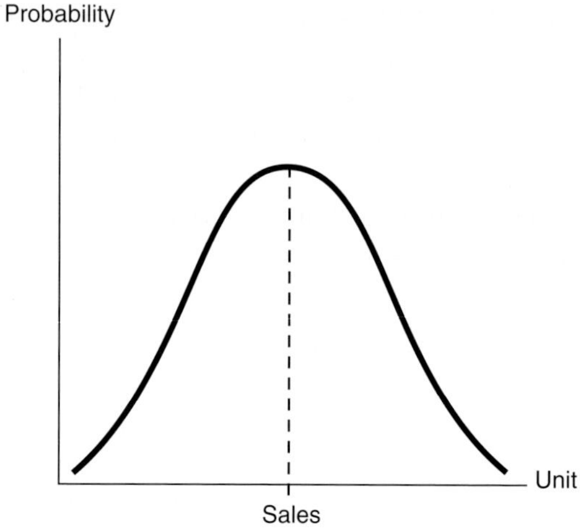

Fig. 2.5. Distribution of sales.

prices, variable costs, has a distribution that is determined by imperfections in the input market. This drastically reduces the degree of correlation with the quantity sold.

While the assumption of independence seems to be fairly accurate in some cases, there is need for more research in this area. Hilliard and Leitch (1975) addressed this problem through the use of a log-normal approach to CVP analysis under uncertainty. They have developed an easily implemented model that can handle dependence among input variables, and that should prove to be helpful to the analyst.

Equation (2.12) can be generalized to allow Q, P, and V to be stochastic variables. Profits also become a stochastic variable, as represented in Eq. (2.16):

$$\text{Operating profit} = \text{EBIT} = Q^{\pi}(P^{\pi} - V^{\pi}) - F. \tag{2.16}$$

This formulation for CVP analysis under uncertainty is very important for the decision-maker. It is becoming increasingly important to move from point (certainty) to interval (uncertainty) estimates, particularly in today's dynamic business environment, the stochastic nature of this CVP formulation allows one to calculate the point estimate and also the related interval estimate based on the combined probability distributions. This application of probabilistic models greatly enhances the degree of realism. Uncertainty break-even analysis has been generalized by Wei (1979) and Yunker (1982) to take into account the crucial elements of random demand and the level of production in the determination of actual sales and resulting profits.

Besides the applications discussed in this section, both CVP and break-even analysis can be integrated with the net present value method of capital budgeting decisions to do financial analysis. Reinhardt (1973) uses this approach to do break-even analysis for Lockheed's Tri Star Program. The Lockheed Tri Star Program uses net present value type of break-even analysis and will be explained later in detail in Chapter 13. The major difference between the net present value (NPV) type of break-even analysis and the "naive" break-even analysis is that the latter does not take into account the cost of capital. This will be explored in the capital budgeting under certainty chapter in detail.

2.6. Accounting Income Versus Economic Income[6]

There are three ways of describing income: accounting earnings, economic income, and finance income. Accounting earnings are based upon recording transactions according to GAAP using accruals and deferrals, rather than cash flows. Accountants measure the change in stockholders' wealth due to the operations of the firm. Economic earnings are more abstract than accounting earnings. Economic income measures the change in wealth based upon both realized and unrealized gains and losses.

Finance income is based on cash flow changes in wealth. Cash income is cash revenues less cash expenses. Finance income defines changes in wealth as net cash flow, or net cash income less cash investment outlays. Technically, economic income, rather than accounting earnings, should be used to determine the value of a firm. However, theoretical economic income is not directly observable, so accounting earnings are generally used as proxy for them. Conceptually, the relationship between accounting earnings and economic income can be defined as

$$E_t = A_t + P_t, \tag{2.17}$$

where

E_t = Economic income,
A_t = Accounting earnings, and
P_t = Proxy errors.

[6]This section is based, in part, on Haley and Schall (1979, pp. 8–10).

In estimating the cost of capital for the utility industry, Miller and Modigliani (1966) take accounting earnings as a proxy for economic income, using instrumental-variable technique, to remove the proxy errors. Instrumental-variable technique can be found in Appendix 25.A of this book. Finance income (cash flows instead of accounting income) will be used to evaluate alternative capital budgeting decisions, which are discussed in Chapters 9 and 10. The main difference between accounting income and cash flows (finance income) is that the former does not focus on cash flows when they occur, while the latter does. The cash flows, for example, correctly deduct the entire expenditure for investment in plant and equipment at the time the cash outflows occur.

2.7. Summary

In this chapter, the usefulness of accounting information in financial analysis is conceptually and analytically evaluated. Both statistical methods and regression analysis techniques show how accounting information can be used to perform active financial analysis for the pharmaceutical industry.

In these analyses, static ratio analysis is generalized to dynamic ratio analysis. In addition, both deterministic and stochastic CVP analyses are examined. The potential applications of CVP analysis in financial analysis and planning are discussed in some detail. Overall, this chapter gives readers a good understanding of basic accounting information and econometric methods, which are needed for financial analysis and planning.

Problem Set

1. What is the value of accounting information in the process of financial analysis and planning? What are the components to annual and quarterly accounting information and their respective advantages and disadvantages for financial analysis and planning?
2. Define the following terms:

   (a) Real versus financial market
   (b) M_1 and M_2
   (c) Leading economic indicators
   (d) NYSE, AMEX, and OTC
   (e) Primary versus secondary stock market
   (f) Bond market
   (g) Options and futures markets.

3. What are limits related to the use of accounting information? What are differences that can result from using accounting, economics, and finance information? How can these limits and differences be overcome?
4. Discuss the major difference between linear and non-linear break-even analysis.
5. What can ratio analysis contribute to financial planning and analysis? What are the determinants of the dynamic adjustment process? How are target ratios derived?
6. What is the relationship between CVP and ratio analysis? How can it be used in financial analysis and planning?
7. Briefly discuss the issue related to net income (EAIT) in financial analysis and planning.
8. A market model is defined as

$$R_{jt} = A_j + B_j R_{mt} + \in_j,$$

where R_{jt}, R_{mt} are the rates-of-return for jth security and market rates-of-return respectively; A_j is the intercept and B_j is the slope. Use the Ordinary Least Squares (OLS) theory and method discussed in Appendix A of this chapter to show how A_j and B_j can be estimated.
9. Parts of financial records for Company XYZ are:

Anticipated sales = \$400,000
Degree of financial leverage = 4/3
Variable cost = \$200,000
Combined leverage effect = 2
Quantity sold = \$100,000 units
Profit margin = 5%
Total debt = \$200,000
Leverage ratio = 1/2
Common stock outstanding = 10,000 shares
Current price per share = \$40
Retention rate = 1/2
IRR = 8%

Calculate the following:

(a) The total interest expense.
(b) The total fixed cost.
(c) The degree of operating leverage.
(d) The break-even quantity.

(e) The EAIT.
(f) Total corporation income tax expense.
(g) The return on net worth.
(h) The return on total asset.
(i) The EPS.
(j) The P/E ratio for common stock.
(k) The pay-out ratio for dividend.
(l) The growth rate for the common stock.
(m) The required rate-of-return.
(n) Total asset turnover.
(o) Analyze the financial situation of Company XYZ.
(p) If the probabilistic concepts are applied to break-even analysis, how should the analyses in (o) be revised?

10. Use the ratio information listed in Table 2.5 of the text to estimate the partial ratio adjustment model for GM and interpret the related results.
11. ABC Company's financial records are as follows:

Quantity of goods sold = 10,000
Price per unit sold = $20
Variable cost per unit sold = $10
Total amount of fixed cost = $50,000
Corporate tax rate = 50%

(a) Calculate EAIT.
(b) What is the break-even quantity?
(c) What is the DOL?
(d) Should the ABC Company produce more for greater profits?

12. ABC Company's predictions for next year are as follows:

	Probability	**Quantity**	**Price ($)**	**Variable Cost/Unit ($)**	**Corporate Tax Rate**
State 1	0.3	1,000	10	5	0.5
State 2	0.4	2,000	20	10	0.5
State 3	0.3	3,000	30	15	0.5

In addition, we also know that the fixed cost is \$15,000. What is next year's expected EAIT?

13. Use an example to discuss four alternative depreciation methods.
14. XYX, Inc. currently produces one product that sells for \$330 per unit. The company's fixed costs are \$80,000 per year; variable costs are \$210 per unit. A salesman has offered to sell the company a new piece of equipment which will increase fixed costs to \$100,000. The salesman claims that the company's break-even number of units sold will not be altered if the company purchases the equipment and raises its price (assuming variable costs remain the same).

    (a) Find the company's current break-even level of units sold.
    (b) Find the company's new price if the equipment is purchased and prove that the break-even level has not changed.

15. Consider the following financial data of a corporation:

    Sales = \$500,000
    Quantity = 25,000
    Variable cost = \$300,000
    Fixed cost = \$50,000

    (a) Calculate the DOL at the above quantity of output.
    (b) Find the break-even quantity and sales levels.

16. On the basis of the following firm and industry norm ratios, identify the problem that exists for the firm:

Ratio	**Firm**	**Industry**
Total Asset Utilization	2.0	3.5
Average Collection Period (days)	45	46
Inventory-Turnover (times)	6	6
Fixed Asset Utilization	4.5	7.0

17. The financial ratios for Wallace, Inc., a manufacturer of consumer household products, are given below along with the industry norm:

	Firm			
Ratio	**1986**	**1987**	**1988**	**Industry**
Current Ratio	1.44	1.31	1.47	1.2
Quick Ratio	0.66	0.62	0.65	0.63
Debt to Assets	0.56	0.54	0.46	0.50
Debt to Equity	1.24	1.14	0.84	1.00
Times Interest Earned	2.75	5.57	7.08	5.00
Day's Sales in Receivable (Average Collection Period)	33	37	32	34
Inventory-Turnover	7.86	7.62	7.72	7.6
Fixed Asset Turnover	2.60	2.44	2.56	2.80
Total Asset Turnover	1.24	1.18	2.8	1.20
Profit Margin	0.02	0.05	0.05	0.05
ROA	0.02	0.06	0.07	0.06
ROE	0.06	0.12	0.12	0.13

Analyze Merck's ratios over the 3-year period for each of the following categories:

(a) Liquidity
(b) Asset utilization
(c) Financial leverage
(d) Profitability

18. Below are the Balance Sheet and the Statement of Earnings for Johnson and Johnson:

Balance Sheet for Johnson and Johnson on 12/30/12	
Assets	
Cash and Cash Equivalent ($)	$14,911
Marketable Securities	6,178

(Continued)

(*Continued*)

Account Receivable	11,309
Inventory	7,495
Deferred Taxes on Income	3,139
Prepaid Expenses and Other Receivable	3,084
Total Current Assets	$46,116
Marketable Securities — Non-current	—
PP&E, Net	16,097
Intangible Assets, Net	51,176
Deferred Taxes on Income	4,541
Other Assets	3,417
Total Assets	$121,347
Liabilities and Stockholder's Equity	
Loans and Notes Payable	$4,676
Account Payable	5,831
Accrued Liabilities	7,299
Accrued Rebates, Returns, and Promotion	2,969
Accrued Salaries, Wages, and Commissions	2,423
Taxes on Income	1,064
Total Current Liabilities	$24,262
Long-Term Debt	11,489
Deferred Tax Liability	3,136
Employee Related Obligations	9,082
Other Liabilities	8,552
Stockholder's Equity	
Preferred Stock–without Par Value	—
Common Stock — Par Value $1.00	3,120
Net Receivable from Employee Stock Plan	—
Accumulated Other Comprehensive Income	−5,810
Retained Earnings	85,992
Less: Common Stock Held in Treasury	18,476
Total Stockholder's Equity	$64,826
Total Liabilities and Stockholder's Equity	$121,347

(*Continued*)

(Continued)

Statement of Earnings for Johnson and Johnson for Year Ending 12/30/12	
Sales to Customers	$67,224
Cost of Products Sold	21,658
Gross Profit	45,566
Selling, Marketing, and Administrative expense	20,869
R&D Expense	7,665
In-process R&D	1,163
Interest income	−64
Interest Expense, net of	532
Other (income) expense, Net	1,626
Earnings before Provision for Taxes on Income	$13,775
Provision for Taxes on Income	3,261
Net Earnings	$10,853

(a) Calculate the following ratios for Johnson and Johnson.

		J&J	*Industry*
(1)	Current Ratio	1.9	3.40
(2)	Quick Ratio	1.34	2.43
(3)	Cash Ratio	0.87	
(4)	Net working-capital to total asset	0.18	
(5)	Debt-to-Asset	0.45	88.65
(6)	Debt-to-Equity	0.84	6.46
(7)	Equity Multiplier	1.87	4.41
(8)	Times Interest Paid	26.89	1.12
(9)	Log-term Debt Ratio	0.15	0.34
(10)	Cash Coverage Ratio	33.78	5.25
(11)	Day's Sales in Receivables (Average Collection Period)	61.40	12.00
(12)	Receivable Turnover	5.94	0.12
(13)	Day's Sales in Inventory	126.31	0.18
(14)	Inventory-Turnover	2.89	0.12

(Continued)

(*Continued*)

		J&J	*Industry*
(15)	Fixed Asset Turnover	1.00	
(16)	Total Asset Turnover	0.55	
(17)	Net Working-Capital Turnover	3.08	
(18)	Profit Margin	16.14%	
(19)	ROA	8.94%	
(20)	ROE	16.74%	
(21)	Price-earnings ratio	17.63	
(22)	Market-to-book ratio	1.58	
(23)	Earnings yield	5.67%	
(24)	Dividend yield	3.45%	
(25)	PEG Ratio	269.49	
(26)	Enterprise value — EBITDA ratio	12.96	

(b) Identify Johnson and Johnson's strengths and weaknesses relative to the industry norm.

19. **Please describe the procedure of using the indirect method to compile the cash flow statement based upon the 2011 financial data of JNJ. (Please refer to Appendix 2 of this Chapter to answer this question).**

Appendix 2.A: Simple and Multiple Regression

2.A.1. *Introduction*

Algebra, basic calculus, and linear regression topics are usually required for both undergraduate and graduate business students. This appendix reviews simple regression and multiple regression. This appendix enables the reader to use the available standard multiple regression and simultaneous equation statistic packages (i.e., North Carolina State University's SAS and University of Illinois SOUPAC) to estimate and interpret the empirical results of financial analysis and planning.

2.A.2. *Simple Regression*

If we want to explain the variation of the CR for JNJ Company in period t $[Y_t]$, given the auto industry's CR in period $t-1[X_{t-1}]$, we can choose either a linear or a log-linear model, as defined below:

$$Y_t = a + bX_{t-1} + \varepsilon_t, \tag{2A.1a}$$

$$\log Y_t = a' + b' \log X_{t-1} + \varepsilon'_t, \tag{2A.1b}$$

where ε_t and ε'_t are error terms representing the difference between actual CRs and the predicted CRs. The choice between Eqs. (2A.1a) and (2A.1b) depends on whether the related variables, Y_t and X_{t-1}, are normally or log-normally distributed.

In order to obtain the best linear model to predict Y_t, given X_{t-1}, we want to find the equation that minimizes the squared error terms. The error terms $(\hat{\varepsilon}_t)$ represent the difference between the actual and current ratio (Y_t) and the current ratio predicted by the estimated linear model $(\hat{Y}_t)$. The estimated current ratio can be defined as $Y = \hat{a} + \hat{b}X_{t-1}$. The theory and method of estimating a and b are one of the main issues of this appendix.

In Eq. (2A.1a), if the unconditional probability distribution of Y_t is normally distributed with mean $\overline{Y}$ and variance σ_Y^2, the conditional probability distribution of $Y_t, \tilde{Y}_t|X_{t-1}$ will be a normal distribution with mean $(a + b\overline{X}_{t-1})$ and variance σ_ε^2.

Applying the variance operator to both sides of Eq. (2A.1a) we have

$$\begin{aligned} Var[Y_t] &= Var[a + bX_{t-1} + \varepsilon_t] \\ &= Var[a] + Var[bX_{t-1}] + Var[\varepsilon_t] + 2\text{cov}[a, bX_{t-1}] \\ &\quad + 2\text{cov}[a, \varepsilon_t] + 2\text{cov}[bX_{t-1}, \varepsilon_t], \end{aligned} \tag{2A.2a}$$

$$Var\left[Y_t\right] = b^2 Var\left[X_{t-1}\right] + Var\left[\varepsilon_t\right]. \tag{2A.2b}$$

The conditions for obtaining Eq. (2A.2b) are

(i) Both a and b must be constants. Equation (2A.1) is a fixed coefficient model instead of a random coefficient model.
(ii) X_{t-1} must be uncorrelated with ε_t. This implies that there is no errors-in-variables problem inherent in the raw data associated with the independent variable.

Equation (2A.2b) implies that the total variance Y_t, Var$[Y_t]$, can be decomposed into two components: (1) explained variance, $b^2 Var[X_{t-1}]$ and (2) unexplained variance, $Var[\varepsilon_t]]$. If X_{t-1} has any explanatory power, then

$\text{Var}[Y_t]$ will be larger than $Var[\varepsilon_t]$. The degree of explanatory power X_{t-1} can be defined as

$$\begin{aligned} R^2 &= \frac{\text{Variation explained by the explanatory variable}}{\text{Total variation in the dependent variable}} \\ &= \frac{b^2 Var\left[X_{t-1}\right]}{Var\left[Y_t\right]}. \end{aligned} \tag{2A.3}$$

To obtain the best estimates of a and b, we want to find the equation that minimizes the error sum of squares (ESS) as defined below:

$$ESS = \sum_{t=1}^{n} \left[Y_t - \hat{Y}_t\right]^2 = \sum_{t=1}^{n} \left[Y_t - \hat{a} - \hat{b}X_{t-1}\right]^2. \tag{2A.4}$$

ESS evaluates the predicted relationship by summing the squares of the differences between actual and predicted values of the dependent variable, Y_t. In order to minimize the value of ESS, we must take the derivative of ESS with respect to $\hat{a}$ and $\hat{b}$ and set the results equal to zero, as shown in Eqs. (2A.5a) and (2A.5b):

$$\frac{\partial(ESS)}{\partial a} = -2\sum_{t=1}^{n} \left(Y_t - \hat{a} - \hat{b}X_{t-1}\right) = 0, \tag{2A.5a}$$

$$\frac{\partial(ESS)}{\partial b} = -2\sum_{t=1}^{n} X_{t-1} \left(Y_t - \hat{a} - \hat{b}X_{t-1}\right) = 0. \tag{2A.5b}$$

In order to jointly solve for estimates of the parameters a and b, Eqs. (2A.5a) and (2A.5b) are used to formulate a two-equation simultaneous system as follows:

$$\hat{a}n + \hat{b}\sum_{t=1}^{n} X_{t-1} = \sum_{t=1}^{n} Y_t, \tag{2A.6a}$$

$$\hat{a}\sum_{t=1}^{n} X_{t-1} + \hat{b}\sum_{t=1}^{n} X_{t-1}^2 = \sum_{t=1}^{n} X_{t-1}Y_t. \tag{2A.6b}$$

In these normal equations, two parameters are to be solved for from the given information: $\sum_{t=1}^{n} X_{t-1}$; $\sum_{t=1}^{n} Y_t$; $\sum_{t=1}^{n} X_{t-1}^2$ and $\sum_{t=1}^{n} X_{t-1}Y_t$. By

Cramer's rule (see also Chapter 3), we have

$$\hat{b} = \frac{\begin{vmatrix} n & \sum_{t=1}^{n} Y_t \\ \sum_{t=1}^{n} X_{t-1} & \sum_{t=1}^{n} X_{t-1}Y_t \end{vmatrix}}{\begin{vmatrix} n & \sum_{t=1}^{n} X_{t-1} \\ \sum_{t=1}^{n} X_{t-1} & \sum_{t=1}^{n} X_{t-1}^2 \end{vmatrix}} = \frac{n\left(\sum_{t=1}^{n} X_{t-1}Y_t\right) - \left(\sum_{t=1}^{n} X_{t-1} \sum_{t=1}^{n} Y_t\right)}{n\sum_{t=1}^{n} X_{t-1}^2 - \left(\sum_{t=1}^{n} X_{t-1}\right)^2}, \tag{2A.7a}$$

$$\hat{b} = \frac{Cov[X_{t-1}, Y_t]}{Var[X_{t-1}]}, \tag{2A.7b}$$

$$\begin{aligned}\hat{a} &= \frac{\begin{vmatrix} \sum Y & \sum X_{t-1} \\ \sum X_{t-1}Y_t & \sum X_{t-1}^2 \end{vmatrix}}{\begin{vmatrix} n & \sum X_{t-1} \\ \sum X_{t-1} & \sum X_{t-1}^2 \end{vmatrix}} \\ &= \frac{\left(\sum_{t=1}^{n} Y_t\right)\left(\sum_{t=1}^{n} X_{t-1}^2\right) - \left(\sum_{t=1}^{n} X_{t-1}\right)\left(\sum_{t=1}^{n} X_{t-1}Y_t\right)}{n\sum_{t=1}^{n} X_{t-1}^2 - \left(\sum_{t=1}^{n} X_{t-1}\right)^2} \\ &= \frac{\left(\sum_{t=1}^{n} Y_t/n\right)\left[n\left(\sum_{t=1}^{n} X_{t-1}^2\right) - \left(\sum_{t=1}^{n} X_{t-1}\right)^2\right] - \left(\sum_{t=1}^{n} X_{t-1}/n\right)\left[n\left(\sum_{t=1}^{n} X_{t-1}Y_t\right) - \left(\sum_{t=1}^{n} X_{t-1}\right)\left(\sum_{t=1}^{n} X_{t-1}\right)\right]}{n\sum_{t=1}^{n} X_{t-1}^2 - \left(\sum_{t=1}^{n} X_{t-1}\right)^2},\end{aligned} \tag{2A.8a}$$

$$\hat{a} = \overline{Y} - \overline{X}\hat{b}. \tag{2A.8b}$$

Equations (2A.7b) and (2A.8b) can be used to estimate the parameters of Eq. (2A.1a). For JNJ's CR and the related industry average data, we have:

$$\overline{X} = 1.730 \qquad Var[X_{t-1}] = 0.0481$$
$$\overline{Y} = 1.587 \qquad Var[Y_{t-1}] = 0.0967$$
$$Cov[Y_t, X_{t-1}] = 0.0402$$
$$b = 0.8358 \qquad \hat{a} = 0.1411$$

Before the estimated $\hat{a}$ and $\hat{b}$ are used, they should be tested to determine whether they are statistically different from zero or not. To perform the null hypothesis test, the variance of $\hat{b}$ and $\hat{a}$ should be derived.

Variance of $\hat{b}$

Equation (2A.7b) implies that

$$\hat{b} = \sum_{t=1}^{n} \frac{(x_{t-1}y_t)}{\sum_{t=1}^{n} x_{t-1}^2} = \sum_{t=1}^{n} W_{t-1}y_t, \tag{2A.7c}$$

where

$$x_{t-1} = X_{t-1} - \overline{X}$$
$$y_t = Y_t - \overline{Y}$$
$$W_{t-1} = \frac{x_{t-1}}{\sum_{t=1}^{n} x_{t-1}^2}$$

Substituting $y_t = bx_{t-1} + \varepsilon_t$ into Eq. (2A.7b), we have

$$\hat{b} = \sum_{t=1}^{n} W_{t-1}bx_{t-1} + \sum_{t=1}^{n} W_{t-1}\varepsilon_t. \tag{2A.7d}$$

Through the application of the variance operator on Eq. (2A.7d), we have

$$\begin{aligned} Var(\hat{b}) &= E(\hat{b} - b)^2 \\ &= E\left(\sum_{t=1}^{n} W_{t-1}bX_{t-1} + \sum_{t=1}^{n} W_{t-1}\varepsilon_t - b\right)^2 \end{aligned}$$

$$= E\left[\left(\sum_{t=1}^{n} W_{t-1}x_{t-1} - 1\right)b + \sum_{t=1}^{n} W_{t-1}\varepsilon_t\right]^2$$

$$= E\left(\sum_{t=1}^{n} W_{t-1}\varepsilon_t\right)^2, \quad \text{since } \sum_{t=1}^{n} W_{t-1}x_{t-1} = 1.$$

Therefore,

$$Var(\hat{b}) = E[(W_0\varepsilon_1)^2 + 2(W_0W_1\varepsilon_1\varepsilon_2) + (W_1\varepsilon_2)^2 + \cdots]. \tag{2A.9}$$

If ε_t is serially uncorrelated, that is, $E[\varepsilon_t, \varepsilon_{t-1}] = 0$, then Eq. (2A.9) implies that

$$Var(\hat{b}) = E(W_0\varepsilon_1)^2 + E(W_1\varepsilon_2)^2 + \cdots$$
$$= W_0^2E(\varepsilon_1^2) + W_1^2E(\varepsilon_2^2) + \cdots.$$

In generalized form,

$$Var(\hat{b}) = \sum_{t=1}^{n} W_{t-1}^2 E(\varepsilon_t^2)$$
$$= \sigma_\varepsilon^2 \sum_{t=1}^{n} W_{t-1}^2$$

But

$$\sum_{t=1}^{n} W_{t-1}^2 = \frac{\sum_{t=1}^{n} x_{t-1}^2}{\left(\sum_{t=1}^{n} x_{t-1}^2\right)^2} = \frac{1}{\sum_{t=1}^{n} x_{t-1}^2}.$$

Therefore,

$$Var(\hat{b}) = \frac{\sigma_\varepsilon^2}{\sum_{t=1}^{n} x_{t-1}^2}. \tag{2A.10}$$

Using a similar derivation, we can derive $Var(\hat{a})$ and $Cov(\hat{a}, \hat{b})$:

$$Var(\hat{a}) = \sigma_\varepsilon^2 \frac{\sum_{t=1}^{n} x_{t-1}^2}{n\sum_{t=1}^{n} x_{t-1}^2}. \tag{2A.11}$$

$$Cov(\hat{a}, \hat{b}) = -\sigma_\varepsilon^2 \frac{\overline{X}}{\sum_{t=1}^{n} x_{t-1}^2}. \qquad (2A.12)$$

Multiple Regression

If the current ratio for JNJ in period $t[Y_t]$ is a function of the pharmaceutical industry's current ratio in period $t-1[X_{1,t-1}]$ and the pharmaceutical industry's LR in period $t-1[X_{2,t-1}]$, the linear relationship can be defined as

$$Y_t = a + bX_{1,\,t-1} + cX_{2,\,t-1} + \varepsilon_t. \qquad (2A.13a)$$

The ESS can be defined as

$$ESS = \sum \hat{\varepsilon}_t^2 = \sum (Y_t - \hat{Y}_t)^2,$$

where

$$\hat{Y}_t = \hat{a}_t + \hat{b}X_{1,\,t-1} + \hat{c}X_{2,\,t-1}.$$

To obtain the least-squares estimates of the parameters a, b, and c, we can minimize ESS by calculating its partial derivatives with respect to these three unknown parameters, equating each to zero, and solving:

$$\frac{\partial ESS}{\partial a} = 0 \quad \text{or} \quad \sum Y_t = na + b\sum X_{1,\,t-1} + c\sum X_{2,\,t-1}, \qquad (2A.14a)$$

$$\frac{\partial ESS}{\partial b} = 0 \quad \text{or} \quad \sum X_{1,\,t-1}Y_t = a\sum X_{1,\,t-1} + b\sum X_{1,\,t-1}^2 + c\sum X_{1,\,t-1}X_{2,\,t-1}, \qquad (2A.14b)$$

$$\frac{\partial ESS}{\partial c} = 0 \quad \text{or} \quad \sum X_{2,\,t-1}Y_t = a\sum X_{2,\,t-1} + b\sum X_{1,\,t-1}X_{2,\,t-1} + c\sum X_{2,\,t-1}^2. \qquad (2A.14c)$$

Substituting $y_t = Y_t - \hat{Y}$, $x_{1,\,t-1} = X_{1,\,t-1} - \hat{X}$ and $x_{2,\,t-1} = X_{2,\,t-1} - \hat{X}$ for Y_t, $X_{1,\,t-1}$ and $X_{2,\,t-1}$, Eqs. (2A.14a), (2A.14b), and (2A.14c), respectively, can be rewritten as

$$0 = \text{na} + \text{b}(0) + \text{c}(0), \tag{2A.15a}$$

$$\sum x_{1,\,t-1}y_t = a(0) + b\sum x_{1,\,t-1}^2 + c\sum x_{1,\,t-1}x_{2,\,t-1}, \tag{2A.15b}$$

$$\sum x_{2,\,t-1}x_t = a(0) + b\sum x_{1,\,t-1}x_{2,\,t-1} + c\sum x_{2,\,t-1}^2. \tag{2A.15c}$$

The important conditions used to obtain Eq. (2A.15) are

(i) $\sum y_t = 0$,
(ii) $\sum x_{1,\,t-1} = 0$,
(iii) $\sum x_{2,\,t-1} = 0$.

Equation (2A.15a) implies that $a = 0$. Therefore, we can use Eqs. (2A.15b) and (2A.15c) to solve $\hat{b}$ and $\hat{c}$. Based upon Cramer's rule, we have

$$\hat{b} = \frac{\sum x_{1,\,t-1}y_t(\sum x_{2,\,t-1}^2) - \sum x_{2,\,t-1}y_t\sum x_{1,\,t-1}x_{2,\,t-1}}{(\sum x_{1,\,t-1}^2)(\sum x_{2,\,t-1}^2) - (\sum x_{1,\,t-1}x_{2,\,t-1})^2}, \tag{2A.16a}$$

$$\hat{c} = \frac{\sum x_{2,\,t-1}y_t(\sum x_{1,\,t-1}^2) - \sum x_{1,\,t-1}y_t\sum x_{1,\,t-1}x_{2,\,t-1}}{(\sum x_{1,\,t-1}^2)(\sum x_{2,\,t-1}^2) - (\sum x_{1,\,t-1}x_{2,\,t-1})^2}. \tag{2A.16b}$$

Substituting Eqs. (2A.16a) and (2A.16b) into Eq. (2A.14a), and dividing both sides of Eqs. (2A.14a) by n, we have

$$\hat{a} = \hat{Y} - \hat{b}\overline{X}_1 - \hat{c}\overline{X}_2. \tag{2A.17}$$

Using the concept of estimating standard errors of regression parameters as discussed earlier, standard errors of $\hat{a}$, $\hat{b}$ and $\hat{c}$ (S_a, S_b, and S_c, respectively) can be estimated. The empirical results for JNJ's ratio are listed in Eq. (2A.13b).

The multiple regression result associated with JNJ's dynamic CR adjustment process is

$$\begin{aligned} Y_t = {} & -0.2837 + 0.7564X_{1,\,t-1} + 0.2990X_{2,\,t-1} \\ & (0.4323) \qquad\quad (0.3288) \qquad\qquad (0.2240) \end{aligned}. \tag{2A.13b}$$

Figures below the regression coefficients are standard errors of estimated regression coefficients.

Substituting related estimates into (2A.17), we obtain

$$\begin{aligned} \hat{a} &= 1.7071(0.7564)(1.8448)\ (0.2990)(1.6904) \\ &= 0.2837. \end{aligned}$$

There exists a similar coefficient of determination (R^2) for the multiple regression.

The difference between $Y\frac{1}{2}t$ and its mean, $Y^{\mathrm{TM}\sim}$, can be broken down as

$$(Y_t - \overline{Y}_t) = (Y_t - \hat{Y}_t) + (\hat{Y}_t - \overline{Y}_t), \tag{2A.18}$$

where

$$\hat{Y}_t = \hat{a} + \hat{b}X_{1,\,t-1} + \hat{c}X_{2,\,t-1}. \tag{2A.19}$$

Note that $\hat{Y}$ is the estimated dependent variable and Y_t is the actual dependent variable; $Y_t - \hat{Y}$ is the residual term for the tth period, and $(\hat{Y}_t - \overline{Y})$ represents the difference between the overall mean and the estimated dependent variable in period t (conditional mean). Squaring both sides of Eq. (2A.18) and summing over all observations (1 to n), we obtain

$$\underset{\text{TSS}}{\sum(Y_t - \overline{Y}_t)^2} = \underset{\text{ESS}}{\sum(Y_t - \hat{Y}_t)^2} + \underset{\text{RSS}}{\sum(\hat{Y}_t - \overline{Y}_t)^2}, \tag{2A.20}$$

where

TSS = Total sum of squares;
ESS = Residual sum of squares; and
RSS = Regression sum of squares.

The R^2 can now be defined as

$$R^2 = \frac{\text{RSS}}{\text{TSS}} = \frac{\sum(\hat{Y}_t - \overline{Y}_t)^2}{\sum(Y_t - \overline{Y}_t)^2} = 1 - \frac{\sum \hat{\varepsilon}_t^2}{\sum(Y_t - \overline{Y}_t)^2}. \tag{2A.21}$$

Here R^2 measures the portion of variation in Y that is explained by multiple regression. The term R^2 is often informally interpreted as a measure of "goodness-of-fit" and used as a statistic for comparison of the validity of the regression results under alternative specifications of the independent variables of the model.

The difficulty with R^2 as a measure of "goodness-of-fit" is that R^2 pertains to the explained and unexplained variation in Y: therefore, it does not account for the number of degrees of freedom in the problem. Originally there are n degrees of freedom in a sample of n observations, but one degree of freedom is used up in calculating $\overline{Y}$; thus, leaving only $n - 1$ degrees of freedom for residuals $(Y - \overline{Y})$ to calculate $Var(Y_t)$. Similarly, k degrees of freedom are used up in calculating k regressors; thus, leaving only $n - k$

degrees of freedom for calculating $Var(\hat{\varepsilon}_t)$. To correct this problem, the corrected R^2 ($\overline{R}^2$) is defined as

$$R^2 = 1 - \frac{\sum \hat{\varepsilon}_t^2}{Var(Y_t)}, \tag{2A.22}$$

where

$$Var(\hat{\varepsilon}_t) = \sigma_\varepsilon^2 = \frac{\sum \hat{\varepsilon}_t^2}{n-k},$$

$$Var(Y_t) = \frac{\sum (Y_t - \overline{Y})^2}{n-1}.$$

and $k =$ the number of independent variables.

Even though the ESS will decrease (or remain the same) as new explanatory variables are added, the residual variance may not decrease. From Eqs. (2A.21) and (2A.22), the relationship between R^2 and $\overline{R}^2$ can be defined as

$$\overline{R}^2 = 1 - (1 - R^2)\frac{n-1}{n-k}. \tag{2A.23}$$

Some implications of Eq. (2A.23) are

(a) If $k = 1$, then $R^2 = \overline{R}^2$;
(b) If $k > 1$, then $R^2 > \overline{R}^2$;
(c) $\overline{R}^2$ can be negative.

The R^2 and $\overline{R}^2$ associated with Eq. (2A.13b) are 0.4901 and 0.4350, respectively. If the error, $\hat{\varepsilon}_t$, is normally distributed, t-tests can be applied to test the regression coefficient because $(\hat{a} - a)/S_a$, $(\hat{b} - b)/S_b$ and $(\hat{c} - c)/S_c$ are all t-distributions with $n - k$ degrees of freedom. The t-statistics associated with $\hat{a}$, $\hat{b}$, and $\hat{c}$ are -0.6565, 2.3005, and 1.3345, respectively. The estimated regression coefficients, the standard errors and t-statistics, and $\overline{R}^2$ are printed out by most regression programs.

In addition to the t-statistics, the regression program also prints F-statistics, R^2 and $\overline{R}^2$. The relationship between the F-statistic and R^2 can be defined as

$$F(k-1, n-k) = \frac{R^2}{1-R^2}\frac{n-k}{k-1},$$

where $F(k-1, n-k)$ represents F-statistic with $k-1$ and $n-k$ degrees of freedom.

Strictly speaking, the $F(k-1, n-k)$ F-statistic allows us to test the hypothesis that none of the explanatory variables help explain the variation of Y about its mean. In other words, the F-statistic is used to test the joint hypothesis, H (0): $a = b = c = 0$. The F-statistic for JNJ's current ratio is $F(2, 24) = 11.7689$. This statistic is significantly different from zero at the 95% confidence level. The multiple regression explored here will be used in the chapters on cost of capital and dividend policy.

Appendix 2.B: Using Indirect Method to Compile Cash Flow Statement

It is important to note that the preparation of the cash flows statement is different from the other three basic financial statements — it is not prepared from the adjusted trial balance sheet, since the statement requires information concerning changes in account balances over a period of time. The information used to prepare this statement comes from comparative balance sheets as shown in Table 2.1, the current income statement as shown in Table 2.2) and selected transaction data to determine how the company used cash during the period.

A review of the income statement reveals information that would be used in preparing the SCF. There are two important facts to be noted about the income statement: One is that the company does not report any depreciation on the statement; and Second is that interest revenue is included in operating income. In most cases, companies place interest received in the investing section but interest paid is shown in the operating section. Similarly, most firms place depreciation and gain or loss from sale of assets in the operating section but cash paid for operating assets is shown in the investing section. As shown below in the SCF, JNJ shows both interest received and interest paid as operating activities and shows all asset related transactions, including depreciation, in the investing section.

Table 2B.2 shows the statement of cash flows for JNJ as submitted to the SEC. Note that, like most other submitted statements, J&J also uses the **indirect method**.

Table 2B.1. Comparative Balance Sheets JNJ.

	2012	2011	Change
Cash/Equivalents	14,911,000.00	24,542,000.00	**−9,631,000.00**
Marketable Securities	6,178,000.00	7,719,000.00	−1,541,000.00
Accounts Receivables — Gross	11,309,000.00	10,581,000.00	728,000.00
Doubtful Account	−466,000.00	−361,000.00	−105,000.00
Raw Materials	1,416,000.00	1,206,000.00	−210,000.00
Goods in Process	2,262,000.00	1,637,000.00	625,000.00
Finished Goods	3,817,000.00	3,442,000.00	375,000.00
Deferred Taxes	3,139,000.00	2,556,000.00	583,000.00
Prepaid & Others	3,084,000.00	2,633,000.00	451,000.00
Total Current Assets	**46,116,000.00**	**54,316,000.00**	**-8,200,000.00**
Land Improvement	793,000.00	754,000.00	39,000.00
Buildings	10,046,000.00	9,389,000.00	657,000.00
Machinery & Equipment	21,075,000.00	19,182,000.00	1,893,000.00
Construction	2,740,000.00	2,504,000.00	236,000.00
Depreciation	−18,557,000.00	−17,090,000.00	−1,467,000.00
Goodwill	22,424,000.00	16,138,000.00	6,286,000.00
Intangible — Gross	18,755,000.00	8,716,000.00	10,039,000.00
Amortization of Intangible	−4,030,000.00	−3,432,000.00	−598,000.00
Deferred Taxes	4,541,000.00	6,540,000.00	−1999,000.00
Other Assets	3,417,000.00	3,773,000.00	−356,000.00
Total Assets	**121,347,000.00**	**113,644,000.00**	**7,703,000.00**
Loans and Notes Payable	4,676,000.00	6,658,000.00	−1,982,000.00
Accounts Payable	5,831,000.00	5,725,000.00	106,000.00
Accrued Liabilities	7,299,000.00	4,608,000.00	2691,000.00
Accrued Compensation	2,423,000.00	2,329,000.00	94,000.00
Accrued Rebates	2,969,000.00	2,637,000.00	332,000.00
Income Taxes	1,064,000.00	854,000.00	210,000.00
Total Current Liabilities	**24,262,000.00**	**22,811,000.00**	**1,451,000.00**
Long-term debt	11,489,000.00	12,969,000.00	−1,480,000.00
Total Long Term Debt	11,489,000.00	12,969,000.00	−1,480,000.00
Deferred Taxes	3,136,000.00	1,800,000.00	1,336,000.00
Employee Oblig.	9,082,000.00	8,353,000.00	729,000.00
Other Liabilities	8,552,000.00	10,631,000.00	−2,079,000.00
Total Liabilities	**56,521,000.00**	**56,564,000.00**	**−43,000.00**
Common Stock	3,120,000.00	3,120,000.00	0.00
Retained Earnings	85,992,000.00	81,251,000.00	4,741,000.00
Compreh. Income	−5,810,000.00	−5,632,000.00	178,000.00
Treasury Stock	−18,476,000.00	−21,659,000.00	−3,183,000.00
Total Equity	**64,826,000.00**	**57,080,000.00**	**7,746,000.00**
Total Liabilities & Shareholders' Equity	**121,347,000.00**	**113,644,000.00**	**7,703,000.00**

Table 2B.2. Statement of Cash Flows (JNJ).

Johnson & Johnson (JNJ) Company Statement of Cash Flow for the year ended December 30, 2012	
Net Income/Starting Line	**10,514,000.00**
Depreciation	3,666,000.00
Depreciation/Depletion	3,666,000.00
Deferred Taxes	−39,000.00
Other Non-Cash Items	754,000.00
Non-Cash Items	754,000.00
Accounts Receivable	−9,000.00
Inventories	−1,000.00
Other Assets	−2,172,000.00
Payable/Accrued	2,768,000.00
Other Liabilities	−2,555,000.00
Changes in Working-Capital	−2,059,000.00
Cash from Operating Activities	**15,396,000.00**
Purchase of Fixed Assets	−2,934,000.00
Capital Expenditures	−2,934,000.00
Acquisition of Business	−4,486,000.00
Sale of Fixed Assets	1,509,000.00
Sale/Maturity of Investment	14,797,000.00
Purchase of Investments	−13,434,000.00
Other Investing Cash Flow	38,000.00
Other Investing Cash Flow Items, Total	−1,576,000.00
Cash from Investing Activities	**−4,510,000.00**
Cash Dividends Paid — Common	−6,614,000.00
Total Cash Dividends Paid	−6,614,000.00
Repurchase/Retirement of Common	−12,919,000.00
Common Stock, Net	−12,919,000.00
Options Exercised	2,720,000.00
Issuance (Retirement) of Stock, Net	−10,199,000.00
Short-Term Debt Issued	3,268,000.00
Short-Term Debt Reduction	−6,175,000.00
Short-Term Debt, Net	−2,907,000.00
Long-Term Debt Issued	45,000.00
Long-Term Debt Reduction	−804,000.00
Long-Term Debt, Net	−759,000.00
Other*	−83,000.00
Issuance (Retirement) of Debt, Net	−3,749,000.00
Cash from Financing Activities	**−20,562,000.00**

(Continued)

Table 2B.2. (*Continued*)

Foreign Exchange Effects	45,000.00
Net Change in Cash	**−9,631,000.00**
Net Cash − Beginning Balance	24,542,000.00
Net Cash − Ending Balance	14,911,000.00
Cash Interest Paid	616,000.00
Cash Taxes Paid	2,507,000.00

*The net cash inflow or outflow from other financing activities. This element is used when there is not a more specific and appropriate element in the taxonomy.

2.B.1. *Cash Flow from Operating Activities*

In the above statement, the company started with the net income, as reported in the income statement, and adjusted it for all:

1. Non-cash revenues and expenses (For example, depreciation expense).
2. Increases (decreases) in the balances of all operating assets are subtracted (added): For example, when accounts receivable increase during the year, it implies that cash receipts were lower than revenues. JNJ's accounts receivable increased by $9,000 during the year. This amount will be deducted from the net income to arrive at the amount of cash from operations. Similarly, increase in inventories, or any other operating asset, represents an operating use of cash, even though it is not an expense. This will also be deducted from net income to arrive at the cash flow from operations.
3. Increases (decreases) in the balances of all operating liability accounts are added (subtracted). For example, when accounts payable increase during the year, it means the company paid less cash than the expenses incurred. JNJ's accounts payable increased by $2,768,000 during the year. This amount will be added back to net income to arrive at the amount of cash from operations. A similar adjustment is made for the increase in deferred taxes or any other expenses payable, which keeps cash in the business.

A correct procedure to arrive at the amount of net cash flow from operations is to measure change in each operating account on the balance sheet to determine whether any changes in balance sheet accounts caused an increase or decrease in cash. A few important points should be noted here:

1. Changes in operating accounts shown on JNJ's SCF do not equal the balance sheet changes. For example, the SCF shows that accounts receivables increased by $9,000. However, the balance sheet reports an increase of only $728,000. Similarly, accounts payable increase by $2,768,000 as per the SCF but the balance sheet shows an increase of $106,000 in accounts payable. It is not clear what accounts for these and other discrepancies in operating assets and liabilities. Perhaps the company has made some adjustments and aggregations, but they are not explained.
2. The SCF shows an increase of deferred taxes of $39,000. A careful look at the balance sheet reveals that deferred taxes are reported thrice: in current assets, in long-term assets and also in long-term liabilities. Moreover, the total of the three is not equal to the amount reported in the SCF.
3. JNJ reports an increase in almost all of its long-term assets in the balance sheet, (land, building, machinery and equipment, construction and goodwill all went up significantly) but the SCF provides only a single number of additions to PP&E of $2,934.000, which does not add up to all the increases in assets. Moreover, the SCF reports proceeds from sale of assets in the investing section, but which assets were sold and whether they were sold at a gain or a loss is not revealed. The company also reports significant transactions in investments and in short term debt instruments in the SCF, but the balance sheet does not even have a category named investments in its asset section. Moreover, the short-term debt does not match the short-term loans payable in the balance sheet. Why is this information not deemed important and why the cash paid for operating assets is not shown in the operating section are major concerns that FASB should address.

2.B.2. *Cash Flow from Investing Activities*

Capital expenditures for long-term assets such as plant, property and equipment, land and buildings are the primary component of investing cash flow. Capital expenditures may be reported net or gross of proceeds from the sale of these assets. However, trends in gross capital expenditures contain useful insight into management plans. The JNJ cash flow statement reports only a net figure for all plant property and equipment, without providing details about changes in their composition.

Other components of cash flow from investing activities include consequences of acquisitions, investments in affiliates and joint ventures. However, segregating operating assets and liabilities acquired in acquisitions may provide useful information about payments made in cash. The JNJ cash flow statement reports a capital expenditure of $2,934,000 for purchase of various fixed assets. Moreover, they report a cash outflow of $4,486,000 for acquisition of business and another cash outflow of $1,576,000 as "Other cash outflow". It is clear that the company engaged in significant acquisition activity during the year. Since most of the company's long-term assets went up during the year, it is impossible to figure out how much of the increase in assets is due to purchase of new assets and how much is due to acquisition of another business and its assets and liabilities. This is probably the reason why the changes in the balance sheet accounts do not correspond to changes in the cash flow statement.

Please note, the information from comparative balance sheets and the current income statement are not enough to compile the cash flow statement as indicated in Table 2B.2. In other words, we need to get information from either foot note or financial statement or information from JNJ's internal financial reports. Therefore, most accounting textbooks use hypothesized data to compile a cash flow statement in terms of indirect method.

References for Chapter 2

Bodie, Z, A Kane, and A Marcus (2011). *Investments*, 9th ed. New York: McGraw-Hill Book Company.

Brealy, RA, SC Myers, and F Allen (2013). *Principles of Corporate Finance*, 11th ed. New York: McGraw-Hill Book Company.

Brigham, EF and MC Ehrhardt (2007). *Financial Management-Theory and Practice*, 12th ed. Hinsdale, OH: South-Western College Pub.

Copeland, TE, JF Weston, and K Shastri (2004). *Financial Theory and Corporate Policy*, 4th ed. Reading, Massachusetts: Addison-Wesley Publishing Company.

Deakin, EB (1976). Distribution of financial accounting ratios. *The Accounting Review*, 51, 90–96.

Gentry, JA and CF Lee (1983). Measuring and interpreting time, firm and ledger affect. In *Financial Analysis and Planning: Theory and Application — A Book of Readings*, CF Lee (ed.), Boston: Addison-Wesley Publishing Company.

Hilliard, JE and RA Leitch (1975). Cost–Volume–Profit analysis under uncertainty: A log-normal approach. *The Accounting Review*, 51, 69–80.

Hong, H (1977). Inflation and market value of the firm: Theory and test. *Journal of Finance*, 32, 1031–1048.

Lee, CF and AC Lee (2013). *Encyclopedia of Finance*, 2nd ed. New York, NY: Springer.

Lee, CF and JK Zumwalt (1981). Associations between alternative accounting profitability measures and security returns. *Journal of Financial and Quantitative Analysis*, 16, 71–93.

Lev, B (1969). Industry averages as targets for financial ratios. *Journal of Accounting Research*, 290–299.

Manes, R (1966). A new dimension of break-even analysis. *Journal of Accounting Research*, 4, 87–100.

Reinhardt, UE (1973). Break-even analysis for lockheed's tri-star: An application. *Journal of Finance*, 28, 821–838.

Ross, S, RW Westerfield, and J Jaffe (2012). *Corporate Finance*, 10th ed., McGraw-Hill Education, New York.

Penman, SH (2010). Financial statement analysis and security valuation, 5th ed. McGraw-Hill/Irwin, New York.

Wei, S (1979). A general discussion model for cost–volume–profit analysis under uncertainty. *The Accounting Review*, 54, 687–706.

Yunker, JA and PJ Yunker (1982). Cost–Volume–Profit analysis under uncertainty: An integration of economic and accounting concepts. *Journal of Economics and Business*, 34, 21–37.

Chapter 3

Discriminant Analysis and Factor Analysis: Theory and Method

3.1. Introduction

Financial ratios are widely used in all financial analysis and planning. Banks use a firm's current and quick ratio to determine acceptability, for commercial loans; the leverage ratio is used as a proxy for a firm's capital measure in predicting bankruptcy and to analyze the impact of leverage on the market value of a firm. Furthermore, for financial planning and forecasting, firm managers use activity ratios, that is, the asset turnover ratio and the inventory-turnover ratio, to determine the total amount of assets required to sustain a level of activity. In financial analysis and planning determination, lenders or managers need to measure a customer's (either an individual's or a firm's) short-term or long-term financial position. The well-known statistical techniques of factor analysis and discriminant analysis can be used in such instances to identify important financial ratios and to construct an overall financial indicator, that is, a "financial z-score."

Although the measurement of financial z-scores is a compromise between theory and practice, z-scores have been used extensively by practitioners and academicians in credit analysis, financial distress determination, and bankruptcy prediction. Factor analysis has been used to determine important financial ratios and in testing other finance-related issues. Two-group discriminant analysis and k-group discriminant analysis have been applied to bond-rating analysis as well. Other multivariate analysis techniques gaining wide acceptance in both investment analysis and financial management are principal components and cluster analysis.

The theory and methodology of factor analysis and discriminant analysis are explored in this chapter, and applications of these two statistical methods will be discussed in the next chapter. In Section 3.2, the linear algebra needed for factor analysis, discriminant analysis, and portfolio analysis (which will be explored in Chapter 7) are reviewed in accordance with the basic concepts of algebra. In Section 3.3, the theory and methodology of two-group discriminant analysis will be explored in accordance with both the dummy-regression method and the analysis-of-variance (eigenvalue) method. Section 3.4 will discuss the theory and methodology of k-group discriminant analysis. In Section 3.5, the theory and the methodology of principal component and factor analysis are investigated. Finally, in Section 3.6, the results of this chapter are summarized.

3.2. Important Concepts of Linear Algebra

In performing financial analysis and planning, the most important concepts of linear algebra that are needed are: (i) linear combination and its distribution, (ii) operation of vectors and matrices, and (iii) the linear-equation system and its solution.

3.2.1. *Linear Combination and its Distribution*

If $x_1, x_2, \ldots, x_n$ are one set of variables, then a linear combination of these variables is:

$$Y = a_1x_1 + a_2x_2 + \cdots + a_nx_n. \tag{3.1}$$

In financial analysis, $x_1, x_2, \ldots, x_n$ can be used to represent amounts of i products ($i = 1, 2, \ldots, n$) to be purchased. The a_i coefficients ($i = 1, 2, \ldots, n$) can be used to represent the net profit of producing one unit of product i; Y can be used to represent the total profit of a firm. The variables of linear combination will be used as an objective function (the function to, be minimized or maximized) for (i) portfolio analysis, (ii) linear programming in performing capital rationing (Chapter 12), and (iii) financial analysis, planning, and forecasting (Chapters 21, 22, and 23). In both factor analysis and discriminant analysis, the variables used to obtain a linear combination are generally random instead of deterministic. Hence, the distribution of a linear combination is required for performing empirical analysis.

Linear discriminant analysis, which will be discussed in Sections 3.3 and 3.4, is a linear combination of a set of random variables.

In calculating the financial z-score, Eq. (3.1) can be rewritten as:

$$\tilde{z} = a_1\tilde{x}_1 + a_2\tilde{x}_2 + \cdots + a_m\tilde{x}_m, \tag{3.1$'$}$$

where the $\tilde{x}_i$'s $(i = 1, 2, \ldots, m)$ represent the related financial ratios; $\tilde{z}$ is the financial z-score. The financial ratio discussed in Chapter 2, which are used to compute the financial z-core, can be either normally or log-normally distributed. If the $\tilde{x}_i$'s are normally distributed, then Anderson (2003) and others show that i is normally distributed. If $\bar{x}_i$, σ_i^2 are the mean and the variance *for* $\tilde{x}_i$, respectively, and ρ_{ij} is the correlation coefficient between $\tilde{x}_i$ and $\tilde{x}_j$, then the mean and variance of $\tilde{z}$ can be defined as:

$$\bar{z} = \sum_{i=1}^{m} a_i \bar{x}_i, \tag{3.2a}$$

$$\sigma_{\tilde{z}}^2 = \sum_{i=1}^{m} a_i^2 \sigma_i^2 + 2\sum\sum_{i>j} a_i a_j \rho_{ij} \sigma_i \sigma_j, \tag{3.2b}$$

where the symbol $\sum\sum_{i>j}$ denotes summation over all possible pairs of i and j values in the range *from* 1 through m, with the restriction that i is at least one greater than j. If $i = 2$, then:

$$\sigma_z^2 = a_1^2\sigma_1^2 + a_2^2\sigma_2^2 + 2a_1a_2\rho_{12}\sigma_1\sigma_2 \quad (\rho_{12}\sigma_1\sigma_2 = \sigma_{12}). \tag{3.2b$'$}$$

If $i = 3$, then:

$$\begin{aligned} \sigma_z^2 =& a_1^2\sigma_1^2 + a_2^2\sigma_2^2 + a_3^2\sigma_3^2 + 2a_1a_2\rho_{12}\sigma_1\sigma_2 \\ &+ 2a_1a_3\rho_{32}\sigma_1\sigma_{32} + 2a_3a_2\rho_{23}\sigma_3\sigma_2. \end{aligned} \tag{3.2b$''$}$$

3.2.2. *Vectors, Matrices, and Their Operations*

In estimating financial z-scores, we need time-series ratio data in order to estimate the coefficients $a_1, a_2, \ldots, a_m$. Under this circumstance, the X_i's $(i = 1, 2, \ldots, m)$ are vectors. If the current ratio (X_l) and the leverage ratio (X_2) are the only two ratios to be used in estimating z, then time-series financial ratio data can be written in terms of vectors as

$$X_1 = \begin{bmatrix} X_{11} \\ X_{12} \\ \vdots \\ X_{1n} \end{bmatrix} \quad \text{and} \quad X_2 = \begin{bmatrix} X_{21} \\ X_{22} \\ \vdots \\ X_{2n} \end{bmatrix},$$

where X_{ij} represents the ratio i in time period j. Vector X_1 and vector X_2 can be used to formulate a matrix of the ratios used in computing the financial z-score:

$$X = \begin{bmatrix} X_{11} & X_{12} \\ X_{12} & X_{22} \\ \vdots & \vdots \\ X_{1n} & X_{n2} \end{bmatrix}.$$

A matrix is a rectangular array of numbers. Matrix X is an $n \times 2$ matrix because it has n rows and two columns.

To represent all observations of financial ratios for either factor or discriminant analysis, Matrix X can be generalized as

$$X = \begin{bmatrix} X_{11} & X_{21} & \cdots & X_{11} \\ X_{21} & X_{22} & \cdots & X_{1m} \\ \vdots & \vdots & \cdots & X_{2m} \\ X_{n1} & X_{12} & \cdots & X_{nm} \end{bmatrix}. \tag{3.3}$$

Since, X is now $n \times m$ matrix, the computer will generally use this type of matrix to store ratio information for performing related analyses.

In portfolio analysis (which will be discussed in Chapter 7), the variance of a portfolio can be written as Eq. (3.2b″). In vector and matrix notation, Eq. (3.2b″) can be written as

$$\sigma^2 = \underset{1\times 3}{\overset{A'}{[a_1 a_2 a_3]}} \underset{3\times 3}{\overset{B}{\begin{bmatrix} \sigma_1^2 & \sigma_{12} & \sigma_{13} \\ \sigma_{21} & \sigma_2^2 & \sigma_{23} \\ \sigma_{31} & \sigma_{32} & \sigma_3^2 \end{bmatrix}}} \underset{3\times 1}{\overset{A}{\begin{bmatrix} a_1 \\ a_2 \\ a_3 \end{bmatrix}}}, \tag{3.2b‴}$$

where B is a 3×3 covariance matrix, σ_{ij} represents the covariance between x_i and x_j.

In Eq. (3.2b‴), A is a 3×1 coefficient vector and A' is the transposition of A. A *transpose* of a matrix A is defined to be a matrix obtained by interchanging the corresponding rows and columns *of* A. That is, first with first, second with second, and so on. Here we have only one row and three columns, so taking the transpose of A is a fairly simple operation. For example, if

$$B = \begin{bmatrix} 3 \\ 5 \\ 6 \end{bmatrix},$$

then B′ = (3, 5, 6). Similarly, if

$$A = \begin{bmatrix} a_1 \\ a_2 \\ a_3 \end{bmatrix},$$

then A′ = $(a_1,\ a_2,\ a_3)$;

The multiplicative rule of matrices and vectors is used to show that Eq. (3.2b‴) is indeed equal to Eq. (3.2b″). The rule for matrix multiplication requires "row–column multiplication".

In order for any two matrices to be multiplied together, the number of columns in one must be equal to the number of rows in another. For example:

$$\underset{(1\times3)}{A = [2 \quad 1 \quad 0]}, \quad B = \underset{(3\times2)}{\begin{bmatrix} 2 & 0 \\ 0 & 3 \\ -1 & 0 \end{bmatrix}},$$

These two matrices can be multiplied together. An element in the ith row and j^{th} column of the product AB is obtained by multiplying the ith row of A by the jth column of B. Therefore:

$$AB = [2 \quad 1 \quad 0] \begin{bmatrix} 2 & 0 \\ 0 & 3 \\ -1 & 0 \end{bmatrix} = [4 \quad 3].$$

We obtained the first element of AB from $(2 \times 2) + (1 \times 0) + (-1 \times 0) = 4$. To see how this is done for Eq. (3.2b‴),

Step 1: multiply A' by B; we then have

$$C = \big[(a_1\sigma_1^2 + a_2\sigma_{21} + a_3\sigma_{31}),\ (a_1\sigma_{12} + a_2\sigma_2^2 + a_3\sigma_{32}),$$
$$(a_1\sigma_{31} + a_2\sigma_{23} + a_3\sigma_3^2)\big],$$

Step 2: Multiply C by A, and we get:

$$\sigma^2 = a_1(a_1\sigma_1^2 + a_2\sigma_{21} + a_3\sigma_{31}) + a_2(a_1\sigma_{12} + a_2\sigma_2^2 + a_3\sigma_{32})$$
$$+ a_3(a_1\sigma_{31} + a_2\sigma_{23} + a_3\sigma_3^2)$$
$$= a_1^2\sigma_1^2 + a_2^2\sigma_2^2 + a_3^2\sigma_3^2 + 2(a_1a_2\sigma_{12} + a_1a_3\sigma_{13} + a_2a_3\sigma_{23}),$$

3.2.3. *Linear-Equation System and its Solution*

A general linear-equation system can be defined as

$$\begin{aligned} a_{11}X_1 + \cdots + a_{1m}X_m &= b_1 \\ &\vdots \\ a_{n1}X_1 + \cdots + a_{nm}X_m &= b_n. \end{aligned} \tag{3.4}$$

In matrix formulation, Eq. (3.4) can be written as $AX = b$, or

$$\begin{bmatrix} a_{11} & \cdots & a_{1m} \\ \vdots & & \vdots \\ a_{n1} & \cdots & a_{nm} \end{bmatrix} \begin{bmatrix} X_1 \\ \vdots \\ X_m \end{bmatrix} = \begin{bmatrix} b_1 \\ \vdots \\ b_n \end{bmatrix}.$$

In general, there are four alternative methods to solve an equation system. These methods are (i) Substitution Methods, (ii) Cramer's Rule, (iii) Matrix Method, and (iv) Excel Matrix Inversion and Multiplication. For details please refer to Appendix 3.A.

The solution of Eq. (3.4) can be obtained either by the derivation of the inversion of A or by using Cramer's rule.

In order to take the inverse of a matrix, the matrix must be a non-singular square matrix. That is, the number of rows must equal the number of columns. Then the following condition must be satisfied:

$$A^{-1}A = I, \quad \text{where } I \text{ is the identity matrix.}$$

An identity matrix is a matrix such that:

$$I = \begin{bmatrix} 1 & 0 & \cdots & 0 \\ 0 & 1 & & 0 \\ \vdots & & & \vdots \\ 0 & & \cdots & 1 \end{bmatrix}.$$

If the inversion of coefficient matrix A is used, then, the solution of X can be defined as

$$X = A^{-1}b, \tag{3.5}$$

A^{-1} can generally be obtained by using a computer program. Alternatively, Cramer's rule can be used to obtain the solution as defined in Eq. (3.6):

$$X_i = \frac{\left|\hat{A}_i\right|}{|A|}, \tag{3.6}$$

where $\hat{A}_i$ is the matrix obtained from A by replacing the ith column with the constant vector. Both $|\hat{A}_i|$ and $|A|$ represent the determinants. A determinant of a matrix is the value of a matrix. An example is:

$$A = \begin{bmatrix} a_{11} & a_{12} \\ a_{21} & a_{22} \end{bmatrix}, \quad |A| = a_{11}a_{22} - a_{12}a_{21}.$$

If both $\hat{A}_i$ and A are square matrices, then the determinants of $\hat{A}_i$ and A are unique numbers associated with these matrices. Numerically, if

$$A = \begin{bmatrix} 2 & 8 \\ 7 & 6 \end{bmatrix},$$

then $|A| = (2)(6) - (7)(8) = -44$.

The application using Cramer's rule to estimate simple regression coefficients can be found in Appendix 3.B of Chapter 3. This technique can also be used to estimate optimal portfolio weights.

Equation (3.4) is a general equation system. If all elements of $(b_1 \ldots b_n)$ are zero, then it is a homogeneous equation system. A special case of homogeneous equation systems can be defined as

$$(A - \lambda I)X = 0, \tag{3.7}$$

where A and X are identical to those defined in Eq. (3.4). A is an unknown scalar quantity and I is an $n \times m$ matrix with all unity elements in the diagonal elements. There is a trivial solution ($X = 0$) and a non-trivial solution ($(A - \lambda I)X = \hat{0}$) for this set of homogeneous equations.

Tatsuoka (1988), Moore (1968), Anton (2004), and others show that the condition of Eq. (3.7) poses a non-trivial solution that is

$$|A - \lambda I| = 0, \tag{3.8}$$

which is called the *characteristic* equation of Matrix A.

Conceptually, the existence of this characteristic equation can be justified as follows:

If $|A - \lambda I| \neq 0$, then $A - \lambda I$ is not a singular matrix, and hence it possesses an inverse; then pre-multiplying both sides of Eq. (3.7) by $(A - \lambda I)^{-1}$ will yield $X = (A - \lambda I)^{-1}\, 0 = 0$; that is, the trivial solution is the only solution of the equation. We therefore conclude that in order for a set of homogeneous equations to possess a non-trivial solution, there must exist a characteristic solution as defined in Eq. (3.8).

To obtain the non-trivial solution, we should first find the unknown scalar quantity A. The scalar A is called an eigenvalue of A, and X is said to be an eigenvector corresponding to A. One of the meanings of the word "eigen" in German is "proper"; eigenvalues are also called proper values, characteristic values; or latent roots, by some writers.

A numerical example is now used to show how eigenvalue can be calculated. The eigenvalue is the characteristic root associated with $|A - \lambda I| = 0$. To find the eigenvalue of the matrix

$$A = \begin{bmatrix} 3 & 2 & 4 \\ 2 & 0 & 2 \\ 4 & 2 & 3 \end{bmatrix},$$

we note that the characteristic equation of A is :

$$\begin{bmatrix} 3-\lambda & 2 & 4 \\ 2 & -\lambda & 2 \\ 4 & 2 & 3-\lambda \end{bmatrix} = 0.$$

This determinantal equation can be easily reduced to $(1 + \lambda)^2 = 0$ or $(\lambda - 8) = 0$. This implies that there are three roots for A: $\lambda_1 = -1$, $\lambda_2 = -1$, and $\lambda_3 = 8$. This concept and this method of eigenvalues and the eigenvector are useful in understanding discriminant analysis and principal-components analysis.

As an example, we will show how the eigenvector associated with $\lambda_3 = 8$ can be calculated: (a) To find A – 8I:

$$A - 8I = \begin{bmatrix} 3-\lambda & 2 & 4 \\ 2 & -\lambda & 2 \\ 4 & 2 & 3-\lambda \end{bmatrix}.$$

(b) To find the adjoint of the above matrix:

(i) Calculate the cofactor of A – 8I:

$$\text{Cofactor of:} \quad A - 8I = \begin{bmatrix} \begin{matrix} 1+1 \\ (-1)(36) \end{matrix} & \begin{matrix} 1+2 \\ (-1)(-18) \end{matrix} & \begin{matrix} 1+3 \\ (-1)(36) \end{matrix} \\ \begin{matrix} 2+1 \\ (-1)(-18) \end{matrix} & \begin{matrix} 2+2 \\ (-1)(9) \end{matrix} & \begin{matrix} 2+3 \\ (-1)(-18) \end{matrix} \\ \begin{matrix} 3+1 \\ (-1)(36) \end{matrix} & \begin{matrix} 3+2 \\ (-1)(-18) \end{matrix} & \begin{matrix} 3+3 \\ (-1)(36) \end{matrix} \end{bmatrix}.$$

$$= \begin{bmatrix} 36 & 18 & 36 \\ 18 & 9 & 18 \\ 36 & 18 & 36 \end{bmatrix}.$$

(ii) Adjoint of $A - 8I = \begin{bmatrix} 36 & 18 & 36 \\ 18 & 9 & 18 \\ 36 & 18 & 36 \end{bmatrix}$.

Note that all these columns are proportional, which offers a partial check on the calculation. (In this case, the first and third columns are identical, but this will not be true in general.) Before carrying out the last step, the reader should verify that:

$$(A - 8I)\begin{bmatrix} 36 \\ 18 \\ 36 \end{bmatrix} = 0 \quad \text{or that } A\begin{bmatrix} 36 \\ 18 \\ 36 \end{bmatrix} = 8I\begin{bmatrix} 36 \\ 18 \\ 36 \end{bmatrix}.$$

The eigenvector is one vector solution of x corresponding to the eigenvalue 8.

(c) In order to have x satisfy the limit norm condition, $x'x = 1$, we divided each element of

$$\begin{bmatrix} 36 \\ 18 \\ 36 \end{bmatrix},$$

by $\sqrt{36^2 + 18^2 + 36^2} = 54$, and obtain:

$$x' = \left(\frac{36}{54} \quad \frac{18}{54} \quad \frac{36}{54}\right) = [0.6667 \quad 0.3333 \quad 0.6667].$$

This example has shown how the solution of a special kind of homogeneous-equation system [as indicated in Eq. (3.7)] can be solved. This kind of equation system differs in two respects from the regular equation system of Eq. (3.4). First; the vector of constraint on the right-hand side is a null vector. Second, the matrix of coefficients on the left-hand side, $A - \lambda I$, involves an unknown scalar quantity A. Therefore, in order to solve x, we should first solve λ by using the characteristic equation of matrix A' as indicated in Eq. (3.8).

Alternatively, x can be solved by the equation system as:

$$\begin{aligned} -5x_1 + 2x_2 + 4x_3 &= 0, \\ 2x_1 - 8x_2 + 2x_3 &= 0, \\ 4x_1 + 2x_2 - 5x_3 &= 0. \end{aligned}$$

The solution of this equation system is: $2x_1 = x_2 = 2x_3$. Hence, (2d, d, 2d) is the eigenvector associated with the eigenvalue $\lambda = 8$ (where d is a constant). This implies that one element in the eigenvector is arbitrary. We may normalize the vector by setting its length at unity, $x_1^2 + x_2^2 + x_3^2 = 1$, and obtain the normalized solution as indicated above.

The concepts and methods of solving for eigenvalue and eigenvectors discussed in this section are important to understand both discriminant analysis and factor analysis, which will be discussed in later sections of this chapter.

Now the inversion of matrix A is discussed, by the definition:

$$A^{-1} = \frac{1}{|A|} \text{ (Adjoint A);} \tag{3.9}$$

by using the previous example, we have:

$$|A| = \begin{vmatrix} 3 & 2 & 4 \\ 2 & 0 & 2 \\ 4 & 2 & 3 \end{vmatrix} = (0 + 16 + 16) - (0 + 12 + 12) = 8.$$

$$\text{Cofactor of A} = \begin{bmatrix} (-1)^{1+1}(-4) & (-1)^{1+2}(-2) & (-1)^{1+3}(4) \\ (-1)^{2+1}(-2) & (-1)^{2+2}(-7) & (-1)^{2+3}(-2) \\ (-1)^{3+1}(4) & (-1)^{3+2}(-4) & (-1)^{3+3}(-4) \end{bmatrix}$$

$$= \begin{bmatrix} -4 & 2 & 4 \\ 2 & -7 & 2 \\ 4 & 4 & -4 \end{bmatrix}.$$

$$\text{Adjoint of A} = \begin{bmatrix} -4 & 2 & 4 \\ 2 & -7 & 4 \\ 4 & 2 & -4 \end{bmatrix}.$$

And therefore,

$$A^{-1} = \begin{bmatrix} -\frac{1}{2} & \frac{1}{4} & \frac{1}{2} \\ \frac{1}{4} & -\frac{7}{8} & \frac{1}{2} \\ \frac{1}{2} & \frac{1}{4} & -\frac{1}{2} \end{bmatrix}.$$

3.3. Two-Group Discriminant Analysis

Following Eq. (3.1), a linear two-group discriminant function can be defined as

$$Y_i = a_1 x_{1i} + a_2 x_{2i} + \cdots + a_m x_{mi}, \tag{3.10}$$

where Y_i is a binary variable and is used to indicate two alternative options, and $x_{1i}, x_{2i}, \ldots, x_{mi}$ are explanatory variables. In credit analysis, Y_i can be used to represent good and bad accounts in corporate bankruptcy analysis, to represent bankrupt and non-bankrupt firms and in banking analysis, to present the problem and non-problem banks. Two different methods can be used to estimate the coefficients of Eq. (3.10). These two methods are the dummy regression method or the eigenvalue method.

It is important for readers to understand the relationship between the logic of two-group discriminant analysis and the multiple-regression technique to estimate related discriminant-function parameters.

The purposes of discriminant analysis are (1) to test for mean group differences and to describe the overlaps among the groups and (2) to construct a classification scheme based upon a set of m variables in order to assign previously unclassified observations to appropriate groups. For example, in a study of corporate bankruptcy, Altman (1968) used data from a sample of failed firms and a sample of existing firms to determine whether, on average, bankrupt firms had significantly different financial ratios prior to failure than did solvent firms. When his, statistical tests indicated significant differences between the two groups, Altman then developed a classification rule that used financial ratios to predict potential corporate failures.

Following Tatsuoka (1988), Johnston and Dinardo (1996), and Eisenbeis and Avery (1972), the basic equation of discriminant analysis as derived in Appendix A can be defined as

$$(\mathrm{B} - \mathrm{EC})\mathrm{A} = 0,\ D' = [\overline{X}_{1,1} - \overline{X}_{1,2} \ldots, \overline{X}_{m,1} - \overline{X}_{m,2}], \tag{3.11}$$

where

$B = DD'$, between-group variance;
C = Within-group variance;
A = Coefficient vector representing the coefficients of Eq. (3.8);
E = Ratio of the weighted between-group variance to the pooled within variance.

Table 3.1. Roster of liquidity and leverage ratios. For two groups with two predictors and a "dummy" criterion variable Y.

Group 1 [$N_1 = 6$]			Group 2 [$N_2 = 8$]		
x_{1i}	x_{2i}	Y_i	x_{1i}	x_{2i}	Y_i
2.0	0.50	1	1.8	0.35	0
1.8	0.48	1	1.9	0.34	0
2.3	0.49	1	1.7	0.42	0
3.1	0.41	1	1.5	0.49	0
1.9	0.43	1	2.2	0.36	0
2.5	0.44	1	2.8	0.38	0
			1.6	0.55	0
			1.4	0.56	0
$\sum x_{1i} = 13.6$	$\sum x_{2i} = 2.75$		$\sum x_{1i} = 14.9$	$\sum x_{2i} = 3.45$	
$\sum x_{1i}^2 = 32$	$\sum x_{2i}^2 = 1.2671$		$\sum x_{1i}^2 = 29.19$	$\sum x_{2i}^2 = 1.5447$	
$\sum x_{1i}x_{2i} = 6.179$			$\sum x_{1i}x_{2i} = 6.245$		

Since Eq. (3.11) is similar to Eq. (3.7), the characteristic equation associated with Eq. (3.10) is

$$(C^{-1}B - EI)A = 0. \tag{3.12}$$

In order to use the linear discriminant function (LDF) for empirical analysis, one must estimate the coefficients of Eq. (3.11). To illustrate the computation of two-group discriminant functions as a multiple regression equation and the eigenvalue method of discriminant analysis, we shall use a numerical example as indicated in Table 3.1. Table 3.1 shows the number scores of two groups on two predictor variables, X_1 [liquidity ratio], and X_2 [leverage ratio], and on a dummy variable Y. All members of group I are assigned $Y = 1$ and all members of group 2 are given $Y = 0$.

There are two alternative methods, the dummy regression and the eigenvalue method, to estimate the discriminant function.

(i) Dummy Regression Method:

If $m = 2$, then Eq. (3.10) can be written as

$$Y_i = a_1X_{1i} + a_2X_{2i}. \tag{3.13}$$

This equation can be rewritten as

$$y_i = a_1x_{1i} + a_2x_{2i}, \tag{3.14}$$

where $y_i = Y_i - \overline{Y}$, $x_{1i} = a_1X_{1i} + a_2\overline{X}_1$ and $x_{2i} = X_{2i} - \overline{X}_2$.

Following Appendix A of Chapter 2, the equation system used to solve a_1 and a_2 can be defined as:

$$Var(x_{1i})a_1 + Cov(x_{1i}, x_{2i})a_2 = Cov(x_{1i}, y_i), \tag{3.15a}$$

$$Cov(x_{1i}, x_{2i})a_1 + Var(x_{2i})a_2 = Cov(x_{2i}, y_i). \tag{3.15b}$$

Following the data listed in Table 3.1, $Var(x_{1i})$, $Var(x_{2i})$, $Cov(x_{1i}, x_{2i})$, $Cov(x_{1i}, y_i)$, and $Cov(x_{2i}, y_i)$ are calculated as follows:

$$\begin{aligned}
Var(x_{1i}) &= \frac{\sum X_{1i}^2}{n} - \left(\frac{\sum X_{1i}}{n}\right)^2 \\
&= \frac{32 + 29.19}{n} - \left(\frac{13.6 + 14.9}{n}\right)^2 \\
&= \frac{61.19}{14} - \left(\frac{28.5}{14}\right)^2 \\
&= 4.3707 - 4.144 = 0.2267; \\
Var(x_{2i}) &= \frac{\sum X_{2i}^2}{n} - \left(\frac{\sum X_{2i}}{n}\right)^2 \\
&= \frac{1.2671 + 1.5447}{14} - \left(\frac{2.75 + 3.45}{14}\right)^2 \\
&= \frac{2.8122}{14} - \left(\frac{62}{14}\right)^2 \\
&= 02008 - 0196 = 0.0048; \\
Cov(x_{1i}, x_{2i}) &= \frac{12.424}{14} - (2.0357)(0.4428) \\
&= 0.8874 - 0.9014 \\
&= -0.014; \\
Cov(x_{1i}, y_i) &= \frac{\sum X_{1i}Y_i}{n} - (\overline{X}_1)(\overline{Y}) \\
&\quad \frac{13.6}{14} - (2.0357)(0.4285) \\
&= 0.9714 - 0.8722 \\
&= 0.0992;
\end{aligned}$$

$$Cov(x_{2i}, y_i) = \frac{\sum X_{2i} Y_i}{n} - (\overline{X}_2)(\overline{Y})$$

$$\frac{2.75}{14} - (0.4428)(0.4288)$$

$$= 0.1964 - 0.1897$$
$$= 0.00668.$$

Following Cramer's rule, a_1 and a_2 can be estimated as:

$$a_1 = \frac{\begin{vmatrix} 0.0992 & -0.0140 \\ 0.0066 & 0.0048 \end{vmatrix}}{\begin{vmatrix} 0.2267 & -0.0140 \\ -0.0140 & 0.0048 \end{vmatrix}}$$

$$= \frac{0.00047616 + 0.0000924}{0.0010886 - 0.000196} = \frac{0.00056886}{0.0008926} = 0.63697;$$

$$a_2 = \frac{\begin{vmatrix} 0.2267 & 0.00992 \\ -0.0140 & 0.0066 \end{vmatrix}}{\begin{vmatrix} 0.2267 & -0.0140 \\ -0.0140 & 0.0048 \end{vmatrix}} = \frac{0.00149 + 0.00138}{0.00108 - 0.00019} = \frac{0.00288}{0.00089} = 3.2359;$$

Normalizing the regression coefficient by dividing a_2 into a_1, we obtain

$$\begin{bmatrix} \frac{a_1}{a_2} \\ 1 \end{bmatrix} = \begin{bmatrix} \frac{0.63697}{3.2359} \\ 1 \end{bmatrix} = \begin{bmatrix} 0.1968 \\ 1 \end{bmatrix}$$

(ii) Eigenvalue Method:

For the eigenvalue method, the elements of C and B can be calculated as:

$$C_{11} = 32 - \frac{(13.6)^2}{6} + 29.19 - \frac{(14.9)^2}{8} = 2.612;$$

$$C_{22} = 1.2671 - \frac{(2.75)^2}{6} + 1.5447 - \frac{(3.45)^2}{8} = 0.0636;$$

$$C_{12} = 6.179 - \frac{(13.6)(2.75)}{6} + 6.245 - \frac{(14.9)(3.45)}{8} = -0.2350;$$

$$B_{11} = 6\left[\frac{13.6}{6} - 2.0357\right]^2 + 8\left[\frac{14.9}{8} - 2.0357\right]^2 = 0.5601;$$

$$B_{22} = 6\left[\frac{2.75}{6} - 0.4428\right]^2 + 8\left[\frac{3.45}{8} - 0.4428\right]^2 = 0.0025;$$

$$B_{12} = 6\left(\frac{13.6}{6} - 2.0357\right)\left(\frac{2.75}{6} - 0.4428\right)$$
$$+8\left(\frac{14.9}{8} - 2.0357\right)\left(\frac{3.45}{8} - 0.4428\right) = 0.03753;$$

Following the above-mentioned information, the matrices C and B can be written as:

$$C = \begin{bmatrix} 2.612 & -0.2350 \\ -0.2350 & 0.0636 \end{bmatrix} \quad \text{and} \quad B = \begin{bmatrix} 0.5601 & 0.03753 \\ 0.03753 & 0.0025 \end{bmatrix}.$$

Based upon the matrix inversion and multiplication rules, we can obtain:

$$C^{-1}B = \begin{bmatrix} 0.4007 & 0.0268 \\ 0.0268 & 0.1384 \end{bmatrix}$$

and the matrix to be substituted in Eq. (3.12). The characteristic equation, $\left|C^{-1}B - EI\right| = 0$, is found to be $E^2 - 0.5391E = 0$, whose single non-zero root is $E_1 = 0.5391$. The adjoint of $C^{-1}B - E_1I$ is:

$$\text{Adjoint of } C^{-1}B - E_1I = \begin{bmatrix} -0.4007 & -0.0268 \\ -0.2071 & -0.1384 \end{bmatrix}.$$

To find the adjoint of a matrix, take the transpose of the cofactor. The cofactor of $C^{-1}B - E_1I$ is:

$$\text{Cofactor of} \quad C^{-1}B - E_1I = \begin{bmatrix} \overset{1+1}{(-1)}(-0.4007) & \overset{1+2}{(-1)}(2.071) \\ \overset{2+1}{(-1)}(0.0268) & \overset{2+2}{(-1)}(-0.1384) \end{bmatrix}$$
$$= \begin{bmatrix} -0.4007 & -2.071 \\ -0.0268 & -0.1384 \end{bmatrix}$$

and the transpose is:

$$\begin{bmatrix} -0.4007 & -0.0268 \\ -2.071 & -0.1384 \end{bmatrix};$$

hence the eigenvector of $C^{-1}B$, with larger elements set equal to unity, is:

$$A_1 = \begin{bmatrix} -0.4007 - 2.071 \\ 1 \end{bmatrix} = \begin{bmatrix} 0.1935 \\ 1 \end{bmatrix},$$

when the vector of regression weights obtained earlier is similarly rescaled, we find:

$$a = \begin{bmatrix} 0.63697065/3.2359 \\ 1 \end{bmatrix} = \begin{bmatrix} 0.1968 \\ 1 \end{bmatrix}.$$

This agrees, within rounding errors, with the A_1 just obtained by the general method of discriminant analysis mentioned above.

Alternatively, the non-zero root, $E_1 = 0.5391$, can be substituted into Eq. (3.11), yielding:

$$\begin{bmatrix} -0.4007 - 0.5391 & -0.0268 \\ -2.071 & -0.1384 - 0.5391 \end{bmatrix} \begin{bmatrix} a_1 \\ a_2 \end{bmatrix} = 0. \tag{3.16}$$

Equation (3.12) implies that:

$$-0.1384\mathrm{a}_1 + 0.0268\mathrm{a}_2 = 0,$$

$$2.071\mathrm{a}_1 - 0.4007\mathrm{a}_2 = 0;$$

that is:

$$2.071\mathrm{a}_1 - 0.4007\mathrm{a}_2 = 0$$

In this case, one element in the characteristic (eigen) vector is arbitrary. We may normalize the vector by setting its length at unity, that is, by making $\mathrm{a}_1^2 + \mathrm{a}_2^2 = 1$. When this is combined with the fact that $\mathrm{a}_1 = 0.1936\mathrm{a}_2$, it gives these results: at $= 0.1901$ and $\mathrm{a}_2 = 0.9819$. From these figures, we have:

$$a = \begin{bmatrix} 0.1907/0.9818 \\ 1 \end{bmatrix} = \begin{bmatrix} 0.1935 \\ 1 \end{bmatrix}.$$

This result is identical to the result obtained by solving the eigenvector.

3.4. *k*-Group Discriminant Analysis

The two-group discriminant analysis theory that we have discussed can be readily generalized to the k-group case. Assume there are k samples $(\mathrm{G} = 1, 2, \ldots, k)$ of size N. The linear discrimination function is similar to that defined in Eq. (3.10), but we now have k groups instead of two. The k-group discriminant function can be defined as:

$$Y_j = a_{j1}X_1 + a_{j2}X_2 + \cdots + a_{jm}X_m \quad (j = 1, 2, \ldots \mathrm{k}). \tag{3.17}$$

The k-group analogy to the two-group case of maximizing the ratio E is to find the set of $(m \times 1)$ vectors $A_1, A_2, \ldots A_m$, that maximizes the ratio:

$$E_j = \frac{A'BA}{A'CA}, \tag{3.18}$$

where:

$$A' = [A_1, A_2, \ldots A_m],$$

B is the matrix of the weighted among-group deviation sums of squares of X, and

C is the matrix of pooled within-group deviation sums of squares of X.

Following Tatsuoka (1988), and Appendix A, the optimum discriminant function can be defined as Eq. (3.19):

$$(C^{-1}B - EI)A = 0. \tag{3.19}$$

In sum, the theory and methodology of two-group discriminant-function analysis can be easily extended to k-group analysis. Both eigenvalues and eigenvectors can be solved in accordance with the procedure discussed in Section 3.3.

Following Tatsuoka (1988), the discriminant functions associated with Eq. (3.13) can be explicitly defined as:

$$Y_1 = a_{11}X_1 + a_{12}X_2 + \cdots + a_{1m}X_m, \tag{3.20a}$$

$$Y_2 = a_{21}X_1 + a_{22}X_2 + \cdots + a_{2m}X_m, \tag{3.20b}$$

$$Y_3 = a_{31}X_1 + a_{32}X_2 + \cdots + a_{3m}X_m, \tag{3.20c}$$

$$\vdots \quad \vdots \quad \vdots \quad \vdots$$

$$Y_r = a_{r1}X_1 + a_{r2}X_2 + \cdots + a_{rm}X_m, \tag{3.20r}$$

where $r < k$. These equations can be used to perform r-group discriminant analysis. The implications of these equations need further explanation.

To obtain the equations indicated in Eqs. (3.20a)–(3.20r), we need r discriminant-criterion values, denoted as $E_1, E_2, \ldots E_r$ in descending order of magnitude, and r associated eigenvectors $A_1, A_2, \ldots A_r$. The eigenvectors are determined only up to an arbitrary multiplier, because if A satisfies Eq. (3.19) for some E, it is clear that d A also satisfies the equation for some E (where d is an arbitrary constant). It is customary to choose the multiplier for each eigenvector in one of two ways: (i) so that its norm will be unity (that is, $A_p'A_p = 1$, for each p) or (ii) so that its largest element will be unity.

Eigenvalues E_r are, by definition, the values assumed by the discriminant criterion for linear combinations using the elements of corresponding eigenvectors A_m as combining weights. Therefore, it is clear that the eigenvector provides a set of weights such that the transformed variable [as indicated in Eq. (3.20a)] has the largest discriminant criterion, E_1, achievable by any linear combination of the m predictor variables.

It is clear that the weights of the linear combination as indicated in Eq. (3.20b) are the elements of A_2. It can be shown that Y_2 has the discriminant criterion value E_2, which is the largest achievable by any linear combination of the X's that is uncorrelated with Y_1. Similarly, Y_3, as indicated in Eq. (3.20c), has the largest discriminant criterion value (E_3) among all linear combinations of the X's that are uncorrelated with Y_1 and Y_2, and so on. Y_r, using the elements of A_r as weights, has the largest possible discriminant criterion value among linear combinations that are uncorrelated with all the preceding linear combinations $Y_1, Y_2, \ldots, Y_{r-1}$. The linear combinations $Y_1, Y_2, \ldots, Y_{r-1}$ are called the first, second, ..., rth (linear) discriminant functions for optimally differentiating among the k given groups. Pinches and Mingo (1973) used four discriminant functions in analyzing industrial bond ratings. Statistical tests of these discriminant values will be discussed in the next chapter.

We have discussed the theory and methodology for fitting a LDF over the analysis sample. The estimated LDF can be used to investigate the group difference. After the LDF is estimated, the estimated LDF can also be used to do either descriptive or predictive analyses. As argued by Joy and Tollefson (1975), predictive analysis (ex-post discrimination) refers to cross validation, which is classifying members of a time-coincident holdout or validation sample. Joy and Tollefson (1975) argued that prediction requires intertemporal validation (testing predictive results over time), whereas explanation requires only cross validation. Classification procedures are needed to do either explanation or prediction.

Following Eisenbeis and Avery (1972) and Altman and Eisenbeis (1978), the discriminant-function coefficients are derived either (a) to minimize the expected overall error rate R or (b) to minimize the overall costs of misclassification. Using Altman's (1968) bankruptcy analysis for an example, R and C can be defined as:

$$R = q_1 p(1|2) + q_2 p(2|1), \tag{3.21a}$$

$$R = q_1 p(1|2)C_{12} + q_2 p(2|1)C_{21}, \tag{3.21b}$$

where:

q_1 = Prior probability of being classified as bankrupt,
q_2 = Prior probability of being classified as non-bankrupt,
$p(2|1)$ = Conditional probability of being classified as non-bankrupt when, in fact, the firm is bankrupt,
$p(1|2)$ = Conditional probability of being classified as bankrupt when, in fact, the firm is non-bankrupt,
C_{12} = Cost of classifying a bankrupt firm as non-bankrupt,
C_{21} = Cost of classifying a non-bankrupt firm as bankrupt.

If $p(1|2) = 0.20$, $p(2|1) = 0.40$, $q_1 = 0.01$, and $q_2 = 0.99$, then

$$\mathrm{R} = (0.01)(0.20) + (0.99)(0.40) = 0.3962,$$

$$\mathrm{C} = 0.0002C_{12} + 0.3960C_{21}.$$

Application of the above-mentioned classification procedure will be discussed further in the next chapter.

3.5. Factor Analysis and Principal-Component Analysis

Factor analysis was developed by psychologists and has only recently been applied in marketing, finance, and accounting. Anderson (2003), Tatsuoka (1988), Green and Tull (1978), and Churchill and Iacobucci (2004) have argued that factor analysis is one of the more popular "analyses of interdependence" techniques. In studies of interdependence, all variables have equal footing and the analysis is concerned with the whole set of relationships among variables that characterize the objects. In factor analysis two key concepts, factor scores and factor loadings, should be explained first.

3.5.1. *Factor Score*

A factor score is simply a linear combination (or linear composite) of the original variables. It can be defined as:

$$f_i = b_1Y_1 + b_2Y_2 + \cdots + b_jY_j + b_pY_p, \tag{3.22}$$

where f_i is the ith factor score, $Y_j (j = 1, 2, \ldots, \mathrm{p})$ are original variables. For example, Johnson and Dinardo (1996) used factor analysis to classify 61 financial ratios into eight groups (factors) [see Chapter 4 for detail]. In Eq. (3.22) the coefficients (weights) $b_1, b_2, \ldots, b_p$, are parameters to be estimated.

3.5.2. *Factor Loadings*

A factor loading is defined simply as the correlation (across objects) of a set of factors with the original variables. In Johnson's case (1979), he used 306 primary manufacturing firms and 159 retailing firms to calculate eight factors. For manufacturing firms, he used 306 original variables for each factor. For retailing firms, he used 159 original variables for each factor. By using the simple correlation-coefficient formula, he calculated 61 factor loadings for each industry.

Following Anderson (2003), the basic model of factor analysis can be defined as

$$Y = \mu + \beta f + U, \tag{3.23}$$

where f is an m-component vector of (non-observable) factor scores, μ is a fixed vector of means, and U is a vector of (non-observable) errors (or errors plus specific factors).

The $p \times m$ matrix β consists of factor loadings (m $<$ p). When f is random, we assume $\mathrm{E}(f) = 0$, $\mathrm{E(U)} = 0$, $E(f'f) = M$, $\mathrm{E(UU')} = \Sigma$, a diagonal matrix, and $f\mathrm{U}' = 0$. Then $\mathrm{E(Y)} = \mu$, and the covariance matrix of the observable Y is

$$\mathrm{E}(\mathrm{Y} - \mu)(Y - \mu)' = \beta \mathrm{M} \beta' + \Sigma. \tag{3.24}$$

There are two alternative models in estimating the factor score, which are the principal-component method and the maximum-likelihood method. The principal-component method for extracting factors or calculating the coefficient matrix to meet the foregoing statistical assumption can be found in both Johnson and Dinardo (1996) and Tatsuoka (1988). The maximum-likelihood method can be found in Lawley (1940), Lawley and Maxwell (1963), and Joreskog (1967). The principal-component method is discussed in Appendix 3.C.

3.6. Summary

In this chapter, method and theory of both discriminant analysis and factor analysis needed for determining useful financial ratios, predicting corporate bankruptcy, determining bond rating, and analyzing the relationship between bankruptcy avoidance and merger are discussed in detail. Important concepts of linear algebra, which are linear combination and matrix operations, required to understand both discriminant and factor analysis are discussed.

Notes

1. Principal-component analysis is one of the major factor-analytic techniques for summarizing multivariate data. Cluster analysis is an appropriate set of techniques for summarizing multivariate data as well as to partition the data set into homogeneous subsets of objects. See Green and Tull (1978) for detail.
2. The procedure of inversion will be discussed in the example in this section.

Problem Set

1. Briefly discuss the basic concepts of linear combination for both deterministic and stochastic variables. Why are these concepts needed for financial planning and forecasting?
2. What is the purpose of discriminant analysis?
3. What techniques are used to derive the coefficients in MDA? What is the objective in deriving them?
4. For what purpose is principle-component analysis used?
5. (i) Estimate the eigenvalue and related eigenvector for:

$$A = \begin{bmatrix} 3 & 2 & 4 \\ 2 & 0 & 2 \\ 4 & 2 & 3 \end{bmatrix},$$

   (ii) Discuss how the procedure of (i) can be used to estimate the two-group LDF.
6. Please discuss four alternative methods to solve a simultaneous equation system. (Please refer to Appendix 3.A for information.)

Appendix 3.A. Four Alternative Methods to Solve System of Linear Equations

Method 1: Substitution methods

(Reference: Wikipedia)

The simplest method for solving a system of linear equations is to repeatedly eliminate variables. This method can be described as follows:

1. In the first equation, solve for one of the variables in terms of the others.
2. Substitute this expression into the remaining equations. This yields a system of equations with one fewer equation and one fewer unknown.

3. Continue until you have reduced the system to a single linear equation.
4. Solve this equation and then back-substitute until the entire solution is found.

For example, consider the following system:

$$\begin{aligned} x + 3y - 2z &= 5, \\ 3x + 5y + 6z &= 7, \\ 2x + 4y + 3z &= 8. \end{aligned} \tag{3.A.1}$$

Solving the first equation for x gives $x = 5 + 2z - 3y$, and plugging this into the second and third equation yields

$$\begin{aligned} -4y + 12z &= -8, \\ -2y + 7z &= -2. \end{aligned} \tag{3.A.2}$$

Solving the first of these equations for y yields $y = 2 + 3z$, and plugging this into the second equation yields $z = 2$. We now have:

$$\begin{aligned} x &= 5 + 2z - 3y, \\ y &= 2 + 3z, \\ z &= 2. \end{aligned} \tag{3.A.3}$$

Substituting $z = 2$ into the second equation gives $y = 8$, and substituting $z = 2$ and $y = 8$ into the first equation yields $x = -15$. Therefore, the solution set is the single point $(x, y, z) = (-15, 8, 2)$.

Method 2: Cramer's rule

Explicit formulas for small systems (Reference: Wikipedia)
Consider the linear system

$$\begin{cases} a_1 x + b_1 y = c_1 \\ a_2 x + b_2 y = c_2, \end{cases} \tag{3.A.4}$$

which in matrix format is

$$\begin{bmatrix} a_1 & b_1 \\ a_2 & b_2 \end{bmatrix} \begin{bmatrix} x \\ y \end{bmatrix} = \begin{bmatrix} c_1 \\ c_2 \end{bmatrix}. \tag{3.A.5}$$

Assume $a_1b_2 - b_1a_2$ non-zero. Then, x and y can be found with Cramer's rule as

$$x = \begin{bmatrix} c_1 & b_1 \\ c_2 & b_2 \end{bmatrix} \Big/ \begin{bmatrix} a_1 & b_1 \\ a_2 & b_2 \end{bmatrix} \frac{c_1b_2 - b_1c_2}{a_1b_2 - b_1a_2} \tag{3.A.6}$$

and

$$y = \begin{bmatrix} a_1 & c_1 \\ a_2 & c_2 \end{bmatrix} \Big/ \begin{bmatrix} a_1 & b_1 \\ a_2 & b_2 \end{bmatrix} \frac{a_1c_2 - c_1a_2}{a_1b_2 - b_1a_2}. \tag{3.A.7}$$

The rules for 3×3 matrices are similar. Given

$$\begin{cases} a_1x + b_1y + c_1z = d_1 \\ a_2x + b_2y + c_2z = d_2, \\ a_3x + b_3y + c_3z = d_3 \end{cases} \tag{3.C.8}$$

which in matrix format is

$$\begin{bmatrix} a_1 & b_1 & c_1 \\ a_2 & b_2 & c_2 \\ a_3 & b_3 & c_3 \end{bmatrix} \begin{bmatrix} x \\ y \\ z \end{bmatrix} - \begin{bmatrix} d_1 \\ d_2 \\ d_3 \end{bmatrix}. \tag{3.A.8}$$

Then the values of x, y, and z can be found as follows:

$$x = \frac{\begin{vmatrix} d_1 & b_1 & c_1 \\ d_2 & b_2 & c_2 \\ d_3 & b_3 & c_3 \end{vmatrix}}{\begin{vmatrix} a_1 & b_1 & c_1 \\ a_2 & b_2 & c_2 \\ a_3 & b_3 & c_3 \end{vmatrix}}, \quad y = \frac{\begin{vmatrix} a_1 & d_1 & c_1 \\ a_2 & d_2 & c_2 \\ a_3 & d_3 & c_3 \end{vmatrix}}{\begin{vmatrix} a_1 & b_1 & c_1 \\ a_2 & b_2 & c_2 \\ a_3 & b_3 & c_3 \end{vmatrix}}, \quad \text{and } z = \frac{\begin{vmatrix} a_1 & b_1 & d_1 \\ a_2 & b_2 & d_2 \\ a_3 & b_3 & d_3 \end{vmatrix}}{\begin{vmatrix} a_1 & b_1 & c_1 \\ a_2 & b_2 & c_2 \\ a_3 & b_3 & c_3 \end{vmatrix}}. \tag{3.A.9}$$

And then you need to use determinant calculation, which will be discussed in next session.

Determinant Calculation

3 × 3 matrices

The determinant of a 3×3 matrix is defined by

$$\begin{vmatrix} a & b & c \\ d & e & f \\ g & h & i \end{vmatrix} = a\begin{vmatrix} e & f \\ h & i \end{vmatrix} - b\begin{vmatrix} d & f \\ g & i \end{vmatrix} + c\begin{vmatrix} d & e \\ g & h \end{vmatrix} \tag{3.A.10}$$

$$= a(ei - fh) - b(di - fg) + c(dh - eg)$$

$$= aei + bfg + cdh - ceg - bdi - afh.$$

We use the same example as we did in the first method:

$$x = \frac{\begin{bmatrix} 5 & 3 & -2 \\ 7 & 5 & 6 \\ 8 & 4 & 3 \end{bmatrix}}{\begin{bmatrix} 1 & 3 & -2 \\ 3 & 5 & 6 \\ 2 & 4 & 3 \end{bmatrix}}, \quad y = \frac{\begin{bmatrix} 1 & 5 & -2 \\ 3 & 7 & 6 \\ 2 & 8 & 3 \end{bmatrix}}{\begin{bmatrix} 1 & 3 & -2 \\ 3 & 5 & 6 \\ 2 & 4 & 3 \end{bmatrix}}, \quad z = \frac{\begin{bmatrix} 1 & 3 & 5 \\ 3 & 5 & 7 \\ 2 & 4 & 8 \end{bmatrix}}{\begin{bmatrix} 1 & 3 & -2 \\ 3 & 5 & 6 \\ 2 & 4 & 3 \end{bmatrix}} \tag{3.A.11}$$

$$\begin{aligned} y &= \frac{1*7*3+5*6*2 +(-2)*3*8-(-2)*7*2-5*3*3-1*6*8}{1*5*3+3*6*2 +(-2)*3*4-(-2)*5*2-3*3*3-1*6*4} \\ &= \frac{21+60-48+28-45-48}{15+36-24+20-27-24} = \frac{-32}{-4} = 8 \end{aligned} \tag{3.C.12}$$

$$\begin{aligned} z &= \frac{1*5*8+3*7*2+5*3*4 -5*5*2-3*3*8-1*7*4}{1*5*3+3*6*2 +(-2)*3*4-(-2)*5*2-3*3*3-1*6*4} \\ &= \frac{40+42+60-50-72-28}{15+36-24+20-27-24} = \frac{-8}{-4} = 2. \end{aligned} \tag{3.C.13}$$

Method 3: Matrix Method

Using the example above, we can derive the following matrix equation:

$$\begin{bmatrix} x \\ y \\ z \end{bmatrix} = \begin{bmatrix} 1 & 3 & -2 \\ 3 & 5 & 6 \\ 2 & 4 & 3 \end{bmatrix} * \begin{bmatrix} 5 \\ 7 \\ 8 \end{bmatrix}. \tag{3.A.14}$$

The inversion of matrix A is, by the definition

$$A^{-1} = \frac{1}{\det A} * (Adj\ \mathrm{A}). \tag{3.A.15}$$

The Adjoint A is defined by the **transpose** of the cofactor matrix. First we need to calculate the cofactor matrix of A. Suppose the cofactor matrix is:

$$\text{cofactor matrix} = \begin{bmatrix} A_{11} & A_{12} & A_{13} \\ A_{21} & A_{22} & A_{23} \\ A_{31} & A_{32} & A_{33} \end{bmatrix},$$

$$A_{11} = \begin{bmatrix} 5 & 6 \\ 4 & 3 \end{bmatrix} = -9, \quad A_{12} = -\begin{bmatrix} 3 & 6 \\ 2 & 3 \end{bmatrix} = 3, \quad A_{13} = \begin{bmatrix} 3 & 5 \\ 2 & 4 \end{bmatrix} = 2,$$

$$A_{21} = -\begin{bmatrix} 3 & -2 \\ 4 & 3 \end{bmatrix} = -17, \quad A_{22} = \begin{bmatrix} 1 & -2 \\ 2 & 3 \end{bmatrix} = 7, \quad A_{23} = -\begin{bmatrix} 1 & 3 \\ 2 & 4 \end{bmatrix} = 2,$$

$$A_{31} = \begin{bmatrix} 3 & -2 \\ 5 & 6 \end{bmatrix} = 28, \quad A_{32} = -\begin{bmatrix} 1 & -2 \\ 3 & 6 \end{bmatrix} = -12, \quad A_{33} = \begin{bmatrix} 1 & 3 \\ 3 & 5 \end{bmatrix} = -4,$$

Therefore,

$$\text{Cofactor matrix} = \begin{bmatrix} -9 & 3 & 2 \\ -17 & 7 & 2 \\ 28 & -12 & -4 \end{bmatrix}. \tag{3.A.16}$$

Then, we can get the Adjoint A:

$$\text{Adj A} = \begin{bmatrix} -9 & -17 & 28 \\ 3 & 7 & -12 \\ 2 & 2 & -4 \end{bmatrix}. \tag{3.A.17}$$

The determinant of A we have calculated in Cramer's rule:

$$\text{Det A} = \begin{bmatrix} 1 & 3 & -2 \\ 3 & 5 & 6 \\ 2 & 4 & 3 \end{bmatrix} = -4,$$

$$A^{-1} = \frac{1}{(-4)} * \begin{bmatrix} -9 & -17 & 28 \\ 3 & 7 & -12 \\ 2 & 2 & -4 \end{bmatrix} = \begin{bmatrix} \frac{9}{4} & \frac{17}{4} & -\frac{28}{4} \\ -\frac{3}{4} & -\frac{7}{4} & -3 \\ -\frac{1}{2} & -\frac{1}{2} & 1 \end{bmatrix}. \tag{3.A.18}$$

Therefore,

$$\begin{bmatrix} x \\ y \\ z \end{bmatrix} = \begin{bmatrix} \frac{9}{4} & \frac{17}{4} & -\frac{28}{4} \\ -\frac{3}{4} & -\frac{7}{4} & -3 \\ -\frac{1}{2} & -\frac{1}{2} & 1 \end{bmatrix} * \begin{bmatrix} 5 \\ 7 \\ 8 \end{bmatrix}$$

$$= \begin{bmatrix} \frac{9}{4} * 5 + \frac{17}{4} * 7 + \left(-\frac{20}{4}\right) * 8 \\ \left(-\frac{3}{4}\right) * 5 + \left(-\frac{7}{4}\right) * 7 + 3 * 8 \\ \left(-\frac{1}{2}\right) * 5 + \left(-\frac{1}{2}\right) * 7 + 1 * 8 \end{bmatrix} = \begin{bmatrix} -15 \\ 8 \\ 2 \end{bmatrix}. \quad (3.A.19)$$

Method 4: Excel Matrix Inversion and Multiplication

1. Using minverse () function to get the A inverse. Type "Ctrl + Shift + Enter" together you will get the inverse of A.

Matrix A		Matrix A		
1	3	1	3	−2
3	5	3	5	6
2	4	2	4	3
Matrix A Inverse		Matrix A Inverse		
2.25		= minverse (B20:D22)		
−0.75				
−0.5				

2. Using mmult () function to do the matrix multiplication and type "Ctrl + Shift + Enter" together, you will get the answers for x, y, and z.

Matrix A Inverse				Vector D		Vector_(x,y,z)
Matrix A Inverse				Vector D		Vector_(x,y,z) :F27)
2.25	4.25	−7		5		−15
−0.75	−1.75	3	*	7	=	8
−0.5	−0.5	1		8		2

Appendix 3.B. Relationship between Discriminant Analysis and Dummy Regression Analysis

3.B.1. Derivation of the Discriminant Function

Data composed of two samples of size N_1 and N_2 for two-group discriminant analysis must meet the following assumptions: (1) that the groups being investigated are discrete and identifiable; (2) that each observation in each group can be described by a set of measurements on m characteristics or variables; and (3) that these m variables have a multivariate normal distribution in each population. In vector notation, the nth observation can be represented as an $m \times 1$ column vector of the form

$$X'_n = (X_{1n}, X_{2n}, \cdots, X_{mn}),$$

where $n = 1, \ldots, N_1$, or $n = 1, \ldots, N_2$.

Under these assumptions, the linear discriminant function can be defined as Eq. (3.10) of the chapter text (repeated here for convenience)

$$Y_i = a_1 X_{1i} + a X_{2i} + \cdots + a_m X_{mi} \tag{3.B.1}$$

The a_i's were then chosen to maximize the ratio of the weighted between-group variance to the pooled within-group variance. Ladd (1966) has proposed a discriminant criterion E, as defined as Eq. (3.A.2) or Eq. (3.18) of the text, to determine the coefficients $a_1, a_2, \ldots, a_m$:

$$E \frac{A'DD'A}{A'CA} = \frac{A'BA}{A'CA}, \tag{3.B.2}$$

where

$$A' = [a_1, a_2, \ldots, a_m];$$
$$D' = [\overline{X}_{1,1} - \overline{X}_{1,2}, \overline{X}_{2,1} - \overline{X}_{2,2}, \overline{X}_{m,1} - \overline{X}_{m,2}];$$
$$C = \text{Within-group variance matrix;}$$
$$DD' = \text{Between-group variance matrix.}$$

There are two alternative methods that can be used to derive the basic equation of discriminant analysis as defined in Eq. (3.B.3) later in this Appendix.

a) Subsequent Vector Derivation Method

Symbolically, we may find the derivative of E with the respect to the column vector of A and equate the result to the $(m \times 1)$ vector (see Tatsuoka (1971), 160–161). The vector equation thus obtained is

$$\frac{\partial E}{\partial A} = \frac{2[(BA)(A'CA) - (A'BA)(CA)]}{(A'CA)^2} = 0.$$

Dividing both numerator and denominator of the middle member by A'CA and using the definition of E in Eq. (3.B.2), this equation reduces to

$$\frac{2[BA - ECA]}{A'CA} = 0,$$

which is equivalent to

$$(B - EC)A = 0. \tag{3.B.3}$$

b) Long-hand Method

If $m = 2$, then Eq. (3.B.2) can be rewritten as

$$E = \frac{b_{11}a_1^2 + b_{22}a_2^2 + 2b_{12}a_1a_2}{c_{11}a_1^2 + c_{22}a_2^2 + 2c_{12}a_1a_2}, \tag{3.B.2a}$$

Where b_{11}, b_{22}, and b_{12} are elements of B, and c_{11}, c_{21}, and c_{12} are elements of C.

Taking the partial derivative of E with respect to a_1, we obtain:

$$\begin{aligned}\frac{\partial E}{\partial a_1} &= \big[(2b_{11}a_1 + 2b_{12}a_2)(C_{11}a_1^2 + C_{22}a_2^2 + 2C_{12}a_1a_2 \\ &\quad - (b_{11}a_1^2 + b_{22}a_2^2 + 2b_{12}a_1a_2)(2C_{11}a_1 + 2C_{12}a_2)\big] \\ &\quad \times (C_{11}a_1^2 + C_{22}a_2^2 + 2C_{12}a_1a_2)^{-2} \\ &= 2[b_{11}a_1 + b_{12}a_2) - E(C_{11}a_1 + C_{12}a_2)] \\ &\quad \times (C_{11}a_1^2 + C_{22}a_2^2 + 2C_{12}a_1a_2)^{-1}.\end{aligned}$$

Setting this equation equal to zero and simplifying, we get:

$$b_{11}a_1 + b_{12}a_2 = E(C_{11}a_1 + C_{12}a_2).$$

Using vector notation, we have:

$$[b_{11}, b_{12}]A = E[C_{11}, C_{12}]A. \tag{3.B.4}$$

Similarly, it can be shown that, upon equating $\partial E/\partial a_2$ to zero and simplifying, we get:

$$[b_{21}, b_{22}]A = E[C_{21}, C_{22}]A. \tag{3.B.5}$$

It is evident that Eqs. (3.B.4) and (3.B.5) can be written as a single matrix equation:

$$\begin{bmatrix} b_{11} & b_{12} \\ b_{21} & b_{22} \end{bmatrix} A = E \begin{bmatrix} C_{11} & C_{12} \\ C_{21} & C_{22} \end{bmatrix} A$$

or

$$(B - EC)A = 0. \tag{3.B.3}$$

Equation (3.B.3) can be used to formulate the characteristic equation for solving eigenvector A as indicated in the text.

If A^* maximizes the function shown in Eq. (3.B.1), then so does any $A^{**} = KA^*$, where K is a scalar. Substituting A^{**} for A^* simply multiplies both the numerator and denominator by K^2. Because the coefficients themselves are not unique, there are several methods of calculating the discriminant function. Johnston and Dinardo shows (1996), for example, that the vector A^* that maximizes the ratio E is proportional to the vector A (that is, $A = KA^*$), which maximizes $G = A'DD'A$ subject to the constraint that $L = A'CA$, where L is an arbitrary constant.

Let λ be a Lagrange multiplier and define

$$F = A'DD'A - \lambda[A'CA - L]. \tag{3.B.6}$$

Setting the derivatives of F with respect to A equal to zero yields

$$\frac{\partial F}{\partial A} = 0 = 2DD'a - 2\lambda CA, \tag{3.B.7}$$

where $D'A$ is a scalar, say H. Hence, Eq. (3.A.7) can be rewritten as $(\lambda/\mathrm{H})CA = D$, and thus a solution is

$$A\left(\frac{\lambda}{H}\right) = C^{-1}D = A_1, \quad \text{say}, \tag{3.B.8}$$

which is proportional to A. It can be seen that Al is a solution to Eq. (3.B.3):

$$(DD' - \lambda C)A_1 = (DD' - \lambda C)A\left(\frac{\lambda}{H}\right) = 0.$$

Alternatively, a new objective function can be developed as follows: From Eq. (3.A.3) we have

$$BA = ECA. \tag{3.B.9}$$

Add EBA to both sides of Eq. (3.A.9), obtaining

$$(1 + E)BA = E(B + C)A$$

or

$$(B - E'S)A = 0, \tag{3.B.10}$$

where $E' = E/(1 + E)$. This implies that Eq. (3.B.10) can be used as an alternative discriminant function of Eq. (3.B.3). Under this circumstance, an alternative objective function can be defined as

$$E' = \frac{A'DD'A}{A'SA},$$

where $S = [S_{ij}] = \mathit{the}\ m \times m$ matrix of S_{ij}, and S_{ij} is the sum of cross products of the deviations of X_i, and X_j about the overall means.

Following the same procedure mentioned above, we can obtain

$$A\left(\frac{\lambda}{H}\right) = S^{-1}D = A_2. \tag{3.B.11}$$

Ladd (1966) has shown that A_2 is proportional to A_1.

These results imply that the parameters of a two-group discriminant function can be estimated by using the related data of S and D.

If we let $Y = 1$ for observations in group 1 and $Y = 0$ for those in group 2, then, following the multiple regression technique, Ladd (1966) showed that the regression coefficient vector is

$$A = S^{-1}MD, \tag{3.B.12}$$

where $M = [N_1N_2]/[N_1 + N_2]$, and N_1 and N_2 are total observations in group 1 and group 2, respectively.

A comparison of Eq. (3.B.11) with Eq. (3.B.12) shows that the parameters obtained from the eigenvalue method differ from those of the dummy regression method only by a constant M.

The implications of Eqs. (3.B.11) and (3.B.12) can be discussed as follows: If $m = 2$, then Eq. (3.B.l) can be defined as

$$Y_i = a_1X_{1i} + a_2X_{2i}. \tag{3.B.1$'$}$$

Equation (3.B.1') can be written in derived form as

$$y_i = a_1x_{1i} + a_2x_{2i}. \tag{3.B.13}$$

where $y_i = Y_i - \overline{Y}$, $x_{1i} = X_{1i} - \overline{X}_1$, $X_{2i} = X_{2i} - \overline{X}_2$. Following the regression method discussed in Appendix A of Chapter 2, the equation system used to solve a_1 and a_2 can be defined as

$$\left(\sum x_{1i}^2\right)a_1 + \left(\sum x_{1i}x_{2i}\right)a_2 = \sum x_{1i}y_i, \tag{3.B.14a}$$

$$\left(\sum x_{1i}x_{2i}\right)a_1 + \left(\sum x_{2i}^2\right)a_2 = \sum x_{2i}y_i. \tag{3.B.14b}$$

Since Y_i is a dichotomous variable, we write

$$\begin{aligned}\sum X_1V_1y &= \sum X_1Y - N\overline{X},\overline{Y}\\ &= N_1\overline{X}_{11} - \left(\frac{N_1\overline{X}_{11} + N_2\overline{X}_{12}}{N_1 + N_2}\right)\left(\frac{NN_1}{N_1 + N_2}\right). \quad (3.B.15)\\ &= \left(\frac{N_1N_2}{N}\right)(\overline{X}_{11} - \overline{X}_{12}) = \left(\frac{N_1N_2}{N}\right)(D_1)\end{aligned}$$

Similarly, we can show that

$$\sum x_2 y = \left(\frac{N_1 N_2}{N}\right)(\overline{X}_{21} - \overline{X}_{22}) = \left(\frac{N_1 N_2}{N}\right)(D_2). \tag{3.B.16}$$

From Eqs. (3.B.14), (3.B.15), and (3.B.16), we obtain

$$A = S^{-1} MD,$$

where $A' = (a_1, a_2)$, $D' = (D_1, D_2)$, $M = N_1 N_2 / N$, and

$$S = \begin{bmatrix} \sum x_{1i}^2 & \sum x_{1i} x_{2i} \\ \sum x_{2i} x_{1i} & \sum x_{2i}^2 \end{bmatrix}.$$

References for Appendix 3.B

Eisenbeis, RA and RB Avery (1972). *Discriminant Analysis and Classification Procedures: Theory and Applications.* Lexington: D. C. Heath and Company.

Johnston, J and J Dinardo (1996). Econometrics Methods 4th ed. New York: McGraw-Hill.

Ladd, GW (1964). Linear probability functions and discriminant functions, *Econometrica* 34, 873–885.

Tatsuoka, MM (1988). *Multivariate Analysis: Techniques for Educational and Psychological Research*, 2nd ed. New York: John Wiley & Sons, Inc.

Appendix 3.C. Principal-Component Analysis

3.C.1. Introduction

Following Anderson (2003), principal components are linear combinations of random or statistical variables that have special properties in terms of variances. For example, the first principal component is the normalized linear combination (that is, the sum of squares of the coefficients being one) with maximum variance. In effect, transforming the original vector variable to the vector of principal components amounts to a rotation of coordinate axes to a new coordinate system that has inherent statistical properties.

The principal components turn out to be the eigenvectors of the covariance matrix, as discussed in the chapter text. Thus the study of principal components can be considered as putting into statistical terms the usual developments of eigenroots and eigenvectors (for positive and semidefinite matrices).

From the point of view of statistical theory, the set of principal components yields a convenient set of coordinates, and the accompanying variances of the components characterize their statistical properties. In statistical practice, the method of principal components is used to find the linear combinations with large variance. In many empirical studies, the number of variables under consideration is too large to handle. A way of reducing the number of variables to be treated is to discard the linear combinations that have small variances and to study only those with large variances.

For example, a physical anthropologist may make dozens of measurements of each of a number of individuals, measurements such as ear length, ear breadth, facial length, facial breadth, and so forth. He may be interested in describing and analyzing how individuals differ in these kinds of physiological characteristics. Eventually he will want to "explain" these differences, but first he wants to know what measurements or combinations of measurements show considerable variation; that is, which should need further study. The principal-components approach provides a set of linearly combined measurements. It may be that most of the variation from individual to individual resides in two linear combinations; if so, the anthropologist can direct his study to these two quantities. Other linear combinations may vary so little from one person to the next that study of them will tell the researcher little about individual variation.

Using Johnson's (1979) financial ratio study as an example, we have data matrix Y of 306 observations on 61 variables.

$$Y = \begin{bmatrix} Y_{11} & \cdots & Y_{1n} \\ Y_{21} & & Y_{2n} \\ \vdots & & \vdots \\ Y_{p1} & \cdots & Y_{pn} \end{bmatrix} \quad \begin{pmatrix} n = 1, 2, \ldots, 306 \\ p = 1, 2, \ldots, 61 \end{pmatrix}.$$

Following Johnston and Dinardo (1996), the procedure of estimating principal components can be described as follows: We express the observations of Y's as deviations from the sample means, for we are concerned with studying the variation in the data.

The method of principal components may be approached in a number of ways. One is to ask how many dimensions or how much independence there really is in the set of p variables. More explicitly, we consider the transformation of the Y's to a net set of variables that will be pairwise uncorrelated and of which the first will have the maximum possible variance, the second the maximum possible variance among those uncorrelated with the first, and so forth. Let

$$f_{1t} = b_{11}y_{1t} + b_{21}y_{2t} + \cdots + b_{p1}y_{pt}, \quad (t = 1, \ldots, n),$$

denote the first new variable. In matrix form

$$f_1 = yb_1, \tag{3.C.1}$$

where f_1, is an n-element vector and b_1 a p-element vector. The sum of squares of f_1, is

$$f_1' f_1 = f_1' Y' Y f_1. \tag{3.C.2}$$

We wish to choose b_1 to maximize $f_1' f_1$. Clearly, some constraint must be imposed on b_1, or $f_1' f_1$, could be made infinitely large, so let us normalize by setting

$$b_1' b_1 = 1. \tag{3.C.3}$$

The problem now is to maximize Eq. (3.C.2) subject to Eq. (3.C.3). Define ϕ as

$$\phi = b_1' Y' Y b_1 - \lambda_1 (b_1' b_1 - 1),$$

where λ_1, is a Lagrange multiplier. Thus

$$\frac{\partial \phi}{\partial b_1} = 2Y'Yb_1 - 2\lambda_1 b_1.$$

Setting $\partial\phi/\partial b_1 = 0$ gives

$$(Y'Y)b_1 = \lambda_1 b_1. \tag{3.C.4}$$

Thus b_1 is a latent (eigen) vector of $X'X$ corresponding to the root of λ_1. From Eq. (3.C.2) and (3.C.4) we see that

$$f_1' f_1 = \lambda_1 b_1' b_1 = \lambda_1,$$

and so we must choose λ_1, as the largest latent root of $Y'Y$. The $Y'Y$ matrix, in the absence of perfect collinearity, will be positive definite ($Y'Y > 0$) and thus have positive latent roots. The first principal component of Y is then f_1.

Now define $f_2 = Yb_2$. We wish to choose b_2 to maximize $b_2'Y'Yb_2$ subject to $b_2'b_2 = 1$ and $b_1'b_2 = 0$. The reason for the second condition is that f_2 is to be uncorrelated with f_1. The covariation between them is given by

$$\begin{aligned} b_2'Y'Yb_2 &= \lambda_1 b_1' b_2 \\ &= 0 \quad \text{if and only if } b_1'b_2 = 0. \end{aligned}$$

Define

$$\phi = b_2'Y'Yb_2 - \lambda_2(b_2'b_2 - 1) - \mu(b_1'b_2),$$

where λ_2 and μ are Lagrange multipliers:

$$\frac{\partial \phi}{\partial b_2} = 2Y'Yb_2 - 2\lambda_2 b_2 - \mu b_1 = 0.$$

Premultiply by b_1',

$$2b_1'Y'Yb_2 - \mu = 0.$$

But from $(Y'Y)b_1 = \lambda_1 b_1$,

$$b_2'(Y'Y)b_1 = \lambda_1 Y_1'Y_1 = 0.$$

Thus $\mu = 0$, and we have

$$(Y'Y)b_2 = \lambda_2 b_2, \tag{3.C.5}$$

and λ_2 should obviously be chosen as the second largest latent root of $Y'Y$. We can proceed in this way for each of the p roots of $Y'Y$, and assemble the resultant vectors in the orthogonal matrix:

$$B = \begin{bmatrix} b_1 & b_2 & \ldots & b_p \end{bmatrix}. \tag{3.C.6}$$

The p principal components of Y are then given by the $n \times p$ matrix F,

$$F = YB. \tag{3.C.7}$$

Moreover,

$$F'F = B'Y'YB = \Lambda = \begin{bmatrix} \lambda_1 & 0 & \cdots & 0 \\ 0 & \lambda_2 & \cdots & 0 \\ \vdots & \vdots & & \vdots \\ 0 & 0 & \cdots & \lambda_p \end{bmatrix}, \tag{3.C.8}$$

showing that the principal components are indeed pairwise uncorrelated and that their variances are given by

$$f_i' f_k = \lambda_i \quad (i = 1, \ldots, p). \tag{3.C.9}$$

This appendix has already shown the major concepts and procedures of principal-component analysis. For further detail, we suggest that readers consult Anderson (2003), Johnston and Dinardo (1996), and Stuart (1982).

References for Appendix 3.C

Anderson, TW (2003). *An Introduction to Multivariate Statistical Analysis*, 3rd ed. New York: John Wiley and Sons.

Johnson, WB (1979). The cross-sectional stability of financial ratio patterns. *Journal of Financial and Quantitative Analysis* 14, 1035–1048.

Johnston, J and J Dinardo (1996). *Econometrics Methods*, 4th ed. New York: McGraw-Hill.

Stuart, M (1982). A geometric approach to principal-components analysis, *The American Statistician*, 36, 365–367.

References for Chapter 3

Altman, EI (1968). Financial Ratios, Discriminant Analysis, and the Prediction of Corporate Bankruptcy, *Journal of Finance*, 23, 589–609.

Altman, EI and RA Eisenbeis (1968). Financial Applications of Discriminant Analysis: A Clarification, *Journal of Financial and Quantitative Analysis*, 13, 185–195.

Altman, EI, R Haldeman, and P Narayanan (1977). ZETA Analysis, A New Model for Bankruptcy Classification, *Journal of Banking and Finance*, 29–54.

Anderson, TW (2003). *An Introduction to Multivariate Statistical Analysis*, 3rd ed. New York: John Wiley and Sons.

Anton, H (2004). *Elementary Linear Algebra*, 9th ed. New York: John Wiley & Sons.

Churchill, GA, Jr. and D Iacobucci (2004). *Marketing Research: Methodological Foundations*, 9th ed. OH: South-Western College Pub.

Eisenbeis, RA and RB Avery (1972). *Discriminant Analysis and Classification Procedure*. Lexington, Massachusetts: Lexington Books.

Green, PE (1988). *Research For Marketing Decisions* 5th ed. Englewood Cliffs, New Jersey: Prentice-Hall.

Johnson, WB (1979). The Cross-Sectional Stability of Financial Patterns, *Journal of Financial and Quantitative Analysis*, 14, 1035–1048.

Johnston, J and J Dinardo (1996). *Econometrics Methods* 4th ed. New York: McGraw-Hill.

Joreskog, KG (1967). Some Contributions to Maximum-Likelihood Factor Analysis, *Psychometrika*, 32, 443–482.

Joy, OM and JO Tollefson (1975). On the Financial Applications of Discriminant Analysis, *Journal of Financial and Quantitative Analysis*, 10, 723–739.

Joy, OM (1978). Some clarifying comments on discriminant analysis, *Journal of Financial and Quantitative Analysis*, 13, 197–200.

Ladd, GW (1966). Linear probability functions and discriminant functions, *Econometrica* 34, 873–885.

Lawley, DN (1940). The Estimation of Factor Loadings by the Method of Maximum Likelihood. *Proceedings of the Royal Society of Edinburg, Series A*, 62, 64–82.

Lawley, DN and AE Maxwell (1963). *Factor Analysis as a Statistical Method.* London: Butterworth.

Moore, JT (1968). *Elements of Linear Algebra and Matrix Theory.* New York: McGraw-Hill Book Company.

Penman, SH (2010). *Financial Statement Analysis and Security Valuation*, 5th ed. New York: McGraw-Hill/Irwin.

Pinches, GE and KA Mingo (1973). A multivariate analysis of industrial bond ratings. *Journal of Finance*, 28, 1–18.

Tatsuoka, MM (1988). *Multivariate Analysis: Techniques for Educational and Psychological Research*, 2nd ed. New York: John Wiley & Sons, Inc.

Chapter 4

Application of Discriminant Analysis and Factor Analysis in Financial Management*

4.1. Introduction

The theoretical and methodological results of discriminant analysis and factor analysis, which were discussed in the previous chapter, can be used to analyze financial data and perform related financial decision making. Section 4.2 discusses how discriminant analysis caned in loan credit analysis. Section 4.3 applies discriminant analysis to bankruptcy and financial distress analysis, as well as possible problems faced in using discriminant analysis are discussed. Section 4.4 demonstrates how the factor-analysis technique can be used to select useful financial ratios. Section 4.5 discusses how k-group discriminant-analysis methods can be used to forecast bond ratings. Also explored in this section is the method of combining factor analysis and discriminant analysis in financial analysis application. Section 4.6 explores the issues related to bond quality ratings and the change of quality rating for the electric utility industry. Section 4.7 discusses other models for estimating default probability. Finally, Section 4.8 summarizes the results of this chapter.

4.2. Credit Analysis

Two-group multiple discriminant analysis (MDA) can be used to determine whether a customer's credit should be authorized or not, or to determine the financial soundness of an industrial firm, a bank, or an insurance company.

In determining the trade credit policy of a firm, Mehta (1974) and Van Horne (2001) proposed a two-group discriminant-analysis model to identify

*This chapter is jointly written by Cheng-Few Lee, Lili Sun, and Bi-Huei Tsai.

the "good account" from the "bad account." A linear discriminant function similar to Eq. (3.8) of Chapter 3 is defined as

$$Y_I = AX_{1i} + BX_{2i}, \tag{4.1}$$

where Y_i is the index value for the ith account; X_{1i} ith firm's quick ratio; X_{2i} ith firm's total sales/inventory ratio; and A and B are the parameters or weights to be determined.

For purposes of formulating the original model, we extend open-book credit to all new credit applicants for a sample period, recording for each account the quick ratio and the total sales/inventory ratio and whether or not the account defaults in payment after a specified length of time. If the account defaults, it is classified as a bad account and the index is assigned the value of zero. If the account pays on time, it is classified as a good account and the index is assigned the value of one. With this information, we are able to apply a linear discriminant analysis (as discussed in Chapter 3) with two independent variables. Based upon the sample data of X_1 and X_2, the coefficients A and B can be calculated by the following procedure.

Following Appendix A of Chapter 3, two equations used in solving for A and B of Eq. (4.1) are defined as:

$$S_{11}A + S_{12}B = D_1, \tag{4.2}$$

$$S_{12}A + S_{22}B = D_2. \tag{4.3}$$

Using Cramer's rule (defined in Chapter 3), we obtain

$$A = \frac{S_{22}D_1 - S_{12}D_2}{S_{22}S_{11} - S_{12}^2}, \tag{4.4a}$$

$$B = \frac{S_{11}D_2 - S_{12}D_1}{S_{22}S_{11} - S_{12}^2}, \tag{4.4b}$$

where

S_{11} = Variance of X_1;
S_{22} = Variance of X_2;
S_{12} = Covariance between X_1 and X_2;
D_1 = Difference between the average of X_1's for good accounts and the average of X_1's for bad accounts; and
D_2 = Difference between the average of X_2 for good accounts the average of X_2 for bad accounts.

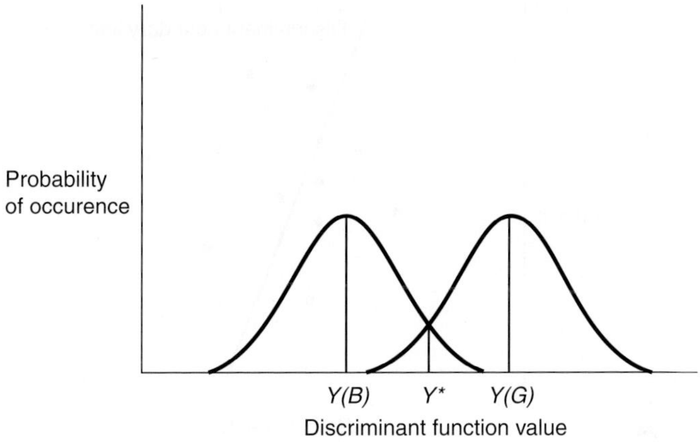

Fig. 4.1. Universes of good and bad accounts.

Table 4.1. Status and index values of the accounts.

Account Number	Account Status	Y_i
7	Bad	0.81
10	Bad	0.89
2	Bad	1.30
3	Bad	1.45
6	Bad	1.64
12	Good	1.77
11	Bad	1.83
4	Good	1.96
1	Good	2.25
8	Good	2.50
5	Good	2.61
9	Good	2.80

Based upon the estimated parameters, A and B, we need to determine the minimum cutoff value of the discriminant function. The aim here is to refuse credit to accounts with a value of Y below the cutoff value and to extend credit to accounts with a Y value above the cutoff. Theoretically, we wish to find the discriminant-function value that is denoted by Y^* in Fig. 4.1, where $Y(\mathrm{B})$ and $Y(\mathrm{G})$ are average discriminant function values for bad and good accounts, respectively.

Following Van Horne (2001), we start by calculating the Y_I for 12 accounts, as shown in Table 4.1, in ascending order of magnitude.

We see that there is an area of overlap for accounts 6, 2, 11, and 4, as shown graphically in Fig. 4.1. We know that the cutoff value must lie

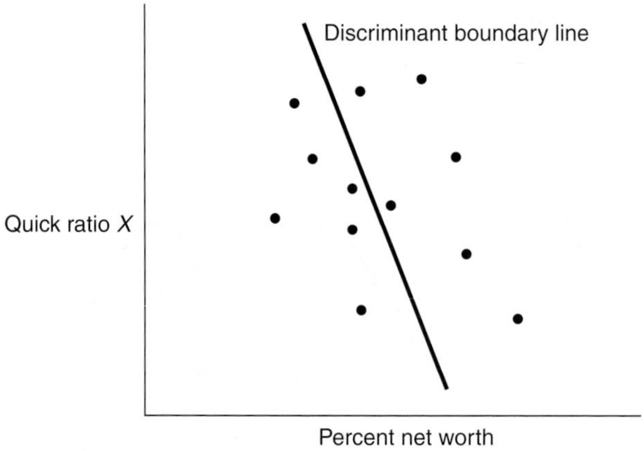

Fig. 4.2. Discriminant analysis of accounts receivable.

between 1.64 and 1.96. For simplicity, we may want to use the midpoint, 1.80, as our cutoff value. In Fig. 4.2, we are able to draw a discriminant boundary that most accurately classifies accounts into good and bad categories. Note, however, that two of the accounts, 11 and 12, are misclassified, given the cutoff value. Account 11 is classified by the graph as a good account when, in fact, we know it to be a bad account, while account 12 is classified as a bad account when, in fact, it was a good account.

These are Type I classification errors and Type II classification errors, respectively. Type I errors involve the rejection of the null hypothesis when it is actually true, while Type II classification errors involve the acceptance of the null hypothesis when it is actually false. For the sake of practicality, the analysis should assume an area of possible misclassification for indexes between 1.64 and 1.96. Accounts or firms falling within this range require further investigation and analysis.

If one has reason to believe that new credit applicants will not differ significantly from past ones whose performance has been analyzed, discriminant analysis can be used to select and reject credit sales customers. Using a minimum cutoff value, we reject all credit sales if the Y value for the credit applicant is less than 1.78. Using a 32-point range, we accept all credit sales where the prospective customer has a Y-value over 1.96, and reject applicants with Y-values below 1.64. For applicants with Y-values lying between those two values, we might want to obtain additional credit information, along with information as to the profitability of the sale, before making a decision.

In this credit analysis, Mehta (1974) used the quick ratio and the inventory-turnover ratio to construct the index. He shows that there are four tasks to be faced by the manager in using the MDA for credit analysis. They are:

(i) Determining significant factors.
(ii) Selecting the sample.
(iii) Assigning weights to factors in order to develop an index.
(iv) Establishing cutoff values for the index.

Mehta regards the discriminant approach, the decision-tree approach, and the conventional method as the three major approaches generally used by the credit department of a firm in making the credit-granting decision.

In assessing the risk of a request for credit, the conventional approach regards the three C's as relevant: character, capital, and capacity. This is a subjective credit-analysis method and it generally gives indeterminate and misleading results. Both the discriminant approach and the decision-tree approach can supply financial mangers with objective credit-analysis results, and therefore are generally more useful than the conventional method in credit analysis. However, these two methods use a static analytic framework and assume that collection measures are given.

4.3. Bankruptcy and Financial Distress Analysis

For the past 15 years, academicians and practitioners have used the linear discriminant function to analyze bankruptcy and financial distress for both industrial and financial firms. Here we will discuss only the three most important studies: (1) Altman's (1968) bankruptcy analysis for industrial firms, (2) Sinkey's (1975) study of identifying problem banks from non-problem banks, and (3) Trieschmann and Pinches' (1973) analysis of the financial insolvency of insurance companies.

Altman's study included 33 manufacturers who filed bankruptcy petitions under Chapter X of the Bankruptcy Act during 1946–1965. These 33 firms were paired with 33 non-bankrupt firms on the basis of similar industry and asset size. Asset size ranged between \$1 million and \$25 million. For each firm, 22 variables were initially chosen for analysis on the basis of their popularity in the literature and their potential relevance to the study. These ratios were classified into five categories: liquidity, profitability, leverage, solvency, and activity. One ratio from each category was chosen for inclusion in the discriminant model. The variables used to obtain

Table 4.2. Mean ratios of bankrupt/Non-bankrupt firms.

Ratio	Bankrupt Group Mean	Non-bankrupt Group Mean
X_1	−0.061	0.414
X_2	−0.626	0.355
X_3	−0.318	0.153
X_4	0.401	2.477
X_5	1.500	1.900

Source: From Altman, EI (1968). Financial ratios, discriminant Analysis, and the prediction of corporate bankruptcy. *Journal of Finance*, 23, 596; Table I. Reprinted with permission from EI Altman and *Journal of Finance*.

the final results are:

X_1 = Working-capital/Total assets;
X_2 = Retained earnings/Total assets;
X_3 = EBIT/Total assets;
X_4 = Market value of equity/Book value of total debt; and
X_5 = Sales/Total assets.

The mean ratios of the two groups of firms 1 year prior to the filing for bankruptcy are listed in Table 4.2.

Altman's final estimated discriminant function is:

$$Y_i = 0.012X_1 + 0.014X_2 + 0.033X_3 + 0.006X_4 + 0.999X_5. \tag{4.5}$$

His results show that this discriminant function has done well in predicting non-bankrupt firms.

Using (i) the formula for the overall cost of misclassification (E) and (ii) the expected error rate as discussed in the previous chapters, Altman classified the initial sample. He concluded that all firms having a z-score greater than 2.99 clearly fall into the non-bankrupt sector, while those firms having a z-score below 1.81 are all bankrupt. The area between 1.81 and 2.99 will be defined as the zone of "ignorance" or the "*gray*" *area*.

Sinkey's study of problem banks is another example of the use of a discriminant function in financial analysis. Sinkey draws a profile of characteristics associated with banks that may be in danger of failing, in an attempt to develop an early warning system to help predict problem banks. The Federal Deposit Insurance Corporation wants to predict problem banks as early as possible in order to be able to advise banks of necessary

Table 4.3. Three classes of problem banks.

Class	Size of Sample	Definition
1. PPO	2(1.8%)	Serious problem-potential payoff. An advanced problem bank that has at least 50% chance of requiring financial assistance in the near future.
2. SP	14(12.7%)	Serious problem. A bank whose financial condition threatens ultimately to obligate financial outlay by the FEIC unless drastic changes occur.
3. OP	94(85.5%)	Other problem. A bank with some significant weakness, with vulnerability less than class 2, but still calling for aggressive supervision and extraordinary concern by the FEIC.
Total	110(100%)	

Source: From Sinkey, JF (1975). A multivariate statistical analysis of the characteristics of problem banks. *Journal of Finance*, 30; Table 2. Reprinted with permission.

financial-management changes in time for them to maintain solvent operations. "Problem" banks are categorized according to the likelihood of their financial assistance needs. The three classes of problem banks and the composition of the firms studied are presented below.

Of the 110 banks analyzed, 90 were identified as "problems" in 1972 and 20 in 1973. Each problem bank was matched with a non-problem bank similar to it by (1) geographic market area, (2) total deposits, (3) number of banking offices, and (4) Federal Reserve membership status.

Over 100 variables were initially examined to see if there was a significant difference between the ratios of problem and non-problem banks on a univariate basis. Table 4.3 presents a profile analysis (mean ratios for each group) of five ratios found to be highly significant over the 1969–1972 period. These five variables represent the following dimensions of bank finances: (1) loan volume, represented by loans/assets; (2) capital adequacy, by loans/capital plus reserves; (3) efficiency, by operating expense/operating income; (4) sources of revenue, by loan revenue/total revenue; and (5) uses of revenue, by other expenses/total revenue.

Sinkey then applied the MDA technique to classify the banks on the basis of their financial ratios. Separate discriminant functions were estimated for each year from 1969 through 1972. In general, six or seven variables were included in each function. Recall that a type I error represents the prediction of a problem bank as a non-problem one, and that a type II error represents the prediction of a non-problem bank as a problem one. Obviously, from the viewpoint of financial outlay, a type I error is more

Table 4.4. Profile analysis for problem banks.

Financial Ratio	1969	1970	1971	1972
Loans/Assets				
1. Problem bank	53.9	55.4	56.9	56.0
2. Non-problem bank	49.3	48.9	47.8	47.8
Loans/Capital plus Reserves				
1. Problem bank	648.3	692.2	768.9	838.6
2. Non-problem bank	564.5	562.5	562.4	577.5
Operating Expense/Operating Income				
1. Problem bank	83.9	85.5	89.3	94.1
2. Non-problem bank	78.5	78.6	81.8	82.4
Loan Revenue/Total Revenue				
1. Problem bank	64.7	65.8	68.8	69.8
2. Non-problem bank	59.3	59.2	59.9	59.6
Other Expenses/Total Revenue				
1. Problem bank	15.8	16.0	16.3	16.4
2. Non-problem bank	12.3	13.0	13.2	13.7

Source: From Sinkey, JF (1975). A multivariate statistical analysis of the characteristics of problem banks. *Journal of Finance*, 30; Table 3. Reprinted with permission. This paper was written while the author was a Financial Economics at the Federal Deposit Insurance Corporation, Washington, D.C. He is currently the Professor of Banking and Finance at College of Business Administration, University of Georgia.

costly to the FDIC. The prediction results for each year are presented below.

Year	Type I Error (%)	Type II Error (%)	Total Error (%)
1969	46.36	25.45	35.91
1970	42.73	27.27	35.00
1971	38.18	24.55	31.36
1972	28.15	21.36	24.76

In the years closer to a bank's classification as a problem bank, the discriminant model becomes better able to classify banks that were termed problems in 1971 and 1972. It is apparent that the potential exists for the banking agency to more efficiently allocate resources and analyze pre-examination data through the implementation of an effective early warning system.

A third example of the application of a discriminant function in financial analysis is Orgler's (1970, 1975, Chapter 4) dummy regression model for examining loan quality. His research sample contained 75 criticized loans and 225 non-criticized loans. The validation sample contained 40 criticized loans and 80 non-criticized loans. A final regression model is:

$$\begin{aligned} Z_i = {} & 1.1018 + 0.1017X_{1i} - 0.3966X_{2i} - 0.0916X_{3i} \\ & - 0.1573X_{4i} - 0.0199X_{5i} - 0.4533X_{6i}, \end{aligned} \tag{4.6}$$

where:

$$\begin{aligned} X_1 &= 0\text{: Unsecured loan,} \\ &\quad\ 1\text{: Secured loan;} \\ X_2 &= 0\text{: Past interest payment due,} \\ &\quad\ 1\text{: Current loan;} \\ X_3 &= 0\text{: Not audited firm,} \\ &\quad\ 1\text{: Audited firm;} \\ X_4 &= 0\text{: Net loss firm} \\ &\quad\ 1\text{: Net profit firm} \\ X_5 &= \text{Working-Capital/Current Assets;} \\ X_6 &= 0\text{: Loan criticized by bank examiner,} \\ &\quad\ 1\text{: Loan not criticized by bank examiner.} \end{aligned}$$

Orgler used two cutoff points to classify loans: $C_1 = 0.08$ and $C_2 = 0.25$. These two cutoff points gave three predicted categories for commercial loans:

$$\begin{aligned} \hat{Z}_i > C_2 &= \text{“Bad” loans,} \\ C_1 \le \hat{Z}_i \le C_2 &= \text{“Marginal” loan,} \\ \hat{Z}_i \le C_1 &= \text{“Good” loan.} \end{aligned}$$

A fourth example of the application of a discriminant function in financial analysis is Trieschmann and Pinches' (1973) multivariate model for predicting financially distressed Property-Liability (P-L) insurers. Their paper is concerned with insurance company insolvency and the identification of firms with a high probability of financial distress. They use MDA to classify firms into two groups (solvent or distressed). The model was able to classify correctly 49 out of 52 firms in the study. One solvent firm was classified as being distressed, while two of the distressed firms were classified as being solvent. Of the 70 variables the researchers felt might be important, the final model included only six. The discriminant model for identifying P-L firms with a high potential for financial distress is:

$$Z = -11.08576X_1 - 1.50752X_2 + 3.53606X_3 \\ - 2.49824X_4 - 2.45352X_5 - 0.24492X_6, \quad (4.7)$$

where:

X_1 = Agents' balances/Total assets; a measure of the firms' accounts receivable management;
X_2 = Stocks at cost (preferred and common)/Stocks at market (preferred and common); measures investment management;
X_3 = Bonds at cost/Bonds at market; measures the firm's age;
X_4 = (Loss adjustment expenses paid + underwriting expenses paid)/ Net premiums written; a measure of a firm's funds flow from insurance operations;
X_5 = Combined ratio; traditional measure of underwriting profitability; and
X_6 = Premiums written direct/Surplus; a measure of the firm's sales aggressiveness.

The final discriminant model has an F-ratio of 12.559, which, with the appropriate degrees of freedom (6 and 45), is significant beyond the 0.005 level. Once it is established that the model does discriminate between distressed and solvent P-L insurance firms, the individual contribution of each of the variables can be examined through the use of the t-test. The individual contribution is dominated by X_6, which is significant at the 0.0005 level; X_1, which is significant at the 0.005 level; and X_2 and X_4, which are significant at the 0.025 level. The discriminant model has been proved to be quite applicable to this sort of analysis. With further development of data bases for analysis, future regulators should be in a better position to step in and to help potentially distressed firms well before bankruptcy threatens.

4.4. Applications of Factor Analysis to Select Useful Financial Ratios

Farrar (1962) and King (1966) have used the factor-analysis technique to determine the important factors for security rates-of-return determination.

King (1965) found that there are market factors, industry factors, and other factors, that determine stock price behavior over time. Lloyd and Lee (1975) have used factor analysis to identify the subgroups for the Dow-Jones 30 industrial firms and to test the existence of Block Recursive Systems in asset pricing models. To test the existence of their arbitrage pricing theory (APT), Roll and Ross (1980) have used factor loadings of individual securities to show that many factors are involved in the return-generating process.

In financial ratio analysis, Johnson (1979) has used the information factor loadings to test the cross-sectional stability of financial ratio patterns; Pinches and Mingo (1973) have used factor loading information to determine which variables should be used to estimate their n-group multivariate discriminant analysis for industry bond ratings. More recently, Chen and Shimerda (1981) used factor analysis in the empirical determination of useful financial ratios.

The properties and characteristics of financial ratios have received considerable attention in recent years, with interest focused primarily on determining the predictive ability of financial ratios and related financial data. Principal areas of investigation have included (i) prediction of corporate bond ratings as explored by Horrigan (1966), Pinches and Mingo (1973), and Pogue and Soldofsky (1969); (ii) prediction of financial ratios by Lev (1969) and Frecka and Lee (1983); (iii) prediction of the suitability of the firm to merge, through an examination of the characteristics of merged firms by Simkowitz and Monroe (1971) and Stevens (1973); and (iv) anticipation of financial impairment by Altman (1968), Beaver (1968), Blume (1974), Tinsley (1970), and Wilcox (1971).

Using the information from factor loadings, Johnson (1979) classified 61 financial ratios for 306 primary manufacturers and 159 retailers into eight financial groups as indicated in Tables 4.5 and 4.6. The results of Johnson's study, and results obtained by Pinches, Mingo, and Caruthers (1973) [PMC], and Pinches, Eubank, and Mingo (1975) suggest that meaningful, empirically based classifications of financial ratios can be isolated, and that the composition of these financial ratio groups is reasonably stable over the time periods investigated and across the two industry classifications examined. Similarly, Chen and Shimerda (1981) used factor loadings to study useful financial ratios, obtaining conclusions similar to those obtained by Johnson (1979). Two tables constructed by Chen and Shimerda are very useful to readers. The financial ratios incorporated in predictive studies are indicated in Table 4.7, and factor classification of

Table 4.5. Cross-sectional comparison of financial ratios and factor loadings defining eight financial ratio categories for industrial firms.

		Factor Loadings			
		1972		1974	
		Primary		Primary	
Ratio Number	Ratio Name	Mfg.	Retail	Mfg.	Retail
Factor 1 — Return on Investment					
4	Earnings/Sales	0.88	0.63*	0.75	0.81*
7	Earnings/Net Worth	0.79	0.94*	0.95	0.95*
12	Earnings/Total Assets	0.93	0.89*	0.85	0.87*
13	Cash Flow/Total Assets	0.92	0.85*	0.84	0.84*
14	Cash Flow/Net Worth	0.50	0.88*	0.79	0.93*
15	EBIT/Total Assets	0.89	0.85*	0.77	0.84*
16	EBIT/Sales	0.89	0.61*	0.70	0.77*
17	Cash Flow/Total Capital	0.94	0.90*	0.85	0.93*
18	Earnings/Total Capital	0.94	0.90*	0.88	0.94*
19	Cash Flow/Sales	0.79	0.59*	0.87	0.74*
41	EBIT/Net Worth	0.79[a]	0.92*	0.95	0.97*
47	Cash Flow/Total Debt	0.81	0.73*	0.84	0.70*
48	Earnings/Total Debt	0.87	0.78*	0.86	0.73*
53	Operating Funds/Total Assets	0.88	0.82*	0.45	0.82*
54	Operating Funds/Net Worth	0.25	0.75	0.63[a]	0.86
55	Operating Funds/Total Capital	0.83	0.81	0.33	0.88
Factor 2 — Financial Leverage					
2	Net Worth/Total Assets	−0.80	−0.85*	−0.82	−0.69[a]*
5	Long-Term Debt/Total Assets	0.87	0.85	0.85	0.87
11	Long-Term Debt/Net Worth	0.88	0.90	0.91	0.93
29	Long-Term Debt/Net Plant	0.85	0.81	0.80	0.81
30	Long-Term Debt/Total Capital	0.89	0.92	0.94	0.91
31	Total Debt/Net Worth	0.79	0.85	0.83	0.71[a]
32	Total Debt/Total Assets	0.81	0.85*	0.79	0.74*
50	Total Debt and Preferred Stock/Total Assets	0.79	0.85*	0.78	0.68*
Factor 3 — Capital Intensiveness					
3	Sales/Net Worth	0.66	0.85*	0.70[a]	0.78*
6	Sales/Total Assets	0.78[a]	0.81*	0.75	0.79*
19	Cash Flow/Sales	−0.44	−72[a]*	—	—
20	Current Liabilities/Net Plant	0.81	0.49*	0.81	0.43[a]
22	Current Assets/Total Assets	0.88	0.46*	0.84	0.41
26	Sales/Net Plant	0.94	0.78*	0.91	0.79*
27	Sales/Total Capital	0.85	0.91*	0.86	0.83*
Factor 4 — Inventory Intensiveness					
1	Working-Capital/Sales	0.72[a]	0.44*	0.69[a]	0.81*
20	Current Liabilities/Net Plant	0.33	0.71*	—	—

(*Continued*)

Table 4.5. (*Continued*)

Ratio Number	Ratio Name	Factor Loadings 1972 Primary Mfg.	1972 Primary Retail	1974 Primary Mfg.	1974 Primary Retail
21	Working-Capital/Total Assets	0.40	0.76	0.46	0.85
22	Current Assets/Total Assets	0.39	0.83*	0.45	0.84
24	Current Assets/Sales	0.92	0.74*	0.92	0.74*
25	Cost of Goods Sold/Inventory	−0.91	−0.92*	−0.94	−.93*
28	Inventory/Sales	0.87	0.93*	0.94	0.93*
Factor 5. Cash Position					
42	Cash/Total Assets	0.91	0.93	0.89	0.81
43	Cash/Current Liabilities	0.84	0.88	0.83	0.87
44	Cash/Sales	0.93	0.86*	0.88	0.89*
46	Cash/Fund Expenditures	0.91	0.86*	0.88	0.89*
Factor 6. Receivables Intensiveness					
23	Quick Assets/Total Assets	0.52	0.89*	0.68[a]	0.89*
33	Receivables/Inventory	0.94	0.84*	0.80[a]	0.82*
34	Inventory/Current Assets	−0.75[a]	−0.70*	−0.64	−0.76*
35	Receivables/Sales	0.72[a]	0.83*	0.81	0.83*
37	Quick Assets/Sales	0.58	0.86*	0.78	0.88*
40	Quick Assets/Current Liabilities	0.40	0.76*	0.46	0.81*
45	Quick Assets/Fund Expenditures	0.55	0.85*	0.75	0.87*
Factor 7. Short-Term Liquidity					
21	Working-Capital/Total Assets	—	—	0.73	−0.35
36	Inventory/Working-Capital	—	—	−0.79	0.16*
38	Current Liabilities/Net Work	—	—	−0.55[a]	0.80
39	Current Assets/Current Liabilities	0.91	0.64*	0.90	−0.61
40	Quick Assets/Current Liabilities	0.77	0.37*	0.76	−0.31*
49	Current Liabilities/Total Assets	—	—	−0.64[a]	0.78*
51	Net Defensive Assets/Fund Expenditures	0.55	0.74*	0.75	−0.52[a]*
Factor 8. Decomposition Measures					
56	Asset Decomposition	0.68	0.74	—	—
58	Equity Decomposition	0.84	0.84	0.86	0.87
60	Non-current Items Decompostion	0.83	0.78	0.87	0.85
61	Time Horizon Decompostion	—	—	0.62	0.70

Source: From Johnson, WB (1979). The cross-sectional stability of financial ratio patterns. *Journal of Financial and Quantitative Analysis*, 14; Table 2. Reprinted with permission from WB Johnson and *JFQA*.

[a]Indicates variables having a within-sample cross-loading of between 0.50 and 0.70 on one other factor.

*t-test of untransformed data significant at $p < 0.05$.

Table 4.6. Cross-sectional congruency coefficients for eight financial-ratio dimensions for 1974.

Factor: Primary Manufacturing Firms	Factor: Retail Firms							
	One	Two	Three	Four	Five	Six	Seven	Eight
One — Return on Investment	0.95	−0.41	−0.13	−0.05	0.14	0.05	−0.25	−0.26
Two — Financial Leverage	−0.40	0.95	0.11	−0.17	−0.17	−0.05	0.45	0.07
Three — Capital Intensiveness	−0.15	−0.00	0.84	0.28	−0.14	−0.16	0.55	0.04
Four — Inventory Intensiveness	−0.13	−0.02	−0.27	0.87	−0.01	0.15	0.08	0.08
Five — Cash Position	0.20	−0.15	−0.21	0.00	0.88	0.46	−0.29	0.15
Six — Receivables Intensiveness	0.01	−0.06	−0.42	0.11	0.29	0.92	−0.24	0.10
Seven — Short-term Liquidity	0.19	−0.34	−0.17	0.30	0.38	0.39	0.76	−0.01
Eight — Decomposition Measures	−0.20	0.16	0.06	0.06	0.01	0.05	0.27	0.84

From Johnson, WB (1979). The cross-sectional stability of financial ratio patterns. *Journal of Financial and Quantitative Analysis*, 14. Table 3. Reprinted with permission from WB Johnson and *JFQA*.

important ratios for predicting firm failure, as found in recent studies, is indicated in Table 4.6. Overall, the above-mentioned empirical studies indicated that factor-loading information can be objectively used to determine which ratios are useful for security analysis and financial management.

4.5. Bond Rating Forecasting

Pinches and Mingo (1973) (P&M) have developed and tested a factor-analysis/multiple discriminant model for predicting bond ratings. They used factor analysis to screen the data in the manner discussed earlier. This technique has been discussed in previous chapters. Here, we will use P&M's multiple discriminant results to show how a k-group discriminant function can be used to analyze the performance of bond ratings and predict future bond ratings.

The following six variables estimate the final discriminant functions:

X_1 = Subordination; the legal status of bonds;
X_2 = Years of consecutive dividends; indicates the stability of the firms' earnings;

Table 4.7. Financial ratios incorporated in predictive studies.

Firm Failure	NW/TL	NI/TA	QA/CL	NI+DDA/TD(1)	TD/TA	WC/TA	CA/CL	No Cr.Inter(2)	EBIT/TA	S/TA	RE/TA	CA/S	WC/S	NI + DDA/CL(1)	NW/S	CL/NW	Inv/S	QA/Inv	Quick Flow(3)	CA/TA	C + MS/TA	NI + DDA/S(1)	NI + DDA/TA(1)	NI/S	OI/S	LTD/TA	NI+Int/Int	Div Ratio
1966 Tamari	*	*					*						*				*											
1966 Beaver		*	X	*	*	*	*	*		X		X	X		X		X			X	X	X	X	X		X		
1968 Altman	X				X	*	X		*	*	*		X				X							X		X		
1972 Deakin		*	*	*	*	*	*					*	*							*	*							
1972 Edmister	X		*	X		X	X			X			*	*	*	*	*											
1974 Blum	*			*														*	*									
1975 Libby		*	X	X	X	X	*					*	X							*	*							
1975 Elam	*		*	*	*		*		X	*			X		X		X					*	*	*	*			
Bond Ratings																												
1966 Horrigan	*		X				X		X	X			*		*		X							X	*			
1969 Pogue & Soldofsky		*																								*	*	
1970 West	*																											
1973 Pinches & Mingo		*								X			X		X									X		*	*	
Market Return																												
1971 Martin				*																					*			X
1973 O'Connor	*									X			*															X
Mergers																												
1973 Stevens	X	X			X	*			X	*			X											X	*	*		X
Beta																												
1973 Breen & Lerner	X				X																							*
Sub- Found Useful*	6	6	3	5	3	4	5	1	1	3	1	2	5	1	2	1	2	1	1	2	2	1	1	1	4	3	2	1
Total Mentioned	10	7	6	7	7	6	8	1	4	8	1	3	11	1	5	1	6	1	1	3	3	2	2	6	4	5	2	4
Prior to 1965																												
1932 Fitzpatrick	X																											
1935 Winakor & Smith	X					X																						
1942 Merwin	X					X	X																					
1945 Chudson							X														X					X		
1958 Hickman																								X			X	
1958 Saulnier	X						X																					
1961 Moore & Atkinson	X					X	X																					
1962 Jackendoff	X					X	X																	X				
1962 Wojenlower	X					X	X																					
1963 Jen		X			X																							
Subtotal	7	1			1	5	6														1			2		1	1	
Total Found Useful	12	7	3	5	4	9	11	1	1	3	1	2	5	1	2	1	2	1	1	2	3	1	1	3	4	4	3	1

*Ratio found useful in study; (X) Ratio mentioned in study; (1) Net Income plus Depreciation, Depletion, Amortization; (2) No Credit Interval = Quick Assets minus CL/Operating Expense minus Depreciation, Depletion, Amortization; (3) Quick Flow = C + MS + AR + (Annual Sales divided by 12)/[CGS = Depreciation + Selling and Administration + Interest] divided by 12]; (4) Cash Interval = C + MS/Operating Expense minus Depreciation, Depletion, Amortization;

Table 4.7. (*Continued*)

CL/Inv	NI/NW	NI+DDA/ # Shs(1)	NW/FA	NW/TA	S/AR	LTD/FA	C+ MS/CL	CL/TA	NI + DDA/NW(1)	NI / TD	QA/TA	S/C + MS	S/QA	C Inter(4)	Def. Inter(5)	S/FA	GP/S	EBT/S	NI + Int/TA	GGS/Inv	S/CL	Inv/WC	CA/TD	NW + LTD/FA	EBT/TA	EBT/NW	OI/Int	NW / LTD	Cap Exp/S(6)	NI/EBT	OI/TD	LTD/CA	LTB/TA	Int/C + MS	EPS	Non OI BT/S(7)	NI/CE
					X	X																															
	X				X		X	X	X	X	X	X	X	X	X																						
							X	X				X				X	X	X	X	X	X																
							*				*	*	*																								
			X													X		X				X	X	X	X	X											
																																					*
							X				X	X	X																								
	*		X		X		*	*	*			X	X			X											X	X			X	*					
	X		X		X		X									X											X	X									
	X			X																								X							X		
	*																												X								
*	*	*																												X						X	
	X												X				X	X		X													X	X			
1	3	1					2	1	1		1	1	1																			1					1
1	7	1	3	1	4	1	6	3	2	1	3	5	5	1	1	4	2	3	1	2	1	1	1	1	1	1	2	3	1	1	1	1	1	1	1	1	1
	X																																				
			X																																		
				X																																	
	X																																				
	2		1	1																																	
1	5	1	1	1			2	1	1		1	1	1																								

(5) Defensive Interval = QA/Operating Expense Minus Depreciation, Depletion, Amortization; (6) Capital Expenditure/Sales; (7) Non-operating Income before Taxes/Sales.
Source: From Chen, KH and TA Shimerda (1981). An empirical analysis of useful financial ratios, *Financial Management*; Table 4.7. Reprinted with permission.

Table 4.8. Factor classification of import ratios for predicting firm failure, as found in recent empirical studies.

Factor	Ratio	Study by						
		Beaver	Altman	Deakin	Edmister	Blum	Elam	Libby
Return on Investment	Net Income/Sales*						X	
	Funds Flow/NW						X	
	Funds Flow/TA						X	
	Net Income/TA	X		X				X
	Net Income/NW						X	
	EBIT/Sales						X	
	EBIT/TA		X					
	NI/Common Equity**					X		
Capital Turnover	QA/TA			X				
	Funds Flow/Sales						X	
	Current Assets/TA			X				X
	Net Worth/Sales				X			
	Sales/TA		X				X	
	WC/TA*	X	X	X				
Financial Leverage	Total Liabilities/TA	X		X			X	
	Total Liabilities/NW					X	X	
	Long-Term Debt/CA**						X	
	Funds Flow/TD**	X		X		X	X	
	Funds Flow/CL**				X			
	Retained Earnings/TA**		X					

(*Continued*)

Table 4.8. (*Continued*)

Factor	Ratio	Study by						
		Beaver	Altman	Deakin	Edmister	Blum	Elam	Libby
Short-Term Liquidity	Current Assets/CL*	X		X			X	X
	Quick Assets/CL			X	X		X	
	Current Liabilities/NW				X			
	Current Liabilities/TA						X	
Cash Position	Cash/Sales			X				
	Cash/Total Assets			X				X
	Cash/Current Liabilities			X			X	
	No Credit Interval**	X						
	Quick Flow**					X		
Inventory-Turnover	Current Assets/Sales			X				X
	Inventory/Sales				X			
	Sales/Working-Capital			X	X			
Receivables Turnover	Quick Assets/Inventory**					X		
	Quick Assets/Sales			X				

Source: From Chen, KH and TA Shimerda (1981). An empirical analysis of useful financial ratios. *Financial Management*, Table 4.8. Reprinted with permission.

*Ratio not included in the final factors of the PEMC studies.

**Ratio not in the 48 ratios included in the PEMC study.

X_3 = Issue size; reflects the size of the firm;
X_4 = (Net income + interest)/interest: 5-year mean; indicates the ability of the firm to meet debt obligations;
X_5 = Long-term debt/total assets: 5-year mean; a measure of the capital structure of the firm; and
X_6 = Net income/total assets; a measure of management's ability to earn a satisfactory return on investment.

These variables were chosen from a group of 35 through factor analysis. In all, 180 bonds were analyzed and randomly assigned to one of two sample groups — 132 forming the original sample for model development and 48 forming a holdout sample for testing purposes. P&M's model includes three discriminant functions that were significant at the 0.001 level (based upon Barlett's v-statistic).[1] The structural form of these three functions is presented below:

$$Y_1 = -0.329X_1 + 0.107X_2 + 0.100X_3 + 0.005X_4 - 0.270X_5 + 0.893X_6,$$

$$Y_2 = 0.046X_1 + 0.218X_2 - 0.212X_3 - 0.264X_4 - 0.505X_5 - 0.762X_6,$$

$$Y_3 = -0.128X_1 - 0.044X_2 - 0.138X_3 + 0.001X_4 + 0.320X_5 - 0.928X_6.$$

The overall discriminating power of the model was determined by testing the equality of the group means. The calculated F-value for the MDA model is 17.225. As the tabled value (0.001) is 2.13, the calculated F-value permits rejection of the null hypothesis that the bonds came from the same population. With the overall conclusion that, *a priori*, the groups of bonds are significantly different, the six variables entering the final MDA model can be examined. The individual discriminating ability of each of the variables and their rank of importance in the various discriminant functions is presented in Table 4.9.

The MDA model correctly rated 92 of the 132 bonds in the original sample, which corresponds to a correct prediction rate of 69.7%; this is analogous to the coefficient of determination (R^2) in regression analysis. If an analyst were interested only in the ability of the model to predict ratings within one classification (either higher or lower) of the actual rating, the model performed very accurately, classifying all but two of the bonds within one rating of the actual rating.

[1]Scaled coefficients for these three discriminant functions can be found in Appendix A.

Table 4.9. Variable means, test of significance, and import ranks.

	Bond Rating						Function Ranks		
Variable	AA	A	BAA	BA	B	F-Ratio	One	Two	Three
X_1	0.000	0.077	0.520	1.000	1.000	—	1	6	2
X_2	1.634	1.581	1.260	1.058	0.486	25.45***	2	2	5
X_3	1.869	1.657	1.275	1.354	1.250	13.97***	3	3	1
X_4	1.138	0.606	0.560	0.511	0.707	6.05***	6	1	6
X_5	0.091	0.162	0.154	0.151	0.215	4.06**	5	4	4
KX_6	0.099	0.075	0.066	0.075	0.069	2.68*	4	5	3

Source: From Pinches, GE and KA Mingo (1973). A multivariate analysis of industrial and bond ratings. *Journal of Finance*, 28, Table 3. Reprinted with permission.
***Significant at 0.001 level.
**Significant at 0.01 level.
*Significant at 0.05 level.

In another test of validity, the model was applied to the holdout sample. With this group, the model correctly rated 31 of 48 bonds (64.58%) and rated all 48 bonds within one rating higher or lower than the actual rating. In order to further validate the MDA model, a stratified random sample of 48 companies issuing bonds during the first 6 months of 1969 was gathered. The MDA model (developed from a sample of newly rated bonds issued in 1967 and 1968) was employed to predict the ratings on the new bonds issued in 1969. About 27 of the 48 bonds were rated correctly, indicating that the model possesses future predictive ability.

The subordination status of a corporate bond [represented by a binary (0-1) variable] appears to be the most important variable among those that were examined in this study. If one were interested only in rating bonds as investment quality (AA, A, and BAA) or non-investment quality (BA and B), the best single predictor is the subordinated status of the bond. Based on this variable alone, correct ratings (investment versus non-investment quality) would have occurred 88.6% of the time for the original sample (117/132) and 83.3% of the time for the holdout sample (40/48).

The model performed very poorly for BAA-rated bonds. An analysis of the multiple range tests indicated that the inability of the MDA model to accurately predict BAA-rated bonds appears to be due to a lack of statistically significant differences in the quantifiable variables included in the model. Overall, though, the model's ability to discriminate between different bond rating is fairly good, and it shows potential for application to the prediction of future bond ratings.

There are two major technical differences between the methods and procedures used in this section and those used in Section 4.3. First, the MDA used in this section is a k-group instead of two-group analysis. Secondly, Pinches and Mingo's MDA analysis is predictive instead of descriptive in nature. Joy and Tollefson (1974) argue that MDA can be used for either predictive or descriptive purposes. They regard Altman's (1968) MDA application as a descriptive instead of a predictive analysis. This comment can also apply to both Sinkey's and Trieschmann and Pinches' (1973) MDA analysis. Other related arguments can be found in Joy and Tollefson (1978) and Altman and Eisenbeis (1978).

4.6. Bond Quality Ratings and the Change of Quality Ratings for the Electric Utility Industry

The multivariate-analysis technique developed by Pinches and Mingo for analyzing industrial bond ratings has also been used to determine bond quality ratings and their associated changes for electric utilities. Pinches, Singleton, and Jahakhani (1978) (PSJ) used this technique to determine whether fixed coverages were a major determinant of electric utility bond ratings. Bhandari, Soldofsky, and Boe (1979) (BSB) investigate whether or not a multivariate discriminant model that incorporates the recent levels, past levels, and the instability of financial ratios can explain and predict the quality rating changes of electric utility bonds.

PSJ (1978) found that fixed coverage is the *only* (and not the dominant) financial variable that apparently influences the bond ratings assigned to electric utility firms. Other important variables are the climate of regulation, total assets, return on total assets, growth rate or net earnings, and construction expenses/total assets.[2] The major finding of BSB's study is that the MDA method can be more successful in predicting bond rating *changes* than it had been predicting the bond ratings themselves. These results have shed some light for the utility regulation agency on the determinants of bond ratings and the change of bond ratings for electric utility industries.

---

[2]To validate their MDA model, PSJ use the Lachenbruch's (1967) Jackknife procedure to do the empirical analysis. They concluded that the MDA analysis is relatively effective in determining bond rating prediction for the electric utility industry. The Jackknife method and its application to MDA are discussed in Appendix A.

4.7. Other Model for Estimating Default Probability

4.7.1. *Ohlson's and Shumway's Methods for Estimating Default Probability*[3]

Beginning in the 1980s, more complex estimation methods such as Logit and Probit were used to determine the likelihood of company bankruptcy. Logit model is a methodology that uses maximum likelihood estimation, or so-called conditional logit model. Two well-known models using Logit models to estimate the probability of bankruptcy are Ohlson (1980) and Shumway (2001), which we will discuss next. Ohlson discusses the following econometric advantages of logit model over MDA used for the development of Altman Z-score. MDA imposes certain statistical requirements on the distributional properties of the predictors, violation of which will result in invalid or poor approximations. For example, MDA assumes the same variance–covariance matrices of the predictors for both failed and non-failed group; it also requires normal distributions of failure predictors which bias against the use of indicator independent variables. Moreover, the output of MDA model is a score which has little intuitive interpretation. The matching procedure which is typically used in MDA technique can result in losing useful information such as losing meaningful predictors. The use of logistic regression, on the other hand, essentially overcomes the weaknesses of MDA discussed above.

Ohlson (1980) used data available prior to the date of bankruptcy to ensure the strict forecasting relationships. His sample included 105 bankruptcies and 2,058 non-bankruptcies from the 70s (1970–1976). Among the 105 bankrupt firms, 8 firms are traded in New York Stock Exchange, 43 are traded in American Stock Exchange, and 54 are traded over-the-counter market or regional exchanges. Nine variables defined below are used to develop the logit model.

X_1 = Natural log of (Total Assets/GNP Implicit Price Deflator Index). The index assumes a base value of 100 for 1968;
X_2 = (Total Liabilities/Total Assets);
X_3 = (Current Assets — Current Liabilities)/Total Assets;
X_4 = Current Assets/Current Liabilities;
X_5 = One if total liabilities exceeds total assets, zero otherwise;
X_6 = Net income/total assets;

[3]This section was written by Professors Lili Sun and Bi-Huei Tsai.

X_7 = Funds provided by operations/total liabilities;
X_8 = One if net income was negative for the last 2 years, zero otherwise; and
X_9 = (Net income in year t − Net income in t − 1)/(Absolute net income in year t + Absolute net income in year t − 1).

Three sets of coefficients are estimated using data 1 year prior to bankruptcy and or 2 years prior to bankruptcy. Intuitively, the model with estimates computed using data 1 year prior to bankruptcy performs the best, which is expressed as follows:

$$Y = -1.32 - 0.407X_1 + 6.03X_2 - 1.43X_3 + 0.0757X_4 - 2.37X_5 - 1.83X_6 + 0.285X_7 - 1.72X_8 - 0.521X_9, \tag{4.8}$$

where $Y = \log[P/(1-P)]$, P = the probability of bankruptcy.

Thus, the probability of bankruptcy (P) is calculated as $\exp(Y)/[1+\exp(Y)]\exp$, and the model becomes relatively easy to interpret.

Ohlson found that using a probability cutoff of 3.8% for classifying firms as bankrupt minimized type I and type II errors of the model presented in Eq. (4.8). At this probability cutoff point, the model correctly classified 87.6% of his bankrupt firm sample and 82.6% of the non-bankrupt firms. Begley *et al.* (1996) applied Ohlson's logit model (1980) to predict bankruptcy for a holdout sample of 65 bankrupt and 1,300 non-bankrupt firms in the 1980s. They found substantially higher type I and type II error rates than those in the original studies. They re-estimated the coefficients for each model using data for a portion of their 1980s sample. However, they found no performance improvement for the re-estimated Ohlson Model.

The logit model used by Ohlson (1980) is single-period static logit model. Shumway (2001) employed a discrete hazard model or multiple-period dynamic logit model. The concept of discrete-time hazard model originates from the survival model and is widely used in biological medication field. It was not until recent years that social science researchers started using it for analyzing variables' effect upon survival (e.g., Lancaster (1992). Cox and Oakes (1984) calculate hazard rate to estimate the likelihood of survival and survival time. Shumway (2001) elaborates the econometric advantages of a hazard model over a static binary logit model. First, hazard models control for each firm's period at risk, while static models do not. Secondly, hazard models exploit each firm's time-series data by including annual observations as time-varying covariates. Thirdly, hazard models produce more efficient out-of-sample forecasts by utilizing much more data. Shumway (2001) proves that a multi-period logit model is equivalent to a discrete-time hazard model. Therefore, his model used multiple years of data for each sample firm, and treated each firm as a single observation.

Moreover, Shumway (2001) also corrected the problem in the traditional approaches of bankruptcy forecasting, that is, previous studies used only most of the accounting ratios used in the previous bankruptcy studies are found not significant. Shumway (2001) incorporated not only financial ratios but also market variables such as market size, past stock returns, and idiosyncratic returns variability as bankruptcy predictors.

The dependent variable in the prediction models is each firm-year's bankruptcy status (0, 1) in a given sample year. In a hazard analysis, for a bankrupt firm, the dependent variable equals 1 for the year in which it files bankruptcy, and the dependent variable equals 0 for all sample years prior to the bankruptcy-filing year. The non-bankrupt firms are coded 0 every year they are in the sample.

The Shumway (2001) study employed all available firms in a broad range of industries, resulting in a sample of 300 bankrupt firms for the period of 1962–1992. The study found that a multi-period logit model out-performed MDA and single-period logit models, and that a combination of market-based and accounting-based independent variables out-performed models that were only accounting-based. The Shumway model with incorporation of market-based and accounting-based predictors is expressed as follows:

$$Y = -13.303 - 1.982X_1 + 3.593X_2 - 0.467X_3 - 1.809X_4 + 5.79X_5, \tag{4.9}$$

where $Y = \log[P/(1 - P)]$, P = the probability of bankruptcy;

X_1 = Net Income/Total Assets;
X_2 = (Total Liabilities/Total Assets);
X_3 = The logarithm of (each firm's market capitalization at the end of year prior to the observation year/total market capitalization of NYSE and AMEX market);
X_4 = Past excess return as the return of the firm in year t − 1 minus the value-weighted CRSP NYSE/AMEX index return in year t − 1; and
X_5 = idiosyncratic standard deviation of each firm's stock returns. It is defined as the standard deviation of the residual of a regression which regresses each stock's monthly returns in year t − 1 on the value-weighted NYSE/AMEX index return for the same year.

To evaluate the forecast accuracy of the Hazard model presented in Eq. 4.9, Shumway (2001) divided the test sample into 10 groups based upon their predicted probability of bankruptcies using the model. The hazard model classifies almost 70% of all bankruptcies in the highest bankruptcy probability decile and classifies 96.6 of bankrupt firms above the median probability. Following Shumway (2001), researchers of bankruptcy prediction have been using multiple-period logit regression. For instance, Sun (2007) developed a multi-period logistic regression model and found this model outperforms auditors' going concern opinions in predicting bankruptcy.[4]

4.7.2. *KMV-Merton Model*

The KMV Corporation developed the KMV-Merton model, which now sees frequent use in both practice and academic research. This model is an application of Merton's model in which the equity of the firm is a call option on the underlying value of the firm with a strike price equal to the face value of the firm's debt. The KMV-Merton Model estimates the market value of debt by applying the Merton (1974) bond-pricing model. The Merton model makes two particular important assumptions. The first is that the total value of a firm follows geometric Brownian motion. The second critical assumption is that the firm has issued only one discount bond maturing in T periods. Based on these assumptions, the equity of the firm is a call option on the underlying value of the firm with a strike price equal to the face value of the firm's debt and a time-to-maturity of T. The Black–Scholes–Merton Formula can describe the value of equity as a function of the total value of the firm. By put-call parity, the value of the firm's debt equals the value of a risk-free discount bond minus the value of a put option written on the firm, again with a strike price equal to the face value of debt and a time-to-maturity of T. If the assumptions of the Merton model hold, the KMV-Merton model should give accurate default forecasts.

Bharath and Shumway (2004) examined two hypotheses: (i) the probability of default implied by the Merton model is a sufficient statistic for forecasting bankruptcy; and (ii) the Merton model is an important quantity to consider when predicting default. This study hypothesizes that a reasonable set of simple variables cannot completely replace the information in Π_{KMV} (The KMV-Merton probability), or that a sufficient statistic for default probability cannot neglect Π_{KMV}.

[4]Saunders and Allen (2002) and Saunders and Cornett (2006) have discussed alternative methods for determining credit risk.

Bharath and Shumway (2004) incorporated Π_{KMV} into a hazard model that forecasts default from 1980 through 2003. Using this hazard model, they compared Π_{KMV} to a naive alternative (Π_{Naive}), which is much simpler to calculate, but retains some of the functional form of Π_{KMV}.

In conclusion, they examined the accuracy and the contribution of the KMV-Merton default-forecasting model. Looking at hazard models that forecast default, the KMV-Merton model does not produce a sufficient statistic for the probability of default, and it appears to be possible to construct a sufficient statistic without solving the simultaneous non-linear equations required by the KMV-Merton model.

4.7.3. *Empirical Comparison*

Mai's dissertation (2010) have re-examined the four most commonly employed default prediction models: Z-score model (Altman (1968), logit model (Ohlson (1980)), probit model (Zmijewski (1984)), and hazard analysis (Shumway (2001)). Her empirical results show that the discrete-time hazard model adopted by Shumway (2001), combined with a new set of accounting-ratio and market-driven variables improves the bankruptcy forecasting power.

By using a hand-collected business default events from *Compustat* Annual Industrial database and publicly available press-news, Mai's (2010) has constructed a sample of publicly-traded companies in one of the three U.S. stock markets between 1991 and 2006. With cautiously chosen cutoff at 0.021 implied bankruptcy probability level, the out-of-sample hazard model with stepwise methodology results in classifying 82.7% of default firms and 82.8% of non-default firms. Comparing to the best results in Shumway (2001), which provides 76.5% classification of default firms, 55.2% in Altman (1993), 66.1% in Ohlson (1980), and 65.4% in Zmijewski (1984). It can be concluded that resolve from her dissertation did better than the other 4 models.

The specification of Logit and Probit Models can be found in Appendix 4.B, and SAS Code for Hazard Model in Bankruptcy Forecasting can be found in Appendix 4.C.

4.8. Summary

In this chapter, we have discussed applications of two multivariate statistical methods in discriminant analysis and factor analysis. Examples of using two-group discriminant functions to perform credit analysis, predict corporate bankruptcy, and determine problem banks and distressed P-L insurers were discussed in detail. Basic concepts of factor analysis were presented, showing their application in determining useful financial ratios. In addition, the combination of factor analysis and discriminant analysis to analyze industrial bond ratings was discussed. Finally, Ohlson's and Shumway's methods for estimating default probability were discussed.

In sum, this chapter shows that multivariate statistical methods can be used to do practical financial analysis for both managers and researchers.

Notes

1. Scaled coefficients for these three discriminant functions can be found in Appendix A.
2. To validate their MDA model, PSJ use the Lachenbrach's (1967) jackknife procedure to do the empirical analysis. They concluded that the MDA analysis is relatively effective in determining bond rating prediction for the electric utility industry. The Jackknife method and its application to MDA are discussed in Appendix A.
3. Saunders and Allen (2002) and Saunders and Cornett (2006) have discussed alternative methods for determining credit risk.

Problem Set

1. Describe the application of two-group discriminant analysis to a real-world problem. For each step involved, discuss the rationale and ramifications.
2. Of what value is factor loading to the financial analyst? What are some examples of factor loading?
3. How did Pinches and Mingo combine the factor analysis and discriminant analysis in the bond-rating forecasting? How was their discriminant analysis different from previous examples?
4. Describe how Mehta and Van Horne used two-group discriminant analysis for credit analysis. How is the proper cutoff point determined? What tasks is the manager responsible for in doing credit analysis?
5. Briefly discuss the classification errors in Question 4 and their implications to this type of analysis.
6. Describe the application of factor analysis and factor loadings to classify financial ratios, as in the Johnson study of industrial firms. How are the factor scores determined?

7. Please describe Ohlson's (1980) and Shumway's (2001) model for estimating default probability in detail.
8. Briefly describe the jackknife method described in Appendix A of Chapter 4. What are the benefits of its use in multidiscriminate analysis?
9. Use the dummy regression method to estimate the financial z-scores for the data listed in Tables 4.P.1a and 4.P.1b. In these tables, X_1, X_2, X_3, X_4, and X_5 represent Working-Capital/Total Assets, Retained Earnings/Total Assets, EBIT/Total Assets, Market Value of Equity/Book Value of Debt, and Sales/Total Assets, respectively. (Printouts of these tables are provided in the *Solutions Manual*.) This data was supplied by Moyer (1978); the author is grateful for his contribution. A more detailed discussion of this sample can be found in Moyer's 1977 article.
10. Use the factor analysis to classify Pinches and Mingo's (1973) financial ratio data as listed in Table 4.P.2 into five groups and then interpret the related results. Here there are 18 columns and 264 rows, as shown by the printouts in the *Solutions Manual*. This data set represents the financial information for 132 bonds. Each bond's data is indicated by two rows. Therefore, column (a) represents subordination, and column (s) represents the five different bond ratings. The definition of the other 34 variables can be found in the appendix of Pinches and Mingo's (1973) *Journal Finance* paper.
11. Use the results of Question 9 to do multivariate analysis of industrial bond ratings in accordance with Pinches and Mingo's (1973) procedure. (*Hint*: To answer Questions 9 and 10, students should carefully read and understand the Pinches and Mingo paper.)
12. Please discuss the similarities and differences among Altman's (1968), Ohlson's (1980), and Shumway's (2001) approaches for credit analyses.

Appendix 4.A. Jackknife Method and its Application in MDA Analysis

The jackknife statistic is a general method for reducing the bias of an estimator while providing a measure of the resulting estimator by sample reuse (Crask and Perreault, 1977). The result of applying a jackknife procedure is an unbiased, or nearly unbiased, estimator, along with its approximate confidence interval.

The jackknife is a general technique in that it can be applied to any linear estimator. To describe it in its general form, consider a random sample of size N, with an observed variable X for each of the N sampling units. If the sample is partitioned into M subsets, each of size k (such that $kM = N$), a new random sample can be formed by deleting any one of the size k subsets from the original sample.

Pseudovalues can be formed by (1) estimating θ'_I using only $N-k$ sample values (i.e., after deleting one of the M subsets). Thus, M pseudovalues can be obtained by deleting each of the M subsets in turn, and forming a weighted combination of θ and the θ'_I such that

$$J_i(\theta) = M\theta - (M-1)\theta'_i \quad (i = 1, \dots, M). \tag{4.A.1}$$

The jackknife statistic is thus

$$J(\theta) = \left[\sum_{i=1}^{M} \frac{J_i(\theta)}{M}\right] = M\theta - (M-1)\bar{\theta}'_i, \tag{4.A.2}$$

which is the simple mean of the pseudovalues (Crask and Perreault, 1977).

The pseudovalues can be considered as independently distributed random variables (Tukey, 1958). Thus confidence intervals can be computed for the jackknife estimates and these can be tested using the Student's t-distribution. The bias of the jackknife estimate has been shown to be less than the bias in the original sample estimate θ, and frequently approaches zero (Gray and Schucany, 1972).

One set of procedures that can be used to apply the jackknife technique is described below (based on the BMDP program):

1. Means, standard deviations, and coefficients of variation are computed for each variable in each group for all groups. The pooled (within-groups) standard deviation is

$$\left[\frac{\sum (N_k - 1)S_k^2}{\sum (N_k - 1)}\right]^{\frac{1}{2}}. \tag{4.A.3}$$

where S_k^2 is the variance and N_k is the sample size of the kth group.

2. The F-to-enter for each variable is computed. The F-to-enter corresponds to the F-statistic computed from a one-way analysis of variance (ANOVA). The degrees of freedom correspond to those of one-way ANOVA, that is, $(g-1)$ and $\sum (N_k - 1)$, where g is the number of groups.

3. The variable with the highest F-to-enter is entered into the discriminant functions. This is the variable that discriminates the best between groups.

   At this step, the following are computed:

   (i) F-to-enter for each variable in the equation (this is equal to the F-to-enter at step 2).
   (ii) F-to-enter for each variable not in the equation.
   (iii) Wilk's lambda or University-statistic (this is a multivariate analysis-of-variance statistic that tests the equality of group means for the variable(s) in the discriminant function).
   (iv) Approximate F-statistic (this is a transformation of Wilk's lambda that can be compared with the F-distribution).
   (v) F-matrix (this contains F-values computed from the Mahalonobi's D^2-statistics that test the equality of group means for each pair of groups; the test is for only the variables in the discriminant function).
   (vi) Classification functions (the classification function can be used to classify cases into groups; the case is assigned to the group with the largest value of the classification function).

The jackknife technique classifies each case into a group according to the classification functions computed from all the data *except* the case being classified. Mahalanobi's D^2 and the posterior probabilities are computed for each case after the final step of the discriminant analysis, D^2 is the distance from each case to each group mean. Both the group mean and the cross-products matrices use the case in the computation of the cross products.

Table 4.A.1. Original and Jackknifed (Standardized) Discriminant Functions.

	Discriminant Function					
	1		2		3	
Variable	Coefficient	Jackknifed* Coefficient	Coefficient	Jackknifed* Coefficient	Coefficient	Jackknifed* Coefficient
X_1	−0.936	−0.882**	0.131	0.102	−0.365	−0.361**
X_2	0.528	0.461**	1.073	0.863**	−0.216	−0.017
X_3	0.360	0.352**	−0.758	−0.541	−0.493	−0.516**
X_4	0.023	0.041	−1.284	−0.888**	0.006	0.012
X_5	−0.283	−0.171	−0.529	−0.544**	0.335	0.421**
X_6	0.327	0.302**	−0.280	−0.067	−0.340	−0.320**

In the jackknife technique, each case is eliminated in turn from the computation of the group means and cross products. Then Department and the posterior probability are computed for the distance from the case to the groups formed by the remaining cases. The jackknife method discussed in this appendix has been applied to Lee and Howell (1984) to the Pinches and Mingo (1973) bond rating data. Both original and jackknifed (scaled) discriminant functions are listed in Table 4.A.1. The main advantage of jackknifed discriminant functions is that t-statistics can be used to test whether the estimated coefficients are significantly different from zero or not.

References for Appendix 4.A

Crask, MR and WD Perrault (1977). Validation of discriminant analysis in marketing research. *Journal of Marketing Research*, 14, 60–65.

Dixon, WT, Chief Editor, BMDP *Statistical Software 1981*, University of California Press, pp. 519–537.

Gray, HL and WR Schucany (1972). *The Generalized Jackknife Statistic.* New York: Marcel & Dekker.

Lee, CF and RD Howell (1984). *Jackknife discrimination method for bond rating analysis.* Mimeo.

Tukey, JW (1958). Bias and confidence in not-quite-large samples. *Annals of Mathematical Statistics*, 29, 614–625.

Appendix 4.B. Logistic Model and Probit Model

The likelihood function for binary sample space of bankruptcy and non-bankruptcy is

$$l = \prod_{i \in s_1} P(X_i, \beta) \prod_{i \in s_2} (1 - P(X_i, \beta)), \tag{4.B.1}$$

where P is some probability function, $0 \leq P \leq 1$; and $P(X_i, \beta)$ denotes probability of bankruptcy for any given X_i and β.

Since it is not easy to solve the selecting probability function P, for simplicity, one can solve the likelihood function in (4.B.1) by taking the natural logarithm. The logarithm of the likelihood function then is

$$L(l) = \sum_{i \in s_1} \log P(X_i, \beta) + \sum_{i \in s_2} \log(1 - P(X_i, \beta)), \tag{4.B.2}$$

where S_1 is the set of bankrupt firms; and S_2 is the set of non-bankrupt firms.

The maximum likelihood estimators for β_s can be obtained by solving $\underset{\beta}{Max}\, L(l)$.

In Logistic model, the probability of company i going bankrupt given independent variables X_i is defined as

$$P(X_i, \beta) = \frac{1}{1 + \exp(-\beta' X_i)}. \qquad (4.B.3)$$

The two implications here are (1) $P(.)$ is increasing in $\beta' X_i$ and (2) $\beta' X_i$ is equal to $\log\left[\frac{P}{(1-P)}\right]$.

We then classify bankrupt firms and non-bankrupt firms by setting a "cut-off" probability attempting to minimize Type I and Type II errors.

In Probit models, the probability of company i going bankrupt given independent variables X_i is defined as

$$P(X_i, \beta) = \int_{-\infty}^{(X_i,\beta)} \frac{1}{\sqrt{2\pi}} e^{-\frac{z^2}{2}} dz, \qquad (4.B.4)$$

the cumulative standard normal distribution function.

Maximum likelihood estimators from Probit model can be obtained similarly as in the Logistic models. Although Probit models and Logistic models are similar, Logistic models are preferred to Probit models due to the non-linear estimation in Probit models (Gloubos and Grammatikos, 1998).

Appendix 4.C. SAS Code for Hazard Model in Bankruptcy Forecasting

```
libname  jess 'D:\Documents and Settings\MAI\Desktop\sas code';
*test modified model's performance in the test sample;
*** Logistic Regression Analysis ***;
options pageno=1;
* Add prediction data set to original data;
data jess._prddata;
   _FREQ_ = 1;
   set jess.train_winsor1 jess.test_winsor1(in=inprd);
   _inprd_ = inprd;
   * set freq variable to 0 for additional data;
   if inprd then _FREQ_ = 0;
run;

proc logistic data=jess._prddata DESCEND;
   freq _FREQ_;
```

```
   model BPTSTATUS = NITA CASALES CACL CATA CASHTA LTDTA LSALES CAR LNMCP/
    ctable pprob=0.001 to 0.99 by 0.01;
** Create output data set for predictions **;
   output out=jess.pred p=phat;
run;

proc means data=jess._prddata;
var NITA CASALES CACL CATA CASHTA LTDTA LSALES stress3 CAR LNMCP;
run;

data jess.out_sample;
set jess.pred;
if _FREQ_ = 0;
run;

data jess.count1_1;
set jess.out_sample;
if phat >=0.021 and bptstatus = 1;
run;

data jess.count1_2;
set jess.out_sample;
if  bptstatus =1;
run;

data jess.count2_1;
set jess.out_sample;
if phat < 0.021 and bptstatus = 0;
run;

data jess.count2_2;
set jess.out_sample;
if  bptstatus =0;
run;
```

References for Chapter 4

Altman, EI (1968). Financial ratios, discriminant analysis, and the prediction of corporate bankruptcy. *Journal of Finance*, 23, 589–609.

Altman, EI, R Haldeman, and P Narayanan (1977). ZETA analysis, a new model for bankruptcy classification. *Journal of Banking and Finance*, 29–54.

Altman, EI and TP McGough (1974). Evaluation of a company as a going-concern. *Journal of Accounting*, 50–57.

Altman, EI (1982). Accounting implications of failure prediction models. *Journal of Accounting, Auditing, Finance*, 4–19.

Altman, EI (1984). The success of business failure prediction models. An international survey. *Journal of Banking and Finance*, 8(2), 171–198.

Altman, EI (1989). Measuring corporate bond mortality and performance. *Journal of Finance*, 44(4), 909–922.

Altman, EI (1993). *Corporate Financial Distress and Bankruptcy: A Complete Guide to Predicting and Avoiding Distress and Profiting from Bankruptcy.* New York: Wiley.

Altman, EI (2000). Predicting financial distress of companies revisiting the Z-score and ZETA models. Working paper.

Altman, EI, G Marco, and F Varetto (1994). Corporate distress diagnosis: Comparisons using linear discriminant analysis and neural networks. *Journal of Banking & Finance*, 18, 505–529.

Amemiya, T (1981). The qualitative response models: A Survey. *The Journal of Economic Literature*, 1483–1536.

Anandarajan, M, P Lee, and A Anandarajan (2001). Bankruptcy prediction of financially stressed firms: An examination of the predictive accuracy of artificial neural networks. *International Journal of Intelligent Systems in Accounting, Finance and Management*, 10, 69–81.

Anderson, JA (1972). Separate sample logistic discrimination. *Biometrika*, 59, 19–35.

Barth, ME, WH Beaver, and WR Landsman (1998). Relative valuation roles of equity book value and net income as a function of financial health. *Journal of Accounting & Economics*, 25, 1–34.

Beaver, WH (1968a). Market prices, financial ratios and prediction of failure. *Journal of Accounting Research*, 6(2), 179–192.

Beaver, WH (1966). Financial ratios as predictors of failure. *Journal of Accounting Research*, 4, 71–111.

Beaver, WH (1968b). Alternative accounting measures as predictors of failure. *The Accounting Review*, 43, 113–122.

Beaver, WH, MF McNichols, and J Rhie (2005). Have financial statements become less informative? Evidence from the ability of financial ratios to predict bankruptcy. *Review of Accounting Studies*, 10(1), 93–122.

Begley, J, J Ming, and S Watts (1996). Bankruptcy classification errors in the 1980s: An empirical analysis of Altman's and Ohlson's models. *Review of Accounting Studies*, 1, 267–284.

Bhandari, SB, RM Soldofsky, and WJ Boe (1979). Bond quality rating changes for electric utilities: A multivariate Analysis. *Financial Management*, 8, 74–81.

Bharath, ST and T Shumway (2004). *Forecasting default with the KMV-Merton model.* Working paper, the University of Michigan.

Billings, B (1999). Revisiting the relation between the default risk of debt and the earnings response coefficient. *Accounting Review*, 74(4), 509–522.

Blume, MP (1974). The failing company doctrine. *Journal of Accounting Research*, 43, 1–25.

Bonn, Jeff and Crosbre Peter (2003). Modeling Default Risk: Modeling Methodology. Moody's KMV Company.

Chen, KH and TA Shimerda (1981). An empirical analysis of useful financial ratios. *Financial Management*, 51–60.

Cielen, A, L Peeters, and K Vanhoof (2004). Bankruptcy prediction using a data envelopment analysis. *European Journal of Operational Research*, 154(2), 526–532.

Clark, K and E Ofek (1994). Mergers as a means of restructuring distressed firms: An empirical investigation. *Journal of Financial & Quantitative Analysis*, 29(4), 541–565.

Cox, DR and D Oakes (1984). *Analysis of Survival Data*. New York: Chapman & Hall.

Denis, D, D Denis, and A Sarin (1997). Ownership structure and top executive turnover. *Journal of Financial Economics*, 45, 193–221.

Diamond. Jr H (1976). *Pattern recognition and the detection of corporate failure.* Ph.D. dissertation, New York University.

Dichev, I (1998). Is the risk of bankruptcy a systematic risk? *Journal of Finance*, 53, 1131–1148.

Dimitras, AI, SH Zanakis, and C Zopounidis (1996). Theory and methodology: A survey of business failure with an emphasis on prediction methods and industrial applications. *European Journal of Operational Research*, 90, 487–513.

Duffie, D and K Singleton (1999). Modeling term structures of defaultable bonds. *Review of Financial Studies*, 12, 687–720.

Drehmann, M, AJ Patton, and S Sorensen (2005). *Corporate defaults and large macroeconomic shocks.* Working paper.

Falkenstein, Eric G, Boral, Andrew and Carty, Lea V (2000). Riskcalc for Private Companies Moody's Default Model. Global Credit Research.

Farrar, FS (1962). *The Investment Decision Under Uncertainty.* Englewood Cliffs, NJ: Prentice Hall, Inc.

Fitzpatrick, P (1932). A comparison of the ratios of successful industrial enterprises with those of failed companies. *The Accountants Publishing Company.*

Foster, G (1998). *Financial Statement Analysis*, 2nd ed. Englewood Cliffs, NJ: Prentice Hall, Inc.

Foster, B, T Ward, and J Woodroof (1998). An analysis of the usefulness of debt defaults and going concern opinions in bankruptcy risk assessment. *Journal of Accounting, Auditing & Finance*, 13(3), 351–371.

Frecka, T and CF Lee (1983). Generalized ratio generation process and its implications. *Journal of Accounting Research*, 308–316.

Glennon, D and P Nigro (2005). Measuring the default risk of small business loans: A survival analysis approach. *Journal of Money, Credit, and Banking*, 37(5), 923–947.

Hillegeist, SA, EK Keating, and DP Cram (2004). Assessing the probability of bankruptcy. *Review of Accounting Studies*, 9, 5–34.

Hol, S, S Westgaard, and N Wijst (2002). *Capital structure and the prediction of bankruptcy.* Working paper.

Honjo, Y (2000). Business failure of new firms: An empirical analysis using a multiplicative hazards model. *International Journal of Industrial Organization*, 18(4), 557–574.

Hopwood, WS, JC Mckeown, and JP Mutchler (1989). A test of the incremental explanatory power of opinions qualified for consistency and uncertainty. *The Accounting Review*, 64, 28–48.

Hopwood, W, JC Mckeown, and JF Mutchler (1984). A reexamination of auditor versus model accuracy within the context of the going-concern opinion decision. *Contemporary Accounting Research*, 10, 409–431.

Horrigan, JO (1965). Some empirical bases of financial ratio analysis. *The Accounting Review*, 40, 558–586.

Johnson, WB (1979). The cross-sectional stability of financial ratio patterns. *Journal of Financial and Quantitative Analysis*, 14, 1035–1048.

Jones, F (1987). Current techniques in bankruptcy prediction. *Journal of Accounting Literature*, 6, 131–164.

Jones, S and DA Hensher (2004). Predicting firm financial distress: A mixed logit model. *Accounting Review*, 79(4), 1011–1038.

Joy, OM and JO Tollefson (1975). On the financial applications of discriminant analysis. *Journal of Financial and Quantitative Analysis*, 10, 723–739.

Kiefer, NM (1988). Economic duration data and hazard functions. *Journal of Economic Literature*, 26, 646–679.

King, BF (1966). Market and industry factors in stock price behavior. *Journal of Business*, 139–190.

Lachenbruch, PA (1967). An almost unbiased method of obtaining confidence intervals for the probability of misclassification in discriminant analysis. *Biometrics*, 639–645.

Lancaster, T (1992). *The Econometric Analysis of Transition Data.* New York: Cambridge University Press.

Lane, WR, SW Looney, and JW Wansley (1986). An application of the cox proportional hazards model to bank failure. *Journal of Banking and Finance*, 10, 511–531.

Lau, AHL (1987). A five-state financial distress prediction model. *Journal of Accounting Research*, 18, 109–131.

Lloyd, WP and CF Lee (1975). Block recursive systems in asset pricing models. *Journal of Finance*, 31, 1101–1113.

Mai, JS (2010). Alternative Approaches to Business Failure Prediction Models. Essay I of Dissertation, Rutgers University.

Mehta, DR (1974). *Working Capital Management.* Englewood Cliffs, NJ: Prentice-Hall, Inc.

Merton, RC (1974). On the pricing of corporate debt: The risk structure of interest rates. *Journal of Finance*, 29, 449–470.

Molina, CA (2005). Are firms underleveraged? An examination of the effect of leverage on default probabilities. *Journal of Finance*, 3, 1427–1459.

Moyer, RC (1977). Forecasting Financial Failure: A Re-examination. *Financial Management*, 11–117.

Ohlson, JS (1980). Financial ratios and the probabilitistic prediction of bankruptcy. *Journal of Accounting Research*, 19, 109–131.

Orgler, YE (1970). A credit-scoring model for commercial loans. *Journal of Money, Credit and Banking*, 2, 435–445.

Orgler, YE (1975). *Analytical Methods in Loan Evaluation.* Lexington, MA: Lexington Books.

Penman, SH (2006). *Financial Statement Analysis and Security Valuation.* 3rd ed. New York: McGraw-Hill/Irwin.

Pinches, GE and KA Mingo (1973). A multivariate analysis of industrial bond ratings. *Journal of Finance*, 28, 1–18.

Pinches, GE, AA Eubank, and KA Mingo (1975). The hierarchical classification of financial ratios. *Journal of Business Research*, 3, 295–310.

Pinches, GE, KA Mingo, and JK Caruthers (1973). The stability of financial patterns in industrial organizations. *Journal of Finance*, 28, 389–396.

Pinches, GE, JC Singleton, and A Jahankhani (1978). Fixed coverage as a determinant of electric utility bond ratings. *Financial Management*, 8, 45–55.

Pogue, TF and RM Soldofsky (1969). What's in a bond rating? *Journal of Financial and Quantitative Analysis*, 201–228.

Rao, CR (1952). *Advanced Statistical Methods in Biometric Research.* New York: Wiley.

Roll, R and SA Ross (1980). An empirical investigation of the arbitrage pricing theory. *Journal of Finance*, 35, 1073–1103.

Saretto, AA (2005). *Predicting and pricing the probability of default.* Working paper.

Sarkar, S and RS Sriram (2001). Bayesian models for early warning of bank failures. *Management Science*, 47(11), 1457–1475.

Saunders, A and L Allen (2002). *Credit Risk Measurement: New Approaches to Value at Risk and Other Paradigms.* 2nd ed. New York: Wiley.

Saunders, A and MM Cornett (2013). *Financial Institutions Management: A Risk Management Approach.* 8th ed. New York: McGraw-Hill/Irwin.

Scott, J (1981). The probability of bankruptcy: A comparison of empirical predictions and theoretical models. *Journal of Banking and Finance*, 5, 317–344.

Shumway, T (2001). Forecasting bankruptcy more accurately: A simple hazard model. *The Journal of Business*, 74, 101–124.

Simkowitz, MA and RJ Monroe (1971). A discriminant analysis function for conglomerate targets. *Southern Journal of Business*, 1–16.

Singer, JD and JB Willett (1993). It's about time: Using discrete-time survival analysis to study duration and the timing of events. *Journal of Educational Statistics*, 18, 155–195.

Sinkey, JF (1975). A multivariate statistical analysis of the characteristics of problem bank. *Journal of Finance*, 30, 21–36.

Stevens, DL (1970). Financial characteristics of merged firms: A multivariate analysis. *Journal of Financial and Quantitative Analysis*, 5, 36–62.

Tam, KY and MY Kiang (1992). Managerial applications of neural networks: The case of bank failure redictions. *Management Science*, 38(7), 926–947.

Trieschmann, JS and GE Pinches (1973). A multivariate model for predicting financially distressed P-L insurers. *Journal of Risk and Insurance*, 327–338.

Van Horne, JC (2001). *Financial Management and Policy.* 12th ed. Englewood Cliffs, NJ: Prentice Hall Inc.

Venuti, EK (2004). The going-concern assumption revisited: Assessing a company's future viability. *CPA Journal.*
Vuong, Q (1989). Likelihood ratio tests for model selection and non-nested hypotheses. *Econometrica*, 57(2), 307–333.
Wilcox, JW (1971). A simple theory of financial ratios as predictors of failure. *Journal of Accounting Research*, 389–395.
Zavgren, CV (1983). The prediction of corporate failure: The state of the art. *Journal of Accounting Literature*, 2, 1–38.
Zmijewski, ME (1984). Methodological issues related to the estimation of financial distress prediction models. *Supplement to Journal of Accounting Research*, 22, 59–68.

Chapter 5

Determination and Applications of Nominal and Real Rates-of-Return in Financial Analysis

5.1. Introduction

The utilization of interest factors in the process of business decision making is discussed extensively in most introductory economics, accounting, and finance courses. The determination and forecasting of future interest rates, an important input in the financial analysis and planning process generally has not been carefully explored in these introductory texts. We therefore find it appropriate to discuss various measures of return and averaging processes, and then consider how they relate to the term structure of interest rates. We introduce the methods of calculus to allow for the examination of various measures of return and averaging processes in a continuous time framework. Notably, we exclude a discussion of present- and future-value factors and their derivation, because it would require too many assumptions. For a review of these concepts, we have included Appendix A on the mechanics of discounting and compounding.

The term structure of interest rates is the relationship between yield and maturity on securities differing only in length of time-to-maturity. Following this theoretical discussion of the term structure of interest rates and relevant measures of return, the empirical estimation of the term structure is presented, which should yield more information to the financial planner. Taking the term structure as given, we then consider how it may be used to forecast future inflation rates and relative risk premiums between bonds and equities. Also of interest is how stock returns relate to general economic activity and the effect inflation has on all the relevant variables. The relationship between stock prices, interest rates, inflation, and the real sector, an issue we will devote considerable attention to in the latter portion of the chapter. Section 5.2 discusses theoretical justifications of interest payments. Section 5.3 defines rate-of-return measurement and alternative methods for estimating averages of these returns. Section 5.4 explores theories of the term structure and its application. The relationship between an interest-rate change and a change in price level is investigated in Section 5.5. The alternative hypotheses used in exploring the impacts of inflation on the value of the firm are reviewed in Section 5.6. Finally, results of this chapter are summarized in Section 5.7.

5.2. Theoretical Justification of Paying Interest

When attempting to explain why interest is paid to lenders of funds, even in a default-free situation, we generally find two related rationales, which are the liquidity preference and time preference theories. The liquidity preference theory asserts that rational people prefer more liquid assets to those that are less liquid. Cash or currency is the most liquid asset. Cash holders must be offered some premium to lend and relinquish their liquidity position, hence the term liquidity premium. Startz (1982) used 1-month Treasury bill rates to show that one- to two-thirds of the variation in the difference between forward notes and realized spot notes is due to variation in term premiums. The longer the time for which money is to be lent, the larger the liquidity premium required before lenders will commit themselves to the loan. The time-preference theory states that lenders are sacrificing current consumption for greater (nominal) units of currency than they relinquished in the hope of obtaining greater real consumption levels or degrees of satisfaction, and therefore they require a premium for doing so.

In most theoretical developments, the returns from such loans are assumed to be riskless. With such assumptions, for nominal returns, it is considerably less difficult to show that basic interest rates must be positive. When we extend the analysis to include uncertainty, risk premium is included The risk premium is a complicated factor and may be influenced by business risk, or inflation risk. Business risk is the risk of the inherent uncertainty and variability of expected pretax returns on the firm's "portfolio" of assets. Financial risk is the risk induced by the use of financial leverage. Inflation risk is risk related to the change of purchasing power. We will consider this risk premium after a detailed examination of the determination of riskless interest rates.

5.3. Rate-of-Return Measurements and Types of Averages

Rate-of-return measurement and different types of averages are important arithmetic tools for financial analysis and planning. In this section, we will discuss two different rates-of-return measurements and four different types of averages.

5.3.1. *Discrete Rates-of-Return and Continuous Rates-of-Return*

Both discrete and continuous rates-of-return are important measurements for determining the performance of an investment. In the discrete compounding case, the holding-period yield (HPY) can be rewritten as

$$HPY = \frac{P_t + D_t}{P_{t-1}} - 1 = \frac{P_t - P_{t-1}}{P_{t-1}} + \frac{D_t}{P_{t-1}}, \tag{5.1}$$

where

HPY_D = Discrete holding-period yield,
P_t = Price per share in period t,
P_{t-1} = Price per share in period $t-1$,
D_t = Individual dividends per-share in period t.

Equation (5.1) indicates that the capital gain yields $[(P_t - P_{t-1})/P_{t-1}]$ and the dividend yield $[D_t/P_{t-1}]$ are the two components in determining the HPY. Dividend yield is also an important variable for testing the impact of dividend policy on the value of a firm (see Chapter 16).

Following the continuous compounding process discussed in Appendix A of this chapter, the continuous version of HPY can be written as

$$HPY_c = \ln\left(\frac{P_t + D_t}{P_{t-1}}\right), \tag{5.2}$$

where $(P_t + D_t)/P_{t-1}$ is the holding period rate-of-return (HPR). It is the notation for the natural logarithm, and P_t, P_{t-1}, and D_t are identical to those defined in Eq. (5.1).

As can be verified by the use of a Taylor-series expansion,[1] a higher-stated annual rate is required to make the discrete HPR equal to the continuously compounded HPR.

Intuitively we expect this, since the continuous case receives more interest on the interest through the more frequent compounding.

The HPR is a very useful concept for analyzing past trends of a security. Possibly its greatest virtue is that it is greater than zero in all but the oddest circumstances. This is important in the calculation of averages as we shall see shortly, because the negative yields are properly factored into the average. By now the relationship between holding period returns and holding period yields should be obvious;

$$HPR = HPY_D + 1 = \frac{P_t + D_t}{P_{t-1}}. \tag{5.3}$$

With respect to the discrete or continuous compounding issue, many empirical studies have shown that security-return distributions tend to display some (non-trivial) degree of positive skewness.[2] Hence, a log-normal distribution may describe security returns better than the normal distributions; or a logarithmic transformation could be performed on the return data, thus yielding a normal distribution of returns. However, if the return period is relatively short, say a week or less, between times t and $t-1$, the normal distribution usually proves to be a good approximation of the actual return distribution. Therefore, the choice of discrete- or continuous-based return measurement should depend largely on the extent on the time interval being considered, regardless of whether equities or bonds are the financial instrument of interest. The relationship between $e^x$and X, as indicated in Appendix B, can be used to show the relationship between normally distributed and log-normally distributed rates of return.

5.3.2. *Types of Averages*

Both the arithmetic mean and the geometric mean are used frequently by the finance profession. The harmonic mean is used mainly in theoretical finance. Because of its limited professional use, we will not devote much time to it. In the deterministic case, the harmonic mean is the smallest, followed by the geometric mean, which is smaller than the arithmetic mean;

$$\overline{X}^H \leq \overline{X}^G \leq \overline{X}^A. \tag{5.4}$$

In addition, the geometric mean is less sensitive to extreme values (outliers) than the arithmetic mean. The geometric mean is as popular as the arithmetic mean, despite its greater difficulty of calculation.

We can denote these three means as follows:

$$\overline{X}^A = \sum_{i=1}^{N} \frac{X_i}{N} \quad \text{(arithmetic)}; \tag{5.5}$$

$$\overline{X}^G = \left[\prod_{J=1}^{N} X_J\right]^{\frac{1}{N}} \quad \text{(geometric);} \tag{5.6}$$

$$\overline{X}^H = \frac{N}{\displaystyle\sum_{j=1}^{N} \frac{1}{X_J}} \quad \text{(harmonic).} \tag{5.7}$$

We can denote the population standard deviation as follows:

$$\sigma_x = \sqrt{\frac{1}{N}\left[\sum_{J=1}^{N} (X_J - \overline{X})^2\right]}, \tag{5.8}$$

where $\overline{X}$ is any of the averages we have discussed. If we are calculating the standard deviation for a sample, the divisor of the sum of squares would be $N - 1$, instead of N.

In using the arithmetic or geometric mean of one-period returns to predict the long-term expected rates-of-return, we must consider whether either statistic is an unbiased estimator, i.e., equal to the true population expected rates-of-return.

Assume, for example, that our historical data consists of T monthly relatives. A relative is the ratio of the value at the end of 1 month (P_t) to the value at the end of the previous month (P_{t-1}):

$$HPR_t = \frac{P_t}{P_{t-1}}. \tag{5.9}$$

Next, if we want to determine the expected increase in the value of the asset after we have held it for N months, we would want an N-period price relative. An N-period price relative is the ratio of the terminal value to the initial value.

Because we have only a sample of the entire population of monthly price relatives, we cannot directly observe the true population values. Therefore, we must rely upon the sample statistics to estimate the population values. From a historical data set of T 1-month price relatives, we can calculate the arithmetic and geometric means, described in Eqs. (5.5) and (5.6). We could then compound this same mean (as discussed in Appendix A) over N periods, to determine the value of the asset after we had held it for N periods.

The question then becomes, what mean should we compound? As we have noted above, the geometric mean is less sensitive to outliers and therefore would be a more conservative estimate than the arithmetic mean. This, however, is not the issue here. The major issue is that we want an unbiased estimator of the population statistic for investment-performance determination. Blume (1974) found that, for any period longer than one, that is, $N > 1$, the arithmetic mean is generally an upward-biased estimator of the true population value. In addition, Blume showed that, for any value of N less than T, the geometric mean was a downward-biased estimator.

To clarify Blume's results, let us examine the implications of the biases of forecasting. To be upwardly biased implies that the arithmetic average would predict a value for the N-period relative higher than its true value for the N-period relative. To be downward biased, the geometric mean would predict a value for the N-period relative lower than the true value. Obviously, the true value is somewhere between the arithmetic and geometric means. To resolve the biases associated with sample mean estimates, Blume suggested four types of adjustment methods to obtain an unbiased estimator. The most robust and the easiest method to calculate is the weighted unbiased estimator. We will call this estimator the mixed average and denote it as follows:[3,4]

$$\overline{X}^M = \frac{T-N}{T-1}\overline{X}^A + \frac{N-1}{T-1}\overline{X}^G. \tag{5.10}$$

It is easily seen that the weighting factors sum to one and we have an average that is between the arithmetic and geometric mean and also, as Blume proved, an unbiased estimator of the N-period relative. If N were to be equal to one, then only the arithmetic average would be used. The arithmetic average would be weighted by one, while the geometric mean would be weighted by zero. The reason for this is, as mentioned above, that the arithmetic mean is an unbiased estimator of a one-period relative.

When N = T all the weight is be given to the geometric mean, because at this point the geometric mean is an unbiased predictor of the N-period relative (the reader should verify these statements as far as the weighting goes). The assumption underlying this mixed-average estimator process is that the successive 1-month relatives are independent. Because the mixed average is fairly robust, slight dependencies will not affect the unbiasedness of the mixed average. There is an even more fundamental assumption underlying this entire forecasting process, which is that the past is a valid basis for predicting the future. We will have more to say about this very important assumption in later chapters.

Table 5.1. JNJ stock price and dividend data.

Year	Closing Price	Annual Dividend	Annual HPR	Annual HPY
1997	\$27.94	\$0.43	—	—
1998	36.04	0.49	1.307	30.7%
1999	40.54	0.545	1.140	14.0
2000	46.31	0.31	1.150	15.0
2001	52.8	0.7	1.155	15.5
2002	48.64	0.795	0.936	−6.4
2003	47.63	0.925	0.998	−0.2
2004	59.62	1.095	1.275	27.5
2005	57.61	1.275	0.988	−1.2
2006	64.78	1.455	1.150	15.0

We offer the following example to illustrate how the definitions and concepts discussed in this section can be used in real-world decision making. The data of Johnson & Johnson (JNJ) during 1997–2006, shown in Table 5.1, is used to perform the related empirical analysis.

In order to calculate the HPR for 2002, we must add the terminal value of stock (\$48.64) to the dividend received during 2002 (\$0.795) and divide the sum by the initial value of the stock (\$52.8) (closing price in 2001):

$$HPR_{2002} = \frac{\$48.64 + \$0.795}{\$52.8} = \frac{\$49.44}{\$52.8} = 0.936$$

By using the same method, we can calculate all other HPR estimates, which are listed in the fourth column of Table 5.1. By using the relationship between HPR and HPY as indicated in Eq. (5.3), we can obtain HPY estimates, as listed in the fifth column of Table 5.1.

In accordance with Eqs. (5.5), (5.6), and (5.10), we can calculate $\overline{X}^A$, $\overline{X}^G$, and $\overline{X}^M$ for HPR of JNJ as

$$\overline{X}^A = \frac{10.10}{9} = 1.1221, \tag{5.11a}$$

$$\overline{X}^G = \sqrt[9]{2.6781} = 1.1157, \tag{5.11b}$$

$$\begin{aligned}\overline{X}^M &= \frac{9-5}{9-1}(1.1221) + \frac{5-1}{9-1}(1.1157)\\ &= 0.5611 + 0.5578 = 1.1189.\end{aligned} \tag{5.11c}$$

In Eq. (5.11c), we assume that N = 5 and T = 9. One of the most important implications is that $\overline{X}^M$ is smaller than $\overline{X}^A$ and larger than $\overline{X}^G$.

If we wished to argue that the average rate-of-return earned on equity was a good proxy for the long-run required rate-of-return on JNJ's stock, we would claim 11.89% per year was the relevant figure; this is to be interpreted much like a hurdle rate in the capital-budgeting decision. The consequences of using either the geometric or arithmetic figure (in terms of firm value maximization) should be obvious. The alternative concepts and methods of HPY's can be used to determine appropriate rates-of-return measures in public-utility rate case testimonies.

5.3.3. *Power Means*

Rothstein (1972) has shown that the power mean of order r includes both geometric and arithmetic means as special cases. The power mean of order $r(\overline{X}^r)$can be defined as

$$\overline{X}^r = \left(\frac{1}{N}\sum_{1}^{N} X_j^r\right)^{\frac{1}{r}}, \tag{5.12}$$

where r is any real number (≥ 0); $\overline{X}$ and X_i are defined previously. If $r = 1$, then Eq. (5.12) reduces to the arithmetic average as defined in Eq. (5.5). Rothstein has also shown that $\overline{X}^r$approaches the geometric average as defined in Eq. (5.6) when r approaches zero. The power mean has been used by Fisher (1966), to compile further stock indices. The exact relationship between $\overline{X}^r$ and $\overline{X}^M$ is still to be investigated, but we should notice the distinct similarity between the two formulations. The Blume mixed-average estimator is a reasonably accurate estimator of true long-run rates-of-return, and is nowhere near as computationally difficult as the power mean.

5.4. Theories of the Term Structure and Their Application

Now that we have examined the methods by which returns on various assets can be measured, we can proceed to the theoretical discussion concerning required rates-of-return on debt and equity. Beginning with debt obligations, it is most common to relate bond yields to one another through the concept of the yield curve. A yield curve is a cross-sectional, graphical representation of required yields to maturity and term to maturity, while holding default risk constant as closely as possible. Table 5.1 provides the Daily Treasury Yield Curve Rates published by the U.S. Department of the Treasury.

When discussing yield curve, we usually center attention on a government-security yield curve, since the default risk is most nearly uniform through all maturities. Examining risk classes of bonds and inferring the risk structure of interest rates is a much trickier business; therefore, we will not cover this topic in detail. For more information refer to Van Horne (2000), in which other topics such as tax effects, call premium, and bond strategies are discussed in detail.

The data from Table 5.2 represents Treasury Market Bid Yields at Constant Maturities: Bills, Notes, and Bonds from May 7, 2015. Using the data from Table 5.2 we can draw the Fig. 5.1 Treasury Yield Curve in terms of the nominal rate and the real rate, respectively.

In general there are three alternative explanations to this shape, the segmented-markets theory, the liquidity-preference theory, and the unbiased (or pure) expectations theory. We will now examine each of these theories.

Table 5.2. Treasury market bid yields at constant maturities: Bills, notes, and bonds.

04/01/15	0.02	0.03	0.12	0.27	0.55	0.86	1.32	1.65	1.87	2.23	2.47
04/02/15	0.02	0.02	0.10	0.25	0.55	0.87	1.35	1.69	1.92	2.29	2.53
04/03/15	0.04	0.02	0.10	0.21	0.49	0.80	1.26	1.60	1.85	2.24	2.49
04/06/15	0.02	0.03	0.10	0.21	0.51	0.83	1.31	1.67	1.92	2.31	2.57
04/07/15	0.02	0.02	0.10	0.22	0.52	0.85	1.32	1.66	1.89	2.27	2.52
04/08/15	0.02	0.03	0.10	0.22	0.54	0.86	1.35	1.68	1.92	2.28	2.53
04/09/15	0.02	0.03	0.10	0.22	0.56	0.89	1.40	1.73	1.97	2.35	2.61
04/10/15	0.01	0.02	0.09	0.24	0.57	0.91	1.41	1.73	1.96	2.33	2.58
04/13/15	0.02	0.03	0.11	0.23	0.54	0.89	1.38	1.71	1.94	2.33	2.58
04/14/15	0.02	0.02	0.10	0.23	0.53	0.85	1.34	1.67	1.90	2.29	2.54
04/15/15	0.02	0.02	0.08	0.23	0.51	0.85	1.33	1.66	1.91	2.30	2.55
04/16/15	0.03	0.02	0.08	0.22	0.50	0.81	1.31	1.64	1.90	2.31	2.56
04/17/15	0.03	0.01	0.08	0.23	0.51	0.84	1.31	1.63	1.87	2.26	2.51
04/20/15	0.03	0.03	0.10	0.24	0.55	0.86	1.33	1.65	1.90	2.31	2.56
04/21/15	0.02	0.03	0.09	0.23	0.55	0.86	1.35	1.67	1.92	2.33	2.58
04/22/15	0.01	0.03	0.10	0.23	0.57	0.91	1.41	1.75	1.99	2.42	2.66
04/23/15	0.01	0.03	0.09	0.24	0.55	0.87	1.37	1.70	1.96	2.38	2.63
04/24/15	0.03	0.03	0.10	0.24	0.54	0.84	1.34	1.68	1.93	2.36	2.62
04/27/15	0.01	0.02	0.10	0.25	0.54	0.87	1.36	1.69	1.94	2.36	2.61
04/28/15	0.00	0.02	0.09	0.24	0.56	0.90	1.39	1.75	2.00	2.42	2.68
04/29/15	0.00	0.01	0.07	0.25	0.56	0.91	1.43	1.80	2.06	2.49	2.76
04/30/15	0.00	0.01	0.06	0.24	0.58	0.91	1.43	1.79	2.05	2.49	2.75
05/01/15	0.00	0.01	0.05	0.25	0.60	0.97	1.50	1.87	2.12	2.57	2.82
05/04/15	0.01	0.02	0.08	0.25	0.60	0.96	1.51	1.90	2.16	2.62	2.88
05/05/15	0.01	0.01	0.08	0.24	0.62	1.00	1.54	1.92	2.19	2.64	2.90
05/06/15	0.02	0.02	0.08	0.25	0.65	1.03	1.58	1.97	2.25	2.72	2.98

Source: U.S. Department of the Treasury.

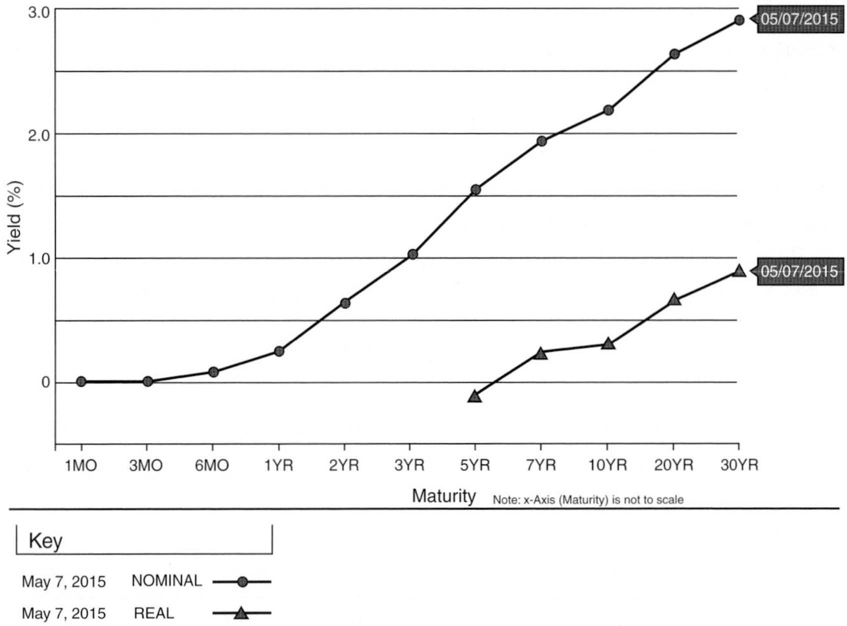

Fig. 5.1. Treasury yield curve.

The segmented-market hypothesis suggests that there are different markets for different maturity ranges, because of either individual preferences or institutional requirements. Most often these maturity ranges are classified as short-term, intermediate, and long-term. Such a phenomenon as segmentation can be created and maintained only if investors viewed these different maturities as imperfect substitutes for one another. To some extent, this implies that the yield curve is non-continuous (a point that is technically correct because of the finite number of maturities available), but the question that still remains to be answered is to what extent, if any, the market for bonds is segmented.

As we will discover in the following paragraphs, there appears to be little evidence to support this hypothesis. This a reasonable conclusion for the reason that arbitrageurs, or others not so restricted to specific maturities, would exploit such opportunities by purchasing those maturities least preferred by others while selling bonds with the most heavily desired maturities, thus capturing a preference premium of some form. The degree of efficiency of the bond markets is the major concern in attacking this issue and will be addressed shortly.

The liquidity-preference theory is somewhat aligned with the segmented-markets theory. Hicks (1946) is generally credited with the thorough development of this theory, which also asserts that short- and long-term securities are imperfect substitutes. However, the rationale underlying this theory is based primarily on economics. Hicks argued that risk aversion suggests that borrowers would prefer to obtain long-term loans, assuming long-term needs for such loans, to lock in financing costs. This same attribute, risk aversion, would leave lenders with a propensity to maintain short positions due to a desire to remain liquid. If such conditions prevailed, this would leave a large excess of demand for long-term funds and set into action the wheels of an adjustment process. Long-term borrowers would be inclined to offer greater returns on funds lent, in effect paying a premium to induce lenders to sacrifice their liquidity positions. Such liquidity premiums are probably an increasing function of the term-to-maturity of the loan rather than a stepwise process, as the segmented markets hypothesis seems to suggest.

The final theory to be considered is that of the unbiased-expectations camp. This theory denies that any such preference of liquidity premiums exists and concludes that any long-term rate must be the geometric average of the relevant short-term forward rates over the life of the long-term bond of interest. To better illustrate this concept, let us define a forward rate, F_t, as the rate of interest expected to prevail on a 1-year government security at time t. Likewise, denoting the expected yield-to-maturity on an N-year-to-maturity government bond as YTM_N, we can express this relationship as follows:

$$YTM_N = \left\{ \prod_{t=1}^{N} (1 + F_t) \right\}^{\frac{1}{N}} - 1. \tag{5.13}$$

where each interest rate of interest can itself be thought of as the product of a real component, inflation premium, and a default-risk premium, as Fisher (1930) asserted.[5]

Given the relationship in Eq. (5.13), we can infer from the government yield curve what the future rates are expected to be. Allowing F_t to be our 1-year forward rate of interest, we can solve for F_t $(t = N)$,

$$(1 + YTM_N)^N = (1 + F_1)(1 + F_2)\ldots(1 + F_N). \tag{5.14}$$

$$\frac{(1 + YTM_N)^N}{(1 + F_1)(1 + F_2)\ldots(1 + F_{t-1})} = 1 + F_N, \tag{5.15}$$

or by recognizing $(1+F_1)(1+F_2)\ldots(1+F_{t-1}) = (1+YTM_{N-1})^{N-1}$ by the assumption of the pure-expectations approach:

$$1 + F_N = \frac{(1+YTM_N)^N}{(1+YTM_{N-1})^{N-1}}. \tag{5.16}$$

The more convenient arithmetic approximation of Eq. (5.16) can be defined as:

$$F_N = (N)(YTM_N) - (N-1)(YTM_{N-1}). \tag{5.16$'$}$$

Equation (5.16) can be used to estimate forward rate if we know the yield to maturity of (YTM_N) and (YTM_{N-1}). If (YTM_N) and (YTM_{N-1}) are 0.0487 and 0.0491, respectively. If we also know $N = 2$, then the 2 year forward rate can be estimated as 0.0483.

The pure-expectations theory has great intuitive appeal since it prevents arbitrageurs from engaging in strategies of buying long-(short-)-term and selling short-(long-)-term to reap any profits. We should also recognize that its strict validity depends upon the ability of individuals to costlessly roll over short-term positions to ultimately enjoy the same ending wealth position as that person who chose a longer-term instrument.

The pure-expectations theory assumes that arbitrage would work to force equilibrium where no windfalls can be obtained. This assumption is also essential in proving the Modigliani and Miller Proposition I as indicated in Chapter 7, and in deriving the arbitrage pricing theory explored in Chapter 9.

Now that these assorted term-structure theories have been examined, it becomes clear that they cannot all be correct. To the extent we intend to utilize the term structure as an indicator of required rates-of-return on bonds, an input to most cost-of-capital formulations, we must consider tests of these theories to ascertain what approach is appropriate in modeling and estimating the required rate-of-return on debt.

Meiselman's (1962) book provides possibly the most comprehensive test of the liquidity-preference and unbiased-expectations theories, where we consider the segmented-markets hypothesis as a special case of the Hicksian liquidity-preference hypothesis. The test itself was specifically designed to test the pure-expectations hypothesis through an adaptive model. Since expectations are unobservable, we are left to examine changes in interest rates (unexpected) from their previous implied forward-rate levels, and how these unanticipated changes are then incorporated into longer-term rates through the revision of expectations. From Eq. (5.16), we can compute the

1-year rates expected to prevail going forward, and compare them with the actual rate that prevails, r_t, to derive the forecast error E_t:

$$E_t = r_t - F_t. \tag{5.17}$$

Because a long-term rate is expected to be the geometric average of short-term rates, we would expect unanticipated changes in long-term rates to be positively related to the unanticipated short-term rate change, The size of this long-term rate change is inversely related to the term-to-maturity of the long-term bond in question.

Meiselman tested his model using annual observations on the yield curve from the years 1901–1954, examining the changes in long-term rates up to 8 years into the future and utilizing a variant of Eq. (5.17) as shown by Eq. (5.18),

$$\Delta R_t = A + BE_t, \tag{5.18}$$

where ΔR is the change in the long-term rate in question, E_t is the forecast error in period t, A is the intercept and B is the slope. If all of the change in the long-term rate is explained by the forecast error in the 8-year forward rate, the intercept term should be approximately zero; but if any liquidity premium exists as Hicks asserted, we would expect the liquidity premium to decrease and thus the intercept term would be negative.

The results of this test were very striking; the correlations between changes in long-term rates and the forecasting error were all high and positive, and these correlations decreased smoothly as Meiselman examined the changes in successively longer-term rates. Since the regression results showed that the regression coefficients of E_t (B's) decreased in size, and none of the intercepts (A's) were significantly different from zero, it could be concluded that the changes in long-term rates following a forecast error decreased in a systematic fashion with term-to-maturity of the bond. This evidence shows that a liquidity premium is not imbedded in interest-rate formulations and that interest rates on a long-term basis are simply the geometric average of future short-term rates. This simply states that the unbiased-expectations hypothesis explanation of the term structure holds. Meiselman's method of empirically testing the pure expectations hypothesis is quite similar to that of Fama (1975) who shows how to derive inflation forecasts, given that this hypothesis holds. We will examine the Fama study in the next section.

In addition to the pure-expectation theory and the liquidity-premium theory mentioned above, there exists a market-segmentation theory, which takes into consideration both price variability and investment (or income) risk. To blend the theories of expectations, liquidity preference, and market segmentation, Modigliani and Swatch (1966, 1967) developed their "preferred habitat" hypothesis. Empirically, they concluded that interest-rate expectations are based upon the recent trend in interest rates, and the "normal" level of interest rates is based upon long-run experience.

5.5. Interest Rate, Price-Level Changes, and Components of Risk Premium

There is a strong relationship between interest-rate and price-level changes. Irving Fisher (The Theory of Interest) has summarized four empirical relationships between interest rates and price levels:

1. Interest rates tend to be high when prices are rising and low when prices are falling.
2. Interest-rate movements lag behind price-level changes; this tends to obscure the relationship between them.
3. There is a market relationship between interest rates and the weighted average of past price-level changes, reflecting effects that are distributed over time.
4. High interest rates accompany high prices and low interest rates accompany low prices.

In financial analysis and planning, financial managers need information about future interest rates and inflation rates. Hence, relationships (1), (2), and (3) are of the greatest interest to financial managers. The first relationship derives from the fact that, if lenders and borrowers could perfectly foresee future price level movements, lenders would hedge against changes in the real value of their loan principal by adding the percentage change in prices over the life of the loan to the interest charge. Borrowers, expecting money income to change in proportion to prices, would readily accept the higher rates.

Fisher attributed the second and third relationships to imperfect foresight about future prices and the resulting inclination to extrapolate from past price-level changes in order to adjust interest rates for expected price-level changes. He devised the concept of "distributed lag" to explain the way information about the past affects expectations of the future. The "distributed lag" model is a model in which lagged explanatory variables are explicitly included in the model specification. This kind of model can be used to take care of some amount of time lapse between the movement of the independent variables and the response of the dependent variable.

Yohe and Karnosky's (1969) empirical results will demonstrate the imperfect-foresight case and Fama's (1975) results will demonstrate the "perfect-foresight" case. These results will give financial managers some insight into how interest rates and inflation rates can be forecasted.

5.5.1. *Imperfect-Foresight Case*

The late 1970s provide a good example of how imperfect foresight affects extrapolation of past prices into the future. Furthermore, the "distributed lag" effect played a key role during this time in the adjustment of interest rates to account for expected price changes. Once the effects of the second oil embargo by the OPEC nations had been fully realized in the U.S. economy, inflation easily surpassed the double-digit barrier. Since this inflationary period was believed by many to be just a temporary reaction, interest rates adjusted only slightly. After repeated reports of double-digit inflation and the resulting realization that this level of inflation was not temporary, interest rates began to more fully reflect the losses in purchasing power which, it appeared, were going to continue. The reaction of interest rates was to begin to climb, and in 1980 the prime rate exceeded 20%.

Yohe and Karnosky (1969) present an interesting analysis of the interaction between inflation and interest rates. They attempt to estimate the lag time before the full impact of price-level changes is felt in the rate of interest for different maturities. The equations estimated were of the following form:[7]

$$rn_t = \alpha_0 + \sum_{j=0}^{N} a_{j+1}\dot{P}_{t-j} + \beta_1 Y_t^* + \beta_2 \Delta Y_t^* + \beta_3 \Delta M_t^*, \tag{5.19}$$

where

$\dot{P}$ = Annual rate of change in the GNP deflator;
Y^* = Level of real GNP;
ΔY^* = Rate of change in real GNP;
ΔM^* = Average change in the real money stock (nominal money stock deflated by the GNP deflator);

and rn_t = Nominal interest rate; it includes nominal rate on four-to-six month commercial paper (rn^s), and nominal rate on corporate AAA bonds (rn^l).

The authors found that the explanatory power of price-level changes was only slightly affected as the equations became more fully specified. For example, in the equations for the long-term rate rn^l, when the current real GNP (Y^*) and the real change in the money supply (M^*) were added to the regression, two relevant structural changes took place: (1) the sum of the coefficients on current and lagged rates of price change rose from 0.80 to 0.86, and (2) the mean lag time for the effect of price changes on nominal rates increased from 3.2 quarters to 5.5 quarters. In other words, recent price changes alone tend to overstate the necessary adjustment of nominal rates to account for the Fisher effect. Furthermore, the coefficients on current and lagged rates of price changes were redistributed toward the past in the expanded equations, since the current and last quarter's price levels implicitly enter into the newly added independent variables. The authors estimated Eq. (5.19) without the current price level change and found that β_3 declined in absolute value by 10%.

Yohe and Karnosky found that the estimated mean lag time for the full impact of price-level changes to be reflected in nominal interest rates was about 2 years for corporate AAA bonds, while the adjustment of commercial paper rates took place immediately. When the constant terms in the equations were suppressed, the mean lag was lengthened by three-quarters and one-quarter, respectively. The authors also found that in the expanded equation for the long-term nominal interest rate, price-level changes were the most important variables in their relative contribution to the regression. The beta coefficient for price-level changes is nearly three times as large as that for real GNP, which ranks second in importance. Therefore, it appears that the effect of price expectations on interest rates has increased greatly since 1960, as has the speed at which they are formed. In fact, the most significant finding is that price-level changes, rather than "real" rates, account for nearly all the variation in nominal interest rates since 1961 regardless of the inclusion of variables in the regressions to explicitly account for the "real" rate components of nominal rates. The addition of these variables did not appreciably alter the findings.

There are many who would feel that this was a reasonable finding. The real rate adds little explanatory power, as it is frequently assumed to be relatively stable over time and invariant to inflation. While this contention of a constant real rate is not universally accepted, causal impacts of historical inflation and interest rates show the two do tend to move together and by approximately the same magnitude. We will have more to say about this relationship when we examine Fama's findings on short-term interest rates and inflation.

Yohe and Karnosky argue, with empirical results to back their contentions, that the speed of adjustment of long-term interest rates to actual inflation is not particularly rapid. This is in direct contrast to what the rational-expectations school of economic thought tells us should happen. Rational expectation implies that the future is predictable, or at least unbiased estimates of the future are possible, so that market participants are on average correct about what future inflation rates will be. We will consider this as the perfect-foresight case and examine its supporting evidence, which relies upon many of the same basic characteristics as the efficient-markets hypothesis and the degree of the market's efficiency.

5.5.2. *Perfect-Foresight Case*

Fama (1975) found the almost universal acceptance of the inflation-induced rate-lag finding to be a puzzling phenomenon. Fama did admit that the market has not done a perfect job of predicting inflation, but he argued that that is not a strict requirement for the market to be considered efficient. If the bond markets are reasonably efficient they should, on average, reflect inflation expectations in prices. Furthermore, if the bond markets are efficient, their inflationary expectations should be realized. Fama chose to utilize short-term Treasury bills to examine the ability of the market to predict inflation, this seemed to be a reasonable choice as the Treasury bill market may be the most efficient market of those we study. Another pleasant feature of this market is the fact that default-risk premiums are usually not an element of Treasury bill required returns; therefore, the inflationary effect will not be polluted with any varying risk-premium effects.

With Treasury bills being priced on a discount basis, their nominal return is certain once this discount is known. We can write this nominal return as,

$$R_t = \frac{B_t - B_{t-1}}{B_{t-1}}, \tag{5.20}$$

where

R_t = Nominal rate-of-return in period t,
B_t = Price of the bill in period $t-1$,

and

B_{t-1} = the price of the bill period $t-1$.

If we allow P_t to be the price level at time t, we can express each nominal dollar-denominated Treasury bill in real terms:

$$r_t = \frac{P_t^v B_t - P_{t-1}^v B_{t-1}}{P_{t-1}^v B_{t-1}}, \tag{5.21}$$

where r_t = Real return on the bill, and $P_t^v = 1/P_t$, a real-value factor.

Alternatively we could decompose this real return r into the nominal return and the loss in purchasing power:

$$r_t = R_t + C_t, \tag{5.22}$$

where

$$C_t = \frac{p_t^v - p_{t-1}^v}{p_{t-1}^v},$$

and we ignore the cross-product term because of its relative insignificance.

Fama set up two models for empirical testing, as described by Eqs. (5.23) and (5.24):

$$C_t = B_0 + B_1 R_t, \tag{5.23}$$

$$C_t = B_0 + B_1 R_t + B_2 C_{t-1}, \tag{5.24}$$

where C_{t-1} is included in the model described in Eq. (5.24) as a test to see if information about past price-level changes adds explanatory power to the extinction of current price-level changes. This can be viewed as a partial test of market efficiency. Fama also explained that the real rate was constant; hence the use of the intercept term to estimate the real return component.

Using monthly data for 1-month bills for the time period 1953–1971, the following estimates were obtained;[8]

	$\mathbf{B_0}$	$\mathbf{B_1}$	$\mathbf{B_2}$
(5.23)	0.0007	−0.98	—
	(0.003)	(0.10)	
(5.24)	0.00059	−0.87	0.11
	(0.0003)	(0.12)	(0.07)

where standard errors appear below each coefficient.

Having computed autocorrelations at lags up to 12 months, Fama found them to be close to zero and, as we see above (B_2), not even the most recent price-level change adds significant explanatory power to the model. From the results presented above, Fama concluded that the nominal interest rate was an accurate prediction of forthcoming price-level changes. Upon further study of the autocorrelations of B_0 and the residual error term, and utilizing subsamples of his data set, Fama also concluded that the real rate was constant over time.

If one is to believe Fama's results, the government-security yield curve could be utilized to estimate future inflation rates. As we shall see in future chapters, the rate of inflation is an important input in the determination of the cost of capital and in estimating future cash flows in the capital-budgeting process. Unfortunately, Fama's results and conclusions have been challenged on several grounds. On a practical basis, this means that our ability to estimate future inflation rates is severely hampered. We will examine each of these criticisms in turn.

Carlson (1977) and Joines (1977) both contend that Fama was incorrect in asserting that the real rate was constant and that all past information was already incorporated into the market nominal rate-setting function, but through different techniques. Carlson argues that supply and demand factors may, in the short run, dominate pure expectations in the sense that the real rate is constant. Expectations may incorporate assessments of these supply and demand factors, which is exactly what Carlson wished to show. Utilizing data from the Livingston survey, which is a semi-annual survey of business and academic economists' expectations for price indices, amongst other items, Carlson calculated the expected real return on 6- and 12-month Treasury bills. He did this by subtracting the average expected price-level change from the survey from the yields on bills of the appropriate maturity. While the trend in nominal yields was found to correspond to the trend in expected inflation rates, the real rate varied greatly in the cases of both the 6- and 12-month bills. For 6-month bills the expected real return reached a low of -0.33% and a high of 4.28%, while the low and high for the 12-month bills were 0.15 and 4.51, respectively. This is quite striking, since yields on these securities edged slightly higher than 8% on only a few occasions and were usually within 4% to 6% yield levels. If the Livingston survey is representative of general market expectations, the constant real-rate assertion is certainly questionable.

Joines provided a joint form of a test in which he included lagged wholesale prices for three past periods along with the nominal rate variable as independent variables. He found that all were statistically significant in explaining the variation in monthly consumer-price-index changes. Moreover, the coefficient on the nominal return variable was significantly less than 1.0 (at the 95% level). From this, we can infer that nominal rates do not fully reflect future inflation and that the real return is not constant. Carlson's test of the underspecified model hypothesis added the ratio of employment to population at lags of 1, 2, and 3 months, and yielded findings similar to those of Joines. This new employment-to-population coefficient was highly significant and negatively related to changes in the loss of purchasing power using all three separate lags. As with Joines' test the coefficients on the nominal rate variable changed drastically, so that we can't accept them as being equal to −1. Additionally, many of the real rate figures were statistically different from zero, which is a disconcerting finding.

Having dealt with the misspecification problems, we can now confront the final criticism of Fama's paper, which is one of statistical methodology. Fama was able to accept the constant-example, real-rate hypothesis because the ex-post-real return autocorrelation function showed virtually no autocorrelation at any lags. Nelson and Schwert (1977) point out that this may be due simply to the large variance of errors in expectations of inflation, which serves to drive all of the autocorrelation figures to zero. Despite this potential problem, Nelson and Schwert credited the Fama analysis with a great step forward in the interest-rate-inflation area by shifting the emphasis from past data analysis to that of an expectations basis. Lastly, in his rejoinder Fama (1976) reviewed these criticisms and admitted that the exact model specification of inflation estimation was still unknown. To finish the interest/inflation-rate controversy on a bright note, as Fama noted, nominal interest rates are still the best indicators of future inflation rates, since they contribute the greatest explanatory value to the various model specifications.

Forecasting future inflation rates is admittedly not a trivial exercise in statistical model building, but at least we seem to be moving in the proper direction.

Having covered the state of the art in inflation forecasting, and the relationship between nominal interest rates and inflation, we must turn our attention to the related but separate problem of determining the relationship between equity values, or required rates-of-return on equity and inflation.

5.6. Three Hypotheses About Inflation and the Value of the Firm: A Review

Following Bernard (1982) and Gilmore (1982), some tests of theories about the relationship between inflation and stock prices are reviewed in this section. Here we are concerned with the impact of inflation at the level of the individual firm. The review encompasses research on the debtor–creditor hypothesis, the tax-effects hypothesis, and the impact of inflation upon profits from operations.

5.6.1. *The Debtor–Creditor Hypothesis*

Economic theory suggests that unanticipated inflation should redistribute wealth from creditors to debtors because the real value of fixed monetary claims falls. This theory is well articulated by Kessel and Alchian (1962) and is assumed by many economists to be true. But surprisingly, evidence on this issue offers very little support for the theory.

The debtor–creditor hypothesis has been examined by many economists. Kessel (1956) noted that, during the inflationary period of 1942–1948, stock price changes of 16 banks and 30 industrials were inversely correlated with net monetary positions, where a net creditor position was considered positive. A significant positive correlation was found during the deflationary period of the depression. However, when similar approaches were used by Bach and Ando (1957) to study the 1939–1952 period, little support for the hypothesis was found. They concluded that "other forces, especially sales volume, but perhaps . . . the lead-lag effects of various costs and prices apparently exercised more dominant effects, relegating the debtor–creditor effects to a relatively minor role." Broussalian (1960) obtained results that do not support, and in some cases contradict, the hypothesis over the 1949–1956 period, using a sample of 200 firms. DeAlessi (1964) did show the predicted association between market returns and net monetary position during years of high inflation; however, this study is based on United Kingdom data. Bach and Stephenson (1974), whose association tests over the 1952–1970 period provided little support for the hypothesis, draw an interesting conclusion. They believe that stock market prices fail to reflect debtor–creditor effects because accounting reports reflect these effects at very long lags, if at all. Finally, a study by Johnson, Cogger, and Huffman (1980), who used an empirical approach essentially like those of the early studies, found no support for the debtor–creditor hypothesis over the 1965–1972 period.

Bradford (1974) developed a model that has served as the basic framework for most subsequent tests of the debtor–creditor hypothesis. Bradford employed a cross-sectional regression of market returns against scaled values of firms' net monetary positions and a proxy for firms' depreciation tax shields, which are in essence monetary assets. Tax shields are discussed below. Over the 1949–1955 period, Bradford was unable to reject the hypothesis of no debtor–creditor effect. A model developed by Hong (1977) also included a control for systematic risk, but again the net monetary position offered very little explanatory power.

Some more recent research studies do test the debtor–creditor hypothesis in a way that distinguishes between expected and unexpected inflation. One of these (Baesel and Globerman (1977)) suffers from other important methodological weaknesses. Dietrich (1981) demonstrated that returns to corporate bondholders were negatively correlated with unexpected inflation, but he was unable to detect a corresponding increase in wealth of common shareholders of the 36 firms that had issued the bonds.

A study by Gilmer (1982) found mixed support for the hypothesis over the July 1978–June 1981 period. Certain tests of Gilmer's indicated the existence of a debtor–creditor effect when changes in nominal interest rates were used as proxies for changes in expected inflation. The results are difficult to interpret, since the interest-rate proxy used is based on an assumed constant real rate of interest over a period characterized by volatile real rates of interest. Thus, it is difficult to determine whether the wealth effects detected were in response to changes in expected inflation or changes in real interest rates. Notably, the employment of an alternative inflation forecast model "resulted in an almost complete lack of support" for the debtor–creditor hypothesis.

The two most powerful tests of the debtor–creditor hypothesis to date were conducted by French, Ruback, and Schwert (1983) and Summers (1981). Both studies pool cross-sectional and time-series data on market returns, net monetary position, and tax shields. Using generalized least squares (GLS), French, Ruback, and Schwert did not find support for the debtor–creditor hypothesis over the 1947–1979 period. They conclude that "if anything, the wealth effects seem to go in the opposite direction of theoretical predictions." Nevertheless, when simple paired-comparison tests were used instead of GLS, results were in the predicted direction. Of particular interest here is that all coefficients assumed the predicted signs in the 1964–1979 sub-period.

Summers' approach is similar to that of French, Ruback, and Schwert. However, instead of focusing on unexpected inflation, Summers tested for the impact of changes in expected inflation. Summers' test results for the entire 1963–1978 period were mixed. However, results were in the expected direction for all tests in the 1972–1978 subperiod, and again were significant in three of five cases.

5.6.2. *The Tax-Effects Hypothesis*

Since depreciation and inventory tax shields are based on historical costs, their real values decline with inflation. This, in turn, reduces the real value of the firm. The magnitude of these tax effects could be huge. Feldstein and Summers (1979) estimated that the use of historical-cost-based depreciation and inventory accounting raised corporate tax liabilities by $26 billion in 1977. Despite increases in the investment-tax credit and liberalization of depreciation allowances, they estimate that the effective corporate income tax rate rose from 52% in 1964 to 66% in 1977.

Several of the above-mentioned studies included tests of the tax-effects hypothesis. Bradford (1974) and Hong (1977) found strong and significant negative associations between market returns and proxies for tax shields over "inflationary" periods. However, both studies can be criticized for a failure to identify the unexpected component of inflation and for failing to distinguish between the tax basis of assets and their book values. Furthermore, cross-sectional correlation in studies of this kind could have caused overstatement of t-statistics by 40–80%. Nevertheless, the results of both studies are so strong that they may very well hold even after compensating for the weaknesses.

Summers failed to observe the predicted effect of depreciation tax shields over the 1963–1978 period, but did obtain significant results for the 1974–1978 sub-period. Summers concludes that the market suffered from inflation illusion until the 1970's. Gilmer found mixed support for the tax-effects hypothesis. Both Summers and Gilmer failed to note the (often very large) difference between tax basis and book values. This difference arises because most firms use different accounting methods for tax purposes and financial reporting purposes. The only study to date that makes that distinction is that of French, Ruback, and Schwert. They obtained results inconsistent with the tax-effects hypothesis for the overall 1947–1979 period when GLS was used, but test statistics had the right sign for the 1964–1979 sub period and were statistically significant when paired-comparison tests were used.

Gonedes (1981) tested the tax-effects hypothesis using aggregate economic data and a time-series regression of "real" tax rates against expected and unexpected inflation. Although Gonedes failed to find evidence of an association, it is doubtful that such a design is as powerful as those discussed above. Furthermore, that study does not address directly the issue of concern here, which is the differential impact of unexpected inflation across firms.

To summarize, while there is some support for the debtor–creditor hypothesis and the tax-effects hypothesis when recent data is studied, the effects do not appear large and may be overwhelmed by other factors. Whether or not the hypotheses can be shown to explain wealth redistributions due to inflation appears to depend on the empirical approach used. Of course, such a conclusion is not very comforting to those who must set economic policy, including tax policy. The calculations of Feldstein and Summers suggest that inflation-induced wealth transfers caused by the use of historical cost are extremely large. On the other hand, French, Ruback, and Schwert conclude that "the wealth effects caused by revaluation of nominal contracts (including tax shields) due to unexpected inflation are small compared with other factors that affect stock values." (Emphasis added.)

5.6.3. *Operating-Income Hypothesis*

According to the traditional view of economics, wealth transfers caused by general inflation are due primarily to those effects discussed above. Parties gain or lose only when forced to comply with nominal contracts, the terms of which fail to anticipate inflation. Since relative prices should not be affected by general inflation, price-cost ratios should not be affected, except by nominal contracts, and corporate profits before consideration of interest and taxes should not be affected. This view predominates throughout Kessel and Alchian's article, "Effects of inflation": "Factors that affect relative prices have comparatively little impact on the general level of prices, and conversely."

Empirical evidence indicates that inflation is not neutral in its impact on real profits. Corporate profitability has covaried negatively with inflation, at least over the past two decades (Terbough (1974), Cagen and Lipsey (1978), Modigliani and Cohn (1979), Moosa (1980), Fama (1981), Hasbrouck (1984)). Hasbrouck concluded that "The linear regressions with allowance for a full 5-year time lag point to about 11% depressant effect on real economic earnings as a 'result' of a one-percentage-point sustained increase in the annual rate of inflation." Furthermore, the decline in corporate profitability cannot be explained solely by the effect of the taxation of nominal profits.

There exist several potential explanations for the observed negative relationship between profitability and inflation. Fama (1981) suggests that the inverse relationship is spurious. He asserts that price changes are negatively correlated with profitability only because changes in the money supply have failed to fully accommodate changes in real activity. A second explanation involves government regulation. Inflation may bring about political pressure for restrictive economic policies which, in turn, dampen corporate profitability. This explanation is consistent with the observed lagged reaction of profits apparent in Hasbrouck (1984), and in Fama (1981). A final explanation is based on frictions in markets, which could prevent co-movement of all prices (including the price of labor). For example, see Moore (1977). Such frictions may explain the existence of an inverse relationship between overall corporate profitability and inflation, and certainly could explain the existence of a differential impact across industries.

The research on corporate profitability discussed above is generally based on macroeconomic data; but if aggregate profitability is affected by inflation, then differing reactions of profits across firms may well explain much of the differential reaction of the market values of individual firms to unexpected inflation. Bernard (1982) finds cross-sectional differences in the reactions of corporate operating income to inflation, and such differences can be generally used to predict the reaction of the value of individual firms to unexpected inflation.

5.6.4. *The Relationship among the Three Hypotheses*

In order to determine the relative importance of the three factors discussed above, it is useful to turn to some theory. A model of the impact of unanticipated inflation on the value of common stocks was developed by Van Horne and Glassmire (1972). The model is not concerned with expected inflation. An efficient market should compound the effect of expected inflation in current prices, and thus future returns should not be influenced by expected inflation, unless underlying real interest rates or risk premiums are affected. In the Van Horne–Glassmire model, unanticipated inflation affects the firm in the three ways listed above. That is, the value of the firm is affected through impacts on operating income, the real value of the monetary position, and the real value of depreciation tax shields. But while almost all empirical research at the individual firm level concentrates on the last two influences, Van Horne and Glassmire posit that it is the impact of unexpected inflation on operating income that is the dominating factor:

> It is found that for most situations the dominant factor affecting value is the sensitivity of prices, wages, and other costs to the unanticipated change in inflation.
> Only extreme, and usually unrealistic, parameters for debt and depreciation will result in those terms being dominant.

These conclusions were reached by substituting hypothetical parameters into the Van Horne–Glassmire model. Some empirical evidence on the association of market returns on individual equity securities and unexpected inflation is also available. Bernard (1982) carefully investigated the relationship between unanticipated inflation and the value of the firm. He has empirically developed a model to predict cross-sectional differences in the reaction of firm values to unexpected inflation. Hendershott (1981) thoroughly investigated the joint impacts of taxation, valuation errors, and profitability, on the decline in aggregate share values. In addition, he also considered the simultaneous determination of debt and equity yield and the trade-off between the financial-asset and the real-asset investments. Overall, Hendershott and some other authors believe that the debtor–creditor hypothesis, the tax-effects hypothesis, and the operating-income hypothesis are interrelated. In summary, the theories and empirical evidence discussed in this section are very useful in doing the financial analysis, planning, and forecasting in Chapters 6, 7, 8, 13, and 23.

5.7. Summary

In this chapter, we have examined several concepts that will be of importance later. Determination of appropriate interest rates and risk premiums is very important in capital budgeting (Chapters 12 and 13), leasing (Chapter 14), and cost of capital determinations (Chapter 11). The mathematical concepts of arithmetic, geometric, and mixed means will also be important for estimating growth of dividends (Chapter 16) and financial planning and forecasting (Chapters 22 and 23). A basic understanding about the relationships between various types of risks (inflation, liquidity, and default) will be necessary for analyzing alternative risk premiums in financial analysis, planning, and forecasting.

Notes

1. The basic concepts and formulas of calculus used here can be found in Appendix A of this chapter.

2. Linter (1972), Hagerman (1978), and others have found that log-normal is generally a more suitable distribution than normal distribution in describing the distribution of stock rates-of-return.
3. Blume (1974) also proposed a regression method to estimate the unbiased mean estimator. However, the regression type of unbiased estimator is more complicated to calculate than that defined in Eq. (5.10).
4. If investors have homogeneous beliefs, then they all have some lines in an efficient set called Capital Market Line (CML). Chapter 7 will discuss these concepts in detail. In investing the relationship between risk-premium curve and Capital Market Line (CML), Rogaliski and Tinic (1978) have used the mixed average to obtain unbiased estimates for some AAA corporate bonds.
5. If the fluctuation of forward rates is low, the yield (geometric average) defined in Eq. (5.13) can be approximated by the arithmetic average.
6. Two other factors, the ability to reinvest intermediate payments at the yield-to-maturity, and taxes may also play a role in the pricing of some bonds but these particular effects are not clear-cut by any means, and we will, by and large, attempt to avoid these issues.
7. The term $\sum_{j=1}^{n}(\alpha_{j+1}\dot{P}_{t-j})$ represents the lag structure of the change of the GNP deflator. It is strongly suggested that readers see Yohe and Karnosky (1969) for the detailed empirical results associated with Eq. (5.19)
8. Bubnys and Lee (1985) and Lee and Bubnys (1984) have applied Fama's model to international interest rate and inflation data.

Problem Set

1. Why is interest charged on money borrowed? Explain the components of interest, and factors that determine the shape of the yield curve. How do price levels and expectations affect interest rates?
2. What are the components of HPY? Explain the relationship, including differences, advantages, and applicability of:

$$\mathrm{HPY_C} \quad \text{and} \quad \mathrm{HPY_D}$$

and

$$\text{HPY} \quad \text{and} \quad \text{HPR.}$$

3. Why are (sample) means used? What types are available? What types of bias can be encountered? When? How can they be eliminated?

4. Explain the various processes by which unexpected inflation can affect the value of the firm. Does empirical evidence support these processes?
5. Discuss three possible hypotheses in explaining the impact of inflation on the value of a firm. Are these hypotheses justified? What other explanations can be given?
6. Discuss the four relationships between interest rates and price levels as suggested by Fisher. How are these relationships justified?
7. Explain how depreciation and inventory can affect the value of the firm during inflationary periods. How can differing accounting methods affect this explanation?
8. Use the geometric-series formula to show how present-value annuity tables can be derived.
9. Use integration methods to show how compounded-value annuity and present-value annuity problems can be analyzed.
10. Use the Taylor-expansion formula to show the relationship between discrete compounding and continuous compounding.
11. What is the relationship between the normal distribution and log-normal distribution? How can these two concepts be used to analyze rate-of-return of common stocks?
12. Calculate Company XYZ's expected interest rate 1 year hence in accordance with the information listed in Tables 5.P.1 and 5.P.2.
13. Use GM's monthly rates-of-return as indicated in Table 5.P.3 during the period that included the first quarter of 1977, up to and including

Table 5.P.1. Treasury bill rate 1 year hence.

Treasury Bill Rate (%)	Probability (%)
7	40
9	60

Table 5.P.2. EBIT for next year and associated risk premiums expected on next year's renewal of short-term credit.

EBIT	Risk Premium (%)	Probability (%)
5 million	5	30
15 million	3	40
20 million	2	30

Table 5.P.3. Monthly Treasury bill rate, Market rate-of-return, and rates-of-return for automobile manufacturers.

		A	B	C	D	E	F	G	H	I	J	K
1977	1	0.004	−0.040	0.032	0.012	−0.003	−0.049	−0.045	0.028	0.008	−0.007	−0.053
	2	0.004	−0.017	0.063	−0.029	−0.043	−0.041	−0.020	0.059	−0.033	−0.047	−0.044
	3	0.004	−0.011	0.176	−0.088	−0.065	−0.057	−0.015	0.173	−0.092	−0.069	−0.060
	4	0.004	0.004	−0.075	−0.007	0.044	0.024	0.000	−0.079	−0.011	0.040	0.021
	5	0.004	−0.012	−0.108	−0.063	−0.020	0.001	−0.017	−0.112	−0.067	−0.024	−0.003
	6	0.004	0.051	−0.030	−0.008	0.078	0.041	0.047	−0.034	−0.012	0.073	0.037
	7	0.004	−0.016	0.031	−0.081	−0.034	−0.018	−0.020	0.027	−0.065	−0.038	−0.022
	8	0.005	−0.014	−0.030	−0.008	−0.020	0.007	−0.019	−0.035	−0.013	−0.024	0.002
	9	0.005	0.001	0.000	0.066	0.060	0.042	−0.004	−0.005	0.061	0.055	0.038
	10	0.005	−0.039	−0.051	−0.101	−0.056	−0.048	−0.044	−0.036	−0.106	−0.061	−0.053
	11	0.005	0.042	0.129	−0.043	0.009	0.000	0.037	0.124	−0.048	0.004	−0.005
	12	0.005	0.005	−0.171	−0.073	0.058	−0.018	0.000	−0.176	−0.078	0.053	−0.023
1978	1	0.005	−0.057	0.103	0.020	−0.067	−0.074	−0.063	0.098	0.014	−0.073	−0.079
	2	0.005	−0.012	0.051	−0.107	0.006	0.019	−0.018	0.026	−0.112	0.001	0.014
	3	0.005	0.032	0.212	0.022	0.080	0.054	0.027	0.207	0.017	0.075	0.048
	4	0.005	0.033	−0.075	−0.043	0.143	0.065	0.078	−0.080	−0.049	0.138	0.060
	5	0.005	0.019	0.270	0.080	−0.032	−0.046	0.014	0.265	0.074	−0.037	−0.051
	6	0.006	−0.013	−0.064	−0.065	−0.058	−0.027	−0.019	−0.069	−0.070	−0.064	−0.032
	7	0.006	0.057	0.000	0.011	−0.010	0.051	0.051	0.006	0.006	−0.016	0.045
	8	0.006	0.038	0.136	0.080	−0.026	0.014	0.032	0.130	0.074	−0.033	0.008
	9	0.007	−0.007	0.000	0.032	0.034	0.014	−0.013	−0.007	0.026	0.028	0.008
	10	0.007	−0.102	−0.200	−0.177	−0.101	−0.073	−0.109	−0.207	−0.184	−0.108	−0.080
	11	0.007	0.031	0.025	−0.015	0.028	−0.013	0.024	0.018	−0.023	0.021	−0.020
	12	0.008	0.017	−0.073	−0.104	0.024	−0.027	0.009	−0.081	−0.112	0.017	−0.035

(Continued)

Table 5.P.3. (*Continued*)

		A	B	C	D	E	F	G	H	I	J	K
1979	1	0.008	0.047	0.289	0.217	−0.008	0.049	0.039	0.282	0.210	−0.016	0.041
	2	0.008	−0.029	−0.020	−0.086	0.006	−0.031	−0.037	−0.028	−0.093	−0.002	−0.039
	3	0.008	0.062	0.542	0.079	0.067	0.061	0.054	0.554	0.071	0.059	0.053
	4	0.008	0.007	−0.095	−0.049	0.040	0.026	−0.001	−0.103	−0.057	0.032	0.018
	5	0.008	−0.015	−0.179	−0.131	−0.048	0.018	−0.023	−0.187	−0.139	−0.056	0.010
	6	0.008	0.043	−0.036	0.090	0.003	0.028	0.037	−0.044	0.082	−0.005	0.021
	7	0.008	0.015	0.094	−0.095	0.009	−0.025	0.007	0.087	−0.104	0.001	−0.033
	8	0.008	0.063	0.138	0.030	0.027	0.054	0.055	0.150	0.022	0.019	0.047
	9	0.008	−0.000	−0.045	−0.015	0.014	0.044	−0.009	−0.054	−0.023	0.006	0.035
	10	0.010	−0.069	−0.102	−0.119	−0.134	−0.116	−0.079	−0.111	−0.129	−0.144	−0.126
	11	0.010	0.060	−0.071	−0.119	−0.169	−0.057	0.051	−0.081	−0.129	−0.179	−0.066
	12	0.010	0.023	0.069	0.038	0.045	−0.012	0.013	0.059	0.028	0.035	−0.022
1980	1	0.010	0.062	0.273	0.500	0.086	0.098	0.052	0.263	0.490	0.076	0.087
	2	0.011	−0.003	−0.043	−0.111	−0.095	−0.056	−0.014	−0.054	−0.122	−0.107	−0.067
	3	0.013	−0.108	−0.260	−0.519	−0.045	−0.089	−0.121	−0.273	−0.332	−0.058	−0.102
	4	0.012	0.049	−0.102	0.163	−0.129	−0.014	0.037	−0.114	0.152	−0.140	−0.025
	5	0.008	0.059	−0.023	−0.070	0.005	−0.003	0.051	−0.030	−0.078	−0.022	−0.011
	6	0.006	0.034	−0.023	0.019	0.005	0.039	0.028	−0.029	0.013	−0.001	0.033
	7	0.007	0.068	−0.024	0.093	0.170	0.126	0.061	−0.031	0.086	0.163	0.120
	8	0.008	0.020	0.122	0.254	−0.031	0.033	0.012	0.114	0.247	−0.038	0.025
	9	0.009	0.029	−0.087	−0.014	0.000	−0.014	0.021	−0.096	−0.022	−0.009	−0.023
	10	0.010	0.020	−0.071	−0.096	−0.057	−0.069	0.010	−0.081	−0.106	−0.067	−0.078
	11	0.012	0.107	−0.128	−0.152	−0.131	−0.084	0.096	−0.140	−0.163	−0.143	−0.096
	12	0.013	−0.034	−0.088	−0.304	−0.106	0.014	−0.047	−0.101	−0.317	−0.119	0.001

(*Continued*)

Table 5.P.3. (*Continued*)

		A	B	C	D	E	F	G	H	I	J	K
1981	1	0.012	−0.044	0.065	0.154	0.003	0.022	−0.056	0.052	0.142	−0.010	0.010
	2	0.012	0.018	−0.030	−0.044	−0.005	0.103	0.006	−0.043	−0.057	−0.019	0.090
	3	0.011	0.042	0.094	0.256	0.223	0.055	0.031	0.083	0.245	0.212	0.044
	4	0.011	−0.015	−0.057	−0.037	−0.097	0.021	−0.027	−0.069	−0.048	−0.108	0.010
	5	0.014	0.009	−0.030	−0.019	0.076	0.041	−0.005	−0.044	−0.033	0.062	0.028
	6	0.012	−0.009	0.000	0.039	0.038	−0.047	−0.021	−0.012	0.027	0.026	−0.059
	7	0.012	0.001	−0.094	−0.057	−0.082	−0.031	−0.012	−0.106	−0.069	−0.094	−0.043
	8	0.013	−0.056	−0.069	−0.160	−0.087	−0.086	−0.069	−0.082	−0.173	−0.100	−0.099
	9	0.012	−0.057	−0.037	−0.119	0.000	−0.038	−0.069	−0.049	−0.132	−0.012	−0.050
	10	0.012	0.058	−0.115	−0.108	−0.162	−0.162	0.047	−0.127	−0.120	−0.174	−0.194
	11	0.009	0.045	−0.087	−0.030	0.023	0.030	0.036	−0.096	−0.040	0.014	0.021
	12	0.009	−0.028	−0.095	−0.156	0.008	0.041	−0.037	−0.104	−0.165	−0.002	0.031

the fourth quarter of 1981, to forecast the HPR for 1982 by using three alternative averaging methods. Column A corresponds to the Risk-Free Rate; B is the Market Rate-of-Return (S&P 500); C, D, E, and F correspond to the AMC, Chrysler, Ford, and GM stock rates-of-return, respectively; G is the Market Rate-of-Return minus the Risk-Free Rate; and H, I, J, and K correspond to the Stock Rate-of-Return minus the Risk-Free Rate for AMC, Chrysler, Ford and GM, respectively.

14. Use three kinds of T-bill rates, form those listed in Table PR.I.6 (a–g) in Project I,* to estimate the liquidity premium.
15. Please update the T-Bill rate data described in Table 5P.3 until fourth quarter of 2008. In addition, please also collect monthly stock rate-of-return from January 1977 to December 2008 for Johnson & Johnson Inc. and Merck & Co. Inc. Please do the following.

    (a) Redo the answer as discussed in problem 13.
    (b) Please calculate the mean, standard deviation, skewness, kurtosis, and coefficient of variation by using the data which you have collected.
    (c) Discuss the possible implication of the estimated statistics which you have calculated in (b).

Appendix 5.A. Compounding and Discounting Processes and their Applications

5.A.1. *Single-value Case*

(a) Compound Future Sum (Terminal Value)

The theoretical justification of the liquidity and time preferences led to universal acceptance of a positive rate of forward interest. It is necessary to develop a means of equating present and future amounts of capital if resources are to be efficiently allocated within our economy over time. Since positive interest rate is a "natural" phenomenon, future sums will be larger than present values. Two variables determine how large this difference between present values and future sums will be: the anticipated interest rate (i) and the length of time (N) over which an interest rate will be in effect.

In the discrete case, compounding occurs only at specified intervals of time (i.e., daily, monthly, quarterly, or annually). Equation (5.A.1) indicates the nature of the relationship between the original amount P(0) and its terminal value P(N).

$$P_D(N) = P(0)(1 + i)^N. \tag{5.A.1}$$

To show the mechanics of this relationship, assume \$1,000 in the bank today (P(0) = \$1,000), to earn simple annual interest at 10%. At the end of the first year, you will receive the principal of \$1,000 plus interest of 10%, or \$100. Therefore, the amount at the end of year 1 is represented by $P(0)(1 + i)$. Assuming both the original amount of \$1,000 and the interest earned in the first year (\$100) are left in the bank, 10% will be earned on \$1,100 in the second year. The amount at the end of the second year is represented by P(0)(1 + i)(1 + i) or $P(0)(1 + i)^2$. This process continues as N gets larger.

	End of Year 1	End of Year 2	End of Year 3	End of Year N
Amount	P(0)(1+i)	P(0)(1+i) (1+i)	P(0)(1+i) (1+i)(1+i)	
Received	P(0)(1+i)	$P(0)(1+i)^2$	$P(0)(1+i)^3 \ldots$	$P(0)(1+i)^N$

The original value P(0), the rate of interest (i), and the length of time (N) are all the information necessary to calculate a future sum. Interest can be compounded at various interest rates and times (see Table I at end of book). If we were to calculate the compound sum for the previous example, at a 10% interest rate, we see that, after 5 years, \$1 would grow to \$1,611:

$$\text{P(N)} = \text{P(0)(interest factor)} = \$1{,}000(1.611) = \$1{,}611.$$

If borrowing and lending rates are equal, an individual should be indifferent between receiving \$1,000 today or \$1,610.50 in 5 years if the interest rate remains constant at 10%.

With discrete compounding, it is assumed that value changes only at specific intervals. As this interval gets shorter and shorter, the discrete compounding process approaches continuous compounding.

There are many applications of the compounding/discounting process in evaluating firms for which the original, discrete formulation is inadequate.

In order to derive the formula for the continuously compounded sum, Eq. (5.A.2) is used as an intermediate equation:

$$P_D(N) = P(0)\left(1 + \frac{i}{m}\right)^{m \cdot N}. \tag{5.A.2}$$

where m is the frequency of compounding in each year and N is the number of years. If $m = 4$, Eq. (5.A.2) can be used to describe the quarterly compounding process. If m approaches infinity, the equation can be used to describe the continuous compounding process. Based upon the well-known definition of e, presented in Eq. (5.A.3),

$$\lim_{m \to \infty}\left(1 + \frac{1}{m}\right)^{m} = e = 2.7183, \tag{5.A.3}$$

Eq. (5.A.2) can be rewritten as shown in Eq. (5.A.3a):

$$P_C(N) = \lim P(0)\left(1 + \frac{i}{m}\right)^{\left(\frac{m}{i}\right)iN} = P(0)e^{iN}P_c. \tag{5.A.3a}$$

Equation (5.A.3a) is obtained using the definition of e and the technique of redefining a new variable. With this formulation, we can determine the terminal value P(N) of an original amount P(0) that is continuously compounded at the i rate of interest for N years. If a \$1,000 asset were appreciating in value at the annual rate of 10%, after 5 years it would be worth \$1,648.72 (as shown below). Note the difference from the discrete case.

$$\mathrm{P(N) = P(0)(interest\ factor) = \$1000(2.7183)(0.10)(5) = \$1648.72.}$$

(b) Present Value

Present value is the opposite side of the coin. We must discount a known future amount back to determine its present value. Information on the variables i and N, as well as the future amount (P_N), is all that is necessary for this calculation. When discounting future amounts, we need to *divide* the future interest factor, which is shown in Eqs. (5.A.4) and (5.A.5) for the discrete and continuous cases, respectively:

$$P_D(0) = \frac{P(N)}{[(1+i)^N]}, \tag{5.A.4}$$

$$P_C(0) = \frac{P(N)}{e^{iN}}. \tag{5.A.5}$$

As an example, assume that you just opened a 5-year time deposit account in order to save for a future vacation. You want to have \$3,000 in the account at maturity for a trip to Europe, and the bank agrees to pay you interest at the annual rate of 10%. The computations, for both discrete and continuous cases, are presented below.

$$P_D(0) = \frac{\$3000}{(1+0.10)^5} = \$1862.76,$$

$$P_C(0) = \frac{\$3000}{(2.718)(0.10)(5)} = \$1819.59.$$

Note that the continuously discounted present value is less than the discrete value. Interest is more of a factor when it is compounded continuously. The present-value table (Table II at end of book) presents interest rates or discount rates for various years, along with the discount factor by which one multiplies the future value in order to arrive at the present value.

These numbers are the reciprocal of the interest factor of $(1+i)^N$. The compound future sum and the present-value computations are two different ways of looking at the same relationship.

5.A.2. *Annuity Case*

An annuity is a series of payments, in a fixed dollar amount, made over a period of time. The annuity is just one example of a frequently encountered compound-interest problem. Suppose a firm sells goods that will be paid for in installments. The seller would like to know what the present value of those installment payments is. In another case, a firm needs to know the present value of the future cash inflows from an investment to determine whether the investment is worthwhile. Or perhaps an employee needs to know the size of monthly payments into an annuity that will produce a particular income after retirement. In this instance, one must determine the present value of payments after retirement at the time of retirement, and then determine the size of payments necessary while working.

(a) Compound Future Sum of An Annuity

To pursue the last case, let us determine the amount available for the employee's retirement. This is an application of the concept of the compound future sum of an annuity. The equations for the discrete and continuous cases for this compound sum application are:

N

$$CFSA_D = \sum_{t=1}^{N} C(t)[(1+i)^{N-t+1}], \tag{5.A.6}$$

$$CFSA_C = \int_{t=1}^{N} C(t)[e^{iT}]dt. \tag{5.A.7}$$

Following the previous example, assume that an employee pays \$5,000 annually into an annuity, which pays interest of 10% for 15 years. This is a very cumbersome calculation:

$$\begin{aligned} CSFA_D &= 5000[(1+0.10)^1] + 5000[(1+0.10)^2] + \cdots + 5000[(1+0.10)^{15}] \\ &= 5000[(1+0.10)^1 + (1+0.10)^2 + \cdots + (1+0.10)^{15}] \\ &= 5000[31.772] \\ &= \$158{,}860. \end{aligned}$$

Instead, one can use an annuity table (as in Table III) which shows the summation of interest factors for n years compounded at the i rate of interest. For cases of variable payments, the annual payments must be compounded individually and summed over the life of the annuity.

(b) Present Value of An Annuity

Applications for the discounting of future cash flows frequently surface in the areas of capital budgeting and analysis of investment projects. The firm wants to know the value today of the future stream of earnings to be generated by the project. If the present value of these future cash flows is less than the cost of the investment, the company would be receiving less than it is paying out (i.e., in present-value terms), and therefore it should not invest in the project. Equations (5.A.8) and (5.A.9) present the formulas for the calculation of the present value of annuity (PVA), in the discrete and continuous-compounding cases, respectively.

$$PVA_D = \sum_{t=1}^{n} \frac{C(t)}{(1+i)^t}, \tag{5.A.8}$$

$$PVA_C = \int_{t=1}^{n} \frac{C(t)}{[e^{it}]dt}. \tag{5.A.9}$$

As an illustration, assume that a firm will receive cash flow of \$10,000 per year for 25 years, and that the appropriate discount rate is 6%. How much should this firm be willing to pay for an investment in order to receive this stream of cash flows? The calculation is as follows:

$$\begin{aligned}PVA_D &= 10{,}000(1+0.06)^{-1} + 10{,}000(1+0.06)^{-2} \\ &\quad + \cdots + 10{,}000(1+0.06)^{-25} \\ &= 10{,}000[(1+0.06)^{-1} + (1+0.06)^{-2} + \cdots + (1+0.06)^{-25}] \\ &= 10{,}000(12.783) = 127{,}830.\end{aligned}$$

In order to break even on the investment, the firm should not pay more than \$127,830. Obviously, they would like to pay much less than this for the project. For this type of calculation another table is available which presents the summation of the annual discount factors for various values of i and n (see Table IV at end of book). Furthermore, as with the compounding process, the annual cash flows must be discounted individually over intervals of constant rates if either the size of the cash flow or the discount rate changes over time.

Appendix 5.B. Taylor-Series Expansion and its Applications to Rates-of-Return Determination

Calculus provides methods for approximating complex functions, such as ln X, or e^x. One of these methods is a special type of power series called a Taylor-series expansion. Conceptually, the Taylor-series attempts to approximate the function in question by converging on the true value through the use of an increasing degree of polynomial. Mathematically, the Taylor-series expansion is written:

$$\begin{aligned}F_n(x) &= F(a) + F'(a)(x-a) + \frac{F''(a)}{2!}(x-a)^2 \\ &\quad + \cdots + \frac{F^{(n)}(a)}{n!}(x-a)^n + \cdots,\end{aligned} \tag{5.B.1}$$

where

$F_n(x)$ is the function we are approximating;
$F'(a)$ is the first derivative of the function;
$F^{(n)}(a)$ is the nth derivative of the function;
$n!$ is the factorial value of n [$n! = (n)(n-1)\ldots(2)(1)$];

And a is the value near which we are making the approximation to the function F(x).

If we wish to approximate the ln(x) through the use of the Taylor-series expansion, we must first define the derivative of the natural logarithm.

$$F'(a) = \frac{d}{dx}\ln(x)|_{x=a} = \frac{1}{a}, \quad a > 0, \tag{5.B.2a}$$

$$F''(a) = -a^{-2}, \tag{5.B.2b}$$

$$F'''(a) = 2a^{-3}, \tag{5.B.2c}$$

$$F''''(a) = -6a^{-4}. \tag{5.B.2d}$$

$$\vdots \qquad\qquad \vdots$$

$$-(n-1)!a^{-n}, \quad \text{if n is even,}$$

$$\text{or} \quad +(n-1)!a^{-n}, \quad \text{if n is odd.} \tag{5.B.2n}$$

The importance of looking at the nth-order derivative is that when compared to the nth term of the Taylor-series expansion,

$$\frac{F^n(a)}{n!}(x-a)^n. \tag{5.B.3}$$

And substituting the actual derivative of ln(x) (assuming that the preceding sign is positive in our notation, for the sake of simplicity) result in

$$\frac{(n-1)!}{n!} \cdot \frac{1}{a^n} \cdot (x-a)^n. \tag{5.B.4}$$

Note that the first component reduces to $1/n$. Making this simplification and rearranging the term yields:

$$\frac{1}{n}\left[\frac{x}{a} - 1\right]^n, \tag{5.B.5}$$

for the nth term of the Taylor-series expansion of the natural logarithm.

Thus the full expansion:

$$F(x) = \ln(a) + \left[\frac{x}{a} - 1\right] - \frac{1}{2!}\left[\frac{x}{a} - 1\right]^2 + \cdots + \frac{1}{n}\left[\frac{x}{a} - 1\right]^n \tag{5.B.6}$$

If we let $a = 1$, that is, we are taking the Taylor-series expansion around one, then

$$F(x) = \ln(1) + [x-1] - \frac{1}{2!}[x-1]^2 + \cdots + \frac{1}{N!}[x-1]^n. \tag{5.B.7}$$

Next, define the holding-period yield for the discrete case

$$HPY_D = \left[\frac{P_t + D_t}{P_{t-1}} - 1\right]. \tag{5.B.8}$$

And the holding-period yield for the continuous case

$$HPY_C = \left[\frac{P_t + D_t}{P_{t-1}}\right]. \tag{5.B.9}$$

In order to show $HPY_C < HPY_D$, let

$$x = \frac{P_t + D_t}{P_{t-1}}. \tag{5.B.10}$$

Then

$$\ln x = HPY_C. \tag{5.B.11}$$

If we look at the Taylor-series expansion of ln x, we see that the first term, $x - 1$, is the HPY_D. Also note that, as the order of the terms increases, the contribution each term makes to the approximation declines rapidly since $x - 1$ is, in most cases, less than one. Based on this reasoning, we can limit our examination to the first two terms:

$$HPY_C = \ln x = (x - 1) - \frac{1}{2}(x - 1)^2. \tag{5.B.12}$$

As we have mentioned, $(x-1) = HPY_D$. Substituting this into the equation, we have

$$HPY_C = HPY_D - \frac{1}{2}(x - 1)^2. \tag{5.B.13}$$

Thus, as we have stated, the continuously compounded *HPY* is less than the discrete case of the *HPY*. This should have been intuitively obvious.

There is a special case of the Taylor-series, the *McLaurin series*, which is used when we wish to approximate a function near zero (that is, $a = 0$):

$$F_n(x) = F(0) + F'(0)(x) + \frac{F''(0)}{2!}(x)^2 + \cdots + \frac{F^{(n)}(0)}{n!}(x)^n + \cdots. \tag{5.B.14}$$

We can use the McLaurin-series expansion to approximate the natural antilog function, $F(x) = e^x$. Since every derivative of $F(x) = e^x$ is

$F'(x) = F''(x) = F^n(x) = e^x$ and since $e^a = e^0 = 1$, the McLaurin-series expansion becomes

$$e^x = 1 + \frac{x}{1!} + \cdots + \frac{x^n}{n!} + \cdots. \tag{5.B.15}$$

This expansion can be used to help is understand the relationship between the normal and log-normal distribution. If x is a normally distributed variable — (that is, $x \sim N(\mu, \sigma^2)$) — then $y = e^x$ is a log-normally distributed variable. A log-normal distribution, as discussed in Chapter 2, is positively skewed.

If we take the expected value of $e^x = y$ o Eq. (5.B.15), we find that

$$E(y) = E(e^x) = E\left(1 + x + \frac{1}{2}x^2\right) = 1 + E(x) + \frac{1}{2}\sigma^2 + \frac{1}{2}(E(x))^2,$$

where $E(\bullet)$ represents the expected value of a variable.

It is important for us to note that the mean of a log-normally distributed variable incorporates not only the mean of the related normally distributed variable but also the variance. We are dealing with rates-of-return; the term with $n \geq 3$ are insignificant and are dropped from the analysis. This technique can also help us shed some light on the issue of horizon. If we let $y = HPR$, then

$$y_{t+1} = \frac{P_{t+1} + D_t}{P_t}.$$

Empirical studies have shown that the holding-period return is positively skewed. Because of this positive skewness, the log-normal distribution is better than the normal distribution in describing the distribution of the holding-period returns.

If we calculate the holding-period return based on different time periods, e.g., daily or weekly, the magnitudes of the HPR differ. As the length of time between observations decreases, the magnitude of the HPR decreases.

To repeat, the McLaurin expansion of the natural log is

$$y = e^x = 1 + x + \frac{x^2}{2!} + \cdots + \frac{x^n}{n!}. \tag{5.B.16}$$

If the time horizon is very short, daily or weekly, than all orders of the expansion except the first order becomes insignificant, and the log-normally distributed variable y is then equal to

$$y = 1 + x. \tag{5.B.17}$$

Rearranging the terms, we have

$$y = 1 - x. \tag{5.B.18}$$

By Eq. (5.B.16),

$$y = e^x. \tag{5.B.19}$$

and therefore,

$$x = \ln y. \tag{5.B.20}$$

But $y = HPR = (P_{t+1} + D_t)/P_t$, then

$$x = \ln\left(\frac{P_{t+1} + D_t}{P_t}\right) \tag{5.B.21}$$

and x is therefore the HPY_C. Equation (5.B.18) can be restated as $y - 1 = HPY_C$.

Substituting the equivalent value for y $[y = (P_{t+1}+D_t)/P_t]$, we arrive at

$$\frac{(P_{t+1} + D_t)}{P_t} - 1 = HPYc. \tag{5.B.22}$$

The left-hand term is just the HPY_D. This means that

$$HPY_D = HPY_C, \tag{5.B.23}$$

$$y - 1 = x. \tag{5.B.24}$$

This conclusion, we must remember, is predicated on the assumption that the time period is extremely short. The importance of this conclusion extends far beyond the simple close approximation of the discrete and continuous case of the holding-period yields. As we noted above, y is log-normally distributed and x is normally distributed.

The conclusion we can draw form this is that, for short time horizons, it is valid to assume normality of the distribution of the returns.

References for Chapter 5

Bach, GL and A Ando (1957). The redistributional effects of inflation. *Review of Economics and Statistics*, 39, 1–13.

Bach, GL and J Stephenson (1974). Inflation and the redistribution of wealth. *Review of Economics and Statistics*, 56, 1–13.

Baesel, J and S Globerman (1978). Unanticipated inflation and wealth distribution among business firms: Additional evidence. *Journal of Economics and Business*, 82–88.

Bernard, V (1986). Unanticipated inflation and the value of the firm. *Journal of Financial Economics*, 15(3), 285–321.

Blume, M (1974). Unbiased estimations of long-run expected rates of return. *Journal of the American Statistical Association*, 69, 634–638.

Bradford, W (1974). Inflation and the value of the firm. *Southern Economic Journal*, 40, 414–427.

Broussalian, VA (1961). Unanticipated Inflation: A Test of the Creditor-Debtor Hypothesis. Unpublished doctoral dissertation, University of California at Los Angeles.

Cagen, P and R Lipsey (1978). The Financial Effects of Inflation, NBER General Series No. 103, Ballinger Publishing Company, Cambridge, Massachusetts.

Carlson, J (1977). Short-term interest rates as predictors of inflation: Comment. *American Economic Review*, 67, 469–475.

Chang, RP, BM Lord, and SG Rhee (1985). Inflation-caused wealth-transfer: A case of the insurance industry. *The Journal of Risk and Insurance*, 52(4), 627–643.

Chu, QC, DN Pittman, and Lee (1995). Inflation risk premium. *Journal of Business, Finance and Accounting.*

DeAlessi, L (1964). Do business firms gain from inflation? *Journal of Business*, 37, 162–166.

Dietrich, JR (1980). Wealth-Transfer Hypothesis: Testable Implications and Confounding Effects: Empirical Results, Chapter 3 of Unpublished doctoral dissertation, Carnegie-Mellon University.

Dietrich, JR (1981). Wealth-Transfer Hypothesis: Testable Implications and Confounding Effects: Empirical Results, Chapter 5 of Unpublished doctoral dissertation, Carnegie-Mellon University.

Ecols, E and JW Elliot (1976). A quantitative yield curve model of estimating the term structure of interest rate. *Journal of Financial and Quantitative Analysis*, 11, 80–90.

Fama, E (1975). Short-term interest rates as predictors of inflation. American Economic Review, 269–282.

Fama, E (1976). *Foundations of Finance.* New York: Basic Books, Inc.

Fama, E (1981). Stock returns, real activity, inflation, and money. *American Economic Review*, 545–565.

Feldstein, M and L Summers (1979). Inflation and the taxation of capital income in the corporate sector. *National Tax Journal*, 445–470.

Fisher, I (1930). The Theory of Interest. New York: The Macmillan Company.

Fisher, L (1966). Some new stock market indexes. *Journal of Business*, 39, 191–225.

French, K, R Ruback, and W Schwert (1983). Effects of nominal contracting on stock returns. *Journal of Political Economy*, 91, 70–96.

Gonedes, N (1981). Evidence on the 'tax effects' of inflation under historical cost-accounting methods. *Journal of Business*, 54, 227–270.

Hasbrouck, J (1984). Stock returns, inflation, and economics activity: The survey evidence. *Journal of Finance*, 39(5), 1293–1310.

Hendershott, P (1981). The decline in aggregate share values — Taxation, valuation errors, risk, and profitability. *American Economic Review*, 71, 909–922.

Hicks, J (1946). *Value and Capital*, 2nd ed. London: Oxford University Press.

Hong, H (1977). Inflation and the market value of the firm: Theory and tests. *Journal of Finance*, 32, 1031–1048.

Ibbotson, R and RA Sinquefield. Stocks, Bonds, Bills, and Inflation: 2006 Yearbook, annual updates work by RG Ibbotson and RA Sinquefield (Chicago: Ibbotson Associate).

Johnson, G, K Coggor, and W Huffman (1980). An empirical investigation of the debtor–creditor hypothesis. *Review of Business and Economic Research*, 64–76.

Joines, D (1977). Short-term interest rates as predictors of inflation: Comment. *American Economic Review*, 67, 469–475.

Kessel, R (1956). Inflation-caused wealth redistribution: A test of a hypothesis. *American Economic Review*, 128–141.

Kessel, R and A Alchian (1962). Effects of inflation. *Journal of Political Economy*, 70, 521–537.

Lee, CF and AC Lee (2006). *Encyclopedia of Finance*. New York: Springer.

Meiselman, D (1962). *The Term Structure of Interest Rates*. Englewood Cliffs, New Jersey: Prentice-Hall, Inc.

Modigliani, F and R Cohn (1979). Inflation, rational valuation, and the market. *Financial Analysts' Journal*, 24–44.

Modigliani, F and R Swatch (1966). Innovations in interest rate policy. *American Economic Review*, 56, 178–197.

Modigliani, F and R Swatch (1967). Debt management and the term structure of interest rates: An empirical analysis of recent experience. *Journal of Political Economy*, 75, 569–589.

Moore, G (1977). Cost-price relations in the business cycle. NBER Reporter, 4–16.

Moosa, S (1980). Inflation and stock prices. *Journal of Financial Research*, 115–128.

Nelson, C and W Schwert (1977). Short-term interest rates as predictors of inflation: On testing the hypothesis that the real rate of interest is constant. *American Economic Review*, 478–486.

Rogalski, R and S Tinic (1978). Risk-premium curve vs. capital market line: A re-examination. *Financial Management*, 7, 73–84.

Rothstein, M (1972). On geometric and arithmetic portfolio performance indexes. *Journal of Finance and Quantitative Analysis*, 7, 1983-1982.

Startz, R (1982). Do forecast errors or term premia really make the difference between long and short rates? *Journal of Financial Economics*, 10, 323–329.

Summers, LH (1981). Inflation and the Valuation of Corporate Equities. National Bureau of Economics Research, Working Paper No. 824.

Terbough, G (1974). Inflation and profits. *Financial Analysts' Journal*, 19–23.

U.S. Department of Treasury, Office of Domestic Office, Daily Treasury Yield Curve Rates. http://www.treasury.gov/offices/domestic-finance/debt-management/interest-rate/yield.shtml.

Van Horne, JC (2000). *Financial Market Rates and Flows*, 6th ed. Englewood Cliffs, New Jersey: Prentice-Hall, Inc.

Van Horne, J and W Glassmire (1972). The impact of unanticipated changes in inflation on the value of common stocks. *Journal of Finance*, 1081–1092.

Yohe, W and D Karnosky (1969). Interest rates and price-level changes, 1952–1969. Federal Reserve Bank of St. Louis Review, 2–25.

Project I

Analyses of Accounting, Market and Economic Data

Part II

Alternative Finance Theories and their Application

Chapter 6

Valuation of Bonds and Stocks

6.1. Introduction

The main purpose of this chapter is to discuss how to use time value of money concepts and methods to determine the valuation of bonds and stocks. Some bonds pay coupon interest annually, some semiannually, and some pay no coupon interest at all. Some stocks pay no dividends, others pay the same dollar amount each year as a dividend, and some pay dividends that change every year. How much should investors be willing to pay for these securities? And what price can issuing corporations expect to receive in selling them? Fortunately, basic techniques exist to help us to value, or determine a price on these assets. In the next chapter, we will use the valuation of bonds and stocks to discuss capital structure and other related issues.

We know how the process of discounting allows us to determine the present value of a future cash flow. This technique can be applied to the valuation of any asset: real or financial. In Chapter 6, our aim is to apply this discounting principle to the valuation of financial assets, such as bonds, preferred stocks, and common stocks. We begin with Section 6.2 discussing bond valuation, followed by Section 6.3, which explores stock valuation. Section 6.4 discusses risk, return, and market efficiency, and exchange rates and investing overseas is discussed in Section 6.5. Finally, Section 6.6 gives several examples and Section 6.7 summarizes the chapter.

6.2. Bond Valuation

A bond represents a liability of a firm or government entity that arises from borrowing money. A typical bond pays a set amount of interest each year and repays the principal amount of the loan at maturity. The valuation principle states that the bond's value equals the present value of these expected future cash flows.

Four factors affect bond valuation: the bond's yield-to-maturity (YTM), par value, maturity date, and coupon rate. The YTM is the effective annual rate-of-return demanded by investors on bonds of a given maturity and risk. The face value of a bond is called the **par value**. In general, this is the amount of money that the issuer has initially borrowed and promised to repay at a future **maturity date**. Most U.S. corporate bonds have a par value of $1,000 per bond. The **coupon interest rate** is the percentage of the par value to be paid annually, as interest, to the bond holder.

Most U.S. corporate bonds make interest payments semiannually, that is, every 6 months. **Eurobonds**, which are bonds denominated in U.S. dollars issued by firms in financial markets outside the United States, typically pay interest annually. A bond's maturity date, par value, and coupon rate are all disclosed to investors prior to purchase; for the most part, these items are fixed and do not change over the life of a bond issue. The YTM changes, however, depending upon economic and financial trends, market expectations, and firm-specific information affecting risk.

Suppose that a bond with par (face) value F is purchased today and that the bond matures in N years. Let us assume that interest payments of dollar amount I are to be made at the end of each of the next N years. The bondholder will then receive a stream of N annual payments of I dollars, plus a payment of F dollars at the end of the Nth year. Using the rate of interest k to discount future receipts, the present value of the bond is

$$PV = \sum_{t=1}^{N} \frac{I}{(1+k)^t} + \frac{F}{(1+k)^N}. \tag{6.1}$$

The first term on the right-hand side of Eq. (6.1) is the present value of the stream of interest payments, while the second term is the present value of the future receipt of the par amount.

6.2.1. *Present Value of Future Cash Flows*

Cash flows arise from the receipt of coupon interest every 6 months and from the par value at maturity. Thus, cash flows from a bond have two components. First, the coupon interest payments resemble an annuity that occurs every 6 months over the bond's life. Second, the par value payment is a lump sum or single payment made when the bond matures.

The annual interest payments on a bond equal the coupon rate multiplied by the par value. Thus, the amount of each semiannual coupon payment is half of this amount. For example, a 10% coupon bond pays annual interest of 0.10 times \$1,000, or \$100; each semiannual coupon payment is half of \$100, or \$50.

The easiest way to compute the present value, or price, of a bond is to divide the analysis into two simpler present value problems that we already know how to solve. The complex cash flow pattern shown can be separated into two familiar cash flow patterns: (1) an annuity (the coupon payments), and (2) a lump sum (the principal payment). The first step in determining a bond's price is to compute the present value of the coupon annuity; the second part of the analysis involves computing the present value of the par value. The price of the bond will be the sum of these two present value calculations, as shown in Eq. (6.2):

$$\text{Bond price} = \text{PVAN(Coupon)} + \text{PV(Par Value)}. \tag{6.2}$$

EXAMPLE 6.1

Eurobonds–Annual Coupons

Q: A Eurobond with a coupon rate of 8% pays interest annually, has a par value of \$1,000, and matures 7 years from now. What current market price would we expect for this bond, assuming that bonds of similar risk and maturity have a 10% YTM?

A: To find the price of the bond, first find the present value of the coupon annuity and add it to the present value of the par value. With an 8% coupon rate, annual interest payments for the bond are 0.08 times \$1,000, or \$80; with interest paid annually, the size of the coupon annuity is \$80 per year. With 7 years until maturity and a 10% YTM, the present value of the coupon annuity is:

$$\begin{aligned}\text{PVAN(Coupon)} &= (\$80) \times [\text{PVIFA } (10\%, 7 \text{ periods})] = \$80 \times 4.86842\\ &= \$389.47.\end{aligned}$$

The present value of the par value is:

$$\begin{aligned}\text{PV (Par)} &= (\$1{,}000) \times [\text{PVIF } (10\%, 7 \text{ periods})] = \$1{,}000 \times 0.51316\\ &= \$513.16.\end{aligned}$$

Thus, the current market price of the bond should be \$389.47 plus 513.16, or \$902.63.

6.2.1.1. *Semiannual coupon payments*

Semiannual coupon payments would change our analysis in Example 6.1. We know that when cash flows occur more frequently than once a year, adjustments must be made to n, the number of periods, and to r, the discount rate. The number of periods, n, becomes the number of years multiplied by the number of cash flows per year. The interest rate also will need to be adjusted to determine the appropriate periodic interest rate. The method by which we compute the periodic interest rate depends, however, upon which type of annual interest rate is quoted. Bonds can have two interest rates that reflect their annual returns: they can be based on the effective annual rate (EAR), or they can be quoted based upon the annual percentage rate (APR) concept. We discuss each of these in turn.

EAR or YTM. When the EAR is quoted for bonds, it is called the bond's YTM or market interest rate. To properly discount the semiannual coupons, we must determine the periodic interest rate that corresponds to the EAR.

We can calculate the effective annual rate as:

$$EAR = YTM = (1 + \text{Periodic interest rate})^m - 1,$$

in order to solve for the periodic interest rate:

$$\text{periodic interest rate} = (1 + YTM)^{\frac{1}{m}} - 1.$$

If the YTM is given as 10% for a bond that makes coupon payments semi-annually, the appropriate discount rate is:

$$(1 + 0.10)^{\frac{1}{2}} - 1 = 0.04881 \quad \text{or} \quad 4.881\% \text{ per period.}$$

Let's use this in an example.

EXAMPLE 6.2

Computing Price Using the YTM

Revise Example 6.1 to assume semiannual coupon payments, which is the norm with most bonds issued in the U.S. Let's assume a YTM of 10%. Recall that the bond has an 8% coupon rate and par value of $1,000; it matures in 7 years.

What is the present value (i.e., the current market price) of this bond?

Annual interest payments for this bond are \$80, so the periodic cash flow is \$40. The number of periods is 14 (7 years times 2). Since the YTM is given, the periodic interest rate is:

$$(1 + 0.10)^{\frac{1}{2}} - 1 = 0.044881\% \text{ per period.}$$

The present value of the coupon annuity is:

$$\begin{aligned} PVAN(coupon) &= \$40 \times [PVIFA(4.881\% \text{ 14 periods})] \\ &= \$40 \left[\frac{1 - \dfrac{1}{(1 + 0.04881)^{14}}}{0.04881} \right] \\ &= \$40 \times 9.97439 = \$398.98. \end{aligned}$$

The present value of the par value is:

$$\begin{aligned} PV(Par) &= (\$1,000) \times [PVIF(4.881\% \text{ 14 periods})] \\ &= \$1,000 \times 0.51316 = \$513.16. \end{aligned}$$

Thus, the current market price of the bond should be \$398.98 plus 513.16, or \$912.14. This is higher than the price of the bond in Example 6.1, since one-half of each year's coupon payments occurs earlier. Since some cash flows arrive sooner, their present value is higher when they are discounted at the same YTM.

It is important to note that the present value of the par value is \$513.16 in both Examples 6.1 and 6.2. Regardless of the frequency of the coupon cash flows, the present value of the part value remains the same. When the effective annual rate is 10%, a \$1,000 lump sum cash flow seven years from now is worth \$513.16 in present value terms, regardless of the frequency of the coupon payments.

Annual Percentage Rate or Stated Annual Interest Rate. When the bond interest rate is quoted as an APR, it is called a **stated annual interest rate** or **nominal interest rate**. Given an annual percentage rate, the periodic interest rate is APR/m, where m represents the number of periods or cash flows in a year. Recall that the APR assumes no period-by-period compounding of cash flows, so it fails to account for interest-on-interest. If a bond has a coupon rate of 8% with semiannual coupon payments and has a nominal interest rate of 10%, the bond's periodic cash flows should be discounted at 10%/2% or 5% per 6-month period.

EXAMPLE 6.3

Computing Price with a Stated Annual Rate

Suppose the bond in Example 6.2 had 10% stated annual interest rate. What should its price be?

With no other facts changing, the bond will still pay $40 every 6 months over the next 14 periods (7 years). It will repay its $1,000 par value at maturity. Since the stated annual rate is equivalent to an APR, the periodic interest rate will be APR/m, that is, 10%/2% or 5%. The present value of the coupon annuity is:

$$40 \times PVIFA(5\%,\ 14 \text{ periods}) = \$40 \times 9.8986 = \$395.94.$$

The present value of the par value is:

$$\$1,000 \times PVIF(5\%,\ 14 \text{ periods}) = \$1{,}000 \times 0.5051 = \$505.10.$$

The current market price of the bond will be $395.94 plus $505.10, or $90,104.

Why is the market price of the bond in Example 6.3 less than the $912.14 price found in Example 6.2? Because in Example 6.2, the 10% market interest rate represents an effective annual rate. In Example 6.3, the 10% stated rate (or APR) is equivalent to a YTM (or effective annual rate) of:

$$\begin{aligned} EAR &= (1+r)^m - 1 \\ &= (1+0.102)^2 - 1 = (1+0.05)^2 - 1 = 0.1025 \quad \text{or} \quad 10.25\%. \end{aligned}$$

It is well known that higher discount rates lead to lower present values; in Example 6.3, a higher effective annual rate or YTM of 10.25% leads to a lower price.

6.2.2. *Interest Rate, YTM, and Bond Price*

A bond that sells below par value, such as the one in Example 6.2, is said to be selling at a discount and is called a **discount bond**. Someone who purchases the discount bond in Example 6.2 today and holds it to maturity will receive, in addition to the stream of coupon interest payments, a gain of $87.86, the difference between the bond's price ($912.14) and its principal repayment ($1,000).

A bond's price will reflect changes in market conditions while it remains outstanding with its fixed 8% coupon rate. The bond in the above example will no longer be attractive to investors when alternative investments yield

10%. The bond's market price will have to fall in order to offer buyers a combined return of 10% from the coupon payments and the par value.

If the market YTM falls, to say 6.09%, the price of the 7-year bond in Example 6.2 will rise to $1,112.96 (check this on your own!), a price above the par value. The price of a discount bond will rise as it nears maturity if the market rate remains the same, since at maturity its price will equal par value. When a bond's price exceeds its par value, it is said to be selling at a premium, and it is called a premium bond. The price of a premium bond will fall as ıt nears maturity if the market rate remains the same, since at maturity its price will equal its par value. The investor who holds the bond until maturity will receive the above-market coupon payments of 8% per year, offset by a loss of $112.96 (the difference between its purchase price and par value). In most cases when the bond sells at a premium, interest rates have fallen after the bond's issue. This bond's 8% coupon rate makes it very attractive to investors; buying pressure increases its price until its overall yield matches the YTM of 6.09% of other bonds of similar risk and maturity.

When they originally are issued, most bonds sell at prices close to par and offer coupon rates close to the market rates on bonds of similar maturity and risk. Over the life of a bond its price will fluctuate as a result of interest rate fluctuations in the economy. Our discussion of discounts and premiums shows that bond prices will vary inversely to, or in the opposite direction of, interest rates. As interest rates rise in the Economy, bond prices fall; as interest rates fall, bond prices rise. Since one rises as the other falls, we call this relationship between bond prices and interest rates the "seesaw effect".

6.2.2.1. *Calculating a YTM*

Bond price quotes are available in the marketplace, either from bond dealers or from the daily price listings found in secondary sources, such as *The Wall Street Journal.* Both investors and financial managers must calculate the YTM on bonds, given known par values, coupon rates, times to maturity, and current prices. The YTM can be determined from the PVIFA and PVIF formulas we used to compute the bond price:

$$\text{Price} = PVAN(Coupon) + PV(\text{Par value}) \quad \text{or}$$

$$\text{Price} = \frac{\$CF}{2}\left[\frac{1-\left(\frac{1}{1+k}\right)^{n}}{k}\right] + Par\left[\frac{1}{(1+k)^{n}}\right], \tag{6.3}$$

[The Relationship Between Interest Rates and Bond Prices
— The Seesaw Effect],

where k represents the periodic interest rate and n is the number of semi-annual periods until the bond matures. The YTM equals $(1+k)^2 - 1$; the stated annual rate equals $k \times 2$. But mathematics offers no simple technique for computing r.

6.2.3. *Credit Risk, Interest Rate Risk, and Reinvestment Rate Risk*

Basically, investors in domestic bonds face three types of risks: credit risk, interest rate risk, and reinvestment rate risk. Inventors in foreign bonds are subject to two additional risks: political risk and exchange rate risk.

6.2.3.1. *Credit risk*

The cash flows received by bond market investors are not certain; like individuals, corporate debtors may pay interest payments late or not at all. They may fail to repay principal at maturity. To compensate investors for this credit or default risk, rates-of-return on corporate bonds are higher than those on government securities with the same terms to maturity. Government securities are presumed to be free of credit risk. In general, as investors perceive a higher likelihood of default, they demand higher default-risk premiums. Since perceptions of a bond's default risk may change over its term, the bond's YTM also may change, even if all else remains constant. Firms, such as Moody's and Standard & Poor's, provide information on the riskiness of individual bond issues.

Examples of bond rating categories are presented in Table 6.1. Higher bond ratings imply a lower risk of default and, given the risk/return tradeoff, lower expected return (ER) to investors. Lower bond ratings imply a higher level of default risk and higher ER. Investment quality bonds have ratings of BBB (or Baa) or higher. They are called investment quality as some institutional investors, such as pension funds and insurance companies, restrict themselves to investing only in these low-default risk issues. Non-investment quality bonds are called junk bonds or high-yield bonds to reflect their higher risk and higher ERs.

For those seeking a quick estimate of the return, the approximation method may be used. Here, the average annual dollar return to the investor

Table 6.1. Examples of bond rating categories.

	Moody's	Standard & Poor's	Former Standard & Poor's
Best quality, smallest degree of risk	Aaa	AAA	AAA
High quality, slightly more long-term risk than top rating	Aa1	AA+	
	Aa2	AA	
	Aa3	AA−	
Upper-medium grade, possible impairment in the future	A1	A+	
	A2	A	A
	A3	A−	
Medium-grade, lack outstanding investment characteristics	Baa1	BBB+	
	Baa2	BBB	BBB
	Baa3	BBB−	
Speculative issues, protection may be very moderate	Ba1	BB+	
	Ba2	BB	BB
	Ba3	BB−	
Very speculative, may have small assurance of interest and principal payments	B1	B+	
	B2	B	B
	B3	B−	
Issues in poor standing, may be in default	Caa	CCC	CCC
Speculative in a high degree, with marked shortcomings	Ca	CC	CC
Lowest quality, poor prospects of attaining real investment standing	C	C	C
		D	D

of a bond that matures in n years is the coupon payment plus a straight-line amortization of the bond's premium (or discount):

$$\text{Average annual dollar return} = \text{annual coupon} + \frac{\text{Price} - \text{Par}}{n}.$$

The average amount invested in the bond is the average of it purchase price and par value:

$$\text{Average investment} = \frac{\text{Par} + \text{Price}}{2}.$$

The approximate YTM is the ratio of the average annual dollar return to the average investment.

$$\text{approximate yield-to-maturity} = \frac{\text{Annual coupon} + \frac{\text{Price}-\text{Par}}{\text{n}}}{\frac{\text{Par}+\text{Price}}{2}}.$$

Calculators and spreadsheets usually use a trial and error method for computing values of r. Various values of k are used until one is found, such that the present value of the cash flows equals the price within some (pre-specified) error range.

6.2.3.2. *Interest rate risk*

The general level of interest rates in an economy does not remain fixed; it fluctuates. For example, interest rates will change in response to changes in investors' expectations about future inflation rates. From the "seesaw effect" shown in Fig. 6.1, a rise in interest rates renders the fixed coupon interest payments on a bond less attractive, lowering its price. Therefore, bond holders are subject to the risk of capital loss from such interest rate changes should the bonds have to be sold prior to maturity.

A long term to maturity, all else being equal, increases the sensitivity of a bond's price to a given change in interest rates, as the discount rate change compounds over a longer time period. Similarly, a lower coupon rate also increases the sensitivity of the bond's price to market interest rate changes. This occurs since lower coupons bonds have most of their cash flow occurring further into the future, when the par value is paid.

Because of interest rate risk, investors will demand a larger risk premium for a bond whose price is especially sensitive to market interest rate changes. Hence, we would expect higher YTM for long-term bonds with low coupon rates than for short-term bonds with high coupon rates. A bond's *duration*

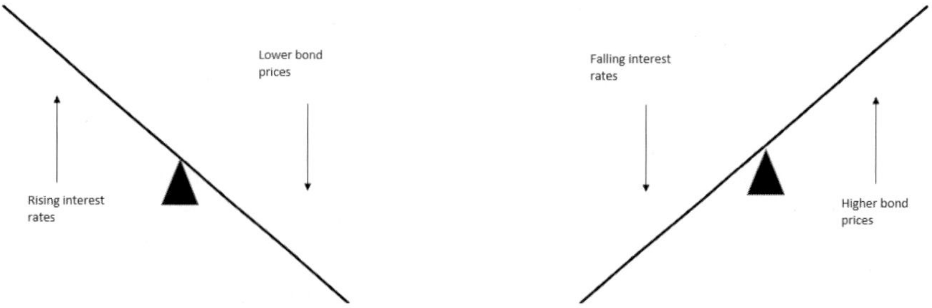

Fig. 6.1. The relationship between interest rates and bond prices: The seesaw effect.

is a measure of a bond's sensitivity to market rate changes that takes maturity coupons and other factors into account. Duration is computed by means of a complicated-looking formula. The concept of duration is now discussed in the following section.

6.2.3.3. *Bond returns and duration*

For a bond, YTM and "total return" are two different concepts. Total return for a fixed-income investment includes not only the income yield but also the interest on reinvested interest and price changes.

Compounded interest is the largest return component for investors that purchase and hold on to long-term bonds until they mature. For short-term investors that buy a bond hoping to sell it quickly at a higher price, fluctuations in a bond's price caused by market interest rate or bond rating changes are the largest return component.

As we've seen in this chapter, a bond's price moves inversely to prevailing interest rates. A measure of the price sensitivity of a bond to interest rate changes is called the *bond's duration.* Higher duration bonds have larger price reactions to interest rate changes; lower duration bonds have smaller price reactions. One method of computing duration calculates it as the weighted average of the time to receive a bond's cash flows; the weights are present values of each cash flow (coupon interest and par value) divided by the bond's price.

The concept of duration has many applications; areas in which duration is used frequently include bank asset and liability management, investment analysis, and pension fund management. A common risk management technique in these areas is to set the duration of a pension fund's asset equal to the duration of its liabilities. This way, as market rates fluctuate, the market value of the asset and liabilities will rise or fall together. By trying to set asset and liability durations equal to each other, the equity, or net worth will be little affected by changing interest rates. Further detail analysis of duration can be found in the Appendix C of this chapter.

6.2.3.4. *Reinvestment rate risk*

The return that an investor receives from a bond investment equals the bond's YTM or effective annual rate only if the coupon payments can be reinvested at a rate equal to the bond's YTM. Recall the form of the interest factor in bond price Equation 6.3: $(1 + k)^n$. This assumes that all the cash flows are reinvested at the periodic rate k. Should future coupons be reinvested at a lower rate, the investor's actual yield will be less than the bond's YTM. Thus, **reinvestment rate risk** occurs when fluctuating interest rates cause coupon payments to be reinvested at different interest rates. Another illustration of reinvestment rate risk occurs when maturing bank CDs are rolled over into new CDs. The risk benefits the investor when the new CD rate is higher than the maturing CD rate; it works against the investor when the new CD rate is lower.

6.2.3.5. *Risk of non-domestic bonds*

Investors in domestic securities face a number of risks beyond those of domestic securities. Among these are political risk and exchange rate risk. **Political risk** can affect a bond investor in a number of ways. A foreign government may block currency exchanges, preventing the investor from repatriating coupon income. Social unrest may lead a foreign corporation to default on its bonds. Of course, exchange rate changes will cause fluctuations in the values of cash flows in terms of U.S. dollars; this is called **exchange rate risk.**

6.2.4. *Zero Coupon Bonds*

Zero coupon bonds pay no coupon interest and provide only one cash flow: payment of their par value upon maturity. Treasury bills are a form of zero coupon debt. An investor purchases a T-bill at a price below par and receives no interest or other cash flows until maturity. At that time, the investor receives the par value of the T-bill. The return on the security is the difference between its discount price and its par value.

There are two reasons for the popularity of zero coupon bonds: (1) the investor does not face a reinvestment rate risk (there are no cash flows to be reinvested, so as interest rates fluctuate the investor is not forced to invest the cash flow at lower rates of interest) and (2) for certain investors (for example, those with IRAs) the tax of the bond return can be deferred until some future date. As these bonds provide no cash flows to reinvest, investors effectively lock in a given YTM. However, under IRS regulations, investors must pay yearly taxes on the *implicit* interest paid by the bonds; the IRS has special rules for determining this value. In essence, investors must pay taxes on income they have not received. Thus, zero coupon bonds are mainly purchased by tax-exempt investors who pay no tax on their investment returns, such as pension funds.

Issuing a zero coupon bond also helps lower borrowing costs for the firm. The original discount can be expensed for tax purposes on a straight-line basis over the life of the bond. Thus, rather than cash outflows from coupon interest payments, the issuing firm receives annual cash inflows from tax savings. However, the issuer must plan for a large capital requirement at the maturity of these bonds.

Present value calculations to determine the price of a zero coupon bond are straight-forward, as the following example illustrates:

EXAMPLE 6.4

Zeroing in on Bonds

A zero coupon bond with a par value of \$1,000 has a maturity date 7 years from now. At what price would this bond provide a YTM to match the current market rate of 10%?

This problem requires finding the present value of a single future cash flow. The price will equal:

$$\begin{aligned} \text{Price} &= \text{Pv(Excepted future cash flow)} \\ &= \$1{,}000 \times \text{PVIF(10 percent, seven years)} \\ &= \$1{,}000 \times 0.51316 = \$513.16. \end{aligned}$$

The current price of this bond should be \$513.16.

6.3. Stock Valuation

We now turn to the valuation of common stock. A stockholder receives income from two sources: (1) dividend payments, and (2) capital gain from the change in stock price (which can, of course, be negative). The price of common stock reflects investors' expectations of these two income sources.

The principle for determining an appropriate stock price is the same as that for determining a bond price: find the present value of expected future cash flows. With bonds, this is a relatively straightforward process; the typical corporate bond has a definite life, fixed coupon payments and par value, and an easily discernible YTM or stated annual interest rate.

Equity offers no such certainty. Common and preferred stocks generally are assumed to have infinite lives. For common stock, relevant cash flows (divided payments) are variable and depend upon firm growth, profitability, and investment opportunities. Finally, each firm can have its own required rate-of-return. Despite these difficulties, in this section we shall see that the present value of all future dividends should equal a stock's current price, and that some simplifying assumptions can make the task of determining stock value much easier. Our discussion in this section focuses on common stock. As we shall see, the method for valuing preferred stock is a special case of common stock valuation.

It may seem rather strange to treat the stock price as nothing more than the present value of all future dividends. Who buys stock with no intention of ever selling it, even after retirement? Investors generally buy stock with the intention of selling it at some future time, ranging from a few hours to 30 years or longer. Despite the length of any one investor's time horizon, we can show that the current price of common stock should equal the present value of all future dividends.

Let the present value, or current market price, of a share of common stock be denoted by P_0. Let $d_0, d_1, d_2, \ldots$ be the successive annual dividends and $P_1, P_2, \ldots$ be the price per share of stock at the end of successive year. Suppose that a share of stock is held for 1 year. At this year's end, after receiving dividend payment d_1, the stockholder could sell the stock for an amount P_1. If these future ERS are discounted at the required rate-of-return, k, the present value of the investor's cash flows comes to:

$$P_0 = \frac{d_1}{(1+k)} + \frac{P_1}{(1+k)}. \tag{6.4}$$

Suppose that someone else purchases the stock at price P_1 at the end of the first year and holds it for 1 year. The purchase price should equal:

$$P_1 = \frac{d_2}{(1+k)} + \frac{P_2}{(1+k)}.$$

Substituting this information into Eq. (6.4) gives us:

$$P_0 = \frac{d_1}{(1+k)^1} + \frac{d_2}{(1+k)^2} + \frac{P_2}{(1+k)^2}.$$

Continuing in this way, looking N years into the future, we have:

$$P_0 = \frac{d_1}{(1+k)^1} + \frac{d_2}{(1+k)^2} + \cdots + \frac{d_n}{(1+k)^n} + \frac{P_n}{(1+k)^n}. \tag{6.5}$$

If we continue this process indefinitely, the time horizon N becomes infinitely large. In that case, the final term on the right-hand side of Eq. (6.5) approaches zero, and we have the final result:

$$P_0 = \sum_{t=1}^{\infty} \frac{d_t}{(1+k)^t}. \tag{6.6}$$

The present value of a share of stock is the sum of all future dividend payments, discounted to the present. It does not depend on the investment horizon of any individual investor.

What if the analyst encounters a corporation that currently pays no dividends and has no plans to pay dividends in the foreseeable future? Is the value of this company's stock zero? Several reasons support the intuitively obvious answer — No! First, just because the firm has no plans to pay dividends does not mean that it never will. To finance rapid growth, young firms often retain all their earnings; when they mature, they often begin paying out a portion of earnings as dividends. Second, at the very least, the firm's stock should be worth the per-share liquidation value of its assets. Otherwise, an arbitrageur could buy all the outstanding stocks to purchase the firm and then make a profit by selling its real assets piece-by-piece. Most firms' values as going concerns exceed their liquidation values; the price of any such firm will reflect its going-concern value.

As it stands, Eq. (6.6) is difficult to use, since it requires estimation of all future dividend payments and investors' required return on the stock. Matters can be simplified considerably if the analyst can assume that the firm's dividends will remain constant or will grow at a constant rate over time.

6.3.1. *Constant Dividend Growth Rate Model*

If the firm's dividends are expected to remain constant, so that $d_0 = d_1 = d_2 \ldots$, we can treat its stock as a perpetuity. This is how we value preferred stock. If a common stock is expected to have constant dividends, the valuation process is identical to that of preferred stock. The present value of a perpetuity is the cash flow divided by the discount rate. For stocks with constant dividends, this means Eq. (6.6) becomes $P_0 = d_0/k$.

Many firms have sales and earnings that increase over time; their dividends may arise, as well. If we assume that a firm's dividends grow at an annual rate of g percent, next year's dividend, d_1, will be $d_0(1+g)$; the dividend in 2 years' time will be $d_0(1+g)^2$. Generalizing,

$$d_t = d_0(1+g)^t.$$

Substituting this into Eq. (6.6) and doing some algebra gives an equation for the present value of all future dividends:

$$P_0 = \frac{d_1}{(k-g)}. \tag{6.7}$$

Derivation of Eq. (6.7) can be found in Appendix 6B.

Where d_1 is equal to the current dividend d_0 times $(1+g)$ or $d_1 = d_0(1+g)$. Or, still more generally, the price at any future time t is given by:

$$P_t = \frac{d_{t+1}}{k-g}, \tag{6.8}$$

where $d_{t+1} = d_t(1+g)$.

This result, known as the **Gordon model** or the **constant dividend growth model**, provides a straightforward tool for common stock valuation. The main assumption of constant growth in dividends may not be realistic for a firm that is experiencing a period of high growth or negative growth (that is, declining revenues). Neither will constant dividend growth be a workable assumption for a firm whose dividends rise and fall over the business cycle. Therefore, a consequence of the Gordon model is that if the dividend growth rate and the discount rate k remain constant, the price per share of stock grows at the same rate as dividend per share (DPS).

The constant dividend growth model reveals that the following three factors affect stock prices, *ceterus paribis*: 1. The higher the dividend, the higher the stock price; 2. The higher the dividend growth rate, the higher the stock price; 3. The lower the required rate-of-return k, the higher the stock price.

The constant dividend growth model also assumes a dividend-paying stock; the model cannot give a value for a stock that does not pay dividends. Also, in the denominations of both Eqs. (6.7) and (6.8), the required rate-of-return, k, must exceed the estimated growth rate, g. Otherwise, the formula gives a nonsense result.

Finally, the constant dividend growth model assumes estimates for k, the required rate-of-return, and g, the dividend growth rate. Some methods for estimating the growth rate, g, will be discussed in this chapter and Chapter 18, including the internal growth rate (the rate at which the firm can grow without raising outside financing) and the sustainable growth rate (the growth that is possible if the firm's debt-to-equity ratio remains constant over time). These estimates must be used circumspectly, however, the dividend growth rate will not necessarily equal the firm's growth rate of assets or sales.

EXAMPLE 6.5

Constant Dividend Growth

A corporation is currently paying dividends of \$5 per share on its common stock, and dividends are expected to grow at an annual rate of 6%. If investors discount future receipts at an annual rate of 10%, compute the stock's price.

Using the notation of Eq. (6.7), we have $k = 0.10$, $g = 0.06$, and $d_0 =$ \$5. Next year's dividend, d_1, is expected to equal \$5 (1 + 0.06) = \$5.30. Substituting these values into Eq. (6.7) gives us:

$$P_0 = \frac{5.30}{0.10 - 0.06} = \$132.50.$$

Under these conditions, the stock should sell for \$132.50 per share.

A shareholder earns returns from both dividend payments and price changes. If dividend payments grow at a constant rate, what happens to the price of the stock? The Gordon model reveals that, if the dividend growth rate and the discount rate remain constant, the price per share of stock will grow at the same rate as dividends per share.

6.3.2. *Rate-of-Return and Required Rate-of-Return*

Share price provides only a step toward fully evaluating a stock investment. The analyst also must compare the investment to others based on rate-of-return. Suppose that share of stock is purchased at price P_0 and sold after 1 year at price P_1. The total return to the investor is the sum of the dividend payment, d_1, and the capital gain, so that:

$$\text{Return} = d_1 + (P_1 - P_0).$$

The annual rate-of-return on this investment is therefore:

$$\text{Rate-of-return} = \frac{d_1 + (P_1 - P_0)}{P_0}. \tag{6.9}$$

We have just seen how the Gordon model implies that stock prices grow at constant rate g, so that:

$$P_1 = (1 + g)P_0.$$

Substituting this information into Eq. (6.9), the required rate-of-return calculation becomes:

$$\begin{aligned} \text{Required rate-of-return} &= \frac{d_1 + [(1 + g)P_0 - P_0]}{P_0} \\ &= \frac{d_1 + gP_0}{P_0} = \frac{d_1}{P_0} + g, \end{aligned} \tag{6.10}$$

which is the same result as solving Eq. (6.7) for r; the discount rate. *This shows that under the Gordon model, the discount rate for future cash flows (Eq. (6.7)) is the investors' expected rate-of-return (Eq. (6.10)).* The required rate-of-return is sometimes called the **market capitalization rate**. From Eq. (6.10), we see that the market capitalization rate is the sum of the **dividend** yield, d_1/P_0, and the dividend growth rate, g, which is the same as the capital gains rate.

EXAMPLE 6.6

Rate-of-Return

A share of common stock currently sells for $120. Current dividends of $6 per share are expected to grow at 7% per year. Find the rate-of-return required by investors in the stock.

Using the notation of Eq. (6.10), we have $P_0 = \$120$, $g = 0.07$, $d_0 = \$6$, and $d_1 = \$6\ (1 + 0.07) = \$6.42$. Substituting this information into Eq. (7.10), we obtain:

$$k = \frac{\$6.42}{\$120} + 0.07 = 0.1235.$$

Hence, the required annual rate-of-return is 12.35%.

Investors in common stocks face a number of risks that bond holders do not. This additional risk leads them to require a higher rate-of-return on a firm's stock than on its debt securities. For example, in the event of corporate failure, the claims of stockholders have lower priority than those of bond holders, so the former face a greater risk of loss than the latter. Dividends can be variable and omitted, whereas bond cash flows have a legal obligation to be met.

If the general level of interest rates rises, investors will demand a higher required rate-of-return on stocks to maintain their risk premium differential over debt securities. From Eq. (6.7), as r rises, the stock price will fall. Therefore, stockholders risk capital loss from any general upward movement of market interest rate.

Also, future dividends, or dividend growth rates, are not known with certainty at the time the stock is purchased. Operating and financial leverage, as we saw in Chapter 5, lead to variations in earnings. If poor corporate performance or adverse general economic conditions lead investors to lower their expectations about future dividend payments, this will lower the present value of shares of the stock, leaving the stockholder with the risk of capital loss. As discussed in more detail in investments courses, stock analysts systematically review economic, industry, and firm conditions in great detail to gain insight into corporate growth prospects and the appropriate level of return that an investor should require of a stock.

The rate-of-return required by investors in a common stock reflects all of these potential risks. The difference in risk as compared to other investments will lead to investors to demand larger risk premiums and therefore higher required returns from common stock investments than from other, less risky investments.

6.3.3. *Supernormal Growth Stocks*

In formulating the Gordon model, it was assumed that dividends per share would grow at a constant rate, strictly less than the market capitalization rate, r. In practice, a corporation in an emerging industry may experience, for an initial period, abnormally high or *supernormal* growth rates. We would not expect these growth rates to be maintained indefinitely; rather, the industry will eventually enter a mature state where constant growth at a lower rate is a reasonable expectation. The Gordon model can be adapted to deal with such supernormal growth stocks. The initial period is treated separately with the constant growth assumption applied only to the mature phase of development.

Suppose, for example, that supernormal growth is expected for 3 years and that, thereafter, dividends are expected to grow at annual rate g. The valuation formula then becomes

$$P_0 = \frac{d_1}{(1+k)^1} + \frac{d_2}{(1+k)^2} + \frac{d_3}{(1+k)^3} + \sum_{t=4}^{\infty} \frac{d_t}{(1+k)^t}. \tag{6.11}$$

Substituting $d_{t+1} = (1+g)d_t$ for $t = 4, 5, 6, \ldots$, we then have

$$P_0 = \frac{d_1}{(1+k)^1} + \frac{d_2}{(1+k)^2} + \frac{d_3}{(1+k)^3} + \frac{d_4}{(1+k)^3(k-g)}. \tag{6.12}$$

EXAMPLE 6.7

Over the next 3 years, a corporation is expected to pay dividends of \$5, \$6, and \$6.75 per share of common stock. Thereafter, dividends per share are expected to grow at an annual rate of 7.5%. If investors require an annual rate-of-return of 12.5%, find the present value of a share of this stock.

In the notation of Eqs. (4.10) and (4.11), we have $r = 0.125$; $g = 0.075$; $d_1 = \$5$; $d_2 = \$6$; $d_3 = \$6.75$; and $d_4 = (1+0.075)(6.75) = \$7.25625$. Using Eq. (4.11), the present value is

$$P_0 = \frac{5}{1.125} + \frac{6}{(1.125)^2} + \frac{6.75}{(1.125)^3} + \frac{7.25625}{(1.125)^3(0.125-0.075)} = \$115.85.$$

Under our assumptions, a share of this stock should sell for \$115.85.

6.4. Growth Rate Estimation and Its Application

The purpose of this section is to show how growth rates can be mathematically estimated. The application of these estimated growth rates is briefly discussed.

6.4.1. *Compound-Sum Method*

One method of estimating the growth rate uses the compounding process. Both discrete and continuous compounding are basic concepts in financial management and investment analysis. These concepts are expressed mathematically in Eqs. (6.14) and (6.15):

$$P_n = P_0(1+i)^n, \tag{6.14}$$

$$P_n = P_0 e^{in}, \tag{6.15}$$

where

P_0 = the price at time zero;
P_n = the price at time n;
i = the compound interest rate; and
e = a constant equal to 2.718.

Equation (6.14) describes a discrete compounding process and Eq. (6.15) describes a continuous compounding process.

The relationship between Eqs. (6.14) and (6.15) can be illustrated by using an intermediate expression such as

$$P_n = P_0\left(1+\frac{i}{m}\right)^{mn}, \tag{6.16}$$

where m is the frequency of compounding in each year. If $m = 4$, Eq. (6.16) is a quarterly compounding process; if $m = 365$, it describes a daily process; and if m approaches infinity, it describes a continuous compounding process. Thus, Eq. (6.17) can be derived from Eq. (3.17) in the following manner. Based upon the definition

$$\lim_{m\to\infty}\left(1+\frac{1}{m}\right)^m = e = 2.718. \tag{6.17}$$

Equation (3.17) can be rewritten as

$$\lim_{m\to\infty} P_n = \lim P_0 \left(1+\frac{1}{\frac{m}{i}}\right)^{\frac{m}{i(in)}} = P_0 e^{in}. \tag{6.18}$$

The growth rate of earnings or dividends can be estimated either mathematically or statistically. Mathematically, the growth rate can be estimated by using either Eq. (6.16) or (6.17). Rewriting Eq. (6.16) using the symbol for growth rate, g, in place of i gives:

$$P_n = P_0(1+g)^n. \tag{6.19}$$

From Eq. (6.19), it is clear that

$$(1+g)^n = \frac{P_n}{P_0}. \tag{6.20}$$

Given values for P_0, P_n, and n, and using a compound sum table, the value of g can easily be obtained. This approach is called the **compound-sum method** for estimating growth rates. While the advantage of this method is its simplicity, it ignores other information points between the first and the last period.

Suppose there are two firms whose dividend payments patterns are as shown in Table 6.2, using the compound-sum method the growth rate of firm ABC can be calculated as

$$(1+g)^m = \frac{P_m}{P_0} = \frac{1.77}{1.00}.$$

Using a compound-sum table where $n = 6$ and interest factor $= 1.77$, $g = 10\%$. The compound-sum method also yields a growth rate of 10%

Table 6.2. Dividend behavior of firms ABC and XYZ in dividends per share (DPS, dollars).

Year	ABC	XYZ
2005	1.00	1.00
2006	1.00	1.10
2007	1.00	1.21
2008	1.00	1.33
2009	1.00	1.46
2010	1.00	1.61
2011	1.77	1.77

for firm XYZ. Yet, it becomes clear that the dividend behavior of these firms is distinctly different when looking at the dividends per share in Table 6.2.

6.4.2. *Regression Method*

To use all the information available to the security analysts, two regression equations can be employed. These equations can be derived from Eqs. (6.16) and (6.17) by letting $i = g$ and taking the logarithm (ln):

$$\ln P_n = \ln P_0 + n \ln(1 + g), \tag{6.21}$$

$$\ln P_n = \ln P_0 + gn. \tag{6.22}$$

Both Eqs. (6.21) and (6.22) indicate that P_n is linearly related to n. Using the data in Table 6.2 for companies ABC and XYZ, we can estimate the growth rates for their respective dividend streams. Graphs of the regression equations for ABC and XYZ are shown in Fig. 6.2. The slope of the regression using Eq. (6.21) for ABC shows an estimated value for growth of about 6%. The estimate for XYZ is 9.5%. If Eq. (6.22) had been used to estimate the growth, then the antilog of the regression slope estimate would equal the growth rate.

6.4.3. *One-Period Growth Model*

Another method of estimating the growth rate involves the use of percentage change in some variable such as earnings per share (EPS), dividend per share, or price per share in a **one-period growth model**. The one-period growth model is the model in which the same growth will continue forever. If b stands for the fraction of earnings retained within the firm,

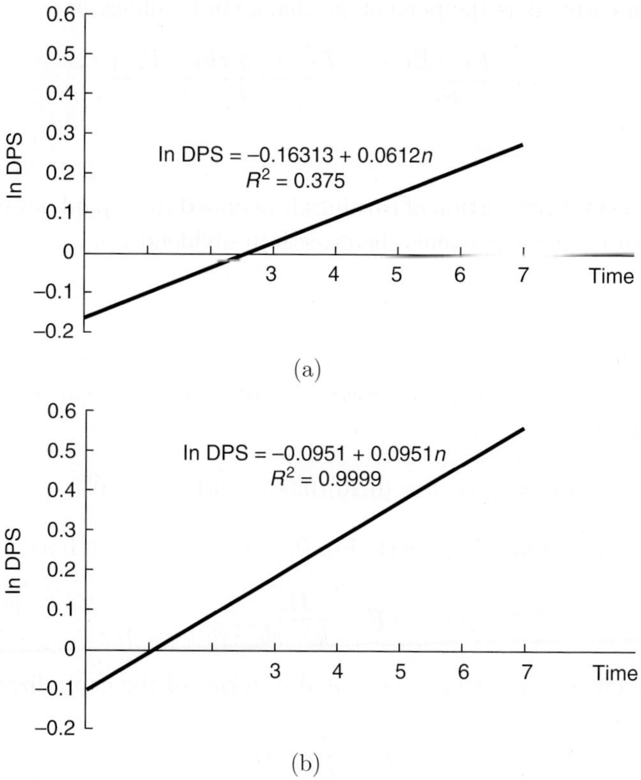

Fig. 6.2. Regression models for ABC and XYZ. (a) ABC, (b) XYZ.

r stands for the rate-of-return the firm will earn on all new investments, and I_t stands for investment at t, a very simple expression for growth is obtained. Growth in earnings arises from the return on new investments. Therefore, earnings can be written as

$$E_t = E_{t-1} + rI_{t-1}, \tag{6.23}$$

where

E_t = earnings in period t; and
E_{t-1} = earnings in period $t-1$.

If the firm's retention rate is constant, then:

$$E_t = E_{t-1} + rbE_{t-1} = E_{t-1}(1 + rb). \tag{6.24}$$

Growth in earnings is the percentage change in earnings, or

$$g = \frac{E_t - E_{t-1}}{E_{t-1}} = \frac{E_{t-1}(1+rb) - E_{t-1}}{E_{t-1}}. \\ = rb \tag{6.25}$$

Since a constant proportion of earnings is assumed to be paid out each year, the growth in earnings equals the growth in dividends, or

$$g_E = g_0 = rb.$$

If firm M has a retention rate of 50% and an average return on investment of 20%, then the expected growth in dividends on earnings can be expressed as

$$g_E = g_0 = rb = (0.20)(0.50) = 0.1 \quad \text{or} \quad 10\%.$$

Using this expression for growth, Eq. (6.8) can be rewritten as

$$P = \frac{D_1}{k - rb}. \tag{6.26}$$

Alternatively, this model can be stated in terms of the capitalization rate:

$$k = \frac{D_1}{P_0} + rb. \tag{6.27}$$

It is worthwhile to examine the implication of this model for the growth in stock prices over time. The growth in stock price is

$$g_P = \frac{P_{t+1} - P_t}{P_t}. \tag{6.28}$$

Recognizing that P_t and P_{t+1} can be defined by Eq. (6.26), with the exception that D_{t+1} must be replaced by $D(1+br)$:

$$g_P = br.$$

Thus, under the assumption of a constant retention rate, for a one-period model, dividends, earnings, and prices are all expected to grow at the same rate.

Investors may use a one-period model in selecting stocks, but future profitability of investment opportunities plays an important role in determining the value of the firm and its EPS and DPS. The rate-of-return on new investments can be expressed as a fraction, c (perhaps larger than one), of the rate-of-return security holders require, or

$$r = ck.$$

Substituting this into Eq. (3.28) and rearranging:

$$k = \frac{(1-b)E}{(1-cb)P_0}. \tag{6.29}$$

If a firm has no extraordinary investment opportunities ($r = k$), then $c = 1$ and the rate-of-return that security holders require is simply the inverse of the stock's price/earnings ratio. On the other hand, if the firm has investment opportunities that are expected to offer a return above that required by the firm's stockholders ($c > 1$), the earnings/price ratio at which the firm sells will be below the rate-of-return required by investors.

An investor could predict next year's dividends, the firm's long-term growth rate, and the rate-of-return stockholders require for holding the stock. Equation (6.7) could then be solved for the theoretical price of the stock that could be compared with its present price. Stocks that have theoretical prices above actual price are candidates for purchase; those with theoretical prices below their actual price are candidates for sale or for short sale. Example 6.8 provides further illustration of the one-period growth model.

EXAMPLE 6.8

The use of the one-period model can be illustrated by using the J&J data from Table 6.3.

Solution

At the end of 2009, J&J's stock was selling for $64.41 a share. The capitalization rate can be calculated using Equation (3.28):

$$k = \frac{d_1}{P_0} + rb, \quad \text{or} \quad k = \frac{d_1}{P_0} + g.$$

The current dividend yield is expressed:

$$\frac{d_1}{P_0} = \frac{\$1.91}{\$64.41} = 0.0297, \quad \text{or} \quad 2.97\%.$$

Table 6.3. Selected financial data for J&J.

Year	Time X_1	*EPS* X_2 ($)	DPS Price X_3	*Price per Share* X_4 ($)
1997	1	2.41	0.93	65.88
1998	2	2.23	0.95	83.88
1999	3	2.94	1.04	93.25
2000	4	3.39	1.22	105.06
2001	5	1.83	0.66	59.10
2002	6	2.16	0.78	53.71
2003	7	2.39	0.91	51.66
2004	8	2.83	1.08	63.42
2005	9	3.46	1.26	60.10
2006	10	3.73	1.44	66.02
2007	11	3.63	1.60	66.70
2008	12	4.57	1.77	59.83
2009	13	4.40	1.91	64.41
Mean ($)		3.0746	1.1962	68.6938
Standard Deviation (SD)		0.8692	0.3849	15.7598
Coefficient of Variation (CV)		0.2827	0.3218	0.2294

Source: Standard & Poor's *Compustat Research Insight*.

If J&J's dividend is expected to grow at 10% per year:

$$k = 2.97 + 10.00,$$
$$k = 12.97.$$

Thus, the required rate-of-return as estimated is 12.97%.

Alternatively, Eq. (6.26) could be used to estimate the theoretical value of J&J stock. If the dividend is expected to stay at \$1.91, and $k = 12.97$, then estimates for the retention rate and the ER for investment are required. For the sake of example, it is assumed that a retention rate of 50% and an ER from investment of 18% yields a value of 9% for b times r. This gives an estimated value for the stock of

$$P = \frac{d_1}{k - br} = \frac{1.91}{0.1297 - (0.5)(0.18)} = \$48.11.$$

While J&J's stock would seem to be overvalued selling at \$64.41 a share, notice the sensitivity of this valuation equation to both the estimate of the appropriate discount rate (required rate-of-return) and the estimate of the long-term growth rate. For example, if J&J's required rate-of-return had been 11.965% rather than 12.97%, its theoretical price would have been \$64.41.

It seems logical to assume that firms that have grown at a very high rate will not continue to do so in the infinite future. Likewise, firms with very poor growth might improve in the future. Although a single growth rate could be found, it is difficult to estimate this single number. In order to give greater flexibility to this technique, in many analysts have turned to multiple period (two or three periods) growth-rate models. Each period has a specific growth rate associated with the firm's prospects in the short run and also in the long run.

6.4.4. *Two-Period Growth Model*

The simplest extension of the one-period model is to assume that a period of extraordinary growth will continue for a certain number of years, after which growth will change to a level at which it is expected to continue indefinitely. This kind of model is called the **two-period growth model**.

If it is assumed that the length of the first period is n year, that the growth rate in the first period is g_1, and that P_n is the price at the end of period n, then the value of the stock can be written as

$$P = \frac{d_1}{1+k} + \frac{d_1(1+g_1)}{(1+k)^2} + \frac{d_1(1+g_1)^2}{(1+k)^3} + \cdots + \frac{d_1(1+g_1)^{n-1}}{(1+k)^n} + \frac{P_n}{(1+k)^n},$$

where

d_1 = the current DPS; and
g_i = the growth rate during period i.

Using the formula for the sum of geometric progression as defined as the sum first term [1 – (common ratio)^n]/(1 – common ratio), where n is the number of terms summed over, the value of the stock can be written as

$$P_0 = d_1 \left(\frac{1 - \left(\frac{1+g_1}{1+k}\right)^n}{k - g_1} \right) + \frac{P_n}{(1+k)^n}. \quad (6.30)$$

After n periods, it is assumed that the firm exhibits a constant growth forever. If g_2 is the growth in the second period and d_{n+1} is the dividend in the $n+1$ period, then:

$$P_n = \frac{d_{n+1}}{k - g_2}.$$

The dividend in the $n+1$ period can be expressed in terms of the dividend in first period:

$$d_{n+1} = d_1(1+g_1)^n(1+g_2).$$

Making substitutions for P_n and d_{n+1} the two-period model becomes:

$$P_0 = d_1\left(\frac{1-\left(\frac{(1+g_1)^n}{(1+k)^n}\right)}{k-g_1}\right) + \frac{d_1}{(k-g_2)}\left(\frac{1+g_1}{1+k}\right)^n(1+g_2). \tag{6.31}$$

This formula can easily be solved for the theoretical price of any stock. For example, Firm OPQ pays a dividend of $1.00 per share which is expected to grow at 10% for 5 years and 5% thereafter. The investors in OPQ require a rate-of-return of 15%. The current price of OPQ stocks using Eq. (6.31) should be

$$\begin{aligned} P &= 1.00\left(\frac{1-\frac{(1+0.10)^5}{(1.15)^5}}{0.15-0.10}\right) + \frac{1.00}{0.15-0.05}\left(\frac{1+0.10}{1+0.15}\right)^5(1+0.05) \\ &= 3.985 + 8.405 \\ &= \$12.39. \end{aligned}$$

6.4.5. *Three-Period Growth Model*

A logical extension of the two-period model is the **three-period growth model**. The three-period growth model implies that there exist three different growth rates for the whole growth valuation process. The resulting model would assume that in the first period growth is expected to be constant at some level. A forecast must be of both the level of growth and the duration of period one. During period two, the growth changes from its value in period one to a different level. Both the duration and the pattern of change of growth in period two must be forecasted. The third and final period is the period of steady-state growth.

Look at Firm OPQ again. If instead of forecasting a growth rate of 5% during the second period, the three-period model is used to forecast at a 7% growth rate during the 6th–10th years and at a 5% growth rate from the 11th year thereafter, the price of OPQ stock can be calculated using Eq. (6.31).

$$P = d_1\left(\frac{1-\dfrac{(1+g_1)^n}{(1+k)^n}}{k-g_1}\right) + d_1(1+g_1)^n(1+g_2)\left(\frac{1-\dfrac{(1+g_2)^{M-n}}{(1+k)^{M-n}}}{k-g_2}\right)$$

$$+\frac{D(1+g_1)^n(1+g_2)^{M-n}(1+g_3)}{(1+k)^M(k-g_3)}, \tag{6.32}$$

where M is the end of the second period and the other terms are defined as before.

$$P = 1.00\left(\frac{1-\dfrac{(1.10)^5}{(1.15)^5}}{0.15-0.10}\right)$$

$$+\,1.00(1.10)^5(1.07)\left(\frac{1-\dfrac{(1.07)^5}{(1.15)^5}}{0.15-0.07}\right) + \frac{1.00(1.1)^5(1.07)^5(1.05)}{(1.15)^{10}(0.15-0.05)}$$

$$= 3.985 + 6.520 + 5.862$$

$$= \$16.05.$$

The additional information about the three periods of OPQ's growth yields a different answer for the theoretical market price of the shares. Since the firm experiences 5 years of growth at 7% during the second period, which is larger than the 5% growth assumed in the two-period model, the market price per share is \$3.66 higher when we use the three-period model.

In Sample Problem 3.3, a set of actual data is employed to show how these concepts can be used to help security analysts and portfolio managers analyze the expected value of a firm.

EXAMPLE 6.9

To demonstrate how the concepts of growth rate and stock-valuation model discussed in the previous sections can analyze securities, the per-share values for price, earnings, and dividends of J&J during 1997–2009 are used (see the Table 6.3). The mean and the SDs of the EPS are higher than the mean and SD of the DPS. As expected, on average J&J earns more per share in earnings than they pay out in dividends; nevertheless, the variability of the earning stream is greater than the variability of the dividend stream. In comparing the dispersion of two different series there generally is a problem with simply comparing the magnitude of the respective SDs. The SD is an absolute measure of dispersion and as such is influenced by the numbers in the series. To compare the dispersion of two series, the CV, is usually employed. The CV is defined as the SD divided by the ER. The larger the CV, the greater the dispersion relative to the mean. In this case, the EPS still has a greater dispersion than the dividend series.

The expected value per share for J&J is determined using the Gordon model as expressed in Eq. (6.31). To use this valuation approach, it is necessary to estimate the dividends per share in the next period, the capitalization rate, and the growth rate of dividends per share. The capitalization rate can be estimated by the earnings yield method, the weighted cost of capital method, or the capital asset pricing model (CAPM) method (discussed in Chapter 9). The following numerical example uses a required return of 16% for J&J and the compound-sum method of computing dividends per share growth rate (use of Eq. (6.32) yields a growth rate of 13%). Substituting these values into Eq. (6.31) yields:

$$P_0 = \frac{1.91}{0.16 - 0.13} = \$63.67.$$

This theoretical value is a higher than the average price for the period ($68.69) and the current price ($64.41). The primary problems associated with this stock-valuation approach involve the adequacy of using averages of past data to estimate the future and using the compound-sum method to estimate the growth rate.

The data from the Table 6.3 can be used to show how the growth rates of dividends and EPS can be estimates by the regression method. To estimate the related regression parameters and to provide a base for discussion of other implications, covariances and correlation coefficients for time, EPS, DPS, PPS, 1n PPS are presented in Tables 6.4(a) and 6.4(b). The covariance matrix in Table 6.4(a) presents variances (elements on the diagonal) and covariances (elements off the diagonal). The correlation matrix in Table 6.4(b) presents correlation coefficients.

Conceptually, both the covariance and the correlation coefficient can be used to measure the extent to which two variables move together. The correlation coefficient is most commonly used because it is a standardized unit-free measure. Correlation coefficients range from −1.0 (perfect negative

Table 6.4. (a) Covariance matrix; (b) Correlation matrix.

Variable		Time 1	EPS 2	DPS 3	PPS 4	1n EPS 5	1n DPS 6	1n PPS 7
Panel A: Covariance matrix								
Time	1	14.00	2.4115	1.1540	−26.2025	0.7596	0.9200	−0.3353
EPS	2		0.6961	0.3048	0.8114	0.2276	0.2547	0.0147
DPS	3			0.1417	0.0710	0.0989	0.1169	0.0034
PPS	4				229.2706	0.4840	0.3867	3.0251
1n EPS	5					0.0756	0.0841	0.0077
1n DPS	6						0.0986	0.0071
1n PPS	7							0.0403
Panel B: Correlation matrix								
Time	1	1	0.7725	0.8193	−0.4625	0.7382	0.7831	−0.4463
EPS	2		1	0.9704	0.0642	0.9920	0.9723	0.0878
DPS	3			0.1752	4.722	−0.0127	0.1069	0.1535
PPS	4				292.4578	1.5915	2.9146	8.7230
1n EPS	5					0.0888	−0.0050	0.0403
1n DPS	6						0.0658	0.0949
1n PPS	7							0.2667

correlation) to +1.0 (perfect positive correlation). The concepts introduced here will be useful in understanding the diversification process discussed later in this book.

Some implications can be drawn from the size and the magnitude of the correlation coefficients in Table 6.4(b). The correlation coefficient between time and price per share (row 1, column 4) is −0.4625, indicating that the price has decreased over time. The coefficient between time and dividends per share (row 1, column 3) is 0.8193, implying that dividends were generally increasing over time. The coefficient of correlation between time and EPS (row 1, column 2) is 0.7725, which is positive, and this implies increased in earnings over time.

Following the format of Eqs. (6.31) and (6.32), the models for regressing X_5 and X_6 on X_1 can be defined:

$$X_5 = a_0 + a_1 X_1 + e_5, \tag{6.33}$$

$$X_6 = b_0 + b_1 X_1 + e_6, \tag{6.34}$$

where

a_0, a_1 and b_0, b_1 = regression parameters; and

e_5 and e_6 = error terms.

The formulas necessary to estimate the slopes a_1 and b_1 are represented by

$$a_1 = \frac{\text{Cov}(X_1, X_5)}{\text{Var}(X_1)}, \tag{6.35}$$

$$b_1 = \frac{\text{Cov}(X_1, X_6)}{\text{Var}(X_1)}. \tag{6.36}$$

Based on the information listed in Table 6.4(a), the estimated slopes are

$$a_1 = \frac{0.7596}{14.00} = 0.0543 \quad (t = 3.6292),$$

$$b_1 = \frac{0.9200}{14.00} = 0.0657 \quad (t = 4.1760).$$

The estimated student's t-statistic, shown in parentheses, is used to show whether the regression estimate is significantly different from zero. Given values of the regression estimate and the degrees of freedom, we see that a_1 is not significantly different from zero and that b_1 is statistically significant. This verifies the aforementioned implications, which were drawn from the correlation matrix — that is, the growth rate of EPS as estimated by a_1 is essentially zero (5.43%) and the growth rate of dividends per share as estimated by b_1 is positive at 6.57%.

Use of the regression-generated growth rate for dividends per share of 6.17% in the valuation equation yields:

$$P_0 = \frac{\$1.91}{0.16 - 0.0657} = \$20.25,$$

which is closer to the average price for the period (\$68.69) than the 2009 price of \$64.41 per share. Thus, use of the regression method in this case is not as useful as the compound-sum method in valuing the shares of J&J.

6.5. Preferred Stock Valuation

Most preferred stock entitles the stockholder to a fixed dividend payment in perpetuity. There is no opportunity for the dividend to grow, so the term $(1+g)^t$ is dropped from the valuation model. Denoting the annual dividend payment by d_0 and the required rate-of-return by r, we can substitute $d_0 = d_t$ for $t = 1, 2, 3, \ldots$ to obtain the preferred stock valuation:

$$P_0 = d_0 \sum_{t=1}^{\infty} \frac{1}{(1+k)^t} = \frac{d_0}{k}. \tag{6.37}$$

EXAMPLE 6.10

A share of preferred stock, yielding annual dividend payments of \$5, sells \$52. Find the rate-of-return required by investors in this stock.

The notation is $P_0 = \$52$ and $d_0 = \$5$. Because Eq. (6.37) implies

$$k = \frac{d_0}{P},$$

it follows that the required rate-of-return is

$$k = \frac{5}{52} = 0.0962.$$

Therefore, investors in the stock require an annual rate-of-return of 9.62%.

In some instances, preferred stock contains a *participation provision*. In these cases, in addition to the fixed dividend, preferred stockholders are allocated a share of any dividend remaining after the common stockholders receive a common share dividend equal to the preferred payment. If there is such a participation provision, Eq. (6.37) is not appropriate for the valuation of preferred stock, because the dividend payments, d, will constitute only a lower limit on the dividend payments stockholders receive. We will not, however, pursue this elaboration in detail here.

An adjustable rate preferred stock (ARPS) is a recently developed financial instrument designed to place the risk of fluctuating interest rates on the investor. The ARPS concept allows the dividend rate on preferred stock to vary, based on changes in the market rate of interest. For example, the ARPS rate may be set each quarter at 30 basis points above the 91-day Treasury bill rate, with an upper and lower bound, called a *collar*, set at some arbitrary level, such as 7–14%. ARPS appeals to corporate managers for two reasons: (1) dividends on ARPS, like the dividends on all preferred issues, enjoy an 80% exclusion from federal income tax, and (2) ARPS reflects current market return because of the quarterly adjustment in interest rates, thereby reducing the fluctuation in stock price.

The valuation of ARPS is different than the valuation shown in Eq. (6.37), as follows:

$$P_0 = \sum_{t=1}^{n} \frac{d_t}{(1+k)^t} + \frac{P_n}{(1+k)^n}. \tag{6.38}$$

The major difference between Eqs. (6.37) and (6.38) is that in the case of preferred stock the d is fixed, whereas for the ARPS the dividend is variable, d_t.

6.6. Risk, Return, and Market Efficiency

This chapter defines the value of an asset as the present value of the expected cash flows that arise from owning that asset. It is the size, timing, and risk of the cash flows that determine the asset value.

To compute a present value, we need to know certain information in addition to the expected future cash flows from owning an asset. For example, we also must know the appropriate discount rate, or the required rate-of-return at which to discount expected cash flows back to the present. Chapter 6 identified three components of required rate-of-return: the real risk-free rate-of-return, inflation expectations, and risk premium.

The first two components of required rate-of-return are the same for all investments; their combined effect is approximated by the yield on a short-term Treasury bill. Required returns differ as a result of different risk premiums; thus, finance professionals say that *risk drives return.* A low-risk investment will have a lower required return than a high-risk investment.

As security prices depend only on future expected cash flows and required returns, it stands to reason that prices should vary only because of changes in these variables. Should unexpected good news occur, such as higher than expected earnings or continued economic growth without expected inflationary pressures, we would expect to see asset prices rise. Should unforeseen bad news occur, such as higher than expected Federal Government budget deficits or lower than expected company sales, asset prices should fall.

Of course, the largest price changes affect the assets that are most sensitive to such news. Since the future cash flows of common stock are much less certain than those of bonds, we would expect common stock prices to be more sensitive than bond prices to news announcements. This sensitivity causes greater price swings and more price variability for stocks than for bonds. As compensation for this higher risk, investors demand higher risk premiums and higher required rates-of-return for common stock than for bonds. This suggests that stockholders should earn higher returns over time than owners of safer investments such as bonds.

6.6.1. *Historical Returns and Fluctuations*

Evidence that higher returns go hand-in-hand with high risk was first presented in Table 6.3, which is reproduced here as Table 6.5. This table reports the average annual returns and SDs for different types of investments. The return distributions for small-company common stocks and all common

Table 6.5. Geometric versus arithmetic average returns: 1926–2011.

Series	Geometric Mean (%)	Arithmetic Mean (%)	SD (%)
Small-company stocks	11.9	16.5	32.5
Large-company stocks	9.8	11.8	20.3
Long-term corporate bonds	6.1	6.4	8.4
Long-term government bonds	5.7	6.1	9.8
Intermediate-term government bonds	5.4	5.5	5.7
U.S. Treasury bills	3.6	3.6	3.1
Inflation rate	3.0	3.1	4.2

stocks have large SDs, indicating much more risk than the bond investments. Clearly, however, investors who undertake such risk earn higher rewards over the long haul, since stock returns reward investors more than conservative bond investments.

For an average risk stock under normal market conditions, the discount rate k for finding the present value of future dividends should be close to the 12% compounded average annual rate-of-return earned by the stock market since 1926.

6.6.2. *Efficient Capital Markets*

Unexpectedly good or bad news can cause assets' prices to change. Good news surprises lead market participants either to reduce the risk premium they demand of an asset (thus decreasing its required return) or to increase their expectations for future cash flows. Either reaction leads to an increase in an asset's price. Bad news surprises lead the market to demand a higher risk premium (and required return) or to reduce its expectations for future cash flows; either reaction results in a falling asset price.

If a market adjusts prices quickly and in an unbiased manner after the arrival of important news surprises, it is said to be an **efficient market**. If the market for IBM stock is efficient, we should see a quick price change shortly after any announcement of an unexpected event that affects sales, earnings, or new products. A quick movement in the price of a stock such as IBM should take no longer than several minutes. After this price adjustment, future price changes should appear to be random. That is, initial price reaction to the news should be unbiased, or, on average, fully reflect the effects of the news. Every time IBM's stock price changes in reaction to new information, it should show no continuing tendency to rise or fall after the price adjustment. After new information hits the market and the price adjusts, no steady trend in either direction should persist.

Any consistent trend in the same direction as the price change would be evidence of an **inefficient market** that does not quickly and correctly process new information to properly determine asset prices. Likewise, evidence of price corrections or reversals after the immediate reaction to news implies an inefficient market that overreacts to news.

In an efficient market, it is difficult to consistently find stocks whose prices do not fairly reflect the present values of future expected cash flows. Prices will change only when the arrival of new information indicates that an upward or downward revision in this present value is appropriate.

This means that in an efficient market investors cannot consistently profit from trades made after new information arrives at the market. The price adjustment occurs so rapidly that no buy or sell order placed after the announcement can, in the long-run, result in return above the market's average return. An order to buy after the arrival of good news may result in large profits, but such a gain will occur only by chance, as will comparable losses. Stock price trends always return to their random ways after initially adjusting to the new information.

Efficient markets result from interactions among many market participants, all analyzing available information in pursuit of an advantage. Also the information flows or news they analyze must be random, both in timing and content (i.e., in an efficient market, no one can consistently predict tomorrow's news). The profit motive leads investors to try to buy low and sell high on the basis of new information and their interpretation of it. Hordes of investors analyzing all available information about the economy and individual firms quickly identify incorrectly priced stocks; resulting market pressures immediately push those stocks to their correct prices. In an efficient market, this causes prices to move in a *random walk*, meaning that they appear to fluctuate randomly over time, driven by the random arrival of new information.

Although some studies refute this contention, the average performance of equity mutual funds usually is worse than that of overall market averages such as the S&P 500 on a year-by-year basis.

Different assumptions about information availability give rise to different types of market efficiency. A market in which prices reflect *all* public and privately available knowledge, including past and current information, is a **strong-form efficient market**. In such an efficient market, even corporate officers and other insiders cannot earn above-average, risk-adjusted profits from buying and selling stocks; even their detailed, exclusive information already is reflected in current stock prices. Few markets can ever pass the test of strong-form efficiency. U.S. laws prohibit *insider trading*, or trading based on important and non-public information. These laws reflect a public perception that it is unfair for someone with access to private information to use that position for their own profit. Remember that corporate officers should try to maximize shareholder wealth. Using inside information to benefit themselves at the expense of unknowing shareholders is a violation of the trust that should exist in the principal–agent relationships.

In a **semistrong-form efficient market**, all *public* information, both past and current, is reflected in asset prices. The U.S. stock market appears to be a fairly good example of a semistrong-form efficient market. For the most part, news about the economy or individual companies appears to produce quick stock price changes without subsequent trends or price reversals.

A **weak-form efficient market** is a market in which prices reflect all past information, such as information in last year's annual reports, previous earnings announcements, and other past news. Some investors, called *chartists* or *technicians*, examine graphs of past price movements, number of shares bought and sold, and other figures to try to predict future price movements. A weak-form efficient market implies that such investors are wasting their time; they cannot earn above-average, risk-adjusted profits by projecting past trends in market variables. Generally, evidence indicates that historical information is not helpful in predicting future stock price performance.

6.6.3. *Implications for Financial Managers*

Much evidence exists that the financial markets are fairly efficient. In terms of the above three categories, most researchers and analysts would conclude that the markets are generally semistrong-form efficient. Evidence shows that higher risk assets do earn higher returns and that stock price reactions to news events generally are rapid and unbiased (that is, no price drift occurs after the announcement).

This means that efficient markets provide valuable information to a firm's managers. Stock price adjustments in reaction to announcements by the firm tell managers if their decisions are perceived by the marketplace to be shareholder-wealth enhancing or destroying. Managers also can base their decisions on current market data, with a high degree of confidence that the interest rates the firm pays and the prices of its bonds and stocks reflect the current market opinion about the firm.

6.7. Exchange Rates and Investing Overseas

Investments outside one's borders are exposed to exchange rate risk and political risk. The result of this exposure is that dollar returns may be higher or lower than the foreign country's local currency returns, depending upon exchange rate fluctuations or political decisions to block/unblock currencies.

In general, a stronger dollar lowers the overseas investment returns to a U.S. investor. For example, suppose the spot exchange rate today is $1 = ¥100. We convert $1 million into ¥100 million and invest it in the Japanese stock market. Over the course of a year, let's assume our investment gains 10% in terms of the yen, so our Japanese investment is worth ¥110 million. But if the U.S. dollar strengthens so that now $1 purchases 105 yen, the value of our ¥110 million converts to (¥110 million/ ¥105/$) or $1,047,619 — a U.S. dollar return of only 4.76%. If the dollar had strengthened even further to, say, ¥115 yen to the dollar, our 10% local currency gain would convert to (¥110 million/¥115/$) or $956,521.74 — a *loss* of over 4.3% in U.S. dollar terms. A stronger dollar can obliterate positive local currency returns. This can happen in both financial market and real asset investments, such as those in overseas subsidiaries.

What helps to increase overseas investment returns in U.S. dollar terms above their local currency returns in a *weaker* dollar. In the above example, if the dollar had weakened to ¥90/$, our ¥110 million would convert to $1,222,222.22. The local currency return of 10% would have resulted in a U.S. dollar gain of over 22%.

Table 6.6 shows returns in a local currency terms and U.S. dollar terms during 1995. The U.S. dollar returns are higher than the local returns in countries such as Austria, Belgium, and Canada, indicating that the dollar weakened against those currencies during 1995. The U.S. dollar returns are lower than the local returns in countries such as Australia and Japan, showing the dollar strengthened against those currencies during 1995.

To an investor in the U.S., the U.S. return on an overseas investment is given by Eq. (6.39):

$$R_{US} = \frac{1 + R_{FC}}{1 + ER} - 1, \tag{6.39}$$

Table 6.6. Local currency and U.S. dollar returns in selected markets December 30, 1994 through November 14, 1995.

	Percentage change in terms of	
Country	Local currency	U.S. dollars
Australia	+11.1%	+6.2%
Austria	−15.5	−7.4
Belgium	+3.1	+12.8
Canada	+8.5	+12.4
Japan	−9.7	−11.3

where R_{FC} and ΔER are the return on investment in the foreign country and the change in the exchange rate, respectively.

For example, using the above example of a 10% return on our Japanese stock investments (¥100–¥110 million) and a 15% rise in the U.S. dollar (spot rate going from ¥100/$ to ¥115/$), the return to a U.S. investors is:

$$R_{US} = \frac{1 + R_{FC}}{1 + ER} - 1 = \frac{1 + 0.10}{1 + 0.15} - 1 = -0.0435$$

or −4.35%.

If we rearrange Eq. (6.39), we can view U.S. market returns from the perspective of non-U.S. investors:

$$(1 + R_{FC}) = (1 + R_{US})(1 + ER). \tag{6.40}$$

A practical implication of Eq. (6.40) is to view it from an "expectational" perspective. That is, let R_{FC} and R_{US} be expected stock or bond market returns and let ΔER represent the *expected* change in the exchange rate. Then we see that foreign investors will purchase U.S. securities only when the ER is favorable relative to the return available in their home currencies, after controlling for exchange rate fluctuations.

Suppose that a Japanese investor can earn 4% on bonds in Japan and that the U.S. dollar is expected to fall 5% against the Japanese yen in the coming year. Equation (6.40) suggests that the Japanese investor will require approximately a 9.5% return on a similar U.S. investment:

$$(1 + R_{FC}) = (1 + R_{US})(1 + ER) = (1 + 0.04) = (1 + R_{US})(1 - 0.05).$$

Solving for R_{US}, we obtain:

$$\frac{(1 + 0.04)}{[1 + (-0.05)] - 1} = 0.0947 \quad \text{or} \quad 9.47\%.$$

The 9.47% U.S. dollar return, after adjusting for the 5% loss in value of the U.S. dollar when the Japanese investor converts dollars back to yen, will equal the 4% return available in Japan.

If the U.S. dollar was expected to lose 7% against the Japanese yen, a Japanese investor would require a U.S. interest rate of 11.83% before investing in U.S. securities.[11] Thus, a falling dollar pushes U.S. interest rates upward and increases the cost for the U.S. government, corporations, and individuals to borrow. Exchange rate fluctuations can affect U.S. interest rates, from rates paid on Treasury bills to home mortgages!

6.8. Application Examples

6.8.1. *Zero Coupon Bond Yield*

Suppose a price quote specifies $250 for a zero coupon bond with a par value of $1,000. The bond matures in 15 years. What is the YTM on the bond, compounded annually?

A: We know that the present value is:

$$PV = \frac{FV}{(1+k)^n}.$$

PV is the current price of $250; the future cash inflow is the par value of $1,000, paid at maturity. The number of years, N, is 15 and r is the unknown. Plugging in the known information and solving for r, we obtain:

$$k = \left(\frac{1.000}{250}\right)^{\frac{1}{15}} - 1 = 1.0968 - 1 = 0.0968 \quad \text{or} \quad 9.68\%.$$

6.8.2. *Valuation*

Calculate the price of the following bond assuming that interest payments are made semiannually and future cash flows are discounted at a 10% nominal annual rate.

Par Value	Coupon Rate	Maturity
$1,000	7%	8 years

A: Since coupons are paid semiannually, the number of periods is 8 years × 2, or 16. The nominal rate of APR of 10% means the periodic interest rate is 10%/2 or 5%. Every 6 months, investors will receive an interest payment of [(0.07 × 1000)/2], or \$35. The bond's price will equal the present value of the coupon annuity plus the present value of the par value:

$$\text{Price} = \$35\left[\frac{1-\left(\frac{1}{1.05}\right)^{16}}{0.05}\right] + \$1{,}000\left(\frac{1}{1.05}\right)^{16}$$

$$= \$35(10.8377) + \$1{,}000(0.45811) = \$837.43.$$

The bond should sell for \$837.43 in the market.

6.8.3. *Stock Valuation*

Ana List estimates that Mertz Company's dividend will grow at 5% a year into the foreseeable future. Mertz's dividend this year is \$1.80 a share.

(a) If stock investors require a 15% return on stocks with Mertz's level of risk, what should the current price of Mertz stock be?

(b) Suppose Mertz's price is \$25 a share and the current dividend is \$1.80 a share. If investors require a 15% return, what is the market's estimate for Mertz's constant dividend growth rate?

A: (a) Since dividends are assumed to grow at a constant rate of 5% annually, we can use the constant dividend growth model. The current dividend is \$1.80; the required return is 15%; and the growth rate is 5%. Our estimate of Mertz's stock price will be:

$$P_0 = \frac{d_1}{k-g} = \frac{(\$1.80)(1.05)}{0.15-0.05} = \frac{\$1.89}{0.10} = \$18.90.$$

According to this data, Mertz's stock should be \$18.90.

(b) Here we are given the current market price and dividend, and the required return. We can work backward to determine the constant growth rate that is constant with this data:

$$P_0 = \frac{d_1}{k-g} = \frac{(\$1.80)(1+g)}{0.15-g} = \$25.$$

Multiplying through and solving for g, the growth rate, we have:

$$\$1.80 + \$1.80(g) = \$3.75 - \$25(g)$$

$$\$26.80(g) = \$1.95,$$

$$g = 0.73 \quad \text{or} \quad 7.3\%.$$

The market anticipates a 7.3% constant growth rate in Mertz's dividend into the foreseeable future.

6.8.4. *Return on Overseas Investment*

Show that if the Japanese interest rate is 4% and the dollar is expected to fall 5% against the yen, a 9.47% U.S. interest rate is needed to offer the investor a 4% return in yen. Assume the current exchange rate is ¥105.0/$.

A: At the current spot rate, the Japanese investor can convert ¥10,500 into $100. 1 year later, the $100 has grown by 9.47% to $109.47. If the dollar does weaken by the expected 5%, the expected exchange rate after 1 year will be ¥99.75/$. If the Japanese investor converts the $109.47 at this expected exchange rate, he receives ($109.47) × (¥99.75/$1), or ¥10,919.93. Thus, the Japanese investor's return is (¥10, 9191.63 – ¥10,500)/¥10,500, which equals 0.0400 or 4.00%.

5. Corporate bonds can be issued either at par, at a discount, or at a premium. ABC Company would like to issue a new corporate bond that will mature in 10 years. The discount rate for this bond is $r = 15\%$. What is the coupon rate needed for this bond to be issued at par. If the par value of this bond is $1,000 and the coupon rate is 10%, then what is the theoretical value of this bond?

6.9. Summary

A variety of factors influence the values of bond and stock issues. In assessing the values of these investments, we can use the notion of present value, discounting future cash flows at some appropriate discount rate. The rate at which the market discounts an investment's expected future receipts depends on its perceived degree of risk. More risk leads the market to demand a higher expected rate-of-return.

An analyst computes the price of a bond from its par value, term to maturity, coupon payments, and periodic interest rate. When computing prices, it is important to distinguish between the stated or nominal annual interest rate on a bond, which is similar to an APR, and the bond's YTM, which is similar to an EAR.

The value of a share of common stock is the present value of all future dividend payments per share. The price of the stock will depend upon investors' perception of its risk and expectations about future dividend growth.

New information affecting future cash flows and investors' required rates-of-return will result in changes in asset prices. How quickly those price changes occur will depend on the efficiency of the market. In a strong-form efficient market, prices reflect all public and private information. In a semistrong-form efficient market, all past and current public information is reflected in current prices. In contrast, a weak-form efficient market reflects only past information.

Exchange rate fluctuations are a major source of risk-and-return when investing overseas. Overseas interest rates and investor expectations about the strength or weakness of the dollar have an effect on U.S. interest rates.

Problem Set

1. Define the following terms.
   (a) Face value or par value of a bond.
   (b) Coupon rate.
   (c) YTM.
   (d) Zero coupon bond.
2. What happens to bonds prices as interest rates rise? Does this relationship change as the term to maturity increases? When will a bond sell for a discount? When will it sell at a premium?
3. What is the relationship between stock prices and the growth rate of dividends?
4. Suppose you wish to value, in U.S. dollar terms, the cash flows from a German bond that is denominated in deutsche marks. How can the process of bond valuation in this chapter be adapted to take non-U.S. dollar cash flows into consideration?
5. What is reinvestment rate risk? How is it related to interest rate risk? How is it different from interest rate risk?
6. Describe what is meant by an "efficient market". What are the expected characteristics on an efficient market? Can a market be weakly efficient by not semistrong efficient? Why or why not?
7. What is insider trading? Why might some argue that insider trading should be illegal? Why might some argue that it should be legal? Why might insider trading be more of a concern for stock investors than bond investors?
8. (CFA Level I exam, 1993) Assuming all other factors remain unchanged, which one of the following would reduce a firm's price/earnings ratio? Explain.

(**a**) The dividend payout ratio increases.
(**b**) Investors become less risk averse.
(**c**) The level of inflation is expected to decline.
(**d**) The yield on Treasury bills increases.

9. (CFA Level I exam, 1993) The semistrong form of the efficient market hypothesis asserts that stock prices:

   (**a**) Fully reflect all historical price information.
   (**b**) Fully reflect all publicly available information.
   (**c**) Fully reflect all relevant information including insider information.
   (**d**) May be predictable.

10. (CFA Level I exam, 1993) Assume that a company announces an unexpectedly large cash dividend to its shareholders. In an efficient market without information leakage, one might expect:

    (**a**) An abnormal price change at the announcement.
    (**b**) An abnormal price increase before the announcement.
    (**c**) An abnormal price decrease after the announcement.
    (**d**) No abnormal price change before or after the announcement.

11. (CFA Level I exam, 1993) Which one of the following would provide evidence against the semistrong form of the efficient market theory? Explain.

    (**a**) About 50% of pension funds outperform the market in any year.
    (**b**) All investors have learned to exploit signals about future performance.
    (**c**) Trend analysis is worthless in determining stock prices.
    (**d**) Low P/E stocks tend to have positive abnormal returns over the long-run.

12. (CFA Level I exam, 1992) List and briefly define the three forms of the efficient market hypothesis.
13. **Bond Valuation.** Yukon Mining Co. bonds have a par value of $1,000 and a 13-year percent coupon rate; they pay interest semiannually. Bonds with similar ratings have a 12% YTM. If the bond has 15 years until maturity, what is its value?
14. **YTM.** Find the YTM on a zero coupon bond that has a $10,000 maturity value, matures in 20 years, and is currently selling for $1,250.
15. **Bond Valuation.** A corporate bond can be issued either at par, at a discount, or at a premium. ABC Company would like to issue a new corporate bond that will mature in 10 years and the discount rate for

this bond is $r = 15\%$. Assume annual coupon payments. (a) What is the coupon rate needed for this bond to be issued at par? (b) If the par value of this bond is \$1,000 and the coupon rate is 10%, then what is the bond's market value?

16. **YTM.** HDTV, Inc., bonds are currently selling for \$776 with a coupon rate of 9% and a maturity of 20 years. What is the YTM, assuming annual coupons?
17. **YTM and the State Annual Rate.** Global Company has a Eurobond issue outstanding. It has a \$900 market value. It matures in 5 years, pays an 8.5% coupon, and has a par value of \$1,000. What is the bond's YTM and its stated annual rate?
18. **Constant Dividends.** Safety, Inc., has a policy of paying dividends of \$5 per share every year. This policy is not expected to change. What is the value of this stock of you require a 15% return?
19. **Stock Valuation.** CD Technologies anticipate constant dividend growth of 15%. The market currently requires a return of 22% on similar securities.
(a) If next year's dividend is predicated to be \$1.75 per share, what is the current price of the stock? (b) What will be the price of the stock in Year 5?
20. **Dividends Per Share.** Reilly Franks has an expected dividend growth rate of 3% and investors require an 11% return on their investment in Reilly's stock. If Reilly's has a current stock price of \$45, what is its current dividend? What is next year's expected dividend?
21. **Required Rate-of-Return.** Suppose ABC Company stock is currently selling for \$50 per share and pays a constant dividend of \$4 per share every year. What is the required return on this stock?
22. **Dividend Yield.** Suppose XYZ, Inc., stock is currently selling for \$72 per share and this year's dividend is \$6.25. What is the dividend yield on this stock?
23. **Growth Rate of Dividend.** Top Spin Tennis, Inc., stock is currently selling for \$100 per share and has just paid a dividend of \$6. Assume stockholders require a 10% return. If dividends are expected to grow at a constant rate, what is the growth rate of Top Spin dividends?
24. **Required Rate-of-Return.** Suppose LMNO Company has just paid a dividend of \$5. Dividends are expected to grow at a constant rate of 6% and the current price of the stock is \$132.50. What is the ER on the stock?

25. **Stock Valuation.** (CFA Level I exam, 1992) Peggy Mulroney recalled from her CFA studies that the constant dividend growth model was one way to arrive at a valuation for a company's common stock. She collected current dividend and stock price data for Eastover, shown below:

	Current Share Price	Current Dividends Per share	1992 EPS Estimate	Current Book Value Per Share
Eastover	\$28	\$1.20	\$1.60	\$17.32

(a) Using 11% as the required rate-of-return (i.e., discount rate) and a projected growth rate of 8%, compute a constant dividend growth model value for Eastover's stock and compare the computed value for Eastover to its stock price indicated above.

(b) Mulroney's supervisor commented that a two-stage constant dividend growth model may be more appropriate for companies such as Eastover. Mulroney believes that Eastover could grow more rapidly over the next 3 years and then settle in at a lower but sustainable rate of growth beyond 1994. Her estimates are shown below:

Projected Growth Rates	
Next 3 years (1992, 1993, 1994)	***Growth Beyond 1994***
12%	8%

Using 11% as the required rate-of-return, compute the two-stage DDM value of Eastover's stock and compare that value to its stock price indicated above. Show calculations.

26. **Required Rate-of-Return.** (CFA Level I exam, 1990) The constant dividend growth model can be used both for the valuation of companies

and for the estimation of the long-term total return of a stock. Assume:

$20 = The price of a stock today.
8% = The expected growth rate of dividends.
$0.60 = The annual dividend 1 year forward.

(a) Using only the above data, compute the expected long-term total return on the stock using the constant dividend growth model.
(b) Briefly discuss three disadvantages of the constant growth dividend discount model.

27. **YTM.** (CFA Level I exam, 1990) What is the YTM of a bond with a 12% coupon, 10 years to maturity, and a price of $880? What assumptions must you make in order to solve for the YTM?
28. **Bond Valuation.** (CFA Level I exam, 1990) Consider a 5-year bond with a 10% coupon that has a present YTM of 8%. If interest rates remain constant, what will be the price of the bond 1 year from now?
29. **Stock Valuation.** The Japanese Motor Company's stock is selling for ¥20,000 and pays a dividend of ¥1,000 annually. The dividend is expected to grow at a 5% annual rate. If the spot exchange rate is ¥110/$, what is the current U.S. price for the stock?
30. **Stock Valuation.** Gordon's Biscuit Company has just paid its shareholders a $5 dividend. Analysts expect the dividend to grow at a 10% rate into the foreseeable future. Investors require a 15% return on this stock.

    (a) What should be the current price of Gordon's stock?
    (b) What is the present value of the dividend over the next 5 years? What percentage is this of Gordon's current price?

31. **Foreign Investment.** (1990 CFA Level II exam) FI is a wholly owned foreign subsidiary of USDS; it is located in the country of Lumbaria. The local currency of Lumbaria is the pont. You are the Treasurer of USDS. One USDS board member has suggested that most of FI's cash be invested in 1 year U.S. Treasury bills to reduce exposure to the pont.

    On January 1, 1990, the yield on 1 year U.S. Treasury bills was 7.1%, while the comparable yield on 1 year Lumbaria Treasury bills was 14.6%; the exchange rate was 4 ponts per 1 U.S. dollar. FI's cash position was such that 60-million ponts could be invested for 1 year without concern that this money would be required for operations.

    Assume that your economist's exchange rate forecast of a 5% decline in the value of the pont (versus the U.S. dollar) by year-end

1990 proves to be correct. Calculate the proceeds to maturity, in U.S. dollars, of a 60-million pont investment in U.S. Treasury bills versus the same investment in Lumbarian Treasury bills.

32. **Foreign Investment.** Given the information below, compute the percentage change in the spot exchange rate during 1995.

	Percent Returns in Terms of	
Country	*Local Currency* (%)	*U.S. Dollar* (%)
Venezuela	+25.84	+25.73
Ireland	+14.17	+19.61
Denmark	+2.52	+14.13
Portugal	−11.82	−5.45
Philippines	−11.67	−17.14

33. **Foreign Investment.** Given the information below, compute the U.S. dollar percentage return.

Country	**Percentage Returns** Local Currency (%)	**Percentage Change** In the Spot Rate (%)
Yelstinia	+10.5	−18.6
Thatcherland	+5.1	+12.3
Georgemark	−12.52	+14.3
Canalistan	−12.8	−4.5

34. **Foreign Investment.** With the following sets of expectations, what U.S. interest rate is needed on a similar maturity instrument in order to convince overseas investors to invest in the U.S. security?

	Home Country Interest Rate (%)	**Expected Spot Rate Change (%)**
(a)	8	5
(b)	12	−3
(c)	2	−7
(d)	15	6

35. Calculate the present value of each of the following bonds, assuming that interest payments are made annually at the end of the year and future receipts are discounted at 10% per annum.

Bond	**Par Value**	**Coupon Rate**	**Maturity**
A	\$1,000	12%	3 years
B	\$1,000	10%	4 years
C	\$1,000	9%	5 years

36. XYZ Company's dividends per share are expected to grow indefinitely by 5% a year.
    (a) If this year's dividend is \$5 payable at year end and the market capitalization race is 10%, what is the current stock price of XYZ Company?
    (b) If this year's dividend is \$7 and the current market price is \$100, what is the market capitalization rate?
37. ABC Company has a retention ratio of 60% of earnings, which is expected to continue. Financial analysts predict that ABC's EPS next year will be \$12 and the company's investments will yield an annual rate-of-return of 20%. ABC's market capitalization rate is 15% per annum,
    (a) What is the payout ratio?
    (b) What is the present value of ABC's stock?
    (c) How much of this present value should be attributed to future productive growth potential?
    (d) What is the growth rate of dividends?
    (e) How much will the expected dividend be 5 years from now?
38. This year, Alvarez, Inc. paid a dividend of \$2 on its common stock. It is predicted that dividends will grow at a rate of 5% a year in perpetuity. If the stockholders require a rate-of-return of 10% on their investment in Alvarez, how much would you pay for this stock?
39. You just bought a 10-year bond from ABC Company, with a par value of \$1,000 and a coupon rate of 10%. If another investor wants to exchange 20 shares of ABC's stock for your bond, what would you do? (Assume the appropriate discount rate is 15%.) The price of stock is equal to \$12 per share.

40. Zelta's bonds have a coupon rate of 10%, a par value of \$1,000, and 5 years remaining until maturity.
    (a) If the bonds have a current (present) market value of \$850, what is the YTM?
    (b) If the bonds have a current YTM of 8% what is the value of the bonds?
41. XYZ's common stock recently paid a dividend of \$1.50 (at $t = 0$) and has a current market price of \$24 per share. Dividends are expected to grow at 8% indefinitely. What is the yield on the stock?
42. Jenner's common stock is currently selling at \$30 per share. Dividends of \$1 are expected to be paid at the end of the year ($t = 1$). The required rate-of-return on this stock is 12%.
    (a) If dividends are expected to grow at a 10% rate indefinitely, find the value of the stock.
    (b) If dividends are expected to grow at a 15% rate over the next 3 years, then at 11% for years 4 and 5, and 6% forever beginning in year 6:
        (1) Find the dividends for years 1 through 6.
        (2) Find the value of the stock at the end of year 5.
        (3) Find the value of the stock at the end of year 3.
        (4) Find the value of the stock now at $t = 0$.
        (5) Does the current value of the stock change if you plan on selling it at the end of year 5? at the end of year 3? Explain.
43. Find the yield on a zero coupon bond which currently sells for \$800 and has 4 years remaining until maturity at which time the holder of the bond will be paid the \$1,000 par value.
44. Carey Smith is considering investing in some preferred stock which pays an 8% dividend on a par value of \$100. If Carey's required rate-of-return on this type of investment is 9%, how much should she be willing to pay for it now?

Appendix 6.A. The Relationship between Exchange Rates and Interest Rates

Exchange rates react to differences in interest rates, inflation rates, and income growth rates between countries. In addition, central bank intervention and trade barriers also influence exchange rates. Fluctuating exchange rates affect returns from overseas investments. This will be true for the company investing in an overseas subsidiary or an individual wanting to buy securities in a foreign market.

In domestic markets, there are two main sources of return: income (such as bond interest or stock dividends) and capital gains or losses from asset price changes. When investing overseas, there is a third source of risk-and-return: the risk of converting foreign currency into domestic currency. If exchange rates vary over time, or currency conversion is blocked by the host country, the returns on foreign investments can be substantially affected. Therefore, changes in exchange rates should be considered before investing overseas.

For example, U.S. corporate treasurers want to invest excess cash in low-risk investments that offer the highest returns. In a global market, treasurers can look beyond Treasury bills or high-quality bank CDs. Suppose the French government offers higher interest rates on its short-term debt than the T-bill rate. U.S. corporate treasurers will use their excess cash to buy francs at the spot rate and invest them at the higher French interest rates. To protect their investment returns from the risk of adverse exchange rate changes, U.S. treasurers will enter into forward market agreements. This allows them to lock in the exchange rate at which they can convert francs back into dollars when the debt instruments mature. The U.S. treasurer will generally be indifferent between investing excess funds in the United States or in France if the extra interest earned by investing at higher French rates is offset by a foreign exchange market loss caused by the difference between the spot and forward market exchange rates.[1]

When this occurs, we have **interest rate parity.** Under interest rate parity, investors are indifferent between investing at home or abroad as far as ER is concerned; any existing nominal risk-free interest rate disparity is offset by spot and forward exchange rate differentials. When interest rate parity exists, the following relationship is true.

$$S_0 \times \frac{(1 + R_{FC})}{F_1} = (1 + R_{US}). \tag{6.A.1}$$

[1]The adjustment process of funds flowing into or out of the U.S. in order to achieve this equilibrium is called *covered interest arbitrage.* The term "covered" refers to the fact that the difference between the current and possible future exchange rate is "locked in" by entering into a forward contract.

The left-hand side of Eq. (6.A.1) reflects the return from converting dollars at the spot rate (S_0), investing them at the foreign rate ($1 + R_{\text{FC}}$), and then converting the currency back into dollars at the forward rate (F_1). The right-hand side reflects the return from investing the dollars in the U.S.

For example, assume that the spot exchange rate is FF 5.2870/\$, the 1-year-forward rate is quoted as FF 5.4930/\$, and the U.S. and French 1-year interest rates are 4% and 8%, respectively. For every \$1 invested in the U.S., the return is \$1 $(1 + 0.4)$ or \$1.04.

In this example, there is interest rate parity. The benefits of investing in France (the left-hand side of Eq. (6.A.1)) equal the benefits of investing in the U.S. (the right-hand side of Eq. (6.A.1)). Both choices lead to a return of \$1.04 for every \$1 invested.

Rearranging Eq. (6.A.1), we obtain the equilibrium relationship between nominal risk-free interest rates, spot rates, and forward rates:

$$F_1 = S_0 \frac{(1 + R_{FC})}{(1 + R_{US})}. \tag{6.A.2}$$

Of course, the nominal risk-free interest rates and forward rate must all refer to the same period of time. The above example used 1-year interest rates and a 1-year forward rate. Shorter or longer time frames also could be used, as long as all the variables used them consistently.

Some forecasters use Eq. (6.A.2) as a means to forecast future exchange rates; that is, they assume the future spot rate will equal the current forward rate. Equations (6.11) and (6.12) in this chapter are based upon the interest rate parity relationship in Eq. (6.A.2), with the change in exchange rate, ΔER, being used in place of the percentage difference between the forward and spot rates.

Appendix 6.B. Derivation of Dividend Discount Model

6.B.1. *Summation of Infinite Geometric Series*

Summation of geometric series can be defined as:

$$S = A + AR + AR^2 + \cdots + AR^{n-1}. \tag{6.B.1}$$

Multiply both sides of Eq. (6.A.1) by R, we obtain

$$RS = AR + AR^2 + \cdots + AR^{n-1} + AR^n. \tag{6.B.2}$$

Subtract Eq. (6.C.1) by Eq. (6.C.2), we obtain

$$S - RS = A - AR^n.$$

It can be shown

$$S = \frac{A(1 - R^n)}{1 - R}. \tag{6.B.3}$$

If R is smaller than 1, and n approaches to ∞, then R^n approaches to 0, i.e.,

$$S_\infty = A + AR + AR^2 + \cdots + AR^{n-1} + \cdots + AR^\infty. \tag{6.B.4}$$

Then

$$S_\infty = \frac{A}{1 - R}. \tag{6.B.5}$$

6.B.2. *Dividend Discount Model*

Dividend Discount Model can be defined as:

$$P_0 = \frac{D_1}{1+k} + \frac{D_2}{(1+k)^2} + \frac{D_3}{(1+k)^3} + \cdots, \tag{6.B.6}$$

where P_0 = present value of stock price per share, D_t = DPS in period t $(t = 1, 2, \ldots, n)$.

If dividends grow at a constant rate, say g, then, $D_2 = D_1(1+g)$, $D_3 = D_2(1+g) = D_1(1+g)^2$, and so on.

Then, Eq. (6.C.6) can be rewritten as:

$$P_0 = \frac{D_1}{1+k} + \frac{D_1(1+g)}{(1+k)^2} + \frac{D_1(1+g)^2}{(1+k)^3} + \cdots \quad \text{or}$$

$$P_0 = \frac{D_1}{1+k} + \frac{D_1}{1+k} \times \frac{(1+g)}{(1+k)} + \frac{D_1}{1+k} \times \frac{(1+g)^2}{(1+k)^2} + \cdots. \tag{6.B.7}$$

Comparing Eq. (6.B.7) with Eq. (6.B.4), i.e., $\mathrm{P}_0 = \mathrm{S}_\infty$, $\frac{D_1}{1+k} = \mathrm{A}$, and $\frac{1+g}{1+k} = R$ as in the Eq. (6.B.4).

Therefore, if $\frac{1+g}{1+k} < 1$ or if $k > g$, we can use Eq. (6.B.5) to find out P_0 i.e.,

$$P_0 = \frac{\dfrac{D_1}{(1+k)}}{1 - \left[\dfrac{(1+g)}{(1+k)}\right]} = \frac{\dfrac{D_1}{(1+k)}}{\left[\dfrac{1+k-(1+g)}{(1+k)}\right]}$$

$$= \frac{\dfrac{D_1}{(1+k)}}{\dfrac{(k-g)}{(1+k)}} = \frac{D_1}{(k-g)} = \frac{D_0(1+g)}{k-g}.$$

Appendix 6.C. Duration Analysis

As mentioned in Section 6.2, we briefly discussed the concept of duration and how it affects bond rate-of-return. In this Appendix, we will discuss duration measurement and its related issues in detail. Section 6.C.1 discusses duration. Section 6.C.2 discusses weighted-average term to maturity and duration. Finally, Section 6.C.3 discusses convexity.

6.C.1. *Duration*

The traditional role of bonds as an asset category has changed over the past 15 years due to surging interest rates and the resultant price volatility. The use of bond maturity to reduce interest-rate risk in bond portfolios through maturity matching has become increasingly inadequate. By the 1970s, several researchers had recognized that maturity is an incomplete measure of the life and risk of a coupon bond.

In 1971, Fisher and Weil recommended a practical measurement tool that could help immunize bond portfolios against interest-rate risk, and in 1973 Hopewell and Kaufman demonstrated that it could also be used as a measure of price risk for bonds. This concept is **duration**, which has emerged as an important tool for the measurement and management of interest-rate risk. Bierwag, Kaufman, and Toevs (BKT) noted in 1983 that only the introduction of beta in the 1960s has generated as much interest in the investment community as has duration.

The purpose of this section is to review briefly the historical development of duration and to examine its potential use by investors in alternative bond-portfolio immunization strategies, as well as to look at certain reservations that should be considered when using duration to immunize bond portfolios.

In 1938, Frederick Macaulay developed the concept of duration as part of an overall analysis of interest rates and bond prices. He was attempting to develop a more meaningful summary measure of the life of a bond that would correlate well with changes in bond price; he arrived at a weighted average of the time to each bond payment, with the weights being the present values of each payment relative to the total present value of all the flows:

$$D = \frac{\sum_{t=0}^{n} t\left[\frac{C_t}{(1+k_d)^t}\right]}{\sum_{t=0}^{n} \frac{C_t}{(1+k_d)^t}}, \tag{6.C.1}$$

where

C_t = the coupon-interest payment in periods 1 through $n-1$;

C_n = the sum of the coupon-interest payment and the face value of the bond in period n;

k_d = the YTM or required rate-of-return of the bondholders in the market; and

t = the time period in years.

Thus, for the first semi-annual payment in the series between 0 and n, t would equal 0.5. The denominator of this equation is equal to the current price of the bond as estimated by the present value of all future cash flows.

The duration of a bond with a fixed maturity date declines just as maturity with the passage of time. The duration of a coupon bond, however, is always shorter than its maturity. Only for pure discount (zero-coupon) bonds will duration equal maturity. Duration is also affected by the size of the coupon and its YTM, decreasing as either increases.

It is useful to place the concept of duration in the perspective of other summary measures of the timing of an asset's cash flow. Because the cash flows from bonds are specific, both as to timing and amount, analysts have derived a precise measure of the timing for bonds. The most commonly used timing measure is term to maturity (TM), the number of years prior to the final payment on the bond. The advantage of TM is that it is easily identified and measured. However, the disadvantage is that TM ignores interim cash flows. Moreover, TM ignores the substantial difference in coupon rates and the difference in sinking funds.

6.C.2. *Weighted-Average Term to Maturity and Duration*

In an attempt to rectify the deficiency of TM, a measure that considered the interest payments and the final principal payment was constructed. The **weighted-average term to maturity** (WATM) computes the proportion of each individual payment as a percentage of all payments and makes this proportion the weight for the year the payment is made:

$$\text{WATM} = \frac{\text{CF}_1}{\text{TCF}}(1) + \frac{\text{CF}_2}{\text{TCF}}(2) + \cdots + \frac{\text{CF}_n}{\text{TCF}}(n), \tag{6.C.2}$$

where

$$\begin{aligned} \text{CF}_t &= \text{the cash flow in year } t; \\ t &= \text{the year when cash flow is received;} \\ n &= \text{maturity; and} \\ \text{TCF} &= \text{the total cash flow from the bond.} \end{aligned}$$

Sample Problem 23.5 provides further illustration.

Sample Problem 6.C.1

Suppose a 10-year, 4% bond will have total cash-flow payments of \$1,400. Thus, the \$40 payment in CF_1 will have a weight of 0.0287 (\$40/\$1,400), each subsequent interest payment will have the same weight, and the principal in year 10 will have a weight of 0.74286 (\$1,040/1,400). Therefore:

$$\begin{aligned} \text{WATM} = {} & \frac{\$40}{\$1400}(1) + \frac{\$40}{\$1400}(2) + \frac{\$40}{\$1400}(3) + \cdots + \frac{\$40}{\$1400}(9) \\ & + \frac{\$1040}{\$1400}(10) = 8.71 \text{ years.} \end{aligned}$$

The WATM is definitely less than the TM, because it takes account of all interim cash flows in addition to the final payment. In addition, a bond with a larger coupon has a shorter WATM because a larger proportion of its total cash flows is derived from the coupon payments prior to maturity — that is, the coupon-weighted average of the larger coupon is larger than the smaller coupon bond. The weighted-average term can be utilized to take into account sinking-fund payments, thus lowering the WATM.

6.C.2.1. *WATM versus duration measure*

A major advantage of WATM is that it considers the timing of all cash flows from the bond, including interim and final payments. One disadvantage is that it does not consider the time value of the flows. The interest payment of the first period is valued the same as the last period.

The **duration measure** is simply a weighted-average maturity, where the weights are stated in present value terms. In the same format as the WATM, duration is

$$\mathrm{D} = \frac{\mathrm{PVCF}_1}{\mathrm{PVTCF}}(1) + \frac{\mathrm{PVCF}_2}{\mathrm{PVTCF}}(2) + \cdots + \frac{\mathrm{PVCF}_n}{\mathrm{PVTCF}}(n), \tag{6.C.3}$$

where,

PVCF_t = the present value of the cash flow in year t discounted at current YTM;

t = the year when cash flow is received;

n = maturity; and

PVTCF = the present value of total cash flow from the bond discounted at current YTM.

The time in the future when a cash flow is received is weighted by the proportion that the present value of that cash flow contributes to the total present value or price of the bond. Similar to the WATM, the duration of a bond is shorter than its TM because of the interim interest payment. Duration is inversely related to the coupon of the bond. The one variable that does not influence the average TM but can affect duration is the prevailing market yield. Market yield does not affect WATM because this measure does not consider the present value of flows. Nevertheless, market yield affects more on both the numerator of WATM and TM. As a result, there is an inverse relation between a change in the market yield and a bond's duration.

Tables 6.C.1 and 6.C.2, taken from Reilly and Sidhu's (1980) article, "The Many Uses of Bond Duration", illustrate the difference between the timing measures. These two tables show the WATM and the duration, respectively. Due to the consideration of the time value of money in the duration measurement, duration is the superior measuring technique.

Table 6.C.1. WATM (assuming annual interest payments).

Bond A: \$1,000, 10 years, 4%				Bond B: \$1,000, 10 years, 8%			
(1) Year	(2) Cash Flow (\$)	(3) Cash Flow/TCF	(4) (1) × (3)	(5) Year	(6) Cash Flow (\$)	(7) Cash Flow/TCF	(8) (5) × (7)
1	40	0.02857	0.02857	1	80	0.04444	0.04444
2	40	0.02857	0.05714	2	80	0.04444	0.08888
3	40	0.02857	0.08571	3	80	0.04444	0.13332
4	40	0.02857	0.11428	4	80	0.04444	0.17776
5	40	0.02857	0.14285	5	80	0.04444	0.22220
6	40	0.02857	0.17142	6	80	0.04444	0.26664
7	40	0.02857	0.19999	7	80	0.04444	0.31108
8	40	0.02857	0.22856	8	80	0.04444	0.35552
9	40	0.02857	0.28713	9	80	0.04444	0.39996
10	1,040	0.74286	7.42860	10	1,080	0.60000	6.00000
Sum	**\$1,400**	**1.00000**	**8.71425**	**Sum**	**\$1,800**	**1.00000**	**7.99980**
WATM = 8.71 years				WATM = 8.00 years			

Source: Reilly and Sidhu (1980).

WATM is always longer than the duration of a bond, and the difference increases with the market rate used in the duration formula. This is consistent with the duration property of an inverse relation between duration and the market rate.

6.C.2.2. *YTM*[2]

Based upon Chapter 5, YTM is an average maturity measurement in its own way because it is calculated using the same rate to discount all payments to the bondholder — thus, it is an average of spot rates over time. For example, if the spot rate for period two, r_2, is greater than that for period one, r_1, the YTM on a 2-year coupon bond would be between r_1 and r_2 — an underestimate of the 2-year spot rate. Likewise, the opposite condition would overestimate the 2-year spot rate. With the high volatility of interest rates that has existed in recent years, the difference can be

[2]Malkiel (1962) and Bodie *et al.* (2011) have carefully discussed the sensitivity of bond prices to changes in market interest rate, i.e., interest rate sensitivity. They have carefully proposed several propositions to describe this kind of relationship. It is well-known that bond characteristics such as coupon rate or YTM affect interest rate sensitivity. Therefore, the YTM discussed in Chapter 5 and this section can be used to analyze the interest rate sensitivity of bond prices.

Table 6.C.2. Duration (assuming 8% market yield).

(1) Year	(2) Cash Flow	(3) PV at 8%	(4) PV of Flow	(5) PV as % of Price	(6) (1) × (5)
Bond A					
1	$40	0.9259	$37.04	0.0506	0.0506
2	40	0.8573	34.29	0.0469	0.0938
3	40	0.7938	31.75	0.0434	0.1302
4	40	0.7350	29.40	0.0402	0.1608
5	40	0.6806	27.22	0.0372	0.1860
6	40	0.6302	25.21	0.0345	0.2070
7	40	0.5835	23.34	0.0319	0.2233
8	40	0.5403	21.61	0.0295	0.2360
9	40	0.5002	20.01	0.0274	0.2466
10	1,040	0.4632	481.73	0.6585	6.5850
Sum			**$731.58**	**1.0000**	**8.1193**
Duration = 8.12 years					
Bond B					
1	$80	0.9259	$74.07	0.0741	0.0741
2	80	0.8573	68.59	0.0686	0.1372
3	80	0.7938	63.50	0.0635	0.1906
4	80	0.7350	58.80	0.0588	0.1906
5	80	0.6806	54.44	0.0544	0.2720
6	80	0.6302	50.42	0.0504	0.3024
7	80	0.5835	46.68	0.0467	0.3269
8	80	0.5403	43.22	0.0432	0.3456
9	80	0.5002	40.02	0.0400	0.3600
10	1,080	0.4632	500.26	0.5003	5.0030
Sum			**$1000.00**	**1.0000**	**7.2470**
Duration = 7.25 years					

dramatic. For example, in Britain during 1977, the 20-year spot rate of interest was approximately 20%, while the YTM on 20-year coupon bonds was only 13%. The reason for the larger discrepancy was that YTM was calculated as an average of the relatively low short-term spot rates and the relatively high long-term spot rates.

Until the 1970s, when interest-rate and bond-price volatility increased dramatically, the significance of the superiority of duration over average-measurement of bond-portfolio risk was required for immunization against interest-rate risk. Studies comparing the success of portfolios immunized with a duration strategy and a maturity strategy have shown that duration outperforms maturity 75% of the time for a variety of planning periods.

Duration also produces lower variances between realized and promised returns than either the maturity strategy or the naïve strategy of annually rolling over 20-year bonds.

The motivation for bond investment is to secure a fixed cash flow over a particular investment horizon. Asset and liability portfolios of financial institutions often generate future cash-flow patterns that must conform to certain solvency and profitability restrictions. For example, insurance companies and pension funds, with definite future commitments of funds, invest now so that their future cash-flow stream will match well with their future commitment stream. Bond-immunization strategies are designed to guarantee the investor in default-free and option-free bonds at rate-of-return that approximates the promised rate (or YTM) computed at the outset of the investment. Nevertheless, the YTM will be equal to the RY only if the interim coupon payments are reinvestable at the YTM. If interest rates change, the RY will be lower or higher than YTM, depending upon the relationship between the bond's measured duration D and the investor's expected holding period H. Babcock (1975) devised a simple formula in which RY is computed as a weighted average of the YTM and the average RR available for coupon payments:

$$\mathrm{RY} = \left(\frac{D}{H}\right)(\mathrm{YTM}) + \left(1 - \frac{D}{H}\right)(\mathrm{RR}). \tag{6.C.4}$$

Therefore, the RY would equal the YTM only if the duration on the bond was kept equal to the time horizon of the investor. An increase in the RR would increase the return from reinvested coupons, but would at the same time decrease the bond value. Only holding the bond to maturity would prevent this value reduction from affecting the RY. Therefore, the overall impact of RR increases depends upon the extent to which the income effect offsets the value reduction. On the other hand, a decrease in the RR will decrease the return from reinvested coupons, but it will increase the bond values in the market. As shown in Eq. (6.C.4), these opposite impacts on RY will exactly offset each other only when D equals H.

If a more complete time spectrum of zero-coupon bonds of all types were readily available, bond-portfolio immunization would be a relatively simple process. Simply by choosing bonds with maturities equal to the length of an investor's investment horizon, the rate-of-return would always be as promised by the YTM, regardless of interest-rate changes. Beginning with Treasury-bond sales of February 15, 1985, the U.S. Treasury has been cooperating with Wall Street firms in the stripping of coupon payments from new Treasury issues through separate registration of coupon and maturity payments, thus manufacturing a series of zero-coupon issues. However, since this applies only to Treasury issues, it is still necessary for investors to use duration models to immunize portfolios of non-Treasury bonds.

To immunize a bond portfolio, investors must match the duration of the portfolio with the length of their investment horizons. This must be accomplished within their assumed stochastic process of interest-rate movements and changes in the yield curve. If the yield curve changes during the holding period, the immunization process will break down and the RY will not equal the YTM as promised.

Since the hoped-for results of the passive duration-immunization method can be upset by interest-rate shifts, some investors may prefer to try to predict interest-rate changes and undertake an active immunization strategy. This would involve the formation of bond portfolios with durations intentionally longer or shorter than the investment-planning period. Since it is usually assumed that the market consensus about future interest rates is the most likely possibility, investors should pursue active strategies only if their forecasts of rates differ from those of the market. The investor, who expects the interest rate to be higher than the market forecast, should form a bond portfolio with a duration shorter than the length of the investment horizon. If successful, the income gains from reinvestment of coupons and maturing bonds will exceed the value loss on unmatured bonds: RY will exceed the YTM promised. If unsuccessful, the reinvestment return will not be enough to offset the value loss and RY will be less than YTM.

If the investor expects interest rates to be lower than the market forecast, the procedure would be the reverse of that described above — that is, to purchase a bond portfolio with a duration longer than the investment horizon. If successful, the lower reinvestment returns will be more than offset by the bond-value gains. Thus, the active immunization strategy relies solely upon the ability of the investor to predict the direction of future interest-rate changes and to take full advantage of market opportunities for realized returns greater than market rates. While this provides the investor with an opportunity for substantial returns, it can also result in substantial losses. Because of this, Leibowitz and Weinberger (LW, 1981) derived a "stop loss" active immunization strategy which they called contingent immunization. In this method, the portfolio manager pursues higher returns through active management unless the value of the portfolio declines to a level that threatens a minimum target return.

At this point, the portfolio is switched into a pure immunization mode designed to provide the minimum target specified at the outset. Other researchers have developed similar strategies that rely on two portfolios — one actively and the other passively immunized. Interest changes could take place that would virtually wipe out the active portfolio, but they would not greatly affect the minimum target return of the two-portfolio combination.

6.C.2.3. *The macaulay model*

The duration model that is still most widely used because of its simplicity is the **Macaulay model**. However, basic limitations affect the use of this model. First, the current and forward spot rates are assumed to be equal over a specific planning horizon — that is, the yield curve is assumed to be flat. This is also one of the basic weakness of the YTM measurement. Second, this model provides an accurate measure of interest-rate risk only when there is a single parallel shift in the term of structure of interest rates — that is, there is only one shift within the holding period and it does not involve a change in yield-curve shape.

Most studies surveyed seem to indicate that the Macaulay model assumptions are unrealistic and too restrictive. Cox *et al.* (1979) noted that it does not take into account the dynamic nature of the term structure observed in the real world, in which yield curves can and do change in shape as well as location. As a result, a number of more complex duration models have been developed to measure risk when multiple term-structure shifts can affect the shape and location of the yield curve. Because the actual underlying stochastic process governing interest-rate changes is not known, only empirical analysis can determine whether the extra complexity of these models justifies their usage. Bierwag *et al.* (1982) extensively tested the Macaulay model along with four more complex duration models and found that duration-matching strategies generated realized returns consistently closer to promised yields than a maturity-matching strategy. Even more interesting, the Macaulay measure appeared to perform as well as the more complex models. Their findings suggest that single-factor duration matching is a feasible immunization strategy that works reasonably well, even with the less complex (and thus less costly) Macaulay model.

Duration appears a better measure of a bond's life than maturity because it provides a more meaningful relationship with interest-rate changes. This relationship has been expressed by Hopewell and Kaufman (1973) as:

$$\frac{\Delta P}{P} = \frac{D}{(1+i)}\Delta i = D^{*}\Delta i, \tag{6.C.5}$$

where Δ = "change in"; P = bond price; D = duration; and i = market interest rate or bond yield.

For example, a bond with 5 years' duration will decline in price by approximately 10% when market yield increases by 2%. Note that $\Delta P/P$ on the left-hand side of Eq. (6.C.5) is the percentage change in price, and Δi is the absolute change in yield level and not percentage change.

Other useful generalizations can be made concerning the relationships of duration to various bond characteristics, as follows.

1. The higher the coupon, the shorter the duration, because the face-value payment at maturity will represent a smaller proportional present-value contribution to the makeup of the current bond value. In other words, bonds with small coupon rates will experience larger capital gains or losses as interest rates change. Additionally, for all bonds except zero-coupon-rate bonds, as the maturity of the bond lengthens the duration at the limit will approach (1 + YTM)/YTM. Table 6.C.3 shows the relationship between duration, maturity, and coupon rates for a bond with a YTM of 6%. At the limit (maturity goes to infinity), the duration will approach 17.667 (i.e., (1 + 0.06)/0.06).

As can be seen in Table 6.C.3, the limit is independent of the coupon rate: it is always 17.667. However, when the coupon rate is the same as or greater than the yield rate (the bond is selling at a premium), duration approaches the limit directly. Conversely, for discount-priced bonds (coupon rate is less than YTM), duration can increase beyond the limit and then recede to the limit. In the case of the bond with the 2% coupon at a maturity

Table 6.C.3. Duration, maturity, and coupon rate.

Maturity (years)	Coupon Rate *0.02*	*0.04*	*0.06*	*0.08*
1	0.995	0.990	0.985	0.981
5	4.756	4.558	4.393	4.254
10	8.891	8.169	7.662	7.286
20	14.981	12.98	11.904	11.232
50	19.452	17.129	16.273	15.829
100	17.567	17.232	17.120	17.064
∞	17.667	17.667	17.667	17.667

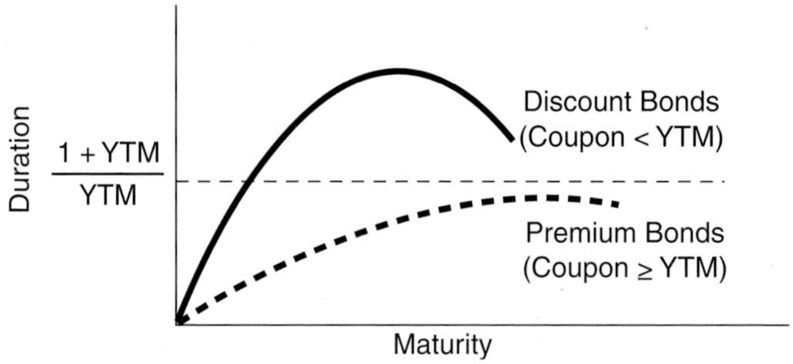

Fig. 6.C.1. Duration and maturity for premium and discount bonds.

of 50 years, the duration is 19.452 — and this approaches the limit as maturity keeps increasing. These relationships are shown in Fig. 6.C.1.

Regardless of coupon size, it is nearly impossible to find bonds with durations in excess of 20 years; most bonds have a limit of about 15 years.

2. The higher the YTM, the shorter the duration, because YTM is used as the discount rate for the bond's cash flows and higher discount rates diminish the proportional present-value contribution of more distant payments. As has been shown, at the limit duration is equal to (1 + YTM)/YTM; in Table 6.C.3 the relationship between duration and YTM is shown.

3. A typical sinking fund (one in which the bond principal is gradually retired over time) will reduce duration. Duration can be reduced by the sinking-fund or call provision. A large proportion of current bond issues do have sinking funds, and these can definitely affect a bond's duration. An example will illustrate this fact. A 10-year 4% bond with a sinking fund of 10% of face value per year starting at the end of the fifth year has a duration of 7.10 years as compared to the duration of 8.12 years of a similar bond without a sinking fund. Table 6.C.5 provides further illustration.

The effect of a sinking fund on the time structure of cash flows for a bond is certain to the issuer of the bond, since the firm must make the payments: they represent a legal cash-flow requirement that will affect the firm's cash flow. However, the sinking fund may not affect the investor since the money put into the sinking fund may not necessarily be used to retire outstanding bonds. Even if it is, it is not certain that a given investor's bonds will be called for retirement.

4. For bonds of less than 5 years to maturity, the magnitudes of duration changes are about the same as those for maturity changes. For bonds of 5 to

Table 6.C.4. Duration and YTM.

YTM	Duration at Limit (maturity $\to \infty$)
0.02	51
0.04	26
0.08	13.5
0.10	11
0.20	6
0.30	4.33
0.50	3

Table 6.C.5. Duration with and without sinking funds (assuming 8% market yield).

	Cash Flow	Present-Value Factor	Present Value of Cash Flow	Weight	Duration
Bond A — No Sinking Fund					
1	$40	0.9259	$37.04	0.0506	0.0506
2	40	0.8573	34.29	0.0469	0.0938
3	40	0.7938	31.75	0.0434	0.1302
4	40	0.7350	29.40	0.0402	0.1608
5	40	0.6806	27.22	0.0372	0.1860
6	40	0.6302	25.21	0.0345	0.2070
7	40	0.5835	23.34	0.0319	0.2233
8	40	0.5403	21.61	0.0295	0.2360
9	40	0.5002	20.01	0.0274	0.2466
10	1,040	0.4632	481.73	0.6585	6.5850
Sum			**$731.58**	**1.0000**	**8.1193**
Duration = 8.12 years					
Bond A — Sinking Fund (10% per year from fifth year)					
1	$40	0.9259	$37.04	0.04668	0.04668
2	40	0.8573	34.29	0.04321	0.08642
3	40	0.7938	31.75	0.04001	0.12003
4	40	0.7350	29.40	0.03705	0.14820
5	140	0.6806	95.28	0.12010	0.60050
6	140	0.6302	88.23	0.11119	0.66714
7	140	0.5835	81.69	0.10295	0.72065
8	140	0.5403	75.64	0.09533	0.76264
9	140	0.5002	70.03	0.08826	0.79434
10	540	0.4632	250.13	0.31523	3.15230
Sum			**$793.48**	**1.00000**	**7.09890**
Duration = 7.10 years					

Source: Reilly and Sidhu (1980).

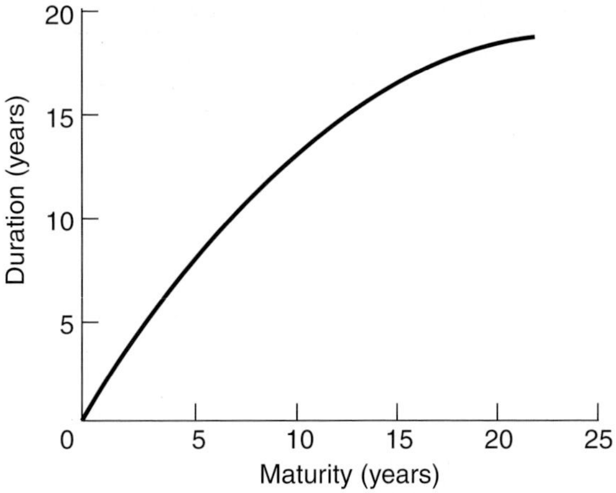

Fig. 6.C.2. Duration versus maturity.

15 years' maturity, changes in the magnitude of duration are considerably less than those of maturity. For bonds with more than 20 years to maturity, changes in the magnitude of duration are very small relative to changes in maturity. As can be seen in Fig. 6.C.2, in the range of 0 to 5 years the relationship between duration and maturity is shown approximately by a straight line with a slope of 45°. In the range of 5 to 10 years, the slope of the line is less, indicating a smaller change in duration for a given change in maturity. And for more than 20 years, the line is almost horizontal, showing a smaller change in duration for a given change in maturity.

5. In contrast to a sinking fund, all bondholders will be affected if a bond is called. The duration of a callable bond will be shorter than a non-callable bond.

When a bond is callable, the cash flow implicit in the YTM figure is subject to possible early alteration. Most corporate bonds issued today are callable, but with a period of call protection before the call option can be exercised. At the expiration of this period, the bond may be called at a specified call price, which usually involves some premium over par.

To provide some measure of the return in the event that the issuer exercises the call option at some future point, the yield to call is calculated instead of the YTM. This computation is based on the assumption that the bond's cash flow is terminated at the "first call date" with redemption of principal at the specified call price. The crossover yield is defined as that yield where the YTM is equal to the yield to call. When the price of the bond rises to some value above the call price, and the market yield declines to value below the crossover yield, the yield to call becomes the minimum yield. At this price and yield, the firm will probably exercise a call option when it is available. When prices go below the call price, the YTM is the minimum yield. Sample Problem 6.C.2 provides further illustration.

Sample Problem 6.C.2

To calculate the crossover yield for a 8%, 30-year bond selling at par with 10-year call protection, the annual return flow divided by the average investment can be used as an approximation for the yield. The implied crossover yield is 8.46%:

$$\text{Crossover yield:} \frac{80 + \dfrac{1080 - 1000}{10}}{\dfrac{1080 + 1000}{2}} = 8.46\%.$$

In 1 year's time the bond's maturity will be 29 years with 9 years to call. If the market rate has declined to the point where the YTM of the bond is 7%, which is below the crossover yield of 8.46%, the bond's yield to call will be 6%.

$$\text{Yield to call} = \frac{80 + \dfrac{1000 - 1123.43}{9}}{\dfrac{1080 + 1123.43}{2}} = 6\%.$$

If a bond-portfolio manager ignored the call option and computed the duration of this bond to maturity at a market yield of 7%, the duration would be 12.49 years. If duration was computed recognizing the call option at a price of $1,080 and using the yield to call of 6%, it would be 6.83 years.

Since a majority of corporate bonds have a call option, the effect of the call option upon a bond's duration could have an effect on the bond manager's investment decision. Therefore, the bond's duration, both disregarding the call option and regarding the call option, must be considered in an investment decision. That is, if interest rates stabilize or continue to rise, the call-option duration is of less importance than the bond's duration disregarding the call option. If interest rates fall, the call-option duration is of more importance.

6.C.3. *Convexity*

The duration rule in Eq. (23.5) is a good approximation for small changes in bond yield, but it is less accurate for large changes. Equation (23.5) implies that percentage change in bond price is linearly related to change in YTM. If this linear relationship is not hold, then Eq. (23.5) can be generalized as

$$\frac{\Delta P}{P} = -D^{*}\Delta i + 0.5 \times \mathit{Convexity} \times (\Delta i)^2, \tag{6.C.6}$$

Where the *Convexity* is the rate of change of the slope of the price-yield curve as follows

$$\begin{aligned} \mathit{Convexity} &= \frac{1}{P} \times \frac{\partial^2 P}{\partial i^2} = \frac{1}{P \times (1+i)^2} \sum_{t=1}^{n} \left[\frac{CF_t}{(1+i)^t}(t^2 + t) \right] \\ &\approx 10^8 \left[\tfrac{\Delta P-}{P} + \tfrac{\Delta P+}{P} \right], \end{aligned} \tag{6.C.7}$$

where CF_t is the cash flow at time t as definition in Eq. (6.C.2); n is the maturity; CF_t represents either a coupon payment before maturity or final coupon plus par value at the maturity date. $\Delta P-$ is the capital loss from a one-basis-point (0.0001) increase in interest rates and $\Delta P+$ is the capital gain from a one-basis-point (0.0001) decrease in interest rates.[3]

In Eq. (6.C.6), the first term on the right-hand side is the same as the duration rule, Eq. (6.C.5). The second term is the modification for convexity. Notice that for a bond with positive convexity, the second term is positive, regardless of whether the yield rises or falls.

The more accurate Eq. (6.C.6), which accounts for convexity, always predicts a higher bond price than Eq. (6.C.5). Of course, if the change in yield is small, the convexity term, which is multiplied by $(\Delta i)^2$ in Eq. (6.C.6), will be extremely small and will add little to the approximation. In this case, the linear approximation given by the duration rule will be sufficiently accurate. Thus convexity is more important as a practical matter when potential inertest rate changes are large. Sample Problem 6.C.3 provides further illustration.

Sample Problem 6.C.3

Figure 23.4 is drawn by the assumptions that the bond with 20-year maturity and 7.5% coupon sells at an initial YTM of 7.5%. Because the

[3]The approximation of convexity is referred to the book by Saunders and Cornett (2010).

coupon rate equals YTM, the bond sells at par value, or \$1000. The modified duration and convexity of the bond are 10.95908 and 155.059 calculated by Eq. (6.C.1) and the approximation formula in Eq. (6.C.7), respectively.

If the bond's yield increases from 7.5% to 8.0% ($\Delta i = 0.005$), the price of the bond actually falls to \$950.9093. Based on the duration rule, the bond price falls from \$1000 to \$945.2046 with a decline of 5.47954%. Equation (6.C.5) as follows

$$\frac{\Delta P}{P} = -D^{*}\Delta i = -10.95908 * 0.005 = -0.0547954, \quad \text{or} \quad -5.47954\%.$$

If we use Eq. (6.C.6) instead of Eq. (6.C.5), we get the bond price falls from \$1000 to \$947.1482 with a decline of 5.28572% by Eq. (6.C.6):

$$\begin{aligned}\frac{\Delta P}{P} &= -D * \Delta i + 0.5 \times \mathit{Convexity} \times (\Delta i)^2 \\ &= -10.95908 \times 0.005 + 0.5 \times 155.059 \times (0.005)^2 \\ &= -0.0528572 \quad \text{or} \quad -5.28572\%.\end{aligned}$$

The duration rule used by Eq. (6.C.5) is close to the case with accounting for convexity in terms of Eq. (6.C.6).

However, if the change in yield are larger, 3% ($\Delta i = 0.03$), the price of the bond actually falls to \$753.0727 and convexity becomes an important

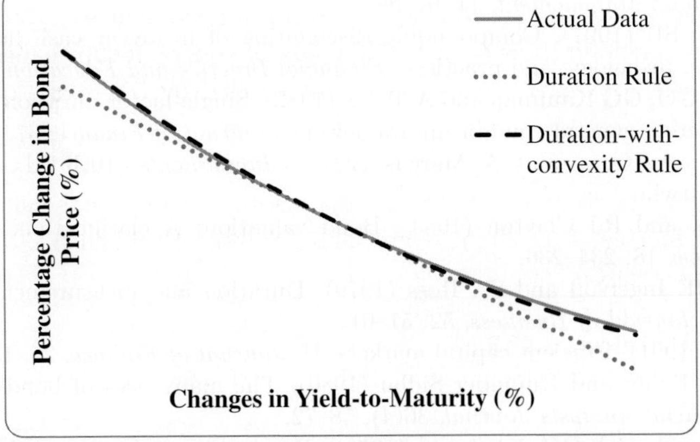

Fig. 6.C.3. The relationship between percentage changes in bond price and changes in YTM.

matter of pricing the percentage change in bond price. Without accounting for convexity, the price of the bond on dash line actually falls from \$1000 to \$671.2277 with a decline of 32.8772% based on the duration rule, Eq. (6.C.5) as follows

$$\frac{\Delta P}{P} = -D * \Delta i = -10.95908 * 0.03 = -0.328772 \quad \text{or} \quad -32.8772\%.$$

According to the duration-with-convexity rule, Eq. (6.C.6), the percentage change in bond price is calculated in following equation

$$\begin{aligned}\frac{\Delta P}{P} &= -D * \Delta i + 0.5 \times Convexity \times (\Delta i)^2 \\ &= -10.95908 \times 0.03 + 0.5 \times 155.059 \times (0.03)^2 \\ &= -0.258996 \quad \text{or} \quad -25.8996\%.\end{aligned}$$

The bond price \$741.0042 estimated by the duration-with-convexity rule is close to the actual bond price \$753.0727 rather than the price \$671.2277 estimated by the duration rule. As the change in interest rate becomes larger, the percentage change in bond price calculated by Eq. (6.C.5) is significantly different from it calculated by Eq. (6.C.6). Saunders and Cornett (2013) have discussed why convexity is important in the risk management of financial institutions.

References for Chapter 6

Babcock, G (1984). Duration as a link between yield and value. *The Journal of Portfolio Management*, 11, 97–98.

Bhandari, SB (1991). Compounding/discounting of intrayear cash flows: Principles, pedagogy, and practices. *Financial Practice and Education*, 1, 87–89.

Bierwag, GO, GG Kaufman and A Toevs (1982). Single-factor duration models in a discrete general equilibrium framework. *Journal of Finance*, 37, 325–338.

Bodie, Z, A Kane, and A Marcus (2013). *Investments*, 10th ed., McGraw-Hill/Irwin.

Chew, IK and RJ Clayton (1983). Bond valuation: A clarification. *Financial Review*, 18, 234–236.

Cox, J, JE Ingersoll and SA Ross (1979). Duration and measurement of basis risk. *Journal of Business*, 52, 51–61.

Fama, E (1991). Efficient capital markets: II. *Journal of Finance*, 25, 1575–1617.

Frank, K Reilly and Rupinder Sidhu (1980). The many uses of bond duration. *Financial Analysts Journal*, 36(4), 58–72.

Hopewell, M and GG Kaufman (1973). Bond price volatility and terms to maturity: A generalized respecification. *American Economic Review*, 63, 749–753.

Hovarth, PA (1985). A pedagogic note on intra-period compounding and discounting. *Financial Review*, 20, 116–118.

Lee, CF, JE Finnerty, J Lee, AC Lee, and D Wort (1990). *Security Analysis and Portfolio Management, and Financial Derivatives.* New York, NY: Harper Collins.

Leibowitz, ML and A Weinberger (1981). The uses of contigent immunization. *Journal of Portfolio Management*, 8, 51–55.

Malkiel, B (1962). Expectations, bond prices, and the term structure of interest rates. *Quarterly Journal of Economics*, 76, 197–218.

Reilly, F and E Norton (1995). *Investments*, 4th ed. Fort Worth, TX: HBJ-Dryden Press, McGraw-Hill/Irwin.

Reilly and Sidhu (1980). The many uses of bond duration. *Financial Analyst Journal*, 36, 60.

Saunders, A and M Cornett (2010). *Management: A Risk Management Approach*, 7th ed., McGraw-Hill/Irwin.

Saunders, A and M Cornett (2013). *Financial Institutions Management: A Risk Management Approach*, 8th ed., McGraw-Hill/Irwin.

Chapter 7

Valuation and Capital Structure: A Review and Integration

7.1. Introduction

The ultimate goal of a financial manager is to maximize the wealth of shareholders. Shareholder wealth can be represented as the value of the firm's collective assets. Therefore, it is necessary for the financial manager to know how to determine the value of the firm. In this chapter, we will examine alternative methods of valuation, their characteristics, and applicability under the various circumstances facing the firm.

It should be noted that there are various definitions of value, depending on the needs and uses of different disciplines. Economics focuses on a concept of long-run equilibrium value, where the market forces of supply and demand intersect to determine a commodity's price. Although, in practice, this theoretical analysis is too difficult to be applied by a manager of a firm, the economic idea of firm value *as income earned from a product sold over a long period of time* has been incorporated into finance. Alternatively, accounting is beginning to focus on the current market value of the firm, that is, the price the firm would bring if sold today in the market. Finance combines these two approaches to valuation. In finance, the value of a firm is the present value of a firm's expected income stream, or the sum, discounted to the present of a firm's expected cash flows from all future periods.

Several additional definitions of value are used in business practice, and should be noted briefly. First, book value as used in accounting represents the historical cost of an asset, or what the firm actually paid to acquire the asset. This can be contrasted both with market value, the price the asset would command in the current market, and with replacement value, the price the firm must pay to buy a replacement (a current model of the asset with approximately similar features) for the asset in question. Secondly, the liquidating value of the firm is that amount which can be realized if all assets of a firm were immediately sold for cash. This can be contrasted to the going-concern value of a firm, or the price a firm would bring if it is sold on the current market as a going concern. Going-concern value includes the worth of such intangibles as firm reputation, goodwill, good customer relations, and so on.

7.1.1. *Components of Capital Structure*

The various financial assets that make up the capital structure of the firm can be valued separately. These financial components include bonds, stock (both common and preferred), and convertible securities. The determination of an asset's value involves, as discussed above, finding the present value of the stream of income which that asset will bring to its owner. Before examining the various methods used to value financial instruments, the basic types of instruments are discussed below.

The bonds of a corporation represent a legal indebtedness of the firm. Essentially, the firm borrows a sum of money (the principal, or face value of the bond) from a creditor for a certain period (the term of the bond) with a promise to pay periodic installments of interest (the coupon) as well as the principal amount at maturity (the end of the term of the bond). As a creditor of the firm, the bondholder has a claim on the assets of the firm, which precedes the claim of stockholders at bankruptcy.

A share of stock represents a claim of ownership in the firm. A share of preferred stock usually entitles the preferred shareholder to a fixed payment each year either as a coupon (e.g., 5% of face value) or as a stated amount (e.g., $2.50 preferred).

The payments from preferred stocks may be either cumulative or non-cumulative. If the preferred stock is non-cumulative, the failure of the firm to make a payment does not create an ongoing liability to preferred shareholders. In the case of cumulative preferred stock, it does, and these payments must be made in future periods before any common shareholders are paid dividends. The same is true upon liquidation of the firm. In rare instances, preferred stock can contain a participating provision, which allocates to the preferred stockholder a fixed dividend, as with other preferred shares, and some share of any dividend remaining after the common shareholders receive a common-share dividend from earnings available for distribution equal to the preferred payment. Thus, for participating preferred shareholders, the fixed dividend payment represents a lower limit on the amount of dividend they may receive in any period, provided that the board of directors votes it. Common stock shareholders are not entitled to fixed dividends, but may receive a dividend if the board of directors of the firm votes to pay one in the current quarter. In bankruptcy proceedings, preferred shareholders take precedence over common.

Finally, both preferred stock and bonds can be issued that are convertible to shares of the common stock of the firm. With these instruments, the holder receives both a fixed income and the opportunity to convert the bond or preferred shares at his discretion into a stipulated number of common shares (see Appendix A for detail).

7.1.2. *Opportunity Cost, Required Rate-of-Return, and the Cost of Capital*

Valuation of any asset requires the determination of the proper discount rate. There are different approaches to defining the discount rate that are conceptually equivalent. For example, economists define the opportunity cost of an asset as either (i) the value of the next most attractive alternative asset or use for which an investor could pay, or (ii) the sacrifice of doing something else. In other words, an asset is not considered in isolation, but must be evaluated in relation to other, similarly attractive alternative uses of an investor's money.

This theoretical concept is closely linked to the financial concept of the required rate-of-return. The required rate-of-return is defined as the minimum rate-of-return necessary to induce an investor to buy and hold an asset. Thus, an asset must bring to its holder at the minimum a given return on his money before he will be willing to invest in it. The rate-of-return required is generally evaluated in terms of what investments similar in risk will yield. For example, if an investor perceives that an ABC Corporation bond has the same risk as a Z Company bond which is yielding a 12% return, he must receive at least 12% return on the ABC Company bond before he becomes willing to buy it instead of buying Z's bond.

Calculation of risk-and-return for an asset have been formalized in finance according to the following equation:

$$E(R_j) = R_f + (E(R_m) - R_f)\beta_j, \tag{7.1}$$

where

$$
\begin{aligned}
E(R_j) &= \text{Expected rate-of-return for asset } j,\\
R_f &= \text{Return on a risk-free asset},\\
(E(R_m) - R_f) &= \text{Market risk premium, or the difference in return on the market as a whole and the return on a risk-free asset},\\
\beta_j &= \text{Beta coefficient for the regression of an individual's security return on the market return; the volatility of the individual security's return relative to the market return.}
\end{aligned}
$$

Equation (7.1) is the capital-asset pricing model (CAPM) developed by Sharpe (1964), Lintner (1965), and Mossin (1966). Chapter 8 of this book will discuss the CAPM indicated in Eq. (7.1) in further detail.

The theoretical foundations for Eq. (7.1) will be discussed at length in Chapter 8. Here, we will simply note that the return on any security can be expressed as the sum of the return from a riskless security (the current return on U.S. Treasury securities is usually used as a proxy) plus a risk premium. Thus, any security must pay at least the return of a security with no risk. The risk premium depends on the market (here expressed in the beta coefficient) as well as the additional return an investor can expect by investing in the risky market (usually proxied by the return on the S&P 500 or the DJ 30). Thus, the required rate-of-return for a security can be approximated from readily available information and used to discount the asset's income stream.

Another valuation procedure uses the cost of capital, which is a financial concept relating the rate-of-return required for an investment project of the firm, with the capital structure (the relative proportions of debt and equity) of the firm and the required rate-of-return of each component of the capital structure. The cost of capital will be discussed at greater length in Chapter 12.

7.2. Bond Valuation

In Chapter 6, we have discussed the cash flow pattern of bond and its present value of future cash flow. Based upon this information we can determine bond valuation. Bond valuation is a relatively easy process, since in the case of riskless asset the income stream that the bondholder will receive is known with certainty. Barring a firm's default, the income stream will consist of the periodic coupon payments and the repayment of principal at maturity. These cash flows must be discounted to the present by the required rate-of-return for the bond. When the cash flow is uncertain, the discount rate needs to be adjusted by a risk premium.

Based upon Eq. (6.1), the basic principles of bond valuation in terms of an explicit formula are represented in the following equation:

$$PV = \sum_{t=1}^{n} \frac{CF_t}{(1+k_b)^t}, \tag{7.2}$$

where

n = Number of periods to maturity,
CF_t = Cash flow (interest and principal) received in period t,
k_b = Required rate-of-return for bond.

7.2.1. *Perpetuity*

The first (and most extreme) case of bond valuation involves a *perpetuity*, a bond with no maturity date, or essentially eternal interest payments. Such bonds do exist: In 1814, the English government floated a large bond issue to consolidate the various smaller issues they had used to pay for the Napoleonic Wars. Such bonds are called *consols*, and the owners are entitled to a fixed amount of interest income annually in perpetuity. In this case, Eq. (7.2) collapses into Eq. (7.3):

$$PV = \frac{CF}{k_b}. \tag{7.3}$$

Equation (7.3) can easily be obtained by applying the formula of infinite geometric series to Eq. (7.2).

Thus, the valuation depends directly on the periodic interest payment and the required rate-of-return for the bond. It can be seen that higher required rates-of-return, necessitated by a higher rate of inflation or an increase in the perceived risk of the bond, will lower the present value of the perpetuity, decreasing the bond's market value. Impacts of inflation on interest rate and equity rates-of-return have been discussed in Chapter 5 in detail.

7.2.2. *Term Bonds*

Most bonds mature at some definite period in time. Thus, Eq. (6.2) expresses the calculation required to find the theoretical value of a bond.

Equation (6.2) can be written as:

$$PV = \sum_{t=1}^{n} \frac{I_t}{(1+k_b)^t} + \frac{P}{(1+k_b)^n}, \tag{7.4}$$

where

I_t = Coupon payment, coupon rate X face value,
p = Principal amount (face value) of the bond,
n = Number of periods to maturity.

Again, it should be noted that the market price of a bond is affected by changes in the rate of inflation. If inflation increases, the discount rate must rise to compensate the investor for the decreases in value of the debt repayment. The present value of each period's interest payment thus decreases, and the price of the bond fails. The bondholder is thus always exposed to interest-rate risk, the variance of bond returns or bond prices due to fluctuations in the level of interest rates. Interest-rate risk, or price volatility of a bond in response to changes in interest-rate levels, is directly related to the term-to-maturity. There exist three types of rate premiums associated with interest-rate risk. The so-called *bond maturity premium* refers to the net return from investing in long-term government bonds rather than bills. Corporate bonds generally possess default risk; therefore, one of the components of corporate-bond rates-of-return is a *default premium.* Empirically, the bond default premium is the net return from investing in long-term corporate bonds rather than long-term government bonds. Finally, the *equity risk premium* is the net return from investing in common stocks rather than bills [see Eq. (7.1)].

Additional features of the bond can affect valuation. Convertible bonds — those bonds with a provision for conversion into shares of common stock — are generally more valuable than a firm's straight bonds for several reasons. First, the investor receives the potential of positive gains from conversion if the stock rises above the conversion price (CP). If the stock price is greater than the CP, the convertible bond will generally sell at or above its conversion value (CV). Secondly, the bondholder also receives the protection of a fixed income payment regardless of the current price of the firm's stock. Thus, the investor is assured that the price of his bond will be at least that of a straight bond if stock prices should fail to rise. Thirdly, the return on a bond is generally greater than that obtainable from a dividend of common stock; thus, the convertible bond would be superior to its converted value until stock dividends rose above a certain return per

Table 7.1. Convertible bond: conversion options.

Advantages	Purchase Price of Bond	Grain
(1) Conversion to stock if price rises above $25.	$1,000	Sell 40 shares at $30 = $1,200, for a return of 12%.
(2) Interest payment if stock price remains less than $25.	$1,000	$100 per year, for a return of 10%
(3) Interest payment versus stock dividend.		Dividend must rise to $2.50 per share before return on stock = 10%.

share. Even then, the convertible bond may be preferred because its interest payment is certain while a dividend may be decreased if earnings decline. The advantages of a convertible bond are summarized in Table 7.1; data in this table are based on a $1,000 face-value bond with 10% coupon rate, convertible to 40 shares of stock at $25 each. The valuation theory of convertible bonds can be found in Appendix 7.A.

A sinking-fund feature may also increase the value of a bond, at least at the time of its issue. A sinking-fund agreement specifies a schedule according to which the firm will amortize the bond issue, by making cash contributions to the sinking fund for use in redeeming bonds. A sinking-fund provision ensures the investor of some potential demand for the bond over its lifetime, thus slightly increasing the liquidity of the investment.

Finally, the possibility that the bond may be called will generally lower the value relative to a non-callable bond. A call provision stipulates that the bond may be retired by the issuer at a certain price, usually above par, or face value. Thus, in periods of large downward interest-rate fluctuations, a company may be able to retire a high-coupon bond in order to issue bonds with a lower interest payment requirement. A call feature, then, increases the risk to an investor in that his expected high interest payments may be called away from him if overall interest-rate levels decline.

Recently, interest has grown in zero-coupon deep discount bonds. Up till now, the bonds we have discussed have all had a coupon — an annual or semiannual interest payment. Zero-coupon bonds, as the name implies, bear no periodic interest payment. The investor is compensated through a deep discount. Much like Treasury bills, the investor buys the bond at a deep discount from face value. Upon maturity, usually 10 years, the investor is paid the full face value of the bond. Because of the income-tax implications, deep-discount zero-coupon bonds are directed at a special institutional clientele rather than individuals.

As an example of a zero-coupon bond, assume that a firm needs \$10 million for a project that has an estimated life of 20 years. Assuming an 8% interest rate and semiannual discounting, the bond would be priced at 0.20828% of par, this being the present-value factor. Therefore, the firm would have to issue approximately \$48 million face value of bonds to obtain the needed \$10 million of capital (\$10 million/0.20828%).

The firm has no cash-flow requirements until the bond matures in 20 years when the firm must pay the \$48 million principal. Corporations could establish a sinking fund to accumulate the funds needed for the principal payment.

This type of bond lowers the borrowing cost for the issuing firm. Since the issuer can expense the original issue discount on a straight-line basis, the firm has annual cash inflows from this tax savings, as opposed to cash outflow of a current-coupon bond required to meet interest payments. However, this does entail large capital requirements at maturity. The investor receives his initial investment plus the accumulated earned interest at maturity. The reinvestment rate for this investor is constant, 8%, in this example. In this kind of investment, there exists no reinvestment risk for this investor (see Reilly and Linke, 1981).

7.2.3. *Preferred Stock*

Since most preferred stock entitles the shareholder to a fixed dividend payment in perpetuity, the valuation of a preferred share is simply an application of Eq. (7.3), the value of a perpetuity, to the circumstances of a share of preferred stock:

$$PV = \frac{d_p}{k_p}, \tag{7.5}$$

where

d_p = Fixed dividend payment, coupon X par on face value of preferred stock;

k_p = Required rate-of-return on the preferred stock.

As mentioned above, the regular dividend payments may be supplemented by a further share of the company's dividends if the preferred stock has a participating feature besides the non-convertible-bond and preferred-stock valuation methods. The methods used to evaluate the convertible bonds and convertible preferred stocks should also be concerned.

7.3. Common-Stock Valuation

7.3.1. *Valuation*

Common-stock valuation is complicated by the uncertainty of cash flows to the investor. The dividends voted to shareholders in each period may change, depending on management's opinion regarding stability of earnings, future prospects for increasing or decreasing earnings, or other factors. The price of the stock may rise or fall, giving rise to capital gains or losses if the shares are sold. Thus, the valuation depends on the ability to forecast both capital gains and the stream of expected dividends. Common-stock valuation requires these future income streams from the stock (both dividends and capital gains) to be discounted at the required rate-of-return for the stock. In their well-known paper "Dividend policy, growth, and the valuation of shares," Professors Miller and Modigliani (1966) have shown that there are four alternative approaches to common-stock valuation, i.e., (1) the stream of dividends approach, (2) the investment opportunity approach, (3) the discounted cash-flow approach, and (4) the stream of earnings approach. They have shown that these four alternative evaluation methods are equivalent. The first two valuation methods are discussed in this chapter.

Following Eq. (6.5) in the last chapter, the stream of dividends approach can be defined as

$$P_o = \frac{d_1}{(1+k)} + \frac{d_2}{(1+k)^2} + \cdots + \frac{P_n}{(1+k)^n}, \tag{7.6a}$$

where

P_0 = Present value, or price of the common stock per share,
d_t = Dividend payment,
k = Required rate-of-return for the stock, assumed to be a constant term,
P_n = Price of the stock in the period when sold.

However, P_n is, in turn, merely the sum of dividends to be received from period n forward into the future, that is,

$$P_n = \sum_{t=n+1}^{\infty} \frac{d_t}{(1+k)^t}.$$

Thus, the value of the stock at the present time can be expressed as an infinite series of dividend payments discounted to the present,

$$P_0 = \sum_{t=1}^{\infty} \frac{d_t}{(1+k)^t}, \tag{7.6b}$$

where d_t = the dividend payment in period t.

Several possibilities exist regarding the growth of dividend payments over time. First, dividends may be assumed to be a constant amount from period to period. In this case, the value of the stock becomes that of an annuity, and the formula for the stock's valuation is simply Eq. (7.5).

Secondly, dividends may be expected to grow at some constant rate, g_n. Thus, a dividend payment is simply the compound value of the present dividend, or $d_t = d_0(1 + g_n)^t$. Under this assumption, the valuation equation can be simplified to[1]:

$$P_0 = \frac{d_1}{(k - g_n)}. \tag{7.6c}$$

This equation represents the Gordon growth model. Note that a crucial condition for this model is that the growth in dividends must be smaller than the required rate-of-return (k). Additionally, Eq. (7.6c) is a more general form, which includes the no-growth assumption as a special case.

Finally, dividends can exhibit a period of supernormal growth (that is, g_s is greater than r) before declining to the normal growth rate in the Gordon model (that is, g is less than k). Supernormal growth can be thought of as the "take-off" phase in a firm's life cycle. That is, a firm may experience a life cycle analogous to that of a product: first, a low-profit introductory phase, then a take-off phase of high growth and high profits, leveling off at a mature plateau, perhaps followed by a period of decline in earnings. For instance, computer and electronic manufacturers experienced a period of supernormal growth in the 1960s, as did semiconductor firms in the 1970s.

The valuation of a super-growth stock requires some estimate of the length of the super-growth period. The current price of the stock will then consist of two components: the present value of the stock during the supergrowth period, plus the value of the stock price at the end of the supergrowth period, discounted to the present. This is expressed in Eq. (7.7):

$$P_0 = \sum_{t=1}^{n} \frac{d_0(1+g_s)^t}{(1+k)^t} + \frac{d_{n+1}}{(r - g_n)} \left(\frac{1}{(1+k)^n}\right), \tag{7.7}$$

where

g_s = Growth rate of dividends during the super-growth period,
n = Number of periods before super-growth declines to normal,
g_n = Normal growth rate of dividends after the end of the super-growth phase,
r = Internal rate-of-return.

A slightly more general form of valuation developed by Modigliani and Miller is treated extensively later, in Section 7.6.

7.3.1.1. *Inflation and common-stock valuation*[2]

Obviously, there are many factors to consider when attempting to forecast dividends, growth rates, and the required rate-of-return. One factor that affects virtually every component of stock valuation is inflation.

If we assume, for the moment, a relatively simple dividend model, i.e., that the dividend payment in any period is some proportion of that period's earnings, we can obtain a clearer understanding of the impact of inflation on the firm. This and other dividend models will be discussed in much greater detail in Chapter 17.

Expressing dividends as a proportion of earnings:

$$d_t = p\text{EPS}_t,$$

where

d_t = Dividend payment per share in period t,
p = Proportion of earnings paid out in dividends (the payout ratio, $0 \leq p \leq 1.0$),
EPS_t = Earnings per share in period t.

Using the definition of EPS as:

$$\text{EPS}_t = \frac{\text{EAIT}_t}{N},$$

where N = the number of common shares outstanding, and EAIT_t = earnings after interest expenses and taxes in period t.

We can obtain an expression for the underlying factors affecting dividend payments:

$$d_t = \frac{p[Q_t(P_t - V_t) - F_t'](1-\tau)}{N}, \tag{7.8}$$

where

Q_t = Quantity of product sold in period t,
P_t = Price of the product in period t,

V_t = Variable costs in period t,
F' = Depreciation and interest expense in period t,
τ = Firm tax rate.

Obviously, then, to gauge inflation's impact on dividend payments, one must further estimate the impact of inflation separately on demand (both quantity and price) and costs (both fixed and variable). Inflation has little effect on the corporate tax rate, which is a constant 46% after the first \$100,000 in corporate earnings.

Estimating changes in price and quantity that may come about through inflation requires an analysis of the elasticity of demand of a particular firm's products. Elasticity of demand estimates for particular industries and products may be generated from past price-quantity data. Generally, necessities will be relatively price-inelastic, while luxuries will be highly elastic.

The cost structure of the firm, whether capital- or labor-intensive, can be embodied in an estimate of the firm's production function. Thus, the stability of costs *vis-à-vis* inflation can be analyzed through the fixed and variable components of the particular factors of production and the relative share of each factor in production as a whole.

Beside considering changes in dividend payments, the financial manager must also estimate the effect of inflation on the required rate-of-return of the firm's stock. The required rate-of-return is composed of the risk-free rate-of-return and a risk premium (Eq. (7.1)). The risk-free rate-of-return is itself the sum of two components, a compensation for the time value of money and the rate of inflation. Thus, the required rate-of-return will change as inflation changes (see Eq. (5.22) in Chapter 5 for detail).

Two aspects concerning the inflation component in the required rate-of-return must be considered: (1) the actual magnitude of the rate of inflation forecast for the period, and (2) any lag in expectations of inflation or adjustments for inflation which may be relevant for the periods in question.

To explicitly take the inflation factor into account, the present value of d_t as defined in Eq. (7.8) can be defined as:

$$\frac{d_t}{(1+k)^t} = \frac{p\{(\text{inflows})_t(1+\eta_i)^t - (\text{outflows})_t(1+\eta_0)^t\}(1-\tau)}{(1+k)^t}, \quad (7.8a)$$

where

$(1+k) = (1+k)(1+\eta)$,
η = Anticipated annual inflation risk,

$$\eta_i = \text{Anticipated annual inflation rate in the cash inflows,}$$
$$\eta_0 = \text{Anticipated annual inflation rate in the cash outflows,}$$
$$(\text{inflows})_t = P_t Q_t, \text{ and}$$
$$(\text{outflows})_t = Q_t V_t + F_t.$$

This kind of inflation-adjustment procedure will be used in Chapter 14 to incorporate the inflation impact on the capital budgeting decision in an inflationary environment.

Lastly, inflation can affect the growth rate of dividends through the growth rate of EPS, or ultimately the difference in growth rates of revenues and costs. Estimating this growth difference requires an analysis of supply and demand, discussed above, as well as some judgment concerning exogenous factors, which may change in importance as a result of the inflationary environment. For instance, imports into the U.S. of a certain product may increase dramatically due to relative differences in inflation rates that develop between countries. Because of currency-exchange rate differences between countries, there is the possibility of a positive return from arbitrage. That is, differences in exchange rates between countries and the existence of multiple currency markets may temporarily result in different prices for the same currency in different exchanges. Simply buying in the lowest market and selling in the highest may result in a positive return after transaction costs. However, as will be discussed in Section 7.6, opportunities for excess profits will be available only for short time periods, as the increasing number of buyers boosts the lower rates, and that of sellers depresses the higher rates. In addition, it should be noted that companies involved in international trade face an additional risk — exchange rate risk — when translating foreign currencies into dollars as part of their business transactions. Another risk of international trade is currency-control risk, such as the one imposed by Mexico in 1982 on dollar-denominated deposits held in Mexican banks.

7.3.1.2. *Growth opportunity and common-stock valuation*

The second valuation model we will consider is the growth-opportunity approach, which can be defined as[3]:

$$V_0 = \frac{\bar{X}_0}{k}\left[1 + \frac{b(r-k)}{k-br}\right], \tag{7.9}$$

where

$\bar{X}_0$ = Current expected earnings per share,
b = Investment (I_t) as a percentage of total earnings (X_t),
r = Internal rate-of-return
V_0 and k = Current market value of a firm and the required rate-of-return, respectively.

Equation (7.9) implies that the market value per share can be decomposed into two components, i.e., the perpetual component, $[\bar{X}_0/k]$, and the growth opportunity component, $[b(r-k)/(k-br)]$.

The criterion that should be used to determine whether the manager of a firm should undertake the future investment opportunity is the magnitude of $(r-k)$. If $(r-k)$ is positive, this implies that undertaking the new investment opportunity will increase the market value of the firm. If $(r-k)$ is negative, then the manager should not undertake the future investment opportunity since it will reduce the market value of the firm. If all sources of funds are due to the retained earnings, then Eq. (7.9) reduces to

$$V_{(0)} = \frac{\bar{X}(0)(1-b)}{k-br} = \frac{D_1}{k-g}, \tag{7.9a}$$

where D_1 is total current dividend payments and g is the growth rate. This is the well-known dividend valuation model. If both sides of Eq. (7.9a) are divided by the total number of common shares outstanding, n, then the equation can be rewritten as

$$P_0 = \frac{d_1}{k-g}. \tag{7.9b}$$

This is the well-known Gordon dividend valuation model. Equation (7.9b) will be used in Chapter 11 in estimating the cost of equity capital. Equation (7.8) can be integrated with the option-pricing model developed by Black and Scholes (1973) to evaluate the market value of a firm. In other words, the growth-opportunity component can be valued in a variety of ways. One method of making this valuation is through the use of the Real Option Theory (Myers, 1977). The real-option theory will be discussed in more detail in Chapter 14.

7.3.1.3. *Growth rate estimation and application*

The purpose of this section is to show how growth rates can be mathematically estimated. The application of these estimated growth rates is briefly discussed.

Compound-sum method

One method of estimating the growth rate uses the compounding process. Both discrete and continuous compounding are basic concepts in financial management and investment analysis. These concepts are expressed mathematically in Eqs. (7.10) and (7.11):

$$P_n = P_0(1+i)^n, \tag{7.10}$$

$$P_n = P_0 e^{in}, \tag{7.11}$$

where

P_0 = the price at time zero;
P_n = the price at time n;
i = the compound interest rate; and
e = a constant equal to 2.718.

Equation (7.10) describes a discrete compounding process and Eq. (7.11) describes a continuous compounding process.

The relationship between Eqs. (7.10) and (7.11) can be illustrated by using an intermediate expression such as

$$P_n = P_0\left(1+\frac{i}{m}\right)^{mn}, \tag{7.12}$$

where m is the frequency of compounding in each year. If $m = 4$, Eq. (7.12) is a quarterly compounding process; if $m = 365$, it describes a daily process; and if m approaches infinity, it describes a continuous compounding process. Thus, Eq. (7.11) can be derived from Eq. (7.12) in the following manner. Based upon the definition

$$\lim_{m\to\infty}\left(1+\frac{1}{m}\right)^{m} = e = 2.718. \tag{7.13}$$

Equation (3.17) can be rewritten as

$$\lim_{m\to\infty} P_n = \lim P_0\left(1+\frac{1}{\frac{m}{i}}\right)^{\frac{m}{i(in)}} = P_0 e^{in}. \tag{7.14}$$

The growth rate of earnings or dividends can be estimated either mathematically or statistically. Mathematically, the growth rate can be estimated by using either Eqs. (7.11) or (7.12). Rewriting Eq. (3.15) using the symbol for growth rate, g, in place of i gives:

$$P_n = P_0(1+g)^n. \tag{7.15}$$

From Eq. (3.20), it is clear that

$$(1+g)^n = \frac{P_n}{P_0}. \tag{7.16}$$

Given values for P_0, P_n, and n, and using a compound sum table, the value of g can easily be obtained. This approach is called the **compound-sum method** for estimating growth rates. While the advantage of this method is its simplicity, it ignores other information points between the first and last period.

Suppose there are two firms whose dividend payments patterns are as shown in Table 7.2, using the compound-sum method the growth rate of firm ABC can be calculated as

$$(1+g)^m = \frac{P_m}{P_0} = \frac{1.77}{1.00}.$$

Using a compound-sum table where $n = 6$ and interest factor $= 1.77$, $g = 10\%$. The compound-sum method also yields a growth rate of 10% for firm XYZ. Yet it becomes clear that the dividend behavior of these firms is distinctly different when looking at the dividends per share in Table 3.2.

Regression method

To use all the information available to the security analysts, two regression equations can be employed. These equations can be derived from Eqs. (7.11) and (7.12) by letting $i = g$ and taking the logarithm (ln):

$$\ln P_n = \ln P_0 + n\ln(1+g), \tag{7.17}$$

$$\ln P_n = \ln P_0 + gn. \tag{7.18}$$

Table 7.2. Dividend behavior of firms ABC and XYZ in dividends per share (DPS, dollars).

Year	ABC	XYZ
2005	1.00	1.00
2006	1.00	1.10
2007	1.00	1.21
2008	1.00	1.33
2009	1.00	1.46
2010	1.00	1.61
2011	1.77	1.77

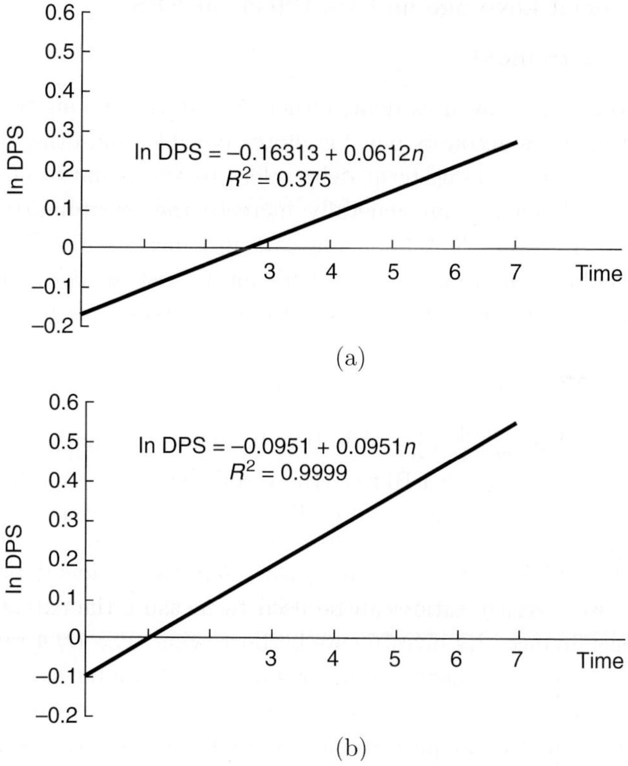

Fig. 7.1. Regression models for ABC and XYZ.

Both Eqs. (7.17) and (7.18) indicate that P_n is linearly related to n. Using the data in Table 7.2 for companies ABC and XYZ, we can estimate the growth rates for their respective dividend streams. Graphs of the regression equations for ABC and XYZ are shown in Fig. 7.1. The slope of the regression using Eq. (7.18) for ABC shows an estimated value for growth of about 6%. The estimate for XYZ is 9.5%. If Eq. (7.17) had been used to estimate the growth, then the antilog of the regression slope estimate would equal the growth rate.

Besides Compound Sum Method and Regression Method, we can also use sustainable growth rate of sales to estimate the growth rate of a firm. This method will be discussed in Eq. (18.1) in Chapter 18. For extensive empirical study using these three alternative growth rate methods can be found in Brick *et al.* (2016).

7.4. Financial Leverage and Its Effect on EPS

7.4.1. *Measurement*

Almost every company uses debt, either short-term or long-term. Short-term debt includes accounts payable, notes payable, and other short-term credit arrangements. Long-term debt refers to the issuance of corporate bonds. Debt financing can generally increase the profitability of equity investment. However, debt financing can also increase the financial risk of equity holders. It appears that there must exist an *optimum mixture* between debt and equity for a given firm. This issue will be explored in more detail in the next section.

Two different methods can be used to measure a firm's capital structure:

(a) $\frac{\text{debt}}{\text{equity}}\left(\frac{D}{E}\right)$ or $\frac{\text{debt}}{\text{assets}}\left(\frac{D}{A}\right)$ ratio (the balance sheet method) and
(b) times interest earned: EBIT/I (the income-statement method), where I = the interest payment, and EBIT = earnings before interest expense and taxes.

These two leverage ratios can be used to measure the extent to which the firm has financed its investments by borrowing. The D/A ratio can be regarded as a balance-sheet leverage ratio and times interest earned as an income-statement leverage ratio. Conceptually, the market value instead of book value of debt and equity should be used to calculate either the D/E or D/A ratio. If they are not available, then the book value of debt and equity can be used as a proxy to calculate the ratios. It should be noted that the proxy measurement does contain proxy error.

Times interest earned is one of several debt-service ratios. These ratios describe how well the firm can service its debt, that is, how easily the firm can pay its interest obligations as they come due. Times interest earned is a kind of "interest coverage" ratio that shows how many times the interest payments are "covered" by funds that are normally available to pay interest expenses.

7.4.2. *Effect*

There are three possible effects of a change in financial leverage on the earnings per share (EPS) of a firm: changes in Financial leverage of a firm can affect the mean of EPS ($\overline{\text{EPS}}$), the standard deviation of EPS (σ_{EPS}), and/or the coefficient of variation of EPS ($\sigma_{\text{EPS}}/\overline{\text{EPS}}$). The impact on each is illustrated below.

One aspect of the net impact of debt usage is its effect upon return on net worth. An expression used to summarize the interrelationships of the relevant variables is:

$$k_e = r + (r - i)\left(\frac{D}{E}\right), \tag{7.10}$$

where

k_e = Return on equity,
r = Return on total assets (return on equity without leverage),
i = Interest rate on outstanding debt,
D = Outstanding debt,
E = Book value of equity.

Here, we do not include tax.

Equation (7.10) is obtained by substituting $A = D + E$ into the basic definition of return on equity

$$k_e = \frac{rA - iD}{E}, \tag{7.11}$$

where A = total assets.

If return on total assets, r, is deterministic, then the increase of the leverage ratio, D/E, can either increase or decrease k_e. If r is larger (or smaller) than i, then the increase in the D/E ratio will increase (decrease) the return on equity. This implies that the change in leverage ratio will affect the return on equity, k_e, and the average EPS. However, the future EBIT is generally uncertain, and therefore r is uncertain. Under this circumstance, Eq. (7.10) should be defined as:

$$\tilde{k}_e = \tilde{r} + (\tilde{r} - i)\left(\frac{D}{E}\right). \tag{7.10a}$$

If r is normally distributed, then k will be normally distributed, with:

$$\text{Mean of } (\tilde{k}) = \bar{k} = \bar{r} + (\bar{r} - i)\left(\frac{D}{E}\right), \tag{7.12a}$$

$$\text{Variance of } (\tilde{k}) = \left(1 + \frac{D}{E}\right)^2 [\text{Var}(\tilde{r})]. \tag{7.12b}$$

Equations (7.12a) and (7.12b) imply that the change in the D/E ratio will affect both the mean and the variance of return on equity. In Eq. (7.12b), the adjustment factor, $(1+D/E)^2$, is larger than one; therefore the variance of return on a leveraged firm will always be larger than a non-leveraged firm. In other words, use of leverage will amplify business risk. This result also implies that leverage has a similar impact on the statistical distribution of EPS.

To investigate the impact of leverage on the variance of EPS, Eq. (7.11) is modified to allow the existence of corporate taxes:

$$k_e = \frac{[(rA - iD) - \tau(rA - iD)]}{E}, \tag{7.10b}$$

where τ = the corporate tax rate, and $\tau(r\text{A} - iD)$ is the total corporate tax payment. Since Eq. (7.10b) can be rewritten with $(1-\tau)(rA - iD/E)$, it can be simplified as:

$$k_e = -\left[r + (r - i)\left(\frac{D}{E}\right)\right](1 - \tau). \tag{7.13}$$

Under the uncertainty case, Eq. (7.13) can be redefined as:

$$\tilde{k}_e = \tilde{r} + \left((\tilde{r} - i)\left(\frac{D}{E}\right)\right)(1 - \tau). \tag{7.14}$$

If $\tilde{r}$ is normally distributed, then $\tilde{k}_e$ will be distributed normally with

$$\text{Mean}(\tilde{k}) = \bar{k}_e = \bar{r} + \left[(\bar{r} - i)\left(\frac{D}{E}\right)\right](1 - \tau), \tag{7.15a}$$

$$\text{Var}(\tilde{k}_e) = (1 - \tau)^2\left(1 + \frac{D}{E}\right)^2 \text{Var}(\tilde{r}). \tag{7.15b}$$

The difference between Eqs. (7.12a) and (7.12b) and Eqs. (7.15a) and (7.15b) is the inclusion of tax factors, $(1-\tau)$, $(1-\tau)^2$.

There is a direct relationship between the return on equity and EPS. Now the impact of leverage on EPS is analyzed in accordance with that for the return on equity. Following the definition of EPS from the previous section, the EPS for a particular firm can be defined as:

$$\text{EPS} = \frac{(rA - iD - \tau(rA - iD))}{N}, \tag{7.16}$$

where N = the total number of shares outstanding.

There exists a proportional relationship between N and E. This proportion can be defined as:

$$h = \frac{E}{N}, \tag{7.17}$$

where h is the dollar value per share.

Based upon Eqs. (7.14), (7.15a) and (7.15b), (7.16), and (7.17), it is clear that the EPS will be normally distributed with mean:

$$\overline{\text{EPS}} = \bar{r}h + \left[(\bar{r} - i)\left(\frac{D}{E}\right)\right](1 - \tau)h \tag{7.18a}$$

and variance:

$$\text{Var(EPS)} = h^2(1 - \tau)^2\left(1 + \frac{D}{E}\right)^2 \text{Var}(\tilde{r}). \tag{7.18b}$$

Equations (7.18a) and (7.18b) imply that leverage will affect both the mean and the variance of EPS. However, if the interest cost is equal to the expected return on total assets, then Eqs. (7.18a) and (7.18b) are reduced to:

$$\overline{\text{EPS}} = \bar{r}h, \tag{7.18c}$$

$$\text{Var(EPS)} = (1 - \tau)^2h^2\left(1 + \frac{D}{E}\right)^2 \text{Var}(\tilde{r}). \tag{7.18d}$$

This implies that a change in the D/E ratio will affect only the variance of EPS. Graphically, normal distributions I and II in Fig. 7.2 represent the distributions of EPS before and after the change in D/E, respectively. Since $i = r$, an increase in D/E only increases the variance of EPS and does not affect the expected EPS.

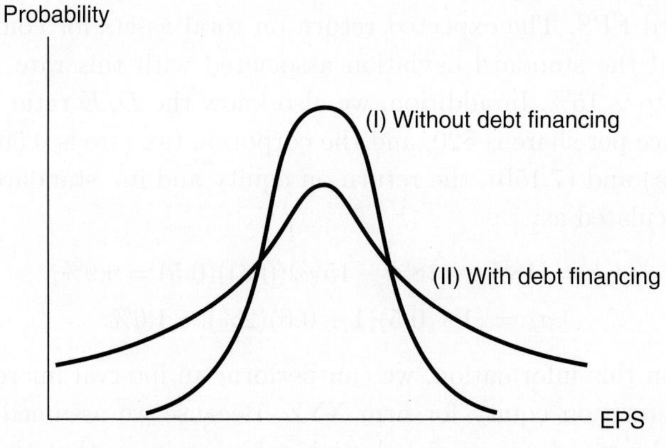

Fig. 7.2. Distribution of EPS.

If r is greater than i, then an increase in leverage will affect both $\overline{EPS}$ and σ^2_{EPS}. A financial manager should use the risk–return trade-off concept to determine whether the increase in the D/E ratio will increase or decrease the firm's market value. This issue will be explored further in the next chapter.

The coefficient of variation instead of the variance of EPS is a unit-less measure. The coefficient of variation of EPS can be defined as:

$$\text{CV}_{\text{EPS}} = \frac{\text{Standard Deviation of EPS}}{\text{Mean(EPS)}} = \frac{\sigma_r\left[1+\left(\dfrac{D}{E}\right)\right](1-\tau)}{\bar{r}_0+(\bar{r}_0-i)\left(\dfrac{D}{E}\right)(1-\tau)}. \tag{7.19}$$

This represents a relative measure of risk for the firm.

The impact of the D/E ratio on the CV of EPS is now analyzed. If the factor $H = [1 + (D/E)](1 - \tau)/[\bar{r}_0 + (\bar{r}_0 - i)(D/E)(1 - \tau)]$ is larger (or smaller) than one, then leverage increases (reduces) the standard deviation of the return on total assets. This relationship can be simplified as

$$\begin{aligned} H \geq 1, \quad \text{if } \frac{D}{E} \leq \frac{1-\bar{r}}{1-\bar{r}+i}, \\ H \leq 1, \quad \text{if } \frac{D}{E} \geq \frac{1-\bar{r}}{1-\bar{r}+i}. \end{aligned} \tag{7.20}$$

Equation (7.20) implies that $1 - \bar{r}/(1 - \bar{r} + i)$ can be used as a critical value for investigating the impact of corporate leverage on the coefficient of variation of EPS.

A numerical example is used to show the impact of corporate leverage on expected EPS. The expected return on total assets for company XYZ is 18% and the standard deviation associated with this rate is 2%. The interest rate is 15%. In addition, we also know the D/E ratio is 0.60, the market price per share is \$20, and the corporate tax rate is 0.50. Following Eqs. (7.15a) and (7.15b), the return on equity and its standard deviation can be calculated as:

$$k = (18\% + (18\% - 15\%)(0.6))(0.5) = 9.9\%,$$
$$\sigma_k = (1 - 0.5)(1 + 0.6)(2\%) = 1.6\%.$$

Based upon this information, we can perform an interval inference on the possible return on equity for firm XYZ. Because we assumed normality, following the standardized distribution table we know that the estimated k will be between 7.49% and 10.69% $[9.09 \pm 1.6]$, with probability 68.27%, and between 5.89% and 12.29% $[9.09 \pm 2(1.6)]$, with 95.45% probability.

Following Eqs. (7.18a) and (7.18b), the expected EPS and its standard deviation can be calculated as:

$$\overline{\text{EPS}} = (18\% + (18\% - 15\%)(0.6))(0.5)(\$20) = \$1.98,$$

$$\sigma_{\text{EPS}} = (\$20)(1 - 0.5)(1 + 0.6)(2\%) = \$0.32.$$

Based upon these values, the confidence interval on future EPS can be estimated. The coefficient of variation of EPS for XYZ Company will be $(0.32/1.98) = 0.1616$. If XYZ Company is without leverage, its $\overline{\text{EPS}}$ and the standard deviation of EPS will be:

$$\overline{\text{EPS}} = (18\%)(1 - 0.5)(\$20) = \$1.80,$$
$$\sigma_{\text{EPS}} = (\$20)(1 - 0.5)(2\%) = \$0.20.$$

Under these circumstances, the coefficient of variation for EPS will be 0.1111 instead of 0.1616.

7.5. Degree of Financial Leverage and Combined Effect[4]

In Chapter 2, we derived an elasticity measure for the relationship of a percentage change in sales to a percentage change in net income. Based upon a similar concept, the degree of financial leverage can be derived.

The degree of financial leverage is defined as the percentage change of EPS over the percentage change of EBIT, or:

$$\frac{\dfrac{\Delta\text{EPS}}{\text{EPS}}}{\dfrac{\text{EBIT}}{\text{EBIT}}} = \frac{\dfrac{\Delta\text{EBIT}}{(\text{EBIT} - iD)}}{\dfrac{\text{EBIT}}{\text{EBIT}}} = \frac{\text{EBIT}}{\text{EBIT} - iD}, \tag{7.21}$$

where iD = interest payment on debt. Using EBIT $= Q(P - V) - F$ Eq. (7.21) can be rewritten as:

$$\text{DFL} = \frac{Q(P - V) - F}{Q(P - V) - F - iD}. \tag{7.22}$$

Combining the DFL with the degree of operating leverage (DOL) defined in Chapter 2, we have

$$\text{CLE} = \text{DFL} \times \text{DOL},$$
$$\text{CLE} = \frac{Q(P - V)}{Q(P - V) - F - iD}, \tag{7.23}$$

where CLE = combined leverage effect.

A numerical example can be used to show how DOL, DFL and CLE can be used to measure the impact of debt financing. If XYZ Company's price is \$100, variable costs = \$40, fixed costs = \$2,000, quantity produced = 100 units, and iD = \$700, then the DFL = \$4,000/(\$4,000 − \$700) = 3.08. Then CLE = \$6,000/\$6,000 − \$2,000 − \$700) = 1.81. In this case, if XYZ increase sales by one percent, EPS will increase by 1.81%. This illustrates the fact that increased financial leverage will increase expected EPS. It should be noted, however, that the variance of EPS will also increase, as indicated in the previous section.

If Q and $(P - V)$ are allowed to be random variables, then the DOL, DFL, and CLE will become random as well:

(a) $$\widetilde{\text{DOL}} = \frac{Q\widetilde{(P-V)}}{\tilde{Q}(P-V) - F},$$

(b) $$\widetilde{\text{DFL}} = \frac{Q\widetilde{(P-V)} - F}{\tilde{Q}(P-V) - F - iD},$$

(c) $$\widetilde{\text{CLE}} = \frac{Q\widetilde{(P-V)}}{\tilde{Q}(P-V) - F - iD}.$$

Following Hilliard and Leitch (1975), a log-normal approach, as discussed in Chapter 2, can be used to analyze the costs, volume, and profit relationship. The interval for DOL, DFL, and CLE can be analyzed. The detailed analysis associated with the stochastic DOL, DFL, and CLE can be found in Hilliard *et al.* (1983).

7.6. Optimal Capital Structure

7.6.1. *Overall Discussion*

The existence of optimal capital structure has become one of the important issues for academicians and practitioners in finance. Classical finance theorists argue that there is an optimal capital structure for a firm. However, the new classical financial theory developed by Modigliani and Miller (1958, 1963) has cast doubt upon the existence of an optimal capital structure for a firm. To establish their theory, they assumed that:

1. Capital markets are perfect (frictionless).
2. Both individuals and firms can borrow and lend at the risk-free rate.
3. Firms use risk-free debt and risky equity.

4. There are only corporate taxes (i.e., there are no wealth taxes or personal income taxes).
5. All cash-flow streams are perpetuities (i.e., no growth).

Using additional concepts [(i) risk class and (ii) home-made leverage], Modigliani and Miller have derived their well-known three alternative propositions. Proposition I is the value proposition; Proposition II is the cost-of-capital determination proposition, and Proposition III is the investment-decision proposition.

If all firms are in the same risk class, then their expected risky future net operating cash flow ($\tilde{X}$) varies only by a scale factor. Under this circumstance, the correlation between two firms' operating cash flows $\tilde{X}_{it}$ and X_{jt} within a risk class should be equal to one. In this case, $\tilde{X}_{it} = C\tilde{X}_{jt}$, where C is the scale factor. The correlation coefficient between $\tilde{X}_{it}$ and $\tilde{X}_{jt}(\delta_{ij})$ can be defined as

$$\delta_{ij} = \frac{\text{Cov}(\tilde{X}_{it}, \tilde{X}_{jt})}{\sigma(X_{it})\sigma(X_{jt})} = \frac{\text{Cov}(CX_{it}, X_{jt})}{C\sigma(X_{it})\sigma(X_{jt})} = 1,$$

where $\delta(\cdot)$ = standard deviation, Cov $(\tilde{X}_{it,}\tilde{X}_{jt})$ = covariance between $\tilde{X}_{it}$ and $\tilde{X}_{jt}$. This implies that the rates-of-return will be equal for all firms in the same risk class, that is

$$\tilde{R}_{it} = \frac{\tilde{X}_{it} - \tilde{X}_{it-1}}{\tilde{X}_{i,t-1}}$$

and because $\tilde{X}_{it} = C\tilde{X}_{jt}$, then

$$\tilde{R}_{jt} = \frac{C\tilde{X}_{jt} - C\tilde{X}_{jt-1}}{C\tilde{X}_{jt-1}} = \tilde{R}_{it},$$

where R_{it} and R_{jt} are rates-of-return for the ith and jth firms, respectively. Therefore, if two streams of cash flow differ by, at most, a scale factor, they will have the same distributions of returns and the same risk, and will require the same expected return.

The homemade leverage is used to refer to the leverage created by individual investors who sell their own debt, while corporate leverage is used to refer to the debt floated by the corporation. Using the assumption that the cost of homemade leverage is equal to the cost of corporate leverage, Modigliani and Miller (1958) have derived their Proposition I with taxes and without taxes. However, the Proposition I with taxes is not correct, and they corrected this result in their 1963 paper. Mathematically, Modigliani and Miller's Proposition I can be defined as

$$V_j = (S_j + D_j) = \frac{\bar{X}_j}{\rho}, \tag{7.24}$$

$$V_j^L = \frac{(1-\tau_j)\bar{X}_j}{\rho^\tau} + \frac{\tau_j I_j}{r} = V_j^U + \tau_j D_j. \tag{7.25}$$

In Eq. (7.24), D_j, S_j, and V_j are the market values of riskless debts, of common shares, and of the firm, respectively; X_j is the expected profit before deduction of interest, and r the required rates-of-return or the cost of capital. In Eq. (7.25), ρ^τ is the required rates-of-return used to capitalize the expected returns net of tax of the jth unleveraged firm with long-run average earnings before tax and interest $(\bar{X}_j)$; τ_j is the corporate tax rate for the jth firm, I_j the total interest expense for the jth firm, r is the market interest rate used to capitalize the sure cash inflows generated by risk-free debt, D_j is total risk-free debt floated by the jth firm, V_j^L and V_j^U are the market values of the leveraged and unleveraged firms, respectively.

Equation (7.24) defines Modigliani and Miller's Proposition I without tax (see next section for the proof) and Eq. (7.25) defines their Proposition I with tax. By comparing these two equations, we find that the advantages of a firm with leverage will increase its value by $\tau_j D_j$, that is, the corporate tax rate times the total debt floated by that firm. One of the important implications of this proposition is that *there is no optimal capital structure* for this firm unless there are bankruptcy costs associated with this firm's debt flotation. If there are bankruptcy costs, then a firm will use its debts until its tax benefit is equal to the bankruptcy cost and, therefore, in this case, there is an optimal structure for this firm. In addition to the bankruptcy costs, information signaling [see Leland and Pyle (1977) and Ross (1977)] and differential expectations between shareholders and bondholders can also be used to justify the possible existence of an optimal structure for a firm.

Traditional financial theorists believe that there is an optimal capital structure for a firm. The principal concept used to justify this argument is that the cost of equity capital increases less than the proportion of the increase of debt/equity ratio. In contrast to the classical arguments associated with cost of capital, Modigliani and Miller (1958, 1963) proposed their Proposition II to define the cost of equity capital for jth firm (k_j) as

$$k_j = \rho + \frac{(\rho - r)D_j}{S_j}, \tag{7.26}$$

$$k_j = \frac{\bar{\pi}^\tau}{S_j} = \rho^\tau + (1 - \tau_j)\frac{[\rho^\tau - r]D_j}{S_j}, \tag{7.27}$$

where ρ, D_j, S_j have been defined in Eq. (7.24), and ρ^t, r, and τ have been defined in Eq. (7.25). In Eq. (7.27), $\bar{\pi}^{1-\tau}$ is the expected net profits after taxes. Applications of Eqs. (7.25) and (7.27) in estimating cost of capital will be explored in Chapter 11.

7.6.2. *Arbitrage Process and the Proof of M&M Proposition I*[5]

The arbitrage process is generally used to explain how the foreign exchange market value is determined. Professors Modigliani and Miller (1958, 1963) have used this concept to prove their Proposition I with and without taxes. We shall discuss both cases below.

(a) Without Tax

Assume two firms in the same risk class and with the same expected net operating cash flow, $\bar{X}$. The only difference between these two firms is that Company 1 is financed entirely with common stock while Company 2 has some debt in its capital structure. Modigliani and Miller argued that the market value of Company 1 (V_1) should be equal to that of Company 2 (V_2). If the market value of these two firms is different because their capital structure is different, then the investor can use "homemade leverage" and an "arbitrage strategy" to increase his return.

There are two possible cases, (i) $V_2 > V_1$ and (ii) $V_1 > V_2$, which should be considered in proving Modigliani and Miller's Proposition I without taxes.

An investor, using his own dollars of saving, can buy the common stock of either Company 2 or Company 1. The return of these two possible investments can be defined as

$$Y_2 = \frac{s_2}{D_2 + S_2}(X_2 - rD_2) = \alpha_2(X - rD_2), \tag{7.28}$$

$$Y_1 = \frac{s_1}{S_1}X_1 = \alpha_1 X, \tag{7.29}$$

where Y_2 and Y_1 are the returns associated with the stock of Company 2 and Company 1, respectively; S_2 and S_1 are the total numbers of shares of common stock issued by Company 2 and Company 1, respectively; s_2 and s_1 are the amounts of common stock of Company 2 and of Company 1, respectively, that are owned by the investor. In Eq. (7.28), rD_2 is the total interest expense of Company 2 (r is the interest rate and D_2 is the total debt issued by Company 2). Lastly, α_2 and α_1 are the percentages of V_2 and V_1, respectively, owned by the investor.

In a state of market equilibrium, we must have $V_2 = V_1$. If V_2 is not equal to V_1, then the market is not in an equilibrium condition; therefore, there are arbitrage opportunities for the investor.

If the market value of the leveraged firm (V_2) is larger than the market value of the unleveraged firm (V_1), then the investor could sell his s_2 (αS_2) worth of Company 2 shares and acquire instead an amount $s_1 = \alpha_2(S_2+D_2)$ of the shares of Company 1. The money used to buy the s_1 dollars of shares of Company 1 comes from two different sources: (i) $\alpha_2 S_2$ dollars is realized from the sale of his initial holding of Company 2's common shares, and (ii) $\alpha_2 D_2$ dollars is due to his personal credit, pledging his new holdings in Company 1 as collateral. Making proper allowance for the interest payments on his personal debt, $\alpha_2 D_2$, the return of the new portfolio, Y_1', is given by:

$$Y_1' = \frac{\alpha_1(S_2 + D_2)}{S_1}X - r\alpha_1 D_2 = \alpha_1 \frac{V_2}{V_1}X - r\alpha D_2. \tag{7.30}$$

Comparing Eq. (7.28) with Eq. (7.30) we see that as long as $V_2 > V_1$, we must have $Y_1 > Y_2$; therefore, it is worthwhile for the investors of Company 2's common shares to sell their stocks and buy the common shares of Company 1. This kind of arbitrage process will depress the value of S_2, and hence V_2, and will increase the value of S_1 and thus V_1. Overall, Modigliani and Miller conclude that the investors can use "homemade leverage" and "the arbitrage process" to bring the market value of the leveraged firm equal to the market value of the unleveraged firm.

If an investor holds initially an amount s_1 of shares of Company 1, then his return will be Y_1, as indicated in Eq. (7.29). If the market value of V_2 is smaller than the market value of V_1, then this investor can exchange his s_1 dollars of the first company's stocks for the second company's stock and bonds. Then the investor's returns will be

$$\begin{aligned} Y_2' &= \frac{s_2}{S_2}(X - rD_2) + rd \\ &= \frac{s_1}{V_2}(X - rD_2) + r\frac{D_2}{V_2 s_1} = \frac{s_1}{V_2}X = \alpha_1\frac{s_1}{V_2}X, \end{aligned} \tag{7.31}$$

where $s_2 = (S_2/V_2)s_1$ = the percentage of Company 2's stock owned by the investor, and $(D_2/V_2)s_1 = d_2$, the amount of the second company's bonds owned by the investor. Comparing Y' with Y_1, if $V_2 < S_1 = V_2$, then Y_2' will exceed Y_1, and then it is worthwhile for the investor to exchange Company 1's shares for a mixed portfolio continuing an appropriate fraction of the shares of Company 2.

We shall now illustrate arbitrage with a numerical example. Suppose that Companies 1 and 2 are in the same risk class and generate the same expected annual net operating income (X) of \$50. Company 1, which is all equity-financed, has a total market value of \$500, whereas Company 2, financed with a combination of debt and equity, has a total market value of \$600.

Company 1, which is all equity-financed with a combination of debt and equity, has a total market value of \$600 (see left half of Table 7.3). Since these values are in disequilibrium with $V_2 > V_1$, Modigliani and Miller's Proposition I states that it would be profitable for shareholders of Company 2 to sell their shares and use the proceeds to acquire shares in Company 1.

If an investor owns 20% or \$120 worth of the shares in Company 2, then his return can be calculated in terms of Eq. (7.28) as 0.20(\$50 – \$21), or simply \$5.80. Next suppose that this investor sells all his shares for \$120 and augments this sum by borrowing another \$120 from a bank at the going interest rate of 7%. From this transaction, the investor has created a \$240 "homemade" balanced fund, made of \$60 debt and \$60 equity. If he

Table 7.3. Valuation of two companies in accordance with Modigliani and Miller's Proposition 1.

	Initial Disequilibrium		Final Equilibrium	
	Company 1	*Company 2*	*Company 1*	*Company 2*
Total Market Value (V_j)	\$500	\$600	\$550	\$550
Debt (D_j)	0	300	0	300
Equity (S_j)	500	300	550	250
Expected Net Operating Income ($\bar{X}$)	50	50	50	50
Interest ($r_j D_j$)	0	21	0	21
Net Income ($\bar{X} - r_j D_j$)	50	29	50	29
Cost of Common Equity (k_j)	10.00%	9.67%	9.09%	11.6%
$W_1 = D_j/D_jV_j$	0	$\frac{1}{2}$	0	$\frac{6}{11}$
$W_2 = S_j/V_j$	1	$\frac{1}{2}$	1	$\frac{5}{11}$
Average Cost of Capital (p_j)	10.00%	8.34%	9.09%	9.09%

invests his balanced fund of \$240 in the shares of the unlevered Company 1, the financial leverage of the investor's new portfolio will be equivalent to that in his old portfolio. The return on his old portfolio can be calculated in terms of Eq. (7.30) as (240/500)(\$50) – (0.07)(\$120), or simply \$15.60. Since the two portfolios are perfect substitutes for one another in the M&M theory, the investor holding shares in Company 2 would find it profitable to shift his investments to shares in Company 1. The process of arbitrage will continue until the value of Company 2 is equivalent to that of Company 1. It is obvious that if $V_1 > V_2$, it would be profitable for investors to exchange shares in Company 1 for those in Company 2.

Finally, assume that both Companies 1 and 2 have a net operating income ($\bar{X}$) of \$50 and the same risk characteristics. The equilibrium values of these two firms are both assumed to be \$550. Since Company 1 has no debt, its common stock must be \$275 and its yield on equity of 9.09% becomes identical to ρ_k (see right half of Table 7.3). Company 2, however, has \$300 of debt on which it pays \$21 in interest. Company 2's stock therefore must be worth only \$250(\$550 – \$300). This implies that the cost of equity capital (i_2) is 11.6 (29/250)%. Note that this cost of equity capital can also be calculated in terms of Eq. (7.26). Thus in the Modigliani and Miller model, although Company 2 finances more than half of its assets with "low cost" debt, the increase in financial risk drives up the cost of equity financing by such an amount that ρ_k, the average cost of capital, remains unchanged at the rate of 9.09%.

(b) With Tax

Modigliani and Miller (1958, 1963) have shown that the value of the leveraged firm will be equal to the value of the unleveraged firm, plus an adjustment term, $\tau_j D_j$, as indicated in Eq. (7.25). In his well-known presidential address paper, Professor Miller (1977) modified the results of Eq. (7.25) by introducing personal as well as corporate taxes into the model, and obtaining[6]

$$V_j^L = V_j^U + \left[1 - \left[\frac{(1-\tau_j^C)(1-\tau_j^{PS})}{1-\tau_j^{PD}}\right]\right] D_j, \qquad (7.32)$$

where V_j^L, V_j^U, and D_j have been defined in Eq. (7.25); τ_j^C, τ_j^{PS}, and τ_j^{PD} are the corporate tax rate, the personal tax rate on equity income, and the personal tax from bond income, respectively, for the jth firm. By comparing

Eq. (7.32) with Eq. (7.25), we find that

$$\left[1 - \frac{(1-\tau_j^C)(1-\tau_j^{PS})}{(1-\tau_j^{PD})}\right] < \tau_j^C.$$

Therefore, the advantage of using debt in a case with both corporate tax and personal tax will be smaller than that with only corporate tax. Using Eq. (7.32), Miller has also derived some extreme conditions in which the advantage of debt vanishes completely. These conditions are: (i) personal tax on equity is zero, and (ii) supply rates-of-return for bonds is equal to the demand rates-of-return for bonds.

Arguments used to support condition (i) are: (1) no one has to realize a capital gain until after death; (2) capital gains and capital losses in well-diversified portfolios can entirely offset each other; (3) the first seven hundred dollars of dividend income received by individuals is not taxed; (4) 85% of dividends received by taxable corporations can be excluded from taxable income, of (5) many types of investment funds (e.g., non-profit organizations, pension funds, trust funds, etc.) pay no tax at all. If condition (i) holds, then the second term of Eq. (7.32) reduces to

$$\left[1 - \frac{(1-\tau_j^C)}{(1-\tau_j^{PD})}\right] D_j. \tag{7.33}$$

If the bond's supply rate-of-return is equal to its demand rate-of-return, as indicated in Eq. (7.34), then the tax advantage will certainly vanish:

$$r_s = \frac{r_0}{1-\tau_j^C} = r_d = \frac{r_0}{1-\tau_j^{PD}}, \tag{7.34}$$

where r_0 is the rate paid on the debt of a tax-free institution (municipal bonds, for example). The relationship can be graphically portrayed in Fig. 7.3. The acceptance of this analysis has recently been critically discussed by Shelton (1981), Hamada (1986), and Kim (1982).

If the tax advantage is zero, then the procedure under Modigliani and Miller's Proposition I is essentially identical to that discussed in the previous section. If the tax advantage does not vanish, then following their (1958, 1963).

Proposition I with tax does not hold, and their theory implies (i) $V^L - t^C D^L < V^U$ or (ii) $V^L - t^C D^L > V^U$. Case (i) implies that the unleveraged firm is overranked. The logic used to prove the Proposition I with tax is identical to that used to prove the Proposition I without tax. However, the after-tax return can be decomposed into two components: (i) an uncertainty

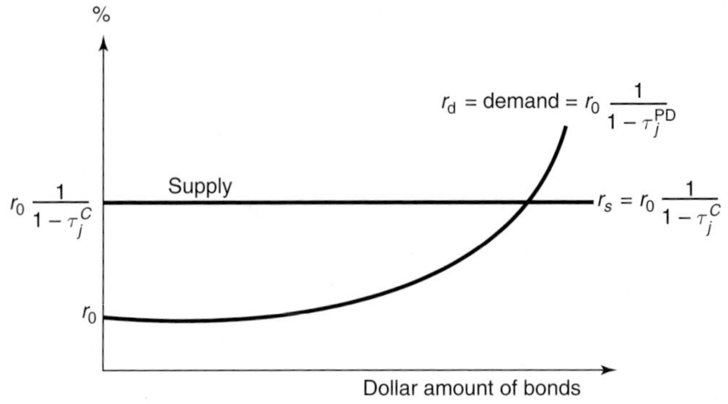

Fig. 7.3. Aggregated supply and demand for corporate bonds (before tax rates). From Miller (1977). Reprinted by permission.

component and (ii) a certainty component:

$$\bar{X}^\tau = (1-\tau^C)(X-R) + R = (1-\tau^C)X + \tau^C R = (1-\tau^C)\bar{X}Z + \tau^C R, \tag{7.35}$$

where $\bar{X}$ is the expected value of X, R is the interest payment and $Z = X/\bar{X}$, having the same value for all firms in a risk class, k, drawing from a distribution, say $f_k(z)$. (We drop the sub and superscripts on τ for simplicity of presentation.) If the variance of Z is equal to σ_z^2, then

$$\begin{aligned}\mathrm{Var}(\bar{X}^\tau) &= \mathrm{Var}[(\bar{X}^\tau - \tau^C R)Z + \tau^C R] \\ &= \mathrm{Var}\left[\bar{X}^\tau\left(1 - \frac{\tau^C R}{\bar{X}^\tau}\right)Z + \tau^C R\right] \\ &= \sigma_z^2(\bar{X}^\tau)\left(1 - \tau^C\frac{R}{\bar{X}^\tau}\right)^2. \end{aligned}\tag{7.36}$$

Equation (7.36) indicates the variance of total return, interest plus net profit; it implies that the higher τ^C and the degree of leverage $R/\bar{X}^\tau$, the smaller the variability of after-tax total returns. This degree of leverage $R/\bar{X}^\tau$ can replace debt/equity ratio to measure the capital structure. Based upon the definition of $\bar{X}^\tau$, as indicated in Eq. (7.35) and the logic used to prove Proposition I without tax, Proposition I with tax can be easily proved as follows:

If $V^L - \tau^C D^L < V^U$, and an investor holds m dollars of stock in the overvalued unleveraged firm, then he or she will have the uncertain income

$$Y^U = \left(\frac{m}{V^U}\right)(1-\tau^C)\bar{X}Z, \tag{7.37}$$

where m = dollars of stock.

Now it will be shown that this investor can improve his or her income by selling the common stock of unleveraged firms to exchange for Company 2's common stocks and bonds. If this investor sells m dollars of Company 1's common shares and buys $m[S^L/(S^L+(1-\tau^C)D^L)]$ dollars of Company 2's common stock and $m[(1-\tau^C)D^L/(S^L+(1-\tau^C)D^L)]$ dollars of Company 2's bonds, then the total return for this investor will be

$$Y^L = \left[\frac{m}{(S^L+(1-\tau^C)D^L)}\right][(1-\tau^C)\bar{X}Z]. \tag{7.38}$$

This will dominate the uncertain income Y^U as indicated in Eq. (7.37) if and only if

$$S^L+(1-\tau^C)D^L = S^L+D^L-\tau^C D^L = V^L-\tau^C D^L < V^U.$$

If this situation exists, then the investor can sell the common shares in the unleveraged company and purchase the shares (and bonds) of the leveraged company. If $V^L-\tau^C D > V^L$, then the investor who holds the leveraged company's stock can sell those shares and use homemade leverage to buy those of the unleveraged firm, to improve the uncertain income, as shown by Modigliani and Miller (1963). The important assumptions used to prove Proposition I with tax are: (1) There is no transaction cost; (2) homemade leverage is equal to corporate leverage; (3) corporate debt is riskless; and (4) there is no bankruptcy cost. Overall, Proposition I implies that there exists no optimal capital structure. If there are taxes, then the corporation will use either tax-free debt or 100% debt, depending upon whether there exists tax advantage or not. Shelton (1981) has contested Modigliani and Miller's assumption that homemade leverage is equal to corporate leverage. Shelton calls this equal access. Corporations have better access to the debt markets than do individuals. Individuals must pay a premium in the market because of the unevenness of information regarding their capacity and willingness to repay.

Kim (1978, 1982) showed that, in a perfect market with costly bankruptcies, debt capacity occurs at less than 100% debt financing and firms have optimal capital structures. These structures have debt financing at a level below their debt capacity, since firms are shareholder-wealth-maximizing entities. The market value of a firm increases at the lower levels of debt and it decreases at the higher levels of debt. The approach taken was within a theoretical framework based on capital market equilibrium. This optimal level of capital structure is reached when the present value of the tax advantages of debt usage just offsets the present value of bankruptcy costs.

Meanwhile Haugen and Senbet (1978) are of the opposite viewpoint. They state that "The irrelevance of capital structure in the absence of corporate taxes and the denomination of debt in the capital structure in the presence of corporate taxes can both be demonstrated under the framework of perfect markets and associated costless bankruptcy."

They show that the present value of bankruptcy costs is "highly unlikely" to significantly offset the tax benefits of debt usage. They also show that Kim's and others' proposition of an optimal capital structure with a ceiling on debt capacity is true only if: (1) capital market participants are irrational in not being able to profit from arbitrage and therefore eliminate it in equilibrium, or (2) the market environment is such that investors expect to buy or sell securities only at unfavorable terms.

This unequal access, combined with the fact that individuals in differing tax brackets benefit in varying ways from the corporate leverage, makes Modigliani and Miller's analysis become less acceptable. The implication is that individuals cannot recreate the same leverage position by buying the unlevered firm and issuing their own debt as by buying the stock of a levered firm. Modigliani and Miller's assumptions generally do not hold; it generally can be shown that there is an optimal amount of debt for a corporation. Barnea *et al.* (1981) [BHS] used market imperfections and agency costs to show that the optimal capital structure does exist for a firm, which is consistent with classical financial theory.[7] Hence, the choice of optimal debt is an important issue in financial analysis and planning.[8]

7.7. Possible Reasons for Optimal Capital Structure

Our theoretical discussion, earlier in this chapter, on optimal capital structure did not take us very far toward producing a useful prescription for practical management decision-making. We know that greater financial leverage can yield higher expected earnings per share, but that this is accompanied by greater risk. Modigliani and Miller argue that as a result of investors' ability to create homemade leverage, a firm's market value will not depend on its capital structure. However, introducing corporate taxes into their analysis provides a possible tax shield for investors. Consequently, it becomes advantageous to issue debt to increase the firm's market value, according to this model. However, according to Miller's irrelevance argument, the picture changes again when personal taxes enter the discussion. Because individual investors have differing marginal personal tax rates, the cost of aggregate corporate borrowing will be an increasing function of the total amount borrowed. Therefore, in the aggregate, there will be an equilibrium optimal capital structure for all firms. However, no individual firm is sufficiently powerful for its actions alone to disturb this market equilibrium cost of capital, so that for the individual firm, capital structure is again irrelevant to its market value.

Theoretical models such as those just discussed are valuable analytical tools. However, in general, theoretical development is possible only on the basis of assumptions that, at best, are idealizations of the real world and that may altogether neglect certain realities. In this section, we explore various factors not yet considered and see that such considerations may indeed suggest the existence of an optimal capital structure for the firm.

7.7.1. *The Traditional Approach of Optimal Capital Structure*

Durand (1952) proposed an approach to explain why there is an optimal capital structure for a firm. Called the *traditional approach,* it suggests that "moderate" amounts of debt do not noticeably increase the risks to either the debtholders or the equityholders. Hence, both cost of debt (i) and cost of equity (r_E) are relatively constant up to some point. However, beyond some critical amount of debt used, both i and r_E increase. These increases in both the cost of debt and equity begin to offset the decrease in the average cost of capital because of cheaper debt. Therefore, the average cost of capital (r_A), as indicated in Equation (7.20), initially falls and then increases. This allows for a minimum value for the average cost of capital function. If the average cost of capital is at the minimum, then the firm's value

$$V = \frac{(1 - \tau_c)\text{EBIT}}{r_A},$$

is maximized. This implies that there is an optimal capital structure for the firm.

7.7.2. *Bankruptcy Costs*

Earlier in this chapter, we saw in the M&M analysis that in the presence of corporate taxes, the value of the levered firm (V_L) exceeds the value of the otherwise comparable unlevered firm (V_U). The difference can be viewed as an increment to present value derived from the tax shelter ($\tau_c B$). Therefore, we can write

$$V_L = V_U + \tau_c B. \tag{7.39}$$

One issue not considered in deriving this result is the possibility of corporate bankruptcy. Obligations to bondholders constitute a first claim on a company's assets. However, under U.S. law, stockholders, who are the owners of public companies, have only limited liability. Their personal assets, other than holdings in the firm, are protected from the claims of bondholders. If operating performance is sufficiently poor, stockholders can avoid obligations to bondholders through the firm's declaring bankruptcy. Essentially, bankruptcy turns over the firm to its debtholders. Bankruptcy proceedings can be very costly. Heavy legal fees must be paid, assets must often be sold at "bargain basement" prices, frequently following lengthy and expensive disputes among competing claimants. Taken together, these bankruptcy costs may be far from negligible, and the possibility of these costs being incurred must be considered in assessing a firm's market value.

On whom do bankruptcy costs fall? After bankruptcy, the firm belongs to its creditors, who must therefore bear these costs. However, purchasers of corporate bonds will be aware of this and will charge a higher price — that is, demand a higher interest rate — for debt. This, in turn, reduces the amount of earnings available for distribution to stockholders, reducing the value of shares. Hence, before bankruptcy, costs are carried by stockholders as reductions in the value of their equity holdings.

How much does the possibility of bankruptcy lower the firm's value? Two factors must be considered: (1) the costs incurred in the event of bankruptcy and (2) the likelihood, or probability, of bankruptcy occurring. For example, suppose that bankruptcy costs are estimated at \$5 million, and it is believed that there is one chance in ten of bankruptcy occurring. Then,

$$\begin{aligned}&\text{Expected bankruptcy cost}\\&\quad= \text{(probability of bankruptcy) (bankruptcy cost)}\\&\quad= (0.1)(5{,}000{,}000)\\&\quad= \$500{,}000.\end{aligned}$$

All other things equal, the greater the amount of debt a firm has, the more likely it will fail to meet its obligations and be driven to bankruptcy. Therefore, seeing this risk, bondholders will demand higher rates of interest the larger the debt, as suggested in Example 7.1. Thus, expected bankruptcy cost is an increasing function of the proportion of debt in a firm's capital structure.

Taking into account the possibility of bankruptcy and its effect on firm value, we can augment Eq. (7.9) as follows:

$$V_L = V_U + \tau_c B - \text{ present value of bankruptcy costs.} \tag{7.40}$$

The higher the level of debt, the greater the present value of the tax shield. As we saw in Eq. (7.9), the effect is linear, in the sense that the value of the tax shield is a constant multiple τ_c (the corporate tax rate) of the debt value. However, as Eq. (7.23) indicates, we must now subtract the present value of bankruptcy cost. This, too, is an increasing function of the debt level, reflecting the increase in the probability of bankruptcy that attaches to increasing debt levels.

We have seen that increasing debt yields a positive increment to firm value through the tax shield and a negative increment through bankruptcy costs. If these factors operate in conjunction, as illustrated in Fig. 7.4, then an optimal capital structure results. We see for the unlevered firm, zero values for the tax shield and bankruptcy costs. Each increases with the level

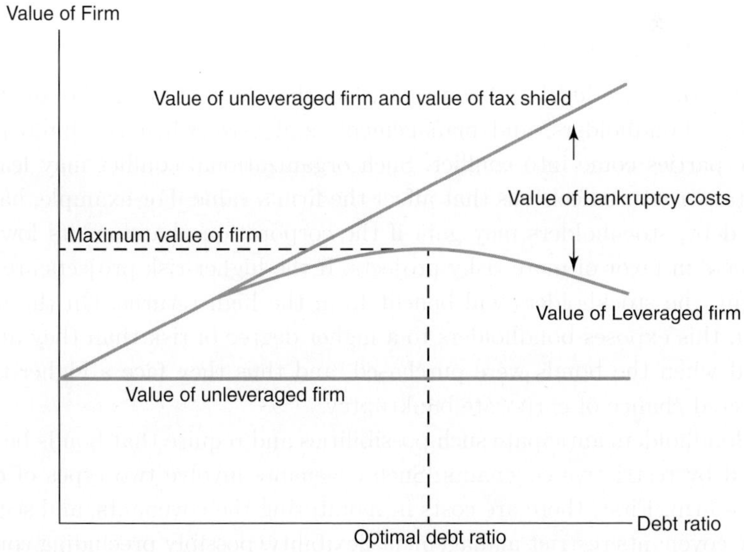

Fig. 7.4. Possibility of optimal debt ratio when allowing for present value of bankruptcy costs.

of debt issued, the net effect being a relationship between firm value and debt level that shows a maximum value for a debt level well below 100% of total value.

Myers (1984) called the optimal capital structure discussed in this section the *static trade-off theory*. He also proposed a *pecking-order theory* to contrast to the static trade-off theory. The pecking-order theory is based on the following:

1. Firms prefer internal finance.
2. Firms adapt their target dividend payout ratio to investment opportunities. (The target dividend payout ratio is discussed in Chapter 12.)
3. If internally generated cash flows are less than investment outlays, the firm first draws down its cash balance or marketable securities portfolio.
4. If external financing is required, the firm issues the safest security first. That is, the firm first issues debt, then hybrid securities such as convertible bonds, then equity as a last resort.

Looking at the behavior of firms in the marketplace, investment outlays are predominantly financed by debt issues and internally generated funds. New stock issues play a relatively small and infrequent part in raising new capital. This indicates that management follows a pecking-order approach.

7.7.3. *Agency Costs*

Agency costs are legal and contract costs that protect the rights of stockholders, bondholders, and management, and arise when the interests of these parties come into conflict. Such organizational conflict may lead to capital structure decisions that affect the firm's value. For example, having sold debt, stockholders may gain if the corporation abandons its low-risk projects in favor of more risky projects. If the higher-risk projects are successful, the stockholders will benefit from the high returns. On the other hand, this exposes bondholders to a higher degree of risk than they anticipated when the bonds were purchased, and thus they face a higher-than-expected chance of corporate bankruptcy.

Bondholders anticipate such possibilities and require that bonds be protected by restrictive covenants. Such covenants involve two types of costs to the firm. First, there are costs in monitoring the covenants, and second, these covenants restrict management flexibility, possibly precluding courses of action that would raise the firm's market value. These costs are borne by stockholders, resulting in a lower market value for equity.

In general, we might expect that agency costs of this sort will be greater the higher the debt. If there is little debt, bondholders will consider their investments relatively secure and demand only modest, fairly inexpensive protection of their interest. At higher debt levels, more stringent assurances will be required. Thus, agency costs affect firm value in much the same way as bankruptcy costs. The greater the debt, the greater the agency cost against firm value. This is illustrated in Fig. 7.5, which extends Fig. 7.4 by allowing for agency cost. At any level of debt above 0, agency cost causes a decrease in market value; the greater the debt level, the larger the agency cost factor. Hence, agency cost yields a lower optimal amount of debt in the capital structure than would otherwise prevail.

How does our discussion of bankruptcy and agency costs square with Miller's irrelevance argument? Under Miller's thesis, the competitive market will drive up the cost of debt to the point where it balances the gain in market value derived from issuing debt. However, for the individual firm, the concept of a single price for debt may be an oversimplification. Rather, bankruptcy and agency costs will raise the price of debt as the level of debt increases. Therefore, there is indeed the possibility of an optimal capital structure.

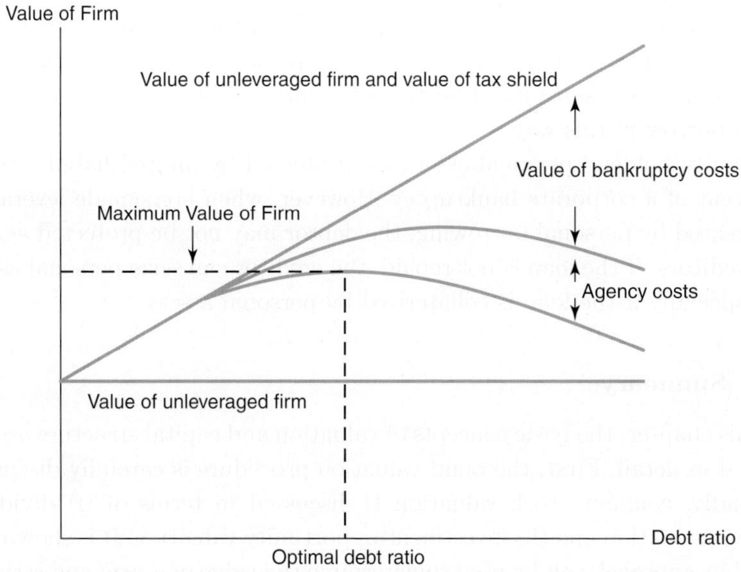

Fig. 7.5. Possibility of optimal debt ratio when allowing for present value of bankruptcy and agency costs.

7.7.4. *Imperfect Markets*

The theoretical analysis of Modigliani and Miller is based on assumptions often characterized as perfect capital market behavior. In evaluating M&M's conclusions on the irrelevance of capital structure, it is natural to look for real-world departures from these assumptions. As we have seen, one important source of imperfection arises if, as a result of bankruptcy costs and agency costs, a firm must pay increasingly higher interest rates the greater the proportion of debt in its capital structure. When this negative impact of debt on firm value is taken in conjunction with the positive impact of the tax shield derived from corporate taxation, there is the possibility of an optimal capital structure.

These are the most common sources of market imperfections. Others come to mind when we recall the requirement, needed to establish the Modigliani and Miller proposition, that investors can substitute homemade leverage for corporate financial leverage. However, three factors that suggest that the two may not be perfect substitutes:

1. In practice, individuals and corporations may face different interest rates for loans. Generally, larger corporations can borrow funds at lower rates than individuals can obtain for personal loans.
2. Institutional factors may stand in the way of the creation of homemade leverage. For example, life insurance companies and pension funds, which account for a substantial portion of equity holdings, are not permitted to borrow in this way.
3. Equity holders' personal assets are protected by limited liability in the event of a corporate bankruptcy. However, when homemade leverage is created by personal borrowing, the debtor may not be protected against creditors. If the loan is not repaid, the creditor can seize personal assets, especially if the loan is collaterized by personal assets.

7.8. Summary

In this chapter, the basic concepts of valuation and capital structure are discussed in detail. First, the bond-valuation procedure is carefully discussed. Secondly, common-stock valuation is discussed in terms of (i) dividend-stream valuation and (ii) investment-opportunity valuation. It is shown that the first approach can be used to determine the value of a firm and estimate the cost of capital. The second method has decomposed the market value of a firm into two components, i.e., perpetual value and the value associated with growth opportunity. The criteria for undertaking the growth opportunity are also developed.

An overall view on the optimal capital structure has been discussed in accordance with classical, new classical, and some modern finance theories. Modigliani and Miller's Proposition I with and without tax has been reviewed in detail. It is argued that Proposition I indicates that a firm should use either no debt or 100% debt. In other words, there exists no optimal capital structure for a firm. However, both classical and some of the modern theories demonstrate that there exists an optimal capital structure for a firm. In summary, the results of valuation and optimal capital structure will be useful for financial planning and forecasting.

The applications of the CAPM, the arbitrage pricing model, and option-pricing theory to the estimation of market value and the determination of optimal capital for a firm will be discussed in the following chapters.

Following a surveyed paper by Graham and Harvey (2001), there is some support for the pecking-order and trade-off capital structure hypotheses but little evidence that executives focus on asset substitution, asymmetric information, transaction costs, free cash flows, or personal taxes.

Notes

1. The proof of Eq. (7.6c) is as follows. We rewrite Eq. (7.6b) as:

$$P_0 = d_0 \left[\sum_{t=1}^{\infty} \frac{(1+g_n)^t}{(1+k)^t} \right]; \tag{1}$$

multiplying both sides of Eq. (1) by $(1+k)/(1+g_n)$, we have

$$\left[\frac{(1+k)}{(1+g_n)} - 1 \right] P_0 = d_0 \left[1 + \sum_{t=1}^{\infty} \frac{(1+g_n)^{t-1}}{(1+k)^{t-1}} \right]. \tag{2}$$

Subtracting Eq. (1) from Eq. (2), we obtain:

$$\left[\frac{(1+k)}{(1+g_n)} - 1 \right] P_0 = d_0. \tag{3}$$

Assuming $k > g_n$, Eq. (3) implies that

$$P_0 = d_0 \left[\frac{1+g_n}{k-g_n} \right] = \frac{d_1}{k-g_n}.$$

In Appendix 7.C, we have proposed a more detailed derivation of this model.

2. Impacts of inflation on capital-budgeting decisions will be explored in Chapter 13.
3. Equation (7.9) can be derived by the following steps:

Step 1. Determine the present value of the perpetual stream of profit generated from this investment in point t, I_t,

$$\sum_{t=1}^{\infty} \frac{I_t r}{(1+k)^t} = \frac{I_t r}{k}. \tag{1}$$

Step 2. Let $I_t = bX_t$ and write I_t as

$$\begin{aligned} I_t = bX_t &= X_{t-1} + rI_{t-1} \\ &= bX_{t-1}(1+br) \\ &= bX_0(1+br)^t. \end{aligned} \tag{2}$$

Step 3. Determine the present value of future "good will associated with all future investment opportunities:

$$\sum_{t=1}^{\infty} \frac{I_t(r-k)}{(1+k)^t} = \sum_{t=0}^{\infty} \frac{bX_0(1+br)^t(r-k)/k}{(1+k)^{t+1}}. \tag{3}$$

Step 4. Add the present value of the (uniform perpetual) earnings X_0 on the asset currently held to Eq. (3); we then have

$$\begin{aligned} V_0 &= \frac{X_0}{k}\left[1 + \frac{b(r-k)}{(1+k)} X \sum_{t=0}^{\infty} \frac{(1+br)^t}{(1+k)}\right] \\ &= \frac{X_0}{k}\left[1 + \frac{b(r-k)}{k-br}\right]. \end{aligned}$$

4. For the derivation of DOL, DFL, and CLE can be found in Appendix 7.B.
5. In this section, we assume that the debts issued by the firms are riskless. If the debt is risky, Resek (1970) argued that the arbitrage process discussed in this section generally does not hold. Most recently, Hellwig (1981) showed that two conditions for the Modigliani and Miller theorem under the risky debt case to be true are either (1) short sales of all securities are permitted, or (ii) securities issued by individuals as well as securities issued by firms serve as collateral.

6. Errunza and Senbet (1981) have generalized Modigliani and Miller's (1963) tax-adjusted domestic-firm valuation to binational-firm valuation as:

$$V^L = (V^U + \tau^d D) + \alpha_f V^U \left(\frac{\tau^d - \tau^f}{1 - \tau^d}\right) + \theta_f D(\tau^f - \tau^d), \qquad (7.32a)$$

where

V^L = Value of leveraged binational firm,
τ^d, τ^f = Proportional domestic and foreign corporate tax, respectively,
D = Market value of debt,
$V^U + \tau^d D$ = Value of the levered domestic firm,
α_f = Portion of income attributable to foreign investment,
$\theta_f D$ = Value of foreign borrowing.

7. Protective covenants can be thought of as a way for creditors to monitor the actions of stockholders, to preclude the erosion in value of their claims; monitoring requires the expenditure of resources, and the costs involved are one form of agency cost.
8. By introducing the existence of non-debt tax shields (i.e., depreciation and investment tax credit), DeAngelo and Masulis show that interior optimal debt levels which are unique to each firm obtain in equilibrium.

Problem Set

1. Discuss the relationships between opportunity costs, required rate-of-return, and cost of capital. Why are these concepts needed for financial planning and analysis?
2. Define the following terms:
   (a) EPS, DPS, and PPS.
   (b) DOL, DFL, and CLE.
   (c) M&M proposition I with tax.
   (d) Miller's proposition.
   (e) Agency cost.
   (f) Pecking order theory.
3. Discuss the relationship between term, perpetuity, discount, and convertible bonds. How can the theoretical values of these bonds be determined?
4. Discuss how optimal capital structure can be theoretically determined.

5. What are the four alternative methods to common-stock valuation? Compare the theoretical relationship between the stream-of-dividends approach and the investment-opportunity approach.
6. Define the concepts: (a) Degree of Operating Leverage; (b) Degree of Financial Leverage, and (c) the combined effect of the two. How can these concepts be used to perform financial analysis?
7. Discuss Modigliani and Miller's three propositions with and without taxes. How can Proposition I (without-tax case) be proved? How does Miller (1977) generalize Proposition I by incorporating personal taxes?
8. Does there exist any optimal capital structure for a firm? Please justify your answers, theoretically and empirically.
9. Company XYZ wants to double its assets in anticipation of increasing market demand. New financing alternatives are:

   (i) Common Stock to net \$50 a share (price/earnings ratio 25 times).
   (ii) Straight 8% debt (price/earnings ratio 20 times).

Current Balance Sheet

	⋮	Debt (6%)	\$10,000
		Common Stock (\$10 par)	30,000
	⋮	Surplus	10,000
Total Assets	\$50,000	Total Claims	\$50,000

   (iii) In addition, assume that EPS = \$6, total fixed cost = \$5,000, and the tax rate is 50%. Please answer the following questions.
      (a) What are the expected EPS for Alternative (i) and the expected EPS for Alternative (ii)?
      (b) What are the expected market prices for both Alternative (i) and Alternative (ii)?
      (c) What is the current degree of financial leverage for this company?

10. Here are some items from the income statement and balance sheet of ABC Company:

    Value of assets = \$2,000 million
    Value of liabilities = \$1,200 million
    Number of shares outstanding = 20 million

Operating income = \$800 million
Corporate tax rate = 40%
Interest paid on debt = \$120 million

(a) Find the effective interest rate on debt.
(b) Find net income and EPS.
(c) Find the rate-of-return on assets.

11. Use the EPS and DPS data of IBM during 2010–2015 to determine the theoretical value of the price of IBM's stocks in terms of the (i) dividend-stream method and (ii) growth-opportunity method.
12. You are going to buy either Company A's stock or Company B's stock. If you are risk-average and your only concern is return and risk of EPS, which company would you choose under the following conditions:

	Company A	Company B
Expected return on assets (r)	10%	11%
Var (r)	0.3%	0.2%
Price per share	\$100	\$100
Debt–equity ratio	$\frac{1}{3}$	$\frac{2}{3}$
Interest rate on debt	7%	11%
Corporate tax rate	34%	34%

13. Stocks in the utility industry currently provide an expected rate-of-return of 15%. A large utility company ABC will pay a year-end dividend of \$3 per share. Assume that the stock is selling \$40 per share.

    (a) What must be the market expectation of the growth rate of ABC dividend?
    (b) If dividend growth forecasts for ABC are revised downward to 3% per year, what will happen to the price of ABC stock? What will qualitatively happen to the company's price–earnings ratio?

14. XYZ Corp. has an ROE of 15% and a retention rate of 45%. If the coming year's earnings are expected to be \$3 per share, at what price will the stock sell? Assume that the market capitalization rate is 14%.

15. The market consensus is that company ABC has an ROE = 12%, has a beta of 1.1, and plans to maintain indefinitely its traditional retention rate of 2/3. This year's earnings were \$2 per share. The annual dividend was just paid. The consensus estimate of the coming year's market return is 12%. Assume that the T-bill currently offers a 5% return.

    (a) What is the price at which ABC stock should sell?
    (b) Please calculate the P/E ratio.
    (c) Please calculate the present value of growth opportunities.
    (d) Assume that your financial advisor tells you that company ABC will announce momentarily that it will immediately reduce its retention rate to 1/3. Please calculate the intrinsic value of the stock.

16. If the expected return of the market portfolio is 17% and a stock with a beta of 1.0 pays a dividend yield of 6%, what must the market believe is the expected rate of price appreciation on that stock?
17. The company XYZ's dividends per share are expected to grow indefinitely by 7% per year.

    (a) If this year's year-end dividend is \$10 and the market capitalization rate is 12% per year, what must the current stock price be according to the DDM?
    (b) If the expected earning per share is \$15, what is the implied value of the ROE on future investment opportunities?
    (c) How much is the market paying per share for growth opportunities (i.e., for an ROE on future investments that exceeds the market capitalization rate)?

18. The stock of the company DEF is currently selling for \$14 per share. Earning per share in the coming year is expected to be \$3.5. The company has a policy of paying out 60% of its earnings each year in dividends and the rest is reinvested in projects that earn a 25% rate-of-return per year. Assume that the current market price reflects its fundamental value as computed using the constant-growth DDM. What rate-of-return do company DEF's investor require?
19. Assume that the stock of AAA Corporation has a beta coefficient of 1.5. Further, the risk free rate-of-return is 6% and the expected rate-of-return on the market portfolio is 12%. AAA Corporation pays out 50% of its earning in dividends and the latest earning announced were \$10 per share. Dividends were just paid and are expected to be paid

annually. The market consensus is that AAA Corporation will earn an ROE of 25% per year on all reinvested earnings forever.

(a) Please calculate the intrinsic value of AAA Corporation stock.
(b) If the market price of a share is currently $200 and you expect the market price to be equal to the intrinsic value 1 year from now, please calculate the expected 1-year holding period return of AAA stock.

20. BBB Corporation pays no cash dividends currently and is not expected to for the next 5 years. Its latest EPS was $8, all of which was reinvested in the company. The company's expected ROE for the next 5 years is 20% per year, and during this time it is expected to continue to reinvest all of its earnings. Starting 6 years from now the company's ROE on new investment is expected to fall to 6% and the company is expected to start paying out 50% of its earnings in cash dividends which it will continue to do forever after. BBB's market capitalization rate is 14% per year. What is the intrinsic value of BBB stock?
21. Company CCC just paid a dividend of $1.2 per share. The dividend is expected to grow at a rate of 20% per year for the next 3 years and then level off to 3% per year forever. Assume the market capitalization rate is 20% per year.

(a) What is the estimate of the intrinsic value of a share of stock?
(b) If the market price is equal to the intrinsic value of the share, what is the expected dividend yield?
(c) What is the price expected to be 1 year from now?

22. Company DDD pays no cash dividends currently and is not expected to for the next 4 years. Its most recent EPS was $4, all of which was reinvested in the company. The firm's expected ROE for the next 3 years is 15% per year, during which time it is expected to continue to reinvest all of its earnings. Starting 4 years from now, the firm's ROE on new investment is expected to fall to 10% per year. The firm is also expected to distribute 50% of its earnings per year to the shareholders starting 4 years from now. Assume that the market capitalization is 15% per year.

(a) What is the estimate of the intrinsic value per share?
(b) What can be expected to happen to its price over the next year if the current market price is equal to its intrinsic value?

23. Calculate the degree of operating leverage, the degree of financial leverage, and the total leverage of TTT company, using the following items:

Quantity sold = 20,000
Price per unit = \$10
Variable cost per unit = \$7
Fixed cost = \$30,000
Interest payments = \$10,000

24. The Moonglow Company has total assets of \$100 million. Given the following B/A ratios and interest rates on debt, calculate Moonglow's rate-of-return on equity for each B/A ratio. (Assume that operations income is \$25 million, and corporate tax rate is 50%.)

B/A Ratio	Interest Rate
0%	—
10%	10%
30%	12%
50%	15%

25. Consider the following items for a fishing business:

Total market value of a firm = \$50,000
Value of debt = \$20,000
Rates-of-return on equity = 12%
Interest payment = \$2,000
Corporate tax rate = 34%

a. Find the value of stockholder's equity.
b. Find the weighted average cost of capital (WACC).
c. Find the net income.
d. If the firm issues more debt, what is the effects on WACC?

26. ABC Company wants to double its assets because of increased market demand. New financing alternatives are for common stock to net \$15

a share or straight debt of 10%. The current balance sheet is as follows:

		Current Balance Sheet	
		Debt (8%)	\$10,000
		Common stock (\$10 par)	15,000
		Retained earnings	5,000
Total assets	\$30,000	Total claims	\$30,000

EPS = \$5
Total fixed cost = \$5,000
Corporate tax rate = 34%

a. Calculate current EBIT.
b. Find expected EPS for the two alternatives.
c. Calculate DFL and DOL.

27. Financial records for ABC Company include the following:

Anticipated sales = \$600,000
Degree of financial leverage = $\frac{4}{3}$
Variable cost = \$300,000
Combined leverage effect = 2
Quantity sold = 100,000
Profit margin = 10%
Total debt = \$200,000
Leverage ratio = $\frac{1}{2}$
Common stock outstanding = 10,000 shares
Current price per share = \$50
Pay-out ratio = $\frac{1}{3}$
IRR = 12%

Find the following:

a. Total interest payment.
b. Total fixed cost.
c. Degree of operating leverage.
d. Break-even quantity.
e. EAIT (Earnings After Interest and Taxes).

f. Corporate tax payment.
g. Return on net worth.
h. Return on total assets.
i. EPS.
j. P/E ratio for common stock.
k. Retention rate.
l. Growth rate for common stock.
m. Required rate-of-return.

28. Here is ABC Company's next year's prediction:

Economy	Probability	ROA (%)	Debt	Equity	Tax Rate (%)	Interest Rate (%)
State 1	0.1	12	\$500	\$1,000	40	8
State 2	0.5	14	\$500	\$1,000	40	8
State 3	0.4	15	\$500	\$1,000	40	8

a. Calculate next year's expected after-tax return on equity.
b. How much is the after-tax return on equity?
c. Assume the debt prediction was wrong. Instead, debt will increase to \$1,000 next year, answer Questions a and b.
d. Compare your results under each scenario. How sensitive are the results to errors in the forecasted level of debts?

29. Assume that you are in Miller and Modigliani's world of no corporate taxes with perfect capital markets. There are two companies L and U that have identical expected EBIT (net operating income) of \$10,000. Assume that the value of the shares of the levered company L is \$5,000 and the value of L's debt is \$5,000 which carries a 10% interest rate. The value of the shares of the unlevered company is \$9,000. If an investor currently owns 1% of the shares of the levered firm, numerically demonstrate the arbitrage transactions that would take place to drive the market value of L to equal that of U.
30. Assume that the world is that of Miller and Modigliani in which corporate taxes exist, but otherwise all of the prior assumptions of the no tax case hold. Two firms X and Y have the same expected EBIT of \$10,000. However, Firm X is unlevered and the total market value of

its stock is \$9,500. Firm Y is levered with debt valued at \$5,000. The corporate tax rate is 40%. The market is in equilibrium.

a. Find the value of the levered firm.
b. Find the value of the levered firm's stock.

31. How would your answer to the previous question change if we expand the world and allow for a personal tax rate on stock income of 30% and a personal tax rate on debt income of 30%?
32. Assume that the value of a levered firm's stock is \$4,000 and that of an unlevered firm is \$9,000. Also assume that the value of the debt of the levered firm is \$3,000 with a 10% interest rate. The corporate tax rate is 40% and all other taxes are non-existent. Explain the arbitrage process that will take place to drive the values of the two firms back into equilibrium if the investor owns 2% of the unlevered firm at the present time.
33. You are supplied with the following income statement for L&S, Ltd. for last year:

Sales	\$30,000
Variable costs	10,000
Fixed operating costs	5,000
EBIT	\$15,000
Interest expense	7,000
Earnings before taxes	\$8,000
Taxes (40%)	3,200
Net income	\$4,800

a. Find the degree of operating leverage for the above level of sales and interpret its meaning.
b. Find the degree of financial leverage and interpret its meaning.
c. Find the degree of combined leverage and interpret its meaning.
d. If L&S pays preferred dividends of \$1,200 per year, what is its degree of financial leverage and its degree of combined leverage? (*Note*: To put preferred dividends on a before-tax basis so that they are comparable to interest, preferred dividends must be divided by (1-corporate tax rate)).

34. Fritzer, Inc. is trying to estimate its cost of equity by using a proxy company that has a beta of 1.2. The proxy has a 40% tax rate and B/S ratio of 0.8. Fritzer's tax rate is 30%. The risk-free rate of interest is 6% and the expected return on the market is 14%.

    a. If Fritzer uses no debt financing, what is its cost of equity?
    b. If Fritzer has a B/S ratio of 1.00 and before-tax cost of debt of 10%, find its cost of equity and its overall cost of capital.

35. Danco is a levered company; however, if it were unlevered the value of its stock based on operating income alone would be $10,000. The market value of its debt is $6,000, and the interest rate on debt is 10%. Its corporate tax rate is 40%, the personal tax rate on debt income is 30%, and the personal tax rate on stock income is 25%. The company's debt to equity ratio is 3,00. In the event of bankruptcy it is estimated that the associated costs will be $10,000 and the probability of bankruptcy is 0.5. Find the value of Danco.

Appendix 7.A. Convertible Security Valuation Theory

Convertible bonds are long-term debt securities that can be converted into a specified number of shares of common stock at the option of the bond-holder. The ratio of exchange can be expressed either in terms of a conversion ratio (CR), which is simply the number of shares into which one bond is convertible — for example, 20 shares per bond — or in terms of a CP, which is equal to the bond's face value (FV) divided by the CR.

$$\mathrm{CP} = \frac{\mathrm{FV}}{\mathrm{CR}}. \tag{7.A.1}$$

With a face value of $1,000 and a CR of 20, the CP is $1,000/20 or $50.

Often these basic conversion terms change over the life of the convertible-bond issue. For example, the conversion price may increase in discrete stages — that is, $50 for the first 5 years, $55 for the next 5 years, and so on. The reason the issuer might employ such a strategy is to shorten the time before conversion if the common-stock price increased enough to make conversion otherwise likely.

The conversion price should not be confused with the bond's conversion value (CV), the total market value of the bond in terms of the stock into which it is convertible. The CV can be computed by multiplying the CR by the price of the firm's common stock, P_S:

$$\text{CV} = (\text{CR})(P_S). \tag{7.A.2}$$

For the current example, if the price of the stock is \$40 per share, the conversion value would be (20)(\$40) = \$800. Because it would otherwise cause arbitrage opportunities, the convertible bond will not sell in the market for less than its CV.

The convertible bond also provides the investor with a fixed return in the form of its coupon payments. The present value of these periodic coupons (usually paid semiannually, as for regular non-convertible bonds) plus the present value of the face value to be paid at maturity will equal what is called the investment value (IV) of the convertible bond:

$$\text{IV} = \sum_{t=1}^{n} \frac{I}{(1+k)^t} + \frac{FV}{(1+k)^n}, \tag{7.A.3}$$

where

FV = the face value of the bond;
I = the periodic coupon payment;
k = the investor's required rate-of-return; and
n = the number of periods until the maturity of the issue.

Because a convertible bond is effectively a hybrid security with some of the features of bonds and some of common stock, its value both as a bond and as a common stock must be considered in order to value it. When the conversion value exceeds the investment value, the convertible-bond price (P_{CV}) is related primarily to the CV; and when the conversion value is less than the investment value, P_{CV} is related primarily to the investment value. Figure 7.A.1 provides further illustration.

A convertible bond will ordinarily sell at a premium over the investment value, primarily because of the conversion option, and will sell at a premium above the conversion value because of the floor established by its investment value. This IV floor is not constant over time, but will actually vary with interest-rate movements and perceived changes in the financial risk of the issuing company. For example, if interest rates increase or the firm's financial risk increases (possibly accompanied by a lower bond rating) the floor can decrease, thus providing less protection to the convertible bondholder. If the face value of the convertible is higher than the IV (as it ordinarily would be at the time of issue because of the bond's conversion

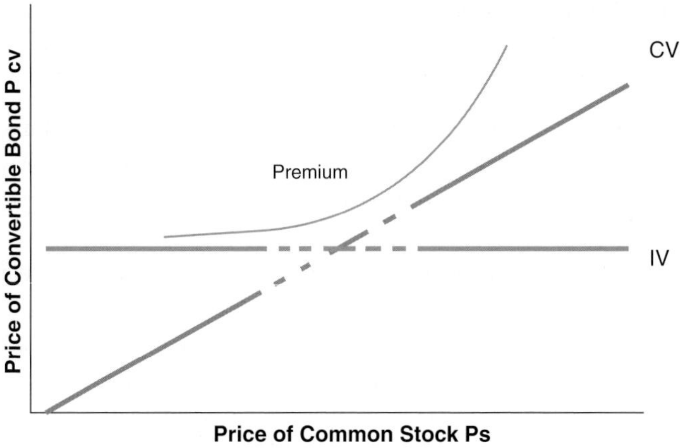

Fig. 7.A.1. IV, CV, and the price of a convertible bond.

potential), the investment value will increase over time, while other things are held constant. This is true because the ultimate price is always the face value at maturity. The size of the premiums reflected in the convertible-bond's price would be larger the more volatile the underlying stock price is if the bond had a significant conversion potential.

As indicated above, the convertible bond actually has two types of premiums, the premium over IV and the premium over CV. At relatively common-stock prices, the value of the investment floor becomes negligible and the IP becomes insignificant: the bond is selling at price very close to its CV. Another factor causing P_{CV} to closely approximate CV at high stock prices is that if the conversion value exceeded the call price of the bond, the firm could exercise its call option and effectively force conversion. Upon conversion, the convertible bond would be worth only its conversion value. If, on the other hand, the convertible-bond price were close to the investment value, it would be an indication that the conversion potential of the bond is negligible.

The main reason for convertible-bond premium is the hybrid nature of the security. It offers downside protection against stock-price declines at the same time that it provides upside price-appreciation potential similar to straight common-stock investment. However, other factors also influence the size of the premiums to some extent. For example, transaction costs charged for convertible-bond purchases are ordinarily lower than for common-stock purchases. This should increase the convertible-bond premiums, other things held constant. Another factor that might have an upward influence is the fact that certain regulated financial institutions are more restricted in their common-stock investment than in their purchase of convertible bonds (see Brigham, 1966). An additional factor taken into account by convertible-bond investors is the comparison of the common-stock dividend yield (d/P_S) and the current yield (I/P_{CV}) of the convertible bond. The greater the common stock's dividend yield is relative to the convertible bond's interest yield, the less attractive the convertible and the lower the premiums on it.

With the definitions of investment value, conversion value, and the premiums associated with them in hand, it is possible to take a more rigorous approach to the convertible bonds. Using the simplifying assumptions of a single-period investment horizon and a constant term structure of interest rates over that horizon, convertible bonds can be separated into two categories: (1) those for which IV > CV and (2) those for which CV > IV.

For convertible bonds in which IV > CV, investors set prices for these securities primarily for their bond value and only secondarily because of their conversion potential. The single-period cash flows could be expressed as the sum of the face value (FV), the coupon payment (I), and the expected gain upon conversion. This last flow is a function of the stock price per share in state i at period 1 (P_{si1}). For all values of P_{si1} greater than the corresponding values of IV/CR:

$$\text{Expected conversion profit} = \sum_{i=1}^{m}[(P_{si1})(\text{CR}) - \text{IV}_{i1}]\left[\prod_{i1}\right], \tag{7.A.4}$$

where

$$(P_{si1})(\text{CR}) = \text{CV}_1$$

$$\prod_{i1} = \text{the probability of occurrence for } P_s \text{ values at time } i.$$

Therefore:

$$\text{Expected CV} = \text{FV}_1 + I_1 + \sum_{i=1}^{m}[(P_{si1})(\text{CR}) - \text{IV}_{i1}]\left[\prod_{i1}\right]. \tag{7.A.5}$$

Using the k_d, the required rate-of-return for straight debt investments, and k_s, the required rate-of-return for straight common-stock investments, the value of the debt-denominated convertible bond (IV > CV) can be expressed as follows:

$$P_{CVD} = \frac{\text{FV}_1 + I_1}{(1 + k_d)} + \frac{\sum_{i=1}^{m} [(P_{si1})(\text{CR}) - \text{IV}_{i1}] \left[\prod_{i1}\right]}{(1 + k_s)}. \quad (7.A.6)$$

Since $\text{FV}_1 + I_1/(1 + k_d)$ is equal to IV_0, Eq. (7.A.6) can be written as:

$$P_{CVD} = \text{IV}_0 + \frac{\sum_{i=1}^{m} [(P_{si1})(\text{CR}) - \text{IV}_1] \left[\prod_{i1}\right]}{(1 + k_s)}. \quad (7.A.7)$$

The price of a convertible bond with IV > CV is equal to its current investment value and the present value of the expected conversion profit. Since $P_{\text{CVD}} - \text{IV}$ is equal to the current premium over investment value, IP,

$$\text{IP} = \frac{\sum_{i=1}^{m} [(P_{si1})(\text{CR}) - \text{IV}_{i1}] \left[\prod_{i,1}\right]}{(1 + k_s)}. \quad (7.A.8)$$

That is, IP is equal to the present value of the expected conversion profit.

For convertible bonds in which CV > IV, investors set prices for these securities primarily for their conversion potential and secondarily for their IV floor protection. This floor protection is also a function of the common-stock price probability distribution. For all values of P_{si1} larger than or equal to the corresponding value of IV_1/CR:

$$\text{Expected floor protection} = \sum_{i=1}^{m} [\text{IV}_{i1} - (P_{si1})(\text{CR})] \left[\prod_{i1}\right]. \quad (7.A.9)$$

Therefore:

$$\text{Expected } CV_1 = (\text{CR})\,[E(P_{si1})] + I_1 + \sum_{i-1}^{m} [\text{IV}_{i1} - (P_{si1})(CR)] \left[\prod_{i1}\right]. \quad (57.A.10)$$

Discounting at the appropriate rates, the value of the stock-denominated convertible bond (CV > IV) can be expressed as:

$$P_{CVS} = \frac{(\text{CR})[E(P_{si1})] + \sum_{i=1}^{m} [\text{IV}_{i1} - (P_{si1})(\text{CR})] \left[\prod_{i1}\right]}{(1 + K_s)} + \frac{I}{(1 + k_d)}. \quad (7.A.11)$$

Since the current price of common stock, P_{s0}, can be written in terms of the present value of the sum of the expected period-1 price P_1 and the expected period-1 dividends d:

$$P_0 = \frac{E(P_1) + E(d_1)}{(1 + k_s)}, \qquad (7.A.12)$$

it can also be shown that

$$\frac{(\text{CR})[F(P_{oi1})]}{(1 + k_s)} = (\text{CR})(P_0) - \frac{(\text{CR})[E(d_1)]}{(1 + k_s)}. \qquad (7.A.13)$$

Substituting into Eq. (7.A.11):

$$P_{\text{CVS}} = (\text{CR})(P_0) + \frac{I}{(1 + k_d)} - \frac{E(d_1)(\text{CR})}{(1 + k_s)} + \frac{\sum_{i=1}^{m} \text{IV}_1 - [(\text{CR})(P_{si1})]\left[\prod_{i1}\right]}{(1 + k_s)}. \qquad (7.A.14)$$

Thus, with $(\text{CR})(P_0) = \text{CV}_0$:

$$P_{\text{CVS}} = \text{CV}_0 + \left\{\frac{I_1}{(1 + k_d)} - \frac{E(d_1)(\text{CR})}{(1 + k_s)}\right\} + \frac{\sum_{i=1}^{m} \text{IV}_{i1} - (\text{CR})(P_{si1})\left[\prod_{i1}\right]}{(1 + k_s)}. \qquad (7.A.15)$$

The price of a convertible bond with CV > IV is then equal to the sum of its current conversion value, the present value of the difference between the coupon interest payments on the bond and the expected dividend that would be paid upon conversion, and the present value of the expected floor protection.

Since $P_{CVS} - \text{CV}$ is equal to the current premium over investment value, CP:

$$\text{CP} = \left\{\frac{I_1}{(1 + k_d)} - \frac{E(d_1)(\text{R})}{(1 + k_s)}\right\}^t + \frac{\sum_{i=1}^{m} \text{IV}_{i1} - [(\text{CR})(P_{si1})]\left[\prod_{i1}\right]}{(1 + k_s)}. \qquad (7.A.16)$$

That is, CP is equal to the present value of the income-stream differential between the bond and an equivalent amount of common stock, and the present value of the floor protection.

Even though the preceding analysis of convertible-bond valuation was made under simplifying assumptions, the removal of each of them could be shown to uphold the basic logic and results that were found. Empirical testing by Walter and Que (1973) and West and Largay (1972) essentially shows that the relationships developed here seems to hold up in the markets for convertible bonds. For example, Walter and Que note that for bonds with CV $>$ IV, premiums decline at a decreasing rate as the difference between CV and IV increases. They also note that the premiums are positively correlated with the difference between bond coupon and stock dividends. For bonds with IV $>$ CV, Walter and Que find that the premium declines at a decreasing rate as the CV/IV ratio declines, that is, as the probability of profitable conversion decreases. West and Largay study's results basically agree with those of Walter and Que. However, neither study finds conclusive results concerning the impact of systematic risk on bond premiums. An alternative way of viewing convertible bonds is presented by Brennan and Schwartz (1977, 1980). In their view, a convertible bond is a combination of a regular bond and a call option. Chapters 10 and 11 discuss option theory and apply option theory to valuing convertibles.

In this Appendix, we use single-period method to evaluate convertible bonds. In Appendix 11.B of Chapter 11 we will discuss alternative multi-period approaches to evaluate the convertible bond. These approaches include the graphical, calculus, option-pricing, and numerical approaches.

Appendix 7.B. Derivation of DOL, DFL, and CML

I. DOL

$$\begin{aligned}\text{Let Sales} &= P \times Q' \\ \text{EBIT} &= Q(P - V) - F, \\ Q' &= \text{new quantities sold.}\end{aligned}$$

The definition of DOL can be defined as:

$$\begin{aligned}\text{DOL} &= \frac{\text{Percentage Change in Profits}}{\text{Percentage Change in Sales}} \\ &= \frac{\Delta\text{EBIT}/\text{EBIT}}{\Delta\text{Sales}/\text{Sales}} \\ &= \frac{\{[Q(P-V)-F]-[Q'(P-V)-F]\}/Q(P-V)-F}{(P\times Q - P\times Q')/(P\times Q)}\end{aligned}$$

$$= \frac{Q(P-V) - Q'(P-V)/Q(P-V) - F}{P \times (Q-Q')/P \times Q}$$

$$= \frac{(Q-Q')(P-V)/[Q(P-V) - F]}{P(Q-Q')/P \times Q}$$

$$= \frac{\cancel{(Q-Q')}(P-V)}{Q(P-V) - F} \times \frac{\cancel{P} \times Q}{\cancel{P}\cancel{(Q-Q')}}$$

$$= \boxed{\frac{Q(P-V)}{Q(P-V) - F}}$$

$$= \frac{Q(P-V) - F + F}{Q(P-V) - F} = \frac{Q(P-V) - F}{Q(P-V) - F} + \frac{F}{Q(P-V) - F}$$

$$= 1 + \frac{F}{Q(P-V) - F}$$

$$= 1 + \frac{\text{Fixed Costs}}{\text{Profits}}.$$

II. DFL

Let

i = interest rate on outstanding debt
D = outstanding debt
(or iD = interset payment on dept)

N = the total number of shares outstanding

τ = corporate tax rate

$$\text{EAIT} = [Q(P-V) - F - iD](1-\tau)$$

The definition of DFL can be defined as:

DFL (Degree of financial leverage)

$$= \frac{\frac{\Delta\text{EPS}}{\text{EPS}}}{\Delta\text{EBITEBIT}}$$

$$= \frac{(\Delta\text{EAIT}/N)/(\text{EAIT}/N)}{\Delta\text{EBIT}/\text{EBIT}} = \frac{\frac{\Delta\text{EAIT}}{\text{EAIT}}}{\frac{\Delta\text{EAIT}}{\text{EAIT}}}$$

$$= \frac{\dfrac{[Q(P-V)-F-iD](1-\tau)-[Q'(P-V)-F-iD](1-\tau)}{[Q(P-V)-F-iD](1-\tau)}}{\dfrac{[Q(P-V)-F]-[Q'(P-V)-F]}{[Q(P-V)-F]}}$$

$$= \frac{\dfrac{[Q(P-V)](1-\tau)-[Q'(P-V)](1-\tau)}{[Q(P-V)-F-iD](1-\tau)}}{\dfrac{[Q(P-V)]-[Q'(P-V)]}{[Q(P-V)-F]}}$$

$$= \frac{[\cancel{(Q-Q')(P-V)}](\cancel{1-\tau})}{[Q(P-V)-F-iD](\cancel{1-\tau})} \times \frac{Q(P-V)-F}{\cancel{(Q-Q')(P-V)}}$$

$$= \boxed{\frac{Q(P-V)-F}{Q(p-V)-F-iD}} \left(= \frac{\text{EBIT}}{\text{EBIT}-iD}\right).$$

III. DCL

(degree of combined leverage)

$$\frac{Q(P-V)}{\cancel{Q(P-V)-F}} \times \frac{\cancel{Q(P-V)-F}}{Q(P-V)-F-iD} = \frac{Q(P-V)}{Q(P-V)-F-iD}.$$

References for Chapter 7

Barnea, ARA Haugen, and LW Senbet (1981). Market imperfections, agency problems, and capital structure: A review. *Financial Management* 10, 7–22.

Berger, PGE Ofek, and DL Yermack (1997). Managerial entrenchment and capital structure decisions. *Journal of Finance*, 52(4), 1411–1438.

Black, F and M Scholes (1973). The pricing of options and corporate liabilities. *Journal of Political Economics*, 637–654.

Brennan, MJ and ES Schwartz (1977). Convertible bonds: Valuation and optimal strategies for call and conversion. *Journal of Finance*, 32(5), 1699–1715.

Brennan, MJ and ES Schwartz (1980). Analyzing convertible debentures. *Journal of Financial and Quantitative Analysis*, 15(4), 907–929.

Brick, IE, H-Y Chen, C-H Hsieh, and C-F Lee (2016). A comparison of alternate models for estimating firm's growth rate. *Review Quantitative Finance and Accounting*, forthcoming.

Brigham, Eugene F (1966). An analysis of convertible debentures. *Journal of Finance*, 21(1), 35–54.

Brigham, EF and MC Ehrhardt (2007). *Financial Management-Theory and Practice*, 12th ed. Hinsdale, OH South-Western College Pub.

Copeland, TE and JF Weston (2003). *Financial Theory and Corporate Policy*, 4th ed., Reading, MA: Addison-Wesley Publishing Company.

DeAngelo, H and RW Masulis (1980). Optimal capital structure undercorporate and personal tax. *Journal of Financial Economics*, 7, 3–29.

Durand D (1952). Costs of debt and equity funds for business: Trends and problems of measurement. In *Conference on Research in Business Finance*, pp. 215–262, NBER.

Errunza, VK and LW Senbet (1981). The effect of international operations on the market value of the firm: Theory and evidence. *Journal of Finance*, 36, 401–417.

Frank, M and V Goyal (2003). Testing the pecking order theory of capital structure. *Journal of Financial Economics*, 67(2), 217–248.

Friend, I and LHP Lang (1988). An Empirical test of the impact of managerial self-interest on corporate capital structure. *Journal of Finance*, 47, 271–281.

Graham, JR and CR Harvey (2001). The theory and practice of corporate finance: Evidence from the field. *Journal of Financial Economics*, 60(2–3), 187–243.

Hamada, RS (1986). Differential taxes and the structure of equilibrium rates-of-return: Managerial implications and remaining conundrums. *Advances in Financial Planning and Forecasting*, II.

Harris, M and A Raviv (1988). Corporate control contests and capital structure. *Journal of Financial Economics*, 20, 55–86.

Haugen, HA and LW Senbet (1978). The insignificance of bankruptcy costs to the theory of optimal capital structure. *Journal of Finance*, 33, 383–393.

Hellwig, MF (1981). Bankruptcy, limited liability, and the Modigliani–Miller theorem. *American Economic Review*, 155–170.

Hilliard, JE and RA Leitch (1975). Cost-volume analysis under uncertainty: A log-normal approach. *The Accounting Review*, 69–80.

Hilliard, JECF Lee, and RA Leitch (1983). Stochastic analysis of DOL, DFL, and the coefficients of variation: A log-normal approach. *Financial Review*, 220–233.

Kim, EH (1978). A mean–variance theory of optimal structure and corporate debt capacity. *Journal of Finance*, 32, 45–63.

Kim, EH (1982). Miller's equilibrium, shareholder leverage clienteles and optimal capital structures. *Journal of Finance*, 37, 301–323.

Krainer, RE (1977). Interest rates, leverage, and investor rationality. *Journal of Financial and Quantitative Analysis*, 12, 1–16.

Leland, H and D Pyle (1977). Information asymmetrics, financial structure, and financial intermediation. *Journal of Finance*, 33, 371–387.

Lee, CF and AC Lee (2006). *Encyclopedia of Finance*. New York: Springer.

Lee, CF (2009). *Handbook of Quantitative Finance and Risk Management*. New York: Springer.

Lintner, J (2009). The valuation of risk assets and the selection of risky investments in stock portfolios and capital budgets. *Review of Economics and Statistics*, 47, 13–37.

Miller, M (1977). Debt and taxes. *The Journal of Finance*, 29, 261–275.

Miller, MH and F Modigliani (1966). Dividend policy, growth, and the valuation of shares. *The Journal of Business*, 34, 411–433.

Modigliani, F and MH Miller (1958). The cost of capital, corporation finance, and the theory of investment. *American Economic Review*, 48, 261–297.

Modigliani, F and MH Miller (1963). Corporate income taxes and the cost of capital: A correction. *American Economic Review*, 53, 433–443.

Mossin, J (1966). Equilibrium in capital asset market. *Econometrica*, 34, 768–783.

Myers, SG (1977). Determinants of corporate borrowing. *Journal of Financial Economics*, 4, 147–175.

Myers, Stewart C (1984). Capital structure puzzle. *Journal of Finance*, 39(3), 575–592.

Penman, SH *Financial Statement Analysis and Security Valuation*, 3rd ed. New York: McGraw-Hill/Irwin.

Rajan, RG and L Zingales (1995). What do we know about capital structure? Some evidence from international data. *Journal of Finance*, 50, 1421–1460.

Reilly, F and C Linke (1981). The appealing economics of zero-coupon and mini-coupon bonds. *Faculty Working Paper No. 810*, University of Illinois at Urbana-Champaign, Bureau of Economic and Business Research, 1–20.

Resek, RW (1970). Multidimensional risk and the Modigliani–Miller hypothesis. *Journal of Finance*, 25, 47–52.

Ross, SA (1977). The determination of financial structure: The incentive-signaling approach. *Bell Journal of Economics*, 8, 23–40.

Sharpe, WF (1964). Capital asset prices: A theory of market equilibrium under condition of risk. *Journal of Finance*, 19, 425–442.

Shelton, J (1981). Equal access and Miller's equilibrium. *Journal of Financial and Quantitative Analysis*, 16, 603–625.

Shyam-Sunder, L and SC Myers (1999). Testing static tradeoff against Pecking order models of capital structure. *Journal of Financial Economics*, 51, 219–244.

Titman, S and R Wessels (1988). The determinants of capital structure. *Journal of Finance*, 43(1), 1–19.

Van Horne, JC (2001). *Financial Management and Policy*, 12th ed., Englewood Cliffs, N.J.: Prentice Hall Inc.

Walter J and A Que (1973). The valuation of convertible bonds. *Journal of Finance*, 28(3), 713–732.

West, R and J Largay (1972). Premiums on convertible bonds. *Journal of Finance*, 27(5), 1156–1162.

Zwiebel, J (1996). Dynamic capital structure under managerial entrenchment. *American Economic Review*, 86(5), 1197–1215.

Chapter 8

Risk Estimation and Diversification

8.1. Introduction

This chapter presents the basic concepts of risk in the context of business operations, corporate financing decisions, and diversification. Methods of measuring risk are explained by using basic statistical procedures. Also included are the concepts and applications of the dominance principle and portfolio theory.

We begin the chapter by discussing the types and classifications of risk in Section 8.2. This is followed by Section 8.3 on the concepts of portfolio analysis and its applications. In Section 8.4, we discuss the calculations of the market rate-of-return and the market risk premium. Determination of the commercial lending rate in accordance with risk and return concepts is discussed in Section 8.5. Section 8.6 discusses the dominance principle and the necessity of using performance measures to compare the performance of different portfolios. Finally, in Section 8.7, the results of this chapter are summarized. Appendix 8.A discusses the estimation of market risk premium, while Appendix 8.B explores the normal distribution.

8.2. Risk Classification

Earlier, we discussed the rates-of-returns on stocks. In this chapter, we discuss the risk associated with the rate-of-return. Risk is defined as the probability of success or failure, where success is making a profit and failure is losing money on an investment. In finance and accounting, we refer to risk as the degree of fluctuation associated with either return on investment (ROI) or the rates-of-return on securities. Depending on its sources, risk can be classified as business risk or financial risk. Sources of risk are useful for both corporate managers and shareholders to determine and assess a firm's market value.

8.2.1. *Business Risk*

Business risk, sometimes called operating risk, refers to the degree of fluctuation of net income and cash flow associated with different types of businesses and operating strategies. The fluctuation of operating income represents a business risk. Business risk to shareholders generally arises from uncertainty about the firm's product markets, input markets, or operations. Business risk also can be inherent in the firm's commercial activities. If a firm is entirely equity funded, then the fluctuation of ROI, earnings per share (EPS), and rate of equity (ROE) can be used to determine business risk. (In Chapter 8, we will discuss the variables that affect business risk.)

The possible ROIs of General Motors (company A) and Ford (company B) for the coming year are listed in Table 8.1.

In Table 8.1, we see that there is a 20% chance of a boom economy in the coming year, in which both GM and Ford will have a high ROI; and a 20% chance of a recession, which will mean low ROI for both GM and Ford.

The expected ROI and the variance of ROI for these two auto manufacturers can be calculated by Eqs. (8.1) and (8.2):

$$\text{Expected ROI} = \overline{X} = \sum_{i=1}^{n} X_i P_i. \tag{8.1}$$

$$\text{Variance of ROI} = \sigma^2 = \sum_{i=1}^{n} (Xi - \overline{X})^2 P_i, \tag{8.2}$$

where P_i = probability of occurrence of the ith state of the economy, and X_i = ROI in the ith state of the economy.

Table 8.1.

State of Economy	State Occurring (p_i)	ROI (A_1) of GM(X_{AI}) (%)	ROI (B_i) of Ford (X_{Bi}) (%)
Boom	0.20	15	14
Normal	0.60	12	11
Recession	0.20	4	3

Substituting the data of Table 8.1 into Eqs. (8.1) and (8.2), we have

$$\begin{aligned}
\text{GM: } \overline{X}_{\text{A}} &= (0.15)(0.2) + (0.12)(0.6) + (0.4)(0.2) = 11\%,\\
\text{Ford: } \overline{X}_{\text{B}} &= (0.14)(0.2) + (0.11)(0.6) + (0.3)(0.2) = 10\%,\\
\text{GM: } \sigma_{\text{A}}^2 &= (0.15 - 0.11)^2(0.2) + (0.12 - 0.11)^2(0.6) + (0.4 - 0.11)^2(0.2)\\
&= 0.00136,\\
\text{Ford: } \sigma_{\text{B}}^2 &= (0.14 - 0.10)^2(0.2) + (0.11 - 0.10)^2(0.6) + (0.3 - 0.1)^2(0.2)\\
&= 0.00136.
\end{aligned}$$

These results show that the expected ROIs are 11% for GM and 10% for Ford, with a variance of ROI for both firms of 0.00316. Thus, the absolute business risk is about the same for both firms.

To simultaneously compare these firms in terms of expected returns and risk, we use the coefficient of variation (CV) as indicated in Eq. (8.3):

$$\text{CV} = \frac{\sigma}{\overline{X}}. \tag{8.3}$$

The CV for GM and Ford is determined as follows:

$$\text{GM: } \text{CV}_{\text{A}} = \frac{\sqrt{0.00136}}{0.11} = \frac{0.369}{0.11} = 0.3353,$$

$$\text{Ford: } \text{CV}_{\text{B}} = \frac{\sqrt{0.00136}}{0.10} = \frac{0.0369}{0.10} = 0.3690.$$

These CVs show that the risk per unit of return for Ford is greater than the risk per unit of return for GM. That is, even though both companies face the same business risk, when we simultaneously consider both risk and return, GM is superior. It should be noted that this result does not necessarily hold in a portfolio context, where the appropriation risk measure is not only the variance or the CV but is also the correlation coefficient. (This is discussed in greater detail later in this chapter.)

If the probability distribution of the firms' ROI is normal, then the mean and standard deviation of ROIs for both GM and Ford can be used to calculate the probability that ROI will be greater or less than a certain amount. We will now discuss the method that is used to standardize the distribution in order to determine how many standard deviations a specific ROI is from the mean. Suppose we want to know the probability that the actual ROI for GM will be greater than 15.44%. In standardizing the distribution (see Appendix 7.A), we obtain:

$$Z = \frac{15.44\% - 11\%}{3.69\%} = 1.20 \text{ Standard deviations.}$$

Referring to the normal distribution table found in the appendix at the end of this book, we find that there is a 0.885 probability that actual ROI will be greater than 15.44%.

For a normal distribution, the actual ROI will lie within ±1 standard deviation of expected ROI 68.27% of the time the actual ROI will be within ±2 standard deviation of expected ROI 95.45% of the time and the actual ROI will lie within ±3 standard deviation of expected ROI 99.73% of the time. These interval estimates of ROI for both GM and Ford are shown below:

	Interval	Chance of Occurrence (%)
GM	$0.11 - 0.037 < X < 0.11 + 0.037$	68.27
	$0.11 - 0.074 < X < 0.11 + 0.074$	95.45
	$0.11 - 0.111 < X < 0.11 + 0.111$	99.73
Ford	$0.10 - 0.037 < X < 0.10 + 0.037$	68.27
	$0.11 - 0.074 < X < 0.11 + 0.074$	95.45
	$0.11 - 0.111 < X < 0.11 + 0.111$	99.73

This information is useful for investors because it enables them to make risk comparisons between GM and Ford. In this case, the standard deviations of ROI for both companies are the same, implying that the risk for each is the same. Hence, GM is preferable because it has a higher return for the same level of risk.

8.2.2. *Financial Risk*

Financial leverage is the magnification of profit or loss through the use of debt financing. Financial risk refers to the risk of not being able to meet the fixed cash flow requirement of debt financing, which could lead to bankruptcy. Hence, financial risk is related to financial leverage. The amount of financial leverage is determined by the amount of short- and long-term debt that the firm employs in its capital structure. One of the ways to measure financial risk is by the firm's debt/equity ratio. The

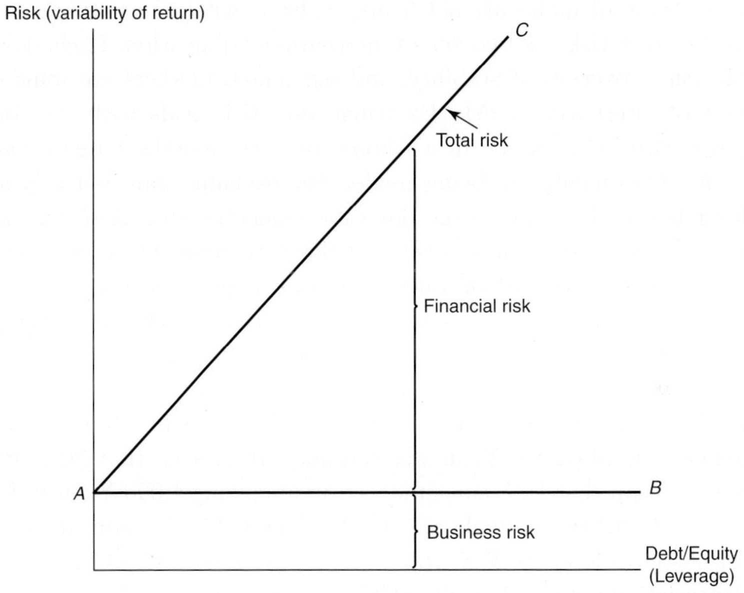

Fig. 8.1. Relationship of total risk to financial leverage.

relationship between total risk and financial leverage (debt/equity) is indicated in Fig. 8.1. Business risk is unrelated to the amount of financial leverage, as shown by line AB. But financial risk is directly related to the amount of leverage, as shown by line AC. The sum of business risk and financial risk is the firm's total risk. The combination of business risk and financial risk plays a central role in the theory and practice of corporate finance.

Business risk and financial risk are not necessarily constant over time. Both can be affected by fluctuations of the business cycle or by changes in the federal government's fiscal policy and the Federal Reserve System's monetary policy. Hence, economic information is relevant to the financial manager when assessing the riskiness of a given situation.

8.2.3. *Total Risk*

Total risk refers to the combined effects of business risk and financial risk, as indicated in Fig. 8.1. Total risk is defined as:

$$\text{Total risk} = \text{Business Risk} + \text{Financial Risk}.$$

In the case of multinational firms, or firms with international investments, business risk can take on an international dimension. Exchange rate fluctuations, government stability, and segmented markets are some components of international risk. Exchange rate risk deals with the foreign exchange rate between the firm's home country and the foreign country where its investments are being made. The exchange rate is the price of foreign currency in terms of the domestic monetary unit. A change is the price of foreign currency in terms of the domestic monetary unit. A change in the exchange rate will produce a change in price of foreign goods in terms of domestic currency, as well as a proportionate change in the price of domestic goods in terms of the foreign currency.

For example on September 24, 2007, the exchange rate between the U.S. dollar and the Chinese Yuan was \$0.1331 to 1 Yuan. Suppose that on September 25, 2007, the Yuan was devalued 10%, such that \$0.1198 was equal to 1 Yuan. For U.S. consumer, an item costing 1,000 Yuan in China would cost \$133.1 on September 24. On September 25, this same item would be \$119.8. Therefore, the U.S. will import more goods from China because the depreciation in the value of the Chinese currency makes Chinese exports cheaper. For the Chinese consumer, an item worth \$133.1 would cost 1,000 Yuan on September 24 and 1,110 Yuan on September 25. This increase in price, caused by the Yuan depreciation, would result in a decreased demand for American imports. Therefore, an appreciation in the Yuan would cause an opposite effect, an increase in demand for imports. It is apparent that firms with business dealings in foreign countries must be aware of foreign exchange fluctuations. A profit made in a foreign country could be easily translated into a loss with a sudden appreciation in the U.S. dollar.

A second type of international business risk is political risk, which refers to the political climate and conditions of the country. For instance, a country with an unstable government may experience wild fluctuations in interest rates because of a lack of confidence from the business community. Or there may be a chance that the government will expropriate plant and equipment or negate contracts. These are all political risks that a firm must include in its risk analysis when it operates internationally. Such risks are also included in the business risk component of total risk.

8.3. Portfolio Analysis and Application

A portfolio is any combination of assets or investments. Portfolio analysis is used to determine the return and risk characteristics for any combination of assets. As first described by Harry Markowitz (1959), portfolio analysis involves the identification of specific statistical characteristics that enable managers or investors to systematically reduce risk through diversification; that is, holding more than a single asset in a portfolio.

8.3.1. *Expected Rate-of-Return on a Portfolio*

The rate-of-return on a portfolio is simply the weighted average of the returns of individual securities in the portfolio. This is a linear relationship. For example, suppose 40% of the portfolio is invested in security a, which has a 10% in security c with a 12% expected return. The expected rate-of-return on this portfolio is:

$$\begin{aligned}\overline{R}_P &= W_a\overline{R}_a + W_b\overline{R}_b + W_c\overline{R}_c \\ &= (0.4)\ (0.1) + (0.3)\ (0.05) + (0.3)\ (0.12) \\ &= 0.091,\end{aligned}$$

where W_a, W_b, and W_c are the propositions of the portfolio invested in securities a, b, and c. The summation of these weights equals 1. $\overline{R}_a$, $\overline{R}_b$, and $\overline{R}_c$ represent expected rates-of-return on securities a, b, and c. $\overline{R}_p$ represents the expected rate-of-return for the portfolio, which is the weighted average of the securities' expected rates-of-return. In general, the expected return on an n-asset portfolio is defined by Eq. (8.4):

$$\overline{R}_p = \sum_{i=1}^{n} W_i\overline{R}_i \left(\text{where } \sum_{i=1}^{n} W_i = 1\right), \tag{8.4}$$

where W_i is the proportion of the individual's investment allocated to security i, and $\overline{R}_i$ is the expected rate-of-return for security i.

If an investor chooses not to invest the entire portfolio in financial assets, then one of the investor's assets will be cash. Hence, the individual investor must hold 100% of his or her financial wealth in some form of profitable assets and cash.

8.3.2. *Variance and Standard Deviation of a Portfolio*

A portfolio's risk is measured by its standard deviation, or variance. The standard deviation is the square root of the variance. To calculate a portfolio's standard deviation, we should first identify the covariance among the securities in the portfolio. The covariance between two such securities is defined as follows:

$$\begin{aligned}COV(W_1R_1, W_2R_2) &= \frac{1}{N}\sum_{t=1}^{N}(W_1R_{1t} - W_1\overline{R}_1)(W_2R_{2t} - W_2\overline{R}_2)\\ &= \frac{W_1W_2}{N}\sum_{t=1}^{N}(R_{1t} - \overline{R}_1)(R_{2t} - \overline{R}_2)\\ &= W_1W_2\,Cov(R_1, R_2),\end{aligned} \tag{8.5}$$

where R_{1t} is the rate-of-return for the first security in period t and R_{2t} is the rate-of-return for the second security in period t. $\overline{R}_1$ and $\overline{R}_2$ are average rates-of-return for the securities, while COV(R_1, R_2) represents the covariance between R_1 and R_2.

$$\begin{aligned}\sigma_P^2 &= VAR(W_1R_{1t} + W_2R_{2t})\\ &= \frac{1}{N}\sum_{t=1}^{N}\left[(W_1R_{1t} + W_2R_{2t}) - (W_1\overline{R}_1 + W_2\overline{R}_2)\right]^2,\\ &= W_1^2\sigma_1^2 + W_2^2\sigma_2^2 + 2W_1W_2\,COV(R_1, R_2).\end{aligned} \tag{8.6}$$

Now that we have shown how to find covariance and variance of a portfolio, we proceed to the standard deviation of returns for a portfolio, which is determined as follows:

$$\sigma_P = \sqrt{\frac{1}{N}\sum_{t=1}^{N}(R_{pt} - \overline{R}_P)^2}, \tag{8.7}$$

where σ_p is the standard deviation of the portfolio's return, R_{pt} is the portfolio's rate-of-return in period t, and $\overline{R}_p$ is the average portfolio rate-of-return. Figure 8.2 illustrates two possible distributions for two portfolios with the same expected return but with different degrees of risk. Portfolio B's variability is larger than portfolio A's. Consequently, investors regard portfolio B as riskier than portfolio A. Therefore, portfolio A is more attractive than portfolio B because it offers less risk with the same expected return.

8.3.3. *The Two-asset Case*

To explain the fundamental aspect of portfolio risk diversification, we consider the two-asset case. Following Eqs. (8.6) and (8.7), we define σ_p

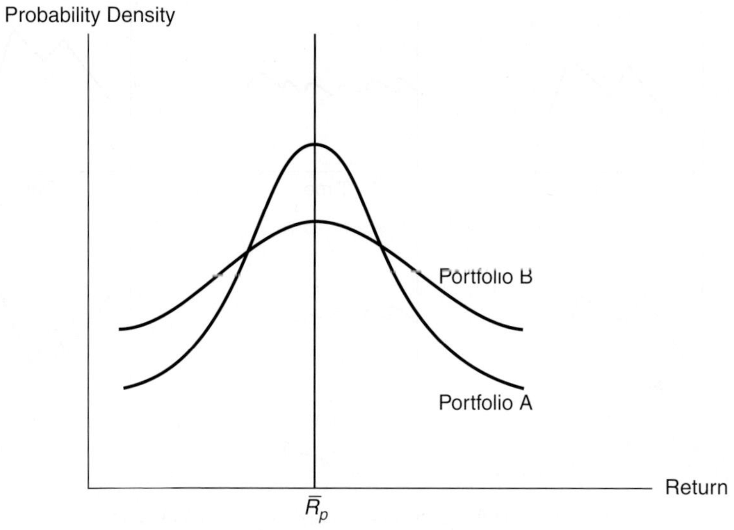

Fig. 8.2. Probability distribution of returns for two portfolios.

as follows:

$$\sigma_P = \left[W_1^2\, VAR(R_1) + W_2^2\, VAR(R_2) + 2W_1W_2\, COV(R_1, R_2)\right]^{\frac{1}{2}}, \qquad (8.8)$$

where $W_1 + W_2 = 1$. The covariance term can be expressed in terms of the correlation coefficient between R_1 and R_2 and the respective standard deviations of R_1 and R_2:

$$COV(R_1, R_2) = \rho_{12}\sigma_1\sigma_2. \qquad (8.9)$$

The correlation coefficient measures the degree of similarity of movement for a time-series. The ρ_{ij} is defined over the range of +1 to −1. Figure 8.3 depicts various values of ρ_{ij}. At $\rho_{ij} = 1$, the fluctuation of returns for both series over time is identical; at $\rho_{ij} = 0$, the returns are unrelated; and at $\rho_{ij} = -1$, the fluctuations are moving in opposite directions.

Equation (8.7) is a quadratic equation, and some value of W_1 minimizes σ_p. To obtain this value,[1] we differentiate Eq. (8.8) with respect to W_1

[1]In Appendix 8.C, we have shown how to obtain optimal weights for a two-security portfolio.

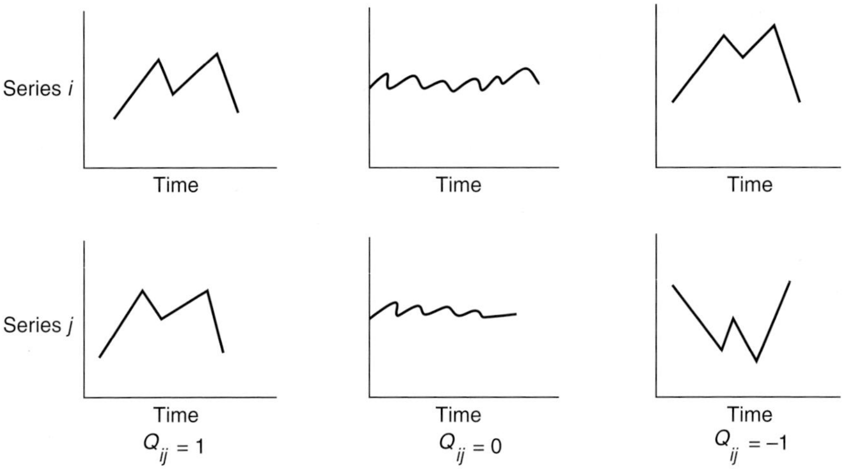

Fig. 8.3. Different types of correlation coefficients.

and set this derivative equal to 0 to solve for W_1:

$$W_1 = \frac{\sigma_2(\sigma_2 - \rho_{12}\sigma_1)}{\sigma_1^2 + \sigma_2^2 - 2\rho_{12}\sigma_1\sigma_2}. \tag{8.10}$$

Equation (8.10) can be used to estimate the optimal weight of security 1. From the constraint $W_1 + W_2 = 1$, the optimal weight of security 2 can also be estimated. From estimated W_1 and W_2, we can estimate $\overline{R}_p$ and σ_p for a two-security minimum variance portfolio.

8.3.4. *The N-asset Case*

An expanded form of Eq. (8.8) for a portfolio of N securities is ρ_{ij}, the correlation coefficient between i and j, and n is the number of securities included in the portfolio.

$$\sigma_p = \sqrt{\sum_{i=1}^{n} W_i^2\sigma_i^2 + \sum_{j=1}^{n}\sum_{i=1}^{n} W_iW_j\rho_{ij}\sigma_i\sigma_j} \quad i \neq j, \tag{8.11}$$

where W_i and W_j are the investor's investment allocated to securities, i and j. ρ_{ij} is the correlation coefficient between i and j, and n is the number of securities included in the portfolio.

Since Eq. (8.11) has n securities, there are n variance terms (that is, $W_i^2\sigma_i^2$) and $(n^2 - n)$ covariance terms (that is $W_iW_j\rho_{ij}\ \sigma_i\sigma_j$). If $n = 20$, Eq. (8.11) will have 20 variance terms and 380 covariance terms.

Using a matrix notation, we can express these terms as follows:

$$\begin{bmatrix} W_1^2\sigma_1^2 & \cdots & \cdots & W_1W_{20}\sigma_{1,20} \\ \vdots & W_2^2\sigma_2^2 & \vdots & \vdots \\ \vdots & \vdots & \ddots & \vdots \\ W_{20}W_1\sigma_{20,1} & \cdots & \cdots & W_{20}^2\sigma_{20}^2 \end{bmatrix}.$$

This is a variance–covariance matrix for portfolio analysis.

8.3.5. *The Efficient Portfolios*

Under the mean–variance framework, by definition, a security or a portfolio will be efficient if

1. No other portfolio has the same expected return at a lower risk.
2. No other portfolio has a higher expected return at the same risk.

These two rules are called the *dominance principle*, which we discuss in detail later in this chapter.

This suggests that given two investments, A and B, A is preferred to B if

$$E(A) > E(B) \quad \text{and} \quad \text{var}(A) = \text{var}(B)$$

or

$$E(A) = E(B) \quad \text{and} \quad \text{var}(A) < \text{var}(B),$$

where $E(A)$ and $E(B)$ are the expected returns of investments A and B, and var(A) and var(B) are their respective variances, or risk. The mean return and standard deviation of an investment can be calculated and plotted as a single point on a mean–standard deviation diagram, as shown in Fig. 8.4.

All points below curve EF represent possible portfolio combinations. All points above EF are combinations of risk and returns that do not exist. Point D represents a portfolio of investments with return R_{D} and risk σ_{D}. Therefore, point B represents a risk-and-return combination that cannot be obtained with any combination of existing investment opportunities.

The EF curve is also called the efficient frontier, because all points below the curve are dominated by a point found on the curve. The efficient frontier is defined as the set of portfolios that has the maximum return for every given level of risk or the minimum risk for every level of return. Suppose

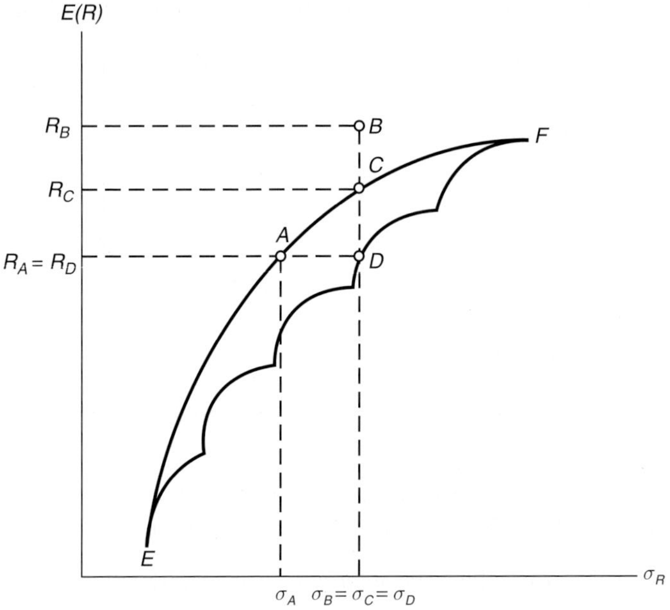

Fig. 8.4. Efficient frontier in portfolio analysis.

a firm is willing to assume a maximum risk σ_D. It can obtain a return of R_D with portfolio D or move to point C on the frontier and receive a higher return of R_C with that portfolio at the same level of risk. Therefore, portfolio C dominates portfolio D because it is preferred to portfolio D.

A similar argument could be made in terms of risk. If the firm wants to achieve a return of R_A, it would select portfolio A over D, because A represents the same return at a lower level of risk or standard deviation: $\sigma_A < \sigma_D$. Therefore, point D is not efficient but points A and C are. A decision-maker following these arguments would, therefore, select any point on the frontier as being preferable to any interior point.

The amount of curvature of the efficient frontier depends on the correlation between the two assets. If the correlation between assets equals +1, the combinations lie on the straight line. The lower the correlation coefficient, the more curved the efficient frontier.

EXAMPLE 8.1

To show how the portfolio concepts and methods discussed in this section can be used in practical analysis, we will evaluate the monthly

Table 8.2. Variance-covariance matrix.

	MRK	JNJ
MRK	σ^2_{MRK} 0.006206	$\sigma_{MRK,JNJ}$ 0.001069
JNJ	$\sigma_{JNJ,MRK}$ 0.001069	σ^2_{JNJ} 0.001645

rates-of-return during January 2010–December 2014 for Johnson & Johnson (JNJ) and Merck & Co. Inc. (MRK). The basic statistical estimates for these two firms are average monthly rates-of-return and the variance–covariance matrix. The average monthly rates-of-return are 0.002101 ($\overline{R}_{MRK}$) for MRK and 0.004233 ($\overline{R}_{JNJ}$) for JNJ. The variance and covariance are listed in Table 8.2.

From Eq. (8.10), we have

$$W_{MRK} = \frac{0.001645 - 0.001069}{0.006206 + 0.001645 - 2(0.001069)} = 0.1007,$$
$$W_{JNJ} = 1 - W_{MRK} = 0.8993.$$

Using the weight estimates and Eqs. (8.5) and (8.8),

$$\begin{aligned}
E(R_P) &= (0.1007)(0.002101) + (0.8993)(0.004233) \\
&= 0.004018, \\
\sigma_p^2 &= (0.1007)^2(0.006206) + (0.8993)^2(0.001645) \\
&\quad + 2(0.1007)(0.8993)(0.001069) \\
&= 0.001587, \\
\rho_{12} &= \frac{\sigma_{MRK,JNJ}}{\sigma_{JNJ}\sigma_{MRK}} = \frac{0.001069}{(0.006206)^{\frac{1}{2}}(0.001645)^{\frac{1}{2}}} \\
&= \frac{0.001069}{(0.078781)(0.040554)} = \frac{0.001069}{0.003195} \\
&= 0.334695.
\end{aligned}$$

When ρ_{12} is less than 1, the combination of the two securities results in a total risk less than the sum of their weighted risk. This is the diversification effect. When ρ_{12} equals to 1, the combination of the two securities has no diversification effect at all.

For the correlation coefficient of $\rho_{12} = 0.334695$, we see that a portfolio that combines JNJ and MRK shows a greater diversification effect and a substantial reduction in risk then would holding each of the securities separately.

Depending on the correlation coefficient between securities, as long as the securities are not positively correlated, the risk of a portfolio as measured by the standard deviation of return will be less than the weighted average of the risks (standard deviations) of the individual securities. In notational form,

$$\sigma_P < W_1\sigma_1 + W_2\sigma_2 \quad \text{if } \rho_{12} \neq 1.$$

This will always be true and represents a significant fact that investors and managers must keep in mind when making financial decisions.

8.3.6. *Corporate Application of Diversification*

The effects of diversification are not necessarily isolated to security analysis and portfolio management but may have wider applications at the corporate decision-making level. Managers often justify undertaking multi-product lines because of the effects of diversification. Instead of putting "all eggs in one basket", the investment risks are spread out among many lines of services of products in hopes of reducing overall risk and maximizing returns. To what degree this diversification takes place in other types of corporate decisions depends on the decision-maker's preference for risk and return. The overall goal is to reduce business risk fluctuations of net income.

This type of corporate diversification can also be taken to the multinational level. For example, General Motors has overseas divisions throughout the world that all produce the same product — autos and auto parts. Because GM is a multinational corporation, it can take advantage of diversifying effects of different exchange rates and political and economic climates, because each overseas division is less than perfectly positively correlated with each other.

The strategy of diversifying at the corporate level has been criticized because shareholders can attain diversification in their own portfolios, which makes corporate diversification redundant. There is the agency theory argument that corporate diversification is in fact a form of risk-sharing between stockholders and bondholders, where the bondholders have less risky fixed-income securities due to corporate diversification and the shareholders suffer a loss in the value of their equity position. Finally, there is a reduction in the risk/return deals with options, which deals with mergers and divestitures.

8.4. The Market Rate-of-Return and Market Risk Premium

The market rate-of-return is the return expected from the market portfolio. This portfolio consists of all risky assets, such as stocks, bonds, options, bullion, real estate, and coins. Because risky assets are included, the market portfolio is a completely diversified portfolio. All unsystematic risks related to individual assets would, therefore, be diversified away. In general, *unsystematic risk* refers to those risks that are related uniquely to the firm (this topic is covered in more detail in Chapter 9). *Systematic risk* influences the rate-of-return for all risky assets.

The market rate-of-return can be calculated using one of several types of market indicator series, such as the Dow Jones 30, Standard and Poor's (S & P) 500, or the New York Stock Exchange Index, using the equation:

$$\frac{I_t - I_{t-1}}{I_{t-1}} = R_{mt}, \tag{8.12}$$

where R_{mt} = market rate-of-return; I_t = market index at t; and I_{t-1} = market index a $t-1$.

R_{mt} is the market rate-of-return using the index I_t. This equation calculates the percent change in the market index during period t and the previous period $t-1$. This change is the rate-of-return an investor would expect to receive in t had he invested in $t-1$.

8.4.1. *The Risk Premium*

A risk-free investment is one in which the timing and amount of income streams are known. However, for most investments, investors are uncertain as to the timing and amount of income. Investment risk can be quite broad, ranging from relatively riskless Treasury bills to highly risky speculative stocks.

The rational investor dislikes risk and uncertainty and thus requires an additional return on the investment to compensate for this uncertainty. This is called the *risk premium* and is added to the nominal risk-free rate. The risk premium should always be positive. This means that investors will not accept a lower return for investments with higher risk. When trying to estimate the correct risk premium, we cannot always rely on historic data. In actuality, risky investments do lose money and hence experience a negative risk premium. However, just because investments have lost money in the past does not mean that they will do so in the future.

EXAMPLE 8.2

The market rate-of-return using S & P 500 was calculated using Eq. (8.12) to derive average quarterly returns. These returns are given in Table 8.3. The T-bill rate was deducted from the market return rate $(R_m - R_f)$ to derive the risk premium. For example, in the first two quarters of 2004, the risk premiums were low because of the low market returns. This allowed the T-bill rate to earn a higher return that the market and resulted in a negative risk premium. On the other hand, when the market return rates are higher than the riskless rates, the market premium is positive.

Theoretically, it is not possible to have an ex ante negative risk premium, because taking on additional risk requires an increase in expected return. However, using short-run estimators, as in Table 8.3, may result in negative figures, which are not good estimators because they reflect the short-run fluctuations of the market, thus demonstrating that the ex ante expectations of market participants may not be realized *ex post.*

Table 8.3. Market returns and T-bill rates by quarters 2004–2006 $\frac{I_t - I_{t-1}}{I_{t-1}}$.

Year	Quarter	S&P 500 Index	(A) Market Return	Annualized 3-month T-bill Rates	(B) Quarterly 3-month T-bill Rates	(A − B) Quarterly Rates Premium
03	4	164.92				
04	1	159.17	−3.49	9.52	2.38	−5.87
	2	153.17	−3.77	9.87	2.47	−6.24
	3	166.09	8.44	10.37	2.59	5.84
	4	167.23	0.69	8.06	2.02	−1.33
05	1	180.65	8.02	8.52	2.13	5.89
	2	191.84	6.19	6.95	1.74	4.46
	3	182.07	−5.09	7.10	1.78	−6.87
	4	211.27	16.04	7.10	1.78	14.26
06	1	238.90	13.08	6.56	1.64	11.44
	2	250.84	5.00	6.21	1.55	3.45
	3	231.32	−7.78	5.21	1.30	−9.08
	4	242.17	4.69	5.53	1.38	3.31
Mean		195.36	3.50	7.58	1.90	1.61

In Appendix 8.A, we discuss long-run risk premium, which more accurately estimates future risk premiums. In later chapters we will use the risk premium to calculate a firm's cost of capital.

8.5. Determination of Commercial Lending Rates

In this section, we explain the process of estimating a lending rate that a financial institution would extend to a firm, or a borrowing rate a firm would feel is reasonable. The loan officers of the bank and the financial analysts of the firm need to consider the firm's business, financial, and total risks to make a fair analysis of the cost of borrowing for the firm or the rate the bank should charge when lending money to the firm.

The lending rate is based in part on the risk-free rate. Therefore, we must forecast the risk-free rate (R_f) for boom, normal, and recession economies.

The second component of the lending rate is the risk premium (R_p), which is calculated individually for each firm by examining the change in EBIT under the three economic conditions. The EBIT is an indicator to the lender as to the ability of the potential borrower to repay borrowed funds.

Tables 8.4 and 8.5 provide the information required for the analysis. In Table 8.4, column B lists probabilities relating to economic conditions for the entire economy, and column D lists probabilities of various levels of EBIT for the firm.

There are nine possible lending rates for the three economic conditions. The probabilities of these rates for the three economic conditions are elaborated in Table 8.5.

These tables show that during a boom the risk-free rate is 10%, but the risk premium can take on different values. There is a 40% chance that

Table 8.4. Input information.

Economic condition	R_t	(A) Probability	(B) EBIT	(C) Probability	(D) R_p
Boom	10%	0.25	\$2.5m	0.40	2%
			1.5	0.30	3
			0.5	0.30	5
Normal	9	0.50	\$2.5m	0.40	2
		0.50	1.5	0.30	3
		0.50	0.5	0.30	5
Poor	8	0.25	\$2.5m	0.40	2
			1.5	0.30	3
			0.5	0.30	5

Table 8.5. Calculation table.

Economic condition	(A) R_t	(B) Probability	(C) R_p	(D) Probability	(B × D) Probability of Occurrence	(A + C) Lending Rate
Boom	10%	0.25	2%	0.40	0.100	12%
			3	0.30	0.075	13
			5	0.30	0.075	15
Normal	9	0.50	2	0.40	0.200	11
			3	0.30	0.150	12
			5	0.30	0.150	14
Poor	8	0.25	2	0.40	0.100	10
			3	0.30	0.075	11
			5	0.30	0.075	13
					1.000	

the risk premium will be 2%, a 30% chance it will be 3%, and a 30% chance it will be 5%. By multiplying the two probabilities, R_f and R_p, we get the joint probability of occurrence. Therefore, there is a 10% chance of receiving a 13% or 15% rate. This process also applies for normal and recession conditions.

For the problem set up in Table 8.5, the weighted average lending rate is

$$\begin{aligned}\overline{R} &= (0.100)(12\%) + (0.75)(13) + (0.075)15 + (0.200)11 + (0.150)(12)\\ &\quad + (0.150)(14) + (0.100)10 + (0.074)(13\%)\\ &= 12.2\%,\end{aligned}$$

with a standard deviation of

$$\begin{aligned}\sigma &= \big[(0.100)(12 - 12.2)^2 + (0.075)(13 - 12.2)^2 + (0.075)(15 - 12)^2\\ &\quad + (0.200)(11 - 12.2)^2 + (0.150)(12 - 12.2)^2 + (0.150)(14 - 12.2)^2\\ &\quad + (0.100)(10 - 12.2)^2 + (0.075)(11 - 12.2)^2 + (0.075)(13 - 12.2)^2\big]^{0.5}\\ &= (0.004 + 0.048 + 0.588 + 0.288 + 0.006\\ &\quad + 0.436 + 0.484 + 0.108 + 0.048)^{0.5}\\ &= 1.42\%.\end{aligned}$$

If the lending rate distribution is normal (as discussed in Appendix 8.B). Given the mean and standard deviation for such a distribution, in Fig. 8.5 we see that 68.3% of the observations of a normal distribution are within a

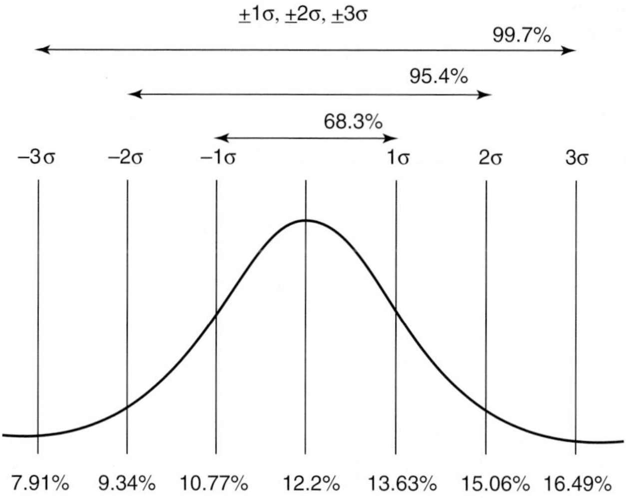

Fig. 8.5. Probability distribution of lending rate.

standard deviation of 1 of the mean, 95.4% are within a standard deviation of 2, and 99.7% within a standard deviation of 3.

Based on the mean and standard deviation of the estimated lending rate, we depict the expected lending rate and its standard deviation in Fig. 8.5. The percentages in Fig. 8.5, along with the mean and standard deviations, illustrate the normal distribution. The average lending rate is normally distributed with a mean of 12.2% and a standard deviation of +1.43%. This implies that almost all (99.7%) of the rates lie in the range from 7.91% to 16.49%. We also know 68.3% of the rates lie in the range of 10.77–13.63%.

This example is based on expected values for determining required rates-of-return. From a financial theory view point, equilibrium models such as capital asset pricing model (CAPM) and option-pricing model (OPM) are superior for determining required rates-of-return.

8.6. The Dominance Principle and Perfomance Evaluation

The *dominance principle* can be used to understand the risk/return trade-off. When making financial decisions, we are dealing with two-dimensional analysis — risk and return. The dominance principle allows us to hold one variable constant while we make comparisons based on the other variable. However, in some cases this may not be sufficient. When dealing

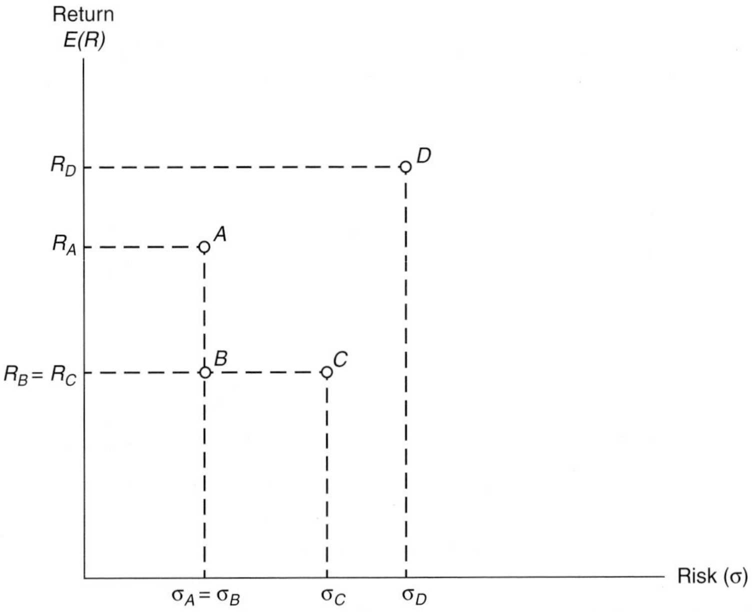

Fig. 8.6. The dominance principle in portfolio analysis.

simultaneously with different levels of risk and return, we need to use the method of *performance evaluation.*

As with efficient frontier analysis, we must assume an investor prefers returns and dislikes risks. For example, as depicted in Fig. 8.6, if prepared to experience the risk associated with σ_A, an investor can obtain a higher expected return with portfolio $A(\overline{R}_A)$ than with portfolio $B(\overline{R}_B)$. Thus, A dominates B and would be preferred. Similarly, if satisfied with a return of $\overline{R}_B$, an investor would select portfolio B over C because the risks associated with B are less: $\sigma_{\mathrm{B}} < \sigma_C$. Points B and C were directly comparable because of a common return, $R_B = R_C$. How about portfolio D? How does its risk versus return compare with other portfolios in the figure, especially B? Portfolio D is not directly comparable using the dominance principle, and this is a basic limitation: portfolios without a common risk or return factor are not directly comparable. The problem can be solved using a technique called *stochastic dominance*, which is a subject covered in advanced corporate finance or investment courses. Stochastic dominance allows for joint consideration of the mean and variance.[2]

[2]Complete coverage of this topic can be found in a text by Levy and Sarnat (1984).

A simplified approach for comparing portfolios A and D is to use a performance measure. Basically, there are three portfolio performance measures: the Sharpe, Treynor, and Jensen methods. Here, we elaborate on the Sharpe measure, which is the most basic of the three. Using this method, we can compare the relative risk–return trade-off performance of portfolios B and D as follows:

$$SP^D = \frac{\overline{R}_D - R_f}{\sigma_D},$$

$$SP^B = \frac{\overline{R}_{\mathrm{B}} - R_f}{\sigma_{\mathrm{B}}},$$

where SP^D and SP^B = Sharpe performance measures; $\overline{R}_D$ and $\overline{R}_{\mathrm{B}}$ = average return of each respective portfolio; R_f = average risk-free rate; and σ_D and σ_{B} = respective standard deviation of returns of each portfolio.

Because the numerator is the average return reduced by the risk-free rate, it represents the average risk premium of each portfolio. Dividing the risk premium by the total risk per portfolio results in a measure of the unit return (premium) per unit risk for each portfolio. The Sharpe performance measure equation would, therefore, allow direct comparison of any portfolio given its risks and returns.

EXAMPLE 8.3

An insurance firm is considering two investment funds. From past performance, they calculate the average returns and variables for both funds, as listed in Table 8.6. The T-bill rate is 9.5%, which the firm uses as a measure of the risk-free rate.

Using this information, the Sharpe performance measure is calculated as

$$SP_S = \frac{0.18 - 0.095}{0.2} = 0.425,$$

$$SP_J = \frac{0.16 - 0.095}{0.15} = 0.433.$$

Table 8.6. Information for two mutual funds.

	Smith Fund (%)	Jones Fund (%)
Average return ($\overline{R}$)	18	16
Standard deviation (σ)	20	15
Risk-free rate = R_f = 9.5%		

From these calculations, we see that the Jones fund will have a slightly better performance and thus would be the better alternative of the two investments.

8.7. Summary

In Chapter 8, we defined the basic concepts of risk and risk measurement. Based on the relationship of risk and return, we demonstrated the efficient portfolio concept and its implementation, as well as the dominance principle and performance measures. Interest rates and market rates-of-return were used as measurements to show how the commercial lending rate and the market risk premium are calculated. Following a surveyed paper by Graham and Harvey (2001), we discussed in this chapter that management evaluates firm risk, rather than project risk, when evaluating new investment opportunities. Also, firms focus on financial flexibility and credit ratings when issuing debt and EPS dilution and recent stock price appreciation when issuing equity.

Problem Set

1. Define the following terms:
   (a) Business risk, financial risk, and total risk.
   (b) CV.
   (c) Diversification.
   (d) Market risk premium.
   (e) Probability.
   (f) Efficient portfolio and efficient frontier.
   (g) Dominance principle.
2. How can diversification concepts and methods be used in financial management?
3. Discuss the concepts and methods used to determine the commercial lending rate that are developed in detail in the text.
4. The average monthly rate-of-return, variance and covariance for GE and General Foods (GF) during the period 1982–1987 are listed as follows:

	E(r)	σ^2	σ_{12}
GE	0.01	0.0035	0.0008
GF	0.008		

If the optimal weights used to calculate the portfolio are $W_1 = 0.6$ and $W_2 = 0.4$, then calculate the mean and standard deviation of this portfolio.

5. For each of the following investments, which would always be preferred by a rational investor?
   (a) portfolio A: $r = 10\%$ $\sigma = 20\%$.
       portfolio B: $r = 14\%$ $\sigma = 15\%$.
       portfolio C: $r = 15\%$ $\sigma = 15\%$.
   (b) portfolio D: $r = 20\%$ $\sigma = 30\%$.
       portfolio E: $r = 20\%$ $\sigma = 25\%$.
       portfolio F: $r = 22\%$ $\sigma = 27\%$.

6. Here is variance–covariance matrix of companies X and Y.

	σ x^2	σ_{xy}
X	0.005	0.0012
	$\sigma_{xy}\sigma$	y^2
Y	0.0012	0.004

(Assuming that $E(r)$ of X and Y are 0.02 and 0.01 respectively).

   (a) Calculate the optimal weights to construct an efficient portfolio.
   (b) Find the mean and the standard deviation of the portfolio.
   (c) Determine the coefficient of correlation.

7. An insurance company wants to choose between two investment opportunities. The company calculates the average returns and variances for two investments shown below. Using the Sharpe performance measure, choose the better investment opportunity for the insurance company.

	1	2
Average return	14%	20%
Variance	10%	15%

8. An investor puts 50% of his money in stock A and the balance in stock B, the standard deviation of returns on A is 10% and on B is 20%. Calculate the variance of portfolio returns when
   (a) The correlation between the returns is 0.
   (b) The correlation is 0.5.

(c) The correlation is 1.
(d) The correlation is −1.

9. The probability distribution of returns on two assets are given as follows.

Asset X		Asset Y	
Probability	Return (%)	Probability	Return (%)
0.3	−5	0.2	−7
0.4	3	0.6	0
0.3	15	0.2	8

(a) Calculate the mean and variance of the returns for securities X and Y.
(b) If you had to choose either X or Y, which would you prefer?
(c) If the correlation coefficient of the returns of the two securities is 0.2, what is the covariance of returns for X and Y?
(d) Given the covariance value you computed in part c, find the mean and variance for a portfolio comprised of 30% of X and 70% of Y.

10 An investor is considering between portfolios A and B. Portfolio A has an expected return of 0.20 and a Sharpe Performance measure of 0.5, while B has an expected return of 0.16 and a Performance measure of 0.4. The risk-free rate of interest is 5%.

(a) Which security would you prefer based on Sharpe's Performance measure? Explain this measure.
(b) Find the standard deviation for each of the two portfolios.

11. Zallex, Inc. is attempting to qualify their business risk for the coming year. Based on different states of the economy, their chief economist has devised the following forecasts:

State of Economy	Probability of State Occurring	ROI in State (%)
Recession	0.3	10
Normal	0.4	16
Boom	0.3	20

(a) Find the mean (Expected) ROI.
(b) Find the standard deviation of the ROI distribution.

12. Below are the mean and standard deviation of returns for securities K, L, and N.

Security	Mean	Standard Deviation
L	0.30	0.10
K	0.20	0.06
N	0.16	0.04

The correlation coefficient between L and K is 0.5; that for L and N is 0.2; and that for K and N is 0.3.

Find the expected return and standard deviation for a portfolio in which L and K each makeup 30% and portfolio N accounts for 40% of the total portfolio.

13. Given the information in the Problem # 12, answer the following:
    (a) Find the optimal weights for a portfolio of only securities K and L. Find the mean and the standard deviation of returns for the portfolio using these optimal weights.
    (b) Find the optimal weights for a portfolio of only securities K and N. Find the mean and the standard deviation of returns for the portfolio using these optimal weights.
    (c) Find the optimal weights for a portfolio of only securities L and N. Find the mean and the standard deviation of returns for the portfolio using these optimal weights.
    (d) Would you prefer portfolio KL, KN, or LN? Explain.
    (e) Draw the opportunity set and explain how the efficient frontier (set) is identified from the opportunity set.

14. Consider a risky portfolio. The end-of-year cash flow derived from the portfolio will be either \$90,000 or \$170,000 with equal probabilities of 0.5. The alternative risk-free investment in T-bills pays 5% per year.
    (a) How much would an investor pay for the portfolio if he requires a risk premium of 10%?
    (b) Assume the portfolio can be purchased by the amount calculated in (a). What is the expected rate-of-return on the portfolio?
    (c) Suppose that the investor's required risk premium increases to 15%. How much would this investor pay for the portfolio now?

(d) Based on the answers in (a), (b), and (c), please discuss the relationship between the required risk premium on a portfolio and the price at which the portfolio will sell.

15. Suppose the utility function of John is $U = E(r) - 0.5A\sigma^2$. He is considering a portfolio that offers an expected rate-of-return of 10% and standard deviation of 15%. The T-bill rate is 5%. Please calculate the maximum level of risk aversion for which the risky portfolio is still preferred to the T-bill.
16. Alice is managing a risky portfolio with expected return of 16% and standard deviation of 25%. Assume the T-bill rate is 6%.

    (a) One of Alice's clients chooses to invest 60% of a portfolio in your fund and 40% in a T-bill money market fund. What is the expected value and standard deviation of the rate-of-return of his portfolio?
    (b) Suppose Alice includes the following three stocks in the given proportion:

    Stock A 41%,
    Stock B 28%,
    Stock C 31%.

    What are the investment proportion of the client's overall portfolio, including the position in T-bills?
    (c) What is the reward-to-variability ratio of Alice's risky portfolio? The client's?

17. Given the information in question 16, suppose that the client decides to invest in Alice's portfolio a proportion y of the total investments budget so that the overall portfolio will have an expected return of 15%.

    (a) What is the investment proportion y?
    (b) What is the client's investment proportion in Alice's three stocks and the T-bill fund?
    (c) What is the standard deviation of the rate-of-return of the client's portfolio?

18. Given the information in question 16, suppose that the client wants to invest in Alice's portfolio a proportion of y that maximizes the expected return on the complete portfolio subject to the constraint that the complete portfolio's standard deviation will not be greater than 15%.

    (a) What is the investment proportion y now?
    (b) What is the expected rate-of-return on the complete portfolio?

19. Suppose that the client's utility function is $U = E(r) - 0.5A\sigma^2$ and the degree of risk aversion A is equal to 4.

    (a) What proportion of y of the total investment should be invested in Alice's fund?
    (b) What is the expected value of standard deviation of the rate-of-return on the client's optimized portfolio?

20. Gordon is managing a risky portfolio and a risk-free asset with the following information.

$$E(r_P) = 14\% \quad \sigma_P = 18\% \quad r_f = 6\%.$$

    (a) One of Gordon's clients wants to invest a proportion of her total investment budget in Gordon's risky fund to provide an expected rate-of-return on her overall or complete portfolio equal to 10%. What proportion should she invest in the risky portfolio P and what proportion in the risk-free asset?
    (b) What will be the standard deviation of the rate-of-return on her portfolio?
    (c) Another client wants the highest return possible subject to the constraint that you limit his standard deviation to be no more than 12%. Which client is more risk averse?

21. Amanda is managing a risky portfolio with an expected rate-of-return of 16% and a standard deviation of 18%. Suppose the borrowing rate your client face is 8%. Assume that the S & P 500 index has an expected return of 15% and standard deviation of 20%. The risk-free rate is 6%. What is the range of the risk aversion for which a client will neither borrow nor lend, that is, for which $y = 1$?
22. Daniel is managing a risky portfolio with an expected rate-of-return of 12% and a standard deviation of 16%. Assume that the S & P 500 index has an expected return of 16% and standard deviation of 30%. Also, the risk-free rate is 6% but the borrowing rate Daniel's client faces is 9%. What is the largest percentage fee that a client who currently is lending ($y < 1$) will be willing to pay to invest in Daniel's fund? What about a client who is borrowing $y > 1$?
23. Suppose that the risk premium $(E(r_M) - r_f)$ for the S & P 500 over T-bill from 1980–2005 is 8.5% and the standard deviation of this risk premium is 20%. Suppose that the S & P 500 is your portfolio.

(a) If your risk-aversion coefficient is 3 and you believe that the entire 1980–2005 period is representative of future expected performance, what fraction of your portfolio should be allocated to T-bills and what fraction to equity?

(b) If your financial advisor tells you that the risk premium of S & P 500 in this period should be 8.7% and you take his advice (assume that the standard deviation of the risk premium is still 20%). What is your answer to part (a) now? Please draw comparison between this two scenarios.

Appendix 8.A. Estimation of Market Risks Premium

To estimate the market risk premium, we used historical returns for 1926–2006 for stocks and bonds; these are shown in Table 8.A.1. The arithmetic risk premium estimated us based on this data is 7.88%, as shown in Fig. 8.A.1. This is calculated as the difference between stock returns of 11.64% and T-bill returns of 3.75%. The long-run market risk premium is one of the key inputs to estimating the cost of equity capital.

The risk premiums calculated by this method are used by both practitioners and academicians. The major potential weakness, however, is that these premiums assume the variance of market return and the risk-free rate are stationary over time. To deal with this problem, Merton (1980) has used the concept of Sharpe's performance measure, as discussed earlier, to generalize the above results. In general, Merton's method obtains a long-run risk premium that is greater than the above results.

Table 8.A.1. Summary statistics of annual returns (1926–2006).

Series	Geometric Mean	Arithmetic Mean (%)	Standard Deviation
S & P 500 Index	9.78	11.64	19.30
U.S. Treasury Bills (3 Months)	3.71%	3.75	3.13%
Long-Term Corporate Bonds (20 Year)	7.04%	7.08	3.07%
Long-Term Government Bonds (20 Year)	5.57%	6.00	9.97%

Sources:

(1) The Center for Research in Security Prices, Wharton School of Business, The University of Pennsylvania.

(2) Federal Reserve Economic Data, The Federal Reserve Bank of St. Louis.

Series	Geometric Mean	Arithmetic Mean	Standard Deviation	Distribution
Equity risk premia (stock–bills)	5.95%	7.88%	19.34%	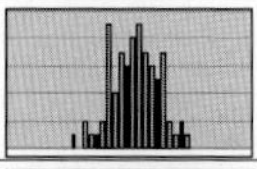
Default premia (LT corps–LT govts.)	0.9	1.39	9.67	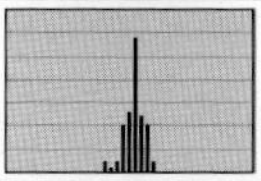
Horizon premia (LT govts.–bills)	1.18	1.63	9.76	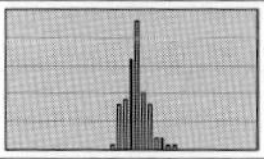
Real interest rates (bills–inflation)	0.55	0.64	4.12	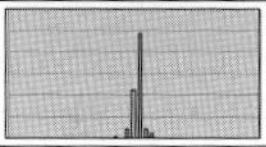

Fig. 8.A.1. Derived series: Summary statistics of annual component returns (1926–2006).

Appendix 8.B. The Normal Distribution

In Chapter 8, we introduced the idea of thinking about the uncertainty involved in future corporate returns on assets by regarding such returns not as fixed numbers but rather as random variables. Specifically, we briefly discussed the possibility of using the normal distribution for this purpose. The normal distribution is generally described by its probability density function. If the random variable X follows such a distribution function, the probability density function is:

$$f_x(x) = \frac{1}{\sigma\sqrt{2\pi}} e^{\frac{-(x-\mu)^2}{2\sigma^2}},$$

where μ is the mean, or expected value of X, and σ^2 its variance. Here, $\pi = 3.14158$ and $e = 2.71828\ldots$ are physical constants.

Figure 8.B.1 shows a graph of this probability density function, exhibiting a characteristic "bell shape" centered on the mean. Probability density functions are constructed in such a way that the area under the curve, between any two possible values of the random variable, measures the probability that the random variable will take a value in the corresponding range, illustrated in Fig. 8.B.1.

The mean of a normal distribution determines the center of the distribution, but does not influence its dispersion. Therefore, two normally distributed random variables with the same variance but different means

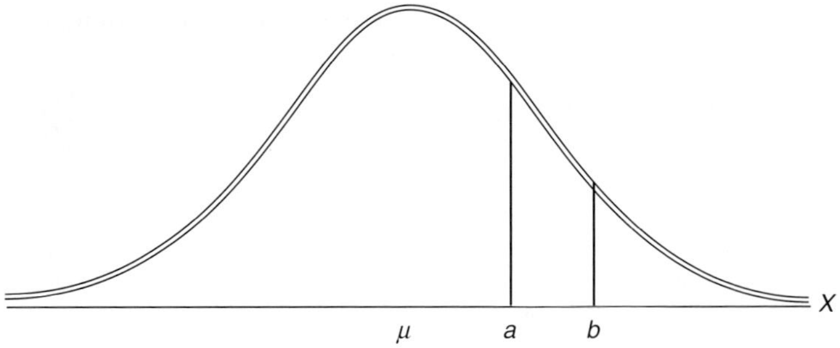

Fig. 8.B.1. Probability density function for a normal distribution, showing the probability that a normal random variable lies between a and b (shaded area).

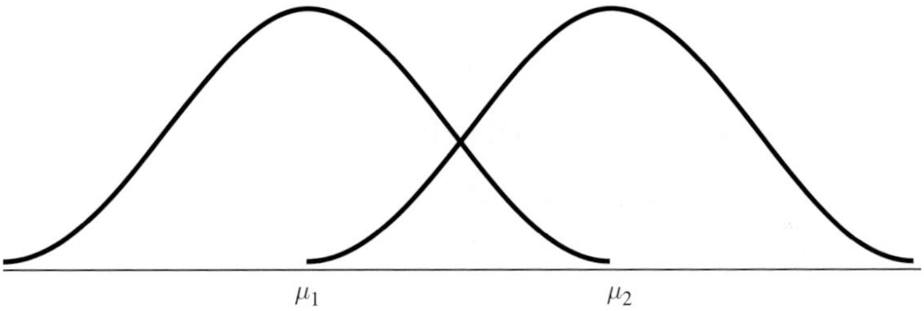

Fig. 8.B.2. Probability density function of normal random variables with equal variances: mean μ_2 is greater than μ_1.

will have identical probability density functions, except that one will be shifted to the right of the other. This is shown graphically in Fig. 8.B.2.

The variance of a normal distribution determines the spread, or dispersion, about the mean, but does not affect the center of the distribution. The higher the variance, the greater is the dispersion. Figure 8.B.3 shows the probability density functions of two normal distributions with identical means but different variances.

It follows that the greater the variance, the larger the probability that a normally distributed random variable differs from its mean by any fixed amount. For this reason, we associate variance with risk when considering the distribution of possible rates-of-return.

In fact, using the normal distribution table listed at the end of the book, it is possible to calculate the probability that a normally distributed random variable lies in any specified range. For convenience, we tabulate some useful values in Table 8.B.1. The table shows the probability that a random variable lies between $\mu - \text{K}$ and $\mu + \text{K}$ for particular values of

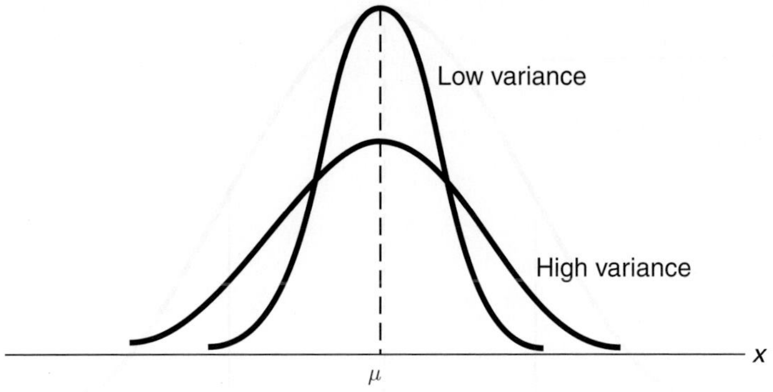

Fig. 8.B.3. Probability density functions of normal distributions with equal means and different variances.

Table 8.B.1. Probability, P, that a normal random variable with mean μ and standard deviation σ lies between $K - \sigma$ and $K - \sigma$.

P	K/σ
0.50	0.674
0.60	0.842
0.70	1.036
0.80	1.281
0.90	1.645
0.95	1.960

K/σ, where the standard deviation is σ, as depicted by the shaded area in Figure 8.B.4.

EXAMPLE 8.B.1

An investor is interested in the prospects of a particular corporation. The investor expects the corporation to achieve a rate-of-return on assets of 12% next year, and believes there is a 50% probability. If this uncertainty can be expressed as a normal distribution, find the mean and variance of that distribution.

The mean is the expected return, so that we have

$$\mu = 12.$$

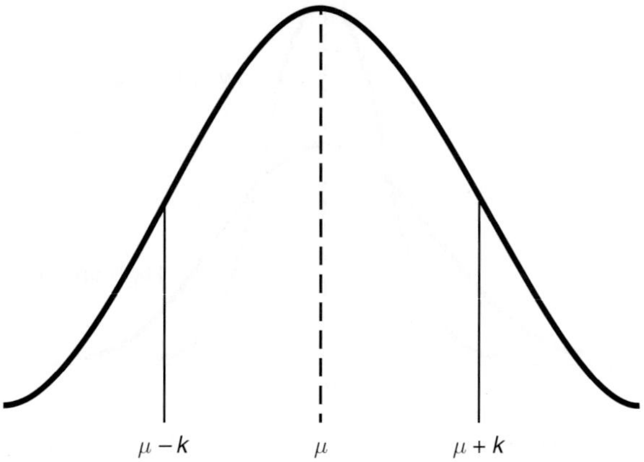

Fig. 8.B.4. Probability that a normal random variable is between μ − K and μ + K (shaded area).

According to this investor, the probability is 0.50 that the actual return will be between 10.5 and 13.5%, so that, in our notation,

$$K = \frac{13.5 - 10.5}{2} = 1.5.$$

From Table 8.B.1, we have

$$\frac{K}{\sigma} = 0.674,$$

so that

$$\sigma = \frac{K}{0.674} = \frac{1.5}{0.674} = 2.2255.$$

Finally, the variance is the square of the standard deviation, hence

$$\sigma^2 = (2.2255)^2 = 4.95.$$

This is illustrated in Fig. 8.B.5.

You might want to extend these calculations to demonstrate that variance does indeed provide a useful measure of uncertainty. Suppose our investor is less uncertain about future prospects. This could be reflected in one of two ways:

1. The investor may believe there is a 70% chance that next year's return on assets will lie between 10.5 and 13.5%.
2. The investor may believe there is a 50% chance that next year's return on assets will be between 11 and 13%.

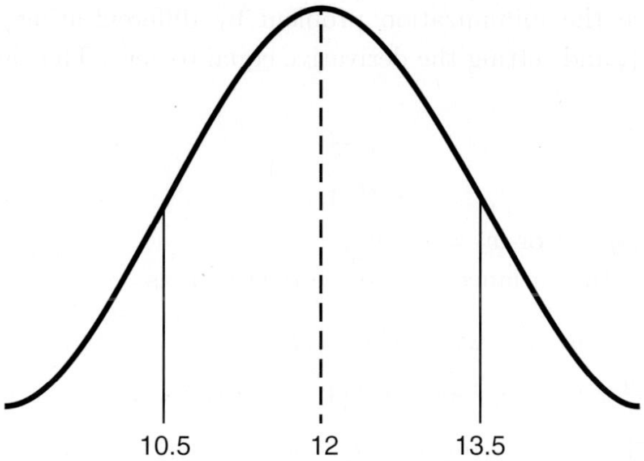

Fig. 8.B.5. For a normal random variable with mean 12, standard deviation 4.95, the probability is 0.5 of a value between 10.5 and 13.5.

It is left as an exercise to the reader to verify that, in either case, assuming a normal distribution, this uncertainty will be described by a distribution with a mean of 12 and a variance of less than 4.95.

One important property of a normal distribution is that any linear function of a normal random variable also has a normal distribution. Specifically, suppose that the random variable X has a normal distribution with mean μ and variance σ^2, and we define the random variable Y as

$$Y = c + dX,$$

where c and d are any constant fixed numbers. Then it can be shown that Y has a normal distribution with mean $(c + d\mu)$ and variance $d^2\sigma^2$.

Appendix 8.C. Derivation of Minimum-Variance Portfolio

If there is a two-security portfolio, its variance can be defined as

$$\sigma_p^2 = w_1^2\sigma_1^2 + w_2^2\sigma_2^2 + 2w_1w_2\text{Cov}(r_1, r_2), \tag{8.C.1}$$

where w_1 and w_2 are weight associated with securities 1 and 2 respectively; σ_1^2 and σ_2^2 are variance of securities 1 and 2 respectively.

The problem is choosing optimal w_1 to minimize the portfolio variance, σ_p^2

$$\underset{w_1}{Min} \times \sigma_P^2. \tag{8.C.2}$$

We can solve the minimization problem by differentiating the σ_p^2 with respect to w_1, and setting the derivative equal to zero. That is, we want to solve

$$\frac{\partial \sigma_p^2}{\partial w_1} = 0. \tag{8.C.3}$$

Since, $w_1 + w_2 = 1$ or $w_2 = 1 - w_1$.

Therefore, the variance, σ_p^2, can be rewritten as

$$\begin{aligned}\sigma_p^2 &= w_1^2\sigma_1^2 + w_2^2\sigma_2^2 + 2w_1w_2\text{Cov}(r_1, r_2)\\ &= w_1^2\sigma_1^2 + (1-w_1)^2\sigma_2^2 + 2w_1(1-w_1)\text{Cov}(r_1, r_2)\\ &= w_1^2\sigma_1^2 + \sigma_2^2 - 2w_1\sigma_2^2 + w_1^2\sigma_2^2 + 2w_1\text{Cov}(r_1, r_2) - 2w_1^2\text{Cov}(r_1, r_2).\end{aligned}$$

Now, the first-order conditions of equation (8.C.3) can be written as

$$2w_1\sigma_1^2 - 2\sigma_2^2 + 2w_1\sigma_2^2 + 2\text{Cov}(r_1, r_2) - 4w_1\text{Cov}(r_1, r_2) = 0.$$

Rearrange the above equation

$$\begin{aligned}w_1\sigma_1^2 + w_1\sigma_2^2 - 2w_1\text{Cov}(r_1, r_2) &= \sigma_2^2 - \text{Cov}(r_1, r_2),\\ [\sigma_1^2 + \sigma_2^2 - 2\text{Cov}(r_1, r_2)]w_1 &= \sigma_2^2 - \text{Cov}(r_1, r_2).\end{aligned}$$

Finally, we have

$$\boxed{w_1 = \frac{\sigma_2^2 - \text{Cov}(r_1, r_2)}{\sigma_1^2 + \sigma_2^2 - 2\text{Cov}(r_1, r_2)}.}$$

Appendix 8.D. Sharpe Performance Approach to Derive Optimal Weight

Solution for the weights of the optimal risky portfolio include two securities can be found by solving the following maximization problem:

$$\underset{w_1}{Max}\, S_p = \frac{E(r_p) - r_f}{\sigma_p},$$

where

$E(r_p)$ = expected rates-of-return for portfolio P.

r_f = Risk free rates-of-return.

S_p = Sharpe performance measure.

σ_p as defined in Eq. (8.C.1) of Appendix 8.C.

We can solve the maximization problem by differentiating the S_p with respect to w_1, and setting the derivative equal to zero. That is, we want to solve

$$\frac{\partial S_p}{\partial w_1} = 0. \tag{8.D.1}$$

In the case of two securities, we know that

$$E(r_p) = w_1 E(r_1) + w_2 E(r_2). \tag{8.D.2}$$

$$\sigma_p = [w_1^2\sigma_1^2 + w_2^2\sigma_2^2 + 2w_1w_2\text{Cov}(r_1, r_2)]^{\frac{1}{2}}. \tag{8.D.3}$$

$$w_1 + w_2 = 1. \tag{8.D.4}$$

From above Eqs. (8.D.2), (8.D.3), and (8.D.4), we can rewrite $E(r_p) - r_f$ and σ_p as

$$\begin{aligned} E(r_p) - r_f &= w_1E(r_1) + w_2E(r_2) - r_f = w_1E(r_1) + (1 - w_1)E(r_2) - r_f \\ &\equiv f(w_1), \end{aligned} \tag{8.D.5}$$

$$\begin{aligned} \sigma_p &= [w_1^2\sigma_1^2 + w_2^2\sigma_2^2 + 2w_1w_2\text{Cov}(r_1, r_2)]^{\frac{1}{2}} \\ &= [w_1^2\sigma_1^2 + (1 - w_1)^2\sigma_2^2 + 2w_1(1 - w_1)\text{Cov}(r_1, r_2)]^{\frac{1}{2}} \\ &\equiv g(w_2). \end{aligned} \tag{8.D.6}$$

Equation (8.D.1) becomes

$$\frac{\partial S_p}{\partial w_1} = \frac{\partial \frac{f(w_1)}{g(w_2)}}{\partial w_2} = \frac{f'(w_1)g(w_2) - f(w_1)g'(w_2)}{[g(w_2)]^2} = 0, \tag{8.D.7}$$

where

$$f'(w_1) = \frac{\partial f(w_1)}{\partial w_1} = E(r_1) - E(r_2), \tag{8.D.8}$$

$$\begin{aligned} g'(w_1) = \frac{\partial g(w_1)}{\partial w_1} &= \frac{1}{2} \times [w_1^2\sigma_1^2 + (1 - w_1)^2\sigma_2^2 + 2w_1(1 - w_1)\text{Cov}(r_1, r_2)]^{\frac{1}{2} - 1} \\ &\quad \times [2w_1\sigma_1^2 + 2w_1\sigma_2^2 - 2\sigma_2^2 + 2\text{Cov}(r_1, r_2) - 4w_1\text{Cov}(r_1, r_2)] \\ &= [w_1\sigma_1^2 + w_1\sigma_2^2 - \sigma_2^2 + \text{Cov}(r_1, r_2) - 2w_1\text{Cov}(r_1, r_2)] \\ &\quad \times [w_1^2\sigma_1^2 + (1 - w_1)^2\sigma_2^2 + 2w_1(1 - w_1)\text{Cov}(r_1, r_2)]^{\frac{1}{2}}. \end{aligned} \tag{8.D.9}$$

From Eq. (8.D.7),

$$f'(w_1)g(w_1) - f(w_1)g'(w_1) = 0, \quad \text{or} \quad f'(w_1)g(w_1) = f(w_1)g'(w_1). \tag{8.D.10}$$

Now, plugging $f(w_1), g(w_1), f'(w_1)$, and $g'(w_1)$ [Eqs. (8.D.5), (8.D.6), (8.D.8) and (8.D.9)] into Eq. (8.D.10), we have

$$\begin{aligned}
&[E(r_1) - E(r_2)] \times [w_1^2\sigma_1^2 + (1-w_1)^2\sigma_2^2 + 2w_1(1-w_1)\text{Cov}(r_1,r_2)]^{\frac{1}{2}} \\
&\quad = [w_1E(r_1) + (1-w_1)E(r_2) - r_f] \\
&\qquad \times [w_1\sigma_1^2 + w_1\sigma_2^2 - \sigma_2^2 + \text{Cov}(r_1,r_2) - 2w_1\text{Cov}(r_1,r_2)] \\
&\qquad \times [w_1^2\sigma_1^2 + (1-w_1)^2\sigma_2^2 + 2w_1(1-w_1)\text{Cov}(r_1,r_2)]^{\frac{1}{2}}. \qquad (8.D.11)
\end{aligned}$$

Multiplying by $[w_1^2\sigma_1^2 + (1-w_1)^2\sigma_2^2 + 2w_1(1-w_1)\text{Cov}(r_1,r_2)]^{-\frac{1}{2}}$ on both hand sides of equation (8.D.11), we have

$$\begin{aligned}
&[E(r_1) - E(r_2)] \times [w_1^2\sigma_1^2 + (1-w_1)^2\sigma_2^2 + 2w_1(1-w_1)\text{Cov}(r_1,r_2)], \\
&\quad = [w_1E(r_1) + (1-w_1)E(r_2) - r_f] \\
&\qquad \times [w_1\sigma_1^2 + w_1\sigma_2^2 - \sigma_2^2 + \text{Cov}(r_1,r_2) - 2w_1\text{Cov}(r_1,r_2)]. \qquad (8.D.12)
\end{aligned}$$

Rearrange all terms on both hand sides of Eq. (8.D.12). i.e.,

Left hand side of Eq. (8.D.12):

$$\begin{aligned}
&[E(r_1) - E(r_2)] \times [w_1^2\sigma_1^2 + (1-w_1)^2\sigma_2^2 + 2w_1(1-w_1)\text{Cov}(r_1,r_2)] \\
&\quad = [E(r_1) - E(r_2)] \times [w_1^2\sigma_1^2 + \sigma_2^2 - 2w_1\sigma_2^2 + w_1^2\sigma_2^2, \\
&\qquad + 2w_1\text{Cov}(r_1,r_2) - 2w_1^2\text{Cov}(r_1,r_2)], \\
&\quad = [E(r_1) - E(r_2)] \times \{w_1^2[\sigma_1^2 + \sigma_2^2 - 2\text{Cov}(r_1,r_2)] \\
&\qquad + 2w_1[\text{Cov}(r_1,r_2) - \sigma_2^2] + \sigma_2^2\}, \\
&\quad = [E(r_1) - E(r_2)] \times \{w_1^2[\sigma_1^2 + \sigma_2^2 - 2\text{Cov}(r_1,r_2)]\} \\
&\qquad + [E(r_1) - E(r_2)] \times \{2w_1[\text{Cov}(r_1,r_2) - \sigma_2^2]\} \\
&\qquad + [E(r_1) - E(r_2)] \times \sigma_2^2, \\
&\quad = [E(r_1) - E(r_2)] \times [\sigma_1^2 + \sigma_2^2 - 2\text{Cov}(r_1,r_2)]w_1^2 \\
&\qquad + 2[E(r_1) - E(r_2)] \times [\text{Cov}(r_1,r_2) - \sigma_2^2]w_1 + [E(r_1) - E(r_2)] \times \sigma_2^2.
\end{aligned}$$

Right-hand side of Eq. (8.D.12)

$$\begin{aligned}
&[w_1E(r_1) + (1-w_1)E(r_2) - r_f] \\
&\qquad \times [w_1\sigma_1^2 + w_1\sigma_2^2 - \sigma_2^2 + \text{Cov}(r_1,r_2) - 2w_1\text{Cov}(r_1,r_2)]
\end{aligned}$$

$$
\begin{aligned}
&= [w_1 E(r_1) + E(r_2) - w_1 E(r_2) - r_f] \\
&\quad \times [w_1\sigma_1^2 + w_1\sigma_2^2 - 2w_1\mathrm{Cov}(r_1, r_2) - \sigma_2^2 + \mathrm{Cov}(r_1, r_2)] \\
&= \{w_1[E(r_1) - E(r_2)] + [E(r_2) - r_f]\} \\
&\quad \times \{w_1[\sigma_1^2 + \sigma_2^2 - 2\mathrm{Cov}(r_1, r_2)] + \mathrm{Cov}(r_1, r_2) - \sigma_2^2\} \\
&= w_1[E(r_1) - E(r_2)] \times w_1[\sigma_1^2 + \sigma_2^2 - 2\mathrm{Cov}(r_1, r_2)] \\
&\quad + w_1[E(r_1) - E(r_2)] \times [\mathrm{Cov}(r_1, r_2) - \sigma_2^2] \\
&\quad + [E(r_2) - r_f] \times w_1[\sigma_1^2 + \sigma_2^2 - 2\mathrm{Cov}(r_1, r_2)] + [E(r_2) - r_f] \\
&\quad \times [\mathrm{Cov}(r_1, r_2) - \sigma_2^2] \\
&= [E(r_1) - E(r_2)] \times [\sigma_1^2 + \sigma_2^2 - 2\mathrm{Cov}(r_1, r_2)]w_1^2 \\
&\quad + [E(r_1) - E(r_2)] \times [\mathrm{Cov}(r_1, r_2) - \sigma_2^2]w_1 \\
&\quad + [E(r_2) - r_f] \times [\sigma_1^2 + \sigma_2^2 - 2\mathrm{Cov}(r_1, r_2)]w_1 \\
&\quad + [E(r_2) - r_f] \times [\mathrm{Cov}(r_1, r_2) - \sigma_2^2].
\end{aligned}
$$

Subtracting $[E(r_1) - E(r_2)][\sigma_1^2 + \sigma_2^2 - 2\mathrm{Cov}(r_1, r_2)]w_1^2$ and $[E(r_1) - E(r_2)][\mathrm{Cov}(r_1, r_2) - \sigma_2]w_1$ from both hand sides of Eq. (8.D.12), we have

$$
\begin{aligned}
&[E(r_1) - E(r_2)] \times [\mathrm{Cov}(r_1, r_2) - \sigma_2^2]w_1 + [E(r_1) - E(r_2)] \times \sigma_2^2 \\
&\quad = [E(r_2) - r_f] \times [\sigma_1^2 + \sigma_2^2 - 2\mathrm{Cov}(r_1, r_2)]w_1 + [E(r_2) - r_f] \\
&\quad \times [\mathrm{Cov}(r_1, r_2) - \sigma_2^2]. \qquad (8.D.13)
\end{aligned}
$$

Moving all the terms with w_1 on one side and leaving the rest terms on the other side from Eq. (8.D.13), we have

$$
\begin{aligned}
&[E(r_1) - E(r_2)] \times \sigma_2^2 - [E(r_2) - r_f] \times [\mathrm{Cov}(r_1, r_2) - \sigma_2^2] \\
&\quad = [E(r_2) - r_f] \times [\sigma_1^2 + \sigma_2^2 - 2\mathrm{Cov}(r_1, r_2)]w_1 - [E(r_1) - E(r_2)] \\
&\quad \times [\mathrm{Cov}(r_1, r_2) - \sigma_2^2]w_1. \qquad (8.D.14)
\end{aligned}
$$

Rearrange Eq. (8.D.14) in order to solve for w_1, i.e.,

$$
\begin{aligned}
&[E(r_1) - E(r_2) + E(r_2) - r_f] \times \sigma_2^2 - [E(r_2) - r_f]\mathrm{Cov}(r_1, r_2) \\
&\quad = \{[E(r_2) - r_f]\sigma_1^2 + [E(r_2) - r_f]\sigma_2^2 - [E(r_2) - r_f][2\mathrm{Cov}(r_1, r_2)] \\
&\quad - [E(r_D) - E(r_E)]\mathrm{Cov}(r_1, r_2) + [E(r_1) - E(r_2)]\sigma_2^2\}\, w_1, \\
&\quad = \{[E(r_1) - r_f]\sigma_2^2 + [E(r_2) - r_f]\sigma_1^2 - [E(r_1) - r_f + E(r_2) - r_f] \\
&\quad \times \mathrm{Cov}(r_1, r_2)]\}\, w_1.
\end{aligned}
$$

Finally, we have the optimum weight of security 1 as

$$w_1 = \frac{[E(r_1) - r_f]\sigma_2^2 - [E(r_2) - r_f]\text{Cov}(r_1, r_2)}{[E(r_1) - r_f]\sigma_2^2 + [E(r_2) - r_f]\sigma_1^2 - [E(r_1) - r_f + E(r_2) - r_f]\text{Cov}(r_1, r_2)}.$$

In this appendix, we discussed Sharpe Performance Measure approach in terms of two securities case. This kind of method can be extended to n securities case. Chiou *et al.* (2008) have used this approach to investigate whether international diversification is beneficial to investors.

References for Appendices 8.A–8.D

Bodie, Z, A Kane, and A Marcus (2006). *Investments* 7th ed. New York: McGraw-Hill Book Company.

Chiou, WJP, AC Lee, and CA Chang (2008). Do investors still benefit from international diversification with investment constraint? Forthcoming in *Quarterly Review of Economics and Finance.*

Lee, CF and AC Lee (2006). *Encyclopedia of Finance*, New York: Springer.

References for Chapter 8

Ben-Horim, M and H Levy (1980). "Total risk, diversifiable risk, and non-diversifiable risk: A pedagogic note," *Journal of Financial and Quantitative Analysis*, 15, 289–295.

Bodie, Z, A Kane, and A Marcus (2006). *Investments 7th ed.*, New York: McGraw-Hill Book Company.

Bowman, RG (1979). The theoretical relationship between systematic risk and financial (accounting) variables. *Journal of Finance*, 34, 617–630.

Chu, CC and F Cheng Lee (1986). Alternative methods for market risk premium estimation and forecasting: implied vs. historical variance approach. *Journal of Midwest Finance Association*, 15, 30–46.

Cochrane, JH (2005). *Asset Pricing.* NJ: Princeton University Press.

Elton, EJ, MJ Gruber, SJ Brown, and WN Goetzmann (2006). *Modern Portfolio Theory and Investment Analysis*, New York: John Wiley & Sons.

Evans, JL and SH Archer (1968). "Diversification and the reduction of dispersion: An empirical analysis. *Journal of Finance*, 23, 761–767.

Francis, J and R Ibbotson (2001). *Investments: A Global Perspective.* Englewood Cliffs, NJ: Prentice Hall.

Francis, JC and SH Archer (1979). *Portfolio Analysis*, Englewood Cliffs, NJ: Prentice-Hall.

Graham, JR and CR Harvey (2001). The theory and practice of corporate finance: Evidence from the field. *Journal of Financial Economics*, 60(2–3), 187–243. Web.

Ibbotson, R and RA Sinquefield. *Stocks, Bonds, Bills, and Inflation: 2006 Yearbook, Annual Updates work by Roger G. Ibbotson and Rex A.* Chicago: Ibbotson Associate.

Levy, H and M Sarnet (1984). *Portfolio and Investment Selection*, Englewood Cliffs, NJ: Prentice-Hall.

Lee, CF and AC Lee (2006). *Encyclopedia of Finance*, Springer: New York.

Luenberger, DG (1997). *Investment Science*, New York: Oxford University Press.

Maginn, JL, DL Tuttle, JE Pinto, and DW McLeavey (2007). *Managing Investment Portfolios: A Dynamic Process (CFA Institute Investment Series)* 3rd ed., New York: John Wiley & Sons.

Markowitz, HM (1959). *Portfolio Selection: Efficient Diversification of Investments*, New York: John Wiley & Sons.

Merton, RC (1980). Eliminating the expected return on the market. *Journal of Financial Economics*, 8, 323–361.

Modigliani, F and GA Pogue (1974). An introduction to risk and return. *Financial Analysts Journal*, 30, 69–86.

Robicheck, AA and RA Cohn (1974). The Economic determinants of systematic risk. *Journal of Finance*, 29, 439–447.

Schall, LD (1972). Asset valuation, firm investment, and firm diversification. *Journal of Business*, 45, 11–28.

Thompson, DJ (1976). Sources of systematic risk in common stocks. *Journal of Business*, 49, 173–88.

Tobin, J (1958). Liquidity preference as behavior toward risk. *Review of Economic Studies*, 25, 65–86.

Chapter 9

Risk and Return Trade-off Analysis

9.1. Introduction

In this chapter, we discuss the risk–return trade-off and the economic relationships between risk and return, using the risk estimation and diversification concepts presented in Chapter 8. We also explain how the market model can be used to estimate the systematic risk and Jensen performance measure. Applications of the beta coefficient and the economic relationships between risk and return are also discussed.

In Section 9.2, we discuss the capital market line (CML), the efficient-market hypothesis (EMH), and the capital asset pricing model (CAPM). In Section 9.3, we define the market model and show how the beta coefficient can be estimated. In Section 9.4, we discuss the empirical evidence for the risk–return relationship. Section 9.5 shows why the beta coefficient is important in financial management. Section 9.6 discusses the determination of systematic risk. In Section 9.7, we discuss the applications and implications of the CAPM. Section 9.8 discusses the impact of liquidity and CAPM. Section 9.9 discusses the generalized capital asset pricing model-arbitrage pricing theory (APT). Finally, in Section 9.10, the results of this chapter are summarized.

9.2. CML, EMH and CAPM

Based on the risk–return trade-off principle and the portfolio diversification process (discussed in Chapter 7), Sharpe (1964), Lintner (1966), and Mossin (1966) developed an asset pricing model that not only determines the value of an efficient portfolio, but also the value of an individual security. They focused on the pricing implications of those areas of risk that can be eliminated through diversification as well as those that cannot.

Systematic risk is the part of total risk that results from the tendency of stock prices to move together with the general market. *Unsystematic risk* is the result of variations peculiar to a firm or industry; for example, a labor strike or resource shortages.

Systematic risk, also referred to as *market risk*, reflects the fluctuations and changes of the general market. Some stocks and portfolios are sensitive to movements in the market, while others show more independence and stability. A measure of a stock or portfolio's relative sensitivity to the market, based on its past record, has been designated by the Greek letter *beta* (β). The estimation and application of beta is discussed in the following section.

9.2.1. *Lending, Borrowing, and the Market Portfolio*

In Chapter 8, we assumed the efficient frontier was constructed with risky assets only. In Fig. 9.1, this is shown by the curve AM_pB. If there are both risk-free and risky assets, then investors have the choice of investing in either type of asset or in combinations of the two types.

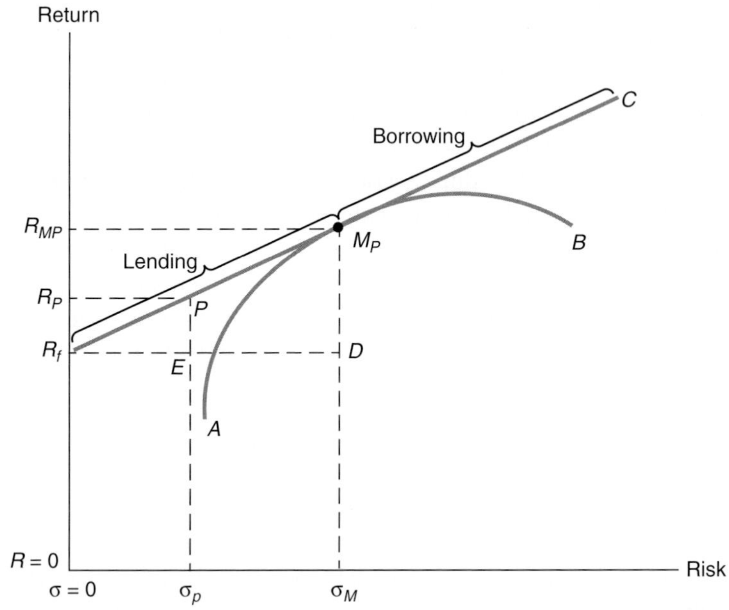

Fig. 9.1. The CML.

In general, risk-free assets refer to government securities, such as Treasury bills (T-bills). These assets are backed by the federal government and are default free and hence riskless; the cash flows are certain. An investor's portfolio can be comprised different sets of investment opportunities including the risk-free asset with a return of R_f. The riskless asset has zero risk and is a point on the vertical axis of the risk-and-return area as shown in Fig. 9.1.

With the additional opportunity to invest in risk-free assets that yield a return of R_f, the investor can create new combinations of portfolios that combine the risk-free asset with risky assets. The investor is thus able to achieve any combination of risk and return that lies along the line connecting R_f and a point tangent to M_p, the market portfolio. All portfolios along the line R_fM_pC are preferred to the risky portfolio opportunities on the curve AM_pB because of the dominance principle. Therefore, the points of the line R_fM_pC represent the best attainable combinations of risk and return.

At point R_f, an investor has all available funds invested in the riskless asset and expects to receive the return of R_f. The portfolios along the line R_fM_p are *lending portfolios* and contain combinations of investments in the risk-free asset and investments in a portfolio of risky assets, M_p. In a sense, the investor is lending the government money at the risk-free rate R_f; hence, the name lending portfolio.

At point M_p, the investor holds only risky assets; all the investor's wealth is in the risky-asset portfolio, which is the market portfolio. At M_p, investors receive a rate-of-return R_m and undertake risk σ_m.

If investors can borrow money at the risk-free rate R_f and invest this money in risky portfolio M_p, they will be able to construct portfolios with higher rates-of-return but with higher risks along the line extending beyond M_p. The extent to which this is possible is regulated by the margin requirements imposed by the government. The higher the margin requirement, the shorter the line M_pC. The amount of money that can be borrowed by investors may also be limited by considerations of the creditworthiness of borrowers. The portfolios along segment M_pC are called *borrowing portfolios*, because the investor must borrow funds to achieve these risk-and-return combinations. The new efficient frontier becomes R_fM_pC and is referred to as the CML. In short, the CML describes the relationship between expected return and total risk for efficient portfolios with the existence of risk-free assets.

9.2.2. *The CML*

We have just given a graphical illustration and verbal explanation of the CML. In equation form, the CML is:

$$E(R_P) = R_f + [E(R_m) - R_f]\frac{\sigma_P}{\sigma_m}, \tag{9.1}$$

where R_f = the risk-free rate; R_m = return on market portfolio M_p; R_p = return on the portfolio consisting of combinations of the risk-free asset and portfolio M_p; σ_p and σ_m = standard deviations of the portfolio and the market; and the operator E denotes expectations.

The interpretation of Eq. (8.1) can be explained geometrically. An investor has three investment choices: R_f, the riskless asset; M_p, the market portfolio' and any other efficient portfolio along the efficient frontier, such as portfolio P in Fig. 9.1.

The riskless asset offers a return of R_f, the market portfolio an average return of R_m and risk of σ_m, and portfolio P an average return of R_p with risk of σ_p. The difference between R_m and R_f $(R_m - R_f)$ is called the *market risk premium.*

The investor in portfolio P only needs to take on risk of σ_p, so the risk premium is $(R_p - R_f)$, which is less than the risks of an investor who holds portfolio M_p.

By geometric theory, triangles $R_f PE$ and $R_f M_p D$ are similar and are, therefore, directly proportional. Thus,

$$E(R_p) - R_f = [E(R_m) - R_f]\frac{\sigma_p}{\sigma_m}. \tag{9.2}$$

In equilibrium, all investors will want to hold a combination of the risk-free and risky assets at the tangency portfolio M_p. At equilibrium, prices are such that the demand for all marketable assets equals their supply; therefore, tangency portfolio M_p must present the market portfolio. An individual security's proportional makeup in the market portfolio is the ratio of its market value (its equilibrium price times the total number of shares outstanding) to the total market value of the securities in the market, or

$$x = \frac{\text{market value of an individual asset}}{\text{market value of all asset}}. \tag{9.3}$$

Thus, at equilibrium, prices are such that supply is equated to demand and all securities in the market will be represented in the market portfolio according to their market value.

9.2.3. *EMH*

Some critical assumptions which will be discussed in deriving the capital asset pricing model are concerned with the efficiency of capital markets. Therefore, the basic concepts of the EMH are discussed next. In the EMH, it is assumed all investors cannot predict the future or direction of capital markets based upon past actions; that is, the short-run changes in stock prices cannot be predicted.

Following Fama (1970, 1976), there are several assumptions that must hold for the efficient-market theory to be accepted. First, there must be a large number of profit-maximizing investors who operate independently for each other. Second, new information must enter the market randomly and independently over time. Third, all investors adjust security prices accordingly when they receive new information, as quickly as possible. It is assumed that price adjustment would occur rapidly because of the large volume of investors participating in the market.

The last assumption is that any point in time, security prices reflect unbiasedly all available information. This hypothesis arises because stock prices are supposed to reflect all available public information at any given time.

Therefore, an efficient market is one in which security prices adjust rapidly with the introduction of new information, and stock prices always reflect all currently available information, including all risks. In conclusion, the returns expected from any given security are consistent with the risk reflected in its price.

9.2.4. *Weak-Form EMH*

This hypothesis assumes that all current stock prices fully reflect all historical and current stock market information. This includes information on prices, price sequences, and volume. The main conclusion is that there is no relationship between past price changes and future price changes, and all price changes are independent.

9.2.5. *Semistrong-Form EMH*

This hypothesis states that security prices adjust rapidly after the release of any new public information and that prices reflect all of this information. This hypothesis is inclusive of the theory also, because public information includes market information as well as non-market information such as economic and political news, earnings, stock splits, and other fundamental corporate information.

The major implication of this hypothesis is that investors who act on public information after it is released will not be able to earn above-average profits, because security prices will already have changed to reflect this information.

9.2.6. *Strong-Form EMH*

This hypothesis encompasses both the weak and semistrong forms in that it contends stock prices fully reflect all information — public, private, or otherwise. Therefore, no group of investors will ever be able to consistently derive above-average profits. As a requirement, therefore, the strong form states that market must be perfect in that all information must be available to everybody at the same time. Since, all information is available to all groups, the strong-form hypothesis contends that no group will have monopolistic access to information and derive above-average profits.

A lot of empirical work has been done in the last two decades to test which EMH is valid. Fama (1976) and others have concluded that the semistrong hypothesis best describes market behavior. Finnerty (1976) and Jaffee (1975) have shown that the stock market is not strong-form efficiency. In recent years, this has led to an increase in inside-trading prosecution by the Securities and Exchange Commission. All these issues can be found in investment textbooks, such as Francis (2013).

9.2.7. *CAPM*

To derive the CAPM we must first list a few assumptions concerning the investors and the securities market:

1. Investors are risk-averse.
2. The CAPM is a single-period model because it is assumed that investors maximize the utility of their end-of-period wealth.
3. All investors have the same efficient frontier; that is, they have homogeneous expectations concerning asset returns and risk.
4. Portfolios and securities are characterized by their means and variances.
5. There is a risk-free asset with an interest rate R_f. This rate is available to all investors to either borrow or lend. The borrowing rate is equal to the lending rate.
6. All assets are remarkable are perfectly divisible, and their supplies are fixed.

7. There are no transaction costs.
8. Investors have all information available to them at no cost.
9. There are no taxes or regulations associated with trading.

Given these assumptions and the derivation presented in Appendix 8.A, the CAPM is defined as

$$E(R_i) = R_f + \beta_i[E(R_m) - R_f], \tag{9.4}$$

where $E(R_i)$ = the expected rate-of-return for asset i; R_f = the risk-free rate; β_i = the measure of systematic risk (beta) for asset i; and $E(R_m)$ = the expected return on the market portfolio.

Equation (9.4) implies that an asset's systematic risk (β_i) is the only relevant risk measure of capital asset pricing for both individual asset and portfolio. Figure 9.2 depicts the risk–return trade-off relationship for the CAPM. This risk–return trade-off is also called the *security market line* (SML).

With the CAPM, we must assume that utility-maximizing investors will attempt to be somewhere along the CML and will attempt to put some portion of their wealth into the market portfolio of risky assets.

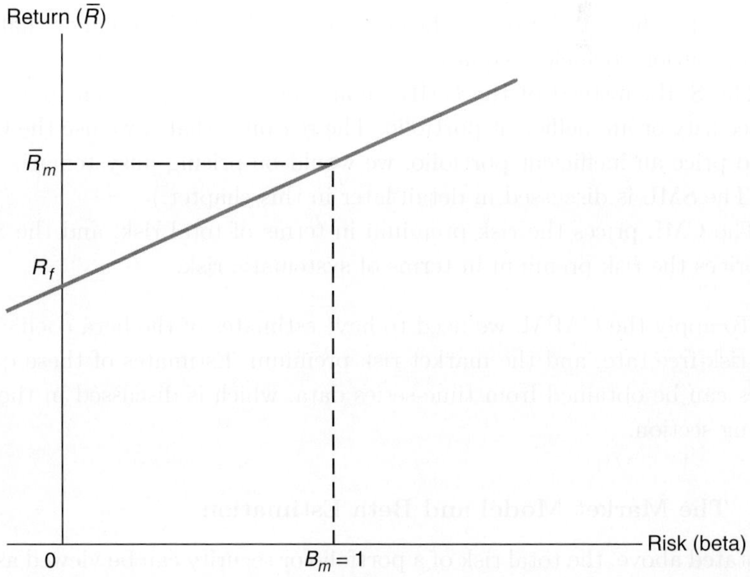

Fig. 9.2. CAPM (SML).

The CAPM implies that the market portfolio is the only relevant portfolio of risky assets. Hence, the relevant risk measurement of any security is its covariance with the market portfolio, the systematic risk of the market.

The relationship between the CML and the CAPM can be shown by starting with the definition of the beta coefficient:

$$\beta = \frac{\mathrm{COV}(R_i, R_m)}{\mathrm{VAR}(R_m)} = \frac{\rho_{i,m}\sigma_i\sigma_m}{\sigma_m^2} = \frac{\rho_{i,m}\sigma_i}{\sigma_m}, \tag{9.5}$$

where σ_i = standard deviation of ith security's rate-of-return; σ_m = standard deviation of the market rate-of-return; and $\rho_{i,m}$ = the correlation coefficient of R_i and R_m.

If $\rho_{i,m} = 1$, then Eq. (9.4) reduces to

$$E(R_i) = R_f + \frac{\sigma_i}{\sigma_m}[E(R_m) - R_f]. \tag{9.6}$$

If $\rho_{i,m} = 1$, this is an efficient portfolio, or for an individual security, the returns and risks associated with the asset are similar to the market as a whole. The implications of this comparison are as follows:

1. Equation (9.4) is a generalized case of Eq. (9.2), because Eq. (9.4) includes the correlation coefficient, whereas Eq. (9.2) assumes that the correlation coefficient equals 1.
2. The SML, instead of the CML, should be used to price an individual security or an inefficient portfolio. The reason is that if we use the CML to price an inefficient portfolio, we would be pricing unsystematic risk. (The SML is discussed in detail later in this chapter.)
3. The CML prices the risk premium in terms of total risk, and the SML prices the risk premium in terms of systematic risk.

To apply the CAPM, we need to have estimates of the beta coefficient, the risk-free rate, and the market risk premium. Estimates of these quantities can be obtained from time-series data, which is discussed in the following section.

9.3. The Market Model and Beta Estimation

As stated above, the total risk of a portfolio or security can be viewed as the sum of its systematic and unsystematic risks. The equation that expresses these concepts states that the return on any asset at time t can be expressed as a linear function of the market return at time t plus a random error component. Thus, this relationship, called the *market model*, is

$$R_{i,t} = \alpha_i + \beta_i R_{m,t} + \varepsilon_{i,t}, \tag{9.7}$$

where $R_{i,t}$ = the return of the ith security at time t; α_i = the intercept of the regression; β_i = the slope coefficient of the regression; $R_{m,t}$ = the market return at time t; and $\varepsilon_{i,t}$ = the random error term.

This regression equation describes the risky asset's return relationship with the market portfolio return. Equation (9.7) is also called the *characteristic line* and is a statistical tool employed to measure systematic and unsystematic risk. The term α_i is called *alpha coefficient* for security i. This is the intercept point where the characteristic line intercepts the y-axis. Since beta is the slope coefficient for this regression (market model), it demonstrates how responsive returns for the individual assets are to the market portfolio.

Alternatively, a market model can be defined as follows:

$$R_{i,t} - R_{f,t} = \alpha_i + \beta_i(R_{m,t} - R_{f,t}) + \varepsilon_{i,t}, \tag{9.8}$$

where $R_{f,t}$ is the risk-free rate. All variables of Eq. (8.8) can be estimated from observed data. Equation (9.8) is the risk premium form of the market model and is similar to the market model indicated in Eq. (9.7).

The CAPM shown by Eq. (9.4) has R_f as the intercept term. In Eq. (9.8), the intercept term of the characteristic line in terms of risk premium is α_i, which has investment performance implications. The estimated α_i, is called the Jensen performance measure. The α_i is defined as

$$\hat{\alpha}_i = (\overline{R}_i - \overline{R}_f) - \beta_i(\overline{R}_m - R_f), \tag{9.9}$$

where $\overline{R}_i$, $\overline{R}_m$, and $\overline{R}_f$ represent the average rate-of-return for security i; average market rate-of-return, and the risk-free rate. (The use of α_i for evaluating investment performance is covered in the section that discusses the Sharpe, Jensen, and Treynor performance measures.)

EXAMPLE 9.1

To show how Eqs. (9.7) and (9.8) can be applied, we use estimates from Johnson & Johnson (JNJ), Merck & Co. Inc. (MRK), and Procter & Gamble Co. (PG) monthly returns for the period from January 2002 to December 2006. Average return, variance, and covariance for these companies are provided in Table 9.1, as is the market average return and the variance of market return.

Table 9.1. Descriptive statistics for firms and stock index.

	Average Return ($\overline{R}_i$)	Variance (σ_i^2)	Covariance [COV (R_i, R_m)]
JNJ	0.0042	0.00162	0.000407
MRK	0.0021	0.00610	0.000974
PG	0.0105	0.00124	0.000244
Market	0.0043	0.00126	

From the definition of the slope of the regression line, defined in Appendix 8.B of Chapter 2, we have:

$$\beta_i = \frac{\text{cov}(R_i, R_m)}{\sigma_m^2}.$$

We calculate the beta of JNJ to be

$$\beta_{JNJ} = \frac{\text{cov}(R_{JNJ}, R_m)}{\sigma_m^2} = \frac{0.000407}{0.00126} = 0.3246,$$

the beta of MRK to be

$$\beta_{MRK} = \frac{\text{cov}(R_{MRK}, R_m)}{\sigma_m^2} = \frac{0.000974}{0.00126} = 0.7763$$

and the beta of PG to be

$$\beta_{PG} = \frac{\text{cov}(R_{PG}, R_m)}{\sigma_m^2} = \frac{0.000244}{0.00126} = 0.1943.$$

To compare these three firms, we have various methods available. In a mean-and-variance framework, the three firms are related as you would expect; which is the higher the risk, the higher the return. This is shown in Fig. 9.3.

In a systematic risk-and-return framework, we find that the higher the beta, the higher the return. This is shown in Fig. 9.4.

Using the Jensen performance measure, we can calculate the relative performance of each firm. If $R_f = 0.004$, then:

$$\hat{\alpha}_{JNJ} = (0.0042 - 0.004) - (0.3255)(0.0043 - 0.004) = 0.0001,$$
$$\hat{\alpha}_{MRK} = (0.0021 - 0.004) - (0.7790)(0.0043 - 0.004) = -0.0021,$$
$$\hat{\alpha}_{PG} = (0.0105 - 0.004) - (0.1941)(0.0043 - 0.004) = 0.0064.$$

The relative risk–return ranking shown by the Jensen measure ranks PG first, JNJ second, and MRK third. In this case, the three methods yield the same relative rankings; however, this may not always be the case. If we have

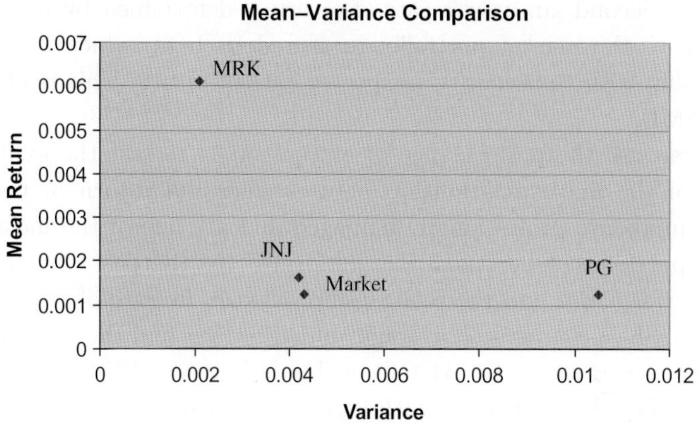

Fig. 9.3. Mean–variance comparison.

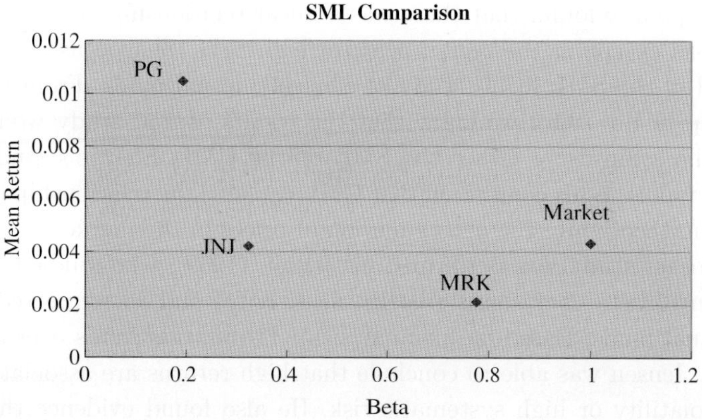

Fig. 9.4. SML comparison.

divergent rankings, the best method to rely on is the Jensen performance measure.

9.4. Empirical Evidence for the Risk–Return Relationship

The validity of the CAPM can be shown through observations of actual portfolios held in the marketplace. As discussed in Chapters 7 and 8, there are two primary observations about the relationship between risk and return. First, the rate-of-return of efficient portfolios is a linear function of their riskiness as measured by their standard deviation and illustrated by the CML. Second, an asset's rate-of-return is determined by its risk contribution to the market portfolio, measured by beta, which has a linear relationship with the security's expected rate-of-return. This is illustrated by the SML.

We can use the performance of mutual funds to test the explanatory powers of the linear relationship between risk and return of the CML. Mutual funds are professionally managed and are one of the most visible type of portfolios. One study was performed by Sharpe (1966) to test a fund's performance and the relationship between its rate-of-return to risk over time. Sharpe computed average annual returns and the standard deviation on these returns for 34 mutual funds between 1954 and 1963. His model implies that portfolios with higher risks will receive higher returns. Sharpe found this to be true for all 34 funds. He calculated a correlation between average returns and their standard deviations to be 0.836, so that greater than 80% of the difference in returns was due to differences in risk.

Sharpe also found that there was a linear relationship between returns and risks except in the region of extra high risks. Sharpe used the CML instead of the SML in his study of efficient mutual funds. From the relationship in Eq. (9.6), we know that the results of that study would have been the same using either the SML or the CML. Sharpe's study gives basic support to his contention that CML explains the relationship between portfolio theory and the determination of prices in the market.

Another study was performed by Jensen (1969), who studied the correlation of beta coefficients (market sensitivity) and the expected return of mutual funds. Based on his analysis of 115 mutual funds over a 9-year period, Jensen was able to conclude that high returns are associated with high volatility or high systematic risk. He also found evidence that beta coefficients were a valid and accurate measure of risk.

Both the Sharpe and Jensen studies on the risk-and-return relationship of mutual funds show that there is an empirical risk–return relationship among mutual funds. However, Sharpe used the CML to perform his empirical tests, while Jensen used the SML, which was derived by Sharpe (1964).

The second implication of the risk–return relationship is that the risk premium on individual assets depends on the contribution of each asset to the riskiness of the entire portfolio and can be algebraically explained by the CAPM and written as

$$E(R_i) - R_f = [E(R_m) - R_f]\beta_i, \tag{9.10}$$

Where

$$\beta_i = \frac{\sigma_{im}}{\sigma_m^2} = \frac{\rho_{i,m}\sigma_i}{\sigma_m}. \quad (9.5)$$

The first equality of Eq. (9.5) states that the riskiness of each asset depends on the covariance of the return between the security i and the market rate-of-return ($\sigma_{i,m}$), and the market variance (σ_m^2). From the second equality of Eq. (9.5) we can analyze how the correlation coefficient between the rate-of-return of security i and market rate-of-return ($\rho_{i,m}$) can be used to analyze the magnitude of beta coefficient. If the correlating coefficient is equal to 1, then the beta coefficient is equal to σ_i/σ_m. If the correlation coefficient is 0, then the beta is equal to 0 and the risk premium is equal to 0 because the asset does not add any additional systematic risk to the portfolio.

To test the CAPM, a problem must first be resolved. The CAPM utilizes *expected* returns, whereas we can observe *actual* returns. The first step is to transfer non-measurable expected returns into a form that utilizes observable data. The empirical model used to test the CAPM is defined as

$$\overline{R}_p - \overline{R}_f = r_0 + r_1\beta_p + e_p, \quad (9.11)$$

where $R_p - R_f$ = the observed excess return on portfolio p; β_p = the estimated beta for portfolio p; and e_p = the residual term associated with the cross-sectional regression.

Equation (9.11) predicts the following:

1. The intercepts, r_0, will not be significantly different from 0. If it were, the CAPM might be misspecified.
2. The relationship with respect to beta is linear.
3. The estimated r_1 would be equal to $(R_m - R_f)$.

Another problem that is prevalent with testing whether theoretical models are valid representatives of real-world phenomena is the "joint hypothesis" problem. When we evaluate real-world problems using theoretical models, we can not be sure that the conclusions reached are accurate or affected by a misspecification of the model used to perform the evaluation. Are the results obtained from using a correct model or are the results obtained because the model is incorrect?

Major empirical tests performed on the CAPM are Blume and Friend (1970, 1973); Black *et al.* (1972); and Fama and Macbeth (1973). Their results were mixed. The empirical results of these researchers were summarized in Copeland and Weston (1988). Roll (1977, 1978) provided a critique on both the CAPM and the Jensen performance measure.

9.5. Why Beta is Important in Financial Management

Beta is used as a measurement of risk by gauging the sensitivity of a stock or portfolio relative to the market. A beta of 1 is characteristic of a broad market index, such as the NYSE index or the S&P 500. A beta of 2 indicates that the stock is expected to swing twice as far in either direction, given a fall or rise in the market average. If the market is expected to gain 15%, a security of beta equal to 2 is expected to gain 30%. Conversely, if the market is expected to fall 15%, then the stock is expected to fall 30%.

A beta of 0.5 indicates that the stock is more stable than the market and is expected to move half as much as the market. For example, if the market is expected to lose 20%, a stock with beta equal to 0.5 is expected to fall only 10%, while if the market is expected to gain 20%, the stock is expected to gain only 10%. High-beta stocks have been classified as *aggressive*, while low-beta stocks are referred to as *defensive*.

The CAPM approach requires a long-run view of decision-making. If the manager consistently follows the indications of the CAPM, short-run errors will tend to cancel out and the expectations will be realized. However, for any single decision, the *a priori* expectations may be very different from the actual results because of various random factors. Therefore, any judgment or evaluation of the efficiency of this method must be carried out over relatively long periods and numerous usages.

The CAPM has shown that risks are associated with portfolios. For instance, the relevant (systematic) risk of a security is dependent on the security's effect on portfolio risk. Therefore, the CAPM equation, $E(R_{i,t}) = R_f + \beta_i[E(R_{m,t}) - R_{f,t}]$, represents a description of how rates-of-return are established in the marketplace assuming that investors behave according to the model's assumptions. Thus, a stock's beta measures its contribution of risk to the portfolio and therefore is a measure of the stock's riskiness relative to the market.

In the previous section, we found that stock i is presumed to bear a linear relationship with the market, as described by Eq. (9.7):

$$R_{i,t} = \alpha_i + \beta_i R_{m,t} + \epsilon_{i,t}. \tag{9.7}$$

The regression coefficient β_i is a market sensitivity index and is a measure of the volatility of stock i against the market. This risk component is the stock's market or *non-diversifiable* risk. Therefore, the size of beta indicates the amount of systematic risk. The greater the beta, the greater the stock's market or non-diversifiable risk.

There is a distinction between the market risk premium and an individual stock's risk premium. The CAPM asserts that the market risk premium is common to all stocks. However, the beta coefficient multiplied by the market risk premium determines the stock's risk premium. Hence, because each stock has a different beta, it will also have a unique risk premium.

The use of beta is of great importance to the financial manager because it is a key component in the estimation of the cost of capital. A firm's expected cost of capital can be derived from $E(R_i)$, where $E(R_i) = R_f + \beta_i[E(R_m) - R_f]$. This assumes that the manager has access to the other parameters, such as the risk-free rate and the market rate-of-return. (This is explored in more detail in Chapter 12.)

Beta is also an important variable because of its usefulness in security analysis. In this type of analysis, beta is used to measure a security's response to a change in the market and so can be used to structure portfolios that have certain risk characteristics.

9.6. Systematic Risk Determination

As mentioned above, systematic risk is non-diversifiable because it occurs in all industries and companies and affects entire markets. Systematic risk is comprised of several components, which we will now discuss.

There are two dimensions of risk that affect a firm's systematic risk. The first is *business risk*, which is the riskiness of a firm's operations if the firm takes on no debt. This is related to the types of investment the firm makes; which could be capital intensive or labor intensive. The second is *financial risk*, which is the additional risk placed on the firm and its stockholders due to the firm's decision to be levered (taking on debt).

Business risk is inherent in a firm's operations. It can also be defined as the uncertainty inherent in the projection of future operating income or earnings before interest and taxes (EBIT). Fluctuations in EBIT are caused by a number of factors. On the national level, these can be economic factors such as inflationary or recessionary periods. At the industry level, factors such as the level of competition between similar industries, natural or man-made catastrophes during production, labor strikes, and price controls can cause EBIT fluctuation. There are a host of possibilities, all of which are reflected in the increase or decrease of EBIT.

Uncertainty regarding future income flows is caused by the company's business risk, which may fluctuate between industries, among firms, and over time. The extent of business risk is dependent on the firm and industry. Cyclical industries, such as steel and automobiles, have especially high business risks because they are dependent on the cycles of the economy. The retail food industry is considered stable because food is a necessary good and will be purchased regardless of the state of the economy.

Business risk is dependent on numerous factors; some of the most important factors are as follows:

1. *Demand variability*: Stable demand levels for the firm's product reduce business risk.
2. *Sales price variability*: Highly volatile prices result in high-risk volatile markets. Therefore, price stability reduces business risk.
3. *Supplier price variability*: Firms whose input prices are highly variable are exposed to higher levels of risk.
4. *Output price flexibility relative to input prices*: Because of inflation, a firm that raises its output prices with increasing input costs minimizes its business risk.

Financial risk refers to the use of fixed-charge securities such as debt or preferred stock. Financial leverage affects a firm's return on equity (ROE) and the riskiness of these returns, as well as the firm's earnings per share and stock price.

9.6.1. *Business Risk and Financial Risk*

A firm's capital structure affects the riskiness inherent in the company's common stock and thus affects its required rate-of-return and stock price. A company's capital structure policy requires choosing between risk and return. Taking on increasing levels of debt increases the riskiness of the firm's earning stream but results in a higher expected rate-of-return. High levels of risk tend to lower a stock's price, but high levels of expected rate-of-return tend to raise it. Therefore, striking a balance between risk and return affects the stock's price. (This issue of capital structure is discussed in Chapter 7.)

When a firm uses debt, or financial leverage, business risk and financial risk are concentrated on the stockholders. For example, if a firm is capitalized only with common equity, then the investors all share the business risk in proportion with their ownership of stock. However, if a firm is 50% levered (50% of the corporation financed by debt, the other half by common equity), then the investors who put up the equity will have to bear all business and financial risk as a result of leverage.

A generalization of the effects of leverage upon return on assets (ROA) and ROE and its effect on the stockholders can be summarized as follows:

1. Leverage, or debt, generally increases ROE.
2. The standard deviation of ROA (σ_{ROA}) measures business risk, while the standard deviation of ROE (σ_{ROE}) measures the risk borne by stockholders. $\sigma_{ROA} = \sigma_{ROE}$ if the firm is not levered; otherwise, with the use of debt, $\sigma_{ROE} > \sigma_{ROA}$, an indication that business risk is being borne by the stockholders.
3. The difference between σ_{ROA} and σ_{ROE} is the actual risk stockholders face and a measure of the increased risk due to financial leverage:

$$\text{risk of financial leverage} = \sigma_{ROE} - \sigma_{ROA}.$$

9.6.2. *Other Financial Variables*

Besides leverage, other financial variables are associated with the firm that can affect the beta coefficient. These are the growth rate, accounting beta, and variance in EBIT.

The growth rate is measured in terms of the growth in total assets or the growth in sales, and is determined by the percentage change between two periods. For example:

$$g_s = \frac{\text{Sales}_t - \text{Sales}_{t-1}}{\text{Sales}_{t-1}} \times 100\%$$

or

$$g_{TA} = \frac{\text{total assets}_t - \text{total assets}_{t-1}}{\text{total assets}_{t-1}} \times 100\%.$$

These equations give the firm's percentage growth. (Chapter 12 discusses other methods of measuring growth rates.)

The accounting beta is calculated from earnings per share data. Using EPS as an example, the accounting beta is calculated as follows:

$$EPS_{i,t} = a_0 + a_1 EPS_{m,t} + E_{i,t}, \tag{9.12}$$

where $EPS_{i,t}$ = earnings per share of firm i at time t and $EPS_{m,t}$ = earnings per share of market average at time t. The estimate of a_1 is the EPS type of accounting beta.

The variance of $EBIT$ can be defined as

$$\sigma^2(EBIT) = \frac{\sum_{t=1}^{N}(EBIT_t - \overline{EBIT})^2}{N-1},$$

where $EBIT_t$ = earnings before interest and taxes in period t. The variance of EBIT can be used to measure the overall fluctuation of a firm's accounting earnings. In general, the more stable the firm's earnings, the better for the investors.

9.6.3. *Capital Labor Ratio*

Both capital (K) and labor (L), are two important inputs for the firm's production process. Mathematically, the relationship between the quantity produced and these two inputs is described in Eq. (9.13):

$$Q = f(K, L), \tag{9.13}$$

where K = the machine (that is, capital) usage during a period (machine/year can be used to measure the amount of capital used) and L = hours of labor input. The capital–labor ratio, K/L, and be used to measure the degree of capital intensity.

Corporations often choose between increasing their capital intensity by installing computers, using robotics in place of labor, or increasing their labor inputs. Small industries specializing in hand-crafted goods will have to increase their capital ratio to increase production. However, the trend in recent years for many growth-oriented firms, whether manufacturers or other members of the business sector, is to increase efficiency through increased investments in capital. Auto manufacturers are finding that robots can assemble cars of high and consistent quality at only a fraction of the cost of assembly-line labor. Hence, many automobile firms are increasing their capital intensity ratio to be more profitable.

Capital intensity increases total risk and generally results in an increase in beta. Large investments are often needed to make a plant fully automated or a financial institution completely computerized. Taking on debt or issuing securities to finance these capitalizations increases the financial risk. If the capital–labor ratio is less than 1, then there is a reduction in capital intensity and a shift toward human resource investments. Firms with capital intensity ratios greater than 1 tend to have high betas, as shown by Subrahmanyam and Thomadakis (1980) and Mandelker and Rhee (1984).

9.6.4. *Fixed Costs and Variable Costs*

Business risk depends on the extent to which a firm builds fixed costs into its operations. Fixed costs do not decline when demand falls off. If fixed costs are high, then a slight drop in sales can lead to large decline in EBIT. Therefore, the higher a firm's fixed costs, the greater its business risk.

Firms with a high percentage of fixed costs have a high degree of operating leverage (as discussed in Chapter 2). An example of such costs is the highly skilled workers of an engineering firm. The firm cannot easily hire and fire experienced and highly skilled workers, so these workers must be retained and paid during periods of slack activity when revenues are low. Therefore, a firm that is highly levered can be characterized as one for which a small change in sales causes a large change in operating income.

Variable costs have the opposite effect because they are adjustable in meeting the changes in revenues that a firm may face. Should a drop in sales occur, variable costs can be reduced to meet the lower output demand.

The extent to which firms can control their operating leverage depends on the type of product or service they provide. Companies that require large investments in fixed assets (such as steel mills, auto manufacturers, and airlines) have large fixed costs and operating leverage. Therefore, the extent to which a company is willing to take on operating leverage must be considered during the capital budgeting decision. If the firm is risk averse, it may opt for alternatives with smaller investments and fixed costs, or it may use different types of financing arrangements (such as leases) to shift the burden of ownership and thereby reduce the investment required.

A company with a large percentage of fixed costs generally uses more capital-intensive types of technology in production. For example, an automobile manufacturer such as Ford has a higher percentage of fixed costs than a company in the food industry such as Coca-Cola. Therefore, Ford's capital–labor ratio is expected to be higher than Coca-Cola's. The implication is that Coca-Cola is expected to have a lower beta than Ford.

9.6.5. *Market-Based versus Accounting-Based Beta Forecasting*

Market-based beta forecasts are based on market information alone. The firm's historical betas are used as a measure of the firm's future beta.

Table 9.2. Regression results for the accounting beta.

$\beta = a_0 + a_1X_1 + a_2X_2 + \cdots + a_nX_n$	Coefficients	t Values
Intercept (a_0)	0.911	11.92
Financial leverage (a_1)	0.704	5.31
Dividend payout (a_2)	−0.175	−3.50
Sales beta (a_3)	0.03	3.02
Operating income beta (a_4)	0.011	2.18

On the other hand, accounting-based beta forecasts rely on the relationship of accounting information — such as the growth rate, EBIT, and leverage — as a basis for forecasting beta. To use accounting information in beta forecasts, we first relate the historical beta estimates cross-sectionally with accounting information:

$$\beta = a_0 + a_1X_1 + a_2X_2 + a_3X_3 + \cdots + a_nX_n, \tag{9.14}$$

where X_j = jth accounting variables for individual firms ($j = 1, 2, \ldots, n$); a_j = the coefficient associated with the jth variable; and a_0 = the intercept.

Lee *et al.* (1986), with the use of accounting information, have shown a relationship between beta and accounting variables. Over the period 1961 to 1980, for a sample of 250 manufacturing firms, they estimated the regression equation shown in Table 9.2.

From these results, we can conclude that accounting information is related to the firm's measure of systematic risk. This information can be used to estimate the cost of capital or the risk-adjusted discount rate for those firms that are not actively traded and therefore do not have market data available. The accounting beta is discussed in Chapter 13 as a method of determining the risk-adjusted discount rate for projects or divisions of a firm faced with capital budgeting decisions. It is also discussed in Chapter 12 as a means of determining the firm's cost of capital.

9.7. Some Applications and Implications of the CAPM

In this section, we will discuss both applications and implications of CAPM. First we will discuss some applications of CAPM. Then we will discuss the implications of CAPM, especially the relationship between liquidity and CAPM.

9.7.1. *Applications*

Since its development, the uses of the CAPM have extended into all areas of financial analysis and planning. These specific uses are discussed in detail in subsequent chapters and are given a general overview here. The CAPM can be applied to the capital budgeting problem in determining the cost of capital (Chapter 12) and in assessing the riskiness of a project under consideration (Chapter 14). The CAPM can also be useful in a real asset problem, such as the lease–buy decision (Chapter 15).

The use of the CAPM can be extended into the valuation of the entire firm. Because of its impact on firm valuation, the CAPM has been of great use in the merger analysis area of financial analysis (Chapter 16). The CAPM has also been used to test various financial theories. By including a dividend term and considering its effects, the CAPM can be used to test the effects of the firm's dividend policy on the value of the firm's shares (Chapter 17). An area that has received a great deal of attention is the use of the CAPM in testing the EMH.

An application of the CAPM to the capital budgeting process concerns the valuation of risky projects. If accurate estimates can be made about the systematic risk of a project, then the CAPM can be used to determine the risk-adjusted discount rate necessary to compensate the firm for the project's risk. If the sum of the estimated cash flows discounted by the CAPM-calculated required rate-of-return is positive, then the firm should undertake the project. This is one method that can be used to handle uncertainty. A more detailed discussion of this risk-adjusted-discount rate method as well as the certainty equivalent method is presented in Chapter 14.

Rubenstein (1973) demonstrated how the CAPM could be used to value securities and to calculate their risk-adjusted equilibrium price. First, the CAPM must be converted to price variables instead of expected returns, as follows:

$$E(R_i) = \frac{E(P_1) - P_0}{P_0}, \tag{9.15}$$

where $E(R_i)$ = the expected returns of the CAPM model; P_1 = price of stock in period 1; and P_0 = price of stock in the previous period. Thus, the CAPM becomes

$$\frac{E(P_1) - P_0}{P_0} = R_f + [E(R_m) - R_f]\beta_i, \tag{9.16}$$

or rearranging 9.16

$$P_0 = \frac{E(P_1)}{1 + R_f + [E(R_m) - R_f](\beta_i)}. \tag{9.17}$$

Thus, the rate-of-return used to discount the expected end-of-period price contains a risk premium dependent on the security's systematic risk. (Eq. (9.16) is used in Chapter 14 to determine risk-adjusted discount rates for capital budgeting decisions under uncertainty.)

The CAPM can be used to choose between alternative projects under uncertainty. For example, the capital budgeting and business strategy relationship matrix, as used in Chapter 14, can be solved by using the CAPM relationship.

If the SML is identified as shown in Fig. 9.5, then the acceptance or rejection of projects A, B, C, D, E, and F can be easily determined. Projects A, B, and D should be accepted because they offer a higher level of return for a given risk level than currently available in the market. Projects C, E, and F should be rejected because their returns are not sufficient to justify the amount of risk that each entails.

The Sharpe approach, used in Chapter 8, consists of drawing a CML and then evaluating the risk-and-return trade-off of each project. The difference between the CML and the SML is the selection of either total risk or systematic risk as the appropriate risk measure.

CAPM has also been applied in the analysis of mergers. It has been shown that portfolio risk can be substantially reduced with the inclusion of securities whose returns are not perfectly correlated. This principle also

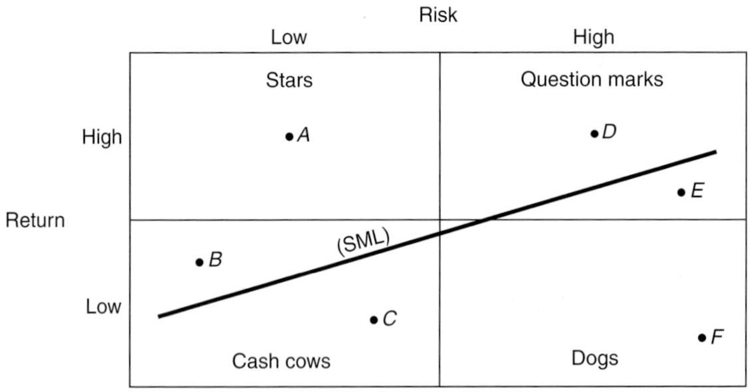

Fig. 9.5. Capital budgeting and Business Strategy Matrix.

applies with respect to mergers between firms. The merger of two firms with different product lines is considered a conglomerate merger. The managers of the merging firms consider the benefits of diversification for these types of firms to be positive. Suppose that one firm sells a product that is recession-resistant, while the other firm's product is highly cyclical. A decrease in earnings of one division of the conglomerate will be offset by the steady earnings of another division during changes in the business cycle. The overall result will be a relatively stable income stream despite shifting trends in the economy.

The application of the CAPM form of analysis in a perfect market setting is governed by the *value additivity principle* (VAP). According to the VAP, in equilibrium the total market value of any set of income streams received by investors in the market is the same regardless of how that set of streams is combined or divided into the debt or equity stream of one or more firms. In our merger discussion, we apply the CAPM form of the analysis, but we assume that real-world markets (both financial and product) in which the manager must operate are not perfect (VAP may not hold). This real-world approach will be stressed in the remainder of the text.

9.8. Liquidity and CAPM

Cochrane (2005) has introduced the liquidity factor into the CAPM model. In accordance with the liquidity effect, Acharya and Pedersen (2005) proposed the following model for liquidity considering the impact of liquidity risk on security pricing.

$$E(R_i) = kE(C_i) + \lambda(\beta + \beta_{L1} - \beta_{L2} - \beta_{L3}), \tag{9.18}$$

where

$E(C_i)$ = expected cost of liquidity,
k = adjustment for average holding period over all securities,
λ = market risk premium net of average market liquidity,
β = systematic market risk,
$\beta_{L1}, \beta_{L2}, \beta_{L3}$ = liquidity betas.

In their model, Acharya and Pedersen (2005) suggests that the overall risk of a security account for three kinds of liquidity risks are defined as follows.

$$\beta_{L1} = \frac{\text{Cov}(C_i, C_M)}{\text{Var}(R_M - C_M)},$$

$$\beta_{L2} = \frac{\text{Cov}(R_i, C_M)}{\text{Var}(R_M - C_M)},$$

$$\beta_{L3} = \frac{\text{Cov}(C_i, R_M)}{\text{Var}(R_M - C_M)},$$

where

$$R_M = \text{market rate-of-return,}$$

$$C_M = \text{market average liquidity premium.}$$

First, β_{L1} measures the sensitivity of security illiquidity to market illiquidity. In general, investors demand higher premium for holding an illiquid security when the overall market liquidity is low. Further, β_{L2} measures the sensitivity of security's return to market illiquidity. Investors are willing to accept a lower average return on security that will provide higher returns when market illiquidity is higher. Finally, β_{L3} measures the sensitivity of security illiquidity to the market rate-of-return. In general, investors are willing to accept a lower average return on security that can be sold more easily.

Liquidity is an important subject in finance research. It has been found liquidity will affect the asset pricing determination. Readers can refer this issue to Cochrane (2005) and Acharya and Pedersen (2005).

9.9. APT

Ross (1976, 1977) has derived a generalized capital asset pricing relationship called APT. To derive the APT, Ross assumed the expected rate-of-return on ith security $[E(R_{it})]$ be explained by k independent influences (or factors) as

$$[E(R_{it})] = a + b_{j1}(\text{factor } 1) + b_{j2}(\text{factor } 2) + \cdots + b_{jk}(\text{factor } k), \quad (9.19)$$

where b_{ij} is a sensitivity indicator that measures how responsive returns from asset i are to factor (index) j for $1, 2, \ldots, k$ factors. The theory doesn't say what factors should be used to explain the expected rates-of-return. These factors could be interest rates, oil prices, or other economic factors. The market portfolio itself might be a factor.

Using Eq. (8.18), Ross has shown that the risk premium of jth security can be defined as

$$E(R_i) - R_f = [E(F_i) - R_f]b_{i1} + \cdots + [E(F_k) - R_f]b_{ik}, \quad (9.20)$$

where $E(F_i)-R_f$ represents the risk premium associated with the ith factor and measures the market price of risk for whatever risk is measured by b_{ij}. If $b_{i1}=1$, and $b_{i2}=b_{i3}=\cdots=b_{ik}=0$, and the first factor is the market, then Eq. (9.19) reduces to the CAPM as

$$E(R_i)-R_f[E(R_m)-R_f]\beta_i.$$

By comparing Eq. (9.19) with the CAPM equation, we can conclude that the APT is a generalized CAPM. Therefore, it is one of the most important models for students of finance to understand. Generally, this model is discussed in upper-level financial management or investment courses.

9.10. Summary

In Chapter 9, we have discussed the basic concepts of risk and diversification and how they pertain to the CAPM, as well as the procedure for deriving the CAPM itself. It was shown that the CAPM is an extension of the CML theory. The possible uses of the CAPM in financial analysis and planning were also indicated. According to a surveyed paper by Graham and Harvey (2001), larger firms rely on present value techniques and the capital asset pricing model, while smaller firms rely on the payback criterion. The paper also discusses how firms are concerned about financial flexibility and credit ratings when issuing debt. However, when issuing equity, firms focus on earnings per share dilution and recent stock appreciation.

The concept of beta and its importance to the financial manager were introduced. Beta represents the firm's systematic risk and is a comparative measure between a firm's security or portfolio risk and market risk. Systematic risk was further discussed by investigating the relationship between the beta coefficient and other important financial variables.[1]

Problem Set

1. Define the following terms:
   (a) Systematic versus non-systematic risks.
   (b) CML versus SML.
   (c) Sharpe versus Jensen performance measures.

[1]Since $\Delta PR_fE \cong \Delta M_pR_fD$ therefore,

$$\frac{E(R_p)-R_f}{E(R_m)-R_f}=\frac{\sigma_p}{\sigma_m}.$$

From this equation, we obtain Eq. (8.2).

(d) Strong versus weak form market efficiency.
(e) Market model and characteristic line.
(f) Aggressive versus defensive stock.

2. What is the relationship between the CAPM and the APT?
3. Briefly discuss the key variables used to describe the beta coefficient.
4. The risk-free interest rate of an investment is 5% and the expected return on the market is 11%. Answer these questions on the basis of CAPM.

   (a) What is the risk premium on the market?
   (b) XYZ Company has a beta of 2. What is the required rate-of-return on an investment made with the XYZ Company?
   (c) If an investment with a beta of 1.5 is supposed to yield an expected rate-of-return of 11%, does the investment have positive *NPV*?

5. If the standard deviation of the market return is 15%, answer the following:

   (a) What is the standard deviation of return on a well-diversified portfolio (zero non-systematic risk) with a beta of 1.2?
   (b) A portfolio still has some non-systematic risks. If its standard deviation is 30% and its beta is 1.7, what is the non-systematic risk portion?
   (c) How much is the systematic risk of the portfolio in question b?

6. ABC Company is a manufacturing firm that buys rare raw materials from other countries. However, the supply of these materials is very unstable, causing wide fluctuations in ABC's income. If the expected market rate-of-return is 10% and ABC Company's beta is 2, what is the company's expected rate-of-return?
7. Stock X has a beta of 1.2 and its expected price at time 1 is \$100. Find its equilibrium price at time 0. (Assume $R_m = 12\%$ and $RF = 6\%$).
8. If the stock's expected price at time 1 is \$100 with certainty, what will be the price of X in question 7 at time 0?
9. Here is a firm's data on business and financial risk:
   variance of ROA = 5%
   variance of ROE (with debt) = 7%

   (a) How much is business risk?
   (b) How much is financial risk?
   (c) How much is the variance of ROE without debt?

10. Below are the statistics on the returns from the three securities, the market, and the risk-free rate:

Security	Mean Return	Variance	Covariance
Sellnex	0.20	0.15	0.08
Kally	0.10	0.06	0.03
Nikita	0.13	0.10	0.05
Market	0.15	0.06	
Risk-free Rate	0.05		

    (a) Find the betas for the three securities.
    (b) Find the required rate-of-return for the three securities according to the SML.
    (c) What is the average risk premium for the market return?
    (d) Find the average risk premium for each of the three securities.
    (e) Find Jensen's Performance Measure, alpha, for each of the three securities.
    (f) Plot the mean and variance of the three securities. Does any one security dominate the other two?
    (g) Plot the mean return against the expected rate-of-return along the Security Market Line. Which securities are "good" investments?

11. Graph the Security Market Line and the CML. Then discuss how they are similar and how they differ.
12. AXEL, Inc. has security returns which have a correlation coefficient with the market of 0.6. The standard deviation of AXEL's returns is 5% while that for the market is 8%.

    (a) Find AXEL's beta.
    (b) If the risk-free rate of interest is 5% and the expected (mean) return on the market is 14%, what is the required rate-of-return for AXEL? (Use the CAPM.)
    (c) If an investor analyzes AXEL's stock and estimates an expected rate-of-return of 12%, is it a good investment?

13. A firm has a standard deviation of its ROE equal to 4%.

    (a) What is its business risk if no debt financing is use?
    (b) What is its business and financial risk if the standard deviation of ROA is 2%?

14. Joe's stock is expected to have a market price of \$70 at the end of 1 year ($t = 1$). The stock's beta is 1.3, the return on the market is 14%, and the risk-free rate is 6%. What is the value of the stock now?
15. Compare and contrast SML and the characteristic line. How are they similar and how do they differ?
16. The return on the market portfolio is 16% and its standard deviation is 6%. The risk-free rate of interest is 5%.

    (a) Find thc return and risk of an investment strategy in which the investor lends 40% of his/her investment at the risk-free rate and invests the remaining 60% in the market portfolio.
    (b) Find the risk-and-return of an investment strategy in which the investor puts 130% of his/her investment in the market portfolio by borrowing at the current risk-free rate.
    (c) Would the risk-averse investor prefer the strategy in part a or part b? Explain.

17. Assume that the current market price for a security is \$70. Its expected return is 15%. The risk-free rate and the market risk premium are 5% and 7.5% respectively. What will be the market price of the security if its correlation coefficient with the market portfolio doubles (and all other variables remain unchanged)? Assume that the security is expected to pay a constant dividend in perpetuity.
18. The following table gives a security analyst's expected return on two stocks with two particular market returns:

Market Return (%)	**Stock A (%)**	**Stock B (%)**
7	−5	8
26	30	14

    (a) Calculate the betas of the two stocks.
    (b) Calculate the expected return on each stock if the market return is equally likely to be 7% and 26%.
    (c) Assume that the risk-free rate is 5%. Calculate the alphas of each stock.

19. Assume the CAPM is valid. Please explain if the following two situations are possible.

(a)

Portfolio	Expected Return	Standard Deviation
A	40	45
B	50	20

(b)

Portfolio	Expected Return	Standard Deviation
Risk Free	12	0
Market	15	26
A	21	20

20. Assume that the risk-free rate is 5% and the expected rate-of-return of the market is 15%. The current market price of stock A is $50 today. It is expected to pay a dividend of $6 at the end of the year. Further, the stock's beta is 1.5. What do investors expect stock A to sell at the end of the year?
21. An investment firm is buying a manufacturing firm with an expected perpetual cash flow of $1200 but is not sure of its risk. If the investment firm thinks the beta of the firm is 0.8 when the beta is actually 1, how much more the investment firm will offer for the firm than it is truly worth. Assume that the risk-free rate is 6% and the market return is 16%.
22. A mutual fund manager is considering buying a stock with an expected return of 7%. Assume that that risk-free rate is 6% and the market rate-of-return is 15%. Calculate the stock's beta.
23. Assume the zero-beta version of the CAPM holds. The expected rate-of-return of the market portfolio is 15% and that of the zero-beta portfolio is 10%. Please calculate the expected return on a portfolio with a beta of 0.8.
24. Assume a mutual fund has an expected return of 16% with a beta of 0.7. Further, the current risk-free rate is 5% and the return on the market portfolio is 16%. Should investors invest in this mutual fund? What is this mutual fund's alpha?

25. Consider the same mutual fund described in the previous question. What passive portfolio comprised of a market index portfolio and a money market account would have the same beta as the fund? What is the expected return of this portfolio?
26. An investor is considering two investment advisers. The first adviser averaged a 20% rate-of-return and the second one a 15% rate-of-return. The beta of the first adviser is 1.8 whereas the beta of the second investor is 1.2.

    (a) Can the investor tell which adviser is a better selector of individual stocks (aside from the market general movement)?
    (b) Assume the risk-free rate is 5% and the market rate-of-return is 15%. Which adviser would be a superior stock selector?
    (c) Consider part (b) again if the risk-free rate is 6% and the market rate-of-return is 18%.

27. Assume the rate-of-return on the short-term government securities is about 6%. Furthermore, the rate-of-return required by the market for a portfolio with beta of 1 is 15%. If the CAPM is valid, then

    (a) What is the expected return on the market portfolio?
    (b) What is the expected rate-of-return on a stock with beta equal to 2?
    (c) An investor is buying a stock at $50. The stock is expected to pay $3 dividend next year and the investor is expected to sell the stock then for $53. The stock has a beta equal to −0.8. Determine whether this stock is overpriced or underpriced.

28. A consultant at a large steel manufacturer is considering a project with the following net after-tax cash flow ($billion):

Years From Now	**After-Tax Cash Flow**
0	−50
1–10	20

    Assume that the risk-free rate is 6% and the rate-of-return on a market portfolio is 16%. Further, the project's beta is 1.6.

    (a) What is the net present value of the project?
    (b) What is the highest possible beta estimate for the project before its NPV becomes negative? (Assume that the IRR is 38%).

29. Suppose that the risk premium on the market portfolio is estimated at 10% with a standard deviation of 25%. What is the risk premium on a portfolio invested at 30% in Microsoft and 70% in Dell if they have betas of 1.2 and 1.5 respectively?

Appendix 9.A. Mathematical Derivation of the CAPM

Using the assumptions of efficient and perfect markets, stated earlier in Chapter 8, we can show how Sharpe derived the CAPM.

Sharpe (1964) used a general risky asset that did not lie on the CML and dubbed it I. The combinations of risk and return possible by combining security I with the market portfolio, M, are shown by Fig. 9.A.1. The average return and standard deviation for any I–M combination can be approached in the same way as for a two-asset case:

$$E(R_P) = w_i E(R_i) + (1 - w_i) E(R_m), \tag{9.A.1}$$

$$\sigma_P = [w_i^2 \sigma_i^2 + (1 - w_i)\sigma_m^2 + 2(1 - w_i) w_i \sigma_{im}]^{\frac{1}{2}}, \tag{9.A.2}$$

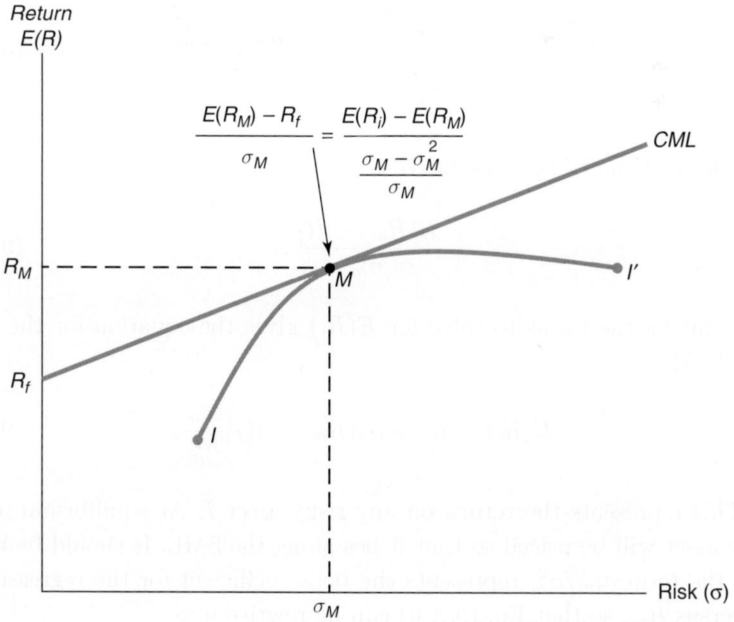

Fig. 9.A.1. The opportunity set provided by combinations of risky asset and/or market portfolio, M.

where w_1 represents excess demand for I or demand greater than its equilibrium weight in portfolio M, and σ_{im} is the covariance of i and m.

The change in mean and standard deviation as the proportion w_1 changes are the partial derivatives

$$\frac{\partial E(R_P)}{\partial w_i} = E(R_i) - E(R_m), \tag{9.A.3}$$

$$\frac{\partial(\sigma_P)}{\partial w_i} = \frac{1}{2}[w_i^2\sigma_i^2 + (1-w_i)^2\sigma_m^2 + 2w_i(1-w_i)]^{-\frac{1}{2}}$$
$$\times (2w_i\sigma_i^2 - 2\sigma_m^2 + 2w_i\sigma_m^2 + 2\sigma_{im} - 4w_i\sigma_{im}).$$

When $w_i = 0$, the security is held in proportion to its total market value and there is no excess demand for security I. This is the key insight to Sharpe's paper, for when $w_i = 0$, it is possible to equate the slope of the curve *IMI*' with the CML and thus obtain an expression for the return on any risky security I. At equilibrium when $w_i = 0$, the slope along the *IMI*' curve will equal

$$\frac{\partial E(R_P)}{\partial(\sigma_P)} = \frac{\dfrac{\partial E(R_P)}{\partial w_i}}{\dfrac{\partial(\sigma_P)}{\partial w_i}} = \frac{\dfrac{E(R_i) - E(R_m)}{\sigma_{im} - \sigma_m^2}}{\sigma_m}. \tag{9.A.4}$$

The slope of the CML at point M is

$$\frac{E(R_m) - R_f}{\sigma_m}. \tag{9.A.5}$$

Rearranging the terms to solve for $E(R_i)$ gives the equation for the SML or CAPM

$$E(R_i) = R_f + [E(R_m) - R_f]\frac{\sigma_{im}}{\sigma_m^2}. \tag{9.A.6}$$

This represents the return on any risky asset I. At equilibrium, every risky asset will be priced so that it lies along the SML. It should be noted that the term σ_{im}/σ_m^2 represents the beta coefficient for the regression of R_i versus R_m, so that Eq. (9.A.6) can be rewritten as

$$E(R_i) = R_f + [E(R_m) - R_f]\beta_i. \tag{9.A.7}$$

Appendix 9.B. Arbitrage Pricing Model

An alternative to the CAPM has been developed by Ross (1976, 1977), which is a more generalized form of an equilibrium relationship such as is found in the CAPM. First, Ross proposed that the returns on a security can be explained by k factors:

$$R_j = E(R_j) + b_{1j}\delta_1 + b_{2j}\delta_2 + \cdots + b_{kj}\delta_k + \varepsilon_j, \tag{9.B.1}$$

where

$$\delta_{1,\ldots,k} = \text{the common return-generating factors and}$$
$$b_{1j,\ldots,kj} = \text{the sensitivity of security } j \text{ to factors 1 through } k.$$

Certain assumptions are then made concerning an arbitrage portfolio. The general idea behind an arbitrage portfolio is that it is constructed with no new wealth invested, as well as a beta of zero. Thus, it has no risk. In general, if an asset involves no risk, then it must pay the risk-free rate-of-return. If this were not so, if the return on the zero-beta portfolio were greater than the risk-free rate-of-return, then an arbitrage opportunity exists. Positive excess returns will be available to any investor who invests in this risk-free, excess-return portfolio. As more investors attempt to transfer their funds to take advantage of this opportunity, the price of the portfolio rises relative to others available, and its return declines. This process will continue until the return on this risk-free portfolio is such that no further arbitrage opportunity exists. At this point, the portfolio is priced to yield the risk-free rate-of-return.

To construct such an arbitrage portfolio, we first assume:

$$\sum b_{kj}X_j = 0, \tag{9.B.2}$$

where X_j, is a portfolio weight for the jth security, and b_{kj} is the sensitivity of the security, for each of the k factors. This condition says that the total beta of the arbitrage portfolio is zero.

Next, it is assumed that the portfolio involves no new investment, or

$$\sum_{j=1}^{n} X_j = 0. \tag{9.B.3}$$

The conditions that the portfolio has no risk (zero beta) and invests no wealth means that its expected return must be zero:

$$\sum X_j \dot{R}_j = 0. \tag{9.B.4}$$

where $\dot{R}_j$, is the expected rate-of-return.

Stating these conditions in another way, the security weight vector is orthogonal to the vector of betas, the vector of 1's, and the vector of expected returns. Therefore, the expected return vectors can be expressed as a linear combination of the constant vector and the beta vectors:

$$E(R_j) = \lambda_0 + \lambda_1 b_{j1} + \lambda_2 b_{j2} + \cdots + \lambda_k b_{jk}, \qquad (9.B.5)$$

where $\lambda_0, \ldots, \lambda_k$ = the $(k+1)$ factor weights for security j.

Thus, the assumption of an arbitrage portfolio and a multifactor, return-generating process can be combined to give a multifactor SML which allows for more complex factors as part of the return-generating process. Note that Eq. (9.B.5) is a more general form of the SML, which contains the SML as a special case where $k = 1$.

This pricing relationship Eq. (9.B.5) is the central conclusion of the APT, and it is the cornerstone for Roll and Ross's (1980) empirical test. It is important to ask what interpretation can be given to the λ_j factor risk premiums. By forming portfolios with unit systematic risk for each factor and no risk on other factors, each λ_j can be interpreted as:

$$\lambda_i = E_i - E_0,$$

the excess-return or market-risk premium on only systematic j risk. Then Eq. (9.B.5) can be rewritten as:

$$E(R_j) - E_0 = (E_1 - E_0)b_{j1} + \cdots + (E_k - E_0)b_{jk}. \qquad (9.B.6)$$

Ross (1977) shows that Eq. (9.B.6) can reduce to the CAPM if there is only one factor. Roll and Ross (1980) argue that a market factor might serve substitute for one of the factors.

To perform the empirical test of the APT of Eq. (9.B.5), Roll and Ross (1980) use the factor-analysis technique discussed in Chapter 3, to obtain the factor loadings as estimates for b_{it} ($i = 1, 2, \ldots, k$). Then the cross-sectional regression estimates are used to determine the numbers of factors needed in determining the capital-asset pricing process. Roll and Ross found that there are either three or four factors needed to determine the Capital Asset Pricing Process as indicated in their Tables II and III. Results of their Table III were obtained by running cross-sectional, generalized least-squares regressions of Eq. (9.B.6). For 42 groups of 30 individual securities per group, 1962–1972 daily returns were used to calculate the arithmetic-mean sample return and factor loadings needed to do the empirical analysis.

Roll and Ross's empirical test has been carefully reexamined by Dhrymes Friend and Gultekin (1984) and Cho *et al.* (1984).

Most recently Jobson (1982) and Lee *et al.* (1991) [LWC] have used linear combination concepts as an alternative method for testing the APT. This alternative model can be defined as:

$$R_{jt} = a_0 + a_1 R_{1t} + \cdots + a_{i-1} R_{i-1t} + a_{i+1} R_{i+1t} + a_k R_k + \varepsilon_{it}, \qquad (9.B.7)$$

where R_{jt} $(j = 1, 2, \ldots, n)$ is the rate-of-return for the jth security in period t. LWC have also shown that Eq. (9.B.7) can be used to theoretically justify Lloyd and Lee's (1976) Block Recursive systems in asset pricing.

Theoretically, the applications of APT in financial analysis and planning should be similar to those of the CAPM. Bower *et al.* (1985) have used APT to estimate cost of capital and investment decisions for the electric utility industry. It is obvious that the usefulness of APT in both financial management and investment analysis are growing. Fogler (1982) recently discussed the common sense of CAPM, APT, and correlated residuals. He concluded that both APT and the multi-index model can be used to improve investment analysis and portfolio management. Possible relationships between the APT and the multi-index model have been discussed by Roll and Ross and LWC in some detail.

References for Appendix 9.B

Cho, DC, EJ Elton, and MJ Gruber (1984). On the robustness of the roll and ross arbitrage pricing theory. *The Journal of Financial and Quantitative Analysis*, 19(1), 1–10.

Dhrymes, JP, I Friend, and NB Gultekin (1984). A critical reexamination of the empirical evidence on the arbitrage pricing theory. *Journal of Finance*, 39(2), 323–426.

Francis, JC and D Kim (2013). *Modern Portfolio Theory: Foundation, Analysis, and New Developments*. New York: John Wiley and Sons, Inc.

Lee, CF, KCJ Wei, and AH Chen (1991). Multivariate regression tests of the arbitrage pricing theory: The instrumental-variables approach. *Review of Quantitative Finance and Accounting*, 1, 191–208.

Roll, R and SA Ross (1980). An empirical investigation of the arbitrage pricing theory, *Journal of Finance*, 35(5), 1073–1103.

Ross, SA (1976). Arbitrage theory of capital asset pricing. *Journal of Economic Theory*, 8, 341–360.

Ross, SA (1977). Return, risk and arbitrage. *Risk and Return in Finance*, 1, 187–208.

References for Chapter 9

Acharya, VV and LH Pedersen (2005). Asset pricing with liquidity risk. *Journal of Financial Economics*, 77(2), 375–410.

Black, F, MC Jensen, and M Scholes (1972). The Capital asset pricing model: Some empirical test, reprinted in *Studies in the Theory of Capital Markets*. New York: Praeger 79–124.

Blume, M and I Friend (1970). Measurement of portfolio under uncertainty. *American Economics Review*, 60, 561–575.

Blume, M and I Friend (1973). A new look at the capital asset pricing model. *Journal of Finance*, 28, 19–34.

Chen, KC, CF Lee, and KT Liaw (1995). Systematic risk, wage rates, and factor substitution, (with K.C. Chen and K. Thomas Liaw). *Journal of Economics and Business*, 47, 267–279.

Copeland, TE and JF Weston (2003). *Financial Theory and Corporate Policy* 4th ed., Reading, Mass, Addison-Wesley Publishing Company.

Cochrane, JH (2005). *Asset Pricing*. Princeton: Princeton University Press.

Elton, EJ and MJ Gruber (2006). *Modern Portfolio Theory and Investment Analysis* 7th ed. New York: John Wiley & Sons.

Fama, EF (1970). Efficient capital market: A review of theory and empirical work. *Journal of Finance*, 25, 383–405.

Fama, EF (1976). *Foundations of Finance*. New York: Basic Books.

Fama, EF and J MacBeth (1973). Risk, return and equilibrium: Empirical tests. *Journal of Political Economy*, 31, 607–636.

Finnerty, J (1976). Insiders and market efficiency. *Journal of Finance*, 31, 1141–1148.

Jaffe, J (1974). The effect of regulation changes on insider trading. *The Bell Journal of Economics and Management Science*, 5, 93–121.

Jensen, MC (1969). Risk, the pricing of capital assets, and the evaluation of investment portfolio. *Journal of Business*, 42, 167–247.

Lee, CF, WP Chen, H Chung, and W Liao (2007). Corporate governance and equity liquidity: Analysis of S&P transparency and disclosure rankings. *Corporate Governance*, 15(4), 644–660.

Luenberger, DG (1997). *Investment Science*, Oxford University Press.

Mandelker, G and S Rhee (1984). The impact of the degree of operating and financial leverage on systematic risk of common sotck. *Journal of Financial and Quantitative Analysis*, 14, 45–57.

Roll, R (1977). A critique of the asset pricing theory's test. *Journal of Financial Economics*, 4, 128–176.

Roll, R (1978). Ambiguity when performance is measured by the securities market line. *Journal of Finance*, 33, 1051–1069.

Ross, SA (1976). Arbitrage theory of capital asset pricing. *Journal of Economic Theory*, 8, 341–360.

Ross, SA (1977). Return, risk and arbitrage. *Risk and Return in Finance*, 1, 187–208.

Rubinstein, ME (1973). A mean–variance synthesis of corporate financial theory. *Journal of Finance*, 18, 167–187.
Sharpe, WF (1963). A simplified model for portfolio analysis. *Management Science*, 2, 277–293.
Sharpe, WF (1964). Capital asset prices: A theory of market equilibrium under conditions of risk. *Journal of Finance*, 19, 425–442.
Sharpe, WF (1966). Mutual fund performance. *Journal of Business* 9, 119–138.
Subrahmanyam, M and S Thomadakis (1980). Systematic risk and the theory of the firm. *Quarterly Journal of Economics*, 39, 437–451.

Chapter 10

Options and Option Strategies

10.1. Introduction

The use of stock options for risk reduction and return enhancement has expanded at an astounding pace over the last twenty years. Among the causes of this growth, two are most significant. First, the establishment of the Chicago Board Option-Exchange (CBOE) in 1973 brought about the liquidity necessary for successful option trading, through public listing and standardization of option contracts. The second stimulus emanated from academia. In the same year that the CBOE was established, Professors Fischer Black and Myron Scholes published a paper in which they derived a revolutionary option-pricing model. The power of their model to predict an option's fair price has since made it the industry standard.

The development of option-valuation theory shed new light on the valuation process. Previous pricing models such as CAPM were based on very stringent assumptions, such as there being an identifiable and measurable market portfolio, as well as various imputed investor attributes, such as quadratic utility functions. Furthermore, previous theory priced only market risk since investors were assumed to hold well-diversified portfolios. The strength of the Black–Scholes and subsequent option-pricing models is that they rely on far fewer assumptions. In addition, the option-valuation models price total risk and do not require any assumptions concerning the direction of the underlying securities price. The growing popularity of the option concept is evidenced by its application to the valuation of a wide array of other financial instruments (such as common stock and bonds) as well as more abstract assets including leases and real estate agreements.

This chapter aims to establish a basic knowledge of options and the markets in which they are traded. It begins with the most common types of options, calls, and puts, explaining their general characteristics and discussing the institutions where they are traded. In addition, the concepts relevant to the new types of options on indexes and futures are introduced. The next focus is the basic pricing relationship between puts and calls, known as put-call parity. The final study concerns how options can be used as investment tools. The chapter on option valuation that follows utilizes all these essential concepts to afford a deeper conceptual understanding of valuation theory.

10.2. The Option Market and Related Definitions

This section discusses option-market and related definitions of options, which are needed to understand option valuations and option strategies.

10.2.1. *What Is an Option?*

An **option** is a contract conveying the right to buy or sell a designated security at a stipulated price. The contract normally expires at a predetermined time. The most important element of an option contract is that there is no obligation placed upon the purchaser: it is an "option". This attribute of an option contract distinguishes it from other financial contracts. For instance, while the holder of an option has the opportunity to let his or her claim expire unused if so desired, futures and forward contracts obligate their parties to fulfill certain conditions.

10.2.2. *Types of Options and Their Characteristics*

A **call option** gives its owner the right to buy the underlying asset while a **put option** conveys to its holder the right to sell the underlying asset.

An option is specified by five essential parts.

1. The type (call or put).
2. The underlying asset.
3. The exercise price.
4. The expiration date.
5. The option price.

While the most common type of underlying asset for an option is an individual stock, other underlying assets for options exist as well. These include futures contracts, foreign currencies, stock indexes, and U.S. debt instruments. In the case of common stock options (on which this discussion is exclusively centered), the specified quantity to which the option buyer is entitled to buy or sell is one hundred shares of the stock per option.

The **exercise price** (also called the **striking price**) is the price stated in the option contract at which the call (put) owner can buy (sell) the underlying asset up to the expiration date, the final calendar date on which the option can be traded. Options on common stocks have expiration dates three months apart in one of three fixed cycles.

1. January/April/July/October.
2. February/May/August/November.
3. March/June/September/December.

The normal expiration date is the third Saturday of the month. (The third Friday is the last trading date for the option.)

As an example, an option referred to as an "ABC June 25 call" is an option to buy 100 shares of the underlying ABC stock at \$25 per share, up to its expiration date in June. Option prices are quoted on a per-share basis. Thus, a stock option that is quoted at \$5 would cost \$500 (\$5 × 100 shares), plus commission and a nominal SEC fee.

A common distinction among options pertains to when they can be exercised. Exercising an option is the process of carrying out the right to buy or sell the underlying asset at the stated price. American options allow the exercise of this right at any time from when the option is purchased up to the expiration date. On the other hand, European options allow their holder the right of exercise only on the expiration date itself. The distinction between an American and European option has nothing to do with the location at which they are traded. Both types are currently bought and sold in the United States. There are distinctions in their pricing and in the possibility of exercising them prior to expiration.

Finally, when discussing options, the two parties to the contract are characterized by whether they have bought or sold the contract. The party buying the option contract (call or put) is the option buyer (or holder), while the party selling the option is the option seller (or writer). If the writer of an option does not own the underlying asset, he or she is said to write a naked option.

Table 10.1 shows a listing of publicly traded options for Johnson & Johnson at September 21st, 2007.

Table 10.1. Options quotes for Johnson & Johnson on February 25, 2015.

Calls						
Strike	Contract Name	Last	Bid	Ask	Volume	Open Interest
Stock Price on February 25, 2015 = $100.45						
Call Options Expiring Fri. Feb. 27, 2015						
∵ Filter						
91	JNJ150227C00091000	7.35	9.15	9.75	11	0
92	JNJ150227C00092000	8.4	8.15	8.75	1	0
95.5	JNJ150227C00095500	5.25	4.6	5.2	840	0
96	JNJ150227C00096000	3.3	4.15	4.7	1	0
96.5	JNJ150227C00096500	3.95	3.65	4.2	4	0
97	JNJ150227C00097000	3.2	3.15	3.7	20	20
97.5	JNJ150227C00097500	2.17	2.67	3.2	1	1
98	JNJ150227C00098000	3	2.23	2.74	2	5
98.5	JNJ150227C00098500	1.85	1.7	2.26	10	20
99	JNJ150227C00099000	1.6	1.29	1.65	2	82
99.5	JNJ150227C00099500	1.02	0.93	1.13	27	160
100	JNJ150227C00100000	0.66	0.65	0.71	42	611
101	JNJ150227C00101000	0.2	0.17	0.21	382	1044
102	JNJ150227C00102000	0.07	0.03	0.15	481	1258
103	JNJ150227C00103000	0.05	0	0.07	8	384
104	JNJ150227C00104000	0.06	0	0.04	11	92
105	JNJ150227C00105000	0.03	0	0.04	50	217
106	JNJ150227C00106000	0.03	0	0.04	5	50
107	JNJ150227C00107000	0.01	0	0.04	8	116
108	JNJ150227C00108000	0.15	0	0.03	53	53
109	JNJ150227C00109000	0.57	0	0.03	24	24
110	JNJ150227C00110000	0.11	0	0.03	402	306
111	JNJ150227C00111000	0.18	0	0.03	1	12
112	JNJ150227C00112000	0.19	0	0.03	9	9
113	JNJ150227C00113000	0.24	0	0.03	1	2
114	JNJ150227C00114000	0.17	0	0.03	2	2
Puts						
Strike	Contract Name	Last	Bid	Ask	Volume	Open Interest
Put Options Expiring Fri. Feb. 27, 2015						
∵ Filter						
85	JNJ150227P00085000	0.04	0	0.03	140	140
90	JNJ150227P00090000	0.01	0	0.03	1	246
91	JNJ150227P00091000	0.14	0	0.03	13	92
92	JNJ150227P00092000	0.12	0	0.04	6	55
93	JNJ150227P00093000	0.06	0	0.04	50	162
94	JNJ150227P00094000	0.08	0	0.04	5	54
95	JNJ150227P00095000	0.01	0	0.02	15	132
95.5	JNJ150227P00095500	0.32	0	0.03	4	198
96	JNJ150227P00096000	0.03	0	0.03	5	762

(*Continued*)

Table 10.1. (*Continued*)

Puts						
Strike	Contract Name	Last	Bid	Ask	Volume	Open Interest
∵ Filter						
96.5	JNJ150227P00096500	0.14	0	0.17	10	32
97	JNJ150227P00097000	0.07	0	0.11	20	4848
97.5	JNJ150227P00097500	0.02	0.01	0.21	10	191
98	JNJ150227P00098000	0.04	0	0.23	14	501
98.5	JNJ150227P00098500	0.09	0	0.09	4	302
99	JNJ150227P00099000	0.1	0.05	0.15	10	373
99.5	JNJ150227P00099500	0.21	0.12	0.18	10	169
100	JNJ150227P00100000	0.27	0.24	0.31	60	554
101	JNJ150227P00101000	0.74	0.73	0.91	35	230
102	JNJ150227P00102000	1.58	1.39	1.84	20	112
103	JNJ150227P00103000	3.6	2.36	2.83	18	70
104	JNJ150227P00104000	3.73	3.25	3.85	1	14
105	JNJ150227P00105000	4.77	4.25	4.85	1	8
106	JNJ150227P00106000	5.05	5.25	5.85	1	36
107	JNJ150227P00107000	5.92	6.25	6.8	21	3
108	JNJ150227P00108000	8.61	7.25	7.8	7	0
110	JNJ150227P00110000	5.55	9.25	9.8	3	0

10.2.3. *Relationships Between the Option Price and the Underlying Asset Price*

A call (put) option is said to be **in the money** if the underlying asset is selling above (below) the exercise price of the option. An **at-the-money** call (put) is one whose exercise price is equal to the current price of the underlying asset. A call (put) option is out of the money if the underlying asset is selling below (above) the exercise price of the option.

Suppose ABC stock is selling at \$30 per share. An ABC June 25 call option is in the money (\$30–25 > 0), while an ABC June 35 call option is out of the money (\$30–35 < 0). Of course, the expiration dates could be any month without changing the option's standing as in, at, or out of the money.

The relationship between the price of an option and the price of the underlying asset indicates both the amount of intrinsic value and time value inherent in the option's price, as shown in Eq. (10.1):

$$\text{Intrinsic value} = \text{Underlying asset price} - \text{Option exercise price}. \quad (10.1)$$

For a call (put) option that is in the money (underlying asset price > exercise price), its intrinsic value is positive. And for at-the-money and out-of-the-money options the intrinsic value is zero. An option's time value is the amount by which the option's premium (or market price) exceeds its intrinsic value. For a call or put option:

$$\text{Time value} = \text{Option premium} - \text{Intrinsic value}, \tag{10.2}$$

where intrinsic value is the maximum of zero or stock price minus exercise price. Thus an option premium or market price is composed of two components, intrinsic value, and time value. In-the-money options are usually most expensive because of their large intrinsic-value component. An option with an at-the-money exercise price will have only time value inherent in its market price. Deep out-of-the-money options have zero intrinsic value and little time value and consequently are the least expensive. Deep in-the-money cases also have little time value, and time value is the greatest for at-the-money options. In addition, time value (as its name implies) is positively related to the amount of time the option has to expiration. The theoretical valuation of options focuses on determining the relevant variables that affect the time-value portion of an option premium and the derivation of their relationship in option-pricing.

In general, the call price should be equal to or exceed the intrinsic value:

$$\mathrm{C} \geq \mathrm{Max}(S - E, 0),$$

where
C = the value of the call option;
S = the current stock price; and
E = the exercise price.

Figure 10.1 illustrates the relationship between an option's time value and its exercise price. When the exercise price is zero, the time value of an option is zero. Although this relationship is described quite well in general by Fig. 10.1, the exact relationship is somewhat ambiguous. Moreover, the identification of options with a mispriced time-value portion in their total premium motivates interest in a theoretical pricing model.

One more aspect of time value that is very important to discuss is the change in the amount of time value an option has as its duration shortens. As previously mentioned, options with a longer time-to-maturity and those near to the money have the largest time-value components. Assuming that a particular option remains near to the money as its time-to-maturity diminishes, the rate of decrease in its time value, or what is termed the effect of time decay, is of interest. How time decay affects an option's premium is an important question for the valuation of options and the application of option strategies. To best see an answer to this question refer to Fig. 10.2.

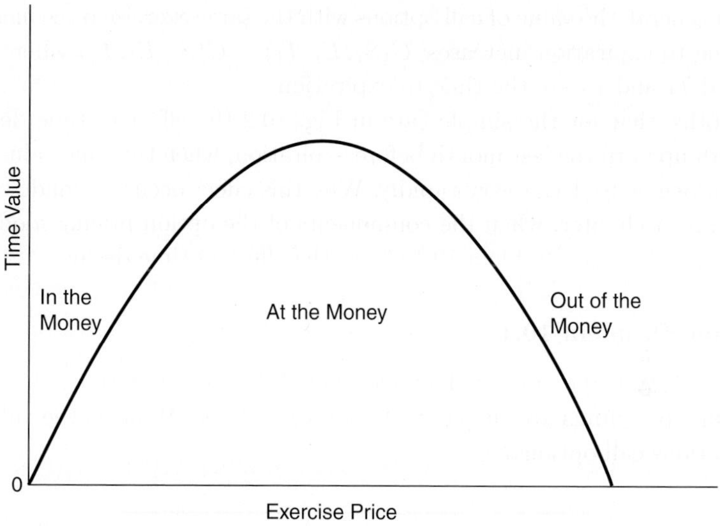

Fig. 10.1. The relationship between an option's exercise price and its time value.

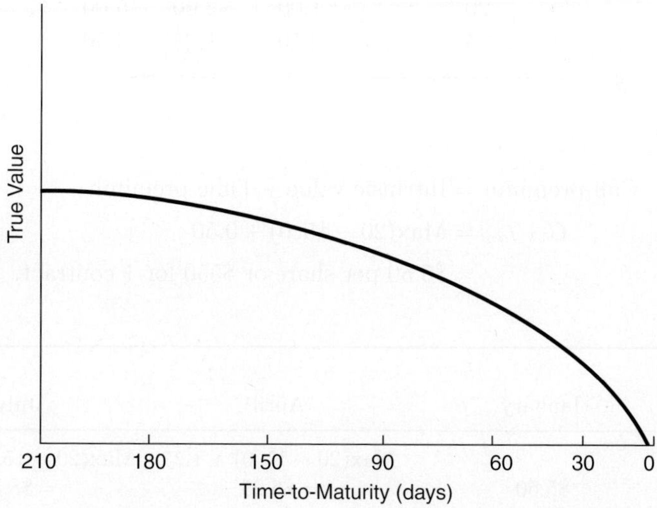

Fig. 10.2. The relationship between time value and time-to-maturity for a near-to-the-money option (assuming a constant price for the underlying asset).

In general, the value of call options with the same exercise price increases as time to expiration increases: $C(S_1, E_1, T_1) \leq C(S_1, E_1, T_2)$ where $T_1 \leq T_2$ and T_1 and T_2 are the time to expiration.

Notice that for the simple care in Fig. 10.2 the effect of time decay is smooth up until the last month before expiration, when the time value of an option begins to decay very rapidly. Why this effect occurs is made clearer in the next chapter, when the components of the option-pricing model are examined. Sample Problem 10.1 shows the effect of time decay.

Sample Problem 10.1

It is January 1, the price of the underlying ABC stock is $20 per share, and the time premiums are shown in the following table. What is the value for the various call options?

Exercise Price X	January	April	July
15	\$0.50	\$1.25	\$3.50
20	1.00	2.00	5.00
25	0.50	1.25	3.50

Solution

$$\begin{aligned} \text{Call premium} &= \text{Intrinsic value} + \text{Time premium} \\ C_{15,Jan} &= \text{Max}(20 - 15, 0) + 0.50 \\ &= \$5.50 \text{ per share or } \$550 \text{ for 1 contract.} \end{aligned}$$

Exercise Price X	January	April	July
15	\$5.50	$\text{Max}(20 - 15, 0) + 1.25 = \$6.25$	$\text{Max}(20 - 15, 0) + 3.50 = \$8.50$
20	$\text{Max}(20 - 20, 0) + 1.00 = \$1.00$	$\text{Max}(20 - 20, 0) + 2.00 = \$2.00$	$\text{Max}(20 - 20, 0) + 5.00 = \$5.00$
25	$\text{Max}(20 - 25, 0) + 5.0 = \$0.50$	$\text{Max}(20 - 25, 0) + 1.25 = \$1.25$	$\text{Max}(20 - 25, 0) + 3.50 = \$3.50$

Other values are shown in the table above.

10.2.4. *Additional Definitions and Distinguishing Features*

Options may be specified in terms of their classes and series. A **class of options** refers to all call and put options on the same underlying asset. For example, all AT&T call and put options at various exercise prices and expiration months form one class. A **series** is a subset of a class and consists of all contracts of the same class (such as AT&T) having the same expiration date and exercise price.

When an investor either buys or sells an option (that is, is long or short) as the initial transaction, the option exchange adds this opening transaction to what is termed the **open interest** for an option series. Essentially, open interest represents the number of contracts outstanding at a particular point in time. If the investor reverses the initial position with a closing transaction (that is, sells the option if he or she originally bought it or vice versa) then the open interest for the particular option series is reduced by one.

While open interest is more of a static variable, indicating the number of outstanding contracts at one point in time, **volume** represents a dynamic characteristic. More specifically, volume indicates the number of times a particular option is bought and sold during a particular trading day. Volume and open interest are measures of an option's liquidity, the ease with which the option can be bought and sold in large quantities. The larger the volume and/or open interest, the more liquid the option.

Again, an option holder who invokes the right to buy or sell is exercising the option. Whenever a holder exercises an option, a writer is assigned the obligation to fulfill the terms of the option contract by the exchange on which the option is traded. If a call holder exercises the right to buy, a **call writer** is assigned the obligation to sell. Similarly, when a put holder exercises the right to sell, a **put writer** is assigned the obligation to buy.

The seller or writer of a call option must deliver 100 shares of the underlying stock at the specified exercise price when the option is exercised. The writer of a put option must purchase 100 shares of the underlying stock when the put option is exercised. The writer of either option receives the premium or price of the option for this legal obligation. The maximum loss an option buyer can experience is limited to the price of the option. However, the maximum loss from writing a naked call is unlimited; the maximum loss possible from writing a naked put is the exercise price less the original price of that put. To guarantee that the option writer can meet these obligations, the exchange clearinghouse requires margin deposits.

The payment of cash dividends affects both the price of the underlying stock and the value of an option on the stock. Normally, no adjustment is made in the terms of the option when a cash dividend is paid. However, strike price or number of shares may be adjusted if the underlying stock realizes a stock dividend or stock split. For example, an option on XYZ Corporation with an exercise price of $100 would be adjusted if XYZ Corporation stock split two for one. The adjustment in this case would be a change in the exercise price from $100 to $50, and the number of contracts would be doubled. In the case of a non-integer split (such as three for two), the adjustment is made to the exercise price and the number of shares covered by the option contracts. For example, if XYZ Corporation had an exercise price of $100 per share and had a three-for-two split, the option would have the exercise price adjusted to $\$66\frac{2}{3}$, and the number of shares would be increased to 150. Notice that the old exercise value of the option, $10,000 ($\$100 \times 100$ shares), is maintained by the adjustment ($\$66\frac{2}{3} \times 150$ shares).

10.2.5. *Types of Underlying Asset*

Although most people would identify common stocks as the underlying asset for an option, a variety of other assets and financial instruments can assume the same function. In fact, options on agricultural commodities were introduced by traders in the United States as early as the mid-1800s. After a number of scandals, agricultural commodity options were banned by the government. They were later reintroduced under tighter regulations and in a more standardized tradable form. Today, futures options on such agricultural commodities as corn, soybeans, wheat, cotton, sugar, live cattle, and live hogs are actively traded on a number of exchanges.

The biggest success for options has been realized for options on financial futures. Options on the S&P 500 index futures contracts, NYSE index futures, foreign-currency futures, 30-year U.S. Treasury bond futures, and gold futures have all realized extraordinary growth since their initial offerings back in 1982. Options on futures are very similar to options on the actual asset, except that the futures options give their holders the right (not the obligation) to buy or sell predetermined quantities of specified futures contracts at a fixed price within a predetermined period.

Options on the actual asset have arisen in another form as well. While a number of options have existed for various stock-index futures contracts, options now also exist on the stock index itself. Because of the complexity of having to provide all the stocks in an index at the spot price should a call holder exercise his or her buy right, options on stock indexes are always settled in cash. That is, should a call holder exercise his or her right to buy because of a large increase in the underlying index, that holder would be accommodated by a cash amount equal to the profit on his contract, or the current value of the option's premium. Although the options on the S&P 100 stock index at the Chicago Board Options Exchange (CBOE) are the most popular among traders, numerous index options are now traded as well. These include options on the S&P 500 index, the S&P OTC 250 index, the NYSE composite and AMEX indexes (computer technology, oil and gas, and airline), the Philadelphia Exchange indexes (gold/silver), the Value Line index, and the NASDAQ 100 index.

10.2.6. *Institutional Characteristics*

Probably two of the most important underlying factors leading to the success of options have been the standardization of contracts through the establishment of option exchanges and the trading anonymity brought about by the Option Clearing Corporations and clearinghouses of the major futures exchanges.

An important element for option trading is the interchangeability of contracts. Exchange contracts are not matched between individuals. Instead, when an investor or trader enters into an option contract, the Option Clearing Corporation (or clearinghouse for the particular futures exchange) takes the opposite side of the transaction. So rather than having to contact a particular option writer to terminate an option position, a buyer can simply sell it back to the exchange at the current market clearing price. This type of anonymity among option-market participants is what permits an active secondary market to operate.

The sources of futures options traded on the various futures exchanges mentioned earlier are determined by the **open-auction bidding**, probably the purest form of laissez-faire price determination that can be seen today. With the open-auction-bidding price mechanism there are no market makers, only a large octagonal pit filled with traders bidding among themselves to buy and sell contracts. While some traders buy and sell only for themselves, many of the participants are brokers representing large investment firms. Different sides of the pit usually represent traders who are dealing in particular expiration months. As brokers and other pit participants make trades they mark down what they bought or sold, how much, at what price, and from whom. These cards are then collected by members of the exchange who record the trades and post the new prices. The prices are displayed on "scoreboards" surrounding the pit.

While stock options and options on commodities and indexes are traded in a similar fashion, one major difference prevails-the presence of **market makers**. Market makers are individuals who typically trade one type of option for their own account and are responsible for ensuring that a market always exists for their particular contract. In addition, some option ex-changes utilize **board brokers** as well. These individuals are charged with the maintenance of the book of limit orders (orders from outside investors that are to be executed at particular prices or when the market goes up or down by a prespecified amount). Essentially, market makers and board brokers on the options exchanges share the duties performed by the specialists on the major stock exchanges.

Although stocks can be bought with as little as 50% margin, no margin is allowed for buying options-the cost of the contract must be fully paid. Because options offer a high degree of leverage on the underlying asset, additional leveraging through margins is considered by regulators to be excessive. However, if more than one option contract is entered into at the same time — for instance, selling and buying two different calls — then, of course, a lower cost is incurred, since the cost of one is partially (or wholly) offset by the sale of the other.

10.3. Put-Call Parity

This section addresses a most important concept, called **put-call parity** (for option valuation). The discussion includes European options, American options, and future options.

10.3.1. *European Options*

As an initial step to examining the pricing formulas for options, it is essential to discuss the relationships between the prices of put and call options on the same underlying asset. Such relationships among put and call prices are referred to as the *put-call parity theorems*. Stoll (1969) was the first to introduce the concept of put-call parity. Dealing strictly with European options he showed that the value of a call option would equal the value of a portfolio composed of a long put option, its underlying stock, and a short discounted exercise price. Before stating the basic put-call parity theorem as originally devised by Stoll, it must be assumed that the markets for options, bonds, and stocks (or any other underlying asset we choose) are frictionless.

Theorem 10.1. *Put-Call Parity for European Options with No Dividends.*

$$C_{t,T} = P_{t,T} + S_t - EB_{t,T}, \tag{10.3}$$

where

$C_{t,T}$ = *value of a European call option at time t that matures at time $T(T > f)$;*

$P_{t,T}$ = *value of a European put option at time t, that matures at time T;*

S_t = *value of the underlying stock (asset) to both the call and put options at time t;*

E = *exercise price for both the call and put options;*

$B_{t,T}$ = *price at time t of a default-free bond that pays \$1 with certainty at time T (if it is assumed that this risk-free rate of interest is the same for all maturities and equal to r — in essence a flat-term structure — then $B_{t,T} = e^{-r(T-t)}$, under continuous compounding), or $B_{t,T} = 1/(1+r)^{T-t}$ for discrete compounding.*

Equation (10.3) uses the following principle. If the options are neither dominant nor dominated securities, and if the borrowing and lending rates are equal, then the return patterns of a European call and a portfolio composed of a European put, a pure discount bond with a face value equal to the options exercise price E, and the underlying stock (or asset) are the same.[1]

In understanding why the put-call parity theorem holds, and to support the theorem, two additional properties of option-pricing must be provided:

Property 10.1. At maturity (time T) the call option is worth the greater of $S_T - E$ dollars or zero dollars:

$$C_T = \text{Max}(0, S_T - E). \tag{10.4}$$

As an example, suppose that the call option has an exercise price of \$30. At maturity, if the stock's (asset's) price is \$25, then the value of the call is

[1] Any security x is dominant over any security y if the rate-of-return on x is equal to or greater than that of y for all states of nature and is strictly greater for at least one state. For an expanded discussion of this subject, see Merton (1973) and Smith (1976).

the maximum of $(0, 25-30)$ or $(0, -5)$, which of course is zero. If an option sells for less than $(S, -E)$, its intrinsic value, an arbitrage opportunity will exist. Investors would buy the option and short sell the stock, forcing the mispricing to correct itself. Consequently, this first property implies that a call option's value is always greater than zero. An equivalent property and argument exist for the value of a put option as well.

Property 10.2. At maturity, the value of a put option is the greater of $E - ST$ dollars or zero dollars:

$$P_T = \text{Max}(0, E - S_T). \tag{10.5}$$

Using the same line of reasoning and argument as for the call option, the second property also implies that the value of a put option is never less than zero. Table 10.2 provides proof of this first put-call parity theorem. Suppose at time t, two portfolios are formed: portfolio B is just a long call option on a stock with price S_t an exercise price of E, and a maturity date at T. Portfolio A consists of purchasing one hundred shares of the underlying stock (since stock options represent one hundred shares), purchasing (going long) one put option on the same stock with exercise price E and maturity date T, and borrowing at the risk-free rate an amount equal to the present value of the exercise price or $EB_{t,T}$ with face value of E. (This portion of the portfolio finances the put, call, and stock position.)

At maturity date T, the call option (portfolio B) has value only if $S_T > E$, which is in accordance with Property 10.1. For portfolio A, under all these conditions the stock price and maturing loan values are the same, whereas the put option has value only if $E > S_T$. Under all three possible

Table 10.2. Put-call parity for a european option with no dividends.

	Time T (Maturity)		
Time t Strategy	$S_T > E$	$S_T = E$	$S_T < E$
Portfolio A			
1. Buy 100 shares of the stock (S_t)	S_T	S_T	S_T
2. Buy a put (P_t, maturity at T with exercise price E)	0	0	$E - S_T$
3. Borrow $EB_{t,T}$ dollars.	$-E$	$-E$	$-E$
Portfolio A value at time T	$(S_T - E)$	0	0
Portfolio B			
1. Buy a call (C_t maturing at T with exercise price E)	$(S_T - E)$	0	0

outcomes for the stock price S_T, it can be seen that the values of portfolios A and B are equal. Proof has been established for the first put-call parity theorem. Sample Problem 10.2 provides further illustration.

Sample Problem 10.2

A call option with 1 year to maturity and exercise price of $110 is selling for $5. Assuming discrete compounding, a risk-free rate of 10%, and a current stock price of $100, what is the value of a European put option with a strike price of $110 and 1-year maturity?

Solution

$$P_{t,T} = C_{t,T} + EB_{t,T} - S_t,$$

$$P_{0,1yr} = \$5 + \$110\left(\frac{1}{(1.1)^1}\right) - \$100,$$

$$P_{0,1yr} = \$5.$$

10.3.2. *American Options*

Of course, this first put-call parity theorem holds only under the most basic conditions (that is, no early exercise and no dividends). Jarrow and Rudd (1983) gave an extensive coverage of the effects of more complicated conditions on put-call parity. These authors demonstrate that the effect of known dividends is simply to reduce, by the discounted value (to time t) of the dividends, the amount of the underlying stock purchased. In considering stochastic dividends, the exactness of this pricing relationship breaks down and depends on the degree of certainty that can be maintained about the range of future dividends. Put-call parity for American options is also derived under various dividend conditions. Jarrow and Rudd demonstrate that as a result of the American option's early exercise feature, strict pricing relationships give way to boundary conditions dependent on the size and certainty of future dividends, as well as the level of interest rates and the size of the exercise price. To summarize, they state that for sufficiently high interest rates and/or exercise prices it may be optimal to exercise the put prior to maturity (with or without dividends). So the basic put-call parity for an American option with no dividends and constant interest rates is described by the following theorem.

Theorem 10.2. *Put-Call Parity for an American Option with No Dividends*

$$P_{t,T} + S - EB_{t,T} > C_{t,T} > P_{t,T} + S_t - E. \tag{10.6}$$

Increasing the generality of conditions results in increasing boundaries for the equilibrium relationship between put and call options. The beauty of these arguments stems from the fact that they require only that investors prefer more wealth to less. If more stringent assumptions are made, then the bounds can be made tighter. For an extensive derivation and explanation of these theorems see Jarrow and Rudd (1983). Sample Problem 10.3 provides further illustration.

Sample Problem 10.3

A put option with one year to maturity and an exercise price of \$90 is selling for \$15; the stock price is \$100. Assuming discrete compounding and a risk-free rate of 10%, what are the boundaries for the price of an American call option?

Solution

$$\begin{aligned}
&P_{t,T} + S - EB_{t,T} > C_{t,T} > P_{t,T} + S_t - E,\\
&\$15 + \$100 - \$90\left(\frac{1}{(1.1)^1}\right) > C_{t,T} > \$15 + \$100 - \$90,\\
&\$33.18 > C_{t,1yr} > \$25.
\end{aligned}$$

10.3.3. *Futures Options*

As a final demonstration of put-call parity the analysis is extended to the case where the underlying asset is a futures contract. The topic of futures contracts and their valuation will be more fully examined in the next chapter. Nevertheless, this chapter takes time to apply put-call parity when the options are on a futures contract because of the growing popularity and importance of such futures options. A futures contract is a contract in which the party entering into the contract is obligated to buy or sell the underlying asset at the maturity date for some stipulated price. While the difference between European and American options still remains, the complexity of dividends can be ignored since futures contracts do not pay dividends. Put-call parity for a European futures option (when interest rates are constant) is as follows:

Theorem 10.3. *Put-Call Parity for a European Futures Option.*

$$C_{t,T} = P_{t,T} + B_{t,T}(F_{t,T} - E), \tag{10.7}$$

where $F_{t,T}$ is the price at time t for a futures contract maturing at time T (which is the underlying asset to both the call and put options).

Option-pricing Properties 1 and 2 for call and put options apply in an equivalent sense to futures options as well. However, to understand this relationship as stated in Eq. (10.7) it must be assumed that the cost of a futures contract is zero. While a certain margin requirement is required, the majority of this assurance deposit can be in the form of interest-bearing securities. Hence, as an approximation a zero cost for the futures contract is not unrealistic.

Again, the easiest way to prove this relationship is to follow the same path of analysis used in proving Theorem 10.1. Table 10.3 indicates that the argument for this theorem's proof is similar, with only a few notable exceptions. The value of the futures contract at time T (maturity) is equal to the difference between the price of the contract at time T and the price at which it was bought, or $F_{TT} - F_{t,T}$. This is an outcome of the fixed duration of a futures contract as opposed to the perpetual duration of common stock. Second, because no money is required to enter into the futures contract, the exercise price is reduced by the current futures price and the total is lent at the risk-free rate. (Actually this amount is either lent or borrowed

Table 10.3. Put-call parity for a European futures option.

	Time T (Maturity)		
Time t Strategy	$F_{TT} > E$	$F_{TT} = E$	$F_{TT} < E$
Portfolio A			
1. Buy a futures contract ($F_{t,T}$)	$F_{TT} - F_{t,T}$	$F_{TT} - F_{t,T}$	$F_{TT} - F_{t,T}$
2. Buy a put ($P_{t,T}$ on $F_{t,T}$ with exercise price E and maturity T)	0	0	$E - F_{TT}$
3. Lend $EB_{t,T}(F_{t-T} - E)$ dollars.	$F_{t,T} - E$	$F_{t,T} - E$	$F_{t,T} - E$
Portfolio A's value at time T	$F_{TT} - E$	0	0
Portfolio B			
1. Buy a call ($C_{t,T}$ on $F_{t,T}$, with exercise price E and maturity T)	$F_{TT} - E$	0	0

depending on the relationship between $F_{t,T}$ and E at time t. If $F_{t,T} - E < 0$, then this amount will actually be borrowed at the risk-free rate.)

Why are there options on spot assets as well as options on futures contracts for the spot assets? After all, at expiration the basis of a futures contract goes to zero and futures prices equal spot prices; thus, options in the spot and options on the future are related to the same futures value, and their current values must be identical. Yet, a look at the markets shows that options on spot assets and options on futures for the same assets sell at different prices. One explanation for this is that investors who purchase options on spot must pay a large sum of money when they exercise their options, whereas investors who exercise an option on a future need only pay enough to meet the initial margin for the futures contract. Therefore, if the exercise of the option is important to an investor, that investor would prefer options on futures rather than options on spot and would be willing to pay a premium for the option on the future, whereas the investor who has no desire to exercise the option (remember, the investor can always sell it to somebody else to realize a profit) is not willing to pay for this advantage and so finds the option on spot more attractive.

10.3.4. *Market Applications*

Put options were not listed on the CBOE until June 1977. Before that time, brokers satisfied their clients' demands for put option risk–return characteristics by a direct application of put-call parity. By combining call options and the underlying security, brokers could construct a **synthetic put**.

To illustrate, the put-call parity theorem is used when a futures contract is the underlying asset. Furthermore, to simulate the option broker's circumstances on July 1, 1984, the equation is merely rearranged to yield the put's "synthetic" value:

$$P_{t,T} = C_{t,T} - B_{t,T}F_{t,T} + B_{t,T}E. \tag{10.8}$$

So instead of a futures contract being purchased, it is sold. Assume the following values and use the S&P 500 index futures as the underlying asset.

$C_{t,T} = \$3.35$;
$F_{t,T} = 154.85$ (September contract);
$E = 155.00$; and
$B_{t,T} = 0.9770$ (current price of a risk-free bond that pays \$1 when the option and futures contract expire, average of bid and ask prices for T-bills from *The Wall Street Journal*).

According to Eq. (10.8), the put's price should equal the theorem price: $P_{t,T} = \$3.497$. The actual put price on this day (July 1, 1984) with the same exercise price and expiration month was $P_{t,T} = \$3.50$. With repeated comparisons of the theorem using actual prices, it becomes clear that put-call parity is a powerful equilibrium mechanism in the market.

10.4. Risk–Return Characteristics of Options

One of the most attractive features of options is the myriad of ways in which they can be employed to achieve a particular combination of risk-and-return. Whether through a straight option position in combination with the underlying asset or some portfolio of securities, options offer an innovative and relatively low-cost mechanism for altering and enhancing the risk–return tradeoff. In order to better grasp these potential applications this section analyzes call and put options individually and in combination, relative to their potential profit and loss and the effects of time and market sentiment.

10.4.1. *Long Call*

The purchase of a call option is the simplest and most familiar type of option position. The allure of calls is that they provide the investor a great deal of leverage. Potentially, large percentage profits can be realized from only a modest price rise in the underlying asset. In fact, the potential profit from buying a call is unlimited. Moreover, the option purchaser has the right but no obligation to exercise the contract. Therefore, should the price of the underlying asset decline over the life of the call, the purchaser need only let the contract expire worthless. Consequently, the risk of a long call position is limited. Figure 10.3 illustrates the profit profile of a **long call** position. The following summarizes the basic risk–return features for a long-call position.

Profit potential: Unlimited,
Loss potential: Limited (to cost of option),
Effect of time decay: Negative (decrease option's value),
Market expectation: Bullish.

As the profit profile indicates, the time value of a long call declines over time. Consequently, an option is a wasting asset. If the underlying asset's price does not move above the exercise price of the option E by its expiration

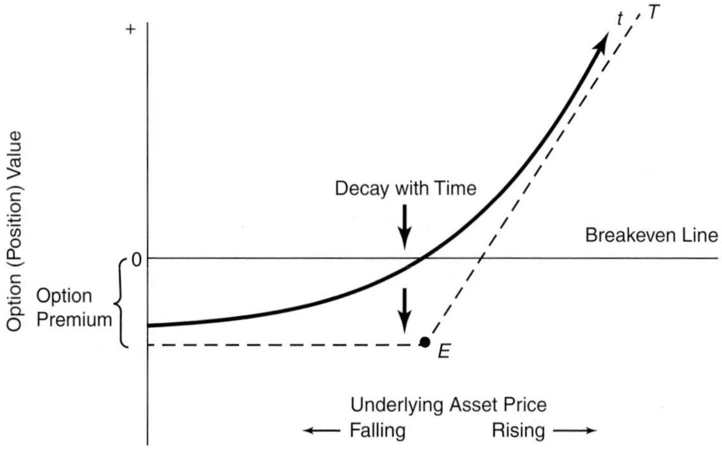

Fig. 10.3. Profit profile for a long call.

date T, the buyer of the call will lose the value of his initial investment (the option premium). Consequently, the longer an investor holds a call, the more time value the option loses, thereby, reducing the price of the option. This leads to another important point — taking on an option position. As with any other investment vehicle, the purchaser of a call expresses an opinion about the market for the underlying asset. Whereas an investor can essentially express one of three different sentiments (bullish, neutral, or bearish) about future market conditions, the long call is strictly a bullish position. That is, the call buyer only wins if the underlying asset rises in price. However, depending on the exercise price of the call, the buyer can express differing degrees of bullishness. For instance, since out-of-the-money calls are the cheapest, a large price increase in the underlying asset will make these calls the biggest percentage gainers in value. So, an investor who is extremely bullish would probably go with an out-of-the-money call, since its intrinsic value is small and its value will increase along with a large increase in the market.

10.4.2. *Short Call*

Selling a call (writing it) has risk-reward characteristics, which are the inverse of the long call. However, one major distinction arises when writing calls (or puts) rather than buying them. That is, the writer can either own the underlying asset upon which he or she is selling the option (a **covered**

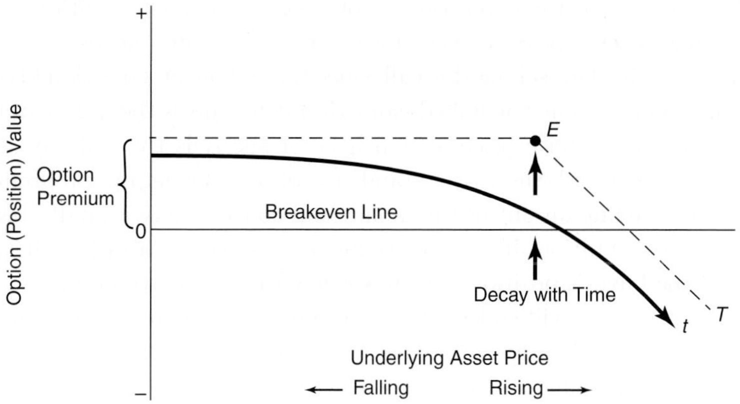

Fig. 10.4. Profit profile for a short call.

write), or simply sell the option without owning the asset (a **naked write**). The difference between the two is of considerable consequence to the amount of risk-and-return taken on by the seller. Let us first examine the profit profile and related attributes of the naked **short call**, displayed in Fig. 10.4.

When the writer of a call does not own the underlying asset, his or her potential loss is unlimited. Why? Because if the price of the underlying asset increases, the value of the call also increases for the buyer. The seller of a call is *obliged* to provide a designated quantity of the underlying asset at some prespecified price (the exercise price) at any time up to the maturity date of the option. So if the asset starts rising dramatically in price and the call buyer exercises his or her *right*, the naked-call writer must go into the market to buy the underlying asset at whatever the market price. The naked-call writer suffers the loss of buying the asset at a price S and selling it at a price E when $S > E$ (less the original premium collected). When common stock is the underlying asset, there is no limit to how high its price could go. Thus, the naked-call writer's risk is unlimited as well. Of course, the naked-call writer could have reversed position by buying back the original option he sold — that is, zeroing out the position — however, this also done at a loss. The following summarizes the basic risk–return features for a naked short-call position.

Profit potential: Limited (to option premium),
Loss potential: Unlimited,
Effect of time decay: Positive (makes buyer's position less valuable),
Market expectation: Bearish to neutral.

The naked short-call position is obviously a bearish position. If the underlying asset's price moves down, the call writer keeps the entire premium received for selling this call, since the call buyer's position becomes worthless. Once again, the naked-call writer can express the degree of bearishness by the exercise price at which he or she sells the call. By selling an in-the-money call, the writer stands to collect a higher option premium. Conversely, selling an out-of-the-money call conveys only a mildly bearish to neutral expectation. If the underlying asset's price stays where it is, the value of the buyer's position, which is solely time value, will decay to zero; and the call writer will collect the entire premium (though a substantially smaller premium than for an in-the-money call).

While the passing of time has a negative effect on the value of a call option for the buyer, it has a positive effect for the seller. One aspect of an option's time value is that in the last month before the option expires, its time value decays most rapidly. Why? Time value is related to the probability that the underlying asset's price will move up or down enough to make an option position increase in value. This probability declines at an accelerating (exponential) rate as the option approaches its maturity date. The consideration of time value, then, is a major element when investing in or hedging with options. Unless an investor is extremely bullish, it would probably be unwise to take a long position in a call in its last month before maturity. Conversely, the last month of an option's life is a preferred time to sell since its time value can more easily and quickly be collected.

Now consider the other type of short-call position, covered-call writing. Because the seller of the call owns the underlying asset in this case, the risk is truncated. The purpose of writing a call on the underlying asset when it is owned is twofold. First, by writing a call option, one always decreases the risk of owning the asset. Second, writing a call can increase the overall realized return on the asset. The profit profile for a covered short call (or a covered write) in Fig. 10.5 provides further illustration. The following summarizes the basic risk–return features for the covered short-call position.

Profit potential: limited (exercise price − asset price + call premium),
Loss potential: limited (asset price − call premium),
Effect of time decay: positive,
Market expectation: neutral to mildly bullish.

By owning the underlying asset, the covered-call writer's loss on the asset for a price decline is decreased by the original amount of the premium

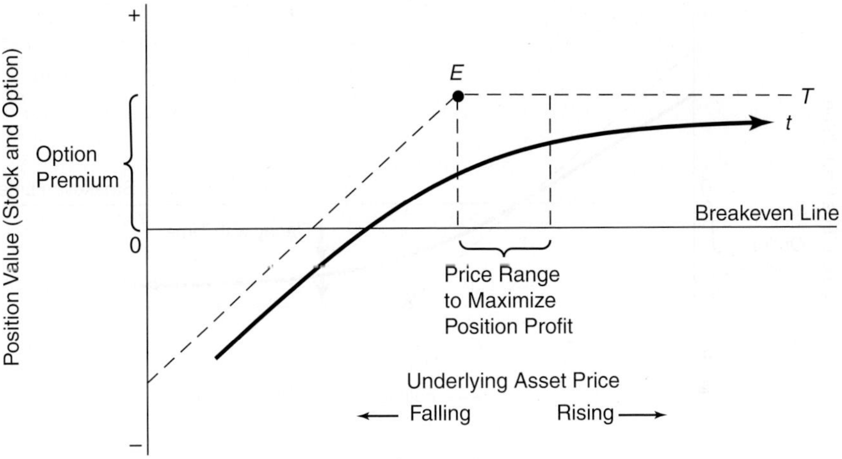

Fig. 10.5. Profit profile for a covered short call.

collected for selling the option. The total loss on the position is limited to the extent that the asset is one of limited liability, such as a stock, and cannot fall below zero. The maximum profit on the combined asset and option position is higher than if the option was written alone, but lower than simply owning the asset with no short call written on it. Once the asset increases in price by a significant amount the call buyer will very likely exercise the right to purchase the asset at the pre specified exercise price. Thus, covered-call writing is a tool or strategy for enhancing an asset's realized return while lowering its risk in a sideways market.

10.4.3. *Long Put*

Again, the put option conveys to its purchasers the right to sell a given quantity of some asset at a prespecified price on or before its expiration date. Similar to a long call, a **long put** is also a highly leveraged position, but the purchaser of the put makes money on the investment only when the price of the underlying asset declines. While a call buyer has unlimited profit potential, a put buyer has limited profit potential since the price of the underlying asset can never drop below zero. Yet, like the long-call position, the put buyer can never lose more than the initial investment (the option's premium). The profit profile for a long put is seen in Fig. 10.6. The following summarizes the basic risk–return features for the profit profile of a long-put position.

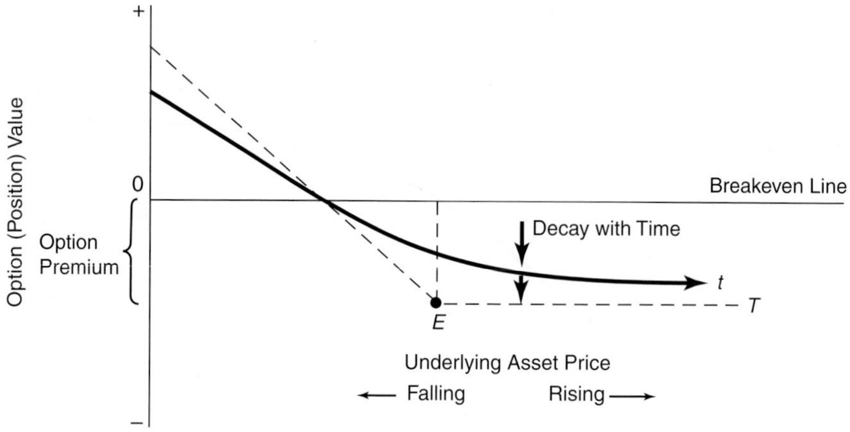

Fig. 10.6. Profit profile for a long put.

Profit potential: limited (asset price must be greater than zero),
Loss potential: limited (to cost of put),
Effect of time decay: negative or positive,
Market expectation: bearish.

An interesting pricing ambiguity for this bearish investment is how the put's price is affected by the time decay. With the long call there is a clear-cut relation — that is, the effect of the time decay is to diminish the value of the call. The relationship is not so clear with the long put. Although at certain prices for the underlying asset the value of the long-put position decreases with time, there exist lower asset prices for which its value will increase with time. It is the put's ambiguous relationship with time that makes its correct price difficult to ascertain. (This topic will be further explored in Chapter 11.)

One uniquely attractive attribute of the long put is its negative relationship with the underlying asset. In terms of the capital asset pricing model, it has a negative beta (though usually numerically larger than that of the underlying asset, due to the leverage affect). Therefore, the long put is an ideal hedging instrument for the holder of the underlying asset who wants to protect against a price decline. If the investor is wrong and the price of the asset moves up instead, the profit from the asset's price increase is only moderately diminished by the cost of the put. More on hedging and related concepts is discussed in Chapter 11.

10.4.4. *Short Put*

As was true for the short-call position, put writing can be covered or uncovered (naked). The risk–return features of the uncovered (naked) **short put** are discussed first.

For taking on the obligation to buy the underlying asset at the exercise price, the put writer receives a premium. The maximum profit for the uncovered-put-writer is this premium, which is initially received. Figure 10.7 provides further illustration.

While the loss potential is limited for the uncovered-put-writer, it is nonetheless still very large. Thus, someone neutral on the direction of the market would sell out-of-the-money (lower exercise price) puts. A more bullish sentiment would suggest that at-the-money options be sold. The investor who is convinced the market will go up should maximize return by selling a put with a larger premium. As with the long put, the time-decay effect is ambiguous and depends on the price of the underlying asset. The following summarizes the basic risk–return features for the profit profile of an uncovered short-put position.

Profit potential: limited (to put premium),
Loss potential: limited (asset price must be greater than zero),
Effect of time decay: positive or negative,
Market expectation: neutral to bullish.

Referring again to Fig. 10.5 for the combined short-call and long-asset position, notice the striking resemblance of its profit profile at expiration

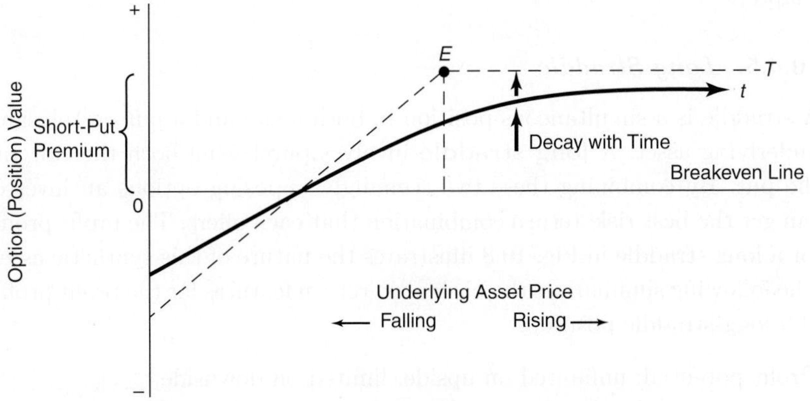

Fig. 10.7. Profit profile for an uncovered short put.

to that for the uncovered short put. This relationship can be seen mathematically by using put-call parity. That is, the synthetic put price $P_T = E_c + C_T - S_T$, or at expiration the value of the put should equal the exercise price of the call option plus the call option's value minus the value at time T of the underlying asset. Buying (writing) a call and selling (buying) the underlying asset (or vice versa) allows an investor to achieve essentially the same risk–return combination as would be received from a long put (short put). This combination of two assets to equal the risk-and-return of a third is referred to as a synthetic asset (or synthetic option in this case). Synthesizing two financial instruments to resemble a third is an arbitrage process and is a central concept of finance theory.

Now a look at covered short puts is in order to round out the basics of option strategies. For margin purposes and in a theoretical sense, selling a put against a short-asset position would be the sale of a covered put. However, this sort of position has a limited profit potential that is obtained if the underlying asset is anywhere below the exercise price of the put at expiration. This position also has unlimited upside risk, since the short position in the asset will accrue losses while the profit from the put sale is limited. Essentially, this position is equivalent to the uncovered or naked short call, except that the latter has less expensive transaction costs. Moreover, because the time value for put options is generally less than that of calls, it will be advantageous to short the call.

Strictly speaking, a short put is covered only if the investor also owns a corresponding put with exercise price equal to or greater than that of the written put. Such a position, called a spread, is discussed later in this chapter.

10.4.5. *Long Straddle*

A straddle is a simultaneous position in both a call and a put on the same underlying asset. A **long straddle** involves purchasing both the call and the put. By combining these two seemingly opposing options an investor can get the best risk–return combination that each offers. The profit profile for a long straddle in Fig. 10.8 illustrates the nature of this synthetic asset. The following summarizes the basic risk–return features for the profit profile of a long-straddle position.

Profit potential: unlimited on upside, limited on downside,
Loss potential: limited (to cost of call and put premiums),
Effect of time decay: negative,
Market sentiment: bullish or bearish.

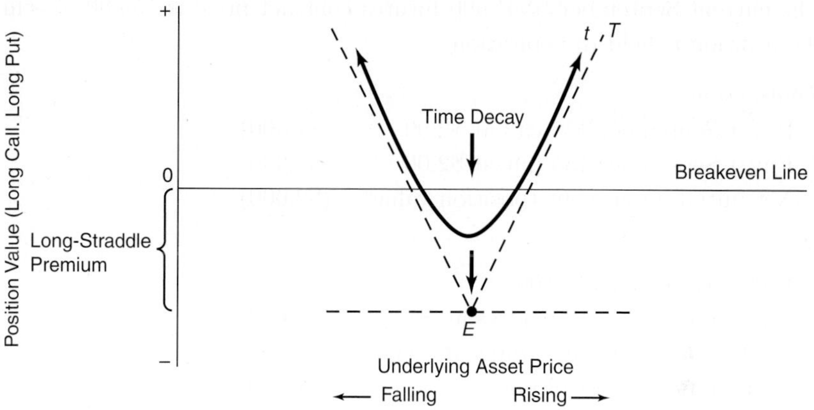

Fig. 10.8. Profit profile for a long straddle.

The long straddle's profit profile makes clear that its risk-reward picture is simply that of the long call overlapped by the long put, with each horizontal segment truncated (represented by the horizontal dashed lines on the bottom). An investor will profit on this type of position as long as the price of the underlying asset moves sufficiently up or down to more than cover the original cost of the option premiums. Thus, a long straddle is an effective strategy for someone expecting the volatility of the underlying asset to increase in the future. In the same light, the investor who buys a straddle expects the underlying asset's volatility of price to be greater than that imputed in the option price.

Since time decay is working against the value of this position, it might be unwise to purchase a straddle composed of a call and put in their last month to maturity when their time decay is greatest. It would be possible to reduce the cost of the straddle by purchasing a high-exercise-price call and a low-exercise put (out-of-the-money options); however, the necessary up or down movement in the asset's price in order to profit is larger. Sample Problem 10.4 provides further illustration.

Sample Problem 10.4

Situation: An investor feels the stock market is going to break sharply up or down but is not sure which way. However, the investor is confident that market volatility will increase in the near future. To express his position the investor puts on a long straddle using options on the S&P 500 index, buying both at-the-money call and put options on the September contract.

The current September S&P 500 futures contract price is 155.00. Assume the position is held to expiration.

Transaction:

1. Buy 1 September 155 call at $2.00.	($1,000)
2. Buy 1 September 155 put at $2.00.	($1,000)
Net initial investment (position value)	($2,000)

Results:

1. If futures price = 150.00:	
(a) 1 September call expires at $0.	($1,000)
(b) 1 September put expires at $5.00.	$2,500
(c) Less initial cost of put	($1,000)
Ending position value (net profit)	$ 500
2. If futures price = 155.00:	
(a) 1 September call expires at $0.	($1,000)
(b) 1 September put expires at $0.	($1,000)
Ending position value (net loss)	$2,000
3. If futures price = 160.00:	
(a) 1 September call expires at $5.00	$2,500
(b) 1 September call expires at $0.	($1,000)
(c) Less initial cost of put	($1,000)
Ending position value (net profit)	$ 500

Summary:

Maximum profit potential: unlimited. If the market had contributed to move below 150.00 or above 160.00, the position would have continued to increase in value.

Maximum loss potential: $2,000, the initial investment.

Break-even points: 151.00 and 159.00, for the September S&P 500 futures contract.[2]

[2]Break-even points for the straddle are calculated as follows:

$$\begin{aligned}
\textit{Upside BEP} &= \text{Exercise price} + \text{Initial net investment (in points)} \\
159.00 &= 155.00 + 4.00. \\
\textit{Downside BEP} &= \text{Exercise price} - \text{Initial net investment (in points)} \\
159.00 &= 155.00 + 4.00, \\
151.00 &= 155.00 - 4.00.
\end{aligned}$$

Effect of time decay: negative, as evidenced by the loss incurred, with no change in futures price (result 2).

10.4.6. *Short Straddle*

For the most part, the short straddle implies the opposite risk–return characteristics of the long straddle. A short straddle is a simultaneous position in both a short call and a short put on the same underlying asset. Contrary to the long-straddle position, selling a straddle can be an effective strategy when an investor expects little or no movement in the price of the underlying asset. A similar interpretation of its use would be that the investor expects the future volatility of the underlying asset's price that is currently impounded in the option premiums to decline. Moreover, since the time decay is a positive effect for the value of this position, one appropriate time to set a short straddle might be in the last month to expiration for the combined call and put. Figure 10.9 shows the short straddle's profit profile, and Sample Problem 10.5 provides further illustration. The following summarizes the basic risk–return features for the profit profile of a short-straddle position.

Profit potential: limited (to call and put premiums),
Loss potential: unlimited on upside, limited on downside,
Effect of time decay: positive,
Market expectation: neutral.

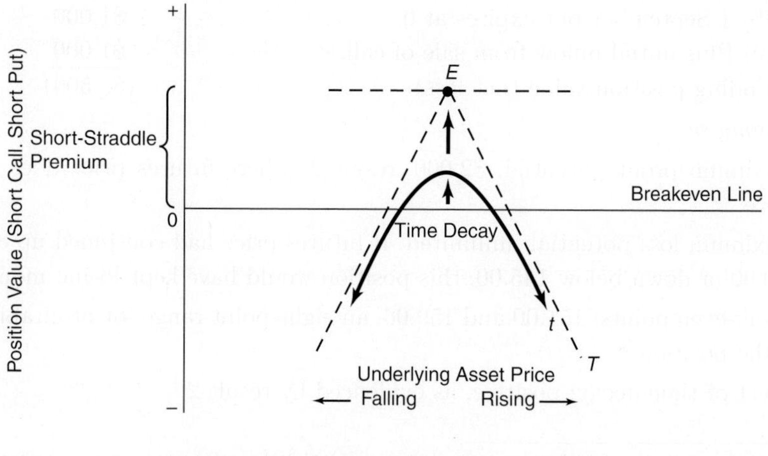

Fig. 10.9. Profit profile for a short straddle.

Sample Problem 10.5

Situation: An investor feels the market is overestimating price volatility at the moment and that prices are going to remain stable for some time. To express his opinion, the investor sells a straddle consisting of at-the-money call and put options on the September S&P 500 futures contract, for which the current price is 155.00. Assume the position is held to expiration.

Transaction:

1. Sell 1 September 155 call at \$2.00 (× \$500 per point).	\$1,000
2. Sell 1 September 155 put at \$2.00.	\$1,000
Net initial inflow (position value)	\$2,000

Results:

1. If futures price = 150.00:	
(a) 1 September 155 call expires at 0.	\$1,000
(b) 1 September 155 put expires at \$5.00.	(\$2,500)
(c) Plus initial inflow from sale of put.	\$1,000
Ending position value (net loss).	(\$ 500)
2. If futures price = 155.00:	
(a) 1 September 155 call expires at 0.	\$1,000
(b) 1 September 155 put expires at 0.	\$1,000
Ending position value (net profit).	\$2,000
3. If futures price = 160.00:	
(a) 1 September 155 call expires at \$5.00.	(\$2,500)
(b) 1 September put expires at 0.	\$1,000
(c) Plus initial inflow from sale of call.	\$1,000
Ending position value (net loss).	(\$ 500)

Summary:

Maximum profit potential: \$2,000, result 2. where futures price does not move.

Maximum loss potential: unlimited. If futures price had continued up over 160.00 or down below 145.00, this position would have kept losing money.

Break-even points: 151.00 and 159.00, an eight-point range for profitability of the position.[3]

Effect of time decay: positive, as evidenced by result 2.

[3]Break-even points for the short straddle are calculated in the same manner as for the long straddle: Exercise price plus initial prices of options.

10.4.7. *Long Vertical (Bull) Spread*

When dealing strictly in options, a spread is a combination of any two or more of the same type of options (two calls or two puts, for instance) on the same underlying asset. A vertical spread specifies that the options have the same maturity month. Finally, a long vertical spread designates a position for which one has bought a low-exercise-price call (or a low-exercise-price put) and sold a high-exercise-price call (or a high-exercise-price put) that both mature in the same month. A long vertical spread is also known as a **bull** spread because of the bullish market expectation of the investor who enters into it. Actually, the long vertical spread (or bull spread) is not a strongly bullish position, because the investor limits the profit potential in selling the high- exercise-price call (or high-exercise-price put). Rather, this is a popular position when it is expected that the market will more likely go up than down. Therefore, the bull spread conveys a bit of uncertainty about future market conditions. Of course, the higher the exercise price at which the call is sold, the more bullish the position. An examination of the profit profile for the long vertical spread (see Fig. 10.10) can tell more about its risk–return attributes. The following summarizes the basic risk–return features for the profit profile of a long-vertical-spread position.

Profit potential: limited (up to the higher exercise price),

Loss potential: limited (down to the lower exercise price) Effect of time decay: mixed,

Market expectation: cautiously bullish.

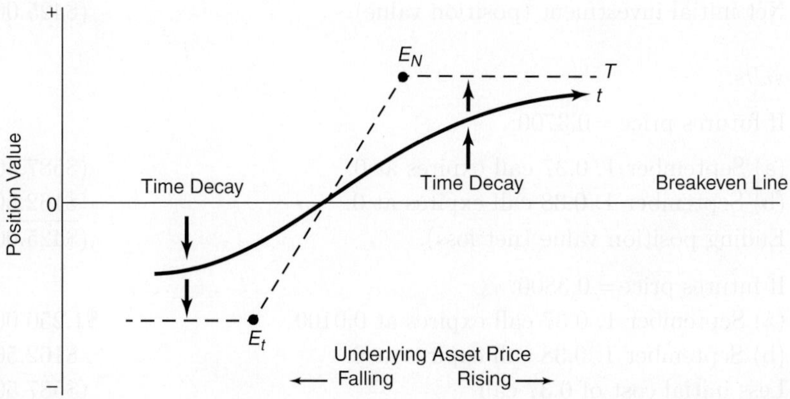

Fig. 10.10. Profit profile for a long vertical spread.

Although profit is limited by the shorted call on the upside, the loss potential is also truncated at the lower exercise price by the same short call. There are other reasons for this being a mildly bullish strategy. The effect of time decay is ambiguous up to the expiration or liquidation of the position. That is, if the asset price, S_t, is near the exercise price of the higher-price option E_H, then the position acts more like a long call and time-decay effect is negative. Conversely, if S_t is near the exercise price of the lower-price option E_L, then the bull spread acts more like a short call and the time-decay effect is neutral.

Consequently, unless an investor is more than mildly bullish, it would probably be unwise to put on a bull spread with the low exercise price call near the current price of the asset while both options are in their last month to expiration. Sample Problem 10.6 provides further illustration.

Sample Problem 10.6

Situation: An investor is moderately bullish on the West German mark. He would like to be long but wants to reduce the cost and risk of this position in case he is wrong. To express his opinion, the investor puts on a long vertical spread by buying a lower-exercise-price call and selling a higher-exercise-price call with the same month to expiration. Assume the position is held to expiration.

Transaction:

1. Buy September 1, 0.37 call at 0.0047 (× 125.000 per point).	($587.50)
2. Sell September 1, 0.38 call at 0.0013.	$162.50
Net initial investment (position value).	($425.00)

Results:

1. If futures price = 0.3700:

(a) September 1, 0.37 call expires at 0.	($587.50)
(b) September 1, 0.38 call expires at 0.	$162.50
Ending position value (net loss).	($425.00)

2. If futures price = 0.3800:

(a) September 1, 0.37 call expires at 0.0100.	$1,250.00
(b) September 1, 0.38 call expires at 0.	$162.50
Less initial cost of 0.37 call	($587.50)
Ending position value (net profit)	$825.00

3. If futures price = 0.3900:

(a) September 1, 0.38 call expires at 0.0200.	$2,500.00
(b) September 1, put expires at 0.	($1,250.00)
Less initial premium of 0.37 call	($587.50)
Plus initial premium of 0.38 call.	$162.50
Ending position value (net profit).	$825.00

Summary:

Maximum profit potential: $825.00, result 2.

Maximum loss potential: $425.00, result 1.

Break-even point: 0.3734.[4]

Effect of time decay: Mixed. Positive if price is at high end of range and negative if at low end.

10.4.8. *Short Vertical (Bear) Spread*

The **short vertical spread** is simply the reverse of the corresponding long position. That is, an investor buys a high-exercise-price call (or put) and sells a low-exercise-price call (or put), both having the same time to expiration left. As the more common name for this type of option position is bear spread, it is easy to infer the type of market sentiment consistent with this position. The profit profile for the short vertical spread is seen in Fig. 10.11.

As the profit profile indicates, this strategy is profitable as long as the underlying asset moves down in price. Profit is limited to a price decline in the asset down to the lower exercise price, while risk is limited on the upside by the long-call position. From the time-decay effects shown, a mildly bearish investor might consider using options in the last month to expiration with the E_L option near the money. The following summarizes the basic risk–return features for the profit profile of a short-vertical-spread position.

Profit potential: limited (down to E_L),

Loss potential: limited (up to E_H),

Effect of time decay: mixed (opposite to that of long vertical spread),

Market sentiment: mildly bearish.

[4] Break-even point for the long vertical spread is computed as lower exercise price plus price of long call minus price of short call ($0.3734 = 0.3700 + 0.0047 - 0.0013$).

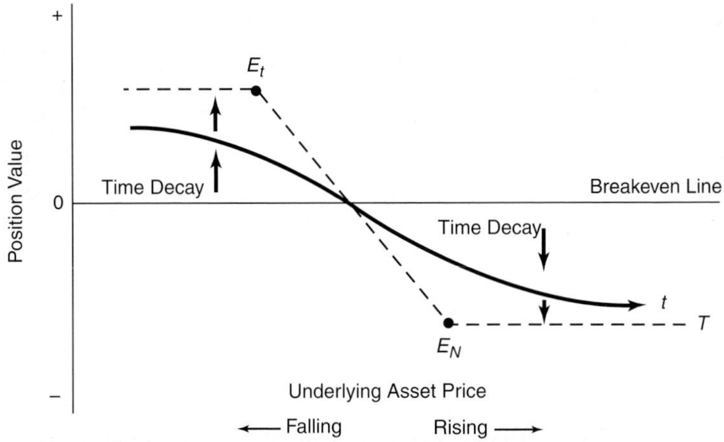

Fig. 10.11. Profit profile for a short vertical spread.

10.4.9. *Calendar (Time) Spreads*

A **calendar spread** (also called a **time** or **horizontal spread**) consists of the sale of one option and the simultaneous purchase of another option with the same exercise price but a longer term to maturity. The objective of the calendar spread is to capture the faster erosion in the time-premium portion of the shorted nearer-term-to-maturity option. By taking a position in two of the same type options (two calls or two puts), both with the same exercise price, the investor utilizing this strategy expresses a neutral opinion on the market. In other words, the investor is interested in selling time rather than predicting the price direction of the underlying asset. Thus, a calendar spread might be considered appropriate for a sideways-moving or quiet market. However, if the underlying asset's price moves significantly up or down, the calendar spread will lose part of its original value. Figure 10.12 displays the calendar spread's profit profile and related risk–return attributes.

The profit profile shows that this strategy will make money for a rather narrow range of price movement in the underlying asset. While similar in nature to the short straddle (both are neutral strategies), the calendar spread is more conservative. The reason? It has both a lower profit potential and lower (limited) risk than the short straddle. The lower potential profit is the result of only benefiting from the time decay in one option premium instead of two (the call and the put) for the short straddle. Moreover, taking

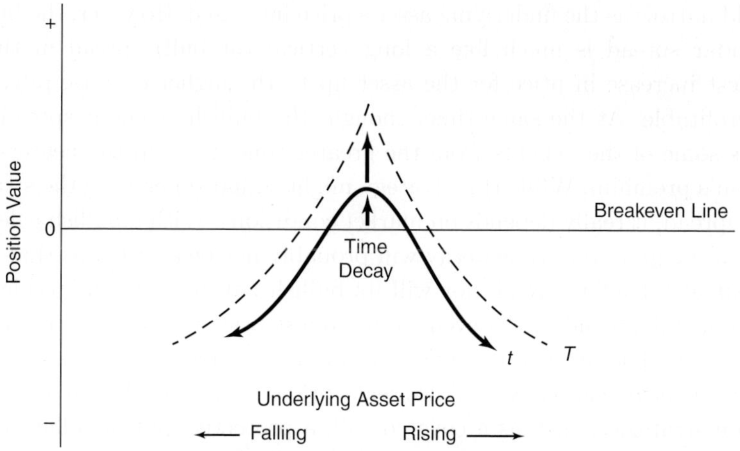

Fig. 10.12. Profit profile for a neutral calendar spread.

opposite positions in the same type of option at the same exercise price adds a loss limit on each side against adverse price moves. The following summarizes the basic risk–return features for the profit profile of a neutral calendar-spread position.

Profit potential: limited,

Loss potential: limited (to original cost of position),

Effect of time decay: positive. (Option sold loses value faster than option bought.)

Market sentiment: neutral.

The calendar spread does not have to be neutral in sentiment. By diagonalizing this spread it is possible to express an opinion on the market. For instance, by selling a near-term higher-exercise-price option and purchasing a longer-term lower-exercise-price option, the investor is being bullish in position. Such a position is thus referred to as a bullish calendar spread. Why is it bullish? Remember that with the neutral calendar spread we are concerned solely with benefiting from the faster time decay in the premium of the shorted near-term option. Any significant movement in price upwards, for instance, would have not been profitable because it would have slowed the time decay and increased the intrinsic value of the shorted near-term option. In fact we would eventually lose money because the difference in premiums between the near-term and the longer-term options (the spread) would narrow as the underlying asset's price increased. However, the bullish calendar spread is much like a long vertical (or bull) spread in that a modest increase in price for the asset up to the higher exercise price will be profitable. At the same time, though, the bullish calendar spread also reaps some of the benefits from the greater time decay in the nearer-term option's premium. While this strategy might sound superior to the straight bull spread, it really depends on market conditions. With a bullish calendar spread, its gain from time decay will probably not be as great as that from a neutral calendar spread, nor will its bullish nature be as profitable as a straight bull spread in the event of a modest price increase for the underlying asset. The real world application will be discussed in the next section.

In the next section, we will use real world data to show how to construct option strategies, such as a covered call, a protective put, a collar, a long straddle, a short straddle, a long vertical (bull) spread, and a short vertical (bear) spread.

10.5. Examples of Alternative Option Strategies

In this section, we are considering several option strategies and using the options of the International Business Machines Corporation (IBM) in the following examples. Below is the information published on December 20, 2014 for all options that will expire in January 2014. IBM stock closed at \$161.53 on December 20, 2014.

10.5.1. *Protective Put*

Assume that an investor wants to invest in the IBM stock on December 20, 2014 but does not desire to bear any potential loss for prices below \$160. The investor can purchase IBM stock and at the same time buy the put option IBM with a strike price of \$160. Let S_0, S_T, and X denote the stock purchase price, future stock price at the expiration time T, and the strike price, respectively. Given $S_0 = \$161.53$, $X = \$160$, and the premium for the put option \$2.09, Table 10.5 shows the values for Protective Put at different stock prices at time T. The profit profile of the Protective Put position is constructed in Fig. 10.13.

The definitions and calculations to find the payoff, profit, and break-even point are as follows. The payoff is the difference between the exercise price and the stock price. The profit for buying long is defined as stock price − exercise price − premium. The profit for buying short is defined as

Table 10.4. Call and put option quotes for IBM on December 20, 2014.

Strike	Contract Name	Last	Bid	Ask	Change	%Change	Volume	Open Interest	Implied Volatility (%)
∵ Filter									
140	IBM141220C00140000	48.03	20.8	22.2	0	0.00%	0	0	36.91
145	IBM141220C00145000	16.8	15.55	18.05	0	0.00%	3	0	38.27
150	IBM141220C00150000	11.85	11.45	12.2	0	0.00%	11	63	22.85
155	IBM141220C00155000	7.1	7.1	7.25	−0.4	−5.06%	34	264	15.87
160	IBM141220C00160000	3.37	3.4	3.5	−0.04	−1.01%	347	1792	14.26
165	IBM141220C00165000	1.15	1.16	1.18	−0.08	−5.44%	614	5594	13.33
170	IBM141220C00170000	0.29	0.28	0.31	0	0.00%	368	5772	13.53
175	IBM141220C00175000	0.09	0.08	0.1	0	0.00%	327	3972	14.94
180	IBM141220C00180000	0.03	0.01	0.05	0	0.00%	66	1770	17.19
185	IBM141220C00185000	0.02	0	0.05	0	0.00%	5	1040	20.80
190	IBM141220C00190000	0.02	0	0.02	0	0.00%	1	1543	21.68
195	IBM141220C00195000	0.02	0.01	0.02	0	0.00%	11	1633	24.61
200	IBM141220C00200000	0.02	0	0.03	0	0.00%	3	951	28.91
205	IBM141220C00205000	0.01	0	0.01	0	0.00%	20	973	28.13
210	IBM141220C00210000	0.01	0	0.02	0	0.00%	2	272	33.20
215	IBM141220C00215000	0.02	0	0.02	0	0.00%	5	328	35.55
220	IBM141220C00220000	0.09	0	0.02	0	0.00%	10	53	38.28
225	IBM141220C00225000	0.21	0	0.03	0	0.00%	0	12	42.19
230	IBM141220C00230000	0.13	0	0.03	0	0.00%	0	21	44.92
235	IBM141220C00235000	0.12	0	0.03	0	0.00%	0	2	47.27
240	IBM141220C00240000	0.04	0	0.03	0	0.00%	2	4	49.61
245	IBM141220C00245000	0.04	0	0.03	0	0.00%	0	1	51.76
250	IBM141220C00250000	0.04	0	0.03	0	0.00%	35	35	50.78
260	IBM141220C00260000	0.03	0	0.03	0	0.00%	1	1	54.69

(*Continued*)

Table 10.4. (*Continued*)

Puts Strike	Contract Name	Last	Bid	Ask	Change	%Change	Volume	Open Interest	Implied Volatility (%)
∵ Filter									
90	IBM141220P00090000	0.04	0	0.03	0	0.00%	1	11	68.75
95	IBM141220P00095000	0.07	0	0.03	0	0.00%	10	10	63.28
100	IBM141220P00100000	0.01	0	0.03	0	0.00%	3	3	57.03
110	IBM141220P00110000	0.15	0	0.05	0	0.00%	6	3	53.13
115	IBM141220P00115000	0.07	0	0.06	0	0.00%	1	1	48.63
120	IBM141220P00120000	0.01	0	0.06	0	0.00%	5	61	43.16
125	IBM141220P00125000	0.04	0.01	0.07	0	0.00%	5	45	38.48
130	IBM141220P00130000	0.06	0.02	0.11	0	0.00%	2	93	35.55
135	IBM141220P00135000	0.06	0.04	0.13	0	0.00%	2	194	30.96
140	IBM141220P00140000	0.12	0.09	0.15	0	0.00%	5	341	26.17
145	IBM141220P00145000	0.16	0.1	0.2	0.01	7.69%	202	987	21.88
150	IBM141220P00150000	0.35	0.33	0.36	0	0.00%	42	1462	18.60
155	IBM141220P00155000	0.81	0.81	0.83	−0.05	−6.67%	142	2097	16.19
160	IBM141220P00160000	2.07	2.07	2.09	−0.05	−2.65%	407	3246	14.54
165	IBM141220P00165000	4.7	4.75	4.95	−0.08	−1.82%	278	2539	14.71
170	IBM141220P00170000	7.95	8.25	9.2	0	0.00%	22	1775	16.98
175	IBM141220P00175000	13	13.4	14	0.62	5.01%	10	1445	20.78
180	IBM141220P00180000	17.87	18.6	19	0.32	1.82%	12	634	25.90
185	IBM141220P00185000	20.86	22.15	24	0	0.00%	7	253	30.66
190	IBM141220P00190000	26.3	26.35	30.35	0	0.00%	1	164	50.29
195	IBM141220P00195000	33.5	31.65	34.05	0.19	0.59%	51	60	40.28
200	IBM141220P00200000	37.09	36.35	40.35	0	0.00%	1	18	60.43
205	IBM141220P00205000	42.5	41.35	45.35	0	0.00%	1	1	65.11
210	IBM141220P00210000	17.7	46.35	50.35	0	0.00%	0	2	69.58
220	IBM141220P00220000	32.8	56.35	60.35	0	0.00%	0	0	78.00

Table 10.5. Value of protective put position at option expiration.

	Long a Put at strike price E		$160.00	Premium		$2.09
	Buy one share of stock			Current Price		$161.53
Stock (P)	One Share of Stock (P)		Long Put at Strike Price E		Protective Put Value	
Price	*Payoff*	*Profit*	*Payoff*	*Profit*	*Payoff*	*Profit*
$135	$135.00	−$26.53	$25.00	$22.91	$160.00	−$3.62
$140	$140.00	−$21.53	$20.00	$17.91	$160.00	−$3.62
$145	$145.00	−$16.53	$15.00	$12.91	$160.00	−$3.62
$150	$150.00	−$11.53	$10.00	$7.91	$160.00	−$3.62
$155	$155.00	−$6.53	$5.00	$2.91	$160.00	−$3.62
$160	$160.00	−$1.53	$0.00	−$2.09	$160.00	−$3.62
$165	$165.00	$3.47	$0.00	−$2.09	$165.00	$1.38
$170	$170.00	$8.47	$0.00	−$2.09	$170.00	$6.38
$175	$175.00	$13.47	$0.00	−$2.09	$175.00	$11.38
$180	$180.00	$18.47	$0.00	−$2.09	$180.00	$16.38
$185	$185.00	$23.47	$0.00	−$2.09	$185.00	$21.38

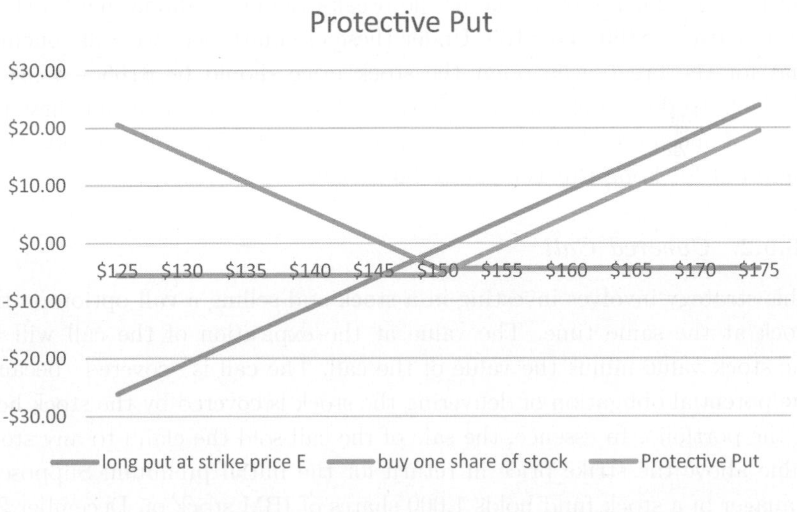

Fig. 10.13. Profit profile for protective put.

stock price − exercise price + premium. To find the break-even point set each of the profit equations equal to zero, respectively.

For example, the profit calculations for Table 10.5 are as follows:

Stock price = $135, Exercise price = $160, Premium = $2.09, Current Price = $161.53

One Share of Stock (P): Profit = \$135 – \$161.53 = –\$26.53
Payoff = \$135.

Long Put at Strike Price E:
Payoff = \$160 – \$135 = \$25,
Profit = \$25 – \$2.09 = \$22.91.

Protective Put Value:
Payoff = \$135 + \$25 = \$160,
Profit = –\$26.53 + \$22.91 = –\$3.62.

Break-even point = Purchase price of underlying + Premium paid = \$161.53 + \$2.09 = \$163.62.

From Table 10.5, if the stock price is \$160 the profit of protective put is –\$3.62, however, if stock price increases to \$165 the profit of the protective put is \$1.38. Therefore, we know the break-even point should have a stock price between \$160 and \$165. Under these circumstances we will conclude that for the break-even point the stock price should be \$165 – \$1.38 = \$163.62. To double check whether this solution is correct or not, first the profit of one share of stock at stock price \$163.62 – \$161.53 = \$2.09. Then the profit for Long Put is equal to \$0 – \$2.09.

10.5.2. *Covered Call*

This strategy involves investing in a stock and selling a call option on the stock at the same time. The value at the expiration of the call will be the stock value minus the value of the call. The call is "covered" because the potential obligation of delivering the stock is covered by the stock held in the portfolio. In essence, the sale of the call sold the claim to any stock value above the strike price in return for the initial premium. Suppose a manager of a stock fund holds 1,000 shares of IBM stock on December 20, 2014 and she plans to sell the IBM stock if its price hits \$165. Then she can write 1,000 share of the call option IBM with a strike price of \$165 to establish the position. She shorts the call and collects premiums. Given that S_0 = \$161.53, X = \$165, and the premium for the call option \$1.16, Table 10.6 shows the values for Covered Call at different stock prices at time T. The profit profile of the Covered Call position is constructed in Fig. 10.14.

Table 10.6. Value of covered call position at option expiration.

Write a call at strike price E		$165.00	**Premium**		$1.16	
Buy one share of stock			**Price**		$161.53	

Stock (P)	One Share of Stock		Written Call at Strike Price E		Covered Call	
Price	*Payoff*	*Profit*	*Payoff*	*Profit*	*Payoff*	*Profit*
$140.00	$140.00	−$21.53	$0.00	$1.16	$140.00	−$20.37
$145.00	$145.00	−$16.53	$0.00	$1.16	$145.00	−$15.37
$150.00	$150.00	−$11.53	$0.00	$1.16	$150.00	−$10.37
$155.00	$155.00	−$6.53	$0.00	$1.16	$155.00	−$5.37
$160.00	$160.00	−$1.53	$0.00	$1.16	$160.00	−$0.37
$165.00	$165.00	$3.47	$0.00	$1.16	$165.00	$4.63
$170.00	$170.00	$8.47	−$5.00	−$3.84	$165.00	$4.63
$175.00	$175.00	$13.47	−$10.00	−$8.84	$165.00	$4.63
$180.00	$180.00	$18.47	−$15.00	−$13.84	$165.00	$4.63
$185.00	$185.00	$23.47	−$20.00	−$18.84	$165.00	$4.63
$190.00	$190.00	$28.47	−$25.00	−$23.84	$165.00	$4.63

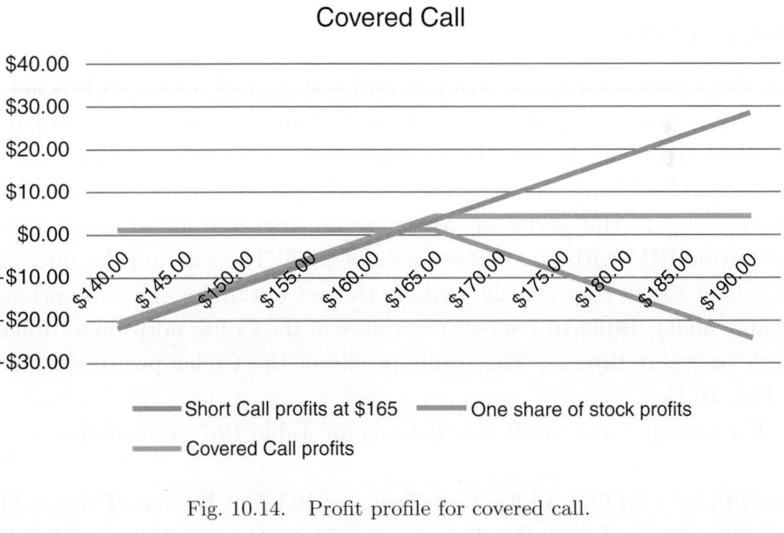

Fig. 10.14. Profit profile for covered call.

For example, the profit calculations for Table 10.6 are as follows:

Stock Price = $140, Exercise Price = $165, Premium = $1.16, Current Price = $161.53.

One Share of Stock:
Profit = $140 − $161.53 = −$21.53.

Written Call at strike price E:

Profit = \$0 + \$1.16 = \$1.16.

Covered Call:

Profit = −\$21.53 + \$1.16 = −\$20.37,

Break-even point = Purchase price of underlying − Premium received = \$161.53 − \$1.16 = \$160.37.

From Table 10.6, if the stock price is \$160 the profit of the covered call is −\$0.37, however, if stock price increases to \$165 the profit of the covered call is \$4.63. Therefore, we know the break-even point should have a stock price between \$160 and \$165. Under these circumstances, we will conclude that for the break-even point the stock price should be \$165 − \$4.63 = \$160.37. To double check whether this solution is correct, first the profit of one share of stock at stock price \$160.37 − \$161.53 = −\$1.16. Then the profit for the written call is equal to \$0 + \$1.16.

10.5.3. *Collar*

A collar combines a protective put and a short call option to bracket the value of a portfolio between two bounds. For example, an investor holds the IBM stock selling at \$161.53. Buying a protective put using the put option IBM with an exercise price of \$160 places a lower bound of \$160 on the value of the portfolio. At the same time, the investor can write a call option IBM with an exercise price of \$165. The call and the put sell at \$1.16 and \$2.09, respectively, making the net outlay for the two options to be only \$0.93. Table 10.7 shows the values of the Collar position at different stock prices at time T. The profit profile of the Collar position is shown in Fig. 10.15.

For example, the profit calculations for Table 10.7 are as follows:

Stock Price = \$140, Call Exercise Price = \$165, Put Exercise Price = \$160, Call Premium = \$1.16, Put Premium = \$2.09, Current Price = \$161.53.

One Share of Stock:

Profit = \$140 − \$161.53 = −\$21.53.

*Written Call at strike price E*1:

Profit = \$0 + \$1.16 = \$1.16.

Table 10.7. Value of collar position at option expiration.

	Write a call at strike price E1		$165.00	**Premium**			$1.16	
	Long a Put at strike price E2		$160.00	**Premium**			$2.09	
	Buy one share of stock			**Current Price**			$161.53	
Stock (P)	One Share of Stock		Written Call at Strike Price E1		Long Put at Strike Price E2		Collar Value	
Price	*Payoff*	*Profit*	*Payoff*	*Profit*	*Payoff*	*Profit*	*Payoff*	*Profit*
$140.00	$140.00	−$21.53	$0.00	$1.16	$20.00	$17.91	$160.00	−$2.46
$145.00	$145.00	−$16.53	$0.00	$1.16	$15.00	$12.91	$160.00	−$2.46
$150.00	$150.00	−$11.53	$0.00	$1.16	$10.00	$7.91	$160.00	−$2.46
$155.00	$155.00	−$6.53	$0.00	$1.16	$5.00	$2.91	$160.00	−$2.46
$160.00	$160.00	−$1.53	$0.00	$1.16	$0.00	−$2.09	$160.00	−$2.46
$165.00	$165.00	$3.47	$0.00	$1.16	$0.00	−$2.09	$165.00	$2.54
$170.00	$170.00	$8.47	−$5.00	−$3.84	$0.00	−$2.09	$165.00	$2.54
$175.00	$175.00	$13.47	−$10.00	−$8.84	$0.00	−$2.09	$165.00	$2.54
$180.00	$180.00	$18.47	−$15.00	−$13.84	$0.00	−$2.09	$165.00	$2.54
$185.00	$185.00	$23.47	−$20.00	−$18.84	$0.00	−$2.09	$165.00	$2.54
$190.00	$190.00	$28.47	−$25.00	−$23.84	$0.00	−$2.09	$165.00	$2.54

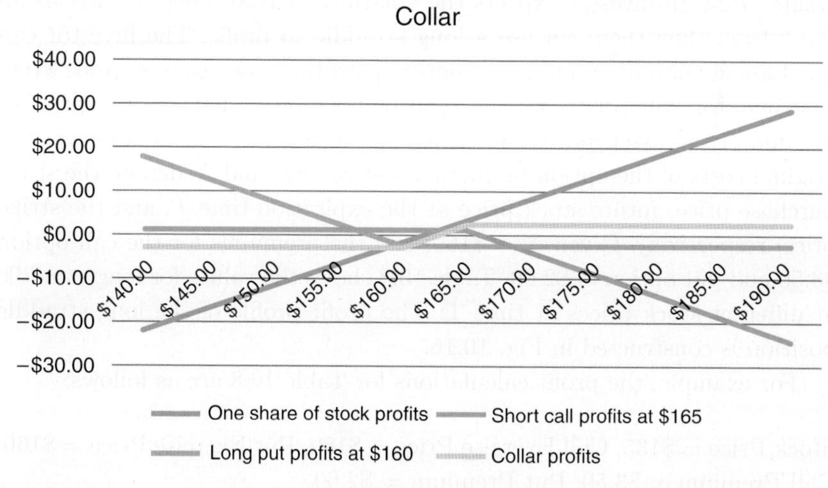

Fig. 10.15. Profit profile for collar.

Long Put at strike price E2:

Profit = $20 − $2.09 = $17.91.

Break-even point = Purchase price of underlying + Net Premium Paid = $161.53 + ($2.09 − $1.16) = $162.46.

Collar Value:

Profit = −\$21.53 + \$1.16 + \$17.91 = −\$2.4.

From Table 10.7, if the stock price is \$160 the profit of the collar is −\$2.46, however, if stock price increases to \$165 the profit of the collar is \$2.54. Therefore, we know the break-even point should have a stock price between \$160 and \$165. Under these circumstances, we will conclude that for the break-even point the stock price should be \$165 − \$2.54 = \$162.46. To double check whether this solution is correct, first find the profit of one share of stock at stock price \$162.46 − \$161.53 = −\$.93. Then the profit for the written call is equal to \$0 + \$1.16 and the profit for the long put is equal to \$0 − \$2.09.

10.5.4. *Long Straddle*

The long straddle strategy is when you long a call and a put option at the same strike price (costs are the ask prices of options). For example, assume that an investor expects the volatility of IBM stock to increase in the future, they then can use a long straddle to profit. The investor can purchase a call option and a put option with the same exercise price \$160. The investor will profit on this type of position as long as the price of the underlying asset moves sufficiently up or down to more than cover the original costs of the option premiums. Let S_0, S_T, and X denote the stock purchase price, future stock price at the expiration time T, and the strike price, respectively. Given $X = \$160$, and the premiums for the call option \$3.50 and put option = \$2.09, Table 10.8 shows the values for long straddle at different stock prices at time T. The profit profile of the long straddle position is constructed in Fig. 10.16.

For example, the profit calculations for Table 10.8 are as follows:

Stock Price = \$135, Call Exercise Price = \$160, Put Exercise Price = \$160, Call Premium = \$3.50, Put Premium = \$2.09.

Long Call at Strike Price E:

Profit = \$0 − \$3.50 = −\$3.50.

Long Put at strike price E:

Profit = \$25 − \$2.09 = \$22.91.

Table 10.8. Value of long straddle position at option expiration.

	Long a Call at strike price *E*	$160.00	**Premium**	$3.50		
	Long a Put at strike price *E*	$160.00	**Premium**	$2.09		
Stock (P)	Long Call at Strike Price E		Long Put at Strike Price E		Long Straddle	
Price	*Payoff*	*Profit*	*Payoff*	*Profit*	*Payoff*	*Profit*
$135.00	$0.00	−$3.50	$25.00	$22.91	$25.00	$19.41
$140.00	$0.00	−$3.50	$20.00	$17.91	$20.00	$14.41
$145.00	$0.00	−$3.50	$15.00	$12.91	$15.00	$9.41
$150.00	$0.00	−$3.50	$10.00	$7.91	$10.00	$4.41
$155.00	$0.00	−$3.50	$5.00	$2.91	$5.00	−$0.59
$160.00	$0.00	−$3.50	$0.00	−$2.09	$0.00	−$5.59
$165.00	$5.00	$1.50	$0.00	−$2.09	$5.00	−$0.59
$170.00	$10.00	$6.50	$0.00	−$2.09	$10.00	$4.41
$175.00	$15.00	$11.50	$0.00	−$2.09	$15.00	$9.41
$180.00	$20.00	$16.50	$0.00	−$2.09	$20.00	$14.41
$185.00	$25.00	$21.50	$0.00	−$2.09	$25.00	$19.41

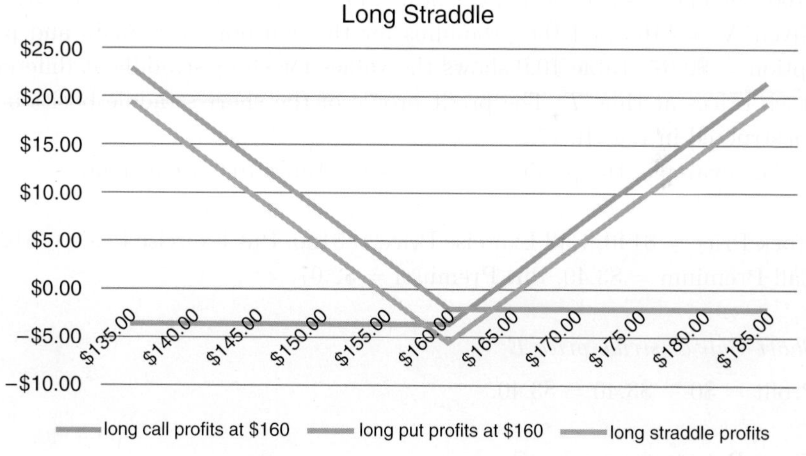

Fig. 10.16. Profit profile for long straddle.

Long Straddle:

Profit = −$3.50 + $22.91 = $19.41.

Upper Break-even point = Strike price of long call + Net Premium paid = $160 + ($3.50 + $2.09) = $165.59.

Lower Break-even point = Strike price of long put − Net Premium Paid = $160 − ($3.50 + $2.09) = $154.41.

From Table 10.8, there are two break-even points. For the first break-even point, if the stock price is \$150 the profit of the long straddle is \$4.41, however, if stock price increases to \$155 the profit of the long straddle is −\$0.59. Therefore, we know the break-even point should have a stock price between \$150 and \$155. Under these circumstances, we will conclude that for the break-even point the stock price should be \$150 + \$4.41 = \$154.41. For the second break-even point, if the stock price is \$165 the profit of the long straddle is −\$0.59, however, if the stock price increases to \$170 the profit of the long straddle is \$4.41. Under these circumstances, we will conclude that for the break-even point the stock price should be \$170 − \$4.41 = \$165.59.

10.5.5. *Short Straddle*

Contrary to the long straddle strategy, an investor will use a short straddle via a short call and a short put on IBM stock with the same exercise price \$160 when he or she expects little or no movement in the price of IBM stock. Given X = \$160 and the premiums for the call option = \$3.40 and put option = \$2.07, Table 10.9 shows the values for short straddle at different stock prices at time T. The profit profile of the short straddle position is constructed in Fig. 10.17.

For example, the profit calculations for Table 10.9 are as follows:

Stock Price = \$140, Call Exercise Price = \$160, Put Exercise Price = \$160, Call Premium = \$3.40, Put Premium = \$2.07.

Short Call at strike price E:

Profit = \$0 + \$3.40 = \$3.40.

Short Put at strike price E:

Profit = −\$25 + \$2.07 = −\$22.93.

Short Straddle:

Profit = \$3.40 − \$22.93 = −\$19.53.

Upper Break-even point = Strike price of short call + Net Premium Received = \$160 + (\$3.40 + \$2.07) = \$165.47.

Lower Break-even point = Strike price of short put − Net Premium Received = \$160 − (\$3.40 + \$2.07) = \$154.53.

Table 10.9. Value of short straddle position at option expiration.

	Write a Call at strike price E		$160.00	Premium	$3.40
	Write a Put at strike price E		$160.00	Premium	$2.07

Stock (P)	Short Call at Strike Price E		Short Put at Strike Price E		Short Straddle	
Price	*Payoff*	*Profit*	*Payoff*	*Profit*	*Payoff*	*Profit*
$135	$0.00	$3.40	−$25.00	−$22.93	−$25.00	−$19.53
$140	$0.00	$3.40	−$20.00	−$17.93	−$20.00	−$14.53
$145	$0.00	$3.40	−$15.00	−$12.93	−$15.00	−$9.53
$150	$0.00	$3.40	−$10.00	−$7.93	−$10.00	−$4.53
$155	$0.00	$3.40	−$5.00	−$2.93	−$5.00	$0.47
$160	$0.00	$3.40	$0.00	$2.07	$0.00	$5.47
$165	-$5.00	−$1.60	$0.00	$2.07	−$5.00	$0.47
$170	-$10.00	−$6.60	$0.00	$2.07	−$10.00	−$4.53
$175	-$15.00	−$11.60	$0.00	$2.07	−$15.00	−$9.53
$180	-$20.00	−$16.60	$0.00	$2.07	−$20.00	−$14.53
$185	-$25.00	−$21.60	$0.00	$2.07	−$25.00	−$19.53

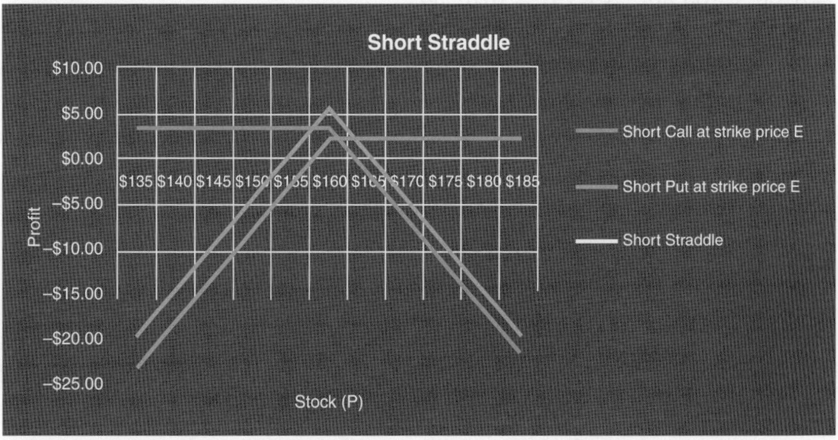

Fig. 10.17. Profit profile for short straddle.

From Table 10.9, there are two break-even points. For the first break-even point, if the stock price is $150 the profit of the short straddle is −$4.53, however, if stock price increases to $155 the profit of the short straddle is $0.47. Therefore, we know the break-even point should have a stock price between $150 and $155. Under these circumstances, we will conclude that for the break-even point the stock price should be

\$155 − \$0.47 = \$154.53. For the second break-even point, if the stock price is \$165 the profit of the short straddle is \$0.47, however, if the stock price increases to \$170 the profit of the short straddle is −\$4.53. Under these circumstances, we will conclude that for the break-even point the stock price should be \$165 + \$0.47 = \$165.47.

10.5.6. *Long Vertical (Bull) Spread*

This strategy combine a long call (or put) with a low strike price and a short call (or put) with a high strike price. For example, an investor purchases a call with the exercise price \$160 and sells a call with the exercise price \$165. Given X_1 = \$160, X_2 = \$165 and the premiums for the long call option is \$3.50 and the short call option is \$1.16, Table 10.9 shows the values for long vertical spread at different stock prices at time T. The profit profile of the long vertical spread is constructed in Fig. 10.18.

Break-even point = Strike price of long call + Net Premium Paid = \$160 + (\$3.50 − \$1.16) = \$162.34.

From Table 10.10, if the stock price is \$160 the profit of protective put is −\$2.34, however, if stock price increases to \$165 the profit of the protective put is \$2.66. Therefore, we know the break-even point should have a stock price between \$160 and \$165. Under these circumstances we will conclude

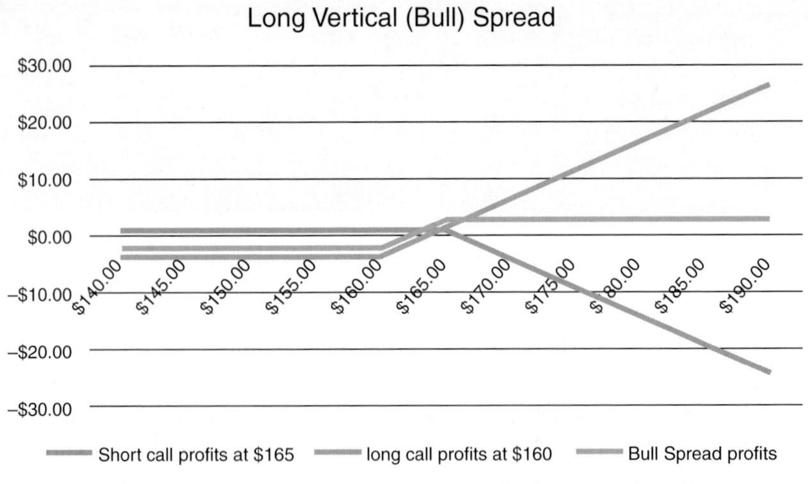

Fig. 10.18. Profit profile for long vertical (Bull) spread.

Table 10.10. Value of long vertical (Bull) spread position at option expiration.

	Write a Call at strike price E1		$165.00	**Premium**	$1.16	
	Long a Call at strike price E2		$160.00	**Premium**	$3.50	
Stock (P)	Write Call at Strike Price E1		Long Call at Strike Price E2		Bull Spread (Call) Value	
Price	*Payoff*	*Profit*	*Payoff*	*Profit*	*Payoff*	*Profit*
$140.00	$0.00	$1.16	$0.00	−$3.50	$0.00	−$2.34
$145.00	$0.00	$1.16	$0.00	−$3.50	$0.00	−$2.34
$150.00	$0.00	$1.16	$0.00	−$3.50	$0.00	−$2.34
$155.00	$0.00	$1.16	$0.00	−$3.50	$0.00	−$2.34
$160.00	$0.00	$1.16	$0.00	−$3.50	$0.00	−$2.34
$165.00	$0.00	$1.16	$5.00	$1.50	$5.00	$2.66
$170.00	−$5.00	−$3.84	$10.00	$6.50	$5.00	$2.66
$175.00	−$10.00	−$8.84	$15.00	$11.50	$5.00	$2.66
$180.00	−$15.00	−$13.84	$20.00	$16.50	$5.00	$2.66
$185.00	−$20.00	−$18.84	$25.00	$21.50	$5.00	$2.66
$190.00	−$25.00	−$23.84	$30.00	$26.50	$5.00	$2.66

that for the break-even point the stock price should be $165 – $2.66 = $162.34.

10.5.7. *Short Vertical (Bear) Spread*

Contrary to a long vertical spread, this strategy combines a long call (or put) with a high strike price and a short call (or put) with a low strike price. For example, an investor purchases a call with the exercise price $165 and sells a call with the exercise price $160. Given $X_1 = \$165$, $X_2 = \$160$ and the premiums for the long call option is $1.18 and the short call option is $3.40, Table 10.10 shows the values for short vertical spread at different stock prices at time T. The profit profile of the short vertical spread is constructed in Fig. 10.19.

Break-even point = Strike price of short call + Net Premium Received = $160 + ($3.40 – $1.18) = $162.22.

From Table 10.11, if the stock price is $160 the profit of protective put is $2.22, however, if stock price increases to $165 the profit of the protective put is −$2.78. Therefore, we know the break-even point should have a stock price between $160 and $165. Under these circumstances we will conclude that for the break-even point the stock price should be $160 + $2.22 = $162.22.

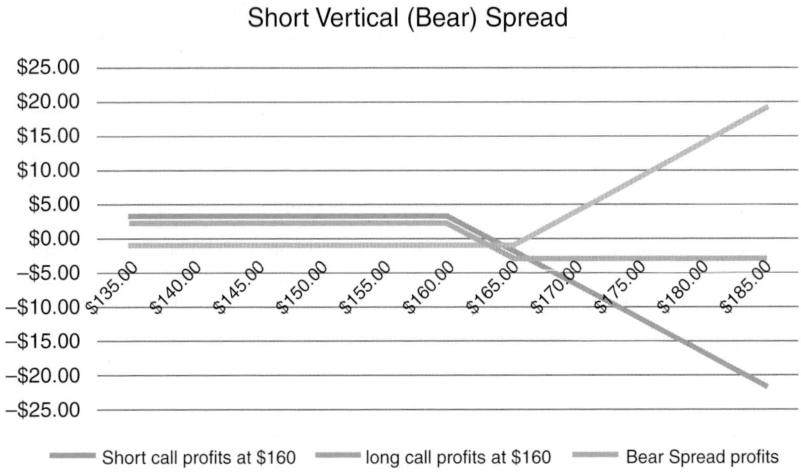

Fig. 10.19. Profit profile for short vertical (Bear) spread.

Table 10.11. Value of short vertical (Bear) spread position at option expiration.

Write a Call at strike price E1	$160.00	**Premium**	$3.40
Long a Call at strike price E2	$165.00	**Premium**	$1.18
E1 < E2			

Stock (P)	Write Call at Strike Price E1		Long Call at Strike Price E2		Bull Spread (Call) Value	
Price	*Payoff*	*Profit*	*Payoff*	*Profit*	*Payoff*	*Profit*
$135.00	$0.00	$3.40	$0.00	−$1.18	$0.00	$2.22
$140.00	$0.00	$3.40	$0.00	−$1.18	$0.00	$2.22
$145.00	$0.00	$3.40	$0.00	−$1.18	$0.00	$2.22
$150.00	$0.00	$3.40	$0.00	−$1.18	$0.00	$2.22
$155.00	$0.00	$3.40	$0.00	−$1.18	$0.00	$2.22
$160.00	$0.00	$3.40	$0.00	−$1.18	$0.00	$2.22
$165.00	−$5.00	−$1.60	$0.00	−$1.18	−$5.00	−$2.78
$170.00	−$10.00	−$6.60	$5.00	$3.82	−$5.00	−$2.78
$175.00	−$15.00	−$11.60	$10.00	$8.82	−$5.00	−$2.78
$180.00	−$20.00	−$16.60	$15.00	$13.82	−$5.00	−$2.78
$185.00	−$25.00	−$21.60	$20.00	$18.82	−$5.00	−$2.78

10.6. Summary

This chapter has introduced some of the essential differences between the two most basic kinds of option, calls and puts. A delineation was made of the relationship between the option's price or premium and that of the underlying asset. The option's value was shown to be composed of intrinsic value, or the underlying asset price less the exercise price, and time value. Moreover, it was demonstrated that the time value decays over time, particularly in the last month to maturity for an option.

Index and futures options were studied to introduce these important financial instruments. Put-call parity theorems were developed for European, American, and futures options in order to show the basic valuation relationship between the underlying asset and its call and put options. Finally, investment application of options and related combinations were discussed, along with relevant risk–return characteristics. A thorough understanding of this chapter is an essential basic tool to successfully study option-valuation models in the next chapter.

Problem Set

1. Define the following terms.

   (a) call option
   (b) put option
   (c) striking price
   (d) straddle
   (e) option
   (f) spread
   (g) exercise price
   (h) put-call parity
   (i) intrinsic value
   (j) European option
   (k) American option
   (l) time value

2. Compare the following pairs of investment strategies

   (a) Which is riskier, buying or selling a call option?
   (b) Which is riskier, writing a naked call option or writing a covered call option?
   (c) Other things being equal, which option has greater value, an American call option or a European call option?
   (d) Other things being equal, which option should have greater value, the option written on a low-beta stock or the option written on a high-beta stock?

3. Plot profit versus the stock price for a call option with an exercise price of \$100 and a premium of \$3.
4. HHH, Inc. is a company doing medical research. It has decided to place all of its resources into finding a cure for AIDS. If HHH is successful, the value of its stock will increase tenfold. If the company is unsuccessful, it will be bankrupt in ten years. (a) If you believe that there is a SO-percent chance of success, is there an investment strategy you

can devise using put and call options to exploit this situation? (b) How might your answer in (a) change if you believe that there is only a 33% chance of success?

5. Carefully explain the difference between a vertical bull spread and a vertical bear spread. When would you use the vertical bull spread? When would you use the vertical bear spread?
6. You would like to purchase a put option on XYZ Company's stock. If only call options exist on XYZ's stock, explain how you could create your own put option.
7. What is the benefit of purchasing a call option over purchasing the underlying stock? What are the disadvantages?
8. Carefully explain why the value of an option can never be negative.
9. Compare an option to a futures contract. How are they similar? How are they different?
10. What is a butterfly spread? When would an investor purchase a calendar spread?
11. Plot the profit opportunities for an investor who purchases a long straddle. Assume that the exercise price on the put and call options is $100.
12. Use the information given in the previous question to plot the profit opportunities for a short straddle. Compare these two positions.
13. Explain what is meant by an option that is:

    (a) In the money.
    (b) At the money.
    (c) Out of the money.

14. Explain how the time value of an option behaves as the option moves closer to expiration.
15. Given a stock valued at $25 on February 1, 1989, and the following information about call-option premiums, what is the time value for each of the options?

Exercise Price	March	June	September
20	$5.75	$6.75	$7.50
25	1.00	2.00	3.00
30	0.25	0.50	0.75

16. What impact does the payment of cash dividends by XYZ Company have on the put options of XYZ? How does it affect the call options of XYZ?
17. Discuss the uses of an option on foreign currencies.
18. Why would you never exercise an index option before the exercise date?
19. Explain the logic behind the put-call parity relationship shown in Table 9.2.
20. A call option with six months to maturity and an exercise price of 20 is selling for \$3. Assuming discrete compounding, a risk-free rate of interest of 8%, and a current stock price of \$19, what is the value of a European put option with a strike price of 20 and one year to maturity?
21. For a stock with a price of \$10, a put option with three months to maturity and an exercise price of \$12 is selling for \$3. Assuming discrete compounding and a risk-free rate of 8 percent, what are the boundaries of the price for an American call option?
22. What are the major advantages of an option on futures over an option on an underlying asset?
23. What is a synthetic put? Why would a synthetic put be useful if you have listed put options?
24. Compare the risk–return features of a long call with a short naked call. If these two types of call positions were to be continued indefinitely, what would be the result?
25. Compare the risk–return features for a short covered call with an uncovered short put. Be sure to discuss the time decay.
26. An investor wants to use a long straddle, the current market index being 150. He buys the three-month 150 call for \$5.00 and the three-month 150 put at \$4.50. If the market rises to 180 at the end of three months, what is the investor's profit or loss? If the market falls to 125 at the end of three months, what is the investor's profit or loss? If the market stays at *150* at the end of 3 month, what is the profit or loss?
27. Calculate the break-even points (upside and downside) for the straddle described in the previous problem.
28. An investor wants to use a short straddle; the current market index is 100. He sells a 1-month 100 call for \$1.50 and a 1-month 100 put for \$1.75. At the end of one month the market index is: (a) 100, (b) 90, or (c) 80. What is the profit or loss for (a), (b), and (c)?
29. If an investor sells a high-exercise-price call and buys a low-exercise-price call of the same month to expiration, what does he hope for the price of the underlying asset?

30. How do you profit from a neutral calendar spread?
31. Firm A's common stock has been trading in a narrow price range for the past month. An investor is convinced that the price is going to break far out of that range in the next 3 month. However, this investor does not know whether the price will go up or down. The current price of the stock is $90 per share and the price of a 3-month call option at an exercise price of $90 is $8.
    (a) Assume the risk-free rate is 6% per year, what is the price of a 3-month put option on firm A's stock at an exercise price of $90? (Assume the stock pays no dividend).
    (b) What would be a simple option strategy to exploit your conviction about the stock price movement in the next 3 months? How far would it have to move in either direction for you to make a profit on your initial investment?
32. Firm B's common stock has been trading in a narrow price range around $60 per share for a while. You believe the price is going to stay in the range for the next 3 month. The price of a 3-month put option with an exercise price of $60 is $5.
    (a) Assume the risk-free rate is 6% per year, what is the price of a 3-month call option on firm B stock at an exercise price of $60 if it is in the money? (Assume the stock pays no dividend).
    (b) What would be a simply option strategy to exploit your conviction about the stock price movement in the next 3 month? What is the most money you can make on this position? How far would it have to move in either direction before you lose money?
33. A manager in firm C receives 10,000 shares of company stock as part of his compensation package. The current market price of the stock is $50 per share. At this current price, this manager would receive $500,000 for the stock. This manager is considering buying a second house in April but is worried about the value of his stock holding. If the value of the stock holding falls below $450,000, he will not be able to come up with the down payment for the house. However, if the value of the stock rises above $550,000, he would be able to have a small cash reserve even after he makes his down payment. Please evaluate the following two strategies with respect to this manager's investment goal. What are the advantage and disadvantage of each strategy.
    (a) Strategy A: Write April call options on firm C's share with strike price $55. These calls are currently selling at $4 each.

(b) Strategy B: Long April put options on firm C's share with strike price \$45. These calls are currently selling at \$4 each.

34. Please discuss why owning a corporate bond is similar to shorting a put option. A call option?
35. An investor is holding the following option portfolio. She is writing an April expiration call option on Dell with exercise price 80. She is also writing an April Dell put option with exercise price 75. The cost of the above options are \$1 and \$0.5 respectively.

    (a) Graph the payoff of this portfolio at option expiration as a function of Dell's stock price at that time.
    (b) What is the profit/loss on this position if Dell is selling at \$78 on the option maturity data? What if Dell is selling at 88?
    (c) At what two stock prices will you just break even on your investment?

36. Consider the following portfolio. An investor writes a put option with exercise price 70 and buys a put option on the same stock with the same maturity date with exercise price 86.

    (a) Graph the *value* of the portfolio at the option maturity date.
    (b) Graph the *profit* of the portfolio. Determine which option costs more.

37. A GM put option with strike price \$50 trading on the Acme options exchange sells for \$3. However, a GM put with the same maturity selling on the Apex options exchange but with strike price \$52 also sells for \$3. If an investor plans to hold the option position to maturity, devise a zero-net-investment arbitrage strategy to exploit the pricing anomaly. Please graph the diagram at maturity for your position.
38. John purchased a stock index fund currently selling at \$500 per share. He also purchases an at-the-money European put option on the fund for \$15 with exercise price \$500 and 3 month time to expiration because he is worried about the losses. Investor A's financial adviser, Alice, points out that he is spending too much money on the put option. The adviser notes that 3 month puts with the strike prices of \$480 cost only \$10 and suggest investor A to use the cheaper put.

    (a) For both John and Alice, draw the profit diagram for the stock-plus-put position for various stock prices in 3 month.
    (b) When does Alice's strategy do better? When does it do worse?
    (c) Which strategy has larger systematic risk?

39. An investment manager writes a call option with strike price \$30 and buys a call option with strike price \$40. The options are on the same stock and have the same maturity date. One of the call sells for \$2 and the other one sells for \$6.

    (a) Draw both payoff and profit graph for this strategy at the option maturity date.
    (b) What is the break even point for this strategy? Is this manager bullish or bearish on the stock?

References for Chapter 10

Amram, M and N Kulatilaka (2001). *Real Options*. USA: Oxford University Press.

Ball, C and W Torous (1983). Bond prices dynamics and options. *Journal of Financial and Quantitative Analysis*, 18, 517–532.

Bhattacharya, M (1980). Empirical properties of the Black–Scholes formula under ideal conditions. *Journal of Financial and Quantitative Analysis*, 15, 1081–1106.

Black F (1972). Capital market equilibrium with restricted borrowing. *Journal of Business*, 45, 444–445.

Bodhurta, J and G Courtadon (1986). Efficiency tests of the foreign currency options market. *Journal of Finance*, 41, 151–162.

Bookstaber, RM (1981). *Option Pricing and Strategies in Investing*. USA: Addison-Wesley Publishing Company.

Brennan, M and E Schwartz (1977). The valuation of American put options. *Journal of Finance*, 32, 449–462.

Cox, JC and M Rubinstein (1985). *Option Markets*. NJ: Prentice-Hall.

Cox, JC and M Rubinstein (1979). Option pricing: A simplified approach. *Journal of Financial Economics*, 8, 229–263.

Eckardt, W and S Williams (1984). The complete options indexes. *Financial Analysts Journal*, 40, 48–57.

Ervine, J and A Rudd (1985). Index options: The early evidence. *Journal of Finance*, 40, 743–756.

Finnerty, J (1978). The Chicago board options exchange and market efficiency. *Journal of Financial and Quantitative Analysis*, 13, 28–38.

Fischer Black (1985). Fact and fantasy in the use of options. *Financial Analysts Journal*, 31, 36–72.

Fischer Black and Myron Scholes (1973). The pricing of options and corporate liabilities. *Journal of Political Economy*, 31, 637–654.

Galai, D and RW Masulis (1976). The option pricing model and the risk factor of stock. *Journal of Financial Economics*, 3, 53–81.

Galai, D, R Geske, and S Givots (1988). *Option Markets*. USA: Addison-Wesley Publishing Company.

Gastineau, G (1979). *The Stock Options Manual*. NY: McGraw-Hill.

Geske, R and K Shastri (1985). Valuation by approximation: A comparison of alternative option valuation techniques. *Journal of Financial and Quantitative Analysis*, 20, 45–72.

Hull, J (2005). *Options, Futures, and Other Derivatives*, 6th ed., NJ: Prentice Hall.

Jarrow, RA and A Rudd (1983) *Option Pricing.* In *An Empirical Examination of the Black–Scholes Call Option Pricing Model*, RD Irwin, J Macbeth and L Merville (eds.), Wiley, American Finance Association.

Jarrow R and S Turnbull (1999). *Derivatives Securities*, 2nd ed., South-Western College Pub.

Liaw, KT and RL Moy (2000). *The Irwin Guide to Stocks, Bonds, Futures, and Options.* New York: McGraw-Hill Companies.

Lee, CF and AC Lee (2006). *Encyclopedia of Finance.* New York: Springer.

Lee, CF (2009). *Handbook of Quantitative Finance and Risk Management*, New York: Springer.

Merton, R (1973). Theory of rational option pricing. *Bell Journal of Economics and Management Science*, 4, 141–183.

McDonald, RL (2005). *Derivatives Markets*, 2nd ed., Boston, Massachusetts: Addison Wesley.

Rendleman Jr, RJ and BJ Barter (1979). Two-state option pricing. *Journal of Finance*, 34, 1093–1110.

Richard M. Bookstaber and Roger G. Clarke (1983). *Option Strategies for Institutional Investment Management.* USA: Addison-Wesley Publishing Company.

Ritchken, P (1987). *Options: Theory, Strategy and Applications.* Scott: Foresman.

Rubinstein, M and H Leland (1981). Replicating options with positions in stock and cash. *Financial Analysts Journal*, 37, 113–121.

Rubinstein, M, H Leland, and J Cox (1985). *Option Markets.* NJ: Prentice-Hall.

Sears, S and G Trennepohl (1982). Measuring portfolio risk in options. *Journal of Financial and Quantitative Analysis*, 17, 391–410.

Smith, C (1976). Option pricing: A review. *Journal of Financial Economics*, 3, 3–51.

Stoll, H (1969). The relationships between put and call option prices. *Journal of Finance*, 24, 801–824.

Summa, JF and JW Lubow (2001). *Options on Futures.* New York: John Wiley & Sons.

Trennepohl, G (1981). A comparison of listed option premium and Black–Scholes model prices: 1973–1979. *Journal of Financial Research*, 4, 11–20.

Weinstein, M (1983). Bond systematic risk and the options pricing model. *Journal of Finance*, 38, 1415–1430.

Welch, W (1982). *Strategies for Put and Call Option Trading.* USA: Winthrop.

Whaley, R (1982). Valuation of American call options on dividend paying stocks: Empirical tests. *Journal of Financial Economics*, 10, 29–58.

Zhang, PG (1998). *Exotic Options: A Guide to Second Generation Options*, 2nd ed., Singapore: World Scientific Pub. Co. Inc.

Chapter 11

Option-Pricing Theory and Firm Valuation

11.1. Introduction

The emergence of options and option-pricing discuss several types of options and how their value is determined. We begin be looking at the basic concepts of options in Section 11.2, then go on to discuss factors that affect the value of options in Section 11.3. Hedging, hedge ratio, and option valuation are discussed in Section 11.4. Section 11.5 discusses how option-pricing theory is used to investigate the capital structure question. We close the chapter with a look as the type of option called the warrant in Section 11.6. Summary of this chapter is discussed in Section 11.7. Appendix 11.A discusses the applications of the binomial distribution to evaluate call options.

11.2. Basic Concepts of Options

In general, there are three types of equity options: (1) warrants, (2) executive stock options, and (3) publicly traded options. A *warrant* is a financial instrument issued by a corporation that gives the purchaser the right to buy a fixed number of shares at a set price for a specific period. There are two major differences between a warrant and a publicly traded option. The first is that the maturity of the warrant is normally less than 9 months. The second difference is that the warrant is an agreement between the corporation and the warrant's buyer. This means that if the warrant's owner decides to exercise his right and purchase stock, the corporation issues new shares and receives the cash from the sale of those shares. The *publicly traded option* is an agreement between two individuals who have no relationship with the corporation whose shares are being optioned. When the publicly traded option is exercised, money is exchanged for shares between individuals and the corporation receives no funds, only a new owner.

Executive stock options are a means of compensation for corporate employees. For services rendered, the manager or the employee has the right to buy a specific number of shares for a set price during a given period. Unlike warrants and publicly traded options, executive stock options cannot be traded. The option's owner has only two choices: exercise the option or let it expire. Like a warrant, should the owner decide to exercise the option, the corporation receives money and issues new shares.

The use of executive stock options for management compensation raises an interesting agency question. The firm's managers may make investment and financing decisions that increase the firm's risk in order to increase the value of their stock options. Such action could have a detrimental effect on the bondholders and other creditors of the firm. Thus, we will see that the value of an option is directly related to the variability or riskiness of the underlying asset, which in this case is in the firm.

Publicly traded options are probably the most widely known of the three types of equity option instruments. An important date in the history of these options is 1973, when the Chicago Board Options Exchange was founded. Although it was possible to trade options over the counter before that time, trading volume was relatively low. This date marks the beginning of a phenomenal growth in the popularity of options as a financial instrument. Indeed, in terms of the value of securities traded, the Chicago Board Options Exchange is running neck and neck with the New York and Tokyo stock exchanges as the world's largest securities market. There are now five options-trading centers in the United States — the Chicago Board Option Exchange, the American Stock Exchange, the Philadelphia Stock Exchange, the Pacific Stock Exchange, and the New York Stock Exchange and there is a steady stream of proposals for new listings on these exchanges.

The share volume of trading and the general acceptance of these financial instruments renders options valuation an important subject for study. However, even more significant for our purposes, the theory of options valuation has important applications in financial management and in the valuation of other financial instruments. Black and Scholes (1973) point out those corporate securities can be viewed as options or contingent claims on firm value. In viewing a firm's securities as options, we need to evaluate the interdependencies of binds and stocks. As we have seen, a bond's price is the present value of future interest and principal payments, and a stock's price is determined by future dividends. The contingent-claims approach to security valuation differs in that it considers the valuation of all of the firm's classes of securities simultaneously. Bonds and stocks are valued in terms on the value placed on the firm's assets; that is, their value is contingent on the firm's assets or investments.

Banz and Miller (1978) developed an approach to making capital budgeting decisions based on a contingent claims framework. They created a method for calculating the NPV of an investment based on estimates derived from using an option valuation model. In this chapter, we consider the question of option valuation and how options are used to make financial management decisions. However, before doing so, we must become acquainted with some of the terminology of options trading.

There are two basic types of options: puts and calls. A *call* gives the holder the right to buy a particular number of shares of a designated common stock at a specified price, called the *exercise price* (or strike price), on or before a given date, known as the *expiration date*. Hence, the owner of shares of common stock can create an option and sell it in the options market, thereby increasing the return or income on his or her stock investment. Such an option specifies both an exercise price and an expiration date. On the Chicago Board of Options Exchange, options are typically created for 3, 6, or 9 months. The actual expiration date is the third Saturday of the month of expiration. A more venturesome investor may create an option in this fashion without owning any of underlying stock. This is called *naked option writing* and can be very risky, especially if the value of the underlying asset has a high degree of variability.

A *put* gives the holder the right to sell a certain number of shares of common stock at a set price on or before the expiration date of the option. In purchasing a put, the owner of shares has bought the right to sell these shares by the expiration rate at the exercise price. As with calls, the creator can own the underlying shares (covered writing) or not (naked writing).

The owner of a put or call is not obligated to carry out the specified transaction, but has the *option* of doing so. If the transaction is carried out, it is said to have been *exercised*. For example, if you hold a call-option on a stock that is currently trading at a price higher than the exercise price, because the stock could be immediately resold at a profit. (Or you could sell the option or hold it in the hope of further gains.) This call-option is said to be "in the money." On the other hand, if the call-option is "out of the money" — that is, the stock is trading at a price — you certainly would not want to exercise the option, as it would be cheaper to purchase the stock directly.

An American option can be exercised at any time up to the expiration date. A simpler instrument to analyze is the European option, which can only be exercised on the expiration date. In this case, the term to maturity of the option is known. Because of this simplifying factor, we will concentrate on the valuation of the European option. The factors determining the values of the two types of options are the same, although, all other things equal, an American option is worth more than a European option because of the extra flexibility permitted the option holder.

Although our discussion is limited to equity options, many kinds of publicly traded options are available. Those include options in stick indexes, options on treasury bonds, options on future contracts, options on foreign currencies, and options on agricultural commodities.

The proceeding discussion presented quite a lot of new terminology. For convenience, we list and define those terms below.

Call: An option to purchase a fixed number of shares of common stock.
Put: An option to sell a fixed number of shares of common stock.
Exercise price contract: Trading price set for the transaction as specified in an option
Expiration date: Time by which the option transaction must be carried out.
Exercise option: Carrying out the transaction specified in an option.
American option: An option in which the transaction can only be carried out at any time up to the expiration date.
European option: An option in which the transaction can only be carried out in the expiration date.
Call-option "in the money": If the stock price is above the exercise price.
Put-option "in the money": If the stock price is below the exercise price.
Call-option "out of the money": If the stock price is below the exercise price.
Put-option "out of the money": If the stock price is above the exercise price.

11.2.1. *Option Price Information*

Each day the previous day's options trading are reported in the press. Exhibit 11.1 is a partial listing of equity options traded on the Chicago Board of Options Exchange. In this exhibit, we have highlighted the option

Exhibit 11.1. Listed options quotations.

		Calls			Puts		
Close Price	Strike Price	Apr	Oct	Jan	Apr	Oct	Jan
JNJ							
102.40	90.00	N/A	13.90	14.20	N/A	1.34	2.19
102.40	91.00	12.30	N/A	N/A	0.14	N/A	N/A
102.40	92.00	N/A	N/A	N/A	0.17	N/A	N/A
102.40	92.50	10.80	11.60	12.10	N/A	1.70	2.64
102.40	93.00	N/A	N/A	N/A	0.20	N/A	N/A
102.40	93.50	9.75	N/A	N/A	0.23	N/A	N/A
MRK							
58.58	51.50	N/A	N/A	N/A	N/A	N/A	N/A
58.58	52.00	6.85	N/A	N/A	0.08	N/A	N/A
58.58	52.50	6.35	7.15	7.55	N/A	1.33	2.06
58.58	53.00	N/A	N/A	N/A	0.10	N/A	N/A
58.58	54.00	4.85	N/A	N/A	0.13	N/A	N/A
58.58	54.50	4.40	N/A	N/A	0.13	N/A	N/A
58.58	55.00	3.90	5.25	5.65	0.17	2.02	2.80
PG							
84.74	74.50	29.70	N/A	N/A	N/A	N/A	N/A
84.74	76.50	24.60	N/A	N/A	N/A	N/A	N/A
84.74	80.00	5.00	6.10	6.65	0.17	2.23	3.15
84.74	81.00	4.00	N/A	N/A	0.22	N/A	N/A
84.74	81.50	3.55	N/A	N/A	0.21	N/A	N/A
84.74	82.00	3.10	N/A	N/A	0.20	N/A	N/A
84.74	82.50	2.61	4.40	5.05	0.25	3.10	4.15
84.74	83.00	2.18	N/A	N/A	0.32	N/A	N/A

for Johnson & Johnson (JNJ). The first 3 months (April, October, and January) are for a call-option contract on JNJ for 100 shares of stock at an exercise price of 102.40 which represents the closing price of Johnson & Johnson shares on the New York Stock Exchange. The numbers in the April column represents the price of one call-option with a April expiration date. Since each option is the right to buy 100 shares, the cost of the call-option with the strike price \$91 is \$1,230 or \$12.30 × 100. The values of the call options for January is somewhat higher, reflecting the fact that if you owned those options you would have a longer time to exercise them. In general, this time premium is reflected in higher prices for options with longer lives. The last three columns (April, October, and January) represent the value of put options on JNJ stock. Again, each put-option contract is for 100 shares and worth 100 times the price, or \$1.70 for the October 92.50 JNJ puts. The specific factors that determine option value are discussed next.

How much should you pay for a put or call-option? The answer is not easy to determine. However, it is possible to list the various factors that determine option value.

We begin with a simple question. How much is a call-option worth on its expiration date? The question is simple because we are in a deterministic world. The uncertain future movement of the price of the stock in question is irrelevant. The call must be exercised immediately or not at all. If a call-option is out of the money on its expiration date, it will not be exercised and the call becomes a worthless piece of paper. On the other hand, if the call-option is in the money on its expiration date, it will be exercised. Stock can be purchased at the exercise price, and immediately resold at the market price, if so desired. The option value is the difference between these two prices. On the call option's expiration date, its value will be either 0 or some positive amount equal to the difference between the market price of the stock and the exercise price of the option. Symbolically, let P = price of stock, V_c = value of call-option, and E = exercise price. Then $V_c = P - E$ if $E \geq P$, and $V_c = 0$ if $P < E$. This relationship can be written as

$$V_c = \mathrm{MAX}(0, P - E),$$

where MAX denoted the larger of the two bracketed terms. For a put-option (V_p), $V_p = E - P$, if $E > P$, and $V_p = 0$ if $E \leq P$. This can be written as

$$V_p = \mathrm{MAX}(0, E - P).$$

The call position is illustrated in Fig. 11.1(a), where we consider a call-option with an exercise price of \$50. The figure shows the option value as a function of stock price to the option holder. For any price of the stock up to \$50, the call-option is worthless and its value increases. The option's value increases as the stock price rises above \$50. Hence, if on the expiration date the stock is trading at \$60, the call-option is worth \$10.

Figure 11.1(b), which is the mirror image of (a), shows the option position from the view point of the writer of the call-option. If the stock is trading below the exercise price on the expiration date, the call-option will not be exercised and the exercise price on the expiration date, the call-option will not be exercised and it seller incurs no loss. However, if the stock is trading at \$60, the seller of the call-option will be required to sell this stock for \$50, which is \$10 below the price that could be obtained on the market.

We have seen that once a call-option have been purchased; the holder of the option has the possibility of obtaining gains but cannot incur losses.

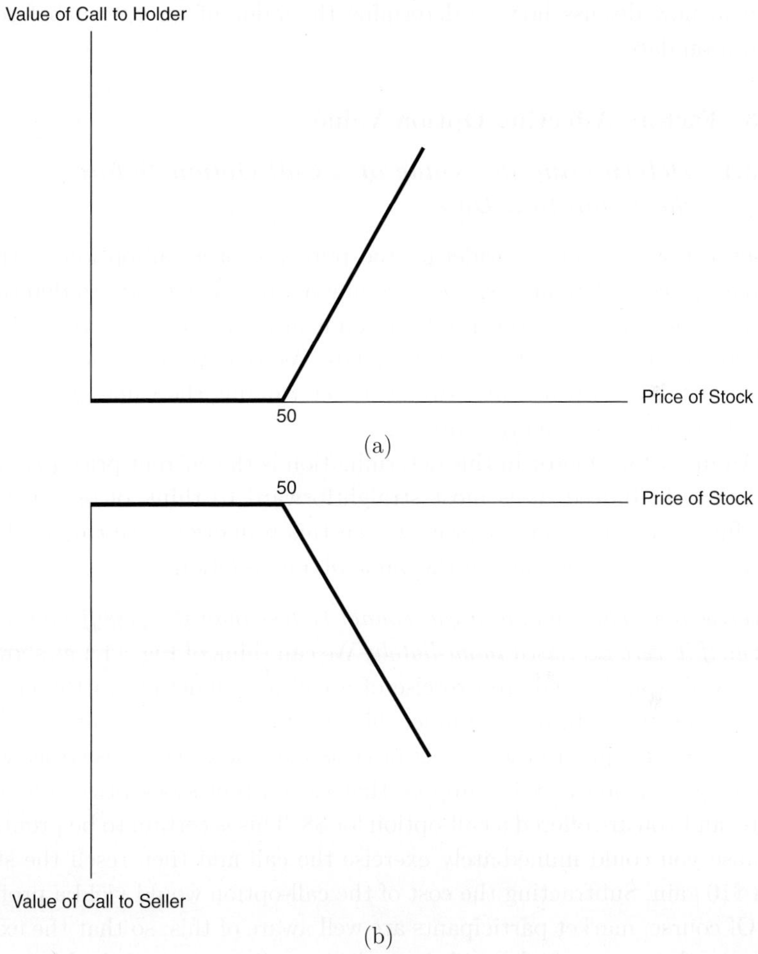

Fig. 11.1. Value of $50 exercise price call-option (a) to holder, (b) to seller.

Correspondingly, the writer of the option may incur losses but cannot achieve any gains after receiving the premium. Further, there is no net gain in the sense that the profit incurred by one will balance the loss of the other. Thus, options are zero sum securities — they merely transfer wealth rather than create it. To acquire this instrument, a price must be paid to the writer, and it is this price that corresponds to the call value. This value is the price paid to aquire the chance of future profit and will therefore reflect uncertainty about the future market prices on the common stock.

We will now discuss how to determine the value of an option before its expiration date.

11.3. Factors Affecting Option Value

11.3.1. *Determining the Value of a Call-Option Before the Expiration Date*

Suppose that you are considering the purchase of a call-option, with an exercise price of $50, on a share of common stock. Let us try to determine what factors should be taken into account in trying to assess the value of such an option prior to the expiration date. As we have seen, the problem is trivial at the expiration date. However, determining the value of an option prior to expiration is more complex.

An important factor in this determination is the current price per share of the stock. Indeed, it is most straightforward to think of option value as a function of the market price. Given this framework, we can see fairly quickly how to set bounds on the value of a call-option.

Lower bound: *The value of a call cannot be less than the payoff that would accrue if it were exercised immediately.* We can think of Fig. 11.1 as showing the payoff from immediate exercise of a call as a function on the current price of the stock. In our example, this payoff is zero for any market price below $50 and equal to the market price less for the $50 exercise price when market price is above $50. Suppose that the current stock price is $60 per share, and you are offered a call-option for $8. This is certain to be profitable because you could immediately exercise the call and then resell the stock at a $10 gain. Subtracting the cost of the call-option would yield a profit of $2. Of course, market participants are well aware of this, so that the excess of demand over supply for such immediate profits are unattainable.

Upper bound: *The value of a call cannot be more than the market price of the stock.*

Suppose that, at the same cost, you are offered two alternatives:

(a) Purchase a share of stock,
(b) Purchase an option on the same share of stock.

Looking into the future, option (b) will either be exercised or discarded as worthless. If the option is exercised, its value will be the difference between the future stock prices less the exercise price. This will be less than the future stock price, which is the value derived from option (a) Similarly, if

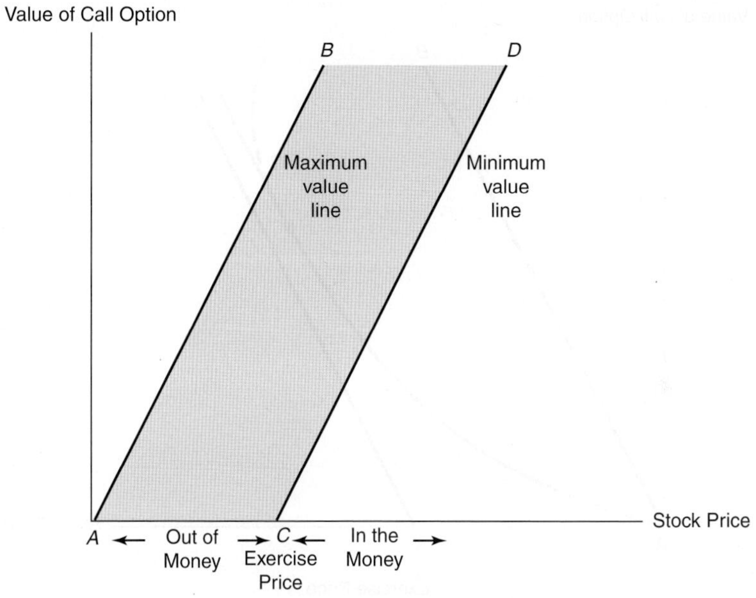

Fig. 11.2. Value of call-option.

the option turns out to have no value, this cannot be preferable to holding the stock, which, while it may have fallen in price, will have retained some value. Therefore, option (b) cannot be preferable to (a), so that the option value cannot exceed the market price of the stock.

These conclusions are illustrated in Fig. 11.2, which relates the call-option value to the market price of the stock. The ACD line shows the payoff that would be obtained if the option were exercised immediately. The AB line is the set of points at which the call value equals the market price of the stock. The call value must lie between these boundaries; that is, in the shaded area depicted in Fig. 11.2.

So far, we have been able to determine a fairly wide range in which the option value must lie for any given value of the market price of the stock. Let us now see if we can be more precise in formulating the shape of the relationship between call-option value and market price stock. The following considerations should help in forming the appropriate picture of Fig. 11.3.

1. *If the market price of the stock 0, the call value will also be 0, as indicated by point* A. This extreme case arises only when there is no hope that the stock will ever have any value, for otherwise investors would be prepared

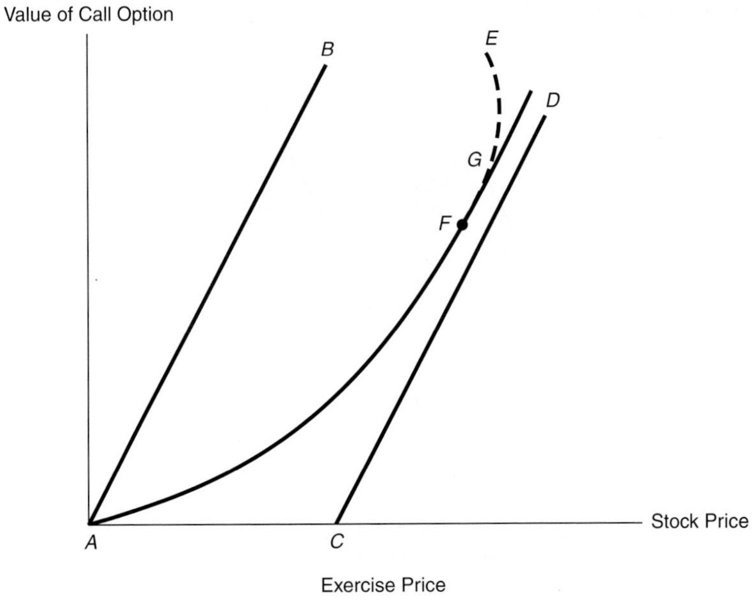

Fig. 11.3. Call-option value as a function of stock price.

to pay some price, however small, for the stock. It follows, in such a dire circumstance, that the call-option will never be exercised, and so it too has no value.

2. *All other things equal, as the stock price increases, so does the call value (see lines* AB *and* CD). A call with an exercise price of \$50 would be worth more if the current market price were \$40 than if it were \$35, all else equal. The probability that the market price will eventually exceed the exercise price by any given amount is higher in the former case than in the latter, and so, consequently, is the payoff expected from the holding call.
3. *If the price of the stock is high in relation to the exercise price, each dollar increase in price induces an increase of very nearly the same amount in the call value (shown by the slope of the line at point* F). Suppose that the market price of the stock exceeds the exercise price of a call by such a large amount that it is virtually impossible for the stock price to fall below the exercise price before the expiration date. Then, any change in stock price will induce a change of the same amount in the payoff expected from the call, since it is certain that the option will be exercised. The point is that if it is known that an option will eventually

be exchanged for stock, this is tantamount to already owning stock. The call holder has effectively purchased the stock without paying the full amount for it right away. The balance owned is the exercise price to be paid at the expiration date. It follows that the value of the call-option is the market value of the stock less the present value of the exercise price. Notice that in our previous notation, this will exceed $P-E$ if the exercise price does not have to be paid until some time in the future, because of the time value of money.

4. *The call value rises at an increasing rate as the value of the stock price rises, as shown by curvature AFG. (NOTE TAKE OUT?)* The segment AF shows that as the stock price increases, the call value increases by a lesser amount. The segment *FE* shows the call price increasing by a larger amount than the increase in the stock price. Theoretically, this is impossible, because if it occurs, eventually the call price would exceed the price of the underlying stock.

Putting these four considerations together, we show in Fig. 11.3(a) typical curve relating call-option value to the market price of a stock. Beginning at the origin, when both quantities are 0, the curve shows call value increasing as market price increases. Eventually, the curve becomes virtually parallel to the two 45° lines, forming the boundaries if the possible-values region. This is a result of the fourth consideration listed above.

The curve graphed in Fig. 11.3 shows the relationship between the call-option value and the market price of the stock, when all other relevant factors influencing call-option value are constant. Next, we must try to see what these other factors might be and assess their impact on call value.

We consider, in turn, five factors that influence the value of a call-option:

1. *Market price of the stock* In Fig. 11.3, we have seen the curvilinear relationship between call-option value and market price of the stock. All other things equal, the higher the market price, the higher the call-option value on the stock. As already noted, the slope of this relationship increases as market price becomes higher, to the point where, eventually, each dollar increase in the stock price translates into an increase of about the same amount in the call-option value on that stock.
2. *The exercise price* offered two otherwise identical call options on the same stock; you would prefer the call with the lower exercise price. This would involve larger gains from any favorable movement in the price of the stock than would an option with a higher exercise price. Therefore,

we conclude that the lower the exercise price, the higher the call-option value, all other things are equal.

3. *The risk-free interest rate* if a call-option is eventually exercised, the holder of the option will reap some of the benefits of an increase in the market value of the stock. However, the holder will do so without having to immediately pay the exercise price. This payment will only be made at some future time when the call-option is actually exercised. In the meantime, this money can be invested in government securities to earn a no-risk return. This opportunity confers an increment of value on the call-option; the higher the risk-free rate of interest, the greater this incremental value or lower the present value of the exercise price. Therefore, we would expect to find, all else equal, that the higher the risk-free rate of interest, the greater the call-option value. Moreover, the longer the exercise of the option is postponed, the greater the risk-free interest earnings. Accordingly, we would expect the risk-free interest rate to determine call-option value in conjunction with the time remaining before the expiration date.
4. *The volatility of the stock price.* Suppose that you are offered opportunity to purchase one of two call options, each with an exercise price of \$50. Table 11.1 lists probabilities for different market prices on the expiration date for each of the two stocks.

   In each case, the mean (expected) future price is the same. However, for the second stock, prices that differ substantially from the mean are far more likely than for the first stock. The price of such a stock is said to be relatively volatile. We now show that the expected price of such a stock is said to be relatively volatile. We now show that the expected payoff on the expiration date is higher for a call-option on the more volatile stock than for a call-option on the less volatile stock. For less volatile stock, the option will not be exercised for prices below \$50, but

Table 11.1. Probabilities for future prices of two stocks.

Less Volatile Stock		More Volatile Stock	
Future Price (\$)	Probability	Future Price (\$)	Probability
42	0.10	32	0.15
47	0.20	42	0.20
52	0.40	52	0.30
57	0.20	62	0.20
62	0.10	72	0.15

for the three higher prices its exercise will result in payoffs of \$2, \$7, and \$12. Therefore, we find

$$\begin{aligned}&\text{expected payoff from call-option on less volatile stock}\\&\quad= (0)(0.10) + (0)(0.20) + (2)(0.40) + (7)(0.20) + (12)(0.10)\\&\quad= \$3.40.\end{aligned}$$

Similarly, for a call-option on more volatile stock,

$$\begin{aligned}&\text{expected payoff from call-option on more volatile stock}\\&\quad= (0)(0.15) + (0)(0.20) + (2)(0.30) + (12)(0.20) + (22)(0.15)\\&\quad= \$6.30.\end{aligned}$$

We find, then, that although the expected future price is the same for the two stocks, the expected payoff is higher from a call-option on the more volatile stock. This conclusion is quite general. For example, it does not depend on our having set the exercise price below the expected future stock price. The reader is invited to verify that the same qualitative finding would emerge if the exercise price were \$55. We can conclude that, all other things remaining the same, the greater the volatility in the price of the stock, the higher the call-option value on that stock.

One useful way to measure volatility is through the *variance* in day-to-day changes in the stock price. Figure 11.4 illustrates our assertion about the influence of stock-price volatility on call-option value. The figure shows the relationship between call value and current market price for three stocks. The three curves have the same general form depicted in Fig. 11.3. However, notice that for any given current market price of the stock, the higher the variance of day-to-day price changes, the greater the call-option value.

The notion of volatility in future stock market prices is related to the length of the time horizon being considered. Specifically, if the variance of day-to-day changes is σ^2, the variance in the change from the present to t days is $\sigma^2 t$ if the price changes are serially independent. Therefore, the further ahead is the expiration date, the greater the volatility in price movements. This suggests that for a European option, which can only be exercised on the expiration date, the relevant measure of volatility is $\sigma^2 t$ where t is the number of days remaining to the expiration date. The larger is this quantity, the greater the call-option value.

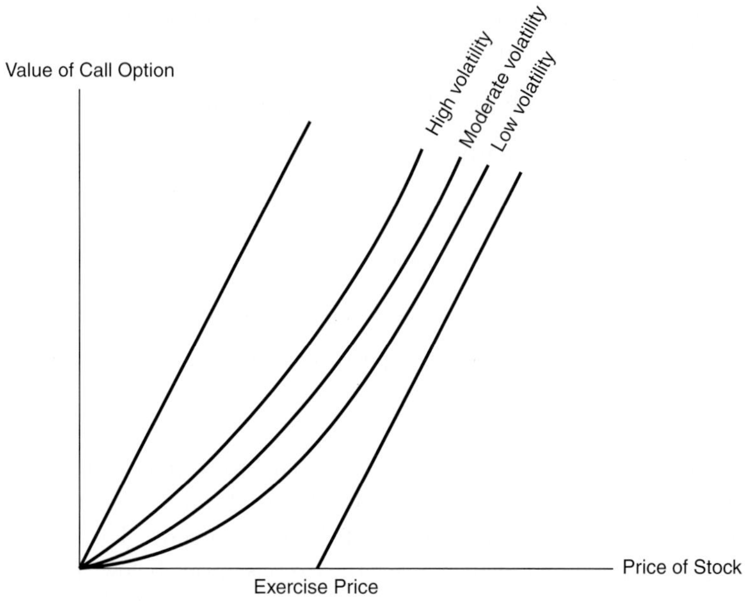

Fig. 11.4. Call-option value as function of stock price for high-, moderate-, and low-volatility stocks.

5. *Time remaining to expiration date* We have seen in factors 3 and 4 more than two reasons to expect that the longer the time remaining before the expiration date, the higher the call-option value, all else equal. The reason is that the extra time allows larger gains to be derived from postponing payment of the exercise price and permits greater volatility in price movements of the stock. These two considerations both operate in the same direction — toward increasing the call-option value.

We have seen that five factors influence the value of a call-option. The interaction of these various factors in determining option value is rather complex.[1] We present a formula that, under certain assumptions, can be shown to determine a call-option value as a function of these five parameters. However, before proceeding to this somewhat complicated relationship, we discuss a simple situation in which option valuation is more straightforward. This is useful in explaining further the dependence of option value on the risk-free rate of interest.

[1]Compared to the CAPM, the option-pricing model (OPM) is a relative pricing approach In the CAPM, the major determinants are risk and return. In the OPM, the return of the asset or the market does not affect the option value.

Our aim here is to show, for a special set of assumptions, that an investor can guarantee a particular return from a combined strategy of holding shares in a stock and writing call options on that stock, even though there is some uncertainty about the future price of the stock. The essential simplifying assumption required to generate this result is that there are only two possible values for the future price per share of the stock. In addition, for convenience we will use European options, with an expiration date in 1 year. Further, we assume that the stock pays no dividend and that there are no transactions costs.

Within this framework, consider the factors in Table 11.2. An investor can purchase shares for \$100 each and write European call options with an exercise price of \$100. There are two possible prices of the stock on the expiration date, with uncertainty as to which will materialize.

In Table 11.3, we list the consequences to the investor for the two expiration-date stock prices. If the higher price prevails, each share of stock will be worth \$125. However, the call options will be exercised, at a cost per share to the writer of the difference between the stock price and the exercise price. In Table 11.3, this is a negative value of \$25 from having written the call-option. If the lower of the two possible stock prices materializes on the expiration date, each share owned will be worth \$85, and it will have cost nothing to write the option because it will not be exercised.

Suppose that the investor wants to form a *hedged portfolio* by both purchasing stock and writing call options, so as to guarantee as large a total value of holdings per dollar invested as possible, whatever the stock

Table 11.2. Data for a hedging example.

Current price per share:	\$100
Future price per share:	\$125 with probability 0.6
	\$85 with probability 0.4
Exercise price of call-option:	\$100

Table 11.3. Possible expiration-date outcomes for hedging example.

Expiration-Date Stock Price	Value per Share of Stock Holdings	Value per Share of Options Written
\$125	\$125	−\$25
\$85	\$85	\$0

price on the expiration date. The hedge is constructed to be riskless, since any profit (or loss) from the stock is exactly offset with a loss (or profit) from the call-option. This is called a *perfect* or *riskless hedge* and can be accomplished by purchasing H number of shares for each option written. We now determine H. If H shares are purchased and one option written, the total value on the expiration date will be \$125H–\$25 at the higher market price and \$85H–\$0 at the lower price. Suppose we choose H so that these two amounts are equal; that is

$$125H - 25 = 85H$$

or

$$H = \frac{25}{40} = \frac{5}{8}.$$

Then, the same total value results whatever the stock's expiration-date market price. This ratio is known as the *hedge ratio* of stocks to options, the implication being that a hedged portfolio is achieved by writing eight options for each five shares purchased. More generally, it follows from the above argument that the hedge ratio is given by

$$H = \frac{P_U - E}{P_U - P_L},$$

where P_U = upper share price; P_L = lower share price; E = exercise price of option; and E is assumed to be between P_U and P_L.

Returning to our example, suppose that five shares are purchased and an option on eight shares is written. If the expiration-date price is \$125, then the total value of the investor's portfolio is

$$(5)(125) - (8)(25) = \$425.$$

If the expiration-date stock price is, \$85, total value is

$$(5)(85) - (8)(0) = \$425.$$

As predicted, the two are identical, so that this value is assured.

Next, we must consider the investor's income from the writing of call options. Let V_c denote the price per share of a call-option. Then, the purchase of five shares costs \$500, but \$8 V_c is received from writing call options on eight shares, so that the net outlay will be \$500 – \$8 V_c. For this outlay, a value 1 year hence of \$425 is assured. However, there is another simple mechanism for guaranteeing such a return. An investment could be made in government securities at the risk-free interest rate. Suppose that this rate is 8% per annum. On the expiration date, an initial investment of \$500 − \$8 V_c will be worth \$1.08(500 − 8 V_c) If this is to be equal to the value of the hedged portfolio, then

$$1.08(500 - 8V_c) = 425,$$

so that

$$H = \frac{Max(0, P_U - E) - Max(0, P_L - E)}{P_U - P_L} = \frac{25 - 0}{125 - 85}.$$

Therefore, we conclude that if the price per share for the call-option is \$13.31, the hedging strategy will yield an assured rate-of-return equal to the risk-free interest rate.

In a competitive market, this is the price that will prevail, and therefore is the value of the call-option. Suppose that the price of the call-option was above \$13.31. By forming a hedged portfolio in the manner just described, investors could ensure a return in excess of the risk-free rate. Such an opportunity would attract many to sell options, thus driving down the price. Conversely, if the price of the option was below \$13.31, it would be possible to achieve a return guaranteed to be in excess of the risk-free rate by both purchasing call options and selling short the stock. The volume of demand thus created for the call-option would drive up its price. Hence, in a competitive market, \$13.31 is the only sustainable price for this option.

Our example shows that a hedged portfolio can achieve an assured rate-of-return of 8%. Notice that our analysis depends on the level of the risk-free rate. If that rate is 10% per annum, the call-option value is \$14.20. This illustrates the dependence of call-option value on the risk-free interest rate.

11.4. Determining the Value of Options

11.4.1. *Expected Value Estimation*

A higher *expected rate-of-return,* as compared with the hedged portfolio, can be achieved by the exclusive purchase either of shares or of call options. Suppose that a single share is purchased for \$100. 1 year hence, the expected value of that share is

$$\text{expected value of share} = (0.6)(125) + (0.4)(85) = \$109.$$

Hence, the expected rate-of-return from a portfolio consisting entirely of holdings of this stock is 9%. Similarly, suppose that a call-option is purchased for \$13.31. The expected value of this option on the expiration date is

$$\text{expected value of call} = (0.6)(25) + (0.4)(0) = \$15.$$

Hence, the expected rate-of-return is

$$\text{expected rate-of-return on call} = \frac{15 - 13.31}{13.31} \times 100 = 12.7\%.$$

The increased expected rates-of-return from holding exclusively these two types of securities should not be surprising. They simply represent increases required by investors for assuming additional risk.

We have shown how call-option valuation can be determined within a simple framework in which only two values for the future market price of a stock are possible. We must move on to more realistic situations that involve a range of future market prices.

The value of a put-option is determined by the same factors that determine the value of a call-option, except that the factors have different relationships to the value of a put than they have to the value of a call. Figure 10.5 shows the relationship between put-option value and stock price.

The value of a put-option is

$$V_P = \text{MAX}(E - P, 0),$$

where V_P = value of the put; E = exercise price; and P = value of the underlying stock. The maximum value of a put is equal to the exercise price of the option when the stock price is O. This is shown by the line "Maxium value of the put" in Fig. 11.5. The minimum value of the put is 0, which occurs when the stock price exceeds the exercise price.

11.4.2. *The Black–Scholes OPM*

The notion that the price of a call-option should be such that the rate-of-return on a fully hedged portfolio is equal to the risk-free rate of interest that has been used by Black and Scholes (1973) to derive a more generally applicable procedure for valuing an option. The assumption that only two future prices are possible is dropped for a more realistic view of future price

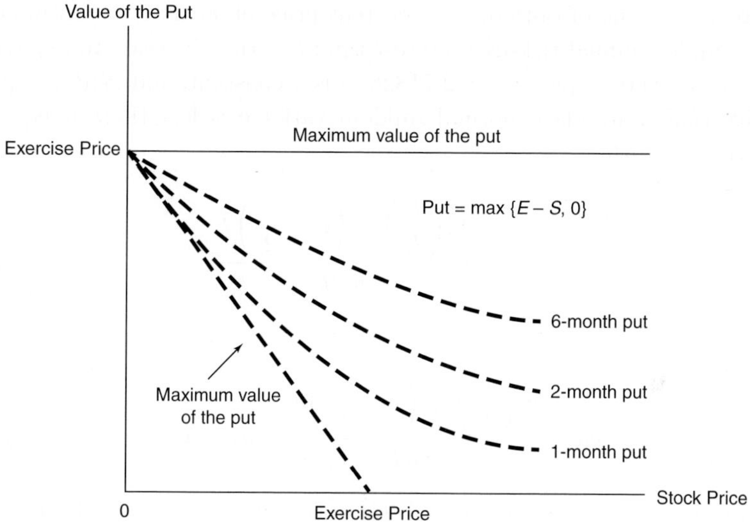

Fig. 11.5. Put-option value.

movements. The complete set of assumptions on which the Black–Scholes formula is based are given below.

- Only European options are considered.
- Options and stocks can be traded in any quantities in a perfectly competitive market; there are no transactions costs and all relevant information is freely available to market participants.
- Short-selling of stocks and options in a perfectly competitive market is possible.
- The risk-free interest rate is known and is constant up to the expiration date.
  Market participants are able to borrow or lend at this rate.
- No dividends are paid on the stock.
- The stock price follows a random path in continuous time such that the variance of the rate-of-return is constant over time and known to market participants. The logarithm of future stock prices follows a normal distribution.

Under these assumptions, Black and Scholes show that the call-option value on a share of stock is given by

$$V_c = P[N(d_1)] - e^{-rt}E[N(d_2)], \tag{11.1}$$

where V = value of option; P = current price of stock; r = continuously compounded annual risk-free interest rate; t = time in years to expiration date; E = exercise price; $e = 2.71828\ldots$ is a constant; and $N(d_1)$ = probability that a standard normal random variable is less than or equal to $d_i(i = 1, 2)$, with

$$d_1 = \frac{\ln\left(\frac{P}{E}\right) + \left(r + \frac{\sigma^2}{2}\right)t}{\sigma\sqrt{t}} \tag{11.2A}$$

and

$$d_2 = \frac{\ln\left(\frac{P}{E}\right) + \left(r - \frac{\sigma^2}{2}\right)t}{\sigma\sqrt{t}} = d_1 - \sigma\sqrt{t}, \tag{11.2B}$$

where σ^2 = variance of annual rate-of-return on the stock, continuously compounded; and logarithms are to base e. A binomial distribution approach to derive the OPM can be found in Appendix 11.A.

Although the specific form of the Black–Scholes option-pricing formula is complicated, its interpretation is straightforward. The first term of Eq. (11.1) is the value of an investor's right to that portion of the probability distribution of the stock's price that lies above the exercise price. This term equals the expected value of this portion of the stock's price distribution, as shown in Fig. 11.6.

The second term in Eq. (11.1) is the present value of the exercise price times the probability that the exercise price will be paid (the option will be exercised at maturity). Overall, the Black–Scholes model involves the present value of a future cash flow, a common concern in finance. The Black–Scholes model equates option value to the present expected value of the stock price minus the present value of the cost of exercising the option. More important for our purposes than the particular formula is the manner in which the model relates option value to the five factors discussed in the previous section. These relationships are as follows:

1. All other things equal, the higher the current market price of the stock, the higher the call-option value.
2. All other things equal, the higher the exercise price, the lower the option value.
3. All other things equal, the higher the risk-free interest rate, the higher the option value.

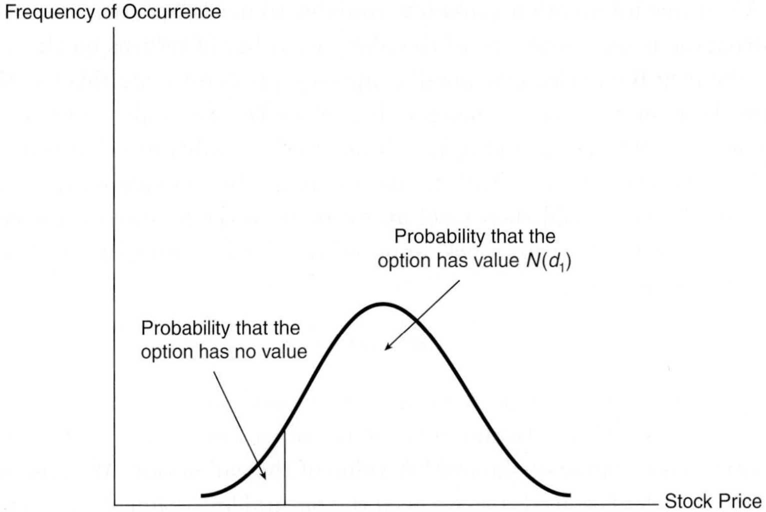

Fig. 11.6. Probability distribution of stock prices.

4. All other things equal, the greater the time to the expiration date, the higher the option value.
5. All other things equal, the greater the volatility of the stock price (as measured by σ^2), the higher the option value.

According to the Black–Scholes model, although the call-option value depends on the variance of rate-of-return, it does not depend on the stock's expected rate-of-return. This is because a change in expected rate-of-return affects stock price but not the relative value of the option and the stock. Recall from our earlier discussion that formation of the hedged portfolio was independent of expected return. For example, changing the two probabilities in Table 11.2 has no effect on call-option value.

The following example illustrates the computation of option value using the Black–Scholes formula.

EXAMPLE 11.1

Suppose that the current market price of a share of stock is \$90 and an option is written to purchase the stock for \$100 in 6 months. The current risk-free rate of interest is 8% per annum. Since the time to the expiration date is half a year, we have, in the notation of the Black–Scholes model, $P = 90$; $E = 100$; $r = 0.08$; and $t = 0.50$.

All of this information is readily available to market participants. More problematic is an assessment of the likely volatility of returns on the stock over the next 6 months. One possible approach is to estimate this volatility using data on past price changes. For instance, we could compute the variance of daily changes in the logarithm of price (daily rate-of-return) over the last 100 trading days. Multiplying the result by the number of trading days in the year would then yield an estimate of the required variance on an annual basis.[2] For this stock, suppose that such a procedure yields the standard deviation

$$\sigma = 0.6.$$

This value or some alternative (perhaps developed subjectively) can then be substituted, together with the values of the other four factors, in Eq. (11.1) to obtain an estimate of the market value of the call-option. We now illustrate these calculations. First, we need the natural logarithm of P/E. This is

$$\ln\left(\frac{P}{E}\right) = ln(0.9) = -0.1054.$$

It follows that

$$\begin{aligned} d_1 &= \frac{\ln\left(\frac{P}{E}\right) + rt + \sigma^2 \frac{t}{2}}{\sigma\sqrt{t}} \\ &= \frac{-0.1054 + (0.08)(0.50) + \frac{1}{2}(0.36)(0.50)}{0.6\sqrt{0.50}} = 0.06. \\ d_2 &= \frac{\ln\left(\frac{P}{E}\right) + rt - \sigma^2 \frac{t}{2}}{\sigma\sqrt{t}} \\ &= \frac{-0.1054 + (0.08)(0.50) - \frac{1}{2}(0.36)(0.50)}{0.6\sqrt{0.50}} \\ &= -0.37. \end{aligned}$$

Using the table of the cumulative distribution function of the standard normal distribution in the appendix at the back of this book, we find the

[2] If we use monthly rate-of-return to calculate the variance, then the annualized variance will be 12 times the monthly variance.

probability that a standard normal random variable less than 0.06 is

$$N(d_1) = N(0.06) = 0.5239$$

and the probability that a standard normal random variable is less than −0.37 is

$$N(d_2) = N(-0.37) = 0.3557.$$

These numbers represent the probability that the stock price will be at least equal to the exercise price — 52% of the time over the life of the option — and the, probability of exercise — 35%. We also require

$$e^{-rt} = e^{-(0.08)(0.5)} = 0.9608.$$

Finally, on substitution into Eq. (11.1), we find

$$\begin{aligned} V_c &= PN(d_1) - e^{rt}EN(d_2) \\ &= (90)(0.5239) - (0.9608)(100)(0.3557) = \$12.98. \end{aligned}$$

Therefore, according to the Black–Scholes model, the call-option should be priced at $12.98 per share.

A further implication of the Black–Scholes model is that the quantity $N(d_1)$ provides the hedge ratio for a hedged portfolio of stocks and written options. We see, then, that to achieve such a portfolio, 0.5239 shares of stock should be purchased for each option written.

11.4.3. *Taxation of Options*

The taxation of option gains, losses, and income are a fairly complex and constantly changing part of the tax law. However, tax treatment can have a large impact on the usefulness of options for the individual investor. Income (premiums) received by the option writer is taxed as normal income, just as if the option writer were providing a service.

Options can be used to defer gains into the future, which reduces the investor's current tax liability. For example, an investor with a short-term gain on a stock can purchase a put to protect against a drop in the stock price. This allows the investor to hold the stock and not realize the gain until sometime in the future, perhaps the next year, thereby deferring the payment of tax from the present until some future period. Hence, the tax position of the investor is also a factor in determining the value or usefulness of options. However, because we do not have a homogeneous tax structure, it is difficult to incorporate the tax effect into a formulation such as the Black–Scholes model.

11.4.4. *American Options*

In our analysis of options, we have assumed the options are European and thus may only be exercised on the expiration date, and that no dividends are paid on the stock before the expiration date. Merton (1973) has shown that if the stock does not pay dividends, it is suboptimal to exercise an American call-option before the expiration date. Therefore, if American and European call options on a non-dividend-paying stock are otherwise identical, they should have the same value.

The effect of dividends on a call-option depends on whether the firm is expected to pay dividends before the option's expiration date. Such action should reduce the option's value — the greater the expected dividend, the larger the reduction in option value. The reason is that a dividend payment amounts to the transfer to stockholders of part of the firm's value, a distribution in which option holders do not share. The larger this reduction in firm value, all other things equal, the lower the expected future price of the stock, because that price reflects firm value at any point in time. Therefore, the higher the dividend, the smaller the probability of any gains from exercising a call-option on common stock and, hence, the lower the value of the option. The extreme case occurs if the firm is liquidated and the entire amount of funds realized from the liquidation is distributed as dividends to common stockholders. Once such a distribution is made, the stock and the call-option have zero value.

If the firm pays dividends, the value of an American call-option on its stock will exceed that of an otherwise identical European option. The reason is that the holder of the American call can exercise the option just before the ex-dividend date and thus receive the dividend payment. If the benefits from such an exercise outweigh the interest income that would, have been earned on the exercise price had the option been held to the expiration date, it benefits the holder of an American call to exercise the option. Since this opportunity is not available to the holder of a European option, the American option should have a higher value.

The solution to valuing an option on a stock that pays dividends can be approximated by replacing P, the stock price in the Black–Scholes formula, with the stock price minus the present value of the known future dividend. This is justified because if the option is not exercised before maturity, the option holder will not receive the dividends, in which case the holder should subtract the present value of the dividend from the stock price.

11.5. Option-Pricing Theory and Capital Structure

In this section, we show how option-pricing theory can be used to analyze the value of the components of a firm's capital structure. Suppose that management of an unlevered corporation decides to issue bonds. For simplicity, we assume these to be zero coupon bonds with face value B to be paid at the maturity date.[3] When the bonds mature, bondholders must be paid an amount B, if possible. If this money cannot be raised, bondholders have a first claim on the firm's assets and will be paid the firm's entire value, V_f which in this case will be less than B. Let us look at this arrangement from the point of view of the firm's stockholders. By using debt, stockholders can be regarded as having sold the firm to bondholders, with an option to purchase it back by paying an amount B at the maturity date of the bonds. Thus, the stockholders hold a call-option on the firm, with expiration date at the date of maturity of the bonds. If the firm's value exceeds the value of the debt on the expiration date, the debt will be retired, so that stockholders will have exercised their call-option. On the other hand, if the firm's value is less than the face value of the debt, stockholders' limited liability allows them to leave the firm in the hands of the bondholders. The call-option will not be exercised, so that the stock will be worth nothing. However, stockholders will have no further obligations to bondholders. Therefore, on the date of expiration, the value of this call-option, or, equivalently, the value of stockholders' equity, will be $V = V_f - B$ if $V_f > B$ and 0 if $V_f < B$. Thus, we can write

$$V = \text{MAX}(0, V_f - B), \tag{11.3}$$

where V = value of stockholders' call-option on the firm; V_f = value of the firm; and B = face value of debt. This relationship is shown in Fig. 10.7. As we can see, this is exactly the relationship shown in Fig. 10.1(a) for the value of a call-option.

We see, then, that the theory of options can provide us with insights into the valuation of debt and stockholders' equity. This analysis indicates that the stockholders own a call-option on the firm's assets. At any time,

[3] These bonds will sell for less than the face value, the difference reflecting interest to be paid on the loan.

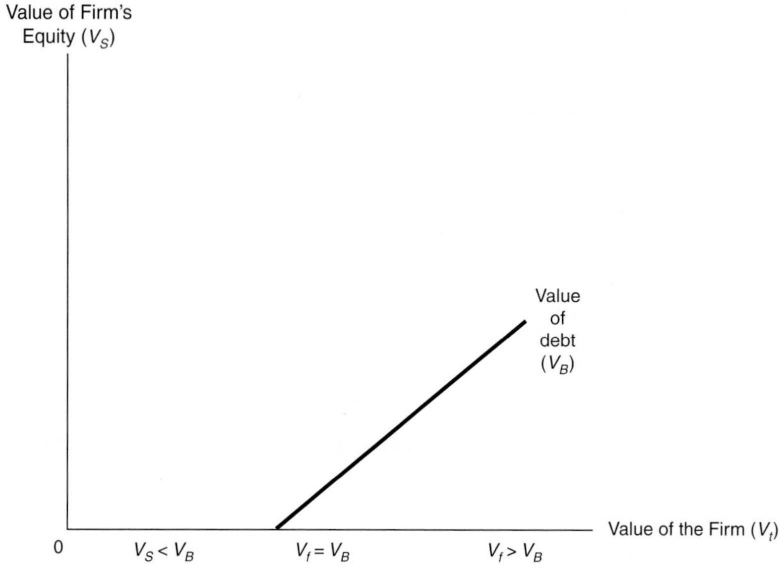

Fig. 11.7. Option approach to capital structure.

they could exercise this option by delivering the face value of the bonds to payoff the bondholders and realize the value of their option. This point is illustrated in the following example, where we employ the Black–Scholes model.

EXAMPLE 11.2

An unlevered corporation is valued at \$14 million. The corporation issues debt, payable in 6 years, with a face value of \$10 million. The standard deviation of the continuously compounded rate-of-return on the total value of this corporation is 0.2. Assume that the risk-free rate of interest is 8% per annum.

In our previous notation, the current market price of the asset (in this case, the firm) is \$14 million, and the exercise price of the option is the face value of the debt. Therefore, we have $P = 14$, $E = 10$, $r = 0.08$, $t = 6$, and $\sigma = 0.2$, where we are measuring value in units of a million dollars.

We will use the Black–Scholes formula, Eq. (11.1), to compute the value of stockholders' equity; that is, the value of the stockholders' call-option on the firm. First, we require the natural logarithm of P/E, so that

$$\ln\left(\frac{P}{E}\right) = \ln(1.4) = 0.3365.$$

Next, we find

$$d_1 = \frac{\ln\left(\frac{P}{E}\right) + rt + \sigma^2 \frac{t}{2}}{\sigma\sqrt{t}},$$

$$= \frac{0.3365 + (0.08)(6) + \frac{1}{2}(0.2)(6)}{0.2\sqrt{6}} = 1.91$$

and

$$d_2 = \frac{\ln\left(\frac{P}{E}\right) + rt - \sigma^2 \frac{t}{2}}{\sigma\sqrt{t}},$$

$$= \frac{0.3365 + (0.08)(6) - \frac{1}{2}(0.2)(6)}{0.2\sqrt{6}} = 1.42.$$

From tabulated values of the cumulative distribution function of the standard normal random variable, we find

$$N(d_1) = N(1.91) = 0.9719$$

and

$$N(d_2) = N(1.42) = 0.9222.$$

We also require

$$e^{-rt} = e^{-(0.08)(6)} = 0.6188.$$

On substitution in Eq. (11.1), we find the value of stockholders' equity

$$V = PN(d_1) - e^{-rt}EN(d_2)$$

$$= (14)(0.9719) – (0.6188)(10)(0.9222) = \$7.90 \text{ million}.$$

Since the total value of the firm is \$14 million, the value of the debt is

$$\text{value of debt} = \$14 – \$7.9 = \$6.10 \text{ million}.$$

Assuming the market is efficient, this firm could sell debt with a face value of \$10 million for \$6.1 million. These receipts could be distributed to stockholders, leaving them with an equity worth \$7.9 million.

We now turn to examine the effects of two factors on our calculations.

11.5.1. *Proportion of Debt in Capital Structure*

Let us compare our results of Example 11.2 with an otherwise identical situation, but where now only \$5 million face value of debt is to be issued. With $E = 5$ so that $P/E = 2.8$, we find $In(P/E)$ to be 1.0296. Using the same procedure as in Example 11.2, $d_1 = 3.33$ and $d_2 = 2.84$, so that $N(d_1) = 0.9996$ and $N(d_2) = 0.9977$. Using Eq. (11.1), the value of stockholders' equity is

$$\begin{aligned} V &= PN(d_1) - e^{-rt}EN(d_2) \\ &= (14)(0.9996) - (0.6188)(5)(0.9977) \\ &= \$10.91 \text{ million.} \end{aligned}$$

Therefore, the value of the debt is

$$\text{value of debt} = 14 - 10.91 = \$3.09 \text{ million.}$$

In Table 11.4, we compare, from the point of view of bondholders, the cases where the face values of issued debt are \$5 million and \$10 million. We see from the table that increasing the proportion of debt in the capital structure decreases the value of each dollar of face value of debt. If all the debt is issued at one time, this phenomenon, which simply reflects the increase in bondholders' risk as debt increases, will result in the demand for correspondingly higher interest rates. As our example illustrates, if the corporation sells only \$5 million of face-value bonds, a price of \$618,000 per million dollars in face value will be paid for these bonds. However, if bonds with face value of \$10 million are to be issued, this price will fall to \$610,000. In such a case, the market for bonds operates such that the risk to bondholders of future default is considered in establishing the price of the zero coupon bonds, or, more generally the interest rate attached to any bonds.

Suppose, however, that our company issues bonds with face value of \$5 million, at a cost to bond purchasers of \$3.09 million. 1 year later, this

Table 11.4. Effect of different levels of debt on debt value.

Face Value of Debt (\$ Millions)	Actual Value of Debt (\$ Millions)	Actual Value per Dollar Debt Face Value of Debt
5	3.09	\$0.618
10	6.10	\$0.610

corporation decides to issue more debt. In valuing this new debt, potential purchasers of bonds will assess the risk of default. One factor taken into consideration will be the *total* level of debt of the corporation; that is, the amount of existing debt as well as the size of the new issue. Hence, the market price for the new bonds will reflect riskiness. Consider, however, the position of existing bondholders. The interest rates to be paid to these holders of old debt has already been established. The issue of new debt is going to increase the chance of default on all loans. Consequently, the value of existing bonds must fall when new bonds are issued. Therefore, the issue of new bonds entails a decrease in the wealth of existing bondholders. The beneficiaries are the stockholders of the company whose wealth increases by a corresponding amount. We see, then, that there is a conflict of interest between existing bondholders and holders of common stock. All other things equal, existing bondholders will prefer that no further debt be issued, while stockholders will prefer to see more debt issued. This provides an illustration of the agency problem discussed in Chapter 11. Purchasers of bonds will require covenants restricting the freedom of action of corporate management in order to protect the value of their investment.

11.5.2. *Riskiness of Business Operations*

Let us return to the corporation of Example 11.2, which is about to issue debt with face value of \$10 million. Leaving the other variables unchanged, suppose that the standard deviation of the continuously compounded rate-of-return on the corporation's total value is 0.4, rather than 0.2. This implies that the corporation is operating in an environment of greater business risk. Setting $\sigma^2 = 0.4$, with all other relevant variables as specified in Example 11.2, we find $d_1 = 1.32$ and $d_2 = 0.34$, so that $N(d_1) = 0.9066$ and $N(d_2) = 0.6331$. From Eq. (11.1), we find the value of stockholders' equity to be

$$\begin{aligned} V &= PN(d_1) - e^{-rt}EN(d_2) \\ &= (14)(0.9066) - (0.6188)(10)(0.6331) \\ &= \$8.77 \text{ million.} \end{aligned}$$

Thus, the value of the debt is

$$\text{value of debt } = 14 - 8.77 = \$5.23 \text{ million.}$$

Table 11.5 summarizes the comparison between these results and those of Example 11.2. We see that this increase in business risk, with its associated

Table 11.5. Effect of different levels of business risk on the value of $10 million face value of debt.

Variance of Rate-of-Return	Value of Equity ($ Millions)	Value of Debt ($ Millions)
0.2	7.90	6.10
0.4	8.77	5.23

increase in the probability of default on the bonds, leads to a reduction from $6.10 million to $5.23 million in the market value of the $10 million face value of debt. To the extent that potential purchasers of bonds are able to anticipate the degree of business risk, the higher interest rate on the bonds reflects the risk involved. The greater the degree of risk, the higher the interest rate that must be offered to sell a particular amount of debt.

However, suppose that having issued debt, corporate management embarks on new projects with a higher level of risk than could have been foreseen by the purchasers of the bonds. As we have just seen, this will lower the value of existing bonds. This decrease in bondholders' wealth accrues as a gain in wealth to holders of common stock. Once again, we find a conflict of interest between stockholders and bondholders. Once debt has been sold, it will be in the interests of stockholders for the firm to operate with a high degree of business risk, while bondholders will prefer lower levels of risk. Thus, the degree of business risk represents another example of an agency problem. Bondholders will want protection against the possibility that management will take on riskier than anticipated projects, and will demand protective covenants against such actions.

Because of this factor, the issue of a large volume of debt is likely to be accompanied by constraints on the freedom of management action in the firm's operation.

11.6. Warrants and Diluted Earnings Per Share (EPS)

11.6.1. *Warrants*

A *warrant* is an option issued by a corporation to individual investors to purchase, at a stated price, a specified number of the shares of common stock of that corporation. Warrants are issued in two principal sets of circumstances:

1. In raising venture capital, either to start a new company or to substantially increase the scope of operations of an existing company, warrants

are often issued to lenders as an additional inducement to the promised interest payments or to purchasers of new stock issues.

2. Often, when issuing bonds, a company will increase the bonds' attractiveness by attaching warrants. Thus, as well as receiving interest payments on the bonds, their purchasers obtain an option to buy stock in the corporation at a specified price. As we have seen, such options will have some value, and so their attachment to bonds should lead to a lowering of the interest rate paid on a fixed quantity of bonds or an increase in the number of bonds that can be sold at a given interest rate.

Since a warrant is essentially a call-option on a specified number of shares of, common stock, the principles underlying the valuation of call options are also applicable to the valuation of warrants. Suppose that a warrant entitles its holder to purchase N shares of common stock at a total cost E. If, at the expiration date, the price per share of common stock is P, then shares of total value NP can be purchased at cost E. If NP exceeds E, the option to purchase will be exercised, and the difference between these quantities is the value of the warrant. On the other hand, if NP is less than E, it will not pay to exercise the option, so that the warrant will be worthless. The warrant's value on the expiration date can then be expressed as

$$V_w = \text{MAX}(0, NP - E),$$

where V = value of warrant; N = number of shares that can be purchased; P = market price per share of stock; and E = exercise price for the purchase of N shares of stock.

Prior to the expiration date, for reasons discussed earlier in this chapter, the warrant's value will exceed this theoretical value. The same factors affecting the value of an ordinary call-option are also relevant here. Thus, all other things equal, warrant value will increase with increases in the volatility of the stock price, in the risk-free interest rate, and in the time to the expiration date. However, the basic version of the Black–Scholes model generally will not be directly applicable, as it pertains to the valuation of warrants. The reason is that, generally, warrants differ in important respects from ordinary call options. These factors are as follows:

1. The life of a call-option typically is just a few months. However, the life of a warrant is several years. While it may not be unreasonable to expect

volatility of rate-of-return to remain constant for a few months, it is less likely that it will do so for several years.

2. Over a period of several years, it is likely that dividends will be paid. As we have seen, dividend payments, which do not accrue to warrant holders, reduce the value of options to purchase stock.
3. For many warrants, the exercise price is not fixed to the expiration date, but changes at designated points in time. It may well pay to exercise the option to purchase shares immediately before such a change.
4. It may be that the number of shares that all warrant holders are entitled to purchase represents a considerable fraction of the total number of shares of the corporation. Thus, if these options are all exercised, and total earnings are unaffected, then EPS will be diluted.

Let us look at this last point in more detail. Since by using warrants, a corporation can extract more favorable terms from bondholders, it follows that, in return, the company must have transferred something of value to these bondholders. This transfer can be visualized as giving the bondholders a stake in the corporation's equity. Thus, we should regard equity comprising both stockholdings and warrant value. We will refer to this total equity, prior to the exercise of the options, as *old equity* so that

$$\text{old equity} = \text{stockholders' equity} + \text{warrants.}$$

Suppose that the warrants are exercised. The corporation then receives additional money from the purchase of new shares, so that total equity is

$$\text{new equity} = \text{old equity} + \text{exercise money.}$$

We denote by N the number of shares outstanding and by N_w the number of shares that warrant holders can purchase. If the options are exercised, there will be a total of $N + N_w$ shares, a fraction $N_w/(N_w + N)$ of which is owned by former warrantholders. These holders then own this fraction of the new equity; that is

$$H(\text{new equity}) = H(\text{old equity}) + H(\text{exercise money}),$$

$$\text{where } H = \frac{N_w}{N_w + N}.$$

Thus, a fraction, $N_w/(N_w + N)$, of the exercise money is effectively returned to the former warrant holders. In fact, they have really spent $[1 - N_w/(N_w + N)] = N/(N_w + N)$ of the exercise money to acquire a fraction, $N_w/(N_w + N)$, of the old equity. Therefore, in valuing the warrants, the

Black–Scholes formula must be modified. We need to make the appropriate substitutions in Eq. (11.1) for the current stock price, P, and the exercise price of the option, E.

$$P = \left(\frac{N_w}{N_w + N}\right) \quad \text{(value of old equity)},$$

$$E = \left(\frac{N}{N_w + N}\right) \quad \text{(exercise money)}.$$

It also follows that the appropriate measure of volatility, σ^2, is the variance of rate-of-return on the total old equity (including the value of warrants), not simply on stockholders' equity.

Suppose that a firm has one million shares outstanding, currently selling at \$100 per share. There are also 500,000 warrants with an exercise price of \$80 per share. The warrants are worth \$20, or the current stock price, \$100, less the exercise price of \$80. The value of the old equity is

$$\text{old equity} = 100(\text{lm}) + 20(0.5\,\text{m}) = \$110 \text{ million}.$$

If the warrants are exercised, the firm will receive \$40 million (\$80 × 0.5 m) of new equity, so that the new equity is

$$\text{new equity} = \$110\,\text{m} + \$40\,\text{m} = \$150 \text{ million}.$$

When they exercise their warrants, the warrantholders will own $\frac{1}{3}$ of the shares outstanding; that is,

$$H = \frac{N_w}{N_w + N} \quad \text{or} \quad \frac{500{,}000}{500{,}000 + 1{,}000{,}000},$$

and the old shareholders will own the remaining 2/3 of the shares outstanding.

The warrantholders now have an investment worth \$50 million, or

$$\frac{1}{3}(150\text{ m}) = \frac{1}{3}(110\text{ m}) + \frac{1}{3}(40\text{ m}) = 50 \text{ million}.$$

It makes sense for the warrantholders to exercise their warrant; they spend \$40 million for shares that are worth \$50 million. In terms of the warrant value, the market should be willing to pay \$20 per warrant for 500,000 warrants, or \$10 million.

In Chapter 7, we discuss convertible bonds. A *convertible bond* is a security that gives its owner the right to exchange it for a given number of shares of common stock any time before the maturity date of the bond.

Hence, a convertible bond is actually a portfolio of two securities: a bond and a warrant. The value of a convertible bond is the value of the bond portion of the portfolio plus the value of the warrant.

11.6.2. *EPS with Warrants and Convertibles*

Warrants and convertible securities can change a firm's EPS and number of shares outstanding. Investors, managers, accountants, and federal and state government agencies all watch the EPS of a corporation. EPS generally means net income after taxes, less preferred stock dividends, divided by the weighted average number of shares of common stock outstanding. In 1969, the Accounting Principles Board, a forerunner of the FASB, issued APB Opinion No. 15, "Earnings per Share." This ruling laid down the rules for calculating the EPS for financial reporting purposes. In 1982, the FASB issued Statement No. 55, "Determining Whether a Convertible Security Is a Common Stock Equivalent." The accounting requirements set out in these rulings provide alternative ways of calculating EPS if a company has outstanding convertible securities, warrants, stock options, or other contracts that permit it to increase the number of shares of common stock.

The EPS for a firm with a simple capital structure is called basic EPS. A simple capital structure has only one form of voting capital and includes no potential equity, such as warrants or convertibles. The existence of non-convertible preferred stock does not create a complex capital structure.

A corporation that has warrants, convertibles, or options outstanding is said to have a **complex capital structure**. The complexity comes from the difficulty of measuring the number of shares outstanding. This is a function of a known amount of common shares currently outstanding plus an estimate of the number of shares that may be issued to satisfy the holders of warrants, convertibles, and options should they decide to exercise their rights and receive new common shares.

Because of the possible dilution in EPS represented by securities that have the potential to become new shares of common stock, the EPS calculation must account for **common stock equivalents** (CSEs). CSEs are securities that are not common stock, but are equivalent to common stock because they are likely to be converted into common stock in the future. Convertible debt, convertible preferred stock, stock rights, stock options, and stock warrants all are securities that can create new common shares and thus dilute (or reduce) the firm's EPS. APB No. 15 mandates the calculation of two types of EPS for a firm with a complex capital structure: primary EPS and fully diluted EPS. It is useful to review the basic accounting concepts dealing with income recognition and ownership at this point.

1. *Basic EPS*. The earnings available to stockholders are divided by the average number of shares actually outstanding during the period.
2. *Primary EPS*. The earnings available to stockholders are divided by average number of common shares plus the CSEs.
3. *Fully diluted EPS*. Earnings are handled in a manner similar to primary EPS, but all warrants and convertibles are assumed to be exercised or converted. In other words, EPS is assumed to be at maximum dilution.

The relationship between these three types of EPS can be presented as follows:

Primary EPS

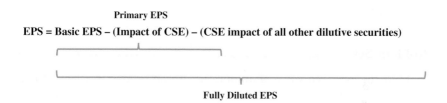

EPS = Basic EPS – (Impact of CSE) – (CSE impact of all other dilutive securities)

Fully Diluted EPS

It is interesting to speculate on whether the market will use primary EPS or fully diluted EPS in valuing shares of stock. If the market expects holders of CSEs to convert them into new equity, then fully diluted EPS is likely to be more meaningful. If the market does not expect conversion, then it is likely to treat convertible bonds like straight debt and focus on primary EPS with no adjustment for new shares. In other words, the market is likely to use basic EPS in such cases.

Convertible bonds that have no chance of being converted are called **hung convertibles**. The idea here is that if investors don't wish to convert their bonds into the firm's equity, the conversion price is hung. The bond is worth more as a bond than it is worth converted into equity. APB No. 15 and FASB No. 55 require a firm to provide EPS information under either circumstance and let the market participant choose which measure is more meaningful.

The financial analyst needs to identify the difference between two firms with a similar primary EPS value and markedly different fully diluted

EPS values. In general, hybrid securities in the capital structure cause the difference.

Concept Quiz

1. How does the issuance of warrants or convertibles affect EPS?
2. What is fully diluted EPS? What is primary EPS?

11.7. Summary

In Chapter 11, we have discussed the basic concepts of call and put options and have examined the factors that determine the value of an option. One procedure used in option valuation is the Black–Scholes model, which allows us to estimate option value as a function of stock price, option-exercise price, time-to-expiration date, and risk-free interest rate. The option-pricing approach to investigating capital structure is also discussed, as is the value of warrants.

Problem Set

1. Find the expected value of an option with an exercise price of $100 at the end of the period, given the following information. (Current stock price is $100.)
2. A riskless hedge position can be constructed by buying a stock and writing options on the stock. Using the information in problem 1: (Assume the risk-free interest rate is 10%.)

   (a) Find the optimal hedge ratio.
   (b) Find the equilibrium option price.

3. The price of Goodsell Company stock on January 1 is $100 per share. A call-option maturing on April 1 has a $100 exercise price. The standard deviation of Goodsell stock is 20% per year. What is the call-option value if the risk-free rate is 10%'
4. Suppose an unleveraged firm is valued at $10 million. The firm issues debt, payable in 9 years, with a face value of $7 million. The standard deviation of the rate-of-return on the total value of this firm is 0.4, and the risk-free interest rate is 8% per annum. Using the option valuation model, calculate the value of stockholders' equity.

5. How does the price of a call-option respond to the following changes, other things equal?
   (a) Stock price increase.
   (b) Exercise price increase.
   (c) Risk-free interest rate increase.
   (d) Extension of the expiration date.
   (e) Volatility of the stock price increase.
6. If a call-option has an exercise price of \$50, then over what stock price range would it be:
   (a) Out of the money?
   (b) In the money?
7. If a put-option has an exercise price of \$50, then over what stock price range would it be:
   (a) Out of the money?
   (b) In the money?
8. Would an American option generally sell at a price higher or lower than a European option? Explain.
9. If a call-option has an exercise price of \$50, how much will it be worth on its exercise date (assuming no transaction costs) if the price of the underlying stock is:
   (a) \$30.
   (b) \$50.
   (c) \$80.
10. If a call-option has an exercise price of \$60 and the price of the stock is \$40, what is the value of the call-option to the
    (a) Holder of the option.
    (b) The seller of the option.
11. Allison Merrick is considering two call options, each having exercise prices of \$20 and being identical in all other respects except for the distribution of underlying stock values. The distributions of the values of the underlying stocks of Companies J and K are given below:
    Find the expected payoff for each and explain which one you would prefer.
12. The current price per share is \$80 which can either go up to \$100 or down to \$60. The probabilities of upward and downward movement of

the stock price is 0.6 and 0.4, respectively. Given an exercise price of \$80 on a call-option and an optimal hedge ratio of 0.4:

(a) Find the lower bound of the stock price.
(b) Find the expected value of the call-option.
(c) Demonstrate that the hedged portfolio is riskless.

13. The standard deviation of the return on the stock of Company A is 0.5 per year. A call-option written on this stock is maturing 6 months from now and has an exercise price of \$80. If the current stock price is \$80 and the risk-free rate of interest is 8%, find the optimal hedge ratio for a portfolio of stocks and options using the Black–Scholes model. (Note: This is equivalent to finding $N(d_1)$in the Black–Scholes model).
14. A firm has outstanding debt of \$12 million which matures in 0.5 years from now. The standard deviation of the rate-of-return of the firm's value is 0.3. The value of another otherwise identical firm with zero debt is \$20 million. Find the value of the firm's outstanding debt, given that the risk-free interest rate is 8%.
15. $S_0 = 100$, $X = 120$, $R_f = 10\%$. There are two possibilities for S_T, \$140 and \$70. Derive a two-state put-option value in this problem.

    (a) Show that the range of S is 70 whereas that of P is 40 across state.
    (b) Form a portfolio of 4 shares of stocks and 7 puts. What is the (non-random) payoff to this portfolio? What is the present value of the portfolio?
    (c) Given the stock is currently selling at 100, solve for the value of the put.

16. Use the Black–Scholes formula to find the value of a call-option on the following stock and then use the put-call parity to calculate the put-option value on the stock in the previous problem with the same exercise price and maturity as the call-option.

Time-to-maturity	6 months
Standard deviation	20% per year
Exercise price	\$50
Stock price	\$50
Interest rate	5%

17. A call-option with strike price \$50 on a stock currently priced at $S =$ \$65 is selling for \$10. Using a volatility estimate of $\sigma = 0.30$, you find

that $N(d1) = 0.6$ and $N(d2) = 0.4$. The risk-free interest rate is 0. Is the implied volatility based on the option price more or less than 0.3? Explain.

18. The hedge ratio of an at-the-money call-option on Dell is 0.3. The hedge ratio of an at-the-money put-option is −0.6. What is the hedge ratio of an at-the-money straddle position on Dell?
19. A collar is established by buying a share of stock for $50, buying a 6 month put-option with exercise price $45, and writing a 6 month call-option with exercise price $55. Based on the volatility of the stock, you calculate that for a strike price of $45 and maturity of 6 month, $N(d1) = 0.7$, whereas for the exercise price of $55, $N(d1) = 0.3$
    (a) What will be the gain or loss on the collar if the stock price increases by $1?
    (b) What happens to the delta of the portfolio if the stock price becomes very large? Very small?
20. John is very bullish on Microsoft, much more so than the rest of the market. In each question, choose the portfolio strategy that will give you the largest dollar profit if John's bullish forecast turns out to be correct. Please briefly discuss your answer.
    (a) Choice A: $20,000 invested in calls with $X = 50$.
    Choice B: $20,000 invested in Microsoft.
    (b) Choice A: 20 call options contracts (for 100 shares each) with $X = 50$.
    Choice B: 2,000 shares of Microsoft stock.
21. Suppose you are a provider of portfolio insurance and are establishing a 3-year program. The portfolio you manage is currently worth $100 million and you hope to provide a minimum return of 0%. The equity portfolio has a standard deviation of 35% per year and T-Bills pay 7% per year. Assume the portfolio pays no dividend. How much of the portfolio should be placed in equity? How much of the portfolio should be placed in bills?
22. Dennis wants to hold a protective put position on stock A to lock in a guaranteed minimum value of $100 at year-end. Stock A currently sells for $100. Over the next year the stock price will increase by 30% or decrease by 10%. The T-bill rate is 7%. Unfortunately, no put options are traded on stock A.
    (a) If the desired put-option were traded, how much would it cost to purchase?

(b) What would have been the cost of the protective put portfolio?
(c) What portfolio position in stock and T-bills will ensure a payoff that would be provided by a protective put with $X = 100$? Please show that the payoff to this portfolio and the cost of establishing the portfolio matches that of the desired protective put.

23. Richard is attempting to value a call-option with an exercise price of \$100 and 1 year to expiration. The underlying stock pays no dividends, its current price is \$100 and Richard believes it has a 50% chance of increasing to \$110 and a 50% chance of decreasing to \$90. The risk-free rate of interest is 6%. Calculate the call option's value using the two-state stock price model.
24. Consider an increase in the volatility of the stock in the previous problem. Suppose that if the stock increases in price, it will increase to \$120, and that if it falls, it will fall to \$80. Show that the value of the call-option is now higher than the value derived previously.
25. Tim believes that market volatility will be 20% annually for the next 3 years. 3 year at-the-money call and put options on the market index sell at an implied volatility of 22%. What options portfolio can Tim establish to speculate on its volatility belief without taking a bullish o bearish position on the market? Using Tim's estimate of volatility, 3 year at-the-money options have $N(d1) = 0.2$.
26. Suppose that call options on IBM stock with time-to-maturity 6 months and strike price \$60 are selling at an implied volatility of 30%. IBM stock currently is \$60 per share, and the risk-free rate is 6%. If you believe the true volatility of the stock is 38%, how can you trade on your belief without taking on exposure to the performance of IBM? How many shares of stock will you hold for each option contract purchased or sold?
27. Suppose a firm sells call options on \$1.6 million worth of a stock portfolio with beta = 1.8. The option delta is 0.6. It wishes to hedge out its resultant exposure to a market advance by buying a market index portfolio.

(a) How many dollars worth of the market index portfolio should the firm purchase to hedge its position?
(b) What if the firm instead uses market index puts to hedge its exposure? Should it buy or sell puts? Each put-option is on 100 units of the index, and the index at current prices represents \$1,000 worth of stock.

28. John is holding call options on a stock. The stock's beta is 0.6, and John is concerned that the stock market is about to fall. The stock is currently selling for \$5 and John holds 1 million options on the stock (i.e. John holds 10,000 contracts for 100 shares each). The option delta is 0.9. How much of the market index portfolio must you buy or sell to hedge your market exposure?
29. Suppose the price of Company A's stock is currently \$100. Now let us assume that from one period to the next, the stock can go up by 15% or go down by 10%. In addition, let use assume that there is a 50% chance that the stock will go up and a 50% chance that the stock will go down. It is also assumed that the price movement of a stock today is completely independent of its movement in the past; in other words, the price will rise or fall today by a random amount. In addition, suppose a call-option has three periods to expiration. The underlying asset is stock A, the exercise price is \$105, and the risk-free rate is 5%.

Please use either the following formula to calculate the call-option value of stock A.

Formula 1:

$$C = \frac{[p^3 C_{uuu} + 3p^2(1-p)C_{uud} + 3p(1-p)^2 C_{udd} + (1-p)^3 C_{ddd}]}{R^3}.$$

Formula 2:

$$C = \frac{1}{R^n}\sum_{k=0}^{n}\frac{n!}{k!(n-k)!}p^k(1-p)^{n-k}\text{Max}[0, u^k d^{n-k}S - X].$$

Appendix 11.A. Applications of the Binomial Distribution to Evaluate Call Options

In this appendix, we show how the binomial distribution is combined with some basic finance concepts to generate a model for determining the price of stock options.

11.A.1. *The Simple Binomial OPM*

Before discussing the binomial option model, we must recognize its two major underlying assumptions. First, the binomial approach assumes that trading takes place in discrete time — that is, on a period-by-period basis. Second, it is assumed that the stock price (the price of the underlying asset) can take on only two possible values each period; it can go up or go down.

Say we have a stock whose current price per share S can advance or decline during the next period by a factor of either u(up) or d (down). This price either will increase by the proportion $u - 1 \geq 0$ or will decrease by the proportion $1 - d$, $0 < d < 1$. Therefore, the value S in the next period will be either uS or dS. Next, suppose that a call-option exists on this stock with a current price per share of C and an exercise price per share of X and that the option has one period left to maturity. This option's value at expiration is determined by the price of its underlying stock and the exercise price X. the value is either

$$C_u = \text{Max}(0, uS - X) \tag{11.A.1}$$

or

$$C_d = \text{Max}(0, dS - X). \tag{11.A.2}$$

Why is the call worth Max $(0, uS - X)$ if the stock price is uS? The option holder is not obliged to purchase the stock at the exercise price of X, so he or she will exercise the option only when it is beneficial to do so. This means the option can never have a negative value. When is it beneficial for the option holder to exercise the option? When the price per share of the stock is greater than the price per share at which he or she can purchase the stock by using the option, which is the exercise price, X. Thus if the stock price uS exceeds the exercise price X, the investor can exercise the option and buy the stock. Then he or she can immediately sell it for uS, making a profit of $uS - X$ (ignoring commission). Likewise, if the stock price declines to dS, the call is worth Max $(0, dS - X)$.

Also for the moment, we will assume that the risk-free interest rate for both borrowing and lending is equal to $r\%$ over the one time period and that the exercise price of the option is equal to X.

To intuitively grasp the underlying concept of option-pricing, we must set up a *risk-free portfolio* — a combination of assets that produces the same return in every state of the world over our chosen investment horizon. The investment horizon is assumed to be one period (the duration of this period can be any length of time, such as an hour, a day, a week, etc.). To do this, we buy h share of the stock and sell the call-option at its current price of C. Moreover, we choose the value of h such that our portfolio will yield the same payoff whether the stock goes up or down.

$$h(uS) - C_u = h(dS) - C_d. \tag{11.A.3}$$

By solving for h, we can obtain the number of shares of stock we should buy for each call-option we sell.

$$h = \frac{C_u - C_d}{(u - d)S}. \tag{11.A.4}$$

Here, h is called the *hedge ratio*. Because our portfolio yields the same return under either of the two possible states for the stock, it is without risk and therefore should yield the risk-free rate-of-return, r %, which is equal to the risk-free borrowing and lending rate, the condition must be true; otherwise, it would be possible to earn a risk-free profit without using any money. Therefore, the ending portfolio value must be equal to $(1 + r)$ times the beginning portfolio value, $hS - C$.

$$(1 + r)(hS - C) = h(uS) - C_u = h(dS) - C_d. \tag{11.A.5}$$

Note that S and C represent the beginning values of the stock price and the option price, respectively.

Setting $R = 1 + r$, rearranging to solve for C, and using the value of h from Eq. (11.A.4), we get

$$C = \frac{\left[\left(\frac{R-d}{u-d}\right)C_u + \left(\frac{u-R}{u-d}\right)C_d\right]}{R}, \tag{11.A.6}$$

where $d < r < u$. To simplify this equation, we set

$$p = \frac{R-d}{u-d} \quad \text{so } 1 - p = \left\{\frac{u-R}{u-d}\right\}. \tag{11.A.7}$$

Thus, we get the option's value with one period to expiration:

$$C = \frac{[pC_u + (1-p)C_d]}{R}. \tag{11.A.8}$$

This is the binomial call-option valuation formula in its most basic form. In other words, this is the binomial valuation formula with one period to expiration of the option.

To illustrate the model's qualities, let us plug in the following values, while assuming the option has one period to expiration. Let

$$\begin{aligned}
X &= \$100,\\
S &= \$100,\\
u &= (1.10), \quad \text{so } uS = \$110,\\
d &= (0.90), \quad \text{so } dS = \$90,\\
R &= 1 + r = 1 + 0.07 = 1.07.
\end{aligned}$$

Table 11.A.1. Possible option value at maturity.

Today			
Stock (S)	Option (C)		Next Period (Maturity)
		$uS = \$110$	$C_u = \text{Max}(0,\ uS - X)$ $= \text{Max}(0, 110 - 100)$ $= \text{Max}(0, 10)$ $= \$10$
\$100	C		
		$dS = \$90$	$C_d = \text{Max}(0,\ dS - X)$ $= \text{Max}(0, 90 - 100)$ $= \text{Max}(0, -10)$ $= \$0$

First, we need to determine the two possible option values at maturity, as indicated in Table 11.A.1.

Next, we calculate the value of p as indicated in Eq. (11.A.7).

$$p = \frac{1.07 - 0.90}{1.10 - 0.90} = 0.85 \quad \text{so } 1 - p = \frac{1.10 - 1.07}{1.10 - 0.90} = 0.15.$$

Solving the binomial valuation equation as indicated in Eq. (11.A.8), we get

$$C = \frac{[0.85(10) + 0.15(0)]}{1.07} = \$7.94.$$

The correct value for this particular call-option today, under the specified conditions, is \$7.94. If the call-option does not sell for \$7.94, it will be possible to earn arbitrage profits. That is, it will be possible for the investor to earn a risk-free profit while using none of his or her own money. Clearly, this type of opportunity cannot continue to exist indefinitely.

11.A.2. *The Generalized Binomial OPM*

Suppose we are interested in the case where there is more than one period until the option expires. We can extend the one-period binomial model to consideration of two or more periods. Because we are assuming that the stock follows a binomial process, from one period to the next it can only go up by a factor of u or go down by a factor of d. After one period, the stock's price is either uS or dS. Between the first and second periods, the

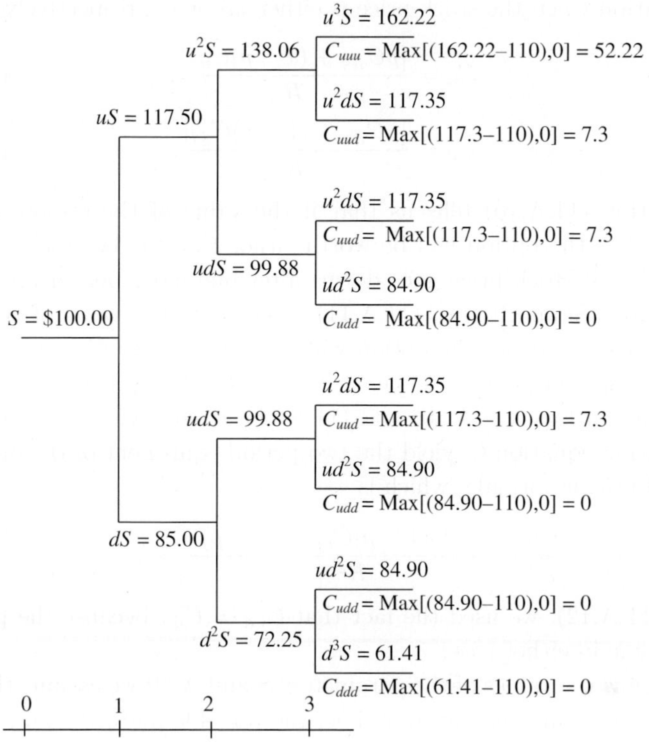

Fig. 11.A.1. Price path of underlying stock and value of call-option.

stock's price can once again go up by u or down by d, so the possible prices for the stock two periods from now are uuS, udS, and ddS. This process is demonstrated in tree diagram from (Fig. 11.A.1) in Example 17.A.1 later in this appendix.

Note that the option's price at expiration, two periods from now, is a function of the same relationship that determined its expiration price in the one-period model, more specifically, the call option's maturity value is always

$$C_T = \text{Max}[0, S_T - X], \tag{11.A.9}$$

where T designated the maturity date of the option.

To derive the option's price with two periods to go ($T = 2$), it is helpful as an intermediate step to derive the value of C_u and C_d with one period to expiration when the stock price is either uS or dS, respectively

$$C_u = \frac{[pC_{uu} + (1-p)C_{ud}]}{R}. \tag{11.A.10}$$

$$C_d = \frac{[pC_{du} + (1-p)C_{dd}]}{R}. \tag{11.A.11}$$

Equation (11.A.10) tells us that if the value of the option after one period is C_u, the option will be worth either C_{uu} (if the stock price goes up) or C_{ud} (if stock price goes down) after one more period (at its expiration date). Similarly, Eq. (11.A.11) shows that the value of the option is C_d after one period, the option will be worth either C_{du} or C_{dd} at the end of the second period. Replacing C_u and C_d in Eq. (11.A.8) with their expressions in Eqs. (11.A.10) and (11.A.11), respectively, we can simplify the resulting equation to yield the two-period equivalent of the one-period binomial pricing formula, which is

$$C = \frac{[p^2C_{uu} + 2p(1-p)C_{ud} + (1-p)^2C_{dd}]}{R^2}. \tag{11.A.12}$$

In Eq. (11.A.12), we used the fact that $C_{ud} = C_{du}$ because the price will be the same in either case.

We know the values of the parameters S and X. If we assume that R, u, and d will remain constant over time, the possible maturity values for the option can be determined exactly. Thus deriving the option's fair value with two periods to maturity is a relatively simple process of working backwards from the possible maturity values.

Based upon Fig. 11.A.1 of Example 11.A.1, we can write C_{uu}, C_{ud}, and C_{dd} as follows:

$$C_{uu} = \frac{[pC_{uuu} + (1-p)C_{uud}]}{R}, \tag{11.A.13a}$$

$$C_{ud} = \frac{[pC_{uud} + (1-p)C_{udd}]}{R}, \tag{11.A.13b}$$

$$C_{dd} = \frac{[pC_{udd} + (1-p)C_{ddd}]}{R}. \tag{11.A.13c}$$

Substituting Eqs. (11.A.13a), (11.A.13b), and (11.A.13c) into Eq. (11.A.12), then we can obtain the three-period model as follows:

$$C = \frac{[p^3C_{uuu} + 3p^2(1-p)C_{uud} + 3p(1-p)^2C_{udd} + (1-p)^3C_{ddd}]}{R^3}. \tag{11.A.14}$$

We here use a numerical example to show how Eq. (11.A.14) can be applied to evaluation call-option in a three-period case.

EXAMPLE 11.A.1

A Decision Tree Approach to Analyzing Future Stock Price and Determining Value of Call-Option

By making some simplifying assumptions about how a stock's price can change from one period to the next, it is possible to forecast the future price of the stock by means of a decision tree. To illustrate this point, let us consider the following example.

Suppose the price of Company A's stock is currently \$100. Now let us assume that from one period to the next, the stock can go up by 17.5% or go down by 15%. In addition, let us assume that there is a 50% chance that the stock will go up and a 50% chance that the stock will go down. It is also assumed that the price movement of a stock (or of the stock market) today is completely independent of its movement in the past; in other words, the price will rise or fall today by a random amount. A sequence of these random increases and decreases is known as a **random walk**.

In addition, suppose a call-option has three periods to be expiration. The underlying asset is stock A, the exercise price is \$110, and the risk-free rate is 16%.

Given this information, we can lay out the paths that the stock's price may take. Figure 11.A.1 shows the possible stock prices for company A for three periods.

Note that in period 1, there are two possible outcomes: the stock can go up in value by 17.5% to \$117.50 or down by 15% to \$85.00. In period 2, there are four possible outcomes. If the stock went up in the first period, it can go up again to \$138.06 or down in the second period to \$99.88. Likewise, if the stock went down in the first period, it can go down again to \$72.25 or up in the second period to \$99.88. Using the same argument, we can trace the path of the stock's price for all three periods.

In addition, we can Eq. (11.A.14) to determine the value of the call-option.

$$p = \frac{R-d}{u-d} = \frac{(1.16)-1.15}{1.175-1.15} = 0.4$$

and

$$1-p = \frac{u-R}{u-d} = \frac{1.175-1.16}{1.175-1.15} = 0.6,$$

$$C = \frac{[p^3 C_{uuu} + 3p^2(1-p)C_{uud} + 3p(1-p)^2 C_{udd} + (1-p)^3 C_{ddd}]}{R^3}$$
$$= \frac{[(0.4)^3 52.22 + 3(0.4)^2(0.6)(7.3) + 3(0.4)(0.6)^2(0) + (0.6)^3(0)]}{(1.16)^3}$$
$$= \frac{[(0.4)^3 52.22 + 3(0.4)^2(0.6)(7.3)]}{(1.16)^3}$$
$$= 3.4880.$$

The cumulative binomial density function can be defined as

$$B(n,p) = \sum_{k=0}^{n} \frac{n!}{k!(n-k)!} p^{n-k}(1-p)^k, \qquad (11.A.15)$$

where

n is the number of periods,
k is the number of successful trials,
$n! = n(n-1)(n-2)\dots(1)$,
$k! = k(k-1)(k-2)\dots(1)$, and
$(n-k)! = (n-k)(n-k-1)(n-k-2)\dots(1)$.

We can use the cumulative binomial distribution as defined in Eq. (11.A.15) to generalize Eq. (11.A.14).

Then we can extend the binomial approach to its more generalized form, with n periods maturity:

$$C = \frac{1}{R^n} \sum_{k=0}^{n} \frac{n!}{k!(n-k)!} p^k (1-p)^{n-k} \text{Max}[0, u^k d^{n-k} S - X]. \qquad (11.A.16)$$

To actually get this form of the binomial model, we could extend the two-period model to three periods, then from three periods to four periods, and so on. Eq. (11.A.14) would be the result of these efforts. To show how Eq. (11.A.13) can be used to assess a call option's value, we modify the example as follows: $S = \$100$, $X = \$100$, $R = 1.07$, $n = 3$, $u = 1.1$ and $d = 0.90$.

First we calculate the value of p from Eq. (11.A.7) as 0.85, so $1 - p$ is 0.15. Next we calculate the four possible ending values for the call-option after three periods in terms of $\text{Max}[0, u^k d^{n-k} S - X]$.

$$C_{uuu} = \text{Max}[0, (1.1)^3(0.90)^0(100) - 100] = 33.10,$$
$$C_{uud} = \text{Max}[0, (1.1)^2(0.90)(100) - 100] = 8.90,$$

$$C_{udd} = \text{Max}[0, (1.1)(0.90)^2(100) - 100] = 0,$$
$$C_{ddd} = \text{Max}[0, (1.1)^0(0.90)^3(100) - 100] = 0.$$

Now we insert these numbers ($C_{uuu}, C_{uud}, C_{udd}$, and C_{ddd}) into the model and sum the terms.

$$C = \frac{1}{(1.07)^3}\left[\frac{3!}{0!3!}(0.85)^0(0.15)^3 X 0 + \frac{3!}{1!2!}(0.85)^1(0.15)^2 X 0\right.$$
$$\left. + \frac{3!}{2!1!}(0.85)^2(0.15)^1 X 8.90 + \frac{3!}{3!0!}(0.85)^3(0.15)^0 X 33.10\right]$$
$$= \frac{1}{1.225}\left[0 + 0 + \frac{3X2X1}{2X1X1}(0.7225)(0.15)(8.90)\right.$$
$$\left. + \frac{3X2X1}{3X2X1X1} X(0.61413)(1)(33.10)\right]$$
$$\frac{1}{1.225}[(0.32513 X 890) + (0.61413 X 33.10)]]$$
$$= \$18.96.$$

As this example suggests, working out a multiple-period problem by hand with this formula can become laborious as the number of periods increases. Fortunately, programming this model into a computer is not too difficult.

Now let us derive a binomial OPM in terms of the cumulative binomial density function. As a first step, we can rewrite Eq. (11.A.15) as

$$C = S\left[\sum_{k=m}^{n} \frac{n!}{k!(n-K)!} p^K (1-p)^{n-k} \frac{u^k d^{n-k}}{R^n}\right]$$
$$- \frac{X}{R^n}\left[\sum_{k=m}^{n} \frac{n!}{k!(n-K)!} p^k (1-p)^{n-k}\right]. \tag{11.A.17}$$

By a form of the central limit theorem, we can show that the option price C converges to Black–Scholes Model as defined in Eq. (11.1). The option price C converges to C below[4]

$$C = SN(d_1) - XR^{-T}N(d_2).$$

[4]See Cox, J., S. Ross, and M. Rubenstein (1979). Option pricing: A simplified approach. *Journal of Financial Economics*, 7, 229–263. For further detail please refer to Lee *et al.* (2015) Alternative Methods to derive option price models: review and comparison. *Review of quantitative finance and accounting* (2015) forthcoming.

This formula is identical to Eq. (17.A.9) except that we have removed the Max operator. In order to remove the Max operator, we need to make $u^k d^{n-k} S - X$ positive, which we can do by changing the counter in the summation from $k = 0$ to $k = m$. What is m? It is the minimum number of upward stock movements necessary for the option to terminate "in the money" (i.e., $u^k d^{n-k} S - X > 0$). How can we interpret Eq. (11.A.16)? Consider the second term in brackets; it is just a cumulative binomial distribution with parameters of n and p. Likewise, via a small algebraic manipulation we can show that the first term in the brackets is also a cumulative binomial distribution. This can be done by defining $P' \equiv (u/R)p$ and $1 - P' \equiv (d/R)(1 - p)$. Thus

$$P^k (1-p)^{n-k} \frac{u^k d^{n-k}}{R^n} = p'^k (1-p')^{n-k}.$$

Therefore, the first term in brackets is also a cumulative binomial distribution with parameters of n and p'. We can write the binomial call-option model as

$$C = SB_1(n, p', m) - \frac{X}{R^n} B_2(n, p, m), \tag{11.A.18}$$

where

$$B_1(n, p', m) = \sum_{k=m}^{n} C_k^n p'^k (1-p')^{n-k},$$

$$B_2(n, p, m) = \sum_{k=m}^{n} C_k^n p^k (1-p)^{n-k}$$

and m is the minimum amount of time the stock has to go up for the investor to finish *in the money* (i.e., for the stock price to become larger than the exercise price).

In this appendix, we showed that by employing the definition of a call-option and by making some simplifying assumptions, we could use the binomial distribution to find the value of a call-option. Lee and Lin (2010) have shown how to use binomial OPM approach to derive the Black–Scholes OPM. In the next chapter, we will show how the binomial distribution is related to the normal distribution and how this relationship can be used to derive one of the most famous valuation equations in finance, the Black–Scholes OPM. In Chapter 27, we have shown how we can use Itô's calculus and normal–lognormal approach to derive the OPM.

Appendix 11.B. Alternative Models for Evaluating Convertible Bond: Review and Integration*

11.B.1. *Introduction*

A convertible bond which entitled to a set of fixed claims is a bond that can be converted into common stocks at the owner's option subject to conditions specified in the indenture. Therefore, convertible bonds are two instruments in one: one is the straight debt instrument, which guarantees a fixed payment for the life of the bond. The second instrument is the equity portion, which allows the bondholder to reap the gains due to increase in the equity value by conversion. By issuing convertible bonds, the firms can lower its cost of debt funding compared to straight debt alone. For investors, convertible bonds offer greater stability of income than common stock.

There are two varieties of convertible bonds: callable versus non-callable convertibles. Usually, callable convertibles have the same provisions as their non-callable counterparts, except they are subject to redemption by the issuing company at the prevailing call price prior to maturity. In most cases, the call provision is standard in indentures and is especially important in case of convertibles. As one can think of a non-callable convertible as a special case of callable convertible with sufficiently large call price, in this study, convertibles with call provision are always assumed.

In general, the price of a convertible is determined by three state variables and four decision variables, respectively. The three state variables are: (1) The price behavior of the firm's market value or common stock; (2) The value of the corresponding straight bond; (3) The credit risk of the issuing firm. The four decision variables are: (1) The call policy of a company with convertibles outstanding as when to announce a call, the call price for redemption payment, the specification of the call notice, ...etc.; (2) The conversion policy includes the date of conversion, the conversion price as how much one share of common stock costs at conversion, or equivalently, the conversion ratio as how many shares of common stocks one debenture is convertible; (3) The put provision that allows the investor to sell the convertible bond to the issuer for specific prices on specific dates prior to maturity; (4) The capital structure of the firms, e.g., whether there are any other senior claims of the firms.

*This appendix is from the *Encyclopedia of Finance*, Second Edition, Chapter 67, edited by Cheng-Few Lee and Alice C. Lee. Published by Springer in 2013.

In literature, various assumptions are employed regarding the aforementioned three state variables. The assumptions spans from deterministic to stochastic. By assuming a constant interest rate r and deterministic stock price growing at a constant rate g, the graphical method of Brigham (1966) is a representative of the deterministic approach. To describe the dynamics of these state variables more rigorously, stochastic models are developed, which can be further divided into calculus and option-pricing approach, respectively. In the calculus approach, one considers the issuing firm's market value (or stock price) on a specific date in the future as a random variable. While in the option-pricing approach, the dynamics of the issuing firm's market value (or stock price) for a time period in the future is modeled as a random process. The representatives of the calculus approach include Baumol *et al.* (1966), Poensgen (1965, 1966), and Frankle and Hawkins (1975). The option-pricing approach dominates the pricing of convertible bonds, which is pioneered by Brennan and Schwartz (1977, 1980) and Ingersoll (1977a, 1977b).

Both the deterministic and calculus approach ignore the possibility of bankruptcy by the issuing firm, therefore the convertible bonds might be mispriced. The option-pricing approach, on the other hand, considers the likelihood of default based on either type of default models: the structural model (Merton, 1974; Black and Cox, 1976) or the reduced-form model (Jarrow and Turnbull, 1995). In the one-factor structural model, the issuing firm's market value follows a geometric Brownian motion. Later Brennan and Schwartz (1980) proposed a two-factor structural model with a stochastic interest rate. Nyborg (1996) extends Brennan and Schwartz's two-factor structural model by including a put provision and floating coupons feature.

In contrast to the structural model, the more recent literature use reduced-form model in which stochastic stock price instead of the firm's market value is modeled. These include the works by Goldman Sachs (1994), Ho and Pfeffer (1996), Tsiveriotis and Fernandes (1998), Davis and Lischka (1999), Takahashi (2001), Ayache *et al.* (2003), Lau and Kwok (2004).

This work reviews the literature on convertible debt valuation including the deterministic, static stochastic, and dynamic stochastic models. The outline of the paper is as follows. In Section 11.B.2, the graphical model with deterministic assumptions is stated. Section 11.B.3 states the calculus models with static stochastic stock price and/or straight bond's price. Section 11.B.4 gives the option-pricing approach by modeling the dynamics of a firm's market value as a stochastic process.

In Section 11.B.5, a numerical approach, e.g., the tree approach, for the valuation of convertible bonds in reduced-form models is given. Section 11.6 concludes.

11.B.2. *Deterministic Model: Graphical Approach*

Brigham (1966) proposed a descriptive graphical model for the valuation of a callable convertible where the stock price is assumed to grow at a constant rate g and therefore the time-t conversion value satisfies

$$C_t = P_0(1+g)^t R, \tag{11.B.1}$$

where R is the conversion ratio, P_0 is the initial stock price. By assuming a constant market interest rate i, the time-t straight-debt value is

$$B_t = \sum_{k=1}^{T-t} \frac{I}{(1+i)^k} + \frac{M}{(1+i)^{T-1}},$$

where M is the par value of the bond, T is the maturity date, and I is the coupon paid each period.

This model is presented in Fig. 11.B.1. Logically, the value of the convertible bond cannot be less than its straight-debt as well as conversion

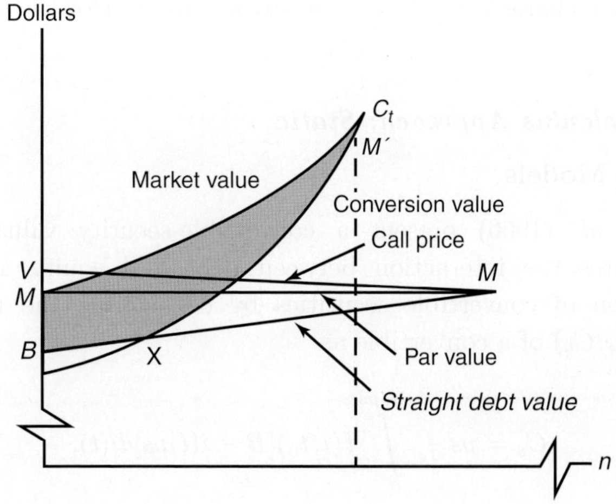

Fig. 11.B.1. Hypothetical model of a convertible bond. (Reprinted by permission from Brigham, EF (1966). An analysis of convertible debentures: theory and some empirical evidence. *Journal of Finance* 21, 37.)

value. Therefore, the higher of the conversion value curve CC_t and straight-debt value curve BM forms a floor curve (BXC_t) for the market value of the convertible represented by the curve (MM'). At relatively low conversion value, the convertible's floor curve is represented by the straight debt value, BX. Above the segment BX, the shaded area refers to the value attached to the conversion feature of the security. Thus, at the lower levels of equity prices, the convertible's market value is a composite of its straight debt value and a premium for the conversion feature. Moving to higher levels of equity prices, there exists a premium between the conversion value XC_t and the convertible's market value MM' due to the risk exposure reduction by holding the convertibles. As the conversion value increases to exceed the call price VM, the convertible's market value approaches M' where the convertible's market value intersects with the conversion value. The reasons for the intersection are three folds: (i) The likelihood of a call increases as the conversion value increases; (ii) Loss protection against interest rate risk diminishes; (iii) The dividend yield of the common stock exceeds the fixed coupon yield of the convertible as the conversion value increases. In summary, a convertible's market price is a complex interaction between its straight debt value and a premium associated with the expected future market price of the underlying equity security. This complex interaction, however, is not explicitly specified in Brigham's work. In the following, the interaction is accounted for by random characterization of the stock price and/or the straight debt value.

11.B.3. *Calculus Approach: Static*

Stochastic Models

Baumol *et al.* (1966) present a convertible-security valuation model that separates the interaction between debt and equity attributes in the valuation of convertible securities by considering the time-t value $C = \max(C_s, C_b)$ of a convertible as

$$C_s = ps + \int_0^{\bar{B}/ps} f(i, t_0)[\bar{B} - i(t)ps]di(t), \tag{11.B.2}$$

$$C_b = \bar{B} + \int_{\bar{B}/ps}^{\infty} f(i, t_0)[i(t)ps - \bar{B}]di(t), \tag{11.B.3}$$

where $\bar{B}$ = equivalent straight debt value; s = number of equity securities issued upon conversion; p = price of the equity security at present t_0; $i(t)$ = date-t to date-t_0 equity security's price relative; $f(i, t_0)$ = subjective probability assessment of $i(t)$ at t_0, when $t > t_0$. Equation (11.B.2) specifies that C_s is composed of two values: the conversion value ps and the insurance value of the debt character as the stochastic price relative $i(t)$ varies between 0 and $\bar{B}/ps$ at the end of time horizon t. Equation (11.A.3) states that C_b is a combination of two values: the straight debt value $\bar{B}$ and the value assigned to the conversion feature as the stochastic price relative $i(t)$ varies between $\bar{B}/ps$ and ∞ at the end of time horizon t.

Later *et al.* (1966) extended their previous model by introducing the *ex ante* notion that the convertible security holder is interested in the future conversion value of the convertible security as follows:

$$C = \int_0^{\infty} i(t)psf(i,t_0)di(t) + \int_0^{\bar{B}/ps} f(i,t_0)[\bar{B} - i(t)ps]di(t). \qquad (11.B.4)$$

In this model, the first term represents the conversion value in all possible states of the price relative $i(t)$ from 0 to ∞, while the second term represents the insurance value of the debt character as the stochastic price relative $i(t)$ varies between 0 and $\bar{B}/ps$.

Both in Brigham (1966) and Baumol *et al.* (1966), the market interest rate is flat and bond's straight debt value was treated as an exogenously determined constant. By including the nature of interest-rate changes, an explicit characterization of the random nature of a convertible security's bond value would lead to a robust model of the market setting of convertible securities. In Poensgen (1965), both the stochastic stock price and stochastic straight debt value are explicitly considered. Be more specific, on an arbitrarily date when conversion is possible, Poensgen (1965) suggests the expected price of the convertible security as

$$E(P) = \int_0^{\infty} \left[y \int_0^{y} h\left(\frac{x}{y}\right) dx + \int_y^{\infty} xh\left(\frac{x}{y}\right) dx \right] g(y)dy, \qquad (11.B.5)$$

where x = the stock price (or conversion value); y = the straight debt value; $h(x/y)$ = the conditional probability of x for a particular bond value y; $g(y)$ = the probability of occurrence of the bond value y (unconditional). Note that the probability of joint occurrence of the stock price x and bond value

y is $h(x,y) = h(x/y)g(y)$. It can be shown that Eq. (11.B.5) is logically equivalent to the following:

$$E(P) = \int_0^\infty \Bigg[\underbrace{\int_0^\infty xh(x,y)dx}_{\text{Expected stock value}} + \underbrace{\int_0^y (y-x)h(x,y)dx}_{\text{Value of floor guarantee}} \Bigg] dy. \quad (11.B.6)$$

$$E(P) = \underbrace{\int_0^\infty yg(y)dy}_{\text{Expected straight debt value}} + \underbrace{\int_0^\infty \int_y^\infty (x-y)h(x,y)dxdy}_{\text{Expected value of the conservation option}}. \quad (11.B.7)$$

Equation (11.B.6) specifies that the value of the convertible security is the expected stock price plus the value attached to the floor guarantee for a stochastic straight debt value, y. This formulation is identical to Eq. (11.B.4) by Baumol, Malkiel, and Quandt's (1966) model except for the assumption by Poensgen (1965) that y is a random variable. Alternatively, in Eq. (11.B.7), the first term evaluates the value of a straight debt, while the second term evaluates the value of a warrant with exercise price y by integrating over all possible straight-debt value, y.

By showing that there was no statistically significant correlation between bond yield variability and stock prices, Poensgen (1965) claims that Eq. (11.B.7) is analytically equal to

$$E(P) = \int_0^\infty yg(y)dy + \int_y^\infty (x-y)f(x)dx, \quad (11.B.8)$$

where $f(x)$ is the probability density function of x. Based on Eq. (11.B.8), Poensgen (1965) suggests that the distribution of stock prices, x, is truncated on the left by the straight-debt value. This assertion facilitates Poensgen's (1965) subsequent empirical work dealing with the truncated distribution of convertible security returns. Nevertheless, the integration in Eq. (11.B.8) does not equal to that in Eq. (11.B.7). Therefore, the subsequent work of Poensgen (1965) on the truncated distribution of convertible security returns is not of great help.

Later, Frankle and Hawkins (1975) adopted Poensgen's valuation model for convertible securities to explore the link between the beta of a convertible security and the beta of the underlying common stock by assuming independence of the stock and straight bond prices so as to obtain

$$E(CB) = \int_0^y yh(y)dx + \int_y^\infty xh(x)dx, \tag{11.B.9}$$

where $E(CB)$ = expected price of the convertible security; y = straight-debt value, x = log of the stock price relative; $h(x)$ = log-normal distribution of stock price relatives. By assuming a constant straight debt value and following the previous direction of Poensgen (1965) by asserting that the probability density function of the log of the stock price relatives are truncated at a constant value a, Frankle and Hawkins (1975) present the expected log return on the convertible bond as:

$$E_{en(i(t))CB} = a\int_{-\infty}^{a} \frac{1}{\sqrt{2\pi\sigma_x}} e^{-(1/2)[(x-\mu_x)/\sigma_x]^2} dx$$

$$+ \int_a^{-\infty} x\frac{1}{\sqrt{2\pi\sigma_x}} e^{-(1/2)[(x-\mu_x)/\sigma_x]^2} dx. \tag{11.B.10}$$

Frankle and Hawkins (1975) proceed to derive an explicit form for the beta of a convertible security based on the beta of the underlying common stock. This relationship is presented as follows:

$$Beta = \rho\frac{\sigma_x}{\sigma_m}\left[1 - \phi\left(\frac{a}{\sigma_x}\right)\right], \tag{11.B.11}$$

where ρ = correlation coefficient between x and the market m; σ_x = standard deviation of common stock return; σ_m = standard deviation of market return; ϕ = the cumulative normal function. It is noted by Frankle and Hawkins that Eq. (11.B.11) implies that the beta of a convertible security is less than or equal to that of its underlying common stock. Thus, Frankle and Hawkins (1975) derive an upper bound for the convertible security's beta. Nevertheless, the result by Frankle and Hawkins (1975) in Eq. (11.B.11) is false as Eq. (11.B.9) is falsely derived. Further efforts need to be done for a valid relationship between the beta of a convertible security and that of its underlying common stock.

The next major advance in convertible-security valuation evolved from the option-pricing theory originated by Black–Scholes (1973) and the risky zero-coupon bond's pricing by Merton (1974). In the option-pricing approach, the firm's market value over time is modeled as a stochastic process, and three possibilities of the termination of a convertible bond are considered: conversions by the bondholders, maturity of the bond, called back or default of the firm. The following Section considers option-pricing approach for the valuation of convertible bonds.

11.B.4. *Option-Pricing Approach: Dynamic Stochastic Model*

When pricing a convertible bond, one needs to consider the conversion and put strategies of bondholders, the call back policy and the default mechanism of the firm. For simplicity, we'll not consider the put-option in this study. Therefore, in the following, we focus on the three decision variables of a convertible bond: the conversion strategy, call back policy, and default mechanism.

Ingersoll (1977a) is the first to derive the optimal conversion strategy for bondholders and optimal call policy for the firm in a perfect, frictionless market with no dividends and constant conversion terms. According to Ingersoll (1977a), for a firm with a capital structure consisting of equities and convertible bonds only, the optimal conversion strategy satisfies the following lemma:

Lemma 11.B.1. *If the perfect market, no dividends, and constant conversion terms assumptions are valid, then a callable convertible will never be converted except at maturity or a call.*

With the additional assumptions of no call notice and flat interest rate, Ingersoll (1977a) gave the optimal call strategy for a company as

Lemma 11.B.2. *If the conditions for the above lemma hold, the optimal call strategy is to call when the firm's market value reaches the call price divided by the dilution factor γ, the fraction of the equity that the bond holders possess if they convert.*

One advantage of Ingersoll's result (1977a) is that it captures the dilution effect as convertible bonds are converted into common stocks (Schönbucher, 2003). With this advantage, Ingersoll (1977a) decomposed the price of a non-callable convertible bond G into a straight discount bond F (with the same principal as the convertible bond) and a warrant W as

$$G(V,\tau;B,0,\gamma) = F(V,\tau;B,0) + W(\gamma V,\tau;B), \qquad (11.B.12)$$

where B is the balloon payment, τ is the time-to-maturity, c is coupon payment, γ is the dilution factor, $W(\gamma V,\ \tau;\ B)$ is the warrant price with underlying price γV and exercise price B. The initial condition for W satisfies

$$W(\gamma V, 0; B) = \max(\gamma V_T - B, 0),$$

where V_T is the firm value at maturity. By assuming the firm's market value V follows a geometric Brownian motion and default occurs if V falls below an exogenously determined barrier (Merton, 1974; Black and Cox, 1976; Longstaff and Schwartz, 1995; Briys and Varenne, 1997), or an endogenously determined barrier due to the strategic decision of the firm (Leland, 1994; Leland and Toft, 1996), Ingersoll (1977a) derived analytically the values of the straight discount bond F and the warrant W using the option pricing theory for a risky debt.

In the case of a callable convertible bond, the bond's price H is decomposed into a straight discount bond F, a warrant W and an additional term representing the cost of the call which reduces the value of the callable convertible bond relative to its non-callable counterpart as

$$\begin{aligned} H(V,\tau;K(\tau),0,\gamma) &= F(V,\tau;B,0) + W(\gamma V,\tau;B) \\ &\quad + Z^{2(r-\rho)/\sigma^2}[F(\gamma V',\tau;B',0) - F(\gamma V',\tau;B'/\gamma,0)], \end{aligned} \tag{11.B.13}$$

where $K(\tau)$ is the call price of the convertible and $Z = K(\tau)/\gamma V$, $B' = Be^{(r-\rho)\tau}$; $V' = Ve^{(r-\rho)\tau}$. In another paper by Brennan and Schwartz (1977), the partial differential equation for the price of a convertible with call provisions and dividends is derived based on the following conversion and call strategies.

Lemma 11.B.3. *It will never be optimal to convert a convertible bond except immediately prior either to a dividend date or to an adverse change in the conversion terms, or maturity.*

Lemma 11.B.4. *The firm's optimal call strategy is to call the bond as soon as its value, if it is not called, is equal to the call price.*

Later, in addition to the simplistic capital structure assumed by Ingersoll (1977a) and Brennan and Schwartz (1977) consisting solely of equity and convertible bonds, Brennan and Schwartz (1980) include senior straight debts in a firm's capital structure and develop a two-factor structure model with stochastic firm's market value and interest rate for the valuation of a convertible bond. Brennan and Schwartz (1980) found that often the additional factor representing stochastic interest rates had little impact on the prices of convertible bonds. Later, Nyborg (1996) extends the two-factor model of Brennan and Schwartz (1980) with a put provision and floating coupons feature.

Nevertheless, due to the complexity of the convertible's contractual provisions so the number of parameters used is large and the firm's market value is unobservable, the aforementioned approach can be impractical and there might be no analytical solutions for the valuation of a convertible bond. Instead, practitioners often use the equity price as the underlying for the valuation of a convertible bond and some numerical approaches are employed. In the following Section, the prevalent numerical approach, i.e., the tree method, is given.

11.B.5. *Numerical Approach: Tree Method*

The most widely used numerical approach for the pricing of a convertible is the tree approach. The approach has the capability to handle various convertible bond provisions. The main procedure of the tree approach for convertible bond pricing is stated as follows:

First, consider the firm's stochastic price S as the underlying, which follows a lognormal Ito process of the form:

$$dS = \mu(S,t)Sdt + \sigma SdW, \tag{11.B.14}$$

where $\mu(S,t)$ is the drift term, σ is the volatility, and W is a standard Brownian motion. A binomial tree is built in a risk neutral world for the development of the stochastic price S in (11.B.14) according to the Cox–Ross–Rubinstein (1979). Each node on the tree represents a possible future stock price. Then a backward induction procedure starting from the maturity is applied, a maximum convertible bond value on each node is decided according to the stock price and the action taken according to the provisions, e.g., convert, put, call, hold or redeem the bond. Finally the current value of convertible bond can be calculated. The credit risk of the convertible bond is considered by setting a risky discount rate with the credit spread of the issuer (Goldman Sachs, 1994) or adding a default node (Hull, 2009) with the default probability which is decided by the default intensity of the issuer.

More complex model with multi-factors, such as adding a stochastic interest rate, or with time-varying default intensity, volatility, and interest rate is also applicable with tree model (Ho and Pfeffer, 1996; Hung and Wang, 2002; Ammann *et al.* 2003; Carayannopoulos and Kalimipalli, 2003; Chambers and Lu, 2007). Ho and Pfeffer (1996) employed a two-dimensional binomial tree for the stochastic stock price and interest rate in their two-factor model, in which all the cash flows are discounted at the risky rate (i.e., risk-free plus credit spread). Correlated default intensity and stock price is discussed in Andersen and Buffum (2003). However, Bernnan and Schwartz (1980) and Goldman Sachs (1994) indicated that the major factor which decides the convertible bond value is the equity price. Adding additional factor, such as dynamic interest rate, into consideration had little impact on the value of convertible bond.

11.B.6. *Conclusion*

This article reviews the various models developed for the valuation of callable convertible bonds, which is a dual option problem: on the one hand, the shareholders determine the optimal call and bankruptcy policies so as to maximize the equity value, on the other hand, the bondholders determine the optimal conversion strategy so as to maximize the convertible bond's value. As the bondholders' optimal conversion strategy depends on the firm's call strategy, and the firm's optimal call strategy in turn depends on the bondholders' voluntary conversion strategy, the dual option problem is complex with no simplifying solution on it.

Studies further taking into account of the bankruptcy costs, tax benefits, and capital structure of the bond issuer as well as the refunding costs and a call notice period can be found in Liao and Huang (2006). In Lee *et al.* (2009), the association between investor protection and the security design of convertibles, as measured by the expected probability of converting the convertibles at maturity is examined. For convertible bonds with non-standard features, such as the refix clause that alters the conversion ratio (shares per bond) or conversion price, subject to the share price level on certain days between issue and expiry, the convertible bond's coupons can be allowed to change with time, or at conversion the bondholders receive a combination of shares and cash instead of just shares, more advanced models need to be developed to take into account of the versatile designs of the convertible bonds.

References for Appendix 11.B

Amram, M and N Kulatilaka (2001). *Real Options*. USA: Oxford University Press.

Banz, R and M Miller (1978). Prices for state contingent claims: Some estimates and applications. *Journal of Business*, 51, 653–672.

Bhattachayra, M (1980). Empirical properties of the black-scholes formula under ideal conditions. *Journal of Financial and Quantitative Analysis*, 15, 1081–1105.

Black, F (1972). Capital market equilibrium with restricted borrowing. *Journal of Business*, 45, 444–445.

Black, F and M Scholes (1973). The pricing of options and corporate liabilities. *Journal of Political Economy*, 31, 637–659.

Bookstaber, RM (1981). *Option Pricing and Strategies in Investing*, Reading, MA: Addison-Wesley.

Cox, JC and M Rubinstein (1985). *Option Markets*, Englewood Cliffs, NJ: Prentice-Hall.

Finnerty, J (1978). The chicago board options exchange and market efficiency. *Journal of Financial and Quantitative Analysis*, 13, 29–38.

Galai, D and RW Masulis (1976). The option pricing model and the risk factor of stock. *Journal of Financial Economics*, 3, 53–81.

Hull, J (2005). *Options, Futures, and Other Derivatives*. 5th ed. New York: Prentice Hall.

Jarrow R and S Turnbull (1999). *Derivatives Securities*, 2nd ed. South-Western College Pub.

Liaw, KT and RL Moy (2000). *The Irwin Guide to Stocks, Bonds, Futures, and Options*. New York: McGraw-Hill Companies.

Lee, CF, J Finnerty, J Lee, A Lee, and D Wort (2013). *Security Analysis, Portfolio Management and Financial Derivatives*. Singapore: World Scientific.

Lee, CF, JC Lee, and AC Lee (2013). *Statistics for Business and Financial Economics*, 3rd ed. New York: Springer.

Lee, CF and AC Lee (2006). *Encyclopedia of Finance*, 2nd edn. New York: Springer.

Lee, CF (2009). *Handbook of Quantitative Finance and Risk Management*. New York: Springer.

MacBeth, J and L Merville (1979). An empirical examination of the Black–Scholes call option pricing model. *The Journal of Finance*, 34, 1173–1186.

McDonald, RL (2005). *Derivatives Markets*, 2nd ed. Massachusetts: Addison Wesley, Boston.

Rendleman, RJ, Jr and BJ Barter (1979). Two-state option pricing. *Journal of Finance*, 24, 1093–1110.

Ritchken, P (2001). *Optiom: Theory, Strategy, and Applications*. Glenview, IL: Scott, Foresman.

Summa, JF and JW Lubow (2001). *Options on Futures*. New York: John Wiley & Sons.

Trennepohl, G (1981). A comparison of listed option premia and Black–Scholes model prices: 1973–1979. *Journal of Financial Research*, 11–20.

Zhang, PG (1998). *Exotic Options: A Guide to Second Generation Options*, 2nd ed. Singapore: World Scientific Pub Co Inc.

References for Chapter 11

Amram, M and N Kulatilaka (2001). *Real Options*. New York: Oxford University Press.

Banz, R and M Miller (1978). Prices for state contingent claims: Some estimates and applications. *Journal of Business*, 51, 653–672.

Bhattachayra, M (1980). Empirical properties of the Black–Scholes formula under ideal conditions. *Journal of Financial and Quantitative Analysis*, 15, 1081–1105.

Black, F (1972). Capital market equilibrium with restricted borrowing. *Journal of Business*, 45, 444–445.

Black, F and M Scholes (1973). The pricing of options and corporate liabilities. *Journal of Political Economy*, 31, 637–659.

Bookstaber, RM (1981). *Option Pricing and Strategies in Investing*. Reading, MA: Addison-Wesley.

Chen, SS, CF Lee, and HH Lee (2010). Alternative methods to determine optimal capital structure: Theory and application. In *Handbook of Quantitative Finance and Risk Management*, CF Lee, AC Lee, and J Lee (eds.), 933–951. New York, NY: Springer.

Cox, JC and M Rubinstein (1985). *Option Markets*. Englewood Cliffs, NJ: Prentice-Hall.

Cox, JS Ross, and M Rubenstein (1979). Option pricing: A simplified approach. *Journal of Financial Economics*, 7, 229–263.

Finnerty, J (1978). The chicago board options exchange and market efficiency. *Journal of Financial and Quantitative Analysis*, 13, 29–38.

Galai, D and RW Masulis (1976). The option pricing model and the risk factor of stock. *Journal of Financial Economics*, 3, 53–81.

Hull, J (2005). *Options, Futures, and Other Derivatives*, 6th edn. Upper Saddle River, New Jersey: Prentice Hall.

Jarrow R and S Turnbull (1999). *Derivatives Securities*, 2nd edn. Cincinnati, OH: South-Western College Pub.

Liaw, KT and RL Moy (2000). *The Irwin Guide to Stocks, Bonds, Futures, and Options*. New York: McGraw-Hill Companies.

Leland, HE (1994). Corporate debt value, bond covenants and optimal capital structure. *Journal of Finance*, 49, 1213–1252.

Lee, AC, JC Lee, and CF Lee (2009). *Financial Analysis, Planning and Forecasting: Theory and Application*, 2nd edn. Singapore: World Scientific Publishing Company.

Lee, CF, Y Chen, and J Lee (2015). *Alternative Methods to Derive Option Price Models: Review and Comparison*. Review of Quantitative Finance & Accounting.

Lee, CF and AC Lee (2006). *Encyclopedia of Finance*. 2nd edn. New York, NY: Springer.

Lee, CF, AC Lee, and J Lee (2010). *Handbook of Quantitative Finance and Risk Management.* New York, NY: Springer.

Lee, CF and CSM Lin (2010). Two alternative binomial option pricing model approaches to derive Black–Scholes option pricing model. In *Handbook of Quantitative Finance and Risk Management*, CF Lee, AC Lee and J Lee (eds.), New York, NY: Springer, 409–420.

MacBeth, J and L Merville (1979). An empirical examination of the Black–Scholes call option pricing model. *The Journal of Finance*, 34, 1173–1186.

McDonald, RL (2005). *Derivatives Markets*, 2nd edn. Boston, MA: Addison Wesley.

Merton, R (1973). An inter-temporal capital asset pricing model. *Econometrica*, 41, 867–887.

Rendleman Jr, RJ and BJ Barter (1979). Two-state option pricing, *Journal of Finance*, 24, 1093–1110.

Ritchken, P (2001). *Option: Theory, Strategy, and Applications* Glenview, IL: Scott, Foresman.

Summa, JF and JW Lubow (2001). *Options on Futures.* New York: John Wiley & Sons.

Trennepohl, G (1981). A comparison of listed option premia and Black–Scholes model prices: 1973–1979. *Journal of Financial Research*, 4, 11–20.

Zhang, PG (1998). *Exotic Options: A Guide to Second Generation Options*, 2nd ed. Singapore: World Scientific.

Project II

Application of Useful Finance Theories

Part III

Capital Budgeting and Leasing Decisions

Chapter 12

Alternative Cost of Capital Analysis and Estimation

12.1. Introduction

The determination of a firm's cost of capital is one of the most central issues in finance. Theoretically, the firm should invest in projects, or increase its capital stock, until the marginal rate-of-return on the new investment is equal to its cost of capital. Thus, the optimal allocation of scarce investment resources in the economy depends on the correct assessment of the cost of obtaining those resources. An accurate estimate of a firm's cost of capital is necessary for correctly ranking and selecting investment projects. In addition, the cost of capital can also be used for making financing decisions for the firm. From the theoretical assumptions of the different cost of capital analyses, we come to various conclusions regarding the existence of an optimum capital structure, the effect of varying tax rates on investment, and the proper assessment of growth opportunities for a firm.

In this chapter, we first discuss overview of cost of capital in Section 12.1. Then we discuss average earnings yield versus current earnings yield method, discounted cash flow (DCF) method, and weighted average cost of capital in Sections 12.3, 12.4, and 12.5, respectively. In addition, we discuss the Capital Asset Pricing Model (CAPM) method, M&M cross-sectional method, and chase cost of capital in Sections 12.6, 12.7, and 12.8. Finally, summary and conclusion remarks are discussed in Section 12.9. Appendix 12.A. discusses the derivative of the basic equilibrium market price of stock and its implications.

12.2. Overview of Cost of Capital

From an economic theory viewpoint, a firm's cost of capital represents the opportunity cost of funds. The rate-of-return required by an investor is the opportunity cost to him of investing his limited funds in one project rather than another project with equivalent risk. Various sources of funds, from debt-holders, new common or preferred shareholders, current shareholders (essentially retained earnings), etc., represent varying amounts of risk for the individual investor, requiring varying rates-of-return in compensation. Additionally, a firm must be assured that the value of an investment project undertaken with investors' money will be greater than what the firm pays out for the funds. Thus, the key issue in capital budgeting is to select projects that will compensate the investor of the various sources of funds for the risk undertaken, and increase the wealth of the firm's shareholders. The cost of capital must be calculated in a manner consistent with these objectives.

Modigliani and Miller (M&M) (1966) argued that there are two alternative approaches for estimating the cost of capital: (i) the certainty approach, and (ii) the uncertainty approach. Under conditions of perfect certainty — the assumption on which most of classical economic theory has been developed — the concept of the cost of capital presents no particular difficulty. It is simply the market rate of interest. Under conditions of uncertainty, cost of capital no longer is a directly observable magnitude, and its determination and estimation should be done from a modern finance (economic)-theory viewpoint.

From the finance-theory viewpoint, the cost of capital, in general, consists of two components, a risk-free component and a risk premium. As discussed in Chapter 5, the risk-free component is essentially a compensation for the time value of money, or for the opportunity cost of holding money. The risk premium represents the compensation for the three types of risk a firm and its shareholders face: business risk, financial risk, and inflation risk.

Business risk represents the unexpected fluctuations in cash flow resulting both from the firm's particular operations and from the cyclical nature of general economic activity. Financial risk is strongly related to a firm's use of leverage. It includes the possibility of failure to meet creditors' interest or repayment demands and the ultimate possibility of having inadequate assets to meet the various creditors' claims if the firm becomes bankrupt. Finally, inflation risk originates from the uncertainty surrounding firm costs, revenue, and profit when inflation affects each of those earnings components differently.

The uneven distribution of price increases among firms means that unexpected inflation may reduce a firm's profitability through the inability of the firm to raise its prices along with its increased costs. In addition, unexpected inflation can reduce a firm's purchasing power over time, as well as decrease productivity through insufficient capital replacement.

There are various methods that can be used to estimate the cost of capital for a firm. Six methods will be discussed in this chapter: current earning yield, the DCF, the weighted average cost of capital (WACC), the CAPM, the M&M, and the Chase methods.

Concept Quiz

(1) Why should the cost of capital be computed on an after-tax basis?
(2) Why is incremental or marginal analysis important for determining a firm's cost of capital?
(3) What are flotation costs? How do they affect the firm's cost of capital?
(4) What is the meaning of the term *cost of capital*?

12.3. Average Earnings Yield Versus Current Earnings Yield Method

The average earnings yield method is the most basic method used for estimating the cost of capital. Using the M&M valuation model discussed in Chapter 7, the market value of the firm can be defined as:

$$V = \frac{\overline{x}}{k}, \tag{12.1}$$

where x is the total expected future earnings and k is the cost of capital. Equation (12.1) implies that the cost of capital can be estimated from:

$$k = \frac{\overline{x}}{V}. \tag{12.2}$$

In general, average accounting earnings are used as a proxy for expected earnings in this equation.

The main weakness of this method is that an earnings growth rate is not being directly incorporated into the cost of the capital determination process. However, Lintner (1963) has shown that the current earnings yield is equal to the marginal cost of capital under certainty. Under uncertainty a risk premium should be incorporated into the estimation of the marginal cost of capital (see Lintner (1963), Eq. (9)). Although this method is not very popular in the practical application of cost of capital to investment and financing decisions, it is useful as a linkage between valuation theory and cost-of-capital determination. Lintner (1963) derived the rule for the marginal cost-of-capital decision as:

$$r \geq Y_e, \tag{12.3}$$

where r is the marginal internal rate-of-return (IRR) and $Y_e = Y_0/P_0$, the current earnings yield. Y_0 and P_0 are current earnings per share (EPS) and current price per share, respectively. Equation (12.3) implies that an investment should not be accepted unless r is larger Y_e. In addition, Lintner also shows that Y_e is equal to the discount rate k as indicated in Eq. (12.2) only in the special case where profit opportunities are infinitely elastic throughout, i.e., constant return to scale for investment.[1] Lintner concluded that current earnings yield instead of average earnings yield should be used to estimate the cost of capital.

12.4. DCF Method

The DCF method essentially determines the cost of capital for a firm's retained earnings. The formula to derive the cost of capital using this method is taken from the Gordon growth equation for stock valuation:

$$P_0 = \frac{d_1}{K_e - g}, \tag{12.4}$$

where P_0 and d_1 are current price per share and dividend per share in the next period, respectively, and K_e is the required rate-of-return for common equity, and g is the growth rate of dividends. We can rearrange this to solve for the cost of equity capital, K_e:

$$K_e = \frac{d_1}{p_0} + g. \tag{12.5}$$

While both dividends and price are readily ascertainable, the estimation of a proper growth rate can be a considerable problem. Generally, one of

[1]See Appendix 12.A for this conclusion and the importance of marginal cost of capital in investment decision.

the four methods can be used to estimate the growth rate of earnings. A simple growth rate can be estimated from the percentage change in earnings over a time period. For instance, over 1 year:

$$\hat{g}_t = \frac{X_t - X_{t-1}}{X_{t-1}},$$

where X_t, X_{t-1} = earnings in year t, year $(t-1)$, respectively, and $\hat{g}_t$ = the estimate of the growth rate in period t.

A modification of this method involves an arithmetic average, where annual growth estimates for short periods, say 5 years, are averaged to arrive at one annual average growth estimate for the total period:

$$\frac{\hat{g}_1 + \hat{g}_2 + \hat{g}_3 + \hat{g}_4}{4} = \hat{g},$$

where g_1, g_2, g_3, and g_4 = simple growth-rate estimates for each of the four annual periods.

A slightly more accurate estimate can be obtained by solving for the continuously compounded growth rate:

$$X_0(1+g)^t = X_t$$

or

$$(1+g)^t = \frac{X_t}{X_0},$$

where X_0 and X_t represent earnings in period 0 and t, respectively.

Since compounded interest factors are generally available from finance texts, the compound growth-rate estimate can be solved for by taking the tth root of the interest factor, where t equals the number of periods of growth. This method is called the *compound sum* method of growth-rate estimation.

Finally, growth rates for EPS and DPS can be obtained from an Ordinary Least Squares (OLS) regression by using

$$\log_e \mathrm{EPS}_t = a_0 + a_1 T + \varepsilon_{1t}$$

and

$$\log_e \mathrm{DPS}_t = b_0 + b_1 T + \varepsilon_{2t},$$

where EPS_t and DPS_t are EPS and dividends per share, respectively, in period t, and T is the time indicators, that is, $T = 1, 2, \ldots, n$. The estimated

a_1 and b_1 are estimated growth rates for EPS and DPS, respectively; a_0 and b_0 are intercept terms.

The regression method instead of the compound sum method has taken more available information into account. In addition, a null hypothesis test can be used to determine whether the growth rate obtained from the regression method is statistically significantly different from zero or not. Therefore, the regression method is suggested for estimating the cost of capital. However, logarithms cannot be taken with zero or negative numbers. Under this circumstance, the arithmetic average ($\bar{g}$) is a good alternative.

Both EPS and DPS data of Johnson & Johnson (JNJ) during 1995–2006, as listed in Table 12.1, are needed to show that the regression method can be used to estimate the growth rates of EPS and DPS. The regression results are:

$$\begin{aligned}\log \text{EPS}_t &= 0.910 + 0.015T \\ &\quad (0.026) * (0.020), \\ \log \text{DPS}_t &= -0.137 + 0.022T \\ &\quad (0.145)(0.020).\end{aligned}$$

From these regression results, we can conclude that the growth estimates for EPS and DPS are 1.5% and 2.2%, respectively.

Table 12.1. EPS and DPS of Johnson & Johnson (1995–2006).

Year	EPS_t	DPS_t	$\text{Ln}(\text{EPS}_t)$	$\text{L}(\text{DPS}_t)$	T
1995	3.72	1.28	1.314	0.247	1
1996	2.17	0.74	0.775	−0.308	2
1997	2.47	0.85	0.904	−0.163	3
1998	2.27	0.97	0.820	−0.030	4
1999	3.00	1.09	1.099	0.086	5
2000	3.45	1.24	1.238	0.215	6
2001	1.87	0.70	0.626	−0.357	7
2002	2.20	0.80	0.788	−0.229	8
2003	2.42	0.93	0.884	−0.078	9
2004	2.87	1.10	1.054	0.091	10
2005	3.50	1.28	1.253	0.243	11
2006	3.76	1.46	1.324	0.375	12

*Standard errors are in parentheses.

12.5. Weighted-Average Cost of Capital (WACC)

In this section, we will first discuss the procedure of calculating the WACC and then discuss the theory used to develop and justify the WACC method of calculating the cost of capital.

In order to estimate the WACC, you must: (1) determine the relative proportions of the various financial instruments in a firm's capital structure, and (2) calculate the proper cost of each of these capital components. The determination of the components of a firm's capital structure may be complicated by the existence of convertible securities (both preferred stock and bonds); the possibility and extent of conversion must be estimated in order to adjust for changing proportions due to the exercise of conversion privileges.

Each of the various components of a firm's financial structure has a unique cost, since each component involves a different degree of risk to the supplier of the funds. To derive the explicit cost of debt, we solve for the discount rate k_d that equates the net proceed of debt issued with the present value of interest plus principal payments as indicated in Eq. (12.6):

$$M = \sum_{t=1}^{n} \frac{I_t}{(1+k_d)^t} + \frac{P}{(1+k_d)^n}. \tag{12.6}$$

Equation (12.6) is similar to Eq. (7.4), where I_t, p, and n have been defined in that equation; and M represents the market price of bond. If $M =$ \$922.85, $n = 3$, and $P =$ \$1,000, then by using the IRR method in capital budgeting as indicated in Chapter 12, it can be found that $K_d = 8\%$. If the bond is a perpetuity and $M = P$, then k_d can be defined as

$$k_d = \frac{\text{Interest payment}}{\text{Principle borrowed}}. \tag{12.6$'$}$$

Thus, if XYZ can issue long-term bonds totaling \$1,000,000 with a coupon rate of 7.5%, the before-tax cost of debt capital for XYZ is:

$$k_d = \frac{(0.075)(\$1{,}000{,}000)}{\$1{,}000{,}000} = \frac{\$75{,}000}{\$1{,}000{,}000} = 7.5\%.$$

However, interest payments of a corporation are in effect "subsidized" by the federal government through the deductibility of interest expense before computation of taxes. Thus, the true cost of debt capital to the firm is the after-tax cost of its interest payment, or:

$$K_d^{\tau} = (1 - \tau_c)k_d, \tag{12.7}$$

where τ_c = the marginal corporate tax rate.

For XYZ, with a marginal corporate tax rate of 50%:

$$k_d^{\tau} = (0.075)(1 - 0.50) = 3.75\%.$$

Thus, if the firm borrows funds from debt-holders at 3.75% and earns 3.75% on the investment it undertakes with the funds, the wealth of shareholders will remain unchanged, indicating a marginal cost of debt capital equal to the marginal yield on investment.

The cost of debt must also be adjusted for flotation costs of issuing the debt if they are sufficiently high. In addition, the discount and premium should also be considered in calculating cost of debt. In general, they will be negligible since most debt is placed directly with private debt-holders. However, if flotation costs are substantial, then Eq. (12.6′) is modified to an approximation for flotation costs using per-bond quantities:

$$k_d' = \frac{C_t + \dfrac{(M - M')}{n}}{\dfrac{(M + M')}{2}}, \tag{12.6''}$$

where

M = Price at which the bond is sold in the market;
M' = Issue price of the bond (the price actually received by the issuing company);
$(M - M')$ = Flotation cost;
n = Life of the bond;
C_t = Interest expense per period on one bond.

Hence, Eq. (12.6″) averages the flotation differential (or the flotation cost) over the life of the bond, N, and adds this to the periodic interest payment as a cost of debt; the principal borrowed is represented by an average between the par value and the actual price of the bond received by the issuer.

If XYZ Corporation must pay a 4.5% flotation fee to its underwriter for the 30-year long-term bond mentioned above, making the issue price of the bond (according to XYZ) \$955, their cost of debt capital becomes:

$$k'_d = \frac{\dfrac{[75 + (1000 - 955)]}{30}}{\dfrac{(100 + 955)}{2}} = \frac{75 + \left(\dfrac{45}{30}\right)}{977.5} = 7.8\%.$$

Thus, with a flotation fee of 4.5%, the before-tax cost of debt for XYZ has increased by 3%.

Similarly, Eq. (12.6′) can also be modified to an approximation for discount or premium as:

$$k''_d = \frac{C_t + \left[\dfrac{(M - P)}{n}\right]}{\dfrac{(M + P)}{2}}, \tag{12.6'''}$$

where $M - P$ = discount or premium on the bond.

It should be noted that both Eqs. (12.6″) and (12.6‴) can give us approximate results. To obtain precise results, we can incorporate the flotation cost and discount or premium information into Eq. (12.6), to solve the related cost of debt in terms of the IRR method.

Looking at convertible bonds, we see that they are priced at a slightly lower rate-of-return than debt by the market, due to the decreased risk of price declines (see Chapter 7 for discussion of convertible securities). The cost of capital for a convertible bond, k_{dc}, can be found using the IRR method and the formula for convertible bond value:

$$M = \sum_{t=1}^{N} \frac{C_t}{(1 + k_{dc})^t} + \frac{V}{(1 + k_{dc})^N}, \tag{12.8}$$

where

M_C = Market price of the convertible bond;
C_t = Interest payment on the convertible bond in period t;
N = Time to conversion;
V = Forecast value of the bond on termination.

The approximate formula for k_{dc} is

$$k_{dc} = C_t + \frac{\left(\dfrac{1}{n}\right)(V - M_c)}{\dfrac{1}{2}(V + M_c)}.$$

Another cost of capital component, the cost of retained earnings, as discussed in Eq. (12.5), is the rate-of-return required by a firm's current stockholders on the common shares of the firm. It should be noted that the price of a firm's stock will remain unchanged (or increase) if the firm invests its retained earnings in projects offering the same (or a higher) rate-of-return as the cost of retained earnings.

In general, the cost of retained earnings will always be smaller than the cost of external new equity due to flotation costs involved with issuing new securities.

New common stock issues, or external equity, involve flotation costs, and thus the cost of new equity must be adjusted for the cost of issue. The price of the common stock, used in Eq. (12.5), must be adjusted to represent the net price received by the firm:

$$P_N = P_0(1 - C_f), \tag{12.9}$$

where

P_N = Net price of the stock;
P_0 = Market price of the new stock;
C_f = Percentage flotation cost.

If XYZ must pay a 5% flotation cost on its \$22 stock, the net price becomes:

$$P_N = 22(1 - 0.05) = 20.90.$$

Using the net price, the cost of new common equity capital becomes:

$$K_e = \frac{d_1}{P_N} + g.$$

Thus, for XYZ:

$$k_e = \frac{1.10}{20.90} + 0.05 = 10.3.$$

Thus, flotation costs on new equity raise the cost of new equity to 10.3%, which is greater than the cost of retained earnings, estimated at 10% $(1.1/22 = 0.05)$.

Similarly, the cost of new preferred stock must be adjusted for flotation costs. Using P_p to represent the net price received by the firm for its preferred stock, the cost of preferred capital is:

$$K_P = \frac{D_P}{P_p}. \tag{12.10}$$

For XYZ, which has an outstanding \$1 preferred selling (after flotation costs) at $9\frac{7}{8}\%$ the cost of preferred capital is:

$$k_p = \frac{1.00}{9.875} = 10.127\%.$$

Thus, the cost of preferred stock is somewhat higher than retained earnings, as expected, but slightly lower than new common stock.

The various calculations for the cost of capital components of XYZ financing are shown in Table 12.2. Note that the cost of capital of each component is in proportion to the amount of risk borne by the holder.

In calculating the cost of debt capital, as indicated in Eqs. (12.6), (12.6′), and (12.7), the issues related to risky debt and limited liability. Following Chen (1978) and Chen and Kim (1979), the equilibrium value of cost-of-debt capital can be theoretically determined. In addition, these two papers also discuss the existence of an optimal capital structure under the conditions of both shareholder-wealth maximization and managerial-welfare maximization.

The second set of calculations required to determine the WACC, involve finding appropriate weights for each of the capital components. Each component will be weighted in proportion to its market value and the total

Table 12.2. XYZ financing.

Component	Calculation	Cost of Component (%)
Debt(no flotation cost)	$\frac{\text{Total interest}}{\text{Principal borrowed}} = \frac{\$75{,}000}{\$1{,}000{,}000}$	7.5
After tax	$(1-0.50)(7.5\%)$	3.75
Debt (with flotation cost)	$\dfrac{7.5 + \frac{(100-95)}{30}}{\frac{100+95}{2}}$	7.87
After tax	$(1-0.50)(7.8\%)$	3.9
Retained earnings	$\frac{1.10}{22.00} + 0.05$	10.0
New preferred stock	$\frac{1.00}{9.875}$	10.125
New equity	$\frac{1.10}{20.90} + 0.05$	10.3

assets of the firm:

$$\text{Weight} = \frac{\text{Market value outstanding of component}}{\text{Total assets}}. \tag{12.11}$$

Note that book value weights have often been used to replace market value weights. Thus, for instance, the approximate weight for cost of equity would be calculated as follows:

$$\frac{(\text{Book value of retained earnings}) + (\text{Market value of common stock}).}{(\text{Book value of total assets})} \tag{12.11$'$}$$

To determine the total WACC for a firm, then, the component costs will be weighted by their respective representation in the capital structure of the firm, or:

$$\text{WACC} = \sum_{i}^{n} W_i K_i, \tag{12.12}$$

where i represents convertible debt, regular debt, new preferred stock, new common stock, retained earnings, and current outstanding common stock, where applicable.

It should be noted that Eq. (12.12) can be expanded to include other types of capital such as short-term debt or other types of hybrid securities.

12.5.1. *Theoretical Justification of the WACC*

Using M&M's (1958, 1963) theoretical framework for the value of a levered firm, as discussed in Chapter 6, the weighted average cost of capital can be defined as (for the derivation, see Section 11.6 of this chapter):

$$\text{WACC}^{\tau} = \rho\left[1 - \tau_c\left(\frac{\Delta D}{\Delta A}\right)\right], \tag{12.13}$$

where ΔD and ΔA are the change in risk-free debt and the change in total assets of a firm, respectively; ρ is the required net-of-tax yield for investment with a proportion of debt $\Delta D/\Delta A$, and τ_c is the marginal corporate rate, M&M (1963, p. 441) suggest that the long-run target ratio for total debt-to-value ratio can be used as an approximation for the marginal ratio ($\Delta D/\Delta A$).

Haley and Schall (1979, pp. 346–350) introduce an alternative cost-of-capital definition where target leverage is the ratio of debt to reproduction value. In other words, Eq. (12.13) is rewritten as

$$\mathrm{WACC}^{\tau} = \rho\left[1 - \tau_c\left(\frac{\Delta D}{\Delta V}\right)\right] \tag{12.14}$$

Copeland and Weston (2003) have reconciled the weighted average cost-of-capital concept defined in Eq. (8.12) and those defined in Eqs. (11.13) and (11.14). To do this, Copeland and Weston show that the cost of equity capital can be defined as

$$K_e = \rho + (1 - \tau_c)(\rho - k_d)\left(\frac{\Delta D}{\Delta S}\right), \tag{12.15}$$

where $\Delta D/\Delta S$ = changes in the market value ratio of debt to equity.

If the market-value ratio of debt to equity (D/S) is used to replace $\Delta D/\Delta S$, then Eq. (12.15) can be rewritten as

$$K_e = \rho + (1 - \tau_c)(\rho - k_d)\left(\frac{D}{S}\right). \tag{12.15$'$}$$

Equation (12.15′) is the M&M Proposition II with corporate tax case as discussed in Chapter 7. The difference between Eq. (12.15) and Eq. (12.15′) is the capital structure used to calculate the risk premium associated with leverage. These two are equal only when the firm's average debt-to-equity ratio is the same as its marginal debt-to-equity ratio. This will be true as long as the firm's "target" debt-to-equity ratio is equal to D/S, and it finances its new project so that $D/S = \Delta D/\Delta S$.

Using similar notation, the WACC with only debt and equity can be defined as:

$$\mathrm{WACC}^{\tau} = (1 - \tau_c)K_d\left(\frac{D}{D+S}\right) + K_e\left(\frac{S}{D+S}\right). \tag{12.16}$$

Substituting the M&M expression for K_e as indicated in Eq. (11.15) into Eq. (11.16), we get:

$$\begin{aligned}
\mathrm{WACC}^{\tau} &= (1 - \tau_c)k_d\left(\frac{D}{D+S}\right) + \left[\rho - (1 - \tau_c)(\rho - k_d)\frac{D}{S}\right]\left(\frac{S}{D+S}\right)\\
&= (1 - \tau_c)k_d\left(\frac{D}{D+S}\right) + \rho\left(\frac{S}{D+S}\right) + (1 - \tau_c)\rho\left(\frac{D}{S}\right)\left(\frac{S}{D+S}\right)\\
&\quad - (1 - \tau_c)k_d\left(\frac{D}{S}\right)\left(\frac{S}{D+S}\right)
\end{aligned}$$

$$= (1-\tau_c)k_d\left(\frac{D}{D+S}\right) + \rho\left[\frac{S}{D+S} + \frac{D}{D+S}\right] - \rho\tau_c\left(\frac{D}{D+S}\right)$$
$$- (1-\tau_c)k_d\left(\frac{D}{D+S}\right)$$
$$= \rho\left[1 - \tau_c\left(\frac{D}{D+S}\right)\right],$$

which is the same as Eq. (12.13) if D/V is equal to $\Delta D/\Delta V$. Henderson (1979) has used this concept to defend the WACC. In addition, Henderson has shown that the cost of equity capital from the CAPM method can be used to estimate the cost of equity capital. This issue will be explored in the next section.

One additional issue that should be addressed in the discussion of the WACC method is the effect of varying tax rates on the use of debt by a firm. Given the deductibility of interest expense before taxes are computed, it might seem that firms would be encouraged to expand the use of leverage to take advantage of this government "subsidy" of interest expense. Miller (1977), however, has shown that the existence of differing tax rates for the bond- versus the stockholder may imply a complete loss of the tax advantage of interest deductibility. Using his equation as defined in Chapter 7 for the value of a levered firm:

$$V^{\mathrm{L}} = V^{\mathrm{U}} + \left[1 - \frac{(1-\tau_c)(1-\tau_{ps})}{(1-\tau_{pD})}\right]D, \tag{7.32}$$

where

V^{U} = Market value of unlevered firm;
τ_c = Corporate tax rate;
τ_{ps} = Capital gains tax rate;
τ_{pD} = Tax rate on ordinary income;
D = Market value of debt.

It can be seen that the tax advantage will disappear when

$$(1-\tau_{pD}) = (1-\tau_{ps})(1-\tau_c).$$

Thus, the actual use of leverage by a firm depends on the relative sizes of its corporate tax rate *vis-à-vis* the personal tax rates relevant to its individual bond- and stockholders.

Similarly, the tax deductibility of interest expense is also counterbalanced by the increasing riskiness associated with increasing leverage for a firm. The risk of bankruptcy, which rises as interest expense rises, serves to mitigate the advantage of a firm, using leverage. Therefore, the tax advantage due to interest deductibility may be merely an illusory advantage when consideration of investor tax rates and bankruptcy costs are included in the analysis.

Concept Quiz

(1) How is a firm's cost of capital computed?
(2) When should an analyst use k_{re} as the cost of equity? When should he or she use k_{cs}?
(3) How are the capital structure weights determined? Will they be constant over time?

12.6. The CAPM Method

As discussed in Chapter 9, the CAPM expresses the required rate-of-return for a risky asset or investment. Therefore, the CAPM can be used to determine the required rate-of-return (or the cost of capital) for an investment project undertaken by a firm.

The CAPM possesses an advantage that the WACC method does not: the concept of systematic risk is directly incorporated into the CAPM framework. Each asset or investment project has a beta, which represents the systematic risk associated with undertaking the project or buying the asset. The total return required is therefore a function of both a risk-free rate and the systematic risk of the individual project.

The WACC, on the other hand, implicitly assumes that all risky projects under study have a beta equal to the beta of the firm. Thus, the CAPM and WACC estimates of the cost of capital will coincide only when the firm and the project have equivalent risk (see Fig. 12.1).

As can be seen from Fig. 12.1, some projects, such as A, will be accepted (using the WACC) which are unacceptable according to the risk-adjusted CAPM. Similarly, others (B) will seem to offer a rate-of-return insufficient to increase shareholder wealth, though this is not the case when the systematic risk of the particular project is directly considered in terms of the risk-adjusted CAPM.

When calculating the CAPM cost of capital for a project, the risk-free rate-of-return must be approximated: generally, the rate-of-return on

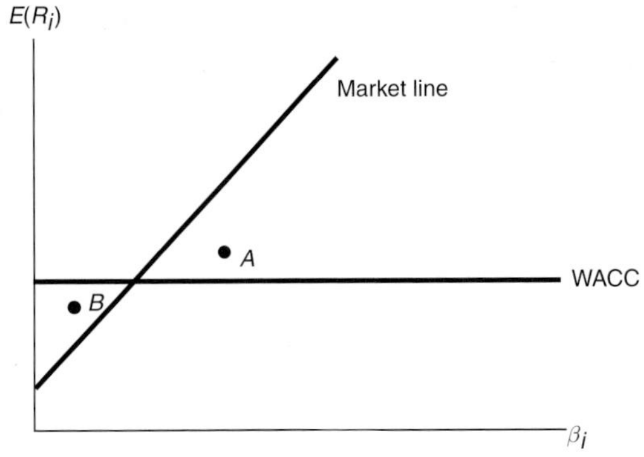

Fig. 12.1. Application of the asset-expansion criterion.

90-day Treasury bills is used. In addition, the risk premium $(R_m - R_f)$ can be approximated by the long-term market return of a market index such as the *Dow Jones 30*, the *Standard and Poor's* 500, or any other acceptable market index measure.

For methods of estimating the market-risk premium $(R_m - R_f)$, see Ibbotson and Sinquefield (1977) [IS] or Merton (1980) for a more sophisticated treatment. The former use a simulation technique to estimate the long-run nominal market-risk premium for 1977 and the period 1977–2000, inclusive. For 1977, this long-run averaging market-risk premium estimate is 9.23%. Merton argues that the IS estimate does not take the level of risk associated with market into account even though the inflation risk has implicitly been considered. Merton uses three alternative reward-to-risk ratio specifications and the data from 1926–1978 to estimate the long-run average market-risk premium. The long-run average market-risk premium estimates are 8.28%, 12.04%, and 10.36% for his model's first, second, and third specifications, respectively. Merton refers to his third model as a state-of-the-art model, which assumes that the average market-risk premium remains relatively stable for appreciable periods of time even though the risk level of the market is changing. The specification of Merton's second and third models directly takes the change of market risk over time into account. Interested readers can refer directly to his original paper. Chu (1984) and Lee and Chu (1984) have empirically generalized Merton's approach to market-risk premium determination.

Substituting the cost of capital obtained from the CAPM into M&M's valuation model, as defined in Chapter 7, Henderson (1979, pp. 60–61) shows that WACC^τ can also be shown as

$$\text{WACC}^\tau = [R_f + \beta(E(R_m) - R_f)]\left[1 - \tau_C\left(\frac{\Delta D}{\Delta A}\right)\right], \qquad (12.17)$$

where $[R_f + \beta(E(R_m) - R_f)]$ is Security Market Line (SML), as defined in Chapter 9.

Equation (12.17) is a specific form of the more general model in Eq. (12.13), where ρ is defined by the SML as $R_f + \beta(R_m - R_f)$.

The traditional CAPM has recently been extended to a more realistic type of CAPM. Brennan (1970) and Litzenberger and Ramaswamy (1979) have derived an after-tax version of CAPM, such that

$$\begin{aligned} E(\tilde{R}_j) = R_f &+ [E(\tilde{R}_m) - R_f]\beta_j \\ &+ E(\tilde{R}_z)(1 - \beta_j) + E(\tilde{R}_h)(d_i - \beta_j d_m), \end{aligned} \qquad (12.18)$$

where R_j, R_m, and β_j are defined in Chapter 6,

$E(\tilde{R}_z)$ = The risk premium on a portfolio having a zero beta and zero dividend yield;
$E(\tilde{R}_h)$ = Expected rate-of-return on a hedge portfolio having zero beta and dividend yield of Unity;
d_i = Dividend yield on stock i; and
d_m = Dividend yield on the market portfolio.

Litzenberger, Ramaswamy, and Sosin (1980) have used Eq. (12.18) to show that the cost of capital obtained from the classical to the traditional version of CAPM may be biased. Conceptually, the bias may occur because the terms $E[\tilde{R}_z](1-\beta_j)$ and $E(\tilde{R}_h)(d_i - \beta_j d_m)$ have been omitted from the traditional CAPM.

An example of using the average earnings yield, the DCF and the CAPM method for estimating the cost of equity capital was shown by Lee, Linke, and Zumwalt (1982) for the utility industry during the period 1967–1976.

The average-earnings-yield cost of capital used a 5-year earnings average of the E/P ratio in order to smooth fluctuations due to short-term disturbances. The DCF model used Gordon's model, as indicated in Eq. (12.5). The CAPM model used the same as presented in Chapter 7.

Three alternative cost-of-capital estimates for the utility industry are listed in Table 12.3. These results indicate that DCF cost-of-capital estimates are always larger than those from averaging the E/P ratio. The

Table 12.3. Means and standard deviations for three estimates of the cost of equity for the electric utility industry (standard deviations in parentheses).

Year	E/P	K_e	R_j
1967	0.0558	0.1033	0.1054
	(0.0077)	(0.0169)	(0.0140)
1968	0.0589	0.1119	0.1063
	(0.0077)	(0.0186)	(0.0149)
1969	0.0663	0.1340	0.1209
	(0.0088)	(0.0225)	(0.0140)
1970	0.0713	0.1451	0.1252
	(0.0092)	(0.0283)	(0.0143)
1971	0.0752	0.1576	0.1010
	(0.0090)	(0.0330)	(0.0133)
1972	0.0788	0.1657	0.1034
	(0.0091)	(0.0354)	(0.0152)
1973	0.0880	0.1891	0.1285
	(0.0088)	(0.0395)	(0.0157)
1974	0.1031	0.2381	0.1313
	(0.0119)	(0.0566)	(0.0156)
1975	0.1115	0.2009	0.1258
	(0.0146)	(0.0388)	(0.0163)
1976	0.1167	0.1905	0.1202
	(0.0166)	(0.0350)	(0.0159)

CAPM method generates cost-of-capital estimates that were always greater than the E/P ratio but smaller than those of Gordon's model in all but the first 2 years.

Besides CAPM method to estimate cost of capital, the Arbitrage Pricing Theory (APT) model can also be used to estimate cost of equity capital. Lee and Cummins (1998) have used both CAPM and APT models to estimate the cost of equity capital for property/casualty insurers. In addition they have also used Granger and Newbold (1978) conditional efficiency model to estimate composite cost of equity estimation methods by combining the cost of capital estimated from CAPM and that from APT.

12.7. M&M's Cross-Sectional Method

M&M (1966) developed a theoretical expression for the value of a firm from which the firm's cost of capital could be derived. This relationship can be used (as it was by M&M for the utility industry) to estimate the cost of capital for an industry or for a group of firms in a similar risk class. The theoretical derivation will be discussed as well as the issues involved in the estimation.

12.7.1. *The Cost of Capital*

M&M assumed a perpetual stream of earnings from real assets, and a constant capitalization rate (ρ), at which the market discounts the uncertain pure (unlevered) equity stream of earnings for some risk classes and perfect markets. With these assumptions, the value of a levered firm can be expressed as:

$$V = \frac{\overline{X}(1 - \tau_c)}{\rho_k} + \tau_c D \tag{12.19}$$

where

V = Sum of the market value of all securities issued by the firm;
$\bar{X}$ = Expected level of average annual earnings generated by current assets;
τ_c = Corporate tax rate;
ρ_k = Cost of unlevered equity capital in a certain designated risk class;
D = Market value of a firm's debt.

The cost of capital for the levered firm can be found by partitioning the value of the firm and its constituent financial sources:

$$V = S + D + P, \tag{12.20}$$

where

S = Common equity;
D = Debt;
P = Preferred equity

and expressing investment in new real assets as:

$$\frac{\Delta V}{\Delta A} = \frac{\Delta S^0}{\Delta A} + \frac{\Delta S^n}{\Delta A} + \frac{\Delta P}{\Delta A} + \frac{\Delta D}{\Delta A} = \frac{\Delta S^0}{\Delta A} + 1, \tag{12.21}$$

where

ΔV = Change of market value of a firm;
$\Delta A = \Delta S^n + \Delta P + \Delta D$ = New investment in real asset;
ΔS^0 = Change in the market value of the shares held by the current owners of the firm;

ΔS^n = Value of any new common stock issued;
ΔP = Value of any new preferred stock issued;
ΔD = Value of any new debt issued.

This solution says that the increase in value of the firm arising from investment in new real assets can involve simultaneous increases in the value of equity, and in new preferred, as well as issuance of new tax-deductible debt. Substituting the definition of value defined in Eq. (12.20) into Eq. (12.21), we obtain

$$\frac{\Delta V}{\Delta A} = \frac{\Delta S^0}{\Delta A} + 1 = \frac{\Delta \overline{X}(1-\tau_c)}{\Delta A \rho_k} + \frac{\tau_c \Delta D}{\Delta A}, \tag{12.22}$$

where τ_c = corporate tax rate.

Since new investment will be undertaken only if the value of current shareholders' equity will increase, $\Delta S^0/\Delta A$ must be positive and:

$$(1-\tau_c)\frac{\Delta \overline{X}}{\Delta A} > \rho_k \left[1 - \tau_c \left(\frac{\Delta D}{\Delta A}\right)\right] = C. \tag{12.23}$$

Thus, since the rate-of-return on a new asset must be greater than the cost of capital, $\rho_k[1-\tau_c(\Delta D/\Delta A)]$ represents the firm's cost of capital or required yield on a tax-adjusted base (C).

Assuming a firm can invest annually an amount equal to $100 \times k\%$ of its tax-adjusted earnings ($\bar{X}(1-\tau)$) on which it will earn a rate-of-return (ρ^*) greater than its cost of capital (C), for a period of years (n), the expression for the value of a firm will be:

$$V = (1-\tau_c)\overline{X} + \tau_c D + K\overline{X}(1-\tau_c)\left[\frac{\rho^* - C}{C(1+C)}\right] n \tag{12.24}$$

where K = investment as a percentage of tax-adjusted earnings ($K \gtreqless 1$).

The added growth term contains three separate components: the level of investment opportunities (represented by ($K\bar{X}(1-\tau_c)$)), the time period over which the investment opportunity will persist (n), and the size of the profitability of the investments represented by $[(\rho^* - C)/(C(1+C))]n$.

Using Eq. (12.24), it is thus possible to estimate the market capitalization rate (and thus the cost of capital) of a group of firms by performing a cross-sectional regression of the market value of the firm's equity on the expected average earnings of the firm, the market value of debt, and the growth resulting from the above-average investment opportunities.

12.7.2. *Regression Formulation and Empirical Results*

The above analysis suggests as a cross-sectional regression:

$$(V - \tau_c D) = a_0 + a_1 \overline{X}(1 - \tau_c) + a_2(\text{growth potential}) + \varepsilon, \tag{12.25}$$

where V, τ_c, D, and $\bar{X}$ are variables as desired earlier; a_0, a_1, and a_2 are regression parameters, and ε is the residual term of a regression.

Several problems must be addressed concerning the specific form of the regression. The problems involved and the solutions provided by M&M illustrate several important issues involved in regression estimation.

First, some quantifiable estimate must be made for the growth-component variable of the firm's value. The variable used by M&M for the investment opportunity level was a linear 5-year average growth rate of assets, multiplied by the current total assets:

$$\Delta \bar{A} = \left(\frac{A_t - A_{t-5}}{A_t} \right) \frac{1}{5} \cdot A_t. \tag{12.26}$$

It should be noted that this proxy was suggested by the stable pattern of investment present in the utility industry at the time in question; it should not be expected to be generally applicable to all types of industries.

Secondly, empirical research (Gordon, 1962) has suggested that market capitalization rates vary systematically with the size of the firm within the same industry. Thus, a constant coefficient a_0 was added to embody the scale effect, and the coefficient of the earnings variable can be considered the marginal capitalization rate of the industry. The size and sign of the constant coefficient therefore contains information concerning the average capitalization rate. If the sign is negative, the marginal rate would be less than the average, leading to the conclusion that the capitalization rate tends to rise with increasing size of the firm.

Thirdly, efficient and unbiased estimates of the OLS coefficients can be obtained only if the variance of the error term is constant, and the covariance between the independent variables and the error term is zero. In the regression shown in Eq. (12.25) the standard deviation of the error term is not a constant, but varies proportionately to the size of the firm. To avoid heteroscedasticity of regression residuals (the variance of residual changes over observations), the equation must be adjusted to compensate for the dominance of the large companies. M&M considered two approaches: (1) to divide through by $(V - \tau_c D)$, expressing the equation in a yield form, or (2) weighting the observations by some adjustment for firm size.

In rejecting approach (1), M&M argued that the stochastic elements in $(V - \tau_c D)$ would be independent of the terms in the numerators, leading to upward bias in the coefficients for growth and firm size, and a resulting downward bias in the estimate of the cost of capital. The second approach (deflating each variable by a scale factor, the book value of total assets) adjusts the standard deviation of the error term to firm size. Thus, M&M adjusted Eq. (12.25) to:

$$\frac{(V - \tau_c D)}{A} = \frac{a_0}{A} + a_1 \overline{X} \frac{(1 - \tau_c)}{A} + a_2 \frac{\Delta \overline{A}}{A} + u. \qquad (12.27)$$

where $u = \varepsilon / A$. With this reformulation, the regression equation is expected to be homogeneous, that is, to have no constant term, and the term A, total assets, is used to avoid heteroscedasticity.

An additional problem beyond that of heteroscedasticity are the possible errors of measurement associated with the earnings term. Since anticipated average earnings are essentially unobservable, accounting-statement estimates of earnings must be used instead. Therefore, the true relation between value and anticipated earnings, when replaced by the observable estimates, implies a simultaneous system of relationships:

$$V_i^* = \alpha X_i^* + \sum_j \beta_j Z_{ij} + u_i, \qquad (12.28')$$

$$X_i = X_i^* + v_i, \qquad (12.28'')$$

$$X_i^* = \sum_j \delta_j Z_{ij} + w_i, \qquad (12.28''')$$

where

$V_i^* = \dfrac{V_i - \tau_c D_i}{A_i}$;

$X_i^* = \dfrac{\overline{X}(1 - \tau_c)}{A_i}$ = (the true anticipated earnings);

α, β_j, and δ_j are regression coefficients;

u_i and w_i are regression residuals;

v_i = Measurement errors associated with current earnings;

X_i = Observable estimate of earnings derived from the accounting statements;

Z_{ij} = Other relevant variables determining earnings.

The firm's values as represented by the system of Eqs. (12.28′–12.28‴) is related to anticipated earnings and a set of explanatory variables which may also be correlated with the firm's anticipated earnings.

In addition, the earnings variable used in the regression only approximates the true value of anticipated earnings, varying by the error of measurement, v_i. The system represents the simultaneous determination of two endogenous variables, V^* and X, by the Z_j exogenous variables. In regressing:

$$V_i^* = \alpha X_i + \sum \beta_j Z_{ij} + U', \tag{12.29}$$

the coefficients will be biased. The coefficient for earnings, α, will have a downward bias.

In an attempt to remedy the simultaneous-equation bias, M&M is used an instrumental-variable approach.[2] In this approach, the endogenous variable X is first regressed against all the instrumental variables, Z_j, to obtain estimates of the various coefficients, $\ddot{a}_j$. These estimates (j) are then used to develop a new variable, X, which is:

$$\hat{X}_i^* = \sum \hat{\delta}_j Z_{ij}. \tag{12.30}$$

Depending on the choice of Z_j, the new estimate of earnings, $\hat{X}_i^*$, should be relatively free of error measurement. It can then be used in the second-stage regression as the earnings variable. The resulting estimates of α and β can be shown to be consistent.

The adjustments are complete, and the regression equation (12.28′) can be used to find and estimate of the pure equity cost of capital for a group of firms in the same risk class. With this estimate, estimates of the cost of debt and the cost of levered equity capital can be made, and the firm's total cost of capital can be ascertained. The M&M's total cost of capital and the usual definition of the weighted cost of capital are equivalent, as indicated in Section 12.4 of this chapter.[3]

Higgins used a valuation model to estimate the cost of equity capital in a way that was similar to M&M's (1961) method. He divided the value of a firm into two components — a perpetual component and a growth component. The perpetual component was represented by Y_0/k, where Y_0

[2]The instrumental-variable approach to eliminate the simultaneous-equation bias is discussed in Appendix 2.B of Chapter 2.

[3]Using the model discussed in this section, M&M (1966) used data of 64 electric utility firms to estimate the average cost of capital for 1954, 1956, and 1957. The results can be found in Table 10 of the 1966 paper.

is the current earnings available to common shareholders, and k is the cost of equity capital. The present value of future growth to equity shareholders can be represented by:

$$\frac{(r-k)\,\pi I_0}{k}\int_0^T e^{(g-k)t}\,dt, \tag{12.31}$$

where k is the cost of equity capital, r is the average return on equity, π is the proportion of total assets financed by equity (constant over time), I_0 is the investment at time 0, and g is the constant exponential growth rate for investment.

Evaluating the integral yields:

$$\left(\frac{1}{g-k}\right)[e^{(g-k)T}-1].$$

If $(g-k)T$ is small, a Taylor-series expression yields $1-e^{(g-k)^T}\approx(k-g)T$; therefore:

$$\left(\frac{1}{g-k}\right)[(-1)(1-e^{(g-k)T})]=\left(\frac{1}{g-k}\right)[(-1)(k-g)T]=T. \tag{12.32}$$

Therefore, the present value of future growth to equity shareholders is:

$$\frac{(r-k)\pi I_0 T}{k} \tag{12.33}$$

and

$$S_0=\frac{Y_0}{k}+\frac{(r-k)\pi I_0 T}{k}, \tag{12.34}$$

where S_0 = market value of equity. Also,

$$k=\frac{Y_0+r\pi I_0 T}{S_0+\pi I_0 T}, \tag{12.35}$$

where $r\pi I_0$ is the amount of income from the new investment and $\pi I_0 T$ is the cost of acquiring this income stream, which is the equity-financed portion of the investment.

To adjust this model to a perpetual-growth model you need only to assume that $T=\infty$ and require all new equity financing to be internal. Assuming $k>g$:

$$\begin{aligned} S_0 &= \frac{Y_0}{k}+\frac{(r-k)\pi I_0}{k(k-g)} \\ &= \frac{Y_0k-\pi I_0k+r\pi I_0-gY_0}{k(k-g)}. \end{aligned}$$

If b = retention rate, and with no external equity financing $bY_0 = \pi I_0$, and $rb = g$, then:

$$r\pi I_0 = rbY_0,$$

$$gY_0 = rbY_0$$

and

$$S_0 = \frac{Y_0 k - \pi I_0 k}{k(k-g)} = \frac{Y_0 - \pi I_0}{k-g}. \tag{12.36}$$

Since $Y_0 - \pi I_0 = D_0$ (where D_0 is the amount of current dividends):

$$S_0 = \frac{D_0}{k-g}. \tag{12.37}$$

Here, we see perpetual growth as a special case of finite growth with $T = \infty$ and all equity financing being internal.

Assuming that k and T are the same for all sample firms, the following model is used for estimating the cost of equity capital:

$$S = a_2 Y + a_3 r\pi I + a_4 \pi I + \mu, \tag{12.38}$$

where $a_2 = 1/k$, $a_3 = T/k$, $a_4 = -T$, and μ = error term. The estimated cost of capital is $1/\hat{a}_2$ or $-\hat{a}_4/\hat{a}_3$. This equation is non-linear in its coefficients since $a_2 = -a_3/a_4$. Therefore, we can get a non-linear estimate of the cost of capital as well.

This model can be added to by including a size variable as a surrogate for omitted risk variables and a constant term, as well as dividing the equation by total assets, A, to reduce heteroscedasticity, gives us:

$$\frac{S}{A} = a_0 + a_1 \frac{1}{A} + a_2 \frac{Y}{A} + a_3 \frac{r\pi I}{A} + a_4 \frac{\pi I}{A} + e, \tag{12.39}$$

where a_0 is the size value and a_1 is the constant term.

The results obtained from using this model for all 81 electric utilities for the period 1960–1968 showed that all the signs of the coefficients were as expected and almost 75% of the variation on the dependent variables was explained. Most of the regression coefficients were statistically significant at the 5% confidence level.

The cost of capital (k) should exceed the bond yield in every period as well as the earnings-to-price ratio, in order to have extraordinary growth ($r > k$), and the results show that it does.

As for the OLS estimation of the cost of capital, it should exceed the bond yield and the earnings-to-price ratio for each period in order to achieve extraordinary growth ($r > k$). This is shown to be true. The cost of capital was, on average, 1.9% greater than the bond yield and 1.2% greater than the earnings-to-price ratio. Also, the cost of capital should vary with the bond yield, and it does on both upturns and downturns.

This model also allowed for a non-linear estimate of the cost of capital. If there is a sizable difference between linear and non-linear estimates, this would imply that the constraint on the coefficients is fundamentally inconsistent with the valuation model and thus we infer that the valuation equation or its specification is in error. This was not the case, as the estimates differ, on average, by a little over 20 points.

Another estimate resulting from this model was of the time horizon in which extraordinary growth is expected. The estimates were stable, ranging from 3.6 to 4.8 years (except for 1967).

Higgins also reran the model with an added variable, D/A, D being total dividends. (Results of this model appear in his Table 3.) The coefficient of this variable was negative in all but 1 year, and when it was positive, it had a t-value of only 0.26. It may not be correct to say that dividends depress equity values, but they do not seem to add to them. This supports M&M's well-known theory that dividends are irrelevant in valuing equity securities.

Turning our attention to M&M's (1966) results, the direct least-squares estimates of the cost of equity capital show good multiple R values, between 0.83 and 0.88 when a constant term is used and between 0.79 and 0.88 when the constant term is constrained to equal zero. Comparing the two estimates of the cost of equity capital, as shown below, we see that the omission of the constant term gives us lower costs of capital:

The direct least squares estimates

	k_e with constant	k_e without constant
1957	0.0637	0.0625
1956	0.0641	0.0602
1954	0.0730	0.0521

The two-stage estimates

	k_e with constant	k_e without constant
1957	0.0617	0.0621
1956	0.0641	0.0599
1951	0.0552	0.0508

These estimates imply that the k_e obtained from the two-stage estimates are smaller than those direct least-squares estimates. We would expect the reduction in bias to be a result of fluctuations in earnings, when the two-stage estimation method is applied.

M&M hypothesized that the constant term was really zero. Below we show the values for the direct least-squares and two-stage estimates:

	Direct	Two-stage
1957	0.164	0.004
1956	0.057	0.054
1954	0.274	0.072

The reduction of bias on the estimates through the use of the two-stage process also seems to support the hypothesis that the constant term is zero. M&M state that the reason the constant term was significantly different from zero for the direct least-squares cases was that the error of measurement for earnings was large. This error is reduced by the two-stage process.

12.8. Chase Cost of Capital

Chase Manhattan Bank (CM) has developed a method for estimating the cost of capital for a firm which is a useful blend of the CAPM method and M&M's firm value relationship.[4] In a three-step process, CM first estimates

[4]Basic concepts of this method can be found in Stein (1980) and Copeland and Weston (2003).

the equity cost of capital of a firm, then adjusts this cost-of-capital figure for financial risk (the use of leverage by the firm) to arrive at an estimate of the unlevered equity cost of capital. Then the total cost of capital is estimated, using the unlevered cost of capital and an estimate of the future long-term debt-to-equity ratio.

To arrive at an estimate of the levered equity cost of capital, CM uses three variables:

(a) A present-period estimate of the long-term government bond yield.
(b) The premium expected to be earned on all stocks on the New York Stock Exchange (NYSE) over the government bond yield to compensate equity investors for the higher risk they bear. This is the risk premium for stocks over long-term bonds.
(c) The expected beta of the company's common shares, which is defined as the index expressing the relative risk of holding the company's shares compared to holding an average of all the stocks on the NYSE.

Thus, CM bases its estimates of the levered equity cost of capital on both past data (the company beta, derived from past market behavior) and forecasts of long-term financial data (the long-term bond yield and risk premium).

In the second step, CM uses a modified version of the M&M valuation equation to arrive at an estimate of the pure equity cost of capital. Starting with an expression for firm value:

$$V = \frac{NOPAT}{C} + \tau_c D, \tag{12.40}$$

where

NOPAT = Unleveraged net operating after-tax profit of the company,
C = Pure equity cost of capital.

CM then substitutes an equivalent expression for value (V):

$$V = E + D, \tag{12.41}$$

where E = the market value of equity. Substituting Eq. (11.40) into Eq. (8.41), they get

$$E + D = \frac{NOPAT}{C} + \tau_c D \tag{12.42}$$

or equivalently,

$$NOPAT = C(E + D - \tau_c D). \tag{12.43}$$

CM then defines the levered cost of equity (Y) as the normalized net earnings (NE) divided by the stockholder's equity (E) or:

$$Y = \frac{NE}{E} = \frac{NOPAT - bD(1 - \tau_c)}{E}, \tag{12.44}$$

where b = average rate of interest on company debt, and τ_c = corporate tax rate. Substituting Eq. (12.43) into Eq. (12.44), they get:

$$Y = \frac{C(E + D - \tau_c D) - bD(1 - \tau_c)}{E}, \tag{12.45}$$

and, solving for the unlevered cost of equity,

$$C = \frac{Y + (1 - \tau_c)\left(\frac{D}{E}\right) b}{1 + (1 - \tau_c)\left(\frac{D}{E}\right)}. \tag{12.46}$$

To calculate Eq. (12.46), CM uses:

(a) The marginal federal and state income tax over the past 5 years of the company's operations;
(b) The historic debt-to-equity ratio or the average short-term plus long-term debt (including capitalized leases) divided by equity, deferred items, and minority interest during the last 5 years;
(c) The average interest rate on short-term and long-term debt (including imputed lease interest) over the last 5 years;
(d) The expected marginal federal and state income-tax rate for the future.

In the last step, CM uses Eqs. (12.13) or (12.23) to arrive at the firm's cost of total capital:

$$C^* = C\left[1 - (\tau_c)\left(\frac{D}{CE}\right)\right], \tag{12.47}$$

where CE = future projected capital employed and D = the target total debt for the firm.

Thus, the CM method involves adjusting the CAPM-derived cost of equity capital to determine a pure (unlevered) equity cost of capital, similar to M&M's ρ as defined in Chapter 7. From this figure, CM then derives a total-firm cost of capital, using essentially M&M's relationship for the firm cost of capital.

Now an example using Staley Corporation will be used to show how the procedure described in Eqs. (12.40) through (12.47) can be used to estimate

(i) leveraged cost equity capital, (ii) unleveraged cost of capital, and (iii) cost of total capital.

If the long-term government bond yield, R, is 8%, the premium required for common stocks over the bond yield, P, is 5%, and the relative risk, β, in holding Staley stock versus average stock is 0.95, then Y, the cost of Staley's equity capital (including historic financial risk), is as follows:

$$\begin{aligned} Y &= R + \beta(P) \\ &= 8\% + 0.95(5\%) = 12.75\%. \end{aligned}$$

This is a forward-looking rate based on a backward-looking risk characteristic.

In the second step, that proportion of the risk attached to the past debt ratio (the financial risk) is removed in order to determine C, the cost of capital based on business risk alone. This cost of equity capital is considered to be a fundamental characteristic of the risk the firm faces in its particular kind of business, and this may be assumed to continue in the future unless the firm's kind of business is changing significantly, or is judged to have a different risk characteristic due to an economic or a technological change. The second three items in the list are needed to calculate this C and the cost of equity capital when debt is zero. The equation necessary to do this is derived from the cost of equity capital given from Step (a) in which the presence of debt financing is the sum of the return required for business risk plus the return required for financial risk or:

$$Y = C + (1 - \tau_c)(C - b)\left(\frac{D}{E}\right), \tag{12.45'}$$

where

τ_c = Marginal tax rate over the past 5 years;
b = Interest rate on all debt over the past 5 years;
D/E = Average total debt to total equity over the past 5 years. (Debt included capitalized leases, and equity includes deferred items and minority interest.)

The above equation must be rearranged to make it explicit in C. The result is:

$$C = \frac{Y + (1 - \tau_c)\left(\frac{D}{E}\right)(b)}{1 + (1 - \tau_c)\left(\frac{D}{E}\right)}.$$

If the marginal tax rate was 50%, D/E averaged 60%, and the interest rate was 7% over the last 5 years, then C, the cost of capital for business risk alone (no debt) is calculated as:

$$\begin{aligned}
C &= \frac{12.75\% + (1-0.5)(0.60)(7\%)}{1+(1-0.5)(0.60)}\\
&= \frac{12.75\% + 2.10\%}{1+0.30}\\
&= \frac{14.85\%}{1.30} = 11.42\%.
\end{aligned}$$

In the third step, the cost of total capital, C^*, is calculated by factoring in the projected financial risk based on the target debt ratio, D/CE, which is expected in the future. The result will always be less than C for prudent levels of debt because the after-tax cost of debt, which is lower than the cost of equity, lowers the total cost of capital, C^*, despite the higher risk due to debt financing. If the target D/CE is expected to be 40%, then C^* is as follows:

$$\begin{aligned}
C^* &= C\left[1-(\tau_c)\left(\frac{D}{CE}\right)\right]\\
&= 11.42\%[1-0.5(0.40)] = 11.42\%(0.80)\\
&= 9.14\% \text{ (all figures are hypothetical)}.
\end{aligned}$$

The target-debt ratio (total debt plus capitalized leases, divided by total debt plus capitalized leases, plus equity, plus deferred items, plus minority interest) for a firm is useful for the investor to know because it is an important factor in setting the cost-of-capital rate, C^*, which the firm will use to discount future earnings in order to estimate the intrinsic value of the company's stock. If the company does not publicly announce its target-debt ratio, the investor must come to his or her own conclusion as to what average debt ratio the company will have in the future. The point is that, without some knowledge of the company's intentions regarding the future debt ratio, or at least some information about future capital spending and dividend payouts, the investor will feel some uncertainty and will discount future earnings more heavily as a result of this uncertainty. Investors may bid down the price of the company's stock more than if information about capital spending, profitability of new investment, and target-debt levels were available to the public.

The initial information needed to calculate the cost of capital is largely market-determined. The estimate of the long-term government bond yield may be obtained from banks and investment houses. The risk premium for average stocks over the bond yield is a judgmental item, based partly on the historic premium over many years, but mostly on current opinions of the future with its additional risks of increased government regulation and higher levels of inflation. Merrill Lynch and Value Line compute betas for stocks listed on the NYSE and sell this information for a fee.

There are some problems associated with cost-of-capital applications. In the paper entitled "Problems with the Concept of the Cost of Capital," Haley and Schall (HS) (1978) indicate that the concept of the cost of capital has historically served three purposes: (i) as a guide for financial decisions, (ii) as a standard for investment decisions, and (iii) as a link between financing and investment decisions. HS carefully investigate the conditions under which certain cost-of-capital concepts can become either misleading or irrelevant. By reviewing M&M's cost-of-capital definitions, HS demonstrate that the WACC can be misleading and inefficient because income streams may not be perpetual, discount rates may change over time and a firm's risk class is not independent of its financial structure. In addition, HS demonstrate that there are two possible problems in using the cost of capital as an indicator for undertaking investment decisions: (1) there may be a different cost of capital for different risk levels and for different time periods, and (2) if the rate-of-return that an investment must earn in order to be accepted differs when calculated for internal and for external financing, a unique cost of capital does not exist for the investment. Empirically, Lee, Linke, and Zumwalt (1981) have demonstrated that the cost of capital estimates obtained from alternative methods as discussed in this chapter are not necessarily highly correlated. Other important references related to total cost of capital and divisional cost of capital include: (1) Arditti (1980), (2) King (1970), (3) Gordon and Halpern (1974), and (4) Fuller and Kerr (1981).

12.9. Summary

Based upon the valuation models and capital structure theories presented earlier, six alternative cost-of-capital determination and estimation methods are discussed in detail. These methods are (i) average earnings yield method, (ii) DCF method, (iii) WACC method, (iv) CAPM method, (v) M&M's cross-section method, and (vi) Chase's method.

The interrelationship among different cost-of-capital estimation methods were explored in some detail. The relative advantages between different estimation methods were also indirectly explored. The six cost-of-capital estimation methods that were discussed in this chapter give managers enough background to choose the appropriate cost-of-capital estimation method for utility-regulation determination, capital-budgeting decisions, and financial planning and forecasting. According to a surveyed paper by Graham and Harvey (2001), a firm's valuation technique depends on its size and firm risk, rather than the project's risk, and the most popular cost of capital methods include CAPM, average stock returns, and multi-beta CAPM.

Problem Set

1. Discuss five alternative methods for cost-of-capital estimation. Use the criteria of theory and practice to evaluate the relative advantages of these methods.
2. How can we integrate CAPM into the M&M valuation model to improve cost-of-capital estimation?
3. Discuss three alternative methods for growth-rate estimation.
4. Can WACC be theoretically justifiable? Why or why not?
5. Discuss how CAPM can be used to estimate the cost of equity capital in terms of the information needed.
6. Company AAA is an all equity firm with a beta of 0.8. The market risk premium is 10% and the risk-free rate is 6%. The company is considering a project that will generate annual after-tax cash flow of $320,000 at year-end for 5 years. The project requires an immediate investment of $1.3 million. If the project has the same risk as the firm as a whole, should Company AAA take the project?
7. The correlation between the returns on Company BBB and the returns on S&P 500 is 0.675. The variance of the returns on Company BBB is 0.004225 and the variance of the returns on S&P 500 is 0.001467. What is the beta of Company BBB stock?
8. Company CCC is a levered firm with a debt-to-equity ratio of 0.25. Assume that the cost of equity is 15% and cost of debt is 8%. The corporation tax rate is 30%. If a new company project has the same risk as the overall firm, what is the weighted average cost of capital for the project?

9. Company DDD has an equity beta of 1.2 and a debt-to-equity ratio of 1.2. The expected return on the market is 15% and the risk-free rate is 6%. The before tax cost of debt capital is 9%. The corporation tax rate is 35%. Please calculate Company's weighted average cost of capital.
10. Calculate the weighted average cost of capital for Company EEE. The book value of Company EEE's outstanding debt is $50 million. Currently the debt is trading at 130% of book value and is priced to yield 10%. The 6 million outstanding shares of Company EEE's stock are trading at $25 per share. The required return on Company EEE's stock is 16%. The tax rate is 35%.
11. Define the following:

    (a) Average earnings yields versus current earnings yield;
    (b) Cost of retained earnings and cost of new equity;
    (c) Weighted cost of capital;
    (d) Marginal cost of capital;
    (e) Unleveraged cost of capital.

12. Discuss three possible methods for estimating the growth rate of DPS.
13. Discuss how the M&M theory and the CAPM can be integrated together to estimate the unleveraged cost of capital.
14. The current stock price of XYZ Company is $100. It is expected that the company will pay a $10 dividend per share in the next period. If growth rate of the dividend is 5%, what is the cost of equity capital?

    (1) How is the investor's required rate-of-return related to the firm's cost of capital?
    (2) How can an analyst use a firm's cost of capital when making financial decisions?
    (3) What effect do taxes have on the firm's cost of capital?
    (4) What effect do flotation costs have on the firm's cost of capital?
    (5) What methods can a firm use to determine its cost of debt?
    (6) Why are there two different costs of equity capita?
    (7) Explain the various ways to estimate the future growth of a firm's dividends.
    (8) What are the advantages and disadvantages of using the constant dividend growth model to calculate the cost of equity capital?
    (9) What are the pros and cons of using the SML to calculate the cost of equity capital?
    (10) Which method — book value or market value — for determining the weights in the WACC calculation is considered appropriate? Why?

(11) How is the riskiness of a project under consideration by a firm related to the cost of capital that the firm uses to evaluate the project?
(12) How can the CAPM help an analyst find a risk-adjusted discount rate?
(13) Why do the break points arise in a firm's marginal cost of capital curve?
(14) Dunbar Corporation is evaluating projects in the following areas. See if you can identify a real firm that can be used in the pure-play approach to assist Dunbar's analysis:

Project A: An educational TV station.
Project B: Computer software development.
Project C: Cellular telephone communications.
Project D: Copier machines.

(15) How can the accounting beta approach be used to help Dunbar evaluate its proposed projects in Question 14?
(16) What are the appropriate conditions for using the weighted average cost of capital as a project's discount rate?
(17) How do fiscal and monetary policies affect a firm's cost of capital?
(18) Explain why the constant dividend growth model and the SML approach, while attempting to measure the same concept, often determine different values for the cost of equity capital.
(19) Comment on the following statement: "Our firm's cost of equity capital is higher than it should be because we increase our dividend every year at a constant rate. According to Eq. 12.6, we can lower our firm's cost of equity capital just by maintaining a constant dividend; in other words, by setting g equal to zero."
(20) What are some of the pros and cons of rationing capital?
(21) Discuss how lowering agency costs may result in a lower cost of capital.

15. Calculate the after-tax cost of debt under each of the following conditions:

(a) Interest rate = 10%; tax rate = 0%.
(b) Interest rate = 10%; tax rate = 50%.
(c) Interest rate = 10%; tax rate = 100%.

16. The information needed to calculate cost of capital for GM is as follows:

Risk-free interest rate = 8.5%
Beta of GM = 0.46

Market rate-of-return = 10.55%
D/E ratio = 0.36
Target D/E ratio = 0.4
Corporate tax rate = 40%
Interest rate on all debt = 10%

(a) Calculate the cost of capital using the CAPM method.
(b) Calculate the cost of capital using the Chase method.

17. ABC Company's capital is as follows:

Capital	Percentage of Capital (%)	Cost (%)
Common stock	60	12
Preferred stock	2	14
Debt	38	10

Calculate the weighted average cost of capital for ABC Company. (Assume the marginal corporate tax rate is 40%.)

18. Sweet Food's stock sells for $100 a share, and it is believed that the current year's dividend on the stock will be $5 per share. The past earnings growth rate is 10%, and it is expected that this will continue. The current interest rate on new debt is 8%. The firm's marginal tax rate is 40%. The firm's capital structure, considered optimal, is as follows.

Debt	$200,000
Common equity	$300,000

Answer these questions:

(a) Calculate the after-tax cost of new debt and of common equity, assuming new equity comes only from retained earnings.
(b) Find the marginal cost of capital, assuming no common stock is sold.
(c) Find the marginal cost of capital if new common stock is sold with a flotation cost of 10%. (The cost of debt is constant.)

19. Walker Public Relations, Inc. has common stock which currently sells for $40 per share. The most recent dividend was $1.50 per share (at $t = 0$) and they are expected to grow at a 10% rate indefinitely. New common stock can be sold to net the company $38 per share.

    (a) Find the cost of internal equity (retained earnings).
    (b) Find the cost of new common stock.

20. The XBC Company can sell debt with an 8% coupon rate, a $1,000 par value and 10 years to maturity. The company will net $975 per bond and has a tax rate of 40%. Find the company's after tax cost of debt.
21. Jackson's Computer Corporation has preferred stock which currently sells on the market for $90 per share. It pays a dividend of 8% on a par value of $100. New preferred stock can be sold with flotation costs of $5 per share. Find the company's cost of preferred stock.
22. White's Cookie Shops, Inc. has a beta of 1.4 and a tax rate of 40%. The risk-free rate of interest is 6% and the expected return on the market is 13%. New common equity can be sold with flotation costs of 5%.

    (a) Find the company's cost of internal equity.
    (b) Find the company's cost of new common stock.

23. Follen, Inc. has the following optimal capital structure which it considers to be optimal:

Debt	$600,000
Preferred stock	200,000
Common stock	1,200,000
Total value	$2,000,000

Currently the company has $15,000 in retained earnings available for capital investments. The company's tax rate is 46%. Investors expect earnings and dividends to grow at a constant rate of 8% for the indefinite future. Follen will pay a dividend of $1 per share in the coming year ($t = 1$).

New capital can be obtained under the terms identified below:

New Common Stock: New common stock can be sold at the current market price of $20 per share. Flotation costs are $2 per share for the first $30,000 of new common stock sold. Any new stock sold above the $30,000 will entail flotation costs of $3 per share.

Preferred Stock: New preferred stock can be sold to the public at a price of $100 per share and paying an annual dividend of $10 per share. Flotation costs are $5 per share regardless of the amount of preferred stock sold.

Debt: Debt can be sold at a before tax cost of 10%. Investors will pay $1,000 per bond with 10 years until maturity. The coupon rate on the bond is 9.6%. The cost of debt does not change as additional debt is sold.

(a) Find the weights for each of the sources of financing.
(b) Find the breaks in the weighted marginal cost of capital curve.
(c) Find the firm's after tax cost of:
    (1) Debt.
    (2) Preferred stock.
    (3) Internal equity (retained earnings).
    (4) New common stock.
(d) How much of the company's common equity financing will come from new common stock if the company needs to raise:
    (1) $30,000 in total financing.
    (2) $50,000 in total financing.
    (3) $100,000 in total financing.
(e) Compute the firm's weighted marginal cost of capital schedule.
(f) Compute the firm's weighted average cost of capital for $100,000 total financing.

24. Lexington, Inc. has the following capital structure which they consider to be optimal:

Debt	$1,200,000
Preferred stock	800,000
Common stock	2,000,000
Total value	$4,000,000

The firm wishes to raise $900,000 in order to undertake several important investment opportunities. The following information on the cost of sources of funds has been gathered:

Debt: \$200,000 of new 10-year bonds can be sold at \$980 to net the company \$960 per bond if they bear a 10% coupon rate. If more than \$200,000 in debt financing is needed, the company will only net \$940 per bond.

Preferred Stock: Preferred stock can be sold at \$77 to net the company \$75 per share if it carries a 7% dividend on a par value of \$100 per share. These terms prevail regardless of how-much preferred stock is sold.

Common Equity: Common stock is expected to pay a dividend of \$2 per share in the coming year ($t = 1$). The stock is currently selling at \$22 per share and will net the company \$20 per share. Dividends are expected to grow at 7% forever. The firm will have \$200,000 available from retained earnings this year for investment in new capital projects.

The company's tax rate is 50%.

(a) Find the firm's after-tax cost of debt.
(b) Find the firm's cost of preferred stock.
(c) Find the firm's cost of retained earnings.
(d) Find the firm's cost of new common stock.
(e) Find the weights for each of the sources of financing.
(f) Find the breaks in the weighted marginal cost of capital curve.
(g) How much of the \$900,000 will be financed from new common stock?
(h) Compute the WMCC schedule and then prepare the corresponding graph.
(i) Compute the WACC of \$900,000 total financing.
(j) Which projects would be accepted given the above WMCC schedule, if the company faces the following investment schedule:

Project	Cost	IRR
A	\$100,000	25%
B	150,000	20
C	50,000	18
D	100,000	15
E	125,000	13
F	200,000	10
G	100,000	9

(1) **Calculating WACC.** The treasurer for Falcon Enterprises wants to know the weighted average cost of capital for the firm, based on the following information:

Target percent of equity = 65%
Target percent of debt = 35%
Cost of equity = 14%
Pretax cost of debt = 11%
Tax rate = 34%
Compute Falcon's WACC for the treasurer.

(2) **Calculating WACC.** Recomputing Falcon Enterprises' WACC using the information given in Problem 11, but assume that the tax rate has fallen to 25%.

(3) **Calculating WACC.** You are the CRO at Mensa & Company. If the target capital structure weights are 505 debt and 50% equity, calculate the firm's WACC, based on the following information:

Two million shares of stock outstanding;
Current market price of stock = $42;
Total face value of bonds = $80 million;
Bonds currently sell for 90% of face value;
Bond's YTM = 10%;
Risk-free rate = 4%;
Expected return on the stock market = 15%;
Beta = 0.95;
New common stock has a 10% flotation cost;
Tax rate = 30%.

(4) **Calculated Weighted Average Cost of Capital.** LMN Corporation's stock sells for $50 per share. Its expected dividend is $2.50 per share and the firm's growth rate is 10%. It is in the 30% tax bracket. The current rate of interest for the firm's bonds, sold at par, is 8%. New bonds can be sold with a flotation cost of $30 per bond. The market value of the firm's capital is:

Debt	$400,000
Equity	$600,000
Total capital	$1,000,000

(a) What are the after-tax costs of debt and equity for this firm?
(b) What is the weighted average cost of capital (WACC) for this firm?
(c) How would this WACC change if the firm runs out of retained earnings and a new stock issue has flotation costs of 5%?

(5) **Calculated Weighted Average Cost of Capital.** Q Corp has the following capital structure, which also is equal to its target capital structure:

Debt	\$1,000,000
Preferred Equity	1,000,000
Common Equity	2,000,000
Total capital	\$4,000,000

Currently, the firm has \$50,000 in retained earnings available for investment. The company's tax rate is 30%. Investors expect the firm's dividend to grow at an 8% rate. It currently pays \$1.00 per share in dividends. Its stock price is \$15 per share.

New capital can be raised under the following conditions:

- New 20 year bonds can be sold at par with a coupon rate of 7% and a par value of \$1,000. Flotation costs for new bond issues are \$50 per bond.
- New preferred stock can be sold to the public at a price of \$50 per share with an annual dividend of 6%. Flotation costs are 10% of the amount of preferred sold.
- New common stock can be sold at a price of \$15 per share. Flotation costs are \$2.00 per share for new equity.

(a) What are the weights for each source of financing?
(b) What is the company's cost of debt, preferred equity, retained earnings, and new common equity?
(c) Where are the break points in the firm's marginal cost of capital curve?
(d) How much new common equity is needed to raise:

(1) \$90,000 of new capital?
(2) \$150,000 of new capital?

(e) What is the marginal cost of capital for each of the levels of financing in Part (d) above?
(f) Draw the firm's marginal cost of capital schedule.

Appendix 12.A. Derivative of the Basic Equilibrium Market Price of Stock and its Implications

Following Lintner (1963), the basic price equilibrium condition can be defined as

$$\frac{y_d + d\ln P_t}{dt} = k_t, \tag{12.A.1}$$

where

$y_d = D_t/P_t$ = dividend yield,
$d\ln p_t/dt = \frac{1}{P}\frac{dP}{dt}$ = Capital gain yield,
k_t = Required rates-of-return.

Equation (12.A.1) is a first-order differential equation; it can be rewritten as

$$\frac{dP_t}{dt} - kP_t = -D_t. \tag{12.A.2}$$

Following Chiang (1974, pp. 436–439), Eq. (12.A.2) is not an exact differential equation; however, it has a known integrating factor $e^{\int -kdt}$. Using this integrating factor and $D_t = D_0 e^{gt}$ (D_0 = dividend per share in current period), we have

$$\begin{aligned} P_t &= e^{\int kdt}\left[-\int D_0 e^{gt} e^{-kt} + C\right] \\ &= e^{kt}\left[-D_0 \int \frac{e^{gt-kt}}{g-k} d(gt-kt) + C\right] \\ &= \begin{cases} e^{kt}\left[\dfrac{D_0}{k-g} e^{gt-kt} + C\right] & \text{(general solution)}, \qquad (12.A.3a) \\[2ex] D_0 \dfrac{e^{gt}}{k-g} & \text{(special solution)}. \qquad (12.A.3b) \end{cases} \end{aligned}$$

Since the constant $C = P_0 - [D_0/(k-g)] = 0$, Eq. (12.A.3b) is the special solution of Eq. (12.A.3a). Note that Eq. (12.A.3b) is a continuous-compounding version of the dividend-stream valuation model as discussed in Section 7.3 of Chapter 7.

For the current price of the stock, p_0, Eq. (12.A.3b) reduces to

$$P_0 = \frac{D_0}{k-g} = \frac{XY_0}{k-g} = \frac{XY_0}{k-(g^*-n)}(k > g), \tag{12.A.4}$$

where X is the payout ratio, Y_0 is the current earnings; g^* is the growth related to earnings, and n is the growth rate of new shares.

When $n = 0$ and $g^* = g$, and letting the retention rate $b = 1 - X$, we have

as

$$\frac{dP_0}{db} = Y_0 \left[-\frac{1}{b} + \frac{\frac{dg}{db}}{k-g} \right] \geq 0,$$

as

$$\frac{dP_0}{db} = r \geq \frac{k-g}{b} = \frac{Y_0}{P_0} = y_e, \tag{12.A.5}$$

where r is marginal rate-of-return on investment. In our present case, $dg/db = r$ (see Lintner (1963) for the justification). Equation (12.A.5) implies that the optimizing decision rule is to accept all investments having $r > y_e$, the current yield. However, the current earnings yield (marginal cost of capital) is equal to the k (average cost of capital) only in the special case where the returns to scale for an investment are constant. Hence, a marginal cost-of-capital estimate might be important in capital-budgeting decisions. Arditti and Tysseland (1973) have carefully discussed three different ways to present the marginal cost of capital. These three methods are: (a) the economic (marginal cost = marginal revenue) approach, (b) the discounted cash-flow approach, and (c) the mathematical approach. The criterion derived from the mathematical approach is:

$$r \geq k_1 + \left(\frac{V_0}{I}\right)[k_1 - k_0], \tag{12.A.6}$$

where r is the expected rate-of-return associated with investment I, and k_0 and k_1 are the firm's average cost of capital and new cost of capital, respectively; V_0 is the total market value of the firm. The implications of Eq. (12.A.6) are identical to those in Eq. (12.3).

References for Appendix 12.A

Arditti, FD and MS Tysseland (1973). Three ways to present the marginal cost of capital. *Financial Management*, 4, 63–67.

Chiang, AC (2005). *Fundamental Methods of Mathematical Economics*, 4th ed. New York: McGraw-Hill Book Company.

Lintner, J (1963). The cost of capital and optimal financing of corporate growth. *Journal of Finance* 18, 292–310.

References for Chapter 12

Arditti, FD (1980). A survey of valuation and cost of capital. *Research in Finance*, 2, 1–56.

Brennan, M (1970). Taxes, market valuation, and corporate financial policy. *National Tax Journal*, 23, 417–427.

Chen, AH (1978). Recent developments in the cost of debt capital. *Journal of Finance*, 33, 863–877.

Chen, AH and EH Kim (1979). Theories of corporate debt policy: A synthesis. *Journal of Finance*, 34, 371–384.

Chu, CC (1984). Alternative methods for determining the expected market-risk premium: Theory and evidence. Dissertation, Graduate College of the University of Illinois at Urbana.

Copeland, TE and JF Weston (2003), *Financial Theory and Corporate Policy*, 5th ed. Reading, Mass.: Addison-Wesley Publishing Company.

Fuller, RJ and HS Kerr (1981). Estimating the divisional cost of capital: An analysis of the pure-play technique. *Journal of Finance*, 36, 997–1009.

Graham, JR and CR Harvey (2001). The theory and practice of corporate finance: Evidence from the field. *Journal of Financial Economics*, 60, 2–3, 187–243.

Glenn, DW and RH Litzenberger (1979). An interindustry approach to the econometric cost of capital estimation. *Research in Finance*, 1, 53–75.

Gordon, M (1962). *The Investment, Financing and Valuation of the Corporation.* Homewood: Richard D. Irwin Inc.

Gordon, MJ and PJ Halpern (1974). Cost of capital for a division of a firm. *Journal of Finance*, 29, 1153–1163.

Granger, CWJ and P Newbold (1973). Some comments on the evaluation of economic forecast. *Applied Economics*, 5, 35–47.

Granger, CWJ and P Newbold (1977). *Forecasting Economic Time Series.* New York: Academic Press.

Granger, CWJ and P Newbold (1980). *Forecasting in Business and Economics.* New York: Academic Press.

Haley, CW and LD Schall (1978). Problems with the concept of cost of capital. *Journal of Financial and Quantitative Analysis*, 13, 847–870.

Haley, CW and LD Schall (1979). *The Theory of Financial Decision.* New York: McGraw-Hill Book Company.

Henderson Jr, GV (1979). In defense of the weighted-average cost of capital. *Financial Management*, 8, 57–61.

Higgins, RC (1974). Growth, dividend policy, and cost of capital in the electric utility industry. *Journal of Finance*, 29, 1189–1210.

Ibbotson, RG and RA Sinquefield (1977). Stocks, bonds, bills, and inflations: The past (1926–1976) and the future (1977–2000). In *The Financial Analysts' Research Foundation*, reprinted in *Readings in Investment*, JC Francis, CF Lee, and DE Farrar (eds.), pp. 723–829. New York: McGraw-Hill Book Company.

King, MA (1970). Taxation and the cost of capital. *Review of Economic Studies*, 41, 21–35.

Lee, Alice and JD Cummins (1998). Alternative models for estimating the cost of equity capital for property/casualty insurers. *Review of Quantitative Finance and Accounting*, 10, 235–267.

Lee, CF and CC Chu (1984). Reward to risk, functional form, and market-risk premium determination: Theory and evidence. Unpublished paper, The University of Illinois at Urbana-Champaign.

Lee, CF, CM Linke, and JK Zumwalt (1981). Alternative cost-of-capital estimation methods: An integration and comparison. Paper presented at 1981 *FMA* annual meeting.

Lintner, J (1963). The cost of capital and optimal financing of corporate growth. *Journal of Finance*, 18, 292–310.

Litzenberger, R and K Ramaswamy (1979). The effect of personal taxes and dividends on capital-asset prices: Theory and empirical evidence. *Journal of Financial Economics*, 7, 163–175.

Litzenberger, R, K Ramaswamy, and CV Rao (1971). Estimates of the marginal rate of time preference and average risk aversion of investors in electric utility shares: 1960–1966. *Bell Journal of Economics and Management Science*, 11, 265–277.

Litzenberger, R, K Ramaswamy, and H Sosin (1980). On the CAPM approach to the estimation of a public utility's cost of equity capital. *Journal of Finance*, 35, 369–387.

Merton, RC (1980). On estimating the expected return on the market. *Journal of Financial Economics*, 8, 323–361.

Miller, MH (1971). Debt and taxes. *Journal of Finance*, 32, 261–275.

Miller, MH and F Modigliani (1966). Some estimates of the cost of capital to the utility industry, 1954–57. *American Economic Review*, 56, 333–391.

Modigliani, F and MH Miller (1958). The cost of capital, corporation finance, and the theory of investment. *The American Economic Review*, 58, 261–297.

Modigliani, F and MH Miller (1961). Dividend policy, growth, and the valuation of shares. *Journal of Business*, 34, 411–433.

Modigliani, F and MH Miller (1963). Corporate income tax and the cost of capital: A correction. *American Economic Review*, 53, 433–443.

Stern, JM (1980). *Analytical Methods in Financial Planning*. New York: Chase Manhattan Bank.

Chapter 13

Capital Budgeting Under Certainty

13.1. Introduction

Having examined some of the issues surrounding the cost of capital for a firm, it is time to address a closely related topic, the selection of investment projects for the firm.

To begin an examination of the issues in capital budgeting, we will assume certainty in both the cash flows and the cost of funds. Later these assumptions will be relaxed to deal with uncertainty in estimation, and with the problems involved with inflation.

First, we will discuss a brief overview of the capital budgeting process in Section 13.2. Issues related to using cash flows to evaluate alternative projects will be discussed in Section 13.3. Alternative capital budgeting methods will be investigated in Section 13.4. Comparison of NPV and IRR methods will be explored in Section 13.5. Problems related to differences in economic life will be investigated in Section 13.6. Equivalent annual NPV and annual cost will be explored in Section 13.7 A linear-programming method for capital rationing will be discussed in detail in Section 13.8. Finally, results of this chapter will be summarized in Section 13.9.

13.2. The Capital Budgeting Process

In his article "Myopia, Capital Budgeting and Decision Making," George Pinches (1982) assesses capital budgeting from both the academic and the practitioner's point of view. He presents a framework for discussion of the capital budgeting process, which we use in this chapter.

Capital-budgeting techniques can be used for very simple "operational" decisions concerning whether to replace existing equipment, or they may be used in larger, more "strategic" decisions concerning acquisition or divestiture of a firm or division, expansion into a new product line, or increasing capacity.

The dividing line between operational and strategic decisions varies greatly depending on the organization and its circumstances. The same analytical techniques can be used in either circumstance, but the amount of information required and the degree of confidence in the results of the analysis depend on whether an operational or a strategic decision is being made. Many firms do not require capital budgeting justification for small, routine, or "production" decisions. Even when capital-budgeting techniques are used for operating decisions, the tendency is not to recommend projects unless upper-level management is ready to approve them. Hence, while operating decisions are important and can be aided by capital budgeting analysis, the more important issue for most organizations is the use and applicability of capital-budgeting techniques in strategic planning.

In a general sense, the capital budgeting framework of analysis can be used for many types of decisions, including such areas as acquisition, expansion, replacement, bond refinancing, lease versus buy, and working capital management. Each of these decisions can be approached from either of two perspectives: the *top-down* approach, or the *bottom-up* approach. By *top-down*, we mean the initiation of an idea or a concept at the highest management level, which then filters down to the lower levels of the organization. By *bottom-up*, we mean just the reverse.

For the sake of exposition, we will use a simple four-step process to present an overview of capital budgeting. The steps are (1) identification of areas of opportunity, (2) development of information and data for decisions regarding these opportunities, (3) selection of the best alternative or courses of action to be implemented, and (4) control or feedback of the degree of success or failure of both the project and the decision process itself. While we would expect these steps to occur sequentially, there are many circumstances where the order may be switched or the steps may occur simultaneously.

13.2.1. *Identification Phase*

The identification of potential capital expenditures is directly linked to the firm's overall strategic objective; the firm's position within the various markets it serves; government fiscal, monetary, and tax policies; and the leadership of the firm's management. A widely used approach to strategic planning is based on the concept of viewing the firm as a collection, or

		Relative Market Share	
		Strong	Weak
Market Growth Rate	High	Stars	Question marks
	Low	Cash cows	Dogs

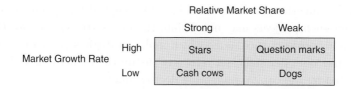

Exhibit 13.1. Boston Consulting Group, Business Strategy Matrix.

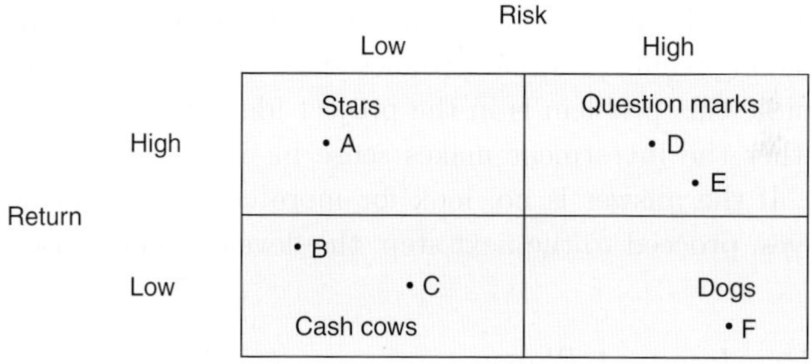

Exhibit 13.2. Capital Budgeting and the Business Strategy Matrix.

portfolio, of assets grouped into strategic business units. This approach, called the Business Strategy Matrix, has been developed and used quite successfully by the Boston Consulting Group. It emphasizes market share and market growth rate in terms of stars, cash cows, question marks, and dogs, as shown in Exhibit 13.1.

Given an organization that follows some sort of strategic planning relative to the Business Strategy Matrix, the most common questions are, How does capital budgeting fit into this framework? and, Are the underlying factors of capital budgeting decisions consistent with the firm's objectives of managing market share?

There are various ways to relate the Business Strategy Matrix to capital budgeting. One of the more appealing is presented in Exhibit 13.2.

This approach highlights the risk-and-return nature of both capital budgeting and business strategy. As presented, the inclusion of risk in the analysis focuses on the identification of projects such as A, which will add sufficient value (return) to the organization to justify the risk that the firm must take. Because of its high risk and low return, project F will not normally be sought after, nor will extensive effort be made to evaluate its usefulness. Marginal projects such as B, C, D, and E require careful scrutiny. In the case of projects such as B, with low risk but also low return, there may be justification for acceptance based on capital budgeting considerations, but such projects may not fit into the firm's strategic plans. On the other hand, projects such as E, which make strategic sense to the organization, may not offer sufficient return to justify the higher risk and so may be rejected by the capital budgeting decision-maker.

To properly identify appropriate projects for management consideration, both the firm's long-run strategic objectives and its financial objectives must be considered. One of the major problems facing the financial decision-maker today is the integration of long-run strategic goals with financial decision-making techniques that produce short-run gains. Perhaps the best way to handle this problem is in the project identification step by considering whether the investment makes sense in light of long-run corporate objectives. If the answer is no, look for more compatible projects. If the answer is yes, proceed to the next step, the development phase.

13.2.2. *Development Phase*

The development, or information generation, step of the capital budgeting process is probably the most difficult and most costly. The entire development phase rests largely on the type and availability of information about the investment under consideration. With limited data and an information system that cannot provide accurate, timely, and pertinent data, the usefulness of the capital budgeting process will be limited. If the firm does not have a functioning management information system (MIS) that provides the type of information needed to perform capital budgeting analysis, then there is little need to perform such analysis. The reason is the GIGO (garbage-in, garbage-out) problem; garbage (bad data) used in the analysis will result in garbage (bad or useless information) coming out of the analysis. Hence, the establishment and use of an effective MIS is crucial to the capital budgeting process. This may be an expensive undertaking, both in dollars and in human resources, but the improvement in the efficiency of the decision-making process usually justifies the cost.

There are four types of information needed in capital budgeting analysis: (1) the firm's internal data, (2) external economic data, (3) financial data, and (4) non-financial data. The actual analysis of the project will eventually rely on firm-specific financial data because of the emphasis on cash flow. However, in the development phase, different types of information are needed, especially when various options are being formulated and considered. Thus, economic data external to the firm such as general economic conditions, product market conditions, government regulation or deregulation, inflation, labor supply, and technological change — play an important role in developing the alternatives. Most of this initial screening data is non-financial. But even such non-financial considerations as the quality and quantity of the work force, political activity, competitive reaction, regulation, and environmental concerns must be integrated into the process of selecting alternatives.

Depending on the nature of the firms business, there are two other considerations. First, different levels of the firm's management require different types of information. Second, as Ackoff (1970) notes, "most managers using a MIS suffer more from an overabundance of irrelevant information than they do from a lack of relevant information."

In a world in which all information and analysis were free, we could conceive of management analyzing every possible investment idea. However, given the cost, in both dollars and time, of gathering and analyzing information, management is forced to eliminate many alternatives based on strategic considerations. This paring down of the number of feasible alternatives is crucial to the success of the overall capital budgeting program. Throughout this process, the manager faces critical questions, such as: Are excellent proposals being eliminated from consideration because of lack of information?; and, Are excessive amounts of time and money being spent to generate information on projects that are only marginally acceptable? These questions must be addressed on a firm-by-firm basis. When considered in the global context of the firm's success, these questions are the most important considerations in the capital budgeting process.

After the appropriate alternatives have been determined during the development phase, we are ready to perform the detailed economic analysis, which occurs during the selection phase.

13.2.3. *Selection Phase*

Because managers want to maximize the firm's value for the shareholders, they need some guidance as to the potential value of the investment projects. The selection phase involves measuring the value, or the return, of the project as well as estimating the risk and weighing the costs and benefits of each alternative to be able to select the project or projects that will increase the firm's value given a risk target.

In most cases, the costs and benefits of an investment occur over an extended period, usually with costs being incurred in the early years of the project's life and benefits being realized over the project's entire life. In our selection procedures, we take this into consideration by incorporating the time value of money. The basic valuation framework, or normative model, that we will use in the capital budgeting selection process is based on present value, as presented in Eq. (13.1):

$$PV = \sum_{t=1}^{N} \frac{CF_t}{(1+k)^t}, \tag{13.1}$$

where PV = the present value or current price of the investment; CF_t = the future value or cash flow that occurs in time t; N = the number of years that benefits accrue to the investor; and k = the time value of money or the firm's cost of capital.

By using this framework for the selection process, we are looking explicitly at the firm's value over time. We are not emphasizing short-run or long-run profits or benefits, but are recognizing that benefits are desirable whenever they occur. However, benefits in the near future are more highly valued than benefits far down the road.

The basic normative model (Eq. (13.1)) will be expanded to fit various situations that managers encounter as they evaluate investment proposals and determine which proposals are best.

13.2.4. *Control Phase*

The control phase is the final step of the capital budgeting process. This phase involves placing an approved project on the appropriation budget and controlling the magnitude and timing of expenditures while the project is progressing. A major portion of this phase is the *post-audit* of the project, through which past decisions are evaluated for the benefit of future capital expenditures.

The firm's evaluation and control system is important not only to the post-audit procedure, but also to the entire capital budgeting process. It is important to understand that the investment decision is based on cash flow and relevant costs, while the post-audit is based on accrued accounting and assigned overhead. Also, firms typically evaluate performance based on accounting net income for profit centers within the firm, which may be inaccurate because of misspecification of depreciation and tax effects. The result is that while managers make decisions based on cash flow, they are evaluated by an accounting-based system.

In addition to data and measurement problems, the control phase is even more complicated in practice because there is a growing concern that the evaluation, reward, and executive incentive system emphasizes a short-run, accounting-based return instead of the maximization of long-run value of cash flow. Thus, quarterly earnings per share, or revenue growth, are rewarded at the expense of longer-run profitability. This emphasis on short-run results may encourage management to forego investments in capital stock or research and development that have long-run benefits in exchange for short-run projects that improve earnings per share.

A brief discussion of the differences between accounting-based information and cash flow is appropriate at this point. The first major difference between the financial decision-maker who uses cash flow and the accountant who uses accounting information is one of time perspective. Exhibit 13.3 shows the differences in time perspective between financial decision-makers and accountants.

As seen in Exhibit 13.3, the financial decision-maker is concerned with future cash flows and value, while the accountant is concerned with historical costs and revenue. The financial decision-maker faces the question, What will I do? while the accountant asks, How did I do?

The second problem is one of definition. The financial decision-maker is concerned with economic income, or a change in wealth. For example, if you purchase a share of stock for \$10 and later sell the stock for \$30, from a financial viewpoint you have gained \$20 of value. It is easy to measure economic income in this case. However, when we look at a firm's actual operations, the measurement of economic income becomes quite complicated.

The accountant is concerned with accounting income, which is measured by the application of generally accepted accounting principles. Accounting income is the result of essential but arbitrary judgments concerning the matching of revenues and expenses during a particular period. For example,

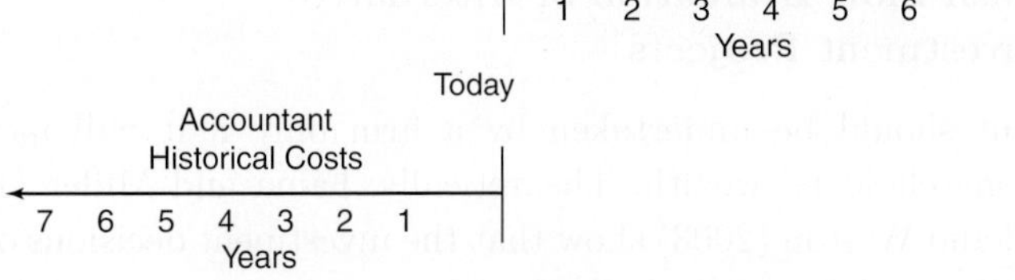

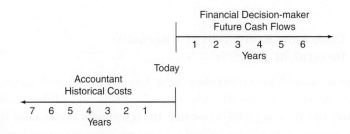

Exhibit 13.3. Relevant time perspective.

revenue may be recognized when goods are sold, shipped, or invoiced, or on receipt of the customer's check. A financial analyst and an accountant would likely differ on when revenue is recognized.

Clearly, over long periods economic value and accounting income converge and are equal because the problems of allocation to particular time periods disappear. However, over short periods there can be significant differences in these two measures. The financial decision-maker should be concerned with the value added over the life of the project, even though the post audit report of results is an accounting report based on only one quarter or 1 year of the project's life. To incorporate a long-run view of value creation, the firm must establish a relationship between its evaluation system, its reward or management incentive system, and the normative goals of the capital budgeting system.

Another area of importance in the control or post audit phase is the decision to terminate or abandon a project once it has been accepted. Too often we consider capital budgeting as only the acquisition of investments for their entire economic life. The possibility of abandoning an investment prior to the end of its estimated useful or economic life has important implications for the capital budgeting decision. The possibility of abandonment expands the options available to management and reduces the risk associated with decisions based on holding an asset to the end of its economic life. This form of contingency planning gives the financial decision-maker and management a second chance to deal with the economic and political uncertainties of the future.

At any point, to justify the continuation of a project, the project's value from future operations must be greater than its current abandonment value. Given the recent increase in the number and frequency of divestitures, many firms now give greater consideration to abandonment questions in their capital budgeting decision-making. An ideal time to reassess the value of an ongoing investment is at regular intervals during the post audit.

13.3. Cash-Flow Evaluation of Alternative Investment Projects

Investment should be undertaken by a firm only if it will increase the value of shareholders' wealth. Theoretically, Fama and Miller (1972) and Copeland and Weston (2003) show that the investment decisions of the firm can be separated from the individual investor's consumption-investment decision in a perfect capital market. This is known as Fisher's (1930) separation theorem. With perfect capital markets, the manager will increase shareholder wealth if he or she chooses projects with a rate-of-return greater than the market-determined rate-of-return (cost of funds), regardless of the shape of individual shareholders' indifference curves. The ability to borrow or lend in perfect capital markets leads to a higher wealth level for investors than they would be able to achieve without capital markets. This ability also leads to optimal production decisions that do not depend on individual investors' resources and preferences. Thus, the investment decision of the firm is separated from the individual's decision concerning current consumption and investment. Investment decision will therefore depend only on equating the rate-of-return of production possibilities with the market rate-of-return.

This separation principle implies that the maximization of the shareholders' wealth is identical to maximizing the present value of their lifetime consumption. Under these circumstances, different shareholders of the same firm will be unanimous in their preference. This is known as the unanimity principle. It implies that the managers of a firm, in their capacity as agents for shareholders, need not worry about making decisions that reconcile differences of opinion among shareholders: All shareholders will have identical interests. In fact, the price system by which profit is measured conveys the shareholders' unanimously preferred production decisions to the firm.

Looked at in another way, the use of investment decision rules, or capital budgeting, is really an example of a firm attempting to realize the economic principle of operating at the point where marginal cost equals marginal revenue to maximize shareholder wealth. In terms of investment decisions, the "marginal revenue" is the rate-of-return on investment projects, which must be equated with the marginal cost, or the market-determined cost of capital.

Investment decision rules, or capital budgeting, involve the evaluation of the possible capital investments of a firm according to procedures that will ensure the proper comparison of the cost of the project, that is, the initial and continuing outlays for the project, with the benefits, the expected cash flows accruing from the investment over time. To compare the two cash flows, future cash amounts must be discounted to the present by the firm's cost of capital. Only in this way will the cost of funds to the firm be equated with the benefits from the investment project.

The firm generally receives funds from creditors and shareholders. Both fund suppliers expect to receive a rate-of-return that will compensate them for the level of risk they take. Hence, the discount rate used to discount the cash flow should be the weighted-average cost of debt and equity. Following Eq. (12.18) of Chapter 12, the weighted-average cost of capital can be defined as:

$$\text{WACC}^{\tau} = (1 - \tau_c)k_d\left(\frac{D}{D+S}\right) + k_e\left(\frac{S}{D+S}\right). \tag{12.18}$$

The weighted-average cost of capital is the same with the market-determined opportunity cost of funds provided to the firm. It is important to understand that projects undertaken by firms must earn enough cash for the creditors and shareholders to compensate their expected risk-adjusted rate-of-return. If the present value of annuity on the cash flow obtained from the weighted-average cost of capital is larger than the initial investment, then there are some gains in shareholders' wealth using this kind of concept. Copeland and Weston (2003) demonstrated that maximizing the discount cash flows provided by the investment project.

Before any capital-budgeting techniques can be surveyed, a rigorous definition of cash flows to a firm from a project must be undertaken. First the decision maker must consider only those future cash flows that are incremental to the project; that is, only those cash flows accruing to the firm that are specifically caused by the project in question. In addition, any decrease in cash flows to the company by the project in question (i.e., the tax-depreciation benefit from a machine replaced by a new one) must be considered as well.

The main advantage of using the cash-flow procedure in capital-budgeting decisions is that it avoids the difficult problem underlying the measurement of corporate income associated with the accrual method of accounting, for example, the selection of depreciation methods and inventory-valuation methods.

Following Copeland and Weston (2003), the equality between sources and uses of funds for an all-equity firm in period t can be defined as:

$$R_t + N_tP_t = N_td_t + \text{WSMS}_t + I_t, \tag{13.2}$$

where

R_t = Revenue in period t,
N_tP_t = New equity in period t,
N_td_t = Total dividend payment in period t,
WSMS_t = Wages, salaries, materials, and service payment in period t,
I_t = Investment in period t.

Equation (13.2) is the basic equation to be used to determine the cash flow for capital-budgeting determination.

Secondly, the definition of cash flow relevant to financial decision making involves finance rather than accounting income. Accounting regulations attempt to adjust cash flows over several periods (e.g., the expense of an asset is depreciated over several time periods); finance cash flows are calculated as they occur to the firm. Thus, the cash outlay (I_t) to purchase a machine is considered a cash outflow in the finance sense when it occurs at acquisition.

To illustrate the actual calculations involved in defining the cash flows accruing to a firm from an investment project, we consider the following situation. A firm is faced with a decision to replace an old machine with a new and more efficient model. If the replacement is made, the firm will increase production sufficiently each year to generate \$10,000 in additional cash flows to the company over the life of the machine. Thus, the before-tax cash flow accruing to the firm is \$10,000.

The cash flow must be adjusted for the net increase in income taxes that the firm must now pay due to the increased net depreciation of the new machine. The annual straight-line depreciation for the new machine over its 5-year life will be \$2,000, and we assume no terminal salvage value. The old machine has a current book value of \$5,000 and a remaining depreciable life of 5 years with no terminal salvage value. Thus, the incremental annual depreciation will be the annual depreciation charges of the new, \$2,000, less the annual depreciation of the old, or \$1,000. The additional income to the firm from the new machine is then the \$10,000 cash flow less the incremental depreciation, \$1,000. The increased tax outlay from the acquisition will then be (assuming a 50% corporate income-tax rate) $0.50 \times \$9{,}000$, or \$4,500.

Adjusting the gross annual cash flow of \$10,000 by the incremental tax expense of \$4,500 gives \$5,500 as the net cash flow accruing to the firm from the new machine. It should be noted that corporate taxes are real outflow and must be taken into account when evaluating a project's desirability. However, the depreciation allowance (dep) is not a cash outflow and therefore should not be subtracted from the annual cash flow.

The calculations of post-tax cash flow mentioned above can be summarized in Eq. (13.3):

$$\begin{aligned}\text{Annual After-Tax Cash Flow} &= \text{ICFBT} - (\text{ICFBT} - \Delta\text{dep})\tau \\ &= \text{ICFBT}(1-\tau) + (\text{dep})\tau, \end{aligned} \tag{13.3}$$

where

ICFBT = Annual incremental operating cash flows,
τ = Corporate tax rate,
Δdep = Incremental annual depreciation charge, or the annual depreciation charges on the new machine less the annual depreciation on the old.

Following Eq. (13.3), ICFBT can be defined in Eq. (13.4) as

$$\text{ICFBT} = \Delta R_t - \Delta\text{WSMS}_t. \tag{13.4}$$

Note that ICFBT is an amount before interest and depreciation are deducted and Δ indicates the change of related variables. The reason is that when discounted at the weighted cost of capital as defined in Eq. (12.18), we are implicitly assuming that the project will return the expected interest payments to creditors and the expected dividends to shareholders.

Alternative depreciation methods will change the time pattern but not the total amount of the depreciation allowance. Hence it is important to choose the optimal depreciation method. To do this, we can use Eq. (13.5) to calculate the net present value (NPV) of tax benefits due to the tax deductibility of the depreciation allowance:

$$\text{NPV(tax benefit)} = \tau \sum_{t=1}^{N} \frac{\text{dep}_t}{(1+k)^t}, \tag{13.5}$$

where dep_t = depreciation allowance in period t and N = life of project; it will depend upon whether the straight-line, double declining balance, or sum-of-years'-digits method is used.

13.4. Alternative Capital-Budgeting Methods

Several methods can be used by a manager to evaluate an investment decision. Some of the simplest methods, such as the accounting rate-of-return or net payback period, are useful in that they are easily and quickly calculated. However, other methods — the NPV, profitability index, and the internal rate-of-return methods — are superior in that explicit consideration is given by them to both the cost of capital and the time value of money.

For illustrating these methods, we will use the data in Table 13.1, which shows the estimates of cash flows for four investment projects. Each project has an initial outlay of \$100, and the project life for the four projects is 4 years. Since they are mutually exclusive investment projects, only

Table 13.1. Input data for capital budgeting decision.

Year	A	B	C	D
0	−100	−100	−100	−100
1	20	0	30	25
2	80	20	50	40
3	10	60	60	50
4	−20	160	80	115

one project can be accepted, according to the following capital budgeting methods.

13.4.1. *Accounting Rate-of-Return*

In this method, a rate-of-return for the project is computed by using average net income and average investment outlay. This method does not incorporate the time value of money and cash flow. The ARR takes the ratio of the investment's average annual net income after taxes to either total outlay or average outlay. The accounting rate-of-return method averages the after-tax profit from an investment for every period over the initial outlay:

$$\text{ARR} = \frac{\sum_{t=0}^{N} \frac{AP_t}{N}}{I}, \tag{13.6}$$

where

AP_t = After-tax profit in period t,
I = Initial investment,
N = Life of the project.

By assuming that the data in Table 13.1 are accounting profits and the depreciation is \$25, the accounting rates-of-return for the four projects are:

Project A: −2.5%.
Project B: 35%.
Project C: 30%.
Project D: 32.5%.

Project B shows the highest accounting rate-of-return; therefore we will choose Project B as the best one.

The ARR, like the payback method, which will be investigated later in this section, ignores the timing of the cash flows by its failure to discount cash flows back to the present. In addition, the use of accounting cash flows rather than finance cash flows distorts the calculations through the artificial adjustment of some cash flows over several periods.

13.4.2. *Internal Rate-of-Return*

The internal rate-of-return (IRR, r) is the discount rate which equates the discounted cash flows from a project to its investment. Thus, one must solve iteratively for the r in Eq. (13.7):

$$\sum_{t=1}^{N} \frac{CF_t}{(1+r)^t} = I, \tag{13.7}$$

where

CF_t = Cash flow (positive or negative) in period t,
I = Initial investment,
N = Life of the project.

The IRR for the four projects in Table 13.1 are:

Project A: IRR does not exist (since the cash flows are less than the initial investment).
Project B: 28.158%.
Project C: 33.991%.
Project D: 32.722%.

Since the four projects are mutually exclusive and Project C has the highest IRR, we will choose Project C.

The IRR is then compared to the cost of capital of the firm to determine whether the project will return benefits greater than its cost. A consideration of advantages and disadvantages of the IRR method will be undertaken when it is compared to the NPV method.

Concept Quiz

1. What does the IRR measure?
2. Why is the NPV method superior to the IRR method?
3. How is the IRR computed?
4. Which of the criteria for judging capital-budgeting techniques does the IRR satisfy?

13.4.3. *Payback Method*

The payback method calculates the time period required for a firm to recover the cost of its investment. It is that point in time at which the cumulative new cash flow from the project equals the initial investment.

The payback periods for the four projects in Table 13.1 are

Project A: 2.0 years.
Project B: 3.125 years.
Project C: 2.33 years.
Project D: 2.70 years.

If we use the payback method, we will choose Project A.

Several problems can arise if a decision maker uses the payback method. First, any cash flows accruing to the firm after the payback period are ignored. Secondly, and most importantly, the method disregards the time value of money. That is, the cash flow returned in the later years of the project's life is weighted equally with more recent cash flows accruing to the firm.

Although there are several problems in using the payback method as a capital-budgeting method, the reciprocal or payback period is related to the internal rate-of-return of the project when the life of the project is very long. For example, assume an investment project that has an initial outlay of I and an annual cash flow of R. The payback period is I/R and its reciprocal is R/I. On the other hand, the internal rate-of-return (r) of a project can be written as follows:

$$r = \frac{R}{I} - \left(\frac{R}{I}\right)\left[\frac{1}{(1+r)^N}\right], \tag{13.8}$$

where r is the internal rate-of-return and N is the life of the project in years. Clearly, when N approaches infinity, the reciprocal of payback period R/I will approximate the annuity rate-of-return. The payback method provides a liquidity measure: i.e., sooner is better than later.

Equation (13.8) is the special case of the internal rate-of-return formula defined in Eq. (13.7). By assuming equal annual net receipts and zero semi-annual value, Eq. (13.7) can be rewritten as:

$$I = \frac{R}{1+r}\left[1 + \frac{1}{(1+r)} + \frac{1}{(1+r)^2} + \cdots + \frac{1}{(1+r)^{N-1}}\right], \tag{13.7'}$$

where $R = CF_1 = CF_2 = \cdots = CF_n$. Summing the geometric series within the square brackets and reorganizing terms, we obtain Eq. (13.8).

13.4.4. *Net Present Value Method*

The net present value of a project is computed by discounting the project's cash flows to the present by the appropriate cost of capital. A net present value of the firm is

$$\text{NPV} = \sum_{t=1}^{N} \frac{CF_t}{(1+k)^t} - I, \tag{13.9}$$

where k = the appropriate discount rate, and all other terms are defined as above.

The NPV method can be applied to the cash flows of the four projects in Table 13.1. By assuming a 12% discount rate, the NPV for the four projects are as follows:

Project A: −23.95991.
Project B: 60.33358.
Project C: 60.19367.
Project D: 62.88278.

Since Project D has the highest NPV, we will select Project D as the best one.

Clearly the NPV method explicitly considers both time value of money and economic cash flows. Based upon the concept of break-even analysis discussed in Chapter 2, we can determine the units of product that must be produced in order for NPV to be zero. If $CF_1 = CF_2 = \cdots = CF_N = CF$ and NPV = 0, the Eq. (13.9) can be rewritten as:

$$\overline{CF}\left[\sum_{t=1}^{N} \frac{1}{(1+k)^t}\right] = I. \tag{13.9'}$$

From the definition of *CF* given in Eq. (13.2) and Eq. (2.12), we can obtain the break-even point (Q^*) for capital budgeting as:

$$Q^* = \left\{ \frac{\dfrac{[I - (\text{dep})\tau]}{(1-\tau)}}{\displaystyle\sum_{t=1}^{N} \frac{1}{[(1+k)^t]}} \right\} \left(\frac{1}{p-v}\right).$$

This equation implies that the break-even point (Q^*) is a function of the discount rate. In Appendix 13.A, we give a real-world example of an application of the NPV method to break-even analysis.

Concept Quiz

1. How does the NPV method satisfy all four criteria for capital budgeting analysis techniques?
2. What decision criterion does the NPV method follow? If two or more mutually exclusive projects under consideration, how does the NPV method suggest choosing among them?

13.4.5. *Profitability Index*

The Profitability Index (PI) is very similar to the NPV method. The PI is calculated by dividing the discounted cash flows by the initial investment to arrive at the present value per dollar outlay:

$$\mathrm{PI} = \frac{\sum_{t=1}^{N} \left[\frac{CF_t}{((1+k)^t)} \right]}{I}. \tag{13.10}$$

The project should be undertaken if the PI is greater than 1; the firm should be indifferent to its undertaking if PI equals one. The project with the highest PI greater than one should be accepted first. Obviously, PI considers the time value of money and the correct finance cash flows, as does the NPV method. Further, the PI and NPV method will lead to identical decisions unless ranking mutually exclusive projects and/or under capital rationing. When considering mutually exclusive projects, the PI can lead to a decision different from that derived by the NPV method.

For example:

Project	Initial Outlay	Present Value of Cash Inflows	NPV	PI
A	100	200	100	2
B	1,000	1,300	300	1.3

Projects A and B are mutually exclusive projects. Project A has a lower NPV and higher PI compared to Project B. This will lead to a decision to select Project A by using the PI method and select Project B by using the NPV method. In the case shown here, the NPV and PI rankings differ because of the differing scale of investment: the NPV subtracts the initial outlay while the PI method divides by the original cost. Thus, differing initial investments can cause a difference in ranking between the two methods.

The firm that desires to maximize its absolute present value rather than percentage return will prefer Project B, because the NPV of Project B ($300) is greater than the NPV of Project A ($100). Thus, the PI method should not be used as a measure of investment worth for projects of differing size where mutually exclusive choices have to be made. In other words, if there exists no other investment opportunities, then the NPV will be the superior method in this case because, under the NPV, the highest-ranking investment project (the one with the largest NPV) will add the most value to shareholders' wealth. Since this is the objective of the firm's owners, the NPV will lead to a more accurate decision.

The manager's views on alternative capital budgeting methods and related practical issues will be presented in Appendix 13.B.

Concept Quiz

1. How is the PI computed? How is it related to NPV?
2. Explain the PI decision rule for accepting or rejecting projects.
3. What advantage does the NPV method offer as compared to the PI method?

13.5. Comparison of the NPV and IRR Method

13.5.1. *Theoretical Criteria*

If projects are mutually exclusive, the ranking of the investment alternatives by a capital-budgeting technique determines which of the projects will actually be undertaken. The IRR and NPV methods may lead to similar accept–reject decisions; in some instances, however, the NPV and IRR methods will provide different ranking for capital investment projects. Some choice must be made as to which method gives the more accurate rankings if projects are mutually exclusive.

Projects have different rankings if the cost of one project is greater than that of another or if the timing of cash flows differs among projects. To show the effect of differing cash-flow patterns, the present-value profile of two projects is shown in Fig. 13.1. The NPV of each project will change depending on the rate-of-return used to discount the periodic cash flows. Thus, when moving along the horizontal axis to higher discount rates,

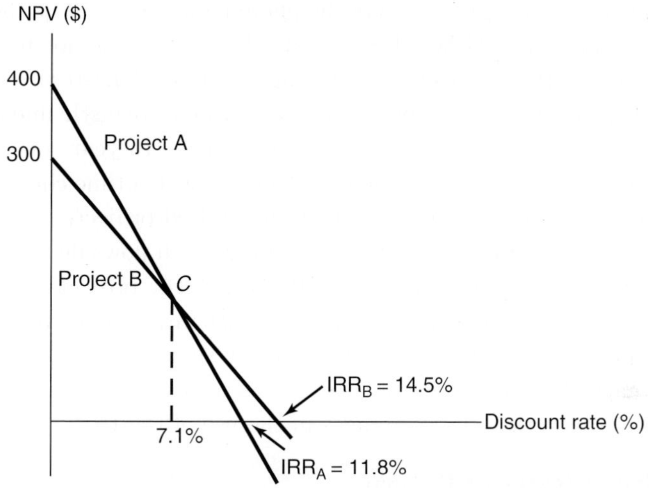

Fig. 13.1. NPVs of Projects A and B at different discount rates.

the NPV of each project will fall. However, the NPV of the project with its largest cash flows in the future will be affected more severely by the increasing discount rate, and thus the NPV for Project A decreases more rapidly than Project B. The point at which the NPV is 0 for a project is the project's IRR.

As shown, the ranking derived from the NPV differs from that of the IRR if the discount rate is below the point C, the cross-over rate. Thus, the conflict between the NPV and IRR rankings on whether the discount rate used by the firm is less than the cross-over rate, or that rate which equates the project's NPVs.

When such a conflict arises, the decision maker should use the NPV-determined rankings. Again, the NPV measures the added value accruing to shareholder wealth when the project is undertaken. The project that maximizes this value (the project with the highest NPV) should be the project that is undertaken.

Although it is typically argued that the NPV is the superior method, the viability of the IRR should not be completely dismissed. Its value depends on certain other assumptions, such as the time horizon used by the firm. For instance, considering two mutually exclusive projects, firm policy sets a planning horizon for the firm of four or 5 years, regardless of what length the investment project's useful life may extend. Projects then must be considered under this time constraint, and the project with the highest terminal value at the end of the planning horizon will be the desired project to undertake. Although obviously the manager is not maximizing shareholder wealth by, in effect, ignoring the more long-term aspects of investment projects, he may be operating in a more realistic and practical manner: many firms feel that planning horizons of 10 years or longer are too fraught with uncertainty to be useful. Given such a time constraint, the IRR method will more accurately judge the desired project.

Since the NPV of projects with large future cash flows decrease rapidly under increasing discount rates, the IRR will favor projects with higher short-term terminal value. That is, projects with larger IRR values will also have time patterns of cash flows with higher short-term terminal values. The existence of such practical constraints as the one above mitigates some of the more theoretical disadvantages in the use of the IRR.

(a) Multiple Rates-of-Return

One of the difficulties with using the IRR is the possibility of multiple rates-of-return. Each time the cash flows change sign (which may be necessitated, for instance, by the requirement to inject additional capital into the project in future years), there will be a new root solution to the IRR problem. For instance, a negative cash flow in the second year would result in a quadratic equation, and consequently multiple roots. For example:

	Year		
	0	1	2
Cash Flow	−50	750	−800

$$\text{NPV} = 0 = -50 + \frac{750}{(1+\text{IRR})} - \frac{800}{(1+\text{IRR})^2},$$

$$-50(1+\text{IRR})^2 + 750(1+\text{IRR}) - 800 = 0;$$

$$50\text{IRR}^2 - 650\text{IRR} + 100 = 0.$$

The solution can be obtained using the quadratic formula:

$$\text{IRR} = 650 \pm \frac{\sqrt{(650)^2 - 4(50)(100)}}{100},$$

$$\text{IRR} = 0.1557 \quad \text{or} \quad 12.84.$$

Thus, use of the IRR would result in an ambiguous capital-budgeting "solution" if the investment under consideration were such as to generate negative cash flows in some years. It is even possible that the IRR method could result in imaginary solutions (involving $\sqrt{-1}$), whose interpretation is problematic at best.

For example:

	Year		
	0	1	2
Cash Flow	−100	250	−160

$$
\begin{aligned}
0 &= -100 + \frac{250}{(1+\text{IRR})} - \frac{160}{(1+\text{IRR})^2},\\
0 &= -100(1+\text{IRR})^2 + 250(1+\text{IRR}) - 160,\\
0 &= -10 - 20\text{IRR} - 10\text{IRR}^2 + 25 + 25\text{IRR} - 16,
\end{aligned}
$$

$$
\begin{aligned}
10\text{IRR}^2 - 5\text{IRR} + 1 &= 0,\\
\text{IRR} &= \frac{5 \pm \sqrt{25-40}}{20},\\
\text{IRR} &= \frac{1}{4} \pm \frac{1}{20}\sqrt{15}i.
\end{aligned}
$$

(b) Reinvestment rate problem

Another of the difficulties involved with the IRR is the underlying assumption of differing reinvestment rates. When discounting cash flows in the NPV method at the cost of capital, the NPV implicitly assumes that the shareholders of the firm can reinvest the periodic cash flows accruing from the project at the cost of capital. With the IRR, however, the implicit assumption is that the shareholder can reinvest the cash flows at the IRR of each project. Thus, the IRR runs into difficulties in two ways: it divorces the discounting process from the cost of capital and it implies that reinvestment rates are contingent on individual projects. In a world of certainty, where each project has the same risk, it is illogical to assume that shareholders

Table 13.2.

(a)

	Year				
Project	0	1	2	3	NPV
A	−100	50	100	500	380.2537
B	−200	600	100	50	451.02269
C	−300	100	700	100	418.49945
A + B	−300	650	200	550	831.27505
B + C	−500	700	800	150	869.52214
A + C	−400	150	800	600	798.75182

(b) Assuming 12% discount rate:

	> IRR
A	1.10438
B	2.18184
C	0.76360
A	1.67275
B + C	1.19227
A + C	0.87172

can invest funds, for instance, at both 14% and 25%, depending on the IRR of the two projects.

(c) Separability of Projects

A third difficulty in using the IRR method is that its use leads to differing decisions when groups of projects are considered. It is desirable that a decision rule allow the manager to choose projects independently of each other; the IRR, however, may lead to the necessity of considering projects in all possible combinations. To illustrate, data for three projects are shown in Tables 13.2(a) and 13.2(b).

Besides the above-mentioned three reasons used to support the NPV, other theoretical justification for NPV can be found in Hirshleifer (1958) and Levy and Sarnat (1995).

13.5.2. *Practical Perspective*

Doenges (1972) takes a closer look at the net-present-value and internal-rate-of-return methods and questions the common assertion that net present value is superior simply because it assumes reinvestment of intermediate funds at a single discount rate. In contrast, a major premise of the internal-rate-of-return method is that intermediate cash flows be reinvested to earn a rate-of-return equal to the internal rate-of-return, without reference to the shareholders' required rate-of-return. The differing foundations upon which each method rests result in frequently conflicting decision signals.

Doenges proceeds to question the assumptions implicit in the "reinvestment problem" concerning the existence of an appropriate single reinvestment rate and the magnitude, duration, and time pattern of net cash flows. Although he questions the assumption of mutually exclusive alternatives caused by capital rationing, other studies have shown that capital rationing is, in fact, prevalent in the business world. If, however, the supply function of funds for the firm is upward sloping, as may be true for many firms, the appropriate discount rate would reflect this rising cost of capital rather than merely an opportunity cost as discussed in Chapter 12.

Doenges also raises a question that has often bothered academics. Although for practicality's sake, the firm's normal planning horizon is often used to evaluate investment alternatives, utilization of the projects' actual expected lives may more accurately reflect the real value of those projects. When the more easily workable time horizons are utilized, the financial analyst should at least recognize the possible effects of this incongruency. This is closely related to the abandonment-versus-retention issue raised in the article, and the effects of these calculations on investment acceptability must also be considered. The project-life problem will be discussed in Section 13.9 and the issues related to the abandonment value will be explored later.

Doenges also raises a very frequently voiced concern about risk and uncertainty. The manner, in which these are accounted for, if at all, in capital-budgeting decisions, may have a tremendous impact on those decisions. The issue of uncertainty will be discussed more completely in a later portion of this section.

The major difference between the net-present-value and internal rate-of-return methods, however, is the assumption by net-present-value theorists that a single reinvestment rate exists. Especially in an economy subject to change such as ours, no one can predict with certainty what returns can be made on funds invested at some future date. Special opportunities can arise in which an alert financier can earn above-average returns. In contrast, recession or depression periods can produce negative returns. Thus, the assumption of limited variability in reinvestment rates can be seen to rest on a fairly tenuous foundation when viewed in a "real-world" perspective.[1]

Doenges presents an alternative that may be feasible in certain cases. When cash inflows from a project currently being considered are earmarked to be used as funding for some future project in the planning horizon, the projected returns from this future project can be considered as the reinvestment rate for the current project. Although this process would involve an abundance of uncertainty and more time-consuming analysis, it could shed new light on alternative projects. In any case, Doenges suggests that several potential reinvestment rates be considered when evaluating projects. This could eliminate some of the uncertainty involved in project analysis. Although Doenges does not say that the internal rate-of-return method is superior to net present value, he does provide some food for thought to net present value supporters.[2] He also questions many of the theoretical and practical assumptions on which capital budgeting decisions are based.

13.6. Different Lives

Up to this section, we assumed that all investment projects have the same life. However, the traditional NPV technique may not be the appropriate criterion to select a project from mutually exclusive investment projects, if these projects have different lives. The underlying reason is that, compared with a long-life project, a short-life project can be replicated more quickly in the long run. In order to compare projects with different lives, we compute the NPV of an infinite replication of the investment project. For example,

---

[1]Based upon a pure "efficient market" hypothesis and the concept of "opportunity cost," Copeland and Weston (2003) have argued that the logic of "reinvestment rates" used by the IRR rule is fallacious. However, if their two unrealistic assumptions do not hold, then their conclusion will not follow. Note that both short-run and long-run economic conditions should be considered in practical capital-budgeting decisions.

[2]Dorfman (1981) has shown that the objective of determining the rate of growth of an enterprise in certain circumstances was best achieved by an IRR criterion instead of a NPV criteria. The reason was that when growth is the objective, the critical consideration in choosing among opportunities is the extent to which they generate funds available for reinvestment, and the best opportunity from this point of view is not necessarily the one with the highest NPV of cash flows.

let Projects A and B be two mutually exclusive investment projects with the following cash flows.

Year	Project A	Project B
0	−100	−100
1	70	50
2	70	50
3		50

By assuming a discount rate of 12%, the traditional NPV of Project A is 18.30 and the NPV of Project B is 20.09. This shows that Project B is a better choice than Project A. However, the NPV with infinite replications for Project A and B should be adjusted into a comparable basis.

In order to compare Projects A and B, we compute the NPV of an infinite stream of constant scale replications. Let $\text{NPV}(N, \infty)$ be the NPV of an N-year project with $\text{NPV}(N)$, replicated forever. This is exactly the same as an annuity paid at the beginning of the first period and at the end of every N years from that time on. The NPV of the annuity is:

$$\text{NPV}(N, \infty) = \text{NPV}(N) + \frac{\text{NPV}(N)}{(1+K)^N} + \frac{\text{NPV}(N)}{(1+K)}2N + \cdots.$$

In order to obtain a closed-form formula, let $(1/[(1+K)^N]) = H$. Then we have:

$$\text{NPV}(N, t) = \text{NPV}(N)(1 + H + H^2 + \cdots + H^t). \qquad (13.11\text{a})$$

Multiplying both sides by H, this becomes

$$H[\text{NPV}(N, t)] = \text{NPV}(N)(H + H^2 = \cdots + H^t + H^{t+1}). \qquad (13.11\text{b})$$

Subtracting Eq. (13.11b) from Eq. (13.11a) gives:

$$\text{NPV}(N, t) - (H)\text{NPV}(N, t) = \text{NPV}(N)(1 - H^{t+1}),$$

$$\text{NPV}(N, t) = \frac{\text{NPV}(N)(1 - H^{t+1})}{1 - H}.$$

And taking the limit as the number of replications, t, approaches infinity gives:

$$\lim_{t\to\infty} \text{NPV}(N,t) = \text{NPV}(N,\infty) = \text{NPV}\left[\frac{1}{1-\left[\frac{1}{(1+K)^N}\right]}\right],$$

$$= \text{NPV}(N)\left[\frac{(1+K)^N}{(1+K)^N-1}\right]. \qquad (13.11)$$

Equation (13.10) is the NPV of an N-year project replicated at constant scale an infinite number of times. We can use it to compare projects with different lives because when their cash-flow streams are replicated forever, it is as if they had the same (infinite) life.

Using Eq. (13.10) for Projects A and B gives us the following:

For Project A:

$$\text{NPV}(2,\infty) = \text{NPV}(2)\left[\frac{(1+0.12)^2}{(1+0.12)^2-1}\right]$$

$$= (18.30)\left[\frac{1.2544}{0.2544}\right]$$

$$= 90.23.$$

For Project B:

$$\text{NPV}(3,\infty) = \text{NPV}(3)\left[\frac{(1+0.12)^3}{(1+0.12)^3-1}\right]$$

$$= 20.09\left[\frac{1.4049}{0.4049}\right]$$

$$= 69.71.$$

Consequently, we would choose to accept Project A over Project B, because, when the cash flows are adjusted for different lives, A provides the greater cash flow.

Alternatively, Eq. (13.11) can be rewritten as an annuity version as:

$$\text{KNPV}(N,\infty) = \frac{\text{NPV}(N)}{\text{Annuity factor}}, \qquad (13.12)$$

where the annuity factor is

$$\frac{[1-(1+K)^{-N}]}{K}.$$

The decision rule from Eq. (13.12) is equivalent to the decision rule of Eq. (13.11).

The different project lives can affect the beta coefficient estimate, as shown by Meyers and Turnbull (1977). This issue will be discussed in the next chapter. For empirical guidance for evaluating capital-investment alternatives with unequal lives, the readers are referred to Emery (1982).

13.6.1. *Mutually Exclusive Investment Projects with Different Lives*

The traditional NPV technique may not be the appropriate criterion to select a project from mutually exclusive investment projects, if these projects have different lives. The underlying reason is that, compared with a long-life project, a short-life project can be replicated more quickly in the long run. In order to compare projects with different lives, we compute the NPV of an infinite replication of the investment project. For example, let Projects A and B be two mutually exclusive investment projects with the following cash flows.

Year	Project A	Project B
0	100	100
1	70	50
2	70	50
3		50

By assuming a discount rate of 12%, the traditional NPV of Project A is 18.30 and the NPV of Project B is 20.09. This shows that Project B is a better choice than Project A. However, the NPV with infinite replications for Project A and B should be adjusted into a comparable basis.

In order to compare Projects A and B, we compute the NPV of an infinite stream of constant scale replications. Let $\text{NPV}(N, \infty)$ be the NPV of an N-year project with $\text{NPV}(N)$, replicated forever. This is exactly the same as an annuity paid at the beginning of the first period and at the end of every N years from that time on. The NPV of the annuity is:

$$\text{NPV}(N, \infty) = \text{NPV}(N) + \frac{\text{NPV}(N)}{(1+K)^N} + \frac{\text{NPV}(N)}{(1+K)^{2N}} + \cdots.$$

In order to obtain a closed-form formula, let $(1/[(1+K)^N]) = H$. Then we have:

$$\mathrm{NPV}(N,t) = \mathrm{NPV}(N)(1 + H + H^2 + \cdots H^t). \tag{13.13}$$

Multiplying both sides by H, this becomes

$$H[\mathrm{NPV}(N,t)] = \mathrm{NPV}(N)(H + H^2 = \cdots + H^t + H^{t+1}). \tag{13.14}$$

Subtracting Eq. (13.14) from Eq. (13.13) gives:

$$\mathrm{NPV}(N,t) - (H)\mathrm{NPV}(N,t) = \mathrm{NPV}(N)(1 - H^{t+1}),$$

$$\mathrm{NPV}(N,t) = \frac{\mathrm{NPV}(N)(1 - H^{t+1})}{1 - H}.$$

And taking the limit as the number of replications, t, approaches infinity gives:

$$\lim_{t\to\infty} \mathrm{NPV}(N,t) = \mathrm{NPV}(N,\infty) = \mathrm{NPV}\left[\frac{1}{1 - \left[\frac{1}{(1+K)^N}\right]}\right]$$

$$= \mathrm{NPV}(N)\left[\frac{(1+K)^N}{(1+K)^N - 1}\right]. \tag{13.15}$$

Equation (13.15) is the NPV of an N-year project replicated at constant scale an infinite number of times. We can use it to compare projects with different lives because when their cash-flow streams are replicated forever, it is as if they had the same (infinite) life.

Using Eq. (13.15) for Projects A and B gives us the following:

For Project A:

$$\begin{aligned}&\mathrm{NPV}(2,\infty)\\ &= \mathrm{NPV}(2)\left[\frac{(1+0.12)^2}{(1+0.12)^2 - 1}\right]\\ &= (18.30)\left[\frac{1.2544}{0.2544}\right]\\ &= 90.23.\end{aligned}$$

For Project B:

$$\begin{aligned}&\mathrm{NPV}(3,\infty)\\ &= \mathrm{NPV}(3)\left[\frac{(1+0.12)^3}{(1+0.12)^3 - 1}\right]\\ &= 20.09\left[\frac{1.4049}{0.4049}\right]\\ &= 69.71.\end{aligned}$$

Consequently, we would choose to accept Project A over Project B, because, when the cash flows are adjusted for different lives, A provides the greater cash flow. Alternatively, Eq. (13.15) can be rewritten as an equivalent annual NPV version as:

$$K \times \text{NPV}(N, \infty) = \frac{\text{NPV}(N)}{\text{Annuity factor}} \tag{13.16}$$

where the annuity factor is

$$\frac{\left[\dfrac{1-1}{(1+K)^N}\right]}{K}.$$

The decision rule from Eq. (13.16) is equivalent to the decision rule of Eq. (13.15).

The different project lives can affect the beta coefficient estimate, as shown by Meyers and Turnbull (1977). This issue will be discussed in the next chapter. For empirical guidance for evaluating capital-investment alternatives with unequal lives, the readers are referred to Emery (1982).

13.6.2. *Equivalent Annual Cost*

Equation (13.16) can be written as

$$\text{NPV}(N) = K \times \text{NPV}(N, \infty) \times \text{Annuity Factor}. \tag{13.17}$$

Corporate Finance by Ross *et al.* (2008) has discussed about Equivalent Annual Cost in p. 193. The Equivalent Annual Cost (C) can be calculated from

$$\text{NPV}(N) = C \times \text{Annuity Factor}. \tag{13.18}$$

From Eqs. (13.17) and (13.18), we obtain

$$C = K \times \text{NPV}(N, \infty). \tag{13.19}$$

Assume company A buys a machine that costs 1,000 and will be maintenance expense of \$250 to be paid at the end of each of the 4 years. To evaluate this investment, we can calculate the present value of the machine. Assuming the discount rate 10%, we have

$$\text{NPV}(A) = 1000 + \frac{250}{1.1} + \frac{250}{(1.1)^2} + \frac{250}{(1.1)^3} + \frac{250}{(1.1)^4} = 1792.47. \tag{13.20}$$

Equation (13.20) shows that payments of (1000, 250, 250, 250, 250) are equivalent to a payment of 1792.47 at time 0. Using Eq. (13.18), we can equate the payment at time 0 of 1749.47 with a 4 year annuity.

$$1792.47 = C \times A^4_{0.1} = C \times 3.1699$$

$$C = 565.47.$$

In this example, following Eq. (13.15), we can find

$$\text{NPV}(N, \infty) = \frac{1749.47 \times (1 + 0.1)^4}{[(1 + 0.1)^4 - 1]} = 5654.71.$$

Then following Eq. (13.19), we obtain

$$C = K^*\text{NPV}(N, \infty) = 0.1 \times 5654.71 = 565.47.$$

Therefore, the equivalent annual cost C is identical to the equivalent annual NPV as defined in Eq. (13.19).

13.7. Capital-Rationing Decision

In this section, we will discuss a capital-budgeting problem that involves the allocation of scarce capital resources among competing economically desirable projects, not all of which can be carried out due to a capital (or other) constraint. This kind of problem is often called "capital rationing." In this section, we will show how linear programming can be used to make capital-rationing decisions.

13.7.1. *Basic Concepts of Linear Programming*

Linear programming is a mathematical technique used to find optimal solutions to problems of a firm involving the allocation of scarce resources among competing activities. Mathematically, the type of problem that linear programming can solve is one in which both the objective of the firm to be maximized (or minimized) and the constraints limiting the firm's actions are linear functions of the decisions variables involved. Thus, the first step in using linear programming as a tool for financial decisions is to model the problem facing the firm into a linear-programming form. To construct the linear-programming model, one must take the following steps.

First, identify the controllable decision variables involved in the firm's problem. Second, define the objective or criterion to be maximized or minimized and represent it as a linear function of the controllable decision variables. In finance, the objective generally is to maximize the profit contribution or the market value of the firm or to minimize the cost of production.

Thirdly, define the constraints and express them as linear equations or inequalities of the decision variables. This will usually involve (a) a determination of the capacities of the scarce resources involved in the constraints, and (b) a derivation of a linear relationship between these capacities and the decision variables.

Symbolically, then, if $X_1, X_2, \ldots, X_n$ represent the quantities of output, the linear-programming model takes the general form:

$$\text{Maximize (or minimize) } Z = c_1X_1 + c_2X_2 + \cdots + c_nX_n, \qquad (13.21)$$

$$\begin{aligned} \text{Subject to: } & a_{11}X_1 + a_{12}X_2 + \cdots + a_{1n}X_n \leq b_1, \\ & a_{21}X_1 + a_{22}X_2 + \cdots + a_{2n}X_n \leq b_2, \\ & \vdots \qquad\qquad\qquad \vdots \\ & a_{m1}X_1 + a_{m2}X_2 + \cdots + a_{mn}X_n \leq b_m, \\ & X_j \geq 0, \quad (j = 1, 2, \ldots, n). \end{aligned}$$

Here, Z represents the objective to be maximized (or minimized), profit or market value (or cost), $c_1, c_2, \ldots, c_n$ and $a_{11}, a_{12}, \ldots, a_{mn}$ are constant coefficients relating to profit contribution and input, respectively; $b_1, b_2, \ldots, b_m$ are the firm's capacities of the constraining resources. The last constraint ensures that the decision variables to be determined are non-negative.

Several points should be noted concerning the linear programming model. First, depending upon the problem, the constraints may also be stated with equal signs (=) or as greater-than-or-equal to. Secondly, the solution values of the decision variables are divisible; that is, a solution would permit $x(j) = 1/2, 1/4$, etc. If such fractional values are not possible, the related technique of integer programming, yielding only whole numbers as solutions, can be applied. Thirdly, the constant coefficients are assumed known and deterministic (fixed). If the coefficients have probabilistic distributions, one of the various methods of stochastic programming must be used. Examples will be given below of the application of linear programming to the areas of capital rationing and capital budgeting.

13.7.2. *Capital Rationing*

The XYZ Company produces products A, B, and C within the same product line, with sales totaling $37 million last year. Top management has adopted the goal of maximizing shareholder wealth, which to them is represented by gain in shareholder price. Wickwire plans to finance all future projects with internal or external equity; funds available from the equity market depend on share price in the stock market for the period.

Three new projects were proposed to the Finance Committee, for which the following net after-tax annual funds flows are forecast:

	Year					
Project	0	1	2	3	4	5
X	−100	30	30	60	60	60
Y	−200	70	70	70	70	70
Z	−100	−240	−200	400	300	300

All three projects involve financing, cost-saving equipment for well-established product lines; adoption of any one project does not preclude adoption of any other. The following NPV formulations have been prepared by using a discount rate of 12%.

Investment	NPV
X	65.585
Y	52.334
Z	171.871

In addition, the finance start has calculated the maximum internally generated funds that will be available for the current year and succeeding 2 years, not counting any cash generated by the projects currently under consideration.

Year 0	Year 1	Year 2
$300	$70	$50

Assuming that the stock market is in a serious downturn, and thus no external financing is possible, the problem is which of the three projects should be selected, assuming that fractional projects are allowed.

The problem essentially involves the rationing of the capital available to the firm among the three competing projects such that share price will be maximized. Thus, assuming a risk-adjusted discount rate of 12%, the objective function becomes:

$$\text{Maximize } V = 65.585X + 52.334Y + 171.871Z + 0C + 0D + 0E.$$

where V represents the total present value realized from the projects, and C, D, and E will represent idle funds in periods 0, 1, 2, respectively. The constraint for period 0 must ensure that the funds used to finance the projects do not exceed the funds available. Thus,

$$100X + 200Y + 100Z + C + 0D + 0E = 300.$$

In this constraint, C represents any idle funds unused in period 0 after projects are paid for. Similarly, for periods 1 and 2,

$$-30X - 70Y + 240Z - C + D + 0E = 70,$$

$$-30X - 70Y + 200Z + 0C - D + E = 50.$$

Here, $-D$ and $-E$ are included in the second and third constraints, ensuring that idle funds unused from one period are carried over to the succeeding period. In addition, to prevent the program from repeatedly selecting only one project (the "best") until funds are exhausted, three additional constraints are needed:

$$X \leq 1, \quad Y \leq 1, \quad Z \leq 1.$$

The solution to the model if $V = \$208.424$, is:

$$X = 1.0, \quad Y = 0.6586, \quad Z = 0.6305.$$

To give an indication of the value of relaxing the funds constraint in any period (the most the firm would be willing to pay for additional financing), the shadow price of the funds constraints are given below[3]:

Funds Constraint	Shadow Price
1st period	0.4517
2nd period	0.4517
3rd period	0.0914

It should be noted that the constraints related to $X \leq 1$, $Y \leq 1$, and $Z \leq 1$ are required in solving capital-rationing problems. If these constraints are removed, then we will obtain $X = 2.4074$, $Y = 0$, and $Z = 0.5926$. This issue has been discussed by Copeland and Weston (2003) and Weingartner (1963, 1977).

Thus, linear programming is a valuable mathematical tool with which to solve capital-budgeting problems when funds rationing is required. In addition, duality has been used by the banking industry to determine the cost of capital of funds. The relative advantages and disadvantages between the linear-programming method and other methods used to fund the cost of capital remain as a subject for further research.

13.8. Summary

Important concepts and methods related to capital-budgeting decisions under certainty were explored in this chapter. Cash-flow estimation methods were discussed before alternative capital-budgeting methods were explored. A comparison of the NPV and IRR methods was investigated in accordance with both theoretical and practical viewpoints. Issues relating different project lives were explored in some detail. Finally, capital-rationing decisions in terms of linear programming were discussed.

Following a survey by Graham and Harvey (2001) what we discussed in this chapter relative to the findings of this survey are present value techniques and firm risk. Furthermore, this survey analyzed how although larger firms use present value techniques and CAPM, however, smaller firms concentrate on the payback criterion. Also the survey findings suggest that

[3]Shadow price is the solution of the duality problem. This price is not a market price; it is the value to be imputed to the resources. These concepts and others, basic concepts of linear programming, will be explored further in Chapter 22.

firms are interested in the firm's risk and financial flexibility when evaluating new investments.

Problem Set

1. Discuss the impact of project cash flows on a firm's market value. Which cash flows should be considered? What effect do accounting regulations have on the estimation of such flows?
2. Define the following terms:

   a. Net cash inflow
   b. Mutual exclusive versus independent project
   c. Opportunity cost versus cost of capital
   d. Accounting rate-of-return method
   e. Reinvestment rate
   f. Profitability index
   g. Capital rationing

3. Discuss the procedures involved in the cash-flow estimation with and without debt.
4. What is the capital budgeting process developed by Professor George Pinches (1982)?
5. What are the advantages and disadvantages of IRR method and NPV method for capital budgeting decisions?
6. Describe how linear programming method can be used to make the capital rationing decision.
7. Briefly discuss the various capital-budgeting methods. Which methods are theoretically and empirically more acceptable? Why?
8. Compare the NPV and IRR methods. Also discuss the situations when there is a conflict between the two results. Why do these conflicts occur?
9. Discuss some of the theoretical arguments against the use of the IRR method. Based upon the literature, are these arguments justifiable?
10. Discuss the effects of inflation on the capital-budgeting decision as suggested by Nelson (1976) in accordance with his five propositions.
11. What major problems in performing capital budgeting are faced by practitioners? In what ways can alternative capital-budgeting techniques be improved?
12. Discuss and explain the processes involved in using linear programming to solve capital-rationing decisions. What assumptions must be made?

13. What are the implications for the capital-budgeting decision when comparing projects with unequal lives? How can we adjust for such a situation?
14. How can the NPV method be incorporated with break-even analysis to make the project decision analysis become more acceptable?
15. ZZZ Company is considering three projects. Which project is the best if the firm uses the accounting rate-of-return method for the selection method?

		Net Income Year			
Project	Cost	1	2	3	4
A	−100	50	50	60	60
B	−100	10	50	60	80
C	−100	120	40	30	10

a. In the question above, which of the three projects is best if ZZZ Company uses the payback method?

16. The ABC Company is considering two mutually exclusive investments. Project A has a cost of $25,000 and will produce after-tax net cash flows of $4,351 per year for 10 years. Project B also has a cost of $25,000, and it is expected to produce cash flows of $6,990 per year for 5 years.

    (a) Assuming that ABC's average cost of capital is 12% and that these two projects are both of average risk, which, if either, should ABC accept?
    (b) Now assume that ABC's cost of capital rises to 14%. What is your decision now?
    (c) Suppose ABC's cost of capital falls to 10%. How does this affect your decision?
    (d) Graph the two projects' NPV profiles. Examine and explain the economic logic of why one project is better than the other.

17. ZZZ Company is considering three projects. Which project is the best if the firm uses the accounting rate-of-return method for the selection method?

Project	Cost	Net Income Year 1	2	3	4
A	−100	50	50	60	60
B	−100	10	50	60	80
C	−100	120	40	30	10

18. In Question 16 above, which of the three projects is best if ZZZ Company uses the payback method?
19. Calculate the internal rate-of-return of Projects A and B:

Project	Cost	Net Income Year 1	2	3	4	5
A	−200	40	60	50	100	1000
B	−200	100	100	50	60	40

20. Let projects X and Y be two mutually exclusive investment projects with a discount rate of 10% and the following cash flows:

Year	Project X	Project Y
0	−100	−100
1	80	20
2	70	30
3		50
4		100

a. Calculate NPV of the two projects.
b. Calculate NPV with infinite replication.

21. Projects A and B both involve the same initial investment and generate the same IRR, which exceeds the opportunity cost of capital. The cash

flows of project A are larger than those of B, but tend to occur later. Which has higher NPV?

22. The cash flows from ZZZ Company's project are $C_0 = 500{,}000$, $C_1 = 400{,}000$, and $C_2 = -1{,}200{,}000$. If the opportunity cost of capital is 12%, should ZZZ accept the project?
23. Lamy Enterprises is a manufacturer of high quality running shoes. Meredith Lamy, President, is considering computerizing the company's ordering, inventory, and billing procedures. She estimates that the annual savings from computerization include a reduction often ten employees with annual salaries of \$15,000 each, \$8,000 from reduced production delays caused by raw materials inventory problems. \$12,000 from lost sales due to inventory stockouts, and \$3,000 associated with timely billing procedures.

    The purchase price of the system is \$200,000 and installation costs are \$50,000. These outlays will be capitalized (depreciated) on a straight-line basis to a zero book salvage value which is also its market value at the end of 5 years. Operation of the new system requires two computer specialists with annual salaries of \$40,000 per person. Also annual maintenance and operating (cash) expenses of \$12,000 are estimated to be required. The corporation's tax rate is 40% and its required rate-of-return (cost of capital) for this project is 12%.

    a. Find the project's initial net cash outlay.
    b. Find the project's operating and terminal value cash flows over its 5-year life.
    c. Evaluate the project using the NPV method.
    d. Evaluate the project using the IRR method.
    e. Evaluate the project using the PI method.
    f. Calculate the project's payback period.
    g. Find the project's cash flows and NPV (*puts* a through c) assuming that the system can be sold for \$25,000 at the end of 5 years even though the book salvage value will be zero.
    h. Find the project's cash flows and NPV (parts a through c) assuming that the book salvage value for depreciation purposes is \$20,000 even though the machine is worthless in terms of its resale value.

24. Thompson's Tree Farm is considering the replacement of its large delivery tractor and trailer. The old truck originally cost \$60,000 when it was purchased 3 years ago. It is being depreciated over a 6-year life to a zero book value. Thompson believes that the useful remaining life

of the old truck is 5 years after which it will have a resale value of zero. The company can sell the old truck now for \$14,000.

The new truck will cost \$90,000 and will be depreciated over a 5-year period to a zero book salvage value. At the end of 5 years, it will be sold for \$20,000. The new truck will produce cash savings of \$8,000 as a result of reduced maintenance and additional savings of \$15,000 from delays caused by breakdowns on deliveries.

The company's tax rate is 40% and it uses straight-line depreciation. The required rate-of-return (cost of capital) for the project is 10%.

a. Find the project's initial net cash outlay.
b. Find the project's operating and terminal value cash flows for years 1–5.
c. Evaluate the project using the NPV.
d. Evaluate the project using the IRR.
e. Evaluate the project using the PI.
f. Calculate the project's payback period.

25. If a project's *PI* is 2.0 and its initial net cash outlay is \$5,000, find its NPV.

26. Stephanie's Tack and Bridle Shop is considering opening a new (additional) store in a nearby city. Fixed operating costs are estimated to be \$25,000 and variable costs will be 30 percent of sales. Annual revenues for the project are forecasted to be \$90,000.

The land for the store currently costs \$40,000 and the building will cost \$80,000 to construct. Depreciable equipment costing \$20,000 must be purchased. The building and equipment will be depreciated over its 10-year life to a zero salvage value. At the end of 10 years, the building and land will be sold for a combined price of \$95,000. (The land value will be \$70,000 and the value of the building will be \$25,000.)

The company's tax rate is 40%. Its required rate-of-return for the project is 14%; and, straight-line depreciation is used.

a. Find the project's initial net cash outlay.
b. Find the project's operating and terminal cash flows.
c. Evaluate the project using the **NPV**, IRR, and PI methods.
d. If the new store reduces annual cash flows at the existing store by \$13,000, would your answers to parts a through c change? Explain.
e. If \$3,000 of Stephanie's existing overhead will be allocated to the new facility for accounting purposes, will your answers to parts a through c change? Explain.

27. AMCG Electric is required to install additional safety control equipment at its northwestern nuclear power plant. There are two different types of equipment that meet government standards. The Alpha equipment costs \$105,000, has a 10-year life over which it will be depreciated to a zero book salvage value. The Gamma equipment costs \$90,000 and will also be depreciated over a 10-year life to a zero book salvage value. The Alpha equipment will require \$10,500 per year in cash operating and maintenance expenses while the Gamma equipment will require only \$9,000. Neither machine will have any resale value at the end of its 10-year life. Given a required rate-of-return of 10% for this investment decision, which type of equipment should be purchased? The corporate tax rate is 40%.

Appendix 13.A. NPV and Break-Even Analysis[4]

A use of the NPV in break-even analysis was shown by Reinhardt (1973) in relation to Lockheed's Tri Star Program. The basic framework is:

$$\mathrm{NPV}(k) = \int_0^T R(t) - C(t)e^{-\rho t}\,dt, \tag{13.A.1}$$

where

$\mathrm{NPV}(k)$ = Net present value of the project discounted at cost-of-capital rate k;
$R(t)$ = Stream of cash revenues at time t;
$C(t)$ = Stream of cash outlays at time t;
T = Investment time horizon;
ρ = Continuously compounded discount rate which is equal to $\ln(1+k)$

The stream of cash outlays is made up of three different but interrelated parts: (1) outlays for research, development, testing, and evaluation (RDTE), which are for the period from the initial design to the evaluation of prototypes; (2) outlays for initial investments and tooling, which are for the setting up of production facilities; and (3) outlays for manufacturing

[4]This appendix has heavily drawn upon Reinhardt's (1973) paper. It is used with permission.

and procuring components and their assembly into the airframe. Parts 1 and 2 are non-recurring costs, and Part 3 the recurring costs.

Looking at the non-recurring costs, a rate for the outlays at time t is:

$$C_t = \frac{R+I}{A} \quad \text{for } 0 < t < A, \tag{13.A.2}$$

where

R = RDTE costs,
I = Total initial outlay on production facilities,
A = Time up to the onset of production.

For this program, $R + I$ was estimated to be between \$800 million and \$1 billion; A was estimated to be 42 months.

We now turn our attention to the recurring costs and their relation to the learning curve — the concept that future productivity is an increasing function of cumulative past output. Past studies of aircraft production have shown that production costs per aircraft decline by a constant percentage for doubled quantities of productions. This leads to the following formulation:

$$Y_Q = Y_1 Q^{-b}, \tag{13.A.3}$$

where

Q = Number of aircraft produced;
Y_Q = Cumulative average production cost for Q aircraft produced;
$b = \ln(\gamma)/\log(2)$;
γ = "Learning coefficient," which remains constant over all Q;
Y_1 = First unit cost of production.

If $Q(t)$ is the number of aircraft produced by the end of period t, and $Y_{Q(t)}$ the associated cumulative average cost of production, then the cumulative total production cost can be written as:

$$TC(t) = Y_1[Q(t)]^{(1-b)} \tag{13.A.4}$$

and the rate of production cost at time t is:

$$C(t) = (1-b)Y_1 Q(t)^{-b}\left(\frac{dQ_t}{dt}\right). \tag{13.A.5}$$

We can rewrite $Q(t)$ in relation to a constant monthly production rate N as:

$$Q(t) = (t - A)N. \tag{13.A.6}$$

The projected time path of recurring costs can now be expressed as:

$$C(t) = (1 - b)Y_1(t - A)^{-b}N^{(1-b)}, \tag{13.A.7}$$

for

$$\begin{aligned} A &= 42, \\ B &= 0.369188, \\ Y_1 &= \$100 \text{ million}, \\ t &> A. \end{aligned}$$

Having discussed the non-recurring and recurring cost estimations, we must also determine a value for k, the cost-of-capital rate. If the goal of the firm is to maximize shareholder wealth, the appropriate k is given by:

$$k = \sum_{j=1}^{n}(W_j)(k_j), \tag{13.A.8}$$

where

k_j = Effective annual after-tax cost per dollar of the jth source of funds;
W_j = Proportion of the jth source of funds in the long-run capital structure.

For Lockheed, historically, this desired capital structure was:

$$k = 0.3k_d + 0.7k_e, \tag{13.A.9}$$

where

k_d = after-tax cost of debt and
k_e = after-tax cost of equity.

In 1968, the year of the adoption of this program, Lockheed's k_d was about 5% and its k_e was 8%, given for the following equation:

$$k_e = \frac{D}{P} + g, \tag{13.A.10}$$

where

D = dividend per share,
P = Net proceeds per share after flotation costs,
g = Average annual compound growth rate

For Lockheed g was approximately 6% to 7%, and D/P was 4.2%. Because of flotation costs, the ratio D/P for new equity is higher and k_e is close to 12%. Inserting this value into Eq. (13.A.9), we obtain Lockheed's overall cost-of-capital rate somewhere between 9% and 10%. It was probably 10% or more due to the marginal business risk the Tri Star project added to Lockheed's overall business risk.

Now we look at the revenues for the Tri Star program. The flow of cash revenues depends on the price of the aircraft, the payment schedule, and the monthly production and delivery of planes.

The base price was estimated to be roughly \$15.5 million. We can state revenues $R_{(t)}$, as:

$$R_{(t)} = PN \quad \text{for } t > A, \tag{13.A.11}$$

where P is the price per aircraft. We can now put the cost and revenue components into an overall NPV for the Tri Star project:

$$\begin{aligned}\text{NPV}_{(k)} = [t - tx]\Bigg[&\text{NP}\int_A^T e^{-\rho t}dt - \frac{R+I}{A}\int_0^A e^{-\rho t}dt \\ &- (1-b)Y_1 N^{(1-b)}\int_A^T (t-A)^{-b}e^{-\rho t}dt\Bigg],\end{aligned} \tag{13.A.12}$$

where

tx = Effective tax rate on corporate profits for Lockheed and
ρ = Discount rate.

The first term in the large brackets is the present value of all future revenues in 1968. The second term in the brackets is the present value of all RDTE and initial investment outlays. The third term is the present value of all production costs. Evaluating the integrals in this equation, we can restate the third term as the product of a set of constants and an integral of the gamma function.[5] Upon evaluation of the remaining integrals in Eq. (12.A.12), the latter becomes:

$$\mathrm{NPV}(k) = [1 - tx]\left[NP\left(\frac{1 - e^{-\rho(T-A)}}{\rho e^{\rho A}}\right) - \left(\frac{R+I}{A}\right)\left(\frac{1 - e^{-\rho A}}{\rho}\right)\right.$$
$$\left. - (1-b)Y_1\left(\frac{N}{\rho}\right)^{(1-b)} e^{-\rho A}\sum_{j=0}^{\infty}\left[\frac{(-1)^j[\rho(T-A)]^{j+1-b}}{j![j+1-b]}\right]\right]. \tag{13.A.13}$$

Figure 12.A.1 has been developed from this equation and the previous parameter estimates. The four curves in this diagram present the estimated net present value of the Tri Star program at alternative sales levels and discount rates. The curves are drawn on the assumption that the total non-recurring costs of the program ($R + I$) are \$900 million; that the average price per aircraft (ρ) is \$15.5 million; that an average of three aircraft per month are produced and sold (N); that the development and initial investment phase (A) is 42 months; that Lockheed faces a 50% tax rate; and that Tri Star program investment will always have positive revenue. These assumptions are indicated in the upper left corner of the

---

[5] Following Reinhardt (1973), the derivation can be written as follows:

The integral $^{-A}(t-A)^{-b}e^{-\rho t}$ in Eq. (12.A.12) can be restated as

$$e^{-\rho A}\int_0^{T-A} t^{-b}e^{-\rho t}dt = e^{-\rho A}\rho^b\int_0^{T-A}(\rho t)^{-b}e^{-\rho t}dt$$
$$= e^{\rho A}\rho^{(b-1)}\int_0^{\rho(T-A)} v^{-b}e^{-v}dv. \tag{1}$$

Where $v = \rho t$. If we denote $z = \rho(T-A)$ and $\alpha = (1-b)$, then

$$\int_0^{\rho(T-A)} v^{-b}e^{-v}dv = \int_0^z v^{\alpha-1}e^{-v}dv = \Gamma(\alpha; z) = \sum_{j=0}^{\infty}\left(\frac{(-1)^j z^{j+\alpha}}{j![j+\alpha]}\right). \tag{2}$$

So that Eq. (1) becomes

$$\int_A^T (t-A)^{-b}e^{-\rho t}dt = e^{-\rho A}\rho^{(b-1)}\sum_{j=0}^{\infty}\left(\frac{(-1)^j[\rho(T-A)]^{j-1-b}}{j![j+1-b]}\right). \tag{3}$$

This expression can be inserted into Eq. (13.A.12) to yield, after evaluation of the other integrals in the expression, Eq. (13.A.13).

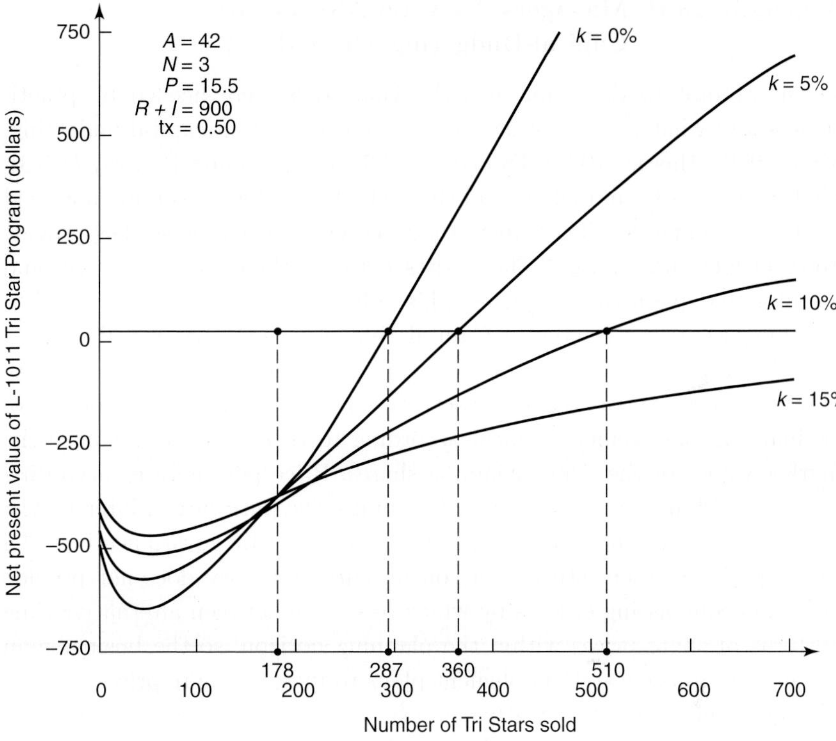

Fig. 13.A.1. Estimated NPV and break-even sales.

Source: From Reinhardt (1973). Reprinted by permission.

diagram. One of the most important implications is that the break-even sales point is a function of discount rates. Figure 13.A.1 indicates that the break-even sales are 287, 360, and 510 aircraft, if discount rates are 0%, 10%, and 15%, respectively. Thus, discount rate is an important factor in dynamic break-even analysis. In addition, Reinhardt analyzed the relationship between: (i) break-even sales and the delivery schedule; (ii) break-even sales and the price per Tri Star, and (iii) break-even sales and non-recurring cost yet to be incurred as of mid-1971. In other words, capacity utilization is introduced into the NPV method of capital-budgeting decisions.

This example has shown how finance theory, accounting information and mathematical tools can be jointly used to make the capital-budgeting decisions more meaningful.

Appendix 13.B. Managers' View on Alternative Capital-Budgeting Methods

In an attempt to determine exactly what tools were needed by practitioners and what methods they were currently using in capital budgeting, Mao (1970), Hastie (1974), Fremgen (1973), Brigham and Pettway (1973), Shall *et al.* (1978), and Oblak and Helm (1980) conducted surveys and field studies of companies. The papers that emerged from these studies provide great insight into the gulf that exists between theory and practice, and attempt to explain the reasons for this gulf.

Mao (1970) in "Survey of Capital Budgeting: Theory and Practice," specifically examines three areas of capital budgeting and the disparity between theory and practice in each area. He first considers the objective of financial management, which, according to theory, is to maximize the market values of the firm's common shares. Price per share is, according to theory, a function of its expected earnings, the pure rate of interest, the price of risk, and the amount of risk as measured by covariance between its return and other returns. Of course, current theory does not provide any all-encompassing criteria by which to choose between alternative time patterns of share prices within the planning horizon, so the businessman has no way to accurately implement plans to increase share price.

Nevertheless, most executives interviewed implied that maximization of the value of the firm was their goal, although they phrased the idea in more operationally meaningful terms. However, in a break from theory, most executives did not consider diversification by investors as having much impact on the value of the firm. According to theory, in a portfolio context only the non-diversifiable risk is relevant. While the major institutional investors, with large staffs of investment analysts, may fit into this portfolio context, many other investors will not. The executives saw consistent growth as a more important factor determining share value.

Mao next considered the theory and practice of risk analysis. The theoreticians measure risk by the variance of returns. Mao suggests, and I agree, that semi variance is a better measure of risk because it measures only downside risk. Management will not see the possibility of excess returns as a risk, but will focus on the risk of failing to earn an adequate return. The executives interviewed also emphasized downside risk and one called the chance of excess returns "a negative risk (a sweetener)." Those interviewed also expressed risk as a danger of insolvency when a large amount of capital was to be invested.

Theory recommends either of two methods for incorporating risk into investment analysis: the certainty-equivalent approach and the risk-adjusted discount-rate approach. When more than one investment may be made, the theory advocates the use of the portfolio approach.

The practitioners depended in general on a risk-adjusted discount rate approach to incorporate risk, although their actual methods may be more rudimentary than the purely theoretical approach dictates. Consideration is given to the human factors of enthusiasm and dedication to the project, qualities that are non-quantifiable. Interviews also disclosed a definitional difference between theorists and practitioners about the word diversification. In theory, every project should be evaluated in terms of its covariance with other projects in the portfolio. In practice, diversification is a much more subjective, long-range process where only major activities and their impact on diversification are considered.

Mao next revives a topic considered earlier: how to measure returns on projects. Theory immediately discounts payback period and accounting profit in favor of internal rate-of-return and net present value. Interview results show that only two of the eight companies use internal rate-of-return alone, whereas six use payback and accounting profit alone or in conjunction with internal rate-of-return. Theorists have advanced two explanations for this incongruence. First, internal rate-of-return and net present value do not consider the effect of an investment on reported earnings. Stability of estimated EPS is important to management and investors alike, and these two criteria do not give management an indication of expected stability of earnings. Many companies neglect the net-present-value method because of the extreme difficulty of determining the appropriate discount rate. Individual company characteristics also determine, to a large extent, which measurement criteria are most appropriate. Lastly, Mao recommends types of research that can make theory more useful and meaningful to practitioners.

Hastie (1974), himself a practitioner, also tries to give the academic world some advice on how to better aid the businessman. According to Hastie, in "One Businessman's View of Capital Budgeting," what is needed is not refinement or multiplication of measurement techniques but a re-evaluation of the assumptions inherent in the capital-budgeting process.

Hastie outlines the major problems practitioners face in capital budgeting. First, most companies are limited by capital rationing, so the problem becomes not one of finding adequate projects, but of choosing from among the acceptable projects. Theory offers no means of ranking projects with different risks, strategic purposes, and quality of analytical support. Ranking *per se* is not an adequate selection method unless the more qualitative criteria can somehow be incorporated into the process.

Judgments enter into any process in which uncertain profits must be estimated. Hastie highlights two types of errors in judgment that can lead to failure to achieve expected returns on projects. The first is caused by excessive pessimism or optimism, with only the second posing a serious problem. Overpessimism is akin to "upside" risk in that the company will not fail to meet its goal. Overoptimism is caused by poor judgment concerning future uncertainties, which in many cases could be cured only by hiring accurate fortune tellers.

Hastie also recognizes that, in many cases, it is not the measurement method but the financial analyst who fails. The financial analyst must have a good grasp of the quantitative and qualitative impacts of each project and must be able to communicate this information to the decision makers. Those preparing expenditure requests should be objective and realistic.

Hastie recommends several methods to improve capital-budgeting techniques. First, corporate strategy must be clarified and communicated so that projects incompatible with this strategy will not be needlessly analyzed. Second, analytical techniques must be evaluated. They should be understood by all who work with them and should generate the type of information used by the company in decision making. Hastie recommends the use of sensitivity analysis to isolate critical variables and give an expanded, more realistic range of estimated profits. What is essential is that those involved in the capital-budgeting process understand corporate strategy and policy and generate realistic data, which can effectively communicate to top-level management.

James Fremgen (1973) in "Capital Budgeting Practices: A Survey," continues the analysis of practitioner use of capital-budgeting techniques, and offers some support for Hastie's position that measurement techniques are not the only important factor in capital budgeting. His survey again finds that payback period and accounting profit are widely used as selection criteria, contrary to theoretical approval of these methods, but also finds strong support for the use of internal rate-of-return. His results, however, do highlight a problem encountered when using the internal rate-of-return method — the multiple internal rate-of-return. His results also give some support to Doenges' recommendation that firms try to predict reinvestment rates for the funds to be received from projects being currently evaluated. Although of the 29% which projected reinvestment rates, the majority used current rates-of-return or costs of capital, some tried to estimate future reinvestment rates based on predicted future rate-of-returns or cost of capital.

A majority of those questioned used some technique to measure risk and uncertainty when analyzing investment projects. Again, however, a problem arises when deciding how to quantify this risk into the analysis. Most firms appear to require an unspecified amount of additional profit for additional risk. Of course, much of the analysis of projects is based on non-financial or non-quantitative judgments, and companies may feel that risk is best handled in this manner.

Fremgen confirmed the previously mentioned conclusion that capital rationing is a major influence on the capital-budgeting process. This rationing, commonly caused by a limitation on borrowing, was dealt with by most of the surveyed companies through ranking of projects. Although Hastie says this is not an adequate method of project selection, Fremgen makes little mention of non-financial, subjective methods of selection. Since project selection must be based on both financial and non-financial data, the results received must be due to wording of the question, which disallowed non-financial answers.

Providing impressive support for Hastie's position, Fremgen next described three stages of capital budgeting, only one of which dealt with financial analysis of the project. The results clearly reveal that financial analysis is considered neither the most critical nor the most difficult stage of the capital-budgeting process. More academic attention should be focused on the stage of project definition and estimation of cash flows, and the implementation and review stage of the process. Although these two stages are more difficult to adapt to quantitative methods, they would be more useful for the practitioner.

One final analysis of capital-budgeting theory and practice deals with a specific, fairly unique industry. Eugene Brigham and Richard Pettway (1973), in "Capital Budgeting by Utilities," studied the practices in this heavily regulated industry. Regulation has a profound effect on capital-budgeting practice, and the theory behind this regulation has become antiquated with the advent of double-digit inflation.

The regulators specify a target rate-of-return for utility companies, which then determine the rates they can charge consumers. However, inflation has caused the actual rate-of-return to fall below the "reasonable" rate-of-return, and, due to the lags in the regulatory process, new targeted rates-of-returns, when implemented, already have fallen behind inflation.

Another unique feature of the utility industry is that, due to legal requirements, they must make "mandatory" investments when needed to provide service upon demand. These mandatory investments, the major component of the capital budget, frequently offer rates-of-return below the utility's cost of capital. Although discretionary investments may provide higher returns, rarely can these excess returns counterbalance the effects of inflated operating costs, rising cost of capital, mandatory investments, and regulatory lags. Thus, the cost of capital exceeds the actual rate-of-return in the capital-investment budget.

Because of this unique situation, utilities must be very cautious when deciding which discretionary projects to accept. Projects with high rates-of-return are needed to help compensate for other losses. For mandatory investments, revenues are disregarded and alternatives evaluated solely on the basis of costs on a discounted cash-flow basis. Due to the urgency of keeping costs as low as possible for mandatory investments, and profits as high as possible for discretionary investments, 94% of the companies use the discounted cash-flow method to project future financial results more accurately. Risk is also formally analyzed by over 50% of the utilities questioned.

Surprisingly, only 49% of these companies indicated that they have experienced capital rationing in the past 5 years, and most of these indicated that their response would be to apply for a rate increase to alleviate the problem. The most serious problem they face is securing permission to build new generating plants, a problem not shared with other industries. Since it is so crucial for rate determination, most utilities have ready cost-of-capital figures to use in capital-budgeting analysis.

Obviously, many of the problems facing the utility industry are unique to the industry, and the managers have developed different perspectives and policies on capital budgeting to cope with these problems. There is a message in this for all those involved with financial management. Regardless of the academician's recommendations, the competition's practices, and the market's signals, capital-budgeting policy and practice must be adapted to suit the individual firm's characteristics and needs. Theory and practice are helpful only to the extent that they can be successfully integrated into the individual company's financial structure. Theorists must try to recognize the needs of financial practitioners, but the practitioners must also realize that no mere formula will guarantee success, and realistic theories will help their financial analysis and planning decisions.

The reader should be aware that, in practice, most firms use a combination of capital-budgeting techniques to arrive at investment decisions.

For instance, in a survey of large firms, Schall *et al.* (1978) found that 17% of those firms responding used four of the capital-budgeting techniques outlined above, and 34% used three of the four in making decisions. More surprisingly, although 86% of the firms used at least one of the discounting methods, the most popular technique was found to be the payback method, despite its disregard of several important factors. Perhaps the continued use of simpler methods combined with the more accurate NPV or IRR, points to the importance of ease of calculation for practitioners. In addition, despite the frequently noted ambiguities accompanying use of the IRR, the method enjoys a substantial and continuing popularity in practice. In their paper "Survey and Analysis of Capital-Budgeting Methods used by Multinationals," Oblak and Helm (1980) found that the IRR method and the payback method are two most popular capital-budgeting methods used by multinational firms. The continued use of IRR may be due to the fact that the rate-of-return of a project has a more intuitive appeal and is therefore easier to explain and justify within the firm than the more esoteric NPV criterion.

The survey conducted by Graham and Harvey (2001) explains the existing and popular methods and processes of corporate finance. This survey also mentioned John Litner's (1956) groundbreaking research and study of the dividend policy. The goal of this survey conducted by Graham and Harvey was to establish new theories as well as alter current views of corporate finance. This survey also hopes to expose how other firms perform by offering recommendations that are not already being fully applied. The overall scope of this survey is very extensive and the concepts of capital budgeting, cost of capital, and capital structure are analyzed and discussed thoroughly. Furthermore, a large sample of about 4,440 firms is selected. Out of this sample, 392 chief financial officers responded to the survey, meaning that this survey has a response rate of about 9%. Another distinguishing factor of this survey, is that the responses are analyzed according to firm characteristics. Overall the approach that this survey implements allows for a balance between clinical studies and large sample analyses.

References for Appendices 13.A and 13.B

Brigham, EF and R Pettway (1973). Capital budgeting by utilities. *Financial Management*, 11–22.

Fremgen, J (1973). Capital-budgeting practices: A survey. *Management Accounting*, 2, 19–25.

Graham, JR and CR Harvey (2001). The theory and practice of corporate finance: Evidence from the field. *Journal of Financial Economics*, 60, 187–243.
Hastie, KL (1974). One businessman's view of capital budgeting. *Financial Management*, 3, 36–44.
Lee, CF and AC Lee (2006). *Encyclopedia of Finance.* New York: Springer.
Litner J (1956). Distribution of incomes and corporations among dividends, retained earnings, and taxes. *American Economic Review*, 46, 97–113.
Mao, JCT (1970). Survey of capital budgeting: Theory and practice. *Journal of Finance*, 349–360.
Oblak, DJ and RJ Helm, Jr (1980). Survey and analysis of capital-budgeting methods used by multinationals. *Financial Management*, 9, 37–41.
Reinhardt, HE (1973). Break-even analysis for Lockheed's Tri Star: An application. *Journal of Finance*, 28, 821–838.
Schall, LD, GL Sundem, and WR Geijsbeek, Jr. (1978). Survey and analysis of capital-budgeting methods. *Journal of Finance*, 281–287.

Appendix 13.C. Derivation of Crossover Rate

Suppose there are two projects under consideration. Cash flows of project A, B and B–A as followed:

Period	0	1	2	3
Project A	−10,000	10,000	1,000	1,000
Project B	−10,000	1,000	1,000	12,000
Cash flows of B–A	0	−9,000	0	11,000

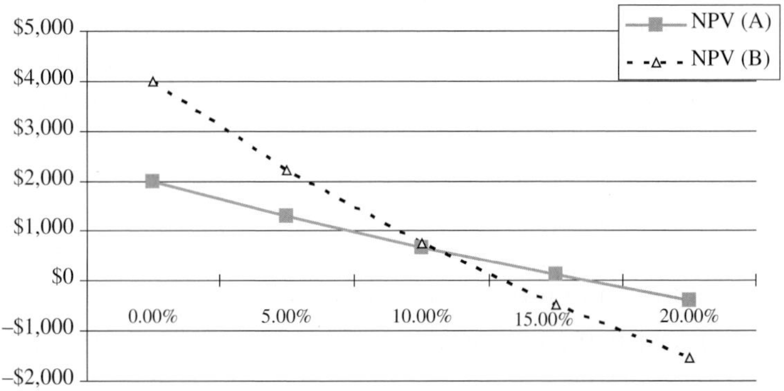

Fig. 13.C.1. Net present value and IRR for mutually exclusive projects.

NPV(B) is higher with low discount rates and NPV(A) is higher with high discount rates. This is because the cash flows of Project A occur early and those of Project B occur later. If we assume a high discount rate, we would favor Project A; if a low discount rate is expected, Project B will be chosen. In order to make the right choice, we can calculate the crossover rate. If the discount rate is higher than the crossover rate, we should choose Project A; if otherwise, we should go for Project B. **The crossover rate, Rc, is the rate such that NPV(A) equals to NPV(B).**

Suppose the crossover rate is Rc, then

$$\text{NPV}(A) = -\frac{10{,}000 + 10{,}000}{(1+Rc)} + \frac{1{,}000}{(1+Rc)^2} + \frac{1{,}000}{(1+Rc)^3}, \quad (13.C.1)$$

$$\text{NPV}(B) = -\frac{10{,}000 + 1{,}000}{(1+Rc)} + \frac{1{,}000}{(1+Rc)^2} + \frac{12{,}000}{(1+Rc)^3}, \quad (13.C.2)$$

$$\text{NPV}(A) = \text{NPV}(B).$$

Therefore,

$$\boxed{\begin{aligned} &-10{,}000 + \frac{10{,}000}{1+R_c} + \frac{1{,}000}{(1+R_c)^2} + \frac{1{,}000}{(1+R_c)^3} \\ &\quad = -10{,}000 + \frac{1{,}000}{1+R_c} + \frac{1{,}000}{(1+R_c)^2} + \frac{12{,}000}{(1+R_c)^3}. \end{aligned}}$$

Rearranging the above equation (moving all terms on the LHS to the RHS), we obtain (13.C.3)

$$\boxed{\begin{aligned} 0 &= [-10{,}000 - (-10{,}000)] + \left[\frac{1{,}000}{1+R_c} - \frac{10{,}000}{1+R_c}\right] \\ &\quad + \left[\frac{1{,}000}{(1+R_c)^2} - \frac{1{,}000}{(1+R_c)^2}\right] + \left[\frac{12{,}000}{(1+R_c)^3} - \frac{1{,}000}{(1+R_c)^3}\right] \cdots \end{aligned}} \quad (13.C.3)$$

Solving Eq. (13.C.3) by trial and error method for R_c.

R_c equals 55%.

In addition, the general equation of (13.C.3) can be defined as

$$\boxed{0 = CF_0(B-A) + \frac{CF_1(B-A)}{1+R_c} + \frac{CF_2(B-A)}{(1+R_c)^2} + \frac{CF_3(B-A)}{(1+R_c)^3},}$$

where

$CF_0(B-A)$ = The different of net cash inflow between Project A and Project B at time 0.
$CF_1(B-A)$ = The different of net cash inflow between Project A and Project B at time 1.
$CF_2(B-A)$ = The different of net cash inflow between Project A and Project B at time 2.
$CF_3(B-A)$ = The different of net cash inflow between Project A and Project B at time 3.

In other word, *Rc* is the IRR of the project (B – A).

References for Chapter 13

Ackoff, Russel L (1970). A concept of corporate planning, Wiley, New York (ch. 1, 2, 3, 7).
Beraneck, W (1978). Some new capital-budgeting theorems. *Journal of Financial and Quantitative Analysis*, 13, 17–31.
Beraneck, W (1980). The AB procedure and capital budgeting. *Journal of Financial and Quantitative Analysis*, 15, 391–406.
Brick, JR and EH Thompson (1978). The economic life of an investment and appropriate discount rate. *Journal of Financial and Quantitative Analysis*, 13, 831–846.
Bierman Jr, H and S Smidt (1988). *The Capital Budgeting Decision* 7th ed., New York: Macmillan Publishing Co., Inc.
Copeland, TE and JF Weston (2003). *Financial Theory and Corporate Policy*, 4th ed. Reading: Addison-Wesley Publishing Co.
Copeland, T, T Koller, and J Murrin (2000). *Valuation: Measuring and Managing the Value of Companies*, 3rd ed., New York: John Wiley & Sons, Inc.
Dorfman, R (1981). The meaning of internal rate-of-return. *Journal of Finance*, 36, 1011–1021.
Doenges, RC (1972). The reinvestment problem in a practical perspective. *Financial Management*, 1, 85–91.
Emery, GW (1982). Some guidelines for evaluating capital investment alternatives with unequal lives. *Financial Management*, 11, 14–19.
Fama, EF and MH Miller (1972). *The Theory of Finance.* New York: Holt, Rinehart and Winston).
Fisher, I (1930). *The Theory of Interest.* New York: MacMillan.
Graham, JR and CR Harvey (2001). The theory and practice of corporate finance: Evidence from the field. *Journal of Financial Economics*, 60(2–3), 187–243.
Haley, CW and LD Schall (1979). *The Theory of Financial Decisions.* New York: McGraw-Hill.
Hirshleifer, JH (1958). On the theory of optimal investment decision. *Journal of Political Economy*, 66, 329–352.

Lee, CF and AC Lee (2006). *Encyclopedia of Finance*. New York: Springer.
Levy, H and M Sarnat (1995). *Capital Investment and Financial Decisions*, 5th ed., Englewood Cliffs, New Jersey: Prentice-Hall International.
Mao, JCT (1966). The internal rate-of-return as a ranking criterion. *Engineering Economists*, 11, 1–13.
Mao, JCT (1969). *Quantitative Analysis of Financial Decisions*. New York: Macmillan Co.
Mayer, RL (1979). A note on capital-budgeting techniques and the reinvestment rate. *Journal of Finance*, 34, 1251–1254.
Modigliani, F and MH Miller (1958). The cost of capital, corporation finance, and the theory of investment. *American Economic Review*, 48, 261–297.
Modigliani, F and MH Miller (1963). Corporate income tax and the cost of capital: A correction. *American Economic Review*, 53, 433–443.
Myers, SC (1974). Interaction of corporate financing and investment decision. *Journal of Finance*, 29, 1–25.
Myers, SC and SM Turnbull (1977). Capital budgeting and the capital-asset pricing model: good news and bad news. *Journal of Finance*, 32, 321–333.
Nelson, CRK (1976). Inflation and capital budgeting. *Journal of Finance*, 31, 923–931.
Pinches, George E. (1982). Myopia, capital budgeting and decision making. *Financial Management*, 11, 6–19.
Reinhardt, UE (1973). Break-even analysis for Lockheed's tri star: an application of financial theory. *Journal of Finance*, 28, 821–838.
Ross, SA, CS Spatt, and PH Dybrig (1980). Present value of internal rates-of-return. *Journal of Economic Theory*, 17, 66–81.
Ross, SA, RW Westerfield, and JF Jaffe (2008). *Corporate Finance*, 8th ed., New York: McGraw-Hill Irwin Publishing Co.
Weingartner, HM (1963). *Mathematical Programming and the Analysis of Capital-Budgeting Problems*. New Jersey: Prentice-Hall, Englewood Cliffs.
Weingartner, HM (1977). Capital rationing: N authors in search of a plot. *Journal of Finance*, 32, 1403–1432.

Chapter 14

Capital Budgeting Under Uncertainty

14.1. Introduction

The information needed for capital budgeting is generally not known with certainty. Therefore, capital-budgeting procedures under conditions of uncertainty should be developed to improve the precision of assessment of the value of risky investment projects. The sources of uncertainty may be either the net cash inflow, the life of the project, or the discount rate. The main sources of uncertainty associated with the net cash inflow were discussed earlier. The uncertainty associated with the life of the project may be due to deterioration or obsolescence. The uncertainty of discount rates may be attributable to changes in market rates-of-return and/or risk-free rates-of-return. In this chapter, Section 14.2 discusses risk-adjusted discount-rate methods, and Section 14.3 discusses the certainty-equivalent method. Section 14.4 investigates the relationship between the risk-adjusted discount-rate method and the certainty-equivalent method. In Section 14.5, three related stochastic methods useful in the making of capital-budgeting decisions are discussed in detail. Section 14.6 introduces the varied impacts that inflation has on the analysis of risky projects, in the assessment of the cash-flow streams, the adjustment of discount rates, and the optimal capital–labor ratio to be employed in the actual undertaking of the project, all of which are explained in detail. In Section 14.7, we introduce the uncertainty of project life and analyses of the product life cycle, and also investigate the potential problems in applying the single-period CAPM to multi-period projects. Lastly, Section 14.8, contains a summary and conclusion to this chapter.[1]

14.1.1. *Why is Net Present Value (NPV) Positive (or Negative)?*

In a competitive economy, positive NPV projects will be difficult to find. The fact that approximately 70% of new businesses fail within 5 years of start-up is strong evidence of this. Analysis of most potential projects should reveal a zero or negative NPV, but a few may fall in the distribution's upper tail with a positive NPV. If initial analysis indicates a positive NPV, managers should remain wary. The project may have a positive NPV for two reasons: it truly may be a wealth-enhancing project, or estimates of the project's cash flows and/or required rate-of-return may be incorrect.[1]

In reality, each period's cash flow can take on a range of values, depending upon assumptions regarding economic and competitive conditions. Cash flow estimates really are point estimates of random variables; they represent the expected values of each period's cash flow: $[E(CF_t)]$. The expected value is based upon the probability distribution of possible cash flows in each period.

An analyst with an optimistic bias or poor ability might evaluate each period's cash flows above their true mean. This would bias the resulting NPV estimate, as well. In this way, a poor project may appear to have a positive NPV. Another way to give the NPV estimate an upward bias is to underestimate the risk of the project and hence used a required return that is too low.

The risk of error in estimating a project's cash flows or required rate-of-return is called **forecasting risk** or **estimation risk**. Table 14.1 reviews some sources of estimation risk.

Concept Quiz

1. Why are project NPVs expected to have a probability distribution?
2. Why are periodic cash flows random variables?
3. What is estimation (or forecasting) risk?

[1]For an interesting insight into other problems associated with capital budgeting under uncertainty, such as capital rationing or analysis in a regulated or international environment, see *Capital Budgeting under Conditions of Uncertainty* (edited by Roy Crum and Frans Derkinderen), Martin Publishing, Boston, 1981.

Table 14.1. Sources of uncertainty.

Expected Cash Flows	Required Rates-of-Return
Political risk:	Real risk-free return:
Blocked currencies	Supply/demand for funds
Tariffs, quotas, embargoes	Macroeconomic consumption patterns
Military conflict	Investor optimism/pessimism
Unstable government	Long-run real economic growth
Fluctuating exchange rates	Expected inflation:
Central bank policy	Monetary policy
Fiscal policy:	Commodity prices
Government spending	Risk premium:
Tax policy	Systematic risk
Inadequate or incorrect:	Political risk
Strategic analysis	Exchange rate risk
Market research	Business risk
Pricing policy	Financial risk
Competitor retaliation	
Construction delays	
Delays in R&D, manufacturing, or production	
Work stoppages or strikes	
Technology obsolescence	

14.1.2. *Break-Even Analysis*

Several subjective and objective methods exist for evaluating the risk of capital budgeting projects. No one method is definitively correct. One method, break-even analysis, will be discussed in this section. Other methods, including scenario analysis, sensitivity analysis, and simulation, will be discussed in the next section.

Break-even analysis is just what the name implies; it determines the quantity of output that a project must sell to break even. There are several ways to evaluate break-even. An analyst may determine the cash break-even point, that is, how much output the project must sell to make the cash it generates equal its cash expenses. Or, the analyst may want a project's accounting break-even point, when its net income is zero. Another break-even quantity, financial break-even, is the quantity that must be sold to make the project's NPV equal to zero. Below, we derive a general formula for break-even analysis, and then we apply it to situations involving cash, accounting, and financial break-even analysis.

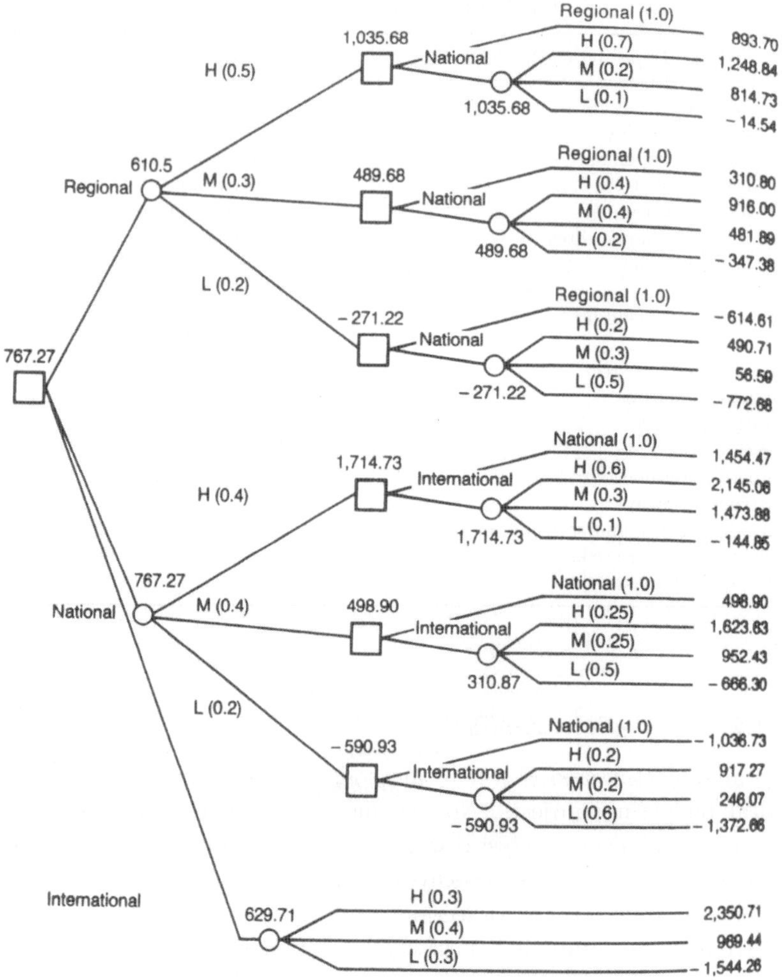

Fig. 14.1. Decision tree. Numbers in parentheses are probabilities; numbers without parentheses are NPV.

14.1.3. *General Break-Even Analysis*

If a firm expects to be able to sell a product for p per unit, total sales revenues will be p per units times Q units, or pQ. If the price is constant, sales revenue is directly related to Q, the total number of units sold.

Total production costs have two components. The first component is variable cost; variable costs rise and fall as output increases and decreases. These costs result mainly from raw material and labor expenses. If each

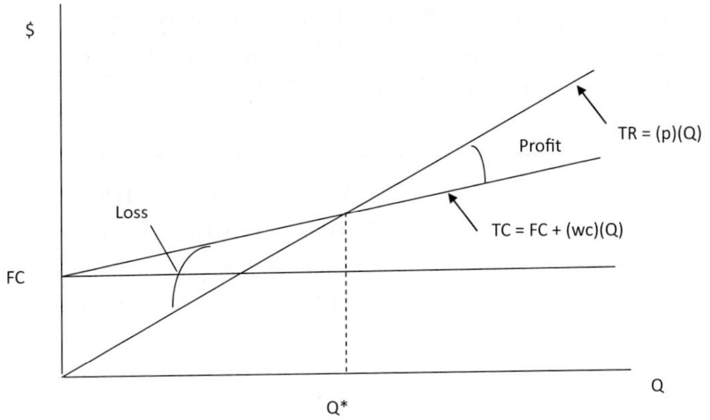

Fig. 14.2. Total revenue and total cost.

output unit has variable production costs of vc per unit, the total variable cost of production is vc times Q units, or vcQ.

The second component of total cost is the fixed cost of production. As we saw in an earlier chapter, fixed costs create operating leverage. Fixed cost is constant at FC, regardless of the level of output.

Total cost is the sum of fixed cost and total variable cost at any level of output. At output level Q, total cost is FC + $(vc)(Q)$.

The lines in Fig. 14.2 represent total revenue and total cost. The vertical distance between the revenue and cost lines represents the project's pretax profit or loss.

Output level Q*, where the revenue and cost lines intersect, represents the break-even point; sales revenue exactly equals cost. At output levels below Q^*, costs exceed revenues and the project loses money. At output levels above Q^*, revenues exceed costs and the project generates a profit.

EXAMPLE 14.1

Revenues Minus Costs

Q: If the forecasted price of a new product offering is \$5, the variable cost-per-unit is \$3, and fixed costs are \$100, what is the profit or loss that results from selling 40 units? 50 units? 100 units?

A: To find the profit or loss, we must first determine the revenues and costs at the different output levels. With a price of \$5 a unit, total revenue at Q units will be \$5Q. Total revenues at 40, 50, and 100 units are \$200, \$250, and \$500, respectively.

Since variable cost is \$3 per unit, total variable cost at Q units will be \$$3Q$. Total cost is the sum of the calculated total variable cost and the fixed cost of \$100. These calculations are show below:

	40 Units	**50 Units**	**100 Units**
Total variable cost	\$120	\$150	\$300
Fixed Cost	100	100	100
Total Cost	\$220	\$250	\$400

The profit or loss is the difference between the total revenue and total cost at each output level:

	40 Units	**50 Units**	**100 Units**
Total Revenue	\$200	\$250	\$500
Total Cost	220	250	400
Profit (loss)	(\$20)	\$0	\$100

The break-even point occurs where revenues equal costs, in this case at 50 units, as represented by Q^* in Fig. 14.2. At output levels less than 50, the project suffers losses; at output levels greater than 50, it generates profits.

With this background, let's derive a general formula to solve for Q^*, the break-even point. As a starting point, let's develop a relationship between output sold, Q, and the project's operating cash flow (OCF). We know that OCF equals sales revenue less expenses less taxes, minus the change in net working-capital. To keep the analysis simple, let's assume that there will be *no changes in net working-capital* and that *taxes are zero*. With these assumptions we have:

$$\text{OCF} = \text{S} - \text{C}.$$

Sales revenue equals price times quantity sold or pQ^* (we use the break-even quantity, Q^*, since this is a break-even situation). Total cost equals fixed cost plus total variable cost, or FC + $(vc)(Q^*)$. Substituting these terms into Eq. (14.1) gives us:

$$\text{OCF} = pQ^* - \text{FC} - (vc)(Q^*).$$

Solving for Q^*, we have a general formula for the break-even quantity, Q^*:

$$Q^* = \frac{\text{FC} + \text{OCF}}{p - vc}. \tag{14.2}$$

The denominator, $p - vc$, or price less the variable cost per unit, is called the **contribution margin.** It measures the contribution of each unit sold toward covering fixed costs. In Example 14.1, price is \$5 and variable cost per unit is \$3. Thus \$2 of the price of every unit sold goes toward covering fixed costs. Since fixed costs in Example 14.1 are \$100, 50 units, each contributing \$2 to cover fixed costs, need to be sold to achieve break-even.

Projects that use production technologies with high fixed costs and high degrees of operating leverage typically have lower variable costs than projects that use technologies with low fixed costs.[2] In other words, there is a tradeoff between fixed cost and variable cost. The effects on profit of a choice between a high fixed-cost technology (for example, robots) and a low fixed-cost technology (more labor-intensive processes) are seen in panels (a) and (b) of Fig. 14.3.

Panel (a) of Fig. 14.3 shows how high fixed cost and low variable cost make the break-even quantity, Q^*_{HFC}, rather large. Panel (a) of Fig. 14.3 reflects a high-business risk, high-return strategy. The use of a high fixed-cost production technology leads to high risk because it increases the amount of output the firm must sell to break even, and the penalty (operating losses) for failing to break even are large due to the negative effects of operating leverage. The rewards, however, also can be quite large. Due to the large contribution margin (price less low variable cost), pretax profits rise rapidly after the project breaks even. In this case, the positive effects of operating leverage cause sales increases to result in large operating profit increases once the break-even point is reached.

The opposite case is shown in panel (b) of Fig. 14.3. Low fixed cost and operating leverage keeps the break-even quantity, Q^*_{LFC}, below that in panel (a). The use of a low fixed-cost production technology leads to low

[2] Theoretical portions of this section should be read for continuity, but it is not necessary for the student to gain complete mastery over such theory as a prerequisite to understanding other portions of this chapter.

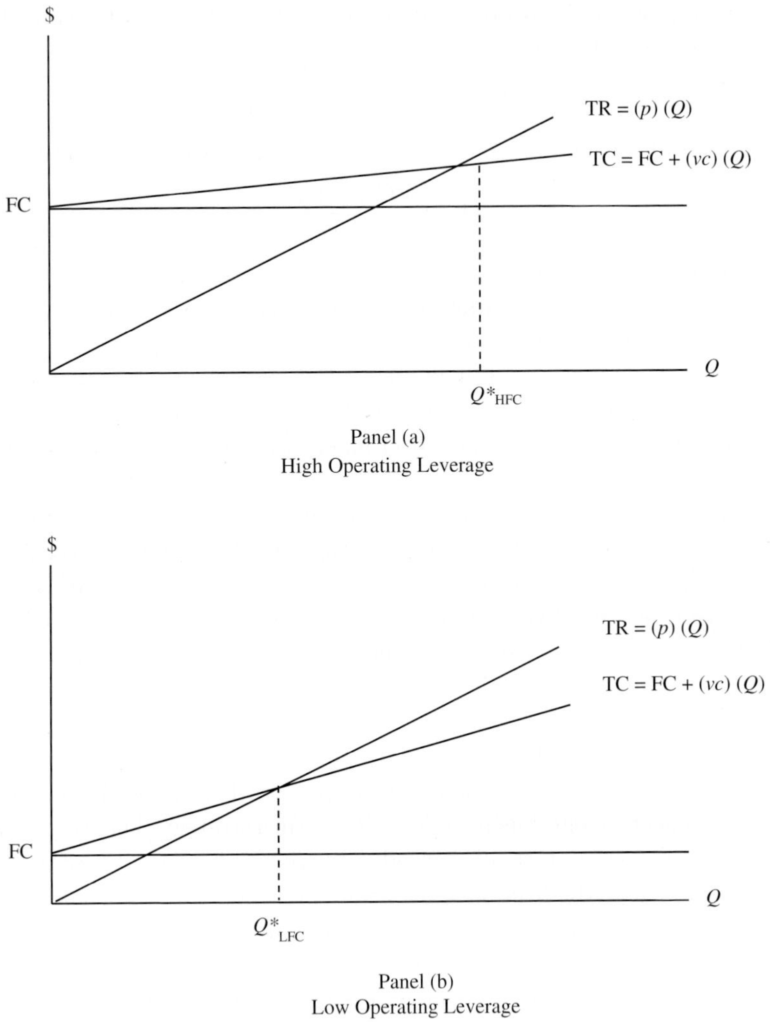

Fig. 14.3. The effect of fixed costs on project break-even.

risk, as the firm must sell output (as compared to panel a) to break even, and the penalty (operating losses) for failure to break even are smaller. The rewards for surpassing break-even, however, also are smaller.

This discussion illustrates the importance of strategic analysis and choice of production technology. Poor strategic analysis of a capital budgeting project can make a decision to use a higher fixed-cost technology harmful to firm value and shareholder wealth if actual sales fall below the forecast.

This discussion also shows why, when the economy begins to recover from a recession, many of the best-performing firms are those with high degrees of operating leverage. Operating leverage can use robust increases in sales to turn a big loser into a very profitable firm.

We now will apply our general break-even formula, Eq. (14.2), to specific situations of cash break-even, accounting break-even, and financial break-even.

Concept Quiz

1. Why is the general break-even formula?
2. How does fixed cost affect the break-even point?

14.1.4. *Cash Break-Even*

Cash break-even occurs when a project's cash inflows equal its cash outflows. Thus, the project's period-by-period OCF is zero. Substituting OCF = \$0 into Eq. (14.2) gives us the formula for the cash break-even point:

$$Q^*_{\text{cash}} = \frac{\text{FC}}{p - vc}. \tag{14.3}$$

Recall from our earlier discussion that we assume taxes are zero. How do taxes affect the cash break-even point? At cash break-even, the firm suffers an accounting loss as a result of non-cash accounting expenses such as depreciation. The resulting tax refund reduces the actual break-even point below Q^*_{cash}.[3]

[3]Substituting Eq. (14.18) into (14.17b) and letting $\rho_{\tau t} = 1$, we have:

$$\begin{aligned}\sigma_{NPV} &= \left[\sum_{t=1}^{N} \frac{\sigma_t}{(1+k)^{2t}} + 2\sum_{\tau=1}^{N}\sum_{t=\tau+1}^{N} \frac{1}{(1+k)^t}\frac{1}{(1+k)^\tau}\sigma_\tau\sigma_t\right]^{\frac{1}{2}} \\ &= \left[\left(\sum_{t=1}^{N} \frac{\sigma_t}{(1+k)^t}\right)^2\right]^{\frac{1}{2}} \\ &= \sum_{t=1}^{N} \frac{\sigma_t}{(1+k)^t}.\end{aligned}$$

EXAMPLE 14.2

Cash Break-Even

Q: For the fruit juice bar, compute the cash break-even point. Basic information about the campus fruit juice bar is given below:

Initial investment in fixed assets = \$10,000;
Project Life = 4 years;
Straight-line depreciation expense per year = \$2,500;
Price per glass = \$1.50;
Variable cost per glass = \$1.10;
Annual fixed cost (license) = \$1,000;
Initial investment in net working-capital = \$3,500;
Recovery of net working-capital in Year 4 = \$3,500;
Salvage value of assets in Year 4 = \$0;
Average tax rate = 40%;
Required rate-of-return = 12%.

Year	Number of Glasses	Net Income	+Depreciation	+NWC	Fixed Assets	Total Cash Flow	PV (12%)
0	0	\$0	\$0	−\$3,500	−\$10,000	−\$13,500	−\$13,500
1	8,750	0	2,500	0	0	2,500	2,232.25
2	17,500	2,100	2,500	0	0	4,600	3,667.12
3	26,250	4,200	2,500	0	0	6,700	4,769.06
4	35,000	6,300	2,500	3,500	0	12,300	7,816.65
						NPV =	\$4,985.08

A: To apply Eq. (14.3), we need to know the project's fixed cost and the product's price and variable cost-per-unit. The annual fixed cost is \$1,000. The price for each glass of fruit juice is \$1.50, and the variable cost is \$1.10 per glass. Substituting these numbers in Eq. (14.3):

$$Q^*_{\text{cash}} = \frac{\$1{,}000}{\$1.50 - \$1.10} = 2{,}500.$$

For the annual OCF to equal zero, the fruit juice bar must sell 2,500 glasses.

At cash break-even, the fruit juice bar's pre-tax profits are:

Revenues	−Variable costs	−Fixed Costs	−Depreciation	
\$1.50(2,500)	−\$1.10(2,500)	−\$1,000	−\$2,500	= −\$2,500

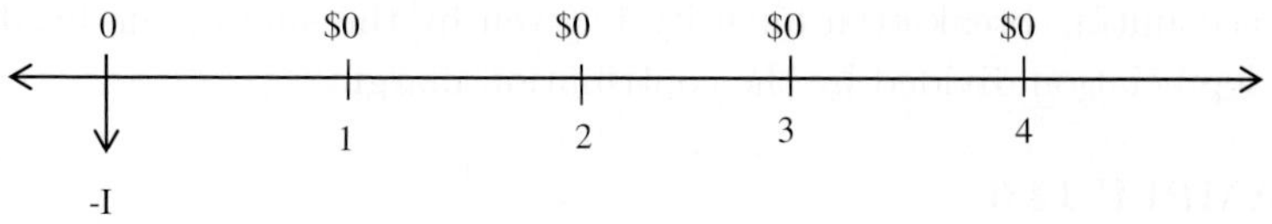

Fig. 14.4. Cash flows for a cash break-even project.

So the stand suffers an accounting loss. The size of the loss equals the size of the non-cash expense, depreciation.

For any project operating at cash break-even, net income (ignoring taxes) will equal depreciation expense. This stands to reason. Ignoring working-capital, we know that OCF equals net income plus depreciation: OCF = NI + Dep. In the case of cash break-even, OCF is zero, so NI = −Dep.

Figure 14.4 shows the cash flow timeline for a project with an initial investment I that operates at its cash break-even. The year 0 cash flow equals $-I$, and the OCF each year is zero.

As the present value of the future cash flows equals $0 and the cost of the investment is I, the net present value for a project operating at cash break-even is $-I$. Since it has no positive OCFs, a project operating at cash break-even has an internal rate-of-return of −100%. As far as the payback period is concerned, the project will never pay for itself.

Concept Quiz

1. What are the components of operating cash flow at cash break-even?
2. How do taxes affect the cash break-even point?
3. What is the relationship between cash break-even and NPV, IRR, and payback?

14.1.5. *Accounting Break-Even*

Accounting break-even occurs when accounting revenues equal accounting expenses so that pretax income (and hence net income) equals zero. Ignoring working-capital effects, Eq. (9.1) defines operating cash flow as OCF = NI + Dep, where NI is net income and Dep is periodic depreciation. At accounting break-even, NI is zero, so OCF equals Dep, the depreciation expense. Substituting this into the general break-even formula, Eq. (14.2), we see that:

$$Q^*_{\text{accounting}} = \frac{\text{FC} + \text{Dep}}{p - vc} = Q^*_{\text{cash}} + \frac{\text{Dep}}{p - vc}. \tag{14.4}$$

The accounting break-even quantity is given by the sum of the fixed cost and depreciation divided by the contribution margin.

EXAMPLE 14.3

Accounting Break-Even

Q: Using the data in Example 14.2, determine the yearly accounting break-even level for fruit juice sales.
A: From the information in Example 14.2, the annual fixed cost is \$1,000, the price-per-glass is \$1.50, and the unit variable cost is \$1.10. Depreciation expense is given as \$2,500 per year. Applying Eq. (10.4) gives us the accounting break-even profit:

$$Q^*_{\text{accounting}} = \frac{\$1{,}000 + \$2{,}500}{\$1.50 - \$1.10} = 8{,}750.$$

To make annual net income equal zero, the juice bar must sell 8,750 glasses. It suffers an accounting loss if it sells less than 8,750 glasses; it generates an accounting profit if it sells more than 8,750 glasses.

Figure 14.5 shows the cash flow timeline for a project that operates continuously at accounting break-even. The initial investment is I and annual cash flows equal the depreciation expense.

The only annual cash flows are from depreciation. Under straight-line depreciation, their annual amount is I/n, where n is the project's life, in years. Over the life of the project, the sum of the depreciation cash flows equals I, the cost of the project. Thus, the payback period of a project operating at accounting break-even exactly equals its life.

The internal rate-of-return of a project operating at accounting break-even is 0%, as the undiscounted sum of the annual OCF equals the initial investment, that is, $\Sigma\text{Dep} = \text{I}$. If the operating cash flows are discounted at any positive discount rate, the NPV of the accounting break-even project will be negative, although the specific NPV will depend upon the discount rate.

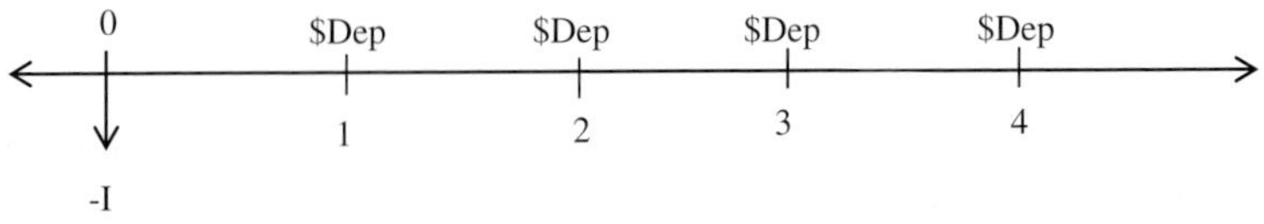

Fig. 14.5. Cash flows for an accounting break-even project.

Concept Quiz

1. What are the components of operating cash flow under accounting break-even?
2. Will the accounting break-even point generally be higher or lower than the cash break-even point? Why?
3. What is the relationship between accounting break-even and NPV, IRR, and payback?

14.1.6. *Financial Break-Even*

Financial break-even occurs when the project breaks even on a financial basis, that is, when it has a net present value of zero. To determine a project's financial break-even point, we must first determine the annual OCF*, that gives it a zero NPV. Substituting this annuity cash flow into Eq. (14.2) gives us the formula for the financial break-even quantity:

$$Q^*_{\text{financial}} = \frac{\text{FC} + \text{OCF}^*}{p - vc} = Q^*_{\text{cash}} + \frac{\text{OCF}^*}{p - vc}. \tag{14.5}$$

Without any calculations, we know intuitively that this break-even quantity should exceed the cash and accounting break-even quantities. OCF* must be sufficiently large to both cover depreciation expense and allow the project to earn its minimum required return. Intuition also tells us that accounting income under financial break-even should exceed that of the accounting break-even point. As OCF* must exceed the depreciation expense, the firm's net income will be positive (as, ignoring working-capital effects, OCF = NI+Dep). Thus, some positive taxable income occurs under financial break-even.[4]

EXAMPLE 14.4

Financial Break-Even

Q: Find the annual financial break-even point of the fruit juice bar described in Example 14.2.

A: The first step in finding the financial break-even quantity is to determine the OCF annuity that results in a zero NPV. We know that the initial investment in fixed assets and net working-capital is \$13,500; the Year 4 net working-capital recovery is \$3,500. Thus, the cash flow timeline for the problem is:

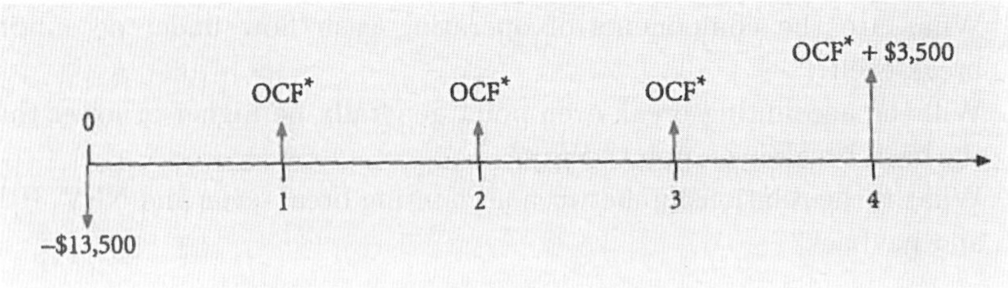

(Figure)

To find the OCF annuity, we first must adjust the timeline so it becomes an annuity problem with one outflow at Time 0 followed by a 4-year annuity. To get the timeline in the appropriate format, we need to find the present value of the net working-capital recovered in Year 4 and add it to the initial investment in Year 0. The present value of \$3,500 in Year 4, discounted at 12% is:

$$\frac{\$3{,}500}{(1/1.12)^4} = \$2{,}224.25.$$

Adding this to the Year 0 cash flow of $-\$13{,}500$ gives a net Year 0 outflow, in present value terms, of $-\$11{,}275.75$. This converts the cash flow timeline to standard annuity format:

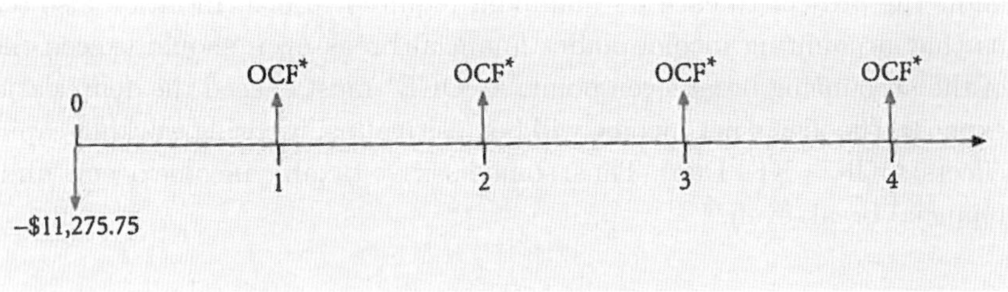

(Timeline diagram)

To find the value of the annuity, we can use the present value of an annuity formula:

$$\text{PVAN} = \text{CF}\left[\frac{1-\left(\frac{1}{1+r}\right)^n}{r}\right] = \$11{,}275.75 = \text{OCF}^*\left[\frac{1-\left(\frac{1}{1.12}\right)^4}{0.12}\right].$$

Which becomes:

$$\text{OCF}^* = \frac{\$11{,}275.75}{3.0373} = \$3{,}712.43.$$

The OCF sufficient for financial break-even is \$3,712.43 per year. The financial break-even point is found by substituting this data into Eq. (14.5):

$$Q^*_{\text{financial}} = \frac{\text{FC} + \text{OCF}^*}{p - vc} = \frac{\$1{,}000.00 + \$3{,}712.43}{\$1.50 - \$1.10} = 11{,}781.08.$$

Since the stand cannot sell fractional units, it must sell 11,782 glasses per year to break even financially.

As expected, the financial break-even quantity and OCF exceed those of the cash and accounting break-even analysis. Note a major difference between financial break-even as compared to cash and accounting break-even: Financial break-even analysis encompasses cash flows from the *entire life* of the project. This is seen in the above example when the present value of the net working-capital recovered in Year 4 is netted against the Year 0 outflow so we can calculate the annuity OCF sufficient for a zero NPV. The cash and accounting break-even analyses are restricted to period-by-period cash flows.

The net present value of a project that breaks even financially is, of course, zero. Since the NPV is zero, the internal rate-of-return equals the project's required rate-of-return. Since the financial break-even OCF*, is an annuity, the project's payback period will equal I/OCF*.

Earlier we discussed how the break-even quantity is affected by the firm's operating leverage; a larger fixed cost results in a higher degree of operating leverage and break-even quantity. In addition, the firm's level of financial risk affects the financial break-even point. Recall that financial risk occurs when debt is used to finance assets. Like fixed costs in the operating structure, the fixed interest obligation must be paid regardless of the firm's sales. As will be discussed later, the proportion of debt and equity in a firm's capital structure affects a project's required rate-of-return. This means the discount rate used to determine the zero NPV OCFs depends upon the firm's financial leverage. Thus, unlike the cash and accounting break-even points, the financial break-even point encompasses the joint effects of the firm's operating and financial leverage.

Table 14.2 summarizes information from the break-even analyses for the fruit juice bar.

14.1.7. *A Final Word on Break-Even Analysis*

The real value of break-even analysis is the number it provides the analyst who must evaluate a project's riskiness. The break-even quantity represents the minimum level of unit sales at which a project can avoid suffering

Table 14.2. Summary of the fruit juice bar's break-even analyses.

Break-Even Method	Operating Cash Flow	Net Income (=OCF – Dep)	Q*
Cash	$0.00	–$2,500.00	2,500
Accounting	$2,500.00	$0.00	8,750
Financial	$3,712.43	$1,212.43	11,782

an operating cash deficit (cash break-even), harming the firm's earnings (accounting break-even), or damaging shareholder wealth and stock price (financial break-even). As the firm should emphasize maximizing shareholder wealth, the most important break-even concept in this analysis is the financial break-even.

By comparing sales forecasts to break-even quantities, analysts and decision makers can determine just how poor sales can be before the project falls to break-even point. A slim margin between the break-even quantity and the sales forecast may induce managers to drop the project or to do additional analysis to try to increase their confidence in the projected sales figures.

Concept Quiz

1. What are the components of OCF under financial break-even?
2. Why will net income be greater than zero at financial break-even? What implications will a tax payment have on a firm's financial break-even point?

14.1.8. *Three Alternative Methods of Analyzing Project Risk*

As we have just reviewed, break-even analysis provides a method of comparing a project's sales forecast to a break-even measure. Several other methods also are available to assist managers in evaluating project risk. Like break-even, these methods result in a subjective evaluation of risk by managers. In this section, we will examine three alternative methods: scenario analysis, sensitivity analysis, and simulation analysis.

14.1.8.1. *Scenario analysis*

Scenario Analysis provides a means to evaluate the potential variability in a capital budgeting project's NPV. Scenario analysis computes several net present values for the project based on different scenarios. The initial capital budgeting analysis using the analyst's estimates of expected cash flows is called the *base-case scenarios.* From this base case, typically at least two other scenarios are developed — a worst-case scenario and a best-case scenario — and NPVs are computed for each. The worst case NPV and the best case NPV gives managers a likely range in which the project's NPV will fall. The purpose of scenario analysis is to examine the joint impact on NPV of simultaneous changes in many different factors.

The worst-case scenario should reflect project results under Murphy's Law: if anything can go wrong, it will. Compared to the base case, the worst-case scenario will have lower sales volume, lower prices, higher costs, shorter product life, lower salvage value, and so on. Rather than being an exercise in disaster forecasting, however, the worst-case scenario should reflect the circumstances that could reasonably be expected should the project be plagued with bad luck or bad analysis. Some of the firm's past failures can be used as models for developing the worst-case scenario. The resulting estimates of cash flows and NPV will reflect this pessimistic perspective.

The best-case scenario should illustrate how the project will turn out if everything works better than expected. The sales figures, prices, costs, and so on should incorporate the upper boundary of *reasonable* optimism. An unrealistic pie-in-the-sky scenario, however, will add little to the analysis. Spreadsheet packages can facilitate the analysis of different scenarios.

The analyst then presents decision makers with three sets of conditions, cash flows, and NPVs. The base-case represents an estimate of the most likely outcome; the worst-case and best-case scenarios illustrate the project's possible extremes. The NPVs of the worst — and best-case scenarios represent the potential range of the project's impact on shareholder wealth. If the worst-case scenario has a large, negative NPV, management may call for more analysis to see if the project can be modified to reduce its potential for severely decreasing shareholder wealth.

Another possibility is that management may decide that the project's best-case scenario is so attractive that it overcomes the project's downside risk. This may be the case for a project with encouraging engineering or market test results or a project that may propel the firm into a position of industry leadership.

Now let us construct worst-case and best-case scenarios for this project. To keep things simple, assume that the worst-case has the income forecast lagged by 1 year so that the bar sells nothing in Year 1; this could occur, for example, if the juice bar were to have difficulty securing the appropriate licenses for zoning variances. Let's assume Year 1 income would then be −$2,500, reflecting depreciation effects. In Year 2, as a result of low sales, price reductions, and/or cost increases, net income would be \$0. Year 3 income would be \$2,100 and Year 4 income would be \$4,200. Assume also that the entrepreneur cannot recover *any* of the original net working-capital investment in Year 4. The cash flows and NPV calculation for the worst-case scenario are presented in Table 14.4. Thus, under the worst-case scenario, the project would reduce the owner's personal wealth by \$3,974.87.

For the best-case scenario, assume that the base-case sales forecast jumps forward a year. Sales would remain at zero during construction in Year 0, but Year 1 income would rise to \$2,100. Similarly, Year 2 income

Table 14.3. Fruit Juice bar–base-case scenario.

Year	# of Glasses	NI	+	Depreciation	+	NWC
0	0	\$0		\$0		−\$3,500
1	8,750	0		2,500		0
2	17,500	2,100		2,500		0
3	26,250	4,200		2,500		0
4	35,000	6,300		2,500		3,500

Year	Fixed Assets	Total Cash Flow	PV (12%)
0	−\$10,000	−\$13,500	−\$13,500.00
1	0	2,500	2,232.25
2	0	4,600	3,667.12
3	0	6,700	4,769.06
4	0	12,300	7,816.65
		NPV =	**\$4,985.08**

Table 14.4. Fruit juice bar — worst-case scenario.

Year	NI	+	Depreciation	+	NWC
0	\$0		\$0		−\$3,500
1	−2,500		2,500		0
2	0		2,500		0
3	2,100		2,500		0
4	4,200		2,500		0

Year	Fixed Assets	Total Cash Flow	PV (12%)
0	−\$10,000	−\$13,500	−\$13,500.00
1	0	0	0.00
2	0	2,500	1,993.00
3	0	4,600	3,274.28
4	0	6,700	4,257.85
		NPV =	**\$3,974.87**

Table 14.5. Fruit juice bar–best-case scenario.

Year	NI	+	Depreciation	+	NWC
0	$0		$0		−$3,500
1	2,100		2,500		0
2	4,200		2,500		0
3	6,300		2,500		0
4	8,400		2,500		3,500

Year	Fixed Assets	Total Cash Flow	PV (12%)
0	−$10,000	−$13,500	−$13,500.00
1	0	4,600	4,107.34
2	0	6,700	5,341.24
3	0	8,800	6,263.84
4	5,000	19,400	12,328.70
			NPV = $14,541.12

would equal $4,200 and Year 3 income would be $6,300. Assume Year 4 income of $8,400. The best-case scenario also will assume that the juice bar can be sold in Year 4 for $8,500 after-tax; $3,500 of this represents recovery of net working-capital and the remainder represents the value of the establishment. The cash flows and NPV calculation for the best-case scenario are presented in Table 14.5.

Under the best-case scenario, the project would increase the owner's personal wealthy by $14,541.12.

The results of the scenario analysis are presented below:

Scenario	**NPV**
Best-Case	$14,541.12
Base-Case	$4,985.08
Worst-Case	−$3,974.87

Under the worst-case scenarios, the estimated NPV of the project is about $9,000 less than the base-case NPV.[5] In the best-case scenario, the estimated NPV is about $9,500 more than the base-case NPV, adding $14,541.12 to the owner's wealth. Based on this analysis, the owner would have to decide whether to launch the project as is, perform additional analysis to try to reduce the downside risk, or reject it as not offering sufficient expected returns given its risk.

Concept Quiz

1. What is scenario analysis?
2. How can it be used to evaluate a project's risk?

14.1.8.2. *Sensitivity analysis*

Scenario analysis simultaneously modifies many variables that affect cash flows and net present value to build different scenarios. **Sensitivity analysis** changes one variable at a time from its base-case value; this isolates the effects on NPV of changes in individual variables. If large changes in NPV occur when the product price assumption or exchange rate assumption changes by, for example, 10%, then additional research may be warranted to better determine the likely market price or exchange rate. On the other hand, if NPV is relatively stable as the assumed salvage value changes, then great effort should not be expended in order to determine a more accurate estimate of salvage value.

One method for doing sensitivity analysis is to change each individual variable from its base-case value by some amount, say 5% or 10%, while holding all other variables constant at their base-case values. The resulting NPVs are computed and then recorded or graphed. A steep NPV graph, such as panel (a) in Fig. 14.6, indicates a variable that has a major impact on project success, especially as the NPV of the project is negative for some reasonable values of the variable. A more gently sloped NPV graph, such as panel (b) of Fig. 14.6, shows that a variable does not have a major influence on NPV, so additional research on likely values of this variable probably is not warranted. Spreadsheet packages allow sensitivity analysis to be done with ease.

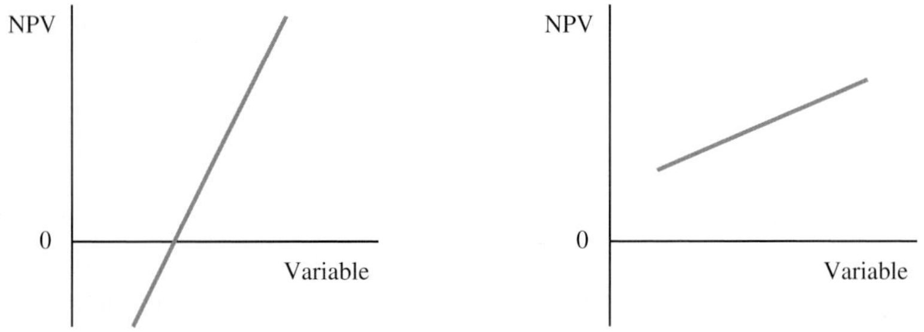

(a) Steep NPV Graph (b) Gently Sloped NPV Graph

Fig. 14.6. Sensitivity analysis graphs.

Rather than arbitrarily changing each variable by some fixed percentage, the analyst might take a cue from scenario analysis and determine best-case and worst-case values for each variable. NPVs can be computed as each variable is adjusted to its best- and worst-case estimates while all other variables are held at their base-case amounts. This combination of sensitivity analysis with scenario analysis can pinpoint which worst-case and best-case values affect NPV by the greatest amount.

Sensitivity Analysis of Price. Let us demonstrate sensitivity analysis of the fruit juice bar problem. The base-case price of each glass is \$1.50; sensitivity analysis might increase or decrease the price by 10%, holding all other factors (unit variable cost of \$1.10, recovery of net working-capital in Year 4, etc.) constant at their base-case values. As before, fixed costs are \$1,000 and depreciation is \$2,500.

Table 14.6 presents a sensitivity analysis of price. If the price-per-glass were to rise by 10%, the project NPV would rise from its base value of \$4,985.08 to \$10,627.29, an increase of \$5,642.21, or 113.18%. If the price were to decline by 10%, the NPV of the project would fall by a similar amount. The fact that NPV changes by 113.18% on a 10% price change may imply a need for additional market research to increase confidence in the price estimate. If competing projects are under consideration, a project with less price sensitivity may be preferred to this project, unless management is highly confident in the base-case scenario.

Although we will end the example analysis here, a complete sensitivity analysis would measure the impact of the remaining variables on project NPV, in order to identify for further analysis the variables causing the greatest changes in NPV.

Concept Quiz

1. What is sensitivity analysis? How does it differ from scenario analysis?
2. How can sensitivity analysis assist capital budgeting risk analysis?

14.1.8.3. *Simulation analysis*

In reality, every variable relevant to the capital budgeting decision can be viewed as a random variable. Scenario analysis and sensitivity analysis limit the randomness aspects of each item by examining only a few values of each variable. **Simulation analysis** attempts to realistically portray the relevant inputs to the capital budgeting project as random variables. Each variable, whether it be price, variable cost, project life, or some other item, is assumed to have a probability distribution with a known mean and

Table 14.6. Sensitivity analysis.

Price Increased by 10% to $1.65/Glass

Year	# of Glasses	NI	+	Depreciation	+	NWC
0	0	$0		$0		−$3,500
1	8,750	787.50		2,500		0
2	17,500	3,675.00		2,500		0
3	26,250	6,562.50		2,500		0
4	35,000	9,450.00		2,500		3,500

Year	Fixed Assets	Total Cash Flow	PV (12%)
0	−$10,000	−$13,500	−$13,500.00
1	0	3,287.50	2,935.41
2	0	6,175.00	4,922.71
3	0	9,062.50	6,450.69
4	0	15,450.00	9,818.48
			NPV = $10,627.29

Price Decreased by 10% to $1.35/Glass

Year	# of Glasses	NI	+	Depreciation	+	NWC
0	0	$0		$0		−$3,500
1	8,750	−787.50		2,500		0
2	17,500	525.00		2,500		0
3	26,250	1,837.50		2,500		0
4	35,000	3,150.00		2,500		3,500

Year	Fixed Assets	Total Cash Flow	PV (12%)
0	−$10,000	−$13,500	−$13,500.00
1	0	1,712.50	1,529.09
2	0	3,025.00	2,411.53
3	0	4,337.50	3,087.43
4	0	9,150.00	5,814.83
			NPV = $657.12

variance. For example, we may assume that the price-per-glass will range from $1.30 to $1.70 and assign each price an equal probability of occurring. The distribution of salvage values may be a skewed distribution, with values lying between $0 and $7,000, with a mean of $1,000.

In each simulation trial, computer analysis uses a random number generator to select values from each variable's probability distribution as the basis for an NPV calculation. This process is repeated many times; each time, numbers are randomly drawn from each probability distribution. After replicating the trials several thousand times, the statistical distribution of the computed NPVs is plotted and the average NPV and its variance are computed. Unlike the NPV point estimates derived from scenario or sensitivity analysis, simulation analysis gives an estimated distribution of potential NPVs.

Of course, the simulation output is only as accurate as the inputs. It is likely that an inaccurate NPV distribution will result if inappropriate probability distributions, means, and variances are used as inputs.

Figure 14.7 presents probability distributions for several fruit bar project variables and the NPV distribution that results from many samplings of these distributions.[6] By the law of large numbers, the NPV

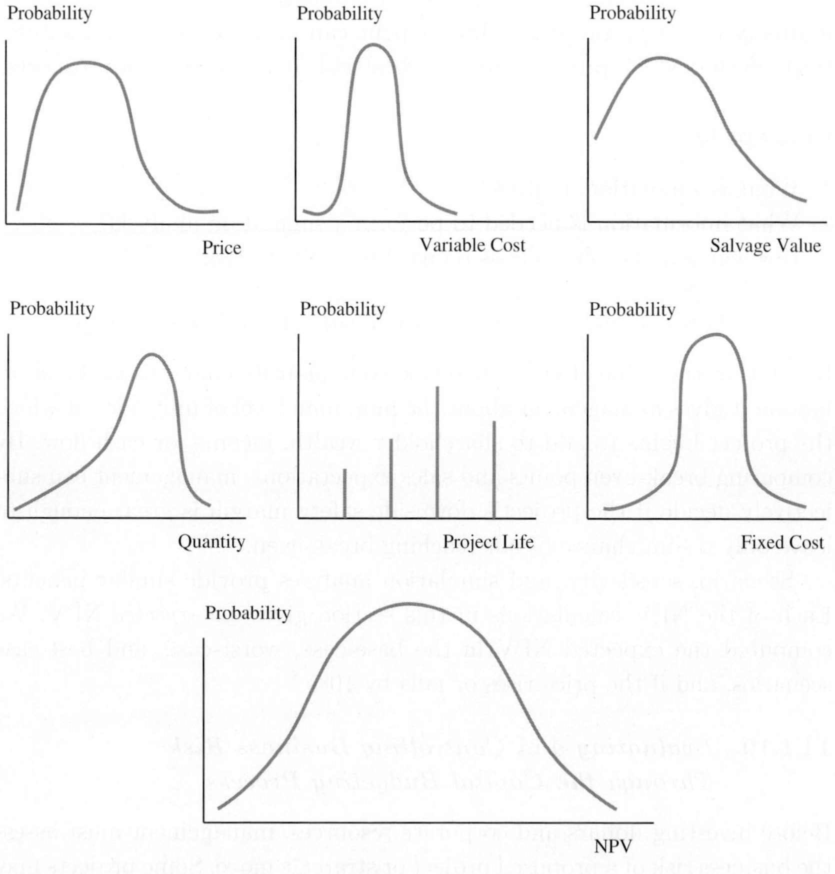

Fig. 14.7. Probability distributions for project variables.

distribution will be approximately normally distributed. Thus, the probability of a project breaking even financially (that is, having an NPV greater than or equal to zero) can be estimated. Let us assume that the simulation indicates an NPV distribution for the fruit juice bar projects with an average NPV of \$7,000 and a standard deviation of \$3,500. This means that the project's actual NPV should fall within \$3,500 and \$10,500 (that is, within one standard deviation of the mean), about 68% of the time. The probability of the project earning an NPV greater than or equal to zero is:

$$\begin{aligned} \text{Prob}(\text{NPV} \geq 0) &= \text{Prob}[\text{z} \geq (\$0 - \$7{,}000)/\$3{,}500] \\ &= \text{Prob}(z \geq -2), \quad \text{or about } 97.5\%.^{7} \end{aligned}$$

These statistics can be computed and compared among competing, mutually exclusive projects. Management can examine them and subjectively decide which project offers the best risk/expected return prospects.

Concept Quiz

1. What is simulation analysis?
2. What information is needed to perform a simulation analysis?
3. How can simulation analysis be used to evaluate risk?

14.1.9. *Some Final Comments on Evaluating Uncertainty*

Recall that the value of knowing break-even quantity comes from the information it gives management about the minimum level of unit sales at which the project begins to add to shareholder wealth, income, or cash flow. By comparing break-even points and sales expectations, management can subjectively decide if the project's downside safety margin is great enough to leave only a slim chance of not reaching break-even.

Scenario, sensitivity, and simulation analyses provide similar benefits. Each of the NPV calculations in this section gives an *expected* NPV. We computed the expected NPV in the base-case, worst-case, and best-case scenarios, and if the price rises or falls by 10%.[8]

14.1.10. *Evaluating and Controlling Business Risk Through the Capital Budgeting Process*

Before investing dollars and corporate resources, management must assess the business risk of a proposed project or strategic move. Some projects may be actively sought because they will help reduce a firm's business risk and its sensitivity to various shocks. For example, by building manufacturing plants overseas to serve overseas customers, a plant's inputs (raw materials, labor, and capital equipment purchases) and outputs both can be denominated in the currency of the same country, thus reducing a firm's exposure to exchange rate risk. In fact, this was a primary concern motivating several Japanese auto manufacturers to locate plants in the United States in the 1980s. This move also helped to mitigate the political risk faced by Japanese auto makers in the U.S., which arose from Japan's growing share of the U.S. auto market.

As another example, 1994, Texaco decided to link the amount of its capital budget to the price of oil. Therefore, the size of its budget would rise when oil prices and revenues were high and shrink when oil prices and revenues were low. By making the capital spending components variable rather than fixed, Texaco was hoping to reduce its fixed costs and business risks somewhat, as well as preserve cash when depressed oil prices hurt cash flow.

The process of risk evaluation also can be seen in Chevron's analysis of oil exploration and pipeline projects. Seeking to expand its oil reserves, the company considered exploring for oil and building pipelines in regions with high degrees of political risk, such as in some of the former Soviet Union republics. Analysis and preliminary exploration led Chevron to cancel the project since routing the oil could be dangerous due to the violence so prevalent in these regions; other alternatives, such as hooking into existing pipeline systems, were financially or politically impossible.

Other firms have been more fortunate when faced with high-risk situations. Firms such as Triton Energy Corporation and British Petroleum have overcome rough terrain and guerrilla attacks from drug traffickers to uncover and develop the largest oil strike in the Western Hemisphere in 20 years — in the country of Colombia.

Meanwhile, other firms seek to direct capital spending toward cost-reduction projects. Such projects, in addition to helping profit margins, help to reduce firm's business risks and their degree of operating leverage by reducing fixed costs and overhead.

These tools focus on NPV's potential range or variability. As such, they help management to evaluate the total risk of a project.

Break-even, scenario, sensitivity, and simulation analyses, as tools, make no decisions by themselves. These tools help management to quantify and better understand the risks of each capital budgeting project.

After analyzing the returns and risks of various projects, management must determine which are likely to add the most to shareholder value.

Management may base this decision on qualitative factors, such as subjective risk preferences and a general "feel" for the marketplace, but there are also methods to quantitatively incorporate risk into net present value analysis and project selection. These methods will be discussed in future chapters.

Concept Quiz

1. What insights do scenario, sensitivity, and simulation analyses give to the decision maker?
2. Will management's attitude toward risk play a role in deciding which capital budgeting projects to accept?

14.1.11. *Management Practices*

Surveys of large U.S. firms have found that over two-thirds of them examine project risk in their analysis of capital budgeting projects, although a smaller percentage seem to have a formal evaluation process.[9] A survey of U.S.-based multinational firms have found that 62% of the respondents consider risk in their capital budgeting analyses.[10] A sample of capital budgeting manuals used by *Fortune* 500 firms found that very few firms explain the concept of measure of risk that their analysts should use. One manual describes it this way:

> ... some investments available to a corporation may be more risky than others, i.e., there is a higher degree of possibility of losses, which in turn forces us to measure relative importance of the possibility of large profits compared with possibility of large losses. It is suggested that management should consciously consider the possibility of not realizing the forecasted results and should incorporate this into the analysis.[11]

Other methods found to be used by 25% or more of large firms include simulations, sensitivity analysis, and the use of probability scenarios to determine expected cash flows.[12] One capital budgeting manual makes the following statement about sensitivity analysis:

> Where sensitivity analysis is required, the objective is to determine those variables to which the returns on the average are most sensitive, such as volume, selling price, capital cost, manufacturing unit cost, project mix, ... etc. The number of sensitivities presented should generally be consistent with the size of the project and the degree of uncertainty in the base-case assumptions over which we will have little or no control.[13]

A survey of cash flow estimation practices by *Fortune* 500 firms found that over one-half of the respondents use sensitivity analysis and simulation as project risk evaluation techniques.[14] Firms with large capital budgets and lengthier forecasting periods were found to be more likely to use sophisticated quantitative techniques to evaluate risk. Similar results were found in a survey of firms in the United Kingdom.[15]

Concept Quiz

1. Are large U.S. firms and multinationals concerned with risk differences among their capital budgeting projects?
2. Why do you think the use of sophisticated risk evaluation techniques is more prevalent in firms with large capital budgets and longer forecasting periods?

14.1.12. *Risk Analysis for Research and Development Projects*

Probably the hardest projects for which to evaluate risk are research and development (R&D) proposals. Standard forecasting tools generally are not appropriate. The more radical and innovative the technology, the more likely the estimates will be wrong. In addition, current R&D can lead to unforeseen R&D opportunities in the future. Investments in R&D allow companies to obtain options on future investments. By doing R&D now, the firm may learn things and develop products that aren't even on today's blackboard. If the firm bypasses the chance to pursue current R&D opportunities, it will forsake these future investment possibilities.

As many R&D projects are long-term in nature, they need to be evaluated for their fit with the corporation's competitive strategy and their interrelationships with the firm's existing products and other R&D projects. Perhaps the best way to develop and manage R&D projects is to follow a portfolio approach. One component of the portfolio should include **development projects**, that is, attempts to develop products and technologies that represent small advances of an already established knowledge base. These "sure things" will be low-risk, low-return investments in R&D. A second R&D portfolio component should represent **applied research**. Applied research is riskier than development projects; it seeks to add to the firm's knowledge base by applying new knowledge to commercial purposes. The third component of the R&D portfolio should be the high-risk/high-reward pursuit of **basic research**, or research to gain knowledge for its own sake. Commercial application of any results may not become evident for a long time, if at all.

One study gives insight into how corporations evaluate R&D projects.[16] About 70% of the responding firms conduct economic analyses of R&D projects. The 30% that do no economic analysis base their decision largely on expected judgment, market potential, and strategic fit.

For those firms that reported completing economic analyses of their R&D projects, the most prevalent methods used to evaluate development and applied research projects were payback and IRR. Accounting rate-of-return was the least favored approach.

Standard discounted cash flow or accounting-based methods were seldom used to evaluate basic research projects. Survey results showed that the project's strategic fit, management's "gut feel", and perceptions of market opportunities and the potential to gain competitive advantage over rivals were important considerations in evaluating applied and basic research projects.

The majority of responding firms reported performing post-audits of R&D projects. About 71% of development projects and 50% of applied projects were reviewed at least twice a year. Only 39% of the firms reported auditing the progress of basic research projects more than once a year.

The most frequent reason given for terminating an R&D project was that the R&D priorities of the firm had changed, presumably because of changing market conditions, technological advances, and windows of opportunity. Few firms terminated projects because they were not technically feasible. This implies that firms do not begin projects unless they are fairly sure that they can achieve the technical goals of their projects.

Concept Quiz

1. What is the purpose of development projects? Applied research projects? Basic research projects?
2. Why are discounted cash flow and accounting-based project evaluation techniques more frequently used for development projects than for basic research projects?

14.1.13. *Summary*

There are many practical methods by which firms evaluate risk in capital budgeting projects and incorporate risk evaluations into NPV analysis.

Break-even analysis allows the firm to estimate the minimum level of unit sales at which a project will not harm the firm's cash position (cash break-even), earnings (accounting break-even), and stock price (financial break-even).

Scenario, sensitivity, and simulation analyses are three methods that examine potential variability in project NPVs. These methods help analysts evaluate the need for additional strategic or market analysis to increase management's confidence in the accuracy of assumed project revenues and costs.

Management practice is consistent with the discussion presented in this chapter. Surveys of financial officers find that firms routinely examine how different revenue and cost assumptions affect the attractiveness of capital budgeting projects. For technology firms, project risk is particularly difficult to evaluate. Current practice is to develop a portfolio of R&D projects; some will be low-risk, low-return "sure things" while others will have more outcomes with high potential returns.

14.2. Risk-Adjusted Discount-Rate Method

With uncertain cash flows, the financial planner will face a distribution of future cash flows rather than a single-point estimate of future cash flow in each period. One of the methods utilized to deal with these uncertain cash flows is that of the risk-adjusted discount-rate method. This method simply extends the cash-flow valuation model under certainty to the uncertainty case. The NPV of this method can be expressed as

$$NPV = \sum_{t=1}^{N} \frac{\overline{X}_t}{(1+r_t)^t} - I_0, \tag{14.6}$$

where

I_0 = Initial outlay of the capital budgeting project;
$\overline{X}_t$ = A location measure such as the median (or the mean) of the expected risky cash-flow distribution X_t in period t;
r_t = Risk-adjusted discount rate appropriate to the riskiness of the uncertain cash flow X_t;
N = Life of the project.

The advantage of the risk-adjusted discount-rate method is that the valuation model gives us a formula that explicitly considers the uncertainty associated with future cash flows. Although the model does not specify exactly what constitutes the risk of the cash flows, it can be used to develop and explore the relationships among the variables of asset-valuation models. For example, an increase in the riskiness of cash flows usually will lead to the selection of a higher discount rate, assuming investors are risk-averse. By using the risk-adjusted discount-rate method, we would expect a higher discount rate to reduce the computed value of the risky project. On the other hand, the disadvantages of the risk-adjusted discount-rate model are clear. The value of r is, at this point, only a subjective estimate, which could well differ from person to person. Therefore, an objective determination of the value of a risky investment project will be almost impossible by simply applying this method. Fortunately, recent developments in the capital-asset pricing model allow us to ultimately arrive at an objective estimate of the appropriate risk-adjusted rate with the knowledge of a capital market equilibrium pricing framework. However, to arrive at such a pricing framework, we must recognize that certain assumptions were required, the more critical of those being the existence of a perfect capital market where all participants develop homogeneous expectations as to the prospects of all securities and projects. These assumptions have been discussed in Chapter 7 in detail. Tuttle and Litzenberger (1968) have investigated the relationship between leverage, diversification, and capital-market effect on a risk-adjusted capital-budgeting framework.

14.3. Certainty Equivalent Method

While the risk-adjusted discount-rate method provides a means for adjusting the basic riskless discount rate, an alternative method, the certainty-equivalent method, adjusts the estimated value of the uncertain cash flows. The underlying rationale is that, given a risky cash flow, the decision maker will evaluate this risky cash flow by attaching an expected utility to that cash flow, that utility estimate being hypothesized to be equal to the utility derived from some certain amount. If the decision maker performs this process for each cash flow, a series of *certainty equivalents* for the risky flows can be obtained. Therefore, the problems of capital budgeting under uncertainty are reduced to those of capital budgeting under certainty, and the decision criteria discussed in the previous chapter can be applied from there. The valuation formula for the certainty-equivalent method is:

$$\text{NPV} = \sum_{t=1}^{N} \frac{C_t}{(1+i)^t} - I_0, \tag{14.7}$$

where

C_t = Certainty-equivalent cash flow at period t;
i = Riskless interest rate;
N = Life of the project.

Now, since C_t is a certain amount, the appropriate discount rate is the risk-free interest rate. It is the convention in economic theory to express C_t as a fraction of the expected value of the cash flow, henceforward. Identifying the expected cash flow as X_t, this allows us to write;

$$C_t = \alpha_t \overline{X}_t, \tag{14.8}$$

and, by substituting Eq. (14.8) into Eq. (14.7), we obtain:

$$\text{NPV} = \sum_{t=1}^{N} \frac{\alpha_t \overline{X}_t}{(1+i)^t} - I_0. \tag{14.7$'$}$$

Both the risk-adjusted discount rate and the ratio α_t reflect the uncertainty associated with the risky cash flow in period t. To obtain an objective method using CAPM, Robichek and Myers (1966) showed that the risk-adjusted rate method tends to lump together the pure rate of interest, a risk premium, and time (through the compounding process), while the certainty-equivalent approach keeps risk and the pure rate of interest separate. This separation gives an advantage to the certainty-equivalent method.

We defined the CAPM as:

$$E(R_i) = R_f + (E(R_m) - R_f)\left(\frac{\sigma_{im}}{\sigma_m^2}\right).$$

By definition, $R_t = \bar{X}_i/V_i$, where V_i is the market value of the ith firm. So

$$\frac{\overline{X}_i}{V_i} = R_f + (E(R_m) - R_f)\text{Cov}\left(\frac{X_i}{V_i}, R_m\right) \Big/ \sigma_m^2.$$

Multiplying both sides of this equation by V_i and rearranging the term, we obtain the market value of the firm as:

$$V_i = \frac{\overline{X}_i - [E(R_m - R_f)][\text{Cov}(X_i, R_m)]/\sigma_m^2}{R_f}. \tag{14.9}$$

For projects, Eq. (14.9) can be redefined as:

$$V_i^0 = \frac{\overline{X}_i^0 - [E(R_m) - R_f][\text{Cov}(X_i^0, R_m)]/\sigma_m^2}{R_f}. \tag{14.9$'$}$$

where V_i^0 and X_i^0 represent market value and cash flow of an individual project. From Eqs. (14.7′) and (14.9′), we have:

$$\text{NPV} = V_i^0 - I_0. \tag{14.7''}$$

If $R_f = 10\%$, $\text{E}(R_m) = 15\%$, $\overline{X} = \$300$, $I_0 = \$2{,}000$, $B_j = 0.80$, $\sigma_m^2 = 0.02$, then $\text{Cov}(X_i^0, R_m) = (0.80)(0.02)(2,000) = 32$, and from Eq. (14.9′) we have:

$$\begin{aligned} V_i^0 &= \frac{300 - [(0.15 - 0.10)(32)]/0.02}{0.10} \\ &= \frac{300 - (2.5)(32)}{0.10} \\ &= \frac{220}{0.10} \\ &= \$2,200. \end{aligned}$$

Since the cost of the project is \$2,000 and the project value is \$2,200, the net present value is \$200. Note that the risk-adjustment factor is \$80, or 0.267 times the expected dollar return. Hence, the certainty-adjustment factor, $\alpha = 1 - 0.267 = 0.733$. Gordon (1986) has discussed this method in detail.

14.4. The Relationship of the Risk-Adjusted Discount-Rate Method to the Certainty-Equivalent Method[2]

If we use the means of the future cash-flow distributions as the location measure, the valuation model under the risk-adjusted discount method is:

$$\text{NPV} = \sum_{t=1}^{N} \frac{\overline{X}_t}{(1 + r_t)^t} - I_0. \tag{14.10}$$

On the other hand, by using a certainty-equivalent method, each future cash flow is converted to its certainty equivalent and is then discounted at the risk-free rate of interest, which allows us to modify Eq. (14.10) to the following;

$$\text{NPV} = \sum_{t=1}^{N} \frac{\alpha_t \overline{X}_t}{(1 + i)^t} - I_0.$$

Since both methods are used to evaluate future uncertain cash flows, the two models should yield the same value for a given stream of cash flows. Moreover, the present value of each period's cash flows should be the same under these two valuation models, that is, for each period t,

$$PV_t = \frac{\alpha_t \overline{X}_t}{(1+i)^t} = \frac{\overline{X}_t}{(1+r_t)^t} \tag{14.11}$$

and from Eq. (14.11) we obtain;

$$\alpha_t = \frac{(1+i)^t}{(1+r_t)^t}. \tag{14.12}$$

Similarly, α_{t+1} can be expressed as;

$$\alpha_{t+1} = \frac{(1+i)^{t+1}}{(1+r_{t+1})^{t+1}}. \tag{14.13}$$

Rearranging Eqs. (14.12) and (14.13), we obtain;

$$r_t = \frac{1+i}{\alpha_t^{1/t}} - 1 \tag{14.14}$$

and

$$r_{t+1} = \frac{1+i}{\alpha_{t+1}^{1/(t+1)}} - 1. \tag{14.15}$$

From Eqs. (14.14) and (14.15), the risk-adjusted discount-rate r_t's will be a function of three variables: the investor's attitude toward risk (measured by α_t); the risk-free interest rate; and the time period t. Under the Arrow (1971) and Pratt (1964) risk-aversion framework, α can be derived as:

$$U(X + E(\tilde{z})\pi) = EU[X + \alpha(E\tilde{z})]$$

$$E(\tilde{z}) - \pi = \alpha E(\tilde{z})$$

$$\alpha = \frac{E(\tilde{z}) - \pi}{E(\tilde{z})},$$

where

$\pi(risk\_premium) = \frac{1}{2}\sigma_z^2 \left[\frac{U''(X)}{U'(X)}\right]$,
E($\tilde{z}$) = Actuarial value of risk;
X is assets; and
U′ (X) and U′(X) are second and first derivatives with respect to utility function U(x).

Therefore, α can be viewed as an indicator of risk for future cash flows. Combining this viewpoint with Eq. (14.6), Pratt and Arrow argue that only if the risk increases at an increasing rate over time will the discount rate be increasing over time. In other words, if $(\alpha_t)^{1/t} > (\alpha_{t+1})^{1/(t+1)}$, then $k_t < k_{t+1}$. This argument is important because in finance literature, we invariably argue that distant cash flows are more risky than near-term cash flows, so the discount rate increases over time. This implicitly assumes that $(\alpha_t)^{1/t} < (\alpha_{t+1})^{1/(t+1)}$. To the contrary, Chen (1967) argues that under a general stochastic process for future dividend flows, the risk will only increase at a decreasing rate, a finding that is in obvious contrast with the usual assumption that discount rates increase over time.

Numerical examples may be helpful to explain the relationship between α_t and r_t. In the following two examples, we will assign a value of 0.06 for the risk-free rate, to be used in all three observed time periods.

EXAMPLE 1

We assume that investors retain the same attitude toward risk over time, that is, $\alpha_1 = \alpha_2 = \alpha_3 = 0.8$. Then the risk-adjusted discount rate for the three periods is:

$$r_1 = \frac{(1+0.06)}{0.8} - 1 = 0.325,$$

$$r_2 = \frac{(1+0.06)}{(0.8)^{\frac{1}{2}}} - 1 = 0.185,$$

$$r_3 = \frac{(1+0.06)}{(0.8)^{\frac{1}{3}}} - 1 = 0.142.$$

Therefore, the risk-adjusted rate decreases over time.

EXAMPLE 2

In the capital-budgeting process, we usually apply a *constant* risk-adjusted discount rate to each period's cash flows, $r_1 = r_2 = r_3$. Assuming that this constant value is 0.185, we have:

$$\alpha_1 = \frac{(1+0.06)}{(1+0.185)} = 0.8945;$$

$$\alpha_2 = \left[\frac{1+0.06}{1+0.185}\right]^2 = 0.80;$$

$$\alpha_3 = \left[\frac{1+0.06}{1+0.185}\right]^3 = 0.716,$$

and we see that the value of the certainty equivalents will decrease over time.

Therefore, the implicit assumption behind the use of the constant discount rate is that investors require greater risk premiums for more distant cash flows.

Considering this issue directly, Gregory (1978) investigated the relationship between the multiplicative risk premium (π) and various popular risk measures used in the finance literature, such as the variance and the coefficient of variation. In order to get a functional form of α, Gregory imposes assumptions on the investor's utility functions and the distributions of each expected cash flow, as listed below. Bernhard (1984) has theoretically investigated these issues in detail.

(a) Under the quadratic utility function and the uniform distribution applied to the cash flows, the multiplicative risk premium will be a convex, decreasing function of cash flows.
(b) Under the exponential utility function and normal distribution for cash flows, the functional form of α can be expressed as;

$$\alpha = 1 - \left(\frac{r}{2}\right) v,$$

where r is the absolute risk-aversion index for the exponential utility function, and v is the coefficient of variation for the risky cash flows.

From this, we see that Gregory has derived equations that express α as a function of the utility-function parameter and the statistical-risk measure of the cash flows. If both the utility parameter and the risk measures of the cash flows can be objectively determined, it will facilitate the process of assigning a multiplicative risk premium to a risky cash flow.

14.5. Three Other Related Stochastic Approaches to Capital Budgeting

Statistical distribution methods, decision tree methods, and simulation methods are three interrelated methods of analysis for capital-budgeting decisions under uncertainty. These three methods are different from both the risk-adjusted discount rate and certainty-equivalent methods because they allow the statistical distributions of the net present values to be explicitly estimated. Under these methods, an interval rather than a point estimate of the expected NPV will be presented. Hence, the methods discussed in this section are generally more objective and general than those discussed earlier.

14.5.1. *The Statistical Distribution Method*

The riskiness of an investment proposal is generally defined as the variability of its possible returns. Decision situations can generally be classified into three types: certainty, risk, and uncertainty. The distinction between risk and uncertainty is that risk involves situations in which the probabilities of a particular event occurring are known, whereas with uncertainty these probabilities themselves are not known. Throughout this chapter, the terms "risk" and "uncertainty" will be used interchangeably, although the strict difference between them is not a matter to be taken lightly.

Economic factors peculiar to investment, competition, technological development, consumer preferences, and labor market conditions are a few of the factors that make it virtually impossible to foretell the future. Consequently, the revenues, costs, and economic life of investment projects are less than certain.

With the introduction of risk, a firm is no longer indifferent between two investment proposals having equal net present values or internal rates-of-return. Both net present value and its standard deviation (σ_{NPV}) should be estimated in performing capital-budgeting analyses under uncertainty. A NPV approach under uncertainty can be defined as

$$\tilde{\text{NPV}} = \sum_{t=1}^{N} \frac{\overline{C}_t}{(1+k)^t} + \frac{S_n}{(1+k)^N} - I_0, \tag{14.16}$$

where C_t is the uncertain net cash flow in period t, k is the risk-adjusted discount rate, S_n is the salvage value, and I_0 is the initial outlay. The mean of the NPV distribution and its standard deviation can be defined as:

$$\overline{\text{NPV}} = \sum_{t=1}^{N} \frac{\overline{C}_t}{(1+k)^t} + \frac{S_n}{(1+k)^N} - I_0, \tag{14.17a}$$

$$\sigma_{\text{NPV}} = \left[\sum_{t=1}^{N} \frac{\sigma_t^2}{(1+k)^{2t}} + \sum_{\tau=1}^{N}\sum_{t=1}^{N} w_t w_\tau \text{Cov}(C_\tau, C_t)\right]^{\frac{1}{2}}, \quad (\tau \neq t), \tag{14.17b}$$

where σ is the variance of the cash flow in the tth period and w_t and w_τ are the discount factors in the tth and τth periods, respectively. The calculation of σ_{NPV} is similar to the standard deviation of a portfolio's returns.

$\text{Cov}(C_\tau, C_t)$ is used to measure the covariability between the cash flow in the tth and τth periods. It is well known that:

$$\text{Cov}(C_t, C_\tau) = \rho_{\tau t}\sigma_\tau\sigma_t, \tag{14.18}$$

where $\rho_{\tau t}$ is the correlation coefficient between the cash flow in the ith period and that in the τth period. In one special case, the cash flows are perfectly correlated over time. If such is the case, then the deviation of the actual cash flow from the mean of its corresponding profitability distribution of expected cash flows for the period gives us the information that cash flows in future periods will deviate in a similar fashion. In other words, Eq. (14.17b) can be rewritten as[3]:

$$\sigma_{\mathrm{NPV}} = \sum_{t-1}^{N} \frac{\sigma_t}{(1+k)^t}. \tag{14.17b$'$}$$

If the cash flows are mutually independent, then Eq. (14.17b′) reduces to:

$$\sigma_{\mathrm{NPV}} = \sqrt{\sum_{t=1}^{N} \frac{\sigma_t^2}{(1+k)^{2t}}}. \tag{14.17b$''$}$$

Hillier (1969) combines the assumption of mutual independence and perfect correlation in developing a model to deal with mixed situations. The model as defined in Eq. (14.19) can be used to analyze investment proposals in which some of the expected cash flows are closely related, and others are fairly independent.

$$\sigma = \sqrt{\sum_{t=1}^{N} \frac{\sigma_{yt}^2}{(1+k)^{2t}} + \sum_{h}^{m} \left(\sum_{t=1}^{N} \frac{\sigma_{zt}^h}{(1+k)^t} \right)^2}, \tag{14.19}$$

where σ_{yt}^2 is the variance for an independent net cash flow in period t, and σ_{zt}^h is the standard deviation for stream h of a perfectly correlated stream of cash flows t. It is clear that Eq. (14.19) is a combination of Eqs. (14.17b′) and (14.17b″). Chen and Moore (1982) have generalized this model by introducing the estimation risk.

They argue that Hiller's (1963) approach is unrealistic due to the assumption of parameter certainty. In reality, the parameters of the probability distribution are never known with certainty and thus the capital budgeting decisions based on Hiller's approach may be potentially misleading because this approach ignores estimation risk. Chen and Moore (1982) hence extend Hiller's approach with a Bayesian framework which leads to the derivation of a predicative distribution that is not conditioned on unknown parameters. Therefore, the effect of estimation risk in capital budgeting decisions can be eliminated in Chen and Moore (1982) approach.

In addition, Wang and Lee (2010) provide the fuzzy real option valuation approach to solve the capital budgeting decisions under uncertainty environment. In Wang and Lee's model framework, the concept of probability is employed in describing fuzzy events and the estimated cash flows are based on the fuzzy numbers which can better reflect the uncertainty in the project. By using a fuzzy real option valuation, the managers can select fuzzy projects and determine the optimal time to abandon the project under the assumption of limited capital budget.

To illustrate the model of Eq. (14.19), suppose that a firm is considering the introduction of a new product with returns expected over the next 5 years. Because the product's market reception is uncertain, management feels that, if initial reception exceeds expectations, actual acceptance in later years will also exceed expectations, in approximately the same proportions. For simplicity, it is believed that the net marketing cash flow (sales less marketing and advertising expenses) can be treated as perfectly correlated over time.

On the other hand, estimates of the initial investment in the project and the production costs are reasonably reliable, so that any deviation from expectations is assumed to be attributable to random fluctuations. Consequently, initial investment and net production cash flows are regarded as being mutually independent over time. The probability information for the introduction of the new product is shown in Table 14.7. We assume that

Table 14.7. Expected cash flow for new product.

Year	Source	Expected Value of Net Cash Flow (in thousands)	Standard Deviation (in thousands)
0	Initial Investment	−\$600	\$50
1	Production Cash Outflow	−250	20
2	Production Cash Outflow	−200	10
3	Production Cash Outflow	−200	10
4	Production Cash Outflow	−200	10
5	Production Outflow — salvage Value	−100	15
1	Marketing	300	50
2	Marketing	600	100
3	Marketing	500	100
4	Marketing	400	100
5	Marketing	300	100

Reprinted by permission of Hillier, F., "The derivation of probabilistic information for the evaluation of risky investments," *Management Science* 9 (April 1963). Copyright 1963 by The Institute of Management Sciences.

each of the probability distributions involved can be regarded as normal. If 10% is used as the risk-free rate, the expected value of the net present value for the proposal is;

$$\begin{aligned}\text{NPV} = \sum_{t=0}^{5} \frac{C_t}{(1.04)^t} &= -600 + \frac{300-250}{(1.04)} + \frac{600-200}{(1.04)^2} + \frac{500-200}{(1.04)^3} \\ &\quad + \frac{400-200}{(1.04)^4} + \frac{300-100}{(1.04)^5} \\ &= \$419.95 = \$420.00.\end{aligned}$$

Following Eq. (14.17b), we can calculate the standard deviation as:

$$\begin{aligned}\sigma_{\text{NPV}} &= \left[50^2 + \frac{20^2}{(1.04)^2} + \cdots + \frac{15^2}{(1.04)^{10}} + \left(\frac{50}{1.04} + \cdots + \frac{100}{(1.04)^5}\right)^2\right]^{\frac{1}{2}} \\ &= \$398.\end{aligned}$$

Thus the expected net present value of the proposal is \$420 and the standard deviation of the distribution relating to NPV is \$398. Using this information, we can express an interval inference for NPV as:

$$\begin{aligned}&\Pr(\$420 \pm \$398) = 68.27\%; \\ &\Pr(\$420 \pm (2)(\$398)) = 95.45\%; \\ &\Pr(\$420 \pm (3)(\$398)) = 99.73\%.\end{aligned}$$

Hillier's approach takes us a long way toward coping with the correlation of cash flows over time, but his method is not always practically applicable. For many investment proposals, cash flows fall into neither of these categories, since in practice they show less than perfect correlation over time. If the correlation is moderate, then the classification suggested by Hillier will not be appropriate. The method suggested by Bonini (1975) and others for handling the problem of moderate correlation is with a series of conditional-probability distributions. Wang and Lee (2010) have expended Bonini's result in terms of fuzzy set and real option approach.

To illustrate the use of this model, we refer to Table 14.8(a), where we consider a project requiring an initial outlay of \$10,000 (Column 1). In each of the following time periods (Columns 3, 5, and 7), the cash flow to be received is not known with perfect certainty, but the probabilities associated with each cash flow in each period are assumed to be known

Table 14.8(a). Illustration of conditional-probability distribution approach.

Initial Outlay Period 0	Initial Probability P(1)	Net Cash Flow	Conditional Probability P(3|2, 1)	Net Cash Flow	Conditional Probability P(3|2, 1)	Cash Flow	Joint Probability
(1)	(2)	(3)	(4)	(5)	(6)	(7)	(8)
					0.2	1,000	0.015
			0.25	2,000	0.5	2,000	0.0375
					0.3	3,000	0.0225
					0.2	2,000	0.03
10,000	0.3	2,000	0.5	3,000	0.5	3,000	0.075
					0.3	4,000	0.045
					0.2	3,000	0.015
			0.25	4,000	0.5	4,000	0.0375
					0.3	5,000	0.0225
					0.3	2,000	0.045
			0.3	3,000	0.4	4,000	0.06
					0.3	6,000	0.045
					0.3	4,000	0.06
	0.5	4,000	0.4	5,000	0.4	5,000	0.08
					0.3	6,000	0.06
					0.3	5,000	0.045
			0.3	7,000	0.4	7,000	0.06
					0.3	9,000	0.045
					0.25	4,000	0.0125
			0.25	5,000	0.5	6,000	0.025
					0.25	8,000	0.0125
					0.25	5,000	0.025
	0.2	6,000	0.5	7,000	0.5	7,000	0.05
					0.25	9,000	0.025
					0.25	7,000	0.0125
			0.25	8,000	0.5	9,000	0.025
					0.25	11,000	0.0125

(Columns 2, 4, and 6), so that we are dealing with a case of risk, and not strict uncertainty. We note that Columns (4) and (6) are conditional-probability figures, where the later periods' expected cash flows depend highly on what occurs in earlier time periods. Given our cash flow and simple probability estimates for the periods 1, 2, and 3, we find 27 possible joint probabilities (Column 8), each of which corresponds to a cash-flow series. Thus in the uppermost path, we find the joint probability 0.015 being associated with a cash flow of \$2,000 in Period 1, followed by cash flows of \$2,000 and \$1,000 in Periods 2 and 3, respectively. This particular path is the worst possible result; in non-discounted dollar terms, there is a 50% loss on the investment. At the other end of the spectrum, we find the best

Table 14.8(b). NPV and joint probability.

PVA	NPV	Probability
4,661.2	−5,338.8	0.015
5,550.2	−4,449.8	0.0375
6,439.2	−3,560.8	0.0225
6,474.76	−3,525.24	0.03
7,363.76	−2,636.24	0.075
8,252.76	−1,747.24	0.045
8,288.32	−1,711.68	0.015
9,177.32	−822.68	0.0375
10,066.32	66.32	0.0225
8,297.84	−1,602.16	0.045
10,175.84	175.84	0.06
11,953.84	1,953.84	0.045
12,024.96	2,024.96	0.06
12,913.96	2,913.96	0.08
13,802.96	3,802.96	0.06
14,763.08	4,763.08	0.045
16,541.08	6,541.08	0.06
18,319.08	8,319.08	0.045
13,948.04	3,948.04	0.0125
15,726.04	5,726.04	0.025
17,504.04	7,504.04	0.0125
16,686.16	6,686.16	0.025
18,464.16	8,464.16	0.05
20242.16	10,242.16	0.025
19,388.72	9,388.72	0.0125
21,166.72	11,166.72	0.025
22,944.72	12,944.72	0.0125

Discount Rate = 4%.
NPV = $2,517.182.
Variance = $20,359,090.9093.
Standard Deviation = $4,512.105.

possible outcome offers a return $12,945 (the last line of Table 14.8(b)) with a joint probability of 0.0125. The returns and joint probabilities can be calculated similarly for the other 25 possible patterns.

While the primary hurdle in this process is in estimating the cash flows and the probabilities, we recognize that it is the NPV figures we are ultimately interested in. Table 14.8(b) gives the present value of the cash flows and the net present value of the project for each cash-flow series, where a constant 4% discount rate was employed. When we multiply each joint probability by the expected net present value associated with that probability, we obtain the expected net present value for the project as a whole, there shown to be \$2,517.18. Also, from all 27 expected net-present-value figures, we can calculate the variance and the standard deviation for the project as a whole, shown in the lower portion of Table 14.8(b) as \$20,359,090.91 and \$4,512.11, respectively, where these figures can be used to assess the riskiness of the project.

The use of this form of conditional-probability distribution enables us to take account of the dependence or correlation in the cash flows over time. In the above example, the cash flow in Period 3 depends upon the size of the cash flow in Periods 2 and 1. Given the cash flow in Period 1, the cash flow in Period 2 can vary within a range, but more of a known range than if we did not know the cash flow in Period 1. Similarly, the cash flows in Period 3 are allowed to vary within a range of values, the range being determined in part by the realized cash flow in the prior period. Most importantly it should be noted that we assume we know what the distribution of each cash-flow figure is, and the probabilities associated with each flow, and, further, that once we make the investment decision we more or less have locked ourselves into the project. In the following section, we relax this latter assumption and allow sequential decisions to be introduced into the conditional-probability decision framework.

14.5.2. *The Decision-Tree Method*

A decision-tree approach to capital-budgeting decisions can be used to analyze some investment opportunities involving a sequence of investment decisions over time. The decision tree is an analytical technique used in sequential decisions, where various decision points are studied in relation to subsequent chance events. This technique enables one to choose among alternatives in an objective and consistent manner. To illustrate this method, let us suppose that a firm is considering the introduction of a new product. Initially, it must decide whether to distribute the product either regionally, nationally, or internationally. Regional distribution will require an expenditure of two million dollars for a new plant and the initial market effort. Depending upon demand during the first 2 years, the firm would then decide whether or not to expand to national distribution. If it goes to national (from regional) distribution, the company will be required to spend an additional million dollars for expanding the plant to meet the increased demand from the national market. Similarly, the firm can distribute nationally at the outset of the project, and then decide whether or not to expand to international distribution. If the firm chooses this alternative, it is expected that an additional three million will have to be raised to set up the plant for this national effort, and another one million would have to be invested so as to expand that plant capacity to meet the international demand. The third alternative is that the firm decides to distribute its products on an international basis from the very outset, where this alternative would require an initial influx of four million dollars in capital expenditure. In setting up this example, we implicitly assume that the fixed cost of the plant is relatively high, which precludes the possibility of the firm gearing down its operations from an international setting to that of a purely national setting, or from a national effort to one aimed at the smaller regional distribution system. Also, we assume that the scale of the plant is inflexible; the possibility of expanding a regional distribution to one capable of handling the international market is nil.

There are two stages of decisions for regional and national distribution, and one stage of decisions for international distribution. The decision point for each stage is represented by a square. The circles represent chance-event nodes. If the firm decides to distribute internationally at the outset, there is a 0.3 probability that demand for the product will be high, a 0.4 probability that the demand will be more of a moderate level, and a 0.3 probability that the actual demand will be lower than expected. Similar explanations can be followed to interpret probability distributions of demand if the firm decides on regional or national distribution at the initiation of the project.

Table 14.9 shows the expected cash flows and net present values for each possible path of decisions. The product's life cycle is assumed to be of a 6 year duration, with no expected salvage value at the end of the life cycle. The expansion decision must be made at the end of year two, and the cash flows for year two reflect the alternative decisions made. Assuming a risk-free rate of 4% prevails, the net present value for each path of decisions is shown in the last column of Table 14.9.

The optimal decision path has the property that, whatever the current state is, the remaining decisions must follow an optimal path. In order to obtain the optimal path of decisions, we solve the problem by working backward. In doing so, we determine the second-stage decision first, that is, the decision of going from regional distribution to national distribution versus continuous regional distribution, or the decision of going from national distribution to international distribution versus that of continuous national distribution. For example, if the firm chooses to distribute regionally and faces high demand for the first 2 years, the firm needs to make the decision pertaining to national distribution. Therefore we need to

Table 14.9. Expected cash flows for various branches of the decision tree.

	0	1	2	3	4	5	6	NPV
Regional Distribution Throughout:								
High	−2,000	250	500	600	900	600	500	893.70
Medium	−2,000	0	400	550	800	550	400	310.80
Low	−2,000	−250	200	450	600	450	200	−614.61
National Distribution Throughout:								
High	−3,000	350	700	1,100	1,400	1,000	600	1,454.47
Medium	−3,000	0	500	900	1,200	800	700	498.90
Low	−3,000	−350	100	700	1,000	600	300	−1,036.73
International Distribution Throughout:								
High	−4,000	450	900	1,600	2,200	1,400	800	2,350.71
Medium	−4,000	0	600	1,400	2,000	1,200	600	969.44
Low	−4,000	−450	100	700	1,500	700	400	−1,544.26
High National–High Inter.	−3,000	350	−300	1,600	2,200	1,400	800	2,145.08
High National–Medium Inter.	−3,000	350	−300	1,400	2,200	1,200	600	1,473.88
High National–Low Inter.	−3,000	350	−300	700	1,500	700	400	−144.85
Medium National–High Inter.	−3,000	0	−500	1,600	2,200	1,400	800	1,623.63
Medium National–Medium Inter	−3,000	0	−500	1,400	2,000	1,200	600	952.43
Medium National–Low Inter	−3,000	0	−500	700	1,500	700	400	−666.30
Low National–High Inter.	−3,000	−350	−900	1,600	2,200	1,400	800	917.27
Low National–Medium Inter	−3,000	−350	−900	1,400	2,000	1,200	600	246.07
Low National–Low Inter	−3,000	−350	−900	700	1,500	700	400	−1,372.66
High Region–High National	−2,000	250	−500	1,100	1,400	1,000	600	1,248.84
High Region–Medium National	−2,000	250	−500	900	1,200	800	700	814.73
High Region–Low National	−2,000	250	−500	700	1,000	600	300	−14.54
Medium Region–High National	−2,000	0	−600	1,100	1,400	1,000	600	916.00
Medium Region–Medium National	−2,000	0	−600	900	1,200	800	700	481.89
Medium Region–Low National	−2,000	0	−600	700	1,000	600	300	−347.38
Low Region–High National	−2,000	−250	−800	1,100	1,400	1,000	600	490.71
Low Region–Medium National	−2,000	−250	−800	900	1,200	800	700	56.59
Low Region–Low National	−2,000	−250	−800	700	1,000	600	300	−772.68

compare the expected value of net present value for the two alternatives at this decision point.

The expected net present value is computed by multiplying the probability of demand by the net present value, then summing over high, moderate, and low demand. The actual computation of this figure is shown as follows:

$$\text{NPV} = 0.7(1{,}248.84) + 0.2(814.73) + 0.1(-14.54) = \$1,035.68.$$

Since the expected net present value for national distribution is greater than that of continuous regional distribution, the firm should decide to distribute nationally, given that the firm chooses to distribute regionally from the beginning and faces high demand during the first 2 years.

In a similar fashion, the expected values of net present values for each second-stage decision can be determined. We note that, given a regional distribution plan at the outset, the firm will opt for national distribution regardless of the demand forthcoming in those first 2 years. From the other starting point we can see that, if the firm chooses to distribute nationally at the outset, it will expand the facilities to that required for international distribution if demand is either high or low in the first 2 years, but it will continue along its national distribution path if the initial year's demand is judged to be moderate.

The second step to find the optimal path is to calculate the expected net present value for the first stage. In the first stage, the expected net present value for regional is 0.5 ($1,035, 680) + 0.3 ($489,680) + 0.2 (−$271,220) = $610,500. The same computation shows that the expected net present value for regional, national, and international distributions are $610,500, $767,270, and $629,710, respectively.

The expected net present value represents returns for different decision paths. But the analyst should be wary of using these figures exclusively, since the risks of the different decision paths are also important. The expected net present values and the associated standard deviations for the preceding example are shown as:

Decision Variables For the First Stage	Net Present Value*	Standard Deviation*	Coefficient Of Variation
Regional	610.50	666.98	1.093
National	767.27	1067.20	1.3909
International	629.71	1533.80	2.4357

*Expressed in thousands of dollars.

Since national distribution has both a higher expected net present value and a lower expected standard deviation than the international distribution, the national distribution plan should dominate the international plan, assuming that the management displays risk aversion. The choice between the regional and national distribution systems is less clear, though; while it is true that the national distribution alternative carries a higher expected net present value, it also displays a greater degree of potential variability, both in absolute standard deviation and in relative (coefficient-of-variation) terms, than the regional alternative. Thus, the final decision rests on the risk attitudes of management.

Nonetheless, we find that this method, where sequential decisions are allowed, involves a slightly different type of risk as the firm is not locked into any particular distribution method for the project, unless, of course, it initially decides to distribute internationally. Thus the risk of being locked into a project is less, though the variability of the cash flows over time or across distribution methods may be greater when sequential decisions are allowed, and the computational difficulty can be seen to grow as well.

14.5.3. *Simulation Analysis*

Simulation is another approach to confronting the problems of capital budgeting under uncertainty. Because uncertainty associated with capital budgeting is not restricted to one or two variables, every variable relevant in the capital-budgeting decision can be viewed as a random variable. Facing so many random variables, it may be impossible to obtain tractable results from an economic model. Simulation is a useful tool designed to deal with this problem, and is the closest we can get to modeling in cases of uncertainty.

The following example utilizes the simulation model developed by Hertz (1964, 1979). Here, we consider a firm that intends to introduce a new product where the 11 input factors thought to determine project value are shown in Table 14.10(a). Of these inputs, variables 1–9 are specified as random variables with the ranges listed in Table 14.10(a). It would be possible to add a random element to variables 10 and 11, but the computational complexity and the insights gained do not justify the effort. Also, for ease of modeling, we chose to implement the uniform distribution as that describing the probability of any particular outcome in that specified range. By using a set range for each of the nine random variables, we are not actually allowing the probabilities of each possible outcome to vary, but the spirit of varying probabilities is imbedded in the simulation approach. One further restriction is made in the model, that being the life of the facilities

Table 14.10(a). Variables for simulation

Variables	Range
1. Market size (units)	2,500,000–3,000,000
2. Selling price ($/unit)	40–60
3. Market growth	0–5%
4. Market share	10–15%
5. Total investment required ($)	8,000,000–10,000,000
6. Useful life of facilities (years)	5–9
7. Residue value of investment ($)	1,000,000–2,000,000
8. Operating cost ($)	30–45
9. Fixed cost ($)	400,000–500,000
10. Tax rate	40%
11. Discount rate	12%

Notes: (a) Random numbers from Wonnacott and Wonnacott (1990) are used to determine the value of the variable for simulation.
(b) Useful life of facilities is an integer.

Random number	Year
10–19	5
20–39	6
40–59	7
60–79	8
80–99	9
00	10

is restricted to an integer value, with the range as specified at the bottom of Table 14.10(a).

The uniform distribution density function can be written as;

$$f_x = \begin{cases} \dfrac{1}{\beta - \alpha} \\ 0 \qquad \text{elsewhere} \end{cases}.$$

where β is the upper bound on the variable value and α is the lower bound.[4] With this in mind, we note the way in which the values are assigned. For each successive input variable, a random-number generator selects a value from 01 to 00 (where 00 is the proxy for 100 using a two-digit random-number generator) and then translates that into a variable value by taking account of the specified range and distribution of the variable value by taking account of the specified range and distribution of the variable in question.

For each simulation, nine random numbers are selected. From these random numbers, a set of values for the nine key factors are created. For example, the first set of random numbers as shown in Table 14.10(b) are (39, 73, 72, 75, 37, 02, 87, 98, and 10). The value of the market-size factor for the first simulation can be obtained as follows;

$$\text{Market size: } 2{,}500{,}000 + \frac{[39][3{,}000{,}000 - 2{,}500{,}000]}{[100]} = 2{,}695{,}000.$$

$$\text{Selling price: } \$40 + \frac{[73][\$60 - \$40]}{[100]} = \$54.5.$$

$$\text{Market growth: } 0.00 + \frac{[72][0.05 - 0.00]}{[100]} = 0.036 \text{ or } 3.6\%.$$

$$\text{Market share: } 0.10\% + \frac{[75][0.15 - 0.10]}{[100]} = 0.1375 \text{ or } 12.75\%.$$

Total investment required:

$$\$8{,}000{,}000 + \frac{[37][\$2{,}000{,}000 - \$1{,}000{,}000]}{[100]} = \$8{,}740{,}000.$$

Useful life of facilities: 5 years

Residue value of investment:

$$\$1{,}000{,}000 + \frac{[87][\$2{,}000{,}000 - \$1{,}000{,}000]}{[100]} = \$1{,}870{,}000.$$

$$\text{Operating cost: } \$30 + \frac{[98][\$45 - \$30]}{[100]} = \$44.7.$$

$$\text{Fixed cost: } \$400{,}000 + \frac{[10][\$500{,}000 - \$400{,}000]}{[100]} = \$410{,}000.$$

Similar computations can be used to calculate the values of all variables except the useful life of the facilities. Because the useful life of facilities is restricted to integer values, we impose the following correspondence between random numbers and useful life of facilities;

For each simulation, a series of cash flows and the NPV can be calculated by using the following formula;

$$\begin{aligned}[\text{Sales Volume}]_t &= [(\text{Market Size}) \times (1 + \text{Market Growth Rate})^t] \\ &\quad \times (\text{Share of Market}), \\ \text{EBIT}_t &= [\text{Sales Volume}]_t \times [\text{Selling Price} - \text{Operating Cost}] \\ &\quad - [\text{Fixed Cost}];\end{aligned}$$

Table 14.10(b). Simulation.

Variables	*1*	*2*	*3*	*4*
VMARK 1	(39)2,695,000	(47)2,735,000	(67)2,835,000	(12)2,580,000
PRICE 2	(73)$54.6	(93)$58.6	(59)51.8	(78)55.6
GROW 3	(72)3.6%	(21)1.05%	(63)0.0315	(03)0.0015
SMARK 4	(75)13.75%	(95)14.75%	(78)0.139	(04)0.102
TOINV 5	(37)8,740,000	(97)9,940,000	(87)9,740,000	(61)9,220,000
KUSE 6	(02)5 years	(68)8 years	(47)7 years	(23)6 years
RES 7	(87)1,870,000	(41)1,410,000	(56)1,560,000	(15)1,150,000
VAR 8	(98)$44.7	(91)$43.65	(22)33.3	(58)38.7
FIX 9	(10)$410,000	(80)$480,000	(19)419,000	(93)493000
TAX 10	40%	0.4	0.4	0.4
DIS 11	12%	0.12	0.12	0.12
NPV	$197,847.561	$7,929,874.287	$12,146,989.579	$1,169,846.55
VARIABLES	*5*	*6*	*7*	*8*
VMARK 1	(78)2,890,000	(89)2,945,000	(26)2,630,000	(60)2,800,000
PRICE 2	(61)$52.2	(18)43.6	(47)49.4	(88)$57.6
GROW 3	(42)0.021	(83)0.0415	(94)0.047	(17)0.0085
SMARK 4	(77)0.1385	(08)0.104	(06)0.103	(36)0.118
TOINV 5	(65)9,300,000	(90)9,800,000	(72)9,440,000	(77)9,540,000
KUSE 6	(71)8 years	(05)5 years	(40)7 years	(43)7 years
RES 7	(20)1,200,000	(89)1,890,000	(62)1,620,000	(28)1,280,000
VAR 8	(17)$32.55	(18)$32.7	(47)37.05	(31)$34.65
FIX 9	(48)448,000	(08)408,000	(68)468,000	(06)406,000
TAX 10	0.40	0.4	0.4	0.4
DIS 11	0.12	0.12	0.12	0.12
NPV	$15,306,245.293	−$1,513,820.475	$11,327,171.67	$839,650.211
VARIABLES	*9*	*10*		
VMARK 1	(68)2,840,000	(23)2,615,000		
PRICE 2	(39)$47.8	(47)$49.4		
GROW 3	(71)0.0355	(25)0.0125		
SMARK 4	(22)0.111	(79)0.1395		
TOINV 5	(76)9,520,000	(08)8,160,000		
KUSE 6	(81)9 years	(15)5 years		
RES 7	(88)1,880,000	(71)1,710,000		
VAR 8	(94)44.1	(58)$38.7		
FIX 9	(76)476,000	(56)456,000		
TAX 10	0.4	0.4		
DIS 11	0.12	0.12		
NPV	−$6,021,018.052	$563,687.461		
NPV = 4,194,647.207				

Notes: 1. Definitions variables can be found in Table 14.10(a).
2. NPV calculator procedure can be found in Table 14.10(c).

Random number	01–19	20–39	40–59	60–79	80–99	00
Useful life	5	6	7	8	9	10

$$[\text{Cash Flow}]_t = [\text{EBIT}]_t \times [1 - \text{Tax Rate}];$$

$$\text{NPV} = \sum_{t=1}^{\text{Useful life}} \frac{[\text{CashFlow}]_t}{(1 + \text{DiscountRate})^t} - I_0,$$

where t represents the tth year.

The results in terms of cash flow for each simulation are listed in Table 14.10(c) with each period's cash flows shown separately. The NPVs for each simulation can be found under the input values listed in Table 14.10(b). From these NPV figures, we can again calculate a mean

Table 14.10(c). Cash Flow Simulations.

Period	*1*	*2*	*3*	*4*
1	$2,034,382.335	$3,368,605.531	$4,260,506.327	$2,376,645.064
2	2,116,476.099	3,406,999.889	4,402,631.377	2,380,653.731
3	2,201,525.239	3,445,797.388	4,549,233.365	2,384,668.412
4	2,289,636.147	3,485,002.261	4,700,453.316	2,388,689.114
5	2,380,919.049	3,524,618.785	4,856,436.695	2,392,715.848
6		3,564,651.282	5,017,333.551	2,396,748.622
7		3,605,104.120	5,183,298.658	
8		3,645,981.714		
Period	*5*	*6*	*7*	*8*
1	$4,549,425.961	$1,841,398.655	$1,820,837,760	$4,344,679.668
2	4,650,608,707	1,927,975.899	1,919,614.735	4,383,680.045
3	4,753,916.289	2,018,146.099	2,023,034.228	4,423,011.926
4	4,859,393.331	2,112,058.362	2,131,314,436	4,462,678.127
5	4,967,085.391	2,209,867.984	2,244,683.815	4,502,681.491
6	5,077,038.985		2,363,381.554	4,543,024.884
7	5,189,301.603		2,487,658.087	4,583,711.195
8	5,303,921.737			
Period	*9*	*10*		
1	$439,076.864	$2,097,642.448		
2	464,802.893	2,127,282.979		
3	491,442.196	2,157,294,016		
4	519,027.194	2,187,680.191		
5	547,591.459	2,218,446.194		
6	577,169.756			
7	607,798.082			
8	639,513.714			
9	672,355.251			

Note: 1. NPVs are listed in Table 13.4(b).

NPV figure and variance and standard deviation, from which we can analyze the risk and the return profile of the project.

Furthermore, if we choose to change the range or the distribution of the random variables, sensitivity analysis can be performed to investigate the impact of the change in an input factor on the risk-and-return of the investment project. Also, by way of the sensitivity-analysis approach, we in essence decompose the uncertainty involved in undertaking of any project, thereby highlighting exactly what the decision maker should be primarily concerned with: forecasting in terms of those variables critical to the analysis. The information obtained from the simulation analysis will be valuable in allowing the decision maker to more accurately evaluate risky capital investments.

Concept Quiz

1. What is simulation analysis?
2. What information is needed to perform a simulation analysis?
3. How can simulation analysis be used to evaluate risk?

14.5.4. *Comparison of the Three Alternative Stochastic Methods*

The probability-distribution, decision-tree, and simulation methods are three alternative approaches that are available to deal with the problem of capital budgeting under uncertainty. These methods have explicitly utilized the concepts of probability distributions and statistical distributions to carry out the analysis. If there is only a single accept–reject decision at the outset of the project, then the decision maker can use either statistical-distribution methods or simulation methods. If investment opportunities involve a *sequence* of decisions over time, then a decision-tree method can be used to perform the analysis. The backward-induction process and the basis of dominance are two important criteria used in the decision-tree method of capital budgeting, as was discussed earlier in this section.

The basic concepts used in simulation analysis are almost identical to that of the probabilistic-distribution method of capital budgeting. The probabilistic method uses the information associated with net cash-flow distributions, useful life of facilities, and salvage value, to estimate the distribution of net present value. The simulation method of capital budgeting explicitly uses the distributions of the inputs related to market analysis, investment cost analysis, and the operating and fixed costs anticipated to simulate the distribution of NPV or IRR. The simulation method can explicitly incorporate the detailed information into the decision process. Stochastic methods for capital-budgeting decision making are generally more complicated than those of the risk-adjusted discount-rate method or the certainty-equivalent method. However, the stochastic methods of capital budgeting generally supply more information to the decision makers than either of the two simplified approaches discussed in Sections 14.2 and 14.3.

14.6. Inflationary Effects in the Capital-Budgeting Procedure

With the advent of double-digit inflation in the 1970s, business persons from all disciplines became critically aware of the influence that general price escalation had in their decision-making processes. The financial manager of today must incorporate inflation estimates into the capital-budgeting decision, which, taken at face value, appears to be a rather simple operation. By examining the two major inputs to the capital-budgeting decision and another related variable, the estimated cash flows, appropriate discount rates, and the relative capital intensity level chosen, we intend to show the introduction of inflation vastly increases the complexity of the capital-budgeting procedure. We then discuss how to account for it properly.

Much of the emphasis on inflationary considerations is geared toward the adjustment or estimation of discount rates, while the cash-flow estimates receive little attention in the literature of finance. Van Horne (1971) noted this lack of attention and specified a bias arising in the accept-reject criterion when the cost-of-capital rate contains an element that recognizes expected future rates of inflation and the cash flow estimates do not embody a similar component. When the anticipated inflation rates are relatively high, this bias can cause serious underestimates of the project's true value to the firm.

No rigorous proof need be offered to substantiate the above claim; we need only look at what the firm or its investors value. The returns to the firm from the project, and the dividends received by the investors, are invariably denominated in nominal dollars, and therefore the discount rates employed to find present values should be formulated so as to evaluate nominal returns. If the firm does not attempt to estimate the true nominal cash flows, which, when netted out, may be either higher or lower than they might have been in a non-inflationary environment, then the estimated value of the project is not the best estimate that could be obtained.

In practice, it is not advisable to estimate the inflation effects directly on the net cash-flow figure, as there may be sizable differences in the way in which inflation affects the price of the output produced by a project and the costs incurred. Relative price elasticities could vary with price levels; thus sales and the prices at which sales are consummated could vary, influencing the revenue and expense cash-flow estimates. On the bright side, if contracts pertaining to sales or supply are in place, the forecasting procedure is somewhat simplified, although it is doubtful that all relevant cash flows are stipulated in enforceable contracts, or, for that matter, in contracts that run the full life of the project.

While there is some evidence that future rates of inflation are incorporated into market interest rates (see Fama, 1975), it is not necessarily the case in considering real assets, which can be valued by different criteria. In that respect, present prices for physical goods cannot be viewed as already accounting for future inflation; hence the need for the financial planner or forecaster to derive estimates as to these future unknown inflationary effects.

The recognition of the necessity to augment discount rates, particularly those associated with interest-bearing securities, can be traced back to Fisher (1930), who suggested that the non-inflationary required rate-of-return should be grossed up by the expected rate of inflation, more specifically, (1 + real required rate-of-return) × (1 + expected inflation rate). In practice, the inflation premium is simply added to the real required rate-of-return, leaving out the cross-product terms, (real required rate-of-return) times the expected rate of inflation. Of course, if we were to be as precise as possible, this factor would be included, but in light of the considerable uncertainty associated with the estimates of the real required rate-of-return and the expected inflation rate, this factor may have only negligible effects on the actual accept–reject decision of the firm.

Possibly the most lucid exposition on the proper procedures for capital budgeting under inflation is a short piece by Cooley, Roenfeldt, and Chew (1975). In their article, they show that the use of the traditional risk-adjusted discount-rate method for capital budgeting is formulated in such a manner as to allow for inflation, contrary to the contentions of others. The problem with the risk-adjusted discount-rate method, as we will stress shortly, is in the *proper implementation*.

Typically, the risk-adjusted discount-rate method, as shown in Eq. (14.20) is characterized by the following:

(i) Nominal flows are discounted.
(ii) Revenue and cost sensitivity to inflation are disregarded.
(iii) Depreciation tax shields are of the same risk as the cash flows.
(iv) The appropriate discount rate is constant through time.
(v) The appropriate discount rate implicitly incorporates inflation
(vi) The rate of inflation incorporated in the discount rate is known:

$$\mathrm{NPV}_t = -I_0 + \sum_{t=1}^{N} \frac{C_t}{(1+k)^t}, \tag{14.20}$$

where

k = A real rate-of-return in the absence of inflation (i) plus an inflation premium (η) plus a risk adjustment to a riskless rate-of-return (ρ).

Our discussion in the preceding paragraphs should clarify points (i) and (ii) and, if anything, point (iii) is a downward bias in net present-value calculations, since most firms have other income streams subject to taxation and/or they could, in effect, carry back the tax shield to obtain a tax refund; i.e., the risk of the depreciation tax shield may well be less than that generally attributed to it. We concern ourselves mainly with points (iv) through (vi), although we will make adjustments in the cash flows as they become necessary to complete the analysis.

The relaxation of the constant-risk-premium assumption yields an interesting result; one that we find has not received much attention. If we examine only those net cash flows that occur following the inception of the project, the discussion of the varying-risk-premium issue is somewhat facilitated. The value of the cash flows can be expressed as; or, with respect to each period's cash flows, as:

$$V_0 = \frac{C_t}{(1+k_t)^t}, \tag{14.21a}$$

or, with respect to each period's cash flows, as:

$$V_{t-1} = \frac{C_t}{1+k_t}, \tag{14.21b}$$

where V_{t-1} is simply the risk-adjusted present value of the cash flows in year t at the beginning of year t. To make the above two relations strictly equivalent, we could multiply the V_{t-1} figure by $(1+k_t)/(1+k_t)^t$, obtaining;

$$V_0 = \frac{V_{t-1}}{(1+k_t)^{t-1}}, \tag{14.22}$$

which is a result most textbooks consider correct. A problem arises when comparing this method to the certainty-equivalent method because, by definition, V_{t-1} is already risk-adjusted, so that further discounting at a rate including a risk premium biases the net-present-value figure downward by the amount associated with the compounding of the risk premiums. As should be readily apparent, this bias is particularly large when the risk premiums are large relative to the inflation-adjusted riskless rate-of-return, and/or the project's duration is quite long. To remedy this problem, the proper expression for V_0 would discount the risk-adjusted figure only at the riskless inflation-adjusted rate (i), as shown below;

$$V_0 = \frac{C_t}{(1+k_t)(1+i_i)^{t-1}}, \tag{14.23}$$

and the proper net-present-value formulation would be;

$$\text{NPV} = \sum_{t=1}^{N} \frac{C_t}{(1+k_t)(1+i)^{t-1}} - I_0. \tag{14.24}$$

As such, we could interpret the cash-flow stream of each project as a separate series of t payments, each payment series starting with certainty (though the payment size is not certain), at time $t-1$. From this we see that each payment is adjusted for a real rate-of-return and inflation from the t periods prior to its receipt, and only once for risk, so that it is equivalent to the certainty-equivalent method, which at times has been considered theoretically superior.

Historical evidence indicates that inflation rates vary across time periods, and, from examining yield curves for government securities, we have reason to suspect that inflation is not expected to continue at constant rates. Hence the inflation-adjustment term used in the above equations must be adjusted itself to indicate compounded rates of inflation. While computationally tedious, this is a rather simple procedure as the one-period inflation rates prior to, and including, the period undergoing valuation should each have one added to them and then all be multiplied together so as to find the current compounding factor attributable solely to inflation. A simple averaging procedure of future inflation rates may be warranted if the planning horizon is relatively short; but again as the inflation rate estimates grow increasingly large and the duration of the payments stream grows longer; the estimates will be more and more inaccurate.

So that the approach discussed above is rendered complete, we should add the adjustment of the cash inflows and outflows by their absolute sensitivity to inflation. Letting λ and θ denote the sensitivity of revenues and expenses to inflation, we can show that the full net-present-value model is:

$$\begin{aligned}\mathrm{NPV}_t &= -I_0 \\ &\quad + \sum_{t=1}^{N} \frac{\left[R_t \prod_{j=1}^{t}(1+\lambda_j) - O_t \prod_{j=1}^{t}(1+\theta_j) - F_t\right](1-\tau)}{(1+i+\rho_t)(1+i)^{t-1}\prod_{j=1}^{t}(1+\eta_j)} \\ &\quad + \frac{(\mathrm{dep}_t)(t)}{(1+i)^t}, \qquad (14.25)\end{aligned}$$

where

R_t = Expected growth in cash flow;
O_t = Outflow for variable operating expense;
θ_j = The percentage change in O_t induced by inflation in period j;
F_t = Expected fixed cash charge;
dep_t = Fixed non-cash charge;
τ = Marginal corporate tax rate;
i = Real risk-free rate;
η = Inflation rate;
ρ = Risk premium associated with uncertainty of nominal cash flow.

Not specifically recognized by this model is the uncertainty of the future inflation rates. The Cooley, Roenfeldt, and Chew analysis suggests the addition of a further risk premium to the figure we have termed k. The theoretical validity of this addition is not widely accepted, and, as we will discuss in the chapter concerning dividend policy, the risk associated with the increasing variance of probability distributions projected further into the future is not necessarily a risk that the market grants a return for taking. At this point, we will leave the incorporation of such a risk premium to the judgment of the analyst; though empirical evidence on capital-asset pricing, however, has not shown that any such risk premium is granted to the purchasers of securities or of real assets in our marketplaces.

Recalling the cash-flow inflation-adjusted arguments, we would find that, if cash revenues and expenses were to grow at the rate of inflation while the discount rate applicable to such flows was grossed up accordingly, all inflation effects would nicely wash out. As Nelson (1976) points out, most textbooks choose to forward this idea by working in a framework devoid of tax effects. However, the harsh realities of the real world, with taxes, makes it even more evident that inflation does matter, by way of the effect it has on the tax shield of depreciation of acquired capital goods. With depreciation being based on historic costs, the present value of the depreciation tax shield is less than the actual cash outlay regardless of whether the forthcoming inflation is anticipated or not, and as a result of this factor-it is anticipated that the optimal level of investment in capital equipment for a given project will generally depend on the rate of inflation anticipated. More specifically, we would expect to find an inverse relationship between the capital investment level and the anticipated rate of inflation.

Defining

PV = Present value of a one-period project;

X = Net cash flow received at the end of the period;

I = Net investment outlay at time 0;

r = Risk-adjusted non-inflation-adjusted required rate-of-return;

τ = Tax rate applicable to the firm;

p' = Change in the price level expected to occur over the coming period;

we can show the value of the project prior to inflation to be:

$$PV = -I + \frac{X - \tau(X - I)}{1 + r}, \tag{14.26}$$

and after inflation, which is assumed here to affect X and $(1 + r)$ equally,

$$PV = -I + \frac{(1 + p')X - \tau[(1 + p')X - I]}{(1 + r)(1 + p')}. \tag{14.27}$$

Now, solving for the optimal level of investment given the anticipated change in the price level, we obtain;

$$\frac{dPV}{dI} = -1 + \frac{(1 - \tau)}{(1 + r)}\frac{dX}{dI} + \frac{\tau}{(1 + r)(1 + p')} = 0.$$

If we restate $(1+p')$ as an approximated present-value factor of $(1-p')$, the above becomes;

$$\frac{dPV}{dI} = -1 + \frac{(1-\tau)}{(1+r)}\frac{dX}{dI} + \frac{\tau - \tau p'}{(1+r)}, \tag{14.28}$$

which, in the last term, clearly shows that the higher the anticipated inflation rate, the lower the optimal level of capital investment due to the tax effects, even when inflation is assumed to affect the net operating flows and the applicable discount rate to the same degree.

From this, the reader can easily infer that the higher the expected rate of inflation, the lower the capital–labor ratio employed in the operation of the project. Again, this is due to the latency in the firm's ability to utilize the actual expense as a tax shield, a problem further aggravated when dealing with multi-period problems, assuming labor is paid on a frequent basis and this expense is deductible in full at the date of the nearest tax payment. Thus, in an inflationary environment, other levels of management will be required to develop alternative minimum-cost production plans, and the financial planner will be required to choose, from those alternative plans, the project, if any, that has the largest positive net present value under the current inflationary expectations. Caution must be exercised when ranking these mutually exclusive projects. Net-present-value rankings of mutually exclusive projects of equal duration may change with changes in the rate of anticipated inflation, and the similar rankings of projects of unequal duration will also vary with changes in the rate of anticipated inflation.

Without elaborating on the algebraic proofs, the latter two propositions can be explained on a much more intuitive basis. If we found two investment opportunities of equal net present value at the current level of inflation, both of whose cash flows respond to inflation by the same factor yet one uses either a slower method of depreciation of capital assets or a higher level of capital intensity, the inclusion of a higher inflation expectation would depress the net present value of the project with the slower depreciation method or higher capital intensity level more than that of the other project because of the delay in the recognition of the depreciation tax shield. Alternatively, if we were to consider two projects whose characteristics were similar in all regards except duration, we would instinctively choose the project of shorter duration by observing compounding effects, and if the inflation rate increases, the project that takes longer to write off the initial investment will decrease in present value to a greater degree, again due to the loss of the tax shield in later periods. Since the depreciation tax shield essentially constitutes a net cash inflow, the preceding argument should come as no great surprise; delay in any inflows will result in a decrease in the net present value of a project, and the shift to a higher discount rate for value payments fixed in their timing will also serve to diminish the value of a project.

The intent of the Nelson analysis was to bring to the forefront the effect inflation has upon the present value of the depreciation tax shield, *ceteris paribus*. The other real concern regarding the cash flows, as was originally pointed out by Van Horne, is the net cash-flow adjustment, which may or may not respond in the same manner as the depreciation tax shield. Kim (1979) elaborated on the net effect assumed equal to the rate of inflation by Nelson, and derived his own empirically testable model, which included the relevant variables associated with inflation.

Using the same notation as that of the Nelson discussion, with the exception that D represents depreciation charges, the net present value of a project without inflationary consideration is:

$$\mathrm{NPV}_0 = \sum_{t=1}^{N} \frac{X_t(1-\tau) + D\tau}{(1+r)^t} - I, \tag{14.29}$$

which could be broken into two components, the first year's flows and all that follows, as shown below:

$$\mathrm{NPV} = \frac{X_1(1-\tau) + D\tau}{1+r} + \sum_{t=2}^{N} \frac{X_t(1-\tau) + D\tau}{(1+r)^t} - I. \tag{14.29$'$}$$

Kim then let inflation affect the first year's flows with no net effect on the present value of those flows occurring in later years. Allowing L to represent the sensitivity of the cash flows (net operating income) to inflation in year one, the real NPV under inflation ($\mathrm{NPV}_{P'}$) can be written as:

$$\mathrm{NPV}_{P'} = \frac{X\,L(1-\tau)(1+p') + D\tau}{(1+p')(1+r)} + \sum_{t=2}^{n} \frac{X_t(1-\tau) + D\tau}{(1+r)^t}. \tag{14.30}$$

By subtracting the net present value of the project with no inflation from that of the project with the adjustment for inflation we obtain;

$$\mathrm{NPV}_{p'} - \mathrm{NPV}_0 = \frac{X_1(1-\tau)}{(1+r)} \left[L - 1 - \frac{D\tau p'}{X_1(1-\tau)(1+p')} \right]. \tag{14.31}$$

We know that the effect of inflation on the depreciation tax shield is negative, so, to avoid any net effect on project value from inflation, we must have:

$$L' = 1 + \frac{D\tau p'}{X_1(1-\tau)(1+p')}, \tag{14.32}$$

which also must be greater than one, where L' is the sensitivity coefficient required for the change in net present value to be exactly zero. If the actual sensitivity coefficient were *equal* to one, as Nelson assumed, his result of a decrease in investment caused by inflation follows logically. The more interesting case results when the actual I is *greater* than one, where the change in investment may be either positive or negative, depending on the actual L values. If the forthcoming inflation is known with some degree of certainty, then the "hurdle" L' can be computed with little difficulty, and the net investment result can be inferred from there.

To test empirically for inter-firm differences in investment activity when confronted with expected inflation, the net-present-value equation was divided by total assets to avoid any size effects that may exist. Then, by systematically taking first-order partial derivatives with respect to L, $1+r$, X_1/Total assets, and D/X_1, the expected signs of each coefficient were determined, as shown in Table 14.11.

With the introduction of a dummy variable Z, which takes the values 1, 0, −1, depending on the inflation responsiveness coefficient L, the model ultimately tested was specified as;

$$G_j = a + bL_j + cX\tau A_j Z_j - dr_j Z_j - eDX_j + u_j, \tag{14.33}$$

the Z_j being required in the third and fourth terms to allow the exclusion of these variables in the event $L' = L$.

The model was subsequently tested over the time period 1965–1976, and over the two subperiods 1965–1970, and 1971–1976, with firms and data drawn from the COMPUSTAT tapes. The subperiod breakdown provides

Table 14.11. Inflation effect analysis.

Condition	L	X/TA	$1+r$	D/X
$L > L'$	+	+	−	−
$L = L'$	+	0	0	−
$L < L'$	+	−	+	−

From Kim, M. K. L., "Inflationary effects in the capital-investment process: An empirical examination," *Journal of Finance* **34** (September 1979): Table 1. Reprinted by permission.

Table 14.12. Regression results (Figures in parentheses are t values).

Period	a	b	c	d	e
1965–1976	0.0884	0.0103	0.0957	−1.0007	−0.0545
		(14.74)	(4.88)	(2.35)	(4.42)
1965–1970	0.0882	0.0131	−0.0079	0.0670	−0.0297
		(9.93)	(0.37)	(0.15)	(1.46)
1971–1976	0.1044	0.0097	0.1046	−0.8642	−0.0870
		(5.90)	(4.05)	(1.87)	(5.63)

From Kim, M. K. L., "Inflationary effects in the capital-investment process: An empirical examination." *Journal of Finance* **34** (September 1979): Table 4. Reprinted by permission.

an interesting comparison of the effects a mild and more severe inflationary environment generates, the consumer price index growing at a 3.82% rate and a 6.58% rate on average during the first and second sub period, respectively. From the results in Table 10.6, we find that the L coefficient is always highly significant and positive, indicating the net operating cash flow is favorably affected during times of inflation, possibly due to cost increases lagging somewhat behind revenue increases.

Also of considerable interest are the consistently negative effects that the depreciation figure has on growth in assets, much as Nelson suggested. Examining the three periods' sample coefficients on the depreciation variable, we also see that the negative impact grows as inflation increases; the statistical significance levels increase in relation to the magnitude of these coefficients. While this is not strictly true for the other three cross-sectional variables, the only real surprise is that the results seem to support the model to a large degree.

From these results we find that Van Horne was quite justified in stressing the need to estimate future cash flows by taking inflation into account. Furthermore the Nelson hypothesis that inflation will slow investment activity through its adverse impact on the present value of the depreciation tax shield was also found to be supported; so this portion of the total cash-flow figure should also garner attention when making the capital-budgeting decision. Lastly, it was found that the cash-flow effect excluding depreciation is not necessarily offset by the proper adjustment of the discount rate, and that inter-firm differences in ability to keep up with or stay ahead of inflation play a major role in developing future investment plans.

The implications for financial management from the introduction of inflation are many. Regardless of the risk-adjustment process involved with the proper discount rate, the adjustment for the decrease in the purchasing power of future dollars received is mandatory. The problem in actually making this adjustment lies in determining exactly what the future rates of inflation will be, a task that is more of an art than a science. The cash-flow estimates must be analyzed in many ways. The value of the depreciation tax shield generated by the project must be valued and the operating cash flows from the project must be evaluated given the current inflationary expectations. It is also advisable to derive some estimates as to their relationship to changes in rates of inflation. These operating and depreciation tax-shield cash flows must be jointly determined with the optimal capital–labor ratio employed by the firm, the latter variable itself being affected by anticipated rates of inflation during the lifetime of the project.

In short, inflation greatly increases the complexity of the capital-budgeting decision, and in ways that offer no sure-fire solutions. Little wonder many of the discussions of capital budgeting under uncertainty assume away inflation and its assorted menacing effects.

14.7. Multi-period Capital Budgeting

14.7.1. *Overall Discussion*

The most difficult and realistic extension of the capital-budgeting decision is to multiple periods. All of the complications mentioned previously are compounded by this extension, but all is not lost. The purpose of this section is to introduce and discuss the various forms that these multi-period models assume. The first section utilizes a concept popularized by other business-related disciplines, the product life cycle. The additional information obtained from viewing the capital-budgeting problem is, or should be, of great practical importance to those active in the area of financial planning and forecasting. The second section views the capital-budgeting decision in a more theoretical light, predominantly with respect to the approach based on the CAPM, with which the reader should be relatively comfortable. The third section, the most complicated of the three, casts the problem back into a mean variance framework, reminiscent of our earlier discussion on the application of portfolio theory to corporate finance problems. Numerous efforts have been made to link the capital-budgeting decision back to the pathbreaking developments in finance. Thus it is all the more appropriate for us to dwell on the equivalence of these more widely known mean–variance approaches to capital budgeting.

The product life cycle is a concept that allows us to view a common product or project in a different light, depending on market conditions and the basic nature of the product itself. Frequently this life cycle is broken down into four phases; development, growth, stabilization, and a declining phase. From a finance standpoint, we would be interested in how the cash flows generated by the project vary from phase to phase, and when each portion of the life cycle is about to begin or end. Basically we are viewing each product as generating cash flows that begin at low or negative levels, grow to a point where the project has attained mature status and enjoys its largest positive net cash flows, then taper down to the point where the divestiture decision is made. By generally stating that any change in the product following its inception constitutes a new product and calls for new capital-budgeting decisions, we can break even longer-term projects down into manageable proportions.

Beyond basic cash-flow forecasting, this approach can be utilized in total financial planning, aiding in the determination of financing needs prior to the fact, and sustaining the firm's ability to maintain dividends at newly established levels if such changes are warranted (see Gup, 1980). When projects are viewed in such a light, management has the option to plan investment activity in such a manner as to smooth out net cash flow as a variant of a hedged position, thus eliminating unspecified quantities of the firm's specific or business risk without necessarily facing decreasing returns. The resolution of the risk inherent in a project is the topic of the following paragraphs, in which an analytic method for performing this product-life-cycle analysis is presented.

One of the virtues of the product-life-cycle approach is the manner in which risk is imbedded in the estimated cash flows, and how that risk is resolved as the true state of nature is revealed. Van Horne (1969) put forth the notion that those cash flows associated with the introduction of a product are the most risky, in that the developments that occur in the market during the incidence of these introductory cash flows by and large determine what will follow. As time passes and various cash flow streams are ruled out, those remaining flows become more predictable, i.e., less risky. If this setting is proper for the problem at hand, then a decision-tree solution format is suitable for the valuation of the project. Not only does the decision tree allow us to explicitly recognize alternative cash-flow streams; it also enables us to discount each component at rates commensurate with its risk, rather than at a constant rate that may serve to distort the value of the project (see Robichek and Meyers, 1966).

The actual decision-tree computation method as outlined in Section 14.5 can be rather tedious, and our intent here is to discuss the information this approach makes available, not the procedure itself.

Following the estimation of future cash flows and the probabilities of each cash flow, which are conditional on the prior period's cash flow, a net-present-value figure can be computed, and expected variances during each time period from each possible cash-flow stream can be computed. The latter figures associated with each cash-flow stream should decrease as we move farther into the future and the true demand for the product is revealed. This is desirable from a budgeting standpoint, but these figures have an even further use. If two mutually exclusive projects are being considered, each having approximately the same net-present-value figure, the one that resolves the uncertainty (variance) in the cash flows at the greatest rate would allow for greater control and forecasting ability. The effect the project has on the smoothing of the firm's total cash flows can also be considered; we should be concerned with total firm risk and not necessarily project related variance *per se*. The smoothing effect on the firm's net cash-flow stream allows for greater flexibility in the area of investment decisions, as funds can be managed so as to arrive at times when the firm expects to need them for new expenditure. Thus, as with any tool that allows for greater forecasting ability, the product-life-cycle approach to capital budgeting may be one of the most useful and easily understood techniques available.

14.7.2. *The CAPM and Multi-period Capital-Budgeting Decision Making*

Recalling that CAPM, as derived by Sharpe (1964), Lintner (1965), and Mossin (1966) is a one-period model, we must invent ways to permit its use in a multi-period setting. Bogue and Roll (1974) found such a method when they assumed that investors possess homogeneous expectations relating to the investment project's potential success and that there exist a single price of risk in the market. Then, if there exist perfect markets for physical capital, the multi-period project can be thought of as a series of single-period projects, where the physical capital employed could be sold at its end-of-period market value, of which there is also a market consensus as to that expected value. The firm, of course, retains the right to use the capital goods in future periods if the expected risk-adjusted rate-of-return is viewed as favorable, which, on an expectations basis, makes the project appear all the more beneficial. However, what is important here is the expectation of the one-period return being favorable. If perfect secondary markets do not exist for the capital in question, expected salvage values with expected concessions must be built into the final expected net cash flow. Depending on the degree of the market imperfection, projects may be rejected on the basis of this revised secondary market-value estimate. In these latter cases, further analysis is required but to the extent the capital is resalable at "perfect" market prices, the single-period procedure is an important and viable technique in evaluating investment opportunities.

Starting with a one-period project, the value of the firm before accepting a new project is:

$$V_0 = \frac{E(V_1) - L_0 E[\text{Cov}(V_1, V_{M1})]}{1 + r_f}, \tag{14.34}$$

where

V_1 = Random value of the firm at the end of the time period;

V_{M1} = Random value of the market value of all firms at the end of the time period;

L_0 = Market-determined price of risk;

r_f = Riskless rate-of-return available to all investors.

By undertaking a project with random expected value, or random expected sales price in the secondary market, the value of the firm becomes;

$$V_0 + V_{p1} = \frac{E[V_1 + V_{p1}] - L_0 E[\text{Cov}(V_1 + V_{p1}, V_{M1})]}{1 + r_f}, \tag{14.35}$$

where the firm value increases if the outlay for V_{p0} is less than the certainty-equivalent return it yields, that is;

$$E[V_{p1}] - L_0 E[\text{Cov}(V_{p1}, V_{M1})] - V_{p0} > 0.$$

The risk encountered in the one-period model above is actually twofold. The return during the period is risk-adjusted by the term L_0, and the value of the project (capital) is also uncertain. In extending the analysis to two periods or more, we should drop the assumption of perfect capital markets for physical capital; in that way creating a generalized model that is capable of accounting for any form of secondary physical goods market.

With the extension to multiple time periods, there will still exist one time period when the one-period valuation model can be applied, that being at time period $t-1$. The resulting value of the final net cash flow, C_t, is the incremental value the project adds to the firm value, or;

$$V_{P(t-1)} = \frac{E[C_t] - L_{t-1}E[\text{Cov}(C_t, V_{mt})]}{1 + r_{f(n-1)}}, \tag{14.36}$$

of which all components are random variables that are conditional on the state of nature revealed at time n. We have one more risk premium to consider, that associated with the unknown future, riskless rates of interest is similar in nature to that uncertain future inflation-rate premium discussed earlier (Cooley, Roenfeldt, and Chew), and is exactly the same if we take a real riskless required rate-of-return to be constant over time.

With this adjustment to the one-period CAPM, Bogue and Roll extended their method of capital budgeting as the only one consistent with maximization of shareholders' expected wealth, in which case unbiased estimates of a project's expected cash flows makes no difference because shareholders hold many securities, effectively diversifying this sort of inadmissible risk away.

While the presentation of Bogue and Roll has intuitive appeal, a basic inconsistency with their underlying asset-pricing framework was found by Fama (1977), which leads us to examine the ideal conditions under which the CAPM is a correct specification of the pricing of risky securities. As Fama points out, the original formulations of the CAPM allow certain types of risk, but not others. More specifically, the uncertainty of the various cash-flow streams or the possible variation in the actual payments received, relative to what was originally expected, is perfectly acceptable uncertainty, but we are forced to recognize the stipulation that the parameters of the pricing process be known with certainty by all participants in the market. The Fama criticism is directed mainly at the claim that future riskless rates-of-return are random variables in the pricing equations. We make this point because we chose to explicitly add the expectations-operator term before the covariance terms of the Bogue and Roll equations, to leave open the possibility of uncertain riskiness of assets as well, even though the Bogue and Roll paper assumed that all factors of their final equations were random variables. This is not to be confused with any stipulation that riskless rates-of-return and degrees of riskiness are constant over time, Fama allows these factors to vary over time but insists that these figures must be known by all investors so that they are recognized as true parameters of the system.

From a practical standpoint, it is hard to conceive of all investors knowing the relative riskiness of a security, or the exact rate-of-return on a riskless-asset or zero-beta portfolio, or, further, of being able to borrow or lend at this known certain rate. The investment community and academics alike have not as yet been able to identify true riskless assets or zero-beta portfolios with any degree of consistency, so the Bogue and Roll analysis is well taken. The argument for non-random riskless discount rates would have to follow an argument similar to an expectations hypothesis of the term structure of interest rates, with intermediaries or other market participants being willing to contract for future short-term riskless rates-of-return implied by the term structure of riskless interest rates, again noting the allowance of changing rates over time. If we refer to Merton's (1973) intertemporal asset-pricing model, we must concern ourselves not only with price, but with quantity adjustments over time, since real asset levels will vary, as technological development functions in the general economic framework and security markets.

In discussing the applicability of using CAPM in capital-budgeting decisions, Myers and Turnbull (1977) have obtained both good news and bad news. The good news is that it is possible to evaluate capital investments using relatively simple formulas derived from the CAPM. Also, the traditional procedures give close-to-correct answers, provided that the right asset beta is used to calculate the discount rate. The bad news is that the right asset beta depends on project life, the growth trend of expected cash flows, and other variables that are not usually considered important in assessing business risk. Moreover, for growth firms the right discount rate cannot be inferred from the observed systematic risk of the firm's stock, even if the firm invests only in projects of a single risk class. The reason is that growth opportunities affect observed systematic risk.

In the framework of the multi-period capital-budgeting decision, Myers and Turnbull have shown that beta depends on the cyclicality of the component cash flows, on the growth rate of the cash flows, on the elasticities of expectation, and on the duration of the asset's cash flow. Explicitly, beta can be written as:

$$\beta = \frac{1 + \eta Q_1}{Q_0} \frac{b\sigma_{Im}}{\sigma_m^2}, \tag{14.37}$$

where

η = Elasticity of expectations of future earnings stream;
b = Firm-specific constant measuring sensitivity of the disturbance term to unanticipated changes in the economic index;

σ_m^2 = Variance of the market asset's rate-of-return;
σ_{Im} = $\text{Cov}(\tilde{I}_t, \tilde{R}_{mt})$; $\tilde{I}_t$ represents the unanticipated changes in some general economic index;
R_{mt} = Market return;
Q_t = Cash-flow multiplier for period t.

Using Eq. (14.37), they have empirically shown that, as project life increases, beta will decrease. Second, as the elasticity of expectations increases, beta will generally increase as well. Third, as the growth rate increases, beta will decrease.

This relationship between growth rate and beta is not consistent with other findings. Fewings (1975) has found that beta is undoubtedly a positive function of the rate of growth of expected corporate earnings. To reconcile these conflicting findings, Senbet and Thompson (1982) have derived a more generalized relationship. Essentially, they show that if beta (β) is a linear function of growth (g), it follows that $\partial\beta/\partial g$ (derivative of β with respect to g) may be greater than zero to some point $g = g^*$, after which $\partial v/\partial g$ may be less than zero. Indeed, the way in which β and g are related depends on the way in which the response of cash flows to unanticipated changes in the economy changes with g.

One can view the Bogue and Roll analysis as an extension of the CAPM, not only in terms of multi-period valuation but also to allow further realistic uncertainties to enter into the asset-pricing picture. Our feeling is that further work of this nature is required before we can claim the CAPM as an uniform theory of risky asset-pricing under conditions of uncertainty.

Several mean-variance models applicable to capital budgeting are yet to be discussed. While most reduce to forms resembling the CAPM, their evident basis is portfolio theory, particularly those models of Hamada (1969) and Rubinstein (1973). This section is intended to show the essential equivalence of these two approaches, drawing on the work of Senbet and Thompson (1978), who also showed the basic equivalence between the two aforementioned articles and other papers.

Hamada began his analysis with the statement of the return-generation process for one-period risky assets as;

$$E[R_i] = r_f + L[\text{Cov}(\text{Cov}(R_i, R_m))], \tag{14.38}$$

where

R_i = Rate-of-return on the risky asset i;
r_f = Riskless rate-of-return available to all market participants;
L = Price of risk in the market, $(E(R_m) - r_f)/$[variance of the returns on the market];
R_M = Return on a market portfolio of risky securities.

If we define the return as being comprised of a dividend component and a capital-return component, the current value of a project or share of stock is the current value of the expected returns;

$$P_{0j} = \frac{E(D_j) + E(P_{j1})}{1 + E(R_j)}, \tag{14.39}$$

where, as we saw in the Bogue and Roll analysis, we are able to determine some value corresponding to the final cash flow to be received at the end of the project's life. In order to maximize the shareholder's interest in the firm, projects should be accepted only if the expected return to shareholders is greater than the cost of new equity that would be required to finance the project. Knowing from a preceding equation that the cost of that new equity is given by the market, we can write the necessary condition for project acceptance as the following;

$$\frac{dE(X_i)}{dI} > r_f + \frac{Id\,\mathrm{Cov}(X_i, R_m)}{dI}. \tag{14.40}$$

This is virtually the same formulation as that of Rubinstein, with the exception that emphasis is laid on the manner in which the decision rule is formulated. Rather than analyze all that shown above, Rubinstein proposed a risk-level acceptance criterion based on our L, which stipulated that a project of an expected return pattern was to be accepted only if the risk was less than that prevailing in the market for projects or securities with similar return characteristics. This is little more than a dominance principle based on the two inputs regarded as necessary to perform the capital-budgeting function. Both are important in that they urge us to abandon required rate-of-return measures such as the Weighted Cost of Capital, because they fail to provide adequate adjustment for risk. While others may argue that these two methods are not necessarily in conflict, the additional attention directed toward the appropriate assessment of risk is certainly worth mentioning.

The similarities of the two approaches discussed above and the Bogue and Roll analysis are many, the only difference arising in the course of implementation. The Hamada and Rubinstein methods are immediately solvable following the estimation of the project's cash flows and the market pricing parameters, while the Bogue and Roll method requires the use of dynamic programming. As such, then, no new models are added to the capital-budgeting area, only new techniques for solving these problems and new ways to view the problems, albeit in a slightly different light. Gordon (1989) has used mean-covariance certainty-equivalent approach to discuss multi-period risky project valuation.

14.8. Summary

The preceding discussion outlined three alternative capital-budgeting procedures, each useful when cash flows are not known exactly but only within certain specifications. Depending on the correlation of the cash flows and the number of possible outcomes, they will all yield meaningful results. Simulation was introduced as a tool to deal with those situations in which the most uncertainty existed.

Also discussed were various means of forecasting cash flows, most notably the product life-cycle approach. The emphasis in the later portion of the chapter was on the effects inflation has on the ability to forecast cash flows and on the appropriate discount-rate selection. We stress the importance of this factor as its non-recognition can lead to disastrous results.

In addition, we touched upon more theoretical issues by attempting to apply the CAPM, which created problems, but the basic approach is still applicable.

Lastly we investigated some of the more generalized mean-variance pricing frameworks and found that they were essentially equivalent. The application of these approaches is much the same as that of the CAPM, and further supports the increasing use of this technique in dealing with a very large, if not the largest problem area in applied finance theory, capital budgeting under uncertainty.

The concepts, theory, and methods discussed earlier are essentially based upon a myopic view of capital budgeting and decision making. This weakness can be improved by using Pinches' (1982) recommendations. Concern should be given to how capital budgeting actually interfaces with the firm's strategic positioning decision: to deal with risk effectively; to improve the control phase; and to take advantage of related findings from other disciplines. A broader examination of the capital-budgeting process, along with many effective business/academic interchanges, can go a long way toward improving the capital-budgeting process.

Following a survey by Graham and Harvey (2001) what we discussed in this chapter relative to the findings of this survey is the CAPM. Furthermore, this survey analyzed how although larger firms use present value techniques and CAPM, however, smaller firms concentrate on the payback criterion. Also the survey findings suggest that firms are interested in the firm's risk and financial flexibility when evaluating new investments.

Problem Set

1. Briefly discuss the processes involved in performing the risk-adjusted discount rate and the certainty-equivalent methods. How these methods are theoretically related?
2. Define following terms:
   (a) Risk-adjusted discount rate method.
   (b) Certainty equivalent coefficient.
   (c) Simulation method for capital budgeting.
   (d) Decision tree method for capital budgeting.
3. Discuss the major difference between the risk-adjusted discount rate method and the certainty equivalent method for capital budgeting decisions.
4. Discuss the relationship between the probability-distribution approach and the decision-tree method for solving capital-budgeting decisions. Why are these methods necessary for capital budgeting under uncertainty?
5. In what ways can simulation analysis be used to solve the problems of capital budgeting under uncertainty? Discuss the basic procedure of this method.
6. Analyze in detail the statistical distribution method for capital budgeting decisions.
7. In what ways can inflation affect the capital-budgeting decision? How can we theoretically adjust for such effects?
8. In what ways can the multi-period capital-budgeting decision problem be solved? Briefly discuss two alternative methods for making the multiperiod capital-budgeting decision.

9. Briefly discuss how the time-state preference and the option-pricing models can be jointly used in solving capital-budgeting-under-uncertainty problems.
10. The coefficient of variation for Project A and Project B are 0.2 and 0.4, respectively. In addition, we also know that the weighted average annual cash flow for Projects A and B are \$15,000 and \$25,000, respectively.

    (a) Is project A less risky than Project B? Why?
    (b) If both projects are going to last for 5 years and the initial outlays for Project A and Project B are \$60,000 and \$120,000, respectively, calculate the NPV for average cash inflow and its standard deviation if the discount rate is 10%.
    (c) Make the capital-budgeting decision in accordance with capital-budgeting-under-uncertainty techniques.
    (d) What is the advantage of the capital-budgeting-under- uncertainty method relative to that of capital budgeting under certainty?

11. What is break-even analysis?
12. What are the components of total cost?
13. How is a project's profit or loss related to the break-even point and contribution margin?
14. How is financial break-even affected by higher fixed operating costs? By higher required rates or return?
15. What is the difference between a project's cash, accounting, and financial break-even points?
16. How important are market research and production cost estimates to break-even analysis?
17. Why should management be wary of any project that appears to have a positive NPV?
18. Why is financial break-even a better concept to use that can or accounting break-even?
19. "Simulation analysis is a much more accurate technique to use in order to evaluate a project's risk. I do not see why we should use any other method." Do you agree or disagree? Why?
20. How is sensitivity analysis similar to scenario analysis? How is it different?
21. How might a firm that spends heavily on R&D evaluate projects that are currently under way or that are being proposed?
22. Why is forecasting risk an important issue in break-even analysis?
23. How does operating leverage affect a project's break-even point?

24. What is a project's contribution margin? How does contribution margin influence the break-even point?
25. Briefly explain why the cash break-even point will lead to accounting losses.
26. What is scenario analysis? How is it used to evaluate a project's risk?
27. What is sensitivity analysis? How is it used to evaluate a project's risk?
28. Discuss the relationship between cash, accounting, and financial break-even and a project's NPV, IRR, and payback period.
29. What agency problems may arise during the risk analysis of a project?
30. A firm has an investment opportunity. Find its NPV according to this information:

    Initial investment cost = \$2,000
    Cash flows for 5 years = \$600 per year
    Risk-free rate = 5%
    Risk premium on the investment = 10%

31. A project is under consideration. The risk-free rate is 5%, and market risk premium is 7%. The beta of the project under consideration is 1.8, with expected net income of \$1,000 per year for 3 years. The initial investment cost is \$2,200.

    (a) Using CAPM, find the required rate-of-return on this project.
    (b) Should the project be accepted?
    (c) If the third year's net income is a certain \$1,000, should the project be accepted?

32. Project A's initial cost is \$2,000, and its cash flow at time 1 has the following probability distribution:

Probability	Cash Flows
0.3	1,000
0.4	3,000
0.3	4,000

    (a) If the risk-free rate is 5% and expected market rate-of-return is 10%, and the project's beta is 2, what is the NPV of the project?

(b) If the beta of project B is 0, so that its cash flow is \$2,500 with certainty, how much initial cost is needed for project B for the analyst to be indifferent between project A and B?

33. A firm is considering an investment with the following values and estimates:

Risk-free rate = 5%.
Initial cost = \$6,500.

Cash Flows (Profit on Investment)			
Joint Probability Distribution			
Expected Market Rate-of-Return	\$400	\$600	\$800
0.1	0.2	0.1	0
0.15	0.1	0.2	0.1
0.20	0.0	0.1	0.2

Find the equilibrium market value of the investment. Would you accept or reject the opportunity?

34. A financial manager derived a 15% of required rate-of-return on his project using CAPM (risk-free rate was assumed 5%). If expected cash flow is \$1,000, how much is the certainty equivalent of the risky return?

35. Given the following information, which project is better according to the statistical distribution method?

State of Economy	Probability	Return of A	Return of B
1	0.3	25%	30%
2	0.4	15%	15%
3	0.3	5%	0%

If the expected marker rates-of-return are 20, 10, and 0% for states 1, 2, and 3, and risk-free rate is 7%, what are required rates-of-return on projects A and B?

36. The following are facts about a small firm:

    Risk-free rate = 6%.
    Expected return on the market = 12%.
    Variance of market return = 2%.
    Covariance of the net income of the firm with the market return is \$50.
    Expected net income =\$450.

    (a) Find the firm's value using the certainty equivalent method.
    (b) Find the firm's value using the risk-adjusted discount rate method.
    (c) If the firm's value is considerably below it equilibrium value derived in (a) and (b), what will happen?

37. Below is the probability distribution of cash flows for years 1 and 2 of projects L and K:

Project L		Project K	
Year 1		Year 1	
Probability	Cash Flow	Probability	Cash Flow
0.4	300	0.5	400
0.6	400	0.5	600
Year 2		Year 2	
0.2	200	0.3	400
0.5	500	0.4	600
0.3	700	0.3	800

    (a) Find the expected value of the cash flows for years 1 and 2 for each of the projects.
    (b) Assume that the risk-free rate of interest is 6%, the expected return on the market is 12%, and the beta is 0.9 for L and 1.2 for K.

        (1) Evaluate each of the projects using the risk adjusted discount rate method. Which one would be preferred?
        (2) Find the certainty equivalent coefficients (alpha) that would give the same present value of the mean cash flow in each year of project L's life.

(3) Evaluate the projects using the certainty equivalent form of the Capital Asset Pricing Model.

38. For the cash flow distributions given in the preceding problem, the certainty equivalent cash flows for each project for each year are given below:

Project	Year	Certain Cash Flow
L	1	200
	2	300
K	1	300
	2	400

(a) Find the certainty equivalent coefficients for each year of the projects' lives.
(b) Evaluate project's L and K using the certainty equivalent method, given a risk-free rate of 6%.

39. Under what circumstances will the certainty equivalent method and the risk adjusted discount rate methods give the same present value of cash flows? When they give different present values, which one should be used?
40. Assume you are given the following information concerning the mean and standard deviation of cash flows?

Year	Expected Value of Cash Flow	Standard Deviation of Cash Flow
1	700	200
2	900	300

The project's initial outlay is $500 and the discount rate for this project is 10%.

(a) Find the E (NPV) and standard deviation of NPV given that the cash flows are independent from one another over time.

(b) Find the E (NPV) and standard deviation of *SPV* given that the cash flows are perfectly positively correlated over time.

(c) How does your answer to part b compare to that of part a? Explain.

41. Spider Enterprises is considering two mutually exclusive investment proposals. Both of the projects have 2-year lives with their initial outlay at \$10,000. The probability distribution of cash flows for years 1 and 2 of the projects' lives are identical and given as follows:

Year 1		Year 2	
Probability	Cash Flow	Probability	Cash Flow
0.1	4,000	0.3	4,000
0.8	6,000	0.4	6,000
0.1	8,000	0.3	8,000

Project A has a perfect correlation between the first and second year cash flow distributions while the correlation coefficient between the first and second year's cash flows for project B is 0.5. The discount rate for this project is 8%.

(a) Find the expected NPV and standard deviation of the NPV for projects A and B.

(b) The firm's existing assets have an expected NPV of \$10,000 and a standard deviation of NPV of \$5,000. The correlation coefficient between the cash flows of the existing assets and project A is 0.0 while the correlation coefficient between the existing assets and project B is 0.3. Find the E (NPV) and standard deviation *of NPV* for portfolios of:

(1) Project A and the existing assets.

(2) Project B and the existing assets.

(c) Should either project A or B be accepted? Explain.

42. Alpha Corporation is considering an investment which will be implemented in two stages if profitable. If Phase I is built now at a cost of \$5,000, high cash flows of \$5,000 for years 1 through 3 have an estimated 0.7 probability of occurrence, while low cash flows of \$3,000 for years 1 through 3 have a 0.3 probability. At the end of year 3, Phase II can be implemented at a cost of \$7,000. If the first 3 years' cash flows

are high, it is estimated that Phase II will generate cash flows of $10,000 for years 4 through 10 with a 0.8 probability and $6,000 for years 4 through 10 with a 0.2 probability. On the other hand, if cash flows for years 1 through 3 are low and Phase II is implemented, then cash flows for years 4 through 10 have a 0.5 probability of being $4,000 and a 0.5 probability of being $1,000. If Phase II is not implemented at the end of year 3, then the cash flows earned in years 1 through 3 are estimated to continue for years 4 through 10. Evaluate the project using the decision tree method. The discount rate for this project is 10%.

43. **Calculating Cash Break-Even Point.** A new project for High Jump Shoe Company has a contribution margin of $2.50. If fixed costs for this project are $11,000, what is its cash break-even point?
44. **Calculating Accounting Break-Even Point.** The No Ticket Radar Detector Company's new radar detector has a contribution margin of $15, fixed costs of $3,000, and a depreciation expense of $1,000. Compute the accounting break-even point.
45. **Calculating Cash Break-Even Point.** Find the cash break-even point for the No Ticket Radar Company's new radar detector project described in Problem 44.
46. **Calculating Cash Break-Even Point.** The Fun Toy Company will be selling a new computer game for $29.95. The fixed cost of producing the game is $180,000 and variable cost is $9.25 per unit. Compute the cash break-even point.
47. **Calculating Accounting Break-Even Point.** Use the information given in Problem 4 to find the accounting break-even point for the Fun Toy Company. Assume that depreciation expenses are $50,000.
48. **Calculating Financial Break-Even Point.** The High Tech Software Company is considering offering a new computer recipe program. The program will be sold over a 4-year period for $15 per program. The program will require an initial non-depreciable investment of $5,000 and its copyright will be sold at the end of Year 4 for $500. The project also will require $2,500 in net working-capital (which will be recovered at the end of Year 4), fixed costs of $600, and a variable cost of $4 per unit. If High Tech's required return is 10%, compute the project's financial break-even quantity.
49. **Calculating Financial Break-even Point.** The Sure Time Clock is offering a new grandfather clock. The clocks will be sold over a 10-year period for $1,900 each. The clock project will require an initial investment of $110,000 and will be sold at the end of Year 10 for

$35,000. The project also will require an initial $40,000 investment in net working-capital (to be recovered at project's end), fixed costs of $50,000, and a variable cost of $500 per clock. If Sure Time's required return is 8%, compute the project's financial break-even quantity.

50. **Scenario Analysis.** Jennison Enterprises is evaluating whether it should enter the personal pager market. It feels the pager can generate after-tax cash flows of $215,000 a year for 8 years after initially investing $1.05 million to develop the technology and production facilities. After 8 years, Jennison assumes the salvage value will be zero. Jennison estimates a 12% discount rate is appropriate for this project.
    (a) Should Jennison pursue the project? Why or why not?
    (b) Jennison has developed two other scenarios for its personal pager project. One scenario forecasts that Jennison's innovative technology will result in a higher market share than originally forecast for the pager, with annual cash flows of $350,000 for 8 years. Another scenario is that Jennison will find it difficult to compete in this technology-driven market; the pager will generate cash flows of $175,000, $130,000, $80,000, and $60,000 before the project is terminated at the end of the fourth year. What are the NPVs for these two additional scenarios? Discuss whether Jennison should go ahead with the project or not.

51. **Calculating Three Alternative Break-Even Points.** Peter's Word Processing Service is thinking about expanding to a spot near your college's campus. The firm charges $1.25 per double-spaced page. This cost incorporates the cost of the paper and ink ($0.05 a page) and the typist's salary ($6.00 an hour); the average typist can type 8 pages an hour. Peter is examining a building that would cost $1,000 a month to rent. Up-front costs of renovating the building and purchasing equipment are $250,000, which will be depreciated straight-line over 10 years. Peter uses a 14% discount rate when evaluating college-town expansions and his tax rate is 30%. Assume Peter is examining the project over a 10-year time horizon and that it will have no salvage value at the end of this time frame.
    (a) Ignoring taxes, find Peter's cash, accounting, and financial break-even assuming no salvage value at the end of 10 years.
    (b) Ignoring taxes, estimate Peter's financial break-even if equipment and supplies can be sold for $25,000 (after-tax) at the end of 10 years.

52. **Sensitivity Analysis.** Given the information on Peter's Word Processing Service in Problem 9, compute the following:
    (a) The expected NPV of the project if Peter feels his business will process 160,000 pages a year.
    (b) From past experience, Peter knows he may be able to charge \$1.50 a page if no competitor locates close to him. But if a competitor appears, Peter may have to lower his prices to \$1.00 a page. How sensitive is the project's NPV to this change in price?
    (c) Local word processors may unionize, thus driving Peter's hourly wage rate up to \$10 an hour. On the other hand, university layoffs may allow Peter to hire qualified personnel for only \$5 per hour. Assuming none of these events affect Peter's basic charge of \$1.25 per page, what is their effect on NPV?
53. **Scenario Analysis.** Consider the following scenarios for Peter's Word Processing Service.
    i. Base-Case: the estimates given in Problem 9 are correct, and Peter's processes 160,000 pages each year.
    ii. Best-Case: the estimates given in Problem 9 are correct, except Peter is able to charge \$1.50 a page and hire word processors at \$5 an hour; 160,000 pages are processed each year.
    iii. Worst-Case: the estimates given in Problem 9 are correct, except Peter can charge only \$1.00 a page, and unionized word processors demand \$10 an hour. In addition, only mathematics and engineering students use Peter's services, so his firm only processes 80,000 highly technical pages annually at a rate of 4 pages per hour.
    (a) Find the NPVs of the base-case, best-case, and worst-case scenarios.
    (b) Given the results of this analysis, should Peter's Word Processing Service expand to your town? Why or why not?
54. **Calculating Cash and Accounting Break-Even Points.** Garfield's Lasagna Hut is thinking about setting up a restaurant in Germany. Depending on local conditions, it may be able to charge either DM 10 or DM 15 for a plate of lasagna. The cost of supplies will average either DM 3.5 a plate or DM 4.8 a plate, depending on whether supplies can be purchased in Germany or whether they must be shipped from Italy. Garfield estimates annual labor, rent, and electricity costs of DM 50,000. Garfield estimates it will have to invest DM 500,000 to construct the restaurant. Assume this will be depreciated over 5 years.

After 5 years, Garfield hopes to be able to sell the restaurant for DM 600,000.

(a) Why are the cash and accounting break-even points, assuming a price of DM 15 per serving and a cost of DM 3.5 per serving?
(b) What are the cash and accounting break-even points, assuming a price of DM 10 per servings and a cost of DM 4.8 per serving?
(c) What are the cash and accounting break-even points, assuming a price of DM 15 and a cost of DM 4.8 per serving?
(d) What are the cash and accounting break-even points, assuming a price of DM 10 and a cost of DM 3.5 per serving?
(e) Suppose Garfield estimates it can sell 20,000 servings of lasagna per year. Given your analysis in parts (a) through (d), how risky is the expansion?

55. **Sensitivity Analysis.** Given the information in Problem 12, assume Garfield can serve 30,000 plates of lasagna per year and that is appropriate required rate-of-return on deutsche mark denominated cash flows is 15%. His tax rate is 40%.

(a) Assuming a cost-per-serving of DM 4.8, how sensitive is the project's NPV to the price assumption?
(b) Assuming a per-serving price of DM 15, how sensitive is the project's NPV to the cost assumption?
(c) Assuming a price of DM 10 and a cost-per-serving of DM 4.8, how sensitive is the project's NPV to the selling price assumption in Year 5? Assume a successful restaurant can be sold for DM 600,000, but the equipment of an unsuccessful restaurant can be sold for only DM 100,000.

56. **Scenario Analysis.** Assume the base-case scenario for Garfield's restaurant in Problem 12 has a price-per-serving of DM 10, a cost-per-serving of DM 3.5, and a Year 5 selling price of DM 600,000. Assume 30,000 plates of lasagna are sold in the base-case.

(a) What is the base-case NPV?
(b) Given the information in Problems 12 and 13, what are the price, cost, and salvage value assumptions for the worst-case scenario for Garfield? What is the worst-case NPV? Assume worst-case sales are 10,000 plates.
(c) Given the information in Problems 12 and 13, what are the price, cost, and salvage value assumptions for best-case scenario for

Garfield? What is the best-case NPV? Assume best-case sales are 40,000 plates.

(d) Should Garfield expand to Germany? Explain.

57. **Cash Break-Even Point with Tax.** The text derived a relationship to estimate the cash break-even quantity that assumed a zero tax rate. Since cash break-even occurs when accounting income is negative, the relationship given the text *overstates* the true cash break-even because of tax refunds. Derive a formula for cash break-even that includes the tax effect.
58. **Financial Break-Even Point with Tax.** The text derived a relationship to estimate the financial break-even quantity assuming a zero tax rate. Since financial break-even occurs when accounting income is positive, the relationship given in the text *understates* the true financial break-even because of the tax liability. Derive a formula for financial break-even that includes the tax effect.

Appendix 14.A. Time-state Preference and the Real Option Approaches for Capital Budgeting Under Uncertainty

The time-state preference model is one approach that can be used in capital budgeting under uncertainty. Breeden and Litzenberger (1978) have shown how option-pricing theory can be applied to the time-state preference model in order to be used in capital budgeting under uncertainty. We will first look at a simple time-state preference model and then see how the option-pricing model can be applied to time-state preferences for a single-period case. Then we will look at the multi-period cases.

Using estimates developed by Banz and Miller (1978) and Haley and Schall (1979), we shall use the following model[4,5]:

$$PV = \sum_{s=1}^{n}\sum_{t=1}^{T}(V_{st})(Z_{st}), \tag{14.A.1}$$

[4]This appendix heavily draws upon Haley and Schall (1979, 254–261), with permission from the publisher.

[5]See Haley and Schall (1979, 218–229, and 253–261) for the detailed discussion on the time-state preference model and its related issues.

Table 14.A.1. Expected cash flows for Project, Z_{st}.

State of Economy	Year 1	Year 2	Year 3
Boom	$1000	$500	$300
Normal	$800	$400	$200
Recession	$500	$200	$100

where

V_{st} = current value (price) of a dollar for state s and time t,
Z_{st} = present value of cash flow for state s and time t,
PV = present value of project.

We are considering introducing a new product that is a fad item and will be profitable to produce for only 3 years.

The expected cash flows for three different states of the economy, boom, normal, and recession are shown in Table 14.A.1.

Using state prices developed from the option-pricing model by Banz and Miller (1978) and substituting into Eq. (14.A.1), Haley and Schall obtained:

$$\begin{aligned} \text{PV} &= \$1000(0.1672) + \$800(0.2912) + \$500(0.5398) \\ &\quad + \$500(0.1693) + \$400(0.2915) + \$200(0.5333) \\ &\quad + \$300(0.1686) + \$200(0.2903) + \$100(0.5313) \\ &= \$1{,}140. \end{aligned}$$

If the initial investment is less than $1,140, the project has a positive NPV and should be undertaken.

To see how V_{st}, the time-state prices, are determined using the option-pricing model, we will first look at the single-period case.

We assume we can define "states of the world" that are associated with payoffs from the market portfolio. In the three-state case used earlier, revision is defined as rates-of-return form −86.47% to 0.068%, normal is 0.068% to 20.428%, and boom is 20.428% to 171.83%.

By being able to define states in this manner, we can determine the historical frequency of occurrence of any state, we can have any number of states, and the state definitions are objective and easily understood. Let the current value of the market portfolio be M_0 and V_j an option that pays $1 one period from now ($t = 1$) if $M_1 \geq M_j$ (M_j is a specified level). Breeden and Litzenberger (1978) show that V's value can be derived from the Black–Scholes model as the second partial derivative of the model with respect to the exercise price evaluated at an exercise price M_j. Therefore:

$$V_j = e^{-i} N[d_2(M_j)], \tag{14.A.2}$$

$$d_2 = \frac{\ln\left(\frac{M_0}{M_j}\right) + \left[\frac{(i - S_M^2)}{2}\right]}{S_M}, \tag{14.A.3}$$

where

i = Interest rate,
S_M^2 = Instantaneous variance of the rate-of-return on the market portfolio,
N = Probability of $d_2(M_j)$ obtained from a normal distribution.

The difference between this formula and that of a financial option lies in the differences in the options. This option has no exercise price, and the payoff when $M_0 \geq M_j$ is limited to \$1. Call options pay the differences between the stock price and the exercise price, which is unlimited.

Now to put this model to use, we observe first that:

$$\frac{M_0}{M_j} = \frac{1}{1 + r_{Mj}}, \tag{14.A.4}$$

where

r_{Mj} = Rate-of-return on the market portfolio for the period if

$$M_0 \geq M_j.$$

Therefore, as r_{Mj} becomes negative, M_0/M_j becomes larger and so does ln (M_0/M_j). For a given i and S, the value of the option approaches certainty of paying off \$1 as r_{Mj} approaches -100%. As r_{Mj} gets larger (positive), the option becomes certain of not paying off and V_j value becomes zero.

When state S_j occurs, the option pays off \$1. This state S_j is defined as the range of rates-of-return on the market portfolio from r_{Mj} to $r_{M(j+1)}$. Given the assumption of perfect markets, the value of this option is:

$$\Delta V_j = V_j - V_{j+1}. \tag{14.A.5}$$

Substituting from Eq. (14.A.2), we have

$$V_j = e^{-i}\{N[d_2(M_j)] - N[d_2(M_{j+1})]\} \tag{14.A.6}$$

or, equivalently:

$$v_j = e^{-i}\{N[d_2(r_{M_j})] - N[d_2(r_{M_{j+1}})]\}. \tag{14.A.7}$$

We can rewrite Eq. (13.A.5) as:

$$V_j = v_j + V_{j+1}. \tag{14.A.8}$$

Here, V_{j+1} is the value of the option that pays \$1 if $M_1 \geq M_{j+1}$ or, if the rate-of-return on the market portfolio $\geq r_{M,(j+1)}$, the only variables we need to estimate are i and S as shown by Haley and Schall.

As for the multi-period state prices, we make some additional assumptions:

(a) State definitions are constant for all future periods under consideration.
(b) Transitions from one period to another follow a stationary market process.
(c) Everyone agrees on state definitions and that the transitions follow a stationary process.

These three assumptions mean that the probability that the rate-of-return of a market portfolio will be in a given state in period t depends only on the state into which it fell in period $(t-1)$. Also, the probability of going from state t to state $(t-1)$ does not vary with t.

The matrix of any future T periods is V^T, matrix V taken to the Tth power. A simple example of this is:

		Next-Period State	
		High	Low
Current-Period	High	H_H	H_L
States	Low	L_H	L_L

For example, H_H and H_L are the current prices of \$1 received next period if the present state is high. The subscripts indicate whether the next period is high or low.

Looking at the matrix of status prices two periods from the present, V^2, we get:

$$\begin{aligned} V^2 &= V \cdot V \\ &= \begin{bmatrix} H_H & H_L \\ L_H & L_L \end{bmatrix} \cdot \begin{bmatrix} H_H & H_L \\ L_H & L_L \end{bmatrix} \\ &= \begin{bmatrix} (H_H H_H + H_L L_H) & (H_H H_L + H_L L_L) \\ (L_H H_H + L_L L_H) & (L_H H_L + L_L L_L) \end{bmatrix}. \end{aligned}$$

Thus if the state row is high and it is also high in time 2, the probability of \$1 to be in control two periods from now is given by $(H_H H_H + H_L L_H)$.

The economic explanation is as follows. We must first look at where we could be at time 1. At time 1 we can be high, H_H, or low, L_H. Looking at the present value (at time zero), we see that the right price of H is $H_H H_H + H_L L_H$, as described in the matrix above.

The basic theory of this approach is:

(a) Given perfect capital markets with continuous trading, the state-contingent claims are implicit in option prices that conform to specific valuation equations.
(b) If states can be defined as ranges of the rate-of-return of the market portfolio, and transition from state is a stationary Markov process, state prices for any future period can be calculated from a matrix at single-period prices.
(c) Given the state prices for future periods, the state of payoffs from an investment can be solved using Eq. (14.A.1).

There exist three different approaches to deal with uncertainty: state-preference, arbitrage, and mean–variance. Generally we regard state-preference models as being impracticable for application in real-world decision making. However, option-pricing theory has made the application possible.

One of the major inputs for this type of application is an estimate of the market rate-of-return for each state of nature. Merton's (1980) time-series approach "On Estimating the Expected Return on the Market" can be used to obtain estimates of market rates-of-return and its variances.

Recently Copeland (2003), Amram and Kulatilaka (1999), and others have been using equation (13.A.9) to do real option analysis.

$$V_c = P[N(d_1)] - e^{-rt}E[N(d_2)], \tag{14.A.9}$$

where V = value of option; P = present value annuity of future cash flow; r = continuously compounded annual risk-free interest rate; t = life of the project; E = initial cost of investment; $e = 2.71828\ldots$ is a constant; and $N(d_1)$ = probability that a standard normal random variable is less than or equal to $d_i (i = 1, 2)$, with

$$d_1 = \frac{\ln\left(\frac{P}{E}\right) + \left(r + \frac{\sigma^2}{2}\right)t}{\sigma\sqrt{t}} \tag{14.A.10}$$

and

$$d_2 = \frac{\ln\left(\frac{P}{E}\right) + \left(r - \frac{\sigma^2}{2}\right)t}{\sigma\sqrt{t}} = d_1 - \sigma\sqrt{t}, \tag{14.A.11}$$

where σ^2 = variance of future cash flow and logarithms are to base e.

The real option model defined in Eqs. (14.A.9), (14.A.10), and (14.A.11) is similar to the financial option-pricing model we defined earlier. The contract period for financial option is predetermined and cannot be changed. However, the life time of the project can be modified by decision maker. In other words, the managers can delay the project, i.e., the managers have the flexibility to change the life the project. The further discussion of the application of real option can be found in Ross *et al.* (2008).

References for Appendix 14.A

Amram, M and N Kulatilika (1999). *Real Options: Managing Strategic Investment in an Uncertain World.* Boston: Harvard Business School Press.

Banz, RW and MH Miller (1978). Prices for state-contingent claims: Some estimates and applications. *Journal of Business*, 51, 653–672.

Breeden, DT and RH Litzenberger (1978). Prices of state-contingent claims implicit in option prices. *Journal of Business*, 51, 621–651.

Copeland, T and V Antikarov (2003). *Real Options: A Practitioner's Guide.* Texere.

Haley, CW and LD Schall (1979). *The Theory of Financial Decisions*, 2nd ed. New York: McGraw-Hill Book Company.

Merton, RC (1980). On estimating the expected return on the market: An exploratory investigation. *Journal of Financial Economics*, 8, 323–361.

Ross, SA, RW Westerfield, and J Jaffe (2008). *Corporate Finance*, 8th ed., New York: McGraw-Hill/Irwin.

References for Chapter 14

Arrow, HB (1971). *Essays in the Theory of Risk-bearing.* Chicago, Illinois: Markham Publishing Co.

Bernhard, RH (1984). Risk-adjusted value, timing of uncertainty resolution, and the measurement of project worth. *Journal of Financial and Quantitative Method*, 19, 83–99.

Bogue, MCR and RR Roll (1974). Capital budgeting of risky projects with 'Imperfect' markets for physical capital. *Journal of Finance*, 29, 601–613.

Bonini, CP (1975). Comment on formulating correlated cash-flow streams. *Engineering Economist*, 20, 269–314.

Bleakley, F (1994). As capital spending grows, firms take a hard look at returns from the effort. *The Wall Street Journal*, A2–A6.

Chen, HYC (1967). Valuation under uncertainty. *Journal of Financial and Quantitative Analysis*, 2, 313–325.

Chen, SN and WT Moore (1982). Investment decision under uncertainty: Application of estimation risk in the Hillier approach. *Journal of Financial and Quantitative Analysis*, 17, 425–440.

Cooley, PLJ, RL Roenfeldt, and IK Chew (1975). Capital budgeting procedures under inflation. *Financial Management*, 4, 18–27.

Copeland, T, T Koller, and J Murrin (2000). *Valuation: Measuring and Managing the Value of Companies* 3rd ed. New York: John Wiley & Sons, Inc.

Crum, RL and F Derkinderen (1981). *Capital Budgeting Under Conditions of Uncertainty*, Boston: Martin Publishing Company.

Fama, EF (1975). Short-term interest rates as predictors of inflation. *American Economic Review*, 65, 269–282.

Fama, EF (1977). Risk-adjusted discount rates and capital budgeting under uncertainty. *Journal of Financial Economics*, 5, 3–24.

Fewings, DR (1975). The impact of corporate growth on risk of common stocks. *Journal of Finance*, 30, 525–531.

Fisher, I (1930). *The Theory of Interest*, New York: Macmillan.

Freund, JE (1992). *Mathematical Statistics*. 5th ed. Englewood Cliffs: Prentice-Hall.

Gordon, AS (1986). A Certainty-equivalent approach to capital budgeting. *Financial Management*, 15.

Gordon AS (1989). Multi-period risky project valuation: A Mean-covariance certainty-equivalent approach. *Advances in Financial Planning and Forecasting*, 3, 1–36, ed. by CF Lee, JAI Press.

Graham, JR and CR Harvey (2001). The Theory and Practice of Corporate Finance: Evidence from the Field. *Journal of Financial Economics*, 60(2–3), 187–243.

Web, GD (1978). Multiplicative risk premiums. *Journal of Financial and Quantitative Analysis*, 13, 947–967.

Gup, BEM (1980). Guide to Strategic Planning, New York: McGraw-Hill.

Hamada, RSY (1969). Portfolio analysis, market equilibrium, and corporation finance. *Journal of Finance*, 24, 13–31.

Hertz, DB (1964). Risk analysis in capital investment. *Harvard Business Review*, 42, 95–106.

Hillier, F (1963). The derivation of probabilistic information for the evaluation of risky investments. *Management Science*, 9, 443–457.

Holden, A and A Pasztor (1995). Chevron slashes outlays for kazakhstan oil field. *The Wall Street Journal*, A3.

Kim, MKL (1979). Inflationary effects in the capital-investment process: An empirical examination. *Journal of Finance*, 34, 941–950.

Lee, CF and AC Lee (2013). *Encyclopedia of Finance*, 2nd ed. New York: Springer.

Lee, CF (2009). *Handbook of Quantitative Finance and Risk Management*. New York: Springer.

Lee, CF, JC Lee, and AC Lee (2013). *Statistics for Business and Financial Economics*, 3rd ed. New York: Springer.

Lintner, JP (1965). The valuation of risk assets and the selection of risky investments in stock portfolios and capital budgets. *Review of Economics and Statistics*, 47, 13–37.

Merton, RCT (1973). An inter-temporal capital-asset pricing model. *Econometrica*, 41, 867–887.

Mossin, JQ (1966). Equilibrium in a capital-asset market. *Econometrica*, 34, 768–783.

Myers, SC and SM Turnbull (1977). Capital budgeting and the capital-asset pricing model: Good news and bad news. *Journal of Finance*, 32, 321–333.

Mun, J (2005). *Real Options Analysis*, 2nd ed. New York: John Wiley & Sons, Inc.

Nelson, CRK (1976). Inflation and capital budgeting. *Journal of Finance*, 31, 923–931.

Pasztor, A (1994). Chevron is plunging into foreign projects to build oil reserves. *The Wall Street Journal*, A1.

Pinches, GE (1982). Myopia, capital budgeting, and decision making. *Financial Management*, 11, 6–19.

Pratt, JB (1964). Risk aversion in the small and in the large. *Econometrica*, 32, 122–136.

Robichek, AAN and SC Myers (1966). Conceptual problems in the use of risk-adjusted discount rates. *Journal of Finance*, 21, 727–730.

Rubinstein, MEV (1973). A mean-variance synthesis of corporate financial theory. *Journal of Finance*, 28, 167–181.

Senbet, LW and HE Thompson (1981). The equivalence of alternative mean–variance capital budgeting models. *Journal of Finance*, 33, 395–401.

Senbet, LW and HE Thompson (1982). Growth and risk. *Journal of Financial and Quantitative Analysis*, 17, 331–340.

Sharpe, WFO (1964). Capital-asset pricing: A theory of market equilibrium under conditions of risk. *Journal of Finance*, 19, 425–442.

Sheth, JN, CF Lee, and A Ignatius (1983). Alternative product-life cycles and their implications to capital budgeting under uncertainty. Unpublished Paper, University of Illinois, Urbana-Champaign.

Solomon, C (1994). Texaco to tie capital budget to price of oil. *The Wall Street Journal*, A6.

Sullivan, A (1996). Where others feared to drill, one group hits a gusher of oil. *The Wall Street Journal*, A1–A10.

Tully, S (1993). The real key to creating wealth. *Fortune*, 38–40, 44, 45, 48, 50.

Tuttle, DL and RH Litzenberger (1968). Leverage, diversification, and capital market effect on a risk-adjusted capital-budgeting framework. *Journal of Finance*, 22, 427–443.

Van Horne, JC (1971). A note on biases on capital budgeting introduced by inflation. *Journal of Financial and Quantitative Analysis*, 6, 653–658.

Wang, SW and CF Lee (2010). Fuzzy set and real option approach for capital budget decision. *International Journal of Information Technology & Decision Making*, 09, 695–714.

Wonnacott, TH and RJ Wonnacott (1990). *Introductory Statistics for Business and Economics*, 4th ed. New York: John Willey.

Chapter 15

Leasing: Practices and Theoretical Developments

15.1. Introduction

Buildings and equipments are two types of fixed assets required by firms to allow them to perform in a productive capacity. It is reasonable to assume that earnings are derived from the use of such assets, not necessarily the *ownership* thereof. Therefore, a given firm may use leasing as an alternative to outright purchasing to acquire the use of facilities and other capital assets. Leasing is an arrangement of contractual nature wherein the lessor (owner) allows the lessee (user) the use of an asset in exchange for a promise by the latter to pay a series of lease payments. Leasing has rapidly become a popular alternative to purchasing assets in both private and public sectors.

Fabozzi (1981) has discussed the conventional reasons for leasing in detail. Here, we shall discuss them only briefly.

(a) True lease financing might be cheaper than borrowing or purchasing the asset. This kind of advantage is primarily due to different marginal tax rates faced by the lessor and lessee.
(b) Since leasing generally does not require the firm to make a down payment (as most lending institutions do), the effect is to conserve working-capital. Although generally smaller than those required in most purchase arrangements, lease payments are prepaid and in that sense are like a down payment.
(c) Leasing may preserve the credit and debt capacity of the firm. This, as we shall see, is a result of the accounting conventions in use today.
(d) Leasing can reduce the risk of obsolescence and capital-equipment disposal problems. Almost always the term of the lease is less than the life

of the asset, particularly so in the case of leases that are cancelable at certain times at the option of the lessee.

(e) Leasing is more flexible and convenient than buying an asset. Most lessors deal with leasing arrangements on a regular basis and are used to tailoring these arrangements, within reason, to their client's best interest.

In sum, corporate executives believe leasing may lend itself to creating tax benefits, while also generating a financing advantage and reducing the risk associated with changing technology. These advantages are not definitive, but rather are relative benefits. The valuation theory developed in previous chapters can be used to perform further analysis.

The organization of this chapter follows two lines, *logical progression* and *degree of difficulty*. Sections 15.2 and 15.3 are practitioner-oriented, and are concerned with forms of leasing arrangements and accounting treatments and with cash-flow estimation and related valuation techniques, respectively. Section 15.4 explores the theoretical issues surrounding lease financing; particular attention is paid to the Modigliani and Miller (1963) tax-corrected firm valuation model, and the Miller (1977) personal-tax-recognition model. Section 15.5 deals with further extensions of lease valuation, using Miller and Upton's (1976) capital-asset pricing model, and incorporates cost of capital considerations. This section will also briefly consider the use of option-pricing models for the valuation of those situations where contingent opportunities exist. Section 15.5 explains how options are used to evaluate salvage value in financial leases. A concluding discussion will integrate the theory with practical considerations while outlining the important issues in leasing productive assets. Appendix A of this chapter discusses how to apply the Adjusted Present Value (APV) method to a lease versus buy decision.

15.2. Types of Leasing Arrangements and Accounting Treatments

15.2.1. *Three Leasing Forms*

A lease may take one of a number of different forms; the most prevalent forms are (I) direct leasing, (II) sale and leaseback, and (III) leveraged leasing. A further breakdown is made in all three of these leasing forms, as required for accounting reporting purposes, with a set of breakdowns applicable to the lessor, and another set applicable to the lessee. This latter breakdown may have an impact on which form of leasing the lessee decides to undertake, if any; but this has no economic value *per se*, even though it may have profound effects on the firm's financial statements. We now turn to a general discussion of the three forms of leasing, leaving the accounting treatment of leases to the latter portion of this section.

(a) Direct Leasing

Upon entering into a direct lease contract, the lessee is gaining the use of an asset that it did not possess prior to the transaction, without becoming the lawful owner. The lessor retains the title and ownership of the asset and receives the contracted lease payments from the lessee as remuneration. Frequently, these contracts contain provisions whereby the lessor provides required maintenance services — hence, the frequent term "service lease" — and may also assist in partial financing if deemed necessary. Quite often, a distinguishing feature of a direct lease is the existence of a cancellation clause that may be exercised by the lessee at periodic intervals such as year end, or some other distinct point in time.

The lessors that enter into direct lease contracts may be as varied as the lessees. Manufacturers of computers, such as IBM, and producers of office equipment, such as Xerox, may well be lessors of their own products. However, they are far from being the only parties involved in the business. Trucking firms, such as Ryder, purchase fleets of vehicles and in turn lease them individually or in smaller lots, acting in a near-wholesale capacity. Still other firms make a business of leasing smaller items on a relatively short-term basis. Often financial intermediaries such as commercial banks and insurance companies will purchase capital goods with the intention of leasing these goods, not as an integral part of their business, but instead to afford themselves certain tax advantages. We will elaborate on this tax advantages shortly.

(b) Sale and Leaseback

In sale-and-leaseback arrangements, a firm sells an asset it owns, or conceivably just purchased, to another party, and these two entities enter into a lease such that the original owner leases the asset from the new owner. The new owner retains title to the asset and all the benefits of ownership in terms of tax credits and depreciation allowances, while the lessee receives the funds from the sale of the asset along with the use of the asset. In the majority of cases, the asset of interest is sold by the original owner for the current or fair market value, which takes into consideration trade and volume discounts and current market conditions. As might be suspected, there are sound economic reasons for simultaneous selling and leasing back of assets, the discussion of which we will leave the discussion of the economic reasons until the accounting treatment of leases has been completed.

(c) Leveraged Leasing

The final form of leasing we will discuss is *leveraged leasing*. As the phrase implies, leverage — specifically financial leverage — is an addition to the situation that is not present to the same degree as in the other leasing forms. The major addition is a *lender*, who supplies a large proportion of the funds the lessor requires to purchase the asset it will in turn lease. This form of leasing can be expected to occur when large capital outlays are necessary for the purchase of the assets in question.

To the lessee, no fundamental difference exists between a leveraged lease and the two forms previously discussed. Any differences to the lessee would result from different lease payments required by the lessor due to the degree of leverage employed. The lessor is, however, in a very different position. As a debtor, the lessor is required to make interest payments, which can be quite sizable if a high degree of leverage is employed, and this will affect the size and timing of the net cash flows to the lessor. Again, the accounting treatment of the lease will be a factor for both the lessee and the lessor. We now turn to the accounting treatment of leases.

15.2.2. *Accounting for Leases*

In the previous section, it was mentioned that each form of leasing must be further dichotomized for accounting reporting purposes, with different breakdowns applicable to the lessors and the lessees. In this section, we will see how such distinctions are made and what the respective effects are on the two parties' financial statements. Tax effects, often considered an accounting issue, will by and large be relegated to the following section when decision criteria will be presented in detail.

The 1976 Financial Accounting Standards Board statement (FASB) No. 13 standardized the procedures for lease accounting. Prior to this statement, lease obligations of lessees either were not presented in the firm's financial statements, or were given cursory treatment in a footnote. Hence, leases that closely resembled debt-financed purchase were "hidden", and kept off the balance sheet. FASB 13's largest contribution has been through the requirement that certain leases — capital leases — be shown in the lessee's financial statements much as if the assets were owned by the firm. The reasoning underlying this ruling is as follows: If the lessee contracts in such a way that he acquires virtually all of the risks and benefits associated with the use of an asset, then it should be reflected in the appropriate financial statements.

The following rules apply toward the classification of capital and operating leases by the lessees, but as Fabozzi (1981) illustrates, even within these guidelines there exists a great deal of latitude in classification. From the lessee's standpoint, the lease is a capital lease if it satisfies any of the following four criteria; otherwise it is accounted for as an operating lease.

(I) The lease transfers ownership of the asset to the lessee prior to the expiration of the lease obligation term, including any time covered by bargain renewal options.
(II) The lease contains a bargain purchase option that allows the lessee to purchase the leased asset at a price that is sufficiently lower than the current expected fair market value at the time the option is exercisable.
(III) The lease term is equal to or greater than 75% of the remaining estimated economic life of the leased asset, unless 75% of the assets expected life has already transpired.
(IV) The present value of the minimum lease payments, including any guarantee by the lessee relating to the lessor's debt and other expenses, equals or exceeds 90% of the fair value of the leased asset less any investment tax credit, and less than 75% of the asset's economic life has elapsed. The discount rate to be employed in the present-value computations is to be the smaller of the lessee's marginal cost of borrowing, or the implicit interest rate in the lease, if the implicit rate is determinable.

(a) Capital Lease Treatment

The accounting treatment of a capital lease (a lease that is viewed as a defacto acquisition) is much the same as though the asset was actually purchased by the lessee and financed entirely with debt. Equal entries must be made on both sides of the balance sheet, to reflect the acquisition of the use of the asset, as well as the contractual promise to make the scheduled payments. The problem inherent in this procedure is the determination of the value of the asset. FASB 13 requires that two estimates of the value of the asset be made. The first estimate is made by discounting the minimum lease payments plus any expected profits derived from bargain purchase options included in the lease agreement, less any executory costs that will be incurred by the lessor that are embodied in the lease payments. The discount rate employed is the lower of the lessee's marginal borrowing rate, or the interest rate implicit in the lease. This implicit rate is the rate (IRR) that sets the net outlay for the asset by the lessor equal to the present value of the lease payments to be made plus any net residual value expected to be realized by the lessor at the termination of the lease.

As an example of how to compute the implicit interest rate in a lease, suppose the Docksider Corporation has just leased a crane for 10 years to lift sailboats in and out of the harbor. The lessor is an insurance company that recently purchased the crane itself, with full intention of leasing it. Annual lease payments, prepaid in each year, are \$75,000. At the end of the lease term, Docksider has the right to buy the crane for \$15,000, at which time its expected market value is also \$15,000. Docksider estimates that the crane cost the insurance company \$500,000 and that the full 10% investment tax credit was utilized, making the net cash outlay \$450,000.

The implicit interest rate in the lease is the value of R in the following equation:

$$\$450{,}000 = \$75{,}000 + \sum_{N=1}^{9} \frac{\$75{,}000}{(1+R)^N} + \frac{\$15{,}000}{(1+R)^{10}}. \tag{15.1}$$

Solving for R yields 14% as the implicit interest rate in the lease, the proof of which is left to the reader.

The implicit rate in the lease may well be higher than the lessee's marginal borrowing rate, as it is here when we assume a marginal borrowing rate of 12%. For future use, we also assume that the firm is subject to a 25% tax rate on ordinary income. One might expect the implicit interest rate in the lease to be greater than the lessee's marginal borrowing rate if the lessor is in a position to avail itself of the use of the investment tax credit that is not fully passed along to the lessee in the form of lower lease payments.

As an interesting side note, Crawford *et al.* (1981) conducted a selective survey that revealed lessor passed along any investment tax-credit benefits to the lessee in only 30% of leasing arrangements.

Given that there is a difference in these two interest rates that are relevant to part of the leasing arrangement, it is important to realize that the comparison of these two rates is by no means the correct method for making purchase-versus-lease decisions, especially in light of the fact that the lessor's cost figure is inevitably only an estimate. Rarely, if ever, will the lessor reveal the costs incurred in acquiring an asset to be leased. Note that here, with the lessee's marginal borrowing rate equal to 12%, the present value of the lessee's lease obligations is $479,448.

The second required estimate is the asset's fair market value at the time the lease takes effect. In our examples, we will proceed under the assumption that the fair market value of the crane being leased is $500,000. The lower of these two estimates, here the $479,448 present value, is simply added to the asset side in an account titled Leased Capital Equipment. A further breakdown is required before entries can be made on the liability side. A schedule of interest expense and the balance on the lease obligation must be computed. The amount of each lease payment that is not interest on the balance of the lease obligation (similar in effect to principal repayment on a loan) must be recorded as a current lease obligation in the period prior to its payment. The balance of the lease obligation is carried as a non-current lease obligation.

Tables 15.1–15.5 give the necessary information to compose the financial statements we will ultimately analyze.

These figures may require some explanation because of the timing of cash flows. The year-end 0 figures reflect the signing of the lease prior to the beginning of year 1. The total liability figure increases in year 1 because

Table 15.1. Docksider corporation depreciation schedule.

Year End	Depreciation Expense	Capital Equipment under Leases
0	$0.00	$479,448.00
1	84,445.09	395,002.91
2	76,000.58	319,002.33
3	67,556.07	251,446.26
4	59,111.56	192,334.70
5	50,667.06	141,667.65
6	42,222.55	99,445.11
7	33,778.04	65,667.07
8	25,333.53	40,333.54
9	19,889.02	23,444.52
10	8,444.52	15,000.00
Total Dpe.	$464,448.00	—

Assumption:
1. Asset value is $479,448.
2. Expected value end of year 10 is $15,000.
3. Depreciation method is sum-of-the-ears'-digits.

Table 15.2. Lease amortization schedule.

End of year	Cash payment	Interest on lease	Lease obligation reduction	Outstanding lease obligation
0	$75,000.00	$0.00	$75,000.00	$404,448.00
1	75,000.00	48,533.76	26,466.24	377,981.76
2	75,000.00	45,357.81	29,642.19	348,339.57
3	75,000.00	41,800.75	33,199.25	315,140.32
4	75,000.00	37,816.84	37,183.16	277,957.16
5	75,000.00	33,345.86	41,465.14	236,312.02
6	75,000.00	28,357.44	46,642.56	189,669.46
7	75,000.00	22,760.34	52,239.66	137,429.80
8	75,000.00	16,491.58	58,508.42	78,921.38
9	75,000.00	9,470.57	65,529.43	13,391.94
10	15,000.00	1,670.03	13,392.97	0.00
			$479,488.00	

Assumption:
1. Original lease value of $479,448.
2. Interest rate is 12%.
3. Annual lease payments of $75,000, with final payment of $15,000 on final day of year 10.

Table 15.3. Principal repayment figures on annual basis: Balance Sheets for 10 years of lease arrangement.

End of year	Assets	Current Lease obligation	Non-current Lease obligation	Total Liabilities
0	$479,488.00	$75,000	$0.00	$404,488.00
1	395,002.91	75,000	377,981.76	452,981.76
2	319,002.33	75,000	348,339.57	423,339.57
3	251,446.26	75,000	315,140.32	390,140.32
4	192,334.70	75,000	277,957.16	352,957.16
5	141,667.65	75,000	236,312.02	311,312.02
6	99,445.11	75,000	189,669.46	264,669.46
7	65,667.07	75,000	137,429.80	212,429.80
8	40,333.54	75,000	78,921.38	153,921.38
9	23,444.52	75,000	13,391.95	88,391.95
10	$15,000.00	$15,000	0.00	$15,000.00

Assumptions:

1. Initial asset value of $479,488.
2. Depreciation schedule in Table 15.1 used to update asset value.
3. Total liability figures taken from implicit interest schedule.

of the prepaid lease payments; i.e., interest accrues during the year on the unpaid balance, while the lease payment is not made until the beginning of the next year. Hence, the interest expense appears in the total liability figure because the statement is compiled at year end.

Table 15.4. Income-statement expenses on annual basis — operating lease option.

Year	Lease Payment
1	75,000
2	75,000
3	75,000
•	•
•	•
•	•
9	75,000
10	75,000*
Total expenses	$750,000

*The $15,000 payment for the machine at the end of the lease contract period would have to be amortized as any other asset at this point and is therefore not included as a deduction from income.

Table 15.5. Income statement expenses on annual basis — Capital lease option.

Year	Depreciation Expense	Interest Expense	Total Expenses
1	$84,445.09	$48,553.76	$132,978.85
2	76,000.58	45,357.81	121,358.39
3	67,556.07	41,800.75	109,356.82
4	59,111.56	37,816.84	96,928.40
5	50,667.06	33,354.86	84,021.92
6	42,222.55	28,357.44	70,579.99
7	33,778.04	22,760.34	56,538.38
8	25,333.53	16,491.58	41,825.11
9	16,889.02	9,470.57	26,359.59
10	8,444.52	1,607.03	10,051.55*
			$750,000.00

*Also excluded from the capitalized lease expense option is the purchase price of the asset.

Also noteworthy is the difference between the asset figure and that of the liability side. Even accounting for the timing disparity associated with the lease payment being made the day after the construction of the financial statement, there are equity effects — the increase or decrease of the shareholders' equity account that would result purely from the accounting treatment of leases for reporting purposes. While these equity effects are purely an accounting creation, to the extent that they affect factors of concern to management, such as ratios and return-on-equity figures, they are a real concern.

On the lessee's income statement, both depreciation and the interest expense implicit in the lease payments, as shown above, are deductions from income. The depreciation method used depends on which of the four rules outlining capital leases are satisfied. If rules (I) or (II) are satisfied, i.e., a bargain–purchase option or the lease transfers ownership, then the lessee's normal depreciation policies apply. If rules (I) or (II) are not satisfied, and either rule (III) or rule (IV) is, then the asset must be amortized over the term of the lease contract. Hence, more flexibility in depreciation expense write-off is afforded the lessor if rules (I) or (II) are satisfied.

There are also several reporting requirements that must be disclosed in footnotes. Total assets under lease obligations must be described by type, either by function or by nature of the asset. The minimum lease payments for each of the next 5 years must be presented, as well as the contingent lease payments incurred during the period. Finally, a general description of the leasing arrangement, including any restrictions imposed by the lease contract, must be disclosed.

(b) Accounting for Operating Leases

Operating leases carry the same reporting requirements in terms of footnotes, but do not require inclusion on the balance sheet, and can also be excluded from the income statement in terms of interest expense and depreciation expense. Of course, the lease payments under operating leases are still deductions from income; but the degree of elaboracy of treatment is diminished. Given that there are differing treatments for leases that could in practice be quite similar, the relevant question now becomes, "what difference does it make?"

The most obvious, and probably the first thing executives look at, is the net income figure.

As can be seen from Table 15.6, we see that in the short-term, net income suffers. Although, this is recouped in later years when the depreciation expense plus interest expense becomes smaller than the uniform lease payment.

With the recent emphasis on short-term profitability, managers reasonably make more than token attempts to arrange lease contracts so that the figures are kept out of the body of the firm's financial statements. If the return on equity is a figure of interest, and we assume it is, then another interesting factor enters when we capitalize leases. To the extent that the spread between the lease payment and the depreciation expense is greater than the spread between the total expenses to be deducted from

Table 15.6. Income differential under two different accounting treatments, capitalization and non-capitalization.

Year	Capitalized Expenses	Non-capitalized Expenses	Difference	Cumulative Difference, Capitalized less Non-capitalized
1	$132,978.85	$75,000	$57,978.85	$57,978.85
2	121,385.39	75,000	46,358.39	104,337.24
3	109,356.82	75,000	34,356.82	138,694.06
4	96,928.40	75,000	21,928.40	160,622.46
5	84,021.92	75,000	9,021.92	169,644.38
6	70,579.99	75,000	−4,420.01	165,224.37
7	56,538.38	75,000	−18,461.62	146,762.75
8	41,825.11	75,000	−33,174.89	113,587.86
9	26,359.59	75,000	−48,640.41	64,947.45
10	10,051.55	75,000	−64,947.45	0.00

Assumptions: Income figures from Tables 15.4 and 15.5 used for comparative purposes.

income and the lease payment, the return-on-equity figure will fall further because of an increase in the equity account. This accrues solely as a result of the depreciation method employed and the capitalization required by FASB 13.

We have established the fact that, by and large, capitalization has an adverse effect on reported profitability measures, *ceteris paribus*. What remains to be discussed is the firm's new liquidity and risk appearance. Since current liabilities are increased while current assets are not, net working-capital decreases, as do most of the standard liquidity ratios, making the firm appear as though it has higher default risk. Coverage ratios such as times interest earned and times fixed charges earned, will also deteriorate. This deterioration is because of the higher fixed charges incurred, all of which will be compounded by the lower earnings figure. Debt-to-equity, including capitalized leases as a form of debt financing, will further display a more risky appearance of the firm's condition. These coverage and debt ratios should improve over time, however, in that interest expense decreases with the passage of time while earnings and equity are expected to increase. Ingberman *et al.* (1979) have performed a more extensive yet easily understood analysis on the topic of ratio changes due to capitalization of lease obligations. We refer interested readers to that article.

The importance of the earnings figures provided by financial statements has intuitive appeal in that it is an often-used proxy for the firm's performance over a given period. Ball and Brown (1968) were early pioneers in empirical analysis of the value of accounting information. They found that at least half of the information used to form market-consensus stock prices comes from the annual income figure; hence, managers may have good reason to worry about reported earnings and the effect it may have on the stock price. Since Ball and Brown's study was based on annual earnings figures, the timeliness of such data is subject to question, especially if most of the embodied information is already anticipated by the market. Joy *et al.* (1977) addressed the timing question when they found that unanticipated quarterly earnings announcements can also have significant effects on share prices. These findings tend to imply that capitalizing leases, with the generally depressing effect on earnings, has at least some potentially adverse effects on the shareholders' position.

It should be noted that these studies do not expressly address the question of whether capitalization *per se* has adverse effects on the shareholder's position. Abdel-Khalik *et al.* (1981) conducted a study in which credit analysts were found to contend that they did not view capitalization of leases as bad *per se*, but, when asked to analyze financial statements of similar firms that did not capitalize leases, there was a tendency on the part of the analysts to penalize those firms that did in fact capitalize leases, in terms of financial strength. Nevertheless, the evidence that capitalization has adverse effects on the shareholder's position, and their returns, is an unsettled issue.

The ratio analysis mentioned earlier has important implications if creditors and other outsiders use these ratios in assessing a firm's financial strength, and are important parties in making those assessments of risk, thereby in part determining the firm's cost of capital (or place lower bounds on the relative costs of part of the firm's capital structure). Two of the better-known studies on the determinant bond ratings, one by Pinches and Mingo (1973), and the other by Pogue and Soldofsky (1969), show that certain ratios, not dissimilar to those we discussed earlier, are highly correlated with bond ratings, and thus with the cost of long-term debt financing. Altman's study (1968) on the predictors of bankruptcy showed that ratios similar to those in the bond-rating studies and our earlier discussion were fairly reliable predictors of bankruptcy, far in advance of the fact. Hence, if these ratios are used in evaluating the firm, capitalization of leases may again have adverse effects on the firm.

The major caveat to these conclusions is that creditors and others evaluating the firm do not see through the facade of capitalizing of leases, a topic to which little if any past research has been addressed.

(c) Accounting for Leases from the Lessor's Standpoint

Accounting for leases from the lessor's standpoint is not as complex as it is from the lessee's. Capitalization and off-balance-sheet reporting is not an issue, since the lessor actually owns the asset and must therefore include it in all relevant statements. The recorded value of the asset is determined in much the same manner as was done for the lessee, as required by FASB 13. The only complication arises when the value to be recorded is less than or greater than the cost of the asset, in which case deductions from income or additions to the income figure must be made.

Despite this cursory treatment of the lessors in terms of accounting treatment, their importance in leasing arrangements is not to be underestimated. Lessors are in business to make a profit, and may be in a position to pass certain benefits particular to themselves along to the lessees. Again we refer to Crawford, Harper, and McConnell as an actual example of this phenomenon. This mutual benefit is of considerable interest in the following section, in which the relevant tax advantages are discussed and illustrated.

15.3. Cash-Flow Estimation and Valuation Methods

Like all other decisions confronting the financial analyst, two considerations are of utmost importance in the leasing decision. The timing and size of each cash flow expected to be realized or paid out must be estimated, and the appropriate discount rate at which it should be discounted must also be stated. Most often, leasing decisions are made on a comparison of the leasing cash flows versus those that would be obtained if the asset were purchased and financed entirely with debt; thus, the investment decision is, in effect, separated from the financing decision. In leasing situations, this may lead to incorrect responses on the part of management when profitable opportunities are passed over. This could happen if the leasing opportunity creates a positive net present value when its discounted cash-flow analysis is performed while all other opportunities are not profitable. Therefore, our analysis will be oriented toward the lease-versus-buy decision with the recognition that *both* need not be good investment projects. Our task is not to find the best of two worlds, but to find the best projects. Here, we will hold with the convention of treating the leasing package as 100% financing, although we will examine that implication and its appropriate treatment in alternative valuation models.

Before outlining the cash flows and solution methods, some subtle clarifications must be made. Regardless of the recording treatment of the lease, the only deduction from taxable income is the lease payment. The depreciation and interest-expense figures, so diligently calculated in the previous section, are irrelevant for tax and cash-flow determination purposes. We hope that this sheds some light on the earlier statement that capitalization of leases is of no economic consequence. The major concern with capitalization is whether the Internal Revenue Service accepts the lease arrangement as a true lease and not a disguised sale, under which there would be more rapid write-off of expenses than generally allowed and higher than normal tax shields. The specifics as to what does or does not constitute a true lease can be found in the IRS Revenue Ruling 55–540. For the most part, the critical criteria are concerned with the lessee having a bargain purchase option, using the asset for almost all of its economic life, or making payments totaling the estimated value of the asset. The IRS stance is a very real concern, yet one that we will not devote further attention to here.[1]

Two generally equivalent approaches can be used to perform the discounted-cash-flow analysis of leasing. The analyst can approach the problem with the goal of maximizing the discounted after-tax cash flows, or the goal can be to find the minimum discounted cost flows under the assumption that the revenues generated under the lease-or-buy situations would be equivalent. We opt for the second method, for reasons of computational ease, and we refer to the earlier example given for illustrative purposes as shown in Tables 15.7 and 15.8.

Thus, if only minimally, we find the leasing option to be less expensive than the purchase option. It should be recognized that the investment-tax-credit assumption is crucial to this outcome; if it were allowed, the purchase option would dominate the leasing option. The assumption was made to

[1]The Economic Recovery Tax Act of 1981 (ERTA) was designed to encourage capital investment by liberalizing depreciation allowances and the investment-tax credit for property acquired and placed into service after December 31, 1980. ERTA also makes it easier to sell these benefits through the use of the "safe harbor lease." An unprofitable firm can buy and own an asset while selling, for cash, the tax benefits associated with ownership. This is called a tax-benefit lease, where the firm buying the tax benefits is recognized as the "lessor" and owner of the assets for federal income tax purposes. See Fabozzi and Yarri (1983) for further discussion on this issue.

Table 15.7. Lease cash flows.

Year	Lease Cash Flow	Tax Shield	After-tax Cash Outflows	Present Value of after-tax Outflows
1	$75,000	$18,750	$56,250	$57,789.16
2	75,000	18,750	56,250	53,025.84
3	75,000	18,750	56,250	48,647.56
4	75,000	18,750	56,250	44,630.78
5	75,000	18,750	56,250	40,945.67
6	75,000	18,750	56,250	37,564.83
7	75,000	18,750	56,250	34,463.15
8	75,000	18,750	56,250	31,617.57
9	75,000	18,750	56,250	29,006.95
10	75,000	22,500	67,500	31,364.01
				$409,064.52

Assumptions:

1. The firm's marginal tax is 25%.
2. The before-tax required return on Docksider's debt is 12%.
3. The lease payments are made at the beginning of the indicated year, and the shields from these payments are not recognized.

*Here, we allow deduction of the $15,000 asset price for illustrative purposes, assuming, in a sense, that the present value of the tax shield is not a significant factor, or that it will be written off in a very short time. We also allow the instantaneous deduction in the following purchase-option cash-flow evaluation for perfect comparability.

highlight the important role that the tax status plays in the lease-versus-buy decision, which means that every lease-versus-buy decision must be evaluated by itself.

One point of argument that evolves from this type of treatment is the discount rate used to compute present values. Johnson and Lewellen (1972) argue that double counting is involved when the interest tax shield is recognized as a cash flow and is then discounted at the after-tax cost of debt to the firm. They further argue that it is inappropriate to mix the financing and investment portions of a cash-flow analysis and that no attempt should be made to include the financing-generated portions at all. This was argued as a point against methods forwarded by Vancil (1961), and Bower *et al.* (1966). Both of these articles formulated methods that dissected the cash flows into portions generated by the operating effects and by the financing effect. This latter term is largely attributable to interest tax shields even in light of the exclusion of interest expenses as a cash-flow relevant to the decision.

Table 15.8. Purchase-option cash flows with 100% debt financing.

Year	Cash Payment	Depreciation Expanse	Interest Expanse	Tax Shield	Present value of after-tax flows
1	$78,247.61	$90,909.09	$50,610.29	$35,379.85	$45,789.03
2	78,247.61	81,818.18	47,293.81	32,278.00	44,619.05
3	78,247.61	72,727.27	43,579.35	29,061.66	43,418.51
4	78,247.61	63,636.36	39,419.16	25,763.88	42,169.73
5	78,247.61	54,545.45	34,759.75	22,326.30	40,922.02
6	78,247.61	45,454.55	29,541.20	18,748.94	39,676.20
7	78,247.61	36,363.64	23,696.44	15,015.02	38,442.76
8	78,247.61	27,272.73	17,150.29	11,105.76	37,230.52
9	78,247.61	18,181.82	9,818.62	7,000.11	36,046.79
10	78,247.61 +15,000.00	9,090.91	1,607.14	2,674.52	41,233.79
					$409,548.40

Assumptions:

1. The asset's initial value is $500,000 and the depreciation method is sum-of-the-years-digits.
2. The firm is unable to utilize the investment tax credit.
3. $15,000 final payment still applies.
4. Ten equal, prepaid annual loan repayments will be made.
5. Marginal borrowing rate is 12% and the applicable tax rate is 25%.

No proofs of their contentions were offered, though the following formulas were given for purposes of proper lease-versus-buy decisions.

For the purchase option,

$$NPV_P = -A + \sum_{t=1}^{n} \frac{(R_t - C_t - D_t)(1-\tau_c) + D_t}{(1+k)^t} + \frac{S_n}{(1+k)^n}, \tag{15.2}$$

where

A = Net cash outflow at $t = 0$;
$R_t - C_t$ = Period's net operating inflows;
D_t = Period's depreciation expense;
S_n = Expected salvage value at time n;
t_c = Ordinary income tax rate; and
k = After-tax cost of capital for the firm.

For the lease option,

$$NPV_L = \sum_{t=1}^{n} \frac{(1-\tau_c)(R_t - C_t + O_t)}{(1+k)^t} - \sum_{t=0}^{n-1} \frac{L_t(1-\tau_c)}{(1+r)^t}, \tag{15.3}$$

assuming prepaid lease payments, where the new terms are defined as;

O_t = Executory costs included in the lease payments;
L_t = Lease payment at time t; and
r = Riskless rate of interest.

If only costs were to be analyzed, the R_t's could be eliminated and the objective would be to pick the lesser of the two figures.

Alternatively the NPV_P equation could be subtracted from the NPV_L equation, to obtain the net leasing advantage, as shown below;

$$NPV_L - NPV_P = \sum_{t=1}^{n} \frac{O_t(1-\tau_c) - \tau_c D_t}{(1+k)^t} - \frac{S_n}{(1+k)^t} + A - \sum_{t=1}^{n} \frac{L_t(1-\tau_c)}{(1+r)^t}. \tag{15.4}$$

From the information given in our earlier example, we can compute this value and compare it with the previous result.

15.4. The Modigliani and Miller Propositions and the Theoretical Considerations of Leasing

The first known article dealing with the theoretical issues underlying leasing was by Gordon (1974). Gordon's paper was intended merely as a pedagogical note to Johnson and Lewellen's paper, but is currently viewed as the first attempt at lease valuation under conditions of market equilibrium.

Gordon was concerned with four issues relating to lease valuation and decision methods.

(a) The correct discount rate for risk-less cash flows.
(b) Differences in the lives of the lease contract versus the purchase option.
(c) Risk differences in each cash flow or stream of cash flows.
(d) The financing differences between alternative acquisition plans.

Gordon performs his analysis in the equilibrium framework developed by Modigliani and Miller in 1963, where:

$$V^u = \frac{(1-\tau)X}{k}, \tag{15.5}$$

V^u = Total value of an unleveraged firm,
$(1-\tau)X$ = A perpetual stream of after-tax cash flows, and
k = Investor's required return on equity.

If we have a firm that invests solely in risk-free bonds, M, earning the riskless rate of interest i, then the earnings stream X becomes Mi. Note that i is equal to the return investors require after corporate income tax has been considered, for the simple reason that the individual could buy these same bonds himself and avoid the corporate income tax penalty. Then, if we allow the firm to lever itself by issuing riskless bonds, since all debt is assumed to be riskless in this framework, the value of the firm is restated as:

$$V^L = V^U + \lambda D,$$

where

$$V^U = \frac{(1-l)}{k} Mi; \quad \text{and} \quad \lambda D = \frac{\lambda Mi}{i}. \tag{15.6}$$

Combining these two terms, we obtain

$$V^L = \frac{(1-\tau)Mi}{k} + \frac{\tau Mi}{i}. \tag{15.7}$$

By leveraging the firm we have added as much in assets as we have in debt, so that the value of the firm increases by the same amount, this holds true for any amount of debt added. By differentiating the expression for the value of the leveraged firm with respect to M and setting the result equal to 1, we are able to rearrange terms and solve for k. Shown below, we find k to be;

$$\frac{dV^L}{dM} = \frac{(1-\tau)}{k}\frac{dMi}{dM} + \frac{\tau}{i}\frac{dMi}{dM} = 1,$$

$$\frac{(1-\tau)i}{k} + \tau = 1,$$

$$(1-\tau)i = (1-\tau)k,$$

This shows that the after-tax required return on the firm's investors is the appropriate discount rate to be employed when dealing with a stream of riskless cash flows.

Checking to see what the results would be if the rate used to discount the debt tax shield was the after-tax cost of debt, we find:

$$\frac{dV^L}{dM} = \frac{(1-\tau)}{k}\frac{dMi}{dM} + \frac{\tau}{i(1-\tau)}\frac{dMi}{dM} = 1,$$

this reduces to

$$(1-\tau)i = \frac{(1-2\tau)k}{(1-\tau)}, \tag{15.8}$$

When $\tau = 0.5$, the right-hand side of the final equation is zero, implying that i must also be zero and that a riskless asset yields no return; therefore the cost of riskless debt to the firm is zero. As bothersome as it is to have non-yielding riskless assets, the case where τ is greater than 0.5 yet less than 1 produces an even more unrealistic situation. Either i or k must be negative in such a case so as to satisfy the equilibrium condition, and it is indeed improbable that investors will accept guaranteed negative rates-of-return when holding cash is a feasible alternative.

The previous finding resolves the first issue of what rate is appropriate for discounting riskless cash flows, and sets a lower bound for the discount rate applied to any cash flow.

The resolution of the last three issues can be found in the following formulation of the values of the two alternatives. In the case of the purchase alternative, the net present value is found by solving:

$$NPV_P = -C + \sum_{t=1}^{n} \frac{(1-\tau^c)(R_t) + \tau^c D_t}{(1-\hat{k})^t}, \tag{15.9}$$

where

C = Net initial outlay;
τ^c = Applicable corporate tax rate;
R_t = Cash flows before depreciation and taxes;
D_t = Depreciation expense accruing in time t;
$\hat{k}$ = A weighted discount rate, weighted according to the risk of the component flows; and
n = The life of the project.

The *lease* alternative's net present value can likewise be found by solving:

$$NPV_L = -L_0(1-\lambda^c) - \sum_{t=1}^{j} \frac{(1-\lambda^c)L_t}{(1+i)^t} + \sum_{t=1}^{n} \frac{(1-\lambda^c)R_t}{(1+k)^t}$$
$$+ \sum_{t=1}^{j} \frac{(1-\lambda^c)F_t}{(1+i)^t} - \frac{P_j}{(1+k)^j} + \sum_{t=j+1}^{n} \frac{\lambda^c D'_t}{(1+k)^t}, \tag{15.10}$$

where

L_0 = Lease payment at day 1;
L_t = Lease payment at the end of time period t;
F_t = Executory costs paid by the lessor;

P_j = Purchase price of asset at end of lease term;
D = Depreciation expense in time period t;
i = Discount rate for a riskless cash flow;
k = Discount rate for a risky cash flow; and
j = Term of lease.

By assuming the asset to be purchased at the end of the lease term, in lease-alternative formulation we have eliminated the problem of alternatives with different lives. Also, by explicitly stating k and i we are able to decompose the total cash flows into separate streams of differing risk. In general, any cash flow stipulated in a lease or debt contract is considered riskless, while any flow associated with the earnings stream is discounted at a rate that incorporates risk.

Still, though, we need to neutralize the debt financing implicit in the lease alternative. This can be most easily done by assuming 100% debt financing in the purchase alternative. The C term in the previous purchase equation is transformed into the same form as the lease payment stream. Subsequently, that equation can be rewritten as:

$$NPV_P = -L_0(1-\tau^c) - \sum_{t=1}^{j} \frac{(1-\tau^c)(M_t - A_t) + A_t}{(1+i)^t} + \sum_{t=1}^{n} \frac{(1-\lambda^c)R_t}{(1+k)^t} + \sum_{t=1}^{n} \frac{\lambda^c D_t}{(1+i)^t},$$

where

M_t = Payment of interest and principal on the loan during period t; and
A_t = Amortization of the loan for tax purposes in period t.

By subtracting the NPV purchase equation from the NPV lease equation, we will derive an expression for the net advantage of the lease over the purchase option. This will give us the following equation;

$$NPL_L - NPV_P = \sum_{t=1}^{n} \frac{\tau^c D'_t}{(1+k)^t} - \sum_{t=1}^{j} \left(\frac{(1-\tau^c)(L_t - M_t - F_t) - \tau^c A_t}{(1+i)^t} \right) - \sum_{t=1}^{n} \frac{\lambda^c D}{(1+i)^t} - \frac{P_j}{(1+k)^j}. \tag{15.11}$$

Hence, we find the lease option to be preferable, the higher the depreciation tax shield on the asset when purchased at time j, the lower the lease payments to the periodic outlays if the asset were to be purchased, and the lower the purchase price at time j. The first and last items mentioned are in apparent conflict and require that we find some way to remedy this problem. If, for the moment, we disregard executory costs F_t, differences in the lease term and the asset's life, and discrepancies in the timing of the payment streams, as well as any lease purchase options, Eq. (15.11) simplifies to:

$$NPV_L - NPV_P = \sum_{t=1}^{n} \frac{(1-\tau^c)(M_t - L_t)}{(1+i)^t}, \tag{15.12}$$

where the lease payment size *vis-à-vis* the loan payment size is the key to the proper decision in the lease-versus-buy area.

Mehta and Whitford (1979) analyzed the lease-versus-buy decision in the same Modigliani and Miller framework, but from the side of the financing decision. Their analysis reduces the problem to an examination of the tax shields generated by the two alternatives. Part of the reason for proceeding in this manner is to preserve the basic M&M risk-class provision. The concern is that equivalent cash flows, such as the alternative depreciation expenses, were being capitalized at different rates, as is done in Gordon's analysis. These problems are remedied in the tax shield analysis. Under the assumptions that the pretax cash flows for the two alternatives, lease-versus-buy and borrow, are the same, and the equivalent depreciation tax shield of the lease payments (D_{Lt}) is equal to the lease payment less the interest on the loan, the leasing advantage (A_L) is found to be;

$$A_L = \sum_{t=0}^{n} \frac{\tau^c D_{Lt}}{(1+i)^t} - \sum_{t=0}^{n} \frac{\tau^c D_t}{(1+k)^t}, \tag{15.13}$$

where $\tau^c D_t$, i, and k are equivalent to those defined in Eqs. (15.9) and (15.10).

It should be noted that the discount rate to be employed is subject to some question, possibly more so in the second term than the first, particularly so if the lease is cancelable at the lessee's option.

The simplifying assumption of before-tax cash-flow equality is not to be mistaken for after-tax cash-flow analysis procedures. The major factor skirted over in the analysis just discussed is the timing of the after-tax cash flows. Despite the treatment of the leasing problem in an economically sound framework, the accounting treatments are at the crux of the matter.

Not only are the purchase options depreciation write-offs subject to great timing variability; the lease payments may well be larger than the loan payments over a similar time span, if the lease term is less than the asset's life. Almost all authors disregard this problem and consider only financial leases. This impact on the after-tax cash-flow analysis is of considerable interest in the event of purchase options at less than the expected market value of the asset at the time the option is exercisable.

Brealy and Young (1980) address the problem of timing using Miller's (1977) equilibrium model, where personal taxes on interest receipts and equity returns are considered, and the marginal corporate tax rate in the economy is equal to the marginal personal tax rate on interest income. A potential lessee will lease an asset rather than purchase it outright only when the following condition holds: $V_L > 0$, and

$$V_L = \sum_{t=0}^{n} \frac{P_t(1-\tau^c) + B_t\tau^c}{(1+R^D(1-\tau^c))^t} - \sum_{t=0}^{n} \frac{P_t(1-\tau^*) + B_t\tau^*}{(1+R^D(1-\tau^c))^t}, \tag{15.14}$$

where

P_t = Lease payment at time t;
τ^c = The lessor's marginal tax rate;
B_t = Depreciation expense on the asset at time t;
R^D = Before-tax cost of debt;
$(1-\tau^c)R^D$ = Investor's after-tax required return on debt; and
τ^* = Lessee's marginal tax rate.

The first term represents the cost of purchasing the asset in a world of perfect competition, or the cash-flow stream that makes the net present value of the lease arrangement to the lessor at the margin, equal to zero, as required by Miller's equilibrium. The second term is the after-tax cost of the leasing payments to the lessee. Letting the first term equal A, we can derive an expression for the ratio of the depreciation expense in terms of present value to the initial outlay made by the lessor at time zero. Symbolized by D, this will be;

$$D = \frac{1}{A}\sum_{t=0}^{n} \frac{B_t}{(1+R^D(1-\tau^c))^t}. \tag{15.15}$$

Remembering that the required return on equity (r_e) is equal to the after-tax required rate-of-return on debt, the above becomes;

$$DA = \sum_{t=0}^{n} \frac{B_t}{(1+r_e)^t}. \tag{15.16$'$}$$

Substituting this into the first term of our original equation, A, and rearranging the first term, the lessor's and all other costs of the asset, we find;

$$\sum_{t=0}^{n} \frac{P_t}{(1+r_e)^t} = \frac{A(1-\tau^c D)}{1-\tau^c}, \tag{15.16}$$

which tells us the required level of lease payments the lessor at the margin requires to purchase the asset in question. Performing the same algebraic manipulations as above for the lessee, who is assumed to have a lower marginal tax rate τ^*, we will obtain:

$$\sum_{t=1}^{n} \frac{P_t}{(1+r_e)^t} = \frac{A(1-\tau^* D)}{1-\tau^*}, \tag{15.17}$$

which tells us the tax rate at which the lessor is indifferent between leasing and ownership.

If

$$\frac{A(1-\tau^* D)}{1-\tau^*} > \sum_{t=0}^{n} \frac{P_t}{(1+r_e)^t}, \tag{15.18}$$

then leasing is preferred to purchase. Since

$$\sum_{t=0}^{n} \frac{P_t}{(1+r_e)^t} = \frac{A(1-\tau^c D)}{1-\tau^c},$$

the above equation becomes:

$$\frac{1-\tau^* D}{1-\tau^*} > \frac{1-\tau^c D}{1-\tau^c}. \tag{15.19$'$}$$

Since all logic tells us that lessees have, or should have, lower marginal tax rates than those of lessors, the above condition that defines the case where leasing is preferred to outright purchase, is true only if D is greater than one. The magnitude of the value of the lease over the purchase option is then given by:

$$A\left[\frac{(1-\tau^* D)}{1-\tau^*} - \frac{(1-\tau^c D)}{1-\tau^c}\right]. \tag{15.19}$$

The value of the lease is now easily seen to be a function of the respective tax rates and the level and timing of the depreciation charges, the latter being the most revolutionary finding here.

Also considered in Brealy and Young's analysis was the case of a firm (lessee) with an increasing tax rate over time. In order for leasing to be preferred to the purchase option, the depreciation expenses must be higher than the lease payments in the early years, and vice versa in the later years, so that the tax shield is squandered. With the carryback and carry-forward tax allowances and the variety of depreciation methods available, there seems to be little reason to lease if this framework accurately represents the real world. Unless there is a large difference in the lessor's and lessee's marginal tax rates, leasing will not be a viable alternative. If large tax differences do appear, the analysis should be modified to allow for the introduction of investment tax credits and the like.

15.5. Leases-Versus-Buy Decisions Under Uncertainty: The CAPM Approach

Miller and Upton (1976) analyzed the leasing decision using capital-budgeting techniques under uncertainty, their favored method being that of CAPM analysis. In doing so, they explicitly distinguished between the economists' approach, where the financing decision is of no consequence, and the accountants' approach, where the non-financial elements are seen as irrelevant and the financial advantages are the element of interest. Miller and Upton proceed with their analysis assuming perfectly competitive markets, therefore dismissing the financial advantages, as they would be impounded in the lease-rental payment stream. Before pushing the point, it is worthwhile to note that Miller and Upton recognized that their analysis is not the final word, and that financial advantages might exist in non-perfect markets, so that each lease-versus-buy decision should be based on its own merits.

Miller and Upton begin their analysis in a one-period world. This is another point of departure from other analyses in that it corresponds to our definition of operating leases, whereas those analyses previously discussed assume that, at one time or another, the lease is for the life of the asset, so they deal only with financial leases. The first task we face in this framework is to find the equilibrium risk-adjusted lease payment.

In this one-period framework, the return to the lessor from leasing the asset will be:

$$R_{ij} = \frac{L_{it}}{X_{it}} - d_{it}, \tag{15.20}$$

where

L_{it} = Lease payment at time t;
X_{it} = Asset's purchase price, and
d_{it} = Economic depreciation of the asset in time t.

Here, d_{it} is assumed to be the only uncertain element in this formulation and is quite reasonable in that respect, since lease payments are often prepaid and the purchase price of the asset is also known. We can define this random d_{it} variable as;

$$d_{it} = d'_{it} + B_{it}(R_m - E(R_m)) + e_{it}, \tag{15.21}$$

where d'_{it} is the expected normal depreciation and all the other coefficients are similar to the standard CAPM format. Except the B_{it} corresponds to the unexpected depreciation attributable to excess use or under use of the asset, because of a higher level or lower level of economic activity than anticipated.

Noting that B_{it} is expected to be negative, we can write in expectations form:

$$E(R_{it}) = R_f - B_{it}[E(R_m) - R_f] \tag{15.22}$$

and consolidating Eqs. (15.20)–(15.23) and rearranging the equilibrium lease payment, L_t can be shown to be;

$$L'_{it} = X_{it}[R_f - B_{it}(E(R_m) - R_f) + E(d_{it})]. \tag{15.23}$$

Thus, in equilibrium the lessor should receive the risk-free rate plus the expected normal depreciation plus a premium for the expected economic depreciation that results from market movements. In its present form this is in expectations terms, and is by no means a guaranteed return. Excluded is any possibility of default risk on the lease payments, something that will enter into the picture if some lease payments are not prepaid and are scheduled to be paid during the period of interest.

Now that the lease payments have been stipulated, we should consider the lessee's decision to invest.

Using the CAPM in its standard form is appropriate if we purchase the machine, but it is helpful to redefine some terms slightly for the sake of lease evaluation. If V_{0j} and V_{1j} are assets purchase, and

$$\frac{E(V_{1j})}{V_{0j}} = 1 + R_f + B_j(E(R_m) - R_f), \tag{15.24}$$

then, letting $V_{0j} * B_j = B'_j$,

$$E(V_{ij}) = 1 + R_f + B'_j(E(R_m) - R_f). \tag{15.25}$$

We should now recognize that B'_j is not the risk of owning the asset at this point. Instead, it is the covariance measure of the relationship between the returns derived from using the machine and the lessee's total wealth. Some assets may even have negative betas, depending on when the assets are put to their best use; and others may have very high betas if their returns are amplified when the firm is operating near full capacity. At any rate, the firm accepts any projects whose cost V_{0i} is less than the present value of the expected cash flows, and

$$V_{0i} = \frac{E(V_{it}) - B'_{it}[E(R_m) - R_f]}{1 + R_f}, \tag{15.26}$$

the above being found by rearranging Eq. (15.24).

Now the question of lease-versus-buy crops up. If the strict CAPM assumptions hold, all risk-equivalent projects have equivalent returns and expenses, since, in the lease case, all costs of purchase will be passed along to the lessee, i.e., total cost, C_{it}, will be:

$$C_{it} = [E(R_{it}) + E(d_{it})]X_{it} \tag{15.27}$$

and is equal to the single lease payment.

We can also express this in present-value terms, as was done in previous analyses. The net present value of the lease option is given by:

$$V_L = \frac{E(V_{it}) - B'_{it}(E(R_m) - R_f)}{1 + R_f} - \frac{L'_{it}}{1 + R_f} \tag{15.28}$$

and the net present value of the purchase option can likewise be given by:

$$V_P = \frac{E(V_{it}) - B'_{itt}(E(R_m) - R_f)}{1 + R_f} - \frac{X_{it}(E(R_{it}) + E(d_{it}))}{1 + R_f}, \tag{15.29}$$

where for the time being, we use the risk-free rate as an appropriate discount rate, and the net advantage to leasing can subsequently be shown to be:

$$NA_L = X_{it}[E(R_{it}) + E(d_{it})] - L'_{it}, \tag{15.30}$$

which results from subtracting Eq. (15.29) from Eq. (15.28). The result looks very similar to Eq. (15.27). As we said earlier, $NA_L > 0$ if and only if market imperfections exist.

Extending the analysis to multiple time periods, we can consider cost-of-capital issues. The problem is best handled if we consider the costs of being a lessee as being comprised of two parts. The first is our initial certain lease payment. The second portion is the risk-adjusted compensation the first lessee must offer to a sublessee at the end of the first time period.

The user of the asset will acquire a new asset if the risk-adjusted return is slightly greater than the equilibrium lease payment, L'_{it}. If we let $E(V'_{it})$ be the expected risk-adjusted return from the use of the asset in the first period, and $(E(R_m) - R_f)B'_{it}$ be the risk-adjusted concession granted to the sublessee, so that he will be indifferent between acquiring the used asset or a new comparable asset of similar function, we find:

$$\frac{L_{i't}}{1+R_f} = \frac{E(V_{it})' - B_{i't}[E(R_m) - R_f]}{1+R_f}. \tag{15.31}$$

In a sense this procedure obscures the cost-of-capital question, since the two terms on the right-hand side of Eq. (15.32) are risk-adjusted. There is no attempt to specify a proper risk-adjusted discount rate, which is how most writers make an attempt to specify the cost of capital, or the premium above and beyond the risk-free rate that the project must return.

By making use of Eq. (15.26), and recognizing that, in equilibrium the risk-adjusted lease payments, when discounted at the risk-free rate, are equal to the cost of the asset, we can arrive at a cost of capital services, $C_{it(n)}$, for any n-period lease project as shown below:

$$C_{it}(n) = \frac{1}{1+R_f}[R_f - B_{it}(E(R_m) - R_f) + E(d_{it})]. \tag{15.32}$$

The reader should recognize this expression as the same as Eq. (15.24). This result should not be surprising since all factors are foreseen in a perfect capital market, and is consistent with multi-period versions of the CAPM. As with other analyses, the critical assumption involved is that the lease exists for the same time span as does the asset, and the risks involved with the contractual obligation of the lease are simply transferred amongst the various economic units involved. Depending on the term of the lease, the shorter the lease the more risk is assumed by the lessor, and the shorter the lease term, the more risk is assumed by the lessee. Still, despite the conclusion that leasing and purchasing are equivalent means of acquiring the use of an asset; no financial advantages exist in a framework such as this.

A similar but more general result was also arrived at by Lewellen *et al.* (1976). Using the Modigliani and Miller equilibrium model of market equilibrium, they found no net risk-adjusted advantages to leasing even in the presence of taxation. Miller and Upton also considered the potential effects of taxation, but the existence of a competitive marketplace ensures that this will not change the contention that leasing is a window-dressing activity, although it is no longer true that anyone or any business organization would be involved in leasing activities.

Not considered, however, and a major blow to these analyses, is the situation where non-standard taxation elements occur, such as the existence of Investment Tax Credits that do not have equal value for all firms. Myers *et al.* (1976) allow this tax effect and in very general terms outline the new lease-versus-purchase equalities that would have to be considered. From this analysis, we find that the various market imperfections ignored in capital market theory create the new focal points in the debate on whether the existence of leasing opportunities is of any value to companies considering new asset acquisition.

The Option-Pricing Model originally developed by Black and Scholes (1973) can also be utilized in the analysis of leases, or the components thereof. The obvious application is the valuation of any purchase options during, or at the end of, the lease term as the exercise price is the contracted purchase price in the lease.

Alternatively, multiple-payment leases can be viewed as compound options since each payment is discretionary. McConnell and Schallheim (1983) performed such an analysis under the most difficult circumstances. The leases they considered were cancelable operating leases, at the option of the lessee. It stands to reason the purchase option will not be exercised prior to the expiration date, but if the lease is cancelable at the lessee's option, each payment is an option to continue or maintain the right to all future options.

Computationally, this procedure is extremely complicated, and we need not pursue that issue here. We refer the interested reader to two papers on compound options. The first is by Rubinstein (1976), which evaluates such options in a discrete time framework. The second is by Geske (1977), which is carried out in continuous time. What remains is the ability to value any lease as a contingent claim, and in a sound theoretical framework that is consistent with the other equilibrium frameworks that received greater attention in the development of this chapter.

15.6. Options to Evaluate Salvage Values in Financial Leases

In the last section, we used the CAPM model to evaluate financial leases under uncertainty. Here, we use the model of Lee *et al.* (1982) to show how the option model can be used to evaluate salvage values in a financial lease.

We define the initial purchases price of assets (S_o) to be leased as follows:

S_o = present value of after-tax lease payment $[L(1-\tau_c)]$ + present value of accounting depreciation (capital recovery) tax shelter (DTS) on the asset + after-tax residual value on the leased asset $[S_N(1-\tau_c)]$ at termination of the lease agreement in year N. (15.33)

Lee *et al.* proposed an option-pricing framework to evaluate the present value of the salvage value. To do this, they decompose S_N as

$$S_N = \text{MAX}(\text{O}, S_N - E) + \text{MIN}(S_N, E), \qquad (15.34)$$

where MAX(O, $S_N - E$) = the intrinsic value of a call option to purchase the asset for an exercise price, X, at the end of year T; MIN(S_T, E) = the residual component of S_N after the call option's intrinsic value has been deducted; and MAX (.) and MIN (.) refer to the maximum and minimum value of the arguments.

Since valuation of a call option on a leased asset's value is analogous to the valuation of an option on a dividend payment,[2] Lee *et al.* used Geske's (1978) option-pricing model with stochastic yield to evaluate the present value of MAX (O, $S_N - E$).

The term MIN(S_N, E) is the value of a put option. Once the value of the first term is known (call option), the value of MIN(S_N, E) can be determined using the put-call parity relationships. Adding these two values yields an estimate of the salvage value of the leased asset to the lessor.

15.7. Summary

In this chapter, we have uncovered many of the interesting facets of leasing. The conventional rationales for leasing deal primarily with reducing the

[2]The Black and Scholes (1973) model discussed in Chapter 1 does not take dividend payments into account.

risk of making use of an asset *vis-à-vis* that of actually owning the asset, and with maintaining greater borrowing capacity than would otherwise be possible. The latter rationale is subject to greater questioning, given the recent emphasis, in the field of leasing accounting on making these fixed obligations known to all viewers of the firm's financial statements, rather than allowing quasi-debt instruments to be, for the most part, hidden in footnotes. There still should exist some concern as to the effects that leases have on the various financial statements, for bond covenants and other restrictions may become binding if leases that could conceivably be treated in more than one way for accounting purposes are not optimally treated. The risk factor, the element of lease contracts that attracts most of the attention, raises the question of whether compensating returns must be made between the agreeing parties, while the existence of the various forms of leasing arrangements testify toward a willingness on the parts of these parties to engage in leasing activities, with the knowledge that such risk transfers exist.

In the area of lease valuation, we found that the minimum discount rate applied to the cash flows of a leasing scheme was the risk-free rate and not some other rate deflated by the interest-tax-break percentage so that this figure would be less than the risk-free rate. In confronting the problem of valuation under conditions of market equilibrium, whether it is the specification of Modigliani and Miller or of the more specialized CAPM framework, we found no rationale for leasing in competitive markets. Even including the often troublesome market imperfection known as taxation, this result was seen to hold, and due to the competitive element of the market, no abnormal returns were found to be possible through leasing.

Unfortunately, the types of taxation considered in these market-equilibrium models generally avoid those irregular tax considerations such as investment tax credits. Including irregular tax considerations, greatly complicates the analysis because the element of negotiation is involved. All is not lost though, as the Myers *et al.* formulation shows where such subsidies are taken account of in a general form.

With the existence of specialized leasing companies, either as a subsidiary of a manufacturer or as a separate entity altogether, we find it difficult to accept the restrictive view that leasing offers no net benefit to selected lessor–lessee consortiums. As such, the lease-versus-buy decision does require separate analysis for each leasing opportunity, and analysts must consider each proposal (lease versus buy) separately if they believe there are differences between the net costs and/or benefits from leasing and those of legal ownership.

Problem Set

1. Discuss the conventional reasons for leasing, as discussed by Fabozzi (1981), and give your personal evaluation of these reasons.
2. Discuss the three types of leasing, as well as the accounting breakdown of these types of lease. What are the accounting "rules" for classifying capital and operating leases?
3. Briefly compare the accounting treatment of capital leases with that of operating leases. What assumptions and processes are involved?
4. In what ways can the capitalization of leases affect the value of the firm?
5. Compare accounting treatments of leases from the lessor's and the lessee's standpoints. What are the implications to financial decisions?
6. Discuss the relationship between the M&M propositions and the theoretical considerations of leasing. In what ways do tax rates and timing of depreciation changes affect the value of a lease?
7. In what ways can the CAPM approach be used to analyze lease-versus-buy decisions under uncertainty? What other approaches can be utilized in the analysis of leases?
8. XYZ Reduction Company has just leased a press that calls for annual lease payments of \$50,000 payable in advance. The lease period is 9 years and the leased property is classified as a capital lease. The company's incremented borrowing rate is 8%, whereas the lessor's implied interest rate is 12%. The company depreciates all of its owned assets on a straight-line basis. Using the above information, compute:

   (a) The value of the leased property to be shown on the balance sheet after the initial lease payment.
   (b) The annual lease expense in each year, as it will appear on the accounting income statement.

9. Company AAA is a relatively new firm. Company AAA has experienced enough losses during its early years to provide it with at least 8 years of tax-loss carryforwards. Thus Company AAA's effective tax rate is 0. Company AAA plans to lease equipment from BBB Leasing Company. The term of the lease is 4 years. The purchase cost of the equipment is \$300,000. BBB Leasing Company is in the 35% tax bracket. There are no transaction costs to the lease. Each firm can borrow at 8%.

   (a) What is Company AAA's reservation price?
   (b) What is BBB Leasing Company's reservation price?

10. Company CCC is entering a negotiation for the lease of equipment that has a \$250,000 purchase price. Company CCC's effective tax rate

is 0. Company CCC will be negotiating the lease with DDD Leasing Company. The term of the lease is 5 years. DDD Leasing Company is in the 30% tax bracket. There are no transaction costs to the lease. Each firm can borrow at 10%. What is the negotiating range of the lease?

11. EEE Corporation wants to expand its manufacturing facilities. FFF Leasing Corporation has offered EEE the opportunity to lease a machine for $120,000 for 5 years. The machine will be fully depreciated by the straight-line methods. The corporate tax rate for EEE is 20%, while FFF's corporate tax rate is 30%. The appropriate before tax interest rate is 7%. Assume lease payments occur at year end. What is EEE's reservation price? What is FFF's reservation price? What is the negotiating range of the lease?
12. An asset costs $90. Only straight-line depreciation is allowed for this asset. The asset's useful life is 3 years. It will have no salvage value. The corporate tax rate on ordinary income is 30%. The interest rate on risk-free cash flow is 10%.

    (a) What set of lease payments will make the lessee and the lessor equally well off?
    (b) Show the general condition that will make the value of a lease to the lessor the negative of the value to the lessee.
    (c) Assume that the lessee pays no taxes and the lessor is in the 34% tax bracket. For what range of lease payments does the lease have a positive NPV for both parties?

13. RTC is a furniture manufacturer that is considering installing a milling machine for $380,000. The machine will be straight-line depreciated over 7 years and will be worthless after its economic life. RTC has been financially distressed and thus the company does not appear to get tax shields over the next 7 years. ABC Leasing Company has offered to lease the machine over 7 years. The corporate tax rate of RTC is 30%. The appropriate before-tax interest rate is 8% for both firms Lease payments occur at the beginning of the year. What is RTC's reservation price? What is ABC's reservation price? What is the negotiating range of the lease?
14. WOL corporation has decided to purchase a new machine that costs $6 million. The machine will be worthless after 3 years. Only straight-line method is allowed by the IRD for this type of machine. WOL is in the 35% tax bracket. The GGG Bank has offered WOL a 3-year loan of $2 million and an interest charge of 14% on the outstanding balance of

the loan at the beginning of each year. 14% is the market wide rate of interest. Both principal repayments and interest are due at the end of each year. The HHH Leasing offered to lease the same machine to WOL. Lease payments of $2.1 million per year are due at the end of the 3 years of the lease.

(a) Should WOL buy the machine with the loan or lease it?
(b) What is the annual lease payment that will make WOL indifferent to whether it leases the machine or purchased it?

15. Use the following information to compute the annual lease payment that a lease will require. (Lease payments made at the beginning of the year.)

(a) purchase price of $300,000, interest rate of 15%, 6-year lease period, no residual;
(b) purchase price of $200,000, interest rate of 10%, 10-year lease period, residual value of $20,000;
(c) purchase price of $50,000, interest rate of 12%, 10-year lease period, residual value of $30,000.

16. ZXY Company decides to acquire a piece of equipment for $200,000. If ZXY wants to lease-finance the equipment, the manufacturer will provide such financing over 10 years. If the discount rate is 12%, what is the annual lease payment? Use this information to construct a lease amortization schedule.
17. Assume that I_o = $300,000, $F_t = F$ = $3,000, $R_t = R$ = $80,000, $k = 12\%$, $N = 10$ years, $i = 10\%$, $t_c = 34\%$, and $j = 5$ years. Also, let the terms of lease option be six payments of $50,000 each, with the first payment at $t = 0$ and succeeding payments at the end of each year for 5 years. At the end of 5 years, the asset can be purchased at $50,000, which is the current estimate of the asset's value at that time. Using Eqs. (17.5), (17.6), and (17.7), calculate related present values.
18. The purchase price of a piece of equipment is $100,000. The interest rate is 12%. A lease on this equipment would be for 6 years. The residual value of the asset at the end of the lease is expected to be zero. Find the annual lease payments it the payments are due at the beginning of each year.
19. Rework the previous problem assuming that the equipment has a residual value of $5,000.

20. New equipment costs \$50,000. The equipment can be leased for 4 years with five equal payments, the first being made at $t = 0$ and the subsequent ones at the end of each year for 1–4 years. Using this information, calculate the annual lease payment and construct the lease amortization schedule. The residual value is \$3,000 and the discount rate is 10%.
21. How would you answer the previous problem if the equipment had no residual value?
22. ICAI, Inc. has a lease proposal with the conditions as given below:

    Annual lease payment (advance) = \$15,000
    Life of the lease = 7 years
    Marginal borrowing rate = 15%
    Residual value = \$4,000

    (a) Calculate the estimated value of the capital lease.
    (b) If the implicit interest rate is 14%, find the value of the lease.
    (c) How would your answer change if the implicit rate of interest were 16%?
    (d) What is the relationship between the value of the lease and the appropriate discount rate?

23. GKM Corporation is considering acquisition of new equipment. The specific details associated with purchasing as well as leasing the equipment are given as follows:

    Purchase cost (I) = \$300,000
    Executory costs (F) = \$4,000
    Life of asset = 10 years
    Life of lease = 5 years
    Cash flows before depreciation and taxes = \$70,000
    Corporate tax rate = 30%
    Cost of capital (K) = 13%
    Discount rate for riskless cash flows = 9%
    Annual lease payment = \$60,000
    Residual value at j = \$50,000

    The first lease payment will be made at $t = 0$, and the succeeding payments being made at the end of each year. Using Eqs. (17.5)–(17.7), calculate the NPVs of the lease and buy options. The firm can borrow \$250,000 at an interest rate of 9% to finance the purchase of the equipment, payable in five equal annual installments.

Appendix 15.A. APV Method and Application to Leasing Decision

15.A.1. *Myers APV Method*

Myers (1974) has used Modigliani and Miller's (1963) proposition I with tax and derived APV formulation as:

$$APV = \sum_{t=1}^{N} \frac{(R_t - C_t - dep_t)(1-\tau_c) + dep_t}{(1+\rho)^t} - I + \sum_{t=1}^{N} \frac{\tau_c r D_t}{(1+r)^t}, \quad (15.35)$$

where

R_t = Pretax operating cash revenue gathered by the project during time period t;
C_t = Pretax operating cash expenses due to the project during time period t;
dep_t = Additional depreciation due to the project during time period t;
ρ = The market rate-of-return on unlevered flows of the indicated risk class;
r = The interest rate paid on debt; and
τ_c = Corporate tax rate.

An example involves the simplest case, where a \$1,200 investment project generates operating flows of \$400 per year for all 5 years of the project's life. Debt financing comprises \$600 of the project's total financing and the principal is repaid over the 5 time periods in equal amounts. For this project, the discount rate on unlevered firm is 8%, the interest rate on debt is 4%, and the tax rate is 0.4. The tax shields of levered investment are calculated in Table 15.A.3. By using (15.A.1), we can get the *APV* of the investment project is \$423.40.

$$APV = \sum_{t=1}^{N} \frac{(R_t - C_t - dep_t)(1-\tau_c) + dep_t}{(1+\rho)^t} - I + \sum_{t=1}^{N} \frac{\tau_c r D_t}{(1+r)^t}$$

$$= \sum_{t=1}^{N} \frac{400}{(1.08)^t} - 1200 + \frac{9.60}{(1.04)^1} + \frac{7.68}{(1.04)^2} + \frac{5.76}{(1.04)^3} + \frac{3.84}{(1.04)^4} + \frac{1.92}{(1.04)^5}$$

$$= 423.40.$$

Table 15.A.1. Accounting information for Docksider Corporation.

	Year 0	Year 1	Year 2	Year 3	Year 4	Year 5
Out Standing balance of loan	\$600	\$480	\$360	\$240	\$120	\$0
interest payment		\$24	\$19	\$14	\$10	\$5
Tax deduction on interest		\$9.60	\$7.68	\$5.76	\$3.84	\$1.92
After-tax interest expense		\$14.40	\$11.52	\$8.64	\$5.76	\$2.88
Repayment of loan		\$120	\$120	\$120	\$120	\$120

15.A.2. *Myers APV Method to Leasing*

We have learned that the APV of any project can be expressed as:

$$APV = \text{All-equity value} + \text{Additional effects of debt.}$$

As an example of how to compute the net present value of lease relative to purchase by using Myers *APV* method, suppose the Docksider Corporation can spend \$50,000 purchasing a crane, for lifting sailboats in and out of the harbor. Docksider also can lease the same crane by paying \$12,500 per year for 5 years. The pretax interest rate and tax rate are 6.5% and 0.34. In the context of the lease-versus-buy decision, the APV method can be expressed as:

$$\begin{pmatrix}\text{APV of the lease}\\ \text{relaive to the purchase}\end{pmatrix} = \begin{pmatrix}\text{NPV of the lease}\\ \text{relaive to the purchase}\\ \text{when purchase is financed}\\ \text{by all equity}\end{pmatrix} - \begin{pmatrix}\text{Additional effects when}\\ \text{purchase is financed}\\ \text{with some debt}\end{pmatrix}.$$

For Docksider's example, we know the all-equity value is the NPV of the cash flows discounted at the pretax interest rate. The incremental cash flows for Docksider from leasing instead of purchasing are shown in Table 15.A.2. The calculation shows that the lease is preferred over the purchase by \$529.03 if the purchase is financed by all equity.

$$\text{All-Equity } NPV = \$50{,}000 - \frac{\$9{,}950}{1.065} - \frac{\$9{,}950}{(1.065)^2} - \frac{\$9{,}950}{(1.065)^3} - \frac{\$9{,}950}{(1.065)^4} - \frac{\$9{,}950}{(1.065)^5} = \$8650.99.$$

Table 15.A.2. Leasing information.

Lease Minus Buy	Year 0	Year 1	Year 2	Year 3	Year 4	Year 5
Lease						
Lease Payment		−$12,500	−$12,500	−$12,500	−$12,500	−$12,500
Tax benefit of lease payment		$4,250	$4,250	$4,250	$4,250	$4,250
Buy (minus)	$50,000					
Cost of machine						
Lost depreciation tax benefit		−$1,700	−$1,700	−$1,700	−$1,700	−$1,700
Total	$50,000	−$9,950	−$9,950	−$9,950	−$9,950	−$9,950

Table 15.A.3. Purchasing information.

	Year 0	Year 1	Year 2	Year 3	Year 4	Year 5
Out Standing balance of loan	$50,000	$42,195	$34,055	$25,566	$16,713	$0
Interest payment		$3,250	$2,743	$2,214	$1,662	$1,086
Tax deduction on interest		$1,105	$933	$753	$565	$369
After-tax interest expense		$2,145	$1,810	$1,461	$1,097	$717
Extra cash that purchasing firm gernerates over leasing firm		$9,950	$9,950	$9,950	$9,950	$9,950
Repayment of loan		$7,805	$8,140	$8,489	$8,853	$16,713

If Docksider decides to finance all equity of its purchase, the relative tax shields are calculated in Table 15.A.3. The additional effect of debt, NPV of tax shields is:

$$\frac{\$1{,}105}{1.065} + \frac{\$933}{(1.065)^2} + \frac{\$753}{(1.065)^3} + \frac{\$565}{(1.065)^4} + \frac{\$369}{(1.065)^5} = \$3{,}191.55.$$

Because the tax shield represents interest deductions not available under the lease alternative, the NPV of tax shield must be subtracted from the NPV of the lease relative to the purchase when purchase is financed by all equity. Thus, the APV of the lease relative to the purchase is \$8,650.99 − \$3,191.55 = \$5,459.44. A positive NPV of the lease relative to the purchase indicates that the leasing alternative is preferred to purchase alternative.

References for Appendix 15.A

Modigliani, F and M Miller (1963). Corporation income taxes and the cost of capital: A correction. *American Economic Review*, 53(3), 261–297.

Myers, SC (1974). Interaction of corporate financing and investment decision. *Journal of Finance*, 29, 1–25.

References for Chapter 15

Abdel-Khalik, AR (1981). *The Economic Effects On Lessees of FASB Statement No. 13, Accounting for Leases.* Financial Accounting Standards Board of Financial Accounting Association, Stanford, Connecticut. See also News Reports, *Journal of Accountancy*, 8(4), 10–14.

Altman, E (1968). Financial ratios, discriminant analysis, and the prediction of corporate bankruptcy. *Journal of Finance*, 23(4), 589–609.

Ball, R and P Brown (1968). An empirical analysis of accounting income numbers. *Journal of Accounting Research*, 6(2), 159–178.

Black, F and M Scholes (1973). The pricing of options and corporate liabilities. *Journal of Political Economy*, 81(3), 637–654.

Bower, R, F Herringer, and P Williamson (1966). Lease evaluation. *Accounting Review*, 41, 257–265.

Brealy, R and C Young (1980). Debt, taxes, and leasing — A note. *Journal of Finance*, 35(5), 1245–1250.

Copeland, TE, JF Weston, and K Shastri (2004). *Financial Theory and Corporate Policy*, 4th edn. Reading, Mass.: Addison-Wesley Publishing Company.

Crawford, P, C Harper, and J McConnell (1981). Further evidence on the terms of financial leases. *Financial Management*, 10(4), 7–14.

Fabozzi, F (1981). *Equipment Leasing*, Homewood, Illinois: Dow Jones-Irwin, Inc.

Fabozzi, FJ and U Yarri (1983). Valuation of safe harbor tax-benefit transfer leases. *Journal of Finance*, 38, 595–606.

Financial Accounting Standards Board (1976). *Accounting for Leases.*

Geske, R (1977). The valuation of corporate liabilities as compound option. *Journal of Financial and Quantitative Analysis*, 12(4), 541–552.

Gordon, M (1974). A general solution to the buy-or-lease decision. *Journal of Finance*, 31(1), 245–250.

Ingberman, M, J Ronen, and G Sorter (1979). How lease capitalization under FASB Statement No. 13 will affect financial ratios. *Financial Analysts' Journal*, 35(1), 28–31.

Johnson, R and W Lewellen (1972). Analysis of the lease-vs.-buy decision. *Journal of Finance*, 27(4), 815–823.

Joy, CM, R Litzenberger, and RW McEnally (1977). The adjustment of stock prices to announcements of unanticipated changes in quarterly earnings. *Journal of Accounting Research*, 15(2), 207–225.

Lee, Cheng F and AC Lee (2006). *Encyclopedia of Finance*, New York: Springer.

Lee, Cheng F, JE Finnerty, and EA Norton (1996). *Foundations of Financial Management*, New York: West.

Lewellen, W, M Long, and J McConnell (1976). Asset leasing in competitive markets. *Journal of Finance*, 31(3), 787–798.

McConnell, J and J Schallheim (1983). Valuation of asset-leasing contracts. *Journal of Finance Economics*, 12, 237–262.

Mehta, D and D Whitford (1979). Lease financing and the M&M proposition. *Financial Review*, 12(3), 47–58.

Miller, M and C Upton (1976). Leasing, buying, and the cost of capital services. *Journal of Finance*, 31(3), 761–786.

Miller, M (1977). Debt and taxes. *Journal of Finance*, 32(2), 261–275.

Modigliani, F and M Miller (1963). Corporate income taxes and the cost of capital: A correction. *American Economic Review*, 53(3), 433–443.

Myers, S, D Dill, and A Bautista (1976). Valuation of financial lease contracts. *Journal of Finance*, 31(3), 799–820.

Pinches G and K Mingo (1973). A multivariate analysis of industrial bond ratings. *Journal of Finance*, 28(1), 1–18.

Pogue, T and R Soldofsky (1969). What's in a bond rating? *Journal of Financial and Quantitative Analysis*, 4(2), 201–228.

Rubinstein, M (1976). The value of uncertain income streams and the pricing of options. *Bell Journal of Economics*, 7(2), 407–425.

Vancil, R (1961). Lease or borrow — New method of analysis. *Harvard Business Review*, 39(5), 122–136.

Project III

Capital Budgeting and Leasing Decisions

Part IV

Corporate Policies and Their Interrelationships

Chapter 16

Mergers: Theory and Evidence

16.1. Introduction

In this chapter, we begin the discussion of mergers and divestitures with a brief historical overview of the merger movements that have occurred in the U.S in Section 16.2. Next, we classify the various types of business combinations and discuss the tax, accounting, and legal considerations involved in mergers in Sections 16.3–16.5 respectively. The following Sections (16.6 and 16.7) examine the theoretical rationale for mergers as well as the empirical evidence about them. Here we present a cost–benefit analysis of business combinations from the perspective of the firm. In the final section, we present the integration and summary of this chapter. Appendix 16.A discusses effects of divestiture on firm valuation.

16.2. Overview of Mergers

One of the central problems of financial planning and management is that of expansion. Firms expand *internally* in the normal course of operations in order to meet increasing demand for a product, to replace old or technologically obsolete equipment, and to establish new product lines or service areas. This type of expansion is characterized by the acquisition of assets and was discussed in Chapters 11 and 12 on capital budgeting. Another type of expansion is known as *external* expansion and is characterized by the acquisition of *business operations.* The distinction between internal and external expansion is often one of degree. The term *business combination* is used in the case of external expansions when substantially all of the operations of two firms are combined under a single ownership. Business combinations are the topic of this chapter.

Following The Economist (July 7, 2007), Gaughan (2007), and Ferreira, *et al.* (2007), there have been five major waves of business combinations in the American economy. The first wave was between 1887 and 1904, the second wave was between 1916 and 1929, and the third was peaking in 1968. The fourth merger wave started in the early 1980s. There were 2,395 mergers and acquisitions in 1981 but this is substantially below the peak of 6,107 recorded in 1969. In terms of the total value of combinations, however, 1981 was nearly three and one-half times the amount in 1969. The Fifth wave began in the 1990s and ended in 2001. John *et al.* (2009) find that the number of U.S. public acquisitions was increasing from 1990 and peaked to 282 in 1998.

During the period from 1981 to 1995, there were a large number of mergers, acquisitions, and leveraged buyouts (LBOs). Twenty-six of the largest transactions in terms of cost involving U.S. companies are presented in Table 16.1.

16.3. Classification of Business Combinations

There are several ways to classify business combinations, and the terminology is often very imprecise. In this section, we will discuss classification by corporate structure and classification by economic relationship.

Classification by corporate structure. Assume there are originally two firms, A and B. One possible business combination might result in only B surviving. This type of combination is known as a *merger*, and B is called the *acquiring* firm and A the *acquired* firm or *target* firm. Another type of business combination might result in the formation of a new firm C, which has the assets of both A and B. This type of combination is known as a *consolidation*. Finally, consider a combination in which A exchanges some of its shares for some of the shares of B. This is called an *acquisition*; B is the *parent* and A is the *subsidiary*. Note that one, both, or neither of the original firms may survive after a business combination. The terms merger, consolidation, and acquisition are often used interchangeably.

Classification by economic relationship. Another useful way of classifying business combinations is by the economic relationship of the firms before the combination. If the two firms had performed a similar function in the production or sale of goods and services, then the combination is said to be *horizontal*. Before a horizontal combination, the firms were, or at least had the potential to be, competitors. Another type of combination may involve two firms that are in a supplier–customer

Table 16.1. Largest mergers, acquisitions and LBOs: 1980–1995.

	Acquiring Company	Acquired Company	Price ($ Billions)	Year
1	Kohlberg Kravis Roberts (LBO)	RJR Nabisco	$25.1	1988
2	AT&T	McCaw Cellular Comm. Inc.	18.9	1994
3	Air Touch Communications (merger)	US West Inc.	13.5	1995
4	Chevron	Gulf Oil	13.3	1984
5	Philip Morris	Kraft	13.1	1988
6	Bell Atlantic Corp. (merger) (cellular phone business)	NYNEX Corp. (cellular phone business)	13.0	1995
7	Time Inc.	Warner Communications	12.6	1990
8	Bristol-Myers	Squibb	12.5	1989
9	Texaco	Getty Oil	10.1	1984
10	Martin Mirietta Corp. (merger)	Lockheed Martin Corp.	10.0	1995
11	Viacom Inc.	Paramount Communication Inc.	9.6	1994
12	American home Products Corp.	American Cyanmid Co.	9.6	1989
13	Beecham Group	Smith Kline Beckman	8.3	1989
14	DuPont	Conoco	8.0	1981
15	Viacom Inc.	blockbuster Entertainment Corp.	8.0	1994
16	British Petroleum	Standard Oil Ohio (remaining 45% interest)	7.8	1987
17	AT&T	NCR	7.5	1991
18	Hoechst AG	Marion Merrell Dow Inc.	7.1	1995
19	Upjohn co.	Phamacia AB	7.0	1995
20	Matsushita Electric Industrial Co. Ltd.	MCA, Inc.	6.9	1991
21	GTE	Contel	6.8	1991
22	Kimberly-Clerk Corp.	Scott Paper Co.	6.8	1995
23	Bankers Trust New York Corp.	Cheska Sporitela Savings Banks (40% of Cesky Investichi Fond and Vynosovy Investichi Fond	6.7	1995
24	Campeau	Federated Department Stores	6.5	1988
25	Kohlberg Kravis Roberts (LBO)	Beatrice	6.2	1983
26	Merck & Co.	Medco Containment Services Inc.	6.2	1993

Source: Mergers & Acquisitions, IDD Inc., Philadelphia, Reprinted with permission.

relationship. Such a combination is said to be *vertical*. Finally, a third type of combination may involve firms which have little, if any, product market similarities. These are known as *conglomerate* combinations. The term conglomerate, however, is generally reserved for firms that have engaged in several conglomerate combinations.

Concept Quiz

1. What is meant by the term "business combination"?
2. What were the characteristics of the four merger waves in U.S. history?
3. Explain the difference between merger, consolidation, and acquisition.
4. What is the difference between horizontal, vertical, and conglomerate business combinations?

16.4. Methods of Business Combination

Actual business combinations may take many forms, and there are several techniques that may be used. One technique used in many combinations is direct *negotiation* by the managements and boards of directors of the two firms. After the negotiations have been worked out, the plans are presented to the shareholder groups for approval. In each combination, the items to be negotiated include the identification of what is to be exchanged, the prices, and the method of payment. Assume firms A and B negotiate so that B acquires all the assets (except cash) of A, and pays for these assets with cash. Now A has cash as its only asset and it may pay off its creditors and distribute any remaining cash as a liquidating dividend to its shareholders. If, however, B pays for the assets of A with B stock, then A may sell off the stock of B for cash or distribute it to the shareholders of A. Note that the effect of these negotiations on the balance sheet of B is an increase in the asset accounts to reflect the acquired assets and a decrease in the cash or increase in the capital accounts to reflect the method of payment.

Assume now that B acquires the common stock of A (and not the assets directly); B may acquire the shares for cash, or in exchange for some of its shares, or by some other complicated plan. In the extreme case in which the shareholders of A surrender all their shares for shares of B, firm A ceases to exist and firm B assumes all the assets and liabilities of A. State "blue sky" laws specify that, once a certain percentage of A's shareholders agree to an exchange of shares, all shareholders must comply. Holdout shareholders of A may go to the courts to earn a "fair price" for their shares in the event they are not satisfied with the negotiated price. In a less extreme case,

B may acquire less than all the shares of A and maintain an *interest* in A. In this case, the shares of A are listed as an investment on the balance sheet of B.

The main point in the above two paragraphs is the distinction between the acquisition of assets and the acquisition of stock. The method of payment is much more important for the accounting and tax treatment.

One of the more common results of negotiation is an agreement to exchange shares of common stock. In these cases, the determination of "price" is actually the determination of an *exchange ratio.* The exchange ratio is a matter for negotiation but, for two publicly traded corporations, the range of negotiation can be specified. Larson and Gonedes (1969) presented a model for exchange-ratio determination. The analysis of exchange ratios involves making assumptions about the pre- and post-combination earnings streams and P/E (price-to-earnings) ratios. Assume that the information known about firms A and B before the negotiation is as shown in Table 16.2.

Let ER be the exchange ratio defined as the number of shares of B divided by the number of shares of A traded. The earnings per share after the combination is given by

$$EPS^* = \frac{5,000,000}{2,000,000 + 1,000,000ER} = \frac{5}{2 + ER}$$

and the post-combination price will be

$$P^* = \left(\frac{5}{2 + ER}\right)\left(\frac{P}{E^*}\right),$$

where P/E^* is the post combination P/E ratio.

In order for the shareholders of B to be as well off as before the negotiation, we must have $P^* \geq P_B$; that is,

$$\frac{5}{2 + ER_B}\frac{P}{E^*} \geq 40.$$

Table 16.2. Accounting information.

Firm	Net Income	Shares	EPS	Price	P/E
A	\$1,000,000	1,000,000	\$1.00	\$10	10
B	4,000,000	2,000,000	2.00	40	20

This will happen when

$$ER_B \leq -2 + \frac{\frac{P}{E^*}}{8}.$$

In order for the shareholders of A to be as well off, we must have $P^* \geq P_A/ER$; that is,

$$\frac{5}{2 + ER_A}\frac{P}{E^*} \geq \frac{10}{ER}.$$

Thus will happen when

$$ER_A \geq \frac{4}{\frac{P}{E^*} - 2}.$$

Hence, the acceptance of the negotiated exchange ratio depends on expectations about the post-combination P/E ratio. Graphically, these requirements imply that the range of negotiation lies in the area labeled I in Fig. 16.1. The exact exchange ratio agreed to will depend on the relative bargaining positions of the two firms. Conn and Nielsen (1977) conducted an empirical test of the exchange-ratio model on a sample of 131 combinations over the period 1960–1969. They found that the exchange-ratio model was supported by the tests, but there were cases when the shareholders

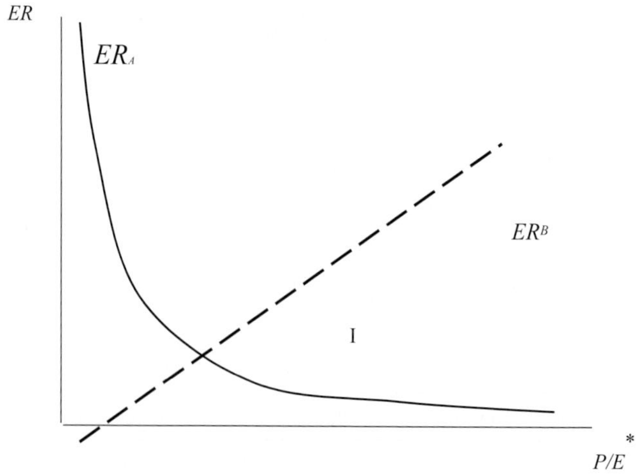

Fig. 16.1. The relation between ER and P/E.

of the acquired firm benefited at the expense of the shareholders of the acquiring firm.

Another technique used in business combinations is the *tender offer*. In a tender offer, the acquiring firm makes its offer directly to the shareholders of the firm it wishes to acquire. This is usually accomplished through the financial press. The acquiring firm offers to pay a fixed amount per share to each shareholder who "tenders" his shares and this price is usually set far enough above the current market price to entice the shareholders of the target firm. Tender offers can be made when negotiation breaks down, or as a surprise move by one firm to catch the management of the other firm off guard. Tender offers may take the form of either a cash and/or stock bid for a block of shares of the target firm. In many large corporations, effective control can be gained with considerably less than 100% of the shares. Hence, an acquiring firm can make a tender offer, gain control, and then proceed with negotiation for the remainder of the shares.

There are several legal requirements placed on tender offers by state and federal law. The bids for shares must remain open for at least 20 days. Moreover, shares that are tendered during this period may be withdrawn during the period. Furthermore, if the original offer price is raised, those shares that were tendered under the original offer are also entitled to the higher price. After one firm makes a tender offer, other firms may also enter the battle for a target firm.

A vigorous battle, for example, was waged in 1982 when Bendix Corporation made a tender offer for shares of Martin Marietta Corporation. The board of Martin Marietta moved quickly to repel the threat of a take-over by Bendix. In such a situation, often a "white knight" enters, a third company by whom the target (Martin Marietta) would rather be acquired. Martin Marietta, however, first countered with a tender offer for Bendix shares, then enlisted the help of United Technological Corporation, which also made a tender offer for a take-over of Bendix. Thus the original "raider" company (Bendix) was forced to seek its own "white knight" (friendly acquirer) and was eventually acquired by Allied Corporation. Soon after the Allied–Bendix merger, the Bendix chairman who had initiated this complex battle was forced out of his position. His departure was cushioned by a "golden parachute" clause in the merger agreements, which provided him with multi-million-dollar compensation for the loss of his job.

The market price of the shares of a target firm generally rises following the announcement of the tender offer. Table 16.3 shows some examples of price effects.

Table 16.3. Selected companies that received offers in 1981.

Acquired Company	Line of Business	Acquired By	Pre-Bid Price	At Acquisition Closing Date: Price	% Premium Over Pre-Bid Price	Price to Book Value	†P/E Ratio
American Microsystems	Semiconductors	Gould	23	$39\frac{7}{8}$	73	3.0	39.4
Applicon	Graphics	*Schlumberger	27	$33\frac{3}{4}$	25	12.8	43.3
Bache Group	Brokerage	Prudential Insurance Co. of Am.	20	32	60	2.0	11.4
Barton's Candy	Candy	American Safety Razor	2	4	100	0.9	d
Beckman Instruments	Health care, anal, instr.	SmithKline	28	$50\frac{1}{2}$	80	3.3	28.7
Buffalo Forge	Machine tools	Ampco-Pittsburgh	16	$37\frac{1}{2}$	134	1.9	13.0
Bunker Ramo	Elect, compon., data systems	Allied Corp.	39	55	41	2.0	13.0
Caldor	Discount stores	Associated Dry Goods	13	$36\frac{5}{8}$	182	3.0	13.8
Cavitron	Dental supplies	Cooper Laboratories	31	$36\frac{1}{2}$	18	4.6	21.5
Coldwell, Banker	Real estate, mtge., brokerage	Sears, Roebuck	21	$39\frac{3}{8}$	88	4.0	29.2
Copeland	Refrig., air cond. equip.	Hillman Co.	27	$38\frac{1}{2}$	43	2.2	11.3
Danty Machine	Stamping presses	Ogden	32	70	119	1.5	10.1
Dean Witter	Brokerage	Sears, Roebuck	27	50	85	2.1	14.0
Diamond Int'l	Packaging & forest products	Generale Occidentale, S.A.	35	$44\frac{1}{2}$	27	1.2	16.6
Fischer Scientific	Laboratory equipment	Allied Corp.	49	55	12	2.6	17.1

(*Continued*)

Table 16.3. (*Continued*)

			At Acquisition Closing Date				
Acquired Company	Line of Business	Acquired By	Pre-Bid Price	Price	% Premium Over Pre-Bid Price	Price to Book Value	†P/E Ratio
Franklin Mint	Specialty minting, collectibles	Warner Communications	19	$27\frac{1}{2}$	45	2.2	14.3
GDV	Homebuilding	City Investing	14	20	43	1.3	11.0
GK Technologies	Electronic components	Penn Central	41	50	22	2.5	9.4
General Steel Indus.	Metal process	Walco National	14	19	36	1.5	16.5
Gino's	Restaurants	Marriott Corp.	7	18	157	1.7	10.8
Gray Drug Stores	Drug & discount dept. stores	Sherwin Williams	10	21	110	1.1	d
Hoban Corp.	Food preparation equip.	Dart & Kraft	19	40	111	2.2	13.8
Iowa Beef Processors	Beef processor	Occidental Petroleum	55	73	33	2.5	14.1
Kennecott Corp.	Copper	Standard Oil of Ohio	24	62	158	1.3	22.2
Kent Moore	Specialty tools, equip.	Sealed Power	23	38	65	1.8	13.5
Lightolier	Lighting fixtures	Bairnco	17	28	65	1.4	15.5
Ludlow	Packaging, furniture	Tyco Laboratories	17	$27\frac{1}{2}$	62	1.9	22.4
Macdonald (E.F.)	Incentive programs	Carlson	7	10	43	1.7	9.8
Mallinckrodt	Chemicals	Avon Products	38	50	32	2.0	13.1
Mayer (Oscar)	Processed meats	General Foods	16	29	81	1.6	21.0
Memorex	Computer equipment	Burroughs	11	14	27	0.7	d
Metpath	Laboratory tests	Corning Glass	15	23	53	2.4	11.5
Nat'l Health Enterp.	Health care	*National Medical Enterp.	13	$22\frac{1}{2}$	73	2.3	12.8
Morris Industries	Building	Kohlberg, Kravis	30	43	44	1.7	17.6

(*Continued*)

Table 16.3. (*Continued*)

			At Acquisition Closing Date				
Acquired Company	Line of Business	Acquired By	Pre-Bid Price	Price	% Premium Over Pre-Bid Price	Price to Book Value	†P/E Ratio
Richardson Co.	Batteries, chemicals	Witco Chemical	17	$27\frac{1}{2}$	62	1.2	35.3
Russell Stover Candies	Candies	Ward Paper	15	20	33	1.6	10.0
St. Joe Minerals	Coal, lead, zinc	Fluor	27	$44\frac{1}{4}$	64	2.1	17.0
Sante Fe lnt'l	Drilling, oil & gas	Kuwait Petroleum	23	51	122	4.3	27.6
Schaefer (F.M.)	Brewing	Stroh Brewery	4	$7\frac{3}{8}$	85	N.A.	3.0
Shearson Loeb Rhodes	Brokerage	American Express	52	$62\frac{3}{8}$	20	3.9	8.9
Sperry & Hutchinson	Trading stamps	Baldwin United	18	36	100	2.3	16.7
Sterndent	Dental supplies	Cooper Laboratories	13	$22\frac{1}{2}$	73	2.3	30.8
Sunbeam	Home appliances	Alleghany lnt'l	21	41	95	1.6	13.0
Teleprompter	CATV systems	Westinghouse	33	38	15	33.3	7.2
Twentieth Century Fox	Film producer, distributor	TCF Holdings	53	$68\frac{5}{8}$	30	62.4	14.0
United Guaranty	Mtge. guaranty insurance	American lnt'l Group	29	36	24	1.8	11.7
Wallace Murray	Building products	Household lnt'l	30	50	67	1.7	10.0

Notes: d = deficit; N.A. = not available; * = Master Fisk stock; † = based on latest full-year earnings. From *The Outlook*, a Standard and Poor's publication (March 1982): 876–879. Reprinted by permission.

There are several options a shareholder might take after a tender offer has been made: he may accept the bid and tender his shares; he may just continue to hold his shares; or he may decide to sell his shares on the market. If a shareholder decides to hold original shares and the offer is otherwise successful, he may end up a minority shareholder, facing an inactive market and the possible delisting of his shares. Shareholders who are not happy with the offered price can resort to a court valuation under state laws, and often this is accomplished by means of a class-action suit.

The effect of tender offers on the returns to shareholders has been empirically investigated. It is important to distinguish the tender-offer tests from tests of completed mergers (these tests are discussed in Section 16.4), because the tender offer can succeed or fail. Dodd and Ruback (1977) provide empirical estimates of the market's reaction to both successful and unsuccessful tender offers. These tests are important because they reflect the market's expectation as to the "value" of the merger. If mergers or acquisitions are preceded by a tender offer, then an appropriate date to use in the study of benefits to shareholders is the first public announcement of the tender offer. Moreover, another important consideration for firms attempting takeovers by tender offers is the probability of success. To consider only the returns to shareholders of successful offers ignores the attempts that fail and the market's reaction to those unsuccessful attempts.

Dodd and Ruback use a sample of firms involved in 172 tender offers, which can be classified as follows:

	Successful	Unsuccessful
Bidding Firm	124	48
Target Firm	136	36

They assume that returns are generated by the market model

$$R_{jt} = \alpha_j + \beta_j R_{mt} + \varepsilon_{jt}, \tag{16.1}$$

where

R_{jt} = Rate-of-return on security j over period t,
R_{mt} = Rate-of-return on a value-weighted market index,
ε_{jt} = Disturbance term with $E(\varepsilon_{jt}) = 0$,
β_j = Measure of the systematic risk of security j, and
α_j = Intercept of the market model for security j.

In order to test for possible shifts in risk that a tender offer might induce, they use a dummy-variable technique and data from months −73 through −14, and from months 14 through 73, where month 0 is the month of the first public announcement of the tender offer. This test assumes that the risk shift occurs at the announcement date. Dodd and Ruback find evidence of significant changes in β_j in 34 out of 184 cases, and hence they calculate market residuals using coefficients estimated before and after the announcement of the tender offer. They then use the Fama *et al.* (1969) technique of event study to calculate average monthly residuals for each month as well as the cumulative average residuals. They follow this with statistical tests similar to Mandelker (1974), which will be discussed below. Their results indicate that the stockholders of target firms earn large positive abnormal rates-of-return in the month of the first public announcement of the tender offer. The average residual in the month of tender offer is 20.58% for successful offers and 19.96% for unsuccessful target firms.[1] Notably, however, the average return residuals for both successful and unsuccessful bidding firms are zero, indicating no abnormal returns. In addition to the effects of the tender-offer announcement, Dodd and Ruback also investigate the returns before and after the announcement. For both successful and unsuccessful bidding firms, there is evidence of significant positive abnormal returns in the 12 months before the tender-offer announcement and normal returns in the months after the announcement (insignificant and negative). For target firms involved in tender offers, there is evidence of positive returns in the 12 months before the tender offer and a normal return in the 5 years following the offer. This indicates that the price changes that take place in the month of the tender offer are permanent. The results of Dodd and Ruback indicate that there are gains from takeovers that could be attributed to the expectation of future gains from the combination.

Kummer and Hoffmeister (1978) also examine the returns to shareholders prior to the announcement of a tender offer. They use 88 firms involved in cash-tender offers between 1956 and 1974. They also use the market model and monthly data to examine the residuals and calculate the cumulative average residuals from −40 months through the announcement

[1]A similar finding that shareholders of the target firm take most of benefit from the *M&A* activity is reported by Bradley *et al.* (1988). They also find that the synergies generated by the enhancement of efficiency of the *M&A* activities is decreasing over the sample period.

month for the target firms and through +20 months for the bidding firms. These findings show that firms subject to take-overs have experienced abnormally low return prior to the take-over announcement. The take-over of these firms is consistent with a competitive market for corporate control. They show that tender offer results in increased shareholder wealth for both target and bidding firms.

More recently, Bradley (1980) studied 258 cash-tender offers between 1962 and 1977. He also used the market model to study the abnormal returns, and found that successful completion of the tender offer results in an increase in value for both the target and the bidding firm. Of 161 successful offers, the bidding firms paid an average premium of 49% to target shareholders relative to the price 2 months prior to the announcement of the offer. Notably, both Kummer and Hoffmeister and Bradley argue for a scenario in which the bidding firm secures control of the target firm and then implements a strategy that will increase the value of both firms, i.e., a *synergy theory*.

In addition to the negotiation of terms or the tender-offer technique, parties to a business combination may form a holding company. A *holding company* is defined as a corporation that owns sufficient voting stock of another (or several firms) to have effective control. Typically, a new corporation is formed, and the shareholders of the firms to be combined exchange shares for shares of the holding company. This type of transaction is advantageous because effective control can be gained with as little as 10% or 20% of the outstanding stock, so a smaller investment is required. What is different about the holding company is that it is formed with its only objective to "hold" other firms.

16.5. Merger Accounting and Tax Effects

In this section, we will address the accounting and tax effects of a merger. First, we will discuss tax implications. Secondly, we will go over the accounting treatment of business combinations. Lastly, we will explain legal considerations.

16.5.1. *Tax Implications*

In addition to any economic or financial motivations for business combinations, both the acquiring and acquired firm should consider the tax consequences of a business combination. Notably, all exchanges are taxable to the *seller unless* specifically exempted by the Internal Revenue Code.

Section 368 of the Code provides for the determination of tax consequences in business combinations. The provisions of the Code that allow for the tax-free status to the seller restrict both the type of acquisition and the terms of payment. The guiding principle in the Code is the determination of whether equity interests have been maintained.

a) **Taxable mergers and acquisitions.** On taxable acquisitions, the acquiring company's tax basis in the stock or assets acquired is equal to the amount paid. Moreover, taxable acquisitions require no limitations on the type of acquisition (stock or assets) or on the terms of payment. For the selling firm, the entire gain (or loss) is recognized immediately and is taxable.

b) **Non-taxable mergers and acquisitions.** On non-taxable combinations, the seller defers recognition of the gain and the acquiring company obtains the seller's basis for the stock or assets acquired. To qualify as a non-taxable acquisition, the type of acquisition and terms of payment must meet certain standards and are usually accomplished by a "statutory" merger or acquisition under a state statute, a stock-for-stock exchange of voting stock, or a stock-for-assets exchange.

Hence, in addition to the various other items to be negotiated, the decision to structure a combination on a taxable or non-taxable basis requires the balancing of two tax factors: (i) the recognition or non-recognition of gain or loss to the seller versus an increase or decrease in the tax basis to the acquiring firm; and (ii) the seller's request to receive the purchase price in cash or stock versus the acquiring firm's ability to pay with cash or its own stock.

16.5.2. *Accounting Treatment of Business Combinations*

The appropriate accounting treatment of business combinations is determined by analyzing the provisions of the negotiated agreement and the factual circumstances involved in the combination. The two accounting procedures are known as the *pooling of interests* method and the *purchase* method. Roughly speaking, a pooling of interest is appropriate when neither shareholder group assumes a dominant position in the combination, nor a purchase is appropriate when one shareholder group emerges in a dominant position. APB Opinions 16 and 17 list a precise set of criteria to be used to distinguish pooling and purchases. A combination that meets the pooling criteria *must* be accounted for as a pooling; if it does not meet the criteria, then it must be accounted for as a purchase. One of the major requirements to use the pooling method is that the method of payment must involve common stock in exchange for "substantially all" the voting common stock of the acquired firm.

Pooling of interests. The general idea motivating the pooling treatment is that the business combination was *not* a purchase-sale transaction but rather a combining of interests. Hence, the prior accounting valuations are maintained and merely added together for the combined firm. Moreover, from an accounting standpoint, the two firms are considered to have been joined from day one, and the accounting reports are restated *as if* they had been joined.

Purchase method. The purchase method of accounting for business combinations corresponds to the basic accounting principles for the acquisition of assets. However, in the case of business combinations, the procedure is complicated because several assets and liabilities may be acquired and more than cash may be given. Also, the excess of the price paid for the acquired asset over its book value is reflected as goodwill on the balance sheet of the acquiring firm and is amortized over a period not exceeding 40 years. Goodwill is not deductible for tax purposes, so the net result of the purchase method is a decrease in accounting earnings without the corresponding tax benefits. Hence, the purchase method is not favored by acquiring firms.

Consolidated statements are the relevant accounting reports when one firm has acquired an interest in the common stock of another firm. The affiliation of parent and subsidiary is treated as a single economic unit and the accounting statements reflect the summations of individual assets and liabilities, as well as revenues and expenses.

As an example of the differences between accounting treatments, consider the following example. Assume that the pre-combination balance sheets of firms A and B are as follows:

Firm B			
Working-Capital	100	Long-term Debt	50
Net Plant	300	Equity	350

Firm A			
Working-Capital	50	Long-term Debt	20
Net Plant	150	Equity	180

Assume that a merger is negotiated in which Firm B exchanges shares of its stock for the net assets of Firm A, and the exchange qualifies as a pooling of interest. Now just add up the respective accounts to reflect the combination, so that the post-combination balance sheet looks like this:

Firm B–A			
Working-Capital	150	Long-term Debt	70
Net Plant	450	Equity	530

At this moment we have not considered the effect of the combination on earnings per share or on market values.

Now assume that the criteria for a pooling of interests is not met, as would be the case if Firm B raises capital by issuing new long-term debt in order to buy the shares of Firm A with cash. Assume they issue debt to raise \$150 to buy the stock with a (new) market value of \$200 and use \$50 of excess cash in working-capital. Then the balance sheet of the combined firms will look like the following:

Firm B–A			
Working-Capital (100 − 50 + 50)	100	Long-term Debt (50 + 20 + 150)	220
Net Plant (300 + 150)	400	Equity	350
Goodwill	20		

Note that nothing happens to equity of Firm B. As far as the equity of Firm A is concerned, it is gone and the shareholders of Firm A have pocketed \$200. Again, the effects on earning per share and market values have not been considered.

Another important issue in business combinations is the effect on financial ratios. Ratios play an important role in the planning and control of financial resources, and a business combination can cause a major change in their levels, trend, or relationship to industry averages. The basic issue is to determine the appropriate way to view the surviving firm(s) using pre- and post-combination data. For some business combinations, the problems may be minimal, as, for example, when two similar firms combine. Berger and Ofek (1995) employ similar concept by using the financial ratios[2] to estimate the expected market values of conglomerates. Their finding supports that the mergers and acquisitions of diverse industries ruin companies' value and essentially cause the conglomerate discount.

The accounting treatments considered here are simplified — real-world business combinations are considerably more complicated and the accounting techniques are also more involved.

16.5.3. *Legal Considerations*

Anytime a firm contemplates increasing its size and market power through the acquisition of a company within its business domain, it faces the possibility of a confrontation with federal antitrust law. Three principal statutes constitute the bulk of these legal constraints. The first of these is the Sherman Act of 1890, which declares that "every contract, combination... or conspiracy, in restraint of trade" is prohibited and that "every person who shall... attempt to monopolize... any part of... commerce" is acting illegally. The Federal Trade Commission Act of 1914 prohibits "unfair methods of competition," and by amendment, "unfair methods of competition," and by amendment, "unfair or deceptive acts or practices." The third and most important antitrust law is the Clayton Act of 1914. The most powerful portion of this statute is Section 7, which forbids the acquisition of assets of stock where "in any line of commerce 'or' in any section of the country" the effect "may be substantially to lessen competition, or to tend to create a monopoly." Most prosecution has occurred under Section 7 of the Clayton Act because of its extension to the prohibition of potential restraints of trade.

[2]The three financial ratios used to evaluate the imputed market value of conglomerate are market value/asset, market value/sales, and market value/earnings of the companies of industrial medians. By using the data of median firms, we have the imputed market values of each firm and can calculate the premium/discount caused by multi-industry diversification.

The antitrust intent of the Justice Department is often interpreted to be "antibusiness" because most antitrust actions occur in cases where one or all of the firms are large. Nevertheless, antitrust actions occur in cases where one or all of the firms are large. Nevertheless, antitrust actions are not instigated because of the absolute size of the principals, but rather because of the relative size and number of companies in the industry after the combination. Thus, the real intent of antitrust law, as applied to mergers, is to restrain movements away from two essential tenets of competition: (1) many competitors, with (2) none being so large that its actions dominate in the market.

Defining the probability of antitrust actions is difficult because many proposed combinations have such unique features that it is hard to classify why one was approved and another not. However, there are general guidelines with which firms can assess their chances of regulatory approval.

For horizontal mergers — that is, where two firms from the same industry attempt to combine — a considerable amount of scrutiny will most likely be applied by the regulatory agency. Some of the prerequisite conditions for approval include (1) a large number of competitors in the field, (2) relatively small market shares between the two principals, (3) no substantial barriers for entry into the industry, (4) the number of competitors in the industry is not declining, and (5) one of the firms involved in the merger is in financial distress.

An additional criteria for evaluation of a "within"-industry combination is the Herfindal index (H index), which the Department of Justice included among the merger guidelines set forth in June 1982. The Herfindal index measures the degree of diversification using the Standard Industrial Classification (SIC) system. The larger the H index, the greater the degree of concentration and the more likely the Justice Department will disallow the merger. Sales figures for each firm segment are used in the computation of the segment's share of total sales.

Vertical combinations can be susceptible to antitrust actions whenever they lessen competition between companies in buyer–seller-related industries. Most importantly, antitrust law is concerned with the effect of excluding competitors from competitive access to supply or customer markets. Relatedly, vertical mergers that could potentially result in reciprocal dealing are also prohibited. *Reciprocal dealing* occurs among firms that are vertically aligned in buyer–supplier relationships. If we assume that firms A and C wish to combine into company AC, this new company AC could then insist that firm B purchase C's (now AC's) original product or else AC would no longer buy B's product. If AC represents a large portion of B's market, B will feel pressure to diminish any ties with other suppliers (such as D and E) and buy primarily from AC. Vertical business combinations that create such situations are prohibited by antitrust law.

As the world marketplace has become more integrated, the definition of *market* in recent years has been extended to include global competition. This broader redefinition of *market* has served to make more mergers possible in terms of their anticompetitive effects and may explain the nature of the business combination environment in the 1980s, which witnessed a massive increase in the frequency and number of approved mergers.

16.5.4. *Tax and Surplus Funds Motives*

Another economic based rationale for merger activity is based on tax differentials. By acquiring a growth firm with a small dividend payout (or none at all) and then later selling it, the acquiring firm can convert current income to capital gains and this reduce its tax rate. Sometimes the unused tax shield of one firm can appear as a merger incentive to another, more profitable firm. An incentive to sell arises for a firm whose growth has slowed to the point where the Internal Revenue Service no longer allows earnings retention. By capitalizing its future earnings, the seller can avoid having to pay out future earnings as dividends, which are taxable as income. In addition, energetic managers are reluctant to shrink their own firms by paying out cash dividends or repurchasing their own shares. Firms with surplus cash often become the takeover targets of other firms. Free-cash-flow theory predicts that mature, "cash cow" companies will be the most likely targets of LBO's.

Nonetheless, a business purpose must be established for such an acquisition to be allowed by the IRS. If alternative methods of achieving equivalent tax benefits are relatively less costly and involve fewer problems, then tax differentials cannot provide much motivation for mergers.

16.5.5. *Undervalued Assets*

The market may undervalue a company for a number of reasons. An ineffective management group may not be operating the company up to its potential, for example. The chance to acquire valuable assets at a low market price may tempt an acquirer to initiate a merger.

Motivation for a merger also may come from potential acquirers' inside information. Firms involved in natural resources industries, for example, must estimate the values of their in-ground reserves, such as oil or minerals. Approximations for these values allow for considerable differences in estimates, fueling speculation on the part of other firms about the assets' real worth. Such a situation arose in the merger of U.S. Steel and Marathon Oil. In fact, although U.S. Steel paid a substantial premium, over market value of Marathon stock, Marathon shareholders threatened suit, all edging that independent appraisals had estimated the current value of Marathon assets at more than double the price paid by U.S. Steel. It was more profitable to search for oil on Wall Street than to drill elsewhere!

16.5.6. *Agency Problems*

Two executive compensation issues may justify or explain merger activity: (1) executive stock options, and (2) golden parachutes. Both of these are related to the field of agency theory, which studies the relationship between various corporate groups, in this case shareholders and management.

If managers' compensation, includes extensive stock options, they are more likely to act in the best interest of the firm's stockholders, since the manager's share the gains of the stockholders. For example, if an outside party makes a bid for the firms stock at $20 per share when the current market price is $15 per share, managers are more likely to support the merger if their own executive stock options will increase in value along with the firm's shares. If the managers have no stock options, they have very little to gain by supporting the merger; in fact, they may view the merger as a threat to their job security.

Along this same line of reasoning, many firms have adopted policies of providing golden parachutes for their managers who face job termination. Again, if the managers' interests are compatible with those of the shareholders, managers are less likely to resist mergers and the possible loss of their jobs.

16.6. Economic Theories and Evidence

In this section, we will break down economic theories and evidence. First, we will discuss economic theories and then we will go over market power.

16.6.1. *Economic Theories*

The literature of economics and finance has advanced many theories to justify business combinations. However, it is unlikely that any business combination occurs because of a single reason — several objectives may act together to motivate the activity.

Economists generally assume that the goal of the firm is to maximize the profits of the firm. In light of this assumption, mergers and acquisitions can be analyzed in terms of operating gains and the effect on earnings. In particular, one theoretical justification is based on *economies of scale* (see Silbertson (1972)). These economies of scale relate to the average-cost of unit output as the output level increases. There is general evidence of U-shaped average-cost curves so that, up to some level, average costs fall as output increases and then remain constant for a range of output levels and eventually increase as diseconomies occur. Sources of these economies of scale include economies in capital costs, the specialization of labor and plant, and the linking of successive stages of production.

Another aspect of earnings maximization involves growth. Once a firm has matured and increased in size to a point where *its* scale economies have been exhausted, any further increase in size will result in diseconomies. However, mergers and acquisitions may provide the acquiring firm with the ability to show growth in its assets and earnings. Note, however, that this is not growth in the social sense, unless there is some sort of synergy or other economies.

16.6.2. *Market Power*

Another economic justification for mergers involves the issue of *market power* and *market share*. These issues are the crux of the arguments that the Justice Department advances against mergers. The basic defense is that mergers do not result in an increase in the level of competition; but that they are only organizational changes and should leave competing forces the same. However, many mergers are opposed or blocked by the Justice Department on the grounds that they are "effectively limiting" competition. The question is whether or not the business combination results in undue concentration in an industry since, if it does, the concentration may result in monopoly returns to the firms even in the absence of any synergy or economies of scale.

The precise relationship between economies of scale and market share is not known. One argument is that increases in market share lead to economies of scale. This would be relevant for a firm that is moving "down" the average cost curve as quantity (market share) increases. Another argument is that economies of scale lead to increased market share, and this is because the competitive forces reward the more efficient firms.

Measurement of the effect of market power on the firm can be made with reference to the accounting aspects or the capital market aspects. Melicher *et al.* (1976) examine shareholder returns with respect to industry concentration levels. Their sample of 495 firms was grouped into nine portfolios on the basis of concentration levels. Using annual data, they found that higher concentration implies higher returns. However on a monthly basis, the relationship was not clear. Using the CAPM and the Sharpe, Jensen, or Treynor measures of portfolio performance, they found no abnormal returns for more highly concentrated firms.

Sullivan (1977) investigated the question of who benefits from the supposed higher profits of powerful firms. He measured profitability as the ratio of net income to the book value of equity. He used the CAPM to adjust for risk differences between his 129 firms. He found that firms with market power do in fact earn superior returns on the book value of equity. However, with respect to the rate-of-return on common stock, it appears that the monopoly profits are fully capitalized in share prices.

Winn (1977) studied the relationship between profitability and market structure. He measured profitability by earnings before interest and taxes divided by total assets. For a sample of 736 firms and data from 1960 through 1968, he found that increased concentration raises both the level and variability of profits.

Another test of the relationship of profits and market structure was done by Thomadakis (1977). He used market value to determine whether market structure implies an ability on the part of the firm to maintain excess profits in the future. Using an argument similar to Myers (1977), he considers assets in place and the value of growth opportunities. In an empirical test of 158 firms, he found that industry concentration levels play a key role in the determination of expected excess profits from currently held assets and those expected from the firm's investment options.

Hence the evidence indicates that market power does lead to higher profitability on assets, but the market is efficient at capitalizing these profits so no excess returns to shareholders are available on a risk-adjusted basis.

Although the economic arguments for economies of scale or market power can be used to explain horizontal and vertical combinations, the arguments for conglomerate mergers is less clear. The *Staff Report* of the Federal Trade Commission of 1972 concluded that conglomerate mergers are dispersed across several industries and have relatively small market shares. The data suggests that conglomerate combinations do not benefit their shareholders.

As an alternative explanation of conglomerate mergers, Mueller (1969) advanced the argument that conglomerates benefit the managers. He argued that managers are motivated to assume less than optimal projects (with respect to the shareholders) in order to increase the size of their firms. It is questionable how long the managers of a firm can follow such a policy and retain their positions. Although Mueller's theory is based on the idea that the manager's consumption of benefits and salary is proportional to the size of the firm, it is doubtful whether this relationship is true. Lewellen and Huntsmen (1970) present evidence that a manager's compensation is related to the firm's profitability and not to size.

16.7. Financial Theories and Evidence

16.7.1. *Diversification and Debt Capacity*

The common assumption of financial theories is that the goal of the firm is to maximize shareholder wealth or maximize the value of that firm. Hence, decisions should be evaluated on the basis of how they affect value, and, more directly, on how they affect the cash-flow stream accruing to the owners and the uncertainty of those cash flows. The point is that financial theories of business combination are based on how they affect the cash flow and risk.

One line of financial theories of business combinations that has been used to explain conglomerate mergers involves the diversification effect. The basic argument follows from portfolio theory: the joining together of two less than perfectly correlated income streams will reduce the relative variability of the streams. Levy and Sarnat (1970) point out that, in a perfect capital market, no economic advantage can be gained by a purely conglomerate merger. They argue that a merger does not create diversification opportunities beyond what was available to an individual investor before the merger. Senbet and Taggart (1984) study the equilibrium of capital structure of mergers and acquisitions and suggest that Levy and Sarnat's argument assumes that capital markets before corporate combination are not complete. In that, in an incomplete capital market, the combining of two firms might provide new opportunities.

In an empirical study of the extent of conglomerate diversification, Westerfield (1970) uses the correlation coefficient between the rates-of-return on conglomerates or mutual funds and a market index as a measure of diversification. He finds that conglomerate firms are less diversified than mutual funds so that the assumed benefits are not as great as expected.

The empirical study using corporate data by Berger and Ofek (1996) also suggests that the value of conglomerate is less than its total expected value of stand-alone sectors that are classified by the four-digit industrial codes. The research of Bradley *et al.* (1988) about mergers and acquisitions also implies the negative impact of takeover activities to acquirers. They find that the shareholders of target firms take the major share of synergies. Also the stockholders lose in takeovers as time goes. In that sense, mergers and acquisitions probably will hurt the value of the bidders. The results of two researches do not completely conflict because Berger and Ofek focus the conglomerates that are diversified in different industries while Bradley, Desai and Kim include broader range of diversifications.

Lewellen (1971) suggests two possible sources of gains in conglomerate mergers, based on financial theory. The first source of gain arises from finding undervalued firms and acquiring them above their current market value but below their intrinsic value. The second source of gain arises from an increase in debt capacity, and hence, all other things equal, lower costs of capital. These gains are based on the "portfolio effect" or diminished relative variability that results from combining less than perfectly correlated income streams. Lewellen argues that lenders will establish new limits to borrowing, which can only exceed the sum of the original limits — hence increased debt capacity. When two firms merge, there are two debt-related effects: (1) the impact of the merger on the value of the existing debt, and (2) the impact of the merger on the capacity of the firm to issue future debt.

Schall (1972) argues that, in perfect capital markets, the opportunities for investor diversification make firm diversification redundant so that a value-addictively principle must hold:

$$V_{\mathrm{AB}} = V_{\mathrm{A}} + V_{\mathrm{B}},$$

where the V's represent the value of the income stream accruing to the firm. Schall provides an arbitrage argument that holds in a multi-period world with taxes, to show that business combinations cannot be justified on the basis of diversification effects alone.

Kim and McConnell (1977) approach the diversification question from the point of view of the bondholders. They argue that, in the absence of any synergistic effects, the diversification argument implies a wealth transfer from the shareholders to the bondholders. Using a paired sample and 39 conglomerates, they find that conglomerates do use a greater amount of leverage (see Weston and Mansinghak (1977) also). They estimate abnormal returns by using a two-index model for bond returns (a bond index *and* a stock index) and find that bondholders do not earn abnormal returns around the time of business combination. Hence, they argue that, if any gains are available in a conglomerate merger, they do not go to the bondholders.

Gahlon and Stover (1979) suggest that what conglomerates may have earned in terms of risk reduction through the "portfolio effect" they may also have lost by utilizing the higher debt capacity. Using a matched-sample approach and 37 conglomerate mergers between 1969 and 1975, they confirm their hypothesis.

The above arguments approached the debt-capacity issue in terms of the surviving entity. Using a different approach, Shrieves and Stevens (1979) present empirical evidence suggesting that one motive for merging is the desire to avoid bankruptcy on the part of one firm. Hence, the act of merging can be viewed as having two effects on value — one effect comes from the avoidance of bankruptcy and the savings of bankruptcy costs as well as the reduction in bankruptcy risk, and the other effect comes from a gain in aggregate debt capacity. Shrieves and Stevens limit their study to the first of these effects but are restricted in making a complete analysis by the lack of data on bankruptcy costs and merger savings from bankruptcy avoidance. Hence they limit their study to the incidence of financially distressed firms involved in mergers. They note, too, that the fact that most firms acquired in a merger are financially sound does not rule out the bankruptcy-avoidance motive for some mergers. In order to determine firms that are on the verge of bankruptcy, Shrieves and Stevens apply Altman's (1968) multiple discriminant analysis of financial ratios to predict bankruptcy:

$$Z = 0.012x_1 + 0.014x_2 + 0.033x_3 + 0.006x_4 + 0.99x_5,$$

where

$$x_1 = \frac{\text{Working-capital}}{\text{Total assets}},$$

$$x_2 = \frac{\text{Retained earnings}}{\text{Total assets}},$$

$$x_3 = \frac{\text{Earnings before interest and tax}}{\text{Total assets}},$$

$$x_4 = \frac{\text{Market value equity}}{\text{Book value of debt}},$$

$$x_5 = \frac{\text{Sales}}{\text{Total assets}}.$$

Altman's results provide a reliable means of classifying firms as likely bankruptcy candidates in the year before their merger. Shrieves and Stevens apply Altman's model to 112 acquired firms and 112 non-acquired firms chosen on a paired-sample basis with the acquiring group. The mergers occurred during the period 1948–1971. Notably, the Altman model for predicting bankruptcy was based on a smaller sample of firms with a limited range of asset size. In order to test for differences in the predictive model due to size, Shrieves and Stevens used a subsample of firms the same asset size as Altman used to test the model's appropriateness. Their results show that, for data for the year prior to merger, Altman's model predicts that 17 of 112 firms in the merging group were near bankruptcy, and this rate is much greater than the failure rate of large firms over the period (15.2% compared to 2.8%). The model predicted bankruptcy for five of 112 firms in the control group; and in three of these firms' financial reorganization subsequently occurred. In one instance the firm apparently survived, and the fifth firm actually acquired another firm to improve its financial condition. Hence, the Shrieves and Stevens study provides evidence consistent with a bankruptcy-avoidance rationale for some mergers. Moreover, this study is an interesting integration of Altman's model with a motive for merger.

The emphasis in the arguments above has been on a "diversification" theory of business combinations. Another line of financial research has investigated the issues of when and to whom any benefits of business combinations accrue. The empirical studies have examined the nature of the benefits as well as the efficiency of the market with respect to merger events. The research has advanced significantly in the type of tests done. In an early study, Hogarty (1970) compares the "investment performance" of 43 firms engaged in mergers between 1953 and 1964, with that of their respective industries, using annual data. He found that only 10 of 43 firms were successful in outperforming their industries. He also compared the growth of earnings per share of these merging firms with that of their industries and found that 16 out of 37 did better. He concluded that we cannot determine whether mergers are profitable. The Hogarty study laid the groundwork for the many studies that followed and attempted to improve the tests. Similar results are also found by Gort and Hogarty (1970) and Lorie and Halpern (1970). Other early studies include Lev and Mandelker (1972), who used a paired-sample technique with 69 active acquirers, and found that these firms outperformed the control group in terms of annual rates-of-return. Shick (1972) studied four merging firms over the 1958–1967 period "as if" no merger had occurred.

Haugen and Udell (1972) investigated the effect of business combinations on the shareholders of the *acquired* companies. They used 44 conglomerate mergers and 44 non-conglomerate mergers between 1961 and 1967, and compared monthly closing prices of the acquired firms with a stock index; the evidence indicates that the shareholders of firms acquired by conglomerates fared better than those acquired by non-conglomerates, but both fared better than the market. They also found that most of the gain accrues at the time of the merger, due to the substantial premium paid by acquirers.

Melicher and Rush (1973) examined both the operating and market-related characteristics of conglomerates. They used a sample of 45 conglomerates between 1965 and 1971 and a matched sample of non-conglomerates and found that the operating performance of the two groups was comparable. The conglomerate group used more leverage and had higher levels of systematic risk, but the same level of total risk. Their evidence suggests "defensive diversification" (see Melicher and Rusk (1974)).

The next three studies indicate the main line of merger research in the 1970's. They all use some model based on the capital-asset-pricing model to describe the normal rate-of-return on a risky asset.

Halpern (1973) improves the methodology used to study the benefits of mergers and investigates the size and distribution of any gains to the merging firms. He notes that there are two problems in estimating the benefits of a merger: (1) choosing the correct dates from which to measure benefits and (2) eliminating the general market influence so that only the merger benefits can be estimated. His sample consists of 78 successful mergers of NYSE-listed firms between January 1950 and July 1965. He required that the method of payment used be the exchange of common stock, or the exchange of common stock for assets. Halpern states that "if the stock market is efficient, the sum of the changes in the values of equity of the companies in the merger will be the market's estimate of the expected economic gain of the merger" (p. 561). He ignores any effect in the market values of any debt. The calculation of the gain to each shareholder group is the change in their stock's price between some base date and the actual date of the merger, and should exclude the market and industry effects. In order to do this, Halpern used a two-factor model such as

$$R_{it}^k = \alpha^k + \beta_i^k R_{mt}^K + \beta_2^k R_{It}^k + \varepsilon_{it}, \tag{16.2}$$

where, R_i^k, R_m^k, and R_I^k are the k-period price relatives for the security, a market index, and an industry index. In particular, the market index excludes companies in the same industry as the subject company, and the industry index is based on the price relatives of other companies in the industry. Using the two-digit SEC industry classification resulting in 18 industry indexes based on 10 or more companies. There were eight industries with an insufficient number of firms to form an index and for these, the single index market model was used. The model was estimated for all periods up to 7 months before the announcement and then used to calculate residuals for each company from 23 months before the announcement to the announcement date. In order to eliminate other individual firm factors, cross-sectional average residuals for each month were calculated and so was the cumulative average residual. By using the residual technique, Halpern is able to identify the average date when information about an impending merger was reflected in security prices as the seventh month before the announcement. Hence, in order to determine the base date to measure merger benefits, he chooses the end of the eighth month before the announcement. Next, Halpern measures the gain from the base date to the announcement date and finds evidence of positive gains to both the shareholder groups involved in the merger. The mean gain in dollar amounts to the larger firm is approximately four times that for the smaller firms, using unadjusted prices, and approximately the same, using the adjustment for the market. This downward adjustment after removing the market effect is due to the fact that mergers usually occur in rising markets. In terms of annualized rates-of-return, the evidence indicates that both firms in a merger have positive returns over the period between 7 months before the announcement and the date of the announcement; the gain to the smaller firms, however, exceeds the gain to the larger firms in terms of rates-of-return. Halpern argues that these results are consistent with a synergistic effect or the replacement of inferior management. One of the major methodological developments of the Halpern study is the use of the residual technique to identify the appropriate base date from which to measure merger benefits.

Mandelker (1974) provides a smaller but more complete analysis, using a CAPM approach. His study considers two basic questions: (1) Does the basic risk and return trade-off hold for merging firms, or are there abnormal returns associated with mergers? (2) Is the capital market efficient with respect to merger information? After a discussion of various theories, Mandelker uses the following model, which is consistent with the capital-asset-pricing model to do empirical analysis:

$$R_{jt} = \gamma_{0t} + \gamma_{1t}\beta_{jt} + \varepsilon_{jt}, \tag{16.3}$$

where R_{jt} = the percentage of return on security j during period t; γ_{0t} and γ_{1t} = market-determined variables representing the export relation between rates-of-return and risk in period t; and ε_{jt} = stochastic disturbance term in the return on asset j at month t. Data for the years 1926–1929 are used to estimate ß$_j$ for each stock on the NYSE by the formula

$$\beta_j = \frac{\text{cov}(R_j, R_m)}{\text{var}(R_m)},$$

where R_m is the return on the market and proxied by Fisher's Index. Each stock is then allocated to one of 20 portfolios by beta ranking. Betas are next recomputed for all firms for the period 1930–1934, and these are used to compute a beta for each of the 20 portfolios. For each of the portfolios, the monthly returns are computed for the period 1935–1938. Then the month-by-month returns of the 20 portfolios are regressed against the portfolio beta estimates as follows:

$$R_{pt} = \gamma_{0t} + \gamma_{1t}\beta_{p(t-1)} + U_{pt}(p = 1, 2, \ldots, 20), \tag{16.4}$$

to determine the estimates for the coefficients. These steps are repeated for other periods by using 7 years of data to form the portfolios, 5 years to compute the initial portfolio beta, and then 4 years to estimate the coefficients. Finally, the estimates of g$_{0t}$ and g$_{1t}$ are used to compute the residuals, which are defined as

$$e_{jt} = R_{jt} - \hat{\gamma}_{0t} - \hat{\gamma}_{1t}\hat{\beta}_{jt'}, \tag{16.5}$$

where $\hat{\beta}_{jt}$ is the jth security's beta, using the prior 60 months' data. (This is the Fama–MacBeth (1973) methodology). This estimating procedure accounts for any change in risk. By defining each firm's merger date as month zero, the residuals for each month can be averaged and accumulated over some period. The sample of mergers used by Mandelker consists of 241 acquiring firms and 252 acquired firms between 1941 and 1962.

The results of the Mandelker study indicate that there are positive abnormal returns to the shareholders of the acquiring firms before the merger and negative returns after the merger. Moreover, the systematic risk of acquiring firms declines over the pre- and post-merger period. For the acquired firms the cumulative average residuals indicate a large, positive, abnormal gain during the last 7 months before the merger. Mandelker also notes that the beta of the acquiring firms' increases during the period between −100 and −20 months, decreases in the period −20 months to the event month, and continues to decrease in the period from the event month to month +40. He argues that these changes in beta may bias the estimates of abnormal returns, and hence he uses a set of beta estimates from months −30 to +30 (that is, past and future data). These betas cause the cumulative average residuals to reach only half the level of those using only past information. The general results of this study imply that the shareholders of the acquired firm earn abnormal gains in the period prior to the merger.

Haugen and Langetieg (1975) test for synergism in mergers by using 59 mergers between 1951 and 1968 and a matched-sample technique to eliminate non-merger-related factors. They found little evidence of merger synergism and argued that an individual could do as well by forming a portfolio of the two stocks involved in a merger.

Another methodological approach was used by Langetieg (1978), who used a three-factor model to measure the gains from business combinations. His goal was to compare the merged firm with an identical non-merged firm, so he uses factors for (1) the market, to account for systematic risk, (2) the industry, to account for any industry-specific factors, and (3) a control group of matched non-merging firms. In the single-factor market model, the residual represents the influence of all extramarket factors including industry effects and firm-specific effects such as mergers. Ideally, any merger analysis by a residual technique should first begin by removing all non-merger influences. Hence, Langetieg uses an industry index based on the two-digit SEC industry classifications, and excludes the industry factor with a procedure similar to Ball and Brown (1968):

$$R_{It} - R_{ft} = \alpha_I + B_I(R_{mt} - R_{ft}) + E_{It}. \tag{16.6}$$

Now assume that the firm's residuals are linearly related to the industry residuals as follows:

$$E_{it} = C_i E_{It} + \mu_{it}. \tag{16.7}$$

Now using this residual relationship in the simple index model results in:

$$\begin{aligned} R_{it} - R_{ft} &= \alpha_i + \beta_i(R_{mt} - R_{ft}) + \varepsilon_{it} \\ &= \alpha_i' + \beta_i(R_{mt} - R_{ft}) + C_i(\varepsilon_{It} - \alpha_I) + \mu_{it}. \end{aligned} \tag{16.8}$$

Now any merger-related excess returns can be written as

$$E_{it} = \alpha_i' + \mu_{it}. \tag{16.9}$$

The third factor Langetieg introduces is a well-matched sample of non-merging firms, where the matching is based on the correlation of the residuals in the market model. Hence, these control firms are similar to the merging firms over the period observed.

Langetieg uses 149 mergers of NYSE firms listed on the CRSP tapes, and estimates the abnormal performance for the acquired, acquiring, and combined firm over three periods. Although he applies various models to the data, he finds little difference between the cumulative excess return estimates. The general results indicate that the acquired firms have significantly negative cumulative average excess returns over the period between 72 and 19 months before the merger and a significantly positive gain over the period between 6 months and 1 month prior to the merger. For the acquiring firm, the empirical results are not so strong: The gain to the shareholders of the acquiring firm is positive but substantially less than that to the acquired firm's shareholders. Langetieg concludes that the merger results in only a slightly positive abnormal return. In terms of the multiple-factor model versus the single-factor model, it appears that inclusion of the industry factor makes a substantial difference in the results. For the combined firm after the merger, Langetieg finds that after adjusting for the control group the excess returns are insignificantly different from zero, indicating a normal rate-of-return to the shareholders of the combined firm.

The following study uses a different approach to the analysis of mergers and does not rely upon the market model or any multiple-factor model to describe the "normal" return generating process. In particular, Shick and Jen (1974) investigate the benefits to shareholders of acquiring firms involved in horizontal acquisitions. They point out that the merger benefit to the shareholders of the acquiring firm is the difference between the return they earn with the merger and the return they would have earned if there had been no merger. However, this difference has two elements — the actual merger benefit and any compensation for the change in risk. Hence to measure the merger benefit, the risk compensation must be removed. Shick and Jen begin by computing the actual rate-of-return for a merging firm for the three 1-year periods following the merger by using market data. They choose the 1-year horizon because they are using annual accounting data and by using only 1-year horizons, they hope to minimize any risk changes. The next step is to calculate the return that would have been earned without the merger. Several alternatives are available, such as the CAPM approach used in the studies cited above, or the use of average industry returns or average returns for an inter industry sample of non-merging firms. In order to determine the hypothetical dividends and stock price, Shick and Jen use a common-stock valuation model (see Shick (1972) and Bower and Bower (1969)) based on Gordon's model:

$$P = \frac{D \cdot \varepsilon}{(k - g)}, \tag{16.10}$$

where P is the stock price, D is the dividend, k is the investor's required rate-of-return, and g is the dividend growth rate; ε is an error term. This model, however, assumes a perpetual constant growth in dividends. Miller and Modigliani allowed for alternative reinvestment rates. The particular model Shick and Jen use allows for short-term growth and long-term growth. Specifically, they use a logarithmic model:

$$\ln P = B_0 + B_1 \ln D + B_2 \ln\left(\frac{g_s}{g_1}\right) + B_3 \ln g_1 + B_4 \ln h$$
$$+ B_5 \ln V + B_6 \ln A + B_7 \ln F + \varepsilon, \tag{16.11}$$

where g_s and g_1 are the short- and long-term growth rates, he is a leverage measure based on debt and preferred stock over the common equity, V is a measure of earnings variability based on 10 years of data for EBIT/book value of equity, A is a size variable, and F is a firm-specific variable based on an exponentially weighted average of the four preceding residuals from the equation without the firm effect term. This model was estimated on a cross-sectional basis for each industry (supplemented with data for non-merging firms in the same industry) and had an average R^2 equal to 0.82. The merger benefits were then measured as the difference between the actual return and the return that would have been earned estimated by using the firm-specific variable in the estimated model.

The sample of firms Shick and Jen use are 24 acquiring firms involved in horizontal mergers between 1958 and 1966. The sample of firms is limited to three industries. The results of the study indicate a significant positive merger benefit of 9.6% during the first year following the merger. Merger benefits for the next 2 years were −2.68% and 2.68%, and both of these were insignificant. Hence, mergers may be beneficial to the shareholders of the acquiring firm but the market is quite efficient in evaluating the merger information and the benefits do not persist for long.

Elgers and Clark (1980) examine a sample of 337 mergers for the period 1957–1975. They also use the market model on monthly returns and a cumulative average residual approach. Their results indicate abnormal gains to acquired firms over the premerger period. Moreover, conglomerate mergers show superior gains for both shareholder groups compared to non-conglomerate mergers. They conclude that the debt-capacity issue does not distinguish conglomerate from other merger types.

With respect to the question of risk changes, Langetieg *et al.* (1980) examine 149 mergers and find increases in systematic risk for merged firms.

Dodd (1980) and Keown and Pinkerton (1981) examine the efficiency of the market with respect to merger information. These studies use daily data around the first public announcement of the merger proposal and they find some leakage of information. Bradley *et al.* (1988) also find that the information impact of mergers and acquisitions, considering the both sides of acquirers and targets, is positive. The shareholders of target firm benefit more than the stockholders of acquirers.

Rajan *et al.* (2000) demonstrate internal-game model in an organization to explain the distribution of resources of a conglomerate after takeover. If a company obtains sections of similar level of endowments and investment chances, the resources will be located to the department that might generate highest profit. However, when the company has more resources and opportunities to expand, due to the organization politics, the divisions of the worst efficiency will obtain the cash flow. In that sense, they suggest the mergers and acquisitions will hurt the firm's value because such activities probably distort resource allocations.

In summary, a vast amount of literatures and empirical researches on business combinations indicate that there is no strong evidence of operating gains in business combinations. With respect to the capital market effects, the evidence suggests that shareholders of the acquired firm earn abnormal returns due to the (anticipated) premium paid by the acquirers. The acquiring firm's shareholders earn a normal risk-adjusted return. Moreover, no wealth transfer occurs between shareholders and bondholders. The unresolved issue is an integration of the operating effects and the capital market effects. Business combinations occur for many reasons and what we need is an integration of the various reasons and their effects on the risk and return combinations offered to the capital markets. Further discussion on this issue can be found in Jensen and Ruback's (1983) review article.

16.8. Summary

Most of the merger studies since 1960 have concentrated on two issues: Are there any real benefits to mergers, and what are the effects on the security holders of the merging firms? Sections 16.3 and 16.4 divided the research roughly along the lines of economic and financial theories of merger. One major shortcoming of the previous research on mergers is the lack of integration of the economics and finance into a more complete model of the firm. From a managerial decision-making point of view, the following decisions must all be made, and none can be considered as exogenous:

(a) The production decision — what product markets should be served and how should the various inputs be combined?
(b) The investment decision — what assets should the firm own?
(c) The financing decision — how should the firms pay for those assets?
(d) The dividend decision — how should any profits be distributed?

The empirical research on mergers has examined the product-market effects and the capital-market effects, but has not integrated the two for a more complete model of the firm. Rather than judge the success or failure of a particular business combination by the *ex post* effects on security holders, a more complete study of business combinations should investigate why some are successful and others are not. A direct link between the product market and the capital market should be studied.

Greenberg *et al.* (1978) provide a theoretical model to link the product and capital markets. They view the product-market decisions of the firm (such as expansion in an industry and diversification between two industries) as altering the risk-and-return combination offered to investors in the capital markets. They explicitly use the capital-asset-pricing model to describe the value of the risky securities offered in the capital markets. One interesting aspect of their model is the "interaction" term, which is derived from the covariance of the firm's cash flows and those available in the market. If the firm's decision alters the set of return distributions available in the capital markets, then there is a diversification effect; and if the firm's decision leaves the set of return distributions unaltered, then there is no diversification effect and the shareholders could have achieved the same benefits by means of home-made diversification. The approach of Greenberg, Marshall, and Yawitz has testable implications for mergers and allows for more specific studies of horizontal, vertical, and conglomerate mergers.

Subrahmanyam and Thomadakis (1980) also integrate product-market factors into a capital-asset-pricing model framework. In particular, they investigate how changes in a firm's monopoly power and capital-to-labor ratio affect the systematic risk of the firm. They provide a theoretical argument to show that increases in monopoly power decrease systematic risk. Their model has testable implications for merger research, since it allows the economic motivation for mergers on the basis of increased monopoly power to be related to capital-market changes in systematic risk.

Fellows (1984) also provides an integration of economics and financial theory with specific reference to mergers. His model integrates the product-market effects of changes in monopoly power and returns to scale with the capital-market effects of systematic risk and debt capacity. These three works provide an explanation for the sources of systematic risk. Future research in this direction can test the empirical implications and extend the range of factors considered.

Another area of financial research that has been extended to mergers is that of option-pricing theory. Galai and Masulis (1976) use the option-pricing model to value the equity of the firm. In this framework, the value of the equity will be an increasing function of the variability of the rate-of-return on the firm's assets. Hence, in a merger or acquisition in which there is a change in the variance of the firm's rate-of-return (i.e., a product-market effect), there will be a change in the market values of equity (and debt). In particular, the merger of two firms with less than a perfect correlation in their rates-of-return will decrease the relative variability of the resulting returns in the absence of any other changes. Hence, the value of equity will decrease and the value of debt will increase if there are no synergistic economic effects. Galai and Masulis discuss how their model explains the debt-capacity arguments by showing the increase in the debt-to-equity ratio of merged firms. Also along similar lines is an article by Myers (1977). He shows that, by considering growth opportunities as "real options," the change in total variance of the firm's rate-of-return causes a wealth transfer between shareholders and bondholders.

As mentioned in Section 16.4, there have been two approaches to valuation used in the analysis of mergers. One approach is the capital-asset-pricing model, and the other is along the lines of the present value of the stream-of-earnings approach. Technically, the use of the capital-asset-pricing model assumes a one-period model and the stream-of-earnings approach allows for multiple time periods. In terms of merger research, the distinction should be made between specific individual acquisitions and programs of acquisition activity over several years. Many of the merger studies using the CAPM limit their samples to firms that follow a single acquisition. Studies of conglomerate mergers, however, should take into account the entire acquisition program and not merely one specific event. Future research could investigate the different effects of merger programs versus individual acquisitions.

Another area for future research is to improve the methodology used in testing for merger benefits. Many of the more recent studies rely upon the Fama *et al.* (1969) residual-analysis technique. Whether a single- or multiple-factor model is used, abnormal behavior is indicated when average residuals differ significantly from zero. Examination of the average residuals gives an indication of whether there is an overall effect for a number of firms, but does not indicate the size of the effect and how the effects are distributed across firms. The analysis of mergers should indicate merger-specific effects since there is no reason why all mergers will have the same effect on the firms involved. This is one problem with the pooling of time-series and cross-sectional data that cannot be completely resolved by use of the cumulative average residual technique. A better analysis of merger effects on security holders would involve using a random coefficient technique in which the coefficients of interest are allowed to vary between firms.

One potential use of financial market data measuring the merger benefit is the specification of goodwill in the purchase method of accounting for acquisitions. Accountants define goodwill as the difference between the price paid and the book value of the acquired assets. Capital market data allow us to measure the market value of the benefit gained from an acquisition. This would be particularly useful when there was not a competitive market for the acquisition.

Another use of merger research is for the analysis of disinvestment or spin offs. Many of the same theoretical issues can be applied to the disposition of assets.

In this chapter, we have reviewed historical merger and acquisition activities in United States and other countries. Then, we have discussed accounting treatment of merger and acquisition. In addition, we also discussed the method to evaluate and forecast merger and acquisition activities.

There are many reasons why firms engage in business combinations and there is much we can learn from empirical research. Mergers and acquisitions provide a rich area for study of the firm because they allow specific events to be analyzed in light of their capital-market effects. An integration of accounting, microeconomics, and financial theory has the potential to provide a more complete theory of the firm.

Problem Set

1. Discuss the various methods and forms of business combinations. Distinguish between the acquisition of assets and the acquisition of stock. How is the exchange ratio determined?
2. Discuss the processes involved in a tender offer. What legal restrictions are there? What effects can a tender offer have on shareholders?

3. Discuss the tax implications and consequences of business combinations. What criteria must be met to qualify a business combination as a non-taxable merger?
4. Discuss the accounting methods used for treating mergers. What are the effects of these methods on the structure of financial statements?
5. Discuss and compare economic and financial theories used to justify business combinations. How can these theories be used by managers to make their decisions?
6. Discuss how Galai and Masulis (1976) use option-pricing theory to consider mergers.
7. Briefly discuss the effects of divestiture on the value of the firm, as mentioned in Appendix 16.A of this chapter.
8. Briefly discuss the effects of divestiture on the value of the firm.
9. Offer some reasons why two firms might be interested in merging.
10. What is a horizontal combination? Why would a firm be interested in a horizontal combination?
11. What is a vertical combination? Why do vertical combinations occur?
12. Briefly explain why a firm that is losing money may be a target for a takeover.
13. Briefly explain why a firm that is losing money may wish to purchase a firm that is making money.
14. The Best Hotels are negotiating a merger with the Dove Inn Motel chain. Consider the following table:

	EPS	D_o	I (%)	P_o	Number of Common Shares
Best	2	\$1.25	8	\$51	4 million
Dove Inn	1	0.75	4	\$13	1 million

Establish the appropriate exchange ratio,

(a) based on current EPS;
(b) based on EPS in 5 years;
(c) based on current market values;
(d) to maintain Best's current EPS;
(e) to maintain Dove Inn's current EPS.

Note: For parts (d) and (e), assume that incremental earnings attributable to synergy equal \$2 million.

15. The Pinewood Corporation plans a merger with the Redbark Company through a $6 million cash purchase. Since Redbark has no debt in its capital structure, Pinewood will acquire it by issuing $6 million of long-term debt at 10% to finance the acquisition.

Pinewood Corporation			
Current Assets	$7,000,000	Debt (19%)	$4,000,000
Fixed Assets	3,000,000	Equity	6,000,000
Total Assets	$10,000,000	Total Claims on Assets	$10,000,000

Redbark Company			
Current Assets	$4,000,000	Debt	$0
Fixed Assets	2,000,000	Equity	6,000,000
Total Assets	$6,000,000	Total Claims on Assets	$6,000,000

Using the M&M $V^L = V^u + \tau^D$ equation as discussed in Chapter 6, determine the incremental value Pinewood will gain by acquiring Redbark. Pinewood has EBIT of $1 million and is in a 50% tax bracket, while Redbark's EBIT of $500,000 is also subject to a 50% tax rate. Also, assume that the capitalization rate for operating earnings (k_s for an unlevered firm) is 12.5% for each company.

16. Company A has a market value of $600 million and 30 million shares outstanding. Company B has a market value of $400 million and 40 million shares outstanding. Now, Company A is attempting to acquire Company B. Company A's CFO concludes that the combined firm will have $1.5 billion synergy and Company B can be acquired at a premium of $200 million.

    (a) If Company A offers $15 million shares to exchange for the 40 million shares of Company B, what will the after-acquisition stock price of Company A be?
    (b) To make the value of a stock offer equivalent to a cash offer of $300 million, what would be the proper exchange ratio of the two stocks?

17. Company A is analyzing the possible acquisition of Company B. Neither firm has debt. The forecasts of Company A show that the purchase would increase its annual after-tax cash flow by $1 million indefinitely. The current market value of Company B is $15 million. The current market value of Company A is $40 million. The appropriate discount rate for the incremental cash flows is 8%. Company A is trying to decide whether it should offer 15% of its stock or $10 million in cash to acquire Company B.

    (a) What is the synergy from the merger?
    (b) What is the value of Company A to Company B?
    (c) What is the cost to Company A of each alternative?
    (d) What is the NPV to Company A of each alternative?
    (e) Which alternative should Company A use?

18. Company A is considering making an offer to purchase Company B. Securities analysts expect the earnings and dividends of Company B to grow at a constant rate of 5% per year. Current dividend of Company B is $1.5 per share. Company A predicts the acquisition would provide Company B with some economies of scale that would improve this growth rate to 8% per year.

	Company A	Company B
Price-Earning Ratio	18	15
Number of Shares Outstanding	2,000,000	300,000
Earnings	$2,000,000	$900,000

    (a) What is the value of Company B to Company A?
    (b) If Company A were to offer 750,000 of its shares in exchange for the outstanding stock of Company B, what would the NPV of the acquisition be?
    (c) Should the acquisition be attempted, and if so, should it be a cash or stock offer?
    (d) Company A's management thinks that 8% growth is to optimistic and that 6% is more realistic. How does change your previous answers?

Appendix 16.A. Effects of Divestiture on Firm Valuation[1]

From a theoretical standpoint, divestment can be defined as the disposal of a portion of a firm's assets. Usually divestments deal with whole business units or divisions of a firm. The usual reason for divestment is that the business unit or division is unprofitable. However, economic, behavioral, and business-portfolio factors may also influence divestment decisions.

Gilmour (1973) thought that behavioral factors influenced the divestment decision. He found that a change in top management preceded divestitures. Duhaime and Grant (1984) found that divisional performance as well as the performance of parent firms in comparison to industry averages were important influences on such decisions. Other influences they found included relationships among a firm's businesses and the size of divested units in relation to their parent firms. Wrigley (1970) and Rumelt (1974) have *also* indirectly discussed this issue.

The conventional theory in regard to a divestiture says that holding the return of the firm constant, the divestiture *should* increase the variability in earnings and cause the value of the firm to increase according to Galai and Masulis (1976).

Galai and Masulis use the option-pricing model to argue that "the stockholders have 'stolen away' a portion of the bondholders' collateral since they no longer have any claim on the assets of the new firm."

We can show that:

$$\dot{V}_t^G = \dot{V}_t^A + \dot{V}_t^B \quad (0 \leq t \leq T), \tag{16.A.1}$$

where

$$\begin{aligned} \dot{V}_t^G &= \text{Value of combined firm } G, \\ \dot{V}_t^A &= \text{Value of division } A, \\ \dot{V}_t^B &= \text{Value of division } B. \end{aligned}$$

This implies:

$$V_0^G = V_0^A + V_0^B. \tag{16.A.2}$$

If division B is divested, this leaves only division A. Therefore, the debtholders of A, who are the debtholders of firm G after the divestiture, find that their claim on assets has been reduced. If C is the face value of debt, the leverage of the firm (V/C) has gone up due to the loss in assets.

[1]Full citations for references in this appendix can be found in the chapter text references.

The variance of the firm's rate-of-return will change. If we assume that the variance is constant, we see that:

$$D_0^A \leq D_0^G, \tag{16.A.3}$$

where

$$D_0^G = \text{Value of G's debt},$$
$$D_0^A = \text{Value of A's debt}$$

and combining this with Eq. (16.A.2)

$$S_0^A + S_0^B > S_0^G, \tag{16.A.4}$$

where

$$S_0^A = \text{Value of } A\text{'s Equity},$$
$$S_0^B = \text{Value of } B\text{'s Equity},$$
$$S_0^G = \text{Value of } G\text{'s Equity}.$$

All of this means that the value of the holdings of the equity holders of G, who are equity holders of A and B, increases at the expense of the debt holders of G, who are the debt holders of A, as a result of the divestiture.

If this divestment decision had been anticipated by the market, there would be no redistribution of wealth. If the market over anticipated the decision, the redistribution of wealth would be reversed from the above case.

With the changing economic and legislative environment of the last few years, divestiture has become an option that has gained in prominence in a firm's decision-making process. The primary reason for divesting a business unit is to get rid of an unprofitable unit.

Finally, the AT&T divestiture was finalized January 1, 1984. How this divestiture can be analyzed in accordance with the theory and methods discussed in this chapter and Chapters 6 is an interesting issue. Interested readers can refer to Linke and Zumwalt (1983).

References for Chapter 16

Agrawal, A and JF Jaffe (2003). Do takeover targets underperform? Evidence from operating and stock returns. *Journal of Financial and Quantitative Analysis*, 38, 721–746.

Akerlof, G (1970). The market for "lemons": Quality uncertainty and the market mechanism. *The Quarterly Journal of Economics*, 84, 488–500.

Aktas, N, E de Bodt, and R Roll (2010). Negotiations under the threat of an auction. *Journal of Financial Economics*, 98, 241–255.
Alanis, E and S Chava (2014). *Shareholder Bargaining Power and Debt Overhang.* Georgia Institute of Technology, Working paper.
Altman, E (1986). Financial ratios, discriminant analysis, and the prediction of corporate bankruptcy. *Journal of Finance*, 23, 589–609.
Andrade, G, M Mitchell, and E Stafford (2001). New evidence and perspective on mergers. *Journal of Economic Perspectives*, 15, 103–120.
Ang, J and N Mauck (2011). Fire sale acquisitions: Myth vs. realty. *Journal of Financial Economics*, 11, 532–543.
Asquith, P (1983). Merger bids, uncertainty, and stockholder returns. *Journal of Financial Economics*, 11, 51–83.
Asquith, P, RF Bruner, and DW Mullins (1983). The gains to bidding firms from merger. *Journal of Financial Economics*, 11, 121–139.
Asquith, P, R Gertner, and D Scharfstein (1994). Anatomy of financial distress — an examination of junk-bond issues. *Quarterly Journal of Economics*, 109, 625–658.
Ball, R and P Brown (1968). An empirical evaluation of accounting income numbers. *Journal of Accounting Research*, 159–178.
Barber, BM and JD Lyon, (1997). Detecting long-run abnormal stock returns: The empirical power and specification of test statistics. *Journal of Financial Economics*, 43, 341–372.
Barth, ME, R Kasznik, and MF McNichols (2001). Analyst coverage and intangible assets. *Journal of Accounting Research*, 39, 1–34.
Bates, TW, DA Becher, and ML Lemmon (2008). Board classification and managerial entrenchment: Evidence from the market for corporate control. *Journal of Financial Economics*, 69, 656–677.
Bates, TW and ML Lemmon (2003). Breaking up is hard to do? An analysis of termination fee provisions and merger outcomes. *Journal of Financial Economics*, 69, 469–504.
Berger, PG and E Ofek (1995). Diversification's effect on firm value. *Journal of Financial Economics*, 39–65.
Berger, PG and E Ofek (1996). Bustup takeovers of value-destroying diversified firms. *Journal of Finance*, 51, 1026–1027.
Betton, S and BE Eckbo (2000). Toeholds, bid jumps, and expected payoffs in takeovers. *Review of Financial Studies*, 13, 841–882.
Bock, B (1970). *Statistical Games and the "200 Largest" Industrials: 1954 and 1968.* New York: National Industrial Conference Board.
Boone, AL and JH Mulherin (2007). How are firms sold? *The Journal of Finance*, 62, 847–875.
Bower, R and D Bower (1969). Risk and the valuation of common stock. *Journal of Political Economy*, 349–362.
Bradley, M (1980). Interfirm tender offers and the market for corporate control. *Journal of Business*, 345–376.
Bradley, M, A Desai, and EH Kim (1988). Synergistic gains from corporate acquisitions and their division between the stockholders of target and acquiring firms. *Journal of Financial Economics*, 3–40.

Brenner, M and D Downes (1979). A critical evaluation of the measurement of conglomerate performance using the CAPM. *Review of Economics and Statistics*, 292–296.

Bris, A, I Welch, and N Zhu (2006). The costs of bankruptcy: Chapter 7 liquidation versus chapter 11 reorganization. *Journal of Finance*, 61, 1253–1303.

Brown, DT, CM James, and RM Mooradian (1994). Asset sales by financially distressed firms. *Journal of Finance*, 49, 1054–1055.

Campa, JM and S Kedia (2002). Explaining the diversification discount. *Journal of Finance*, 57, 1731–1762.

Chang, SY (1998). Takeovers of privately held targets, methods of payment, and bidder returns. *Journal of Finance*, 53, 773–784.

Chava, S and R Jarrow (2004). Bankruptcy prediction with industry effects. *Review of Finance*, 8, 537–569.

Chava, S and A Purnanandam (2010). Is default risk negatively related to stock returns? *Review of Financial Studies* 23, 2523–2559.

Chava, S, C Stefanescu, and S Turnbull (2001). Modeling the loss distribution. *Management Science*, 57, 1267–1287.

Chung, KH and SW Pruitt (1994). A simple approximation of Tobins-Q. *Financial Management*, 23, 70–74.

Coates, JC (2007). The goals and promise of the Sarbanes–Oxley Act. *Journal of Economic Perspectives*, 21, 91–116.

Cohen, DA, A Dey, and tZ Lys (2008). Real and accrual-based earnings management in the pre and post-Sarbanes–Oxley periods. *Accounting Review*, 83, 757–787.

Conn, R and J Nielsen (1977). An empirical test of the Larson–Gonedes exchange ratio determination model. *Journal of Finance*, 749–760.

Coval, JD and TJ Moskowitz (2001). The geography of investment: Informed trading and asset prices. *Journal of Political Economy*, 109, 811–841.

Cremers, KJM, VB Nair, and K John (2009). Takeovers and the cross-section of returns. *Review of Financial Studies*, 22, 1409–1445.

Davidoff, SM (2009). *Gods at War: Shotgun Takeovers, Government by Deal, and the Private Equity Implosion.* Hoboken, N.J: John Wiley & Sons.

Dodd, P (1980). Merger proposals, management discretion, and stockholder wealth. *Journal of Financial Economics*, 105–138.

Dodd, P and R Ruback (1977). Tender offers and stockholder returns: An empirical analysis. *Journal of Financial Economics*, 351–373.

Duhaime, IM and JH Grant (1984). Factors influencing divestment decision making: Evidence from a field study. *Strategic Management Journal*, 5, 301–318.

Dyck, A, A Morse, and L Zingales (2010). Who blows the whistle on corporate fraud? *Journal of Finance*, 65, 2213–2253.

Eckbo, BE and KS Thorburn (2008). Corporate takeovers. In *Handbook of Empirical Corporate Finance*, B. E. Eckbo (ed). Boston Elsevier.

Eckbo, BE and KS Thorburn (2008). Automatic bankruptcy auctions and fire-sales. *Journal of Financial Economics*, 89, 404–422.

Edmans, A, I Golstein, and W Jiang (2012). The real effects of financial markets: The impact of prices on takeovers. *Journal of Finance*, 67, 933–971.

Elbert, J (1976). Mergers, antitrust law enforcement, and stockholder returns. *Journal of Finance*, 715–732.

Eleswarapu, VR, R Thompson, and K Venkataraman (2004). The impact of regulation fair disclosure: Trading costs and information asymmetry. *Journal of Financial and Quantitative Analysis*, 39, 209–225.

Elgers, P and J Clark (1980). Merger types and shareholder returns: Additional evidence. *Financial Management*, 66–72.

Erel, IYJ and MS Weisbach (2013). Do acquisitions relieve target firms' financial constraints? *Journal of Finance.*

Faccio, M and RW Masulis (2005). The choice of payment method in European mergers and acquisitions. *The Journal of Finance*, 60, 1345–1388.

Fama, E and J MacBeth (1973). Risk, return and equilibrium. *Journal of Political Economy*, 607–636.

Fama, E, L Fisher, M Jensen, and R Roll (1969). The adjustment of stock prices to new information. *International Economic Review*, 1–21.

Fama, EF (1998). Market efficiency, long-term returns, and behavioral finance. *Journal of Financial Economics*, 49, 283–306.

Fama, EF and KR French (2002). Testing trade-off and pecking order predictions about dividends and debt. *Review of Financial Studies*, 15, 1–33.

Fee, CE, CJ Hadlock, and S Thomas (2006). Corporate equity ownership and the governance of product market relationships. *Journal of Finance*, 61, 1217–1251.

Fellows, P (1984). Risk returns to scale and monopoly power in horizontal mergers: Theory and evidence. Unpublished Ph.D. Dissertation, University of Illinois.

Ferreira, M, M Massa, and P Matos (2007). Shareholders at the Gate? Cross-Country Evidence on the Role of Institutioinal Investors in Mergers and Acquisitions. *18th Annual Conference on Financial Economics and Accounting.*

Fich, EM, J Cai, and AL Tran (2011). Stock option grants to target CEOs during private merger negotiations. *Journal of Financial Economics*, 101, 413–430.

Gahlon, J and R Stover (1979). Diversification, financial leverage, and conglomerate systematic risk. *Journal of Financial and Quantitative Analysis*, 999–1013.

Galai, D and R Masulis (1976). The option-pricing model and the risk factor of stock. *Journal of Financial Economics*, 53–82.

Garlappi, L and H Yan (2011). Financial distress and the cross-section of equity returns. *Journal of Finance*, 66, 789–822.

Gaughan, PA (2007). *Mergers, Acquisitions, and Corporate Restructuring*, 4th ed., New York: John Wiley & Sons, Inc.

Genesove, D (1993). Adverse selection in the wholesale used car market. *Journal of Political Economy*, 101, 644–665.

Gilmour, SC (1973). The divestment decision process. Unpublished Doctoral Dissertation, Harvard Business School.

Gilson, SC (1989). Management turnover and financial distress. *Journal of Financial Economics*, 25, 241–262.

Gilson, SC (1997). Transactions costs and capital structure choice: Evidence from financially distressed firms. *Journal of Finance*, 52, 161–196.

Gilson, SC and MR Vetsuypens (1993). CEO compensation in financially distressed firms-an empirical-analysis. *Journal of Finance*, 48, 425–458.

Gintschel, A and S Markov (2004). The effectiveness of regulation FD. *Journal of Accounting & Economics*, 37, 293–314.

Gort, M and T Hogarty (1970). New evidence on mergers. *Journal of Law and Economics*, 167–184.

Greenberg, E, W Marshall, and J Yawitz (1978). The technology of risk and return. *American Economic Review*, 241–251.

Hadlock, CJ and JR Pierce (2010). New evidence on measuring financial constraints: Moving beyond the KZ index. *Review of Financial Studies*, 23, 1909–1940.

Halpern, P (1973). Empirical estimates of the amount and distribution of gains to companies in mergers. *Journal of Business*, 554–575.

Harford, J (1999). Corporate cash reserves and acquisitions. *Journal of Finance*, 54, 1969–1997.

Harford, J (2005). What drives merger waves? *Journal of Financial Economics*, 77, 529–560.

Hartzell, JC, E Ofek, and D Yermack (2004). What's in it for me? CEOs whose firms are acquired. *Review of Financial Studies*, 17, 37–61.

Hasbrouck, J (1985). The characteristics of takeover targets Q and other measures. *Journal of Banking & Finance*, 9, 351–362.

Haugen, R and T Langetieg (1975). An empirical test for synergism in merger. *Journal of Finance*, 1003–1014.

Haugen, R and J Udell (1972). Rates-of-return to stockholders of acquired companies. *Journal of Financial and Quantitative Analysis*, 1387–1398.

Heckman, JJ (1979). Sample selection bias as a speculation error. *Econometrica*, 47, 153–161.

Heflin, F, KR Subramanyam, and YA Zhang (2003). Regulation FD and the financial information environment: Early evidence. *Accounting Review*, 78, 1–37.

Heitzman, S (2011). Equity grants to target CEOs during deal negotiations. *Journal of Financial Economics*, 102, 251–271.

Hobarg, G and G Phillips (2010). Real and financial industry booms and busts. *Journal of Finance*, 65, 45–86.

Hogarty, T (1970). The profitability of corporate mergers. *Journal of Business*, 317–327.

Hotchkiss, ES (1995). Postbankruptcy performance and management turnover. *Journal of Finance*, 50, 3–21.

Hotchkiss, ES, K John, RM Mooradian, and KS Thorburn (2008). Bankruptcy and the resolution of financial distress. In *Handbook of Corporate Finance: Empirical Corporate Finance*, BE Eckbo (ed). Amsterdam Elsevier/North-Holland.

Hotchkiss, ES and RM Mooradian (1997). Vulture investors and the market for control of distressed firms. *Journal of Financial Economics*, 43, 401–432.

Hotchkiss, ES and RM Mooradian (1998). Acquisitions as a means of restructuring firms in Chapter 11. *Journal of Financial Intermediation*, 7, 240–262.

Huang, YS and RA Walkling (1987). Target abnormal returns associated with acquisition announcements: Payment, acquisition form, and managerial resistance. *Journal of Financial Economics*, 19, 329–349.

Hubbard, RG and D Palia (1999). A reexamination of the conglomerate merger wave in the 1960s: An internal capital markets view. *Journal of Finance*, 54, 1131–1152.

Jensen, MC and RS Ruback (1983). The market for corporate control: The scientific evidence. *Journal of Financial Economics*, 5–50.

John, K, Z Shangguan, and G Vasudevan (2009). Hot and cold merger markets. Review of *Quantitative Finance and Accounting*.

Jovanovic, B and PL Rosseau (2002). The q-theory of mergers. *American Economic Review*, 92, 198–204.

Kaplan, SN and MS Weisbach (1992). The success of acquisitions — evidence from divestitures. *Journal of Finance*, 47, 107–138.

Kaplan, SN and L Zingales (1997). Do investment-cash flow sensitivies provide useful measures of financing constraints? *Quarterly Journal of Economics*, 112, 169–215.

Karpoff, JM, G Lee, and RW Masulis (2013). Contracting under asymmetric information: Evidence from lockup agreements in seasoned equity offerings. University of Washington.

Keim, DB and A Madhavan (1996). The upstairs market for large-block transactions: Analysis and measurement of price effects. *Review of Financial Studies*, 9, 1–36.

Keown, A and J Pinkerton (1981). Merger announcements and insider trading activity: An empirical investigation. *Journal of Finance*, 855–869.

Kim, E and J McConnell (1977). Corporate mergers and the co-insurance of corporate debt. *Journal of Finance*, 349–363.

Kini, O, W Kracaw, and S Mian (2004). The nature of discipline by corporate takeovers. *Journal of Finance*, 59, 1511–1552.

Kini, O, W Kracaw, and S Mian (1995). Corporate takeovers, firm performance, and board composition. *Journal of Corporate Finance*, 1, 383–412.

Kothari, SP, AJ Leone, and CE Wasley (2005). Performance matched discretionary accrual measures. *Journal of Accounting & Economics*, 39, 163–197.

Kummer, D and J Hoffmeister (1978). Valuation consequences of cash-tender offer. *Journal of Finance*, 505–516.

Lamont, O, C Polk, and J Saa-Requejo (2001). Financial constraints and stock returns. *Review of Financial Studies*, 14, 529–554.

Lang, LHP and RM Stulz (1994). Tobin q, corporate diversification, and firm performance. *Journal of Political Economy*, 102, 1248–1280.

Lang, LHP, RM Stulz, and RA Walkling (1989). Managerial performance, Tobin's q, and the gains from successful tender offers. *Journal of Financial Economics*, 24, 137–154.

Lang, LHP, RM Stulz, and RA Walkling (1991). A test of the free cash flow hypothesis: The case of bidder returns. *Journal of Financial Economics*, 29, 315–335.

Langetieg, T (1978). An application of a three-factor performance index to measure stockholder gains from merger. *Journal of Financial Economics*, 365–384.

Langetieg, T, R Haugen, and D Wichern (1980). Mergers and shareholders' risk. *Journal of Financial and Quantitative Analysis*, 689–717.

Larson, H and N Gonedes (1969). Business combinations: An exchange-ratio determination model. *Accounting Review*, 720–728.

Leary, MT and MR Roberts (2010). The pecking order, debt capacity, and information asymmetry. *Journal of Financial Economics*, 95, 332–355.

Lee, CMC and MJ Ready (1991). Inferring trade direction from intraday data. *Journal of Finance*, 46, 733–746.

Lee, CF, JE Finnerty, and EA Norton (1997). *Foundations of Financial Management*, Minneapolis/St. Paul: West Publishing Co.

Lee, CF and AC Lee (2006). *Encyclopedia of Finance*, New York: Springer.

Lee, G and RW Masulis (2009). Seasoned equity offerings: Quality of accounting information and expected flotation costs. *Journal of Financial Economics*, 92, 443–469.

Lev, B and G Mandelker (1972). The microeconomic consequences of corporate merger. *Journal of Business*, 85–104.

Levy, H and M Sarnat (1970). Diversification, portfolio analysis, and the uneasy case for conglomerate mergers. *Journal of Finance*, 795–802.

Lewellen, W (1971). A pure financial rationale for the conglomerate merger. *Journal of Finance*, 521–545.

Lewellen, W and B Huntsman (1970). Managerial pay and corporate performance. *American Economic Review*, 710–720.

Liao, RC (2010). What drives corporate block acquisitions? The case for financial constraints. Rutgers Business School.

Lichtenberg, FR (1992). Industrial de-diversification and its consequences for productivity. *Journal of Economic Behavior & Organization*, 18, 427–438.

Linck, JS, JM Netter, and T Yang (2009). The effects and unintended consequences of Sarbanes-oxley act on the supply and demand for directors. *Review of Financial Studies*, 22, 3287–3328.

Linke, CM and JK Zumwalt (1983). A theoretical analysis of the AT&T divestiture. Mimeo, unpublished paper, The University of Illinois at Urbana-Champaign.

Lorie, J and P Halpern (1970). Conglomerates: The rhetoric and the evidence. *Journal of Law and Economics*, 149–166.

Maloney, MT, RE McCormick, and ML Mitchell (1993). Managerial decision making and capital structure. *The Journal of Business*, 66, 189–217.

Mandelker, G (1974). Risk and return: The case of merging firms. *Journal of Financial Economics*, 303–335.

Martin, KJ and JJ McConnell (1991). Corporate performance, corporate takeovers, and management turnover. *Journal of Finance*, 46, 671–687.

Matsusaka, JG and V Nanda (2002). Internal capital markets and corporate refocusing. *Journal of Financial Intermediation*, 11, 176–211.
Melicher, R and D Rush (1973). The performance of conglomerate firms: Recent risk-and-return experience. *Journal of Finance*, 381–388.
Melicher, R and D Rush (1974). Evidence on the acquisition–related performance of conglomerate firms. *Journal of Finance*, 141–149.
Melicher, R, D Rush, and D Winn (1976). Degree of industry concentration and market risk–return performance. *Journal of Financial and Quantitative Analysis*, 627–635.
Mitchell, ML and JH Mulherin (1996). The impact of industry shocks on takeover and restructuring activity. *Journal of Business*, 73, 193–229.
Mitchell, ML and E Stafford (2000). Managerial decisions and long-term stock price performance. *Journal of Business*, 73, 287–329.
Moeller, SB, FP Schlingemann, and RM Stulz (2004). Firm size and the gains from acquisitions. *Journal of Financial Economics*, 73, 201–228.
Moeller, SB, FP Schlingemann, and RM Stulz (2007). How do diversity of opinion and information asymmetry affect acquirer returns? *Review of Financial Studies*, 20, 2047–2078.
Morck, R, A Shleifer, and RW Vishny (1990). Do managerial objectives drive bad acquisitions? *The Journal of Finance*, 45, 31–48.
Mueller, D (1969). A theory of conglomerate mergers. *Quarterly Journal of Economics*, 643–659.
Mulherin, H and AL Boone (2000). Comparing acquisitions and divestitures. *Journal of Corporate Finance*, 6, 117–139.
Mulherin, H and SA Simsir (2013). *Measuring Deal Premiums in Takeovers*. University of Georgia.
Myers, SC and NS Majluf (1984). Corporate financing and investment decisions when firms have information that investors do not have. *Journal of Financial Economics*, 13, 187–221.
Myers, S (1977). Determinants of corporate borrowing. *Journal of Financial Economics*, 147–175.
Officer, MS (2003). Termination fees in mergers and acquisitions. *Journal of Financial Economics*, 69, 431–467.
Officer, MS (2007). The price of corporate liquidity: Acquisition discounts for unlisted targets. *Journal of Financial Economics*, 83, 571–598.
Officer, MS, AB Poulsen, and M Stegemoller (2009). Target-firm information asymmetry and acquirer returns. *Review of Finance*, 13, 467–493.
Oler, D and K Smith (2008). The characteristics and fate of take me over firms.
Palpepu, KG (1986). Predicting takeover targets — a methodological and empirical-analysis. *Journal of Accounting & Economics*, 8, 3–35.
Pastena, V and W Ruland (1986). The merger bankruptcy alternative. *Accounting Review*, 61, 288–301.
Prabhala, N and K Li (2008). Self-selection models in corporate finance. In *Handbook of Empirical Corporate Finance*, BE Eckbo (ed).
Pulvino, TC (1998). Do asset fire sales exist? An empirical investigation of commercial aircraft transactions. *Journal of Finance*, 53, 939–978.

Puri, M (1996). Commercial banks in investment banking — conflict of interest or certification role? *Journal of Financial Economics*, 40, 373–401.

Rajan, R, H Servaes, and L Zingales (2000). The cost of diversity: The diversification discount and inefficient investment. *Journal of Finance*, 35–80.

Ross, SA, RW Westerfield, and JF Jaffe. *Corporate Finance*, 8th Ed. New York: McGraw-Hill Irwin Publishing Co.

Rumelt, RP (1974). *Strategy, Structure and Economic Performance.* Cambridge, MA: Harvard University Press.

Sanders, RW and JS Zdanowicz (1992). Target firm abnormal returns and trading volume around the initiation of change in control transactions. *Journal of Financial and Quantitative Analysis*, 27, 109–129.

Schall, L (1972). Asset valuation, firm investment, and firm diversification. *Journal of Business*, 11–28.

Scherer, F (1980). *Industrial Market Structure and Economic Performance.* Boston: Rand McNally, Houghton-Mifflin.

Schlingemann, FP RM Stulz, and RA Walkling (2002). Divestitures and the liquidity of the market for corporate assets. *Journal of Financial Economics*, 64, 117–144.

Schwert, GW (1996). Markup pricing in mergers and acquisitions. *Journal of Financial Economics*, 41, 153–192.

Schwert, GW (2000). Hostility in takeover: In the eyes of the beholder? *Journal of Finance*, 55, 2599–2640.

Senbet, L and R Taggart (1984). Capital-structure equilibrium under incomplete market conditions. *Journal of Finance*, 93–103.

Servaes, H (1991). Tobin's q and the gains from takeovers. *The Journal of Finance*, 46, 409–419.

Shick, R (1972). The analysis of mergers and acquisitions. *Journal of Finance*, 495–502.

Shick, R and F Jen (1972). Merger benefits to shareholders of acquiring firms. *Financial Management*, 45–53.

Shleifer, A and RW Vishny (1992). Liquidation values and debt capacity — a market equilibrium approach. *Journal of Finance*, 47, 1343–1366.

Shrieves, R and D Stevens (1979). Bankruptcy avoidance as a motive for merger. *Journal of Financial and Quantitative Analysis*, 501–516.

Shumway, T (2001). Forecasting bankruptcy more accurately: A simple hazard model. *Journal of Business* 74, 101–124.

Silbertson, A (1972). Economies of scale in theory and practice. *Economic Journal*, 82, 369–391.

Smiley, R (1976). Tender offers, transaction costs and the theory of the firm. *The Review of Economics and Statistics*, 58, 22–32.

Stein, JC (1997). Internal capital markets and the competition for corporate resources. *Journal of Finance*, 52, 111–133.

Subrahmanyam, M and S Thomadakis (1980). Systematic risk and the theory of the firm. *Quarterly Journal of Economics*, 437–451.

Sullivan, T (1977). A note on market power and returns to stockholders. *Review of Economics and Statistics*, 108–113.

Economics and Financial Indicators: Global M&A (2007). *The Economist*, July 7.

Thomadakis, S (1976). A model of market power, valuation, and the firm's return. *Bell Journal of Economics*, 150–162.

Thomadakis, Stavros B (1977). A value-based test of profitability and market structure. *Review of Economics and Statistics*, 59, 179–85

Travlos, NG (1987). Corporate takeover bids, methods of payment, and bidding firms' stock returns. *Journal of Finance*, 42, 943–963.

U.S. Federal Trade Commission, Staff Report: Economic Report on Conglomerate Merger Performance (November, 1972).

Westerfield, R (1970). A note on the measurement of conglomerate diversification. *Journal of Finance*, 909–914.

Weston, F (1970). The nature and significance of conglomerate firms. *St. John's Law Review*, 44.

Weston, J and S Mansinghka (1971). Tests of the efficiency performance of conglomerate firms. *Journal of Finance*, 919–936.

Whited, TM and GJ Wu (2006). Financial constraints risk. *Review of Financial Studies*, 19, 531–559.

Winn, D (1977). On the relations between rates of return, risk, and market structure. *Quarterly Journal of Economics*, 157–163.

Wrigley, L (1970). Divisional autonomy and diversification. Unpublished Doctoral Dissertation, Harvard Business School, 1974.

Chapter 17

Dividend Policy Theory, Practice, and Empirical Evidence

17.1. Introduction

In this chapter, we will discuss the issue of dividend policy in terms of theory, practice, and empirical evidence. In an effort to maximize shareholders' wealth, corporate finance is generally thought to be responsible for three decisions to meet that goal: the investment decision, the financing decision, and the dividend decision. It is on this latter decision that we now focus our attention. If dividend policy can affect the value of the firm, it is reasonable to assume that there is some optimal, or a range of optimal, dividend payouts. This is, in essence, a two-pronged question. Can dividend policy alter the value of a firm? And if so, do firms display a tendency to gravitate toward some optimal payout ratio or optimal dollar-per-share payout? There is reason to believe that practitioners would reply affirmatively to this first question, given the attention that the dividend decision has garnered and all the attempts made to manage the dividend figures. By and large academicians hold that dividend policy does not matter, and have developed rigorous proofs of such claims under various asset-pricing frameworks with very restrictive sets of assumptions.

In this chapter, we will show the development of various methods used to determine the effectiveness of dividend policy and the statistical methods to test the validity of these various analyses. The development of the subsequent sections mirrors the development of finance theory over the past 50 years. We can use Fig. 17.1 to describe the framework of financial theory

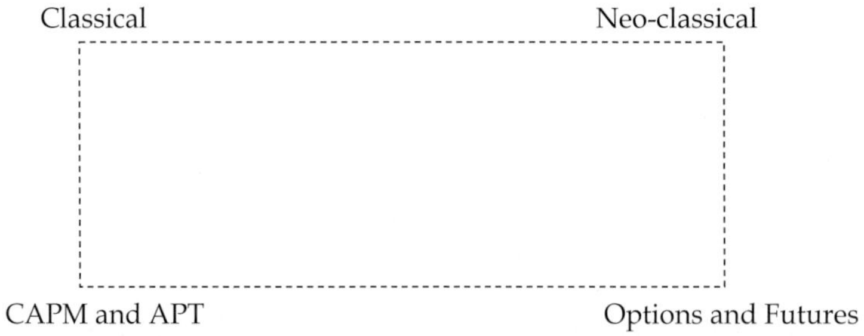

Fig. 17.1. Theoretical framework of finance.

development. We begin with the classical framework, the upper left-hand corner of the Fig. 17.1, with the work of Gordon (1959, 1963).

Breaking away from the classical framework, we go to the neo-classical framework, typified by the monumental work of Miller and Modigliani (1961, 1966), where dividend policy is reduced to a special case of the financing decision. Extending the analysis into multi-periods and uncertainty, the Capital Asset Pricing Model (CAPM), as developed by Sharpe (1964), Lintner (1956), and Mossin (1966), is used to test for dividend significance. Brennan's extended CAPM (1970) is also evaluated to analyze the tax effects as they relate to dividends. Option-pricing theory and its potential use in dividend research will then be discussed, along with two further extended analyses.

The first of these analyses was performed by Litzenberger and Ramaswamy (1979), which derives a version of the CAPM similar to that of Brennan, which is then used to assist in the explanation of security returns. The second extended analysis is by Lee *et al.* (1987), and considers the behavioral aspects of dividend policy and their implications for financial management. In conclusion, a summary will be presented, and remarks on the general conclusions of the cited studies put forth as to the current status of the dividend controversy.

In this chapter, we will discuss how firms pay dividends in Section 17.2. The four approaches on the value of dividend policy to the firm is explored in Section 17.3. We discuss in detail the irrelevance of dividend policy in Section 17.4. Section 17.5 deals with theories and models regarding dividend payment and policy determination, while stock dividends, stock splits, and stock repurchases are explored in Section 17.6. Section 17.7 recognizes factors that influence dividend policy. Section 17.8 presents some issues marring the dividend problem and the behavioral considerations of dividend policy are discussed in Section 17.9. Summary and conclusions are offered in Section 17.10.

17.2. How Firms Pay Dividends

Firms can disburse dividends in many forms, but most make quarterly cash payments. For example, Exxon paid total dividends of $2.91 per share in 1995, in quarterly installments of $0.72, $0.72, $0.72, and $0.75. The dividend payment procedure for the first quarter includes several steps as indicated in Fig. 17.1.

On the **dividend declaration date**, the directors of the firm may issue a sate declaring a regular dividend. The statement might be worded something like, "On January 2, 1996, the directors of this corporation met and declared quarterly dividends to be $0.75 per share payable to the holder of record on January 22; payment will be made on February 7, 1996." With this declaration, the dividend becomes a legally binding obligation to the corporation.

The shareholders whose names appear on the corporation's list of shareholder at 5 p.m. on the **record date** (January 22, 1996, in Fig. 17.2) are entitled to receive the dividend even if they sell their stock before the payment date. The firm mails checks to shareholders on **payment date** (February 7, 1996, in Fig. 17.2).

17.2.1. *Ex-Dividend Date*

A practical problem arises if a shareholder decides to sell a day to two before the record date. Because the brokerage industry requires some time to process the transaction and enter the name of the buyer on the stockholder

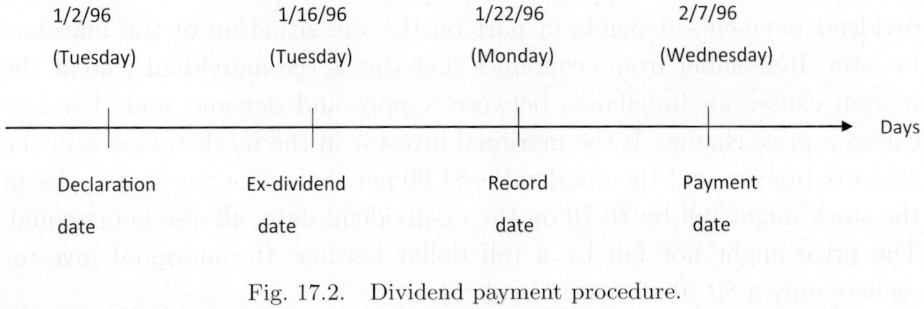

Fig. 17.2. Dividend payment procedure.

list, it has arbitrarily decided that the right to the declared dividend is terminated four business days before the record date. Any sale between this **ex-dividend date** and the record date leaves the seller with the right to the dividend. The term ex-dividend comes from the Latin *ex* meaning *from*, because the dividend has been taken from anyone who buys the stock after ex-dividend date. The ex-dividend date in Fig. 17.1 is Tuesday, January 16, 1996, four business days prior to the January 22 record date. As an example, suppose Investor A buys 200 shares of stock from Investor B. In order to receive dividends with a January 16 ex-dividend date, Investor A must buy the stock by January 15. If A buys the stock on January 16 or later, B will receive the dividend. On the ex-dividend date, the market price of the stock should change to reflect the decrease in its value through the loss of the current dividend.

EXAMPLE 17.1

Dividend Payment Decision

Q: The board of directors of Francis, Inc. has declared a dividend of $1.50 per share to be payable on February 15, 1996, to shareholders of record as of Friday, January 26, 1996. If John C. Lee buys 200 shares of Francis, Inc., on January 19, 1996, what is the ex-dividend date? What other events related to the cash dividend and stock price are likely to occur?

A: The ex-dividend date is four business days before the date of record, January 26, 1996, so the stock will go ex on January 22, 1996. Since John bought the stock before the ex-dividend date, he will receive $\$1.50 \times 200 = \$300$, which will be mailed to him by Francis, Inc., on February 15, 1996. When the stock does go ex on January 22, 1996, its value may drop overnight by about $1.50 per share.

The extent of the appropriate drop in stock prices associated with dividend payments depends in part on the tax situation of the marginal investor. Remember from economics that this is the individual who at the margin causes an imbalance between supply and demand and therefore causes a price change. If the marginal investor in the marketplace is in the 30% tax bracket and the dividend is $1.00 per share, the per-share price of the stock might fall by $0.70 on the ex-dividend date, all else being equal. The price might not fall by a full dollar because the marginal investor realizes only a $0.70 after-tax dividend.

One model has been developed to incorporate tax effects into determining the ex-dividend price[1]:

$$\frac{P_0 - P_x}{D_0} = \frac{1 - T_p}{1 - T_g}, \tag{17.1}$$

where

P_0 = the price just before the stock goes ex
P_x = the ex-dividend share price
D_0 = the amount of the dividend per share (DPS)
T_p = the relevant marginal personal tax rate
T_g = the effective marginal tax rate on capital gains

$$\text{If } T_p = T_g = 0, \quad \text{or} \quad T_p = T_g, \quad \text{then } P_x = P_0 - D_0. \tag{17.1a}$$

EXAMPLE 17.2

Ex-Dividend Stock Price with Taxes

Q: An investor owns a stock that has a market price of \$50 per share and has been paid a cash dividend of \$2 per share. If this investor's $T_p = 30\%$ and $T_g = 25\%$, what is the ex-dividend stock price?

A: Substituting $P_0 = \$50$, $D_0 = \$2$, $T_p = 30\%$, $T_g = 25\%$ into Eq. (17.2), we obtain:

$$P_x = 50 - \frac{(1 - 0.30)(2)}{(1 - 0.25)} = \$48.13.$$

Tax laws require the corporation to mail a copy of Form 1099 to every shareholder at the end of the year to report the amount of dividends the firm paid to that person. The firm also sends a copy of this form to the IRS to report the dividend income it paid to each shareholder during the year. This system of informing the taxing authorities is unique to the United States. Most other nations of the world require that corporations withhold portions of stockholders' dividends and turn these funds over to the government to settle each individual's tax liability on dividend income.

17.2.2. *Dividend Reinvestment Plans*

As we shall see, controversy surrounds the value of paying dividends. One way to resolve the question is to ask whether shareholders want dividends

[1]E. Elton and M. Gruber (1970). Marginal stockholder tax rates and the clientele effect. *Review of Economics and Statistics*, 52, 68–74.

or not. Dividend reinvestment plans (DRIPs) give shareholders the choice of receiving either cash dividends or shares of stock that reflect a reinvestment of those cash dividends in the firm.

Although the exact details of each plan differ, the general characteristics of a DRIP are fairly standard. In a bank-administered DRIP, the corporation sends the participating share-holder's dividend to the trust department of a bank, which maintains an account for each participating shareholder. The trust department purchases the stock of the firm in the secondary market and credits shares proportionally to each participant's account, less any brokerage fees or administrative costs. A second type of DRIP is administered by the firm itself. The firm either issues new shares to the participants or purchases its own shares I the secondary market and distributes them to the plan's participants.

From the firm's viewpoint, a DRIP has two major advantages: it can provide a continuous source of new equity capital to the firm, and it buys support for the firm's common stock I the secondary market. From the shareholder's viewpoint, DRIPs provide for immediate reinvestment of dividends, which takes a full advantage of compounding. The major disadvantage of DRIPs is the tax law provision that the participating shareholder must pay taxes on declared dividends despite receiving no cash flow from the corporation.

Concept Quiz

1. What are the record date and the ex-dividend date? How are they related?
2. How do cash dividend payouts affect the market price of common stock price per share (PPS)?
3. What are the advantages and disadvantages of DRIPs?

17.3. The Value of Dividend Policy to the Firm

17.3.1. *Methods of Determining the Relevance of Dividends*

Gordon's 1959 article, in which he developed the well-known constant-growth formula,

$$P_0 = \frac{D_1}{K - g}, \tag{17.2}$$

where

P_0 = Today's stock price,
K = Investor's required rate-of-return, and
g = Constant growth rate in dividends,

was one of the first attempts to relate share price to the dividend stream in an explicit manner. From Gordon's point of view, the price of a share of stock was primarily dependent upon dividends, in that two of the three arguments in the relation,

$$P_0 = f(D, g, K),$$

are specifically related to dividends.

It is easiest to see the point that the dividend payout does affect share price if we use Gordon's original formulation, where all investment is financed internally, b is the retention rate with respect to earnings, r is the required rate-of-return on equity, and X is the expected earnings figure:

$$P_0 = \frac{(1-b)X}{K-br}. \tag{17.3}$$

Hence, br is the growth rate in dividends. Differentiating Eq. (17.3) with respect to the retention rate,

$$\frac{dP_0}{db} = \frac{X(r-K)}{(K-br)^2}, \tag{17.4}$$

which will be positive if r is larger than K, and/or K is not equal to rb. Since a firm would presumably not invest if the expected rate-of-return on investment was less than the required rate-of-return, we expect Eq. (17.4) to be positive. This is equivalent to saying that the firm should retain enough earnings so as to take on all projects with positive net present values.

Oddly enough, this argument runs somewhat counter to the gist of Gordon's argument. If we differentiate Eq. (17.2) with respect to D, the dividend, we obtain $1/(K-g)$, which must be positive for any meaningful interpretation. This tells us that the share price increases when dividends are increased. If no profitable investment opportunities are foregone as a result of this increased dividend decision, this also seems to be reasonable, although it misses the point forwarded by Gordon. His claim was that not all else would remain constant. Specifically, Gordon felt that the investor's required rate-of-return would increase as a result of increased retention of earnings; and though the future dividend stream would presumably be larger as a result of the increase in investment, the higher discount rate would overshadow this effect. The reason for the increase in the discount rate would be the increased uncertainty of the receipt of the cash flows due to delaying the dividend stream.

If the above-mentioned attitude did in fact prevail, it would imply that investors place a time premium on distant cash flows, this premium being reflected in the discount rate employed, and imbedded in the investors' required rates-of-return. Thus, firms with high payout ratios would be preferred to those with low payout ratios. This concept has come to be known as the "bird-in-the-hand fallacy", the term fallacy being added by Gordon's detractors. This issue has attracted the attention of many empirical and theoretical researchers. The former findings we defer to later in this chapter, and relate now to the opponents of Gordon's view.

Miller and Modigliani (1961), hereafter referred to as M&M, addressed the dividend controversy with the contention that a proper valuation framework was missing. Previously developed valuation formulations were *ad hoc* in nature, and therefore did not pay proper respect to economic theory. They saw it necessary to develop a general valuation format, in which the dividend decision could subsequently be analyzed, and then proceeded to show that dividends were only one of a number of economic variables that could be used in developing the valuation formula, if those elements were properly defined. M&M then sought to explain why such confusion was present by discussing issues related to the dividend decision.

M&M initiated their analysis by making a number of simplifying assumptions. They assumed all-equity firms, so as to eliminate any capital structure effects, and assumed these firms to be members of the same risk class, to avoid having to specify distinct risk–return relationships. They assumed perfect frictionless capital markets, and perfect certainty with regard to the investment decisions made by management and the future earnings stream derived from that investment. Perfect certainty is used here in a broad sense, where the earnings stream is a statistical variable for which the expected value and the distribution of returns are known. If taken in the narrow and stricter sense, meaning that the expected future earnings is some definite number, the risk-class assumption would be redundant, with all flows being certain.

Lastly, and in no sense of least importance, is the assumption of rational investors. By the term "rational investors" M&M not only assume that investors prefer more wealth to less, but also that they are indifferent as

Table 17.1. M&M notation and definitions.

d_{jt}	= DPS received from firm j's stock, at time t;
p_{jt}	= Price of firm j's stock as of time t;
r_{jt}	= Percentage return on firm j's stock during time t;
D_{jt}	= Total dividends paid by firm j during time t;
V_{jt}	= Total market value of firm j at time t;
n_{jt}	= Number of firm j's shares outstanding at time t;
m_{jt}	= Number of new shares issued by firm j at time t;
I_{jt}	= Total investment undertaken by firm j at time t;
X_{jt}	= Total earnings of firm j in time t.

to the form of their return, dividends, or increases in the market value of their security holdings. This assumption explicitly dismisses the question posed by Gordon regarding investors' required rates-of-return dependence upon the timing of the realization of the returns.

For convenience and with the intent to refamiliarize the reader with the symbols used by M&M, we first present the entire notation to be used in the subsequent M&M derivations and proofs, with brief explanations as to their meaning; see Table 17.1.

Given the assumptions, the discounted value of the dividends and capital gains accruing to the shareholder of two firms of equal size and risk must be the same, and from a similar view the rate-of-return earned on the two investments must also be equal. Symbolically these can be shown as;

$$P_{jt} = \frac{D_{jt} + P_{j(t+1)}}{1 + r_{jt}}. \tag{17.5}$$

By rearrangement,

$$r_{jt} = \frac{d_{jt} + P_{j(t+1)} - P_{jt}}{P_{jt}}. \tag{17.6}$$

If the r_{jt}'s were not equal for equally risky shares, then arbitrage opportunities would exist. These simple formulations allow us to answer the question "does dividend policy have any value *per se*?" Since the discount rate used to discount capital gains and dividends is the same, we could probably say "No" and leave well enough along; but it is easy to show in a more rigorous manner what is required to allow this phenomenon.

Taking this analysis one step further, what conditions are necessary if the above conclusion is to hold? Making use of our previously defined notation, we can write the value of the firms in question as:

$$V_{jt} = \frac{D_{jt} + V_{j(t+1)}}{1 + r_{jt}} \tag{17.7}$$

or, equivalently:

$$V_{jt} = \frac{D_{jt} + (n_{jt})(P_{j(t+1)})}{1 + r_{jt}}. \tag{17.7a}$$

If the firm in question wished to increase the dividends and still hold the firm's market value constant, $m(t+1)$ shares would have to be sold at price $P(t+1)$, to new or existing investors; V_{jt} could then be written as:

$$V_{jt} = \frac{[D_{jt} + (n_{jt})(P_{j(t+1)} - m_{jt}p_{j(t+1)})]}{1 + r_{jt}} \tag{17.8}$$

and the outflow of dividends would be equal to the inflow from the sale of new stock. If the new stock were to be sold to existing shareholders in proportion to their current holdings, dividend policy would not affect anyone's position in the least. If the sale of stock was to new investors, then the original investors' claim to the firm falls in direct relation to the increased dividend. Hence, if the dividend payment does not affect the firm's investment decision because funds can be raised externally, the value of the firm should not be affected by the dividend decision.

More explicitly, let us recognize that any earnings not paid out, and new funds raised by the sale of new stock are all used for the known investment that the firm will undertake. By doing so, Eq. (17.7) can become:

$$V_{jt} = \sum_{t=1}^{N} \frac{X_{jt} - I_{jt}}{(1 + r_{jt})^t} + \frac{V_{j,N}}{(1 + r_{jN})^N} \tag{17.9}$$

and dividends no longer appear in the valuation equation. This states that the value of the firm depends on variables other than dividends, namely, the firm's earning ability and investment policy, and again, not the form in which investors receive their returns. Equation (17.9) will be referred to as the *valuation equation* for use in this, the M&M analysis.

As M&M recognize, so long as no information is conveyed by the change in the dividend payout, that is, the future dividend policy is known by the investors, changes in dividend payout are of no value. The information effects so briefly mentioned here will be granted further attention in the empirical discussion soon to follow.

If dividend policy, or changes in dividend payout, is known to have no effect on the general policy, are dividends the only variable that can be used to find the value of the entire firm? If not, then the dividend irrelevance proposition will be strengthened, and that is exactly what M&M had in mind when they showed four different approaches to valuation; discounted cash flow, the current earnings and investment opportunities approach, the dividend-stream approach, and the earnings-stream approach; these could all be reconciled to be equivalent to the basic valuation formula just presented.

17.3.1.1. *The discounted cash-flow approach*

As discussed in almost all finance texts, cash flow should be the object of attention when one is concerned with returns. For that reason, it seems an appropriate place to begin to develop alternative valuation formulas. Using this approach, the value of the firm is equal to the sum of the discounted inflows less the sum of the discounted outflows. Specifically,

$$V_{jt} = \sum_{t=1}^{N} \frac{CI_{jt}}{(1+r_{jt})^t} - \sum_{t=1}^{N} \frac{CO_{jt}}{(1+r_{jt})^t} + \frac{V_j, N}{(1+r_{jN})^N}, \tag{17.10}$$

where CI and CO are defined as cash inflow and cash outflow, respectively, and N is the number of years of operation of the firm.

If we interpret X to be a net cash inflow figure, and I as a net cash outflow (for investment purposes) figure, Equation (17.9) is the same as Eq. (17.10) in perpetuity, when the final term in Eq. (17.9) would asymptotically approach zero. Alternatively, if the firm was not held forever by the same individual, but was sold at time N, then a final term would be required in Eq. (17.10) to represent the sale price of the firm. This final figure, in turn, would be required to be equal to the net present value of the remaining cash flows, and would thereby be formally equal to Eq. (17.9).

17.3.1.2. *The investment opportunities approach*

M&M saw it easiest to describe this approach from the view of an outsider looking to buy out a going concern, questioning the value of the prospective purchase. The investor knows the required return for projects of the given risk, and since it should be the same as that of the market consensus, we will continue to use our symbol r_{jt} to represent that item. The question boils down to what the investor is buying. The investor is obviously buying the returns from the already existing assets, or a normal rate-of-return, but the price of the firm would generally be above the present value of that stream, the difference being labeled "goodwill" by the accounting profession. This goodwill is nothing more than some fair price for future opportunities the firm will confront. The goodwill of any future project can be seen to be the difference between the rate-of-return on the opportunity (here, as in M&M (1961), held constant), and the required rate-of-return times the investment dollar amount, capitalized into perpetuity by the required rate-of-return; see Eq. (17.11):

$$I_{jt}\left[\frac{r_{jt}^{*}-r_{jt}}{r_{jt}}\right]. \tag{17.11}$$

Total goodwill is then simply the summation of the net present values of all future opportunities.

The value of the firm can be expressed as:

$$V_{jt}=\sum_{t=1}^{\infty}\frac{X_{jt}}{(1+r_{jt})^{t}}+\sum_{t=1}^{\infty}\frac{\frac{I_{jt}(r_{jt}^{*}-r_{jt})}{r_{jt}}}{[(1+r_{jt})^{t}]}. \tag{17.12}$$

If the firm will be held only until time N, then the two summations in Eq. (17.12) could be modified, with another residual V_{jN} term added, which would itself contain the present value of the remaining earnings stream and the remaining investment opportunities. This would leave us with exactly the same end product as in Eq. (17.9) once again.

This proof cuts directly to the heart of the M&M contention that dividends in and of themselves do not matter. The regular earnings taken with the all-important growth potential (not in assets but in terms of wealth) dictate, by and large, the value of the firm, and, not so incidentally, the eventual dividend stream that will result.

17.3.1.3. *Stream-of-dividends approach*

Here we see the basic valuation approach forwarded by many: the dividend or stream-of-dividends, to be received determines the value of the firm; or, in short;

$$V_{jt}=\sum_{t=1}^{N}\frac{D_{jt}}{(1+r_{jt})^{t}}. \tag{17.13}$$

If we allow dividends to be defined as the difference between the earnings, X_{jt}, and the level of investment, I_{jt} (negative dividends resulting when more new funds are raised from previous outsiders than the amount of the total dividend paid to old shareholders), then Eq. (17.13) can also be written as

$$V_{jt} = \sum_{t=1}^{N} \frac{X_{jt}}{(1+r_{jt})^t} - \sum_{t=1}^{N} \frac{I_{jt}}{(1+r_{jt})^t}. \quad (17.14)$$

This is readily seen to be equivalent to Eqs. (17.10) and (17.12), both of which are equal to Eq. (17.9); thus we have a third method of valuation that is consistent with the basic valuation concept.

17.3.1.4. *Stream-of-earnings approach*

Earning is an often used, and frequently confused, term. Ordinarily, when one thinks of earnings, it is the accounting earnings figure that is being referred to. Here we need to distinguish between accounting and economic earnings so as to lend credence to this, the fourth approach to valuation.

Economic earnings are those that accrue above and beyond a fair return to the suppliers of capital, or more succinctly, the required rate-of-return, and in that sense are closely aligned with the concept of net present value. Lest there be any misconception, we explicitly wish to deal only with the latter.

Our previous earnings figure, X_{jt}, when discounted at the rate $(1 + r_{jt})$, gives economic earnings when net outlays are zero. If outlays are greater than zero, then we may have accounting earnings without economic earnings. The reason for this is quite simple: the return on investment is less than the required rate that prevailed when the investment capital was raised. Since it is a required return, we should specify exactly what the dollar amount of required return will be. Knowing that r_{jt} is the percentage required return, we can multiply by the amount of investment capital raised, and we obtain the **constant dollar return** required. The summation of all such discounted required payments is then very similar to negative earnings from the standpoint of those residual claimants, or the original shareholders. The value of the firm can now be expressed as:

$$V_{jt} = \sum_{t=1}^{N} \frac{X_{jt}}{(1+r_{jt})^t} - \sum_{t=1}^{N}\sum_{\tau=0}^{t} \frac{r_{jt} I_{j\tau}}{(1+r_{jt})^t}. \quad (17.15)$$

The first term is simply the discounted earnings, while the second term is the summation of all projects over all time periods. If expressed as perpetuity, the second term goes to I_{jT}, and then Eq. (17.15) also converges to our standard valuation Eq. (17.9).

17.4. The Irrelevance of Dividend Policy

As we mentioned previously, debate lingers regarding the effect of dividend policy on the value of the firm. M&M were the first to present an argument for **dividend irrelevance**.[2] M&M's theory that the value of the firm is independent of its dividend policy is similar to their analysis of the irrelevance of capital structure. The theory assumes a world without taxes or transaction costs. In addition, investors are assumed to be rational, with homogeneous expectations, and both corporate management and shareholders are assumed to know the same information about the firm.

17.4.1. *M&M Dividend Policy*

The irrelevance of dividends is best illustrated through the use of an example that considers three alternative policies. Suppose a firm will be in existence for only 2 years. During the first year, the firm generates earnings of \$115,000, from which management can pay dividends or reinvest in company operations. During the second year, the firm will pay out its entire cash flow, \$132,250, to the shareholders in the form of a cash dividend.

Policy I: Pay out all cash flows each year. If the firm's cost of capital is 15%, the value of the firm is the present value of this future cash flows, discounted at the cost of capital:

$$\begin{aligned}\text{Firm Value} &= \sum_{t=1}^{N} \frac{(\text{Cash flow})_t}{(1+\text{WACC})^t} \\ &= \frac{\$115{,}000}{1.15} + \frac{\$132{,}250}{(1.15)^2} \\ &= \$200{,}000. \end{aligned} \tag{17.16}$$

To translate this value of the entire firm to a per-share value, assume that the firm has 20,000 shares outstanding. The firm's value per share, based on its cash flows, is \$10.

[2]M. Miller and F. Modigliani (1961). Dividend policy, growth and the valuation of shares. *Journal of Business*, 43, 411–432.

Policy II: *Pay no dividends and make a short-term investment in the first year.* Suppose, however, that management makes a short-term investment equal to the entire amount of the first-year cash flow at the firm's cost of capital (paying no dividend in that year). It still pays out the entire proceeds in Year 2. Written as an equation, the value of the firm is:

$$\begin{aligned}\text{Firm Value} &= \sum_{t=1}^{N} \frac{(\text{Cash flow})_t(1+\text{Return on investment})^{N-t}}{(1+\text{WACC})^t}\\ &= \frac{0}{1.15} + \frac{\$115{,}000(1+0.15)}{(1.15)^2} + \frac{\$132{,}250}{(1.15)^2}\\ &= \$200{,}000. \end{aligned} \tag{17.17}$$

The per-share value remains at \$10, as in Policy I.

Policy III: *Issue new shares to pay in excess of firm's earnings in the first year.* To pay a dividend during the first year in excess of the firm's \$115,000 earnings, management would have to finance the additional cash required to pay the dividend. We have seen numerous ways for the firm to raise funds. For the sake of this example, assume that management decides to issue 3,500 shares of new equity. At \$10 per share, this stock generates \$35,000 in new capital.[3]

Suppose management declares a dividend of \$150,000 during the first year. The cash flow of \$115,000 and the stock issue proceeds of \$35,000 fund the dividend. The new shareholders expect to earn a 15% return on their investment, so during Year 2 they expect to receive \$40,250 (\$35,000 × 1.15) in the form of a dividend and return of capital. This, the old shareholders will receive a Year 2 dividend of \$132,250 minus \$40,250, or \$92,000. The value of the firm under these conditions becomes:

$$\begin{aligned} &= \frac{\$150{,}000}{(1.15)} + \frac{\$92{,}000}{1.15^2} + \frac{\$40{,}250}{(1.15)}\\ &= \$200{,}000 + \$35{,}000\\ &= \$235{,}000, \end{aligned}$$

[3]Because of the arguments made by M&M on the capital structure of the firm, the form of financing that is chosen really has no effect on the arguments presented here, although the presentation becomes somewhat more complicated as various forms of debt-financing are introduced.

where \$200,000 is cash flow to initial shareholders and \$35,000 is cash flow to new shareholders.

The per-share value of the firm remains at \$10 per share (\$235,000/23,500 shares), because now the firm has 20,000 old shares and 3,500 new shares outstanding. Regardless of the dividend declared by management, the value of the firm in the eyes of the old shareholders remains unchanged. Based on this reasoning, M&M conclude that dividends have no effect on the value of the firm and are therefore irrelevant.

17.4.2. *Homemade Dividends*

The earlier analysis ignores shareholders, who may care deeply about the amount and timing of dividends. However, it turns out that regardless of the size and timing of the firm's declarations of dividends, shareholders can customize their own payout streams either by selling shares or reinvesting dividends. In the earlier example, the firm initially paid \$115,000 in Year 1 and \$132,250 in Year 2 as a dividend for the 20,000 shares outstanding, or \$5.75 per share (\$115,000/20,000) during Year 1 and \$6.6125 per share (\$132,250/20,000) during Year 2. A shareholder with no immediate need for the dividend could reinvest this income in an equally risky investment yielding 15% to receive the cash flow from this investment in Year 2, along with the firm's regular dividend. This investor's cash flow would be zero in Year 1 and \$6.6125 from the new investment (\$5.75 $\times$ 1.15), plus \$6.6125 from the regular dividend, or a total cash flow of \$13.225 per share. This exactly matches the cash flow the investor would have received if the firm had invested its entire earnings, while paying zero dividends in Year 1 and \$264,500 in Year 2.

If the individual preferred a larger cash flow than the company's Year 1 dividend, this person could sell some shares in Year 1. Suppose a sale of shares generated a cash flow in Year 1 equal to \$7.50, made up of \$5.75 in dividends and \$1.75 from the sales of shares. The sale of stock during Year 1 would reduce the amount of Year 2 dividends by \$1.75 plus the rate-of-return the investor would have earned for that year, or a total of \$2.0125 (\$1.75 $\times$ 1.15). The Year 2 dividend would decline to \$6.6125 minus \$2.0125, or \$4.60 a share. This is exactly the amount of dividends the investor would have earned had the corporation issued new shares to generate the same cash flows. The cash flow that belongs to the original shares of \$92,000 in Year 2 divided by 20,000 original shares equals \$4.60 per share.

By this technique, the shareholder creates an equivalent return called **homemade dividends**. Due to the possibility of homemade dividends, no matter what dividend policy managers follow, the investor can achieve a preferred combination of dividend flows, either by investing excess dividends or selling shares. M&M hold that this makes the corporation's dividend policy irrelevant.

Concept Quiz

1. What are the assumptions M&M use to show the irrelevance of dividend policy?
2. What is a homemade dividend? Is this concept similar to the homemade lever age?

17.5. Dividend Payment and Policy Determination

Dividend policy represents one of the most important financial decisions a firm makes. How much a firm chooses to pay out in the dividends and how much it chooses to retain for future investments can affect both the growth of the firm and its stock price.

17.5.1. *Residual Theory*

The most easily understood theory of dividend payment determination is called the **residual theory**. As the name implies, this theory holds that firms pay dividends out of earnings that remain after it meets its financing needs. These are funds for which the firm has no immediate use. The procedure for a residual dividend policy follows several steps:

1. Determine the firm's optimal capital budget.
2. Determine the amount of equity needed to finance that budget.
3. To the extent possible, use the firm's retained earnings to supply the needed equity.
4. Distribute any leftover earnings as dividends.

The basic assumption of residual dividend theory is that shareholders want the firm to retain earnings if reinvesting them can generate higher rates-of-return than the shareholders could obtain by reinvesting their dividends. For example, if a corporation can invest retained earnings in a new venture that generates an 18% rate-of-return, whereas investors can obtain a return of only 10% by reinvesting their dividends, then stockholders would benefit more from the firm reinvesting its profits.

Whether firms actually practice the residual theory is a matter of question. Such a theory would simply erratic dividend payments, especially for fast-growth companies. Firms do seem to try to stabilize their dividend-payout rates, so analysts do not place much faith in the residual theory. However, two alternative theories for the dividend behavior of firms have found considerable empirical support.

17.5.2. *Lintner's Model*

Lintner's model, sometimes referred to as the *partial adjustment model*, assumes that firms adjust their dividend payouts slowly over time and provides another explanation for a firm's dividend policy.[4] In Lintner's model, a firm is assumed to have a desired level of dividends that is based on its expected earnings. When earnings vary, the firm will adjust its dividend payment to reflect the new level of earnings. However, rather than doing so immediately, a firm will choose to spread (or partially adjust) these variations in earnings over a number of time periods. Lambrecht and Myers (2012) have used Lintner's model to determine managerial rents. In addition, they also propose a permanent earning definition for estimating Lintner's model.

17.5.3. *Stable Dividend Policy*

The Lintner study reinforces the notion that dividend policy conveys information to investors. Many financial managers strive to maintain steady or modestly growing dividends and avoid large fluctuations or changes in dividend policies. Reducing dividend fluctuations helps reduce investor uncertainty about future dividends. Lower risk leads to higher stock prices. Managers resist increasing dividends if they do not expect to maintain the increase in the future. This supports a predominant policy of maintaining historical dividends.

If firms hesitate to raise dividends too quickly, they positively abhor the prospect of reducing dividends, for several reasons. First, many individuals

---

[4] J. Lintner (1956). Distribution of incomes of corporations among dividends, retained earnings and taxes. *American Economic Review*, 56, 97–113.

and institutions require large cash flows from their investments. For example, retired people in lower tax brackets generally covet high dividend payments. Tax-exempt institutions, such as endowment funds or pension funds, also need high current income and therefore desire high dividends. M&M argue that these individuals or institutions should ignore a stock's level of dividends because they always can liquidate some of their holdings in order to generate desired cash flows. Unfortunately, in real-world capital markets, this advice would generate substantial transaction costs, especially brokerage fees. In addition to the time involved in deciding to sell securities, investors may exhaust all of their principal, leaving none for future income requirements.

Second, mangers often resist reducing dividends also because a cut in dividends may be interpreted by the investment community as a signal of trouble with the firm or a result of poor management. Even if the reduction is intended to allow the firm to pursue an attractive opportunity, it may adversely affect stock prices.

A third reason that firms resist reducing dividends involves the legal list. Many large, institutional investors are bound by the prudent man rule, or by legislation, to buy only securities that are included on the legal list. One criterion of the list is a long history of continued dividend payments without dividend reductions. Therefore, a firm that reduces or omits a dividend payment faces the risk of being ineligible for purchase by certain institutional investors.

A stable dividend policy can become a sort of self-fulfilling prophecy. An unexpected rise or reduction in dividends can have an announcement effect on the firm's share price. An increase in dividends may lead investors to perceive a promising future and share price may increase. A drop in dividends may lead investors to fear a less promising future, resulting in a drop in share price. These perceptions may be accurate if managers themselves feel it is important to avoid fluctuations, especially cuts. In such a company, investors would be correct in viewing dividend declarations as sources of information.

The DPS, earnings per share (EPS), and PPS data information presented in Table 17.1 illustrates how important managers consider consistent dividends to be. Notice that Johnson & Johnson's (J&J's) dividend continued to increase in 1992, despite a drop in earnings. When earnings fell, J&J managers felt compelled to increase the payout ratio in order to maintain the growth in dividends that investors had come to expect.

Table 17.2. J&J — EPS and DPS.

Year	1995	1994	1993	1992	1991	1990	1989
DPS	$1.28	$1.13	$1.01	$0.89	$0.77	$0.66	$0.56
EPS	3.72	3.12	2.74	1.56	2.19	1.72	1.62
PPS	85.5	54.75	44.875	50.50	57.28	35.875	29.625
Payout ratio	34.41%	36.22%	36.86%	57.05%	35.16%	38.37%	34.57%

In 1993, 1994, and 1995, stronger earnings resulted in payout ratio of between 34% to 36%.

Using the data of Table 17.2, we can calculate the dividend yield (DPS/PPS) and earnings yield (EPS/PPS) as follows:

	1995	1994	1993	1992	1991	1990	1989	Mean
Dividend yield	0.015	0.021	0.023	0.018	0.013	0.018	0.019	0.018
Earnings yield	0.044	0.057	0.061	0.031	0.038	0.048	0.055	0.048

Both dividend yield and earnings yield can be used to show profitability of an investment in a stock.[5] Based upon Value Line, the median of estimated market dividend yields for market low (12/31/74) and market high (9/4/87) are 7.8% and 2.3% respectively.

17.5.4. *Information Content of Dividends — A Synthesis*

Many theorists and practitioners alike believe that the payment of a dividend conveys a signal to the marketplace. In effect, each dividend payment, and especially a change in dividends, carries information to investors about the company. This type of information could be made public in other ways, but managers routinely set dividends to signal to the market that they expect the firm to prosper. "From the Boardroom" feature in this chapter presents a study that indicates that the market does view dividend policy as a source of information.

[5]Statistical analyses of the relationship between (i) DPS and EPS and (ii) dividends yield and earnings yield for J&J are to be done by students (Problem 1 of this chapter).

17.5.5. *Double Taxation*

Tax law complicates dividend decision by imposing the burden of **double taxation**. In effect, income that a firm pays to shareholders as dividends is taxed twice. A corporate income tax is levied on the corporation's profits, and shareholders then pay personal income taxes on the dividends they receive. This is one of the complexities of the U.S. tax laws that affects dividend policy.

The investor has no control over corporate tax effects. It is up to the corporate managers to reduce or defer tax payments as much as possible. However, the investor can influence the amount of personal taxes due on any dividend earnings. Investors can reduce or defer taxes by buying low-dividend, high-growth stocks. Or, if they are tax exempt, investors can buy dividend-paying stocks.

Personal income taxes may affect an investor's preference for dividends or capital gains. When the tax rate on capital gains is substantially lower than the tax rate on personal income, then shareholders should prefer capital gains to dividends. This increases the firm's focus on retained earnings as equity financing. Investors still can realize homemade dividends through capital gains from sales of stock.

Different investors will have different preferences between dividends and capital gains. For example, average investors may prefer dividends because of the need for additional income, while wealthy investors may prefer capital gains because they currently do not need the income. Some large, tax-exempt institutions, such as pension funds, pay no taxes on their investment income, so they may be indifferent between dividends or capital gains. Other tax-exempt institutions, such as foundations and endowments, may favor current income to help meet budget needs.

Investors can defer receiving capital gains by holding stock; gains are received and become taxable only when stock is sold at a profit. Dividends offer less flexibility. Once the firm pays a dividend, the investor must pay taxes on this income. Therefore, the ability to defer taxes on capital gains may bias the investor against cash dividend payments.

Concept Quiz

1. What is the payout ratio?
2. What is the residual theory of dividends?
3. Why does a firm often use stable dividend policy?
4. What is the information content of dividends?
5. What is double taxation?

From the Boardroom

Stock Price and Dividend Policy

In boardrooms across the country, managers have long recognized the impact of dividend policy on their stock's price. Although an early study by M&M in 1961 first suggested that dividends should not matter to shareholders, recent studies by academics have begun to recognize what managers have known all along — that is, that dividends are important signals of the financial well-being of a company.

A number of studies by academics have found that dividend announcements do serve as a source of information to stockholders in the United States. Now, a 1992 study titled "dividend Announcements and Stock Price Performance," by Paul Marsh of the London Business School, finds that British firms and their shareholders behave much like their American counterparts.

Professor Marsh's study looks at the dividend announcements of nearly 6,000 publicly traded firms between January 1989 and April 1992. His findings indicate that firms revealing a large dividend increase saw their share price rise by 1.7% more than those of similar-sized companies. In contrast, the shares of companies that cut their dividends saw their share price fall by 4.3%, while companies that suspended dividend payments saw their price fall by 7.4%.

Professor Marsh's findings are consistent with the idea that dividend announcements serve as a source of information to shareholders. Increases in dividends are a signal that earnings will be sufficient to maintain an increase in dividends. More importantly, decreases in dividends are an even more important signal because managers try not to cut dividends. Therefore, a cut in dividends, or worse still, suspension of the dividend payment altogether, indicates that the firm is in a real financial mess.

One criticism of this and other dividend studies is that too much emphasis is placed on dividends because firms usually announce their dividends along with other information about the firm. Separating out these effects can be difficult. So, the question of how important dividend policy is remains a bit unclear.

Source: Adapted from "Revisiting the Dividend Controversy". *The Economist*. 1992, p. 69.

17.6. Stock Dividends, Stock Splits, and Stock Repurchases

Managers can use stock dividends, stock splits, or stock repurchases to change the firm's number of common shares outstanding. A **stock dividend** is a payout of dividends in the form of stock rather than cash. A stock dividend commonly is expressed as a percentage; for example, a 10% stock dividend means that a stockholder receives one new share for every 10 shares currently owned. A **stock split** is essentially the same thing as a stock dividend, except that a split is expressed as a ratio instead of a percentage. Basically, a stock dividend and a stock split increase the number of shares of stock outstanding without any cash flow to the firm or increase in firm value.

A **stock repurchase** is another way to pay cash to shareholders. It occurs when management uses cash to buy back the stock of the company. As we discussed in an earlier chapter, net equity sales in the United States have been small or negative in recent years. This has occurred because U.S. corporations actually repurchased more stock than they sold. Stock repurchases will reduce the number of common shares outstanding in the equity markets.

17.6.1. *Stock Dividends and Stock Splits*

The major difference between a stock split and a stock dividend is in their accounting treatments. The American Institute of Certified Public Accountants (AICPA) recommends treatment of an increase in shares outstanding of less than 20–25% as a stock dividend and treatment of any increase greater than this as a stock split. The accounting treatment for a stock dividend transfers retained earnings equal to the market value of the new shares to the common stock account. Table 17.3 shows the effect on the firm's equity account of a 10% stock dividend.

Table 17.3 shows that major changes include a capitalization of retained earnings at the current market price of the stock and an increase in the number of shares by the amount of the stock dividend. The value of shareholders' equity, in both an accounting and an economic sense, remains the same. The total equity book value was reported as $123,000 both before and after the stock dividend. The market value of the firm stayed at $100,000 (1,000 shares × $100/share before the split; 1,100 shares at $90.91/share after the split). However, the common stock account rises by $4,000 (100 new shares × $40 per share) paid in capital excess of par becomes $3,000

Table 17.3. Stock dividend and the balance sheet.

Before Dividend:	
Common stock: $40 par value, 1,000 shares issued and outstanding; current market price $100 per share ($40 par × 1,000 shares = $40,000)	$40,000
Paid in capital in excess of par	$ 3,000
Retained earnings	$80,000
Total shareholders' equity	**$123,000**
After a 10% Stock Dividend:	
Common stock: $40 par value, 1,100 shares issued and outstanding; current market price $90.01 per share ($40 par × 1,100 shares = $44,000)	$44,000
Paid in capital in excess of par	$ 9,000
Retained earnings	$70,000
Total shareholders' equity	**$123,000**

+ 100 ($100 − $40) = $9,000; retained earnings' new value is $80,000 − 100 ($100) = 70,000.

The firm accounts for a stock split differently. Table 17.3 shows that a two-for-one stock split causes no changes in any of the equity account balances. The number of shares increases, but each shares has a lower par value. The market price of the shares also changes to reflect the increase in the number of shares outstanding.

There is no economic difference between the effects of a stock split and the effects of a stock dividend. To see why, envision a family of four have an apple pie for dessert. It does not matter if each member of the family gets one piece equal to one quarter of the pie or two pieces equal to one-eighth each. Stock splits and stock dividends change how the firm divides the pie, but they do not affect the percentage of ownership held by shareholders.

Stock splits or stock dividends may be of value for various reasons. For one, these techniques may help the firm maintain an optimal trading range for its stock price. This argument is based on the belief that investors are more likely to purchase a stock if its price falls within a certain range. Above the upper limit of this range, a round lot of stock may cost too much for some investors.[6] Consequently, they are forced to choose between buying odd lots and paying higher commissions, or investing in other securities. Below the trading range, some investors may consider the stock too cheap and not worthy of investment.

[6]Most stock trades occur in "round lots" of 100 shares. "Odd lots" are stock trades involving less than 100 shares. Because of their smaller size, transaction costs on odd-lot trades are higher on a per-share basis than round-lot trades.

Table 17.4. Stock and a partial balance sheet.

Before Split:	
Common stock: $40 par value, 1,000 shares issued and outstanding; current market price $100 per share	$40,000
Paid in capital in excess of par	$3,000
Retained earnings	$80,000
Total shareholders' equity	**$123,000**
After a Two-for-One Stock Split:	
Common stock: $40 par value, 2,000 shares issued and outstanding; current market price $50	$40,000
Paid in capital in excess of par	$3,000
Retained earnings	$80,000
Total shareholders' equity	**$123,000**

The institutionalization of the market casts doubt on the optimal trading range argument. Mutual funds, pension funds, and other institutions usually buy and sell in such large amounts that they care little about optimal trading ranges. Stocks have performed so well in recent years, in fact, that they have attracted a lot of investor attention. Despite these anecdotal arguments, the question of an optimal trading range is still an open issue that needs to be evaluated by further empirical work.

Copeland presents an argument against stock splits and stock dividends and claims that transaction costs are higher after stock splits.[7] Some analysts favor stock splits or stock dividends, however, for the information that such announcements convey to the market. Generally, high-growth firms split their stock or issue stock dividends. If the market were to extend this trend to conclude that all stock splits or stock dividends indicate profitable, high-growth firms, then there would be some merit to the information-content argument. However, Fama, Fisher, Jensen, and Roll report negligible price impacts for stock splits or dividends, unless they are accompanied by earnings or cash-dividend increase.[8]

Until scholars improve their understanding of investor psychology, the value of stock splits and stock dividends will remain an open question. Managers will continue to offer stock splits and dividends, and some investors will readily accept them as valuable, whereas other investors will not.

[7]T. Copeland (1979). Liquidity changes following stock splits. *Journal of Finance*, 34, 115–141.

[8]E. Fama, L. Fisher, M. Jensen, and R. Roll (1969). The adjustment of stock prices to new information. *International Economic Review*, 10, 1–21.

A **reverse stock split**, as its name implies, is a reduction in the number of shares outstanding, with each share increasing in value to keep the total value of the firm unchanged. As with a stock split, theory gives no reason to expect any change in the underlying value of the company that engages in a reverse split. In fact, many investors regard a reverse split as an admission by management that the company faces financial difficulties. This belief is based primarily on the argument that the PPS share is too low to attract serious investors.

EXAMPLE 17.3

Stock Dividends and Stock Splits

Q: Use the information in the "Before Dividend" section of Table 17.2 to answer the following question:

a. If this company announces a 5% stock dividend, how will the equity account be affected?
b. Using Table 17.3, if this company announces a four-for-one stock split, how should the "After Stock Split" section of this table be presented?

A: a. The equity account will change as follows:

i. The amount added to common stock is:

$$(\$40)(5\%)(1{,}000) = \$2{,}000$$

The current stock PPS is $95.24 ($100/1.05).

ii. The amount added to be paid in capital in excess of par is:

$$(\$100 - \$40)(5\%)(1{,}000) = \$3{,}000$$

iii. Retained Earnings will be reduced by $5,000 ($2,000 + $3,000).

b. The statement will be the same except the number of shares outstanding will be 4,000 shares at $10 per share.

17.6.2. *Stock Repurchase*

A **stock repurchase** occurs when management spends corporate funds to buy back the stock of the company. A stock repurchase can benefit both management and shareholders. The repurchased shares become treasury stock and are then available for reissue to executives under stock option plans, to employees as part of profit sharing plans, and to other firms as part of mergers or acquisitions.

Management gains some defensive benefits by way of a stock repurchase. If managers of a cash-rich, low-debt firm fear a takeover, they may finance the stock purchase with the firm's excess cash or use debt, reducing the attractiveness of the firm as a takeover target. In addition, the repurchase program invites any dissatisfied stockholders to sell their shares back to the firm at a favorable price before a potential takeover company can make an offer for the stock. Management also benefits from the reduction in mailing and processing costs for annual reports, dividend payments, proxy statements, and other materials. Some repurchases are aimed directly at small shareholders for precisely this reason.

Shareholders also may benefit from a stock repurchase. Stockholders who want to sell their shares can do so at a favorable price. Stockholders who choose to hold onto their shares may benefit from the reduction in the number of shares outstanding. For example, suppose someone owns 1,000 shares of a company that has 25,000 shares outstanding. This stock represents a 4% (1,000/25,000) stake in the company. If the company repurchases 5,000 of its shares from other investors, then that stockholder's stake in the company increases to 5% (1,000/20,000).

Information related to cash dividends paid, repurchases of common stock, and employee compensation and stock option plans can be found in a firm's (consolidated) statement of common stock, retained earnings, and treasury stock. Table 17.5 presents this information for J&J, Inc. during the period from 1993 to 1995. For example in 1993, J&J distributed

Table 17.5. Consolidated statement of common stock, retained earnings and treasury stock: 1993, 1994, and 1995 (Dollars in millions; shares in thousands).

	Common Stock Issued		
	Shares	Amount	Retained Earnings
Balance, January 3, 1993	767,366	$767	$6,648
Net earnings	—	—	1,787
Cash dividends paid (per share: $1.01)	—	—	(659)
Employee compensation and stock option plans	—	—	(49)
Repurchase of common stock	—	—	—
Other	6	—	—

(*Continued*)

Table 17.5. (*Continued*)

	Common Stock Issued		
	Shares	Amount	Retained Earnings
Balance, January 2, 1994	767,372	767	7,727
Net earnings	—	—	2,006
Cash dividends paid (per share: $1.13)	—	—	(727)
Employee compensation and stock option plans	—	—	(78)
Repurchase of common stock	—	—	—
Other	20	—	38
Balance, January 1, 1995	767,392	767	8,966
Net earnings	—	—	2,243
Cash dividends paid (per share: $1.28)	—	—	(827)
Employee compensation and stock option plans	—	—	(35)
Repurchase of common stock	—	—	—
Acquisitions	—	—	—
Other	20	—	4
Balance, December 31, 1995	767,412	$767	$10,511

	Treasury Stock	
	Shares	Amount
Balance, January 3, 1993	111,970	$2,006
Net earnings	—	—
Cash dividends paid (per share: $1.01)	—	—
Employee compensation and stock option plans	(3,066)	(134)
Repurchase of common stock	15,487	632
Other	—	—
Balance, January 2, 1994	124,391	2,504
Net earnings	—	—
Cash dividends paid (per share: $1.01)	—	—
Employee compensation and stock option plans	(3,855)	(186)
Repurchase of common stock	3,846	185
Other	—	—
Balance, January 1, 1995	124,382	2,503
Net earnings	—	—
Cash dividends paid (per share: $1.01)	—	—
Employee compensation and stock option plans	(4,576)	(309)
Repurchase of common stock	4,582	322
Acquisitions	(4,656)	(199)
Other	—	—
Balance, December 31, 1995	119,732	$2,317

See Notes to Consolidated Financial Statements of J&J 1995 Annual Report.

its net earnings as follows: cash dividends (\$659 million), employee compensation and stock option plans (\$49 million), and retained earnings (\$1,787 − \$659 − \$49 = \$1,079 million). In 1993, J&J paid cash dividends of \$1.01 per share. This statement also reveals that J&J repurchased 15,487 shares of common stock in 1993.

Firms can repurchase stock by two methods. A tender offer is a publicly announced offer by the company to all shareholders to buy a certain number of shares at a specified price during a set period of time. Every shareholder has to decide whether the price offered by the company beats the price the shares will have when the tender offer expires. If stockholders tender more shares than the company intends to repurchase, management may elect to purchase pro rata percentages of the total from each shareholder.

A firm also can reacquire its stock through an **open market repurchase**. Acting through a broker, the corporation purchases shares in the secondary market just like any other investor. A corporation usually announces its intention to engage in an open market repurchase in advance, although the exact amount of shares repurchased and the actual days of the transactions are not known.

The impact of a repurchase on a firm's financing or capital structure can be considered in light of the M&M argument. As the firm repurchases its stock, it may very well increase EPS, but it also increases its financial leverage. The impact of a repurchase on the firm depends on the amount of the firm's initial leverage and how much the repurchase increases this financial leverage.

Concept Quiz

1. What is a stock dividend? What is a stock split? Discuss the similarities and differences between stock dividends and stock splits.
2. What are stock repurchases? What are the methods by which a firm can repurchase its own stock?

17.7. Factors that Influence Dividend Policy

Two broad categories of factors guide financial managers in developing dividend policies. The first is the company's financial position, including the market, economic, and government influences upon the firm. The second is investor preferences, reflecting the influences that shareholders may exert upon management's dividend policy decision.

17.7.1. *Company Financial Situation*

Often, when a firm borrows from a bank or issue a bond to the market, constraints in the debt agreement state that dividends must be paid from earnings generated after the loan agreement has been made. Many debt contracts also stipulate that dividends shall be paid only when the firm can maintain safety levels in certain ratios, such as the current ratio or the times interest earned ratio.

Another legal constraint known as the *impairment of capital rule* is designed to protect the firm's creditors further. It stipulates that dividends cannot exceed the amount of retained earnings listed on the balance sheet. This ensures that the firm retains enough capital to pay its legal obligations.

Most dividends must be paid in cash. This may be a problem for a company with liquidity difficulties. Often, a profitable, high-growth firm will reinvest its earnings back into the firm. Such firms may choose not to pay shareholders dividends (for example, Microsoft, Inc., and Digital, Inc., do not). As discussed earlier, a firm must choose the source of its equity financing carefully. These funds can come either from retained earnings or through a new common stock issue. The overall cost of new common stock depends upon the flotation costs of a new issue. If flotation costs are high, as they are for most smaller firms, then financing through retained earnings may be cheaper than the sale of new common stock. Also, for private companies, issuing new stock means dilution of control, making retained earnings a more desirable means of financing. Of course, any earnings the firm retains for reinvestment reduces the amount it can pay out in dividends.

Another factor in the financing decision is the choice between debt or equity. If debt costs are low, then a firm may choose to raise its debt ratio. This reduces the need for retained earnings and frees up more funds for its dividend payout. If the firm can keep its debt/equity ratio near its target capital structure level, then dividend policy becomes a less important factor in financing decisions.

17.7.2. *Investor Preferences*

Both federal and state governments tax dividend income at ordinary income tax rates. Any differences between capital gains and income tax rates will lead some investors to prefer one or the other for tax reasons. Another influence on dividend policy will be the composition of the firm's shareholders, commonly called its *clientele*.

M&M introduced the **clientele effect** as an imperfection of the market that affects dividend policy. M&M observed that each corporation tends to attract a specific type of clientele that favors the firm's established payout ratio. For example, investors in higher tax brackets tend to hold stocks with lower dividend payouts and higher capital gains yields. This way, they avoid personal taxes on dividend income. On the other hand, retirees, because of their lower tax brackets, tend to invest in companies with larger yields.

Because a firm tends to attract a certain type of investor, management may be reluctant to change its dividend policy. If shareholders have to change their portfolios due to changes in payout ratios, this shift may cause shareholders to incur unwanted transaction costs. In this way, the tax differential favoring capital gains is a systematic imperfection of the market that produces a clientele effect.

Concept Quiz

1. What are the key factors affecting the dividend policy of a firm?
2. How can the clientele effect influence the dividend policy of a firm?

17.8. Issues Marring the Dividend Problem

One point that M&M brought out, and that should become obvious following our discussion of Eqs. (17.3) and (17.4) is that, given the firm's investment policy, dividend policy is irrelevant. The problem of confounding the investment decisions with the dividend-policy decision occurs most often when the analysis assumes an all-internally financed firm, a stringent assumption relaxed by M&M to arrive at their irrelevance proposition. Foregoing profitable investment opportunities for the sake of paying dividends can be a result of the internal-financing case, where capital is limited, all of which makes it appear as though a residual dividend payout of earnings not required for new investment would be the optimal policy, and in a sense a *no dividend* policy, *per se*, is the optimal policy in the world of M&M.

Adding uncertainty does nothing to their conclusions, either, if market rationality is assumed. Hence, discount rates are unaffected by the timing of the flows, since shareholders are concerned only with the *size* of their returns (holding risk constant), and not the *form* in which they arrive. Uncertainty naturally leads to the consideration of information effects as well. But so long as no real variables underlying the situation have changed, investors will see through the change in dividend policy, and no change in perceived firm value will result.

Finally, introducing market imperfections may change the picture. We stress that it may change because the imperfections will have an effect only if a systematic preference for dividends over capital gains develops, or vice versa. The largest effect is thought to be attributable to differential tax rates on dividends and capital gains. Odd as it may seem, this imperfection may be eradicated if clienteles form for all varieties of dividend payouts. Then, within each dividend payout group, market forces will drive prices to their true values, so that a firm's dividend policy does not matter because investors can, in essence, choose their own optimal payout ratios. This assumes a sufficient number of clienteles and participants therein but, given the multitude of securities available and the dispersion of their payout schemes, this seems a harmless assumption, rendering dividend policy irrelevant once again.

17.8.1. *The Classical CAPM*

The CAPM, as originally developed by Sharpe (1964), allowed for uncertainty, a problem ignored in the M&M analysis: this was a very strong assumption, which allowed much of the M&M analysis to flow smoothly. In this framework, the return on a security is determined by the following equation:

$$\tilde{R}_{jt} = R_f + \beta_j(\tilde{R}_{mt} - R_f), \tag{17.18}$$

where at the minimum, the individual security's returns and the returns on the market are random variables. Note that nowhere in this equation is there any delineation between dividend returns and returns attributable to capital gains. The reasons for such an exemption are two-fold: first and foremost, taxes are assumed not to matter — meaning not only corporate taxes, but personal income taxes on capital gains and dividend income as well. This leaves no problems with differential tax rates on these two forms of returns. The second assumption follows from the first, and is somewhat implicit in nature: those investors are assumed to be rational, as in the M&M analysis, and therefore express no preference for capital gains or dividends. In this respect, the basic CAPM approach is very similar to the M&M approach and adds very little to our analysis. Therefore, we leave the basic CAPM approach to investigate one of its extensions, which was the first to allow for taxes affecting investors' security investment decisions, and which did so by assuming that the effective tax rates on the two forms of returns would be different.

17.8.2. *Brennan's CAPM with Taxes*

Brennan (1970) took the first step in allowing for taxation of dividends at rates different than those applicable to capital gains. Furthermore, Brennan sought to allow these tax rates to differ from investor to investor. In light of these relaxations of the original CAPM assumptions, the expected one period after-tax return on an individual's portfolio can be envisioned as:

$$V_i = \sum_{j=1}^{N} X_{ji}[z_j - (z_j - P_j)t_{gi} + d_{ji}(1 - t_{di})] + X_{0i}[q - (q-1)t_{di}], \tag{17.19}$$

where

V_i = Value of the ith person's portfolio;
X_{ji} = Dollar amount of security j in the ith portfolio;
z = Expected end-of-period price of security j;
P_j = Initial equilibrium price of security j;
t_{gi} = Effective capital gains tax on ith investor;
d_j = Dividend payment on security j;
t_{dj} = Effective marginal tax rate applicable to dividend receipt by the ith investor;
q = Expected return on the riskless asset;
X_{0i} = Dollar amount invested in the riskless asset at $t = 0$ by the ith investor.

The difference between this and a no-tax portfolio-return formula is obviously the tax rates applicable to capital gains, dividends, and the riskless return, which also gets taxed as regular income. The portfolio-variance term is likewise affected, in that the returns must be scales down to after-tax figures, taking the form:

$$\sigma_i^2 = \sum_{j=1}^{N}\sum_{k=1}^{N} \sigma_{jk} X_{ji}(1 - t_{gi}) X_{ki}(1 - t_{gi}), \tag{17.20}$$

where

σ_{jk} = Covariance between the returns on security j and security k.

Noticeably missing from the previous equation are the dividend and riskless asset terms, both of which are assumed to be known with certainty at the outset of the period in question, and which in that respect, add nothing to the total variance of returns.

Staying with the original CAPM, we assume, further, that all investors remain fully invested, and face a budget constraint specified by:

$$\sum_{j=1}^{N} P_j(X_{ji} - X_{ji}^0) + (X_{0i} - X_{0i}^0) = 0, \tag{17.21}$$

where

X_{ji}^0 and X_{0i}^0 represent initial endowment of X_{ji} and X_{0i}, respectively and that the utility functions investors seek to maximize can be defined entirely in terms of the first two moments of the return distribution:

$$U_i = U_i(\mu_i, \sigma_i^2). \tag{17.22}$$

In maximizing Eq. (17.19), investors must solve the Lagrangian expression:

$$L = U_i(\mu_i, \sigma_i^2) - \lambda\left[\sum_{j=1}^{N} P_j(X_{ji} - X_{ji}^0) + (X_{0i} - X_{0i}^0)\right], \tag{17.23}$$

which resolves to:

$$(R_j - r) = \beta_j[(R_m - r) + T(r - d_m)] + T(d_j - r), \tag{17.24}$$

the T losing its subscript because of the aggregation of tax rates across all investors, and it represents the aggregated effective market tax rate.

From Eq. (17.24), we see that the return on a security is affected not only be the risk-free rate-of-return and the beta coefficient times some market-risk premium, but also by the weighted average marginal tax rate and the dividend yield on the market portfolio, and the individual security's dividend yield relative to the risk-free rate. The interesting point here is that a security's return is positively related to its dividend yield, yet inversely related to the dividend yield on the market portfolio. One might think that the first dividend-return statement is logical, since dividend yield is a part of total return — the higher the dividend yield, the higher the total return but that misses the point of adding taxes to the model. Those securities paying high dividend yields will have to offer higher returns to investors, to compensate them for the tax burden they will incur, since capital-gains taxes here are assumed to be less than the effective tax rate on dividend income. The inverse correlation with the market dividend yield is the opposite case of that just described because the problem is stated in all relative terms. The higher the market dividend yield relative to some firm's dividend yield, the lower the rate-of-return the given firm must offer to be competitive in a market in which financial assets are priced by their systematic risk, and their return's taxability status.

17.8.3. *The Litzenberger and Ramaswamy CAPM with Taxes*

Litzenberger and Ramaswamy (L&R) (1979) extended the Brennan model and relaxed some of the constraints with the intent of testing for the significance of dividends in security returns. Their paper developed an after-tax version of the CAPM that included a progressive tax system pertaining to dividend and interest income (capital gains effective tax rate assumed to be equal to zero), and riskless borrowing restricted by both investor-related wealth and income. While the final equation appears to be similar to that of Brennan, the interpretation is distinctly different, and it is on that point that we will attempt to focus our attention.

L&R assumed k investors, all seeking to maximize their utility functions given by $f^k(\mu_k, \sigma_k^2)$, which is fully described by the expected after-tax portfolio return and the variance of the after-tax returns, all those mentioned investors exhibiting global-risk tolerance at their respective optimums. All investors are confronted by three constraints: total investment, a borrowing constraint that will allow only as much interest paid on borrowing as that received in dividend income, and a margin constraint that dictates the smallest fraction an investor's net worth can be, relative to his holdings of risky securities.

The optimization problem can then be written as[9]:

$$L^k = f^k(\mu_k, \sigma_k^2) + \lambda_1^k\left(1 - \sum_{i=1}^{N} X_i - X_f^k\right) + \lambda_2^k\left[\sum_{i=1}^{N} X_i^k d_i + X_f^k r_f - S_2^k\right] + \lambda_3^k\left[(1-\alpha)\sum_{i=1}^{N} X_i^k + X_f^k - S_3^k\right], \quad (17.25)$$

[9]The constrained maximization indicated in Eq. (17.22) has used three Lagrange multipliers (λ_1^k, K_2^k, and K_3^k) to take the budget constraint, the income constraint and the margin constraint into account. The essence of the Lagrange-multiplier method is to convert a constrained-optimization problem into a form such that the first-order condition of the non-constrained problem can still be applied. Readers can refer to Appendix A of Chapter 4, which discusses the mathematical procedure of constrained optimization.

where

λ_1^k = Lagrange on the kth investor's budget;
λ_2^k, S_2^k = Lagrange on the kth investor's income and the associated slack variable;
λ_3^k, S_3^k = Lagrange on the kth investor's borrowing and the associated slack variable;
d_i = Dividend yield on security i.

Differentiating with respect to asset weights and solving, L&R find:

$$E(R_j) - r_f = A + B\beta_j + C(d_j - r_f). \tag{17.26}$$

The expected return on security i, the riskless rate-of-return, and the beta associated with security i are all defined in like fashion to the original and Brennan's CAPM, but, as we stated earlier, the other terms merit further scrutiny.

The A, or intercept term, is, in a sense, the excess return on a zero-beta portfolio with a dividend yield equal to the riskless rate of interest, relative to the market portfolio. If the market dividend yield and the riskless rate are not equal, and if the tax implications exist, then A is not the excess return on a zero-beta portfolio. More precisely, A is the margin requirement times the ratio of the non-negative margin requirement times the ratio of the non-negative slack value on the margin constraint on the kth investor's borrowing, to the expected marginal utility of the mean return of the optimal portfolio selection, all multiplied by the ratio of the kth investor's global-risk tolerance to the global-risk tolerance of the market. In this respect the A term is a risk–return relative margin value for the kth investor.

The B term is more easily interpreted, as it is very similar to the market-risk premium concept in the original CAPM. It is defined as the variance of the returns on the market, times the ratio of the market's initial wealth position to the market's global-risk tolerance (θ^m). Alternatively, it can be thought of as the variance of the market "standardized" by the risk tolerance of the market, and scaled up by the wealth of the market and is therefore a risk premium, but expressed in terms of wealth rather than return.

The C term is the most difficult to interpret, since it is comprised of essentially two distinct components. The first term is the summation of investor's marginal tax rates (T^k) times their global-risk tolerances (θ^k) relative to that of the market; the second component is the summation of the investor's global-risk tolerances relative to that of the market, time the value of the income constraint on borrowing, relative to the marginal utility of the optimal portfolio's return. Symbolically displayed, C is:

$$C = \sum_{k=1}^{N} \frac{\theta^k}{\theta^m} \left[\frac{T^k - \lambda_2^k}{f_1^k} \right], \tag{17.27}$$

where

$$f_1^k = \frac{\partial f^k(\mu_k, \sigma_k^2)}{\partial \mu_k}; \quad \theta^m = \sum_k \theta^k.$$

Here C represents a balancing of risks, one of those risks being the tax shield of increased debt, the second of increased return due to being able to borrow greater amounts and purchase the mean optimal portfolio return. We can look at this with the view that there are two clienteles (see Eq. (17.28). For some of those investors, the income margin constraint is binding (b), and for others it is not (n):

$$C = \sum_{k \in n} \frac{\theta^k}{\theta^m} T^k - \sum_{k \in b} \frac{\theta^k}{\theta^m} \frac{\lambda_2^k}{f_1^k}, \tag{17.28}$$

where $k \in n$ and $k \in b$ indicate that k is an element of N and k is an element of B, respectively.

One clientele would prefer more dividends (those for whom the constraint is binding), so that their debt capacity would be increased, and as L&R argue, without increasing their tax liability. In order for this latter point to hold, investors either must be able to utilize dividend exclusion for tax purposes, or must have so little income as to be exempt from income taxes.

The second clientele would prefer capital gains, since the income constraint is not binding, particularly since the effective tax rate of capital gains is assumed to be zero, and taking the extreme case where S is equal to zero, C would become the weighted-average marginal tax rates, weighted by relative risk tolerances, a consideration not present in Brennan's model.

In sum, Eq. (17.26) represents a CAPM family. It includes all other CAPM's as special cases. Here, A, B, C, and S are four important parameters in determining this CAPM family. These alternative special CAPM's can be derived from Eq. (17.26) as follows[10]:

(a) If $A > 0$, $B > 0$, $C > 0$, and $\lambda_2^k = 0$, then Eq. (17.26) reduces to:

$$E(R_j) - T^m d_j = [r_f(1 - T^m) + A](1 - \beta_j) + [E(R_m) - T_m d_m]\beta_j, \tag{17.26a}$$

where $T^m = \sum_k T^k(\theta^k/\theta^m)$ = market marginal tax bracket. This is an after-tax version of zero beta CAPM.

(b) If $A = 0$, $B > 0$, $C > 0$, and $\lambda_2^k = 0$, then Eq. (17.26) reduces to:

$$E(R_j) - T^m d_j = [r_f(1 - T^m)] + [E(R_m) - T^m d^m - r_f(1 - T^m)]\beta_j. \tag{17.26b}$$

This is an after-tax version of Sharpe–Lintner CAPM.

(c) If $A > 0$, $B > 0$, $C = 0$, then Eq. (17.26) reduces to:

$$E(R_j) = (A + r_f)(1 - \beta_j) + E(R_m)\beta_j. \tag{17.26c}$$

This is a before-tax version of zero-beta CAPM.

(d) If $A = 0$, $B > 0$, and $C = 0$, then Eq. (17.26) reduces to:

$$E(R_j) = r_f + [E(R_m) - r_f)]\beta_j. \tag{17.26d}$$

This is a before-tax version of the Sharpe–Lintner CAPM.

17.8.4. *Empirical Evidence*

17.8.4.1. *Gordon's empirical work and its extensions*

Gordon (1959) was interested in the determinants of value. His method of testing for these determinants was one of cross-sectional regression, testing in the first section for the magnitude of the coefficients' differences so as to infer the relative importance of each in the total valuation procedure. The second section of his study involved a more refined model, formulated with regard to previous findings and suspicions to which more comparative analysis was devoted.

Gordon first sought to uncover what it was the market actually capitalized in arriving at stock values, both dividends and earnings — the dividends plus the growth opportunities, where the retained earnings figure was

[10]The derivations of following results can be found in either L&R's paper or Han's (1985) dissertation. In addition, Han has integrated L&R's CAPM model with Bhattacharya's (1979) dividend signaling model and has obtained a joint equilibrium model.

used as a proxy for growth potential, or simply the earnings by themselves. His sample was taken from four industries at two separate points in time, which allowed for analysis of the coefficient's stability and significance over time and across industries, as well as the analysis of the multiple correlations across time. He sought to make only some generalizations, although the results were to some extent inconclusive.

The dividends and earnings model as shown in Eq. (17.29) shows the price of a share of stock to be linearly dependent upon dividends, earnings, and some constant term:

$$P = a_0 + a_1 D + a_2 Y. \tag{17.29}$$

The a_1 and a_2 terms are the point of interest; if a_1 is greater than a_2, then dividends have a relatively larger impact in the valuation procedure than do earnings, and vice versa. The multiple correlations for these eight regressions were quite high, averaging 0.905, with a range from 0.86 to 0.94. Of the dividend coefficients, seven were statistically significant at a 5% level (the only negative value being the insignificant value), while two of the earnings coefficients were not statistically significant. In each case, except that one where the dividend coefficient is insignificant, the dividend coefficient is greater in magnitude than the earnings coefficient. This evidence is shaky proof for dividend preference if one recognizes the multicollinearity problem and the apparent lack of consistency of the coefficients across industries or stability over time periods, even in any relative sense.

The dividend-plus-investment-opportunities approach, which, as we said earlier, uses the retained-earnings figure as a growth proxy, hinting again at an all internally financed firm, is symbolized by Eq. (17.30):

$$P = a_0 + a_1 D + a_2 (Y - D). \tag{17.30}$$

The multiple correlation figures and the constant terms are the same as in the previous test; this might have been expected, since no new variables entered, and none left the formulation, but the relative dividend and retained-earnings coefficients do change in relative values. Actually, the retained-earnings coefficients were the same as the earnings coefficients in the earlier trial, but it is really the difference, or the ratio, of the two that we are interested in. The dividend coefficients also appear to be relatively more consistent from industry to industry and stable in relative terms through time. The new-found stability and consistency is appealing because we would like to believe stocks are priced in some logical and consistent manner, which, given this evidence, indicates that dividends are three to four times as important in the valuation procedure as are growth opportunities. Once again, multicollinearity is a problem that is left unquestioned.

Gordon dismisses the pure-earnings approach with the realization that investors would be indifferent between dividends and increases in market value of their holdings if they valued only earnings, dismissing market imperfections for now. If this were so, then the two relevant coefficients would tend to be equal, and since they were found to be drastically different in the second set of regressions, he discounts this as a viable valuation format.

In refining his model, it appears that Gordon was primarily interested in not allowing short-term aberrations to influence the parameter estimates, although he also adjusted all variables in accordance with a size factor, which, in some respects, could be interpreted as the inclusion of a previously omitted variable that could affect the stability of some of the coefficients. The new model appears as:

$$P = B_0 + B_1\overline{d} + B_2(d - \overline{d}) + B_3(\overline{g}) + E_4(g - \overline{g}), \tag{17.31}$$

where

P = PPS/Book value;
$\overline{d}$ = 5-year average dividend/Book value;
d = Current year's dividend/Book value;
$\overline{g}$ = 5-year average retained earnings/Book value;
g = Current year's retained earnings/Book value.

The multiple correlations from the use of this model are slightly lower than those in the dividend-plus-growth case presented earlier, but most noticeably the constant terms are now quite small, whereas, with the previous models, they were at times quite large, although statistical significance was not discussed. Only the 5-year dividend is significant at a 5% level for all eight regressions with six of the current less the long-run average being significant and five of each of the growth coefficients being significant also, although not as much so as the dividend coefficients.

All things considered, the dividend factors appear to be the predominant influences on share values, although there are certain individual exceptions among the industries surveyed. The evidence presented here in the revised model and in the models presented earlier must be interpreted as supporting Gordon's contention that dividends do matter; in fact, given the methods used here, they are detected as being the most important variable that could be included in the valuation formula.

Friend and Puckett (1964) were concerned with unveiling the limitations to the type of analysis performed by Gordon and others. They pointed out a number of potential problems, the first being the accounting earnings and retained earnings figures and the high degree of measurement error incurred when using these values as proxies for economic or true earnings. Again, it is assumed that investors value economic earnings and not accounting earnings *per se*. Risk measures are also missing from the analysis, as is any awareness of the dynamic nature of corporate dividend policy. In short, we must realize not only a multicollinearity problem and potential specification errors, but that omitted variables must also be accounted for, if the analysis is to be complete.

In a general sense, a composite firm-specific variable, E, could be included in the standard model, which contains dividends and retained earnings, yielding:

$$P = a_0 + a_1 D + a_2 R + F. \tag{17.32}$$

But to have any true economic meaning, this variable should be specified, so multiple statistical trials were run to see which economic variable would be best to include in the analysis. Attempts were also made to alter or adjust the retained-earnings figure so as to more accurately reflect its "true" value, as discussed in a preceding paragraph.

In running the statistical tests, five industry groups were analyzed at two points in time, along the same lines of reasoning as in Gordon's paper. The first trial was run using Eq. (17.31) as the model, without the F coefficient. For each industry the coefficients are relatively stable across time periods, and in two instances the retained-earnings coefficient is greater than the dividend coefficient. In particular, the electrical utility industry is seen to be such a case, and the work was then redone using logarithms, to see if the linearity assumption was responsible for this result. Unsurprisingly, the coefficients change in relative magnitudes; this is due to a combination of the utility industry's high dividend yield and the nature of the logarithmic transformation. Friend and Puckett concede there is no reason to prefer one method versus the other, and leave the functional form issue at that.

Returning to the omitted-variable issue, Friend and Puckett first included the previous period's price as the firm-specific variable. As a result, the retained-earnings coefficients are greater than the dividend coefficients, the latter being negative in six of 10 instances. The multiple R-squared statistics are quite high but, by and large, the significance levels of the retained-earnings coefficients are not. Besides having very little economic rationale for the inclusion of a lagged price variable, the statistics leave sizable uncertainties as to the validity of this approach.

Recognizing that accounting numbers over the short run are subject to sizable measurement error, the authors normalized earnings over 10 years and then ran the regressions again without a firm-specific variable. This rendered all coefficients statistically significant at a 5% level, and the dividend coefficients were consistently higher than the retained-earnings coefficients. This suggests that the same conclusions and interpretation were offered by Gordon. Adding the normalized-earnings price ratio lagged one period, it was found that the intercept or constant terms get very large, as do the dividend coefficients relative to the retained-earnings coefficients, and the R-squared term for each regression is exceptionally high. The earnings/price coefficient was found to be highly negative; all these findings yield questionable results. In a separate analysis of the chemical industry using dividends and normalized earnings, and then further adding the normalized earnings/price ratios, the retained-earnings coefficient was seen to dominate the dividend coefficient. Again, though, the other coefficients were given, and certainly appear to merit some attention.

In summation, Friend and Puckett argue for longer-term measures for variables of accounting nature and earnings-to-price ratios as a sort of risk or firm-specific variable, in that it shows the rate at which the market capitalizes the firm's earnings. In using this variable, it should be recognized that the dependent variable is being used to explain itself. This tends to show the retained-earnings figure as important as or more important in valuation than dividends, thus supposedly invalidating previous results to the contrary. The real question appears to be which approach possesses the best economic grounding. We would like to think theory precedes the empiricism; and to pursue this, one must have an appropriate theory, a question to which Friend and Puckett do not address themselves.

Lee (1976) cited the Friend and Puckett evidence in attacking the issue of functional form, concentrating on the electric utility industry where the risk differential between firms is often seen to be negligible, thereby eliminating a large portion of the firm-specific effects. Using the generalized functional form developed by Box and Cox (1964), the linear and log-linear forms can be tested on a purely statistical basis, and the log-linear form can be tested against a non-linear form.

Quite interestingly, Lee found that the log-linear form was statistically superior to the linear-form model in explaining the dividend effect. The results of this comparison were essentially the same as in Friend and

Puckett's study. Using the linear form, 9 of the 10 years of data examined showed a stronger retained-earnings effect than that for dividends, while, in the log-linear trial, all 10 years showed stronger dividend effects. At this point, the only question remaining is whether either of these models accurately depicts the true functional form.

Using the true functional form from the generalized functional form method to compare the dividend and retained earnings effects, it was found that in only 4 years was there any difference between the two effects; this leads to the conclusion that all models developed in linear or log-linear form, and used to test this particular industry (and possibly other industries as well) are probably misspecified. This is a serious problem, in that the importance of dividends is muddied because the model is not correct. The true value of dividends can be inferred only if the model is correctly specified.

Part of the problem here is due to the nature of the industry, where high payouts are common and external financing is great and unaccounted for. These two factors serve to bias the dividend effect downward in the linear-form models.

The logarithmic-form models reduce the problem of weighting of regression coefficients due to size disparities amongst firms, a problem noticeably existent in the electric utility industry. However, it does have the disadvantage of being unable to cope with negative retained-earnings figures, a phenomenon that is a reality in the current environment.

These caveats to both methods of analysis should evoke more concern from empirical researchers in the future, since misspecification can have drastic effects on the conclusions reached.

17.8.4.2. *M&M empirical work*

M&M (1966) also studied the electric utility industry in depth, but with a different goal in mind. They sought to show the cost of capital in the industry and techniques suitable for that estimation, confronting in that discussion the issue of whether dividends have a role to play in the cost of capital. Since the cost of capital is tautologically the average investor's required rate-of-return before personal taxes, this issue is of great interest to us in determining dividend relevance.

Though the M&M analysis begins in a world of perfect certainty, this restrictive assumption is dropped before the dividend question ever enters into the picture. Assuming perfect capital markets, rational investors, and no tax differentials on income, M&M come to their well-known conclusion that dividend policy does not matter if the investment policy is known and is unaffected by dividend payout. Relaxing the tax and transaction-cost assumptions, they acknowledge that dividend policy can have an effect, though the precise degree of effect is unknown. Also, with the existence of the information effect of dividends, the coefficient attached to this variable will be biased upward since it is intended only to reflect the cash payment. Hence, without some adjustment to alleviate this bias, the dividend term should not be used in the cost-of-capital formulation.

It is not until they confront errors in measurement of expected earnings that M&M return to consider dividends. One way to attempt to obtain truer information on earnings than that provided by the accounting report is through the instrumental-variables approach, and it is here that the dividends enter as an instrumental variable with all their information as to management's expectation of long-run profits. A crucial assumption implicit in this procedure, which deserves and receives recognition from M&M, is that the instrumental variables should not be correlated with the error in measured earnings. M&M assume that this will create few problems for their purposes, or will be met well enough so that an approach such as this is viable.

In the actual procedure of the first-run regression on the instrumental variables, the dividend figure is the most important single factor in earnings. In fact, by adding it to a size, growth, debt, and preferred-stock model of the determinants of earnings, it increases the multiple correlations 1.5, 5.5, and 3.5 times over for the years 1954, 1956, and 1957, respectively. All dividend coefficients found were highly significant and were many times larger (around the order of 20 times) than the other mentioned factors, although they were not particularly stable over time.

Going on to compute the value of the unleveled firms using the newly computed earnings figures, size, and growth, the multiple correlation was virtually as high as those from the trial when measured accounting earnings was used. In both cases, the measured and computed earnings trials, the coefficient on earnings was highly significant and much larger than the size and growth coefficients. Upon further examination of their test M&M found large biases in the measured earnings trials, and left that case to rest. In recognition of the large indirect effect that dividends had in the computed-earnings trial, M&M chose to attempt the instrumental-variables transformation on the dividend figure itself and then attempt to observe the influence it has on valuation.

By itself and compared to the actual dividend figure when added in a simple linear model, dividends are found to have less (or negative) effects in the valuation process. While all the dividend coefficients are negative in the instrumental-variables approach, they are also insignificant, so that to include them in the valuation equation, or argue that they have a positive influence in the valuation process, would be incorrect. The only value that dividends possess in the context presented here is their information content, a conclusion totally in support of the assessment presented in their 1961 paper.

17.8.4.3. *CAPM approach*

Moving to the CAPM framework, we consider the tax versions of the CAPM and the implications found for dividend policy there. Brennan (1970), following his derivation for a CAPM with taxes, tested his model against the standard CAPM model to see if his in fact did yield more explanatory power. As Jensen (1972) shows, Eq. (17.21) can also be written as:

$$E(\tilde{R}_j) = T_2 R_f + \beta_j(E(\tilde{R}_m) - T_1 d_m - T_2 R_f) + T_1 d_j, \qquad (17.33)$$

where

$d_j = D_j/V_j$,
$d_m = D_m/V_m$,
$T_1 = (T_d - T_g)/(1 - T_g)$,
$T_2 = (1 - T_d)/(1 - T_g) = 1 - T_1$,
T_d = Average tax rate applicable to dividends,
T_g = Average tax rate applicable to capital gains.

By substituting the T_1 and T_2 terms into Eq. (17.33), the reader can verify the equivalence of Eqs. (17.21) and (17.30).

Using an instrumental-variables approach, Brennan sought to determine the values of T_1 and T_2. The reason for the instrumental-variables approach was the high degree of correlation between the security's dividend yield and its beta, the instrumental-variables technique being designed to reduce or eliminate the effects of such problems, and also serves to reduce the specification error normally involved in this type of estimation.

To confirm the results from the instrumental-variable approach, Brennan also performed cross-sectional regressions with coefficients on the beta and dividend variables. Almost identical results were obtained using the two different approaches.

From his tests, Brennan argues that the average effective tax rate on dividend income was approximately 63% with an effective tax rate on capital gains of about 5%, which appears to form a large differential in tax rates; but this spread was confirmed by the tests of others. With this evidence in hand, Brennan concludes that the tax effects he incorporated into the standard CAPM are indeed relevant and that his model fits the data for the years 1946–1965 better than the standard CAPM model, which showed lower variance-explained statistics for the various computative tests run.

In running their tests on the improved Brennan model, L&R depart from other empirical researchers in a number of different ways. They used a value-weighted index of all the securities included on the CRSP tapes as a market proxy; they used the monthly rate-of-return on high-grade commercial paper as the rate earned on a riskless asset for the first 20 years of the study (1931–1951) and the monthly return on treasury bills thereafter (1952–1971). Treasury bill rates were unacceptable for use before 1951 because of the Federal Reserve policy of pegging interest rates on government securities at low rates during the time of World War II, so as to minimize the interest burden on the government. This should have little effect on the results, since in his tests Brennan used the rate on 90-day bankers' acceptances as the riskless rate, with no apparent complications. Moving betas were also used, betas being determined by regressing the excess return of the security against the excess return on the market for the 60 months prior to the observation month.

Because there was a 60-month observation period requirement for beta computation and 1936 was the first year in which dividends gained taxable status, 1931 was the first year of observation of prices and was also the first year for which the testing regressions were run. Dividends were included in the return calculations for the various securities, but in a rather complicated manner designed to conform to the assumption that dividends were known at the beginning of each month. Non-recurring dividends not announced in a previous month were not included in the return computations, and those that were recurring and/or announced were computed in the return figure in the month prior to their going ex-dividend.

Analogous to the functional form problem discussed earlier, L&R employed three statistical techniques to estimate the parameters A, B, and C in the after-tax model shown again below:

$$R_{jt} - R_{ft} = A + B\beta_{jt} + C(d_{jt} - R_{ft}). \tag{17.34}$$

The techniques employed were ordinary least-squares, generalized least-squares, and maximum-likelihood estimators, the first two also being applied to provide comparative estimates for the two-factor CAPM of the form;

$$\tilde{R}_{it} - R_m = a_0 + a_1\beta_{it}, \tag{17.35}$$

tested previously by Black, Jensen, and Scholes (1972), and by Fama and MacBeth (1973).

Examining the results, it is striking to note that in the two-factor CAPM, the market-risk premium coefficient is significant at only relatively low levels of confidence. This was explained to be a result of bias and inconsistency in the OLS and GLS estimates, resulting themselves from measurement error in beta.

The Maximum Likelihood Estimation (MLE) technique is more consistent and is favored for that reason, and it also gives the highest t-statistic on the market-risk premium or wealth-risk premium variable, which supports the reasonable contention that most or all investors are risk-averse. The MLE procedure also gives high t-statistics for the excess dividend variable (although the OLS and GLS likewise show high levels of significance), which is consistent with the findings of Brennan just discussed. Also significant and positive is the intercept value, unlike the findings of many others, which could be due to binding margin constraints on a significant number of investors, or misspecification of the model with respect to the exclusion of higher moments of the return distribution, affecting the investor's utility function, or misspecification of the market portfolio.

Returning to the major point of interest of this model, the dividend effect, it was previously mentioned that the dividend variable was highly significant using all three estimation procedures. Also of interest is the finding that the MLE and GLE estimators possessed a standard error approximately 25% smaller than that of the OLS technique, which in itself suggests that previous and future studies could profit from the use of such procedures, or possibly even other estimation techniques, rather than resorting to the standard OLS techniques.

The interpretation of the coefficients on the excess-dividend variable 0.236 is quite straightforward: for every dollar of taxable dividend return, investors require an additional 23 or 24 cents in before-tax return.

Given the long time period over which these parameters were estimated, L&R questioned the stability of the C coefficient over the entire time span. Upon breaking the total time period into smaller subperiods, they found that, in fact, it was rather stable, this result being consistent with evidence on tax rate stability over time. More interestingly they questioned the stability of the C coefficient over the months preceding the dividend payment, dividends presumed to be paid on a quarterly basis. They found that C was not constant through months, its value being highest in the first month of each quarter, approximately 0.289, falling to 0.235 in the second month, and to 0.189 in the third month, the latter being the dividend-paying month. No evidence was found to support the hypothesis that there would be a reversal of the return pattern in non-dividend-paying months following the dividend month; thus the dividend effect appears to stand.

Finally, testing for clientele effects, along the lines of Elton and Gruber (1970), Litzenberger and Ramaswamy find that the excess dividend yield is a decreasing function of total yield, and that the implied tax rate in ex-dividend months falls by 0.069 for every 1% increase in yield. Thus it appears that dividends are not only important in the pricing of securities; they also lead to the formation of clienteles that do not appear to eliminate this phenomenon, all of which makes the modeling process incomplete at this point in time, and increasingly difficult. Lee and Chang (1984) used a generalized Error-Components Model approach to investigate the impacts of dividend policy on CAP and found that dividend policy is important in CAP.

17.9. Behavioral Considerations of Dividend Policy

17.9.1. *Partial Adjustment and Information Content Models*

M&M (1961) showed that dividends were not the only possible focus for valuation of a firm or its equity securities; but, as they found in their 1966 paper on cost of capital, there are other considerations in dividend policy, namely the information effects. To the extent that dividends convey information from the management of the firm to the actual owners, the dividend decision may be extremely important. This section attempts to describe the dividend policies of firms, seeking to uncover rational patterns. A number of long-standing theories as to how the dividend decision is made will be introduced, along with a recent synthesis of the two most elaborate theories. It should become readily apparent that a firm's dividend decision is not some haphazard or ad hoc decision. Firms pursue certain dividend policies for justifiably good reasons, such as the maximization of shareholder wealth subject to some (unspecified) uncertainty constraint.

Probably the most easily understood theory of dividend policy is simply termed the **residual theory of dividends**. As the name implies, dividends, when paid, more or less fall out of the system, since these are funds the firm has no immediate use for. Higgins (1972) supported the contention that dividends were, or should be, a residual payment, when he dispelled the notion that discount rates applicable to dividends would increase as their time to receipt lengthened, due to the added uncertainty induced by the widening of the probability distribution of expected returns. The contrary opinion had been formulated by Gordon (1973). Regardless of the intuitive appeal of the residual dividend theory, its validity or relevance is subject to question in light of the evidence that firms do manage their dividend payout. Primarily because this is so, we now leave the residual theory to consider two alternative explanations of the dividend behavior of firms, both of which have considerably more support on an empirical basis than does the residual theory.

A partial adjustment model of dividend behavior on the part of firms was investigated in some detail by Lintner (1956), as he studied the dividend patterns of 28 well-known, established companies. From his analysis, he concluded that the major portion of the dividend of a firm could be modeled as follows:

$$D^* = rE_t \tag{17.36}$$

and

$$D_t - D_{t-1} = a + b(D(*) - D_{t-1}) + u_t, \tag{17.37}$$

where

D^* = Firm's desired dividend payment;
F_t = Net income of the firm during period t;
r = Target payout ratio;
a = A constant relating to dividend growth;
b = Adjustment factor relating the previous period's dividend and the new desired level of dividends, where b is assumed to be less than one.

From this, we infer that firms set their dividends in accordance with the level of current earnings, and that the changes in dividends over time do not correspond exactly with the change in earnings in the immediate time period. An alternative explanation to the b coefficient being the average-speed-of-adjustment factor, we can interpret the quantity $(1 - b)$ as a safety factor that management observes by not increasing the dividend payment to levels where it cannot be maintained. Together the a and b coefficients can be used to test the hypothesis that management is more likely to increase dividends over time rather than cut them; this obviously contrasts with the major premise of the residual theory.

To eliminate the expectation terms and construct an empirically testable model, Eq. (17.36) is substituted into Eq. (17.37), yielding:

$$D_t - D_{t-1} = a + b(rE_t - D_{t-1}) + u_t, \tag{17.38}$$

which is expressed in difference form because the item of interest is changes in dividend levels and their cause, not the absolute levels themselves. Of the 28 companies followed by Lintner, 26 appeared to have specific predetermined values for r, the target payout ratio, and the vast majority did update their dividend policies annually. While it could be argued that the desired level of dividends depends not only on current earnings but also on expected future levels of earnings, the empirical evidence has borne this theory out [see Brittain (1978) and Fama and Babiak (1968)]. A survey by Harkins and Walsh (1971) found that financial executives are well aware of this factor when they make dividend decisions; this casts doubt on the Lintner model. However, with the partial adjustment coefficient b being included in the model, we essentially have a proxy for expected earnings; this supports the theoretical development of the partial adjustment model.

Following the lines of criticism of Lintner's work, we can specify an adaptive expectations model, where dividends are predetermined, based on estimates of earnings as shown below, with all variables as defined before, the E^* being expected rather than actual earnings:

$$D_t = rE^* + u_t. \tag{17.39}$$

In this light, the dividend is intended to convey information pertaining to management's expectations of earnings and profitability, something akin to a specification of M&M's hypothesis on the informational content of dividends.

Laub (1976) and Pettit (1972) have shown that dividend payments do convey information about future earnings expected by management and that changes in dividends are a result of changes in longer-run expectations. Pettit's 1972 paper examined the returns to investors following dividend announcements, using the CAPM as the equilibrium return-generation process. While it was not clear that investors could obtain abnormal returns on a risk-adjusted basis by buying securities with large deviations in dividends from historical levels, the market was shown to impound the information of these announcements rapidly, particularly so in the case of initial payments. From this, we are forced to the conclusion that the market which appears to be quite efficient, utilizes announcements of changes in dividend policy in the process of valuing a security. Though the dividend announcement may not give perfect information as to management's expectations, it is the best proxy available, and announcements of changes in dividend payments do appear to have informational content.

Returning to Eq. (17.36), we would like to find a way to deal with the expected-earnings figure in the current time period, so we assume:

$$E_t^* = bE_t + (1-b)E_{t-1}^*, \tag{17.40}$$

where b is again a coefficient of expectations, the proportion of the expectational error taken to be permanent. By specifying the transitory element, we now have an expression for expected or permanent level of earnings, partly based on current income, and partly based on the previous period's expected earnings, thus modifying previous expectations.

By substituting Eq. (17.39) into Eq. (17.40), multiplying both sides by $(1-b)$, and lagging by one time period, we obtain:

$$D_t - D_{t-1} = rbE_t - bD_{t-1} + u_t + u_{t-1}(1-b). \tag{17.41}$$

This closely resembles the partial adjustment model presented earlier, although the constant term denoting a reluctance to reduce dividends is missing, and the error term is specified differently. The b coefficient is a profit-expectations coefficient rather than a speed-of-adjustment coefficient, which is the major distinguishing factor of this model. By assumption, D_t^* is subject only to random disturbances given by the u_t in the adaptive expectations model. Due to the conceptual oversights of each model, it is hypothesized that a more general model embodying the essential components from each model should be constructed.

Recognition of this shortfall in each model was initially discussed in Brittain (1978), though his discussion centered around the determinants of the payout ratio rather than the dividend itself, and he did not conduct tests relating to the present controversy. Ang (1975) did test to determine the difference between the two alternative hypotheses of dividend behavior. Using spectral analysis, he argued that his results, derived from quarterly FTC–SEC reports of manufacturing companies, proved that the informational-content theory can be used to explain shorter-run dividend behavior, and that the partial-adjustment hypothesis can be used to explain longer-run dividend policy, both of which seem reasonable approximations. Oddly enough, though neither hypothesis was supported in an intermediate run, all of which reinforces the notion a more generalized model is needed.

17.9.2. *An Integration Model*

Djarraya and Lee (1980) followed the conceptual development of Waud (1966), in embodying the conceptual ingredients of both dividend-behavior rationales, and constructed a more general specification of dividend determination. In a long-run framework, it is expected that the desired level of dividends can be expressed as a percentage of expected earnings, neither variable being observable for practical purposes. Including the major arguments of the partial-adjustment and information-content theories, we can write the following three equations:

$$D^* = rE_t^*, \tag{17.42}$$

$$D_t - D_{t-1} = a + b_1(D^* - D_{t-1}) + u_t, \tag{17.43}$$

$$E_t^* - E_{t-1}^* = b_2(E_t - E_{t-1}^*), \tag{17.44}$$

which, when combined and simplified, were shown to yield:

$$\begin{aligned} D_t - D_{t-1} = {} & ab_2 + (1 - b_1 - b_2)D_{t-1} - (1 - b_2)(1 - b_1)D_{t-2} \\ & + rb_1b_2E_t - (1 - b_2)u_{t-1} + u_t. \end{aligned} \tag{17.45}$$

In performing empirical tests, many varied conclusions can be reached depending on the relevant outcomes. Those most important for the analysis here include:

(i) If the b_2 coefficient of expectations is equal to one, then the generalized model reduces to the simpler partial adjustment model.
(ii) If the speed-of-adjustment coefficient, b_1, equals one and the intercept a equals zero, the model reduces to the alternative simplified model, an adaptive-expectations model of earnings.
(iii) If the intercept term equals zero and the two b coefficients equal one, then dividend policy is actually a residual decision, much as Higgins suggested it should be; and
(iv) If all coefficients are significantly different from zero and/or one, then the two previously discussed simplified models are insufficient to describe corporate dividend policy, and the generalized model offers a much needed explanation.

As for the empirical tests, Djarraya (1980) has shown that the ordinary least-squares regression technique does not allow for the distinction between the b_1 and b_2 coefficients, Doran and Griffiths (1978) have shown that the OLS estimates of b_1 and b_2 are inconsistent. Therefore, the maximum-likelihood estimator techniques required to perform the empirical tests were used in conjunction with Marquardt's (1963) non-linear least-squares regression technique for all 80 industrial firms included in the study.

Using unadjusted quarterly data, it was found that the estimated target payout ratio was between 0 and 1, as expected, with the mean value being 0.43. Breaking the results into deciles, it was found that the relationship between desired DPS and EPS varied from 0.19 for the lowest 10% of the price-earnings ratios to a high of 0.72, on average, for the highest 10% of the price-earnings ratios. In 80% of the firms examined, this relationship was found to be statistically significant, which, roughly translated, implies that the expected or permanent earnings, expressed as a weighted average of the current and previous period's expected earnings, has a significant impact on the desired DPS payout. The a coefficient incorporated from the Lintner model was, somewhat surprisingly, not significantly different from zero in the case of 60% of the firms, and in the lowest two deciles, it was, on average, less than zero. Such evidence supports the suggestion of Fama and Babiak that it should be excluded. As a caveat to taking this suggestion as valid for all tests, it is necessary to realize that firms with higher price-earnings multiples consistently showed positive and statistically significant coefficients for this parameter estimate, and in examining those firms individually, the constant term should probably not be suppressed.

The other factor from the Lintner model, the speed-of-adjustment coefficient, was found to be significantly different from one, with a mean of 0.612; this reveals that dividends, on average, tend to gravitate toward their desired levels in slightly greater than half of 1 year. In greater than 70% of the sample, this coefficient was statistically significant, which should lead to cautious use of the adapted-expectations model by itself as a model of the dividend behavior of corporations.

Examining the coefficient of expectation, a result similar to that above was found, the mean of this estimated parameter being 0.16, where over 60% of the firms in the sample exhibited coefficients-of-expectation significantly different from zero. Again, as with the previous estimates, the higher the value of the P/E ratio, the higher the average level of significance of the coefficient. This systematic result may well come about because of the exclusion of outside influences not included in the model that have a natural dampening effect on P/E ratios; all these findings lend further credence to the generalized model.

In summary, it is reasonable to suggest that neither the partial-adjustment model of dividend behavior nor the adaptive-expectations model adequately explains the dividend behavior of firms. The results of Djarraya and Lee reveal the partial-adjustment and expectations coefficients are significantly smaller than one and greater than zero. In effect, these results confirm the suspicion that a more generalizable model of dividend behavior on the part of firms is necessary, in order to understand the true nature of the dividend decision.

17.9.3. *Optimal Payout Ratio and Optimal Growth Rate*

Lee *et al.* (2011) have examined the Optimal Payout ratio and its implications to dividend policy. They found dividend policy does matter and they conclude that flexibility hypothesis is most suitable for dividend policy decision. Chen *et al.* (2013) have used a Joint Optimization approach to investigate Sustainable Growth Rate, Optimal Growth Rate, and Optimal Payout Ratio. They found that there are optimal growth rate and optimal payout ratio.

17.10. Summary

In this chapter we have addressed the important issue of dividend policy theory, practice and empirical practice. Critical to the issue is whether to pay dividends. Do dividends give value to shareholders? If so, is there an optimal level of dividends? Do dividends increase the value of the firm?

According to the M&M argument, dividends are irrelevant in perfect markets. The introduction of real-world factors, such as taxes, transaction costs, and personal preferences, makes the answer to the question less definite. In some situations, high dividends seem appropriate and, in other scenarios, zero or low dividends seem preferable.

The clientele effect and the information content of dividends provide a framework for the analysis of the importance of dividends. Each consideration may help the analyst determine the value of dividends under a particular set of circumstances. Overall, however, theory can provide no universally applicable rule to guide managers' and shareholders' decisions about dividends. The best that can be said is that the dividend decision depends on specific circumstances.

We also examined many of the aspects of dividend policy from the relevance–irrelevance standpoint, and from multiple pricing–valuation frameworks. From the Gordon growth model, or classical valuation view, we found that dividend policy was not irrelevant, and that increasing the dividend payout would increase the value of the firm. Upon entering the world of M&M where some ideal conditions are imposed, we found that dividends were only one stream of benefits we could examine in deriving a value estimate. However, even in their own empirical work on those other benefit streams, M&M were forced to include dividends, if only for their information content.

Building on the Sharpe, Lintner, and Mossin CAPM derivations, Brennan showed that dividends would actually be detrimental to a firm's cost of capital as they impose a tax penalty on shareholders. While this new CAPM is useful, however, Brennan considered only the effects associated with the difference between the original income tax and the capital-gains tax. L&R extended Brennan's model by introducing income, margin, and borrowing constraints. Their empirical results are quite robust, and show that higher and lower dividends mean different things to different groups of investors.

Option-pricing theory was shown to make dividends a valuable commodity to investors due to the wealth-transfer issue. The theory (and the method) of dividend behavior also showed dividend forecasting to have positive value in financial management. In sum, we conclude that the dividend policy does generally matter, and it should be considered by financial managers in doing financial analysis and planning. Graham and Harvey (2001) surveyed 392 CFO's about cost of capital, capital budgeting, and capital structure. They found that the pecking-order, trade-off capital hypotheses, and Lintner (1956) Partial Adjustment Model have all been used to make their dividend payment decision.

Problem Set

1. Define the following terms:
   a. Declaration date.
   b. Record date.
   c. Ex-dividend date.
   d. Payment date.

2. What is a stock repurchase? By what methods can a firm repurchase shares? Explain why a stock repurchase can be beneficial to stockholders and to management.
3. Suppose XYZ Company's stock currently is selling for $100 and a two-for-one stock split is declared. What will happen to the price of the stock?
4. Briefly explain why a firm's dividend-payout record can be a source of information to the marketplace.
5. Explain the differences between a stock split and a stock dividend.
6. Evaluate the following statement: "When a stock goes ex-dividend, the price of the stock always falls by the amount of the dividend."
7. What are homemade dividends? How do M&M use homemade dividends?
8. What types of companies would be likely to pay little or no dividends? What companies would be likely to pay steady dividends?
9. Briefly explain why a company would choose to repurchase its own stock.
10. Briefly explain why a company might declare a stock split.
11. Suppose the Wagner Corporation has just declared a reverse 1-for-2 split of its stock. If the current price of the stock is $25, what will happen to the stock's price?
12. Explain what is meant by double taxation of dividends.
13. Why do corporations attempt to maintain a stable dividend policy? How do they accomplish this?
14. What is a DRIP? Why would a company institute a DRIP? Why would investors be interested in a DRIP?
15. What information is revealed in a dividend announcement?
16. Why are dividend decisions so important to a firm?
17. How does a firm's access to the capital markets affect its dividend policy?
18. Why would a smaller, fast-growing company be less likely to pay dividends than a larger company that is experiencing moderate growth?
19. Is there any difference between managers buying shares of their firm for themselves and the firm repurchasing its own shares?
20. In establishing a firm's dividend policy, should management consider its compensation (i.e., bonus due to earnings growth) or the need of the shareholders as the primary determinant of how much dividend to pay?
21. Briefly discuss the two competing views on the importance of dividend policy.

22. Why might some bond indentures place restrictions on dividend payments?
23. In the context of the clientele effect, explain what might stop a board of directors from making a major change in the firm's dividend policy to help finance attractive budgeting projects.
24. Kjetsaa Kat Krunchies, Inc., has announced that dividends will be paid on April 3 to holders of record on Friday, March 15.

    a. When is the ex-dividend date?
    b. If the record day is Wednesday, May 13, when is the ex-dividend date?
    c. If the record day is Monday, March 11, when is the ex-dividend date?

25. According to Gordon (1959), are dividends relevant in determining the value of the firm? Explain. How do M&M (1961) view the relevance of dividends? Discuss the four approaches to valuation suggested by them.
26. Discuss the empirical studies of CAPM with taxes and dividends. How can this finding be compared with Gordon (1959) and M&M (1961)?
27. In what ways do behavioral considerations affect a firm's dividend policy? Please use the partial adjustment model to answer this question.
28. How can option-pricing theory be used to determine the relevance of dividends to firm valuation? Explain.
29. How can dividend-policy analysis be used to help financial analysis and planning?
30. Does the presence of corporate taxes have any impact on the importance of a firm's dividend policy to its value? Explain.
31. If personal taxes are irrelevant to the dividend policy of the firm with respect to firm value, how much should the value of a firm's stock change on the ex-dividend date?
32. What is the general relationship between the rate of inflation and the firm's ability to pay dividends from free cash flow?
33. If a firm pays a constant dollar dividend, does this mean that there is no relationship between dividends and earnings? Explain.
34. Use the annual DPS, EPS, and PPS data from Yahoo Finance for J&J, Merck, P&G, and IBM during 1980–2007 to (1) analyze the dividend-earning relationship, (2) to analyze dividend yield-earnings yield relationship, and (3) to forecast dividend payment for all four companies.
35. Use Table 17.2, explain why the payout ratio for J&J is much higher in 1992 than it is for other years.

36. Use the annual DPS, EPS and PPS data of J&J from Yahoo Finance during 1980–2007 to analyze the following:

    a. The dividend-earnings relationship.
    b. The dividend yield-earnings yield relationship.
    c. The DPS, EPS, and PPS.

37. Jennett, Ltd. is paying a dividend with a date of record of April 5, 1988.

    a. If investor A sells the stock to investor B on April 5, 1988, which one is entitled to the dividend?
    b. If investor A sells the stock to investor B on April 1, 1988, which one is entitled to the dividend?
    c. If investor A sells the stock to investor B on March 31, 1988, which one is entitled to the dividend?

38. Tarnell Corporation has the following equity

Common stock (1,000,000 shares at $4)	$4,000,000
Paid in capital	$3,000,000
Retained earnings	$8,000,000
Total net worth	$15,000,000

The current market price of the stock is $15.00.

a. If the company declares a 2-for-l stock split;

    (1) How would the above equity accounts appear?
    (2) What would the EPS be before and after the stock split?

b. If the company pays a 10% stock dividend:

    i. How would Tarnell's equity accounts appear?
    ii. What would the EPS be both before and after the stock dividend?

39. Syntas Systems follows a residual theory of dividends. For the coming year, Syntas has $400,000 in new capital expenditures with rates-of-return above the 12% required by the company's investors. There are currently 100,000 shares outstanding.

    a. If the company currently has $300,000 in internal equity and uses no debt financing, what will dividends per share be?
    b. If the company currently has $500,000 in internal equity and uses no debt financing, what will dividends per share be?

c. Explain the argument against the residual theory concerning investors desire for cur rent income.

40. Reegan's Peanut Corporation has a capital structure consisting of 50% debt and 50% equity. Earnings available to common stockholders (net income) and capital expenditure projections for the next 3 years are given as follows:

Year	Net Income ($)	Capital Requirements ($)
1	500,000	800,000
2	600,000	600,000
3	400,000	700,000

Find the amount of debt, external equity, and total dividends in each year if:

a. The company follows the residual theory of dividends.
b. The company follows a constant payout ratio of 30%.
c. Why is a stable dollar dividend considered by many to result in a higher value than either of the above policies?

41. DPS D&G Corporation maintains a constant payout ratio of 25%. If earnings are $3 per share, what will be D&G's DPS?
42. Payout Ratio A company has just paid a dividend of $4 per share. If earnings are $5 per share, what is the payout ratio?
43. DPS Devito Corporation maintains a constant payout ratio of 45%. If earnings are $8 per share, what will be Devito's DPS?
44. Retention Rate and DPS Lockwood Industries maintains a constant retention rate of 35%. If earnings are $4 per share, what will be Lockwood's DPS?
45. Stock Split The LFN Corporation currently has 1-million shares outstanding with par value of $25. Suppose the company declares a 5-for-1 split.

a. How many shares will be outstanding?
b. What will the new par value be?

46. Stock Dividend Use the information in the "Before Dividend" section of Table 16.2 to construct a new statement after an 8% stock dividend.
47. Stock Splits Use the information in the "Before Split" section of Table 16.3 to construct a new statement for a 5-for-1 stock split.

48. Ex-dividend Price with Tax Miller, Inc., has declared a \$3.00 per share dividend. Miller stock sells for \$55 per share and is about to go ex-dividend. Use Equations 16.2 and 16.2a to answer the following questions:

a. If $T_p = T_g = 0$, what is the ex-dividend price?
b. If $T_p = T_g = 30\%$, what is the ex-dividend price?

If $T_p = 30\%$ and $T_g = 20\%$, what is the ex-dividend price?

49. Stocks Split Suppose ABC Company's stock currently is selling for \$75 per share and a 3-for-2 stock split is declared. What will be the new price of ABC's stock?

Since a 3-for-2 split implies that every two shares will become 3 shares, the new price of ABC Company's stock will be:

$$\$75 \times \frac{2}{3} = \$50.$$

50. Payout Ratio and Ex-dividend Price A company has just paid a dividend of \$2 per share for its stock, which has a price of \$98 per share. If earnings are \$6 per share, what is the payout ratio? What is the ex-dividend stock price if the tax effect is negligible?

$$\text{Payout ratio} = \frac{\text{Dividends per share}}{\text{Earnings per share}}$$

$$= \frac{\$2}{\$6} = \frac{1}{3}, \quad \text{or } 33.3\%$$

The ex-dividend price is \$98 – \$2 = \$96.

References for Chapter 17

Ang, JS (1975). Dividend policy: Informational content or partial adjustment? *Review of Economics and Statistics*, 57, 65–70.

Bhattacharya, S (1979). Imperfect information, dividend policy, and the bird-in-the-hand fallacy. *The Bell Journal of Economics*, 10, 259–276.

Black, F (1976). The Dividend Puzzle. *Journal of Portfolio Management*, 2, 5–8.

Black, F, M Jensen, and M Scholes (1972). The capital-asset pricing model: Some empirical tests. In *Studies in the Theory of Capital Markets*, M. Jensen (eds.), New York: Praeger, 79–124.

Box, GEP and DR Cox (1964). An analysis of transformations. *Journal of Royal Statistical Society, Series B (Methodological)*, 26(2), 211–252.

Brennan, M (1970). Taxes, market valuation, and corporate financial policy. *National Tax Journal*, 417–427.

Brittain, JA (1978). *Corporate Dividend Policy.* Washington, D.C.: Brookings Institute.

Chen, H-Y, MC Gupta, AC Lee, and CF Lee (2013). Sustainable growth rate, optimal growth rate, and optimal payout ratio: A joint optimization approach. *Journal of Banking & Finance*, 37, 1205–1222.

Daniels, K, T Hsin, and CF Lee (1997). The information content of dividend hypothesis: A permanent income approach. *International Review of Economics and Finance*, 6, 77–86.

DeAngelo, H and L DeAngelo (1990). Dividend policy and financial distress: An empirical investigation of troubled NYSE firms. *Journal of Finance*, 45, 1415–1431.

DeAngelo, H and L DeAngelo (2006). The irrelevance of the MM dividend irrelevance theorem. *Journal of Financial Economics*, 79, 293–315.

Djarraya, M (1980). Behavior models of dividend policy and implications to financial management, Dissertation, The University of Illinois at Urbana-Champaign.

Doran, HE and WE Griffiths (1978). Inconsistency of the OLS estimator of the partial-adjustment-adaptive-expectations model. *Journal of Econometrics*, 7, 133–146.

Elton, J. Elton and Gruber, Martin J (1970). Marginal stockholder tax rates and the clientele effect. *The Review of Economics and Statistics*, 52(1), 68–74.

Fama, EF and H Babiak (1968). Dividend policy: An empirical model. *Journal of American Statistical Association*, 63, 1132–1161.

Fama, EF and ID Macbeth (1973). Risk, return, and equilibrium: Empirical tests. *Journal of Political Economy*, 81, 607–636.

Friend, I and ME Puckett (1964). Dividends and stock prices. *American Economic Review*, 54, 656–682.

Gordon, M (1962). The savings investment and valuation of a corporation. *Review of Economics and Statistics*, 44, 37–51.

Gordon, MJ (1988). Why corporations pay dividends. *Studies in Banking and Finance*, 5, 77–96.

Gordon, MJ (1959). Dividends, earnings, and stock prices. *Review of Economics and Statistics*, 41, 99–105.

Gordon, MJ (1963). Optimal investment and financing policy. *Journal of Finance*, 18, 264–272.

Graham, JR and CR Harvey (2001). The theory and practice of corporate finance: Evidence from the field. *Journal of Financial Economics*, 60(2–3), 187–243.

Gupta, MC, AC Lee, and CF Lee (2007). Effectiveness of dividend policy under the capital asset pricing model: A dynamic analysis. *Working Paper*, Rutgers University.

Han, D (1985). Dividend policy under the condition of capital market and signaling equilibria: Theory and evidence. Unpublished Doctoral Dissertation, University of Illinois at Urbana-Champaign.

Harkins, EP and FJ Walsh (1971). Dividend policies and practices. New York: The Conference Board.

Higgins, RC (1972). The corporate dividend saving decisions. *Journal of Financial and Quantitative Analysis*, 7, 1531–1538.

Jensen, MC (1972). Capital markets: Theory and evidence. *Bell Journal of Economics and Management Science*, 3, 357–398.

Kao, C, CF Lee, and C Wu (1991). Rational expectations and corporate dividend policy. *Review of Quantitative Finance and Accounting*, 1, 331–348.

Lambrecht, BM and SC Myers (2012). A Litner model of payout and managerial rents. *The Journal of Finance*, 67, 1761–1810.

Laub, PM (1976). On the informational content of dividends. *Journal of Business*, 49(1), 73–80.

Lee, CF, C Wu, and D Hang (1993). Dividend policy under conditions of capital markets and signaling equilibrium. *Review of Quantitative Finance and Accounting*, 3, 47–59.

Lee, CF, MC Gupta, H-Y Chen, and AC Lee (2011). Optimal payout ratio under uncertainty and the flexibility hypothesis: Theory and empirical evidence. *Journal of Corporate Finance*, 17(3), 483–501.

Lee, CF, T Liaw, and C Wu (1992). Forecasting accuracy of alternative dividend models. *International Review of Economics and Finance*, 261–270.

Lee, CF and WJ Primeaux Jr (1991). Current vs. permanent dividend payment behavior model: Methods and Applications. *Advances in Quantitative Analysis of Finance and Accounting*, I, 109–130.

Lee, CF, DH Wort, and D Han (1987). The relationship between dividend yield and earnings yield and its implication for forecasting. *Advances in Financial Planning and Forecasting*, 2, 155–178.

Lee, CF and RH Gilmore (1986). Empirical tests of Granger proposition on dividend controversy. *Review of Economics and Statistics*, 68, 351–355.

Lee, CF and WJ Primeaux Jr. (1985). Relative importance of current vs. permanent income for dividend payment decision in the electric utility industry. *Journal of Behavior Economics*, 14, 83–97.

Lee, CF and S Forbes (1982). Income measures, ownership, capacity ratios and dividend decision of the non-life insurance industry: Some empirical evidence. *Journal of Risk and Insurance*, 49, 269–289.

Lee, CF and SW Forbes (1980). Dividend policy, equity value, and cost of capital estimates for the property and liability insurance industry. *Journal of Risk and Insurance*, 47, 205–222.

Lee, CF and MC Gupta (1977). An inter-temporal approach to the optimization of dividend with pre-determined investment: A further comment. *Journal of Finance*, 32, 1348–1353.

Lee, CF (1976). Functional form and the dividend effect in the electric utility industry. *Journal of Finance*, 31, 1481–1486.

Lee, CF and HS Chang (1984). On dividend policy and capital market theory: A generalized error components model approach. *Journal of Business Research*, 14, 505–516.

Lee, CF and AC Lee (2006). *Encyclopedia of Finance*. New York: Springer.

Lee, CF and WJ Primeaux, Jr. (1991). Current vs. permanent dividend payments behavioral model: Methods and application. *Advances in Quantitative Analysis of Finance and Accounting*, I.

Lee, CF, M Djarraya, and C Wu (1987). A further empirical investigation of the dividend adjustment process. *Journal of Econometrics*, 267–285.
Lee, CF, MC Gupta, and AC Lee (2007). Effectiveness of dividend policy under the capital asset pricing model: A dynamic analysis. *Working Paper*, Rutgers University.
Lintner, J (1956). Distribution of income of corporations. *American Economic Review* 46, 97–113.
Litzenberger, RH and K Ramaswamy (1979). The effect of personal taxes and dividends on capital-asset prices: Theory and empirical evidence. *Journal of Financial Economics*, 163–195.
Marquardt, D (1963). An algorithm for least-squares estimation of nonlinear parameters. *Journal of SIAM*, 2, 431–441.
Miller, MH and F Modigliani (1961). Dividend policy growth and the valuation of shares. *Journal of Business*, 34, 411–433.
Miller, M and F Modigliani (1966). Some estimates of the cost of capital to the electric utility industry. *American Economic Review*, 334–391.
Miller, MH and MS Scholes (1982). Dividends and taxes: Some empirical evidence. *Journal of Political Economy*, 96, 334–391.
Mossin, J (1966). Equilibrium in a capital-asset market. *Econometrica*, 768–783.
Petit, R (1972). Dividend announcements, security performance, and capital-market efficiency. *The Journal of Finance*, 993–1007.
Rappaport, A (1981). Inflation accounting and corporate dividends. *Financial Executive*, 49, 20–22.
Sharpe, WF (1964). Capital-asset prices: A theory of market equilibrium under conditions of risk. *Journal of Finance*, 19, 425–442.
Soter, D (1979). The dividend controversy — what it means for corporate policy. *Financial Executive*, 47, 38–43.
Waud, RN (1966). Small-sample bias due to misspecification in the "Partial Adjustment" and "Adaptive Expectations" models. *Journal of the American Statistical Association*, 61, 1130–1152.

Project IV

Cost of Capital, Capital Structure, and Dividend Policy for J&J, Inc.

1. Using J&J's growth rate of DPS and dividend yield, which were obtained in Project II, part 4, calculate the cost of equity.
2. Use the CAPM model to estimate the cost of equity for J&J; use the beta estimate obtained in Project III or the beta from the *Value Line Investment Survey.*
3. In 1995, the debt-to-equity ratio for J&J was: D/E=8,828/9045=.98. Using this information and the beta estimate obtained in Project III (or from *Vale Line*), calculate the unlevered beta for J&J.

4. Use J&J's 1995 annual report to discuss J&J's future rental and lease commitments.
5. Using J&J's DPS and EPS data listed in the following table, discuss the dividend policy of this company.

DPS & EPS for J&J

	1995	1994	1993	1992	1991	1990	1989
EPS	3.72	3.12	2.74	1.56	2.19	1.72	1.62
DPS	1.28	1.13	1.01	0.89	0.77	0.66	0.56
	1988	1987	1986	1985	1984	1983	1982
EPS	1.43	1.21	0.46	0.84	0.69	0.64	0.63
DPS	0.48	0.40	0.34	0.32	0.29	0.27	0.24

6. What is J&J's stock repurchase policy?

Chapter 18

Interaction of Financing, Investment, and Dividend Policies

18.1. Introduction

The purpose of this chapter is to discuss the three-way interaction between investment, financing, and dividend decisions. As was shown in previous chapters, there does exist a set of ideal conditions under which there will be no interaction effects between the areas of concern. However, the ideal conditions imposed by academicians to analyze the effects dividend and financing policy have on the investment decision and the value of the firm are not realistic, when one considers financial management in the real world. Thus, an overview of the interactions of financing, investment, and dividend decisions is important for those concerned with financial analysis and planning.

This chapter sequentially addresses the three interaction effects. In Section 18.2, the relation between investment and dividend policy is explored through a discussion of internal-versus-external financing, with the emphasis on the use of retained earnings as a substitute for new equity, or vice versa. The interaction between corporate financing and dividend policies will be covered in Section 18.3, where default risk on debt is recognized. Then in Section 18.4, the interaction between investment and financing policy is discussed; the role of the financing mix in analyzing investment opportunities will receive detailed treatment. Again, the recognition of risky debt will be allowed, so as to lend further practicality to the analysis. The recognition of financing and investment effects are covered in Section 18.5, where capital-budgeting techniques are reviewed and analyzed with regard to their treatment of the financing mix. In this section, several numerical comparisons are offered, to emphasize that the differences in the techniques are non-trivial. Section 18.6 will incorporate a number of current issues by exploring the topic of optimal capital structure, which may be the single most important issue in financial planning. Section 18.7 will discuss implication of different policies on systematic risk determination. Summary and concluding remarks are offered in Section 18.8.

18.2. Investment and Dividend Interactions: The Internal-Versus-External Financing Decision

Internal financing consists primarily of retained earnings and depreciation expense, while external financing is comprised of new equity and new debt, both long- and short-term. Decisions on the appropriate mix of these two sources for a firm are likely to affect both the payout ratio and the capital structure of the firm, and this in turn will generally affect its market value. In this section, an overview of internal and external financing is provided, with the discussion culminating in a summary of the impacts that earnings retention or earnings payout (with or without supplemental financing from external sources) can have on a firm's value and on planning and forecasting. These concerns will be outlined in further detail in later chapters, and also will play an important role in total financial management.

18.2.1. *Internal Financing*

Changes in equity accounts between balance-sheet dates are generally reported in the statement of retained earnings. Retained earnings are most often the major internal source of funds made available for investment by a firm. The cost of these retained earnings is generally less than the cost associated with raising capital through new common-stock issues. It follows that retained earnings, rather than new equity, should be used to finance further investment if equity is to be used and the dividend policy (dividends paid from retained earnings) is not seen to matter. The availability of retained earnings is then determined by the firm's profitability and the payout ratio, the latter being indicative of dividend of dividend policy. Thus we find that the decision to raise funds externally may be dependent on dividend policy, which in turn may affect investment decisions.

The payout ratios indicated in Table 18.1 show that, on average, firms in the S&P 500 retain more than 50% of their earnings after 1971 rather than pay them out in dividends. This is done because of the investment opportunities available for a firm, and indicates that retained earnings are a major source of funds for a firm.

Table 18.1. Payout ratio — composite for 500 firms.

1962	0.580	1974	0.405	1986	0.343	1998	0.234
1963	0.567	1975	0.462	1987	0.559	1999	0.435
1964	0.549	1976	0.409	1988	0.887	2000	0.299
1965	0.524	1977	0.429	1989	0.538	2001	0.383
1966	0.517	1978	0.411	1990	0.439	2002	0.040
1967	0.548	1979	0.380	1991	0.418	2003	0.259
1968	0.533	1980	0.416	1992	0.137	2004	0.311
1969	0.547	1981	0.435	1993	0.852	2005	0.282
1970	0.612	1982	0.422	1994	0.340	2006	0.301
1971	0.539	1983	0.399	1995	0.346		
1972	0.491	1984	0.626	1996	0.327		
1973	0.414	1985	0.525	1997	0.774		

18.2.2. *External Financing*

External financing usually takes one of two forms, debt financing or equity financing. We leave the debt-versus-equity question to subsequent sections, and here directly confront only the decision whether to utilize retained earnings or new common stock to finance the firm.

We have previously shown that the market value of the firm is unaffected by such factors if dividend policy and capital structure are irrelevant. It should also be clear that dividend policy and capital structure can affect market values. Therefore, the consideration of an optimal internal–external financing combination is important in the field of financial management. This optimal combination is a function of the payout ratio, the debt-to-equity ratio, and the interaction between these two decision variables. From this, it can be shown (and this will be the topic of discussion in the following paragraphs) that different combinations of internal and external financing will have different effects on the growth rate of earnings per share (EPS), of dividends per share, and, presumably, of the share price itself.

Higgins (1977) considered the amount of growth a firm could maintain if it was subject to an external equity constraint and sought to maintain certain debt and payout ratios. He was able to show the sustainable growth rate in sales, S^*, to be:

$$S^* = \frac{p(1-d)(1+L)}{t - p(1-d)(1+L)} = \frac{(rr)(ROE)}{1-(rr)(ROE)}, \tag{18.1}$$

where

$p =$ Profit margin on sales,
$d =$ Dividend payout ratio,

L = Debt-to-equity ratio,
t = Total asset-to-sales ratio,
rr = Retention Rate,
ROE = Return on Equity.

Higgins (1977) used 1974 U.S. manufacturing firms' composite financial statement data as an example to calculate $S*$. Using the figures $p = 5.5\%$, $d = 33\%$, $L = 88\%$ and $t = 73\%$, he obtained:

$$S^* = \frac{(0.055)(1 - 0.33)(1 + 0.88)}{0.73 - (0.055)(1 - 0.33)(1 + 0.88)} = 10.5\%.$$

Using this method, we can calculate sustainable growth rate in sales for financial analysts and planning models.

From this, we can see that a firm with many valuable investment opportunities may be forced to forego some of these opportunities due to capital constraints, and the value of the firm will not be maximized as it could have been. Dividend and capital structure decisions relate directly to investment decisions. While it may not be reasonable to assume that the firm could not issue new equity, the question is at what cost it can be raised under such a constraint.

In an even more practical vein, Higgins also incorporated inflation into his model, acknowledging the fact that most depreciation methods that serve to make the depreciation account a source of funds are founded on historical costs and not the replacement values the firm must pay to sustain operations at their current level. Introducing the new variables defined below, it is possible to define sustainable growth in real and nominal terms, the former being the item of interest here.

Let,

c = Nominal current assets to nominal sales,
f = Nominal fixed assets to real sales,
j = Inflation rate.

So real sustainable growth S_r^* is

$$S_r^* = \frac{(1 + j)p(1 - d)(1 + L) - jc}{(1 + j)c + f - (1 + j)p(1 - d)(1 + L)}. \tag{18.2}$$

Using figures from the manufacturing sector and an inflation rate of 10% which at the time of writing was approximately the actual inflation rate then prevailing, it was found that real sustainable growth was only a third of that of the nominal figure; this serves to further emphasize the importance of the interaction between dividend policy and investment decisions, since the former acts as a constraint on the latter. Higgins' (1977) paper has recently been generalized by Johnson (1981) and Higgins (1981).

The usual caveat associated with the dividend-irrelevance proposition is that investment policy is unaffected; i.e., new equity is issued to replace those retained earnings that are paid out. Here we emphasize new equity with the intent of avoiding financing-policy questions. Knowing that the flotation costs involved with new issues could be avoided by employing retained earnings, the effect such a strategy has on firm value is largely an empirical question. Any such tests directed toward this issue must also recognize that there may be a preference for dividends that may dominate or mitigate the flotation-cost effects. With these factors in mind, Van Horne and McDonald (1971) ran cross-sectional regressions on samples of utility stocks and electronics manufacturers to see whether dividend payouts and the rates of new issues of common stocks had significant effects on price–earnings ratios. The utility industry results indicate that, at the lower end of the new-equity issue spectrum, the dividend-preference effect overshadowed the flotation-cost effect, a result that appeared to shift in direction when higher levels of new equity financing were considered. Further analysis into the dividend-preference question has been performed by Litzenberger and Ramaswamy (1979). Using a generalized capital–asset–pricing model, they examined this trade-off between dividend preference and tax effects, all in an effort to justify the contention of an optimal dividend policy. The results presented by Van Horne and McDonald were admittedly tentative (especially since the electronics industry sample yielded few corroborating results), and most of the t-statistics associated with the utility sample new-issue coefficients were quite low. The strongest statement that could be made following this analysis is that there appears to be little detrimental effect on firm valuation from following a strategy of maintaining a high payout rate and financing further investment with new-equity issues.

18.3. Interactions between Dividend and Financing Policies

If we were able to hold the capital structure of firms constant, then we would be able to determine the advantage or disadvantage of internal financing relative to external financing. Van Horne and McDonald, as briefly mentioned before, were able to empirically test for the effects created by either policy, providing the substance for a major part of the following discussion. If we were to go into more depth and specifically consider firms that issue risky debt while maintaining shareholder's limited-liability status, and still keeping to the chosen internal or external equity plan, then the interactions between financing and investment decisions can affect the relative positions of stock and bondholders. Black (1976) argued that a possible strategy a firm could follow to transfer economic resources from bondholders to stockholders is to pay as generous dividends as possible. In this way the internal–external financing plan is predetermined, since paying large dividends jeopardizes the bondholders' position as assets are siphoned away from the firm, all to the gain of the shareholders.

In this section, the interactions between dividend and financing policy will be analyzed in terms of (1) cost of equity capital, and (2) the default-risk viewpoint of debt.

18.3.1. *Cost of Equity Capital and Dividend Policy*[1]

Van Horne and McDonald (1971) chose to develop a cross-sectional model to test for the significance of dividend payouts in the valuation process in the electric utility industry. The use of the electric utility industry proved to be operationally less difficult than other industries because it was desired to hold interfirm differences constant, and independent variable selection to this end was relatively straightforward. Since the authors were interested in capitalization rates, year-end P/E ratios were selected to be the dependent variables. This value was thought to be a function of three variables — growth in assets, dividend payout, and financial risk. The latter variable is considered sufficient for this sample due to the homogeneity of the other aspects of the included firm's risks. The model can be written out and more carefully defined by the following;

$$P/E = a_0 + a_1 g + a_2 p + a_3 R + u, \tag{18.3}$$

where

g = Compound growth of assets over eight previous years;
p = Dividend payout ratio on an annual basis;
Lev = Interest charges/[operating revenues − operating expenses];
u = Error term.

While the growth and risk factors do not correspond exactly to what most capital-market theory tells us is relevant, research with respect to this particular industry lends credence to these variables as defined here (see Malkiel (1970)).

Upon regressing the data for the 86 companies included in the sample, all three independent variables are found to be statistically significant. Of the 86 firms, all of which paid dividends, 37 firms also had new equity issues. Testing to see whether the 37 firms that issued new equity came from the same population as those that did not raise new equity, the researchers found no essential difference. Since we know there are non-trivial flotation costs associated with the issuance of new equity, the finding of no difference between the sub samples implies one of two things: Either the costs associated with new issues are relatively too small compared to the total costs of the firm to be detected (despite their large absolute size, or size relative to the new issue by itself), or a net preference for dividends by holders of electric utility stocks exists which acts to offset the aforementioned expenses.

The main thrust of this paper was to assess the impact of new equity flotation costs on firm value. With the number of firms issuing new equity, Van Horne and McDonald were able to calculate new-issue ratios — that is, new issues/total shares outstanding at year-end — and separate these firms into four groups, leaving those firms issuing new equity in a separate classification, as indicated in the upper portion of Table 18.2. Adding dummy variables to Eq. (18.3), the effect of new issue rates could be analyzed:

$$P/E = a_0 + a_1(g) + a_2 p + a_3(Lev) + a_4(F_1) + a_5(F_2) + a_6(F_3) + a_7(F_4). \quad (18.4)$$

Table 18.2. New-issue ratios of electric utility firms.

	F dummy variable grouping				
	A	B	C	D	E
New-issue ratio interval	0	0.001–0.05	0.05–0.1	0.1–0.15	0.15 and up
Number of firms in interval	49	16	11	6	4
Mean dividend payout ratio	0.681	0.679	0.678	0.703	0.728
Dummy variable coefficient	1.86	3.23	1.26	0.89	N.A.
Dummy variable					
Dummy variable t-statistic	(1.33)	(2.25)	(0.84)	(0.51)	(N.A.)

From Van Horne and McDonald (1971). Reprinted by permission.

where

g = Compound growth rate,
Lev = Financial risk measured by times interest earned, and
F_1, F_2, F_3, F_4 = Dummy variables representing levels of new equity financing.

We would expect negative coefficients on the dummy variables if the flotation costs were to be relevant, but in fact all coefficients were positive, though only one was significant (possibly due to small sample size and small relative differences). Empirical results are indicated in the lower portion of Table 18.2. However, by replacing the dummy variable of Group E for any one of the four dummy variables discussed above, Van Horne and McDonald found that the estimate of its coefficient is negative.

One question pertaining to the figures presented here stems from the interpretation of the significance of the dummy variables. As it turns out, the class B dummy-variable coefficient is greater than the class A coefficient, supposedly because of a preference for dividend payout, while actually that payout was lower in class B. The question is whether the dummy that is intended to substantiate the dividend-preference claim through the new-issue ratio actually tells us that investors instead attach a higher value to higher earnings retention. The finding of higher P/E ratios resulting from earnings retention would be consistent with the Litzenberger–Ramaswamy framework cited earlier, and the new-issue effect is somewhat confounded with the dividend effect.

From the data, we can see that the coefficients did decrease as the new-issue ratios increased, though they were not significant, and, not surprisingly, new-issue ratios were rather highly negatively correlated with dividend payout ratios. From this we can say, although with some hesitation, that external equity appears to be a more costly alternative compared to internal financing when pushed to rather extreme limits. Over more moderate ranges, or those more closely aligned with the industry averages, this claim cannot be made with the same degree of certainty, since we cannot be certain that the payout ratio does not have a positive influence on share price, and therefore an inverse relationship to the cost of equity capital.

18.3.2. *Default Risk and Dividend Policy*

With the development of the Option-Pricing Model, Black and Scholes (1973) have made available a new method of valuing corporate liabilities or claims on the firm. Chen (1978) has reviewed some recent developments in the theory of risky debt, and examines in a more systematic fashion the determinants of the cost of debt capital. Both Resek (1970) and Hellwig (1981) have shown that the Modigliani and Miller (1958, 1963) arbitrage process that renders capital structure irrelevant is generally invalidated if the debt under consideration is risky and the shareholders enjoy limited liability. From this and the 1963 M&M article, we can show that there do exist optimal structures for firms under the more realistic conditions mentioned above.

In the option-pricing framework the two claimants of the firm, the debt holders and the equity holders, are easily seen to have conflicting interests; thus one group's claim can only be put forth at the expense of the other party. The assumption that the total firm value is unchanged is utilized to highlight the wealth-transfer effects, but, as we see in the following section, that need not be the case. It is now necessary to find a way to value corporate debt when default risk is introduced. If the total value of the firm is known or given (this value should be reasonably well known or approximated prior to debt valuation since the former is an upper bound on the latter), then once the debt value is established the total equity value falls out as the residual. It is also required that we know how to perform the transfer of wealth (since the stated goal of corporate finance is to maximize the shareholders' wealth), and learn of any possible consequences that could result from such attempts.

Merton (1974) sought to find the value of risky corporate debt, assuming that the term structure of riskless interest rates was flat and known with certainty. This was an indirect goal, since the true emphasis lay in finding a way to value the equity of the firm as a continuous option. The further assumption of consol-type debt was also employed, in an attempt to avoid the transactions-cost arguments involved with rolling over debt at maturity. Invoking Modigliani and Miller's Proposition I (M&M, 1958) and allowing for risky debt, we find the value of the stock to be the difference between the value of the firm as a whole and the value of the total debt financing employed to support that whole. Explicitly,

$$S = V - \frac{C}{r}(1 - L), \tag{18.5}$$

where

$S =$ Total value of the firm's stock,
$V =$ Total firm value,

C = Constant coupon payment on the perpetual bonds,
r = Riskless rate of interest,
L = A complicated risk factor associated with possible default on the required coupon payment.

The last term of Eq. (18.5) is more often represented by B, the value of the total debt claims outstanding against the firm, stated in a certainty-equivalent form. It should be apparent from this equation that by introducing a greater probability of default on the debt while maintaining firm value, the equity holders gain at the expense of the bondholders.

Rendleman (1978) took Merton's model and adapted it to allow for the tax deductibility of interest charges. As in the Merton article, debt is assumed to be of perpetual type, consols — a justifiable assumption since most firms roll over their debt obligations at maturity. The tax benefit introduced is assumed to be always available to the firm. In instances where the interest expense is greater than earnings before taxes, the carryback provision of the tax code is used to obtain a refund for the amount of the previously unused tax shield and, in the event the 3-year carryback provision is not sufficient to make use of the tax shield, Rendleman suggests that a firm could sell that advantage to another firm by means of a merger or an acquisition, when the other firm involved could use the tax benefit. Thus the coupon (net) to be paid each time period is given by $C(1-T)$.

At first glance, it is apparent that the equity holders gain from this revision, as they are alleged to in the 1963 tax-corrected model of M&M. But something else is at work as well: Since the firm is subject to a lower debt-service requirement, it can build a larger asset base, which serves to act as insurance in the case of default probabilities owing to the small net coupon payment. In short, the risk premium associated with debt is reduced and the value of the stock, given in Eq. (18.5) can be rewritten as below:

$$S = V - \frac{C(1-T)}{r}(1-L^*), \tag{18.6}$$

where all the variables are as defined before and L^* is less than the L given before because of the lessened default risk.

It has been argued above that the bondholders benefit when interest is tax-deductible, excluding the possibility here that an overzealous attempt to lever the firm is quickly undertaken when the tax-deductibility feature is introduced, and Eqs. (18.5) and (18.6) seem to indicate that the value of the shareholders' claim also increases, though we have not yet provided any theoretical justification for such a statement.

Rendleman's analysis gave us the L-value, which is the clue to this seeming problem. Management can act in a way to jeopardize the bondholders' claims by issuing more debt and thus making all debt more risky, or by undertaking projects that are riskier than the average project undertaken by the firm. This is the subject of the next section.

Another possibility is to pay large dividends so as to deplete the firm of its resources, thus paying off the shareholders but hurting the bondholders. Black (1976) goes so far as to suggest that the firm could liquidate itself, pay out the total as a dividend, and leave the bondholders holding the proverbial bag. Bond covenants, of course, prevent this sort of action (hence, agency theory), and if a firm could not sell its growth opportunities not yet exploited in the market, this may not maximize the shareholder's wealth, either, but within bounds it does seem a reasonable possibility.

In their review article, Barnea *et al.* (BHS, 1981) discuss the issues related to market imperfections, agency problems, and the implications for the consideration of optimal capital structures. The authors make use of M&M's valuation theory and option-pricing theory to reconcile the differences between academicians and practitioners about the relevance of financing and dividend policies. They arrive at the conclusion that, without frictionless capital markets, agency problems can give rise to potential costs. These costs can be minimized through complex contractual arrangements between the conflicting parties. Potential agency costs may help to explain the evolution of certain complexities in capital structure, such as conversion privileges of corporate debt and call provisions. If these agency costs are real, then financial contracts which vary in their ability to reduce these costs may very well sell at different equilibrium prices or yields, even if the financial marketplaces are efficient. An optimal capital structure can be obtained when, for each class of contract, the costs associated with each agency problem are exactly balanced by the yield differentials and tax exposures. Overall, BHS show that optimal capital structures can exist and that this is still consistent with the mainstream of classical finance theory.

18.4. Interactions between Financing and Investment Decisions

Myers (1974) has analyzed in detail the interactions of corporate financing and investment decisions and the implications therein for capital budgeting.

He argues that the existence of these interaction effects may be attributable to the recognition of transaction costs, corporate taxes, or other market imperfections. Ignored in his analysis is the probability of default on debt obligations, or, as could otherwise be interpreted, changes in this default risk. As alluded to in the previous section, if we consider possible effects of default risk on the firm's investment and financing decisions, then further analysis must be performed to determine how these interactions can affect the wealth positions of shareholders and bondholders. In this section, we will analyze this issue by considering both the risk-free debt case and the risky debt case.

18.4.1. *Risk-Free Debt Case*

Following Myers (1974), the basic optimization framework is presented in accordance with well-accepted mathematical programming techniques, discussed in the capital-rationing segment of Chapter 13. It is presented as a general formulation; it should be considered one approach to analyzing interactions and not the final word *per se*. Specific results derived by Chambers *et al.* (1982), will be used later to demonstrate the importance of considering alternative financing mixes when evaluating investment opportunities.

We identify a firm Q, which faces several investment opportunities of varying characteristics. The objective is to identify those projects that are in the stockholders' interest (i.e., they maximize the change in the firm's market value ex-dividend at the end of the successive time periods $t = 0, 1, \ldots, T$) and undertake them in order of their relative values. We specify relative values so that project divisibility remains possible, as was assumed by Myers. Required is a financing plan that specifies the desired mix of earnings retained, debt outstanding, and proceeds from the issuance of new equity shares.

Let dV be a general function of four factors in a direct sense: (i) the proportion of each project j accepted, x_j; (ii) the stock of debt outstanding in period t, y_t; (iii) the total cash dividends paid in period t, D_t; and (iv) the net proceeds from equity issued in period t, E_t. For future use, let Z be denoted as the debt capacity of the firm in period t, this being defined as a limit on y_t imposed internally by management or by the capital markets, and C_t is the expected net after-tax cash flow to the firm in time period t. The problem can now be written as:

$$\text{Maximize } dV\,(x_j, y_t, D_t, E_t) = W,$$

Subject to the constraints;

$$\begin{aligned}&\text{(a) } U_j = x_j - 1 \le 0 \quad (j = 1, 2, \ldots, J),\\&\text{(b) } U_t^F = y_t - Z_t \le 0 \quad (t = 1, 2, \ldots, T),\\&\text{(c) } U_t^C = -C_t - [y_t - y_{t-1}(1 + (1 - \tau)r)] + D_t - E_t \le 0,\end{aligned} \tag{18.7}$$

where τ and r are the tax rates and borrowing rates, respectively. Both are assumed constant for simplicity, but in actuality both could be defined as functions of other variables. Constraints (a) and (b) specify the percentage of the project undertaken cannot exceed 100%, and the debt outstanding cannot exceed the debt capacity limit. Constraint (c) is the accounting identity, indicating that outflows of funds equal inflows, and could be interpreted as the restriction that the firm maintain no excess funds.

Constraint (b) can be used to investigate the interaction between the firm's financing and investment decisions by examining the necessary conditions for optimization. If we assign the symbols L_j, L_{ft}, and L_{ct} to be the shadow prices on constraints (a)–(c), respectively, and let $A_j = dW/dx_j$, $F_t = dW/dy_t$, $Z_{jt} = dZ_t/dx_j$, and $C_{jt} = dC_t/dx_j$, we can rewrite Eq. (18.7) in Lagrangian form as the following:

$$\begin{aligned}Max W' =& W - L_j(x_j - 1) - L_{ft}(y_t - Z_t)\\&- L_{ct}\{-C_t - [y_t - y_{t-1}(1 + (1 - \tau)r)]\}\\&+ D_t - E_t).\end{aligned} \tag{18.7$'$}$$

The necessary first-order conditions for the optimum are shown as Eqs. (18.8) through (18.11), with accompanying explanations. For each project:

$$A_j + \sum_{t=0}^{T}[L_{ft}Z_{jt} + L_{ct}C_{jt}] - L_j \le 0. \tag{18.8}$$

This can be interpreted as follows: The percentage of a project undertaken should be increased until its incremental cost exceeds the sum of the incremental value of the project, the latter consisting of the added debt capacity and the value of the cash flows generated by that project. The incremental increase in value of the firm obtained by increasing x_j to this maximum point is termed the Adjusted Present Value, APV ("adjusted" because of the consideration of interaction effects).

We can examine each of these effects in turn. For the debt constraint in each period;

$$F_t - L_{ft} + L_{ct} - L_{c,t-1}[1 + (1 - \tau)r] \le 0. \tag{18.9}$$

For the constraint implied on dividends;

$$\frac{dW}{dD_t} - L_{ct} \leq 0; \tag{18.10}$$

and for the new equity constraint:

$$\frac{dW}{dE_t} + L_{ct} \leq 0. \tag{18.11}$$

While Eqs. (18.8) through (18.11) are all of interest, the focus is on Eq. (18.8), which tells us that the NPV rule commonly put forth should be replaced by the APV rule, which accounts for interaction effects.

Specifically considering the financing constraint, Eq. (18.9), we would like to be able to find the value of this constraint, which is most easily done by assuming for the moment that dividend policy is irrelevant. Combined with Eqs. (18.8) and (18.9) and the definition of APV we obtain[2]:

$$APV_j = A_j + \sum_{t=0}^{T} Z_{jt} F_t, \tag{18.12}$$

which, in the spirit of the M&M with-tax firm-valuation model, tells us that the value of a project is given by the increase in value that would occur in an unlevered firm, plus the value of the debt the project is capable of supporting. This follows from the ability of the firm to deduct interest expenses for tax purposes. This procedure will be further investigated in the following section when we compare it with other well-accepted capital-budgeting techniques.

When dividend policy is not irrelevant, the standard argument arises as to whether the preference for dividends, given their general tax status, outweighs the transaction costs incurred by the firm when dividends are paid and new financing must be raised. In this framework, dividends are viewed as another cash flow and, as such, the issue centers on whether the cash flows from the project plus any increases in the debt capacity of the firm are adequate to cover the cost of financing, through whatever means.

Though we are unable to discern the effect of dividend policy on the value of the firm, it is not outside the solution technique to incorporate such efforts by including the related expenses as inputs to the numerical-solution procedure.

It is generally assumed that these interaction effects exist, so if we are to consider disregarding them, as some would insist, we must know what conditions are necessary for lack of dependence of financing and investment decisions. As Myers points out, only in a world of perfect markets with no taxes is this the case. Otherwise, the tax deductibility of the interest feature of debt suggests that the APV method gives a more accurate assessment of project viability than does the standard NPV method.

18.4.2. *Risky Debt Case*

Rendleman (1978) not only examined the risk premiums associated with risky debt, but also considered the impact that debt financing could have on equity values, with taxes and without. The argument is to some extent based on the validity (or lack thereof) of the perfect-market assumption often invoked, which, interestingly enough, turns out to be a double-edged sword.

Without taxes, the original M&M article claims, the investment decision of a firm should be made independent of the financing decision. But the financing base of the firm supports all the firm's investment projects, not some specific project. From this, we infer that the future investments of a firm and the risk premiums embodied in the financing costs must be considered when the firm takes on new projects. If, for example, the firm chooses to take on projects of higher than average risk, then this may have an adverse affect on the value of the outstanding debt (to the gain of the shareholders), and the converse holds true as well. It follows that the management of a firm should pursue riskier and riskier projects to transfer some of the firm's risk from the shareholders to the bondholders, who do not receive commensurate return for that risk. If the bondholders anticipate this action on the part of management, then it is all the more imperative that management takes the action since the bondholders are requiring, and receiving, a risk premium for which they are not being forced to take the "standard" or market-consensus level of risk.

Myers (1977) presents an argument in which a firm should issue no risky debt. The rationale for this strategy is that a firm possesses certain real options, or investment opportunities, that unfold over time. With risky debt, some of these investment projects available only to the firm of interest may not be undertaken if it is in the interest of the shareholders to default on a near-term scheduled debt payment. In this way, risky debt induces a suboptimal investment policy and firm value is not maximized as it would be if the firm issued no risky debt. One problem here is that we do not have strict equivalence between equity-value maximization and firm-value maximizations, so investment policy cannot be thought of entirely in terms of firm-value maximization. This is a quirk associated with the option-pricing framework when applied to firm valuation, and it clouds the determination of what is suboptimal in the finance area.[3]

While we conceded that we are not entirely sure as to how we should treat the interaction effects of financing and investment policy, we can state with some degree of certainty that, even in the absence of the tax deductibility of interest, these two finance-related decisions are interdependent and, as a result, the financial manager should remain wary of those who subscribe to the idea that financing decisions do not matter.

Allowing the tax deductibility of interest, it is ironic to note that the conclusions are not nearly as clear-cut as before. If the firm undertakes further, more risky projects, the value of debt may actually increase, if the firm does not issue further debt. The shareholders gain from the new project only on its own merits. If no additional debt financing is raised, it is impossible to obtain a larger tax shield and the debt may actually become more secure as a result of the larger asset base. If, however, the firm does issue more debt and in that way acts to jeopardize the currently outstanding debt, the number of considerations multiply, and analysis becomes exceedingly difficult because the value of the project by itself, plus the value of the added tax shield, need to be considered in light of the possible shifting of wealth due to transfers of risk amongst claimants of the firm. Thus it seems that, when we allow the real world to influence the model, as it well should, the only thing we can say for certain about financing and investment decisions is that each case must be considered separately.

18.5. Implications of Financing and Investment Interactions for Capital Budgeting

This section is intended to briefly review capital-budgeting techniques, and explain how each in turn neglects accounting for financing influences in investment-opportunity analysis, and discuss the method by which they do incorporate this aspect of financial management into the decision process. We will draw heavily upon the work of CHP (1982), in making particular distinctions between methods most often covered in corporate-finance textbooks and presumably used in practice, presenting numerical comparisons derived from varying sets of circumstances.

CHP examined four standard, discounted cash-flow models and considered the implications of using each as opposed to the other three. By way of simulation, they were able to deal with differences in financing projects as well as with possible differences in the risk underlying the operating cash flows generated by each project. The problem inherent in this and any project evaluation (not to say that there are not other difficulties) is in concentrating on the specification of the amount of debt used to finance the investment project. Project debt is therefore defined as the additional debt capacity afforded the firm as a result of accepting the project, and can alternatively be described as the difference between the firm's optimal debt level with the project and without it. Conceptually this is a fairly concrete construct, but it still leaves some vague areas when we are actually performing the computations.

As discussed earlier, it is essential to arrive at some value estimate of the estimated cash flows of a project. The CHP analysis considered the following four methods; (i) the Equity Residual method; (ii) the "after-tax Weighted Average Cost-of-Capital (WACC)" method; (iii) the "Arditti–Levy" weighted cost-of-capital method; and (iv) the Myers "APV" method. For simplicity, Table 18.3 contains the definitions of the symbols used in the following discussion, after which we briefly discuss the formulation of each method, and then elaborate on the way in which each method incorporates interacting effects of financing and investment decisions.

18.5.1. *Equity-Residual Method*

The equity-residual method is formulated in Eq. (18.13) in a manner that emphasizes the goal of financial management, the pursuance of the interests

Table 18.3. Definitions of variables.

$R_t =$	Pretax operating cash revenues of the project during period t;
$C_t =$	Pretax operating cash expenses of the project during period t;
$dep_t =$	Additional depreciation expense attributable to the project in period t;
$\tau_c =$	Applicable corporate tax rate;
$I =$	Initial net cash investment outlay;
$D_t =$	Project debt outstanding during period t;
NP $=$	Net proceeds of issuing project debt at time zero;
$r_t =$	Interest rate of debt in period t;
$k_e =$	Cost of the equity financing of the project;
$k_w =$	After-tax weighted-average cost of capital (i.e., debt cost is after-tax);
$k_{AL} =$	Weighted average cost of capital — debt cost considered before taxes;
$\rho =$	Required rate-of-return applicable to unlevered cash-flow series, given the risk class of the project;
r, k_e, and ρ are all assumed to be constant over time.	

of shareholders:

$$NPV(ER) = \sum_{t=1}^{N} \frac{[(R_t - C_t - dep_t - rD_t)(1 - \tau_c) + D_t] - (D_t - D_{t+1})}{(1 + k_e)^t} - [I - NP]. \quad (18.13)$$

The formula presented above can be interpreted as stating that the benefit of the project to the shareholders is the present value of the cash flows not going to pay operating expenses or to service or repay debt obligations.

With these flows identified as those going to shareholders, it is appropriate, and rather easy, to discount these flows at the cost of equity. The only difficulty involved is identifying this cost of equity, a problem embodied in all capital-budgeting methods.

18.5.2. *After-Tax, WACC Method*

The after-tax, WACC method, depicted in Eq. (18.14), has two noticeable differences from the formulation of the equity-residual method:

$$NPV = \sum_{t=1}^{N} \frac{(R_t - C_t - dep_t)(1 - \tau_c) + dep_t}{(1 + k_w)^t} I. \quad (18.14)$$

First, no flows associated with the debt financing appear in the numerator, or as relevant cash flows. Second, the cost of capital is adjusted downward, with k_w being a weighted average of debt and equity costs, the debt expense accounted for on an after-tax basis. In that way, debt financing is reckoned with in an indirect manner. With the assumption that r and k_e are constant over time, k_w can be affected only by the debt-to-equity ratio, a problem most often avoided by assuming a fixed debt-to-equity ratio.

18.5.3. *Arditti and Levy Method*

The Arditti–Levy method is most similar to the after-tax weighted-average cost-of-capital method. This formulation can be written as:

$$NPV(AL) = \sum_{t=1}^{N} \frac{[(R_t - C_t - dep_t - rD_t)(1 - \tau_c) + dep_t] + rD_t}{(1 + k_{AL})^t} - I. \quad (18.15)$$

It was seen as necessary to restate the after-tax, weighted-average, cost-of-capital formula in this manner because the tax payment to the government has an influence on the net cash flows, and for that reason the cash-flow figures would be misleading. To rectify this problem, the discount rate must now be adjusted since the interest tax shield is reflected in the cash flows and double counting would be involved. While the after-tax, weighted-average cost of capital recognized the cost of debt in the discount rate, it was akin to the equity-residual method in considering only returns to equity. The Arditti and Levy formulas imply that a weighted average discount rate including the lower cost of debt could only (or best) be used if all flows to all sources of financing were included; hence the term rD_t is found at the end of the first term. This can be rationalized if one considers the case of a firm where there is one owner. The total cash flow to the owner is the relevant figure, and the discount rate applicable is simply a weighted average of the two individual required rates-of-return.

18.5.4. *Myers Adjusted-Present-Value Method*

This method, derived in Section 18.4, is closely related to the Arditti–Levy method except for the exclusion of the interest-expense flows to the bondholders. In treating the financing mix, Myers implicitly assumes that the tax shield, created by the interest payments and afforded to the equity holders, has the same risk for the equity holders as the coupon or interest payments have for the bondholders. Instead of aggregating all factors and attempting to arrive at a suitable weighted-average discount rate, Myers found it less difficult to leave operating- and financing-related flows separated, and to discount each at an appropriate rate. This formulation can be written as:

$$APV = \sum_{t=1}^{N} \frac{(R_t - C_t - dep_t)(1 - \tau_c) + dep_t}{(1+\rho)^t} - I + \sum_{t=1}^{N} \frac{\tau_c r D_t}{(1+r)^t}. \quad (18.16)$$

This formulation appears to be closely related to the Modigliani and Miller with-tax firm-valuation model, and well it should, given Myers' motivation for this work. We choose not to discuss it here, but the reader should be aware that Myers' emphasis was not solely on the tax advantage of debt, as the last term in the above equation tends to imply.

The four methods are obviously comparable, but usually give different figures for the net present value. The equity-residual, after-tax, weighted-average cost-of-capital and the Arditti–Levy weighted-average, cost-of-capital formulations are comparable if the value of the debt outstanding remains a constant proportion of the remaining cash flows; this is often taken to mean a constant debt ratio. This will not guarantee that the Myers APV method will yield the same results, although the Myers method is equivalent to the other three only if the project life can be described as one period, or as infinite with constant perpetual flows in all periods. By way of numerical examples, we now address the task of determining the factors that create the differences in the net-present-value figures generated by each method.

The first example involves the simplest case, where a \$1,000 investment generates operating flows of \$300 per year for all 5 years of the project's life. Debt financing comprises \$600 of the project's total financing and the principal is repaid over the five time periods in equal amounts. The discount and tax rates employed are included below in Table 18.4 with the results for each of the four methods.

Because the Arditti–Levy method recognizes the acquisition of the debt capital and uses a lower discount rate, as does the after-tax WACC, these two methods give the highest net-present-value figures. The equity-residual method recognizes only the \$400 outflow at time zero, but the higher discount suppresses the net-present-value figure. The Myers APV method, though discounting financing-related flows at the cost of debt, also attains a low net-present-value figure because the majority of the flows are discounted at a higher unlevered cost-of-equity rate.

Basically we can speak of three differences in these methods that create the large discrepancies in the bottom-line figures. The risk factor, reflected in discount rates that may vary over time, is a major element, as was evidenced in the example presented above. The pattern of debt and debt payments will also be an important factor, particularly so when the debt repayment is not of the annuity form assumed earlier. Finally, the recognition and valuation of the debt tax shields will play an important

Table 18.4. Application of four capital-budgeting techniques.

Inputs: (1) $k_e = 0.112$; (2) $r = 0.041$; (3) $\tau_c = 0.46$; (4) $\rho = 0.0802$; (5) $w = 0.6$

Method	NPV Results	Discount Rates
1. Equity-residual	\$230.55	$k_e = 0.112$
2. After-tax WACC	270.32	$k_w = 0.058$
3. Arditti–Levy WACC	261.67	$k_{AL} = 0.069$
4. Myers APV	228.05	$r = 0.041$ and $\rho = 0.0802$

From Chambers *et al.* (1982). Reprinted by permission.

role in net-present-value determination, especially when the constant-debt-repayment assumption is dropped and the interest expenses and associated tax shields grow larger.

In the CHP study, the valuation models described earlier were employed in a simulation procedure that would allow the assessment of the investment proposal. The inputs to the capital-budgeting procedures were varied across simulations, and the effects of the changes in each input were scrutinized from a sensitivity-analysis viewpoint. They considered, but did not dwell upon, the effects of changing discount rates over time or by some scaling factor on the bottom-line valuation figures; further discussion was deferred primarily because of the multitude of possible combinations that would be of interest. Compounding the problem, one would also be interested in different debt–equity combinations and the effects these would have with changing discount rates, since the weighting scheme of the appropriate discount rates plays an integral part in the analysis. In avoiding this aspect of the analysis, the projects evaluated in the forthcoming discussion will be viewed as being of equivalent risk, or as coming from the same risk class. Lest the reader feel shortchanged, it is suggested that one examine each method and verify for him or herself what changes would be produced in the net-present-value figures with varying debt schedules.

More in tune with the basic theme of this chapter, we go on to consider the effects that changing financing mixes, debt-payment patterns, and project lives have on the figures attained for each of the four methods considered, the first (financing mix) being the major issue involved.

In confronting mix effects, we are required to select a model for valuing debt in the Myers APV method because ρ (the unlevered cost of equity capital) is unobservable. In this case, we must choose between numerous alternatives, the most notable being those of Modigliani and Miller (1963), where debt provides an interest-tax shield, and that of Miller (1977), where the inclusion of personal taxes on investor interest income has the effect of perfectly offsetting the tax shield the firm receives, rendering the debt tax advantage moot. In the simulation results of CHP presented in the following paragraphs, the Myers cost of unlevered equity capital is computed using each method, with subscripts denoting the particular method used.

Four projects of varied cash-flow patterns and lives are to be presented and valued, each of which will be simulated with three different debt schedules. Brief descriptions of the projects and debt schedules can be found in Table 18.5, along with the fixed inputs to be used in the actual computations.

Table 18.5. Inputs for simulation.

Project	Net Cash Inflows per Year	Project Life
1	\$300 per year	5 years
2	\$253.77 per year	5 years
3	\$124.95 per year	20 years
4	\$200 per year, years 1–4 \$792.58 in year 5	5 years

For each project the initial outlay is \$1,000 at time $t = 0$, with all subsequent outlays being captured in the yearly flows.

Debt Schedule

(1) Market value of debt outstanding remains a constant proportion of the project's market value.
(2) Equal principal repayments in each year.
(3) Level debt, total principal repaid at termination of project.

Inputs:	$k_e = 0.112$	$r = 0.041$
	$k_w = 0.085$	$\rho_{(M\&M)} = 0.0986$
	$\rho_M = 0.085$	$\tau_c = 0.46$
	$W = 0.3$	

From Chambers *et al.* (1982). Reprinted by permission.

The projects' cash flows, as listed in the table, were actually manipulated in a predetermined way, so that more interesting cases would be presented. Project 1 is simply a base figure, while project 2 has a cash-flow pattern that makes the net present value 0, when using the after-tax, weighted-average cost of capital. Project 3 has a longer life, and thus will serve as a method of determining the effects of increasing project life. Finally, Project 4 has four level payments with a larger final payment in year 5, intended to simulate an ongoing project with terminal value in year 5.

The results of the simulations are presented in Table 18.6. For purposes of comparison, the net-present-value figures of the after-tax, weighted-average cost of capital are reported first, for two reasons. The after-tax weighted-average cost of capital is probably the best-known technique of capital budgeting, and its net present value figures are insensitive to the debt schedule. The initial weights of the debt and equity used to support the project are all that are used in calculating the weighted discount rate, rendering the repayment pattern of debt irrelevant.

As indicated earlier, the after-tax weighted-average cost of capital, Arditti–Levy weighted-average cost of capital, and the equity-residual methods are all equivalent if the debt ratio is held constant. It is also of

Table 18.6. Simulation results.

Project	Capital Budgeting	Net-present-value Under Alternative Debit Schedule		
		Constant Debt Ratio	Equal Principal	Level Debt
1	After-tax WACC	182	182	182
	Arditti–Levy	182	179	187
	WACC	182	167	202
	Equity-Residual	160	157	166
	Myers APV (M&M)	182	182	182
	Myers APV (M)			
2		0	0	0
	After-tax WACC	0	−1	7
	Arditti–Levy	0	−3	32
	WACC	−18	−19	−10
	Equity-Residual	0	0	0
	Myers APV (M&M)			
3	Myers APV (M)	182	182	182
		182	169	186
	After-tax WACC	182	128	194
	Arditti–Levy	138	119	150
	WACC	182	182	182
	Equity Residual			
4	Myers APV (M&M)	182	182	182
	Myers APV (M)	182	174	182
		182	147	183
	After-tax WACC	155	146	156
	Arditti–Levy	182	182	182
	WACC			
	Equity Residual			
	Myers APV (M&M)			
	Myers APV (M)			

From Chambers *et al.* (1982). Reprinted by permission.

interest here that the Myer's APV figures, using the Miller method for determining the cost of capital, are constant over debt schedules; they are, for all intents and purposes, the same as the after-tax, weighted-average cost-of-capital figures, a finding that is reasonable if one believes that the cost of debt capital is the same as that of unlevered equity. Of all the methods cited above, the equity-residual method is the most sensitive to the debt schedule employed, with both principal and interest payments being included in the cash flows, a feature compounded by the higher discount rates included in the computations. The two methods that include the interest tax shield, the Arditti–Levy method and the Myers APV (M&M) method are also sensitive to the amount of debt outstanding, the interest tax shield being of greater value the longer the debt is outstanding. In all cases, the latter method gives the lowest net-present-value figures due to the treatment of the interest tax shield.

In further simulations, CHP showed (and it should be no surprise) that as higher levels of debt are employed and higher tax rates are encountered, the magnitude of the differences is amplified, and the method employed in the capital-budgeting decision takes on greater and greater importance. Even so it was argued that changes associated with changes in the inputs of the longest-lived project, where the changes in the net-present-value figures were the most pronounced, were not that great when compared with the outcomes associated with changing the estimates of the cash flows by as little as 5%. The importance of this finding is that projects that are of short duration and are financed with relatively little debt are not as sensitive to the capital-budgeting technique employed. But, in the case of longer-lived projects, the method selected can have serious implications for the acceptance or rejection of a project, particularly when higher levels of debt financing are employed. Analysts undoubtedly possess their own views as to which method is stronger conceptually, and, in the event of capital-budgeting procedures, should be aware of the debt policy to be pursued. Even in light of these views, it may be prudent to use the Myers APV method with the M&M unlevered-equity cost-determination method as the first screening device for a project or set of projects. Since this method yields the most conservative figures, any project that appears profitable following this analysis should be undertaken, and any project failing this screening can be analyzed using the methods chosen by the financial manager, if further analysis is felt to be warranted.

Since the Myers APV method is recommended, it is worthwhile for us to show the procedure for obtaining the APV, as discussed in Table 18.4. Let the information needed to establish APV be $R_t = \$4{,}000$, $C_t = \$1{,}000$, $dep_t = \$500$, $D_t = \$3600$, E_t (equity financing) $= \$2800$, $I = \$7000$, $k_e = 0.15$, $r = 0.09$, $\tau_c = 0.46$, $w = D/(D+E) = \$4200/\$7000 = 0.6$, $N = 6$.

From this information, we can assemble the information needed to estimate APV as follows:

$$\text{(a) Operating flows} = (R_t - C_t - dep_t)(1 - \tau_c) + dep_t$$
$$= (\$4000 - \$1000 - \$500)(1 - 0.46) + \$500$$
$$= \$1850.$$

$$\text{(b) Financial flows} = \tau_c r D_t$$
$$= (0.46)(0.09)(\$3600)$$
$$= \$149.04.$$

(c) $k_w = wr(1-\tau_c) + (1-w)k_e$
$= (0.6)(0.09)(1-0.46) + (1-0.6)(0.15)$
$= (0.029) + (0.06)$
$= 0.089.$

(d) $\rho = \dfrac{k_w}{(1-\tau_c w)}$
$= \dfrac{0.089}{(1-(0.46)(0.6))}$
$= 0.1229.$

From this information, we can calculate APV as:

$$APV = \$1850\left(\sum_{t=1}^{6} 1/(1+0.1229)^t\right) + \$149.04\left(\sum_{t=1}^{6} 1/(1+0.09)^t\right) - \$7000$$
$$= (\$1850)(4.0784) + (\$149.04)(4.4859) - \$7000$$
$$= \$1213.62.$$

It should be noted that this example has used the concepts discussed in Chapters 8, 12, 13, 14, and 15.

By using appropriate budget constraints, Lambert and Myers (2012) have theoretically shown that investment dividend and financing policy are inter-related. To test this theory developed by Lambert and Myers, Lee *et al.* investigate the interrelationship among investment, financing and dividend decisions using 2SLS, 3SLS, and GMM methods based on the U.S. listed firm annual data between 1965 and 2012. Their results are consistent with Lambrecht and Myers's (2012) theory that dividend and investment decisions are jointly determined. In addition, these three corporate decisions are co-determined and the interaction among them should be taken into account in a simultaneous equation framework.

18.6. Debt Capacity and Optimal Capital Structure[4]

Contrary to the neoclassical theory of Modigliani and Miller and others, developed in the late 1950's and early 1960's, we have argued that the investment, financing, and dividend policies of a firm do interact, and by so doing can affect the market value of the firm and/or the value of the equity of the firm. By way of these interaction effects, the irrelevance propositions cited earlier and so prevalent in the finance literature become themselves invalidated. In being able to outline those interaction effects we are hinting, not very subtly, that firms do have optimal capital structures and certain debt capacities, though they may not necessarily be constant through time. This section more explicitly addresses the debt-capacity issue, and in so doing strives to arrive at optimal capital decisions. Here we assume that the firm's debt capacity is defined at the margin as being the point where the advantage derived from incremental additions of debt to the capital structure of the firm is just offset, or more than offset, by the costs incurred, whether strictly monetary or risk-based costs.

The methods explored in the following discussion are not to be taken as though they were inscribed in stone and handed down from the mountain; they are instead intended to serve as a useful aid to the financial manager in the conduct of financial planning and forecasting. One particular problem embodied in the following is how risk is to be defined so that the cost-benefit analysis can be performed. Total firm risk is one term used, and risk of bankruptcy or insolvency is a viable alternative. Most of the following analysis can be viewed as though we are decomposing total firm risk into two components, business risk and financial risk. Given this and the common assumption firms aim toward target total risk levels (independent of any investor's portfolio decisions), we will be able to show how firms arrive at finance mixes that are considered optimal.

Tuttle and Litzenberger (1968) took the above assumption and applied it to the screening and ranking of investment opportunities, where each project was transformed to be of the same risk as that associated with the existing equity capital of the firm. The ability of the firm to lever or unlever itself at some known borrowing or lending rate is sufficient to allow this to be done, again without consideration of portfolio effects, but first it is necessary to see why a firm would proceed along such lines of investigation.

Let us identify a firm Q, with an expected rate-of-return on the firm's equity denoted as R_Q and the standard error-of-estimate of those returns as S_Q. Given the numerous investment opportunities faced by the firm with expected rate-of-return R_p and standard error-of-estimate of those returns as S_p, we can separate these projects into three groups as characterized in Table 18.7: those accepted without question, those indisputably rejected, and those on which we cannot exercise judgment without the specification of a risk–return trade-off.

By way of a simple dominance principle the "accept" and "reject" decisions should be clear. The concern here is the valuation of those projects that fall into the third category above. Tuttle and Litzenberger allow the

Table 18.7. Acceptance–rejection criteria.

Accept	Reject	Indeterminate
$R_r \geq R_Q^*$	$R_p < R_Q$	$R_p > R_Q$
and	and	and
$S_p \leq S_Q$	$S_p > S_Q$	$S_p > S_Q$
		or
		$R_p < R_Q$
		$S_p < S_Q$

*In the special instance where both relationships are strict equalities the firm is, of course, indifferent in attitude toward the project.

firm to lend or borrow at some constant known rate; in so doing the firm gains the ability to partially offset the risk of a project, making it risk-equivalent with the rest of the firm's projects. Risk being equivalent for all projects, it is a simple task to evaluate the project; the expected return is the sole consideration (if, for the time being, one assumes that the project's cash flows are perfectly correlated with the rest of the firm's cash flows).

We adopt the following notation:

R_e = Expected rate-of-return to equity from the project;
R_d = Yield-to-maturity on long-term debt of similar risk to that of the firm;
R_p = Expected internal rate-of-return offered by the investment project; and
$W = 1 +$ the debt-to-equity ratio.

The levered residual rate-of-return to equity can be shown as:

$$R_e = \mathrm{W}R_p - R_d(W - 1) \tag{18.17}$$

or, alternatively,

$$R_e = R_d + W(R_p - R_d), \tag{18.17a}$$

and the new standard error of equity returns becomes:

$$S_e = WS_p. \tag{18.18}$$

By multiplying the last term of Eq. (18.17a) by S_p/S_p and substituting into Eq. (18.18), we obtain Eq. (18.18):

$$R_e = R_d + \frac{S_e}{S_p}(R_p - R_d). \tag{18.19}$$

Now by differentiating with respect to the risk of equity, we find the linear trade-off between residual return to equity and standard error;

$$\frac{dR_e}{dS_e} = \frac{R_p - R_d}{S_p}. \tag{18.20}$$

By itself Eq. (18.20) could be used to value projects, in much the same way that portfolio-performance measures evaluate portfolio returns on a risk-adjusted basis. In the context of this chapter, however, the task is reduced to finding the factor W' that equates the risk of the equity returns of the project with that of the rest of the equity of the firm; the procedure of solving mix, W', can be defined as:

$$S_{e'} = W'S_p. \tag{18.18a}$$

Then the risk-adjusted rate-of-return on investment project R_e can be written as:

$$R_{e'} = R_d + W'(R_p - R_d). \tag{18.21}$$

At this point, all we need to do is make a simple comparison of the project's levered, expected rate-of-return with the existing ROE for the firm as a whole. We have therefore devised a method for solving all investment-opportunity analysis problems not covered by the dominance rule mentioned earlier.

The assumptions of debt costs being independent of the degree of leverage employed and perfect correlations between cash flows are obviously violated in practice. Tuttle and Litzenberger also showed how both of these factors work into the analysis. By allowing debt costs to be affected in some linear manner, as was the cost of equity, the cost of financing a project (k_p) can be expressed as:

$$k_p = \frac{1}{W'}R_p + \left(1 - \frac{1}{W'}\right)R_d, \tag{18.22}$$

which, when rearranged, appears as:

$$k_p = R_d + \frac{1}{W'}(R_p - R_d). \tag{18.22a}$$

For a project, if R_d, R_p, R_e, S_p, and S_e and 0.05, 0.40, 0.15, 0.60, and 0.30, respectively, then $W' = 0.30/0.60 = 0.50$ and $R_e = 0.05 + (0.50)(0.40 - 0.05) = 0.225$. Since k_p is smaller than R_p, this investment project should therefore be accepted.

As we would expect, the required rate-of-return-to-risk trade-off assumes smaller values when risky debt is allowed. Still, this leaves the method of analysis as viable. By solving for the appropriate W', we make the risk of the project equivalent to all other projects. Then we have only to compare expected rates-of-return with hurdle (cost of capital) rates imposed in the form of the existing ROE. Only in the instance where so much debt has been employed to reduce the risk of a project that the cost of debt for the project exceeds the existing return-on-equity would the firm be unable to evaluate the project in this manner.

Looking at the problem from the portfolio viewpoint, we must also, when assessing its risk, consider the diversification benefits that a project yields, so that the W' is properly selected. By using the equation for the variance between two random variables — the returns on the existing equity of the firm and the returns on the new project — we set the portfolio standard error equal to the existing equity's standard error and vary the financing ratio W (and by so doing, vary the dollar equity investment in the project), until we achieve the stated goal. While computationally this is more difficult than the previous cases, the conclusion is the same: some financing mix exists (in all but the most extreme instances) that will allow us to examine new projects on an equity-risk-equivalent basis, that is being defined as the optimal financing mix.

To explicitly consider the effect of diversification on cost of financing, Tuttle and Litzenberger (1968) generalized Eq. (18.22a) as

$$k'_P = r_d + \frac{\rho_{pe} S_p}{S_e}(R_e - R_d), \tag{18.22a$'$}$$

where

$k'_P =$ Cost of financing a project,
$\rho_{pe} =$ Correlation between R_p and R_e,
$S_p =$ Estimated standard deviation of R_p,
$S_e =$ Estimated standard deviation of R_e.

If $\rho_{pe} = 1$, then Eq. (18.22a′) reduces to Eq. (18.22a). Since k'_P is generally smaller than k_P, diversification associated with capital projects will generally reduce the cost of financing.

This analysis highlights the true meaning of optimal capital structure when target risk levels are set. Optimal capital structure is not some debt-to-equity figure that allows the firm a degree of leverage deemed as safe.

It is a function of the underlying risk of the projects undertaken by the firm. It is almost as though the optimal capital structure decision is given from outside the firm, and the financial manager is the agent pursuing the maintenance of the proper financing mix, given the selection of the projects that themselves add to firm value.

In a later paper, Litzenberger and Sosin (LS) (1979) investigated the capital structure decision for regulated and deregulated firms. They maintain that optimal capital structures do exist (and that firms should actively pursue them), but that an aggressive policy by a regulated industry can be non-optimal from the standpoint of equity investors, and for the consumers of the regulated industry's products. By virtue of being regulated with respect to rates charged, any gains derived by a company by aggressively levering the firm will be passed on to consumers in a rather short time span. If an aggressive leverage policy is followed, the equity holders incur more risk and probably do not receive commensurate return. Since leverage is closely akin to risk, the chance of bankruptcy and disrupted service is increased, and the possibility of the consumer suffering the brunt of the costs through price hikes is likewise increased. The conclusion derived from this analysis is rather straightforward: A regulated firm's debt capacity should not be pushed to its limits in terms of maximizing total firm value. Debt should be used only so long as it is riskless, and the chance of equity holder and consumer loss is minimized. In addition, LS argued that the issuance of non-default-free debt by regulated and non-regulated firms can be socially non-optimal.

Martin and Scott (1976) adopted the insolvency definition of bankruptcy, and broke down the analyst's task into four components: estimation of the before-tax cash flows, estimation of the appropriate discount rate for pure equity streams, estimation of the additional contribution of a project to total firm debt capacity, and computation of the value of the project to the firm. Step 1 is identical to all prior capital-budgeting methods discussed, and should require no further explanation. Step 2 relies heavily on the Hamada (1972) contention that an unlevered beta (β_0) for a firm's equity can be computed as shown below:

$$\beta_0 = \beta \left(\frac{S}{S_0} \right)_{t-1}, \tag{18.23}$$

where β is levered beta, S is the market value of the equity in the firm in time period $(t - 1)$, and S_0 is the market value of the equity if the firm undertook no leverage in period $(t - 1)$. In defining debt capacity, we must specify some accepted probability of insolvency, resulting from the inclusion of financial leverage. Insolvency, based on a flow concept, is defined here as the probability that the operating flows are sufficient to meet the debt financing requirements. In specifying flows, we should be aware that adjustments could be made in cash and marketable securities or in lines of credit so as to avoid insolvency, and are generally not recognized in operating flows. In essence, the argument assumes that these factors are at their optimal points, all other things held constant.

Recognizing portfolio effects, the risk a project adds to the cash-flow variability of the firm is determined by the correlation of the project's cash flows and those of the firm prior to the project's acceptance. If the project's cash flows are positively correlated with those of the firm, the higher the correlation, the less debt its operating cash-flow stream can support. Since no precise estimate exists as to the shareholders' desired leverage, the financial manager is not required to pursue an optimal debt policy by this step. The sole concern here is the establishment of the relevant risk of the project. If we allow C to represent the firm's net cash flow after the financing charges, and E, D, I, SF, and τ denote earnings before interest and taxes, depreciation, interest expenses, sinking-fund requirements, and tax rates, respectively, we can form the following probability statement by assuming that C is distributed normally with variance of 0.02:

$$P(C \leq 0) = P(C \leq \overline{C} - z\sigma_c), \tag{18.24}$$

and Z represents the number of standard normal deviations the expected level of cash flows lies from zero. Clearly, the validity of this procedure hinges on the power of the analysis to compute the proper standard deviation of the firm's cash-flow streams with the new project included (the form of the distribution could be varied according to the analyst's judgment).

By setting the desired insolvency-probability level associated with the firm, the amount of debt a project allows the firm to issue emerges from the analysis, since the allowable increase of interest expense is readily computed by decreasing C until the probability of insolvency is set equal to the prespecified limits. This allowable decrease in C is the allowable increase in interest expense, and by virtue of knowing the required coupon rate on the firm's bond, the amount of debt that can be issued logically follows.

Step 4 of the analysis is the valuation of the project, a process broken into two parts (similar to the Myers analysis cited in earlier sections of this chapter). From the Capital Asset Pricing Model (CAPM), we are able to compute a beta for the project in question, and use that figure to compute a cost of equity capital for unlevered flows, this rate being used to discount the operating cash flows of the project. In knowing the required coupon payment necessary to float the firm's bonds at par, in Step 3, we know the appropriate discount rate to apply to the capitalization of the interest tax shield generated by the debt undertaken as a result of the project's acceptance. Discounting the tax shield generated by the interest payments at the cost of debt, we obtain the present value of the debt capacity attributable to the project, the summation of these two components giving the total value of the project to the firm. Again we see that debt capacity is directly related to the underlying risk of the projects accepted by the firm, and not by any subjective estimate as to what the firm's total debt to equity ratio should be, or some target to which the times-interest-earned figure should revert.

In some respects, the preceding analysis viewed optimal debt capacity in the light of increasing returns to scale. The more highly uncorrelated the flows of those projects undertaken by the firm, given their absolute size, the greater is the debt capacity, or the lower the probability of insolvency. Also of interest is the implicit assumption that insolvency costs are incurred only when the actual event of insolvency occurs. Hong and Rappaport (1978) argue that debt capacity should be expressed as the amount (or percentage) of debt in the firm's capital structure at the point of optimal capital structure, and that insolvency costs are incurred prior to the event of insolvency. In this way, insolvency costs act to offset the advantage of the interest tax shield attained by the amount of interest-paying debt outstanding. The rationale for claiming that insolvency costs are incurred at all levels of debt financing, regardless of the safety of the debt, is by way of agency theory, where the existence of non-trivial monitoring costs decreases the value of obtaining further interest tax shields.

From the Modigliani and Miller analysis (1963), we find few complications in specifying the value of the interest tax shield attributable to increases in debt, particularly so in the case of perpetual debt. The problem of specification arises only when we attempt to examine the insolvency-cost function. If we follow the Hong and Rappaport example and allow insolvency costs to be a linear function of the amount of debt outstanding (an assumption that probably does not generally hold in practice, but does allow for considerable ease in exposition), another term can be added to the standard M&M firm-valuation formula, as shown below:

$$V^L = \frac{NOI(1-\tau)}{k_s} + \frac{rD\tau}{r} - k_i D, \tag{18.25}$$

where NOI, τ, r, k_s, D and V^L have been defined in previous chapters; k_i is average insolvency cost per unit of debt. The insolvency costs are presented in present-value form. Since optimal capital structure also carries with the property that cost of capital overall is at its minimal point, we could express the value of the firm as the present value of the operating inflows discounted at this minimum cost of capital, as shown below in Eq. (18.26):

$$V^L = \frac{NOI(1-\tau)}{k_a}. \tag{18.26}$$

where k_a is the average cost of capital.

By rearranging Eq. (18.26) to read $V^L k_a = \text{NOI}(1-\tau)$ and substituting this into Eq. (18.25) and solving for k_a, we can obtain the following expression for the weighted-average cost of capital:

$$k_a = k_s + \frac{k_s D(k_i - \tau)}{V^L}, \tag{18.27}$$

from which we can see that the overall cost of capital depends heavily on the rates at which k_i and τ change as additional debt is employed. Differentiating with respect to changes in debt outstanding, all else held constant, we find:

$$\frac{dk_a}{dD} = \frac{k_s}{V^L}\frac{(dk_i - \tau)}{dD}, \tag{18.28}$$

where T is assumed constant and k_i, while assumed to be a linear function of the level of debt, may change as the firm attains higher degrees of financial leverage. The financial planner must specify the functional form of k_i to be able to minimize k_a, that is, set Eq. (18.28) equal to zero.

For project valuation, we must consider the optimal debt level at the new level of V^L, which means only that we are again interested in incremental additions of debt, but, unlike the Martin and Scott analysis, this figure is not only dependent on the ability of the firm to utilize interest tax shields; the incremental insolvency costs and the effect on the insolvency-cost function itself must be considered.

The Martin–Scott method of optimizing capital structure subject to an insolvency constraint utilized the CAPM and the Hamada procedure for obtaining unlevered-beta estimates, where the unlevered beta was subsequently used in arriving at unlevered costs of equity capital that are applied in the M&M tax-corrected firm-valuation model. As Conine (1980) points out, the Hamada method applies only when the debt employed is assumed to be risk-free, an assumption that Martin and Scott did not adhere to. This has the effect of overstating the cost of equity capital as equity assumed all of the firm's risk. This bias the total cost of capital upward and may cause incorrect reject decisions to be made when the firm is considering new investment opportunities.

To be consistent with the CAPM, Conine outlines two methods for resolving the problem: The debt can be assumed riskless, or debt could also be priced according to the CAPM, where the Hamada formulation can be rederived with the inclusion of risky debt.[5] With the first proposed solution hardly resolving the problem, Conine showed that the unlevered beta could be computed from:

$$\beta_0 = \frac{\beta S}{S_0} + \frac{D(1-\tau)\beta_D}{S_0}, \tag{18.29}$$

where β_0, β, S, and S_0 have been defined in Eq. (18.23); D and β_D are risky debt and beta of risky debt respectively; τ is the marginal corporate tax rate. This equation shows that the levered beta computed from historical data, most often used as a first approximation to the beta of equity claims, and also reflects the risk of the debt of the firm. In estimating an unlevered beta with the existence of risky debt, the original Hamada method will overestimate the proper beta and should be adjusted by using the Conine method.

While not technically correct, the Martin and Scott method of capital budgeting and the two adjustments to their method provide a solid conceptual basis for evaluating projects under conditions of uncertainty and the existence of valuable tax shields. In making the suggested corrections, the financial manager should be better able to evaluate projects and simultaneously pursue an optimal capital structure [see Conine (1980); Martin and Scott (1980)].

To show how Martin and Scott's (1976) method can be used to estimate debt capacity and perform capital budgeting, we assume that ABC company's current cash flow is normally distributed with mean \$100,000 ($\overline{C}_1$) and a standard deviation of \$80,000 (σ_{c1}). In addition, we also have valuation information for Project X as shown in Table 18.8.

Step 1. We can use the CAPM discussed in Chapters 9 to calculate k_s:

$$k_s = 0.09 + (0.16 - 0.09)(1.5) = 0.195.$$

Step 2. We calculate debt capacity as follows: The combined standard deviation (the firm's cash flow + Project X) can be defined as:

$$\begin{aligned}\sigma_{c'} &= ((80{,}000)^2 + 2(0.5)(80{,}000)(8{,}000) + (8{,}000)^2)^{1/2} \\ &= \$84{,}285.23.\end{aligned}$$

Table 18.8. Valuation information for project X.

A. Project Cash-Flow Information

1. NOI = \$18,000
2. Project maturity = infinity
3. Marginal tax rate for ABC = 45%
4. Initial cash outlay = \$800,000

B. Required Return Information

1. $R_f = 0.09$
2. $R_m = 0.16$
3. $\beta_0 = 1.5$

C. Debt-Capacity Information

1. Standard deviation in project cash flows = \$8,000
2. Correlation between firm and project cash flows = 0.5
3. Cost of new debt, $r = 0.10$

Using this information $\overline{C} = \$100{,}000$, $\sigma_c = \$80{,}000$, we have

$$z = \frac{\overline{C} - 0}{\sigma_c} = \frac{\$100{,}000}{\$80{,}000} = 1.25.$$

From the normal distribution table, as listed at the rear of this book, the z-value 1.25 implies that 10.56% of the area under ABC's cash-flow distribution lies in the tail beyond zero, as indicated in part (a) of Fig. 18.1. This implies that ABC's present risk of insolvency is 10.56%. After the project is undertaken, as indicated in Fig. 18.1(b),

$$z' = \frac{\$118{,}000}{\$84{,}285} = 1.40.$$

This latter z-value (z') indicates (see part (b) of Fig. 18.1) that the risk of insolvency for the firm has been reduced to 8.08%. The reduction of insolvency risk allows the firm to issue new debt up to the point where its insolvency risk is again 10.56%.

The increase in debt capacity can be determined by computing the added interest and before-tax sinking-fund payment ABC could incur without increasing the firm risk of insolvency above its previous level of 10.56%. In this case:

$$z = \frac{(\overline{C} - C')}{\sigma_{c'}} = \frac{(118{,}000 - C')}{84{,}285} = 1.25.$$

This implies that C' equals \$12,643.75.

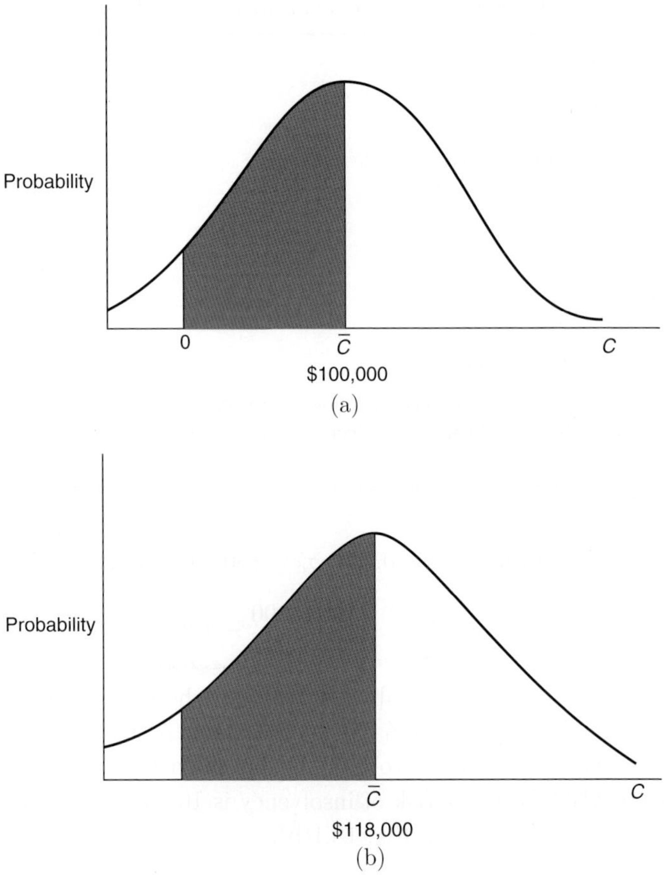

Fig. 18.1. (a) Distribution of unencumbered cash flows for ABC Company, (b) Distribution of unencumbered cash flows after project is undertaken.

The process of inputting the addition to debt capacity can be quite involved where debt has a finite maturity and unequal principal payments. If, however, it is assumed that the addition to debt capacity is permanent, debt service cost (DSC) can be composed entirely of interest expense, so that:

$$D = \frac{DSC}{k_d} = (\$12{,}643.75) \cdot (0.10) = \$126{,}438.$$

Step 3. Using the above-mentioned information, we can make the capital-budgeting decision in terms of the M&M type of valuation model as defined in Eq. (18.25′):

$$V = NOI\frac{(1-\tau)}{k_s} + \frac{rD\tau}{r}. \qquad (18.25')$$

Substituting the related figure into Eq. (18.25′), we obtain:

$$\begin{aligned} V &= \frac{(\$18{,}000)(1-0.45)}{0.195} + \frac{(126{,}438)(0.10)(0.45)}{0.10} \\ &= \$50{,}769 + \$56{,}897 \\ &= \$107{,}666. \end{aligned}$$

Thus, given project X's internal cash outlay of \$80,000, the project is expected to produce a net present value of \$27,666.

Finally, it should be noted that Martin and Scott's model has been generalized by Gahlon and Stover (1979) to incorporate the effect of correlations among the cash flows of all proposed projects. It has also been recently integrated with Myers' (1974) APV model, as discussed in the previous section.

18.7. Implications of Different Policies on the Beta Coefficient

Investment, financing, dividend, and production policy are four important policies in financial management decision. In previous sections, we have discussed investment, financing and dividend policies. In addition, the beta coefficient determination has been discussed in Chapter 8. In this section, we will discuss the impacts of financing, production, and the dividend policy on beta coefficient determination.

18.7.1. *Impact of Financing Policy on Beta Coefficient Determination*

Suppose that the security is a share in the common stock of a corporation. Let us assume that that this corporation increases the proportion of debt in its capital structure, all other relevant factors remaining unchanged. How would you expect this change to affect the firm's beta? We have seen that an increase in the level of debt leads to an increase in the riskiness of stockholders' future earnings. To compensate for this additional risk, stockholders' will demand a higher expected rate-of-return. Therefore, from Eq. (18.30), beta must rise for this company's stock. We see that, all other things equal, the higher the proportion of debt in a firm's capital structure, the higher the beta of shares of its common stock.

$$\beta_L = \beta_U \left(1 + \frac{B(1-\tau_c)}{S}\right) \tag{18.30}$$

where β_L is the leveraged bet; β_U is the unlevered operating beta; B is the amount of debt; S is the amount of equity; and τ_c is the corporate tax rate.

When the market model is used to estimate a firm's beta, the resulting estimate of the beta is the market assessment of both operating and financial risk. This is called leveraged beta. Hamada (1972) and Rubinstein (1973) suggest that Eq. (18.30) can be modified to calculate the unleveraged beta. This beta is an estimate of the firm's operating or business, risk.

We know that Johnson & Johnson's related data are $\beta_L = 0.32$ and average $(B/S) = 0.64$. If $\tau_c = 0.4$, the Johnson & Johnson's unleveraged beta can be calculated as

$$\beta_U = \frac{0.32}{[1 + (0.64)(1-0.4)]} = 0.23.$$

18.7.2. *Impact of Production Policy on Beta Coefficient Determination*

In this section, we will first discuss production policy. Then we will discuss implications of different policies on the beta coefficient determination. Production policy refers to how company uses different input mix to produce its products. The companies' production process can be classified into either capital intensive or labor intensive, which depends upon whether capital labor ratio (K/L Ratio) is larger or smaller than one. We can use either Cobb–Douglas production function or Variable Elasticity of Substitution (VES) production function to show how capital and labor affect the change of the beta coefficient. The Cobb–Douglas production function in two factors, capital (K) and labor (L) can be defined as follows.

$$Q = K^a L^b, \tag{18.31}$$

where Q is firm's output, a and b are positive parameters.

Lee *et al.* (1990) have derived the theoretical relationship between beta coefficient and the capital labor ratio in terms of the Cobb–Douglas production functions as follows in Eq. (18.31).

$$\beta = \frac{(1+r)Cov(\tilde{e}, \tilde{R}_m)}{Var(\tilde{R}_m)\{\phi[1-(1-E)b]\}}, \tag{18.32}$$

where

r = the risk-free rate,
$\tilde{R}_m$ = return on the market portfolio,
$\tilde{e}$ = random price disturbances with zero mean,
$E = -(\partial P/\partial Q)(Q/P)$, an elasticity constant,
b = contribution of labor to total output,
$\phi = 1 - \lambda cov(\tilde{v}, \tilde{R}_m)$,
λ = the market price of systematic risk.

In addition, the VES production function in two factors capital (K) and labor (L) can be defined as follows in Eq. (18.33).

$$Q = K^{\alpha(1-s\rho)}[L + (\rho - 1)K]^{\alpha s\rho}, \tag{18.33}$$

where Q is firm's output and α, s, and ρ are parameters with the following constraints:

$$\alpha > 0,$$
$$0 < s < 1$$
$$0 \leq s\rho \leq 1,$$
$$L/K > (1 - \rho)/(1 - s\rho)^3.$$

Lee *et al.* (1995) have derived the theoretical relationship between beta coefficient and the capital labor ratio in terms of the VES production functions as follows.

$$\beta = \frac{\begin{array}{c}(1+r)\{Cov(\tilde{e}, \tilde{R}_m) - [\Phi(1-\mu E)\alpha s\rho\phi^{-1} \\ -w(pQ)^{-1}(1-\rho)K]Cov(\tilde{v}, \tilde{R}_m)\}\end{array}}{Var(\tilde{R}_m)\{\Phi - [\Phi(1-\mu E)\alpha s\rho - w\phi(pQ)^{-1}(1-\rho)K\}}, \tag{18.34}$$

where

p = expected price of output,
μ = reciprocal of the price elasticity of demand, $0 \leq \mu \leq 1$,
w = expected wage rate,
$\tilde{v}$ = random shock in the wage rate with zero mean,
$\Phi = 1 - \lambda cov(\tilde{e}, \tilde{R}_m)$.
$r, \tilde{R}_m, \tilde{e}, E, \varphi, \lambda$ are as defined in Eq. (18.34).

18.7.3. *Impact of Dividend Policy on Beta Coefficient Determination*

Impact of payout ratio on beta coefficient is one of the important issue in finance research. By using dividend signaling theory, Lee *et al.* (1993) have derived the relationship between the beta coefficient and pay out ratio as follows.

$$\beta_i = \beta_{pi}[1 + \gamma F(d_i)], \tag{18.35}$$

where

β_i = the firm's systematic risk when the market is informationally imperfect and the information asymmetry can be resolved by dividends.

β_{pi} = the firm's systematic risk when market is informaitonally perfect.

γ = a signaling cost incurred if firm's net after-tax operating cash flow X falls below the promised dividend D.

d_i = firm's dividend payout ratio.

$F(d_i)$ = cumulative normal density function in term of payout ratio.

Equation (18.35) implies that beta coefficient is a function of payout ratio.

In sum, this section has shown that how financing, production, and dividend policy can affect the beta coefficient. This information is important for calculating cost of capital equity.

18.8. Summary

In this chapter, we have attacked many of the irrelevant propositions of the neoclassical school of finance theory, and in so doing have created a good news–bad news sort of situation. The good news is that by claiming that financial policies are important, we have justified the existence of academicians and a great many practicing financial managers. The bad news is that we have made their lot a great deal more difficult as numerous tradeoffs were investigated, the more general of these comprising the title of the chapter.

In the determination of dividend policy, we examined the relevance of the internal–external equity decision in the presence of non-trivial transaction costs. While the empirical evidence was found to be inconclusive because of the many variables that could not be controlled, there should be no doubt in anyone's mind that flotation costs (incurred when issuing new equity to replace retained earnings paid out) by themselves have a negative impact on firm value. But if the retained earnings paid out are replaced whole or in part by debt, the equity holders may stand to benefit because the risk is transferred to the existing bondholders — risk they do not receive commensurate return for taking. Thus if the firm pursues a more generous dividend-payout policy while not changing the investment policy, the change in the value of the firm depends on the way in which the future investment is financed.

The effect that debt financing has on the value of the firm was analyzed in terms of the interest tax shield it provides and the extent to which the firm can utilize that tax shield. In Myers' analysis, we also saw that a limit on borrowing could be incorporated so that factors such as risk and the probability of insolvency would be recognized when making each capital-budgeting decision. When compared to other methods widely used in capital budgeting, Myers' APV formulation was found to yield more conservative benefit estimates. While we do not wish to discard the equity-residual, after-tax weighted cost-of-capital method or the Arditti–Levy weighted cost-of-capital method, we set forth Myers' method as the most appropriate starting point when a firm is first considering a project, reasoning that if the project was acceptable following Myers' method, it would be acceptable using the other methods — to an even greater degree. If the project was not acceptable following the APV criteria, it could be reanalyzed with one of the other methods. The biases of each method we hopefully made clear with the introduction of debt financing.

Section 18.6 outlined practical procedures for attaining optimal capital structures subject to probability-of-insolvency constraints or costs incurred attributable to the risky debt financing. If management is able to specify the tolerance for risk, or the rate at which monitoring costs are incurred, then an upper limit on debt capacity can be stated as the amount of interest expense the firm can afford. In the case of regulated firms, we also consider capital structure decisions, in light of the inability of the equity holders to acquire the benefits of the interest tax shield; and we concluded that regulated firms, in the best interests of their shareholders and of society, should issue debt only to the extent it does not jeopardize the equity stake or the existence of the firm. In Section 18.7, we have discussed how different policies can affect the determination of beta coefficient.

In essence, this chapter points out the vagaries and difficulties of financial management in practice. Virtually no decision concerning the finance function can be made independent of the other variables under management's control. Lambrecht and Myers (2012) have shown that investment financing and dividend decision should be jointly determined. Profitable areas of future research in this area are abundant; some have already begun to appear in the literature under the heading "simultaneous-equation planning models". Any practitioner would be well advised to stay abreast of developments in this area.

Graham and Harvey (2001) surveyed 392 CFO's about cost of capital, capital budgeting, and capital structure. What we discussed in this chapter relative to the findings of this survey is the concern for a firm's financial flexibility when issuing debt and earnings. Furthermore, this survey analyzed how although larger firms use present value techniques and CAPM but smaller firms concentrate on the payback criterion. The pecking-order theory and trade-off of capital structure hypothesis were also discussed in this survey.

1. Alderson (1984) has applied this kind of concept to the problem of corporate pension funding. He finds grounds for the integration of pension funding with capital structure decisions. In doing so, he argues that unfunded vested liabilities are an imperfect substitute for debt.
2. If the dividend policy is irrelevant, then $L_{ct} = L_{c,t-1} = 0$; if $\mathrm{dW}/\mathrm{dy}_t = F_t$ is positive, then the constraints U will always be binding, Eq. (18.7b) will be strict equalities, and L_{ft} for all t. Substituting $L_{ct} = 0$ and $L_{ft} = F_t$ into Eq. (18.8), we obtain Eq. (18.12).
3. This statement can be explained by the agency theory. Agency theory was developed by Jensen and Meckling (1976) and was extended by BHS (1981). According to the agency theory and the findings of Stiglitz (1972), the manager might not act out of the equityholders' best interest. For his own benefit, the manager might shift the wealth of a firm from the equityholders to bondholders.
4. By using stochastic-dominance analysis with a linear utility function, Arditti and Peles (1977) demonstrated that these are probability distributions of earnings for which an interior capital structure is optimal for the firm and the leverage varies inversely with the variance of the after-tax cash flow of an all-equity firm. Basic concepts of stochastic dominance and its application to the capital structure with default risk can be found in the appendix of this chapter.
5. CAPM approach of pricing risky debt can be found in Chen (1978).

Problem Set

1. Discuss the potential interaction between investment and dividend decisions. What factors can influence the internal-versus-external financing decision?
2. Briefly discuss the interaction between dividend and financing policy. How can they be analyzed in terms of (1) cost of equity capital, and (2) the valuation on risk debt?

3. Discuss the interaction between financing and investment decisions. How do these interactions affect capital-budgeting decisions?
4. How can the overall theories and methods explored in Chapter 18 be used to justify financial analysis, planning, and forecasting?
5. Please collect the accounting data of Johnson & Johnson, Merck, P&G, and Pfizer from 2004 to 2008 to qualitatively and quantitatively analyze the interrelationship of financing, investment, and dividend decisions.
6. Please discuss implications of different policies on systematic risk determination. In addition, please use the data which you collected in question 5 to estimate both leveraged and unleveraged beta.

Appendix 18.A. Stochastic Dominance and it's Applications to Capital Structure Analysis with Default Risk

18.A1. *Introduction*

Mean–variance approaches were used in previous chapter to derive alternative finance theories, and perform related empirical studies. Besides mean–variance approaches, there is a more general approach, stochastic-dominance analysis, which can be used to choose a portfolio, to evaluate mutual-fund performance, and to analyze the optimal capital structure problem.

Levy and Sarnat (1972), Porter and Gaumwitz (1972), Jean (1975), and Ang and Chua (1982) have discussed the stochastic-dominance approach to portfolio choice and mutual-fund performance evaluation in detail. Baron (1975), Arditti and Peles (1977), and Arditti (1980) have used the theory of stochastic dominance to investigate the optimal capital structure question. In this appendix, we will only discuss how stochastic-dominance theory can be used to analyze the issue of optimal capital structure with default risk.

18.A2. *Concepts and Theorems of Stochastic Dominance*

The expected utility rule can be used to introduce the economics of choice under uncertainty. However, this decision rule has been based upon the principle of utility maximization, where either the investor's utility function is assumed to be a second-degree polynomial with a positive first derivative and a negative second derivative, or the probability function is assumed to be normal. A stochastic-dominance theory is an alternative approach of preference orderings that does not rely upon these restrictive assumptions.

The stochastic-dominance technique assumes only that individuals prefer more wealth to less.

An asset is said to be stochastically dominant over another if an individual receives greater wealth from it in every (ordered) state of nature. This definition is known as first-order stochastic dominance. Mathematically, it can be described by the relationship between two cumulative-probability distributions. If X symbolizes the investment dollar return variable and $F(X)$ and $G(X)$ are two cumulative-probability distributions, then $F(X)$ will be preferred to $G(X)$ by every person who is a utility maximizer and whose utility is an increasing function of wealth if $F(X) \leq G(X)$ for all possible X, and $F(X) < G(X)$ for some X.

For the family of all monotonically non-decreasing utility functions, Levy and Sarnat (1972) show that first-order stochastic dominance implies that:

$$E_F U(X) > E_G U(X), \tag{18.A.1}$$

where $E_F U(X)$ and $E_G U(X)$ are expected utilities. Mathematically, they can be defined as:

$$E_F U(X) = \int_{-x}^{x} U(X) f(X) dx, \tag{18.A.2a}$$

$$E_F U(X) = \int_{-x}^{x} U(X) g(X) dx, \tag{18.A.2b}$$

where $U(X)$ = *the* utility function, X = *the* investment dollar-return variable, $f(X)$ and $g(X)$ are probability distributions of X. It should be noted that the above-mentioned first-order stochastic dominance does not depend upon the shape of the utility function with positive marginal utility. Hence, the investor can either be risk-seeking, risk neutral, or risk-averse. If the risk-aversion criterion is imposed, the utility function is either strictly concave or non-decreasing.

If utility functions are non-decreasing and strictly concave, then the second-order stochastic-dominance theorem can be defined. Mathematically, the second-order dominance can be defined as:

$$\int_{-x}^{x} [G(T) - F(t)] dt > 0, \quad \text{where } G(t) \neq F(t) \text{ for some } t. \tag{18.A.3}$$

Equation (18.A.3) specifies a necessary and sufficient condition for an asset F to be preferred over a second asset G by all risk-averters.

Conceptually, Eq. (18.A.3) means that, in order for asset F to dominate asset G for all risk-aversion investors, the accumulated area under the cumulative-probability distribution G must be greater than the accumulated area for F for any given level of wealth. This implies that, unlike first-order stochastic dominance, the cumulative density functions can cross.

Stochastic dominance is an extremely important and powerful tool. It is properly founded on the basis of expected utility maximization, and even more important, it applies to any probability distribution. This is because it takes into account every point in the probability distribution. Furthermore, we can be sure that, if an asset demonstrates second-order stochastic dominance, it will be preferred by all risk-aversion investors, regardless of the specific shape of their utility functions.

Assume that the density functions of EPS for both firm A and firm B are $f(X)$ and $g(X)$, respectively. Both $f(X)$ and $g(X)$ have normal distributions and the shape of these tow distributions are described in Fig. 18.A.1. Obviously the EPS of firm A will dominate the EPS of firm B if an investor is risk-averse because they both offer the same expected level of wealth ($\mu_f = \mu_g$), and because the variance of $g(X)$ is larger than that of $f(X)$.

Based upon both the first-order and the second-order stochastic-dominance theorems mentioned earlier, a new theorem needed for investigating capital structure with default risk can be defined as:

Theorem 18.A.1. *Let F, G be two distributions with mean values μ_1 and μ_2 respectively, such that, for some $X_0 < \infty$, $F \leq G$ for $X \leq X_0$ (and $F < G$ for some $X_1 < X_0$) and $F \geq G$ for some $X \geq X_0$, then F dominates G (for concave utility functions) if and only if $\mu_1 \geq \mu_2$.*

The proof of this theorem can be formed in either Hanoch and Levy (1969) or Levy and Sarnat (1972). Conceptually, this theorem states that if two cumulative distributions, F and G, intersect only once, then if F is below G to the left of the intersection point and has a higher mean than does G, the investment with cumulative distribution F dominates that with cumulative return distribution G on a second-degree stochastic-dominance basis.

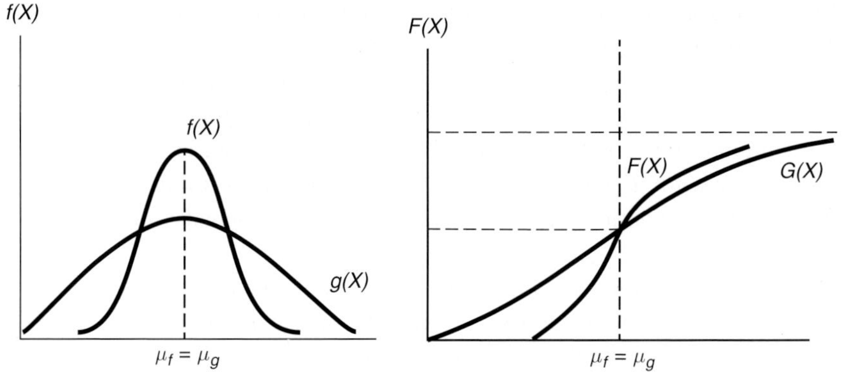

18.A3. *Stochastic-Dominance Approach to Investigating the Capital Structure Problem with Default Risk*

The existence of default risk has been used in Chapter 18 to justify why an optimal capital structure might exist for a firm. To analyze this problem Baron (1975), Arditti and Peles (1977), and Arditti (1980) have used the stochastic-dominance theorem described in the previous section to indicate the effects of debt-financing bonds on relative values of levered and unlevered firms. Baron analyzed the bonds in terms of default risk, tax rates, and debt levels.

Consider two firms, or the same firm before and after debt financing, with identical probability distribution of gross earnings X, before taxes and financial charges, such that, in any state of nature that occurs, both firms have the same earnings. In addition, it is assumed that this random variable X is associated with a cumulative-distribution function $F(X)$. Firm A is assumed to be financed solely by equity, while firm B is financed by both debt and equity. The market value V_1 of firm A equals E_1, the value of its equity, while the market value V_2 of firm B equals the market value of its equity (E_2) plus the value of its debt (D_2). Debt is assumed to sell at its par value and to carry a gross coupon rate of r ($r > 0$).

The firm can generally use the coupon payments as a tax shield and therefore the after-tax earnings for firms A and B can be defined as $X(1-T)$ and $(X - rD_2)(1 - T)$, respectively (where T is the corporate-profit tax rate.) If an investor purchases a fraction of firm A, this investment results in dollar returns of:

$$Y_1 = \begin{cases} 0, & \text{if } X \leq 0, \\ \alpha X(1-T) & \text{if } X > 0, \end{cases} \tag{18.A.4}$$

with cumulative probability function:

$$G_1(Y) = \begin{cases} F(0) & \text{if } Y = 0, \\ F(Y/(1-T) & \text{if } Y > 0. \end{cases} \tag{18.A.5}$$

If the investor purchased a fraction α of the equity and α of the debt of firm B, this dollar return would be:

$$Y_2 = \begin{cases} 0 & \text{if } X \leq 0, \\ \alpha(1-k)X(1-T) & \text{if } 0 < X(1-T) < D_2 + rD_2, \\ \alpha(X(1-T) + TrD_2 & \text{if } x(1-T) \geq D_2 + rD_2, \end{cases} \tag{18.A.6}$$

where k represents the percentage of liquidation cost. Since these bonds comprise a senior lien on the earnings of the firm, failure to pay the promised amount of D_2+rD_2 to bondholders can force liquidation of the firm's assets.

The cumulative distribution associated with Eq. (18.A.6) is:

$$G_2(Y) = \begin{cases} F(0) & \text{if } Y = 0, \\ F[Y/\alpha(1-k)(1-T)] & \text{if } 0 < y \leq \alpha(1-k)[D_2 + rD_2], \\ F[Y/\alpha(1-T) - TrD_2] & \text{if } Y \geq \alpha[D_2 + rD_2]. \end{cases} \tag{18.A.7}$$

Comparing Eq. (18.A.5) with Eq. (18.A.7), it can be found that:

$$G_1(Y) < G_2(Y) \quad \text{if } 0 < Y < \alpha(D_2 + rD_2), \tag{18.A.8}$$

$$G_2(Y) \geq G_2(Y) \quad \text{if } Y \geq \alpha(D_2 + rD_2), \tag{18.A.9}$$

where $\alpha(D_2 + rD_2)$ is the critical income level of bankruptcy.

Equations (18.A.8) and (18.A.9) imply that the levered firm cannot dominate the unlevered firm on a first-degree or second-degree stochastic-dominance basis. From the theorem of stochastic dominance that we presented in the previous section, it can be concluded that the unlevered firm cannot dominate the levered firm because the expected return of the levered firm is generally higher than that of the unlevered firm (otherwise why levered?), and because the $G_2(Y)$ and $G_1(Y)$ curves intersect only once.

Consequently, a general statement using stochastic dominance cannot be made with respect to the amount of debt that a firm should issue. However, these results have indicated the possibility of interior (non-corner) optimal capital structure. By using a linear utility function, Arditti and Peles (1977) show that there are probability distributions for which an interior capital structure for a firm can be found. In addition, they also make some other market observations, which are consistent with the implications of their model. These observations are: (i) firms with low income variability, such as utilities, carry high debt–equity ratios; (ii) firms that have highly marketable assets and therefore low liquidation costs, such as shipping lines, seem to rely heavily on debt financing relative to equity.

18.A4. *Summary*

In this appendix, we have tried to show the basic concepts underlying stochastic dominance and its application to capital structure analysis with default risk. By combining utility maximization theory with cumulative-density functions, we are able to set up a decision rule without explicitly relying on individual statistical moments. This stochastic-dominance theory can then be applied to problems such as capital structure analysis with risky debt, as was shown earlier.

References for Appendix 18.A

Ang, JS and JH Chua (1982). Mutual funds: Different strokes for different folks. *The Journal of Portfolio Management*, 8, 43–47.

Arditti, FD (1980). A survey of valuation and the cost of capital. *Research in Finance*, 2, 1–56.

Arditti, FD and YC Peles (1977). Leverage, bankruptcy and the cost of capital. In *Natural Resources, Uncertainty, and General Equilibrium Systems: Essays in Memory of Rafael Lusky*, A Blinder and P Friedman (eds.). New York: Academic Press.

Baron, DP (December, 1975). Firm valuation, corporate taxes, and default risk. *Journal of Finance*, 30, 1251–1264.

Hanoch, G and H Levy (July, 1969). The efficiency analysis of choices involving risk. *Review of Economic Studies*, 36, 335–346.

Jean, W (1975). Comparison of moment and stochastic-dominance ranking methods. *Journal of Financial and Quantitative Analysis*, 10, 151–162.

Lambrecht, BM and SC Myers (October 2012). A Lintner model of payout and managerial rents. *Journal of Finance*, 67, 1761–1810.

Levy, H and M Sarnat (1972). *Investment and Portfolio Analysis.* New York: John Wiley and Sons.

Porter, RB and JE Gaumwitz (June, 1972). Stochastic dominance vs. mean–variance portfolio analysis: An empirical evaluation. *American Economic Review*, 57, 438–446.

References for Chapter 18

Alderson, MJ (1984). Unfunded pension liabilities and capital structure decisions: A theoretical and empirical investigation. Ph.D. dissertation, The University of Illinois at Urbana-Champaign.

Arditti, FD and YC Peles (1977). Leverage, bankruptcy, and the cost of capital. In *Natural Resources, Uncertainty and General Equilibrium Systems: Essays in Memory of Rafael Lusky*, A. Blinder and P. Friedman (eds.), pp. 35–51. New York: Academic Press.

Arditti, FD and H Levy (Fall 1977). The weighted-average cost of capital as a cutoff rate: A critical examination of the classical textbook weighted average. *Financial Management*, 6, 24–34.

Barnea, A, RA Haugen, and LW Senbet (Summer 1981). Market imperfections, agency problems, and capital structure: A review. *Financial Management*, 10, 7–22.

Baumol, W and BG Malkiel (November, 1967). The firm's optimum debt–equity combination and the cost of capital. *Quarterly Journal of Economics*, 81, 546–578.

Black, F (winter, 1976). The dividend puzzle. *Journal of Portfolio Management*, 2, 5–8.

Black, F and M Scholes (May–June, 1973). The pricing of options and corporate liabilities. *Journal of Political Economy*, 81, 673–654.

Chambers, DR, RS Harris, and JJ Pringle (Summer 1982). Treatment of financing mix in analyzing investment opportunities. *Financial Management*, 11, 24–41.

Chen, AH (1978). Recent development in cost of debt capital. *Journal of Finance*, 33, 863–877.

Conine Jr, TE (Spring 1980). Debt capacity and the capital budgeting decision: A comment. *Financial Management*, 9, 20–22.

DeAngelo, H and L DeAngelo (2006). The irrelevance of the MM dividend irrelevance theorem. *Journal of Financial Economics*, 79, 293–315.

Fama, EF and MH Miller (1972). *The Theory of Finance*. New York: Holt, Rinehart and Winston.

Graham, JR and CR Harvey (2001). The theory and practice of corporate finance: Evidence from the field. *Journal of Financial Economics*, 60(2–3), 187–243.

Gupta, MC and AC Lee (March 2006). An integrated model of debt issuance, refunding, and maturity. *Review of Quantitative Finance and Accounting*, 26(2), 177–199.

Gahlon, JM and RD Stover (Winter 1979). Debt capacity and the capital budgeting decision: A caveat. *Financial Management*, 8, 55–59.

Gupta, MC, AC Lee, and CF Lee (2007). Effectiveness of dividend policy under the capital asset pricing model: A dynamic analysis. Working Paper, Rutgers University.

Hamada, RS (May 1972). The effect of the firm's capital structure on the systematic risk of common stock. *Journal of Finance*, 27, 435–452.

Hellwig, MF (1981). Bankruptcy, limited liability, and the Modigliani–Miller theorem. *The American Economic Review*, 71, 155–170.

Higgins, RC (Fall 1977). How much growth can a firm afford? *Financial Management*, 6, 7–16.

Higgins, RC (Autumn 1981). Sustainable growth under inflation. *Financial Management*, 10, 36–40.

Hong, H and A Rappaport (Autumn 1978). Debt capacity and the capital-budgeting decision: A caveat. *Financial Management*, 7–11.

Jensen, M and W Meckling (1976). Theory of the firm: managerial behavior, agency costs, and ownership structure. *Journal of Financial Economics*, 3, 305–360.

Johnson, DJ (Autumn 1981). The behavior of financial structure and sustainable growth in an inflationary environment. *Financial Management*, 10, 30–35.

Kim, EH (May 1982). Miller's equilibrium, shareholder leverage clienteles, and optimal capital structure. *Journal of Finance*, 37, 301–319.

Kim, EH (March 1978). A mean–variance theory of optimal capital structure and corporate debt capacity. *Journal of Finance*, 45–64.

Kim, EH, JJ McConnell, and PR Greenwood (June 1977). Capital-structure rearrangements and me-first roles in an efficient capital market. *Journal of Finance*, 32, 811–821.

Lambrecht, BM and SC Myers (2012). A Lintner model of payout and managerial rents. *Journal of Finance*, 67, 1761–1810.

Lee, C-F, W-L Liang, F-L Lin, and Y Yang (2015). Application of simultaneous equation in finance research: Methods and empirical results. Rutgers University, Working Paper.

Lee, CF and AC Lee (2006). *Encyclopedia of Finance*. New York: Springer.

Lee, CF, C Wu, and D Hang (March 1993). Dividend policy under conditions of capital markets and signaling equilibrium. *Review of Quantitative Finance and Accounting*, 3, 47–59.

Lee, CF, S Rahman, and KT Liaw (August 1990). The impacts of market power and capital–labor ratio on systematic risk: A Cobb–Douglas approach. *Journal of Economics and Business*, 42(3), 237–241.

Lee, CF, KC Chen, and KT Liaw (August 1995). Systematic risk, wage rates, and factor substitution. *Journal of Economics and Business*, 47(3), 267–279.

Litzenberger, RH and K Ramaswamy (1979). The effect of personal taxes and dividends on capital-asset prices: Theory and empirical evidence. *Journal of Financial Economics*, 7, 163–195.

Litzenberger, RH and HB Sosin (1979). A comparison of capital-structure decision of regulated and nonregulated firms. *Financial Management*, 8, 17–21.

Malkiel, BG (Spring 1970). The valuation of public-utility equity. *Bell Journal of Economics and Management Science*, 1, 143–160.

Martin, JD and DF Scott (Summer 1976). Debt capacity and the capital budgeting decision. *Financial Management*, 7–14.

Martin, JD and DF Scott, Jr (Spring 1980). Debt capacity and the capital budgeting decision: A revisitation. *Financial Management*, 23–26.

Merton, RC (1974). On pricing of corporate debt: The risk structure of interest rates. *Journal of Finance*, 29, 449–70.

Miller, MH (1977). Debt and taxes. *Journal of Finance*, 32, 261–275.

Modigliani, F and M Miller (June 1963). Corporation income taxes and the cost of capital: A correction. *American Economic Review*, 261–297.

Modigliani, F and M Miller (June 1958). The cost of capital, corporate finance, and theory of investment. *American Economic Review*, 48, 261–297.

Myers, SC (1977). Determinants of corporate borrowing. *Journal of Financial Economics*, 5, 147–175.

Myers, SC (1974). Interaction of corporate financing and investment decision. *Journal of Finance*, 29, 1–25.

Rendleman Jr, RJ (Spring 1978). The effects of default risk on firm's investment and financing decisions. *Financial Management*, 45–53.

Reseck, RW (1970). Multidimensional risk and the Modigliani–Miller hypothesis. *Journal of Finance*, 25, 47–51.

Rhee, SG and FL McCarthy (Summer 1982). Corporate debt capacity and capital-budgeting analysis. *Financial Management*, 11, 42–50.

Rubinstein, ME (March 1973). A mean–variance synthesis of corporate financial theory. *Journal of Finance*, 28, 167–87.

Stiglitz, J (Autumn 1972). Some aspects of pure theory of corporate finance: Bankruptcies and take-overs. *Bell Journal of Economics and Management Science*, 3, 458–482.

Tuttle, L and RH Litzenberger (June 1968). Leverage, diversification, and capital-market effects on a risk-adjusted capital-budgeting framework. *Journal of Finance*, 23, 427–443.

Van Horne, JC and JD McDonald (1971). Dividend policy and new equity financing. *Journal of Finance*, 26, 507–519.

Project IV

Corporate Policies and Their Interrelationships

Part V

Short-term Financial Decision

Chapter 19

Short-Term Financial Analysis and Planning

19.1. Introduction

Short-term financial management and planning begins with cash. The financial manager must understand the firm's sources and uses of cash. With an understanding of the environment in which the company operates, the manager can then apply various cash management, budgeting, and planning techniques to accomplish specific organizational goals.

The day-to-day management of a firm's cash flow is often considered a somewhat routine and low-level operation in the overall spectrum of corporate activity. However, the entire organization is directly affected by such short-term activity. Indeed, an organization's success, although helped only marginally by good short-term planning and management, can be severely affected by poor or non-existent short-term financial analysis and planning.

Cash is only one of the critical variables that must be managed in short-term financial analysis and planning. The other components of working-capital, such as accounts receivable (AR), marketable securities, and accounts payable, must also be managed properly in the short-term. We begin Chapter 19 by discussing the components of working-capital in Section 19.2. We then show how the concept of cash flow is used in short-term financial planning, compare the concept of cash flow and funds flow, discuss ways a firm can organize for short-term financial planning, present principles of short-term financial planning, and explain the cash flow cycle and measurement techniques in Sections 19.3, 19.4, 19.5, and 19.6. The final sections (19.7, 19.8, 19.9, 19.10, 19.11, and 19.12) of the chapter discuss the entire process of forecasting, budgeting, and planning and include a case study to demonstrate the interrelated nature of the process. Summary is offered in 19.13.

19.2. The Components of Working-Capital

Working-capital is the dollar amount of an organization's current assets, which include cash, marketable securities, AR, and inventories. These current assets are considered to be liquid because they can be converted into cash within a short period. Each of the separate components of working-capital is affected by the activities of various parts of the organization. Production, pricing, distribution, marketing, wage contracts, and financing decisions are just a few of the diverse activities within the firm that can affect not only the amount of working-capital but also how quickly the individual assets can be converted into cash. Additionally, the external environment in which the firm operates (product markets, investment markets, and financial markets) can also affect the amount and the rate of change of a firm's working-capital. In a highly seasonal industry, the typical scenario is for inventory to increase dramatically. As demand for the product increases, inventory will decrease as AR increases. The cycle is completed when the AR are collected in cash. For many organizations, the level of working-capital is subject to seasonal and cyclical forces, which can cause a high degree of variability.

Working-capital can be further defined as either permanent or temporary. *Permanent working-capital* is the dollar amount of working-capital that remains fixed over time regardless of seasonal or cyclical variations in sales. *Temporary working-capital* consists of the additional funds required to meet the seasonal or cyclical variations in sales over and above permanent working-capital.

The concept of short-term financial planning is much broader than that of working-capital asset management because it involves the management of current assets and current liabilities and their interrelationship. In practice, little or no distinction is made between investment decisions involving current assets and financing decisions involving current liabilities. Current assets and current liabilities are often closely related, as in the spontaneous financing of current assets such as inventory when the firm purchases goods or supplies on credit. Both assets and liabilities are increased simultaneously, providing financing — at least in the short run — for the investment.

Net working-capital is the difference between current assets and current liabilities and is a financial indicator that can be used in conjunction with

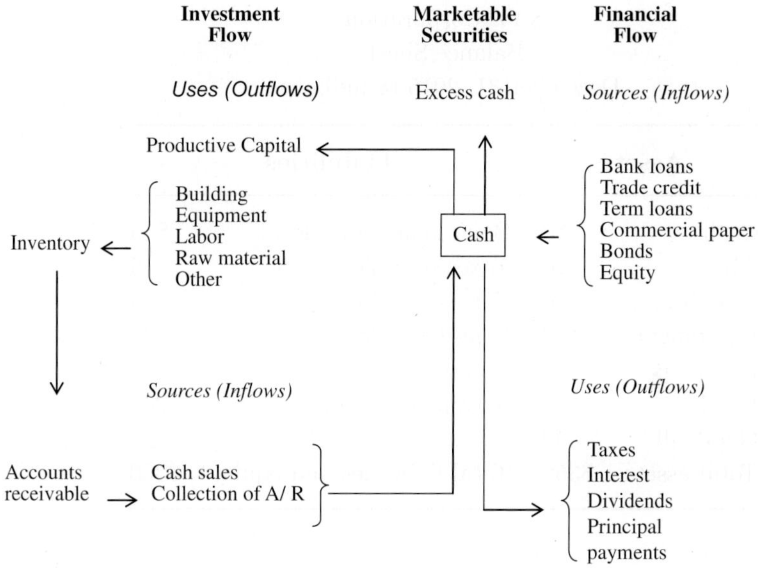

Fig. 19.1. Flow of funds.

ratio analysis to gauge a firm's liquidity. In general, an abundance of net working-capital is considered desirable because it suggests that the firm has ample liquidity to meet its short-term obligations. As we shall see, this may not always be the case. In fact, one of the objectives of short-term financial planning is to reduce excess or redundant working-capital to a minimum, which in turn reduces the cost of carrying idle assets.

As the firm operates, funds flow continuously from one type of asset to another in a circular fashion. Figure 19.1 shows how funds flow through an organization. The time it takes these funds to complete a full cycle reflects the average time that the organization's cash is invested in inventory and AR, both of which are non-earnings assets. Therefore, it is in the organization's best interest to keep this cycle as short as possible while remaining competitive.

EXAMPLE 19.2

Question 1. Given the balance sheet of XYZ Corporation, what is the firm's amount of working-capital? What is its amount of net working-capital? Does XYZ have a potential cash flow problem?

XYZ Corporation
Balance Sheet
December 31, 2015 ($ millions)

Assets		Liabilities	
Cash	$10	Bank loans payable	$15
AR	10	Taxes payable	15
Inventory	10	Wages payable	15
Equipment	100	Long-term debt	30
Buildings	100	Common stock	75
Land	70	Retained earnings	200
Goodwill	50		
Total assets	$350	Total liabilities and equity	$350

Answer:

$$\begin{aligned}\text{Working-capital} &= \text{Cash} + \text{AR} + \text{Inventory}\\ &= \$10 + \$10 + \$10\\ &= \$30 \text{ million.}\\ \text{Net working-capital} &= \text{Cash} + \text{AR} + \text{Inventory} - \text{Payables}\\ &= \$10 + \$10 + \$10 - \$15 - \$15 - \$15\\ &= -\$15 \text{ million.}\end{aligned}$$

Company XYZ has a potential liquidity or cash flow problem because its current assets are less than its current liabilities. The firm either must refinance short-term (borrow additional short-term funds), liquidate or sell long-term assets, or refinance long-term (issue new long-term debt or equity).

Concept Quiz

1. What is working-capital?
2. What is net working-capital?
3. What is meant by spontaneous financing?

19.3. The Concept of Cash Flow

The nature of cash flow varies widely among different types of organizations.

The controlling factors that relate cash flow to short-term financial planning are (1) projecting the cash flow cycle and (2) managing the investment and financing of working-capital.

Today, one of the most critical issues for financial managers is *liquidity* — the organization's ability to pay its debts and expenses in a timely fashion. In the 1960's, financial management stressed growth and profitability. The reason is that during this period, inflation ranged from less than 1% to slightly more than 5% per year, and the prime lending rate of banks ranged from 2 1/4 to 8 1/2%. Because of the stability of the economic environment, financial managers accented growth and profitability rather than liquidity. Even less-skillful managers were able to remain in business simply by riding the economic growth curve.

However, in the mid-1970s, the economic environment changed significantly. Whereas the average rate of inflation was 2.3% in the 1960s, it ranged from 3.3% to 12% in the 1970s, while the prime rate exceeded 20% at times. In the 1980s, the economic condition changed as dramatically as the 1970s. Uncertainty replaced prosperity as economic conditions changed. The significance of all of this change is that financial managers can no longer only stress growth and profitability, but must also consider liquidity. Thus, survival and liquidity are of much greater importance today, when we are facing high interest rates, uncertainty about government policy, and an increase in the magnitude of the variability of cash flows.

FROM THE BOARDROOM: Managing Cash

Managing cash is critical to the treasury executive. At Johnson & Johnson, we have taken three steps to make effective use of corporate cash:

1. We have reduced bank credit risk.
2. We have improved the flow of cash through the corporation.
3. We have established an international coordination center to streamline the flow of funds throughout our operations worldwide.

To achieve the first of these objectives, [we have followed] a policy of only dealing with banks who were rated BAA or better. [Our] Cash Management Improvement Program (CMIP) was created in the United States to improve cash flow, eliminate unnecessary balances and costs, and as a side effect, reduce bank credit exposure. Less money tied up in our cash flow leads directly to less exposure to bank failure.

What was the effect of CMIP? We reduced the number of banks. We reduced balances from $25 million to $3 million, and we expect to move this value even closer to zero in the future. In sum, we achieved three major results. We reduced our bank exposure. We reduced outstanding bank balances via zero balance accounts and fees *in lieu* of balance. And we increased efficiency and communication via automation.

To achieve tax-efficient intercompany lending and cost-efficient worldwide netting, Johnson & Johnson established a Belgian coordination center (BCC). Each portion of the three part program described here has contributed to greater cash flow hboxmanagement efficiency. The success of managing cash at Johnson & Johnson depends on the integrated efforts of all three of these steps.

19.4. Cash Flow Versus Funds Flow

Liquidity and cash flow are closely related. However, cash flow and funds flow are concepts that have origins and uses in two different disciplines: finance and accounting. The concepts of profitability, net working-capital, net income, and funds flow that accountants normally deal with are not cash-based concepts. These accounting concepts are affected by the accruals and deferrals associated with the accounting cycle, which are made to match historical costs and revenues associated with a specific period. Financial managers, bankers, creditors, and investors are more interested in current or future cash flows, because they want to know how much cash will be available for reinvestment, interest, principal, and dividends.

Profitability involves the relationship between revenues and expenses during a given time interval and thus would seem to be a cash-based concept. However, because revenues include credit sales and deferrals, while expenses include payables and accruals, the concept of profitability is also funds-based.

Net working-capital is a funds-based concept. It is the quantity of excess current assets over current liabilities at a single point in time. Net working-capital is strictly a quantitative concept that reveals nothing about the *quality* of current assets or current liabilities. Since the concept of net working-capital deals with current assets, and current assets should eventually be converted into cash, there is a relationship between the firm's net working-capital and its cash flow. However, this relationship can be imprecise and is the function of the timing of the conversion to cash (hence the word *flow*). Only when the timing of current assets conversion into cash or the timing of the payment of current liabilities is considered can we discuss planning cash flow, which is a dynamic concept.

Calculating net income plus depreciation is usually a fund-based operation, although there are two cases in which net income plus depreciation equals cash flow and therefore is cash-based. The first case involves an all-cash business, such as a liquor store or a fast-food outlet. The second case involves a static firm operating on a cash or accrued basis and having no changes in any balance sheet items from one period to another. In such a firm, net income plus depreciation equals the cash flow for the period. However, it is difficult to imagine such a static firm in the real world.

In any short-term financial analysis and planning, the financial manager must understand the difference between cash flow (a financial concept) and funds flow (an accounting-based concept). In planning short-term cash now, the cash budget is the basic tool of analysis and provides the framework that is used for planning. The main purposes of planning cash flows are (1) to predict what demands will be made on the organization on the future, (2) to assess the financial impact of those demands, (3) to generate and choose from alternative courses of action to meet those demands. Forecasting future cash flows is critical because certain aspects of future operations can be predicted with a great degree of accuracy. These aspects tend to be in the area of expenses. Salaries, for example, are a fairly predictable expense; if the work force is to be expanded by 10 employees, the cost can be predicted with a high degree of accuracy. On the other hand, customer demand for products or services and the effect of competitors' actions on the revenue stream are not as easy to predict with any degree of accuracy. To handle these types of difficult forecasting problems, the cash flow manager must generate "what if" scenarios: what if customer demand rises 20%? What if it falls 5%? What if the chief competition cuts prices? In effect, the cash flow manager makes and tests assumptions about customer behavior and competitors' actions and converts these assumptions into cash flow numbers.

After various scenarios have been identified and the appropriate cash flow statements have been prepared, planning can begin. Basically, cash flow planning deals with two areas: (1) the investment of surplus cash balances and (2) the use of short-term borrowing to meet cash flow deficits. Given the wide range of money market investments and the numerous sources and techniques of short-term financing available, the cash flow manager is faced with the problem of identifying the highest return, lowest risk investments for surplus cash and the cheapest, most dependable sources of short-term financing to meet the deficit. (Chapters 19 and 20 provide a detailed look at these issues).

EXAMPLE 19.2

Question 2. The income statement of Jofin Corp. is presented below. What is the relationship between Jofin's net income and its cash flows, assuming that all revenues and expenses except depreciation represent exchanges of cash?

Jofin Corporation
Income Statement
Dec. 31, 2015 (millions)
Accounting data

	(Used for tax purposes)	**Cash Flow Data**
Revenues	\$100	\$100
Cost of goods sold	50	50
General administrative and selling expense	10	10
Depreciation	10	—
Operating income	\$30	\$40
Interest	10	10
Taxable income	\$20	\$30
Tax (30%) (Actual tax paid based on reported income)	6	6
Net income	\$14	Cash flow \$24

Answer: Since depreciation is a non-cash expense of \$10, no cash flow leaves the firm for this expense. Thus, the firm has a \$24 million cash inflow, as shown by the cash flow statement, rather than the \$14 million shown by the standard income statement.

Concept Quiz

1. How does the importance of cash flow planning change with the business cycle?

2. How do cash flows differ from funds flows?
3. How does depreciation relate to cash flow?

19.5. Organizing for Short-Term Financial Planning

The way an organization structures and staffs the resources devoted to short-term financial analysis and planning is primarily a question of the size of the firm. Table 19.1 shows typical resources for small, medium, and large organizations. In a small organization, officers may hold dual titles, such as president and treasurer, and may have a very small staff or no staff responsible for cash planning and management. In a medium-sized firm, specialization begins to occur, and an internal staff becomes necessary for cash management. Given that sizable amounts of money flow through large organizations, they may find it profitable to have a staff devoted exclusively to cash planning and management and may even have cash managers in their regional offices.

Short-Term Financial Planning Principles

The goals for effective short-term financial management are (1) to meet production schedules, (2) to satisfy sales demand, (3) to minimize financing costs, and (4) to provide liquidity for the firm. These goals are best achieved by matching the maturity of the financing sources of funds with the maturity of the assets being held, as indicate in Fig. 19.2. If the maturities are not matched, the firm will be subject to unnecessary risks and the burden of additional costs. If long-term assets are financed with short-term liabilities, the manager will have to refinance continually, which increases the risk the firm faces because the necessary cash may be unavailable or available at substantially higher costs. Additionally, repeated refinancing involves increased transaction costs in terms of dollars and executive time. On the other hand, if short-term needs are financed with long-term liabilities, the cost of long-term financing will be higher than the returns earned on the short-term asset investment, and this negative spread will adversely affect profits.

Table 19.1. Cash planning and management resources.

Size of Organization	Officers in Charge	Staff Size
Small	President/Treasurer Vice President/Controller	0–2
Medium	Treasurer Assistant Treasurer	1–10
Large	Assistant Treasurer	Over 10

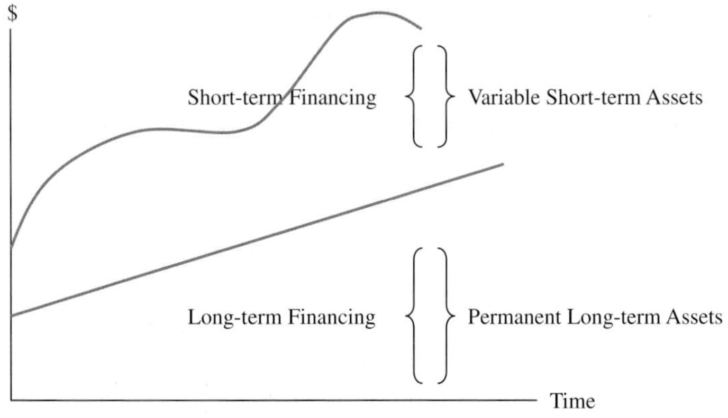

Fig. 19.2. Matching maturities of financing sources and assets.

Liquidity is required and, as we have seen, is becoming more important not only to meet the firm's expected obligations, but also to take advantage of unforeseen opportunities. Therefore, the short-term financial planner must balance liquidity requirements against the opportunity costs of foregoing profitable working-capital investments. Table 19.2 identifies the types of problems financial managers face as they try to balance liquidity and profitability.

In applying the matching principle in practice, each manager may take a somewhat different approach depending on whether the manager wants to be conservative or aggressive. In certain circumstances, deliberately creating a mis-match between current liabilities and current assets could lead to a low-cost financing plan. However, the lowering of cost usually is attendant with higher risk.

Concept Quiz

1. What are the goals of short-term financial management?
2. Why should a manager try to match the maturities of the firm's assets and liabilities?
3. What problems might the firm encounter if a current asset account is too large or too small?

19.6. The Cash Flow Cycle and its Calculation

The time it takes for cash to flow through the working-capital accounts and return to cash is a measurable quantity of time called the *cash flow cycle*.

Table 19.2. Problems associated with balancing liquidity and profitability.

Working Capital Component	Forms	Problem If Component is Too Small	Problem If Component is Too Large
Cash	Dollars Demand Deposits	Risk of running out of cash: illiquidity, insolvency	Loss of return from money market investments
Marketable Securities	Money market Investments (T-bills, CDs, commercial Paper, etc.)	Insufficient safety margin to meet expected and unexpected cash requirements	Misuse of scarce investor capital needed for real investment
AR	Open-book accounts of customers	Credit policy may be too strict and non-competitive Demand for product or services is falling	Credit policy may be over-generous Collection problems Costly use of resources
Inventory	Raw Materials Work in process Finished goods	Inability to meet demand Loss of sales Production interruptions	Costs of carry: storage insurance and handling will be higher than necessary Risk of obsolescence
Short-Term Financing	Bank loans Lines of credit Commercial paper	Not able to carry sufficient short-term assets to meet demand or operating requirements	Very costly; may be financing many idle assets that may not be productive

Essentially, the cycle begins when the organization pays cash for investment in current assets and ends when cash flows back to the organization as payment for the goods or service rendered. To be more specific, the cash flow cycle equals the average age of current assets or inventory plus the average of AR minus the average of accounts payable (AP). The first task of the short-term financial planner is to identify the firm's cash flow cycle. The next step is to focus on how to speed up the inflows and slow down the outflows in the most cost-effective fashion.

The cash flow cycle is defined as follows:

$$\begin{aligned}\text{Cash flow cycle} &= \text{average age of inventory}\\ &\quad + \text{average age of AR}\\ &\quad - \text{average age of AP}\end{aligned}$$

$$
\begin{aligned}
&= \text{number of days in the planning period} \\
&\quad \times \left(\frac{\text{average inventory}}{\text{cash operating expenditures}} + \frac{\text{average AR}}{\text{sales}} \right. \\
&\qquad \left. - \frac{\text{average AP}}{\text{cost of goods sold}} \right), \qquad (19.1)
\end{aligned}
$$

where average inventory = (beginning inventory + ending inventory)/2; average AR = (beginning AR + ending (AR)/2; and average AP = (beginning AP + ending AP)/2.

The managerial actions that affect the duration of the various cash flow components are defined as follows:

$$
\begin{aligned}
&\text{managerial actions} \\
&\quad = \text{inventory financing, collateral for loans, liquidation} \\
&\qquad + \text{factoring, pledging, altering credit terms, tightening collection,} \\
&\qquad\quad \text{policies, speeding up billing procedures} \\
&\qquad - \text{change payment frequency, stretch out payables} \\
&\qquad\quad \text{(forego discounts).} \qquad (19.2)
\end{aligned}
$$

To demonstrate the calculation of the cash flow cycle, we will consider a maintenance service organization called Speedy Maintenance, which provides cleaning services for offices and commercial and industrial buildings. One important aspect of this type of firm is that all work is done on the customers' premises, which means there is little need for speedy to have a large investment in fixed assets. An administrative office and a garage to store vehicles, supplies, and equipment are all that is required. The major expense of doing business is labor. Most employees work on an hourly basis and are unskilled or semi-skilled. Most of Speedy's business is rendered repetitively, usually under a flat-rate contract with extra fees for special services. Two areas of potential concern for Speedy's management are liability and casualty insurance and adequate supervision of its widely dispersed work force. These areas could have a dramatic impact on cash flow. If an employee damages or steals property in the building being cleaned, Speedy could be held liable for a large replacement cost.

Table 19.3. Speedy maintenance, Inc., financial statement.

	Balance Sheet				
	31 December 2014	31 December 2015		31 December 2014	31 December 2015
Cash	$10,000	$15,000	Wages payable	$15,000	$15,000
Marketable securities	5,000	5,000	AP	45,000	55,000
AR	65,000	85,000	Mortgage payable	25,000	25,000
Inventory			Bank note payable	130,000	130,000
Cleaning supplies	18,000	21,000	Common stock	50,000	50,000
Cleaning equipment	50,000	54,000	Retained earnings	8,000	25,000
Trucks (net)	80,000	75,000			
Building (office and garage)	45,000	45,000			
Total Assets	$273,000	$300,000	Total Liabilities + Equity	$273,000	$300,000

Income Statement (for year ending 31 December)	19XX	19X1
Sales	$379,000	$430,500
Cost of services supplied		
Labor	250,222	290,000
Supplies	70,000	70,000
Operating expenses	50,000	50,000
Taxable income	9,600	20,500
Income tax	1,600	3,500
Net income	$8,000	$17,000

Service concerns like Speedy must monitor two levels of cash flow: the *overall cash flows* from the entire operation and the *specific cash flows* from each individual contract. Speedy's financial statement for the past 2 years is presented in Table 19.3, which provides all of the information necessary to calculate Speedy's cash flow cycle. Substituting related information from Table 19.3 into Eq. (19.1), we obtain:

$$\begin{aligned}\text{cash flow cycle} &= 365\left(\frac{\frac{18,000+21,000}{2}}{70,000}\right)+365\left(\frac{\frac{65,000+85,000}{2}}{430,500}\right)\\ &\quad -365\left(\frac{\frac{45,000+55,000}{2}}{360,000}\right)\\ &= 102 \text{ days} + 64 \text{ days} - 51 \text{ days}\\ &= 115 \text{ days.}\end{aligned}$$

To estimate the cost of this cash flow cycle to Speedy, interest rates for short-term financing sources must be used. Table 19.4 presents cost calculation for Speedy's cash flow cycle assuming financing interest rate of 10%, 16%, and 20% per year. These calculations reflect what the costs would be if funds had to be borrowed at these assumed rates to finance the cash flow cycle. The objective of the cash flow manager is to keep these costs to a minimum.

Calculating the cost of financing an organization's cash flow cycle is a useful starting point for the cash flow manager, who can then begin to evaluate whether the firm's resources are being used efficiently and effectively. In turn, this evaluation serves as a starting point for weighing the trade-offs between the costs of carrying a given cash flow cycle and the benefits derived from it. Suppose, for example, that Speedy's management

Table 19.4. Financing costs of speedy's cash flow cycle.

Assets	Average Amount Invested [(being+end)/2]	Average Investment Period in Days	Estimated Cost of Financing (Average Investment × Days × Interest Rate/365) 10%	15%	20%
Cleaning supplies	$19,500	102	$545	$817	$1,090
AR	$75,000	64	1,315	1,973	2,630
AP	$50,000	51	(699)	(1,048)	(1,397)
Total cost to finance		115	$1,161	$1,742	$2,323

Table 19.5. Speedy maintenance contract XYZ.

Total contract = \$120,000 for 1 year
Payment terms = \$10,000 on the last day of each month
Cost of supplies per month = \$2,000
Cost of labor per month = \$7,500 (workers paid weekly)
Cash flow cycle = average age of inventory + average age of AR − average age of AP

$$= 30\left(\frac{\frac{2,000+0}{2}}{2,000}\right) + 30\left(\frac{\frac{0+10,000}{2}}{10,000}\right) - 30\left(\frac{\frac{2,000+7,500/4}{2}}{9,500}\right)$$

$$= 15 \text{ days} + 15 \text{ days} - 6 \text{ days}$$
$$= 24 \text{ days}$$

Assets	Average Amount Invested	Average Investment Period in Days	Estimated Cost of Financing at 15%
Cleaning supplies	\$1,000	15	\$6.16
AR	5,000	15	30.82
AP	1,938	6	(4.78)
Total cost to finance			\$32.20
			×12
Total cost per year			\$386.40

Yearly Cost − Suggested Modifications	Effects
Make payments weekly	Reduce A/R
Make payments bimonthly	Increase A/R
Pay workers bimonthly	Increase A/P
Pay workers monthly	Increase A/P

believes the cost of maintaining AR is too high. Since most of Speedy's AR reflects services provided under contract, Speedy's management could alter the payment terms at contract renewal time to reduce the amount of funds tied up in receivables. However, this cost reduction could be outweighed by the loss of contracts that might be incurred if some customers switch to another maintenance firm. A more appropriate course of action might be to minimize this cost subject to not losing the contract. Table 19.5 shows the cash flow cycle for one of Speedy's contracts, estimates the cost per month to finance the cycle, and lists the effects that several possible modifications to the contract would have on the cash flow.

As in all problem-solving and decision-making, there is more than one way to approach the situation. Short-term financial planning is no different.

The cash flow cycle and cash flow planning are based on the use of a cash budgeting statement. We will now look at this approach to cash flow planning, keeping in mind that these various techniques are meant to be complementary to each other, not substitutes.

19.7. Cash Flow Forecasting, Budgeting, and Planning

Forecasting, budgeting, and planning are the basic components of what has come to be called the *corporate planning process.* As a general rule, planning contributes to higher profits, improved decision-making, and a reduction of critical mistakes. The three-step process of planning involves making decisions and taking actions today that will affect the future of the firm. Because no one can predict the future with any consistent degree of accuracy, the planning process must be continuous and ongoing. The three steps of forecasting, budgeting, and planning must be consistently revised to fit each new situation based on the continued inflow of new information. Hence, this constantly changing environment makes for an unending task of constantly reworking the plan.

Because the future changes so frequently, plans made at any one point in time should not be expected to work precisely as initially formulated. Plans should be amended to reflect new information about the firm's environment that will alter circumstances and decisions. An environment can change yearly, quarterly, monthly, or even daily. Hence, the planner must use a flexible tool to evaluate and analyze the potentially volatile situation.

The three-step procedure of forecasting, budgeting, and planning can be viewed as a set of building blocks that are mutually supportive. We will discuss the planning process as if each of the three steps is performed in sequence. However, each step must constantly be revised in light of new information about the firm's business environment or new information from the other steps. Thus, rather than being sequential, the three steps in the planning process are dealt with simultaneously. Envision the planning process as a three-legged stool; without one of the three legs — forecasting, budgeting, planning — the stool serves no useful function.

19.8. The Cash Budget

A *cash budget* shows the cash flow that is anticipated in the coming planning period given various scenarios. This budget goes beyond a simple summation of cash receipts and disbursements by attempting to forecast the actual timing of the cash flows into and out of the business. The precision of the budget depends on the characteristics of the organization, the degree of uncertainty about the business environment, and the ability of the planner to accurately forecast the future cash flows.

The budget process is characterized by five steps:

1. Forecasting sales;
2. Projecting all cash inflows, including forecasted receipts;
3. Projecting all cash outflows;
4. Interrelating the inflows and the outflows subject to policy decisions of the firm's management;
5. Determining the excess or shortage of cash during the planning period.

It is step 5 that leads from the forecasting and budgeting preparation into the planning process.

All cash budgets begin with a forecast of sales, which is normally supplied to the financial planner by the firm's marketing function. However, the primary source of cash inflows is not sales, but the collection of AR. In addition, the firm may raise cash from external sources through short- or long-term financing or the sale of assets. These inflows are also part of the cash budget.

The collection history of AR is used as the starting point in estimating the cash flow from sales. If the firm has made any changes in its credit terms or policies, or if the firm's customer base has changed, then the manager must incorporate the impact of these changes in estimating cash collections. The planner must look closely at any variation from the normal collection pattern to fully understand the impact the change is having on the firm's cash flow. An example of the relationship between sales and collection of cash is shown in Table 19.6.

The arrows in Table 19.6 indicate the interrelationship between the month in which the sales are generated and the month in which the cash is actually received. For example a total of \$60,000 is collected in March. This consists of 20% cash collection of current month sales on $\$75,000 \times 0.2 = \$15,000$; 70% collection of the sales which were made in the previous month or $\$50,000 \times 0.70 = \$35,000$; and 10% collection of the sales which were made two months previous or $\$100,000 \times 0.10 = \$10,000$.

Most of the cash outflows, or disbursements, are one of four types: (1) payments for purchases of raw materials, (2) payments for wages, rent, maintenance, and other operating expenses, (3) payments to short- and long-term suppliers of financing in the form of interest, principal, and dividends, and (4) taxes.

Table 19.6. Sales and cash flow.

	Nov.	Dec.	Jan.	Feb.	Mar.	Apr.	May.
Sales	$100,000	$100,000	$100,000	$50,000	$75,000	$100,000	$100,000
Cash sales (20% of current months sales)			$20,000	$10,000	$15,000	$20,000	$20,000
Collection of A/R (70% of previous months)			70,000	70,000	35,000	52,500	70,000
Collection of A/R (10% of months t–2)			10,000	10,000	10,000	5,000	7,500
Cash from collection of Sales and A/R			$100,000	$90,000	$60,000	$77,500	$97,500

Operating expenses may be related to the forecasted level of sales and may vary with the changes in expected revenues. The payments to the suppliers of capital, interest, and principal represent contractual obligations that must be met to avoid bankruptcy and are unrelated to sales in the short run. Hence, a portion of the cash outflow is fixed and unrelated to revenues, that is sales fall or do not reach expected levels, the change in cash flow will usually be less than the change in revenues. Note that depreciation and other non-cash expenses do not appear in the firm's cash budget. This is because they represent accrued expenses for which there is no cash outflow during the planning horizon.

Interrelating the starting level of cash, cash inflows, and cash outflows allows the financial manager to determine the amount of excess cash available or the deficit that must be financed by borrowing. It is this surplus or deficit that will determine the type of cash management plans formulated for the planning period.

The final step in the planning process is the most creative, as the cash flow manager tries various strategies to meet the cash shortfall or to invest the cash surplus. If the cash deficit falls below some predetermined limit (minimum cash balance), the cash manager must take corrective action such as raising funds by borrowing, altering the firm's payment pattern, or changing the credit policy to reduce the level of AR and thereby speed up the inflow of cash. Any one or a combination of these options would allow the cash manager to meet the cash shortfall. If there is excess cash, the cash manager must invest this surplus, which raises the question of what type of investment is best.

By experimenting with various alternatives and asking the "what if" question, the cash flow planner is better able to argue convincingly for a certain course of action, whether it be with creditors or other managers within the organization. By anticipating problems before they occur or become serious, cash flow managers act in a proactive fashion that puts them in a much stronger position to perform their job effectively. Failing to foresee problems that may occur and reacting in a hasty fashion once they have occurred puts the cash flow manager in a defensive position, with little room to bargain.

Usually, the cheapest and easiest solution to meeting a cash shortage is to arrange for a line of credit of sufficient size to cover the largest cash deficit the firm might incur. This borrowing can be repaid with excess levels of cash when they occur. However, by anticipating the deficits and surpluses in advance, the cash flow planner may be able to initiate other, more positive actions that will eliminate the problem without the aid of external financing. For example, the manager may convince the marketing department that a reduction in the level of AR, accomplished through a more restrictive credit policy or tighter collection policy, will eliminate the need for external financing and be the cheapest means of meeting the cash shortfall.

In certain cases, the organization may find it cost-effective to finance "on the trade" by extending or delaying payment of its own disbursements. This strategy must be evaluated to gauge the impact that slower payment will have on the firm's overall credit rating.

Whatever strategy is chosen, the cash flow planner must work closely with other managers in the firm and with the firm's creditors must carefully coordinate the information available and correctly define the problem at hand to act effectively. The major contribution of the cash flow manager to the firm's success is that he or she knows the extent, severity, and duration of the problem to be solved.

19.9. Demand-Driven, Capital-Driven, and Cost-Driven Cash Budgets

Budgets must be designed and implemented to suit the organization. Therefore, the approach used in developing the budget should be adapted to the environment and characteristics of the individual organization. For example, in some businesses, success or failure is more closely related to demand or revenues; for other businesses, capital expenditure is most important; for still others, the cost structure is a crucial characteristic.

A *demand-driven* business is typified by a service-oriented firm. The budgeting process begins with a sales forecast, which estimates the level and timing of the cash inflows. Given the amount and timing of the flows, the cash manager has freedom to experiment with various strategies on how these flows will be financed or how the expenses will be met.

A *capital-driven* business, such as a manufacturing firm, must produce substantial cash flows to service long-term financing requirements. In this case, the receipt of revenue and the disbursement for expenses is somewhat flexible, and the cash flow planner can experiment with these components of the cash budget.

A *cost-driven* business is one in which business or operating expenses are the biggest factor in determining the cash budget. Such firms tend to be labor-intensive or governmental in nature. Because such organizations have some difficulty varying the disbursement pattern because of legal or contractual obligations, expenses become the most critical element in the cash flow planning process. The major challenge in managing these organizations is controlling expenses. For example, in most government organizations, the expenses of necessary service is estimated and tax legislation is then passed to cover it. Budgeting for this type of enterprise should begin with outflows, or expenses, which can then be used to justify or determine the necessary inflows.

19.10. Users of Cash Forecasts and Business Plans

In addition to preventing the company's cash balance from falling below an acceptable minimum level and predicting the availability of surplus cash for investment, cash forecasts serve several other purposes, including the following:

- *Using cash efficiently.* A cash manager who accurately forecasts cash balances can often use available cash efficiently and avoid borrowing heavily one week and then having a surplus the following week.
- *Financing seasonal business fluctuations.* An accurate cash forecast helps the manager predict the firm's seasonal need for cash.
- *Borrowing short- and long-term.* By knowing cash needs in advance, a cash manager can select the best combination of short-term and long-term financing to minimize overall interest costs.

- *Paying maturing obligations.* Cash forecast includes provisions for the repayment of large loans or maturing bond issues.
- *Providing financing for expansion.* An accurate forecast helps the cash manager arrange loans and stock issues for expansion well in advance of need. The forecast can also help avoid borrowing money earlier than necessary.
- *Taking advantage of cash discounts.* A company that knows it will have surplus cash available can safely take advantage of trade discounts. A company with surplus cash may also save money by buying materials and supplies on sale or in larger-than-normal quantities, given the consideration of the overall cost impact.
- *Estimating debt capacity.* Cash forecast shows a company's ability to pay interest and therefore shows the amount of debt that the company can safely incur.
- *Formulating dividend policy.* Cash forecasts help to ensure that adequate cash will be available to pay dividends to shareholders.

19.11. Planning Horizons and Time Intervals of Cash Budgets

Cash flow planning is essentially short-term. All of the assets and liabilities that make up net working-capital are also short-term in that they normally turn over several times a year. The purpose of cash flow planning is to identify and deal with temporary shortages or surplus. Permanent or long-term funds are the subject of the capital structure decision. Capital budgeting covers the long-term investment decision.

Few companies undertake cash flow budgeting and planning for more than a year in advance. Sometimes it is advisable to plan for more than a year, such as in the case of a construction company where projects require 18 months to 3 years to complete. But from most manufacturing, trading, and service companies, 1 year is a sufficient planning horizon, and 6 months or less may well be adequate.

Since cash flow planning is concerned with fluctuations in cash balances, the time interval used for planning is often a more important consideration than the length of the overall planning period. The most common planning interval is 1 month; that is, a financial management forecasts cash inflows and outflows over 1 month, then calculates beginning and ending cash balances. This procedure is repeated for each of the other 11 months of the year if the overall planning horizon is 1 year. Using a 1-month time interval has the advantage of coinciding with the payment and receipt patterns of most firms. However, many companies use a shorter interval, and some large firms even use weekly or daily intervals. Why is such a short interval necessary? If the company forecasts by the month and shows adequate cash balances at the end of the month, isn't it a waste of time to use a shorter interval? The answers to the questions depend on the circumstances of the company. Suppose a firm uses a planning interval of 1 month. Its cash flow plan for 1 month might look like A in Table 19.7.

Just looking at the monthly cash flow plan, everything appears to be fine. The company's cash balance stays steady at $30,000. However, if we look at the weekly cash flow interval, we see that the firm needs some short-term financing during the first three weeks of the month. In this case, the firm would do well to choose a planning interval no longer than one week, and perhaps even shorter. The reason this firm should use a weekly planning interval is to ensure that arrangements can be made to meet the cash shortfalls that occur during the first three weeks.

Several additional factors should be taken into consideration when deciding on the length of the planning interval for the cash budget. These include the following:

- *Inflations rates and opportunity costs.* When inflation rates are high, the firm wants to minimize the amount of idle cash it is holding and also minimize the amount of short-term financing that is used.
- *Size of cash flows.* Companies that plan their cash flows by the day usually have very large cash flows. For example, $1 million invested at an annual rate of 12% yields $328.75 per day, a sum that makes it worth while to plan to invest cash daily. In contrast, $10,000 at 12% yields $3.28 per day. A company could not justify spending valuable time and effort to earn this sum.
- *Executive time available for cash flow planning and management.* Executive time is one of the scarcest resources of most companies. Thus, the returns earned from daily cash management may not justify the time spent in achieving them. Such a situation would dictate a longer planning interval.
- *Predictability of cash flow timing and size.* The predictability of the timing and the size of cash flows will have a great impact on the appropriate planning interval. The more unpredictable the size and timing of the cash flow, the shorter should be the planning interval.
- *Size of required cash balances.* From the point of view of avoiding insolvency, the size of the minimum cash balance in relation to the cash flow

Table 19.7. Cash flow budgets and planning intervals.

A. Monthly Planning Interval

Beginning cash balance	$30,000	
Cash inflows		
A/R collections	55,000	
Licensing fee collections	25,000	
Sale of surplus assets	15,000	
Total cash inflow	$95,000	
Total cash available		$125,000
Cash outflows		
Salaries and wages	$24,000	
Raw material purchases	19,500	
Supplies	5,000	
Rent	14,000	
Income tax payment	25,000	
Payroll taxes	7,500	
Total cash outflows	$95,000	
Cash at end of month		$30,000

B. Weekly Planning Interval

	Week 1	Week 2	Week 3	Week 4
Beginning cash balance	$30,000	($2,250)	($9,500)	($2,250)
Cash inflows				
A/R collections	$12,000	$15,000	$11,000	$17,000
Licensing fee collections				25,000
Sale of surplus assets			10,000	5000
Total cash inflow	$12,000	$15,000	$21,000	$47,000
Total cash available	$42,000	$12,750	$11,500	$44,750
Cash outflows				
Salaries and wages	$6,000	$6,000	$6,000	$6,000
Raw material purchases	5,500	5,000	4,000	5,000
Supplies	1,250	1,250	1,250	1,250
Rent	6,500	2,500	2,500	2,500
Income tax payment	25,000			
Payroll taxes		7,500		
Total cash outflows	$44,250	$22,250	$13,750	$14,750
Cash at end of month	($2,250)	($9,500)	($2,250)	$30,000

has a bearing on the planning interval. If cash balances are large, temporary variations within a long planning interval are unlikely to place a firm in jeopardy. But if a company is operating on small or marginal balances, a large cash outflow over only a few days may bring balances down to unacceptable levels. In such circumstances, a short planning interval is necessary for survival, even if it is not economically justified.

19.12. From Forecasting to Budgeting to Planning

The first step in forecasting the cash budgeting is to make a detailed list of the assumptions concerning the inflows and outflows for the planning period. Table 19.8 lists some common assumptions.

The second step is to develop the schedule of receipts and disbursements for at least the three scenarios of worst, most likely, and best cases. The selected estimates are then put on the schedule. The magnitude and timing of these figures will be very sensitive to the individual scenario. Any figures that appear to be out of line should be reevaluated to ensure that the figures and the assumptions make sense. Table 19.9 shows the general format of the cash flow forecast for a most likely case, a worse case, and a best case.

Once cash inflows and disbursements have been forecasted, the planner can then forecast the cash balances at the beginning and end of each interval in the planning period; the results appear as the top and the bottom lines of the schedules. These figures, showing the cash surpluses or deficits, are the main reason for going through the forecasting exercise. They will be used by management in determining the short-term financial plan for the planning period.

If we compare the cash balances under the three scenarios, we notice that under the worst case there is no need for external financing, while the greatest cash shortage is experienced under the best case. This is quite usual for most firms because the increased level of activity under the "best" periods requires more external financing.

Table 19.8. Assumptions for cash inflows and outflows.

	Worst Case	Most Likely	Best Case
Revenues	5% decline	Same as last year	10%increase
Credit sales	95% of sales volume	90% of sales volume	85% of sales volume
Collection experience	80% in 30 days	85% in 30 days	100% in 30 days
	10% in 60 days	10% in 60 days	
	10% in bad debts	5% in bad debts	
Expenses	5% increase	Same as last year	3% decline
Capital expenditures	$0	$100,000 in February	$150,000 in February

Table 19.9. 6-month cash flow forecast.

	Most Likely Case					
	January	February	March	April	May	June
Beginning cash balance	$20,000	$16,000	($63,000)	($3,000)	($5,000)	$25,000
Cash sales and collection of A/R	50,000	65,000	75,000	65,000	75,000	65,000
Insurance claims			25,000			
Dividends and interests	5,000	2,000		5,000		2,000
Total cash inflows	$55,000	$67,000	$100,000	$70,000	$75,000	$67,000
Total cash available	$75,000	$83,000	$37,000	$67,000	$70,000	$92,000
Cash Outflow						
Labor wages	$23,000	$25,000	$25,000	$25,000	$25,000	$25,000
Salary	5,000	5,000	5,000	5,000	5,000	5,000
Raw material payment	4,000	16,000	10,000	15,000	15,000	10,000
Dividends	2,000			2,000		
Income taxes	25,000			25,000		
New equipment		100,000				
Total cash outflow	$59,000	$146,000	$40,000	$72,000	$45,000	$40,000
Cash at end of month	$16,000	($63,000)	($3,000)	($5,000)	$25,000	$52,000
	Worst Case					
	January	February	March	April	May	June
Beginning cash balance	$15,000	$12,500	$26,500	$82,500	$83,500	$109,500
Cash sales and collection of A/R	47,500	62,000	70,000	62,000	70,000	62,000
Insurance claims			25,000			
Dividends and interests	5,000	2,000		5,000		2,000
Total cash inflows	$52,500	$64,000	$95,000	$67,000	$70,000	$64,000
Total cash available	$67,500	$66,500	$121,500	$149,500	$153,500	$173,500
Cash Outflow						
Labor wages	$25,000	$25,000	$26,000	$26,000	$26,000	$26,000
Salary	5,000	5,000	5,000	5,000	5,000	5,000
Raw material payment	3,000	10,000	8,000	13,000	13,000	10,000

(*Continued*)

Table 19.9. (*Continued*)

	Worst Case					
	January	February	March	April	May	June
Dividends	2,000			2,000		
Income taxes	20,000			20,000		
New equipment		—				
Total cash outflow	$55,000	$40,000	$39,000	$66,000	$44,000	$41,000
Cash at end of month	$12,500	$26,500	$82,500	$83,500	$109,500	$132,500
	Best Case					
	January	February	March	April	May	June
Beginning cash balance	$25,000	$17,000	($112,000)	($49,000)	($55,000)	$29,000
Cash sales and collection of A/R	55,000	70,000	85,000	73,000	78,000	73,000
Insurance claims			25,000			
Dividends and interests	6,000	3,000		6,000		3,000
Total cash inflows	$61,000	$73,000	$110,000	$79,000	$78,000	$76,000
Total cash available	$86,000	$90,000	($2,000)	$30,000	$23,000	$47,000
Cash Outflow						
Labor wages	$25,000	$27,000	$27,000	$27,000	$27,000	$27,000
Salary	5,000	5,000	5,000	5,000	5,000	5,000
Raw material payment	6,000	20,000	15,000	20,000	20,000	15,000
Dividends	3,000			3,000		
Income taxes	30,000			30,000		
New equipment		150,000				
Total cash outflow	$69,000	$202,000	$47,000	$85,000	$52,000	$47,000
Cash at end of month	$17,000	($112,000)	($49,000)	($55,000)	$29,000	$0

The cash budget, as shown in Exhibit 19-9, serves a number of purposes. It can be used as a starting point of the cash planning process. It can act as a standard of behavior against which the performance of the company can be evaluated. It can serve as a control mechanism in that any deviation from the standard can be isolated and corrective action taken if needed. The cash budget can also be used as a starting point in "what if" or sensitivity analysis. For example, what if revenues grow at a rate different than assumed? How will this affect the amount of short-term financing required?

So far, we have been talking about cash forecasting and cash budgeting, which serve as a starting point for cash flow planning. Cash flow planning is the way the organization determines how to adjust its cash balances to an optimum level. The two steps in cash flow planning are (1) determining an appropriate cash level and (2) determining how to bring the organization's cash balance to this optimal level. Dividing a company's need for cash into three categories yields (1) cash for day-to-day transactions, (2) reserve cash to meet contingencies, and (3) cash for compensating balance requirements. The required level of day-to-day transaction cash depends on the number, frequency, and amount of anticipated transactions. The only requirement for this element of the cash balance is that it can be large enough to cover the checks written against it.

To estimate reserve cash requirements, the cash flow manager can tabulate the daily or weekly changes in the cash account. These changes will range from some very large changes to small fluctuations. Because the major problem is running short of cash, the cash flow manager is especially interested in the large decreases and thus might select a reserve balance that would allow for all but the largest cash decreases to be met.

Finally, the organization needs to maintain compensating balances required by the bank. To determine the appropriate minimum cash balance, a cash flow manager simply adds together the three segments just estimated. If the budgeted balance is significantly higher than the minimum balance, the organization can use the excess cash to purchase marketable securities. On the other hand, if cash balance falls below the desired level, the organization can plan to borrow short-term funds or to sell marketable securities. To complete the transition from cash budget to cash flow plan, the manager must show how the cash balance will be adjusted to meet the minimum cash balance.

At this point, we have a cash flow budget, not a short-term financial plan. Planning is the mental process of visualizing a set of future events that the financial planner is determined to make happen in the future, not just a summary of what the planner expects to happen. But given the cash budget in Exhibit 18-9 and the minimum cash balance requirements, we can begin planning.

Some of the cash balances at the end of each planning interval may be higher than needed, while others may be too low or even negative. Financial planners first determine how to invest any excess cash to earn the maximum return. This decision depends on the amount of excess cash and the length of time it will be available. Next, the planner decides how to cover temporary cash shortages discovered by the forecast. We will discuss various means of doing this in detail in later chapters, but here we point out that we are not limited to putting the money in the bank or borrowing from the bank. Other options are delaying purchases or payments until a later period, deciding to eliminate or reduce certain expenditures, selling marketable securities or other assets, and accelerating collections.

The results of this kind of planning are shown in Table 19.10 for the most-likely case. In this example, the planner has decided to postpone the

Table 19.10. 6-month most-likely cash flow plan.*

	January	February	March	April	May	June
Beginning cash balance	$20,000	$10,000	$10,000	$10,000	$10,000	$10,000
Cash inflows						
Collection of A/R	50,000	65,000	75,000	65,000	75,000	65,000
Insurance claims			25,000			
Dividends and interests	5,000	2,000		5,000		2,000
Maturing marketable securities*		10,100	43,531		498	30,803
Total cash inflows	$55,000	$77,000	$143,531	$70,000	$75,498	$97,803
Total cash available	$75,000	$87,100	$153,531	$80,000	$85,498	$107,803
Cash Outflow						
Labor wages	$23,000	$25,000	$25,000	$25,000	$25,000	$25,000
Salary	5,000	5,000	5,000	5,000	5,000	5,000
Raw material payment		4,000	16,000	10,000	15,000	15,000
Dividends	2,000			2,000		
Income tax	25,000			25,000		
Payoff line of credit**				2,506		
New equipment			100,000			
Total cash outflow	$55,000	$34,000	$146,000	$69,506	$45,000	$45,000
Cash available	20,000	53,100	7,531	10,494	40,498	62,803
Minimum cash balance	10,000	10,000	10,000	10,000	10,000	10,000
Marketable securities at 12%/year	$10,000	$43,100		$494	$30,498	$52,803
Short-term borrowing at 18%/year			$2,469			

*It is assumed that the marketable securities are invested for 1 month at 1% interest (12%/12 months = 1%/month)10,000 × 1.01 = $10,100 for February.
**It is assumed that the borrowing is done for 1 month at 1.5% interest (18%/12 months = 1.5%/month) 2,469 × 1.015 = $2,506 for April.

expenditure for new equipment from February to March and to stretch out the payables for raw material by an additional 30 days. The planner has also decided to invest cash balances in excess of $10,000 in 30-day T-bills. Any shortages of cash would be covered by establishing a line of credit with a commercial bank. Various other alternatives should also be considered before the final plan is formulated.

Through this plan, the financial planner has kept minimum cash balance of $10,000 and reduced borrowing on the firm's line of credit to $2,469 in March. Also, the cash manager was able to invest in the money-market surplus cash balances during the months of February, March, May, and June. This is only one possible alternative that the financial planner may wish to consider before finalizing the cash flow plan. Thus, once the manager has determined how to invest excess cash and meet cash shortages, the results of these decisions are incorporated into the cash flow budget, which then becomes the cash flow plan. The manager's remaining responsibility is to ensure, to the extent possible, that this plan is put into effect and is mirrored by actual results.

The accuracy of the forecast used in preparing the cash flow plan is of critical importance first in creating the budget and then in developing a plan that is a useful management tool to implement the budget. The less reliable the forecast or the less certain the cash flow manager is about events that may affect the cash flows, the larger the minimum cash balances, lines of credit, or a combination of both that are required. GIGO (garbage-in, garbage-out) is an appropriate acronym in this case. If the planner does not have much confidence in the forecast, the resulting plan will be of little value to the organization.

Concept Quiz

1. What are the major uses of the cash budget?
2. What is the best time interval for cash flow planning?
3. Why should a cash flow plan evaluate three scenarios (worst case, most likely, and best case)?
4. What are the three categories of cash needs for a corporation?

19.13. Summary

In Chapter 19, we have identified and defined cash flow and related it to the accounting-based concept of funds flow. The short-term financial manager is much more concerned with the actual cash flowing through the firm on a day-to-day basis than the long-term funds flow perspective.

A three-scenario approach to short-term financial planning (using worst, most-likely, and best-case scenarios) is recommended because future events cannot always be forecasted with accuracy. For this reason, the initial step of the planning process involves making educated guesses about future cash flows that cover a reasonable range of possible situations. In both budgeting and planning, the cash flow manager should ask the following questions: Dose this plan makes sense in light of my own experiences? Does it coincide with what I expect to happen during the coming year?

Throughout the planning process, there should be a feedback mechanism that enables the short-term financial planner to update the forecast in light of new information and/or a new understanding of the situation that may come about from actually preparing the budget and the plan. Cash flow managers must understand that the process itself is the most important aspect of short-term financial management. The final plan is not definitive. It serves only to guide future courses of action and decisions and is subject to continual revision.

The final part of the chapter demonstrated the interrelationship of forecasting, budgeting, and planning. Once the problems have been defined, a financial planner must generate alternatives that will lead to satisfactory solutions. The material in the next two chapters expands on the possible alternatives available to the financial planner. In most cases, there is more than one way to solve a problem. Sometimes, it is worth the extra effort to look for the optimal solution; sometimes it is not. With experience, the financial manager learns when to use a satisfactory solution that may not be the best one theoretically. It makes little sense to spend a lot of time and make many improvements on a plan that will only marginally improve performance.

Problem Set

1. Define the following:

   a. Cash flow versus funds flow.
   b. Variable short-term asset.
   c. Cash flow cycle.
   d. Cost-versus demand-driven cash budget.
   e. Trend-cycle component of sales.

2. What are major problems associated with balancing liquidity and profitability?
3. Discuss the method of calculating the cash flow cycle.
4. How are cash budgets and business plans used in short-term financial management?
5. Describe the cash budgeting procedure.
6. What are the components of working-capital? Why is working-capital important?
7. What is net working-capital? Why is it important?
8. Below is the balance sheet for RLM Corporation.

RLM Corporation
Balance Sheet
December 31, 19XX (millions)

Assets		**Liabilities**	
Cash	\$70	Bank loans payable	\$25
AR	50	Taxes payable	20
Inventory	25	Wages payable	70
Equipment	75	Long-term debt	50
Buildings	75	Common stock	100
Land	100	Retained earnings	165
Goodwill	35		
Total assets	**430**	**Total liabilities and equity**	**430**

a. Find RLM's working-capital.
b. Find RLM's net working-capital.

9. What does it mean when a company has a negative value for net working-capital?
10. Why is it important for managers to calculate the cash conversion cycle?
11. What can management do to shorten the cash conversion cycle?
12. What risks occur if long-term assets are financed with short-term liabilities?
13. What problems are associated with too much working-capital?
14. To slow down the outflow of cash, should a manager fail to sign a check in payment to a supplier, knowing the bank will not honor an unsigned check?

15. Is there anything wrong with using the excuse "The check is in the mail" when a creditor asks to be paid?
16. A retailer knowingly writes checks to its supplier without sufficient funds in the bank. Is this an ethical or legal issue?
17. When an accountant calculates a funds flow, what information is used? When a financial manager calculates a cash flow, what information is used? Why are the funds flow and the cash flow different?
18. Can a firm be profitable and still have cash flow problems? Give an example of such a firm.
19. XYZ Company's financial data for calculating the cash conversion cycle is listed below. Given this information, calculate the cash conversion cycle and related financial ratios.

	1983	1984	1985	1986	1987
Sales	$1,849	$1,645	$1,375	$1,254	$1,211
Cost of Sales*	$1,164	$1,023	$846	$771	$756
Depreciation	13	12	11	10	9
Administration and other expenses*	623	533	446	389	356
Total operating expenses	$1800	$1,568	$1,303	$1,170	$1,121
Net operating income	$49	$77	$72	$84	$90
Cash and marketable securities	$46	$31	$50	$34	$33
AR	599	543	477	420	368
Inventories	451	399	299	260	222
Other	7	7	5	5	5
Total current assets	$1,103	$980	$831	$719	$628
AP and accrued expenses	$104	$104	$116	$105	$95
Taxes payable	0	8	9	14	10
Commercial paper	453	390	238	246	182
Total current liabilities	$557	$502	$363	$365	$287

*Assumed to be cash operating expenditures

20. Assume cash inflows and outflows are as following:

	Worst Case	Most Likely	Best Case
Revenue	10% decline	Same as last year	5% increase
Credit Sales	90% of sales volume	80% of sales volume	85% of sales volume
Collection experience	80% in 30 days	85% in 30 days	100% in 30 days
	10% in 60 days	10% in 60 days	
	10% in bad days	5% in bad days	
Expenses	5% increase	Same as last year	3% decline
Capital expenditure	$0	$100,000 in February	$150,000 in February

Sales last year were:

Nov.	Dec.	Jan.	Feb.	Mar.	Apr.	May	June
100,000	80,000	100,000	30,000	150,000	80,000	100,000	80,000

a. Prepare a cash budget for each of the three scenarios.

21. The following financial data have been taken from the annual report of RSM Corporation:

Particulars	**1987**	**1988**
Current Assets:		
Cash and marketable securities	$40,000	$43,000
AR	410,000	455,000
Inventory	280,000	305,000
Total Current Assets	$730,000	$803,000
Current Liabilities:		
AP	$215,000	$238,000
Short-term borrowings	150,000	140,000
Total Current Liabilities	$365,000	$378,000

(*Continued*)

(*Continued*)

Particulars	1987	1988
Sales	$1,168,000	$1,314,000
Cost of goods sold*	760,000	825,000
Depreciation	25,000	23,000
Administrative and other expenses*	235,000	246,000
Total Operating Expenses	$1,020,000	$1,094,000

*Cash operating expenses

Using the above information, calculate the following data:

a. Average age of inventory.
b. Average age of AR.
c. Average age of AP.
d. Cash flow cycle.

22. Using the data in the previous problem, calculate the cost of financing the cash flow cycle if RSM Corporation's annual rate of interest on borrowings is:

a. 10%.
b. 12%.
c. 15%.

23. UCI Company's projected sales for the first 4 months in 1989 are given below:

Month	Sales
January	$55,000
February	50,000
March	60,000
April	70,000

The collection schedule is as following:

10% in cash,
60% in 1 month,
25% in 2 months,
5% in bad debts.

Sales for November and December 1988 were \$50,000 and \$75,000 respectively. The firm buys materials 30 days in advance; that is, the materials for consumption in January are bought by the beginning of the preceding month, December, and are paid by the end of the month (The end of December in this example). Materials costs are 60% of the sale price.

Wages for the months of January, February, and March are projected to be \$5,000 per month. Wages are paid twice in a month, on the 1st and 16th. Wages payable as of December 31 were \$2,400. Other monthly expenses amount to \$5,000 per month and are paid in cash. Taxes due for an earlier quarter are paid in the second month of the succeeding quarter. The taxes due for the quarter ended December 31, 1988 were \$8,850.

The company plans to buy a new vehicle in January for \$15,000. The old vehicle is expected to be sold for a net amount of \$1,900. A note of \$10,750 will be due for payment on February 29, 1989. The firm can either withdraw cash deposits or borrow to pay the note. A quarterly loan installment of \$9,000 is also due for payment in March.

The opening cash balance on January 1 is \$5,000. The company policy is to maintain a minimum cash balance of \$5,000. If the cash flow projections show a deficit from a particular month, the firm either withdraws cash from its short-term deposits or borrows at the beginning of the month to meet the expected short fall. The interest rate on such loans is 15% per year. Interest is paid at the end of every month. Such borrowings are paid off in the next month if the funds are available. Excess cash balance (over \$5,000) is put in short-term deposits paying 1% interest per month.

Determine the monthly collections and disbursements and prepare a cash budget for the next 3 months.

24. Raymond Corporation's yearly sales are \$2 million and the average collection period is 25 days. 90% of sales are on a credit basis. Assuming a 360-day year, determine the firm's investment in AR.
25. If Raymond Corp. extends its credit period to 30 days, the sales on credit could increase by 25%.

    a. Calculate the additional investment in AR.
    b. Find the additional expenditure on interest if the cost of financing AR is 15% per year.

26. A firm's annual credit sales are \$2.7 million. If its ARs are \$375,000, what is the firm's average collection period? (Use a 360-day year.)
27. Century's projected cash inflows and outflows for the second quarter in 1989 are as given below:

Month	Receipts	Disbursements
April	$10,000	$12,000
May	12,020	10,000
June	10,000	10,500

The opening cash balance is $1,000 which is also the minimum balance that the company must maintain at all times. The short-term interest rate is 12% per year and interest is paid on a monthly basis. These loans are repaid monthly to the extent that excess cash is available.

Prepare a monthly cash budget for each of the 3 months.

1. **Fund and Cash Flow Statements**

   Assume all sales are for cash and all expenses except depreciation will be paid in cash in January 1997. Given the following information, prepare a funds flow and a cash flow statement for December 1996.

Cost of goods sold	$100	Revenues	$500
Marketing expense	100	Depreciation	25
Utilities	25		
Interest	20		
Tax rate: 30% (Tax paid in December 1996)			

2. **Cash Conversion Cycle**

   Calculate the cash conversion cycle for XYZ Corp.

XYZ Corporation
Income Statement for Period
Ending 31 December, 19XX

Revenues	$2,000
Cost of goods sold	1,000
Depreciation	200

(*Continued*)

(*Continued*)

Administrative expenses	200
Operating income	$600
Interest	100
Taxable income	$500
Tax (30%)	150
Net income	$350

RLM Corporation
Balance Sheet
December 31, 19XX (millions)

Assets		Liabilities	
Cash	$500	Bank loans payable	$800
AR	1,000	Tax payable	200
Inventory	1,000	Commercial paper	1,500
Current assets	$2,500	Current liabilities	$2,500

3. **Costs to Finance Cash Conversion Cycle**

Given the cash conversion cycle from Problem 2, what are the costs to finance this cash conversion cycle for XYZ, if interest rates are expected to be 5%, 10%, or 15%?

4. **Statement of Cash Inflow**

Construct a statement for the first quarter (January–March) that shows the relationship between revenues and cash flows given the following information:

Cash sales 10% of current sales (t)
Collection of AR 80% of previous month ($t - 1$)
Collection of AR 10% of month ($t - 2$)

Revenues

November	December	January	February	March	April
$10,000	$11,000	$12,000	$13,000	$41,000	$15,000

5. **Cash Analysis**

During the month of June, the M&D Corp. has the following cash budget:

June	
Beginning cash balance	$100,000
Cash inflows	
AR collections	100,000
Interest earned	10,000
Sales of assets	40,000
Total cash inflows	$150,000
Total cash available	$250,000
Cash outflows	
Salaries and wages	$80,000
Raw material purchases	50,000
Supplies	10,000
Rent	10,000
Taxes	20,000
Total cash outflows	$170,000
Cash at end of month	$80,000

All cash flows are equally spaced over the month (i.e., the same amount is spent per week except interest earned, sale of assets, and taxes, which occur at the end of the month). Will M&D have enough cash during the month to pay its bills?

6. **Cash Conversion Cycle and Financial Ratios**

Financial data for XYZ Company appears in the table below. Given this information, calculate the firm's cash conversion cycle and its related financial ratios for each year. Has the firm changed over time?

	1999	**1998**	**1997**	**1996**	**1995**
Sales	$1,849	$1,645	$1,375	$1,254	$1,211
Cost of sales	1,164	1,023	846	771	756
Depreciation	13	12	11	10	9

(Continued)

(*Continued*)

	1999	**1998**	**1997**	**1996**	**1995**
Administrative and other expenses	623	533	446	389	356
Total operating expenses	1,800	1,568	1,303	1,170	1,121
Net operating income	$49	$77	$72	$84	$90
Cash and marketable securities	46	31	50	34	33
AR	599	543	477	420	368
Inventories	451	399	299	260	222
Other current assets	7	7	5	5	5
Total current assets	$1,103	$980	$831	$719	$628
AP & accrued expenses	104	104	116	105	95
Taxes	0	8	9	14	10
Commercial paper	453	390	238	238	182
Total current liabilities	$557	$502	$363	$357	$287

7. **Cash Budget Analysis**

Assume cash inflows and outflows for July 1996 are as follows:

Revenue	10% decline	Same as last year	5% increase
Credit sales	90% of sales volume	80% of sales volume	85% of sales volume
Collection experience	80% in 30 days; 10% in 60 days; 10% bad debts	85% in 30 days; 10% in 60 days; 5% bad debts	100% in 30 days
Expenses	5% increase	Same as last year	3% decline
Capital expenditure	$0	$100,000 in February	$150,000 in February

Sales during November 1995 through June 1996 were:

	Sales last year	**Expenses last year**
November	$100,000	$75,000
December	$80,000	$55,000
January	$100,000	$80,000
February	$30,000	$15,000
March	$150,000	$135,000
April	$80,000	$65,000
May	$100,000	$75,000
June	$80,000	$70,000

Prepare a cash budget for each of the three scenarios for July 1996. The beginning cash flow is $50,000.

8. **Cash Conversion Cycle**

The following financial data has been taken from the annual report of RSM Corporation:

	1995	1996
Current assets:		
Cash and marketable securities	$40,000	$43,000
AR	410,000	455,000
Inventory	280,000	305,000
Total current assets	$730,000	$803,000
Current liabilities:		
AP	$215,000	$238,000
Short-term borrowings	150,000	140,000
Total current liabilities	$365,000	$378,000
Sales	$1,168,000	$1,314,000
Cost of goods sold	760,000	825,000
Depreciation	25,000	23,000
Administrative and other expenses	235,000	246,000
Total operating expenses	$1,020,000	$1,094,000

Using the above information, calculate the following data:

a. Average age of inventory.
b. Average age of AR.
c. Average age of AP.
d. Cash flow cycle.

9. **Estimated Cost of Financing**

Using the data in Problem 8, calculate the cost of financing the cash flow cycle if RSM Corporation's annual rate of interest on borrowings is:

a. 10%.
b. 12%.
c. 15%.

10. **Cash Budget**

UCI Company's projected sales for the first 4 months in 1997 are given below:

Month	**Sales**
January	$55,000
February	$50,000
March	$60,000
April	$70,000

The firm expects to collect 10% in immediate cash, 60% in 1 month, and 25% in 2 months, with 5% in bad debts. Sales for November and December 1996 were $50,000 and $75,000, respectively.

The firm buys raw materials 30 days in advance of sales; that is, the materials for January production are bought by the beginning of December, with payment due by the end of the month. (The end of December in this example). Materials costs are 60% of sale prices.

Wages for the months of January, February, and March are projected to be $5,000 per month. Wages are paid twice monthly, on the 1st and 16th. Wages payable as of December 31 were $2,400. Other monthly expenses amount to $5,000 per month and are paid in cash. Taxes due for an earlier quarter are paid in the second month of the succeeding quarter. The taxes due for the quarter ended December 31, 1996, were \$8,850.

The company plans to buy a new vehicle in January for \$15,000. The old vehicle is expected to be sold for a net amount of \$1,900. A note of \$10,750 will be due for payment on February 28, 1997. The firm can either withdraw deposited cash or borrow to pay the note. A quarterly loan installment payment of \$9,000 also is due in March.

The opening cash balance on January 1 is \$5,000. The company policy is to maintain a minimum, cash balance of \$5,000. If the cash flow projections show a deficit for a particular month, the firm either withdraws cash from its short-term deposits or borrows at the beginning of the month to meet the expected shortfall. The interest rate on such loans is 15% per year. Interest is paid at the end of every month. Such borrowings are paid off in the next month if the funds are available. Any excess cash balance (over \$5,000) is transferred to short-term deposits that pay 1% interest per month.

Determine UCI's monthly collections and disbursements and prepare a cash budget for January, February, and March.

Appendix 19.A. Time-Series Components of Sales

One of the most important and difficult tasks facing the financial managers is forecasting. Since financial managers are interested in the future and are interested in making decisions about the future, they must necessarily have some meaningful estimate of future activity. The purpose of this appendix is to shed some light on how the financial planner can realistically forecast working-capital requirements in a systematic fashion.

The main characteristic of a time-series of numbers is that its observations have some dependency on time. There are at least three forms that this time dependency can take, as shown in Fig. 19.A.1.

Figure 19.A.1 (a) shows a time-series with an upward trend; (b) shows a time-series with a quarterly pattern, repeated identically every year; and (c) shows a random or irregular time-series of auto correlated or serially correlated terms (each successive value is related to the preceding value with a random disturbance element added).

If the real-world data that we are using to forecast followed only one of these patterns, there would be no problem in forecasting the future patterns.

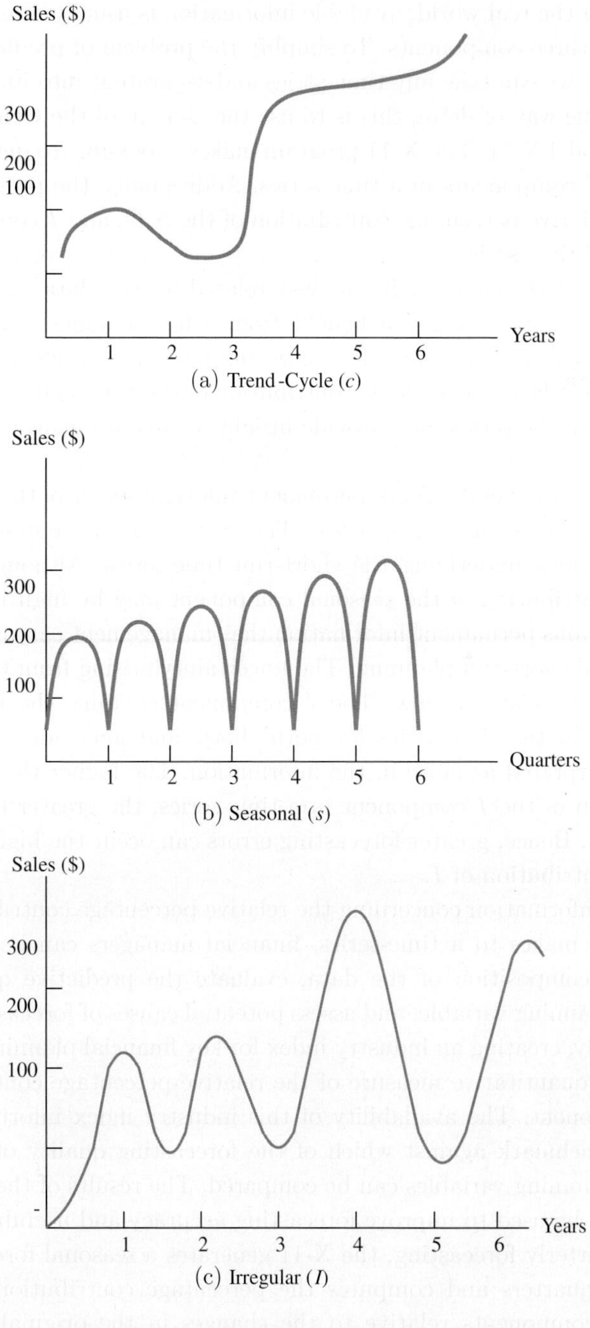

Fig. 19.A.1. Time-series components of sales.

However, in the real world, available information is usually a mixture of at least these three components. To simplify the problem of predicting future movements, we can take any time-series and separate it into its three components. One way of doing this is to use the Bureau of the Census decomposition model X-11. The X-11 program makes it possible to determine the S, C, and I components in a time-series. Additionally, the program calculates the relative percentage contribution of the S, C, and I components to the original time-series.

If future performance is in any way related to past data, then financial planning and forecasting will benefit from a better understanding of the components of the past data. Decomposing past time-series data and discovering the relative percentage contribution of the S, C, and I components to changes in the series may provide insight for management and financial planners.

The C component reflects permanent information in both a short-run and long-run economic time-series. The S component represents a permanent pattern underlying the short-run time-series. Although the percentage contribution of the seasonal component may be high in the short run, it contains permanent information that management can use for intermediate and short-run planning. The uncertainty arising from the seasonal component is relatively low. The I component contains the randomness that exists in the time-series for both short- and long-run analyses and can be interpreted as noise in the information. The higher the percentage contribution of the I component in a time-series, the greater the noise or uncertainty. Hence, greater forecasting errors can occur the higher the percentage contribution of I.

Given information concerning the relative percentage contribution each component makes to a time-series, financial managers can better understand the composition of the data, evaluate the predictive quality of a financial planning variable, and assess potential causes of forecasting errors. Additionally, creating an industry index for key financial planning variables provides a quantitative measure of the relative percentage contribution of each component. The availability of this industry index information provides a benchmark against which of the forecasting quality of the firm's financial planning variables can be compared. The results of these comparisons could be used to improve forecasting accuracy and usefulness.

For quarterly forecasting, the X-11 generates a seasonal forecast of the next four quarters and computes the percentage contribution of the C, S, and I components relative to the changes in the original data. The relationship is defined as

$$\bar{O}_t^2 = \bar{I}_t^2 + \bar{C}_t^2 + \bar{S}_t^2, \tag{19.A.1}$$

where each symbol represents the mean of the absolute quarterly changes, as follows: $\bar{O}_t^2$ = the original series; $\bar{I}_t^2$ = the random components; $\bar{C}_t^2$ = the trend-cycle component; and $\bar{S}_t^2$ = the seasonal series. The relative contribution of the changes in each component for each time span is given by the ratios $\bar{I}_t^2/\bar{O}_t^2, \bar{C}_t^2/\bar{O}_t^2$, and $\bar{S}_t^2/\bar{O}_t^2$. To illustrate the statistical computation of the relative contribution of each C, S, and I components to the percentage change in the original time-series, let us consider the quarterly sales of IBM from the first quarter of 1969 to the fourth quarter of 1982, as shown in Table 19.A.1.

The relative contribution of each component for one quarter is calculated in the following manner. The first step is to determine the absolute change in the original sales series (0_t) between each quarter. For example, sales in the first and second quarter (O_1 and O_2) of 1969 were \$1,685 million and \$1,832 million, so the absolute change in sales between the first and second quarters was \$147 million $(0_1 - 0_2)$. The absolute difference in sales between the third and fourth quarters $(0_3 - 0_4)$ was \$125 million $(\$1,778 - \$1,903)$. Thus, for the original sales series (O_t) the X-11 routine calculates the absolute change in sales between each of the 56 quarters; that is, $O_1 - O_2, O_2 - O_3, O_3 - O_4, \ldots, O_{54} - O_{55}, O_{55} - O_{56}$. The mean of the percent changes in

Table 19.A.1. Original quarterly sales data for IBM, 1969 to 1982 (\$ millions).

Original Series Year	1st quarter	2nd quarter	3rd quarter	4th quarter	Total
1969	1,685	1,832	1,778	1,903	7,198
1970	1,721	1,874	1,914	1,996	7,505
1971	1,870	1,942	2,082	2,380	8,274
1972	2,312	2,365	2,334	2,522	9,533
1973	2,451	2,547	2,756	3,240	10,994
1974	3,002	3,260	3,125	3,288	12,675
1975	3,272	3,496	3,600	4,068	14,436
1976	3,815	4,014	3,957	4,519	16,305
1977	4,090	4,419	4,586	5,038	18,133
1978	4,432	4,921	5,284	6,439	21,076
1979	5,295	5,355	5,384	6,829	22,863
1980	5,748	6,181	6,481	7,805	26,215
1981	6,461	6,895	6,721	8,993	29,070
1982	7,066	8,053	8,171	11,074	34,364

Table 19.A.2. Mean of the absolute average percent changes in sales related to trend-cycle, seasonal, and irregular components for one-, two-, three-, and four-quarter time span, 1969 to 1982 (in percent).

Span in Quarters	Original	Trend-Cycle	Seasonal	Irregular
1	9.25	3.19	7.29	1.9
2	9.54	6.31	6.26	1.44
3	12.73	9.47	7.59	1.57
4	12.89	12.78	0.44	1.45

the original sales for time spans of two, three, and sales for 9.25%, which is shown in Table 19.A.2.

The X-11 routine also calculate the absolute change in the original sales for time spans of two, three, and four quarters because the computation methodology is similar for each time span, we will use the four-quarter time span to illustrate the technique. The absolute change in sales every four quarters is calculated by the model. All possible four-quarter time period combinations of changes in sales are composed: $O_1 - O_5, O_5 - O_9, O_9 - O_{13}, \ldots, O_{45} - O_{49}, O_2 - O_6, O_6 - O_{10}, \ldots, O_{46} - O_{50}, O_3 - O_7, \ldots, O_{47} - O_{51}, O_4 - O_8, \ldots, O_{52} - O_{56}$. The same procedure is used to calculate two- and three-quarter time spans. The means of the changes in the original series (0_t) for two-, three-, and four-quarter time spans were 9.54%, 12.73%, and 12.89%. These values are presented in Table 19.A.2.

THE CONTRIBUTION OF EACH COMPONENT

The next step in the forecasting process is to calculate the mean absolute percent change in the final adjusted time-series for C, I, and S. The X-11 model computes a final adjusted table for each component. We now compute the relative contribution of each component to changes in the original IBM sales series for a one-quarter time span. Using Eq. (19.A.1) and the appropriate values from Table 19.A.2 produces

$$(\bar{O})^2 = (0.0190)^2 + (0.0319)^2 + (0.0729)^2$$
$$= (0.08076)^2.$$

For a one-quarter time span, the relative contribution of each component is

$$I \text{ component} = \frac{\bar{I}^2}{(\bar{O}')^2} = \frac{0.00035}{0.006523} = 5.38\%.$$

Table 19.A.3. Relative Contributions of Components to Changes in IBM Sales for One-, Two-, Three-, and Four-quarter Time Spans, 1969 to 1982 (in percent)

Span in Quarters	Trend-Cycle	Seasonal	Irregular	Total
1	15.13	80.82	4.03	100
2	45.51	51.73	2.76	100
3	58.46	40.35	1.19	100
4	98.40	0.14	1.46	100

$$C \text{ component} = \frac{\bar{C}^2}{(\bar{O}')^2} = \frac{0.00068}{0.006523} = 15.19\%.$$

$$S \text{ component} = \frac{\bar{S}^2}{(\bar{O}')^2} = \frac{0.005180}{0.006523} = \frac{79.42\%}{100.00\%}.$$

INTERPRETATION

The above data indicates that the irregular component contributed slightly over 5% of the change in the original sales of IBM for the period from the first quarter of 1969 to the second quarter of 1982. Additionally, 15% of the change in the original sales series was related to the trend-cycle component and 79% was represented by the seasonal component. Permanent information signals contributed 95% of the change in past quarterly sales of IBM, and random events account for 5%.

Table 19.A.3 shows the relative contribution of each component to changes in IBM's original sales series for one-, two-, three-, and four-quarter time spans. The irregular component went from 4.3% to 1.46% as the time spans increased. The relatively low I component for the four separate time spans suggests that the size of the forecasting error should be relatively small for aggregate forecasts of IBM's sales.

For a more detailed discussion of forecasting, see "Financial Forecasting and the X-11 Model" by Gentry and Lee (1987).

References for Chapter 19

Bergevin, PM (2002). *Financial Statement Analysis: An Integrated Approach.* Upper Saddle River, New Jersey: Prentice Hall.

Campbell, T and LC Brendsel (March 1977). The impact of compensating balance requirements on the cash balances of manufacturing corporations. *Journal of Finance*, 32, 31–40.

Chu, QC and DN Pittman (2006). Treasury inflation-indexed securities. In *Encyclopedia of Finance*, C-F Lee and AC Lee (eds.), pp. 359–363. New York: Springer.

Fabozzi, F and LN Masonson (1985). *Corporate Cash Management Technique and Analysis*. Homewood, IL, U.S.: Dow-Jones, Irwin.

Finerty, JE (2006). Working capital and cash flow. In *Encyclopedia of Finance*, C-F Lee and AC Lee (eds.), pp. 393–404. New York: Springer.

Frost, PA (December 1970). Banking services, minimum cash balances, and the firm's demand for money. *Journal of Finance*, 25, 1029–1039.

Gallinger, GW and PB Healey (1991). *Liquidity Analysis and Management*, 2nd ed. Reading, PA: Addition-Wesley.

Genrty, J and CF Lee (1987). Financial forecasting and the X-11 model: Preliminary evidence. *Advance in Financial Planning and Forecasting*, 2, 27–49.

Gottesman, AA (2006). Loan contract terms. In *Encyclopedia of Finance*, C-F Lee and AC Lee (eds.), pp. 428–434. New York: Springer.

Hill, NC and WL Sartoris (1994). *Short Term Financial Management*, 3rd ed. New Jersey: Prentice Hall.

Lee, CF and AC Lee (2006). *Encyclopedia of Finance*. New York: Springer.

Palepu, KG and PM Healy (2007). *Business Analysis & Valuation: Using Financial Statement*, 4th ed. South-Western College Publishing.

Penman, SH (2006). *Financial Statement Analysis and Security Valuation*, 3rd ed. New York: McGraw-Hill/Irwin.

Robinson, TR, P Munter, and J Grant (2003). *Financial Statement Analysis: A Global Perspective*. New Jersey: Prentice Hall.

Stigum, ML (1978). *The Money Market: Myth, Reality, and Practice*. Homewood, IL: Dow Jones-Irwin.

Stone, BK (Spring 1972). The use of forecasts for smoothing in control-limit models for cash management. *Financial Management*, 1, 72–84.

Soffer, LC and RJ Soffer (2002). *Financial Statement Analysis: A Valuation Approach*. Upper Saddle River, New Jersey: Prentice Hall.

Tan, P and G Yeo (2006), Accounting scandals and implication for directors: Lessons from enron. In *Encyclopedia of Finance*, C-F Lee and AC Lee (eds.), pp. 643–648. New York: Springer.

Van Horne, JC (2000). *Financial Market Rates and Flows*, 6th ed. Englewood Cliffs, New Jersey: Prentice-Hall.

Vander Weide, JH and SF Maier (1985). *Managing Corporate Liquidity: An Introduction to Working Capital Management*. New York: John Wiley.

Chapter 20

Credit, Cash, Marketable Securities, and Inventory Management

20.1. Introduction

Chapter 20 extends some of the generally discussed concepts of Chapter 19 into a more focused examination of a specific aspect of short-term financial analysis and planning: the management of credit. More precisely, we are going to look at the terms, costs, benefits, and methods of evaluation that relate to trade credit. In addition, cash, marketable securities, and inventory management will be discussed in this chapter.

On the balance sheet of nearly any company, accounts receivable are listed on the assets side and accounts payable on the liability side. These categories represent credit extended to other companies (accounts receivable) and credit extended by other companies (accounts payable). Thus, trade credit is a form of short-term financing for the buying company. For the selling company, trade credit is a means to increase overall sales and must be evaluated in terms of the incremental gain per unit of additional risk. Because many firms have a lot of capital tied up or extended to them in the form of trade credit, decisions involving the management of credit can have great impact on such concerns as cash flow, cost of capital, sales growth, and debt capacity.

Based on a firm's future cash needs, the financial manager can determine whether too much or too little cash is on hand at present. Surplus funds, if available, can be invested temporarily in short-term, high quality securities or can be used for other corporate purposes such as dividends or inventory purchase. Conversely, a cash shortage will make it necessary for the firm to either sell current holdings of securities or borrow from the financial markets.

This process is called cash management and represents an important aspect of the firm's operations. Idle funds represent management inefficiency, as they add nothing to firm value. However, enough liquidity must be maintained for the firm to pay its bill and meet emergencies.

Therefore, in examining the characteristics of effective credit, cash, marketable securities and inventory management, Section 20.2 discusses key terms and concept related to trade credit. In Section 20.3, we look at the cost of short-term debt and the factors that must be considered when discerning the true costs and benefits of trade credit. Among some of the selling company's major concerns are to whom should credit be extended and how to make this decision. Sections 20.4 and 20.5 discuss various quantitative methods and qualitative concerns over these decisions, and the credit decision in the context of the firm's collection policies. Section 20.6 looks at two methods to determine the optimal cash balance, or range that allows the firm to meet all obligations as they come due. In Section 20.7, to maximize efficiency and return on the cash flow, we will examine various cash collection systems. Since there will most likely be times when the firm has short-term cash deficits, it is necessary to understand the uses and functioning of bank credit lines, which are covered in Section 20.8 along with a review of the determination of the costs of bank credit. In Section 20.9, we discuss courses of action that the financial manager can follow to effectively invest and manage surplus funds. Section 20.10 covers optimal inventory management. Summary is offered in Section 20.11. Appendix 20.A presents the derivation of optimal amount of cash holdings.

20.2. Trade Credit

Trade credit is credit the seller provides the buyer by allowing the buyer to postpone payment while still taking possession of the goods or services. From an accounting point of view, this kind of credit is listed on the seller's balance sheet as accounts receivable and on the buyer's balance sheet as accounts payable.

Although there is a wide variety of arrangements for transactions involving credit between different industries, credit terms are usually based on the same logic: to induce customers to pay before the final date, it is common to offer a cash discount for prompt settlement. Thus, a company may require final payment within 20 days but offer a 2% discount to customers who pay within 10 days, an arrangement stated as 2/10, net 20.

Other arrangements for credit transactions include special terms for recurrent purchases and seasonal accounts. When a company buys many items on a recurrent basis, it is common to account for all sales during the month as occurring at the EOM, thereby eliminating the inconvenience of requiring separate payment for each delivery. The specific terms relating to this type of arrangement are 5/10, EOM, net 60; that is, by paying the bill within 10 days of the EOM, the customer will receive a 5% discount. Otherwise, full payment is due within 60 days of the invoice date. Manufacturers who produce seasonal goods often encourage customers to take early delivery by allowing them to delay payment until the normal order season, a type of credit arrangement known as *season dating*.

While the terms of sale stipulate the amount of credit granted, they specify nothing concerning the nature of the contract. In many instances, the contract between buyer and seller is only implicit, particularly when the two parties have a well-established relationship. These types of repetitive sales are made on open account simply involving book entries and an implicit contract so stated. However, there are many other types of contractual arrangements, due to such factors as the parties being unfamiliar with each other, the order being very large, customized orders, and international customers. Those more formal types of trade-credit agreements include promissory notes, commercial drafts, bank acceptances, and irrevocable letters of credit.

Basically, a *promissory note* is an IOU, whereby the buyer promises to pay the seller a certain amount by a specified date for a designated order, all in writing and signed by the buyer.

A *commercial draft* is similar in nature to a promissory note. However, its workings are somewhat different. First, the seller draws a draft ordering payment by the customer and sends this draft to the customer's bank along with any shipping documents. This commercial draft is a *sight draft* if immediate payment is required; otherwise, it is a *time draft* on which the customer's signature and the word *accepted* must be added. In either case, the advantage of this trade-credit instrument is that the seller obtains a commitment from the buyer before any goods are delivered. This commitment is the money that the seller receives ahead of time or the trade acceptance the buyer signs, which the bank returns to the seller.

Sometimes the seller knows little of the customer's creditworthiness and thus will require a stronger guarantee of the customer's debt. Such assurance can be constructed by asking the customer to arrange for his or her bank to accept the time draft. This arrangement and the resulting more-negotiable instrument is called a *banker's acceptance.*

An *irrevocable letter of credit* may be requested by an exporter who requires greater certainty of payment. First, the customer's bank sends the exporter a letter stating that it has established a line of credit for the customer with some bank in the U.S. The exporter can then collect payment ahead of delivery from the U.S. bank, which then forwards the appropriate documents to the customer's bank.

For the seller, accounts receivable is the key balance sheet item to analyze for evaluating how much net credit the company has outstanding. Moreover, the balance of accounts receivable is a multidimensional item in terms of time and composition. Current accounts receivable can be defined to satisfy the following relationship:

$$AR_t = AR_{t-1} + AR_t^N - AR_t^0, \tag{20.1}$$

where AR_t = the current balance of accounts receivable outstanding; AR_{t-1} = the balance of accounts receivable outstanding remaining from previous period; AR_t^N = new accounts receivable added during the current period; and AR_t^0 = past accounts receivable collected in the current period.

Typically, this relationship is evaluated for efficiency by using the average-collection-period ratio. In addition, because we could expand Eq. (20.1) in terms of the AR_{t-1} variable $[AR_{t-1} = AR_{t-2} + AR_{t-1}^N - AR_{t-1}^0]$, it is possible and worthwhile to examine the relative age of accounts receivable. This type of analysis can be pursued through an aging-of-accounts receivable table, such as Table 20.1. In this table, notice a decline in the quality of accounts receivable from January to February. This sort of breakdown allows analysis of the cross-sectional composition of accounts over time. An even more in-depth determination of the risk associated with

Table 20.1. Aging of accounts receivable.

	January		February	
	Accounts Receivable	% of Total	Accounts Receivable	% of Total
0–30 days	\$250,000	25.0%	\$250,000	22.7%
31–60 days	500,000	50.0%	525,000	47.8%
61–90 days	200,000	20.0%	250,000	22.7%
Over 90 days	50,000	5.0%	75,000	6.8%
Total accounts receivable	\$1,000,000	100.0%	\$1,100,000	100.0%

accounts receivable is a breakdown by customer, associating probabilities of payment with the dollar amount owed.

The importance of accounts receivable goes beyond the evaluation of the firm's trade credit, to the point of having significant implications for the firm's overall risk. This impact on risk is particularly evident when accounts receivable make up a large portion of the firm's current assets. In such instance, the quality of accounts receivable can lead to misleading conclusions concerning the firm's liquidity ratios. For example, Johnson & Johnson's balance sheet for December 2005 shows accounts receivable of nearly $7 billion, representing about 22% of the total current assets of $31.39 billion. With total current liabilities of $12.64 billion, the firm shows a current ratio of 2.48 and working-capital of $18.75 billion. Yet, just as an example, if Johnson & Johnson's accounts receivable were mostly overdue accounts with low probability for payment, then we would probably be safer in our analysis of their liquidity to disregard the short-term variability of this item as a cash equivalent. If we delete accounts receivable, Johnson & Johnson's current ratio falls to 1.93 and its working-capital to $11.75 billion. This adjustment yields a markedly less-favorable perspective of the company's liquidity position.

Another factor for the financial manager to consider is the relative costs versus the relative benefits of maintaining large accounts receivable. As previously noted, accounts receivable can favorably affect a firm's current ratio, thus making the firm appear more liquid. The effect of a higher current ratio can be multidimensional, influencing the firm's debt capacity and the cost of debt, its stock price, and its credit relations with other companies. Nevertheless, the maintenance of a high current ratio by means of the accounts receivable has its costs, such as the expense of financing the large receivable in terms of the firm's cost of capital; additional collection, investigation, and bad-debt costs; and possibly the cost tying up more of the firm's working-capital in a liquid form, thereby increasing bankruptcy risk.

The trade-credit position of the buyer can be examined in much the same light as that of the seller. For the buyer, we look to the other side of the balance sheet and evaluate the accounts payable. The analysis of this account can be pursued both cross-sectionally in terms of relative size, average payment period, and aging of accounts payable, and overtime by looking at the changes in the cross-sectional characteristics.

There is considerable disagreement over the extent to which firms should utilize trade credit to finance their operations. On one side are those who associate no cost with the credit obtained through accounts payable and believe therefore that the firm should maximize its use of this cheap source of capital. In particular, advocates of this view would advise the firm to maximize the length of time between receiving the goods and paying for them. Yet, there are those in the academic and business domains who believe that using accounts payable as a source of capital involves considerable costs. As mentioned earlier, most trade-credit terms involve a discount on the purchase price for paying earlier. Thus, if the firm does not take this discount, it may actually be incurring an opportunity cost that can be determined as follows.

Suppose you purchase \$100 worth of goods on terms of 5/10, net 30; the cash discount allows you to pay \$95 instead of \$100. If you do not take the discount, you are essentially getting a 20-day loan from the seller. However, you would pay $5/95 = 5.26\%$ more for your goods. By dividing $365/20 = 18.25$, we get the number of 20-day periods at 5.26% per year. Thus, 5.26% per period times 18.25 periods per year = 96% per year, which is a 96% yearly cost on the original loan.

Viewed in this manner, accounts payable is not the cheap financing source it might have originally appeared to be. Surely the firm can raise capital at a lower cost than 96% per annum.

Other costs that must be considered when evaluating accounts payable are those associated with maintaining low liquidity ratios and, relatedly, bankruptcy costs. Moreover, the thorough evaluation and management of a firm's trade credit must consider accounts receivable and accounts payable together, as discussions affecting one will have consequent effects on the other. To better understand this relationship and evaluate the costs of trade credit, we now turn to a more explicit determination of the involved costs.

20.3. The Cost of Trade Credit

The decisions of how much trade credit to issue (seller) or use (buyer) must be made on the basis of the relative costs. This section identifies the costs of trade credit and related issues in the cost estimation–determination process.

20.3.1. *The Seller's Perspective*

For the seller, the cost of granting trade is not a straightforward calculation. Much of what can be considered a cost related to trade credit has to be estimated or forecasted. Furthermore, the seller should really be interested in the incremental cost or, correspondingly, the incremental gain associated with increasing or decreasing trade credit.

First, let us identify the additional costs that the company would bear for extending trade credit to its customers. Changes in accounts receivable can be evaluated according to three dimensions, each related to cost. First, by either granting trade credit to new customers or easing existing terms so that current customers purchase more, the seller incurs the additional expense of financing a larger absolute size of receivable. Second, by easing credit terms, such as by lengthening the credit period, thus increasing the period over which accounts receivable are financed. Third, as credit terms are eased or more trade credit is granted, there is a greater probability of having more bad accounts to write off.

Most obvious, perhaps, is the incremental gain in additional sales that will result from easing credit terms or increasing trade credit granted. We can compute this incremental change in profits that would arise from any change in the seller's credit policy, but to do so we must estimate the additional (or detrimental) sales that will occur as well as the increase in the size of accounts receivable, the average collection period, and the relevant discount rate.

As an example of computing incremental costs, we will examine the impact from an increase in the credit period granted to customers. First, we will define the following terms and their initial values:

S_0 = Current sales = \$1 million per year.

S = Incremental sales = \$250,000.

V = Variable costs as a percentage of sales = 70%. V includes the cost of administering the credit department and all other costs except bad-debt losses and financing costs (interest charges) associated with carrying the investment in receivables. Costs of carrying inventories are included in V.

$1 - V$ = Contribution margin = 30% or equivalently, the percentage of each sales dollar that goes toward covering overhead and increasing profits.

k = The cost of financing the investment in receivables = 12%. k is the firm's cost of new capital when the capital is used to finance receivables.

ACP_0 = Average collection period prior to a change in credit policy = 20 days.

ACP_N = New average collection period after the credit policy change = 30 days. In this example, we assume that customers pay on time, thus ACP = specified collection period).

Given this information, we seek to computer values for ΔI(incremental change in the level of the firm's investment in accounts receivable) and ΔP (incremental change in profits). We can calculate ΔI as follows:

$$\begin{aligned}
\Delta I &= \text{(increased investment in receivables associated with original sales)} + \\
&\quad \text{(additional investment in receivables associated with new sales)} \\
&= \text{(change in collection period) (old sales per day)} + V(ACP_N) \times \\
&\quad \text{incremental sales per day)} \\
&= (ACP_N - ACP_0)\left(\frac{S_0}{360}\right) + \left[V(ACP_N)\left(\frac{S}{360}\right)\right] \\
&= (30 - 20)\left(\frac{1{,}000{,}000}{360}\right) + \left[0.7(30)\left(\frac{250{,}000}{360}\right)\right]. \\
&= \$42{,}361. \qquad (20.2)
\end{aligned}$$

From this information, we can now determine ΔP, the incremental profit associated with the proposed credit period change:

$$\begin{aligned}
\Delta P &= \text{[(new sales) (contribution margin)]} \\
&\quad - \text{(cost of carrying new receivables)} \\
&= \Delta S\,(1 - V) - k(\Delta I) \\
&= \$250{,}000\,(0.3) - 0.12\,(42{,}361) \\
&= \$69{,}917. \qquad (20.3)
\end{aligned}$$

The result indicates that increasing the credit period from 20 to 30 days can be expected to raise pretax profit by \$69,917. Thus, the new credit policy should be adopted.

Note that two simplifying assumptions were made in this analysis: (1) that all customers paid on time (ACP = credit period) and (2) that no bad-debt losses were incurred. However, in both cases, adjustments to the calculation procedures can be made quite easily. For instance, instead of using the credit period in Eq. (20.2), we can use the present average collection period and period estimated for the new credit policy. We can also adjust fro bad-debt losses by estimating the percent of total sales that they will encompass B — say, 5% — and subtract this amount from ΔP. Thus, we modify Eq. (20.3) as

$$\begin{aligned}
\Delta P &= \text{(new sales)(contribution margin)} \\
&\quad - \text{(cost of carrying new receivables)} - \text{(bad-debt losses)} \\
&= \Delta S\,(1 - V) - k\,(\Delta I) - B\,(S)
\end{aligned}$$

$$= \$250{,}000\ (0.3) - 0.12\ (42{,}361) - 0.05\ (\$1{,}250{,}000)$$
$$= \$7.417. \tag{20.4}$$

Alternatively, bad-debt losses could be estimated as a percentage of incremental sales, and this amount is then subtracted from the change-in-profit function.

Capital Ideas: The Effect of the Economy on Credit Ratings

During the 1980s, credit management decisions were like "easy fishing". Everybody — no matter how skilled — could catch a fish. The economy was healthy, firms were growing, and financing was available. Then, with the 1990s, conditions changed dramatically. The economy sank into recession, the S&L crisis deepened, and real estate prices collapsed, which left many banks in very exposed positions and dried up sources of financing. The surge of bankruptcies in 1990 became a flood in 1991 that swept away many of the familiar landmarks in the credit stream. For credit managers, the days of easy fishing came to an abrupt end.

As an unsettled economy became awash in business failures in recent years, merchants were compelled to cast about for new accounts. In many cases, they unwittingly found themselves extending new credit to high risk accounts that had already run up unpaid balances elsewhere. The hard fact is that in a recessionary environment, new business is increasingly likely to consist of rogue elements already once discarded.

But just as it takes a combination of luck, skill, and science to successfully ply a trout-filled stream, surely there is more luck to identifying creditworthy customers and managing existing accounts. For starters, it requires knowledge and the systems capable of approximating knowledge.

Knowledge-based systems assimilate economic, financial, demographic, and geographic information as well as the merchant's own customer history. By drawing on statistically derived analytic models, such systems can identify the most desirable prospective accounts by scoring each account according to degrees of risk. For existing accounts, knowledge-based tools provide early warning systems to identify firms that are likely to become problem accounts unless immediate actions are taken.

Of course, an experienced angler would know never to wade up to his or her waist in an icy brook without first measuring not only the channel's current, but also its depth. Likewise, the perceptive merchant must consider every dimension of the prospective market, its upside and downside, before venturing too far into the churning credit system.

20.3.2. *The Buyer's Perspective*

For the buyer, determining the cost of using trade credit can be approached from various angles, depending on one's viewpoint. For instance, some practioners and academicians argue that there is no cost associated with using trade credit and thus it is essentially a form of free financing. That is, the buyer pays nothing extra for the purchased goods or services by waiting until the last payment day. Therefore, trade credit costs nothing to the buyer and should be used to the maximum extent possible.

Yet, as demonstrated in the previous section, it is possible to identify an opportunity cost to the buyer for not taking the offered trade discounts. In fact, as our example pointed out, foregoing this opportunity to acquire goods or services at a discount to the originally agreed-on price can be a very expensive form of financing for the buyer. Consequently, the opportunity-cost perspective would advocate taking all trade discounts to maximize profitability and, hence, firm value as long as firm's cost of capital is less than the imputed cost of not taking the discount.

Another argument against the view that trade credit has no cost for the buyer relates to bankruptcy costs. In the case where the buyer maximized its use of accounts payable as a form of financing, increasing accounts payable and stretching out payments as much as possible, the risk of illiquidity may increase. The impact of such implicit bankruptcy risk would be to increase the cost of other sources of capital, as creditors would perceive this increased risk and expect to be compensated for it. Moreover, the buyer's extensive accounts payable position could adversely affect relations with other suppliers, resulting in less-advantageous credit terms.

At this point, there seems to be considerable support for the principle that trade credit as a source of financing involves significant costs. In fact, much has been written advocating direct comparison between the cost of trade credit, such as computed under the opportunity-cost perspective, with the cost of alternative sources of capital. However, this view fails to account for the impact of tax timing differences among firms. Brick and Fung (1984) contend that the rate at which firms turn over inventory interacts with the accounting procedure to induce a tax-timing difference between cash and credit transactions, which makes credit tractions less costly.

20.4. Financial Ratios and Credit Analysis

In analyzing the credit of a potential or current customer, we can apply a range of qualitative and quantitative approaches. While a number of outside sources can provide valuable information to aid in this process, we defer our discussion of these sources until the next section. Instead, we discuss here a number of quantitative methods that the seller can use when doing credit analysis. Before going on, one important point must be stressed. Any type of quantitative methodology that is used to aid the decision process is just that — an aid — and not the sole criterion for making the decision. Quantitative methods and models rarely allow consideration of all the information relevant to a problem. Therefore, any outcome from quantitative approaches must be considered in light of aspects that cannot be modeled.

20.4.1. *Financial Ratio Analysis*

While a complete analysis of a customer's present and future financial condition is usually too expensive to conduct, significant evidence of a firm's creditworthiness can be derived from its financial statements. Using key financial ratios and some analytical methodology, the seller can make a reasonable estimate of the customer's financial status.

This investigation might focus on the liquidity ratios and their trend over time. In this case, the analyst would be trying to determine whether the firm is liquid enough to meet its short-term obligations. Additionally, calculating the relative size of the customer's accounts payable to other liabilities, as well as the change in the proportion of accounts payable/sales, should also yield information as to whether the customer will be able to pay its bills. Relatedly, the composition of current assets and their change over time is significant, because if the buying firm has low cash levels but large inventory and accounts receivable balances, it may have a cash flow problem and thereby greater credit risk. The statement of changes in financial position can reveal more detailed knowledge of the customer's cash flow and therefore might be examined as well. Finally, comparisons of the customer firm's financial ratios with industry averages can provide further discrimination of the buyer's credit status.

20.4.2. *Numerical Credit Scoring*

Using financial ratio analysis to evaluate credit risk is certainly helpful. Yet, the decision that must be made following the examination of such data can be complicated by the difficulty of interpreting conflicting ratios. Different ratios often imply different predictions for the same firm. To overcome such ambiguity, information from several financial ratios can be combined into a single index. The resulting multivariate financial model will yield a single number for classifying the firm in terms of credit risk.

When considering how to construct such a multivariate model, there are several areas of concern:

1. What form should the model take (for example, linear or multiplicative)?
2. What variables should be included?
3. What weights should applied to the variables?

These questions have no straightforward answers, for there is an widely accepted economic theory of financial distress to serve as a guide for such decisions. However, researchers have found that statistical tools of *factor analysis* and *linear discriminant analysis* to be of great help in advising financial risk indexes.

As a technique for deriving composite financial variables to classify firms by risk group, discriminant analysis has two purposes: (1) to test for mean group differences and describe the overlap between groups, and (2) to construct a classification scheme based on a set of m variables in order to assign previously unclassified observations to appropriate groups. This composite financial variable by which firms are classified is sometimes called a financial *z score*. Linear discriminant analysis has been applied extensively by practitioners and academicians in financial distress determination, bankruptcy prediction, bond rating analysis, and, as we are most interested in here, credit analysis.

A number of studies have developed models to help determine a firm's trade-credit policy. Notably, Mehta (1974) and Van Horne (2001) proposed a two-group discriminant-analysis model to identify the "good" account from the "bad" account. To implement this type of classification methodology, Mehta utilized a linear discriminant function of the form

$$Y_i = AX_{1i} + BX_{2i}, \qquad (20.5)$$

where Y_i = index value for the ith account; X_{1i} = ith firm's quick ratio; X_{2i} = ith firm's total sales/inventory ratio; and A and B-parameters or weights to be determined.

To formulate the original model, Mehta suggests the following steps. First, extend open-book credit to all new credit applicants for a sample period, recording for each account defaults in payment after a specified period. If the new account defaults, it is classified as a bad account and the index (Y_i) is assigned a value of 0; if the account pays on time, it is classified as a good account and the index is assigned a value of 1. with this information the linear discriminant analysis can be undertaken with two independent variables. Based on the sample data of X_{1i} and X_{2i}, the coefficients can be estimated by either of two methods.

On the derivation of the discriminant model, the minimum cutoff value must be determined. The objective here is to refuse credit to those accounts with a Y value below the cutoff value and to extend credit to those with a Y value above the cutoff.

To demonstrate, we can modify the work of Van Horne (2001). After calculating Y, 12 accounts are arranged in ascending order of magnitude, as shown in Table 20.2.

Observing the overlap area for accounts 6, 12, 11, and 4, we can thus determine that the cutoff value must lie between 1.64 and 1.96. If we arbitrarily choose the midpoint 1.80 as the cutoff value, we will misclassify accounts 11 and 12, as seen graphically in Fig. 20.1. Given the cutoff value, Fig. 20.1 classifies accounts 11 as a good account when, in fact, we know it is a bad account; account 12 is classified as a bad account when it is actually a good account. These are type I and type II classification errors, respectively.

Type I errors involve the rejection of the null hypothesis when it is actually true, while type II errors involve the acceptance of the null hypothesis when it is actually false. For the sake of practicality, the analysis should assume an area of possible misclassification for indexes between

Table 20.2. Status and Index Values of the Accounts.

Account Number	Account Status	Y_i
7	Bad	0.81
10	Bad	0.89
2	Bad	1.30
3	Bad	1.45
6	Bad	1.64
12	Good	1.77
11	Bad	1.83
4	Good	1.96
1	Good	2.25
8	Good	2.50
5	Good	2.61
9	Good	2.80

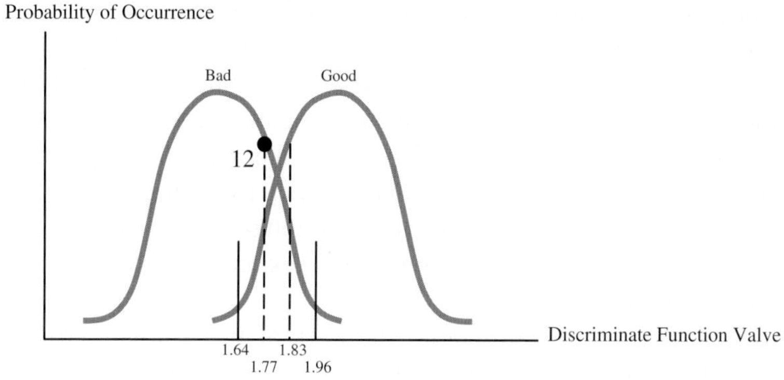

Fig. 20.1. Distributions of good and bad accounts.

1.64 and 1.95. Accounts or firms falling within this range require further investigation and analysis.

If the manager has reason to believe that new credit applicants will not differ significantly from past applicants, whose performance was the basis for the model formulation, then discriminant analysis can be used to select and reject credit sales customers. Moreover, by eliminating the need to spend time investigating customers with a definite reject or select classification (that is, ≤ 1.64 and ≥ 1.96), valuable search costs can be reduced and focused on those accounts in the range of uncertainty ($1.64 < Y_i < 1.96$).

As described by Mehta (1974), the manager faces four tasks to effectively apply linear discriminant analysis to the credit decision:

1. Determining significant factors.
2. Selecting the sample.
3. Assigning weights to factors to develop an index.
4. Establishing cutoff values for the index.

As previously mentioned, factor analysis can also be a valuable quantitative tool for credit analysis. In particular, factor analysis can be used to determine the most important or representative data relevant to the decision at hand. For credit analysis, where the analyst must choose among various feasible indicators and financial ratios in determining creditworthiness, factor analysis can simultaneously take into account all the interdependencies among the variables and help isolate those that best help explain the dependent variable.

Two key concepts related to factor analysis are factor scores and factor loadings. A *factor score* is simply a linear combination (or linear composite) of the original variables and is defined as

$$F_i = b_1Y_1 + b_2Y_2 + \cdots + b_jY_j + b_pY_p, \tag{20.6}$$

where F_i is the ith factor score; $Y_j(j = i, 1, 2, \ldots, p)$ are the original variables; and $b_1, \ldots, b_p$ are the coefficients to be estimated.

A factor loading is simply the correlation (across object) of a set of factors with the original variables. Using the factor loading, one can identify which of the original variables correlate most closely with each of the indicative factor scores. In this way, the credit analyst could derive a general, more efficient set of explanatory variables to use in the decision-making process. Moreover, factor analysis can be combined with discriminant analysis to pinpoint, in a more objective manner, the significant factors to use.

20.4.3. *Benefits of Credit-Scoring Models*

The process of deciding whether to grant trade credit to a customer, and how much, is complicated, requiring significant information search and assimilation time and, in the end, money. Moreover, it is no easy task to identify the costs related to such a process. However, we can highlight some of the potential benefits from implementing a *credit-scoring model*, which can also make related costs easier to identify. These potential benefits are as follow:

1. Quantification of risk.
2. Identification of predictor variables.
3. Consistency of credit decision.
4. More efficient allocation of credit analyst's time and resources.

Related to the quantification of risks in the credit decision, Ewert (1977) and Foster (1998) examined the credit records of a manufacturing firm and classified the accounts into categories of "good" and "bad". Bad accounts were defined as those placed for collection with an outside agency or written off in the company's book. Based on their availability and popularity, the eventual list of predictor variables was narrowed down and modeled using a stepwise regression procedure.

Table 20.3. Distribution of credit scores.

Credit Score from Scoring Model	Cumulative Frequencies "Goods"	"Bads"
−0.200	0%	0%
0.208	0	35
0.226	2	36
0.245	3	40
0.356	6	58
0.543	16	76
0.577	17	82
0.596	20	85
0.699	34	97
0.763	49	99
0.898	75	100
1.200	100	100

From the results of his model, Ewert (1977) presented the following cumulative frequency distribution of good and bad accounts for the 200 firms in his holdout sample[1]:

From this presentation of the results, we could develop a decision rule. For example, to make a credit decision based on Ewert's model, the rule might be to extend trade credit if the score for an applicant is equal to or greater than 0.577. This cutoff point will result in approximately 18% of good and 18% of bad accounts being misclassified. From observing these percentages and the costs of each misclassification, management can make a more concrete, objective decision on the desired risk level.

20.4.4. *Outside Sources of Credit Information*

In addition to internal methods of evaluating credit worthiness, a number of outside sources can provide valuable information. Probably the most important piece of information an outside source could offer is whether potential customers have paid their debts promptly in the past.

For a new customer, checking with a credit agency will probably be the easiest and most efficient way for the seller to evaluate creditworthiness. The largest and most well-known of these agencies is Dun and Bradstreet: its regular reference book provides credit ratings on nearly 3 million domestic and foreign firms. Figure 20.2 shows the key for interpreting these ratings.

[1]The holdout sample refers to the sample having not been used to estimate the empirical results.

Key to Ratings

ESTIMATED FINANCIAL STRENGTH				COMPOSITE CREDIT APPRAISAL			
				HIGH	GOOD	FAIR	LIMITED
5A	$ 50,000,000		and over	1	2	3	4
4A	$ 10,000,000	to	49,999,999	1	2	3	4
3A	1,000,000	to	9,999,999	1	2	3	4
2A	750,000	to	999,999	1	2	3	4
1A	500,000	to	749,999	1	2	3	4
BA	300,000	to	499,999	1	2	3	4
BB	200,000	to	299,999	1	2	3	4
CB	125,000	to	199,999	1	2	3	4
CC	75,000	to	124,999	1	2	3	4
DC	50,000	to	74,999	1	2	3	4
DD	35,000	to	49,999	1	2	3	4
EE	20,000	to	34,999	1	2	3	4
FF	10,000	to	19,999	1	2	3	4
GG	5,000	to	9,999	1	2	3	4

GENERAL CLASSIFICATION

ESTIMATED FINANCIAL STRENGTH			COMPOSITE CREDIT APPRAISAL		
			GOOD	FAIR	LIMITED
1R	$ 125,000	and over	2	3	4
2R	$ 50,000 to	$ 124,999	2	3	4

EXPLANATION
When the designation "1R" or "2R" appears, followed by a 2,3 or 4, it is an indication that the Estimated Financial Strength, while not definitely classified, is presumed to be in the range of the ($) figures in the corresponding bracket, and while the Composite Credit Appraisal cannot be judged precisely, it is believed to fall in the general category indicated.

ABSENCE OF RATING (--) THE BLANK SYMBOL
A blank symbol - - should not be interpreted as indicating that credit should be denied. It simply means that the information available to Dun & Bradstreet does not permit us to classify the company within our rating key and that further inquiry should be made before reaching a credit decision

EMPLOYEE RANGE DESIGNATIONS IN REPORTS ON NAMES NOT LISTED IN THE REFERENCE BOOK
Certain businesses do not lend themselves to a Dun & Bradstreet rating and are not listed in the Reference Book. Information on these names, however, continues to be stored and updated on the D&B Business Information File. Reports are available on such businesses and instead of a rating they carry and Employee Range Designation (ER) which is indicative of size in terms of number of employees. No other signification should be attached

KEY TO THE D&B PAYDEX (PAYMENT INDEX)

PAYDEX	PAYMENT
100	ANTICIPATE
90	DISCOUNT
80	PROMPT
70	SLOW TO 15 days
50	SLOW TO 30days
40	SLOW TO 60 days
30	SLOW TO 90 days
20	SLOW TO 120 days
UN/0	UNAVAILABLE

KEY TO EMPLOYEE RANGE DESIGNATIONS

ER1	1000 or more	Employees
ER2	500 - 999	Employees
ER3	100 - 499	Employees
ER4	50 - 99	Employees
ER5	20 - 49	Employees
ER6	10 - 19	Employees
ER7	5 - 9	Employees
ER8	1 - 4	Employees
ERN		Not available

Dun & Bradstreet Credit Services

ΔB A company of The Dun & Bradstreet Corporation

1988

1 Diamond Hill Road
Murray Hill, N.J. 07974-0027

18B7 (8801)

Fig. 20.2. Key to Dun and Bradstreet ratings.

As an additional service, Dun and Bradstreet provide a full credit report on a potential customer.

The Credit Interchange Service of the National Association of Credit Management provides a clearing house for the collection and dissemination of information relating to the customer experience of other firms. Of course, one could simply contact these firms directly to get this information.

Another source of credit information is the customer's bank. Usually, the seller's bank makes a credit check through the customer's bank to obtain information on the applicant's average bank balance, access to bank credit, and general reputation.

If the customer is a public company with outstanding securities on the secondary markets, Moody's or Standard and Poor's provide ratings for the customer's outstanding bonds. Moreover, comparing these bond prices with those of similar firms, along with an examination of recent movements in the customer's stock price, can offer additional clues to future financial performance.

20.5. Credit Decision and Collection Policies

So far, we have discussed how trade credit is defined for both seller and buyer, what costs should be considered and how they can be measured and quantitative methods to facilitate the seller's decision whether to grant credit. Although the use of numerical credit-scoring methods can assist the manager in the credit-granting decision, additional facets to credit policy need to be determined:

1. If the credit request is acceptable, for what amount is it safe to grant credit?
2. Should the applicant be offered the incentive of a cash discount for early payments?
3. What collection measures are appropriate for a delinquent customer?

The initial credit-granting decisions and these three additional credit policy decisions are all related and affect (1) sales level, (2) collection cost and bad-debt losses, and (3) the form of investment (inventories, accounts receivable, or cash).

The amount of credit to grant can be determined by a comparative evaluation of the new account and its related risk, to established accounts having a similar level of financial ability and willingness to pay. A more quantitative flows from the new account and then determining the net present value of those cash flows. Primary considerations are the probability of delinquency or default, how this probability will increase, and its rate of increase as the amount of credit allowed is increased.

The actual credit terms, such as the length of the payment period and the size and availability of a cash discount, are generally determined by industry practices. Major deviation from these practices usually result in reprisal from competitors, low profit margins, or lost sales.

Another factor to consider when deciding whether and to what extent to grant credit is the possibility of repeat orders. In some instances, it might be profitable over the long run to take on a customer with an expected negative NPV of cash flows from the first order. Such would be the decision where the seller could estimate with a reasonable amount of certainty that the customer would eventually develop into a good, reliable account.

20.5.1. *Collection Policy*

The actions a firm takes when an account becomes delinquent constitute its *collection policy*. A collection policy involves two dimensions to which the firm can allocate its collection efforts. The first dimension is time. When an account is not paid within the allowed credit period, it is considered delinquent. As the account becomes more delinquent, the firm intensifies its collection efforts. For example, an account in its first month of delinquency might be sent an impersonal, mild reminder. If this first notice does not produce result, a stronger reminder may be sent during the second month of delinquency, perhaps followed up by a phone call. If the delinquency continues, more forceful and harsh measures may be pursued, such as turning the account over to a collection agency.

The second dimension of collection policy is account quality, which is inversely related to account risk. An account's quality risk is reflected in the probabilities of bad debt, expected future business, or both. Low risks of this nature would entail mild collection policies.

Although related, time and quality dimensions may not necessarily coincide. Marginal firms may pay early, while high-quality customers such as government agencies may be slow in their payment habits. Nevertheless, because both of these dimensions measure some aspect of risk in accounts receivable, both should be considered when formulating a collection policy.

Another important aspect regarding collection policy is that each successive step may only yield a partial degree of success. Thus, for a given category of accounts, sending the first letter may, on average, produce

50% payment on the outstanding balance. The implication is that a series of collection efforts will yield a series of partial payments. Consequently, various collection policies produce different timing of cash flows over several reporting periods. In this light, the evaluation of collection policies can be seen within the framework of a capital budgeting problem.

As discussed in earlier chapters, one of the more accepted criteria for selecting capital budgeting alternatives is the maximization of the net present value of cash flows (the NPV method). Applying this evaluation method to the collection policy decision, three related estimates must be made:

1. What relevant cash flows will arise and when?
2. How measurement or estimation will be carried out?
3. What discount rate should be used?

The appropriate discount rate to use is the cost of capital, of which estimation methods were discussed earlier. Included among the relevant cash flows are collection receipts, collection costs, and bad-debt costs.

20.5.2. *Factoring and Credit Insurance*

Factoring and *credit insurance* are two other alternatives that can be considered in formulating the collection policy, particularly for the smaller firm. For the large firm, there are definite advantages in actively managing its accounts receivable. Divisions may be able to pool information on customer creditworthiness, and economies of scale may arise in the record-keeping, billing, and pursuit of delinquent accounts. But the smaller firm is perhaps disadvantaged in that it may not be able to hire or properly train someone for the specialized debt-collection function. However, the small firm (and large firms as well) can farm out a good portion of these duties to a third party called a *factor*.

Essentially, under the factoring process, the firm sells its trade credit to a factor. Initially, the factor and the client firm agree on credit limits and the average collection period for each customer, thereby allowing the factor to identify the risk involved. Next, the client firm notifies each customer that the factor has purchased the debt. From this point, the client firm sends the factor invoices from all sales and, subsequently, the customer makes payment directly to the factor. The factor pays the selling firm on the basis of the agree-on average collection period, regardless of whether the customer has paid. Of course, reducing the uncertainty of accounts receivable in this manner has its costs. Typically, the factor charges a fee of 1 to 2% of the value of the invoice.

An alternative route for achieving protection against bad debts and their associated costs is to obtain credit insurance. Generally, the credit-insurance company imposes a maximum amount that it will cover for accounts with a particular credit rating. In many cases, the seller can collect not only if the customer actually becomes insolvent, but also if an account is overdue.

20.6. The Baumol and Miller–Orr Model

Like the firm's real inventories, cash is just another raw material that is needed to carry on the firm's operations. Moreover, the availability of cash determines to a significant extent the firm's liquidity position. All other assets have less liquidity than cash in the sense that their transformation into cash requires time, cost, or both. Marketable securities are considered less liquid than cash because, although they can usually be disposed of immediately, their conversion to cash requires transaction costs. The rate-of-return from this investment represents the opportunity cost of liquidity to the holder of cash.

Consequently, the problem of determining an optimal level for the cash balance can be considered a cost-minimization problem. That is, the financial manager's job in this area is to minimize the relative costs of having a cash surplus versus having a cash deficit. As a starting point for analyzing this problem, we turn to the application of Baumol's economic inventory ordering quantity (EOQ) model for cash management.

20.6.1. *Baumol's EOQ Model*

The EOQ model strives to equate the two opposing marginal costs associated with ordering and holding inventory, thereby minimizing total costs. For our purposes, we can consider cash to be a manageable inventory for which we want to minimize the sum of the following costs:

1. Ordering or transactions costs from converting securities into cash and vice versa.
2. Carrying or opportunity costs equal to the foregone rate-of-return that the holder of cash incurs.

Figure 20.3 shows the relationships among transaction cost (AB), opportunity cost (CD), and total *cost* (EF).

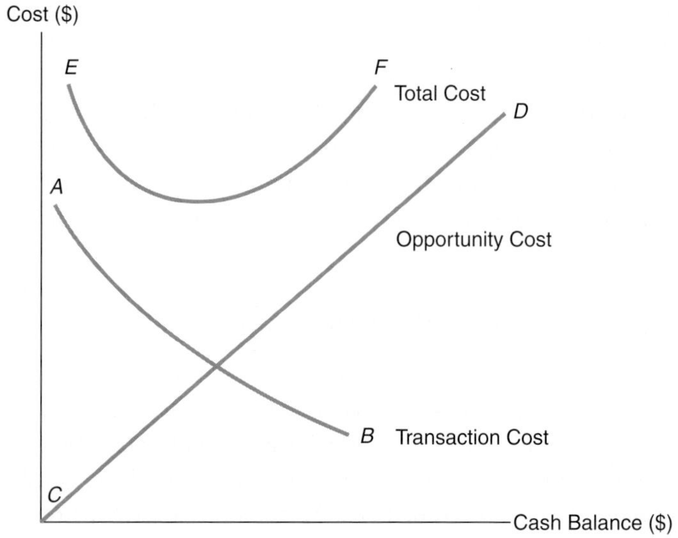

Fig. 20.3. Determining the optimal cash balance as a cost-minimization problem.

In applying the EOQ model to our optimal cash balance problem, we must be aware of the underlying assumptions about cash flows:

1. Cash outflows occur at a constant rate.
2. Cash inflows occur periodically when securities are liquidated.

These assumed cash flow patterns are shown in Fig. 20.4.

We now present the EOQ model, apply its mechanism to a sample problem, and interpret the result. The specific cash flow patterns we assume are (1) the firm uses cash at a steady, predictable rate, say $1 million per week; (2) the firm's cash inflows from operations also occur at an even, forecastable rate, say, $700,000 per week; and (3) the firm's net cash outflows also occur at a similarly predictable rate of $300,000 per week. Based on these assumptions, the EOQ model for determining the optimal cash balance, C*, can be stated as follows[2]:

$$EOQ = C^* = \sqrt{\frac{2FT}{k}}, \tag{20.7}$$

where C^* = optimal cash holdings to be transferred from marketable securities or borrowed; $C^*/2$ = optimal average cash balance (ACB);

[2]Appendix 20.A gives the derivation of Eq. (20.1).

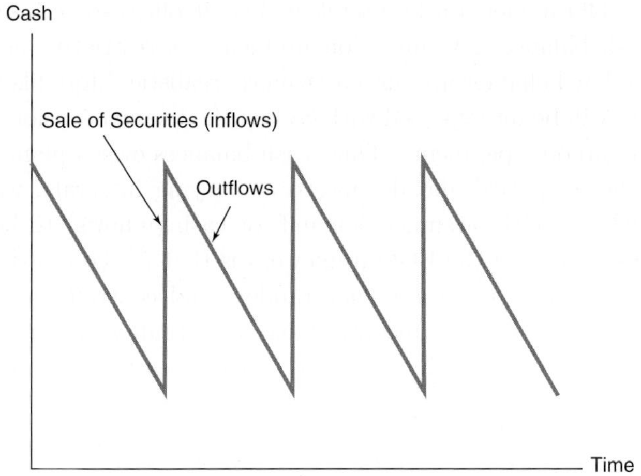

Fig. 20.4. The assumed cash flow patterns using Baumol's EOQ model.

F = fixed-transactions costs of making a securities trade or borrowing money; T = total amount of net new cash needed for disbursements over the entire period (usually a year); and k = the opportunity cost of holding cash (equal to the foregone rate-of-return on marketable securities or the cost of borrowing).

EOQ is positively related to F and T and inversely related to k. By taking the square root of FT/k, the relationship with EOQ is less than proportionate. If the value of fixed-transactions costs (F) doubles, then EOQ will increase by only 1.41 times.

For example, we assume the following values: $F = \$120$; $T = 52$ weeks $\times$ \$300,000/week = \$1,560,000; and $k = 12\% = 0.12$. With these values, we can calculate the value of C^* as

$$C^* = \sqrt{\frac{2(\$120)(\$1{,}560{,}000)}{0.12}} = \$55{,}857.$$

As the firm's cash balance approaches 0 (or some minimum acceptable level), \$55,857 worth of securities should be sold to replenish this account. The frequency with which this process should occur can be calculated as $\$1{,}560{,}000/\$55{,}857 = 27.9 \approx 28$ times during the year or, equivalently, $365/28 =$ every 13 days. Finally, the firm's ACB would be

$$\frac{C^*}{2} = \frac{\$55{,}857}{2} = \$27{,}928.50.$$

While the EOQ model can be useful in that, it offers some insight to the optimal cash balance determination problem, its restrictive assumptions about cash flow behavior are not particularly realistic. More likely, a firm's cash inflows will be interspersed with cash outflows and occasionally exceed the flow of outgoing payments. Thus, cash balances over a planning period will move both upward and downward at varying intervals, whereas the EOQ model implicitly assumes demand for cash (inflows) to be positive. Another problem with the EOQ framework is that the conventional model assumes production (inflows) is non-random and controllable while sales (outflows) are random and uncontrollable. In actuality, we cannot characterize cash flows in this fashion, because control over inflows and outflows is seldom absolute.

20.6.2. *Miller–Orr Model*

The Miller and Orr model for cash management improves on the EOQ methodology in significant ways. Miller and Orr start with the assumption that there are only two forms of assets: cash and marketable securities. Also, the Miller–Orr model allows for cash balance movement in both positive and negative directions and for the optimal cash balance to be a range of values rather than a single point estimate. This model is even more useful for firms that are unable to predict day-to-day cash inflows and outflows.

Figure 20.5 shows the functioning of the Miller–Orr model. Notice in this figure that the cash balance is allowed to meander undisturbed as long as it remains within the predetermined boundary range shown by H and L. However, at point B, the cash balance reaches the maximum allowable level. At this point, the firm could purchase marketable securities of an amount equal to the dashed line, which would lower the cash balance to the "return point" from which it is again allowed to fluctuate freely. At point S, the firm's cash balance reaches the minimum allowable level. At this point, the firm could sell marketable securities to investors or borrow to bring the cash level back up to the return point.

In how much of a range $(H-L)$ should the cash balance be allowed to fluctuate? According to the Miller–Orr model, the higher the day-to-day variability in cash flows and/or the higher the fixed transactions costs associated with buying and selling securities, the farther apart the control limits should be set. On the other hand, if the opportunity cost of holding cash (the foregone interest from marketable securities) is high, the limits

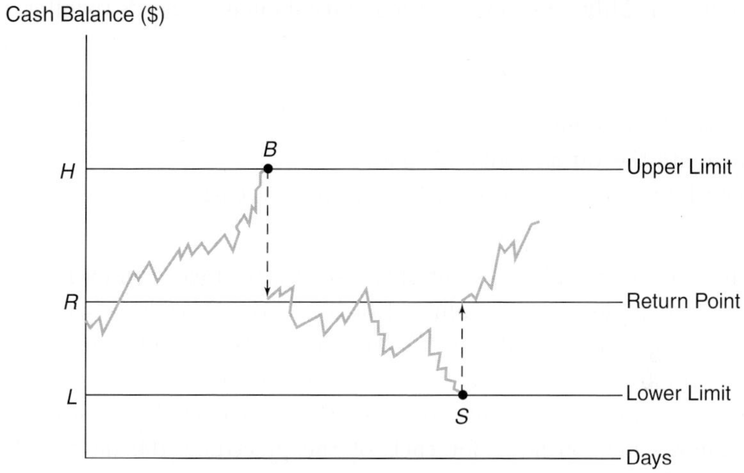

Fig. 20.5. The workings of the Miller–Orr model.

should be set closer together. Management's objective is to minimize total costs associated with cash. By use of minimization procedures, the spread between the upper and lower cash limit (S), the return point (R), the upper limit (H), and ACB are

$$S = 3\left[\frac{3F\sigma^2}{4k}\right]^{\frac{1}{3}}, \tag{20.8}$$

$$R = \frac{S}{3} + L, \tag{20.9}$$

$$H = S + L, \tag{20.10}$$

$$ACB = \frac{4R - L}{3}, \tag{20.11}$$

where L = lower limit; F = fixed-transactions cost; k = opportunity cost on a daily basis; and σ^2 = variance of net daily cash flow.

The firm always returns to a point one-third of the spread between the lower and upper limits. With the return point set, the firm will likely bump up against its lower limit more frequently than its upper limit. While this lower point does not minimize the number of transactions and their resulting cost (as the middle point would), it is an optimum point in that it minimizes the sum of transactions costs and interest costs, the latter of which are incurred from holding excessive cash.

To use the Miller–Orr model, the financial manager needs to follow three steps:

1. Set the lower limit.
2. Estimate the variance of cash flows.
3. Determine relevant transactions and interest costs.

Setting the lower limit is essentially a subjective task. However, common sense and experience are helpful. Most likely, the lower limit will be some minimum safety margin above 0. An important consideration in setting this limit is any bank requirement that must be satisfied.

To estimate the variance of cash flows, one could record the net cash inflows and outflows for each of the preceding 100 days and then compute the variance of those 100 observations. This approach would require updating, particularly if net cash flows were unstable over time. One additional aspect to consider in this calculation is the impact of seasonal effects, which might also require adjustments to the variance estimate.

To determine the relevant transactions costs, the financial manager need only observe what the firm currently pays to buy or sell a security. Interest costs can be derived from current available market returns on short-term, high-grade securities. The financial manager may want to use a forecasted interest rate for the planning period if a significant change from current interest rate levels is expected.

We now demonstrate the actual calculations for the Miller–Orr model. First, assume the following:

Minimum cash balance = \$20,000
Variance of daily cash flows = \$9,000,000 (hence, the Standard deviation, σ = \$3,000 per day)
Interest rate = 0.0329% per day
Transactions cost (average) for buying or selling one Security = \$20

Utilizing this data, we first compute the spread between the lower and upper limits:

$$\begin{aligned}\text{spread} &= 3\left(\frac{3 \times 20 \times 9{,}000{,}000}{4 \times 0.000329}\right)^{\frac{1}{3}}\\ &= \$22{,}293.\end{aligned}$$

Next, we compute the upper limit and return point

$$\begin{aligned}
\text{upper limit} &= \text{lower limit} + \text{spread} \\
&= \$20{,}000 + \$22{,}293 \\
&= \$42{,}293. \\
\text{return point} &= 20{,}000 + \left(\frac{22{,}293}{3}\right) \\
&= \$27{,}431. \\
\text{average cash balance} &= \frac{4\,(\$27{,}431) - \$20{,}000}{3} \\
&= \$29{,}908.
\end{aligned}$$

Based on our assumed input values and model calculations, we can establish the following rule:

If the cash balance rises to \$42,293, invest \$42,293 − \$27,431 = \$14,862 in marketable securities; if the cash balance falls to \$20,000, sell \$27,431 − \$20,000 = \$7,431 of marketable securities to restore the cash balance to the return point.

While the Miller–Orr model is an improvement on the EOQ model, we still must make an evaluation of its assumptions. Most important is the assumption that cash flows are random, which in many cases is not completely valid. Under certain circumstances and at particular times of the year, consecutive periods of cash flows may be dependent, the volatility of net cash flows may sharply increase, or a trend in cash balances may arise. The frequency and extent of these events will affect the Miller–Orr model's effectiveness. Actual tests using daily cash flow data for various firms indicate that the model did as well or better than the intuitive decisions of these firms' financial managers. However, other studies have shown that simple rules of thumb have performed just well. Consequently, the Miller–Orr model can be considered more valuable because of the insight it offers concerning optimal cash balance determination rather than as an operating rule.

As a final observation, let us compare the results from the Baumol and Miller–Orr models. The Baumol EOQ model suggests that for each five-day period, 3 × \$72,111 worth of securities should be sold to cover cash needs. The ACB was determined to be \$36,056. The Miller–Orr model suggests the return point should be \$27,431. However, the number of transactions depends on how often the cash balance reaches the boundaries of the allowed spread (\$20,000 and \$42,293). Thus, using the Miller–Orr results, we would maintain a lower average cash balance, thus freeing up more funds to be invested. Also, allowing the balance to float within the prescribed spread should result in a smaller total number of transactions — buying or selling securities — thereby decreasing this cost relative to the EOQ's result.

20.7. Cash Management Systems

Another aspect to cash management involves the efficiency with which money owed to the company is collected. The sooner the company can collect its money, the sooner the money can be put to work, thereby enhancing firm value. There are a number of systems to improve the cash collection process. However, before discussing these systems, we must consider the float concept.

20.7.1. *Float*

In banking terms, *float* is defined as cash items that are in the process of collection. Another way to think of float is the difference between the balance shown in a firm's (or an individual's) checkbook and the balance on the bank's books. For instance, suppose that, on average, a firm writes \$10,000 worth of checks each day. If it takes five days for these checks to clear and be deducted from the firm's bank account, then the firm's checking records will show a balance \$50,000 less than the bank's records. Conversely, if the firm, on average, receives \$10,000 worth of checks each day, but it takes only three days for these checks to be deposited and cleared, the firm's books will show a balance of \$30,000 above the balance on the bank's records. The difference between the \$50,000 positive float and the \$30,000 negative float, −\$20,000, is called the firm's *net float*. It is conceivable that a firm could consistently have a negative cash balance on its books, as long as it can accurately forecast its positive and negative clearings.

Float management can be seen as an integral component of the cash management system. To understand how float can be analyzed and forecasted, we need to look at the five different types of float:

1. *Invoicing float* is the time it takes for a firm to bill receivables. The company's internal accounting and the efficiency of its billing procedures both affect this type of float.
2. *Mail float* is the time the firm's bill spends in the mail once it is sent to the customer and the time the customer's check spends in the mail coming back to the firm.

3. *Processing float* is the time between receipt of payment by the billing firm and deposit of the check for collection.
4. *Collection float* is the time from when the check is deposited to when the funds are made available in the firm's checking account.
5. *Disbursing float* is the time between when a check is written on available bank account funds and the check actually clears with the corresponding dollar amount deducted from the firm's bank balance.

The first four floats hinder the firm's ability to turn collection items into cash and therefore are negative floats, while the disbursing float is positive float because it reduces cash needs. The benefits of reducing float by one day or from increasing the firm's net float are particularly significant when interest rates are high. Suppose a company with annual credit sales of $250 million can make $684,932 available by reducing negative float by one day, ($250,000,000/365). If the firm's borrowing cost is 15%, then $102,740 in interest costs (before taxes) per year could be saved by the float reduction.

As discussed below, mail float is generally hard to control, but it can be controlled to some degree through the use of *lock boxes*. Processing and invoicing float can be monitored and fine-tuned for efficiency. Collection and disbursement float can be enhanced for the firm's benefit by implementing cash collection and disbursement services provided primarily by the banking system; this is an area of discussion to which we now turn.

20.7.2. *Cash Collection and Transference Systems*

One way to speed up the collection of payments from customers is through *concentration banking.* Using this collection system, customers in a particular location make payment to a local branch office rather than to company headquarters. The branch office then deposits the checks into a local bank account. Surplus funds are transferred at some periodic interval to one of the firm's principal banks, called *concentration banks.*

The advantage of this system is that it reduces both mailing and collection float. However, concentration banking involves some additional costs, such as higher administrative costs, compensation to the local bank for its services, and the cost associated with transferring the funds from the local bank to the concentration bank. (Methods of cash transference are examined in a later section.)

A related cash collection technique is the combining of concentration banking with a *lock-box system.* The primary distinguishing feature of a lock-box system is that the firm pays the local bank to take on the administrative chores. Instead of customers mailing their payments to one of the company's mailing addresses, all payments are sent directly to a post office box. One or more times a day, a bank will collect checks from the box and deposit them for collection. Among the advantages of a lock-box arrangement is the potential reduction in mail float and, significantly, processing float. More sophisticated advanced arrangements between banks and firms involve having the banks capture daily invoice data on magnetic tape and forward this data to the company's central office, thereby reducing the burden on the firm's accounts receivable staff. Figure 20.6 displays a flow diagram of the lock-box system. Numbers in parentheses represent days of float lost to the selling company. As the figure shows, the lock-box system could save three days of float.

Another type of cash collection arrangement, which is perhaps more useful to firms such as insurance, finance, leasing, and mortgage companies, is a *preauthorized check* (PAC). The PAC is a commercial instrument that is used to transfer funds between demand deposit accounts. Through such a preauthorized indemnification agreement, the collecting firm is authorized to draw a check at specified intervals and in specified amounts on the customer's demand deposit account. In terms of float reduction, the PAC

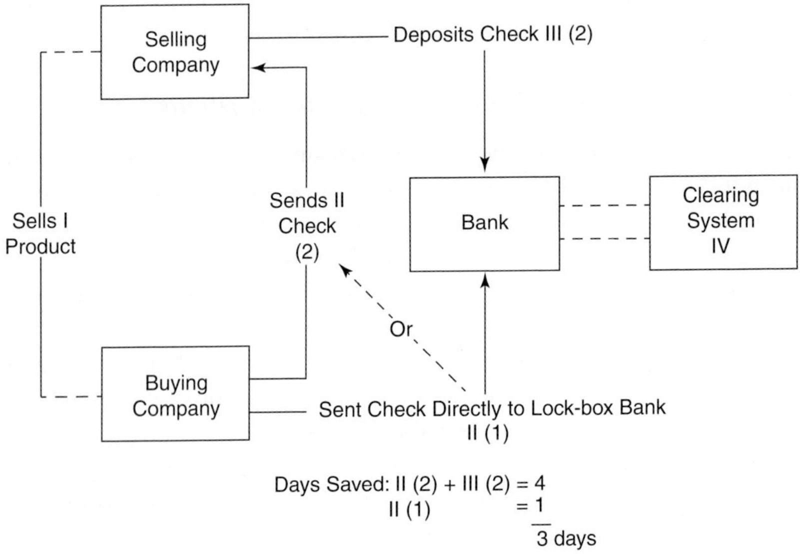

Fig. 20.6. Flow diagram of lock-box system.

reduces both mail and collection float and ensures that the company gets its money by a specified date.

20.7.3. *Cash Transference Mechanism and Scheduling*

Once the company has a cash collection system in place, it must decide how to transfer monies from the selected decentralized points as well as when to simultaneously minimize costs and maximize liquidity. There are three mechanisms for transferring money between accounts at two different banks: wire transfers, depository transfer checks (DTC), and electronic transfers.

Wire transfers involve an electronic bank-to-bank transfer of funds. Large cash balances can be transferred within an hour and made available to the firm immediately. While wire transfer is the fastest method available to move funds, it is also the most costly.

A DTC is an ordinary check restricted "for deposit only" at a designated bank. Hence, the designated collection bank completes a DTC for the daily deposits into the firm's checking account and then submits the DTC to the collection system. Although the DTC is less expensive than a wire transfer, it is also slower.

An *electronic transfer*, or automated DTC, is essentially the DTC mechanism in high-tech form. To reduce the time involved, an electronic check image is processed through automated clearinghouses rather than through a wire network. An electronic transfer is cheaper than a DTC and usually has a one-business-day clearing time.

Although probably more than 80% of the 1,200 largest industrial firms make a daily transfer of each day's reported deposits, the scheduling of when to transfer funds can be a problem. In fact, a growing number of progressive companies are realizing considerable cost savings by adopting various rules of thumb by which to manage the scheduling of cash transfers. We now discuss several of these methods: managing about a target balance, anticipation, dual balance, and weekend timing.

Managing about a target balance is illustrated in Figs. 20.7 and 20.8. Figure 20.7 depicts daily cash transfers that leave a $20,000 target closing balance. Figure 20.8 illustrates the technique of managing about the $20,000 target balance.

Initially, the account balance starts at 0 and then builds above the target up to the point where the average closing balance is $20,000 over the transfer period. However, while both schedules yield the same average balance, the schedule in Fig. 20.8 involves only one-fifth of the transfers.

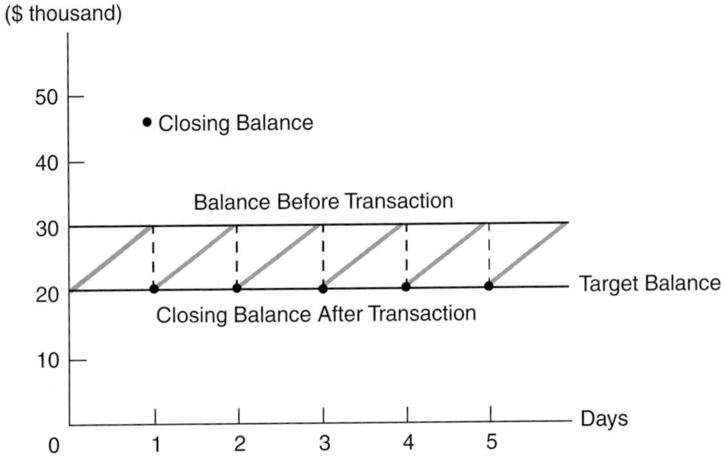

Balance Table ($ thousands)

Day	1	2	3	4	5
Starting balance	20	20	20	20	20
Deposit inflow	10	10	10	10	10
Transfer amount	10	10	10	10	10
Closing balance	20	20	20	20	20

$$\text{Average closing balance} = \frac{20 + 20 + 20 + 20 + 20}{5} = 20$$

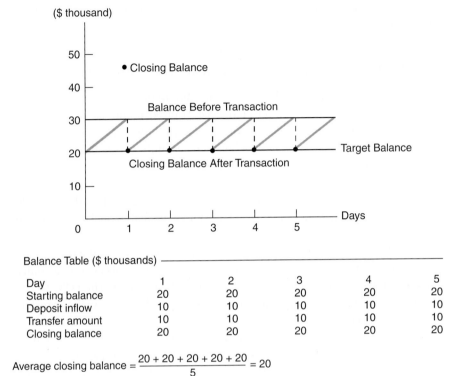

Fig. 20.7. Daily transfer of each day's deposits.

Source: Stone and Hill (1980).

This example has been simplified by ignoring transfer-time delays and weekends (when banks are closed and hence transactions do not occur) and assuming a uniform deposit schedule. However, it does suggest the potential for significant cost savings. Moreover, in addition to reducing transfers, managing about the target balance allows the firm to withdraw its initial investment in the target balance (which is replenished by the deposit flow). Thus, managing about a target means more cash sooner.

Anticipation is a system whereby a cash transfer is initiated before formal notice of a balance addition is received from the depository bank. The benefit of this scheduling technique is that it can eliminate delays arising from communication, processing, and/or clearing. Consequently, it can reduce or eliminate excess balances, accelerating transfers by one to three day's deposits.

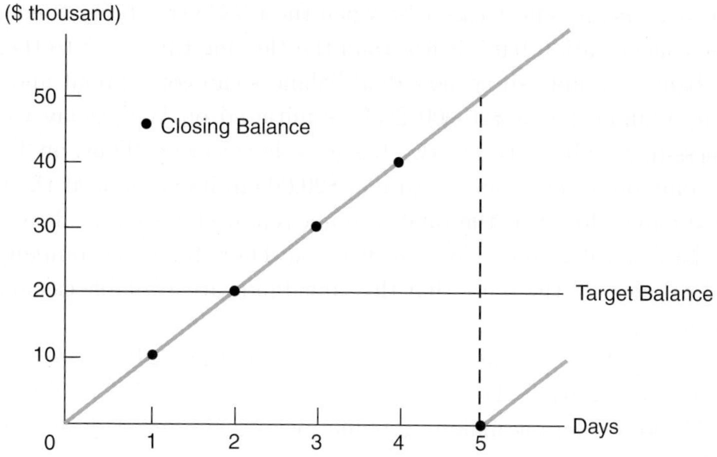

Balance Table ($ thousands)

Day	1	2	3	4	5
Starting balance	0	10	20	30	40
Deposit inflow	10	10	10	10	10
Transfer amount	0	0	0	0	50
Closing balance	10	20	30	40	0

$$\text{Average closing balance} = \frac{10 + 20 + 30 + 40 + 0}{5} = 20$$

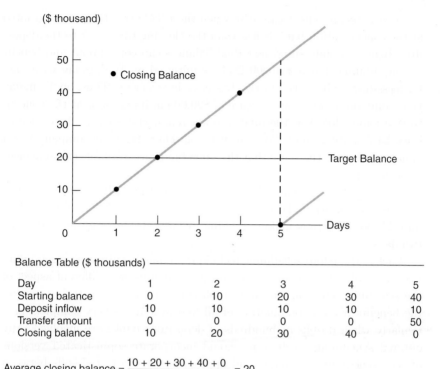

Fig. 20.8. Managing about the target balance.
Source: Stone and Hill (1980).

To illustrate more precisely how anticipation works, we will employ an example of the *adjusted field target* technique, the most common use of anticipation. Assume that your firm wants to maintain an average field balance $10,000. However, from communication, processing, and clearing delays, an average of $8,000 of deposits is left in the process of being transferred. Hence, the actual average balance is $18,000. To achieve the $10,000 target balance, the (manager makes a one-time transfer of $8,000 from the field bank and goes with an adjusted field target, or *effective field target*, of $2,000. Yet, because of the $8,000 average transfer-in-process, the actual average balance is the desired $10,000 target level.

The viability and effectiveness of this technique will be limited by the variability of deposits and the cash manager's ability to accurately forecast deviation in the assumed pattern and level of deposits.

A *dual balance* effect can arise when the DTC availability time granted at the concentration bank is less than the clearing time back to the depository bank. To understand how dual balances can come about and benefit a firm, assume that a $20,000 DTC is initiated on Wednesday with one-business-day availability but two-business-day clearing. Thus, on Thursday your company receives an increase of $20,000 in its account at the concentration bank. However, the funds are not removed from your firm's depository bank until Friday. Consequently, on Thursday your company has a "dual balance" in the sense that the same funds are available cash balances in both banks.

The benefit of a dual balance can be accentuated by *weekend timing.* That is, by initiating the transfer on Thursday, the DTC would not clear until Monday, thereby making the dual balance available for an additional two days.

Each of these four scheduling techniques-managing about a target, anticipation, dual balances, and weekend timing-focuses on a different aspect of the scheduling costs arising from cash transfers. However, trying to reap the benefits from a combination of all four systems is very complex, particularly when dozens or hundreds of depository banks are involved. Any optimal scheduling mechanism should incorporate sophisticated versions of each scheduling technique and appropriately reflect trade-offs between direct transfer costs, excess balances, and any dual balances. To handle such a, task, Stone and Hill (1980) have formulated this problem in a linear programming model. Field tests of their model show it to be an effective means for achieving additional cost reduction in the scheduling of cash transfers.

20.8. Credit Lines and Bank Relations

In the previous section, we examined methods by which firms can improve the efficiency of their cash collection systems. Despite such efforts, seasonal effects or other unpredictable events might cause the firm to occasionally need short-term funds to maintain day-to-day operations. Thus arises the need for, and importance of, establishing good bank relations along with a credit line to fill in for sudden or seasonal "cash gaps". This section examines various aspects of the credit line from both the borrower's and lender's points of view, within the general framework of bank relations.

The most common type of short-term loan by banks to firms is the working-capital credit line, which is extended to financially strong borrowers. The purpose of this credit line is to help firms cover cash gaps in their working-capital requirements that are caused by seasonal swings or some unexpected event. Through the credit line commitment, a bank specifies its intention to honor borrowings up to the amount of the established credit line. This amount is determined on the basis of the firm's pro forma peak funding requirement and assures the firm of the availability of funds to finance disparities in working-capital as sales expand and contract.

The cost of using or having available a line of credit usually has two components. First, loan interest is charged on only the amount actually borrowed, and the loan may be repaid as reflows of cash occur to the firm. Typically, because the loan is short-term, the interest rate is fixed in the line-of-credit agreement. However, because the usual agreement requires that the firm be out of debt to the bank for some period during the year, the bank can renegotiate the terms of the agreement should interest rates change significantly. Part of this requirement is precautionary to ensure the firm's financial viability, because credit lines are often unsecured.

The second cost associated with the availability of a credit line arises when the firm is required to hold compensating balances with the bank. Compensating balances usually take the form of demand deposits or low-interest time deposits and must average an agreed-on percentage of the loan amount. From one point of view, compensating balances essentially increase the effective cost of money borrowed through a line of credit. Let us use an example.

Suppose that your firm sets up a line of credit with ABC Bank for \$1 million, available at an interest rate of 14%. However, as part of the loan agreement, ABC Bank requires your firm to maintain compensating balances in the form of demand deposits equal to 20% of the loan. This is equal to \$200,000 that your firm essentially cannot use. That is, if your company borrowed all \$800,000 for the entire year, it would incur an interest cost of \$112,000. However, there is the additional opportunity cost from having \$200,000 sit idle in the bank vault. Assuming that this money could have been put to work to earn at least the bank's interest rate of 14%, this compensating balance essentially costs the firm an additional \$28,000. Therefore, the incremental cost from the compensating balances can be calculated as follows:

$$\frac{\$112{,}000}{\$800{,}000} = 14\% \qquad \frac{0.14 \times \$200{,}000}{\$800{,}000} = 3.5\%.$$

Therefore:

$$\frac{(\$112{,}000 + \$28{,}000)}{\$800{,}000} = 17.5\%.$$

If the firm borrows the extent of the credit line for the entire year, the additional cost of the compensating balances is 3.5%. Therefore, the firm's effective interest expense is 17.5%, not 14%.

In general, we can state the following:

$$\text{elective interest cost} = \frac{(\text{interest expense} + \text{implicit interest expense})}{(\text{line of credit limit} - \text{compensating balances})}.$$

However, compensating balances have other uses. In particular, firms often use compensating balances to pay the bank for such services as operating lock-boxes, processing the firm's checks without charge, and providing price advice on various business matters.

Before leaving our discussion of credit lines, we should mention the impact of credit lines from the bank's perspective. In general, establishing credit lines for financially sound firms is a profitable investment for the bank. In terms of current interest earned and the heightened potential for additional business from the firm in the future, the bank can view their credit lines as sound assets. However, the bank also faces a number of concerns.

In particular, an overextension of assets in the form of credit lines can bring peril to the bank's liquidity position. The nature of a credit line is short-term, yet the source of funds for this investment is typically a liability with a longer maturity. This disparity in maturities between assets and liabilities is referred to as a *maturity gap*. Thus, should there be a higher-than-forecasted demand on the total available lines of credit, or if enough firms become unable to pay back their credit line to the bank, the bank will find itself in a liquidity crunch.

Another concern for the bank is to analyze how the firm plans to use the credit line. For instance, the banker might think twice about extending a credit line to a firm that plans to use the funds to attempt a leveraged buyout. Such considerations affect the terms of the credit line agreement and consequently the bank's financial health.

20.8.1. *Bank Relations*

Large corporations that are financially sound are not necessarily so dependent on a strong bank relationship. When in need of short-term funds, these corporations can often go directly to the market and issue commercial paper at a lower interest cost. However, for smaller firms or those less financially adept, a good relationship with the bank is an important component in the cash management plan. The importance of these relations, as we have just discussed, can take the form of a credit line. Thus, the future availability of funds can be made less uncertain by establishing and maintaining good bank relations. This nurturing process can take place through such actions as maintaining compensating balances and repaying credit lines on time every year.

20.9. Marketable Securities Management

So far in this chapter, we have focused on determining an optimal cash balance, making cash collection more efficient, and using bank credit lines. This section looks at short-term excess cash balances and how they can be used to maximize firm value yet not endanger liquidity. We will examine criteria for investment of excess cash balances, types of marketable securities, and strategies and hedging considerations.

20.9.1. *Investment Criteria for Surplus Cash Balances*

When deciding on a financial instrument in which to invest short-term excess cash balances, the cash manager must realize that these funds may be needed in the near future for the firm's operations. Therefore, we suggest the following four criteria by which to evaluate investments for short-term surpluses: (1) certainty of principal, (2) maturity, (3) liquidity, and (4) yield.

First and foremost, the firm must consider the level of risk it can afford when investing surplus cash. Because these funds most likely will be needed relatively soon, the financial instrument should be high grade, short-term, and liquid. In determining the value of this investment, we focus on two types of risk: default risk and interest rate risk.

Default risk is the possibility that the company that issues the debt will be unable to make interest payments or to repay the principal amount on schedule. For U.S. Treasury securities, default risk is considered negligible, while for some corporate issues of commercial paper it can be significant. Various rating services such as Standard and Poor's and Moody's rate bonds, commercial paper, and other debt instruments for degree of quality in terms of default risk.

Interest rate risk is the variation in the debt security's price arising from changes in interest rates. The degree of this risk depends on the stability of the instrument. Long-term bonds are more sensitive to shifts in interest rates than are the prices of short-term securities. To understand more clearly how interest rates can affect bond prices, recall our valuation formula from earlier:

$$\text{bond price} = \sum_{t=1}^{n} \frac{\text{fixed interest payment}}{(1+i)^t} + \frac{\text{principal}}{(1+i)^n}.$$

As the market interest rate (i) increases, the present discounted value of the sum of all future interest payments and principal decreases. Moreover, the longer the remaining time before maturity, the more severely the higher i will affect the bond's price by discounting future flows at a higher rate. Thus, there is good reason for the cash manager to avoid default and interest rate risks by choosing short-term-maturity instruments.

Typically, the longer a security's term to maturity, the higher the interest rate the security will pay, for the reasons mentioned above. That is, longer-term bonds have a higher propensity for default and interest rate risks. However, because of supply and demand conditions, economic conditions, and inflation concerns, the term structure of interest rates does not always conform to this pattern. Nevertheless, the cash manager cannot afford to take on high levels of default or interest rate risk and therefore should primarily consider short-term debt instruments for investments.

Another reason for using primarily short-maturity investments is that the firm can usually sell the instrument quickly at a price close to its market value, a quality you will recognize as liquidity. Treasury bills (T-bills) are highly liquid — they have a broad market with many participants, low commission costs, and a price determined primarily by market interest rates. Somewhat less-liquid investments include bank-negotiable certificates of deposit (CD) and commercial paper. An example of an illiquid investment is real estate, which typically has a thin market, high transactions costs, and prices determined to a great extent by the relative bargaining position of buyer and seller.

Finally in maximizing the use of surplus cash, the cash manager should consider the various yields available on different marketable securities relative to the other criteria already mentioned. Since safety of principal is the primary criterion for investment of excess cash, yield should be considered only after the other criteria have been met.

20.9.2. *Types of Marketable Securities*

In classifying financial instruments as marketable securities, the distinction typically is based on maturity and, to a lesser extent, on liquidity. Investment instruments with a maturity of 1 year or less and that are traded to some extent in the secondary markets are called *money-market securities*. Conversely, the market for securities with more than 1 year to maturity, such as stocks, bonds, and mortgage bonds, is called the *capital market*.

U.S. T-bills are the most widely traded and, consequently, the most important money-market instrument. New issues of T-bills are auctioned off by the Federal Reserve every Monday, with maturities of 91 or 182 days. Once a month, T-bills with 365-day maturities are offered as well. Denominations range from \$10,000 to \$100,000 per bill. Further, all obligations for repayment rests with the U.S. government.

Although T-bills are usually the lowest-yielding of all marketable securities, they are also the most riskless in terms of liquidity and default. Moreover, the weekly issuance of T-bills, along with their large outstanding quantities, enables the cash manager to choose a highly precise maturity. The price of a T-bill is determined on a discount basis; that is, its price is the face value, say \$10,000, less the total value of the interest payments to be received, say \$500. Thus, this T-bill would be sold by the Federal Reserve for \$9,500, and its yield can be computed by applying the following equation:

$$\begin{aligned}\text{annual yield} &= \frac{\$10{,}000 - \text{price}}{\text{price}} \times \frac{365 \text{ days}}{\text{days to maturity}} \\ &= \frac{\$10{,}000 - 9{,}500}{9{,}500} \times \frac{365}{182} = 0.1055.\end{aligned}$$

Repurchase agreements (repos) are not actual securities in themselves, but rather contracts to acquire immediately available funds through the sale of securities together with a simultaneous agreement to repurchase those securities at a later date. Repos are most commonly made for one business day and nearly always involve a Treasury or other government agency security.

For example, suppose your company has \$1 million in excess cash available for two days. Instead of buying T-bills and then selling them two days later, your company could create a repurchase agreement with the bank, in which your company would agree to "purchase" \$1 million worth of T-bills and then "sell" them back to the bank after two days for the original $1 million plus two days of interest. No actual transfer of physical securities is made; rather, the entire transaction consists of bookkeeping entries on the two parties accounts.

There are two distinct advantages to using repos for short-term surplus cash. First, maturity can be tailored to the exact period of fund availability, from overnight to 30 days or more. Second, because the selling price of the securities is predetermined by agreement between buyer and seller, interest rate risk can be avoided. The yield on repos is similar but slightly lower than that of T-bills.

Negotiable CDs are financial instruments offered by banks to customers to deposit funds for a fixed period at a fixed and pre-specified rate of interest. CDs are issued in denominations of $100,000 or more, with maturities ranging from 1 to 18 months.

Yields on CDs are higher than yields of T-bills for two reasons. First, CDs are substantially less liquid than T-bills (that is, their secondary market is very thin). Second, CDs have higher default risk because they represent unsecured debt obligations of the issuing bank. However, the spread between CD and T-bill yields will vary depending on economic conditions, supply and demand forces, and investor attitudes.

Commercial paper is defined as the unsecured short-term promissory notes sold by large, financially sound companies. Maturities typically range from 30 to 270 days. While commercial paper is usually sold as bearer securities at a discount (like T-bills), some corporations sell paper that repays the principal plus interest at maturity.

Because of its unsecured nature and heterogeneity, commercial paper is traded infrequently on the secondary markets and hence is somewhat illiquid. However, because only the firms with the highest credit ratings are able to generate enough demand for their paper, yields on commercial paper are similar and sometimes even lower than yields on CDs.

Banker's acceptances are time drafts drawn on and accepted by a bank, usually to secure arrangements between unfamiliar firms. Although we discussed banker's acceptances earlier, we mention them again here because they can also be used for a firm's short-term surplus balances. After generating a banker's acceptance, a bank will typically sell it to an investor at a discount. Maturities range from 30 to 180 days, while denominations vary from $25,000 to over $1 million, depending on the specific transaction the banker's acceptance was originally created to finance. Again, banker's acceptances are relatively illiquid compared to T-bills and carry yields usually higher than on CDs because of their more heterogeneous characteristics.

Developed in 1973, *money-market mutual funds* offer another type of investment, yet today investment in these funds ranges around $200 billion. By pooling investor dollars to buy money-market securities, these funds offer the small investor or firm access to higher market yields at low transaction costs with a large degree of liquidity. Most funds invest only in high-grade marketable securities.

20.9.3. *Hedging Considerations*

In the 1970s and early 1980s, the volatility of market interest rates increased enormously because of increased uncertainty in the financial markets, which requires a higher real return on investment. Nevertheless, under these conditions, the cash manager encounters risks that are substantial in terms of interest rate changes and their resulting impact on portfolio value. How can such risks be addressed?

One aspect of this issue involves the concept of hedging (discussed in Chapter 10). Hedging the current marketable securities portfolio or even some future investment implies that the cash manager is content with current market yield. Thus, hedging attempts to reduce the uncertainty of future conditions by locking-in current parameters (price, interest rate, yield, etc.)

There are various useful financial tools to aid the cash manager in the hedge decision. These include interest rate futures, interest rate options, and options on interest rate futures. Let us consider the application of these instruments to one type of hedge problem.

Suppose your firm holds $10 million in T-bills that it expects to liquidate in 60 days on December 17. According to the forecasts of economists and the firm's cash manager, market interest rates are expected to jump by as much as 1.5% within the next 2 months. This large increase in interest rates will decrease the market value of the firm's T-bills, thus yielding less cash than originally anticipated. With such a variety of hedging instruments, a number of strategies could be employed. In this case, we use options on T-bill futures.

An option on a futures contract is nearly identical to an option on common stock. The obvious difference is that the underlying asset is a futures contract. By exercising a futures option, the holder enters into a long or short futures position, depending on whether the option is a call or put, respectively. Thus, the futures contract is an agreement to buy or sell the commodity at a pre-specified price at some future designated time. However, in using a futures option, one need not necessarily worry about entering into a futures contract. Instead, the hedger earns an offsetting profit (or loss) on the value of the option alone.

For our example, the cash manager could buy the appropriate number of put options on the T-bill futures contract to protect the company against any depreciation in value of its marketable securities. The appropriate number of contracts is the hedge ratio between the option and its underlying asset. However, in this example we use puts, so the hedge ratio for a call option is not the same. Fortunately, there is a simple relationship:

$$\begin{aligned} \text{put hedge ratio} &= 1 - \text{call hedge ratio} \\ &= 1 - \mathrm{N}(d_1), \end{aligned} \tag{20.12}$$

where $\mathrm{N}(d_1)$ is the cumulative normal density function of d_1. The d_1 is

$$\frac{\ln\left(\dfrac{P}{E}\right) + rt + \dfrac{\sigma^2 t}{2}}{\sigma\sqrt{t}},$$

where P and E represent T-bill futures price and strike price; r and t represent risk-free rate and time-to-maturity; and σ is the variance of T-bill futures.

If the cash manager maintains this hedge ratio over time, devaluation of the firm's T-bill holdings, caused by an increase in interest rates, will be offset by the profit in the put options that were bought. On the other hand, if rates remain unchanged or trend downward, the cash manager can simply let the puts expire worthless. The sacrifice of purchase price is a small cost relative to the value and size of the insurance they offer.

20.10. Inventory Management

Inventories are used to link production and sales. A manufacturing firm must maintain a certain amount of inventory during production; that is, goods in process, such as raw materials, finished goods, and inventory in transit.

Raw materials inventory gives the firm flexibility in its purchasing. Without this inventory, the firm must exist on a hand-to-mouth basis, buying raw material strictly in keeping with its production schedule.

Conversely, raw materials inventory may be bloated temporarily because the firm's purchasing department has taken advantage of quantity discounts. *Finished-goods inventory* allows the firm flexibility in production scheduling and marketing. *Inventory in transit* is inventory that is between various stages of production or storage. Management of inventory in transit permits efficient production scheduling and utilization of resources. Without this type of inventory, each stage of production would have to wait for the preceding stage to complete a unit. Resultant delays and idle time give the firm an incentive to maintain a large in-transit inventory.

Inventory management generally concerns (1) inventory loans and (2) inventory economic order quantity (EOQ).

20.10.1. *Inventory Loans*

Both accounts receivable and inventory can be used to secure short-term loans. Inventory loans come in three basic forms: blanket inventory liens, trust receipts, and field warehouse financing.

1. *Blanket inventory lien.* The firm's creditor is given a claim on all inventory held by the firm. The term *blanket* refers to the fact that the firm's entire inventory is "covered" by the lien. If the borrowing firm defaults on the loan, then the lender has the right to seize the collateral (inventory).
2. *Trust receipts.* The firm's creditor is given a claim on specific assets in that the ownership or title of the specific goods belongs to the lender until the loan is paid off. However, actual possession of the goods remains in the hands of the borrowing firm, which is able to use or sell the goods while conducting its normal business.
3. *Field warehouse financing.* In this case, the lender retains title or ownership of the inventory, as in the case of trust receipts, but a third party takes physical possession of the goods. This third party takes control of the inventory and only releases it to the borrower under certain prespecified conditions.
4. *EOQ.* The EOQ for inventory is similar to the Baumol EOQ for cash. The EOQ for inventory is defined as:

$$Q^* = \sqrt{\frac{2SO}{C}}, \tag{20.13}$$

where C = carry cost per unit; S = total usage units of an item of inventory; and O = ordering cost per unit.[3]

Equation (20.13) is known as the economic, lot-size formula. To illustrate its use, suppose that for a specific inventory item, the firm orders 50,000 units during a 200-day period, ordering costs are \$200 per order, and carryings costs are \$20 per unit per 200 days. The optimal EOQ is

$$Q^* = \sqrt{\frac{2(50{,}000)(200)}{20}} = 1{,}000 \text{ units.}$$

For an order quantity of 50,000 units, the firm would order (50,000/1,000), or 50 times during the 200-day period, or every 4 days. Equation (20.13) implies that Q^* varies directly with total usage (S) and order cost (O) and inversely with the carry cost (C). This analysis is similar to the analysis used for EOQ for cash, as discussed earlier in this chapter.

20.11. Summary

The subject of Chapter 20 is the management of trade credit for both buyer and seller. For the buyer, the essential issue is to determine the cost of using trade credit as a form of financing, then compare this cost with the cost of alternative sources of capital. While some argue that accounts payable have no cost, we support the arguments against this view. That is, for the buyer, trade credit involves opportunity costs in the form of foregone discounts, implicit bankruptcy costs for taking on too much accounts payable, and costs associated with the timing of taxes and the accounting procedure used.

The grantor of trade credit, the seller, has a large array of decisions to make. The first of these we discussed was determining the cost of granting trade credit. Next, we examined a numerical credit-scoring method via linear discriminant analysis to make the credit-granting decision more effective in terms of risk and related collection and bad-debt costs. Finally, we discussed the other aspects of the firm's credit policy, including the decision of how much credit to grant, on what terms, and the collection

[3] Q^* is obtained by differentiating the total inventory cost (T), defined as

$$T = \frac{CQ}{2} + \frac{SO}{Q},$$

where C, S, and O are as defined in Eq. (20.13), and Q represents the number of units of inventory. The derivation procedure is the same as that used in Appendix 20.A.

policy procedures to be pursued for delinquent accounts. We noted that the evaluation of various collection policies can be viewed and even carried out in the framework of a capital budgeting problem. Earlier we discussed a number of methods to deal with the capital budgeting problem with uncertainty, including (1) the risk-adjusted discount rate method, (2) the certainty equivalent method, (3) the statistical distribution method, and (4) various simulation methods.

We also discussed the various aspects of cash and marketable security management. Two techniques that can assist in the estimation of an optimal level or range for the cash balance were Baumol's model and the Miller–Orr model.

To make the cash collection system more efficient, the firm can choose from various methods for collecting or transferring cash and deciding when to transfer it. Such cost minimization is ideal for linear programming applications.

The credit line offers the firm a means of handling cash variations caused by seasonal effects or unanticipated events. Establishing good bank relations is an important feature for any cash management system. However, bank services do take on a cost, typically in the form of compensating balances. While credit lines can be a good investment for a bank, they can have detrimental effects on the bank's liquidity that could intensify any maturity gap problems.

Efficient cash management ensures that surplus balances are invested in marketable securities that meet minimum standards for certainty of principal, maturity, liquidity, and yield. In Chapter 20, we considered the hedge decision from the cash manager's perspective and gave various examples of hedging applications. Optimal inventory management was also briefly discussed.

Problem Set

1. Define or explain the following:

    a. Trade credit.
    b. Aging of accounts receivable.
    c. Credit analysis.
    d. Factor score and factor loading.
    e. Collection policy.
    f. Factoring.
    g. Type I and Type II classification errors.

h. Baumol's EOQ model.
i. Invoicing float and disbursement float.
j. Lock-box system.
k. Cash scheduling.
l. Credit line.
m. Effective interest cost.
n. CD.
o. Put hedge ratio versus call hedge ratio.

2. Explain the differences among the three formal types of trade-credit agreements.
3. What is the significance of an aging of accounts receivable schedule to the credit manager?
4. Calculate the annualized cost of not taking a discount if the terms are 2/10, net 30, and the purchase is for \$100. Repeat the calculation for terms of 2/20, net 30, and 2/20, net 60. Explain the relationship of the discount period and the credit period to that of the cost of not taking the discount.
5. From Question 4, cite some possible implications on accounts receivable from the changes in the credit terms. State in terms of the size of the accounts receivable account and the timing of its cash flows.
6. Indicate the effect on sales, accounts receivable, and profits given the following changes on 2/10, net 30, credit terms:

   a. Credit manager changes credit policy to net 60.
   b. Credit manager increases the discount to 5%.
   c. Credit manager lengthens discount period to 20 days.

7. Explain how the credit manager uses ratio analysis to assess a customer's credit risk.
8. What are the limitations of numerical credit scoring?
9. List the alternative sources of obtaining credit information.
10. Outline the interrelationship of trade credit to cash flow, cost of capital, sales growth, and debt capacity.
11. What is a discrimination function? Discuss two methods to estimate this function.
12. What purpose do credit terms serve?
13. What does 3/10, net 60 mean?
14. What does 2/10 EOM, net 30 mean?
15. What is season dating? Why would a company date its invoices?
16. Briefly explain how a commercial draft works.

17. What are the pros and cons of issuing trade credit from the seller's perspective?
18. Briefly explain how factoring can be used to manage accounts receivable.
19. What is an irrevocable letter of credit? Why is it used?
20. How does a banker's acceptance bring together lenders and borrowers? Why is this form of securitization so popular in international transactions?
21. List the reasons that lead firms to hold cash balances.
22. Briefly describe some of the costs associated with holding cash.
23. What costs are associated with holding inadequate cash?
24. What is mail float? How can companies reduce mail float?
25. Check-kiting occurs when a company or individual systematically overdrafts accounts. Why would anyone ever use check-kiting? What are the legal and ethical ramifications?
26. Briefly explain how a company can increase its disbursement float. What are the ramifications of such a strategy? Even though the firm's methods may be legal, are there ethical issues involved?
27. Briefly explain how a company can reduce its collection float.
28. What does the notation "2/10, net 30" mean on a bill?

29. Why is it important for a company to estimate its demand for cash balances?
30. What characteristic of a T-bill make it suitable for a marketable security investment?
31. Compare CDs and commercial paper as possible candidates for marketable security investments.
32. According to the Gentry–De La Garza model, what factors may cause accounts receivable to increase?
33. GTB Inc. has sales of $2 million and a 50-day collection period and is considering loosening its credit standards, a change that is expected to increase sales by $1,000,000. However, the collection period is projected to be 60 days, and added investigation expenses may be $50,000. Bad-debt expenses would be around 5% of the additional sales. The firm's contribution margin is 12%, and the before-tax cost of capital is 15% (using a 360-day year).

    a. What is the total marginal cost associated with a relaxation of the credit standard?

b. What is the marginal benefit of the policy change?
c. Should the change be implemented?

34. Calculate the annualized cost of not taking a discount on the purchase of goods worth $200 for each of the following terms of credit:

    a. 2/15, net 30.
    b. 2/15, net 45.
    c. 3/15, net 60.
    d. 5/30, net 60.

35. RAS, Inc. buys goods on the credit terms of 2/10, net 25. The firm presently does not use the facility of discounts and, instead, pays after 25 days. A new policy has been suggested under which RAS would borrow equivalent money at 20% annual interest rate and use that loan to get the discount benefit. Is it a good proposal? Assume a 360-day year.
36. A company currently discounts 50% of its purchases based on the terms of 3/15, net 30; the balance (the other 50%) is paid in 30 days on the net date. The firm's credit manager has a proposal under consideration to stretch the payables and pay all purchases in 45 days. The expected purchases for next year are $20 million. If the opportunity cost of investment is 15%, demonstrate why the company should or should not implement this policy. Assume a 360-day year.
37. RAJ Company's current annual sales are $1.8 million and the average collection period is 30 days. If the company eases its credit terms, sales would increase to $2.25 million and the average collection period would be 50 days. The variable costs are 80% of sales and the cost of capital is 20%. The bad debts under the new policy would be 4% of new sales. Assuming a 360-day year, calculate the following values and determine if RAJ's policy would be advantageous.

    a. Additional investment in accounts receivable.
    b. Extra costs associated with the new policy.
    c. Incremental net profit contribution.

38. Now assume that the RAJ Company in the previous problem also incurs the following additional expenses:

    Cost of investment = $20,000.
    Increase in the average finished goods inventory = $100,000 (which would be financed at an annual interest rate of 17%).

a. Re-evaluate the decision to ease credit terms.
b. Would the acceptability of the new policy be changed? Explain.

39. Respond to your colleague, who says, "By taking 60 days to pay our suppliers rather than 30 days, we can double our access to zero-cost financing."
40. Indicate the effect of the following changes to initial credit terms of 2/10, net 30, on sales and profits:

    a. Term changes to net 60.
    b. Discount increases to 5%.
    c. Discount period lengthens to 20 days.

41. From Question 39, cite some of the possible implications of these changes on accounts receivable. Respond in terms of the size of the accounts receivable account and the timing of its cash flows.

Problems

1. Suppose the terms of a bill are 1/15, net 30. What is the annual cost of not taking this discount?
2. Show how Miller–Orr's stochastic EOQ model is derived.
3. Briefly discuss cash management systems.
4. Explain how cash managers can hedge the interest rate risk when managing the marketable securities.
5. Given that $F = \$2{,}000$, $T = 52$ weeks $\times$ \$600,000/week $= \$3{,}120{,}222$, and $k = 15\%$, use the Baumol model to calculate the EOQ of cash balance.
6. The standard deviation of JAV Company's daily net cash flows is \$100. The firm pays \$15 in transactions costs to transfer funds into and out of commercial paper that pays 9.5% annual interest. JAV's financial manager uses the Miller–Orr model to set the target cash balance. In addition, JAV decides to maintain a \$20,000 minimum cash balance (lower limit). What are JAV's (a) target balance, (b) upper and lower limits, and (c) expected ACB?
7. Consider the following inventory and storage cost information:

    Orders must be placed in multiples of 100 units
    Requirements for the 50-week year are 50,000 units
    Carrying cost per unit per year is \$0.50
    Ordering cost per order per year is \$20

What is the EOQ of inventory? What is the optimal number of orders to be placed during the year?

8. A firm has the following information regarding its cash flows:

   Fixed transaction costs = \$5 per transaction
   Monthly need for cash = \$1,000
   Opportunity cost of cash = 12%
   Using the Baumol's EOQ Model, compute the optimal cash borrowings or withdrawals and optimal ACB

9. The following data pertain to IRC, Inc.:

   Minimum cash balance = \$10,000
   Annual interest rate = 14.6% (daily rate = 0.04%)
   Variance of daily cash flows = \$1,000,000
   Average transaction cost to buy and sell securities = \$15
   Using the above information and the Miller–Orr Model, calculate:

   a. The spread between the upper and lower limits (S).
   b. The return point (R).
   c. The upper limit (H).
   d. The ACB.

10. Given the results in the previous problem, establish the decision rules for the management of IRC's cash flows.
11. A company writes checks for \$50,000 per day. A customer takes about four days to present these checks to the firm's bank and collect the money. Similarly, the company receives checks of \$60,000 every day, and it takes three days to deposit and clear them. Find the positive, negative and net floats for this firm.
12. MNC International's annual credit sales are \$36.5 billion. If the company is able to reduce negative float by 2 days, how much money would be released? If MNC's cost of financing is 13.5%, calculate the interest expense savings.
13. The Federal Reserve is selling 91-day T-bills with a face value of \$100 for \$96.50. Compute the annualized yield on these T-bills if an investor holds them until maturity
14. HAL, Inc. has a \$10 million line of credit with the Oriental Bank of Commerce. The bank charges an annual interest rate of 13.5%. One of the conditions of the credit line is for HAL to maintain a compensating balance in the form of demand deposits equal to 10% of the loan. If

the company utilizes its full borrowing capacity, what is the effective interest cost of borrowing?

15. BHEL presently handles all its credit customers from its New York City office. Annual credit sales are \$72 million. The company is analyzing the desirability of establishing a lock-box system in selected areas to reduce the negative float. Studies carried out by BHEL's consultants indicate that the lock-box system could possibly reduce float by 4 days. Assuming a 360-day year, find the following:

    a. The extra cash made available by the lock-box system.
    b. If the interest rate is 12.50%, and the charge for the new system is \$80,000 per year, should BHEL adopt this system?

16. Hyper International earns 7.50% interest annually on its investments in marketable securities. If the company adopts a draft disbursing system, disbursement float can be increased by 2 days. Next year's purchases are estimated at \$3.6 million. Individual payments average \$1,000. Assume that there is a 360-day year and that purchases are distributed evenly over 360 days.

    a. Calculate the amount of cash made available by the new proposal.
    b. If each draft issued costs \$0.10, what would be your answer?

17. A firm operates for 250 days out of the year. The total annual consumption of raw materials is 100,000 units. Fixed cost per order is \$180, and the annual, per unit carrying cost of inventory has been estimated at \$9.

    a. Find the optimal EOQ.
    b. How many orders would be placed by the firm during the entire period?

18. Assume in the previous problem that the per order cost is \$225 and the cost of carrying one unit is \$20. Compute the optimal EOQ and explain why the results are so different.
19. A company is holding \$5 million in T-bills, which are to be sold after 45 days on October 15. The firm's treasurer expects an increase of 2% in the market interest rates over the next four to six weeks. Such an increase would lower the market price of T-bill's and would cause a loss to the company. What strategy would you suggest to avoid this loss? Assume that the company uses options on T-bills and the hedge ratio is known.

20. Suppose the terms of a bill are 5/5, net 60. What is the annual cost of not taking this discount?
21. Suppose the terms of a bill are 2/10, net 90. What is the annual cost of not taking this discount?

Appendix 20.A

From Eq. (20.1), the total costs of cash balances are defined as

$$\begin{aligned} \text{total costs} &= \text{holding cost} + \text{transaction cost} \\ &= \frac{C}{2}(k) + \frac{T}{C}(F), \end{aligned} \tag{20.A.1}$$

where C is the amount of cash reinvested by borrowing or selling marketable securities, and k and T are as defined in Eq. (20.1).

To minimize the total cost, we take the partial derivative of Eq. (20.A.1) with respect to C and set the derivative equal to 0:

$$\frac{\partial(\text{total cost})}{\partial C} = \frac{k}{2} - \frac{(T)F}{C^2} = 0. \tag{20.A.2}$$

From Eq. (20.A.2), we solve for C^*, the optimal cash transfer, as

$$\frac{k}{2} = \frac{(FT)}{C^2}; \quad C^* = \sqrt{\frac{2FT}{k}}.$$

This is Eq. (20.1).

References for Chapter 20

Bergevin, PM (2002). *Financial Statement Analysis: An Integrated Approach.* Upper Saddle River, New Jersey: Prentice Hall.

Brick, IF and WKH Fung (1984). The effect of taxes on the trade-credit decision. *Financial Management*, 24–30.

Brigham, EF and MC Ehrhardt (2007). *Financial Management-Theory and Practice*, 12th ed. California: South-Western College Pub.

Chu, QC and DN Pittman (2006). Treasury inflation-indexed securities. In *Encyclopedia of Finance*, C-F Lee and AC Lee (eds.), pp. 359–363. New York: Springer.

Ewert, DC (1977). *Trade Credit Management: Selection of Accounts Receivable Using Statistical Methods.* Atlanta: Georgia State University.

Finerty, JE (2006). Working capital and cash flow. In *Encyclopedia of Finance*, C-F Lee and AC Lee (eds.), pp. 393–404. New York: Springer.

Foster, G (1998). *Financial Statement Analysis*, 2nd ed. Englewood Cliffs, NJ: Prentice-Hall.

Palepu, KG and PM Healy (2007). *Business Analysis & Valuation: Using Financial Statement*, 4th ed. California: South-Western College Publishing.

Gottesman, AA (2006). Loan contract terms. In *Encyclopedia of Finance*, C-F Lee and AC Lee (eds.), pp. 428–434. New York: Springer.

Hamburg, M (1996). *Statistical Analysis for Decision-Making*, 6th ed. Wadsworth Publishing Company: California.

Henderson, GV, GL Trennepohl, and JE Wert (1984). *An Introduction to Financial Management.* Reading, MA: Addison-Wesley.

Hill, NC and WL Sartoris (1994). *Short Term Financial Management*, 3rd ed. Prentice Hall.

Lee, CF and AC Lee (2006). *Encyclopedia of Finance.* New York: Springer.

Mehta, DR (1974). *Working Capital Management.* Englewood Cliffs, NJ: Prentice Hall.

Penman, SH (2006). *Financial Statement Analysis and Security Valuation*, 3rd ed. New York: McGraw-Hill/Irwin.

Robinson, TR, P Munter, and J Grant (2003). *Financial Statement Analysis: A Global Perspective.* Upper Saddle River, New Jersey: Prentice Hall.

Sartoris W and N Hill (May 1983). A generalized cash flow approach to short-term financial decisions. *Journal of Finance*, 38, 349–360.

Soffer, LC and RJ Soffer (2002). *Financial Statement Analysis: A Valuation Approach.* Upper Saddle River, New Jersey: Prentice Hall.

Stone, BK and NC Hill (1980). Cash-transfer scheduling for efficient cash concentration. *Financial Management*, 9 (Autumn), 35–43.

Tan, P and G Yeo (2006). Accounting scandals and implication for directors: Lessons from enron. In *Encyclopedia of Finance*, C-F Lee and AC Lee (eds.), pp. 643–648. New York: Springer.

Van Horne, JC (2001). *Financial Management and Policy*, 12th ed. Englewood Cliffs, NJ: Prentice Hall Inc.

Chapter 21

Short-Term Financing

21.1. Introduction

Corporate issues of commercial paper exceed \$600 billion annually. Commercial loans outstanding were nearly \$2.2 trillion in 1995. Retailers such as Bradlees and Caldor filed for Chapter 11 bankruptcy protection when factors refused to extend short-term financing to them. Commercial paper, bank loans, factors, and others provide a source of short-term financing to firms. Most businesses can't survive very long without short-term financing. Whether it is a loan to finance production in anticipation of seasonal sales or a "bridge" loan to provide funds until a bond issue is sold, firms make frequent use of short-term financing. This chapter reviews the varieties of short-term financing sources that firms can tap.

In earlier chapters, we focused on the asset side of a firm's balance sheet and discussed short-term uses of working-capital. This chapter focuses on the liability side of the balance sheet and describes the various short-term sources of funds that firms commonly use.

Trade credit, bank loans, lines of credit, commercial paper, pledging and factoring of accounts receivable, banker's acceptances, and asset-based types of financing all are available to the firm that needs short-term financing. This chapter looks at the relative costs, advantages, and disadvantages of these various sources and provides a framework for making the short-term financing decision.

In Section 21.2, we will discuss the nature of bank lending, lines of credit and other topics related to bank loans. Section 21.3 further explores the characteristics of bank loans. Short-term financing with trade credit is reviewed in the following Section 21.4. Pledging and factoring receivables into cash is introduced in Section 21.4. We discuss inventory financing and management in Section 21.6 and in Section 21.7, we will go over other non-bank sources of funds. Finally, we will conclude this chapter with a summary.

21.2. Bank Loans

Commercial banks are probably the first source of short-term credit that comes to mind. Yet in terms of volume, they are far from dominating this market; trade credit exceeds total bank credit by a wide margin. The importance of bank credit comes from its availability, however, not just from its volume.

Short-term bank credit is particularly important to the smaller company. Many large, well-established companies make little use of bank credit. When they need working-capital above what is available as trade credit — that is, when they need **negotiated credit**, the term given to all credit that arises from a formal negotiation of funds — they can get attractive terms by borrowing directly from the capital market. This borrowing usually takes the form of selling commercial paper, as shall be described in a later section of this chapter.

A small, recently established business has no such option. Certainly, such a firm makes the maximum possible use of trade credit, but when the need for funds exceeds the supply of trade credit, some other source must be found. Most small companies find that their reputation and credit standing are not well established enough to raise loan funds directly in the capital market. In such cases, the banks are the next best alternative.

Even for the larger company that makes little actual use of bank credit, keeping these funds available is still important. Uncertainty is a feature of all business, as we have stressed throughout this book. Many companies rely on access to bank funds rather than huge cash balances as primary cushions against costly, unexpected events. A company that has not borrowed for a decade may still include maintaining good bank relations as a principal element in its financial strategy.

21.2.1. *The Nature of Bank Lending*

Banks accept funds from the public in the form of deposits, on some of which (savings, time deposits, or negotiable order of withdrawal (NOW) accounts) they pay interest. The banks then put these funds to productive use, either by investing them in government or municipal bonds, or by lending them to business organizations or individuals who wish to borrow. Loans provide higher rates of interest than investments in bonds, and so most banks try to lend as much of their funds as possible, subject to the regulations under which they operate and the level of risk they decide to assume.

Lending operations often expose commercial banks to considerable risk. As we have seen, the companies that borrow bank funds tend to be the smaller, newer enterprises. A bank that lends to such a company assumes more risk, in relation to the return it receives, than a supplier that extends trade credit to the same customer. Suppose, for example, that a small company is buying its raw materials from a supplier on terms of net 30 days with a credit limit of $20,000. If the account is fully used and settled every 30 days, the small company is buying $240,000 of materials a year, and the supplier's profit margin on these sales is probably at least $20,000 (likely much more). Yet the supplier never has more than $20,000 at risk at any one time.

Now compare the position of a bank making a $20,000 loan to the same company. The bank's risk of default is as great as the supplier's. The bank also is committed for the duration of the loan, which is almost certainly more than 30 days, probably between 6 months and 1 year. In return, the bank receives a rate of interest that, even during periods of high interest rates, is unlikely to exceed 20%. Thus, for the same risk, the trade supplier receives returns of $20,000 or more, and the bank earns annual interest of, perhaps, $4,000.

21.2.2. *Self-Liquidating Loans*

In view of this high exposure to risk for a comparatively low return, commercial banks have understandably tried to find ways to protect themselves. Until very recently, this effort led them to lend only short-term funds and only in the form of **self-liquidating loans** — that is, they loaned money only for specific purposes and operations that would produce adequate cash flows to retire the debts quickly. The perfect example of such a self-liquidating situation is a working-capital loan made to a manufacturer or retailer that has a marked seasonal sales pattern.

For example, retail sales of a toy manufacturer's product peak just before Christmas each year. The manufacturer's own sales peak probably comes in August, however, when retailers and toy distributors are building up their inventories for the buying season; to meet this demand, the manufacturer must schedule a high level of production from May through July. In May of each year, therefore, the company takes out a loan from its bank to provide added working-capital to finance the buildup in inventory.

By September, heavy sales draw down the inventory to normal levels. Most of these sales, however, are made on terms of net 30 days, giving the company a large accounts receivable balance, but little cash. Finally, by early November, the customers pay their accounts, and collections of accounts receivable provide enough cash flow to retire the bank loan. Thus, the loan is self-liquidating in 6 months.

This is a classic bank lending situation. The bank knows before it makes the loan exactly how long the funds will be needed. The relatively short life of the loan increases the bank's liquidity. By making a fairly large number of predictable, short-term loans, a bank feels comfortable lending the highest proportion of its funds that regulations permit. In other words, it will want to lend up to its loan limit, or be fully loaned. If a bank finds little demand for self-liquidating, seasonal loans, it may be forced to lend in longer term, less predictable situations. Caution would probably lead this bank to keep a higher proportion of its funds in marketable securities to preserve its overall liquidity.

This traditional scenario has been transformed by important changes in bank practices during recent years. Commercial banks no longer stress the self-liquidating requirement as strongly as they once did. As the suppliers of short-term financing have become more competitive, banks have become more willing to provide longer term funds in the form of term loans. These new practices are creating an increasingly flexible source of short-term and intermediate-term funds for business organizations.

21.2.3. *Lines of Credit*

The loan made to the toy manufacturer in the above example is the simplest form of bank lending; a short-term loan made for a specific time and for a specific, clearly understood need. In other cases, however, a commercial bank may be approached by a company that has no immediate need for the money, in an attempt to fund possible future needs. Such a company may ask for a **line of credit** — an agreement that specifies the maximum amount of unsecured credit the bank will extend to the firm at any time during the life of the agreement. In the past, banks gave lines of credit only to larger, more secure companies. This, too, appears to be changing, however, some commercial banks now provide lines of credit to small, newly formed companies in which they see good growth potential.

In granting a line of credit, a bank is saying, in effect, "It looks as though your position is sufficiently sound to justify a loan, but when the time comes for you to start borrowing, we shall probably want to talk to you again to make sure that everything is going as expected". For example, a company that expects a rapid increase in sales may arrange a line of credit to finance increases in inventory and receivables. Before allowing the company to begin drawing on the line, however, the bank will want to verify that sales actually have increased. If the company has suffered a drop in sales, the bank is unlikely to allow it to use the line of credit to get out of the resulting financial crisis.

Of course, a line of credit has a cost to the borrower. When the loan actually is used, the borrower must pay interest on the funds borrowed. Even before actually accepting any funds, however, the borrower will probably incur a cost. Most banks require borrowers to keep a specified minimum compensating balance in exchange for being granted a line of credit. The compensating balance essentially compensates the bank for the service it provides. Instead of charging a fee for an additional interest rate, however, the bank obliges the borrower to keep an agreed-upon sum in its demand deposit account at all times. Since banks pay no interest on commercial demand deposits, they may then invest the compensating balance in marketable securities or lend them to another borrower; any return the bank earns on these funds is clear profit. In practice, the use of compensating balances has been dwindling. This is especially true for larger firms, which would rather pay fees than hold compensating balances.

21.2.4. *Revolving Credit Agreements*

Banks usually grant lines of credit for specific lengths of time, usually 1 year or less. The parties may, of course, renegotiate the loan to provide the funds for a longer time, if needed. Still, the bank usually expects the borrower to clean up the loan — that is, reduce its debt to the bank to zero — at least once during the year.

A borrower that has a recurring need for funds may instead arrange a **revolving credit agreement**. This type of loan resembles the line of credit, in that the parties agree to a maximum credit level, and the borrower may draw funds up to that limit. The revolving credit agreement, however, meets the borrower's need to borrow the funds, pay off the loans, and then borrow again, time after time. Such a situation may supply funds for a borrowing company that produces a small number of large, high-value products, such as ships or steam turbines; the firm must borrow to finance the construction of each product until it eventually collects the proceeds of the sale. Moreover, a revolving credit agreement is more likely to be guaranteed by the bank than a line of credit.

Because the bank must commit to the agreement for a much longer time than a conventional line of credit would demand, the negotiation process for a revolving credit agreement tends to be more formal. The bank may specify that the borrower must maintain its working-capital above a specified level, forbid any factoring of accounts receivable without the bank's permission, or stipulate that any further borrowing must be subordinated to the revolving credit debt. Commitment fees also are common for large revolving credit agreements. Most banks offer the borrower a choice between a committed line of credit and an uncommitted line of credit. With the *committed line of credit*, the borrower pays an up-front fee which then obliges the bank to lend the firm money under the terms of the line of credit. An *uncommitted line of credit* does not have an up-front fee payment and so the bank is not obliged to lend the firm money. If the bank chooses to lend under the terms of the line of credit, it may do so, but is also may choose not to lend.

21.2.5. *Floor Plan Loans*

FPL finance equipment purchases in an arrangement similar to a revolving credit agreement. Many manufacturers or distributors of machine tools, tractors, and similar heavy equipment supply these items to retailers under a floor plan system, which allows the retailer to pay for the merchandise only after actually selling it. The retailer's inventory therefore is financed by the supplier, either a manufacturer or a distributor. The manufacturer or distributor in turn finances this inventory by setting up a credit arrangement with a bank. Under such an agreement, the bank pays the manufacturer for the equipment as soon as it is shipped. The bank then becomes the official owner of the equipment. When the equipment is sold, the retailer pays the wholesale price plus an interest charge directly to the bank. Alternatively, the retailer may give the manufacturer or distributor a note for the wholesale price of the equipment, which the manufacturer or distributor may then sell to the bank at a discount. This agreement compensates the bank, not by interest payments, but by the difference between the discounted sum it pays to the manufacturer and the full wholesale price it eventually will recover from the retailer.

21.3. Characteristics of Bank Loans

A bank loan, like any other form of negotiated credit, is actually a package of terms and restrictions to which the lender and borrower agree. Although these terms may specify almost anything on which the two parties agree, any loan contract specifies certain key terms and characteristics, including interest rates, security requirements, and the maturity of the loan.

21.3.1. *Interest Rates*

The rates of interest charged by commercial banks vary in two ways: the general level of interest rates varies over time, and, at any given time, different borrowers pay different rates because of varying degrees of creditworthiness. The base rate for most commercial banks traditionally has been the prime rate, although in times of soaring market interest rates, some of the larger banks experiment with marginal pricing schemes. The **prime rate** is the rate that commercial banks charge their most creditworthy business customers for short-term borrowing. The financial press splashes news of any change in this rate across the front page. Congress and the business community speculate about the prime's influence on economic activity, because it is the baseline rate for loan pricing in most loan agreements.

In the latter part of 1971, a large, money-center bank instituted a floating prime rate linked by a formula to the market-determined commercial paper rate. The formula required weekly reviews of the prime rate, with adjustments in minimum steps of one-eighth of a percentage point. The formula kept the prime approximately 50 basis points above the average rate on 90-day commercial paper placed through dealers. The choice of the commercial paper rate reflected the ease of substituting short-term bank loans for commercial paper. Historically, the prime has served as a baseline for loan pricing; a loan contract might state its interest rate as "prime plus two" or "120% of prime".

However, as the banking industry has begun to price its loans and services more aggressively, the prime rate has become less important. As the use of the prime rate has declined, compensating balances have become less popular, as well. The current trend is to price a loan at a rate above the bank's marginal cost of funds, which typically is reflected by the interest rate on a certificate of deposit. The bank adds an interest-rate margin to this cost of funds, and the sum becomes the rate it charges the borrower. This rate changes daily, in line with the bank's money market rates.

In today's environment, as banks rely on borrowing funds in the money market rather than through the depositor, the manner in which bankers price their loans is changing. As liability management becomes more critical for bankers, the pricing of loans will come to depend more on the amount of competition, both domestic and international, that the banker faces in securing loanable funds. Competition for corporate customers and enhanced competition from the commercial-paper market often have allowed large, financially stable corporations to borrow at a rate below prime.

Whether based on the prime rate or not, interest represents the price that the borrower pays to the bank for credit over a specified period of time. The amount of interest paid depends upon a number of factors: the dollar amount of the loan, the length of time involved, the nominal annual rate of interest, the repayment schedule, and the method used to calculate interest.

The various methods used to calculate the amount of interest are basically all variations of the simple interest calculation. Recall from Chapter 6 that simple interest is calculated on the amount borrowed for the length of time the loan is outstanding. If \$1 million is borrowed at 15% and repaid in 1 payment at the end of 1 year, the simple interest would be \$1 million times 0.15 or \$150,000.

Add-on interest is calculated on the full amount of the original principal. The total interest for the entire term of the loan is added immediately to the original principal. Payments are determined by dividing the total of the principal plus interest by the number of payments to be made. When a borrower repays a loan in a single, lump sum, this method gives a rate identical to simple interest. However, when two or more payments are to be made, this method results in an effective rate of interest that is greater than the nominal rate. In our example above, if the million-dollar loan were repaid in two 6-month installments of \$575,000 each, the effective rate would be higher than 15%, since the borrower does not have the use of the funds for the entire year. Putting this into equation form, we see that:

$$\text{PV} = \sum_{t=1}^{\text{N}} \frac{\text{Future flows}}{(1 + \text{Interest rate})^t}, \tag{21.1}$$

where

PV = the present value or loan amount;
t = the time period when the interest and principal repayment occur;
N = the number of periods.

Using the information in the above example, and allowing r to equal the annual percentage rate of the loan, we obtain the following:

$$\$1{,}000{,}000 = \frac{\$575{,}000}{\left(1+\frac{r}{2}\right)^1} + \frac{\$575{,}000}{\left(1+\frac{r}{2}\right)^2}$$

Table 21.1. Installment loan amortization schedule: Add-on loan.

Period	(A) Payment	(B) Beginning Balance	(C) Interest (0.19692) /2 × (B)	(D) Principal Paid (A)−(C)	(E) Ending Loan Balance (B)−(D)
1	\$575,000	\$1,000,000	\$98,460	\$476,540	\$523,460
2	575,000	523,460	51,540	523,460	0
Biannual payment:		\$575,000			
Initial balance:		\$1,000,000			
Initial maturity:		1 year			
APR:		19.692%			

Using a financial calculator, we see that r equals 19.692%. Using this information we can obtain the installment loan amortization schedule as presented in Table 21.1.

Bank-discount interest commonly is charged for short-term business loans. Generally, the borrower makes no intermediate payments, and the life of the loan usually is 1 year or less. Interest is calculated on the amount of the loan, and the borrower receives the difference between the amount of the loan and the amount of interest. In the example, this gives an interest rate of 15%. The interest (\$150,000) is subtracted from the \$1-million loan amount and the borrower has the use of \$850,000 for 1 year. Dividing the interest payment by the amount of money actually used by the borrower (\$150,000 ÷ \$850,000), we find the effective rate is 17.6%.

If the loan were to require a compensating balance of 10%, the borrower would have the use of an even smaller portion of the entire loan amount. This requirement would increase the effective rate of interest to 20% — the interest amount of \$150,000 divided by the funds available, which is \$750,000 (\$1,000,000 − \$150,000 interest, minus a compensating balance of \$100,000).

The effective interest cost on a revolving credit agreement includes both interest costs and a commitment fee. Assume, for example, that the TBA Corporation has a \$1-million revolving credit agreement with a bank. Interest on the borrowed funds is 15% per annum and TBA must pay a commitment fee of 1% on the unused portion of the credit line. If the firm borrows \$600,000, the effective annual interest rate is 15.67%:

$$\frac{(0.15 \times \$600{,}000) + (0.01 \times \$400{,}000)}{\$600{,}000}$$

EXAMPLE 21.1

Loan Costs

A firm has a \$1-million line of credit for the next year. The commitment fee is 1/2% on the unused amount of borrowing, and the interest rate is 12% on the borrowed amount. Additionally, the bank requires a compensating balance of 10% on the total amount of the line of credit. What is the annual effective interest rate for this arrangement if ht firm were to borrow \$750,000 for 9 months?

Since only \$750,000 is borrowed on a \$1-million line of credit, the commitment fee is 1/2% of the \$250,000 that is not borrowed.

Commitment fee $= 1/2\% \times \$250{,}000 = \$1{,}250$
Interest on the used funds $= 12\% \times \$750{,}000 \times 3/4$ year $= \$67{,}500$

$$\begin{aligned}\text{Net funds available} &= \text{Total funds borrowed}\\ &\quad - \text{Compensating balance}\\ &= \$750{,}000 - 0.10(\$1{,}000{,}000)\\ &= \$650{,}000.\end{aligned}$$

$$\begin{aligned}\text{Effective cost} &= \frac{\text{Interest} + \text{Fees}}{\text{Net funds available}}\\ &= \frac{\$67{,}500 + \$1{,}250}{\$650{,}000}\\ &= 10.58\% \text{ for 9 months.}\end{aligned}$$

Thus, the effective annual rate is:

$$r = (1 + 0.0158)^{\frac{4}{3}} - 1 = 14.35\%.$$

Since many factors influence the true rate of interest on a loan, a financial manager should evaluate borrowing costs based strictly on the effective annual rate. Only this standard of comparison can ensure that the actual costs of borrowing will guide the decision.

21.3.2. *Security Requirements*

The previous section discussed installment loan amortization and other terms that banks impose to protect themselves. Yet another way in which a bank can limit its exposure to risk is by requiring the borrower to pledge some valuable assets as **collateral** — that is, security for the loan. For example, a company that produces buildings, locomotives, large generating plants, or other major pieces of equipment may pledge these high-value items as security. On the other hand, if a business mass produces low-value items, it is not practical to give the bank claims against specific items. Instead, a loan may specify a **blanket lien**, or a claim against all work in progress or inventory on hand.

Again, banks face their highest levels of risk in making loans to small companies, and it is not surprising to find that a high proportion of these loans, probably 75%, are secured by collateral. Larger companies present less risk and have stronger bargaining positions, so only about 30% of loans made to companies in this class are secured.

Most banks require **key-person insurance** on the principal officers of the borrowing company to protect their loans. Because the repayment of a loan usually depends upon the managers of the firm running the company profitably, the death or disability of a key manager could jeopardize the safety of the loan. To avoid this uncertainty, the borrower buys a term insurance policy on the life of the key manager for the value of the loan. If he or she should die, the proceeds of the policy would be paid to the bank in settlement of the loan. Key-person insurance is useful for sole proprietorships as well as corporations.

When the needs of a small company exceed its collateral, the bank may decline to make a loan unless the principals of the company pledge personal property as collateral. The bank may demand liens on their houses, personal investment portfolios, and so on. Such a request places these individuals in a very difficult position. If they put up their personal assets, their own exposure to risk is very great, indeed. On the other hand, the bank may resist parting with its money if the risk level is high enough to deter managers from placing their own personal estates on the line. If the individuals concerned have large private fortunes that they have not committed to the venture, the bank may legitimately request that they join it in its risky position.

21.3.3. *Maturity of the Loan*

As we mentioned at the beginning of this chapter, the classic bank loan to a business is a short-term loan, often as short as 90 days and certainly no longer than 1 year. Yet many banks lend funds to companies that quite obviously expect their needs to remain long after their loans' nominal maturities. A company may use bank funds as an almost permanent addition to its current liabilities, for example, by borrowing on a 90-day note and reapplying for the loan every 3 months. Banks have justified this rather unsatisfactory arrangement on the grounds that reapplications allow them to review borrowers' affairs every 3 months to make sure that things are going satisfactorily. This decreases a bank's risk of getting locked into a deteriorating situation. From the borrowing company's point of view, however, the relationship is difficult; with the constant threat that any weakness in the company's financial position will be intensified quickly should the bank decline to renew the short-term note at the next 90-day review.

In practice, this situation is becoming increasingly rare, however, as banks further relax their previous insistence on short-term, self-liquidating loans and expand their use of term loans. Term loans make no pretense as short-term financing. Instead, they specify initial periods of up to 5 or even 10 years, usually with installment payments schedules.

21.4. Short-Term Financing

Almost all businesses use trade credit; few companies pay for their supplies on a cash-and-carry basis. A firm receives invoices for materials, supplies, and services provided by outsiders some days after the materials are delivered or the services are performed. Even if the firm pays the bills as soon as it receives them, the lag between delivery and billing represents credit provided by outside suppliers. A firm can increase this credit by not paying the bills at once. A financial executive's ability to manage these liabilities is as important as the ability to manage assets.

21.4.1. *Stretching Accounts Payable*

The basic mechanics of trade credit were discussed when we looked at the management of receivables — the credit a company extends to its customers. We now look at the same mechanism from the opposite viewpoint, with the company as a user rather than a provider of credit. In fact, both processes go on simultaneously. Almost all companies list both accounts receivable and account payable on their balance sheets, and both provide and use trade credit at the same time.

Companies that find themselves short of cash very commonly respond by paying bills as late as possible. Assuming that the supplies offers standard terms of 2/10, net 30, it is possible to postpone payment until at least 30 days after the date of the invoice. Remember, though, that such funds have a high cost. By paying the bill on the 30th day, the company foregoes a discount of 2% in order to have the use of the funds for just 20 more days. Since the firm would have no incentive to pay prior to the 10th day if it decided to take the discount, it actually would be borrowing funds for 20 days (30−10).

If the firm were to repeat this practice throughout the year, its effective annual interest cost would be equal to approximately 37% ($2/98 \times 365/20$). The finance manager therefore should compare the coast of the foregone discount (37%) to other costs of funds (that is, bank borrowing) and select the least expensive source of funds. Why, then, would a company stretch its accounts payable, exploiting this high-cost source of funds, it had any other alternative?

There are two main reasons. One is that many managers do not recognize the high cost of borrowing funds in this way. Indeed, because the supplier does not charge interest on the unpaid bill, some believe that trade credit costs nothing at all. The other reason is that, although these funds do in fact have a cost, it can be argued that it is nothing like the theoretical 37% because a company that is actively stretching its trade credit is unlikely to pay after 30 days. Table 21.2 shows the theoretical costs of trade credit as a function of how long a firm postpones payment.

The real, practical deadline for trade credit is not the nominal net 30 days, but the point at which further postponement of payment will bring a penalty in the form of damaged relations with the supplier, refusal of further suppliers, a damaged credit rating, interest charges on the unpaid balance, or even a lawsuit. While some financial executives may try to delay payment of bills until the last possible day in order to reduce the implicit cost of financing or to increase outstanding float, they should realize that

Table 21.2. Theoretical cost of trade credit with terms 2/10, net 30.

Payment Date	Number of Days Funds are Used	Theoretical Cost
30th day	20	37.2%
40th day	30	24.8
50th day	40	18.6
60th day	50	14.9
70th day	60	12.4
80th day	70	10.6
90th day	80	9.3

these actions may damage their vendor/customer relations and suggest unethical behavior. One of the benefits of trade credit compared to alternative financing sources is that suppliers often are sympathetic trade credit compared to alternative financing sources is that suppliers often are sympathetic when customers have an occasional problem with the timing of cash flows. However, firms that abuse their suppliers' generosity may find no help available when they need it most.

21.4.2. *Offering Liberal Credit to Increase Sales*

Although it may be difficult to determine exactly how long a supplier will be willing to wait for payment, it almost certainly will be more than the nominal net terms. A supplier's primary objective is to sell products, and it will be very reluctant to do anything that might endanger sales. Few suppliers are monopolists; any supplier who tried to enforce net-30 terms would quickly lose business to competitors, so any company that sells on terms of net-30 days expects some of its customers to stretch their payments beyond that time. If a high percentage of a firm's customers are small companies, which often rely heavily on trade credit, the firm's average receivables probably will exceed 30 days. This may lead the firm to monitor its receivables closely and tighten up collections if average age of receivables increase beyond a certain limit — say, 45 days. However, even this depends to some extent on the policies of rival suppliers.

Some suppliers actively use generous terms of trade credit as a form of sales promotion. This is especially likely when a distributor is trying to enter a new geographic area and must lure customers away from established rivals. In such circumstances, generous credit may well be more effective than an intensive advertising campaign or a high-pressure sales team. The creditor simply may increase the discount and/or extend the period during which it offers the discount or it may modify terms in other ways, such as extending inventory loans. In the most extreme case, the manufacturer or distributor may find no suitable outlets for its product in the new territory, so it may need to encourage local people to startup businesses as company agents. The expanding firm may have to provide almost the entire working-capital of such new ventures in the form of trade credit.

21.4.3. *Trade Credit and Seasonal Business*

Special circumstances arise in highly seasonal businesses. Think of the toy manufacturer discussed earlier in this chapter, whose business is strongest before Christmas. This manufacturer's customers, either toy distributors or retail stores, probably find themselves acutely short of working-capital from August through November of each year, when they must build up their stocks in preparation for Christmas. Even though the toy manufacturer may offer nominal terms of sale of 2/10, net 30, the company may provide extended credit to its customers during this difficult period.

However, the toy manufacturer might be better advised to do whatever it can to encourage customers to start building up their stock well before the August–November peak, to spread toy production over a longer period. As mentioned in Chapter 19, this can be done through seasonal dating, a policy of offering more generous credit terms on orders placed outside usual peak periods. The toy manufacturer may decide to offer terms of net 90 days on June orders, net 60 days on July orders, and net 30 days on orders from August through November. This produces advantages for both the manufacturer and its customers. The toy distributors can start their buying earlier and enjoy longer lead times, without the need to pay for the toys until they have begun to sell them. The manufacturer, on the other hand, can spread toy production for the seasonal peak over a longer period without having to accumulate and store a large inventory of finished goods. This policy clearly has a cost to the manufacturer: a large increase in accounts receivable. As usual, there is a tradeoff between the economics of smoothing production and the cost of financing these receivables.

21.4.4. *Who Pays the Cost?*

This raises another important question. Who, in general, pays the cost of trade credit? Clearly, there is a cost, because funds are tied up in a use that produces no immediate return on investment. The obvious conclusion seems to be that the supplier who extends credit must pay the cost, but this is not always true. A supplier who offers unusually generous credit terms may pass some of the cost on to customers in the form of higher prices, which the customers pay because they have no other source of credit. The extent to which this happens depends upon the supplier's competitive position. If its product is in some way unique, perhaps because it is a powerful brand, the demand will be relatively inelastic, and it may well be possible to pass on some of the cost of trade credit in the form of higher prices. Elastic demand probably would make this impossible. As we have mentioned already, however, the availability of other sources of short-term funds may be more important than the availability of alternative suppliers.

21.4.5. *Advantages of Trade Credit*

Trade credit has two important advantages that justify its extensive use. One is its convenience and ready availability; because terms are standard rather than negotiated individually, trade credit requires no great expenditure of executive time and incurs no legal expense. If a supplier accepts a company as a customer, it automatically extends the usual credit terms, even though the maximum line of credit may be set low at first. The second advantage, closely related to the first, is the fact that the credit available from this source automatically grows as the company grows. As sales expand, production schedules increase. This in turn requires purchases of larger quantities of materials and supplies. If the supplier does not impose limits on credit, the additional credit becomes available automatically, simply by placing orders for extra material. Of course, a buyer will need a separate source of credit if a long manufacturing process leaves a payable outstanding on the supplier's payment deadline while the goods remain unsold. Still, this financing method requires a much smaller amount of credit than the firm would have needed, if no trade credit had been available.

21.5. Turning Receivables into Cash

Accounts receivable consume a major portion of working-capital for most companies. By now, no one should mistake working-capital for cash. Receivables cannot be used to pay bills directly. One way in which a company can increase its cash flow in a financial crisis, however, is to convert receivables into cash more quickly than the normal collection policy would convert them. There are two ways of doing this: pledging and factoring.

21.5.1. *Pledging*

In pledging, the firm offers its receivables as security for a cash advance. The lender who accepts and discounts the receivables may be a commercial bank or a specialized industrial finance company. Figure 21.1 shows schematically the process of pledging accounts receivable.

The first step in setting up a pledging relationship is to negotiate a formal agreement between the borrower and lender. Once the agreement

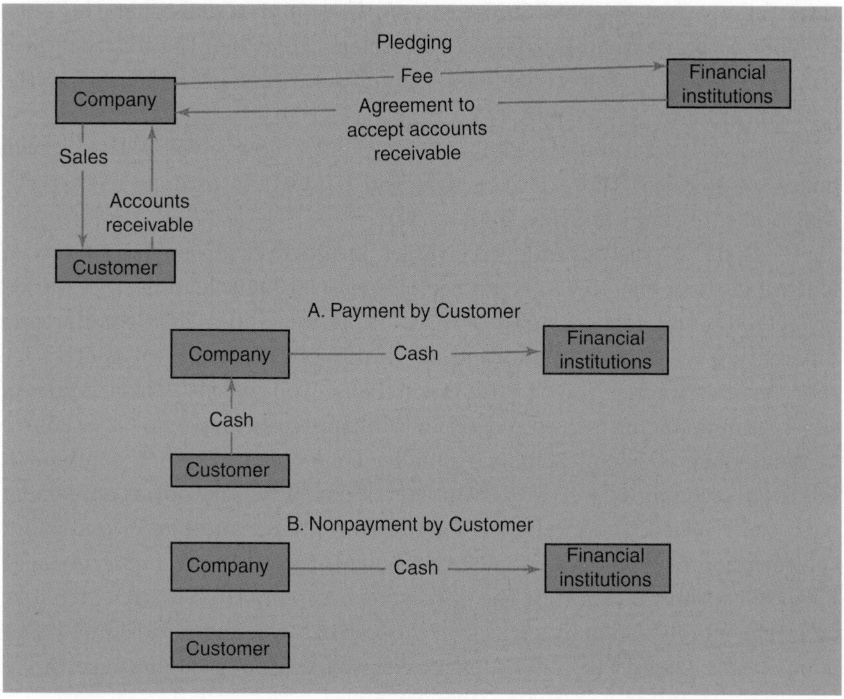

Fig. 21.1. Pledging accounts receivable.

has been reached and a legal contract signed, the borrower can begin to present its receivables. The lender gives the borrower the face value of the invoices less its own charges. That is, the lender buys the invoices at a discount, paying less than the amount it hopes to collect.

Almost all pledging agreements have two important provisions: the lender's right to recourse, and its right to reject invoices. In the event that the customer defaults and fails to pay the sum invoiced, the borrower is obligated to assume responsibility for the outstanding amount. Assume, for example, that the toy manufacturer discussed earlier is short of cash and pledges its receivables with a finance company. One customer, a local department store, buys toys worth $10,000. The toy manufacturer invoices the sale and sends its own copy of the invoice to the finance company. The finance company gives the manufacturer the discounted value of the invoice, probably about $8,500. If all goes well, the department store pays its bill after 30 days or so by sending a check to the manufacturer, which then sends the outstanding amount to the finance company. If the department store fails to pay on time, however, and if inquiry reveals that the store is about to liquidate and will never be able to pay, then the manufacturer still is legally obligated to pay back the full face value of the invoice to the finance company.

The lender also has the right to select only those invoices that it will finance and reject those it considers too risky. It is estimated that the rejection rate could reach as high as 50%.

Pledging, or discounting, receivables is not a cheap source of credit. During most of the 1980s, when the commercial bank lending rate varied between 8% and 15%, the cost of discounting was about 20%. Similar rate differentials exit today. In addition, the lender often charges yet another fee to cover its expenses to appraise credit risks. Consequently, this source of short-term financing is used mostly by companies that have no other source of funds open to them, primarily smaller companies. For such companies, however, pledging offers two advantages. First, after the initial agreement has been reached, the method is fairly informal and automatic, except for the rejection of invoices for bad risk. Second, the customer being invoiced receives no information that the borrowing company is in financial trouble; he or she simply sends in a check in the normal way and never knows that it has been assigned to a third party. For this reason, pledging receivables is sometimes called *non-notification financing.*

21.5.2. *Factoring*

Firms also can convert accounts receivable to cash by a method called factoring. Factoring essentially involves an outright sale of accounts receivable to a finance company or factoring department of a commercial bank. Factoring differs from pledging since it gives the finance company no recourse to the borrower in the case of bad debts. The customer receives notice that the invoice has been sold and is asked to make payment directly to the finance company. Figure 21.2 shows schematically the process of factoring accounts receivable.

This arrangement clearly increases the lender's risk, as compared to pledging. To reduce this risk, the finance company virtually takes over the work of the borrower's credit department. All new customer orders pass through the finance company, which does a credit appraisal. If the finance company rejects the customer as an unacceptable credit risk, the borrower either must turn down the order or fill it for cash.

Factoring, like pledging, is a fairly costly source of credit. This overall cost has a number of distinct components. The factor charges the borrower

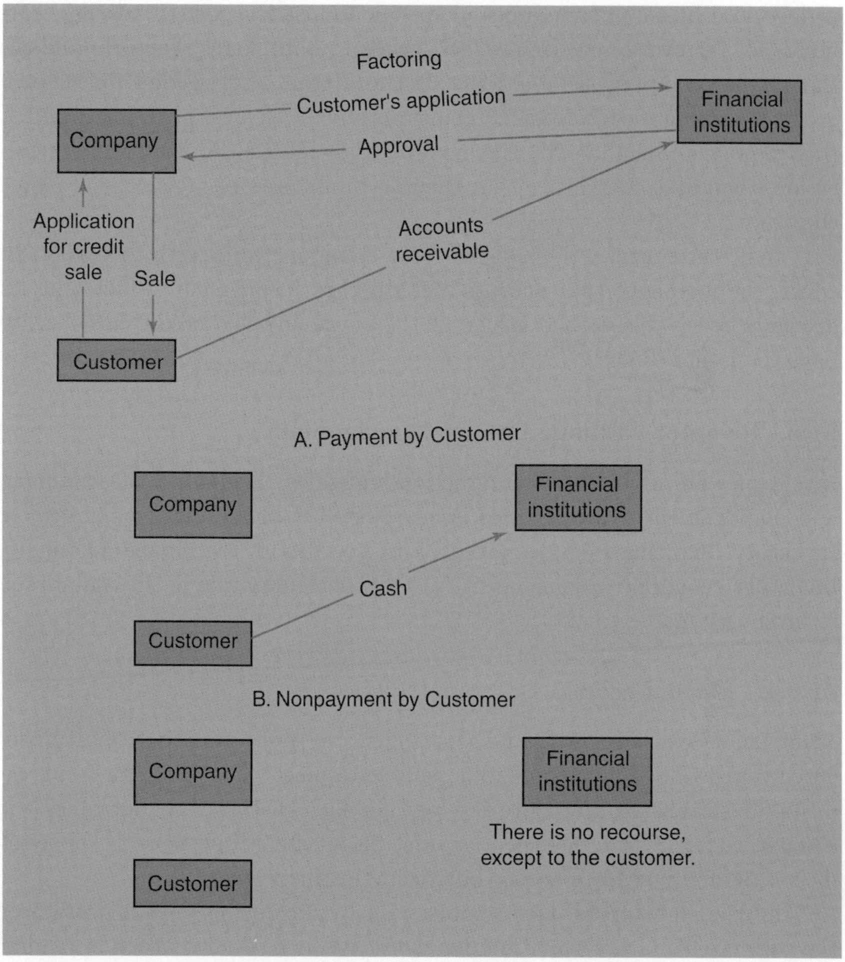

Fig. 21.2. Factoring accounts receivable.

a fee between about 1% and 3% of the face value of the invoices for credit appraisal. The interest charge depends upon whether the finance company has agreed to forward the funds as soon as the good are shipped or only on the receivable's due date at the end of the credit period. For payment at shipment, the interest rate may well rise as high as 15% to 25%.

The advantages of factoring resemble those of pledging; it is a relatively easy and flexible source of funds once the initial negotiations have been completed, and it provides additional funds as the borrower's scale of operations, and therefore its needs, grow. Factoring always has been widely used by small companies in specific industries, such as textiles, garments, or furniture, which may lack access to bank loans. Factoring allows the smaller company to avoid the cost and trouble of setting up its own credit department; this gives factoring one advantage over pledging. Against this, however, must be set the possible damage to the borrower's reputation when customers learn that their accounts have been sold to a finance company.

Credit-card transactions share some common traits with factoring. In effect, the merchant that accepts a credit card in payment is factoring its accounts receivable to the issuer of the card, and the credit-card holder pays the issuer directly.

21.6. Inventory Financing and Management

Inventories are used to link production and sales. Therefore, the financing and management of inventories is a major part of any firm's operations. Inventory financing includes either trust receipts or warehouse financing. Inventory economic order quantity (EOQ) determination is the main issue in inventory management.

21.6.1. *Trust Receipts*

Many businesses lack the financial strength and reputation to support unsecured borrowing. These firms may be able to meet their needs for funds by using physical assets to secure the loan. In such cases, the lender takes out a **trust receipt**, that is, a lien, against these assets. Inventory is the asset most commonly used to secure borrowing in this way.

The lender protects itself against risk by advancing only a portion of the estimated market value of the assets. Where the inventory is readily transferable and salable, the lender may advance as much as 90%. If the inventory is highly specialized, however, the portion is likely to be considerably lower.

Straightforward borrowing by a trust receipt presents a serious disadvantage in that the physical property that secures the loan must be described in detail in the legal documents. This is clearly difficult if various finished goods are being pledged. An alternative called a floating lien give the lender a claim against all the borrower's inventory without listing or specifying individual items. Such an arrangement makes it difficult, however, for the lender to prevent the borrower from running down inventories to a level that gives no real security for the loan; finance companies therefore are usually willing to advance only a small fraction of the estimated market value of the inventory against a floating lien.

21.6.2. *Warehousing*

A warehousing method of financing can reduce the risk of using inventory as collateral to secure the loan. There are two variations of this method: field warehousing and public warehousing.

In field warehousing, the finance company (usually a specialized warehousing organization) takes over the use of a certain part of the borrower's premises. This floor space must be segregated from the borrower's other operations so that it can be kept locked, restricting access only to the warehousing company. The inventory to serve as collateral is transferred to this segregated area, and the warehousing company advances the discounted cash value of the inventory to the borrower. In return, the warehousing company receives a warehouse receipt, which gives it title to the inventory.

This inventory cannot be sold or used without the warehouse company's permission, and this permission is given only when the borrower repays a corresponding portion of the funds advanced. Thus, the lender can ensure that the collateral always is adequate to secure the loan. The warehousing company locates a member of its own staff, the custodian, on the borrower's premises to ensure that its rights are respected.

Public warehousing, sometimes called terminal warehousing, is similar to field warehousing, except that the physical inventory is transferred to and stored in a warehouse operated by an independent warehousing company instead of in a segregated section of the borrower's premises. The mechanics of the financing arrangement remain the same: no inventory is released to the borrower until it repays the corresponding part of the loan. Warehouse financing is very common in the food and lumber industries. Canned goods, in particular, account for almost 20% of all public warehouse loans; however, almost any non-perishable and easily marketable commodity may be used.

Warehousing, like receivables financing, is a flexible source of short-term credit that automatically grows as the company's working-capital needs expansion. Also, like receivables financing, its cost is fairly high. Typically, the warehousing company imposes a service charge, usually a fixed minimum plus 1–2% of the funds loaned, plus an interest rate of 8–12% or sometimes more. The fixed costs of warehousing — the minimum service charge plus the cost of providing the field warehouse facilities or moving goods to a public warehouse — make it unsuitable for very small firms; the minimum feasible inventory size probably is about $100,000.

21.6.3. *Selling*

The simplest way of turning inventory into cash, of course, is simply to sell it. In extreme situations, a discounted bulk sale, fire sale, or distress sale may provide funds, but this source may be very costly, indeed. If the company has finished goods on hand, presumably it has not been able to sell them at the regular price, or it is accumulating them to meet a future seasonal demand. In either case, to sell the goods immediately probably would require more attractive terms of sale, such as lower prices or more attractive credit terms. A company that is short of cash is in no position to offer more credit to its customers. To sell the finished goods, then, the firm probably would have to reduce their price substantially, perhaps to a point where the sale becomes completely unprofitable. This still may be an acceptable strategy, however; in a liquidity crisis, cash flow is much more important than profit.

If the company has an inventory of raw materials in excess of its immediate needs, it may be possible to generate cash by selling some. A chocolate manufacturer, for instance, may have bought large stocks of cocoa bean when its price was unusually low; the firm may be able to resell some of this stock to generate cash. Such a policy is likely to be less expensive than selling off finished goods at "fire sale" prices, and is well worth considering.

Economic Order Quantity

The EOQ for inventory is similar to Baumol's EOQ for cash. The EOQ for inventory is defined as:

where C = Carry cost per unit (e.g., insurance and storage costs); S = Total usage of an item of inventory; and O = Ordering cost per unit. Eq. (21.2) is known as the economic, lot-size formula. The purpose of the formulas is to calculate the optimal order size given various cost considerations.

EXAMPLE 21.2

EOQ for Inventory

Francis Shoes orders 50,000 pairs of hiking boots during a 300-day period, ordering costs are $200 per order, and carrying costs are $20 per unit per 300 days. What is the optimal EOQ?

The optimal EOQ is:

For an order quantity of 50,000 units, the firm would order (50,000/1,000), or 50 times during the 300-day period, or every 6 days.

Equation (21.2) implies that Q^* varies directly with total usage and order cost and inversely with the carry cost. This analysis is similar to the analysis used for the EOQ for cash.

21.7. Other Non-bank Sources of Funds

In the final section of this chapter, we discuss three other non-bank sources of funds. These three sources are commercial paper, banker's acceptances, and asset-backed securities.

21.7.1. *Commercial Paper*

Large companies have another very attractive source of short-term funds open to them: they can sell commercial paper, unsecured promissory notes that trade in the organized money market through a number of recognized dealers. The buyers of the paper are primarily commercial banks looking for safe investments they yield higher returns than U.S. Treasury securities. Other buyers include corporations, pension funds, insurance companies, and others that have temporary surplus funds they wish to put to work safely.

The commercial paper market has grown tremendously in recent decades. Since 1997, the U.S. paper market, the largest in the world, has grown from \$50 billion to over \$600 billion and currently represents approximately 18% of all debt. The commercial paper market now range from 1 to 270 days, typically with extremely large denominations. The average maturity for commercial paper is approximately 22 days and the average denomination is \$100,000. Commercial paper has a maximum maturity of 270 days, because maturities beyond this time need to be registered with the Securities and Exchange Commission (SEC).

Commercial paper is sold in two ways: (1) the issuer may sell the paper directly to the buyer, or (2) the issuer may sell the paper through a dealer firm. Firms prefer to sell directly to save the dealer's fee of approximately one-eighth of a percentage point (12.5 basis points). 100 basis points equal 1%. Thus, if the firm issues \$50 million in commercial paper directly, it can save \$62,500 in dealer's fees (\$50 million $\times$ 0.00125). Commercial paper is sold on a discount basis. Almost half of commercial paper is issued directly, with most of the direct paper being issued by finance companies.

Approximately 75% of all paper (both direct and dealer issues) comes from financial companies, including commercial, savings, and mortgage banking firms, finance leasing, insurance underwriting, and other investment activities. The balance of outstanding paper is issued by non-financial firms, such as utilities and industrial manufacturers. This paper ordinarily is issued by a dealer.

Besides its relative low cost, commercial paper offers three advantages. First, selling the notes is a fairly simple and informal process, certainly simpler than negotiating a bank loan. While it is not as easy as using trade credit, commercial paper is the simplest of all forms of negotiated credit. Second, the ability to sell unsecured promissory notes gives the issuer a degree of prestige. This, in turn, makes it even easier to sell alter issues as the company builds a name for itself in the money market. Third, a commercial paper issue may exceed the legal lending limit of most commercial banks, preventing the need to combine banks to assemble a financing package.

At first sight, commercial paper may seem to be the obvious choice because of its lower cost, but reliance on commercial paper may be a high-risk policy. A company that finances all of its short-term needs through the sale of notes does not build up a good borrowing relationship with a bank. If economic conditions change and the money market becomes tight, such a company may well find itself in difficulties. The banks will give priority to their regular customers; they may not even have enough loanable funds to meet all the needs of their regular borrowers. The company that has relied on the money market when money was easy will have to continue to rely on it when funds are scarce, and the differential between the interest rates of the two sources is likely to shrink dramatically in such circumstances.

21.7.2. *Banker's Acceptances*

The **banker's acceptance** is a comparatively specialized, but still important, credit source largely confined to financing foreign trade (its only major use within the United States had been in financing purchases of raw cotton crops). One of the major difficulties in conducting business overseas is in assessing the creditworthiness of potential customers. This problem is best solved by getting a bank to add its reputation to that of the buyer by accepting, or endorsing, the note payable.

Assume, for instance, that a U.S. manufacturer wants to buy bar steel stock from a Swedish steelmaker. The U.S. manufacturer first goes to its commercial bank and asks it to send a letter of credit to the Swedish company. This letter of credit authorizes the steelmaker to draw a draft, or note payable, against the U.S. bank as soon as it ships the steel.

When the steel is safely aboard ship, the steelmaker sends the draft to the U.S. bank, together with the shipping note, bill of lading, and any other documents required as proof of shipping. The bank receives this draft and accepts it when a bank officer endorses it. This makes the draft a claim against the bank and a readily salable, short-term, money market instrument with a maturity between 30 and 180 days (90 days is average).

Before the draft matures, the U.S. bank may decide to sell it to another bank or company looking for a profitable short-term investment. In the meantime, the U.S. manufacturer enjoys credit. When the draft matures, the seller returns it to the U.S. bank for payment, and the bank in turn recovers the funds from the U.S. manufacturer.

The interest rate on acceptances is quite low, usually at or very slightly above the prime rate. Any bank that performs services of this kind for its customers probably will expect to be compensated in other ways, however, especially through the maintenance of good demand deposit balances.

21.7.3. *Asset-Backed Debt Securities (ABS)*

Recently, issuers of credit have begun following the lead set by mortgage lenders by using asset securitization as a means of raising funds. By securitization, we mean that the firm repackages its assets and sells them to the market. Figure 21.3 shows the basic structure of an **ABS**.

In general, an ABS comes through certificates issued by a grantor trust, which also registers the security issue under the Securities Act of 1933. These securities are sold to investors through underwritten public offerings or private placements. Each certificate represents a fractional interest in one or more pools of assets. The selling firm transfers assets, with or without recourse, to the grantor trust, which is formed and owned by the investors, in exchange for the proceeds from the certificates. The trustee receives the operating cash flows from the assets and pays scheduled interest and principal payments to investors, servicing fees to the selling firm, and other expenses of the trust.

From a legal perspective, the trust owns the assets that underlie such securities. These assets will not be consolidated into the estate of the selling firm if it enters into bankruptcy.

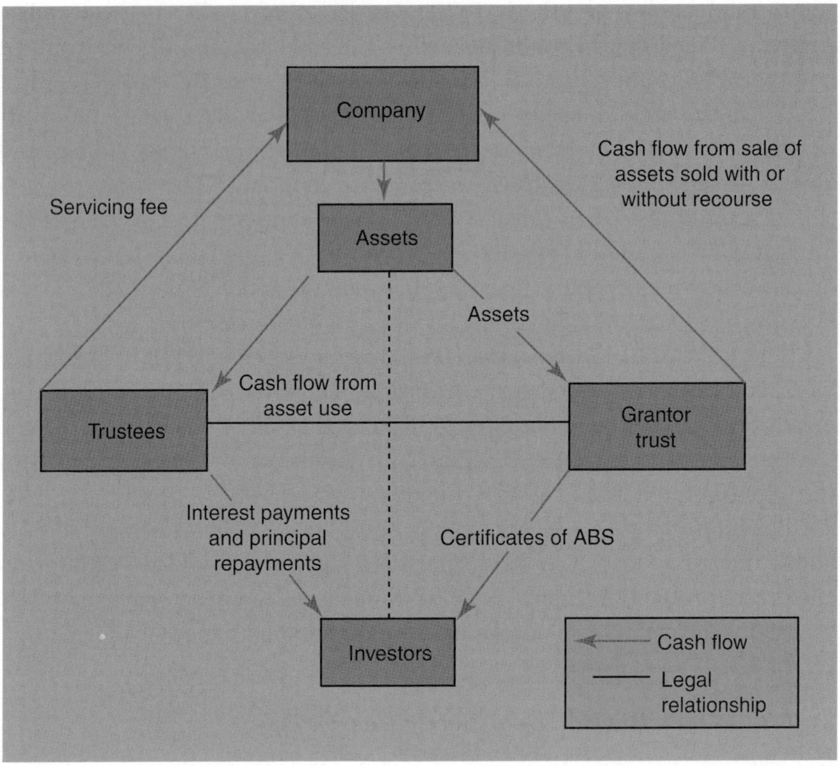

Fig. 21.3. Basic structure of an ABS.

To date, most ABS issues have securitized automobile and credit-card receivables. It is expected that this area will grow into other fields, such as computer leases, truck leases, land and property leases, mortgages on plant and equipment, and commercial loans.

21.8. Summary

In this chapter, we have reviewed the nature and characteristics of bank loans and other sources of short-term financing. Bank loans can be negotiated as the need arises or they can be obtained under regular lines of credit or revolving credit agreements. Because lines of credit and revolving credit agreements offer financing flexibility, they are useful tools for financing short-term asset requirements. Banks calculate interest charges on their loans by three different methods: (1) simple interest, (2) discount interest, and (3) add-on interest. In addition to the stated interest rate, the effective cost of bank credit includes the cost of compensating balance requirements and commitment fees. Interest rate on bank loans depend on the bank's cost of funds, the current market prime rate, and the creditworthiness of the borrower. Firms should choose the banks with which they do business carefully. At a minimum, they should analyze a bank's financial statements to get a picture of its creditworthiness.

Firms also may exploit non-bank sources of short-term funds. Some sources, such as commercial paper and banker's acceptances, are comparatively inexpensive, but access can be difficult for some firms.

Most firms finance large portions of their needs through supplier trade credit. However, improper use of this source may make it expensive; a firm also may create ill among its supplies if it intentionally delays payments. Furthermore, unusually attractive terms of trade credit may conceal higher merchandise prices or lower product quality. In the final analysis, a competitive bid from several suppliers probably will reveal the best overall financing packages.

Problem Set

Set 1:

1. Cost of Alternative Bank Loans A bank has offered to make a loan of \$1 million for 1 year. Which of the following loans is cheaper?

   (a) A simple interest rate of 18%.
   (b) An add-on interest rate of 17% to determine the monthly payment, with monthly payments.
   (c) 171/2% one-payment discount loan.
   (d) A loan for 16% with a 10% compensating balance.

   A: Let's compute the effective annual rate for each loan.

   (a) Simple interest:

$$\begin{aligned}\text{Cost} &= \text{Principal} \times \text{Interest rate} \times \text{Time}\\ &= \$1 \text{ million} \times 0.18 \times 1 \text{ year}\\ &= \$180{,}000.\\ \text{EAR} &= \$180{,}000/\$1{,}000{,}000 = 18\%.\end{aligned}$$

(b) Add-on interest:

$$\begin{aligned}\text{Total interest} &= \text{Principal} \times \text{Interest rate} \times \text{Time}\\ &= \$1\text{ million} \times 0.17 \times 1\text{ year}\\ &= \$170{,}000.\end{aligned}$$

Monthly payment of add-on loan:

$$\frac{1{,}1170{,}000}{12} = \$97{,}500.$$

Substituting related information into Eq. (20.1), we have:

(c) Discount loan.

(d) Compensating balance loan.

2. The EOQ for Inventory Houston Computer Manufacturing orders 45,000 CPUs during a 150-day period. Ordering costs are \$100 per order, and carrying costs are \$1 per unit per 150 days.

   (a) What is the optimal economic order quantity?

   (b) How many times will Houston Computer order CPUs?

   A:

   (a) Substituting $S = 45{,}000$, $O = \$100$, and $C = \$1$ into Eq. (20.2), we obtain:

   (b) For an economic order quantity of 3,000 units, the firm would order (45,000/3,000), or 15 times during the 150-day period, or every 10 days.

Set 2:

1. What is a line of credit? What it is usually used for?
2. What is a revolving credit agreement?
3. What is a floor plan arrangement?
4. What is the prime lending rate?
5. What factors affect the rate that bankers charge for their loans?
6. Why do bankers often require borrowers to put up collateral for a loan?
7. Briefly discuss the two ways commercial paper is sold.
8. Why is the maximum maturity of commercial paper limited to 270 days?
9. Briefly compare pledging to factor.
10. Why does not every firm issue commercial paper?

11. What are the advantages of using trust receipts for inventory financing?
12. Compare field warehousing with public warehousing.
13. Is the reason for collateral in lending and warehousing arrangements to control lender risk or to protect against the agency problem? Explain.
14. Banks have many ways of calculating interest on loans and charging fees. Why do not they simply offer one interest rate?
15. Why should not a firm use the same asset as collateral for different bank loans?

Set 3:

1. *Cost of Alternative Bank Loans*: A bank offers to lend you $5 million for 1 year. Which of the following four alternatives is cheapest?
   (a) 12% simple interest with a single payment.
   (b) Add-on interest rate of $9\frac{1}{2}$% for 1 year, payable in 12 monthly payments.
   (c) Discount loan at 10%.
   (d) A compensating balance loan with a simple interest rate of 10%, with a compensating balance of 10%.
2. *Cost of Factoring*: AR Francis Company factors its account receivables. It pays fees of 2% and is charged interest of 14%. The average collection period for Francis is 36 days. What is the APR and the effective annual rate for this factoring?
3. *Effective Cost of Commercial Paper*: What is the effective cost of commercial paper for First Q? It issues $200 million of 180-day paper at 8%, with a fee of 0.1%.
4. *Cost of Pledging*: AR First Alpha pledges its AR, and the rate is 9% per annum with a handling fee of 1% of the face value of the AR. On average, it pledges $1 million AR per year. What is the cost of this financing?
5. *Effective Cost of Inventory Financing*: A firm uses its inventory for collateral on a 6-month loan. The value of the inventory is $2 million. The field warehouse advances 80% at an interest rate of 7% plus a fixed fee of $15,000 to cover the cost of the field warehouse. What is the effective cost of the loan?
6. *Effective Cost of Commercial Paper*: Compute the cost of a commercial paper issue of $1 million with a maturity of 180 days at a 6% rate. The fee for the issue is $1,000.

7. *Effective Cost of Commercial Paper*: Compute the effective annual cost of a commercial paper issue of $10 million with a maturity of 90 days at an 8% rate. The fee for the issue is $25,000.
8. *The EOQ Inventory Model*: A firm operates for 250 days out of the year. Its total annual consumption of raw materials is 100,000 units. Fixed-costs per order are $180, and the annual per-unit carrying cost of inventory has been estimated at $9.
   (a) Find the optimal economic order quantity.
   (b) How many orders would be placed by the firm during the 250-day period?

References for Chapter 21

For additional information on short-term financing, see:

Finnerty, JE (1992). *Planning Cash Flow*, 2nd ed. New York, NY: American Management Association.

Gallinger, GW and PB Healey (1991). *Liquidity Analysis and Management*, 2nd ed. Reading, MA: Addison-Wesley.

Project V

Short-term Financial Management for Johnson & Johnson, Inc.

Using Johnson & Johnson's 1995 annual report, presented in Appendix B, answer the following questions:

1. Discuss the situation of Johnson and Johnson's liquidity and capital resources.
2. Use J&J's consolidated statement of cash flows to analyze the change of cash and cash equivalents during 1993 to 1995.
3. Discuss J&J's trade credit risk.
4. Discuss how the fair value of J&J's securities has been evaluated.
5. Discuss J&J's borrowing strategy.
6. What are J&J's inventories comprised of? How is the value of inventories determined?

Chapter 22

Elementary Applications of Programming Techniques in Working-Capital Management

22.1. Introduction

This chapter extends our knowledge of programming techniques. In this chapter, we will begin by reviewing the basics of linear programming (LP). Then the LP concept is extended to goal programming (GP), which allows managers to incorporate multiple goals into the quantitative analysis.

Though we will be considering only working-capital applications in this chapter, linear and GP techniques are very useful in many other financial applications. These include capital rationing, as we have seen, and financial planning models, as we will discuss in the next chapter. The programming techniques are helpful because they aid the financial planner/manager in his planning function. It is important to understand that these programming techniques are, of course, an *aid* to planning, not a substitute. Students must be able to interpret the results of the programming techniques, and such interpretation is more important than solving the problem manually. There are a variety of computerized solution methods available to help the financial planner/manager with the process of the numerical solution.

Basic concepts of LP and its applications are discussed in Section 22.2. An example of imposing a liquidity constraint on a firm's profit-maximization decision is presented in Section 22.3, and mathematical solutions and the implications of this example are discussed in some detail.

Applications of a LP model for short-term financial planning are also briefly discussed.

Section 22.4 shows the applications of the GP technique in dealing with the problems of working-capital management. Using the programming technique to handle cash transfer and cash concentration is discussed in Section 22.5. Finally, results of this chapter will be summarized in Section 22.6.

22.2. Linear Programming

LP is a mathematical technique used to find the optimal solution to a problem involving constraint. LP results in an optimal solution by maximizing (or minimizing) an objective function. The objective function is a mathematical expression of the firm's goal. For example, a firm might wish to maximize the value it gains from selling two products. In moving toward an optimal solution, the firm is subject to constraints that limit the ability of the firm to achieve its goal (the firm may have a *finite amount* of production capacity from which to produce the two products). Mathematically, both the equation expressing the firm's objective and the equation(s) expressing the constraints on the firm must be linear functions of the decision variables (the decision variables indicate the amount of some commodity; for example, the number of each of the two products to be sold).

It should be noted that standard LP models optimize only *one* dimension of a problem (e.g., profit, volume, or usage). When two or more dimensions are to be considered, a GP formulation is needed, as will be shown shortly.

To use LP as a tool for financial decisions, the firm's decision must be formulated in a linear manner, as described in the three steps below.

First, identify the controllable decision variables involved in the firm's problem. Second, define the objective or criterion to be maximized or minimized, and represent this objective as a linear function of the controllable decision variables. In finance, generally, the objective is to maximize the profit contribution or the market value of the firm or to minimize the cost of production. Third, define the constraints and express them as linear equations or inequalities of the decision variables. This will usually involve (a) determination of the capacities of the scarce resources involved in the constraints, and (b) derivation of a linear relationship between these capacities and the decision variables.

Symbolically, then, if $x_1, x_2, \ldots, x_n$ represent the quantities of output, the LP model takes the general form:

Maximize (or minimize)

$$Z = c_1x_1 + c_2x_2 + c_3x_3 + \cdots + c_nx_n \quad \text{(Objective function)}, \qquad (22.1)$$

subject to

$$\begin{aligned}
&a_{11}x_1 + a_{12}x_2 + a_{13}x_3 + \cdots + a_{1n}x_n \leq b_1,\\
&a_{21}x_1 + a_{22}x_2 + a_{23}x_3 + \cdots + a_{2n}x_n \leq b_2,\\
&\qquad\qquad\vdots\\
&a_{m1}x_1 + a_{m2}x_2 + a_{m3}x_3 + \cdots + a_{mn}x_n \leq b_m,\\
&x_j \geq 0 \quad (j = 1, 2, \ldots, n).
\end{aligned}$$

In Eq. (22.1), Z represents the objective to be maximized (or minimized) (e.g., profit or market value); $c_1, c_2, \ldots, x_n$ and $a_{11}, a_{12}, \ldots, a_{mn}$ are constant coefficients relating to profit contribution and input quantities, respectively; $b_1, b_2, \ldots, b_m$ are the firm's capacities of the constraining resources. The last constraint ensures that the decision variables to be determined are non-negative.

Several points should be noted concerning the LP model. First, depending upon the problem, the constraints may also be stated with equal sign (=) or greater-than-or-equal-to (≥). Second, the solution values of the decision variables are divisible; that is, a solution would permit $x_1 = \frac{1}{2}, \frac{1}{4}$, etc. If such fractional values are not desirable, the related technique of integer programming, yielding only whole numbers as a solution, can be applied. Third, the constant coefficients are assumed known and deterministic. If the coefficients are probabilistic distributions, one of the various methods of stochastic programming must be used. Although the form necessary to do LP may seem restrictive, the method is useful in a variety of financial decision-making areas. For example, LP can be used to perform capital-budgeting decisions (Carleton, 1967), and portfolio analysis (Sharpe, 1971). It can also be applied to problems in both short-term and long-term financial-planning decisions; GP can be used to analyze different issues related to working-capital management.

22.3. Working-Capital Model and Short-Term Financial Planning

Working-capital management is related to short-term financial analysis and planning, and consists of the deployment of appropriate levels of current assets and current liabilities within the overall company objective of market-value maximization. Specific functions included in this area on the asset side are management of the portfolio of cash and marketable securities, balancing the sometimes conflicting goals of receivables minimization and credit policy, and the complex problem of controlling the levels of various types of inventories. On the liability side, the functions are primarily involved with the use of trade credit from the firm's suppliers and the optimal use of negotiated short-term financing.

According to Mehta (1974), there are three special characteristics associated with current assets. First, the life span of cash, marketable securities, accounts receivables, and inventories does not exceed 1 year. Secondly, each component of current assets is swiftly transformed into other asset forms. Thirdly, the life span of current-asset components depends upon the extent to which three basic activities — production, distribution (sales), and collection — are non-instantaneous and unsynchronized.

Often, because of management's desires or loan agreements, there is a need to have working-capital components set to a certain level, or within an acceptable range. One of the most common working-capital restrictions is the level of current ratio required by loan agreements. In most profit-maximization situations, working-capital concerns play an important part in financial management. It should be noted that there is a cost associated with having inventory and having cash on hand. On a more complex level, if one increases the current liabilities, one must consider the requisite cash flow to repay the payables in the near future.

Overall, working-capital management is an important topic and worthy of careful study, because (i) financial managers generally devote a lot of time to the day-to-day internal operations of the firm; (ii) current assets generally represent more than half the total assets of a business firm; and (iii) the relationship between sales growth and the need to finance current assets is close and direct.

LP is a very useful tool in dealing with working-capital management issues. Applying LP to working-capital management requires that appropriate constraints be imposed on the profit-maximization (of cost-minimization) objective functions. In the following example, one of the constraints limiting the firm's production is a requisite lower level of a liquidity ratio. A more detailed treatment of LP applications to working-capital problems (cash management, in particular) can be found in Mao (1969), Mehta (1974), Smith (1980), and others.

22.3.1. *Questions to be Answered*

ABC Corporation, a small toy manufacturer, produces three lines of toys. Plastic Pistols, Race Cars, and Krazie Kubes. To produce each toy, the component parts must first be molded by machine and then assembled by hand. Machine and assembly times required for each toy are listed in Table 22.1.

Variable costs for the three toys (including labor, materials, and other operating costs) are included in Table 22.2 along with the selling prices and profit contributions.

ABC must also meet certain financial obligations. The firm sells all three of its products on terms of one-period credit; all variable costs, however, must be paid in cash. Management salaries of $10 for period 1 must be paid as well. Finally, a $10 interest payment on ABC debt is due in this period.

ABC has previously financed its day-to-day operations by two short-term bank loans, a $70 loan from a local bank and a $60 loan from an out-of-town bank. Due to increasing tightness in the money market, however, the out-of-town bank will not renew its short-term loan when it expires at the beginning of period 1. In addition, the local bank now insists that, as a provision of its loan renewal, ABC maintain a quick ratio of at least 1. The balance sheet of the ABC Corporation as of the end of period 0 is given in Table 22.3.

Finally, the president would like to drop the Krazie Kube from the firm's product line because of its comparatively low profit margin; however, certain legal restrictions must be taken into consideration before this decision can be made. ABC is prohibited by a new law from producing more than a total of five Plastic Pistols and/or Race Cars. The purpose

Table 22.1. Hours of time spent.

Toy	Machine Time (hours)	Assembly Time (hours)
Krazie Kube	6	5
Plastic Pistol	3	2
Race Car	4	3

Table 22.2. Price, loss and profit.

Toy	Selling Price ($)	Variable Cost ($)	Profit Contribution ($)
Krazie Kube	11	10	1
Plastic Pistol	4	2	2
Race Car	6	3	3

Table 22.3. Balance sheet of the ABC company at the end of period zero.

Assets		Liabilities and Equities	
Cash	$200	Short-term borrowing at	
Receivables		local bank	$70
(collectible during period 0)	50	Short-term borrowing at	
Plant and equipment	250	out-of-town banks*	60
		Long-term debt	290
		Net worth	80
	$500		$500

*Due at beginning of period 1.

behind the law is to encourage indirectly the production of Krazie Kubes, which are considered by the legislature to have a higher educational value as children's toys. Thus, the president and his planning staff are faced with the following specific questions. What is the optimal production schedule for period 1, now that the $60 loan will not be renewed? Will the loss of the loan limit the firm's possible profit for period 1? If it does, by how much will profit be diminished? Finally, how limiting is the new law just passed by the legislature? All of these questions can be answered through LP.

22.3.2. *Model Specification and its Solution*

The first step in modeling the firm's production problem is to identify the controllable decision variables. In this case, the controllable variables are the quantities of Kubes, Pistols, and Cars to be produced in period 1, denoted by x_1, x_2, and x_3, respectively. Second, the primary consideration of the firm's planning staff is profitability. Thus, the objective function will be formulated to maximize the profit contribution of the three products:

$$\text{Max}\,\pi = x_1 + 2x_2 + 3x_3. \tag{22.2}$$

Finally, the capacities of the firm must be identified and related to the number of Kubes, pistols, and cars to be produced. The firm's machine and assembly hours available in period 1 are 100 and 60, respectively. Thus,

$$6x_1 + 3x_2 + 4x_3 \leq 100, \tag{22.3}$$

$$5x_1 + 2x_2 + 3x_3 \leq 60. \tag{22.4}$$

Total production of pistols and/or cars must not exceed five. Therefore,

$$x_2 + x_3 \leq 5. \tag{22.5}$$

The firm's ratio must not fall below 1:

$$\frac{\begin{pmatrix}\text{Cash Available}\\ \text{for Operations}\end{pmatrix} + \begin{pmatrix}\text{Marketable}\\ \text{Securities}\end{pmatrix} + \begin{pmatrix}\text{Accounts}\\ \text{Receivable}\end{pmatrix}}{\begin{pmatrix}\text{Accounts}\\ \text{Payable}\end{pmatrix} + \begin{pmatrix}\text{Loans}\\ \text{Outstanding}\end{pmatrix}} \geq 1 \tag{22.6}$$

$$\frac{(200 - 60 - 10 - 10 - 10x_1 - 2x_2 - 3x_3) + 0 + 50}{0 + 70} \geq 1$$

or, simplifying:

$$10x_1 + 2x_2 + 3x_3 \leq 100. \tag{22.6a}$$

Finally, production must be non-negative:

$$x_i \geq 0 \quad (i = 1, 2, 3). \tag{22.7}$$

The full LP problem becomes:

$$\text{Maximize}\, \pi = x_1 + 2x_2 + 3x_3, \tag{22.8}$$

subject to

$$\begin{aligned} 6x_1 + 3x_2 + 4x_3 &\leq 100,\\ 5x_1 + 2x_2 + 3x_3 &\leq 60,\\ x_2 + x_3 &\leq 5,\\ 10x_1 + 2x_2 + 3x_3 &\leq 100 \quad (x_1, x_2, x_3 \geq 0). \end{aligned}$$

The simplex method is generally used when solving LP problems with more than two variables. Although a treatment of the simplex method is beyond the scope of this chapter, we shall use the final solution obtained by that method to answer the series of questions posed by the ABC planning staff. The final tableau is given in Table 22.4. (For a thorough explanation of the method, see Appendix 22.A.)

Table 22.4. Final tableau of linear programming solution.

	Real Variables			Slack Variables				
	x_1	x_2	x_3	x_4	x_5	x_6	x_7	
x_4	0	$-4/10$	0	1	0	$-22/10$	$-6/10$	29
x_5	0	$-1/2$	0	0	1	$-3/2$	$-1/2$	2.5
x_3	0	1	1	0	0	1	0	5
x_1	1	$-1/10$	0	0	0	$-3/10$	$1/10$	8.5
	Objective-Function Coefficients							
$\Delta\pi$	0	$9/10$	0	0	0	$27/10$	$-1/10$	
	$\pi = 23.5$							

In the final tableau, the solution values for the variables are found in the right-hand column. Thus, $x_1 = 8.5$, $x_2 = 0$, $x_3 = 5$, $x_5 = 2.5$, $x_6 = 0$, $x_7 = 0$, $x_4 = 29$ (x_4 through x_7 represent slack variables introduced into the constraint equations to convert them to equalities prior to use of the simplex method). Profit contribution will be maximized at a total of \$23.5, if the firm produces 8.5 Krazie Kubes, no Pistols, and 5 Race Cars. To obtain an integer solution, integer programming can be used.

22.3.3. *Which Constraints are Causing Bottlenecks?*

If the solution values are substituted into the original constraint equations, it can be seen that there are still 29 hours of surplus machine time and 2.5 hours of surplus assembly time (or similarly, the slack variables $x_4 = 29$, $x_5 = 2.5$). Thus, the constraints effectively limiting profit opportunities for the firm in this instance are the legal and liquidity constraints ($x_6, x_7 = 0$). Hence, these two constraints are causing bottlenecks.

22.3.4. *How Much More Profit is Being Lost Because of Constraints?*

Note that, under the optimal solution, *no* toy pistols will be produced in period 1. That this is indeed the optimal solution can be seen by solving for optimal profit contribution when even one pistol is required to be produced (i.e., a fifth constraint, $x_2 = 1$, is added to the problem formulation). Without showing the calculations, the final solution under this added condition is $x_1 = 8.6$, $x_2 = 1$, $x_3 = 4$, $x_4 = 29.4$, $x_5 = 3$, $x_6 = 0$, $x_7 = 0$, with a total profit contribution of \$22.60. Thus, profit contribution is diminished if even one toy pistol is produced. The reason for this decline in profitability can be seen from the constraints themselves. Production of one toy pistol requires that one less car be produced, so that $x_2 + x_3$ still equals 5. Although this shift in production releases financial resources which enable the firm to produce 0.1 additional Krazie Kubes, the added profit contribution from the Kubes is insufficient to offset the loss in profit contribution from one less car. Therefore, total profit contribution is reduced. The final tableau shows this effect directly. Column x_2 shows that, for the constraint to remain fulfilled, production of an additional pistol requires a corresponding reduction of one unit in x_3, an increase of 0.1 in x_1, and a reduction of \$0.90 in the profit contribution.

22.3.5. *How Do the Constraints Affect the Solution?*

The effect of the legal constraints can be demonstrated by showing the effect of a one-unit relaxation of the law (that is, $x_2 + x_3 \leq 6$). The optimal solution under this new constraint is $x_1 = 8.2$, $x_2 = 0$, $x_3 = 6$, $x_7 = 0$. Thus, the legal and financial constraints are still limiting (x_6, x_7 are still equal to 0), but the profit contribution has increased by \$2.70 to \$26.20. Again, this is depicted in the final tableau, in which a change in profitability of 27/10 is associated with Column x_6. Note that for those constraints (machine and assembly hours, x_4 and x_5) that do not limit production in the optimal solution, the profit contribution associated with the variable column is 0. Similarly, then, the effect of the non-renewed loan can be obtained from the final tableau; that is, according to Column x_7, an increase of \$1 in funds available to the firm would increase profit contribution by \$0.10. Conversely, this indicates that the firm would be willing to pay up to \$0.10 for each new dollar of financing it could obtain (or pay an interest rate of up to 10%) per period. This information enables the firm to evaluate the effect of the terms of any proposed loan on the firm's profitability.

It must be noted, however, that there are limits to the profitability of additional financing (or a relaxation of the legal constraint). These results from the fact that, as credit availability is increased other constraints that previously were not limiting, may in turn become bottlenecks to production. There is a limit, then on how much additional financing the firm can profitably acquire at \$0.10 per period.

This limit can be found by examining the operation of the other constraints as production is increased. Since the law still limits car and pistol production, new financing will be used to produce Krazie Kubes. From Column, it can be seen that each 1/10 increase in Kube production will use

6/10 hour of additional machine time and 1/2 hour of additional assembly time. Remembering that there are only 29 surplus machine hours and 2.5 surplus assembly hours, it is obvious that one of these two constraints will eventually become a limit to increased production in its turn, and additional financing will no longer be effective to increase total profit contribution. To find the limit of financing effectiveness, then, we simply divide 29 (machine hours) and 2.5 (assembly hours) by their corresponding utilization rates, 6/10 and 1/2 hour, obtaining \$48.33 and \$5, respectively. Thus, the small sum \$5 indicates that assembly hours will become limiting first. At this point, this new bottleneck will cause a change in the nature of the optimal solution and a corresponding change in emphasis among the product lines; after \$5 of additional financing is acquired, then the marginal value of more financing becomes 0.

Similarly, it is worthwhile to the firm to ease the legal constraint (perhaps by lobbying the legislature) only up to the point where yet another constraint would limit total profit contribution. If the law is repealed (i.e., the legal constraint is removed from the original problem), the optimal solution becomes $x_1 = 0$, $x_2 = 30$, $x_3 = 0$, $x_4 = 10$, $x_5 = 0$, $x_7 = 40$. There is no x_6 corresponding to the legal constraint. Since $x_2 + x_3$ now equals 30, any ceiling on production imposed by the legislature beyond this maximum of 30 would be superfluous to the firm's production problem; hence, relaxing the legal constraint (or efforts to change the law) has a marginal value of 0 after 30. Thus, the questions originally posed by the planning staff have been answered through the LP solution.

22.3.6. *Duality and Shadow Prices*

Every LP problem has an associated "dual" problem, which provides another way to view the primal solution; that is, (i) the dual solution table has all the same values, but they are in transposed positions, and (ii) dual solution values are, of course, found in the $\Delta\pi$ row of the primal under the slacks.

The standard LP model is:

$$\text{Maximize } z = \sum_{j=1}^{n} c_j x_j. \tag{22.9}$$

Subject to

$$\sum_{j=1}^{n} a_{ij} x_j \leq b_1 \quad (i = 1, 2, \ldots, m),$$

$$x_j \geq 0 \quad (j = 1, 2, \ldots, n).$$

The Dual Model is:

$$\text{Minimize } y = \sum_{i=1}^{m} b_i u_i. \tag{22.10}$$

Subject to

$$\sum_{i=1}^{m} a_{ij} u_i \geq c_j \quad (j = 1, 2, \ldots, n),$$
$$u_i \geq 0 \quad (i = 1, 2, \ldots, m).$$

The economic meaning of the dual problem can be illustrated by using the previous example of the ABC Toy Company. Transforming our original (or primal) problem into its dual gives the following:

$$6u_1 + 5u_2 + 10u_4 \geq 1,$$
$$3u_1 + 2u_2 + u_3 + 2u_4 \geq 2,$$
$$4u_1 + 3u_2 + u_3 + 3u_4 \geq 3,$$
$$u_i \geq 0 \quad (i = 1, 2, 3, 4),$$

for the constraints, and

$$\min y = 100u_1 + 60u_2 + 5u_3 + 100u_4,$$

for the objective function.

Each constraint in the dual problem can be thought of as a simple marginal-cost versus marginal-revenue constraint. In other words, u_1 through u_4 in these constraints are inputted values (or shadow prices, or marginal values) for machine capacity, assembly capacity, legal constraint, and financial constraint, respectively, whose values, when found, are such that their marginal cost is equal to their marginal revenue (or profit contribution) in the optimal solution, and their marginal cost is greater than their marginal revenue for those not in the optimal solution. For instance, $6u_1 + 5u_2 + 10u_4 \geq 2$ ensures that the resources (6 machine hours, 5 assembly hours, and \$10 of liquid resources) necessary for production of one Krazie Kube, when multiplied by their inputted values, will be at least as large as its profit contribution, \$2. Thus, the marginal cost of producing a Krazie Kube will be greater than or equal to its marginal revenue under the constraint. Of course, production of Krazie Kubes will be pushed to the point where its marginal revenue *equals* marginal cost: if MC $\geq$ MR, *no* Kubes will be produced.

The optimal values (u_1 through u_4) must be such as to minimize the objective function, $100u_1 + 60u_2 + 5u_3 + 100u_4$, the total inputted value of the firm's resources. The objective is minimized (the total value of the firm's resources is minimized) because the *minimization* of the opportunity *cost* of resources used in production is equivalent to *maximizing* the *profit* from production.

Solving for the optimal inputted values, $u_1 = 0$, $u_2 = 0$, $u_3 = \$2.70$, and $u_4 = \$0.10$. The inputted value of the legal constraint (u_3) is therefore seen to be \$2.70, as was also found in the optimal primal tableau. Similarly, the shadow price of the two constraints for machine and assembly hours (u_1 and u_2) are equal to 0. As was found previously, the marginal value of additional units of machine or assembly time is 0 because these constraints are not binding in the optimal solution. From economic theory, at the optimum, the marginal value of a factor of production is equal to its average value. Thus, the total inputted value of the firm's factors of production (its total profit contribution) is: $\$2.70 \times 5$ (the inputted value of the legal constraint times its capacity) $+\$0.10 \times 100$, or \$23.50 total.

Thus, the primal-problem formulation can be used to solve for optimal production rates; the dual formulation, in turn, can be used to solve for the inputted value of the resources involved in the firm's production.

22.3.7. *Short-term Financial Planning*

Short-term financial planning generally deals with the interface between the short-run cash requirements of the firm and the times stream of cash available for a firm's long-run financing strategy. This task can be divided into two parts: the acquisition of funds required to supplement long-term funds, and the provision of short-run financing and investment sources to buffer differences in timing of net cash outflows and inflows between successive subperiods.

Both financial-statement simulator and mathematical programming can be used to do short-term financial planning. Stone (1973) used the financial-statement simulator approach to study cash planning and credit-line determination. The statement-simulator approach will be discussed in Chapter 23 in dealing with long-term financial planning. The LP technique has been used by Mao (1967), Robicheck, Teichroew, and Jones (1965), and Pogue and Bussard (1972) to do short-term financial planning. Pogue and Bussard's objective function minimizes the total financing cost. The constraints used by Pogue and Bussard are: (i) constraints on the financing options, (ii) marketable-securities constraints, (iii) sources and uses constraints, (iv) liquidity-reserve constraints, and (v) financial-ratio constraints. The application of LP to long-term financial planning will be discussed in Chapter 23 in detail. Most recently, Sartoris and Hill (1983) have used the capital budgeting method to develop a generalized cash-flow approach for short-term financial decisions.

With the current proliferation of computers, there are a variety of canned programs for solving LP problems. These programs include Lindo, EZLP, MPOS, and others. There are several advantages in these programs. Primarily, they take the drudgery out of solving the problem. These programs also formulate the answer in a way that is easier to understand.

22.4. Goal Programming*

22.4.1. *Introduction*

GP, unlike LP, takes into account more than one goal in arriving at a solution. GP is a satisfying formulation, in which the best compromise of all the goals is made. With all the goals moved into the objective function, only the true constraints remain as constraints. With GP, management can consider multiple goals with different priorities. The priority ranking is of utmost importance when management attempts to "satisfice" incompatible goals. We will consider the mechanics of GP through a working-capital example developed by Sartoris and Spruill (1974).[1]

In contrast to LP, GP does not use only one goal or measure of performance (e.g., profit or cost), which is optimized subject to a set of constraints. Rather, use of GP assumes that there are multiple goals (e.g., attaining (i) a certain level of profitability while attaining (ii) a certain level of utilization of a scarce resource). Then, rather than maximizing or minimizing, an objective function is formulated that measures the absolute deviations from desired goals; *this* objective function is then minimized. In an LP formulation the value of the objective function is found, such that minimum or maximum values of the constraints are not violated. In a GP formulation, constraints can be violated but such violations are penalized based upon the user's priorities.

[1]A major portion of this section is reprinted from Sartoris and Spruill (1974), by permission of the authors and *Financial Management*.

Perhaps an example will best illustrate the concepts of GP. Consider a new company that produces two products, X and Y. The company has a total of 15 production hours available; each unit of product X requires three hours of production time, while each unit of product Y requires one hour. The company will allow the use of overtime, but prefers to use at most 15 hours of production time. The company's marketing department has determined that the company could sell, at most, 10 units of product X and, at most, 6 units of product Y. Since one goal of the new company is market penetration, the company would like to sell as close to the maximum number of units of each product as possible. Finally, each unit of product X generates revenue of \$10, while each unit of product Y generates revenue of \$8. The goal that the company's stockholders consider most important is net revenue. In fact, they expect net revenue of \$75 and are averse to any less.

Three goals can be distinguished: (1) minimizing the amount of overtime; (2) maximizing market penetration; and (3) attaining revenue as close as possible to \$75. In terms of importance to the company, goal (3) is more important than goal (2), which is more important than goal (1).

Let d_i^+ represent an upside deviation from goal i and d_i^- a downside deviation, where both d_i^+ and d_i^- are non-negative numbers. Let the p_1, p_2, and p_3 multipliers in the objective function express the priority relationship described in the preceding paragraph, where (the P values allow us to treat incommensurable goals, that is, those which cannot be compared directly). For a more complete discussion of this, see Lee (1971). With these definitions the model for our problem is:

$$\text{Minimize } Y = P_1 d_1^+ + P_2 d_2^- + P_2 d_3^- + P_3 d_4^-, \tag{22.11a}$$

subject to

$$3X + Y + d_1^+ = 15 \text{ (hours)}, \tag{22.11b}$$

$$X + d_2^- = 10 \text{ (units of product } X), \tag{22.11c}$$

$$Y + d_3^- = 6 \text{ (units of product } Y), \tag{22.11d}$$

$$10X + 8Y + d_4^{--} = 7 \text{ (revenue)}, \tag{22.11e}$$

$$X, Y, d_1^+, d_2^-, d_3^-, d_4^{--} \geq 1. \tag{22.11f}$$

This problem can now be solved using the ordinary simplex method as indicated in Appendix 22.A for solving LP problems. It should be noted that d_i^+ are not slack variables in the usual LP sense, since their coefficients in the objective function are non-zero. The implication is that all constraints in the program are equality constraints, and there is a penalty if the constraints are not met exactly.

22.4.2. *Application of GP to Working-Capital Management*

The following illustration developed by Sartoris and Spruill (1974) uses LP and GP together to develop a one-period financial-decision model that includes both the profitability and the liquidity objectives. One of the goals used in the GP formulation will be derived from a standard LP model used to maximize net present values of the firm, subject only to technical constraints.

The ABC Company manufactures two products, Y and Z, which can be sold either for cash or on credit. The sales can be made either from production during the period or from beginning inventory. See Table 22.5 for information on costs, demand, inventory, and production hours.

The firm has available a maximum of 1,000 hours for production. The company incurs a carrying cost of 10% of the value of the ending inventory. ABC can obtain a loan (secured by the ending inventory) which has a cost of 5% for the period and which can have a maximum value of 75% of the ending inventory. The sale of one unit for cash creates a net cash inflow equal to the production costs plus the credit costs. The carrying cost for the ending inventory is a cash drain for the period. An additional cash inflow of 95% of the value of the loan (the value of the loan minus 5% interest cost) can also be obtained.

ABC managers would like to obtain as much profit during the period as possible. However, they also want an ending cash balance of $75 with downside deviations from this amount being less desirable than upside deviations. At the same time they feel that an opportunity cost of 5% exists for carrying an ending cash balance. In addition, the management would like to obtain an end-of-period current ratio of 2:1 and a quick ratio of 1:1

Table 22.5. Data for ABC company.

	Maximum sales (units)		Price per unit	Cost/unit ($)		Profit/unit ($)		Beginning inventory	Hours used per unit
Product	Cash	Credit	($)	Production cost	Credit cost	Cash	Credit	(units)	produced
Y	150	100	40	35	0.50	5	4.5	60	2
Z	175	250	52.50	45	1.00	7.5	6.5	30	4

with either upside or downside deviations from these goals being possible but undesirable. For simplicity only, the firm presently has $150 in current liabilities; this is not expected to change throughout the period unless the firm obtains an inventory loan.

Before this set of goals can be incorporated in a GP formulation, it is necessary to specify some quantified goal for profit. The managers could choose some arbitrary profit figure as their goal, but this would not be consistent with the actual goal of maximum possible profit. A method of quantifying the profit goal is first to determine the maximum profit that could be obtained if the working-capital goals were not present. An LP formulation is particularly appropriate for this purpose.

For the above illustration the objective function for the LP formulation would be:

$$\begin{aligned}
\text{Max profits} &= \begin{pmatrix}\text{Revenue for}\\ \text{the period}\end{pmatrix} \text{ less } \begin{pmatrix}\text{Any costs charged}\\ \text{to the period}\end{pmatrix}\\
&= \$5\begin{pmatrix}\text{units Y sold}\\ \text{for cash}\end{pmatrix} + \$4.5\begin{pmatrix}\text{units Y sold}\\ \text{for credit}\end{pmatrix}\\
&\quad + \$7.5\begin{pmatrix}\text{units Z sold}\\ \text{for cash}\end{pmatrix} + \$6.5\begin{pmatrix}\text{units Z sold}\\ \text{for credit}\end{pmatrix}\\
&\quad - (0.1)(\$35)\begin{pmatrix}\text{ending inventory}\\ \text{of Y}\end{pmatrix}\\
&\quad - (0.1)(\$45)\begin{pmatrix}\text{ending inventory}\\ \text{of Z}\end{pmatrix}\\
&\quad - (0.05)\begin{pmatrix}\text{value of}\\ \text{loan}\end{pmatrix} - (0.05)\begin{pmatrix}\text{ending cash}\\ \text{balance}\end{pmatrix}.
\end{aligned}$$

This objective function is to be maximized subject to the following constraints: sales $\leq$ production capacity plus beginning inventory; sales $\leq$ maximum demand; ending cash balance ≥ 0; value of the loan $\leq$ (0.75)(value of ending inventory); and the number of units withdrawn from inventory must be less than or equal to number of units sold.

Solution of this LP problem resulted in a profit of $2,698.84 for the period, obtained by selling 150 units of Y for cash, 175 units of Z for cash, and 44.8 units of Z on credit. The ending inventory, cash balance, and loan are all zero. Since the inventory is zero, the current ratio and the quick ratio are equal at a value for 15.69. The maximum profit physically possible for the firm turns out to be $2,698.94, and this becomes the *profit* goal for the GP formulation.

We are now ready to use GP to incorporate into the decision process the conflicting goals specified by ABC management. The firm's goals are: (1) the maximum possible profit of \$2,698.94, (2) an ending cash balance of \$75, (3) an ending current ratio of 2:1, and (4) an ending quick ratio of 1:1. As explained earlier, these goals are incorporated in the model by creation of variables representing deviations from the goal and use of the simplex method to minimize these deviations. For illustration we used three possible sets of priorities: (1) the profit goal has a much higher priority than any of the working-capital goals; (2) the working-capital goals have a much higher priority than the profit goals, and (3) all goals have relatively similar priorities. (See Appendix 22.B for a mathematical formulation of the GP problem for this illustration.)

It should be noted here that in actual practice ABC managers may or may not have a feel for the priority of each goal. If they do have this feel, they could simply assign coefficients for the deviation variables based on these priorities. However, if these priorities do not exist clearly in the minds of the managers, the GP approach is still extremely useful. In a very short period of time, with the aid of a computer, the managers can set an entire range of possible priority situations and associated goal trade-offs. By selecting the solution that best meets their needs, they are implicitly establishing a set of priorities after the fact. Whether before or after the fact, the optimal solution for the managers, determined after examining a set of alternatives and associated goal trade-offs, is useful. Thus, the method can be used for situations where the manager knows the exact weights to be placed on deviation variables, but knows nothing about his priorities. The three sets of priorities chosen to illustrate the method should adequately represent a series of alternatives that would be presented to management.

To show the effects of these three sets of priorities on the profitability and liquidity goals, arbitrary values were assigned to the coefficients of the variables representing deviations from the goals. See Table 22.6 for the values of the coefficients that were used.

The effects of the three different sets of priorities are given in Table 22.7. For set 1, where profit has highest priority, results are identical to the LP solutions. In effect, the priority of the profit goal is so high in relation to the working-capital goals that these lower-priority goals are ignored, in practical effect. When the liquidity goals have much higher priorities than the profit goal, the cash and the quick ratio are at their desired values, while the current ratio is 10% higher and profit is only \$491.25 (see Table 22.7). When the priorities are similar for all goals, the cash balance is equal to

Table 22.6. Coefficients for deviation variables associated with three sets of priorities in GP.

	Coefficient Value		
Deviation variable	Set 1*	Set 2**	Set 3***
Downside profit	999.0	0.05	6.0
Downside cash	4.0	999.0	5.0
Upside cash	3.5	999.0	2.5
Downside current ratio	40.0	999.0	5.0
Upside current ratio	40.0	999.0	5.0
Downside quick ratio	40.0	999.0	5.0
Upside quick ratio	40.0	999.0	5.0

*Profit has a much higher priority than the working-capital goal.
**The working-capital goals have a much higher priority than the profit goal.
***The priorities for all goals are similar.

Table 22.7. Results of the goal-programming solution using three sets of priorities.

	Actual Value		
Goal	Set 1	Set 2	Set 3
Profit = $2,698.94	$2,698.94	$491.25	$857.84
Cash = $75	$0	$75	$75
Current Ratio = 2:1	15.7:1	2.2:1	3.4:1
Quick Ratio = 1:1	15.7:1	1:1	3.4:1

the goal of $75, the quick current ratios have risen to 3.4:1, and the profit is $857.84 (see Table 22.7).

Table 22.8 gives the sales and end-of-period balances resulting from use of the three different sets of priorities in the GP problem. Results generated with the second set of priorities indicate that, to approach the desired values of the current and quick ratios, it is necessary to increase the level of current liabilities. This necessitated some ending inventory to support the inventory loan.

A comparison of the results for set 2 and set 3 indicates that when the priority on the working-capital goals is high, the penalty for upside deviation forces the current and quick ratios down, but it also reduces the profit. At this point the management of ABC might want to reconsider specification of their set of goals, with particular attention being given to the undesirability of too high current and quick ratio.

Table 22.8. Sales and end-of-period balances associated with the three sets of priorities used in the goal programs.

Item	Value		
	Set 1	Set 2	Set 3
Cash sales Y (units)	150.00	40.52	60.00
Credit sales Y (units)	—	19.48	—
Cash sales Z (units)	175.00	—	21.59
Credit sales Z (units)	44.84	3.56	8.41
Ending inventory Y (units)	—	—	—
Ending inventory Z (units)	—	26.42	—
Cash balance ($)	—	75.00	75.00
Loan outstanding ($)	—	891.83	—

22.4.3. *Summary and Remarks on Goal Programming*

For illustration, we have used different sets of priorities to demonstrate their effect on the attainment of profitability and liquidity goals. In a practical application of this technique, managers presumably would have some subjective priorities they would attach to their goals. However, while their priorities might not be so concretely formed that they could specify absolute weights, they would probably be able to specify some relative priorities, such as upside deviations from cash being $\frac{1}{2}$ to $\frac{1}{3}$ as bothersome as downside deviations from the current ratio, and downside deviations from the current ratio being only $\frac{1}{2}$ as important as the downside deviations from profit. The use of relative priorities allows the problem of meeting profitability and liquidity goals to be approached simultaneously, in a manner similar to that employed in this chapter. In other words, managers choose some arbitrary set of values that approximate the importance of various goals, and observe the result when these values are used as coefficients in the objective function of the GP. Then the managers allow these values to change and determine the sensitivity of the final result. The mangers can thus choose the particular mix they feel best achieves their desired goals. This approach may help managers understand which of their specified goals are hardest to attain and may even cause them to reassess their goals and/or priorities.

A logical extension of the simplified model utilized here, but by no means a simple one, would be to make it a multi-period model incorporating discounting for the time value of money. Since a realistic model must deal with uncertainty, it would be necessary to adjust for varying degrees of risk.

A possible, but to our knowledge as yet unexplored, extension would be for different aspects of risk to be employed in a goal framework.

Financial-planning problems with multiple conflicting objectives have received much attention in the finance literature. Two methods that can be applied in such a case are GP and multiple-objective LP. While GP is the solution method most often applied to such problems, its application may result in inefficient decisions. Sealey (1978) has used a banking example with multiple-objective LP to compare the two methods.

22.5. Programming Approach to Cash Transfer and Concentration**

With an increase in the level of interest rates, it becomes even more apparent that cash is a valuable asset, which must be given careful attention. Many firms have short-term lines of credit to help with temporary cash-flow problems; e.g., the bills are due on the 10th but the receivables do not come due until the 20th. Many cash-management problems have been dealt with through the use of LP models.

One area that has received a great deal of attention is the cash-concentration and cash-transfer problem. Cash concentration is the moving of money from the depository bank to the concentration bank. A situation requiring cash concentration usually arises when a company has a main headquarters office and several branch offices, each with some disbursement and receipt authority. The company must balance several factors in transferring funds out of the "local" (depository) bank to the "central" (concentration) bank. Each branch needs a certain amount of working funds, so the headquarters must not transfer out too much money. On the other hand, too much idle cash sitting in a branch's account has an opportunity cost associated with it. The third major factor is that each transfer of funds has a cost associated with it; i.e., there is a bank charge for the transfer.

The goal, then, is to simultaneously minimize the cost of maintaining the depository account and the transfer cost, while maintaining a target level of cash.

Stone and Hill (1980) have addressed this cash-transfer scheduling problem, and a large portion of this section is adapted from their paper. This section presents background for the cash-transfer problem, reviews

**A major portion of this section is reprinted from Stone and Hill (1980), by permission of the authors of *Financial Management*.

contemporary practice and its deficiencies, properly formulates the task as an *optimization* problem, and describes the solution benefits.

22.5.1. *Transfer Mechanisms*

Three mechanisms for moving money between accounts will be considered: wires, depository transfer checks (DTC's), and electronic image transfers. A DTC is an ordinary check restricted "for deposit only" at a designated bank. The third transfer mechanism has only recently come into existence, namely, an electronic check image processed through automated clearing houses rather than through a wire network. It has a one-business-day clearing time rather than the same-day transfer time of wires. It costs less than a DTC and is often called a "paperless DTC" or an "electronic DTC". Readers are referred to Stone and Hill (1981) for more on transfer mechanisms, alternative ways to use them, comparative costs and transfer times, and the procedures to decide on the appropriate mechanism. In this paper, it is assumed that the transfer method and the company's banking system are given. The problem is to specify a schedule of initiation times and amounts.

22.5.2. *Cash-Transfer Scheduling: Contemporary Practice*

Most companies, probably more than 80% of the 1,200 largest industrial firms, make a daily transfer of each day's reported deposits. This is an outgrowth of most of the third-party information-gathering services and most bank-transfer preparation-initiation services. Daily transfer of whatever is deposited is a simple solution to the scheduling problem. This simplicity may, however, be attained at considerable cost.

In recent years, progressive companies have taken advantage of centralized information systems to move away from simple daily-transfer schedules. By using various rules of thumb, such as managing about a target, anticipation and weekend timing, a number of companies have benefited from substantial reductions in scheduling costs. A number of banks have also adapted their transfer-preparation services to accommodate non-daily transfers using some of these rule-of-thumb scheduling procedures.

(a) Managing about a target

Table 22.9 depicts a daily transfer of each day's deposits. It shows a cash build-up during the day and then a transfer that leaves a $20,000 target

Table 22.9. A daily transfer of each day's deposits.

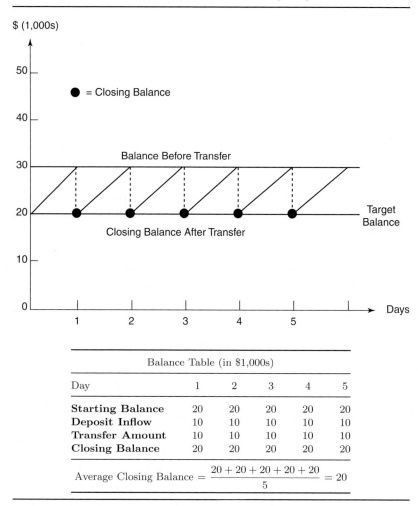

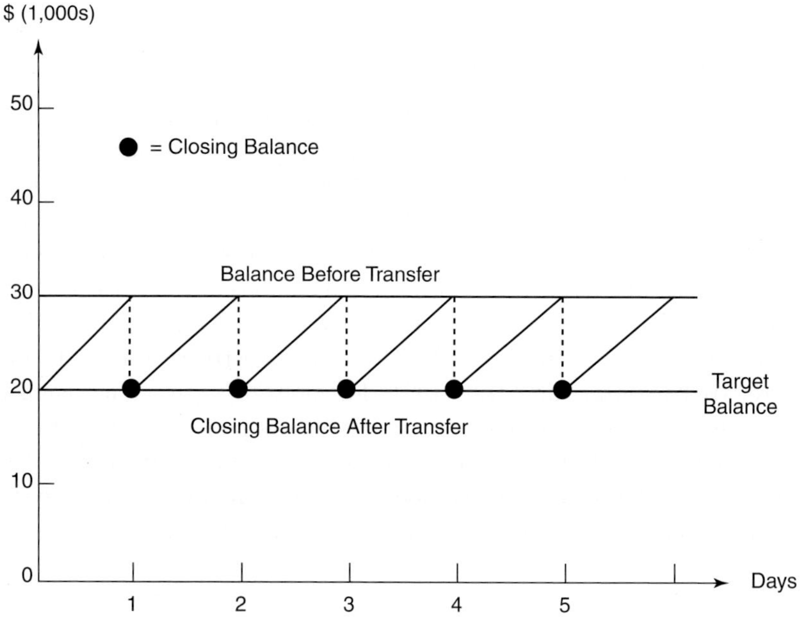

Balance Table (in $1,000s)

Day	1	2	3	4	5
Starting Balance	20	20	20	20	20
Deposit Inflow	10	10	10	10	10
Transfer Amount	10	10	10	10	10
Closing Balance	20	20	20	20	20

$$\text{Average Closing Balance} = \frac{20 + 20 + 20 + 20 + 20}{5} = 20$$

closing balance. Table 22.10 depicts managing about the \$20,000 target balance over the transfer period. Both schedules give the same average balance, but the schedule in Table 22.10 involves one-fifth the transfers. While the illustration is oversimplified in using a uniform deposit schedule and ignoring both transfer-time delays and weekends, it suggests the potential for significant cost reductions. For example, if each transfer cost \$50.00, then the schedule listed in Table 22.9 will cost $\$50.00 \times 5 = \$250.00$ and the schedule listed in Table 22.10 will cost only \$50.00 if the interest

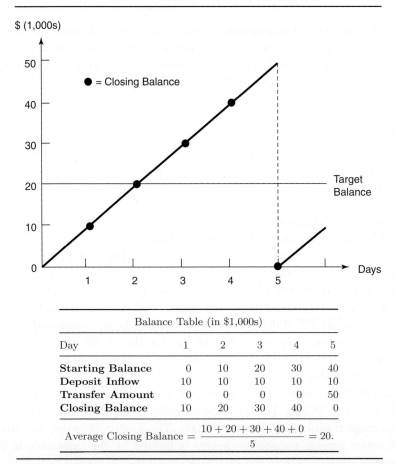

Table 22.10. Managing about the target balance.

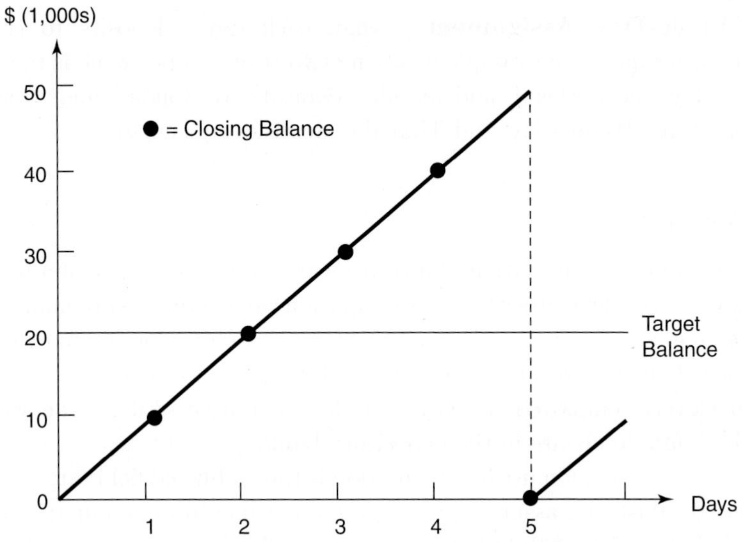

Balance Table (in $1,000s)					
Day	1	2	3	4	5
Starting Balance	0	10	20	30	40
Deposit Inflow	10	10	10	10	10
Transfer Amount	0	0	0	0	50
Closing Balance	10	20	30	40	0

$$\text{Average Closing Balance} = \frac{10+20+30+40+0}{5} = 20.$$

expense is not included. Other methods used to calculate the transfer cost will be discussed later in this section.

Moreover, note that, in addition to reducing transfers, managing about the target enables an initial withdrawal of the company's investment in the target balance. The target balance is then provided, on average, by using the deposit flow. Hence, managing about a target means more cash sooner.

There are several popular variants of managing about a target:

(1) **Trigger Point**. Initiate a transfer whenever cumulative deposits exceed a prespecified level. This procedure is characterized by a trigger point and return point.

(2) **Periodic**. Transfer at periodic intervals — e.g., every third business day.
(3) **Whole-Day Assignment**. Assign each day's deposits to certain transfer days. An example involving two transfers per week is to assign Friday, the weekend, and Monday deposits to Monday, and to assign Tuesday, Wednesday, and Thursday deposits to Thursday.

(b) Anticipation

Anticipation is the initiation of a transfer before formal notice of a balance addition at the depository bank. Anticipation can eliminate communication, processing, and/or clearing delays. Hence, it can reduce or eliminate excess balance. The process can accelerate transfers by one to three days' deposits, when cleverly employed. It may, but does not necessarily, mean writing checks *before* funds are in the depository bank.

The most common use of anticipation is the "adjusted field target" technique. To illustrate, assume that a company wants to maintain an average filed balance of $8,000, but it observes from its bank statement that the combination of communication, processing, and clearing delays leaves, on the average, $7,000 of deposits in the process of being transferred. Hence, its actual average balance is $15,000. To hit the $8,000 target, the cash manager makes a one-time transfer of $7,000 from the field bank and runs with an "adjusted field target" or "effective field target" of $1,000. Because of the $7,000 average transfer-in-process, the actual average balance is the true target of $8,000. This procedure implicitly assumes an average level of average transfer-in-process of $7,000. The ability, however, to extract the entire average transfer-in-process is limited by the variability in the deposits, especially by cycles such as a strong weekly cycle.

An extreme case, suppose that the $15,000 balance was the result of a single deposit of $105,000 on Monday, which is transferred out on Tuesday ($105,000/7 = $15,000). No other deposits are made during the week. It would be impossible to remove the average excess of $7,000 with a one-time transfer, since that would result in an overdraft.

In this case, the company could employ "time-varying anticipation", which reflects variation in the deposit pattern. While there are many versions, most add to the known balance available for transfers of some fraction of the additional deposits expected before the transfer clears. For example, if a weekend deposit of $105,000 is expected to be received at the deposit bank on Monday morning, a DTC for $105,000 could be deposited the previous Friday. By the time the DTC clears, the deposit will have been received.

22.5.3. *Weekend Timing and Dual Balances*

When the DTC availability time granted at the concentration bank is less than the clearing time back to the depository bank, there is an opportunity for a dual-balance benefit. To illustrate, assume a $10,000 DTC transfer initiated on Tuesday with on business-day availability but two business day clearing. On Wednesday, the company receives a $10,000 available addition at the concentration bank, but the funds are not removed from the depository bank until Thursday. The company has a "dual balance" on Wednesday in the sense that the same funds are available balances in two banks. The source of the dual balance might be Federal Reserve float arising from slow check clearings, or it could result from the concentration bank's granting faster availability than its actual clearing.

The dual-balance benefit can be increased by weekend timing. For instance, if the $10,000 DTC transfer were initiated on Thursday, there would be a $10,000 available addition at the concentration bank on Friday with the clearing delayed until Monday. Hence, with Thursday initiation there would be three days of dual balances (Friday, Saturday, Sunday) rather than one.

While the more common situation is for the clearing time to exceed the availability time, the opposite can occur. Clearing time could be faster than granted availability; then the company will have a balance in neither bank. In this case, weekend timing means avoiding weekends.

22.5.4. *Limitations of the Popular Techniques*

Each of the three techniques — meaning about a target, anticipation, and weekend timing — focuses on a different component of the transfer-scheduling cost. Managing about a target primarily reduces transfers, thereby reducing direct transfer costs. Anticipation takes advantage of time delays to get money out faster. It is appropriate when there is an "excess field balance", i.e., greater balance than is necessary to compensate the field bank. (In contrast, managing about a target balance implicitly assumes no excess balance, or at least no significant one.) Weekend timing increases the dual balances that arise from differences between actual clearing times and granted availability times. Such extra balances have value, however, only if they can be removed from the depository bank. Simply adding to an existing excess balance to obtain a larger excess does nothing for a company.

The difference in these objectives points up an obvious need to resolve conflicts. Some of the simpler versions of each technique actually preclude the use of the others. More sophisticated versions, which are not mutually exclusive, conflict. For instance, use of the popular trigger point rules precludes use of weekend timing, because the balance level determines the transfer initiation time. Likewise, use of periodic frequency also precludes systematic use of weekend timing unless the transfer frequency is one week or a multiple of a week. Using the simple adjusted-field-target version of anticipation also precludes using weekend timing, because the same amount as anticipated on each day of the week.

Anyone trying to resolve conflicts between the various versions of each rule-of-thumb technique quickly finds that trial-and-error transfer scheduling is a difficult task, especially when various constraints such as no overdraft and an appropriate average balance are explicitly recognized. The task is, in fact, logically equivalent to finding solutions to a larger number of simultaneous equations and then systematically comparing the solutions.

Finding good solutions is a difficult task even for one single depository bank. Finding good solutions for dozens or hundreds of depository banks clearly requires some kind of systematic procedure. Such a procedure should incorporate sophisticated versions of each scheduling technique and appropriately reflect trade-offs between direct transfer cost, excess balances, and any dual balances.

The mathematical program formulated in the next section is such a procedure. Its solution provides not just a good, but an optimal schedule.

22.5.5. *Mathematical-Programming Formulation*

We have used a one-week period to formulate the problem. Besides being simple for exposition, use of the one-week solution period is consistent with current practice, the often strong weekly cycle in field deposits, and the role of weekends.

(a) The Objective Function

As noted already, there are three considerations in cash-transfer scheduling — the direct-transfer charges, the value of any excess balances, and any dual-balance value. If CPT is the cost per transfer, and I is the appropriate daily interest rate for assessing the value of excess field deposits, the transfer scheduling cost (TSC) is the direct cost plus the interest value of excess field balances less the interest value of any dual balances:

$$\text{TSC} = \text{CPT}\begin{pmatrix}\text{Number of}\\ \text{transfers}\end{pmatrix} + 7 \cdot I(\text{EXCESS} - \text{ADBAL}). \tag{22.12}$$

EXCESS is the average balance over the solution period and ADBAL is the average dual balance. This formulation says a dual balance has value only if it can be removed from the depository bank. The interest rate provides a basis for comparing transfer charges and balances. The seven reflects the one-week solution period.

To express the objective function in terms of the transfer schedule and known parameters, let i be an index denoting days of the week. Further, let i be 1 on Monday, 2 on Tuesday, and so on, up to 7 for Sunday. The decision of cash-transfer scheduling is when to transfer and how much. Let δ_i be a zero-one decision variable that is one only if there is a transfer on day i and zero otherwise. Let T_i be the amount transferred. Of course, T_i must be zero unless δ_i is one. The number of transfers over the week is $\sum_{i=1}^{7} \delta_i$, since δ_i is one whenever there is a transfer and zero otherwise.

To express the average dual balance in terms of the transfer schedule, let A_i denote the number of calendar days (not business days) by which the clearing time exceeds the granted availability time when a transfer is initiated on day i. The A_i's is called *availability advantage coefficients.* To illustrate, assume that the granted availability is one business day and the clearing time is two business days on Monday, Tuesday, Wednesday, and Thursday, but one business day on Friday. Then, the schedule of availability advantage coefficients is $A_1 = A_2 = A_3 = 1$, $A_4 = 3$, and $A_5 = 0$. In addition, we set A_6 and A_7 at zero, since there are no Saturday or Sunday transfers. For wires and electronic DTC's, all the A_i's are zero. For DTC's with faster clearing than granted availability, the A_i's would be negative.

With T_i denoting the amount transferred on day i, the dollar days of availability advantage is A_iT_i. The total dollar days of dual balances from a given week's transfers are the sum from each day's transfers: $\sum_{i=1}^{7} A_iT_i$. The weekly average dual balance is one-seventh this amount.

The objective function of Eq. (22.12) can now be restated. Using $\sum_{i=1}^{7} \delta_i$ for the number of transfers and $(1/7)\sum_{i=1}^{7} A_iT_i$ for the average dual balance gives:

$$\text{TSC} = \text{CPT} \cdot \sum_{i=1}^{7} \delta_{\text{i}} + 7 \cdot I\left(\text{EXCESS} - \frac{1}{7}\sum_{i=1}^{7} A_iT_i\right). \tag{22.13}$$

The objective function is now expressed in terms of cost parameters (CPT and I), parameters of the banking system (the A_i's), and the decision variables characterizing the transfer schedule. The quantity EXCESS will be defined shortly in terms of the compensating balance constraint.

(b) Constraints on transfers include: average balance, flow balance, minimum balance, and maximum transfer.

Assume that a company pays its depository banks for service with balances. Hence, the average balance at the depository bank must be at least as large as the level necessary to pay for services. Let ABAL_i be the available balance on day i. The requirement that the average available balance be at least as large as the required balance for compensation means:

$$\left(\frac{1}{7}\right)\sum_{i=1}^{7}\text{ABAL}_i \geq \text{Required balance.} \tag{22.14}$$

It is necessary to reflect the fact that the required balance depends on the number of transfers. Let TAB denote the average available balance necessary before compensation for transfers. If TCDB is the transfer cost of the depository bank and ECRDB is the earnings credit rate, then TCDB/ECRDB is the required balance per transfer. TAB and (TCDB/ECRDB)(Number of transfers) are the two components of the average balance. Constraint (22.14) can be rewritten as:

$$\frac{1}{7}\sum_{i=1}^{7}\text{ABAL}_\text{i} \geq \text{TAB} + \left(\frac{\text{TCDB}}{\text{ECRDB}}\right)\sum_{i=1}^{7}\delta_i. \tag{22.15}$$

Again, use has been made of the fact that the number of transfers is the sum of the δ_i's.

By definition, EXCESS is the amount by which the average available balance exceeds the required balance. With the additional requirement that EXCESS be non-negative, Constraint (22.15), the average balance constraint, can be written as:

$$\frac{1}{7}\sum_{i=1}^{7}\text{ABAL}_\text{i} - \text{EXCESS} = \text{TAB} + \left(\frac{\text{TCDB}}{\text{ECRDB}}\right)\sum_{i=1}^{7}\delta_i. \tag{22.16}$$

Several special cases are pertinent. When a company pays its depository banks fees for their transfer services, the charge is included in CPT in the objective function, but TCDB is set equal to zero in Eq. (22.16). If balances are not used for compensation at all, set both TAB and TCDB at zero.

In this case, any positive available balance is an excess. By appropriate choice of parameters, Expression (22.16) handles all cases of deposit bank compensation, namely, (1) all balances, (2) some fees and some balances, and (3) all fees.

A stable solution is one in which there is no period-to-period increase or decrease in balances at the depository bank. Requiring a stable solution prevents distortion from building up or drawing down balances. To ensure a stable solution requires that the sum of each week's transfers equals the sum of each week's available additions. This is the flow balance constraint, which can be expressed as:

$$\sum_{i=1}^{7} T_i = \sum_{i=1}^{7} AA_i. \tag{22.17}$$

The ledger balance can never be negative; ledger overdrafts are prohibited. In addition, some banks may even require a positive available balance. Some companies may also want minimum balance restrictions. Let LMIN_i and AMIN_i, respectively, denote the *pro forma* values of the minimum allowable ledger and available balances on day i; and let LBAL_i and ALBAL_i, respectively, denote the ledger balance and available balance on day i. Minimum balance constraints that reflect both bank restrictions and any company policy limits are:

$$\mathrm{LBAL}_i \geq \mathrm{LMIN}_i \quad \text{and} \quad \mathrm{ABAL}_i \geq \mathrm{AMIN}_i. \tag{22.18}$$

In the absence of anticipation, the maximum amount that can be transferred without a *pro forma* violation of the minimum-balance restriction is the closing balance on the previous day, less any transfers made but not yet cleared, less the minimum balance when the transfer clears in c days. The maximum transfer constraint in the absence of anticipation is:

$$T_i \leq \mathrm{LBAL}_{i-1} - (\text{Transfers yet to clear}) - \mathrm{LMIN}_{i+c}. \tag{22.19}$$

The quantity LBAL_{i-1} − (Transfers yet to clear) is an effective start-of-day balance. It is what the company knows about. The amount by which this balance exceeds the minimum on the clearing day is the amount available for transfer before anticipation. It is assumed that deposits for the day i are not know. If known, or if known, in part, these balances would be added to the right-hand side of Eq. (22.19).

Anticipation increases the amount available for transfer so that the maximum transfer constraints become:

$$T_i \leq \text{LBAL}_{i-1}(\text{Transfers yet to clear}) - \text{LMIN}_{i+c} + (\text{Amount anticipated}). \tag{22.20}$$

An analogous constraint can be written in terms of available balances and AMIN.

One possible constraint has not yet been mentioned or included: "whole-day assignment". For reasons of control, implementation ease, or compatibility with current information-control systems, some companies want all the deposits of a given day assigned to a particular transfer day. Alternatively, in the case of multiple deposits per day, they want all the deposits in a given time slot to be assigned to a particular transfer day.

An example of whole-day assignment would be to transfer the Monday and Tuesday deposits on Tuesday, transfer the Wednesday and Thursday deposits on Thursday, and transfer Friday's deposit on Friday. A whole-day restriction would preclude transferring some of Tuesday's deposits on Tuesday and some Thursday. Whole-day assignment considerably complicates the formulation. It means adding a set of integer assignment constraints to the mathematical program.

(c) Formulation Summary

Tables 22.11 and 22.12 summarize notation and the mathematical-programming formulation, adding some technical constraints such as integer restrictions and non-negativity. Additional restrictions such as no Saturday or Sunday transfers and company-specific restrictions are ignored in these exhibits, although there would be no problem in including them in the analysis. This formulation generalizes to an H-day solution horizon by replacing 7 by H.

(d) Deposit Variation

The mathematical-programming formulation develops a transfer schedule for an average deposit pattern, but it can reflect deposit variation. First, the parameters LMIN and AMIN can create a buffer balance to allow for deposit variation. Second, anticipation is generally limited to the fraction of yet-unknown deposits that a company is certain to receive before the

Table 22.11. Notation summary; key variables and parameters.

Active Decision Variables	
δ_i	$\equiv$ 0 – 1 transfer initiation variable for day i
T_i	$\equiv$ Transfer amount on day i
Implicit Decision Variables	
LBAL_i	$\equiv$ Ledger balance for day i
ABAL_i	$\equiv$ Available balance for day i
EXCESS	$\equiv$ Average available balance in excess of the required compensating balance
Objective Function Parameters	
CPT	$\equiv$ Cost per transfer
I	$\equiv$ Interest value of decision horizon
H	$\equiv$ Number of days in decision horizon
A_i	$\equiv$ Expected clearing time less granted availability time in calendar days
Policy Variables	
TAB	$\equiv$ Target average balance before transfer compensation
LMIN_i	$\equiv$ Minimum ledger balance
AMIN_i	$\equiv$ Minimum available balance
Deposit Schedule Parameters	
AA_i	$\equiv$ Available addition on day i
LA_i	$\equiv$ Ledger addition on day i
Other Deposit Bank Parameters	
TCDB	$\equiv$ Direct transfer cost per deposit at the depository bank
ECRDB	$\equiv$ Earnings credit rate at the depository bank
$C(i)$	$\equiv$ Business-day clearing time for transfers initiated on day i

transfer clears, so that anticipation incurs no exposure to an overdraft. Third, with daily deposit reporting, the usual information-control system records the daily error and cumulative variation between actual and *pro forma* deposits before a transfer clears. If any correction is necessary, it can always be done in time. The daily reporting and control means that a company need never be exposed to an overdraft by the schedules developed on the basis of an average deposit schedule, just as no overdraft exposure need occur when companies use any of the rule-of-thumb scheduling techniques for managing about a target. Fourth, translating the mathematical program's solution into transfer procedures includes adaptivity rules to reflect deposit variation. It is, for instance, straightforward either to reduce or to increase a planned transfer by an appropriate amount to reflect deviation from the *pro forma* deposit pattern. Hence, it is possible to have a

Table 22.12. A summary statement of the mathematical program.

$$\text{Minimize TSC} \equiv \text{CPT} \cdot \sum_{i=1}^{H} \delta_{\text{i}} + H \cdot I \cdot \text{EXCESS} - \text{I} \cdot \sum_{i=1}^{H} \text{A}_i \text{T}_i,$$

subject to:

$$(VH) \sum_{i=1}^{H} \text{ABAL}_i - \text{EXCESS} = \text{TAB} + (\text{TCDB/ECRDB}) \sum_{i=1}^{H} \delta_{\text{i}}, \qquad (22.\text{T}.1)$$

$$\sum_{i=1}^{H} T_i = \sum_{i=1}^{H} AA_i, \qquad (22.\text{T}.2)$$

$$\text{LBAL}_i \geq \text{LMIN}_i \qquad I = 1, \ldots, H, \qquad (22.\text{T}.3)$$

$$\text{ABAL}_i \geq \text{AMIN}_i \qquad i = 1, \ldots, H, \qquad (22.\text{T}.4)$$

$$T_i \leq \text{LBAL}_{i-1} - \text{LMIN}_{i+c(i)} - [\text{Transfers YET TO CLEAR}] + [\text{AMOUNT ANTICIPATED}], \qquad (22.\text{T}.5)$$

$$T_i \leq M\delta_i \qquad I = 1, \ldots, H, \qquad (22.\text{T}.6)$$

$$\delta_i = 0 \quad \text{or} \quad \delta_i = 1 \qquad i = 1, \ldots, H, \qquad (22.\text{T}.7)$$

$$\text{EXCESS} \geq 0; \quad T_i \geq 0 \quad I = 1, \ldots, H. \qquad (22.\text{T}.8)$$

Notes:

1. This formulation is for an H-day solution period; for the weekly solution $H = 7$.
2. For any days in which transfers are not permitted, T_i and δ_i are both set at zero in advance.
3. This formulation includes the balances ABAL_i and LBAL_i and Transfers yet to clear. Equations relating these variables to starting balance should be added for completeness, or the defining equations should be substituted for these variables.
4. In an operational formulation, Amount anticipated would be replaced by incorporating anticipation policy — for example, a proportion of ledger additions over the anticipation period.
5. In Eq. (22.T.6), M is a large number that is greater than any possible transfer. This constraint ensures that T_i is zero whenever δ_i is zero and unconstrained when δ_i is one. This constraint could also be $T_i\,(1 - \delta_i)$, which is non-linear but easier to use in a branch-and-bound framework.
6. To eliminate Saturday, Sunday, and holiday transfers, δ_i is set equal to zero for appropriate values of i.

system always tracking the *pro forma* balance of the model solution and, in general, averaging the transfer-scheduling cost of the objective function. Finally, a sense of ability to tolerate deposit variations can be obtained by simulating the solution and adaptivity rules over past deposit data to test robustness and even to make sure that the average improvement in scheduling cost is consistent with the improvement indicated by the objective function.

22.5.6. *Relation of Model Formulation to Current Practice*

Managing about a target balance is accomplished in the model by two constraints — the average balance and flow-balance restrictions. In contrast, a daily transfer to each day's deposits would force the required compensating balance to be provided daily rather than on average; flow balance would also be a daily restriction (e.g., a transfer equal to each day's reported deposits) rather than an average over the solution period.

This mathematical-programming method of managing about a target allows the target balance to adjust to reflect the transfer frequency. It is more general than any of the specific versions such as trigger point or periodic frequency. Typical programming solutions to actual problems rarely have a uniform trigger level. Likewise, they rarely have a periodic frequency except in the unusual case of a single transfer per week. Therefore, the restrictions of these rule-of-thumb methods of scheduling about a target involve some sacrifice in profit.

As already pointed out, anticipation is reflected in the mathematical-programming formulation by the maximum-transfer constraint. By allowing the amount anticipated to vary, the formulation permits the most general form of time-varying anticipation.

Dual balances are counted in the objective function of the mathematical-programming model and, as a result, the model will systematically shift transfers to pick up weekend effects only if the increased balance can be removed from the system and will exceed in value of any increase in transfer costs. This formulation of dual balances is more general than simple weekend timing. It allows for variation in the clearing time over each day of the week. For instance, it can reflect expected differences in Monday and Tuesday clear times. Thus, the formulation actually provides for general dual-balance timing with the usual weekend timing being a special case.

To summarize, the formulation properly trades off the components of transfer-scheduling cost. The model also includes each of the three generic scheduling procedures in their most general form. As a result, the transfer schedule from the mathematical program can never be worse than the schedules obtained from the rule-of-thumb procedures, and it is reasonable to expect model solutions to be significantly better.

(a) Implementation Tests

Stone and Hill have worked with the First National Bank of Chicago to develop a special-purpose solution algorithm and the necessary reports to implement the model. During 1979, the First National Bank of Chicago tested the model on a number of companies. Most of the tests were based on a subsample of each company's banks. Two classes of concentration problems were studied: field concentration and lockbox concentration.

(b) Field Concentration Tests

Field concentration is moving money from depository banks used by cash-generating field units. For companies making daily transfers of each day's deposit and using no systematic scheduling except possibly an adjusted field target, the model solution provided significant improvement over daily transfers. In particular, the model solutions were able to free up the equivalent of at least two days' average deposits.

Several test companies already practiced systematic scheduling. Some had even previously worked with the First National Bank of Chicago in applying the rule-of-thumb scheduling procedures, attaining significant improvement over daily transfers. Therefore, these companies provided at test of the value of the mathematical-programming formulation versus sophisticated use of rule-of-thumb procedures. The model solutions indicated improvements at least equivalent to freeing up one day's average deposits in every case. In some case, improvements equivalent to two days' average deposits were still found beyond those already obtained.

Skilled use of rule-of-thumb procedures was able to obtain only 40% to 60% of the total possible improvement over daily transfers. Moreover, very simple scheduling procedures, such as a trigger point with an adjusted target, typically could obtain only 15–30% of the total possible improvement.

(c) Lockbox Concentration

Lockbox concentration is moving money from a firm's lockbox banks. There were not many tests of lockbox concentration. While the model did generally find opportunities for significant cost improvements, there were also many cases where daily transfers were optimal. Moreover, in other cases, skilful use of rule-of-thumb procedures could produce solutions very close to the optimal solution of the mathematical program.

In another paper, Hill and Stone (1981) extend the cash concentration/transfer analysis. They consider the design of the cash concentration system. In the design stage, the selection of the depository and concentration banks is made.

The goal is two-fold: one, to make optimal selection choices; two, to make the co-assignment of depository banks to their concentration bank. In this system, there can be numerous levels of concentration subsystems. The reason for the leveling may be efficiency, lower total cost, differing responsibility levels within the corporation, or locality. It should be obvious that the middle-level concentration banks are also depository banks in the next level.

22.6. Summary

In this chapter, we have looked at a variety of financial-management problems and their solution through mathematical-programming techniques. As we have seen, LP and goal-programming are very useful. We have also considered certain working-capital problems, including cash concentration and scheduling. In the next chapter we will again be using our LP skills in long-range financial planning. We will use our knowledge gained from this chapter, in combination with other information, as inputs to our financial-planning models.

NOTES

1. Krouse (1974) has suggested a somewhat different multiple-objective programming technique for working-capital management. His procedure utilizes a hierarchical ordering of objectives and requires that they be satisfied sequentially in the implied order. First, the optimal solution is obtained with only the objective having the highest priority being considered. Since it is generally not possible for the other objectives to be satisfied when the first objective is at this optimum level, it is necessary to determine some acceptable suboptimal level. Next, a solution is obtained with consideration being given to the second objective and with the additional requirement that the first objective at least achieve this suboptimal level. If an acceptable solution is not obtainable for both objectives, it is necessary to revise the initial constraining level for the first objective and resolve the problem. When an acceptable solution is obtained for both objectives, an acceptable suboptimal value is specified for the second objective and the solution proceeds to the third objective. This procedure continues until all objectives are considered. In a GP, the user's priority weights establish the importance of the various goals rather than the order in which they must be satisfied; thus, a trade-off

between violations of the different objectives is automatically allowed in the solution.

2. Following Mao (1969) and others, GP can also be very useful in break-even analysis and in situations of inventory variation, varying production proportions, and where management has incompatible goals.
3. There are zero-one decision variables in this model, and thus, only the formulation will be shown. However, readers can, of course, use a zero-one algorithm on such a problem.

Problem Set

1. Briefly describe the basic steps and procedures used in applying LP techniques to working-capital management.
2. Define the following terms: objective function; constraints; shadow price; and "dual" problem.
3. How can GP be more useful than LP in solving financial problems? Please describe the basic procedures of goal-programming formulation and discuss the method of solving the goal-programming formulation.
4. Discuss how mathematical-programming techniques can be used to solve cash concentration and scheduling problems.
5. Briefly describe the procedures of using the simplex method to solve LP problems as discussed in Appendix 22.A of this chapter.
6. How can finance theory, accounting information, and programming techniques be used jointly to solve the working-capital management problems?
7. Let X_1 and X_2 be, respectively, the units of radios and TV sets produced in period 1. In addition, the objective function and constraints are:

   (i) $X_1 + X_2 \leq 4$ (assembly-time constraint);
   (ii) $3x_1 + X_2 \leq 10$ (machine time constraint);
   (iii) $X_1 + 4X_2 \leq 12$ (financial constraint);
   (iv) Maximize $X_1 + 2X_2$ (objective function);
   (v) $X_i \geq 0$ $(i = 1, 2)$ (non-negative conditions).

   (a) Discuss two possible methods to solve this problem.
   (b) Discuss how the LP technique can be used to do financial planning and forecasting.
   (c) How can the objective function for the LP type of financial-planning model be formulated?

Appendix 22.A. The Simplex Algorithm for Solving Eq. (22.8)

The procedure of using the simplex method to solve Eq. (22.8) can be described as follows:

Step 1. To convert inequality constraints into a system of equalities through the introduction of slack variables x_4, x_5, x_6, and x_7 as:

$$\begin{aligned} 6x_1 + 3x_2 + 4x_3 + x_4 &= 100 \\ 5x_1 + 2x_2 + 3x_3 + x_5 &= 60 \\ x_2 + x_3 + x_6 &= 5, \\ 10x_1 + 2x_2 + 3x_3 + x_7 &= 100. \end{aligned} \tag{22.A.1}$$

Step 2. To construct a tableau for representing the objective function and equality constraints.

In Tableau 1, the figures in first, second, ..., seventh column are, respectively, the coefficients of $x_1, x_2, \ldots, x_7$; the first four rows represent four equations in Eq. (22.A.1); the last row represents the objective function. Note that only x_4, x_5, x_6, and x_7 are basic variables in Tableau 1 and that remaining variables x_1, x_2, x_3 have been arbitrarily set equal to zero. With x_1, x_2, and x_3 all equal to zero, the remaining variables take on values as given in the last column of the tableau; that is $x_4 = 100$, $x_5 = 60$, $x_6 = 5$, and $x_7 = 100$. The numbers in the last column always represent the values of basic variables in a particular basic feasible solution.

Step 3. To obtain a new feasible solution. Basic feasible solution of Tableau 1 indicates zero profits for the firm. Clearly, this basic feasible

Tableau 1. Tableau for coefficient of 22.A.1.

		Real Variables			Slack Variables				
		x_1	x_2	x_3	x_4	x_5	x_6	x_7	
Slack Variables	x_4	6	3	4	1	0	0	0	100
	x_5	5	2	3	0	1	0	0	60
	x_6	0	1	1	0	0	1	0	5
	x_7	10	2	3	0	0	0	1	100
	Objective-function coefficients:								
	$\Delta\pi$	1	2	3	0	0	0	0	
			$\pi =$	0					

Tableau 2. Caluculation of feasible solution.

	Real Variables			Slack Variables				
	x_1	x_2	x_3	x_4	x_5	x_6	x_7	
x_4	6	−1	0	1	0	−4	0	80
x_5	5	−1	0	0	1	−3	0	45
x_3	0	1	1	0	0	1	0	5
x_7	10	−1	0	0	0	−3	1	85
$\Delta\pi$	1	−1	0	0	0	−3	0	
				$\pi = 15$				

solution can be bettered, since it shows no profit and profit may be expected from the production of any line of toys. The fact that the largest incremental profit, $\Delta\pi$ is associated with x_3 indicates that x_3 is the variable whose value should be increased from its present level of zero. If we divide the column of figures under x_3 into the corresponding figures in the last column, we obtain quotients 25, 20, 5, and $33\frac{1}{3}$. Since the smallest positive quotient is associated with x_6, the variable x_6 should be assigned a value of zero in the next tableau.

The figures in Tableau 2 are computed by setting the five numbers in the third column, those associated with x_4, x_5, x_3, x_7 and $\Delta\pi$, at 0, 0, 1, 0, 0, respectively. The steps in the derivation are as follows. To eliminate the non-zero terms, we multiply the third row by −4, −3, −3, and −3, and, combining their results with first, second, fourth, and fifth rows, we have

$$\begin{aligned}&(6-0)x_1 + (3-4)x_2 + (4-4)x_3 + (1-0)x_4\\&\quad + (0-0)x_5 + (0-4)x_6 + (0-0)x_7 = 100 - 20,\end{aligned} \tag{22.A.2a}$$

$$\begin{aligned}&(5-0)x_1 + (2-3)x_2 + (3-3)x_3 + (0-0)x_4\\&\quad + (1-0)x_5 + (0-3)x_6 + (0-0)x_7 = 60 - 15,\end{aligned} \tag{22.A.2b}$$

$$\begin{aligned}&(10-0)x_1 + (2-3)x_2 + (3-3)x_3 + (0-0)x_4\\&\quad + (0-0)x_5 + (0-3)x_6 + (1-0)x_7 = 100 - 15,\end{aligned} \tag{22.A.2c}$$

$$\begin{aligned}&(1-0)x_1 + (2-3)x_2 + (3-3)x_3 + (0-0)x_4\\&\quad + (0-0)x_5 + (0-3)x_6 + (0-0)x_7.\end{aligned} \tag{22.A.2d}$$

Coefficients of Eq. (22.A.2(a) through (d)) are those listed in rows 1, 2, 4, and 5 of Tableau 2. Figures of row 3 are identical to the figures of the third row in Tableau 1.

In Tableau 2 we obtain a second basic feasible solution: $x_1 = 0$, $x_2 = 0$, $x_3 = 5$, $x_4 = 80$, $x_5 = 45$, $x_6 = 0$, $x_7 = 85$. Profits now total \$15, and $\Delta\pi$ is positive for x_1, indicating that the firm's profits can be further augmented by increasing the value of x_1 from its present level of zero. Computations similar to the preceding ones reveal that x_7 is the basic variable to be assigned a zero value in the next tableau. The final tableau is Table 22.4 in the text. In this table $\Delta\pi$'s are either zero or negative, and therefore, the firm's profits cannot increase any further.

Appendix 22.B. Mathematical Formulation of Goal Programming*

Following is a list of definitions of all variables used in the GP formulation of the working-capital problem:

x_1 = Unit sales of Y for cash,
x_2 = Unit sales of Y on credit,
x_3 = Unit sales of Z for cash,
x_4 = Unit sales of Z on credit,
x_5 = Unit sales of Y from inventory,
x_6 = Unit sales of Z from inventory,
x_7 = Dollar value of loan secured by inventory,
x_8 = Ending cash balance,
x_9 = Downside difference from profit goal,
x_{10} = Downside difference from cash goal,
x_{11} = Upside difference from cash goal,
x_{12} = Function of downside difference in current ratio.
x_{13} = Function of upside difference in current ratio,
x_{14} = Function of downside difference in quick ratio,
x_{15} = Function upside difference in quick ratio, and

$P_i (i = 1, \ldots, 7)$ = Weights on the deviations from goals.[2]

These weights are defined in Table 22.6 for each of the three sets of priorities.

Using these definitions, the GP problem is formulated as follows:

$$\text{Minimize: } P_1X_9 + P_2X_{10} + P_3X_{11} + P_4X_{12} + P_5X_{13} + P_6X_{14} + P_7X_{15}.$$

[2]This appendix is reprinted from Sartoris and Spruill, by permission of the authors and *Financial Management.*

Subject to:

$$5X_1 + 4.5X_2 + 7.5X_3 + 6.5X_4 + 3.5X_5 + 4.5X_6 - 0.05X_7$$
$$-0.05X_8 + X_9 = 2,698.94$$
$$2X_1 + 2X_2 + 4X_3 + 4X_4 - 2X_5 - 4X_6 \leq 1,000.00$$
$$X_5 \leq 60$$
$$X_6 \leq 30$$
$$X_1 \leq 150$$
$$X_2 \leq 100$$
$$X_3 \leq 175$$
$$X_4 \leq 250$$
$$5X_1 - 35.5X_2 + 7.5X_3 - 46X_4 + 3.5X_5 + 4.5X_6 + 0.95X_7$$
$$+X_{10} - X_{11} = 420.$$
$$26.25X_5 + 33.75X_6 + X_7 \leq 2587.5$$
$$-40X_2 - 52.5X_4 + 35X_5 + 45X_6 + 2X_7 + X_8 + X_{12} + X_{13} = 3,150$$
$$40X_2 + 52.5X_4 - X_7 + X_8 + X_{14} - X_{15} = 150$$
$$5X_1 - 35.5X_2 + 7.5X_3 - 46X_4 + 3.5X_5 + 4.5X_6$$
$$-0.05X_7 - 0.05X_8 + X_9 = 345$$
$$-X_1 + X_2 + X_5 \leq 0$$
$$-X_3 - 6.5X_4 + 4.5X_6 \leq 0$$
$$X_i \geq 0 \quad (i = 1, \ldots, 15).$$

The following list defines the constraint given by each row in the constraint matrix:

Row 1: Profit plus downside deviation = \$2,698.94;
Row 2: Time used in production at most 1,000 hours;
Row 3: At most 60 units of Y drawn from inventory;
Row 4: At most 30 units of Z drawn from inventory;
Row 5: At most 150 units of Y sold for cash;
Row 6: At most 100 units of Y sold on credit;
Row 7: At most 175 units of Z sold for cash;
Row 8: At most 250 units of Z sold on credit;

Row 9: Total cash goals 9;*
Row 10: Inventory loan constraint;*3
Row 11: Current ratio goal;*†
Row 12: Quick ratio goal;†
Row 13: Constraint requiring cash to be non-negative;
Row 14: Sales of Y for cash plus sales of Y for credit must be greater than or equal to Y drawn from inventory;
Row 15: Sales of Z for cash plus sales of Z for credit must be greater than or equal to Z dawn from inventory.

Finally, the following equations represent the goals prior to their being put into appropriate format for the goal program:

$$\text{Cash:}\quad X_8 = 5X_1 - 36X_2 + 7.5X_3 - 47X_4 - 3.5(60 - X_5) - 4.5(30 - X_6) + 0.95X_7 = 75; \tag{22.B.1}$$

$$\text{Current ratio:}\quad \frac{X_8 + 40X_2 + 52.5X_4 + 35(60 - X_5) + 45(30 - X_6)}{150 + X_7} = 2. \tag{22.B.2}$$

$$\text{Quick ratio:}\quad \frac{X_8 + 40X_2 + 52.5X_4}{150 + X_7} = 1. \tag{22.B.3}$$

References for Chapter 22

Beranek, W (1963). *Analysis for Financial Decisions.* Homewood, III: Richard D. Irwin, Inc.
Carleton, WT (1967). Linear-programming and capital-budgeting models: A new interpretation. *Journal of Finance*, 24, 825–833.
Charnes, A and WW Cooper (1961). *Management Models and Industrial Applications of Linear Programming,* Vols. I and II. New York: John Wiley & Sons.
Dantzig, GB (1998). *Linear Programming and Extensions.* Princeton: Princeton University Press.
Dantzig, GB (2003). *Linear Programming 2: Theory and Extensions.* New York: Springer.
Hadley, G and TM Whitin (1963). *Analysis of Inventory Systems.* Englewood Cliffs: Prentice-Hall, Inc.

*The numbers on the right-hand side include not only the goal but also constants carried to right-hand side of the equality from left-hand side.
†Both ratio goals have been linearized by multiplying right-hand side by denominator of ratio.

Ijiri, Y (1965). *Management Goals and Accounting for Control.* Chicago: Rand-McNally & Co.

Knight, WD (1973). Working-capital management — Satisficing versus optimization. *Financial Management*, 1, 33–41.

Krouse, CG (1974). Programming working-capital management. In *Management of Working Capital*, KV Smith (ed.). St. Paul: West Publishing Co.

Lee, S (1971). Decision analysis through goal programming. *Decision Sciences*, 2, 173–185.

Lee, CF and AC Lee (2006). *Encyclopedia of Finance.* New York: Springer.

Luenberger, DG (2003). *Linear and Nonlinear Programming*, 2nd ed. New York: Springer.

Mao, JCT (1967). Application of linear programming to short-term financing decision. *The Engineering Economist*, 13, 221–241.

Mao, JCT (1969). *Quantitative Analysis of Financial Decisions.* New York: Macmilan Co.

Mehta, DR (1974). *Working-Capital Management.* Englewood Cliffs: Prentice-Hall, Inc.

Pogue, GA and RW Bussard (1972). A linear-programming model for short-term financial planning under uncertainty. *Sloan Management Review*, 13, 69–98.

Quirin, CD (1967). *The Capital Expenditure Decision.* Homewood. III: Richard D. Irwin Inc.

Robicheck, AA, D Teichroew, and JM Jones (1965). Optimal short-term financing decision. *Management Science*, 12, 1–36.

Sartoris, WL and NC Hill (1983). A generalized cash-flow approach to short-term financial decision. *Journal of Finance*, 38(May), 349–360.

Sartoris, WL and RS Paul (1973). Lease evaluation — Another capital-budgeting decision. *Financial Management*, (Summer), 46–52.

Sartoris, WL and ML Spruill (1974). Goal programming and working capital management. *Financial Management*, 3, 67–74.

Sealey, CW (1978). Financial planning with multiple objectives. *Financial Management*, 7, 17–23.

Sharpe, WF (1971). A linear-programming approximation for the general portfolio-analysis problem. *Journal of Financial and Quantitative Analysis*, 6, 621–636.

Smith, KV (1980). *Readings on the Management of Working Capital*, 2nd ed., St. Paul: Western Publishing Co.

Soldofsky, RM (1966). A model for accounts receivable management. *Management Accounting*, (January), 55–61.

Stone, BK (1973). Cash planning and credit-line determination with a financial-statement simulator: A case report on short-term financial planning. *Journal of Financial and Quantitative Analysis*, 8, 711–729.

Stone, BK and NC Hill (1980). Cash-transfer scheduling for efficient cash concentration. *Financial Management*, (Autumn), 35–43.

Stone, BK and NC Hill (1981). The design of cash concentration system. *Journal of Financial and Quantitative Analysis*, 16, 301–322.

Stone, BK and NC Hill (1982). Alternative cash-transfer mechanisms and methods: Evaluation frameworks. *Journal of Banking Research*, 13, 7–16.

Stone, BK, DM Ferguson, and NC Hill (1980). Cash-transfer scheduling: An overview. *The Cash Manager*, 3–8.

Vanderbei, RJ (2007). *Linear Programming:Foundations and Extensions*, 3rd ed. New York: Springer.

Weingartner, HM (1974). *Mathematical Programming and the Analysis of Capital Budgeting Problems.* Chicago: Markham Publishing Co.

Part VI

Financial Planning and Forecasting

Chapter 23

Long-Range Financial Planning — A Linear-Programming Modeling Approach

23.1. Introduction

In this chapter, we will combine many of the concepts which have been discussed in previous chapters in considering the total value of a firm. There are two major methods for investigating the long-term financial analysis and planning of a firm. These two methods are a linear-programming method and a simultaneous-equation method. In this chapter, we will discuss Carleton's (1970, 1973) linear-programming model for long-range financial planning.[1] In Chapter 24, we will take up the simultaneous-equation method of performing long-range financial analysis.

Up to this point, our discussion of programming techniques has been confined to fairly simple formulations. We utilized linear programming to perform capital rationing. Then we discussed linear programming as a technique for performing working-capital management and cash transfer. Now we will utilize the techniques of linear programming to create an optimal solution for long-range financial planning.

Carleton's linear-programming model will be defined in Section 23.2. In Section 23.3, General Mills' financial data to be used as inputs for Carleton's

[1]Myers and Pogue's (1974) planning model is similar to Carleton's (1970) model. The major differences between these two models come from three sources: the objective function, the constraints, and the methodology employed. Myers and Pogue's objective function is decomposed into two components, while Carleton's is not explicitly stated. Myers and Pogue include project selection, liquidity, and debt-financing constraints while Carleton does not. Myers and Pogue rely on a mixed integer program to take care of the project selection and the debt-financing constraints. While this model is preferred, it is more difficult to implement.

model will be briefly described. Objective-function development will be discussed in Section 23.4. The procedures for constructing constraints will be developed in Section 23.5. The overall results will be analyzed in Section 23.6, and in Section 23.7 the summary and conclusion will be presented.

23.2. Carleton's Model

Carleton's model is an optimization model. It is composed of an objective function and its constraints. As can be seen from examining Table 23.1, the Carleton model has one objective function and three distinct sets of constraints.

Table 23.1. Carleton's linear-programming model.

I. Objective-Function

$$\text{Max}\ \frac{P_0}{N_0} = \frac{P_0}{N_0} + \sum_{t=1}^{T-1}\left[\frac{D_t}{N_0(1+K)^t} - \frac{\Delta E''_t}{N_0(1+K)^t(1-C)}\right] + \frac{P_T - \Delta E''_t}{N_t(1+K)^t}.$$

II. Constraints

A. *Definitional Constraints*

1. Available-for-Common Definition

$$AFC_t = ATP_t - Pfdiv_t - SA_t;$$

$$ATP_t = (1-\tau)\left\{\pi_t + \Delta eA_t - \Delta aAa_t - \sum_{z=1}^{Z} iz(L_{z,0} + C_{z,t}) - i'_t \sum_{z=1}^{Z} \Delta DL_t\right\}$$

$$+ B_1B_2(I_t + \Delta eA_{t-1}) + (1-\tau)(\Delta aAa_t - \Delta eA_{t-1});$$

$$\pi_t = \pi_{0,t} + \sum_{s=1}^{t} \pi'_s(I_s);$$

$$I_t = \frac{\rho - C_0}{C_t}\left(1 + \frac{\rho - C_0}{C_t}\right)^{t-1} A_0;$$

$$A_t = \left(1 + \frac{\rho - C_0}{C_t}\right)^t A_0.$$

B. *Sources and Uses of Funds Constraints*

1. Sources and Uses of Funds are Equal

$$I_t = AFC_{t-1} - D_{t-1} + \sum_{z=1}^{Z} \Delta CL_{z,t} + \Delta DL_t + \Delta DTL_{t-1} + \Delta E''_t.$$

(*Continued*)

Table 23.1. (*Continued*)

C. *Policy Constrains*

1. Interest Coverage

$$\frac{\pi_t}{\sum_{z=1}^{Z} i_z(L_{z,0} + C_{z,t}) + i\sum_{s=1}^{t} DL_s} \geq X.$$

2. Maximum Leverage

$$\sum_{z=1}^{Z} i_z(L_{z,0} + C_{z,t}) + \sum_{t=1}^{T} \Delta DL_t \leq \left(\frac{S}{1+S}\right) A_t.$$

3. Pre-financing Limitation

$$\sum_{t=1}^{T} \Delta DL_t - \sum_{t=1}^{T-1} \Delta DL_t \leq I_t.$$

4. Minimum Dividend Growth

$$D_t - \alpha_t D_{t-1} \geq 0;$$

$$P_t - \Delta E_t'' \geq \frac{1}{\alpha_t} P_t.$$

5. Payout Restriction

$$D_t \geq \delta_1 AFC_t;$$

$$D_t \geq \delta_2 AFC_t.$$

6. Cumulative Payout Restriction

$$\sum_{t=1}^{T} D_t - \delta \sum_{t=1}^{T-1} AFC_t \leq 0.$$

Note: See Table 23.2 for definitions of notation.

Corresponding to accounting definitions, sources and uses of funds, and alternative financial policies. Policy constraints include: (a) interest coverage, (b) maximum leverage, (c) pre-financing limitation, (d) minimum dividend growth, (e) payout restriction and (f) cumulative payout restriction. Definitions of variables used in Carleton's model are listed in Table 23.2. Variables used in Carleton's model can be divided into unknown variables and parameters provided by the management. Unknown variables include independent variables of the objective function and constraint

Table 23.2. List of unknowns and list of parameters provided by management.

I. Unknown Variables

A. Independent Variables of the Objective Function

(1) D_t = Total dividends paid by the firm in period t;

(2) $\Delta E_t''$ = Net funds received from equity issued in period t.

B. Constraint Variables

(1) AFC_t = Available for common funds;

(2) ΔDL_t = Change in long-term debt (LTD) in year t.

II. Parameters Provided by Management

A. Accounting Parameters

(1) C = Proportion of equity lost to underprising and transaction costs;

(2) N_0 = Number of common shares outstanding;

(3) ATP_t = After-tax profits;

(4) $Pfdiv$ = Preferred dividends;

(5) π_t = Period's EBIT (Earnings before interest and taxes);

(6) Δ_e = Stockholder report depreciation rate of assets;

(7) A_t = Total net assets;

(8) Aa_t = Tax report assets;

(9) $L_{z,0}$ = Initial amount in liability account z;

(10) $C_{z,t}$ = Known cumulative in $L_{z,0}$, as a result of prearranged loan "takedown" amortization schedule, etc. $C_{z,t} = \sum_{\tau=1}^{t} CL_{z,\tau}$. It includes expansion of trade credit and payment of LTD through sinking funds;

(11) ΔCL_z = Change in $C_{z,t}$;

(12) I_t = Net investment;

(13) X = Minimum acceptable interest coverage;

(14) S = Maximum debt/equity ratio;

(15) π_{0t} = The known profit, at time t, associated with the firm's initial stock of assets, A_0;

(16) ΔDTL_{t-1} = The change of deferred corporate income tax.

B. Financial Parameters and Definitions

(1) K = Appropriate discount rate;

(2) SA_t = Special adjustments (SA);

(3) Δ_a = Tax-reported accelerated depreciation;

(4) α_t = 1 + the minimum dividend growth rate;

(*Continued*)

Table 23.2. (*Continued*)

(5) δ_1 = Lower-bound payout ratio.

(6) δ_2 = Upper-bound payout ratio;

(7) δ = Cumulative payout restriction;

(8) ρ = Internal rate-of-return per period earned on I_1 (Growth Profit Margin as a proxy);

(9) D_0 = Total dividend payments in period zero;

(10) P_0 = Theoretical equity value in period zero.

C. Economic Parameters

(1) τ = Corporate tax rate;

(2) i_z = Interest rate of zth liability;

(3) i'_t = Interest rate for new LTD in year t;

(4) B_1 = Investment tax credit (ITC) rate;

(5) B_2 = Proportion of firm's assets on which ITC is applicable;

(6) $\pi_\tau(I_\tau)$ = The level of annual profits resulting from period τ's net investment I_τ;

(7) C_0 and C_1 = Production function parameters associated with $\rho_t = C_0 + C_1 \frac{I_t}{A_{t-1}} (C_0 > 0, C_1 < 0)$;

(8) P_t = Aggregate market value of the firm's equity at the beginning of period t $(t = 0, 1, \ldots, T)$;

(9) N_t = Number of common shares outstanding in period T.

variables. These unknowns will be the outputs of the linear-programming model.

Parameter inputs of this model can be classified as (i) accounting parameters, (ii) financial parameters, and (iii) economic parameters.

Throughout the chapter we will use General Mills' company data as an example to aid us in our understanding of Carleton's model. In Appendix 23.A, we present a complete linear-programming problem and its solution by means of a computer algorithm. While the Carleton model may look complicated at first glance, actually it is not that difficult. The background of concepts, theory, and methods for understanding and using Carleton's model is sufficiently supported by the foundations laid in the previous chapters. It is important for the student to keep in mind that many of these constraints are conflicting, and the first formulation may not result in an optimal solution. Thus, it may take a trial-and-error search procedure to gain a feasible solution.

We should also understand that linear programming is only a mathematical technique; thus it cannot do the financial manager's job for him. Managers must use discretion and judgment in applying the model. In order to use the model, users must have a good comprehension of the underlying concepts of financial theory. They must also know the goals of their organizations and their pertinent policies. These will also be incorporated in the model.

Finally, it is important to note, the model combines many conflicting constraints in arriving at the solution. The financial planner/manager can take advantage of this facet by using the model in a simulation setting to consider the effect that changing the assumptions and constraints would have on the solution and its feasibility.

23.3. Brief Discussion of Data Inputs

To show how Carleton's model can be used to do long-term financial analysis and planning, General Mill's annual financial data from the period 1974 through 1978 will be used as a case study. In order to gain the necessary inputs for the model, we must project certain figures; specifically, EBIT, Total Assets, and Yearly Investment. To project these inputs, we will first project sales for the 5-year period. Then we will project the certain factors based upon their historical ratios to sales. Because general Mills has four distinct segments, which have different characteristics, we will perform our projections on each segment and then combine the figures.

In Part I of Table 23.3 we present the calculations of the EBIT/Sales ratio for each of the divisions for the past 5 years. In the sixth column is our estimate of the ratio value of gross profit margin (GPM) for the next 5 years. A similar calculation is made for the Asset/Sales ratio in part II of the table.

Part III of Table 23.3 lists the historical growth rate on sales for the divisions and our projections for the future. While we have discussed growth-rate estimations before, we have considered some subjective factors in making our estimate. This should serve to put the decision marker on his guard. Pure numerical manipulation is a poor predictor of the future if no tempered by the decision maker's judgment. Part IV of Table 23.3 lists some related corporate segment information.

Table 23.4 contains our initial forecasts. In Part I, we have applied our sales growth-rate figure and then the ratios to get the EBIT, Assets, and Investment levels for each division for the planning horizon. In Part II

Table 23.3. Ratios and sales growth by segment.

I. $\frac{EBIT}{Sales}$ ratio

	Years					
Segment	74 (%)	75 (%)	76 (%)	77 (%)	78 (%)	*GPM Applied* (%)
FOOD PROC.	9.4	8.7	9.4	9.4	9.1	9.2 (Avg. of yrs.)
RESTAURANT	10.5	13.3	13.1	10.7	10.1	10.1 (Most recent)
TOYS, etc.	10.1	10.1	12	13	12.7	12.6 (3-Yr. Avg.)
FASHIONS, etc.	12.1	6.1	7.6	9	9	9 (Most recent)

II. $\frac{Assets}{Sales}$ ratio

Segment	77	78	*Applied*	
FOOD PROC.	0.35	0.36	0.335	(Average of available data — only 77–78 data available)
RESTAURANT	0.68	0.54	0.54	(Most recent, although 0.68 could become more realistic as expansion continues)
TOYS, etc.	0.38	0.68	0.68	
FASHIONS, etc.	0.59	0.62	0.61	(Average of the 2 years)

III. Sales Growth (Compound)

	Period					
Segment	*73–78* (%)	*74–78* (%)	*75–78* (%)	*76–78* (%)	*77–78* (%)	*Applied Growth Figures* (%)
FOOD PROC.	10	8.5	7	6.5	7.3	7.2 Yr.
RESTAURANT	4.5	4.6	4.6	40	47	40, 30, 20, 15, 10
TOYS, etc.	22	18	18	19	22	20
FASHIONS, etc.	19	22	25	19.5	32	25

IV. *Corporate Segment*

Data	*77* (%)	*78* (%)	*Applied Figure* (%)
$\frac{Corp.\ Assets}{Total\ Assets}$ ratio	3.5	4.8	4.8
$\frac{Corp.\ EBIT^*}{Total\ Assets}$ ratio	−0.7	−0.52	−0.6

*Corporate EBIT consisted of unallocated corporate expenses including interest expenses.

Table 23.4. Product-segment planning-horizon summary.

	Years				
	1979	1980	1981	1982	1983
I. Segments					
Food Processing	GPM = 9.2% Assets/Sales = 0.355 Sales Growth = 7%/yr.				
Sales_t	1991	2130	2279	2439	2610
$\text{EBIT}_t = (\prod_t)$	183.2	195.96	209.67	224.4	240.1
Assets_t	706.8	756	809	865.8	926.55
$I_t = (A_t - A_{t-1})$	33	49.35	53	56.8	60.75
Restaurant	GPM = 10.1% Assets/Sales = 0.54 Proj. Growth = 40%, 30%, 20%, 15%, 10%				
Sales_t	496.9	645.47	775.16	891.44	950.58
$\text{EBIT}_t = (\prod_t)$	50.14	65.24	78.29	90.1	99.04
Assets_t	268	348.8	418.6	481.4	529.5
I_t	74.7	80.82	69.8	62.8	48.1
Toys, etc.	GPM = 12.6% Assets/Sales = 0.68 Proj. Growth = 20%/yr.				
Sales_t	590.76	708.9	850.7	1020.8	1225
EBIT_t	74.4	89.3	107.2	128.6	154.4
Assets_t	401.7	482	578.5	694.1	833
I_t	63.9	80.35	96.5	115.6	138.9
Fashions, etc.	GPM = 9% Assets/Sales = 0.61 Proj. Sales Growth = 20%/yr.				
Sales_t	641	769	923	1107	1329
EBIT_t	57.7	69.21	83.07	99.63	119.6
Assets_t	391.01	469	563	675.3	810.7
I_t	61.31	78.08	94	112.3	135.4
Corporate	Assets = 4.8% of Total Sales $\text{EBIT}_t = -0.6\%$ of Corp. Asset				
Assets_t	89.1	103.65	119.45	137	156.3
I_t	10.7	14.55	15.8	17.6	19.3
EBIT_t	−53.5	−62.2	−71.7	−82.2	−93.8
II. Segment totals					
Sales_t	3719.66	4253.87	4827.86	5458.24	6144.58
$\text{EBIT}_t = (\prod_t)$	311.9	537.5	406.53	460.53	519.34
Assets_t (A_t)	1856.6	2159.4	2488.5	2854	3256
I_t	243.6	303.15	329.1	365.1	383.15

of Table 23.4 we have summed the divisional forecasts to get an overall forecast for the entire firm. We will be using these figures in our discussion of this model. In the following sections, we will now proceed with out developments of the Carleton model's objective function, constraints, and solution.

Using the data listed in Tables 23.3 and 23.4, as well as other pertinent data, we will develop a 5-period linear-programming log-term financial planning and analysis model for General Mills.

23.4. Objective-Function Development

The goal of a firm should be to maximize shareholder wealth, usually represented by a proxy-share price. Share price, in turn, has been valued.

In various ways (see Chapter 6); we will use a modified version of the stream-of-dividends approach:

$$\frac{P_0}{N_0} = \sum_{t=1}^{T-1} \frac{D_t}{N_0(1+K)^t} + \frac{P_T}{N_T(1+K)^t}, \tag{23.1}$$

where

D_0 = Total dividend payments in period zero;
P_0 = Theoretical equity value in period zero;
P_T = Aggregate market value of the firm's equity at the end of period T;
N_t = Number of common shares outstanding at the beginning of period t;
D_t = Total dividends paid by the firm in period t;
K = Appropriate discount rate for the firm, assuming constant risk and a constant k;
N_T = Number of common shares outstanding in period T.

(a) That new equity funds will be purchased or sold at the price that obtains after the transaction:

$$\Delta E_t'' = \Delta N \left(\frac{P_t}{N_t}\right). \tag{23.2}$$

(b) That, for mathematical convenience, $E_t'' = 0$, for $t = 1 \ldots j'$, the years in which convertibles are outstanding; and

(c) The inclusion of a parameter, c, representing transaction costs and any new-issue underpricing, so that[2]:

$$\frac{\Delta N_{j+1}}{N_{j+1}} = \frac{\Delta \tilde{E}^n_{j+1}}{P_{j+1}}, \tag{23.3a}$$

where

$$\Delta \tilde{E}^n_{j+1} = \frac{\Delta E^n_{j+1}}{1 - C}$$
$$= \text{Gross funds required to receive } \Delta E^n_t \text{ in new equity.}$$

To linearize, then, from Eq. (23.3a).

$$1 - \frac{N_j}{N_{j+1}} = \frac{\Delta \tilde{E}^n_{j+1}}{P_{j+1}} \quad \text{or} \quad \frac{N_j}{N_{j+1}} = \frac{P_{j+1} - \Delta \tilde{E}^n_{j+1}}{P_{j+1}}. \tag{23.3b}$$

By definition,

$$\frac{P_j}{N_j} = \frac{D_j}{N_j} + \frac{P_{j+1}}{N_{j+1}(1+K)} \quad \text{or} \quad P_j = D_j + \frac{N_j}{N_{j+1}}\left(\frac{P_{j+1}}{1+K}\right).$$

Substituting (N_j/N_{j+1}) in Eq. (23.3b), we have:

$$P_j = D_j + \frac{(P_{j+1} - \Delta \tilde{E}^n_{j+1})}{(1+K)}. \tag{23.4}$$

However, since Eq. (22.4) is valid for all the years of the planning horizon during which convertibles are not outstanding ($t = j', +1 \ldots T$), successive substitutions yield:

$$P_j = D_j + \frac{D_{j+1} - \Delta \tilde{E}^n_{j+1}}{(1+K)} + \frac{D_{j+2} - \Delta \tilde{E}^n_{j+2}}{(1+K)^2} + \cdots + \frac{P_T - \Delta \tilde{E}^n_T}{(1+K)^{T-j}}. \tag{23.5}$$

The original valuation formulation can now be rewritten, recognizing that $\Delta E^n_t = 0$ for $t = 1, \ldots, j'$, in the following manner:

$$\frac{P_0}{N_0} = \frac{D_0}{N_0} + \frac{D_1}{N_1(1+K)} + \cdots + \frac{P_j}{N_j(1+K)^j}.$$

[2]Here, we adopt the Miller and Modigliani's (1961) procedure, amended to include the stock-flotation cost parameter, c, and the present model's dating-of-variables conventions.

Substituting Eq. (22.5) into the above P_j, the valuation becomes:

$$\frac{P_0}{N_0} = \frac{D_0}{N_0} + \frac{D_1}{N_1(1+K)} + \cdots + \frac{D_j}{N_j(1+K)^j} + \frac{D_{j+1} - \Delta\tilde{E}^n_{j+1}}{(1+K)} + \cdots + \frac{P_T - \Delta\tilde{E}^n_T}{(1+K)^{T-j}}. \tag{23.6}$$

Considering, finally, that $N_0 = N_1 \ldots = N_j$ ($\Delta E^n_t = 0$ for $t = 1 \ldots j'$), the above relationship is linear, since we have removed the non-linear variability of N_t.

In the General Mills case, no convertibles are outstanding; therefore $\Delta E^n_t \geq 0$ for each of the planning years. The General Mills objective function then becomes:

$$\begin{aligned} \text{Max}\,\frac{P_0}{N_0} &= \frac{D_0}{N_0} + \frac{D_1}{N_1(1+K)} + - \frac{\Delta E''_1}{N_0(1+K)(1-C)} + \frac{D_2}{N_0(1+K)^2} \\ &\quad - \frac{\Delta E''_2}{N_0(1+K)^2(1-C)} + \frac{D_3}{N_0(1+K)^3} - \frac{\Delta E''_3}{N_0(1+K)^3(1-C)} \\ &\quad + \frac{D_4}{N_0(1+K)^4} - \frac{\Delta E''_4}{N_0(1+K)^4(1-C)} \\ &\quad + \frac{P_3}{N_0(1+K)^5} - \frac{\Delta E''_5}{N_0(1+K)^5(1-C)}. \end{aligned} \tag{23.7a}$$

Given that,

$N_0 = 49.69 =$ Number of General Mills common shares (in millions) outstanding at the beginning of fiscal year 1979;

$C = 0.10 =$ An estimate of the proportion of equity lost to under pricing and transaction costs;

$K = 0.165 =$ The appropriate discount rate calculated using the Chase (CAPM, Modigliani-Miller combination) technique.

The General Mills objective functions is[3]:

$$\begin{aligned} &\text{Max}\, 0.018D1 - 0.0196E1 + 0.015D2 - 0{,}017E2 + 0.013D3 \\ &\quad - 0.0144E3 + 0.011D4 - 0.0125E4 - 0.015E5. \end{aligned} \tag{23.7b}$$

[3]Because of the difficulty of using Δ notation and subscripts on a computer, we will avoid using them or bring subscripts into the variable name. For example, ΔE_1 will be $E1$. This rule will be used to define the empirical results of constraints. In addition, computer notations are used to describe the objective functions and constraints.

In Eq. (23.7b), we do not include the known variable D_0/N_0 and $[P_5/(N_0(1+K)^5]$.

23.5. The Constraints

Various constraints, representing both company policy and accounting relationships, can be included in the model. Policy constraints represent corporate-financing decisions such as the setting of an ideal leverage level (D/E or D/TA), ideal dividend payout, times-interest-earned ratio, etc. Accounting definitional constraints, on the other hand, arise from the necessary relationships of accounting identities on the balance sheet, income statement, and retained earnings statement. The vast quantity of information that can be brought to bear on a financial decision-making model such as the linear-programming formulation can be seen in Fig. 23.1.

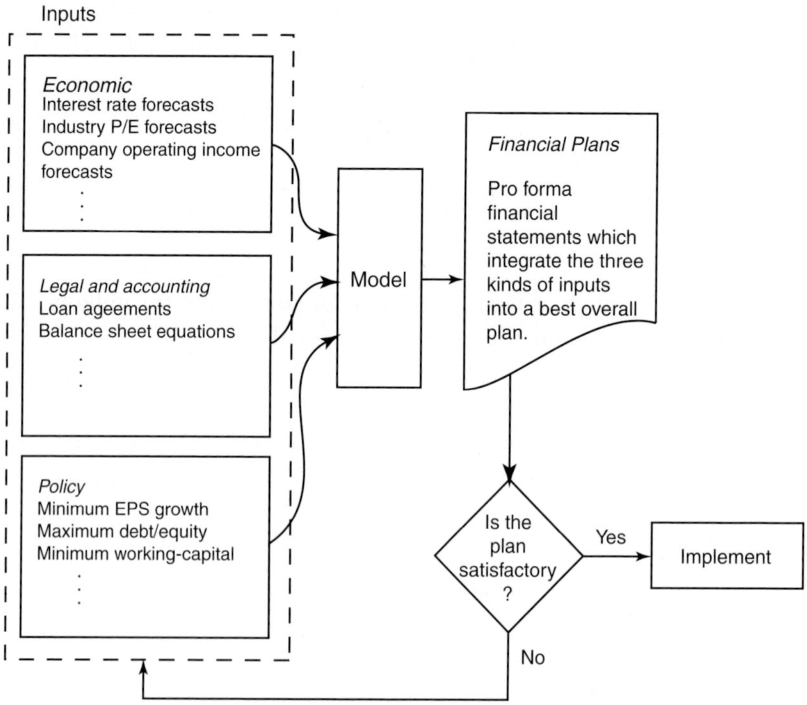

Fig. 23.1. Structure of the optimizing financial planning model. (From WT Carleton, CL Dick Jr, and DH Downes (December 1973). Financial policy models: Theory and Practice. *Journal of Financial and Quantitative Analysis*, Reprinted by permission.)

Certain key policy decisions, accounting relationships, and exogenous economic realities combine in the constraints to define the maximum valuation of share price possible under the various realities facing General Mills' operations. Upon completion of the linear-programming modeling and solution of the problem, pro forma financial statements can be generated to illustrate the company-level implications of the particular solution variables postulated.

23.5.1. *Definitional Constraints*

Two sets of definitional constraints establish the accounting relationships prescribed by the Income Statement and by the Sources and Uses of Funds Statement.

The Balance Sheet shows the value of all company-owned assets (both tangible and intangible) and the claims on these assets. For the purposes of this chapter, the value of total assets (both current and fixed) will be combined and represented as A_t. Liabilities will be shown by three accounts: Accounts Payable and Accrued Expenses, Notes Payable (both current liabilities), and LTD.

The income statement lists all expenses incurred by the corporation, which are in turn subtracted from all revenue earned in the business operations of the company. In our case, total revenues minus expenses (except for taxes and interest payments) will be represented by π_t (or $EBIT_t$). To convert this accounting identity into a usable economic concept, corporate tax must be subtracted, the ITC must be added, and an adjustment made for book-versus-actual tax savings on depreciation (see Eq. (23.8)). These calculations will result in a figure for after-tax profit, which, after preferred dividend payments and extraordinary adjustments to income, is available for investment in the firm.

Finally, the Sources and Uses of Funds Statement are employed. Briefly, this identifies the uses of funds (dividends, stock repurchases) and equates this with its sources, the previously calculated "available for investment" figure, as well as any increase in either equity or liability accounts (see Eq. (23.13)).

To formulate the constraints, we will assume that balance-sheet variables are recorded after investment and its financing, but before the recording of revenues and expenses for the period. In other words, as is apparent in the sources-and-uses equation, the retained earnings in period $(t-1)$ are available for investment in flow, the model assuming that

Investment occurs immediately (no construction or set-up time) and that revenues begin flowing from that investment at the expected rate also immediately. Depending on the planning corporation's investment realities, the above assumption may be modified to include both a start-up time lag and a more S-curve type of returns specification.

(a) **Available-far-Common Definition**

The first set of constraints is derived from the Income Statement in that each period's available-for-common-funds amount (AFC) is identified based upon General Mills' ATP, Pfdiv, and SA to ATP. In equation form,

$$AFC_t = ATP_t - Pfdiv_t - SA_t. \tag{23.8}$$

And,

$$ATP_t = (1-\tau)\left\{\pi_t + \Delta e A_t - \Delta a A a_t - \sum_{z=1}^{Z} i_z (L_{z,0} + C_{z,t}) - i'_t \sum_{s=1}^{t} \Delta DL_s\right\} + B_1 B_2 (I_1 + \Delta e A_{t-1}) + (1-\tau)(\Delta a A a_t - \Delta e A_t). \tag{23.9}$$

Because General Mills has no preferred stock or extraordinary items, AFC = ATP:

τ = Corporate tax rate = 0.51 in the General Mills case (effective rate from the annual report);
π_t = Period's EBIT based upon an estimate of the respective General Mills product segment's sales-growth projections and GPMs, aggregated into a company-wide π figure (Table 23.4);
$\pi_1 = 311.9$; $\pi_2 = 537.5$; $\pi_3 = 406.53$; $\pi_4 = 460.53$; $\pi_5 = 519.34$;
Δ_e = Stockholder-report depreciation rate as of assets = 0.033 for General Mills, based upon 2-year average depreciation/total assets figure;
A_t = Stockholder report assets (total net assets);
$A_1 = 1856.6$; $A_2 = 2159.4$; $A_3 = 2488.5$; $A_4 = 2854$; $A_5 = 3256$;
Δa = Tax-report accelerated depreciation (Not applied to General Mills example because of a lack of necessary information.); $\sim a = 0$;

Aa_1 = Tax-report assets (Also not applied to the General Mills case for the same lack-of-information rationale.); $Aa_1 = 0$;
i_z = Appropriate interest rate for the zth liability;
$L_{z,0}$ = Initial amount in the liability accounts, $z = 1, \ldots, Z$, where z includes all liabilities except deferred taxes;
$C_{z,t}$ = Prearranged takedown or increase of all L_z including expansion of trade credit and payment of LTD through sinking funds;
ΔDL_t = Change in LTD in period t;
i'_t = Interest rate applicable to $\sum_{s=1}^{t} DL_s$.

We can express the appropriate interest payments $\tilde{P}_1$, $\tilde{P}_2$ for the Accounts Payable and Notes Payable, respectively, by the matrix notation of r_1, r_2 and L_1, L_2 for the interest rates, scalar multiplier, and amount of liabilities outstanding, respectively. Following data listed in Table 23.5(a), we have:

$$i_1 = 0,$$

$$i_2 = 0.085,$$

$$L_1 = \begin{bmatrix} 371.32 \\ 431.9 \\ 497.7 \\ 570.8 \\ 651.2 \end{bmatrix},$$

$$L_2 = \begin{bmatrix} 66.8 \\ 77.7 \\ 89.6 \\ 102.7 \\ 117.2 \end{bmatrix},$$

$$\tilde{P}_1 = i_2 L_1 = \begin{bmatrix} 0 \\ 0 \\ 0 \\ 0 \\ 0 \end{bmatrix},$$

Table 23.5. (a) Summary of liabilities. (b) LTD amortization (from Moody's).

(a)

L_1 = Accounts payable and Accrued Expenses,
$i_1 = 0$ No explicit interest costs associated with Accounts payable, etc.,
$L_{1,0} + C_{1,t} = 20\%(A_t)$ based on the 5-year L_1/A_t average,
L_2 = Notes Payable (Foreign Banks, Commercial paper, etc.),
$C_2 = 8.5\%$ based on 5-year weighted average and upon interest-rate projections,
$L_{21,0} + C_{2,t} = 3.6\%(A_t)$ also based on the 5-year average,
L_3 = LTD (from Moody's),

Planning-Horizon Totals	Year				
Liability	1979	1980	1981	1982	1983
L_1, Accts. Pay., etc	371.32	431.9	497.7	570.8	651.2
L_2, Notes Pay.	66.8	77.7	89.6	102.7	117.2
$L_{3,0}$, LTD_0	258.7	234.8	221.9	198.5	185.1
Total	696.82	744.4	809.2	872.0	953.5

(b)

78		Yearly Takedown of $C_{3,t}$				
$L_{3,0}$	i_3 (%)	1979	1980	1981	1982	1983
11	7	—	11	—	—	—
30	4.25	—	—	—	10	—
12.8	8	1.5	1.5	1.5	2	2
20.1	4.875	1.4	1.4	1.4	1.4	1.4
73.1	8.875	—	5	5	5	5
98.7	8	5	5	5	5	5
20.9 (misc.)			No information available			

$$\tilde{P}_2 = i_2 L_2 = \begin{bmatrix} 5.678 \\ 6.6045 \\ 7.616 \\ 8.7295 \\ 9.962 \end{bmatrix}.$$

Because the LTD is several components at different interest rates, it may be easier to evaluate it if we use matrix notation, where L_3 is the matrix of the $L_{3,0} - C_{3,t}$; $t = 1, \ldots, 5$ values for each component; R_3 is the matrix of the interest rates $i_{3,c}$; C is the matrix of yearly takedown. Then we can perform the following calculation in accordance with data listed in Table 23.5(b):

$$
\begin{array}{c}
L_{3,0} - C_{3,t} \\
\begin{array}{ccccc} 79 & 80 & 8 & 82 & 83 \end{array}
\end{array}
$$

$$
L_3 = \begin{vmatrix}
0 & 0 & 0 & 0 & 0 \\
30 & 30 & 30 & 20 & 20 \\
11.3 & 9.8 & 8.3 & 6.3 & 4.6 \\
18.7 & 17.3 & 15.9 & 14.5 & 13.1 \\
73.1 & 68.1 & 63.1 & 58.1 & 53.1 \\
93.7 & 88.7 & 83.1 & 78.1 & 73.1
\end{vmatrix}
$$

$$
R_3 = \begin{bmatrix} 7\% & 4.25\% & 8\% & 4.875\% & 8.875\% & 8\% \end{bmatrix}.
$$

To get the interest payment on LTD

$$
\begin{aligned}
\tilde{P}_3 &= R_3 \cdot L_3 \\
&= \begin{bmatrix} 17.04425 & 16.04225 & 14.96225 & 13.46525 & 12.24475 \end{bmatrix}
\end{aligned}
$$

i'_t = Estimated rate on new LTD (In the General Mills example i' was assumed constant at 9% although variable rates, given interest rate forecasts, would be more appropriate);

$\sum_{s=1}^{t} \Delta DL_s$ = Cumulative change in LTD from the beginning of the planning horizon to $t(DL_t = \Delta DL_t$ is one of the variables we are solving for);

B_1 = ITC = 7% in the General Mills example;

B_2 = Percentage of assets eligible for ITC = 0.36, based upon the General Mills 5-year (fixed assets)/(total assets) ratio average;

I_t = Net investment in year $Bt = A_{t+1} - A_t$ (see Table 23.3 for complete General Mills Product Segment projections, including I_t by segment).

Rewriting the available-for-common constraint equation in matrix form may make it easier to evaluate. We will denote a matrix by a tilde ($\sim$) above the symbol (e.g., for the EBIT, the matrix will be denoted $\tilde{\pi}$). After elimination of the portions of the equation that have no value for this example, we are left with:

$$
AFC = (1 - \tau) \cdot \left[\tilde{\pi} - \sum_{i=1}^{3} \tilde{P}_i - i' \cdot D\tilde{L} \right] + B_1 \cdot B_2 \left[\tilde{I}_1 + \Delta e \tilde{A}^L \right].
$$

Then we can formulate the model in terms of P_2, P_3, $D\tilde{L}$, $\tilde{\pi}$, $\tilde{I}$, and $\tilde{A}^L$ in Table 23.4 as follows:

$$AFC = (1 - 0.51) \overset{\tilde{\pi}}{\begin{bmatrix} 311.9 \\ 357.9 \\ 406.53 \\ 460.53 \\ 519.34 \end{bmatrix}} - \overset{\tilde{P}_2}{\begin{bmatrix} 5.678 \\ 6.6045 \\ 7.616 \\ 8.7295 \\ 9.962 \end{bmatrix}} - \overset{\tilde{P}'_3}{\begin{bmatrix} 17.04425 \\ 16.04225 \\ 14.96225 \\ 13.46525 \\ 12.24475 \end{bmatrix}} - (0.09) \overset{D\tilde{L}}{\begin{bmatrix} DL1 \\ DL2 \\ DL3 \\ DL4 \\ DL5 \end{bmatrix}}$$

$$+ (0.07) \cdot (0.36) \overset{\tilde{I}}{\begin{bmatrix} 243.6 \\ 303.15 \\ 329.1 \\ 365.1 \\ 383.15 \end{bmatrix}} + (0.033) \overset{\tilde{A}^L}{\begin{bmatrix} 1613 \\ 1856.6 \\ 2159.4 \\ 2488.5 \\ 2854 \end{bmatrix}},$$

where $\tilde{A}_t^L$ is the asset matrix $(\tilde{A})$ at lag one period. The value of initial value of assets, A_0 was given by the financial report of current period.

Given this formulation we can solve

$$\begin{bmatrix} AFC1 \\ AFC2 \\ AFC3 \\ AFC4 \\ AFC5 \end{bmatrix} + 0.0441 \cdot \begin{bmatrix} DL1 \\ DL2 \\ DL3 \\ DL4 \\ DL5 \end{bmatrix} = \begin{bmatrix} 149.17 \\ 173.45 \\ 198.22 \\ 226.05 \\ 255.62 \end{bmatrix}$$

and find that:

$$AFC1 + 0.00441DL1 = 149.17, \tag{23.10a}$$

$$AFC2 + 0.00441DL2 = 173.45, \tag{23.10b}$$

$$AFC3 + 0.00441DL3 = 198.22, \tag{23.10c}$$

$$AFC4 + 0.00441DL4 = 226.05. \tag{23.10d}$$

Since $AFC5$ and $DL5$ are assumed to be known parameters in the model, the last row of the matrix is not a constraint.

The critical input in the definition of AFC_t, is the π_t estimation. Carleton (1970) employs an investment-opportunities function that takes the form:

$$\pi_t = \pi_{0,t} + \sum_{s=1}^{t} \pi'_s(I_s), \tag{23.11}$$

where

π_t = EBIT in period t;

$\pi_{0,t}$ = Known profit at time t associated with the firm's initial stock of assets A_0;

$\pi'_s(I_s)$ = Level of annual profit resulting from period s's investment $I_s = \rho_s I_s$;

$\rho_s = C_0 + C_1 \dfrac{I_s}{A_{s-1}}$;

ρ_s = GPM associated with investment opportunities, a function of asset growth;

C_0 = Maximum GPM assuming no growth, $C_0 > 0$;

C_1 = Growth factor representing a return-to-scale factor, $C_1 < 0$;

I_s/A_{s-1} = Asset growth in period t.

Carleton's GPM is thus a decreasing function of growth representing decreasing returns to scale. This representation is consistent with the downward-sloping investment-opportunity curve. Accordingly, Carleton estimates A_t and I_t using the following equations derived from the investment-opportunity specifications,

$$I_t = \left(\frac{\rho - C_0}{C_1}\right)\left(1 + \frac{\rho - C_0}{C_1}\right)^{t-1} A_0, \quad (23.12a)$$

$$A_t = \left(1 + \frac{\rho - C_0}{C_1}\right)^{t} A_0. \quad (23.12b)$$

The approach taken by this chapter, however, in the estimation of π_t, incorporates the General Mills strategy of growth in its existing industries along with average GPM for each industry, assuming constant returns to scale within the segments. GPM data for each product segment was taken from the 1978 annual report and coupled with derived hypothetical sales-growth projections to generate a yearly aggregate π_t. In addition, Assets/Sales ratios were applied, by segment, to the yearly sales projections, to generate a total yearly A_t. The results are summarized in Table 23.4.

Although Carleton (1970) assumed a one-product company for the development of his model, most large corporations at present typically consist of a number of product segments as a result of merger activity. In fact, so common is this phenomenon that the SEC requires accounting reports to be filed for each individual segment within the larger corporation.

Although we will not show constraints for each product segment, it is possible to extend linear programming to include disaggregate constraints for each product segment. In this way, the model can include an analysis of the benefits of separate product lines, as well as the result of the mergers the company has undertaken. The impact of disaggregation of constraints can be explored in future research.

23.5.1.1. *Sources and Uses Definition*

The second set of "definitional" constraints equates the sources and uses of funds in period t (incorporating the aforementioned retained earnings lag). The equation used to describe the change in the left-hand side of the balance sheet and the change in the right-hand side is formulated in this manner:

$$I_t = AFC_{t-1} - D_{t-1} + \sum_{z=1}^{Z} \Delta CL_{z,t} + \Delta DL_t + \Delta DTL_{t-1} + \Delta E_t'', \tag{23.13}$$

where

I_t = Net investment (see Table 23.4);

$\sum_{z=1}^{Z} \Delta CL_{z,t}$ = Change in liability accounts from trade credit expansion or prearranged takedown of debt (see Tables 23.5(a) and 23.5(b));

ΔDL_t = Change in LTD in year;

$t = \sum_{t=1}^{t} \Delta DL_t - \sum_{t=1}^{t-1} \Delta DL_t;$

ΔDTL_{t-1} = Change in deferred tax liability (not incorporated because of information lack);

$\Delta E_t''$ = Net equity received in year t from amount issued.

In matrix notation:

$$\tilde{I}_t = AF\tilde{C}^L - \tilde{D}^L + \sum C\tilde{L}_z + D\tilde{L} - D\tilde{L}^L + DT\tilde{L}^L + \tilde{E},$$

$$AFC^L = \begin{bmatrix} AFC_0 = 105.79 \\ AFC_1 \\ AFC_2 \\ AFC_3 \\ AFC_4 \end{bmatrix}.$$

Rearranging the equation at time $t = 1$, we obtain:

$$AFC_0 - D_0 + \Delta DL_1 + E_1 = I_t - \sum_{z=1}^{Z} \Delta CL_z.$$

From the prior section,

$$AFC_0 - (1 - \tau)[\pi_0 - \sum i_z L_{z,0}].$$

From the Annual Report,

$$\pi_0 = 245.2,$$

and from Moody's, the interest expense was

$$\left[\sum i_z L_{z,0}\right] = 29.3.$$

From the Annual Report,

$$D_0 = 48.2.$$

The change in liability accounts can be determined as follows: From the planning horizon table we can get $\tilde{L}_T$, then

$$CL = \tilde{L}_T - \tilde{L}_T^L.$$

From Table 23.5(a), we have

$$\tilde{L}_T = \begin{bmatrix} 696.82 \\ 744.4 \\ 809.2 \\ 872.0 \\ 953.5 \end{bmatrix},$$

$$\tilde{L}_T^L = \begin{bmatrix} 641.63 \\ 696.82 \\ 744.4 \\ 809.2 \\ 872.0 \end{bmatrix},$$

where the first piece of data in $\tilde{L}_T^L$. [That is, $L_{T,0}$] for 1978 came from the Annual Report. Thus,

$$CL = \begin{bmatrix} 55.19 \\ 47.58 \\ 64.80 \\ 62.80 \\ 81.50 \end{bmatrix}.$$

Then

$$AFC_0 = (1 - 0.51)[254.2 - 29.3] = 105.79.$$

And

$$105.79 - 48.2 + DL_1 + E_1 = 243.6 - 55.19,$$
$$DL_1 + E_1 = 130.82.$$

Thus, the sources and uses constraints are

$$\tilde{I}_t = AF\tilde{C}^L = \tilde{D}^L + \sum C\tilde{L}_z + D\tilde{L} - D\tilde{L}^L + DT\tilde{L}^L + \tilde{E},$$

$$\begin{bmatrix} 243.6 \\ 303.15 \\ 329.1 \\ 365.1 \\ 383.15 \end{bmatrix} = \begin{bmatrix} 105.79 \\ AFC1 \\ AFC2 \\ AFC3 \\ AFC4 \end{bmatrix} - \begin{bmatrix} 48.2 \\ D_1 \\ D_2 \\ D_3 \\ D_4 \end{bmatrix} + \begin{bmatrix} 55.19 \\ 47.58 \\ 64.80 \\ 62.80 \\ 81.50 \end{bmatrix} + \begin{bmatrix} DL1 \\ DL2 \\ DL3 \\ DL4 \\ 488.4 \end{bmatrix}$$
$$- \begin{bmatrix} 0 \\ DL1 \\ DL2 \\ DL3 \\ DL4 \end{bmatrix} + \begin{bmatrix} E_1 \\ E_2 \\ E_3 \\ E_4 \\ E_5 \end{bmatrix}.$$

The value for DL5 is the total liabilities of the firm at the end of the planning horizon. Assuming that the Debt/TA ratio will be at its target level in period 5 ($D/TA = 0.15$).

As we know $A_5 = 3256$; then $\Delta DL_5 = 0.15(3256) = 488.4. = 0.15(3256) = 488.4$. Thus,

$$DL_1 + E_1 = 131.38, \quad (23.10e)$$

$$AFC_1 - D_1 + DL2 - DL1 + E_2 = 255.7, \quad (23.10f)$$

$$AFC_2 - D_2 + DL3 - DL2 + E_3 = 264.3, \quad (23.10g)$$

$$AFC_3 - D_3 + DL4 - DL3 + E_4 = 302.3, \quad (23.10h)$$

$$AFC_4 + D_4 + DL4 - E_5 = 182.15. \quad (23.10i)$$

23.5.2. *Policy Constraints*

The policy constraints designed to limit kt (the cost of capital) and maximize g (growth of dividends) are one of the linear-programming model's strong points. The policy constraints are formulated upon the past 5-year performance of General Mills because of a lack of information regarding the General Mills management's target figures.

(a) Interest Coverage

The first group of policy constraints attempts to limit *kt* by maintaining an "appropriate" or "acceptable" interest-coverage multiplier. Since *kt* is determined by investor/creditor perceptions of the overall riskiness of the corporation, and interest coverage is one measure of risk, "acceptable" is thus defined by the corporation's existing and potential creditors (including shareholders). The communication of the "acceptable" level is not, however, direct, leaving to management the task of discerning the creditors' definition subject to reactions in the capital marketplace. Often management will attempt to maintain the interest-coverage multiplier that will maintain a given bond rating for future issues, or the figure that is "in line" with the industry norm, both benchmarks being used as proxies for creditor preferences.

In the General Mills example offered here, X, the minimum interest-coverage multiplier, was equated to the recent 5-year low of *6.35X*. Assuming a nine-percent interest rate on new debt, the effect of the following yearly constraints is to limit the amount of future LTD issued *vis-à-vis* the interest-coverage figure. In inequality form the specification is:

$$\frac{\Pi_t}{\sum_{z=1}^{Z} i_z(L_{z,0} + C_{z,t}) + i'_t \sum_{s=1}^{t} \Delta DL_s} \geq X, \tag{23.14}$$

where X is the minimum acceptable interest coverage (here 6.35), based upon the minimum interest-coverage figure achieved by General Mills in the recent 5-year period.

As we saw before, $\sum_{z=1}^{Z} i_z(L_{z,0} + C_{z,t})$ can be represented as $\tilde{P}_2 + \tilde{P}_3$ in matrix form,

$$\tilde{P}_2 + \tilde{P}_3 = \begin{bmatrix} 5.678 \\ 6.6045 \\ 7.616 \\ 8.7295 \\ 9.962 \end{bmatrix} + \begin{bmatrix} 17.04 \\ 16.04 \\ 14.96 \\ 13.47 \\ 12.24 \end{bmatrix}.$$

And $i_t' \sum \Delta DL_t$ as $i_t' \tilde{DL}$, or

$$(0.09)\begin{bmatrix} DL1 \\ DL2 \\ DL3 \\ DL4 \\ 488.4 \end{bmatrix}.$$

And Π_t as

$$\tilde{\Pi} = \begin{bmatrix} 311.9 \\ 357.9 \\ 406.53 \\ 460.53 \\ 519.34 \end{bmatrix}.$$

In matrix form, this constraint is

$$\tilde{\Pi} \geq X[\tilde{P}_2 + \tilde{P}_3 + 0.09\tilde{DL}].$$

The minimum interest coverage was set at its 5-year historical low, $X = 6.35$. Thus,

$$\tilde{\Pi} \geq 6.35[\tilde{P}_2 + \tilde{P}_3 + 0.09\tilde{DL}],$$

or

$$\tilde{\Pi} - 6.35[\tilde{P}_2 + \tilde{P}_3] \geq 0.5715\tilde{DL},$$

$$\begin{bmatrix} 311.9 \\ 357.9 \\ 406.53 \\ 460.53 \end{bmatrix} - 6.35\begin{bmatrix} 5.678 \\ 6.6045 \\ 7.616 \\ 8.7295 \end{bmatrix} + \begin{bmatrix} 17.04 \\ 16.04 \\ 14.96 \\ 13.47 \end{bmatrix} \geq 0.5715\begin{bmatrix} DL1 \\ DL2 \\ DL3 \\ DL4 \end{bmatrix}.$$

We consider only the first four constraints because all the values for the fifth are known. Thus:

$$DL_1.LE.284.42,^* \tag{23.15a}$$

$$DL_2.LE.374.1, \tag{23.15b}$$

$$DL_3.LE.460, \tag{23.15c}$$

$$DL_4.LE.558.7. \tag{23.15d}$$

(b) Maximum Leverage

A second restriction on the use *of* debt financing stems from the leverage figure deemed by management to maximize the value *of* the firm. Consistent with the Modigliani–Miller (1963) valuation model, in which the value *of* the firm is increased by increasing leverage.

Management will raise the firm's debt/equity ratio to the point where creditors (including shareholders) view the probability *of* bankruptcy or the variability in earnings as being excessive. At this point *of* high financial and/or operating leverage, the risk-determined discount rate, k in the Gordon valuation model, $P_0 = D_1/(k-g)$ is increased and the value of the firm declines. Thus,

$$\sum_{z=1}^{Z}(L_{z,0}+C_{z,t})+\sum_{z=1}^{Z}\Delta DL_s \leq A_t, \qquad (23.16)$$

where

S = Maximum debt/equity set at 1.25, where, debt = total liabilities − DTL;

$(L_{z,0}+C_{z,t})$ = $\textit{Liabilities}_t + DL_0$;

$\sum_{t=1}^{T}\Delta DL_t$ = Cumulative change in LTD since the beginning of the planning horizon.

Thus,

$$DL_1.LE.243.6 \quad (LE. = \text{“}\leq\text{”}) \qquad (23.17a)$$

$$DL_2 - DL_1.LE.303.15 \quad (GE. = \text{“}\geq\text{”}) \qquad (23.17b)$$

$$DL_3 - DL_2.LE.329.1 \qquad (23.17c)$$

$$DL_4.GE.101.15 \qquad (23.17d)$$

Constraint (23.15a) is redundant, given (23.17a) but is included simply for illustrative purposes. Equation (23.17e) does not include DL_5 because DL_5 is given ($DL_5 = 488.4$).

(d) Minimum Dividend Growth

Many firms find it advantageous to maintain a consistent earnings and dividend growth rate to minimize the level of uncertainty in its shareholder clientele. By minimizing shareholder uncertainty, the firm reduces the cost of equity capital, and increases the value of the firm by reducing the risk-adjusted discount rate applied to the Gordon valuation model. The Carleton model employs a minimum dividends/share growth, which was also included with the General Mills data in this chapter's example. Because of the potential for a new equity issue, two series of growth constraints must be employed, one for dividends, and one for Pr, the total market value of the firm's equity in period t, to ensure that dividends/share grow the desired minimum amount during the planning horizon. In inequality form the two constraints are as follows:

$$D_t - \alpha_t D_{t-1} \geq 0, \tag{23.18a}$$

where $\alpha_t = 1 +$ Minimum Dividend growth (which, in the General Mills example, is 0.06), and

$$P_t - \Delta\tilde{E}_{tt}^{n} \geq \frac{1}{\alpha} P_t. \tag{23.18b}$$

The derivation of Eq. (23.18b) is now discussed. Based upon Carleton (1970), we define

$$\alpha \geq \frac{N_t}{N_{t-1}},$$

And therefore

$$1 - \frac{N_{t-1}}{N_t} \leq 1 - \frac{1}{\alpha}.$$

This relationship also implies that:

$$\frac{\Delta N_t}{N_t} \leq 1 - \frac{1}{\alpha}. \tag{23.18c}$$

Substituting Eq. (23.18c) with Eq. (23.2), we obtain Eq. (23.18b).

To obtain the constraint of Eq. (23.18b), we need to estimate P_1 and P_5. In order to obtain P_5 we assume that the P/E ratio will be 10 in year 5. Since we know $EBIT_5 = 519.34$, interest payment on debt (existing) in period 5 = 22.20, interest payment on debt (new) = 9% (488.4) = 43.96; investments, $I_5 = 383.15$; $A_4 = 2854$, and $A_5 = 3256$. We can solve:

$$\begin{aligned} AFC_5 &= (1-\tau)\left[\pi_5 - \sum_{z=1}^{Z} i_z(L_{z0} + C_{z5}) - i_5'\left(\sum_{s=1}^{5} \Delta DL_s\right)\right] \\ &\quad + B_1 B_2 (I_5 + \Delta e \Delta_4) \\ &= (519.34 - 22.20 - 43.96)(0.49) \end{aligned}$$

$$+ (0.07)(0.36)[383.15 + (0.033)(2854)]$$
$$= 234.087.$$

From the assumption of $P/E = 10$, we have $P_5 = 2340.87 = (10)\,(23.4087)$. Using the definition of objective function and the estimated P_5, we can define P_1 as

$$\begin{aligned}P_1 = D_1 &+ \frac{D_2}{(1+K)} + \frac{D_3}{(1+k)^2} + \frac{D_4}{(1+k)^3}\\ &+ \frac{2340}{(1+k)^4} - \frac{\Delta E_1^n}{(1-c)} - \frac{\Delta E_2^n}{(1-c)(1+k)} - \frac{\Delta E_3^n}{(1-c)(1+k)^2}\\ &- \frac{\Delta E_4^n}{(1-c)(1+k)^3} - \frac{\Delta E_5^n}{(1-c)(1+k)^4}.\end{aligned}$$

Substituting $k = 0.165$, $c = 0.10$ into PI and then substituting P_1 and $\alpha = 1.06$ into modified Eq. (23.18b)

$$\left(\frac{1}{\alpha} - 1\right) P_1 + \frac{\Delta E_1}{1-c} \leq 0.$$

We have,

$$\begin{aligned}&- 0.0566D_1 - 0.0486D_2 - 0.0417D_3 - 0.0358D_4\\ &\quad + 1.174\Delta E_1 + 0.0539\Delta E_2 + 0.0463\Delta E_3 + 0.0387\Delta E_4 + 0.034\Delta E_5\\ &\leq \frac{2340}{(1+0.165)^4}\left(1 - \frac{1}{1.06}\right) = 71.9. \qquad (23.17f)\end{aligned}$$

Using similar procedures, we can estimate the constraint of Eq. (23.18b) for the second, third, fourth, and fifth period. The empirical results are:

$$- 0.0566D_2 - 0.0486D_3 - 0.0417D_4 + 1.1728\Delta E_2$$
$$+ 0.0539\Delta E_3 + 0.0463\Delta E_4 + 0.0387\Delta E_5.LE.83.8.$$
$$- 0.0566D_2 - 0.0486D_3 + 1.1728\Delta E_2 + 0.0539\Delta E_4 + 0.0463\Delta E_5.LE.97.6.$$
$$- 0.0566D_2 + 1.728\Delta E_4 + 0.0539\Delta E_5.LE.113.69.$$
$$1.1728\Delta E_5.LE.132.44.$$

To calculate the constraint of Eq. (16.19), we obtain $D_0 = 48.2$.

General Mills' 1978 financial statement. Substituting $D_0 = 48.2$ and $\alpha_6 = 10.6$ into Eq. (23.18a) and rearranging the terms, we have the values for the first four constraints as:

$$D_1.GE.51.092 \quad (D_0 \text{ is given})$$

$$D_2 - 1.06D_1.GE.0,$$

$$D_3 - 1.06D_2.GE.0,$$

$$D_4 - 1.06D_3.GE.0.$$

The constraint of the fifth period is now discussed. Based upon most recent 5-year payout (1974–1978), we assume the target payout to be $((D_5/AFC_5) = 0.36)$. The estimated $D_5 = 0.36(AFC_5)$. Then AFC_5 can be calculated as follows:

$$\frac{D_5}{AFC_5} = 0.36;$$

$$AFC_5 = (1-\tau)\left[\pi_5 - \sum_{z=1}^{Z} i_z(L_{z0} + C_{z5}) - i_5'\left(\sum_{s=1}^{5} \Delta DL_s\right)\right]$$
$$+ B_1B_2(I_5 + \Delta e\Delta_4),$$

$i_2 = 0.085 \quad b_2 = 117.2 \quad i_2b_2 = 9.962$

i_3	b_3	i_3b_3	
0.0425	20	0.085	
0.08	4.3	0.344	$i_3b_3 = 12.44125$
0.04875	13.1	0.638625	
0.08875	53.1	4.712625	
0.08	73.7	5.886	

$$DL_5 = 488.4$$

$$AFC_5 = (0.49)\{519.34 - 9.962 - 12.44125 - (0.09)(488.41)\}$$
$$+ (0.07)(0.36)\{383.15 + (0.033)(2854)\}$$
$$= 221.96 + 12.03 = 233.99,$$

$$D_5 = AFC_5 \times (0.36) = 84.24.$$

Substituting D_5 into $D_5 - 1.06D_4 \leq 0$, we obtain

$$D_{4.} \leq 79.74 \tag{23.17o}$$

The critical calculations in constraints (23.17f) through (23.17j) are k, the discount rate, and P_5, both of which have a major impact on the resulting solution. We calculated k, using the Staley (combined M&M and CAPM) method, and P_5 was calculated using the Gordon valuation model [see Table 23.6]. We assumed that the post-horizon return on equity, $[\bar{g}/(1 - (D_5/AFC_5))P_5]$, was equal to (as opposed to greater than) the

Table 23.6. Calculation of the year 5 data.

$$AFC_5 = (1-T)\left[\Pi_5 - \sum_{z=1}^{5} i_z(L_{z,0} + C_{z,5}) - i'\sum_{s=1}^{5}\Delta DL_s\right] + B_1B_2(I_5 + \Delta e\Delta_4),$$

where

$$\sum_{s=1}^{5}\Delta DL_s = \sum_{s=1}^{5}\Delta L_s - \sum_{s=1}^{5}\Delta L_{1,s} - \sum_{s=1}^{5}\Delta L_{2,s};$$

$$\sum_{s=1}^{5}\Delta L_s = \left(\frac{m}{1+m}\right)A_5 - L_0;$$

m = Target debt/equity, $L_5/E_5 = 1$;

$$P_5 = \frac{P_5}{k-g}$$ (remembering this model's dating of variables);

$$g = \frac{\left(\frac{1-D_5}{AFC_5}\right)AFC_5}{E_5}$$ (to ensure that the post-horizon return on equity is equivalent to that of the horizon itself; A_5 is given in Table 23.4);

$$E_5 = A_5 - \left(\frac{m}{1-m}\right)A_5;$$

And k is calculated. (See Table 23.7 in general for a list of given parameters.)

With $D_5 = 84.29$, $k = 0.165$, and $g = 0.094$, the resulting P_5 generated an infeasible solution. Checking the implied P/E multiple and comparing it with the historical P/E, we discard the Gordon Valuation Model P_5, and the following formula was used:

$$P_5 = \left(\frac{\text{Proj. } P}{E}\right)(AFC_5).$$

horizon return, AFC_5/E_5.[4] Given a target payout (D_5/AFC_5) of 0.36, based upon most recent 5-year payout, the resulting g, assuming the above condition, becomes 0.094. We then found P_5 to be 1187, in the manner employed by Carleton (see Table 23.4).

However, when $P_5 = 1187$ was incorporated into the linear-programming system, an infeasible solution resulted, indicating an inconsistency in the constraints. Considering that any valuation model is often incongruent with stock-market price realities, $P_5 = 1187$ implied a P/E of 5.07 (given $AFC_5 = 234$), which was compared with the average annual P/E given by *Value Line.* The minimum average annual P/E of General Mills in the past 15 years was 11.5X, registered in 1978. This low figure compares with an overall average of 15.7 from the following year's results:

Year	1970	1971	1972	1973	1974	1975	1976	1977	1978
Average Annual P/E	18	15.3	17.4	20.8	17.8	13.6	13.8	13.2	11.5

The inconsistency in the LP system was assumed therefore to be a result of the inaccurate P_5 generated from the Gordon dividend-valuation model. Estimating conservatively (but consistent with the General Mills P/E history), a $P/E = 10X$ was applied to the $AFC_5 = 234$, to generate a $P_5 = 2340$. This P_5 predictably generated a feasible solution, the results of which are used in this chapter.

(e) Payout Restrictions

The remaining constraints in the model specify an acceptable payout range as a proportion of AFC_t with ρ_1 the minimum and ρ_2 the maximum

[4]The post-horizon retention rate is represented by:

$$\left(1 - \frac{D_n}{AFC_n}\right)$$

and

$$\bar{g} = \frac{\left(\frac{1 - D_n}{AFC_n}\right)(AFC_n)}{E_n}$$

is the growth rate. (See Carleton (1970) for detail.)

percentage of AFC_t deemed "acceptable". Here, again, industry norms often dictate the "acceptable range".

$$D_t - \delta_1 AFC_t \geq 0 \quad (t = 0, \ldots, 5),$$
$$D_t - \delta_2 AFC_t \leq 0 \quad (t = 0, \ldots, 5),$$

where δ_1 and δ_2 are lower bound and upper bound payout ratios, respectively.

Let the estimated ρ_1 and ρ_2 for General Mills be 0.15 and 0.75; then the resulting constraints in Multi-Purpose Optimization System (MPOS) format are the following[5]:

$$D_1 - 0.75AFC_1.LE.0 \quad D_1 - 0.15AFC1.GE.0;$$
$$D_2 - 0.75AFC_2.LE.0 \quad D_2 - 0.15AFC2.GE.0;$$
$$D_3 - 0.75AFC_3.LE.0 \quad D_3 - 0.15AFC3.GE.0;$$
$$D_4 - 0.75AFC_4.LE.0 \quad D_4 - 0.15AFC4.GE.0.$$

We do not show AFC_5 and D_5 in these constraints since they were calculated in Table 23.6. With a target payout for General Mills of 0.36, both of the above constraints are satisfied for $t = 5$.

A second constraint concerns a *cumulative* payout restriction limiting the overall payout of the firm for the entire planning horizon. With estimates of the AFC_t for each of the planning-horizon years and the planning-horizon net investment, the decision maker may, with the cumulative payout restriction, ρ_0 prescribe an approximate internal/external financing mixture. Here sensitivity analysis is a factor, since the model must be rerun with various cumulative payout restrictions included, to obtain an exact internal/external financing breakdown. If the cumulative payout restriction is too strict, the output will be "No feasible solution", since the internal financing requirements are then not consistent with the minimum dividend growth requirements. Following Carleton's (1970), Eq. (26), the cumulative point restriction over the entire planning horizon is as follows:

$$D_1 - \delta_0 AFC_1 + D_2 - \delta_0 AFC_2 + D_3 - \delta_0 AFC_3$$
$$+ D_4 - \delta_0 AFC_4 + D_5 - \delta_0 AFC_5 < 0.$$

[5]MPOS is a computer package of optimization programs. This package was developed by Vogel back Computer Center, Northwestern University (documented in Manual No. 320).

Or, in linear-programming format, using $\delta_0 = 0.4$ and $D_5/AFC_5 = 0.36$, we have

$$D_1 - 0.4AFC_1 + D_2 - 0.4AFC_2 + D_3 - 0.4AFC_3 \\ + D_4 - 0.4AFC_4.LE.9.36. \quad (23.17t)$$

Initially, 0.33 was used as the cumulative maximum consistent with the most recent 5-year maximum. As described above, the output was "no feasible solution" since both the cumulative payout of 0.33 and the dividend growth of 6 percent could not be satisfied. Once the cumulative payout was increased to 0.4, the inconsistency was remedied and a feasible solution was generated.

As previously discussed, the decision maker must also specify a target payout ratio to facilitate the calculation of P_5 and D_5. The target specification is 0.36, based upon the most recent 5-year payout average. A summary of the various parameters that must be specified by the decision maker prior to constraint formulation is given in Table 23.7.

Table 23.7. Summary of parameters and policy inputs.

Parameters	
$L_1 =$	Accounts Payable and Accrued Expenses $i_1 = 0$, $L_{1,t} = 0.2(A_t)$ Based on 5-year average.
$L_2 =$	Note Payable $i_2 = 8.5\%$, $L_{2,t} = 0.036(A_t)$ Based on 5-year average and projecting interest rates
$L_3 =$	LTD (see Table 22.5 for complete information).
$DTL =$	Deferred Tax Liability (Not included in the General Mills example because of a lack of information).
$\tau =$	Corporate tax rate = 0.51 (based on effective rate given in *Annual Report*).
$\Delta e =$	Stockholder Report Depreciation = 0.033 (based on 2-year combined-segment data).
$\Delta a =$	Tax Report Depreciation (Not included because of a lack of information).
$B_1 =$	ITC = 7%
$B_2 =$	Percentage of assets eligible for ITC = 0.36 based upon 5-year (fixed asset)/(total asset) ratio average.
K or $K_t =$	Appropriate risk-adjusted discount rate = 0.165.
$g =$	Post-Horizon Dividend-Growth Rate, assuming that the post-horizon return on equity is equivalent to that of the horizon year = 094. (Used to calculate Ps according to Gordon Valuation Model in Table 22.4).
$D_5/AFC_5 =$	Target Payout Ratio in year 5 = 0.36 (based upon most recent 5-year payout).

(*Continued*)

Table 23.7. (*Continued*)

Parameters

L_5/E_5 = (Liabilities − DTL)/Equity in year 5; the target debt/equity figure. used to calculate P_5 and K.

C = "Equity loss" from transaction costs and underpricing associated with a new equity issue = 0.10; an estimate.

i' = Interest rate on LTD issued during the planning horizon = 9% input could be i_t if variable rates were applied.

Policy Variables

α = Same growth requirement applied to both P_t and D_t to ensure that dividends/share did not decrease. Different growth figures could be applied to P_t and D_t to ensure that dividends/share increased by some minimum percentage. (Management could, using this restriction, equate dividends/share growth with the projected inflation rate to preserve the buying power of the dividend received by the shareholder; or some other similar benchmark could here be applied.)

S = Maximum "acceptable" debt/equity figure during the planning horizon = 1.25 in the General Mills example where debt/equity is defined in the same manner described in L_5/E_5.

X = Minimum "acceptable" interest coverage = 6.35, based upon minimum recent multiple.

δ_0 = Cumulative Payout Maximum = 0.4, an internal financing parameter, which can be varied through sensitivity analysis to generate the desired internal/external financing mix. This figure must not, however, conflict with the dividend-growth figure or as in the General Mills example when 0.33 was applied, an infeasible solution will result.

$\delta_1 = 0.15$ = Lower payout bound.

$\delta_2 = 0.75$ = Upper payout bound. In the General Mills example, both of the payout-range constraints had very little impact on the solution. It is not recommended that these constraints be included, considering the cumulative-payout restriction and the dividend-growth restriction, which eliminate the need for the arbitrary payout-range specification.

23.6. Analysis of Overall Results

The optimal output generated by the simplex algorithm consists of values for each of the variables, AFC_t as $t = 1I \ldots 4$, and D_t as $t = I \ldots 4$; also $\sum_{s=1}^{t} \Delta DL_s$ as $t = I \ldots 4$, and $\Delta E_t''$ as $t = I \ldots 5$.

Using these optimal solutions, A_t as listed in Table 23.3, L_1, L_2, and $L_{3,0}$ as listed in Table 17.5(a), and 1978 retained earnings data, we construct the pro forma General Mills' balance sheet for 1979–1983 as listed in Table 23.8. In Table 23.9, some key financial ratios and their related data

Table 23.8. General mills' pro forma balance sheet.

	As of Year-End				
Item	1979	1980	1981	1982	1983
Assets	1856.6	2159.4	2488.5	2854	3256
Acct. Payable and Accr. Exp. (L_1)	371.32	431.9	497.7	570.8	651.2
Notes Payable (L_2)	66.8	77.7	89.6	102.7	117.2
$LTD_0(L_{3,0})$	258.7	234.8	221.9	198.5	185.1
DL_t	131.38	225.18	297.65	406.89	488.4
Total $LTD_t(L_3)$	390.08	459.98	519.55	605.39	673.5
Equity					
e_{t-1}	727.5	815.1	977.00	1168.83	1366.88
Ret. Earn. $_{t-1}$	87.6	92.29	109.36	127.68	147.26
E_t[a]	—	69.91	82.47	65.37	77.49
Total Equity$_t$	815.1	977.00	1168.83	1361.88	1586.63
Accrd Taxes, Dfd. Taxes and Dfd. Compensation[b]	213.3	374.72	404.65	406.28	452.22
Total Liabilities and Owner's Equity	1856.6	2159.4	2488.5	2854	3256

(Amounts in millions, except ratio and per-share data)
[a]Depicted as ΔE_t on the computer printout.
[b]It is set equal to Total Assets — Total Equity $- L_1 - L_2 - L_3$.

are presented.[6] The procedure of actually constructing Tables 23.8 and 23.9 are left to the students' themselves.[7]

The reader will note that the optimal solution is consistent with the policy restrictions placed on the input, although many of the inequality constraints are not driven to the extreme, "equal to" situation. Inspection of Table 23.6 will also reveal the existence of plug figures, Accrued Taxes,

[6]Interest expenses can be calculated as follows:

$$5.678 + 17.04 + (131.38)\,(0.09) = 34.542 \quad (1979),$$
$$6.605 + 16.04 + (225.18)\,(0.09) = 42.911 \quad (1980),$$
$$7.616 + 14.96 + (297.65)\,(0.09) = 49.365 \quad (1981),$$
$$8.730 + 13.47 + (406.89)\,(0.09) = 58.820 \quad (1982),$$
$$9.962 + 12.24 + (488.40)\,(0.09) = 66.158 \quad (1983).$$

[7]Based upon General Mills' 1983 Annual Report, the actual key financial data for the period 1979–1983 have been compiled and listed in Appendix 23.B. Students can analyze the difference between our forecast results with the actual data listed in Table 23.B.2 for themselves.

Table 23.9. Other financial data and related ratios for General Mills.

Item	Years				
	1979	1980	1981	1982	1983
π_t (EBIT)	311.9	357.9	406.53	460.53	519.34
Interest Expense	34.542	42.911	49.365	58.820	66.158
AFC_t	143.38	163.52	185.09	208.11	234.17
D_{t-1}	48.2	51.09	54.16	57.41	60.85
Debt/Equity[a] L_t/E_t)	1.02	0.83	0.78	0.80	1.05
N_{t-1}	49.69	52.37	55.31	57.48	59.86
ΔN_t^{b}	—	2.68	2.94	2.17	2.38
EPS[c]	2.885	3.122	3.346	3.621	3.912
Estimated PPS	\$27.17	\$28.85	\$31.22	\$33.46	\$36.21
D_1 (total payout)	51.09	54.16	57.41	60.85	84.30
Interest Coverage	9.03	8.34	8.24	7.83	7.85
Payout Ratio	0.356	0.311	0.310	0.292	0.360

(Amounts in millions. except ratio and per-share data)

[a]Debt/Equity figures here are understated because of the exclusion of the plug figure. The target figure of 1 would have been obtained had all but the OTL in the plug figure been included in the numerator.

[b]New Shares Issued $= \Delta\hat{E}_t^n/P_t$ where $E_t^n = \Delta\hat{E}_t^p/P(1-C)$ and $C = 0.10$.

[c]In estimating the PPS_t a constant P/E multiple of $10X$ was applied, consistent with the estimation of P_5, but inconsistent with the Gordon Valuation Model employed as a basic valuation in the LP format.

Deferred Taxes, and Deferred Compensation for accounts, which were not included initially in the General Mills case because of a lack of information.

In the previous analysis, we consider only two potential external sources of funds-common stock and debt. Actually the firm can issue hybrid securities to finance its projects. The hybrid securities are convertible bonds and preferred stock. Convertible bonds and preferred stock issues have enjoyed a great deal of popularity in recent years, in part due to the perceived low corporate growth rate relative to those of competing sources of funds. In particular, their use is widespread as a means of effecting mergers. The preferred stock serves as payment to the owners of the merged firm, which provides them the strong likelihood of capital appreciation while at least temporarily avoiding distribution of the earnings and control of the owners of the acquiring firm. If the firm issues hybrid securities, then no accounting identities should be added to the model to specify the accounting constraints, as discussed by Carleton (1970, pp. 296–298). The conversion of these hybrid securities presents a problem with the number of shares (No) used in the objective function. If a firm issues hybrid (convertible) securities, then there are several different "numbers of shares" in the annual report. We recommend using the number of shares used in calculating primary earnings per share as the value of the variable number. The primary EPS share includes the number of actual shares outstanding during the year, as well as the conversion shares of preferred stock which was issued to yield less than one of the AA corporate bond rating (APB 15, FASB S4). This implies that, if the financial statements mention that such a preferred issue is outstanding, care should be taken in making the correction for conversion of that issue.

For all other convertible securities, the adjustment must be made in the denominator number of shares. In the Carleton model, this adjustment is made by introducing another change in equity account (dE) to account for the conversion. With the exception of forced conversion by calling in the security, the firm usually does not know when conversion will take place. This presents difficulty in incorporating the conversion into the model. To deal with this problem, Carleton suggests that the planner/manager would make the best estimate he can as to the date of conversion. Thus, if there are convertible securities present, then an estimate of their date of conversion is another input to the model.

General Mills presents an interesting illustration of both the three types of mergers and the reasons for merging one company with another. Mergers can take one of three forms. Horizontal mergers involve the combination of two competitors, such as Kenner and Parker Brothers, two toy companies. Vertical mergers include companies either upstream (involving a corporation's suppliers) or downstream (the company's distribution system). General Mills, a food processor, has begun to diversify downstream into restaurants such as the Red Lobster chain. Lastly, conglomerate mergers involve companies with no apparent relationship, such as General Mills' retail clothing additions.

Most conglomerate mergers arise in an effort to diversify (and thus to lessen) some of the risk involved in operating the same kinds of business, a concept related to portfolio diversification in finance theory. The other main reason for mergers is to increase the company's rate-of-return, usually by increasing returns to scale. Again, General Mills accomplishes returns to scale through its acquisition of restaurant capacity in addition to its food-processing capability.

Now that we have completed our discussion of the model, we should step back and look at it. This linear-programming model can be very useful in the determination of an optimal financing solution that maximizes shareholder wealth. However, there are a great many estimates that go into the final solution. It has been shown that the resulting solution is very sensitive to changes in the input values; this can present a problem. If we introduce significant estimation errors into our sales-growth estimates or our input values of EBIT, assets, and investment, the solution from the model will have no real meaning. This problem, however, suggests a good use of the model. The Financial Manager/Planner can use the model in a simulation framework to ask "what if" questions. For example, he or she could ask, "What if EBIT came in under our estimate?"

Carleton's model provides valuable training for the student. The model brings together a variety of concepts from the related disciplines of finance, accounting, and economics, thus allowing the student to review and to reinforce his understanding of these matters. Because the model is based on the accounting sources and uses, the model requires the student to understand how the accounting statements operate and articulate with one another. The student's understanding must extend to comprehension of individual financial statement items.

The interdisciplinary approach includes economic theory. Some of the constraints in the model are based on economic concepts. Thus, the student is allowed the opportunity to review and reinforce his understanding of profit and other economic concepts.

Finance theory plays a large role in the purpose of the model and its constraints. The objective function is based on an M&M (1961) dividend-stream approach. Many of the firm policy constraints are based on finance theory, which defines the relationships and suggests appropriate levels for the constraints, e.g., dividend payout, dividend growth, and interest coverage.

The training the student receives in the mathematic formulation of the model is also very valuable. The actual constraint formulations allow the student further practice in basic algebraic manipulations. Also, by actually getting into the model, in detail, the student is given a better understanding of exactly how the model works and the mathematical concepts pertinent to the linear-programming formulation.

The use of the computer in solving this formulation is an invaluable opportunity for the student to reinforce his computer skills in a learning environment. As we all have discovered, working with a computer can be a frustrating, but eventually rewarding task. Because of the contradictory nature of the constraints, it may take several trial-and-error runs to obtain a mathematically feasible solution. The training the student receives in patience and determination are well worth the time and effort expended.

Throughout this text, we have emphasized a learning-by-doing approach. The learning, however, does not end once the student has arrived at a mathematically reasonable solution. The student should realize that judgment must be exercised. The mathematics of linear programming and the computer solution are only tools. The student also must learn to take the computer output and check it to verify that the solution is satisfactory and reasonable in a qualitative and theoretical framework. Once the student has assumed a position of management responsibility, he will be required to make the judgment, "Does this accurately indicate what we (1) need to do, (2) want to do, and (3) are capable of doing?" This exercise builds the student's ability to answer these questions and proceed from there to the implementation of the resultant decision.

Another important managerial skill is the analysis of alternative courses of action. Carleton's model offers the student an opportunity to reinforce his ability to ask and answer "what if" questions. Through the use of simulation to consider possible scenarios, the student can perform sensitivity analysis. Simulation is a low-risk decision tool for the manager, because it allows him to assess the possible outcome of a series of decisions without concomitant expenditure, and possible loss, of valuable firm resources. The sensitivity analysis allows the manager to estimate with what degree of accuracy he must forecast and make decisions to achieve his desired outcome. In other words, how badly can things deviate from the plan without upsetting the entire applecart? The Carleton model allows the student to perform the process of stimulation and sensitivity analysis.

The Carleton model and the simultaneous-equation model (to be explained in the next chapter) allow the student to consider an interdisciplinary approach to learning-by-doing, in order to prepare him for a job as a financial planner/manager. We have been emphasizing the practical use of Carleton's financial-planning model. We should, however, not overlook its important theoretical implications. The model effectively pulls together concepts from the four corners of our rectangular framework of finance theory, which has been discussed in previous chapters, in formulating the objective function and the constraints. The model allows the student to consider the relationship between the four interrelated policy decisions: the investment decision, the dividend decision, the financing decision, and, to a lesser extent, the production decision. The production decision is embodied in the sales forecast, which the student makes for the planning horizon. While Carleton's model does not explicitly consider either productive capacity (an asset/sales ratio serves to indirectly deal with this problem) or the inventory problem, the student should be able to see a crude relationship between the sales level and the asset level. The sources-and-uses basis allows the student to clearly see the offsetting nature of the investment and dividend decision versus the financing decision.

23.7. Summary and Conclusion

In this chapter, we have considered Carleton's linear-programming model for financial planning. We have also reviewed some concepts of basic finance and accounting. Carleton's model obtains an optimal solution to the wealth-maximization problem and derives an appropriate financing policy. The driving force behind the Carleton model is a series of accounting constraints and firm policy constraints. We have seen that the model relies on a series of estimates of future factors.

In the next chapter, we will consider another type of financial-planning model, the simultaneous-equation models. Many of the concepts and goals of this chapter will carryover to the next chapter. We will, of course, continue to expand our horizons of knowledge and valuable tools.

Problems Set

1. What are the important finance theories used by Carleton to derive his objective function for long-term financial planning? Please briefly describe the procedure of constructing the objective function.
2. What is the basic accounting information needed to do long-term financing planning and forecasting? How can you forecast this information in order to make the long-term financial planning successful?
3. "Available for common definition" and "Sources and uses definition" are two important definitional constraints. Please define these definitions in terms of the income statement and balance sheet information.
4. Please use the financing policy and dividend policy concepts to specify five important policy constraints.
5. Using Carleton's linear-programming model as an example, please discuss how accounting information, finance theory, and programming techniques can be used jointly to do long-term financial planning and forecasting.

Appendix 23.A. Carleton's Linear-Programming Model: General Mills as a Case Study

PROBLEM SPECIFICATION

```
MPOS VERSION 4.0 NORTHWESTERN UNIVERSITY
M P 0 S
VERSION 4.0
MPOS
***** PROBLEM NUMBER 1 *****
MINIT VARIABLES
Dl D2 D3 D4 El E2 E3 E4 E5 AFC1 AFC2 AFC3 AFC4 DL1 DL2 DL3 DL4
MAXIMIZE
0.018Dl−0.0196El+0.015D2−0.017E2+0.013D3−0.0144E3+0.011D4−0.0125E4−0.015E5
CONSTRAINTS
1. AFC1+0.0441DLl .EQ. 149.17
2. AFC2+0.0441DL2 .EQ. 173.45
3. AFC3+0.0441DL3 .EQ. 198.22
4. AFC4+0.0441DL4. EQ. 226.05
5. DL1+E1 .EQ. 131.38
6. AFC1−D1+DL2−DL1+E2 .EQ. 255.7
7. AFC2−D2+DL3−DL2+E3 .EQ. 264.3
8. AFC3−D3+DL4−DL3+E4 .EQ. 302.3
9. −AFC4+D4+DL4−E5 .EQ. 182.15
10. DL1 .LE. 284 .42
11. DL2 .LE. 374.1
12. DL3 .LE. 460
13. DL4 .LE. 558.7
14. DL1 .LE. 243. 6
15. DL2−DL1 .LE. 303.15
16. DL3−DL2 .LE. 329.1
17. DL4−DL3 .LE. 365.1
18. DL4 .GE. 101.15
19. −0.0566D1−0.0486D2−0.0417D3−0.0358D4+1.1740El+0.0539E2+0.0463E3+0.0387E4+0.034E5
    .LE. 71.8
20. −0.0566D2−0.0486D3−0.04 17D4+0.1728E2+0.0539E3+0.0463E4+0.0397E55 .LE.
    83.8
21. −0.0566D3−0.0486D4+1.1728E3+0.0533E4+0.046E5 .LE. 97.6
22. −0.0566D4+1.7280E4+0.0539E5 .LE. 113.69
23. 1.1728E5 .LE. 132.44
24. Dl .GE. 51.092
25. D2−1.06D1 .GE. 0
26. D3−1.06D2 .CE. 0
27. D3−1.06D3 .GE. 0
28. D4 .LE. 79.47
29. D1−0.75AFC1 .LE. 0
30. D2−0.75AFC2 .LE. 0
31. D3−0.75AFC3 .LE. 0
32. D4−0.75AFC4 .LE. 0
33. Dl−0. 15AFC1 .GE. 0
34. D2−0.15AFC2 .GE. 0 ,
35. D3−0.15AFC3 .GE. 0
36. D4−0.15AFC4 .GE. 0
37. Dl−0.4AFCl+D2−0.4AFC2+D3−0.4AFC3+D4−0.4AFC4 .LE. 9.36
```

SOLUTION

MPOS VERSION 4.0 NORTHWESTERN UNIVERSITY
PROBLEM NUMBER
USING MINIT

SUMMARY OF RESULTS

VARIABLE NO.	VARIABLE NAME	BASIC NON-BASIC	ACTIVITY LEVEL	OPPORTUNITY COST	ROW NO.
1	Dl	B	51.0920000	—	
2	D2	B	54.1575200	—	
3	D3	B	57.4069712	—	
4	D4	B	60.8513895	—	
5	El	NB	—	0.0015408	
6	E2	B	69.6152957	—	
7	E3	B	82.4681751	—	
8	E4	B	65.3689022	—	
9	E5	B	77.4902713	—	
10	AFC1	B	143.3761420	—	
11	AFC2	B	163.5195372	—	
12	AFC3	B	185.0936187	—	
13	AFC4	B	208.1059384	—	
14	DL1	B	131.3800000	—	
15	DL2	B	225.1805623	—	
16	DL3	B	297.6503700	—	
17	DL4	B	406.8948203	—	
18	--SLACK	B	153.0400000	—	(10)
19	--SLACK	B	148.9194377	—	(11)
20	--SLACK	B	162.3496300	—	(12)
21	--SLACK	B	151.8051797	—	(13)
22	--SLACK	B	112.2200000	—	(14)
23	--SLACK	B	209.3494377	—	(15)
24	--SLACK	B	256.6301923	—	(16)
25	--SLACK	B	255.8555497	—	(17)
26	--SLACK	B	305.7448203	—	(18)
27	--SLACK	B	69.1612264	—	(19)
28	--SLACK	NB	—	0.0002527	(20)
29	--SLACK	NB	—	0.0018351	(21)
30	--SLACK	NB	—	0.0018840	(22)
31	--SLACK	B	41.5594098	—	(23)
32	--SLACK	NB	—	−0.0087826	(24)
33	--SLACK	NB	—	−0.0089493	(25)
34	--SLACK	NB	—	−0.0069790	(26)
35	--SLACK	NB	—	−0.0039896	(27)
36	--SLACK	B	18.6686105	—	(28)
37	--SLACK	B	56.4401065	—	(29)
38	--SLACK	B	68.4821329	—	(30)
39	--SLACK	B	8l.4132428	—	(31)
40	--SLACK	B	95.2280643	—	(32)

(*Continued*)

(*Continued*)

VARIABLE NO.	VARIABLE NAME	BASIC NON-BASIC	ACTIVITY LEVEL	OPPORTUNITY COST	ROW NO.
41	--SLACK	B	29.5855787	—	(33)
42	--SLACK	B	29.6295894	—	(34)
43	--SLACK	B	29.6429284	—	(35)
44	--SLACK	B	29.6354987	—	(36)
45	--SLACK	B	65.8902139	—	(37)
46	--ARTIF	NB	—	0.0172964	(1)
47	--ARTIF	NB	—	0.0165658	(2)
48	--ARTIF	NB	—	0.0158661	(3)
49	--ARTIF	NB	—	0.0151960	(4)
50	--ARTIF	NB	—	−0.0180592	(5)
51	--ARTIF	NB	—	−0.0172964	(6)
52	--ARTIF	NB	—	−0.0165658	(7)
53	--APTIF	NB	—	−0.0158661	(8)
54	--ARTIF	NB	—	0.0151960	(9)

MAXIMUM VALUE OF THE OBJECTIVE FUNCTION = −1,202792
CALCULATION TIME WAS 0.0670 SECONDS FOR 21 ITERATIONS.

Appendix 23.B. General Mills' Actual Key Financial Data

Table 23.B.1. Sales (in millions).

Year	Consumer Foods	Restaurant	Toys	Fashion	Specialty
1983	$2,792.6	$984.5	$728.3	$616.3	$429.1
1982	2,707.4	839.4	654.8	657.3	453.2
1981	2,514.6	704.0	674.3	580.3	379.0
1980	2,218.8	525.7	647.0	422.5	356.3
1979	2,062.4	436.3	583.9	360.4	302.0

Table 23.B.2. Key financial variables (in millions except per-share or ratios).

Item	1983	1982	1981	1980	1979
Sales	$5,550.8	$5,312.1	$4,852.4	$4,170.3	$3,745.0
EBIT	409.7	406.7	374.4	316.6	263.9
Total Assets	2,943.9	2,701.7	2,301.3	2,012.4	1,835.2
LTD	464.0	331.9	348.6	377.5	384.8
Dividend (PS)	1.84	1.64	1.44	1.28	1.12
Earning (PS)	4.89	4.46	3.90	3.37	2.92
Interest Expense	58.7	75.1	57.6	48.6	263.9
Shares	50.1	50.6	50.4	50.5	50.4
Stockholder Equity*	1,227.4	1,232.2			
Total Liability*	1,716.5	1,469.5			

*Data available only for 1983 and 1982.

References for Chapter 23

Carleton, WT (1970). An analytical model for long-range planning. *Journal of Finance*, 25, 291–315.

Carleton, WT and CL Dick Jr (1973). Financial policy model: Theory and practice. *Journal of Financial and Quantitative Analysis*, 8, 691–709.

Miller, MH and F Modigliani (1961). Dividend policy, growth, and the valuation of shares. *Journal of Business*, 411–433.

Modigliani, F and MH Miller (1963). Corporate income taxes and the cost of capital: A correction. *American Economic Review*, 59, 433–443.

Myers, SC and Pogue, GA (1974). A programming approach to corporate financial management. *Journal of Finance*, 29, 579–599.

Chapter 24

Simultaneous Equation Models for Security Valuation

24.1. Introduction

In Chapter 23, we considered a planning model using a linear-programming format. In this chapter, we will consider two models based upon a simultaneous-equation approach to financial planning. The first model we will consider, in Section 24.2, is the Warren and Shelton (1971) (hereafter, *WS*) model. To certify some of the uses of WS type of simultaneous equation models, we will use a case study of Johnson and Johnson in Section 24.3. The other model in Section 24.4, that of Francis and Rowell (1978) (hereafter, *FR*), is an expansion of the *WS* model. Both models allow the financial planner/manager to analyze important operating and financial variables. Both models are also computer-based and much less complicated for the user than the Carleton model.

In addition, we have discussed Felthan–Ohlson model for determining equity value in Section 24.5. Finally, we have explored the usefulness of integrating WS model and Felthan-Ohlson model to improve the determination of equity value in Section 24.6.

24.2. Warren and Shelton Model[1]

24.2.1. *Percentage of Sales Method for Financial Planning and Forecasting*

Ross, Westerfield, and Jordon (2012) and Lee, Finnerty, Norton (1997) have shown how percentage sales method can be used to develop financial

[1]The case study of the *WS* model by employing the annual report data of Johnson and Johnson will be presented in Section 26.2 in detail.

analysis, planning, and forecasting. Financial planning is the process of analyzing alternative investment, financing, and dividend strategies in the context of various potential economic environments. Planning involves forecasting both the outcomes of different strategies and their risks. Thus, financial planning models are tools to help managers improve their forecasts of important accounts of financial statements and better understand the interactions of investment, financing, and dividend decisions.

In developing a long term financial plan, these three decisions (policies) can be described more explicitly as follows.

1. *The firm's investment decision.* This refers to the amount of cash needed for the firm's investment in a new asset (it is also called the *capital budgeting decision*). In addition, it also refers to the amount of working-capital needed on an ongoing basis (also referred to as the *working-capital decision*).
2. *The firm's financing decision.* This refers to new borrowing or new equity issued for financing the firm's investment in new assets. This decision is influenced by the degree of financial leverage the firm chooses to employ and how it plans to raise the necessary new funds.
3. *The firms dividend decision.* This refers to the amount of cash the firm thinks is necessary and appropriate to pay equity holders as cash dividends.

At the most basic level, a planning model is a tool that uses inputs supplied by managers in the form of economic, accounting, market, and policy information. Depending on its sophistication, the output of the financial planning and forecasting model may include simple estimates of growth rates or complex *pro forma* financial statements, with projected financial statement data, and forecasts of stock price, earnings per share (EPS), dividends per share (DPS), new equity issues, and new debt issues.

The procedure of using percentage sales methods for financial planning and forecasting can be briefly described as follows:

1. Calculate by dividing company sales into both balance sheet and income statement to obtain standardized financial statements.
2. Forecast growth rate and outside financing.
3. Forecast external financing needs.
4. Combine information from steps 1, 2, 3 to obtain *pro forma* financial statements.

5. Use *pro forma* financial statements to perform future financial planning and forecasting.

24.2.2. *Warren and Shelton Model*

Warren and Shelton (1970) expands on the percentage sales method by introducing financing investment and dividend policy into the the planning process. Their model is a 20 equation system, divided into four sections which will be describes in Table 24.1.

Before we discuss the Warren Shelton Model, we will briefly describe the characteristics of a good financial-planning model:

(1) The model results and the assumptions should be plausible and/or credible.
(2) The model should be flexible so that it can be adapted and expanded to meet a variety of circumstances.
(3) It should improve on current practice in a technical or performance manner.
(4) The model inputs and outputs should be comprehensible to the user without extensive additional training.
(5) It should take into account the interrelated investments, financing, dividend, and production decisions and their effect on the market value of the firm.
(6) The model should be fairly simple for the user to operate without extensive intervention of non-financial personnel and tedious formulation of the input.

With the exception of point (6), Carleton's (1970) model fits this framework. In an effort to improve upon Carleton's model, *WS* devised a simultaneous-equation model. The *WS* model has some similarities to Carleton's model. *WS* do take greater account of the interrelation of the financing, dividend, and investment decisions. They rely upon a sales forecast as a critical input to the model. Unlike Carleton, *WS* explicitly used various operating ratios in their model. Carleton had those ratios in his model implicitly through the manner in which the forecasts were made up. The explicit positioning of the ratios means that the *WS* method is computationally less tedious, and thus its use is more time-efficient.

As can be seen from examining Table 24.1, the *WS* model has four distinct segments corresponding to the sales, investment, financing, and return-to-investment concepts in financial theory. The entire model is a

Table 24.1. The *WS* model.

I. Generating of Sales and Earnings Before Interest and Taxes for Period t

(1) $Sales_t = Sales_{t-1} \times (1 + GSALS_t)$,

(2) $EBIT_t = REBIT_t \times SALES_t$.

II. Generating of Total Assets Required for Period t

(3) $CA_t = RCA_t \times SALES_t$,

(4) $FA_t = RFA_t \times SALES_t$,

(5) $A_t = CA_t + FA_t$.

III. Financing the Desired Level of Assets

(6) $CL_t = RCL_t SALES_t$

(7) $NF_t = (A_t - CL_t - PFDSK_t) - (L_{t-1} - LR_t) - S_{t-1} - R_{t-1}$
$-b_t\{(1 - T_t)[EBIT_t - i_{t-1}(L_{t-1} - LR_t)] - PFDIV_t\}$

(8) $NF_t + b_t(1 - T_t)[i_t^e NL_t + U_t^1 NL_t] = NL_t + NS_t$

(9) $L_t = L_{t-1} - LR_t + NL_t$

(10) $S_t = S_{t-1} + NS_t$

(11) $R_i = R_{t-1} + b_t\{(1 - T_t)[EBIT_t - i_t L_t - U_t^1 NL_t] - PFDIV_t\}$

(12) $i_t = i_{t-1}\left(\frac{L_{t-1} - LR_t}{L_t}\right) + i_t^e \frac{NL_t}{L_t}$

(13) $\frac{L_t}{S_t + R_t} = K_t$

IV. Generation of Per Share Data for Period t

(14) $EAFCD_t = (1 - T_t)[EBIT_t - i_t L_t - U_t^1 NL_t] - PFDIV_t$

(15) $CMDIV_t = (1 - b_t)EAFCD_t$

(16) $NUMCS_t = NUMCS_{t-1} + NEWCS_t$

(17) $NEWCS_t = \frac{NS_t}{(1 - U_t^s)P_t}$

(18) $P_t = m_t EPS_t$

(19) $EPS_t = \frac{EAFCD_t}{NUMCS_t}$

(20) $DPS_t = \frac{CMDIV_t}{NUMCS_t}$

The above system is "complete" in 20 equations and 20 unknows. The unknows are listed and defined in Table 24.2, together with the parameters (inputs) that management is required to provide.

Source: Warren and Shelton (1971). Reprinted with permission.

system of 20 equations of a semi-simultaneous nature. The actual solution algorithm is recursive, between and within segments.

Now, we will consider in detail an Excel computer program called FINPLAN, which is used to solve the *WS* model.[2] First, we will consider the inputs to the *WS* model. Second, we will develop into the interaction of the equations in the model. Third, we will look at the inputs to the FINPLAN model.

The 20-equation model appears in Table 24.1, and the parameters used as inputs to the model are demonstrated in the second part of Table 24.2. As in the Carleton model, the driving force of the model is the sales-growth estimates ($GSALS_t$). Equation (24.1) shows that the sales for period t is simply the product of sales in the prior period multiplied by the growth rate in sales for the period t. We then derive earning before interest and taxes (*EBIT*) as a percentage of sales ratio, as in Eqs. (24.3) and (24.4) through the use of the $CA/SALES$ and $FA/SALES$ ratios. The sum of CA and FA is total assets for the period (Eq. (24.5)).

The financing of the desired level of assets is undertaken in Section III of Table 24.1. In Eq. (24.6), current liabilities in period t is derived from the ratio of $CL/SALES$ multiplied by $SALES$. Equation (24.7) is the funds required (NF_t). Like Carleton's model, FINPLAN assumes that the amount of preferred stock is constant over the planning horizon. In determining needed funds, FINPLAN uses accounting identities. As Eq. (24.7) shows, the assets for period t are the basis for financing needs. Current liabilities, as determined in Eq. (24.6), are one source of funds and are therefore subtracted from asset levels. As mentioned above, preferred stock is constant and therefore must be subtracted. After the first parenthesis in Eq. (24.7), we have the financing that must come from internal sources (retain earnings) and long-term external sources (debt and stock issues). The second parenthesis takes into account the remaining old debt outstanding, after retirements, in period t. Then the funds provided by existing stock and retained earnings are subtracted. The last quantity is the funds provided by operations during period t.

Once the funds needed for operations are defined, Eq. (24.8) specifies that new funds, after taking into account underwriting costs and additional

[2]The original FINPLAN is a financial-forecasting model using FORTRAN computer program based upon Warren and Shelton (1971) simultaneous-equation approach to financial planning. The detailed description of the computer program can be found in Appendix 24.B.

Table 24.2. List of unknowns and list of parameters provided by management.

I Unknowns	
1. $SALES_t$	Sales
2. CA_t	Current Assets
3. FA_t	Fixed Assets
4. A_t	Total Assets
5. CL_t	Current Payables
6. NF_t	Needed Funds
7. $EBIT_t$	Earnings before Interest and Taxes
8. NL_t	New Debt
9. NS_t	New Stock
10. L_t	Total Debt
11. S_t	Common Stock
12. R_t	Retained Earnings
13. i_t	Interest Rate on Debt
14. $EAFCD_I$	Earnings Available for Common Dividends
15. $CMDIV_t$	Common Dividends
16. $NUMCS_t$	Number of Common Shares Outstanding
17. $NEWCS_t$	New Common Shares Issued
18. P_t	Price per Share (PPS)
19. EPS_t	Earnings per Share
20. DPS_t	Dividends per Share
II Provided by Management	
21. $SALES_{t-1}$	Sales in Previous Period
22. $GSALS_t$	Growth in Sales
23. RCA_t	Current Assets as a Percent of Sales
24. RFA_t	Fixed Assets as a Percent of Sales
25. RCL_t	Current Payables as a Percent of Sales
26. $PFDSK_t$	Preferred Stock
27. $PFDIV_t$	Preferred Dividends
28. L_{t-1}	Debt in Previous Period
29. LR_t	Debt Repayment
30. S_{t-1}	Common Stock in Previous Period
31. R_{t-1}	Retained Earnings in Previous Period
32. b_t	Retention Rate
33. T_t	Average Tax Rate
34. i_{t-1}	Average Interest Rate in Previous Period
35. i_t^e	Expected Interest Rate on New Debt
36. $REBIT_t$	Operating Income as a Percent of Sales
37. U_t^1	Underwriting Cost of Debt
38. U_t^s	Underwriting Cost of Equity
39. K_t	Ratio of Debt to Equity
40. $NUMCS_{t-1}$	Number of Common Shares Outstanding in Previous Period
41. m_t	Price-Earnings Ratio

Source: Warren and Shelton (1971). Reprinted by permission.

interest costs from new debt, are to come from long-term debt and new stock issues. Equations (24.9) and (24.10) simply update the debt and equity accounts for the new issuances. Equation (24.11) updates the retained earnings account for the portion of earnings available to common shares as a result of operations during period t. The term b_t is the retention rate in period t (i.e., the complement of the payout ratio) and $(1 - T_t)$ is the after-tax percentage, which is multiplied by the earnings from the period after netting out interest costs on both new and old debt. Since preferred stockholders must be paid before common stockholders, preferred dividends must be subtracted from funds available for common. Equation (24.12) calculates the new weighted-average interest rate for the firm's debt. Equation (24.13) is the new debt-to-equity ratio, for period t.

Section IV of Table 24.1 is concerned with the common stockholder, dividends, and market value. Equation (24.14) is the earnings available for common dividends. It is the same as the portion Eqs. (24.11) through (24.15) by using the complement of the retention rate multiplied by the earnings available for common dividends. Equation (24.16) updates the number of common shares for new issues.

As Eq. (24.17) shows, the number of new common shares is determined by the total amount of the new stock issue divided by the stock price after discounting for issuance costs. Equation (24.18) determines the price of the stock through the use of a price-earnings ratio (m_t) of the stock purchase. Equation (24.19) determines *EPS*, as usual, by dividing earnings available for common by the number of common shares outstanding. Equation (24.20) determines DPS in a similar manner. This completes the model of 20 equations in 20 unknowns. Table 24.3 shows the variable numbers and their input format. A sample FINPLAN input is demonstrated, together with a sensitivity analysis.

Sensitivity analysis is accomplished by changing one parameter and noting the effect the change has on the result. FINPLAN allows sensitivity analysis to be built into a single-input deck through the use of the run code. The procedure for performing the sensitivity analysis is indicated in Table 24.3. Sensitivity analysis is very helpful in answering questions about what the results might have been if a different decision had been made.

Since the future cannot be forecast with perfect certainty, the manager/planner must know how a deviation from the forecast will affect his or her plans. The financial manager/planner must also make contingency plans for probable deviations from his or her forecast.

Table 24.3. FINPLAN input format.

Variable* Number	Data**	Variable	Description
21	61897.0	$SALEt - 1$	Net Sales at $t - 1 = 2009$
22	−0.2900	$GCALSt$	Growth in Sales
23	0.6388	$RCAt - 1$	Current Assets as a Percentage of Sales
24	0.8909	$RFAt - 1$	Fixed Assets as a Percentage of Sales
25	0.3109	$RCLt - 1$	Current Payables as a Percentage of Sales
26	0.0000	$PFDSKt - 1$	Preferred Stock
27	0.0000	$PFDIVt - 1$	Preferred Dividends
28	8223.0	$Lt - 1$	Long-Term Debt in Previous Period
29	219.0	$LRt - 1$	Long-Term Debt Repayment (Reduction)
30	3120.0	$St - 1$	Common Stock in Previous Period
31	67248.0	$Rt - 1$	Retained Earnings in Previous Period
32	0.5657	$bt - 1$	Retention Rate
33	0.2215	$Tt - 1$	Average Tax Rate (Income Taxes/Pretax Income)
34	0.0671	$it - 1$	Average Interest Rate in Previous Period
35	0.0671	$i_et - 1$	Expected Interest Rate on New Debt
36	0.2710	$REBITt - 1$	Operating Income as a Percentage of Sales
37	0.0671	U^L	Underwriting Cost of Debt
38	0.1053	U^E	Underwriting Cost of Equity
39	0.1625	Kt	Ratio of Debt to Equity
40	2754.3	$NUMCSt - 1$	Number of Common Shares Outstanding in Previous Period
41	14.5	$mt - 1$	Price–Earnings Ratio

*Variable number as defined in Table 24.2.

**Data obtained from JNJ Balance Sheets and Income Statements.

Historical or Base-Period Input

Balance Sheet

JNJ
TICKER SYMBOL: JNJ
SIC Code: 2834
ANNUAL BALANCE SHEET
($ MILLIONS)

	Dec-09	Dec-08	Dec-07	Dec-06	Dec-05	Dec-04	Dec-03	Dec-02	Dec-01
ASSETS									
Cash and Short-Term Investments	19,425.00	12,809.00	9,315.00	4,084.00	16,138.00	12,884.00	9,523.00	7,475.00	7,972.00
Receivables	9,646.00	9,719.00	9,444.00	8,712.00	7,010.00	6,831.00	6,574.00	5,399.00	4,630.00
Inventories — Total	5,180.00	5,052.00	5,110.00	4,889.00	3,959.00	3,744.00	3,588.00	3,303.00	2,992.00
Prepaid Expense	.	.	.	.	.	.	.	.	.
Other Current Assets	5,290.00	6,797.00	6,076.00	5,290.00	4,287.00	3,861.00	3,310.00	3,089.00	2,879.00
Total Current Assets	39,541.00	34,377.00	29,945.00	22,975.00	31,394.00	27,320.00	22,995.00	19,266.00	18,473.00
Property, Plant, and Equipment — Total (Gross)	29,251.00	27,392.00	26,466.00	24,028.00	19,716.00	18,664.00	17,052.00	14,314.00	12,458.00
Depreciation, Depletion, and Amortization (Accumulated)	14,492.00	13,027.00	12,281.00	10,984.00	8,886.00	8,228.00	7,206.00	5,604.00	4,739.00
Property, Plant, and Equipment — Total (Net)	14,759.00	14,365.00	14,185.00	13,044.00	10,830.00	10,436.00	9,846.00	8,710.00	7,719.00

(*Continued*)

(*Continued*)

	Dec-09	Dec-08	Dec-07	Dec-06	Dec-05	Dec-04	Dec-03	Dec-02	Dec-01
Investments and Advances — Equity Method	0	0	0	0	0	0	0	0	.
Investments and Advances — Other	.	4	2	16	20	46	84	121	969
Intangibles	31,185.00	27,695.00	28,763.00	28,688.00	12,175.00	11,842.00	11,539.00	9,246.00	9,077.00
Deferred Charges	266	136	481	259	1,218.00	1,001.00	1,021.00	959	0
Other Assets — Sundry	8,931.00	8,335.00	7,578.00	5,574.00	2,388.00	2,672.00	2,778.00	2,254.00	2,250.00
TOTAL ASSETS	94,682.00	84,912.00	80,954.00	70,556.00	58,025.00	53,317.00	48,263.00	40,556.00	38,488.00
LIABILITIES									
Debt — Due in 1 Year	34	221	9	9	12	18	224	77	228
Notes Payable	6,284.00	3,511.00	2,454.00	4,570.00	656	262	915	2,040.00	337
Accounts Payable	5,541.00	7,503.00	6,909.00	5,691.00	4,315.00	5,227.00	4,966.00	3,621.00	2,838.00
Income Taxes Payable	442	417	223	724	940	1,506.00	944	710	537
Accrued Expense	9,430.00	9,200.00	10,242.00	8,167.00	6,712.00	6,914.00	6,399.00	5,001.00	4,104.00
Other Current Liabilities	9,430.00	9,200.00	10,242.00	8,167.00	6,712.00	6,914.00	6,399.00	5,001.00	4,104.00
Total Current Liabilities	21,731.00	20,852.00	19,837.00	19,161.00	12,635.00	13,927.00	13,448.00	11,449.00	8,044.00
Long-Term Debt — Total	8,223.00	8,120.00	7,074.00	2,014.00	2,017.00	2,565.00	2,955.00	2,022.00	2,217.00
Deferred Taxes	1,424.00	1,432.00	1,493.00	1,319.00	211	403	780	643	493
Investment Tax Credit	0	0	0	0	0	0	0	0	0
Minority Interest	0	0	0	0	0	0	0	0	0
Other Liabilities	12,716.00	11,997.00	9,231.00	8,744.00	5,291.00	4,609.00	4,211.00	3,745.00	3,501.00

(*Continued*)

(*Continued*)

	Dec-09	Dec-08	Dec-07	Dec-06	Dec-05	Dec-04	Dec-03	Dec-02	Dec-01
EQUITY									
Preferred Stock — Redeemable	0	0	0	0	0	0	0	0	0
Preferred Stock — Non-redeemable	0	0	0	0	0	0	0	0	0
Total Preferred Stock	0	0	0	0	0	0	0	0	0
Common Stock	3,120.00	3,120.00	3,120.00	3,120.00	3,120.00	3,120.00	3,120.00	3,120.00	3,120.00
Capital Surplus	0	0	0	0	0	−11	−18	−25	−30
Retained Earnings	67,248.00	58,424.00	54,587.00	47,172.00	40,716.00	34,708.00	29,913.00	25,729.00	22,536.00
Less: Treasury Stock — Total Dollar Amount	19,780.00	19,033.00	14,388.00	10,974.00	5,965.00	6,004.00	6,146.00	6,127.00	1,393.00
Total Common Equity	50,588.00	42,511.00	43,319.00	39,318.00	37,871.00	31,813.00	26,869.00	22,697.00	24,233.00
TOTAL STOCKHOLDERS' EQUITY	50,588.00	42,511.00	43,319.00	39,318.00	37,871.00	31,813.00	26,869.00	22,697.00	24,233.00
TOTAL LIABILITIES AND STOCKHOLDERS' EQUITY	94,682.00	84,912.00	80,954.00	70,556.00	58,025.00	53,317.00	48,263.00	40,556.00	38,488.00
COMMON SHARES OUTSTANDING	2,754.32	2,769.18	2,840.22	2,893.23	2,974.48	2,971.02	2,967.97	2,968.30	3,047.22

(*Continued*)

Income Statement

JNJ
TICKER SYMBOL: JNJ
SIC: 2834
ANNUAL INCOME STATEMENT COMPARING HISTORICAL AND RESTATED INFORMATION
($ MILLIONS, EXCEPT PER SHARE)

	Dec-09	Dec-08	Dec-07	Dec-06	Dec-05	Dec-04	Dec-03	Dec-02	Dec-01
Sales	61,897.00	63,747.00	61,035.00	53,194.00	50,434.00	47,348.00	41,862.00	36,298.00	33,004.00
Cost of Goods Sold	15,560.00	15,679.00	14,974.00	12,880.00	11,861.00	11,298.00	10,307.00	8,785.00	7,931.00
Selling, General, and Administrative Expense	26,787.00	29,067.00	28,131.00	24,558.00	23,189.00	21,063.00	18,815.00	16,173.00	15,583.00
Operating Income Before Depreciation	19,550.00	19,001.00	17,930.00	15,756.00	15,384.00	14,987.00	12,740.00	11,340.00	9,490.00
Depreciation and Amortization	2,774.00	2,832.00	2,777.00	2,177.00	2,093.00	2,124.00	1,869.00	1,662.00	1,605.00
Interest Expense	552	582	426	181	165	323	315	258	248
Non-operating Income (Expense)	−54	515	551	996	812	316	440	295	513
Pretax Income	15,755.00	16,929.00	II. 13,283.00	14,587.00	13,656.00	12,838.00	10,308.00	9,291.00	7,898.00
Income Taxes — Total	3,489.00	3,980.00	2,707.00	3,534.00	3,245.00	4,329.00	3,111.00	2,694.00	2,230.00
Minority Interest	0	0	0	0	0	0	0	0	0
Income Before Extraordinary Items	12,266.00	12,949.00	10,576.00	11,053.00	10,411.00	8,509.00	7,197.00	6,597.00	5,668.00
Extraordinary Items and Discontinued Operations	0	0	0	0	0	0	0	0	0
Net Income (Loss)	12,266.00	12,949.00	10,576.00	11,053.00	10,411.00	8,509.00	7,197.00	6,597.00	5,668.00

(Continued)

(Continued)

	Dec-09	Dec-08	Dec-07	Dec-06	Dec-05	Dec-04	Dec-03	Dec-02	Dec-01
EPS (Primary) — Excluding Extraordinary Items	4.45	4.62	3.67	3.76	3.5	2.87	2.42	2.2	1.87
EPS (Primary) — Including Extraordinary Items	4.45	4.62	3.67	3.76	3.5	2.87	2.42	2.2	1.87
Common Shares Used to Calculate Primary EPS	2,759.50	2,802.50	2,882.90	2,936.40	2,973.90	2,968.40	2,968.10	2,998.30	3,033.80
EPS (Fully Diluted) — Excluding Extraordinary Items	4.4	4.57	3.63	3.73	3.46	2.84	2.4	2.16	1.84
EPS (Fully Diluted) — Including Extraordinary Items	4.4	4.57	3.63	3.73	3.46	2.84	2.4	2.16	1.84

(Continued)

Statement of Cash Flows

JNJ
TICKER SYMBOL: JNJ
SIC: 2834
ANNUAL STATEMENT OF CASH FLOWS
($ MILLIONS)

	Dec-09	Dec-08	Dec-07	Dec-06	Dec-05	Dec-04	Dec-03	Dec-02	Dec-01
INDIRECT OPERATING ACTIVITIES									
Income Before Extraordinary Items	12,266.00	12,949.00	10,576.00	11,053.00	10,411.00	8,509.00	7,197.00	6,597.00	5,668.00
Depreciation and Amortization	2,774.00	2,832.00	2,777.00	2,177.00	2,093.00	2,124.00	1,869.00	1,662.00	1,605.00
Extraordinary Items and Disc. Operations	0	0	0	0	0	0	0	0	0
Deferred Taxes	−436	22	−1,762.00	−1,168.00	−46	−498	−720	−74	−106
Equity in Net Loss (Earnings)	0	0	0	0	.	.	.	.	.
Sale of Property, Plant, and Equipment and Sale of Investments — Loss (Gain)	0	0	0	0	0	0	0	0	0
Funds from Operations — Other	686	894	2,205.00	1,204.00	331	21	924	183	204
Accounts Receivable — Decrease (Increase)	453	−736	−416	−699	−568	−111	−691	−510	−258
Inventory — Decrease (Increase)	95	−101	14	−210	−396	11	39	−109	−167
Accounts Payable and Incrued Liab. — Increase (Decrease)	−507	−272	2,642.00	1,750.00	−911	607	2,192.00	1,420.00	1,401.00
Income Taxes — Accrued — Increase (Decrease)	.	.	.	.	.	.	.	.	.
Other Assets and Liabilities — Net Change	1,240.00	−616	−787	141	963	468	−215	−993	517
Operating Activities — Net Cash Flow	16,571.00	14,972.00	15,249.00	14,248.00	11,877.00	11,131.00	10,595.00	8,176.00	8,864.00

(Continued)

(Continued)

	Dec-09	Dec-08	Dec-07	Dec-06	Dec-05	Dec-04	Dec-03	Dec-02	Dec-01
INVESTING ACTIVITIES									
Investments — Increase	10,040.00	3,668.00	9,659.00	467	5,660.00	11,617.00	7,590.00	6,923.00	8,188.00
Sale of Investments	7,232.00	3,059.00	7,988.00	426	9,187.00	12,061.00	8,062.00	7,353.00	5,967.00
Short-Term Investments — Change	.	.	.	.	.	.	.	.	.
Capital Expenditures	2,365.00	3,066.00	2,942.00	2,666.00	2,632.00	2,175.00	2,262.00	2,099.00	1,731.00
Sale of Property, Plant, and Equipment	.	.	.	.	.	.	.	.	.
Acquisitions	2,470.00	1,214.00	1,388.00	18,023.00	987	580	2,812.00	478	225
Investing Activities — Other	45	702	−138	439	−187	−36	76	−50	84
Investing Activities — Net Cash Flow	−7,598.00	−4,187.00	−6,139.00	−20,291.00	−279	−2,347.00	−4,526.00	−2,197.00	−4,093.00
FINANCING ACTIVITIES									
Sale of Common and Preferred Stock	882	1,486.00	1,562.00	1,135.00	696	642	311	390	514
Purchase of Common and Preferred Stock	2,130.00	6,651.00	5,607.00	6,722.00	1,717.00	1,384.00	1,183.00	6,538.00	2,570.00
Cash Dividends	5,327.00	5,024.00	4,670.00	4,267.00	3,793.00	3,251.00	2,746.00	2,381.00	2,047.00

(Continued)

(*Continued*)

	Dec-09	Dec-08	Dec-07	Dec-06	Dec-05	Dec-04	Dec-03	Dec-02	Dec-01
Long-Term Debt — Issuance	9	1,638.00	5,100.00	6	6	17	1,023.00	22	14
Long-Term Debt — Reduction	219	24	18	13	196	395	196	245	391
Current Debt — Changes	2,693.00	1,111.00	−2,065.00	3,752.00	483	−777	−1,072.00	1,799.00	−771
Financing Activities — Other	0	0	0	0	0	0	0	0	0
Financing Activities — Net Cash Flow	−4,092.00	−7,464.00	−5,698.00	−6,109.00	−4,521.00	−5,148.00	−3,863.00	−6,953.00	−5,251.00
Exchange Rate Effect	161	−323	275	180	−225	190	277	110	−40
Cash and Cash Equivalents — Increase (Decrease)	5,042.00	2,998.00	3,687.00	−11,972.00	6,852.00	3,826.00	2,483.00	−864	−520
DIRECT OPERATING ACTIVITIES									
Interest Paid — Net	533	525	314	143	151	222	206	141	185
Income Taxes Paid	2,363.00	4,068.00	4,099.00	4,250.00	3,429.00	3,880.00	3,146.00	2,006.00	2,090.00

The above data of financial statements is downloaded from the COMPUSTAT dataset; @NA represents data is not available.

While the *WS* model allows the user a greater control over more details than does the Carleton model, it does not explicitly consider the production segment of the firm. In an effort to deal with the production function and other issues, *FR* have formulated a simultaneous-equation model that expands on the *WS* model.

24.3. Johnson & Johnson (JNJ) as a Case Study

In this section, a case study is used to demonstrate how *WS*'s model set forth in Table 24.1 can be used to perform financial analysis, planning, and forecasting for an individual firm.

24.3.1. *Data Sources and Parameter Estimations*

In this case study, JNJ company is chosen, to perform financial planning and analysis using the *WS* model. The base year of the planning is 2009 and the planning period is 1 year, that is, 2010. Accounting and market data are required to estimate the parameters of *WS* financial-planning model. The *COMPUSTAT* data file is the major sources of accounting and market information. The following paragraphs briefly discuss the parameter-estimation processes. All dollar terms are in millions, and the number of shares outstanding is also millions.

Using these parameter estimates given in Table 24.3, the 20 unknown variables related to income statement and balance sheet can be solved for algebraically. The calculations are set forth in the following subsection.

24.3.2. *Procedure for Calculating WS Model*

By using the data above, we are able to calculate the unknown variables below:

(1) $$\begin{aligned} Sales_t &= Sales_{t-1} \times (1 + GCALS_t) \\ &= 61897.0 \times 0.71 \\ &= 43{,}946.87. \end{aligned}$$

(2) $$\begin{aligned} EBIT_t &= REBIT_{t-1} \times Sales_t \\ &= 0.2710 \times 43{,}946.87 \\ &= 11{,}909.60. \end{aligned}$$

(3) $$\begin{aligned} CA_t &= RCA_{t-1} \times Sales_t \\ &= 0.6388 \times 43{,}946.87 \\ &= 28{,}073.26. \end{aligned}$$

(4) $FA_t = RFA_{t-1} \times Sales_t$
$= 0.8909 \times 43{,}946.87$
$= 39{,}152.27.$

(5) $A_t = CA_t + FA_t$
$= 28{,}073.26 + 39{,}152.27$
$= 67{,}225.53.$

(6) $CL_t = RCL_{t-1} \times Sales_t$
$= 0.3109 \times 43{,}946.87$
$= 13{,}663.08.$

(7) $NF_t = (A_t - CL_t - PFDSK_t) - (L_{t-1} - LR_t) - S_{t-1} - R_{t-1} - b_t \times \{(1 - T_t)[EBIT_t - i_{t-1}(L_{t-1} - LR_t)] - PFDIV_t\}$
$= (67{,}225.53 - 13{,}663.08 - 0) - (8{,}223.0 - 219.0) - 3{,}120.0 - 67{,}248.0 - 0.5657 \times \{(1 - 0.2215) \times [\ 11{,}909.60 - 0.0671 \times\ (8{,}223.0 - 219.0)] - 0\}$
$= -29{,}817.99.$

(12) $i_t L_t = i_{t-1}(L_{t-1} - LR_t) + i^e_{t-1} \times NL_t$
$= 0.0671 \times (8, 223.0 - 219.0) + 0.0671 \times NL_t$
$= 537.0684 + 0.0671 \times NL_t$

(8) $NF_t + b_t(1 - T)[i_{t-1} \times NL_t + U^L_t \times NL_t]$
$= NL_t + NS_t - 29817.99 + 0.5657 \times (1 - 0.2215) \times [0.0671 NL_t + 0.0671 NL_t)$
$= NL_t + NS_t - 29817.99 + 0.0591 \times NL_t$
$= NL_t + NS_t$

(a) $NS_t + 0.9409 NL_t = -29{,}817.99.$

(9) $L_t = L_{t-1} - LR_t + NL_t$

(b) $L_t = 8{,}223.0 - 219.0 + NL_t$
$L_t - NL_t = 8{,}004.$

(10) $S_t = S_{t-1} + NS_t$

(c) $-NS_t + S_t = 3{,}120.0.$

(11) $R_t = R_{t-1} + b_t\{(1 - T_t)[EBIT_t - i_t L_t - U^L_t NL_t] - PFDIV_t\}$
$= 67{,}248.0 + 0.5657 \times \{(1 - 0.2215) \times [11{,}909.60 - i_t L_t - 0.0671 NL_t] - 0\}.$

Substitute (12) into (11)

$$R_t = 67{,}248.0 + 0.5657 \times \{0.7785 \times [11{,}909.60 - (537.0684 + 0.0671 \times NL_t) - 0.0671 NL_t]\}$$
$$= 67{,}248.0 + 5{,}008.4347 - 0.0591 NL_t.$$

(d) $72{,}256.435 = R_t + 0.0591 NL_t$.

(13) $L_t = (S_t + R_t) K_t$

$L_t = 0.1625 S_t + 0.1625 R_t$

(e) $L_t - 0.1625 S_t - 0.1625 R_t = 0$.

(b) − (e) = (f)

$$0 = (L_t - NL_t - 8{,}004) - (L_t - 0.1625 S_t - 0.1625 R_t)$$
$$8{,}004 = 0.1625 S_t + 0.1625 R_t - NL_t.$$

(f) − 0.1625 (c) = (g)

$$8{,}004 - 507 = (0.1625 S_t + 0.1625 R_t - NL_t) - 0.1625(-NS_t + S_t)$$
$$7{,}497 = 0.1625 NS_t - NL_t + 0.1625 R_t.$$

(g) − 0.1625 (d) = (h)

$$7{,}497 - 0.1625 \times 72{,}256.435$$
$$= (0.1625 NS_t - NL_t + 0.1625 R_t) - 0.1625(R_t + 0.0591 NL_t)$$
$$-4{,}244.67 = 0.1625 NS_t - 1.0096 NL_t.$$

(h) − 0.1625 (a) = (i)

$$0.1625 NS_t - 1.0096 NL_t - 0.1625(NS_t + 0.9409 NL_t)$$
$$= -4{,}244.67 + 0.1625(29{,}817.99)$$
$$NL_t = -600.7533/1.1625 = -516.777.$$

Substitute NL_t in (a)

$$NS_t + 0.9409 \times (-516.777) = -29{,}817.99$$
$$NS_t = -29{,}331.755.$$

Substitute NL_t in (b)

$$L_t = 8{,}223.0 - 219.0 - 516.777$$
$$= 7{,}487.223.$$

Substitute NS_t in (c)

$$29{,}331.755 + S_t = 3{,}120.0$$
$$S_t = -26211.755.$$

Substitute NL_t in (d)

$$72{,}256.43 = R_t + 0.0591 NL_t$$
$$R_t = 72{,}256.43 - 0.0591(-516.777)$$
$$R_t = 72{,}286.98.$$

Substitute NL_tL_t in (12)...

$$i_t(7{,}487.223) = 537.0684 + 0.0671 \times (-516.777)$$
$$i_t = 0.0671.$$

(14) $$EAFCD_t = (1 - T_t)(EBIT_t - i_tL_t - U_t^L NL_t) - PFDIV_t$$
$$= 0.7785 \times [11{,}909.60 - (0.0671)(7{,}487.223) - 0.0671(-516.777)]$$
$$= 8{,}907.51.$$

(15) $$CMDIV_t = (1 - b_t)EAFCD_t$$
$$= 0.4343\ (8{,}907.51)$$
$$= 3{,}868.53.$$

(16) $$NUMCS_t = X_1 = NUMCS_{t-1} + NEWCS_t$$
$$X_1 = 2754.3 + NEWCS_t.$$

(17) $$NEWCS_t = X_2 = NS_t/(1 - U_t^E)P_t$$
$$X_2 = -29{,}331.755/(1 - 0.1053)P_t.$$

(18) $$P_t = X_3 = m_tEPS_t$$
$$X_3 = 14.5(EPS_t).$$

(19) $$EPS_t = X_4 = EAFCD_t/NUMCS_t$$
$$X_4 = 8{,}907.5075/NUMCS_t.$$

(20) $$DPS_t = X_5 = CMDIV_t/NUMCS_t$$
$$X_5 = 3{,}868.53/NUMCS_t.$$

(A) = For (18) and (19), we obtain $X_3 = 14.5\ (8{,}907.51)/NUMCS_t = 129{,}158.9/X_1$.

Substitute (A) into Eq. (24.17) to calculate (B)

$(B) = X_2 = -29{,}331.755/[(1 - 0.1053) \times 129{,}158.9/X_1]$

$(B) = X_2 = -0.2538X_1$.

Substitute (B) into Eq. (24.16) to calculate (C)

$(C) = X_1 = 2754.3 - 0.2538X_1$

$(C) = X_1 = 2196.76$.

Substitute (C) into (B)...

$(B) = X_2 = -0.2538 \times 2196.76$

$(B) = X_2 = -557.54$.

From Eqs. (24.19) and (24.20) we obtain X_4, X_5 and X_3

$X_4 = 8{,}907.5075/2196.76 = 4.0548$,

$X_5 = 3{,}868.53/2196.76 = 1.7610$,

$X_3 = 14.5(4.0548) = 58.79$.

The results of the above calculations allow us to forecast the following information regarding JNJ in the 2010 fiscal year (dollars in thousands, except for per share data):

- Sales = \$43,946.87
- Current Assets = \$28,073.26
- Fixed Assets = \$39,152.27
- Total Assets = \$67,225.53
- Current Payables = \$13,663.08
- Needed Funds = (\$29,817.99)
- Earnings before Interest and Taxes = \$11,909.60
- New Debt = (\$516.777)
- New Stock = (\$−29,331.755)
- Total Debt = \$7,487.223
- Common Stock = (\$26211.755)
- Retained Earnings = \$72,286.98
- Interest Rate on Debt = 6.71%
- Earnings Available for Common Dividends = \$8,907.51
- Common Dividends = \$3,868.53
- Number of Common Shares Outstanding = 2196.76
- New Common Shares Issued = (557.54)
- PPS = \$58.79
- EPS = \$4.0548
- DPS = \$1.7610

About 18 out of 20 unknowns are listed in Table 24.4, the actual data is also listed to allow calculation of the forecast errors. In the last column of Table 24.4, the relative absolute forecasting errors ($|(A - F)/A|$) are calculated to indicate the performance of the *WS* model in forecasting important financial variables. It was found that the quality of the sales-growth rate estimate is the key to successfully using the *WS* model in financial planning and forecasting.

By comparing the forecast and actual values in Table 24.4, we find that the forecasting numbers generated by FINPLAN are very close to the ones on actual financial statements. During the financial-planning period, the company's financial policy does not change and the economy is neither in a big recession nor booming. This provides us with an environment in which the historical data are useful for financial planning. From the solution, we know that, under the assumed parameter values, the company must issue both debt and equity. If the company wants to avoid equity financing, *WS*

Table 24.4. The comparison of financial forecast of JNJ: Hand calculation and FINPLAN forecasting.

Category	Manual Calculation	Financial Plan Model	Variance (—(A − F)/A—) (%)
INCOME STATEMENT			
Sales	43,946.87	43,946.87	0.0
Operating Income	11,909.60	11,909.60	0.0
Interest Expense	502.39	502.39	0.0
Income before taxes	11,372.53	11,372.53	0.0
Taxes	2,519.02	2,519.02	0.0
Net Income	8,853.52	8,853.52	0.0
Common Dividends	3,868.53	3,845.08	0.6
Debt Repayments	219.00	219.00	0.0
BALANCE SHEET			
Assets			
Current Assets	28,073.26	28,073.26	0.0
Fixed Assets	39,152.27	39,152.27	0.0
Total Assets	67,225.53	67,225.53	0.0
LIABILITIES AND NET WORTH			
Current Payables	13,663.08	13,663.24	0.0
Total Debt	7,487.22	7,487.20	0.0
Common Stock	(26,211.7)	(26,211.89)	0.0
Retained Earnings	72,286.98	72,286.98	0.0
Total Liabilities and Net Worth	67,225.53	67,225.53	0.0
PER SHARE DATA			
PPS	58.79	58.51	0.5
EPS	4.05	4.04	0.5
DPS	1.76	1.75	0.5

model also enables us to investigate alternative methods to achieve this goal by changing the parameter values. Therefore, the model can answer "*what if*" questions and, hopefully, the company can choose the best alternative. Finally, the model also can help us to understand the impacts of changes in parameters on key financial variables, such as *EPS*, *PPS*, dividend per share (*DPS*), and *EBIT*, through the complicated interactions among the investment, financial, and dividend policies.

To do multi-period forecasting and sensitivity analysis, the program of FINPLAN of Microsoft Excel, as listed in Appendix 24.A, can be used. Using these program provided, the *pro forma* financial statements listed in Tables 24.5 and 24.6 can be produced. The input parameters and the values used to produce the output in Tables 24.5 and 24.6 are listed in Table 24.7.

Table 24.5. *Pro forma* balance sheet of JNJ: 2010–2013.

Item/year	2010	2011	2012	2013
Assets				
Current assets	28,073.26	19,932.01	14,151.73	10,047.73
Fixed assets	39,152.27	27,798.11	19,736.66	14,013.03
Total assets	67,225.53	47,730.12	33,888.39	24,060.76
Liabilities and Net Worth				
Current liabilities	13,663.24	9,700.90	6,887.64	4,890.22
Long-term debt	7,489.12	5,317.28	3,775.27	2,680.44
Preferred stock	0.00	0.00	0.00	0.00
Common stock	−26,214.00	−43,199.96	−55,258.11	−63,817.52
Retained earnings	72,287.17	75,911.90	78,483.59	80,307.61
Total liabilies and net worth	67,225.53	47,730.12	33,888.39	24,060.76
Computed DBT/EQ	0.16	0.16	0.16	0.16
Int. rate on total debt	0.07	0.07	0.07	0.07
Per Share Data				
Earnings	4.04	3.43	2.95	2.54
Dividends	1.75	1.49	1.28	1.10
Price	58.42	49.59	42.68	36.74

Table 24.6. *Pro forma* income statement of JNJ: 2010–2013.

Item/year	2010	2011	2012	2013
Sales	43,946.87	31,202.28	22,153.62	15,729.07
Operating income	11,909.60	8,455.82	6,003.63	4,262.58
Interest income	502.74	356.94	253.43	179.93
Underwriting commission – debt	34.56	131.09	88.81	58.79
Income before taxes	11,372.30	7,967.78	5,661.39	4,023.85
Taxes	2,518.44	1,764.49	1,253.73	891.10
Net income	8,853.87	6,203.29	4,407.65	3,132.75
Preferred dividends	0.00	0.00	0.00	0.00
Available for common dividends	8,853.87	6,203.29	4,407.65	3,132.75
Common dividends	3,845.14	2,694.03	1,914.20	1,360.52
Debt repayments	219.00	219.00	219.00	219.00
Actual funds needed for investment	−29,848.88	−18,938.80	−13,381.16	−9,435.24

The list of these parameters can be found in Table 24.3. To perform the sensitivity analysis, both high and low values are assigned to the growth rate of sales (g), retention rate (b), and target leverage ratio (k). The results of the sensitivity analysis related to *EPS*, *DPS* and *PPS* are demonstrated in Table 24.8. Table 24.8 indicates that the increases in g, b, and k will generally have positive impacts on *EPS*, *DPS*, and *PPS*.

Table 24.7. FINPLAN input.

FINPLAN input 2009 Value of Data	Variable Number*	Beginning Period	Last Period	Description
4	1	0	0	The number of years to be simulated
61897.0000	21	0	0	Net Sales at $t-1$ = 2009
−0.2900	22	1	4	Growth in Sales
0.6388	23	1	4	Current Assets as a Percentage of Sales
0.8909	24	1	4	Fixed Assets as a Percentage of Sales
0.3109	25	1	4	Current Payables as a Percentage of Sales
0.0000	26	1	4	Preferred Stock
0.0000	27	1	4	Preferred Dividends
8223.0000	28	0	0	Long-Term Debt in Previous Period
219.0000	29	1	4	Long-Term Debt Repayment (Reduction)
3120.0000	30	0	0	Common Stock in Previous Period
67248.0000	31	0	0	Retained Earnings in Previous Period
0.5657	32	1	4	Retention Rate
0.2215	33	1	4	Average Tax Rate (Income Taxes/Pretax Income)
0.0671	34	0	0	Average Interest Rate in Previous Period
0.0671	35	1	4	Expected Interest Rate on New Debt
0.2710	36	1	4	Operating Income as a Percentage of Sales
0.0671	37	1	4	Underwriting Cost of Debt
0.1053	38	1	4	Underwriting Cost of Equity
0.1625	39	1	4	Ratio of Debt to Equity
2,754.321	40	0	0	Number of Common Shares Outstanding in Previous Period
14.4700	41	1	4	Price–Earnings Ratio

*Variable numbers except the number of years to be simulated are as defined in Table 24.2.

24.4. Francis and Rowell Model[3]

The model presented below extends the simultaneous linear-equation model of the firm developed by *WS* in 1971. The object of this model is to generate *pro forma* financial statements that describe the future financial condition of the firm for any assumed pattern of sales. Parameters of various equations in the system can be changed to answer "*what if*" question, perform sensitivity analysis, and explore various paths toward some goals or goals that may or

[3]A major portion of this section is reprinted from Francis and Rowee (1978), by permission of the authors and *Financial Management*.

Table 24.8. Results of sensitivity analysis.

Year			2010	2011	2012	2013
$GSALSt = -0.2900$	$bt - 1 = 0.5657$	$Kt = 0.1625$				
$EPS=$			4.04	3.43	2.95	2.54
$DPS=$			1.75	1.49	1.28	1.10
$PPS=$			58.42	49.59	42.68	36.74
$GSALSt = -0.4$	$bt - 1 = 0.5657$	$Kt = 0.1625$				
$EPS=$			3.69	2.88	2.29	1.82
$DPS=$			1.60	1.25	0.99	0.79
$PPS=$			53.47	41.71	33.10	26.27
$GSALSt = 0.09$	$bt - 1 = 0.5657$	$Kt = 0.1625$				
$EPS=$			5.09	5.65	6.23	6.86
$DPS=$			2.21	2.46	2.70	2.98
$PPS=$			73.61	81.81	90.11	99.26
$GSALSt = -0.2900$	$bt - 1 = 0.3$	$Kt = 0.1625$				
$EPS=$			3.97	3.31	2.80	2.37
$DPS=$			2.78	2.32	1.96	1.66
$PPS=$			57.46	47.92	40.52	34.27
$GSALSt = -0.2900$	$bt - 1 = 0.7$	$Kt = 0.1625$				
$EPS=$			4.07	3.49	3.03	2.63
$DPS=$			1.22	1.05	0.91	0.79
$PPS=$			58.90	50.44	43.80	38.03
$GSALSt = -0.2900$	$bt - 1 = 0.5657$	$Kt = 0.1$				
$EPS=$			3.97	3.46	2.99	2.58
$DPS=$			1.72	1.50	1.30	1.12
$PPS=$			57.42	50.02	43.23	37.37
$GSALSt = -0.2900$	$bt - 1 = 0.5657$	$Kt = 0.5$				
$EPS=$			3.94	3.39	2.86	2.42
$DPS=$			1.71	1.47	1.24	1.05
$PPS=$			56.97	49.01	41.40	34.98

may not be optimal. The *FR* model is composed of 10 sectors with a total of 36 equations (see Tables 24.9 and 24.10).

The model incorporates an explicit treatment of risk by allowing for stochastic variability in industry sales forecasts. The exogenous input of sales variance is transformed (through simplified linear relations in the model) to coefficients of variation for *EBIT* and net income after taxes (*NIAT*) (see Table 24.11). These are used in risk–return functions that determine the costs of new financing.

Lee and Rahman (1997) use dynamic optimal control model to discuss the interactions of investment, financing, and dividend decisions. Lee and Rahman's approach can integrate with *FR*'s model.

Table 24.9. List of variables for FR model.

Endogenous		Exogenous	
Sales_t^P	Potential industry sales (units)	GSALS_t	Growth rate in potential industry sales
S_t^{FC}	Full capacity unit output (company)	Sales_{t-1}^P	Previous period potential industry sales (units)
S_t^a	Actual company unit output	S_{t-1}^{FC}	Previous period company full capacity unit output
S_t^P	Potential company unit output	INV_{t-1}	Previous period company finished goods inventory
γ_{1t}	Measure of necessary new investment (based on units)	FA_{t-1}	Previous period company fixed asset base ($)
γ_{2t}	Measure of slack due to underutilization of existing resources	γ_t	Capacity utilization index
K_t	Units of capital stock	c_t	Desire market share
NK_t	Desired new capital (capital units)	θ	Proportionality coefficient of S_t^{RC} to K_t
FA_t	Fixed assets (current $)	P_{kt}	GNP component index for capital equipment
NF_t	Desired new investment (current $)	P	Percentage markup of output price over ratio of $\text{GOP}_t/\text{INV}_t$
P_{ts}	Output price	δ_2	Proportionality coefficient of OC_t to $\$S_t$
$\$S_t$	Sales dollars (current $)	Φ	Proportionality coefficient of D_t to FA_t
COG_t	Cost of goods (current $)	N	Proportionality coefficient of INV_t to $\$S_t$
OC_t	Overhead, selling, cost of goods (current $)	LR_t	Repayment of long-term debt
$OC2_t$	Non-operating income (current $)	T_t	Corporate tax rate
D_t	Depreciation expense (current $)	b_t	Retention rate
INV_t	Inventory (current $)	U_t^L	Underwriting cost of new debt
L_t	Long-term debt	PFDIV_t	Preferred dividend
i_t^L	Cost of new debt (%)	i_{t-1}^A	Previous period weighted average cost of long-term debt
NL_t	New long-term debt needed ($)	L_{t-1}	Previous period long-term debt

(Continued)

Table 24.9. (*Continued*)

Endogenous		Exogenous	
NS_t	New common stock (equity) needed ($)	k	Optimal capital structure assumption
$NIAT_t$	Net income after tax (current $)	α_L, β_L	Coefficients in risk–return tradeoff for new debt
RE_t	Retained earnings	α_s, β_s	Coefficients in risk–return tradeoff for new stock
$EBIT_t$	Earnings before interest and taxes	GOP_{t-1}	Gross operating profit of previous period
i_t^A	Weighted average cost of long term debt	δ_1	Ratio of COG_t to actual net sales
v_{EBIT}	Coefficient of variation of EBIT	δ_3	Ratio of OC2 to net sales
i_t^s	Cost of new stock issue	$\alpha_1, \alpha_2, \alpha_3$	Production function coefficients
v_{NIAT}	Coefficient of variation of NIAT	$\sum_1$	Ratio of CA_t to net sales
TEV_t	Total equity value	$\sum_2$	Ratio of CL_t to net sales
g_t^a	Growth rate in $$S_t$	$\sigma^2_{\text{Sale}\delta}{}^{\rho}_{P}$	Standard deviation of potential industry sales
$EAFCD_t$	Earnings available for common dividend		
$CMDIV_t$	Common dividend		
ΔRE_t	Contributions to RE made in the tth period		
GPO_t	Gross operating profit (current $)		

The model also incorporates some variables external to the firm that are important from a financial-planning viewpoint. These industry or economy-wide variables are introduced in every sector to enable the financial planner to explore their influence on plans. They include: market share, an industry capacity-utilization index, the tax rate, and a GNP component price index for explicit analysis of the effects of inflation.

The *FR* model explicitly allows for divergence between planned (or potential) and actual levels in both sales and production. That is, sales forecasts and production potential are compared to determine the existence of slack or idle capacity and company expansion possibilities. Any positive difference between potential or forecasted company sales and actual company sales is decomposed into the portion facilities. As a result, a forecasted sales increase need not lead to investment in new capital. Likewise, a forecasted

Table 24.10. List of equations for FR model.

1. *Industry Sales*

(1) $\text{Sales}_t^p = \text{Sales}_{t-1}^p(1 + \text{GSALS}_t)$

2. *Company Production Sector*

(2) $\text{S}_t^{FC} = \alpha_1 S_{t-1}^{FC} + \alpha_2\text{INV}_{t-1} + \alpha_3\text{FA}_{t-1}$

(3) $\dfrac{S_t^a}{S_t^{FC}} = \gamma_t \rightarrow S_t^a = \gamma_t S_t^{FC}$

(4) $S_t^p = c_t\text{Sales}_t^p$

3. *Capital Stock Requirements Sector*

(5) $S_t^p - S_t^a = (S_t^{FC} - S_t^a) + (S_t^p - S_t^{FC})$

(6) $S_t^{FC} - S_t^a = \gamma_{2t}$

(7) $S_t^p - S_t^{FC} = \gamma_{1t} \quad (0 \le \gamma_{1t})$

(8) $K_1 = \theta S_t^{FC}$

(9) $NK_t = \theta\gamma_{1t}$

4. *Pricing Sector*

(10) $P_{Kt} \cdot K_t = FA_t$ or $FA_t/K_t = P_{Kt}$

(11) $P_{Kt} \cdot NK_t = NF_t$

(12) $P_{st} \cdot S_t^a = \$S_t^a$

(13) $P_{ts} = p(\text{GOP}_{t-1}/\text{INV}_{t-1})$

5. *Production Cost Sector*

(14) $\text{OC}_t = \delta_2(\$S_t^a)$

(15) $\text{COG}_t = \delta_1(\$S_t^a)$

(16) $\text{GOP}_t = \$S_t^a - \text{COG}_t$

(17) $\text{OC2}_t = \delta_3(\$S_t^a)$

6. *Income Sector*

(18) $\text{INV}_t = N(\$S_t^a)$

(19) $\text{EBIT}_t = \$S_t^a - \text{OC}_\text{t} + \text{OC2}_\text{t} - D_t$

(20) $\text{NIAT}_t = (\text{EBIT}_2 - i_t^A L_t)(1 - T)$

(20′) $\text{CL}_t = \sum_2(\$S_t^a)$

7. *New Financing Required Sector*

(21) $\text{NF}_t + b_t\{(1 - T)[i_t^L \text{NL}_t + U_t^L\text{NL}_t]\} = \text{NLS}_t + \Delta\text{RE}_t + (\text{CL}_t - \text{CL}_{t-1})$

(22) $\text{NLS}_t = \text{NS}_t + \text{NL}_t$

(23) $\Delta\text{RE}_t = b_t\{(1 - T)[\text{EBIT}_t - i_t^A L_t - U_t^L\text{NL}_t] - \text{PFDIV}_t$

(24) $i_t^A = i_{t-1}^A\left[\dfrac{L_{t-1} - \text{LR}_t}{L_t}\right] + i_t^L\dfrac{\text{NL}_t}{L_t}$

(25) $\dfrac{\text{NL}_t}{\text{NS}_t + \Delta\text{RE}_t} = k$

(26) $L_t = L_{t-1} - \text{LR}_t + \text{NL}_t$

8. *Risk Sector*

(27) $\sigma_{\text{ebit}}^2 = \theta_1^2 \cdot \theta_2^2 \cdot \sigma_{\text{Sales}_t^p}^2$

(28) $\sigma_{\text{niat}}^2 = \theta_5^2 \cdot \theta_6^2 \cdot \theta_2^2 \cdot \sigma_{\text{Sales}_t^p}^2$

9. *Costs of Financing Sector*

(29) $i_t^L = \alpha_L + \beta_L v_{\text{EBIT}}$

(30) $v_{\text{EBIT}} = \dfrac{\sigma_{\text{EBIT}}}{\overline{R}_{\text{EBIT}}}$

(31) $i_t^a = \alpha_s + \beta_s v_{\text{NIAT}}$

(32) $v_{\text{NIAT}} = \dfrac{\sigma_{\text{NIAT}}}{\overline{R}_{\text{NIAT}}}$

10. *Valuation of Equity Sector*

(33) $\text{TEV}_t = \dfrac{\text{CMDIV}_t}{i_t^s - g_t^s}$

(34) $\text{EAFCD}_t = (1 - T_t) \times [\text{EBIT}_t - i_t^A L_t - U_t^L\text{NL}_\text{t}] - \text{PFDIV}_t$

(35) $\text{CMDIV}_t = (1 - b_t)\text{EAFCD}_t$

(36) $g_t^a = \dfrac{\$S_t - \$S_{t-1}}{\$S_{t-1}}$

Table 24.11. Transformation of industry sales moments to company *NIAT* and *EBIT* moments.

EBIT

$$\begin{aligned}\text{EBIT}_t &= \$S_t^a - \text{OC}_t - D_t\\ &= \$S_t^a - \delta_2\$S_t^a - \Phi\text{FA}_t\\ &= \$S_t^a - \delta_2\$S_t^a - \Phi P_{kt}\theta\cdot\frac{1}{\gamma_t}\therefore\frac{\$S_t^a}{P_{st}}\\ &= \left\{1-\delta_2-\Phi\left[\left(\frac{P_{kt}}{P_{ts}}\right)\cdot\theta\left(\frac{1}{\gamma_t}\right)\right]\right\}\$S_t^a\\ &= \theta_1\$S_t\end{aligned}$$

If $S_t^p = S_t^{FC}$ then $S_t^{FC} = c_t\text{Sales}_t^p$

$\therefore\ S_t^p = c_t\text{Sales}_t^p$

Since: $S_t^a = \gamma_t S_t^{FC} = \gamma_t[c_t\text{Sales}_t^a]$

so: $P_{ts}S_t^a = \$S_t = P_{ts}\gamma_t[c_t\text{Sales}_t^p]$

and: $\$S_t^a = \theta_2\text{Sales}_t^p$

Hence: $\text{EBIT}_t = \theta_1^2\cdot\theta_2^2\sigma^2_{\text{Sales}_t^p}$

then: $\sigma^2_{\text{EBIT}} = \theta_1^2\cdot\theta_2^2\sigma^2_{\text{Sales}_t^p}$

NIAT

$\text{NIAT}_t = [1-T][\text{EBIT}_t - i^A L_t - U^L\text{NL}_t]$

if $U^I = 0$

also:

$$\begin{aligned}L_t &= \frac{\left[\sum_1 + \frac{P_k\theta_t}{\gamma_t P_{ts}} - \sum_2\right]}{\left[1+\frac{1}{k}\right]}\$S_t^a\\ &= \theta_4\$S_t\end{aligned}$$

$$\begin{aligned}\text{NIAT} &= [1-T][\theta_1\cdot\$S_t^a - i_t^A\theta_4\cdot\$S_t^a]\\ &= [1-T][\theta_1 - i_t^A\theta_4]\$S_t^a\\ &= [1-T][\theta_1 - i_t^A\theta_4]\theta_2\text{Sales}_t^p\\ &= \theta_5\cdot\theta_6\cdot\theta_2\text{Sales}_t^p\end{aligned}$$

(*Continued*)

Table 24.11. (*Continued*)

$\therefore$

$$\text{NIAT}_t = \theta_5 \cdot \theta_6 \cdot \theta_2 \text{Sales}_t^p$$

then

$$\sigma^2_{\text{NIAT}} = \theta_5^2 \cdot \theta_6^2 \cdot \theta_2^2 \cdot \theta^2_{\text{sales}_t^{\text{P}}}$$

where

$$\theta_1 = \left[1 - \delta_2 - \Phi\left(\frac{P_k}{P_{ts}}\right) \cdot \theta\left(\frac{1}{\gamma_t}\right)\right]$$

$$\theta_2 = P_{ts}\gamma_t c_t$$

$$\theta_4 = \left\{ \frac{\left[\sum_1 + \dfrac{\theta_k P_k}{1 + \dfrac{1}{k}} - \sum_2\right]}{\left[1 + \dfrac{1}{k}\right]} \right\}$$

$$\theta_5 = [1 - T_t]$$

$$\theta_6 = \left[\theta_1 - i_t^A \theta_4\right]$$

and

$$CA_t = \sum_1 \cdot \$S_t^a$$

$$D_t = \Phi \text{FA}_t$$

also, parameters δ_2, θ, γ_t, $\sum_2$, are defined in the List of Equations (Table 24.10).

sales downturn would not lead to a divestiture of capital. An advantage of this disaggregation is that it allows for greater realism — that it, it permits both a lagged production response to sales upturns and downturns, as well as lags, overadjustment, and underadjustment in new investment decisions.

The *FR* model offers a disaggregation of the sales equation into separate market share, production, and pricing equations, which has several distinct advantages. It offers the opportunity to treat sales forecast in physical units that can be compared to technical production capabilities in physical units for both potential and actual levels of sales and production. Such disaggregation also allows distinction between physical units of sales and production and dollar units. Therefore, the pricing decision can be treated separately. This feature is helpful in analyzing the effect of changing prices.

Another aspect of the *FR* financial-forecasting model is the econometrical advantage. The *FR* model's risk–return function and its production function are estimated econometrically. Additionally, standard econometric techniques to evaluate goodness-of-fit and predictive power of a simultaneous equation system are reported. In the remaining subsections of this section, the *FR* model is explained in its general form. Then the coefficients of the equations are set to equal to the values that characterize the operations of an existing company, and then the active operations of a well-known firm are simulated, to test this financial model empirically.

24.4.1. *The FR Model Specification*

The *FR* model is composed of 10 sectors: (1) industry sales, (2) production sector, (3) fixed capital-stock requirements, (4) pricing, (5) production costs, (6) income, (7) new financing required, (8) risk, (9) costs of financing, and (10) common stock valuation. These sectors are illustrated in the equation specifications as defined in Table 24.10.

The flowchart conveniently illustrates the simultaneity discussed above. All 10 sectors are portrayed, labeled, and outlined by dot-dash borders with arrows displaying their interaction. This is summarized for sectors one through ten in the interdependence table (Table 24.12). An **"X"** is placed in the table to represent the direction of an arrow (from explaining to explained) on the flowchart.

Looking more deeply reveals that the *FR* model is, to a large extent (but not entirely), recursive between sectors. All entries of the sector-interdependence table, with the exception of one (between sectors seven

Table 24.12. Sector interdependence.

		Earning Sector									
		1	2	3	4	5	6	7	8	9	10
Explained Sector	1										
	2	X									
	3		X								
	4			X							
	5				X						
	6					X					
	7				X		X			X	
	8	X	X	X	X	X	X	X			
	9								X		
	10							X		X	

Table 24.13. Variable interdependence within sector seven.

		Explaining Variables					
		RE_t	L_t	NL_t	NS_t	i_t^A	NLS_t
Explained Variables	RE_t		X	X		X	
	L_t		X				
	NL_t		X		X		
	NS_t			X			X
	i_t^A		X	X			
	NLS_t	X		X			

and nine), are below the diagonal. It has been structures in this manner for the specific purpose of ease of exposition and computation. The simultaneity of the FR model is primarily within each sector's equations. For example, this is illustrated in the variable interdependence table for sector seven, shown as Table 24.13.

SECTOR ONE: INDUSTRY SALES

The primary importance of the industry-sales forecast sector is highlighted by its upper left position on the flowchart in Fig. 24.2. It influences directly the risk sector and production sector and, indirectly, every sector of the model.

The industry sales sector can be any size and is abbreviated here to merely a single equation; (see *FR* example (1) in Table 24.10). The industry-sales equation shows that an industry-sales forecast must be made by some means over a predefined forecast period and given as an exogenous input to the *FR* model.

Although sales remain the driving force for the *FR* model, it is industry instead of the company sales that drive the model, since forecasting experience indicates that industry sales can usually be more accurately forecasted than company sales. In addition, two parameters of the industry sales forecast are employed, the mean and the standard deviation. The mean enters the model in the conventional way, whereas the standard deviation is mathematically transformed to obtain the standard deviation of its derivative quantities, the company's *NIAT* and *EBIT*.[4]

[4]The *FR* model could easily be linked to macroeconomic forecasting model to obtain the sales forecast for the industry and the firm. The expanded macroeconomics and microeconomics model could provide detailed forecasts of the economy, the firm's industry, the firm itself, and the firm's equity returns. A small simultaneous-equation model to explain

SECTOR TWO: COMPANY SALES AND PRODUCTION

Company sales are obtained through a market-share assumption, which is typically a more stable parameter than a company's dollar sales level. Potential company sales is obtained from forecasted industry sales through this market-share assumption. Equation (4) in Table 24.10 shows the relationship explicitly.

The *FR* model distinguishes between potential and actual sales levels; this allows a realistic treatment of slack or idle capacity in the firm. Because of the possibility of directly underutilized assets, it is not necessary that every sales upturn be translated directly into an increase in the asset base. Some or all of the sales upturn can be absorbed by more complete utilization of available resources.

Company production potential is obtained from a production function that defines full-capacity company production. This is determined by previous-period full-capacity production sales, inventory, and fixed assets (see Eq. (24.2) in Table 24.10 for the exact specification). Actual company production is derived from full-capacity production by a capacity-utilization index in Eq. (24.3) of Table 24.10.

The production function allows explicit definition of the company's full-capacity production levels. It serves the useful purpose of relaxing the unrealistic assumption (used in many models) that whatever is produced is sold. Full-capacity production is typically adjusted gradually, or dynamically, over the long run, to upward changes in potential sales and is often not responsive to downturns. The non-proportionality and asymmetry discussed earlier with respect to the distinctions between actual and potential sales also applies to the distinctions between potential full capacity and actual production. For instance, slack (that is, idle capacity) may be decreased to meet a sales upturn without increasing the firm's investment in manufacturing machinery.

SECTOR THREE: FIXED CAPITAL-STOCK REQUIREMENTS

Necessary new investments is not linked directly to company sales in the FR model, but instead results from comparison between potential and actual company sales. Equation (24.7) of Table 24.10 measures the company

a single firm's changes in EPS and stock PPS has been developed by Francis (1977). Francis' model is driven by macroeconomics factors, with some forces from within the firm treated as unexplained residuals (called unsystematic risk). If the Francis quarterly equity-returns model were provided with exogenous input data about aggregate profits and a stock-market index, it could be modified to operate with the FR model and provide detail analysis of period-by-period equity returns.

expansion possibility by the difference between potential company sales (influenced by management's industry-sales forecast and company market-share assumption) and full-capacity sales. The units of required new capital are derived from this difference in Eq. (24.9), shown in Table 24.10.[5]

A capacity–utilization index for the simulated company and industry translates full-capacity output (from the production function) into actual company sales, just as a market-share assumption is used to translate potential industry sales into potential company sales. Any positive difference between potential company sales and actual company sales is decomposed into the contribution due to idle capacity and the contribution due to company expansion possibility, as shown mathematically in Eq. (24.5) of Table 24.10.

SECTOR FOUR: PRICING

The pricing sector of the model plays a key role by relating real or units sector to the nominal or dollar sectors. The real sectors of industry sales, company sales and production, and fixed capital-stock requirements are all denominated in physical units of output. However, the nominal sectors of production costs, income, financing required, and valuation are all dollar-denominated. The real sectors and the nominal sectors are connected by the pricing sector.

This sector separation allows explicit treatment of the product-pricing decision apart from the sales and production decisions. Also, it maintains the important distinction between real and nominal quantities and thus permits an analysis of inflation's impact on the firm (as suggested by the Securities and Exchange Commission (1976)).

FR Eq. (24.13) is a simple formula that generates product price by relating it, through a markup, to the ratio of previous-period gross operating profit to inventory. Real units of company sales are priced out in *FR* Eq. (24.12). Required new capital units are priced out using the average unit capital cost specified in *FR* Eq. (24.11) of Table 24.10.

[5]Through this specification, the *FR* model recognizes the asymmetrical response of the asset base to changes in sales levels. A strict ratio between sales and asset levels, such as those used in other *pro forma* models derived by Pindyck and Rubinfeld (1976) and by Salzman (1967), presume a proportionate and symmetrical response of asset levels to both sales upturns and downturns. The *FR* distinction between actual and potential sales and the concept of slack allows a realistic non-proportionality and asymmetry in the simulation. (For instance, a sales downturn need not and usually does not lead to a reduction in asset levels; instead, it typically causes a decrease in capacity utilization.)

SECTOR FIVE: PRODUCTION COSTS

The production cost sector is similar to previous models; production cost and inventory are related directly to actual company sales dollars. Also, depreciation is linked directly to existing fixed investment.

SECTOR SIX: INCOME

As in the production cost sector, the income-sector ties inventory, earnings before interest and taxes, and *NIAT* directly to actual company sales dollars. This simplicity is preserved here to create a linear-determined income statement that produces *EBIT* as a function of actual company sales (given a few simplifying assumptions). The *NIAT* is derived from *EBIT* after deduction of interest expense (also linearly related to actual sales levels and taxes).

SECTOR SEVEN: NEW FINANCING REQUIRED

The new-financing-required sector is composed primarily of accounting relationships that determine the dollar amount of external financing required from the new capital requirements (Sector Three) and internal financing capability (Sector Six). In *FR* model, Eq. (24.21) obtains this external financing requirement. The retained-income portion of internal financing is derived from *FR* Eq. (24.23) of Table 24.10.

Finally, the breakdown of new external financing into new equity and new debt occurs in *FR* Eq. (24.25), where the notion of optimal capital structure is exploited. The weighted-average cost of debt, *FR* Eq. (24.24), consists of a weighted sum of new debt costs and the cost of existing debt. The cost of the new debt is not exogenous in this model; it is estimated in a simplified risk–return tradeoff from Sector Nine.

SECTOR EIGHT: RISK

The linear derivation of both *EBIT* and *NIAT* in the income sector is used (with simplifying assumptions) in the risk sector to obtain the standard deviation of each income measure. The derivation (presented in Table 24.13) demonstrates how management's judgment as to the variability (i.e., standard deviation) of forecasting industry sales affects the risk character (of both the business and financial risk) of the company. This risk character influences the costs of financing new stock and debt in risk–return tradeoff equations of Sector Nine. In this way, risk is explicitly accounted for as the principal determinant of financing costs, and financing costs are made endogenous to the model. In addition, the risk relationship from the ratio of fixed to variable cost (an operating leverage measures) to the standard deviation of *EBIT*. The debt-to-equity ratio (a financial leverage ratio) also positively influences the *NIAT* standard deviation. Thus, the leverage structure of the firm endogenously influences the costs of financing in a realistic way.

SECTOR NINE: COST OF FINANCING

Market factors enter into the determination of financing costs through the slope (β_1 and β_2) and intercept (α_1 and α_2) coefficients of the risk–return tradeoff functions — namely Eqs. (24.29) and (24.31) of Table 24.10. At the present time, all four coefficients must be exogenously provided by management. However, this is not a difficult task. Historical coefficients can be estimated empirically using simple linear regression. The regression coefficients would establish a plausible range of values that might be used by management to determine the present or future coefficient values.

SECTOR TEN: COMMON STOCK VALUATION

The valuation model used finds the present value of dividends, which are presumed to grow perpetually at a constant rate. This venerable model can be traced from Williams (1938) through more recent analysts. Algebraically reduced to its simplest form, the single-share valuation model is shown below:

$$\text{Share price} = \frac{\text{Cash dividend per year}}{(\text{Equity capitalization rate, } i_{\text{t}}^{\text{s}}) - (\text{Growth rate, } g_{\text{t}}^{\text{a}})}.$$

Equation (24.33) of Table 24.10 differs slightly from the per-share valuation model above because it values the firm's total equity outstanding. This change was accomplished merely by multiplying both sides of the valuation equation shown above by the number of shares outstanding. The remaining equations of this sector are then accounting statements.

24.4.2. *A Brief Discussion of FR'S Empirical Results*

FR (1978) used Anheuser-Busch Company annual reports to perform full simulation experiments, and show one prediction comparison for the *FR* model and the *WS* model.

Overall, *FR* found that their model is very useful in performing financial planning and forecasting. In addition, *FR* also argued that their model has superior explanatory power over a wide range of applications (see Footnote 4). Detailed discussion of *FR*'s empirical results is beyond the scope of this book. Hence it is omitted and left for students' further study. A case study of using both *FR* and Carleton's (1970) models to analyze a forecast General Motors' financial position can be found in Lee (1984).

24.5. Feltham–Ohlson Model for Determining Equity Value

Ohlson Model introduced the clean surplus relations (CSR) assumption requiring that income over a period equals net dividends and the change in book value of equity. CSR ensures that all changes in shareholder equity that do not result from transactions with shareholders (such as dividends, share repurchases or share offerings) are reflected in the income statement. In other words, CSR is an accounting system recognizing that the periodically value created is distinguished from the value distributed.

Let NIAT_t denote the earnings for period $(t-1,t)$, TEV_t denote the book value of equity at time t, R_f denote the risk-free rate plus one, CMDIV_t denote common dividends, and $\text{NIAT}_t^a = \text{NIAT}_t - (R_f - 1)\text{TEV}_t$ denote the abnormal earnings at time t. The change in book value of equity between two days equals earnings plus dividends, so the CSR $\text{TEV}_t = \text{TEV}_{t-1} + \text{NIAT}_t - \text{CMDIV}_t$ implies that

$$P_{ts} = \text{TEV}_t + \sum_{\tau=1}^{\infty} R_f^{-\tau} E_t\left[\text{NIAT}_{t+\tau}^a\right], \tag{24.1}$$

the price of firm's equity (P_{ts}) is equal to its book value of equity adjusted for the present value of expected future abnormal earnings. The variables on the right-hand side of (26.1) are still forecasts, not past realizations. To deal with this problem, Ohlson Model introduced the information dynamics to link the value to the contemporaneous accounting data. Assume $\left\{\widetilde{\text{NIAT}}_t^a\right\}_{\tau\geq 1}$ follows the stochastic process

$$\begin{aligned} \widetilde{\text{NIAT}}_{t+1}^a &= \omega \text{NIAT}_t^a + v_t + \tilde{\varepsilon}_{1,t+1} \\ \tilde{v}_{t+1} &= +\gamma v_t + \tilde{\varepsilon}_{2,t+1}, \end{aligned} \tag{24.2}$$

where v_t is value relevant information other than abnormal earnings and $0 \leq \omega, \gamma \leq 1$. Based on Eqs. (24.1) and (24.2), Ohlson Model demonstrated that the value of the equity is a function of contemporaneous accounting variables as follows.

$$P_{ts} = \text{TEV}_t + \hat{\alpha}_1 \text{NIAT}_t^a + \hat{\alpha}_2 v_t, \quad (24.3)$$

where $\hat{\alpha}_1 = \hat{\omega}/(R_f - \hat{\omega})$ and $\hat{\alpha}_2 = R_f/(R_f - \hat{\omega})(R_f - \hat{\gamma})$. Or equivalently,

$$P_{ts} = \kappa(\varphi x_t - d_t) + (1 - \kappa)\text{TEV}_t + \alpha_2 v_t, \quad (24.4)$$

where $\kappa = (R_f - 1)\hat{\omega}/(R_f - \hat{\omega})$ and $\varphi = R_f/(R_f - 1)$. Equations (24.3) and (24.4) imply that the market value of the equity is equal to the book value adjusted for (i) the current profitability as measured by abnormal earnings and (ii) other information that modifies the prediction of future profitability.

One major limitation of the Ohlson Model is that it assumed unbiased accounting. Feltham and Ohlson (1995) (hereafter *FO*) introduce additional dynamics to deal with the issue of biased (conservative) accounting data. The *FO* Model analyzes how firm value relates to the accounting information that discloses the results from both operating and financial activities. For the financial activities, there are relatively perfect markets and the accounting measures for book value and market value of these assets are reasonably close. However for the operating assets, accrual accounting usually results in difference between the book value and the market value of these assets since they are not traded in the market. Accrual accounting for the operating assets consequently results in discrepancy between their book value and market value and thus influences the goodwill of the firm. Similar to Ohlson Model, the information dynamics in the *FO* Model is

$$\begin{aligned}
\widetilde{ox}_{t+1}^a &= \omega_{10} + \omega_{11} ox_t^a + \omega_{12} oa_t + \omega_{13} v_{1t} + \tilde{\varepsilon}_{1t+1}, \\
\widetilde{oa}_{t+1} &= \omega_{20} + \omega_{22} ox_t^a + \omega_{24} v_{2t} + \tilde{\varepsilon}_{2t+1}, \\
\tilde{v}_{1t+1} &= \omega_{30} + \omega_{33} v_{1t} + \tilde{\varepsilon}_{3t+1}, \\
\tilde{v}_{2t+1} &= \omega_{40} + \omega_{44} v_{2t} + \tilde{\varepsilon}_{4t+1},
\end{aligned} \quad (24.5)$$

where ox_t^a is the abnormal operating earnings, oa_t is the operating assets, v_{1t} and v_{2t} are the other value relevant information variables for firm at time t, respectively. The operating assets and the financial assets are calculated as follows.

$$\begin{aligned}
\text{Operating Assets} &= \text{Total Assets} - \text{Financial Assets}, \\
\text{Operating Liabilities} &= \text{Preferred Shares} + \text{Total Liabilities} \\
&\quad - \text{Financial Liabilities},
\end{aligned}$$

$$\begin{aligned}
\text{Financial Assets} &= \text{Cash and Cash Equivalent} \\
&\quad + \text{Investments and Advancements} \\
&\quad + \text{Short-term Investments}, \\
\text{Financial Liabilities} &= \text{Long-term debt} + \text{Debt in Current Liabilities} \\
&\quad + \text{Notes Payable}, \\
\text{Net Operating Assets} &= \text{Operating Assets} - \text{Operating Liabilities}, \\
\text{Net Financial Assets} &= \text{Financial Assets} - \text{Financial Liabilities}.
\end{aligned}$$

The derived implied pricing function is

$$P_t = y_t + \hat{\lambda}_0 + \hat{\lambda}_1 ox_t^a + \hat{\lambda}_2 oa_t + \hat{\lambda}_3 v_{1t} + \hat{\lambda}_4 v_{2t}, \tag{24.6}$$

where

$$\begin{aligned}
\hat{\lambda}_0 &= \frac{(1+r)\begin{bmatrix} \hat{\omega}_{10}(1+r-\hat{\omega}_{22})(1+r-\hat{\omega}_{33})(1+r-\hat{\omega}_{44}) \\ +\hat{\omega}_{12}\hat{\omega}_{20}(1+r-\hat{\omega}_{33}) + \hat{\omega}_{13}\hat{\omega}_{30}(1+r-\hat{\omega}_{22}) \\ +\hat{\omega}_{14}\hat{\omega}_{40}(1+r-\hat{\omega}_{44}) \end{bmatrix}}{r(1+r-\hat{\omega}_{11})(1+r-\hat{\omega}_{22})(1+r-\hat{\omega}_{33})(1+r-\hat{\omega}_{44})} \\
\hat{\lambda}_1 &= \frac{\hat{\omega}_{11}}{r(1+r-\hat{\omega}_{11})} \\
\hat{\lambda}_2 &= \frac{(1+r)\hat{\omega}_{12}}{(1+r-\hat{\omega}_{11})(1+r-\hat{\omega}_{22})} \\
\hat{\lambda}_3 &= \frac{(1+r)\hat{\omega}_{13}}{(1+r-\hat{\omega}_{11})(1+r-\hat{\omega}_{33})} \\
\hat{\lambda}_4 &= \frac{(1+r)\hat{\omega}_{14}}{(1+r-\hat{\omega}_{11})(1+r-\hat{\omega}_{44})}
\end{aligned} \tag{24.7}$$

Or equivalently,

$$P_t = k(\varphi x_t - d_t) + (1-\kappa) y_t + \hat{\alpha}_2 oa_t + \hat{\lambda}_3 v_{1t} + \hat{\lambda}_4 v_{2t}, \tag{24.8}$$

where $\kappa = (R_f - 1)\hat{\omega}_{11}/(R_f - \hat{\omega}_{11})$ and $\phi = R_f/(R_f - 1)$. The implied valuation function in Eqs. (24.6) and (24.8) is a weighted average of firm's operating earnings, firm's book value, and the other value-relevant information with an adjustment for the understatement of the operating assets resulting from accrual accounting. The major contribution of the *FO* Model is that it considered the accounting conservatism in the equity valuation.

24.6. Combined Forecasting Method to Determine Equity Value

Lee *et al.* (2011) investigate the stock price forecast ability of Ohlson (1995) model, *FO* (Feltham and Ohlson) (1995) model, and *WS* (1971) model. They use simultaneous equation estimation approach to estimate the information dynamics for Ohlson model and *FO* model and forecast future stock prices. Empirical results show that the simultaneous equation estimation of the information dynamics improves the ability of the Ohlson model and *FO* model in capturing the dynaic of the abnormal earnings process.

Lee *et al.* (2011) also find that *WS* model can generate smaller future stock prices prediction errors than those predicted by the Ohlson model and *FO* model, indicating that *WS* model has better forecast ability to determining future stock prices. The superior accuracy comparing to the Ohlsen model and *FO* model are due to the incorporation of both operation and financing decisions of the firms.

Using various time-varying parameters models proposed by Granger and Newbold (1973) and Diebold and Pauly (1987), Lee *et al.* (2011) further examine whether forecast combination provides better prediction accuracy. They also employ the linear and quadratic deterministic time-varying parameters model to produce time-varying weights. The evidence shows that combined forecast method can reduce the prediction errors.

24.7. Summary

Two simultaneous-equation financial planning models were discussed in detail in this chapter. There are 20 equations and 20 unknowns in the *WS* model. Annual financial data from JNJ company were used to show how the *WS* model can be used to perform financial analysis and planning. A computer program of the *WS* model is presented in Appendix 24.B.

The *FR* model is a generalized *WS* financial-planning model. There are 36 equation and 36 unknown in the *FR* model. The two simultaneous-equation financial-planning models discussed in this chapter are an alternative to Carleton's linear-programming model, to perform financial analysis, planning, and forecasting.

In this chapter, we have also briefly discussed Felthan–Ohlson model for determining equity value. In addition, we have explored the usefulness of integrating WS model and Felthan–Ohlson model to improve the determination of equity value.

Problem Set

1. According to Warren and Shelton (1971), what are the characteristics of a good financial-planning model?
2. Briefly discuss the *WS* model of using a simultaneous-equations approach to financial planning. How this model can be used to forecast PPS of the company?
3. How does the *FR* simultaneous model extend the *WS* model? Briefly discuss the *FR* model specification.
4. Please compare the Ohlson model with Feltham and Ohlson model. Which model is more suitable for determining stock PPS? Why?
5. Use a flowchart to interpret the computer program listed in Appendix 24.B of this chapter. Then use these concepts to discuss how the *WS* model can be solved by this computer program.

Appendix 24.A. Procedure of Using Microsoft Excel to Run FINPLAN Program

	A	B	C	D	E	F	G	H	I	J	K
1	FINPLAN input										
2	2009										
3	Value of Data	Variable	Beginning	Last							
4		Number	Period	Period	Value						
5	4	1	0	0	The number of years to be simulated						
6	61897.0000	21	0	0	Net Sales at t-1=2009						
7	-0.2900	22	1	4	Growth in Sales						
8	0.6388	23	1	4	Current Assets as a Percent of Sales						
9	0.8909	24	1	4	Fixed Assets as a Percent of Sales						
10	0.3109	25	1	4	Current Payables as a Percent of Sales						
11	0.0000	26	1	4	Preferred Stock						
12	0.0000	27	1	4	Preferred Dividends						
13	8223.0000	28	0	0	Long Term Debt in Previous Period						
14	219.0000	29	1	4	Long Term Debt Repayment (Reduction)						
15	3120.0000	30	0	0	Common Stock in Previous Period						
16	67248.0000	31	0	0	Retained Earnings in Previous Period						
17	0.5657	32	1	4	Retention Rate						
18	0.2215	33	1	4	Average Tax Rate (Income Taxes / Pretax Income)						
19	0.0671	34	0	0	Average Interest Rate in Previous Period						
20	0.0671	35	1	4	Expected Interest Rate on New Debt						
21	0.2710	36	1	4	Operating Income as a Percentage of Sales						
22	0.0671	37	1	4	Underwriting Cost of Debt						
23	0.1053	38	1	4	Underwriting Cost of Equity						
24	0.1625	39	1	4	Ratio of Debt to Equity						
25	2,754.321	40	0	0	Number of Common Shares Outstanding in Previous Period						
26	14.4700	41	1	4	Price-Earnings Ratio						
27											
28											
29											
30											
31											
32											
33		**Pro forma Income Statement**									
34											
35		2009	2010	2011	2012	2013					
36											
37	Sales	61897.00	43946.87	31202.28	22153.62	15729.07					
38	Operating income	0.00	11909.60	8455.82	6003.63	4262.58					
39	Interest expense	0.00	502.61	356.85	253.36	179.89					
40	Underwriting commission -- debt	0.00	34.69	131.05	88.79	58.77					
41	Income before taxes	0.00	11372.30	7967.91	5661.48	4023.91					
42	Taxes	0.00	2518.44	1764.52	1253.75	891.11					
43	Net income	0.00	8853.87	6203.39	4407.73	3132.80					
44	Preferred dividends	0.00	0.00	0.00	0.00	0.00					
45	Available for common dividends	0.00	8853.87	6203.39	4407.73	3132.80					
46	Common dividends	0.00	3845.23	2694.13	1914.28	1360.58					
47	Debt repayments	0.00	219.00	219.00	219.00	219.00					
48	Actl funds needed for investment	0.00	-29848.90	-18938.76	-13381.13	-9435.22					
49											
50											
51											
52											
53		**Pro forma Balance Sheet**									
54											
55		2009	2010	2011	2012	2013					
56	**Assets**										
57	Current assets	0.00	28073.26	19932.01	14151.73	10047.73					
58	Fixed assets	0.00	39152.27	27798.11	19736.66	14013.03					
59	Total assets	0.00	67225.53	47730.12	33888.39	24060.76					
60	**Liabilities and net worth**										
61	Current liabilities	0.00	13663.24	9700.90	6887.64	4890.22					
62	Long term debt	8223.00	7487.20	5315.91	3774.30	2679.75					
63	Preferred stock	0.00	0.00	0.00	0.00	0.00					
64	Common stock	3120.00	-26212.11	-43198.58	-55257.09	-63816.76					
65	Retained earnings	67248.00	72287.19	75911.89	78483.54	80307.54					
66	Total liabilities and net worth	0.00	67225.53	47730.12	33888.39	24060.76					
67	Computed DBT/EQ	0.0000	0.1625	0.1625	0.1625	0.1625					
68	Int. rate on total debt	0.0671	0.0671	0.0671	0.0671	0.0671					
69	Per share data										
70	Earnings	0.0000	4.0371	3.4269	2.9494	2.5387					
71	Dividends	0.0000	1.7533	1.4883	1.2809	1.1026					
72	Price	0.0000	58.4172	49.5865	42.6783	36.7356					

The program of FINPLAN is available on the Website: http://centerforpbbefr.rutgers.edu/.

Appendix 24.B. Program of FINPLAN with an Example

This program is composed under Visual Basic Application (VBA) environment.

```
Sub FinPlan()
   Dim i As Integer             'Looping control variable
   Dim bNYEARFound As Boolean 'Check if Year Being Simulated is found
   Dim NDATE As Integer         'Year immediately preceeding the first forecasted year
   Dim NUMVR As Integer         'Variable code number
   Dim NYEAR() As Integer       'Year being simulated

   Dim N As Integer             '1 The number of years to be simulated
   Dim SALES() As Double        '21 Sales in the simulation year
   Dim GSALS() As Double        '22 Growth rate of sales
   Dim CARAT() As Double        '23 Ratio of current assets to sales
   Dim FARAT() As Double        '24 Ratio of fixed assets to sales
   Dim CLRAT() As Double        '25 Ratio of current liabilities to sales
   Dim PFDSK() As Double        '26 Preferred stock
   Dim PFDIV() As Double        '27 Preferred dividends
   Dim ZL() As Double           '28 Long term debt
   Dim ZLR() As Double          '29 Debt repayments
   Dim S() As Double            '30 Common stock
   Dim R() As Double            '31 Retained earnings
   Dim B() As Double            '32 Retention rate
   Dim T() As Double            '33 Federal income tax rate
   Dim ZI() As Double           '34 Interest rate on total debt
   Dim ZIE() As Double          '35 Interest rate on new debt
   Dim ORATE() As Double        '36 Operating income rate (EBIT/SALES)
   Dim UL() As Double           '37 Underwriting commission of new debt
   Dim US() As Double           '38 Underwriting commission of new stock
   Dim ZK() As Double           '39 Desired debt to equity ratio
   Dim ZNUMC() As Double        '40 Cummulative number of common stock shares outstanding
   Dim PERAT() As Double        '41 Price / Earnings ratio


   Dim O() As Double            'Operating income
   Dim CA() As Double           'Current assets
   Dim FA() As Double           'Fixed assets
   Dim A() As Double            'Total assets
   Dim CL() As Double           'Current liabilities
   Dim ZNF() As Double          'Estimated needed funds
   Dim ZNL() As Double          'Value of new debt issued
   Dim EXINT() As Double        'Interest expense
   Dim DBTUC() As Double        'Debt underwriting commission
   Dim EAIBT() As Double        'Earnings after interest and before tax
   Dim TAX() As Double          'Federal income taxes
   Dim EAIAT() As Double        'Earnings after interest and after tax
   Dim EAFCD() As Double        'Earnings available for common dividends
   Dim COMDV() As Double        'Common stock dividends
   Dim ZNS() As Double          'Value of new common stock issued
   Dim TLANW() As Double        'Total liabilities and net worth
   Dim COMPK() As Double        'Computed debt to equity
   Dim ANF() As Double          'Actual needed funds
   Dim P() As Double            'Per share market price of common stock
```

```
Dim ZNEW() As Double        'Value of new common stock shares issued
Dim EPS() As Double         'Common stock EPS
Dim DPS() As Double         'Common stock DPS

On Error GoTo ErrorHandler

Columns("a").ColumnWidth = 29     'Set default column A width

Range("a2").Select                'Get the year being simulated from cell A2
NDATE = ActiveCell.Value

Range("b5").Select                'Get the variable code number from cell B5
NUMVR = ActiveCell.Value

bNYEARFound = False
While NUMVR <> Empty And Not bNYEARFound
   If NUMVR = 1 Then              'If the number of years to be simulated is found
      N = ActiveCell.Previous.Value + 1
      bNYEARFound = True
   End If

   ActiveCell.Offset(1, 0).Activate
   NUMVR = ActiveCell.Value
Wend

If Not bNYEARFound Then N = 5     'If the number of years to be simulated is not found
                                  'then set the default of N as 5
ReDim NYEAR(N)
ReDim SALES(N)
ReDim GSALS(N)
ReDim ORATE(N)
ReDim T(N)
ReDim CARAT(N)
ReDim FARAT(N)
ReDim CLRAT(N)
ReDim ZL(N)
ReDim ZI(N)
ReDim ZIE(N)
ReDim ZLR(N)
ReDim PFDSK(N)
ReDim PFDIV(N)
ReDim S(N)
ReDim ZNUMC(N)
ReDim R(N)
ReDim B(N)
ReDim ZK(N)
ReDim PERAT(N)
ReDim UL(N)
ReDim US(N)

NYEAR(1) = NDATE
For i = 2 To N
   NYEAR(i) = NYEAR(i - 1) + 1
Next
```

```
Range("b5").Select
NUMVR = ActiveCell.Value

While NUMVR <> Empty
   Select Case NUMVR

      Case 21
         SALES(1) = ActiveCell.Previous.Value

      Case 22
         For i = ActiveCell.Next.Value + 1 To ActiveCell.Next.Next.Value + 1
            GSALS(i) = ActiveCell.Previous.Value
         Next

      Case 23
         For i = ActiveCell.Next.Value + 1 To ActiveCell.Next.Next.Value + 1
            CARAT(i) = ActiveCell.Previous.Value
         Next

      Case 24
         For i = ActiveCell.Next.Value + 1 To ActiveCell.Next.Next.Value + 1
            FARAT(i) = ActiveCell.Previous.Value
         Next

      Case 25
         For i = ActiveCell.Next.Value + 1 To ActiveCell.Next.Next.Value + 1
            CLRAT(i) = ActiveCell.Previous.Value
         Next

      Case 26
         For i = ActiveCell.Next.Value + 1 To ActiveCell.Next.Next.Value + 1
            PFDSK(i) = ActiveCell.Previous.Value
         Next

      Case 27
         For i = ActiveCell.Next.Value + 1 To ActiveCell.Next.Next.Value + 1
            PFDIV(i) = ActiveCell.Previous.Value
         Next

      Case 28
         ZL(1) = ActiveCell.Previous.Value

      Case 29
         For i = ActiveCell.Next.Value + 1 To ActiveCell.Next.Next.Value + 1
            ZLR(i) = ActiveCell.Previous.Value
         Next

      Case 30
         S(1) = ActiveCell.Previous.Value

      Case 31
         R(1) = ActiveCell.Previous.Value

      Case 32
         For i = ActiveCell.Next.Value + 1 To ActiveCell.Next.Next.Value + 1
            B(i) = ActiveCell.Previous.Value
         Next
```

```
      Case 33
         For i = ActiveCell.Next.Value + 1 To ActiveCell.Next.Next.Value + 1
            T(i) = ActiveCell.Previous.Value
         Next

      Case 34
         ZI(1) = ActiveCell.Previous.Value

      Case 35
         For i = ActiveCell.Next.Value + 1 To ActiveCell.Next.Next.Value + 1
            ZIE(i) = ActiveCell.Previous.Value
         Next

      Case 36
         For i = ActiveCell.Next.Value + 1 To ActiveCell.Next.Next.Value + 1
            ORATE(i) = ActiveCell.Previous.Value
         Next

      Case 37
         For i = ActiveCell.Next.Value + 1 To ActiveCell.Next.Next.Value + 1
            UL(i) = ActiveCell.Previous.Value
         Next

      Case 38
         For i = ActiveCell.Next.Value + 1 To ActiveCell.Next.Next.Value + 1
            US(i) = ActiveCell.Previous.Value
         Next

      Case 39
         For i = ActiveCell.Next.Value + 1 To ActiveCell.Next.Next.Value + 1
            ZK(i) = ActiveCell.Previous.Value
         Next

      Case 40
         ZNUMC(1) = ActiveCell.Previous.Value

      Case 41
         For i = ActiveCell.Next.Value + 1 To ActiveCell.Next.Next.Value + 1
            PERAT(i) = ActiveCell.Previous.Value
         Next

   End Select

   ActiveCell.Offset(1, 0).Activate
   NUMVR = ActiveCell.Value
Wend

ReDim O(N)
ReDim CA(N)
ReDim FA(N)
ReDim A(N)
ReDim CL(N)
ReDim ZNF(N)
ReDim ZNL(N)
ReDim EXINT(N)
```

```
ReDim DBTUC(N)
ReDim EAIBT(N)
ReDim TAX(N)
ReDim EAIAT(N)
ReDim EAFCD(N)
ReDim COMDV(N)
ReDim ZNS(N)
ReDim TLANW(N)
ReDim COMPK(N)
ReDim ANF(N)
ReDim P(N)
ReDim ZNEW(N)
ReDim EPS(N)
ReDim DPS(N)

For i = 2 To N                              'Solve simultaneous equations for N periods
   SALES(i) = SALES(i - 1) * (1 + GSALS(i))
   O(i) = ORATE(i) * SALES(i)
   CA(i) = CARAT(i) * SALES(i)
   FA(i) = FARAT(i) * SALES(i)
   A(i) = CA(i) + FA(i)
   CL(i) = CLRAT(i) * SALES(i)
   ZNF(i) = (A(i) - CL(i) - PFDSK(i)) - (ZL(i - 1) - ZLR(i)) - S(i - 1) - R(i - 1) _
          - B(i) * ((1 - T(i)) * (O(i) - ZI(i - 1) * (ZL(i - 1) - ZLR(i))) - PFDIV(i))
   ZNL(i) = (ZK(i) / (1 + ZK(i))) * (A(i) - CL(i) - PFDSK(i)) - (ZL(i - 1) - ZLR(i))
   ZL(i) = (ZL(i - 1) - ZLR(i)) + ZNL(i)
   ZI(i) = ZI(i - 1) * ((ZL(i - 1) - ZLR(i)) / ZL(i)) + ZIE(i) * (ZNL(i) / ZL(i))
   If ZNL(i) <= 0 Then ZI(i) = ZI(i - 1)
   EXINT(i) = ZI(i) * ZL(i)
   DBTUC(i) = Abs(UL(i) * ZNL(i))
   EAIBT(i) = O(i) - EXINT(i) - DBTUC(i)
   TAX(i) = T(i) * EAIBT(i)
   EAIAT(i) = EAIBT(i) - TAX(i)
   EAFCD(i) = EAIAT(i) - PFDIV(i)
   COMDV(i) = (1 - B(i)) * EAFCD(i)
   R(i) = R(i - 1) + B(i) * ((1 - T(i)) * (O(i) - ZI(i) * ZL(i) - UL(i) * _
        ZNL(i)) - PFDIV(i))
   S(i) = ZL(i) / ZK(i) - R(i)
   ZNS(i) = S(i) - S(i - 1)
   TLANW(i) = CL(i) + PFDSK(i) + ZL(i) + S(i) + R(i)
   COMPK(i) = ZL(i) / (S(i) + R(i))
   ANF(i) = ZNF(i) + B(i) * (1 - T(i)) * (ZI(i) * ZL(i) + UL(i) * _
          ZNL(i) - ZI(i - 1) * (ZL(i - 1) - ZLR(i)))
   P(i) = (PERAT(i) * EAFCD(i) - ZNS(i) / (1 - US(i))) / ZNUMC(i - 1)
   ZNEW(i) = ZNS(i) / ((1 - US(i)) * P(i))
   ZNUMC(i) = ZNUMC(i - 1) + ZNEW(i)
   EPS(i) = EAFCD(i) / ZNUMC(i)
   DPS(i) = COMDV(i) / ZNUMC(i)
Next

Range(ActiveCell.Offset(0,-1), ActiveCell.Offset(70, N)).Clear 'Clear the report area

ActiveCell.Offset(6, 0).Activate    'Select the Income Statemet Starting Cell

With ActiveCell.Font
   .Bold = True
```

```
   .Size = 11
End With

ActiveCell.Value = "Pro forma Income Statement"     'Generate Income Statement
ActiveCell.Offset(2, -1).Activate
For i = 1 To N
   ActiveCell.Offset(0, i).Value = NYEAR(i)
Next

ActiveCell.Offset(2, 0).Activate
Range(ActiveCell, ActiveCell.Offset(15, N)).NumberFormat = "###0.00"

ActiveCell.Value = "Sales"
For i = 1 To N
   ActiveCell.Offset(0, i).Value = SALES(i)
Next

ActiveCell.Offset(1, 0).Activate
ActiveCell.Value = "Operating income"
For i = 1 To N
   ActiveCell.Offset(0, i).Value = O(i)
Next

ActiveCell.Offset(1, 0).Activate
ActiveCell.Value = "Interest expense"
For i = 1 To N
   ActiveCell.Offset(0, i).Value = EXINT(i)
Next

ActiveCell.Offset(1, 0).Activate
ActiveCell.Value = "Underwriting commission -- debt"
For i = 1 To N
   ActiveCell.Offset(0, i).Value = DBTUC(i)
Next

ActiveCell.Offset(1, 0).Activate
ActiveCell.Value = "Income before taxes"
For i = 1 To N
   ActiveCell.Offset(0, i).Value = EAIBT(i)
Next

ActiveCell.Offset(1, 0).Activate
ActiveCell.Value = "Taxes"
For i = 1 To N
   ActiveCell.Offset(0, i).Value = TAX(i)
Next

ActiveCell.Offset(1, 0).Activate
ActiveCell.Value = "Net income"
For i = 1 To N
   ActiveCell.Offset(0, i).Value = EAIAT(i)
Next

ActiveCell.Offset(1, 0).Activate
ActiveCell.Value = "Preferred dividends"
For i = 1 To N
```

```
   ActiveCell.Offset(0, i).Value = PFDIV(i)
Next

ActiveCell.Offset(1, 0).Activate
ActiveCell.Value = "Available for common dividends"
For i = 1 To N
   ActiveCell.Offset(0, i).Value = EAFCD(i)
Next

ActiveCell.Offset(1, 0).Activate
ActiveCell.Value = "Common dividends"
For i = 1 To N
   ActiveCell.Offset(0, i).Value = COMDV(i)
Next

ActiveCell.Offset(1, 0).Activate
ActiveCell.Value = "Debt repayments"
For i = 1 To N
   ActiveCell.Offset(0, i).Value = ZLR(i)
Next

ActiveCell.Offset(1, 0).Activate
ActiveCell.Value = "Actl funds needed for investment"
For i = 1 To N
   ActiveCell.Offset(0, i).Value = ANF(i)
Next

ActiveCell.Offset(5, 1).Activate                'Generate Balance Sheet
With ActiveCell.Font
   .Bold = True
   .Size = 11
End With

ActiveCell.Value = "Pro forma Balance Sheet"
ActiveCell.Offset(2, -1).Activate
For i = 1 To N
   ActiveCell.Offset(0, i).Value = NYEAR(i)
Next

ActiveCell.Offset(1, 0).Activate
ActiveCell.Font.Bold = True
ActiveCell.Value = "Assets"

ActiveCell.Offset(1, 0).Activate
Range(ActiveCell, ActiveCell.Offset(9, N)).NumberFormat = "###0.00"
Range(ActiveCell.Offset(10, 0), ActiveCell.Offset(15, N)).NumberFormat = "###0.0000"

ActiveCell.Value = "Current assets"
For i = 1 To N
   ActiveCell.Offset(0, i).Value = CA(i)
Next

ActiveCell.Offset(1, 0).Activate
ActiveCell.Value = "Fixed assets"
For i = 1 To N
   ActiveCell.Offset(0, i).Value = FA(i)
Next
```

```
ActiveCell.Offset(1, 0).Activate
ActiveCell.Value = "Total assets"
For i = 1 To N
   ActiveCell.Offset(0, i).Value = A(i)
Next

ActiveCell.Offset(1, 0).Activate
ActiveCell.Font.Bold = True
ActiveCell.Value = "Liabilities and net worth"

ActiveCell.Offset(1, 0).Activate
ActiveCell.Value = "Current liabilities"
For i = 1 To N
   ActiveCell.Offset(0, i).Value = CL(i)
Next

ActiveCell.Offset(1, 0).Activate
ActiveCell.Value = "Long term debt"
For i = 1 To N
   ActiveCell.Offset(0, i).Value = ZL(i)
Next

ActiveCell.Offset(1, 0).Activate
ActiveCell.Value = "Preferred stock"
For i = 1 To N
   ActiveCell.Offset(0, i).Value = PFDSK(i)
Next

ActiveCell.Offset(1, 0).Activate
ActiveCell.Value = "Common stock"
For i = 1 To N
   ActiveCell.Offset(0, i).Value = S(i)
Next

ActiveCell.Offset(1, 0).Activate
ActiveCell.Value = "Retained earnings"
For i = 1 To N
   ActiveCell.Offset(0, i).Value = R(i)
Next

ActiveCell.Offset(1, 0).Activate
ActiveCell.Value = "Total liabilities and net worth"
For i = 1 To N
   ActiveCell.Offset(0, i).Value = TLANW(i)
Next

ActiveCell.Offset(1, 0).Activate
ActiveCell.Value = "Computed DBT/EQ"
For i = 1 To N
   ActiveCell.Offset(0, i).Value = COMPK(i)
Next

ActiveCell.Offset(1, 0).Activate
ActiveCell.Value = "Int. rate on total debt"
```

```
    For i = 1 To N
       ActiveCell.Offset(0, i).Value = ZI(i)
    Next

    ActiveCell.Offset(1, 0).Activate
    ActiveCell.Value = "Per share data"

    ActiveCell.Offset(1, 0).Activate
    ActiveCell.Value = "Earnings"
    For i = 1 To N
       ActiveCell.Offset(0, i).Value = EPS(i)
    Next

    ActiveCell.Offset(1, 0).Activate
    ActiveCell.Value = "Dividends"
    For i = 1 To N
       ActiveCell.Offset(0, i).Value = DPS(i)
    Next

    ActiveCell.Offset(1, 0).Activate
    ActiveCell.Value = "Price"
    For i = 1 To N
       ActiveCell.Offset(0, i).Value = P(i)
    Next

    Exit Sub    ' Exit to avoid ErrorHandler.

ErrorHandler:  ' Error-handling routine.
    Select Case Err.Number  ' Evaluate error number.
       Case 9
          MsgBox "'The number of years to be simulated' does not match your " & _
          "'Last Period' input.", vbExclamation
       Case 11
          MsgBox Str$(Err.Number) & ", " & Err.Description & Chr$(10) & _
          "'The number of years to be simulated' does not match your " & _
          "'Last Period' input.", vbExclamation
       Case Else
          MsgBox Str$(Err.Number) & ", " & Err.Description
    End Select
End Sub
```

References for Chapter 24

Brealey, RA and SC Myers (2000). *Principles of Corporate Finance*, 6th ed. Burr Ridge, IL: McGraw-Hill.

Carleton, WT (May 1970). An analytical model for long-range financial planning. *Journal of Finance*, 25, 291–315.

Davis, BE, GJ Caccappolo, and MA Chandry (Spring 1973). An econometric planning model for american telephone and telegraph company. *The Bell Journal of Economics and Management Science*, 29–56.

Diebold, FX and P Pauly (January–March 1987). Structural change and the combination of forecasts. *Journal of Forecasting*, 6, 21–40.

Elliott, WJ (March 1972). Forecasting and analysis of corporate financial performance with an econometric model of the firm. *Journal of Financial and Quantitative Analysis*, 1499–1526.

Feltham, GA and JA Ohlson (1995). Valuation and clean surplus accounting for operating and financial activities. *Contemporary Accounting Research*, 11, 689–731.

Francis, JC (Spring/Summer 1977). Analysis of equity returns: A survey with extensions. *Journal of Economics and Business*, 181–192.

Francis, JC and DR Rowell (1978). A simultaneous-equation model of the firm for financial analysis and planning. *Financial Management*, 7, 29–44.

Gershefski, GW (July/August 1969). Building a corporate financial model. *Harvard Business Review*, 61–72.

Granger, CWJ and P Newbold (March 1973). Some comments on the evaluation of economic forecasts. *Applied Economics*, 5, 35–47.

Lee, AC, JC Lee, and CF Lee (2009). *Financial Analysis, Planning and Forecasting: Theory and Application*, 2nd ed. Singapore: World Scientific Publishing Company.

Lee, CF (1984). *Alternative Financial Planning and Forecasting Models: An Integration and Extension.* Mimeo: The University of Illinois at Urbana-Champaign.

Lee, CF, JE Finnerty, and EA Norton (1997). *Foundations of Financial Management*, 3rd ed. Minneapolis/St. Paul: West Publishing Co.

Lee, CF, JC Lee, and AC Lee (2000). *Statistics for Business and Financial Economics.* Singapore: World Science Publishing Co.

Lee, CF, WK Shih, and HY Chen (2011). Alternative equity valuation models. Working Paper.

Lee, CF and S Rahman (1997). Interaction of investment, financing, and dividend decisions: A control theory approach. *Advances in Financial Planning and Forecasting*, 7.

Lerner, E and WT Carleton (September 1964). The integration of capital budgeting and stock valuation. *American Economics Review*, 54, 683–702.

Myers SC and A Pogue (May 1974). A programming approach to corporate financial management. *Journal of Finance*, 29, 579–599.

Ohlson, JA (1995). Earnings, book values, and dividends in equity valuation. *Contemporary Accounting Research*, 11, 661–687.

Pindyck, RS and DL Rubinfeld (1976). *Econometric Models and Economic Forecasts.* New York: McGraw-Hill Book Co.

Ross, SA, RW Westerfield, and JF Jaffe (2013). *Corporate Finance*, 106th ed. Boston, MA: McGraw-Hill Irwin Publishing Co.

Ross, SA, RW Westerfield, and BD Jordon (2012). *Fundamentals of Corporate Finance.* 10th ed. Boston, MA: McGraw-Hill Higher Education.

Salzman, S (August 1967). An econometric model of a firm. *Review of Economics and Statistics*, 49, 332–342.

Securities and Exchange Commission, Release No. 5695 (1976). Notice of Adoption of Amendments to Regulations S-X Requiring Disclosure of Certain Replacement Cost Data, March 23.

Securities and Exchange Commission, Release No. 33–5699 (1976). April 23.
Warren, JM and JP Shelton (December 1971). A simultaneous-equation approach to financial planning. *Journal of Finance*, 26, 1123–1142.
Williams, JB (1938). *The Theory of Investment Value*. Cambridge, MA: Harvard University Press. Websites http://finance.yahoo.com.

Chapter 25

Time-Series: Analysis, Model, and Forecasting

25.1. Introduction

In the first 24 chapters of this book, we used both time-series and cross-section data to show how statistical analysis techniques can be used in economic and business decision-making.

Time-series data are any set of data from a quantifiable (or qualitative) event that are recorded *over time*. For example, we read newspapers every day and, can obtain the Dow Jones Industrial Average (DJIA) index over time. The series of DJIA index values, ordered through time, constitutes time-series data. Other types of time-series data are based on the rate of inflation, the consumer price index, the balance of trade, and the annual profit of a firm.

Cross-section data are observations made on individuals, groups of individuals, objects, or geographic areas *at a particular time*. For example, price per share for N firms in 1991 is a set of cross-section data. On the other hand, price per share for General Motors over time, P_t $(t = 1, 2, \ldots, T)$, is a set of time-series data.

The purpose of this chapter is to describe components of time-series analyses and to discuss alternative methods of economic and business forecasting in terms of time-series data. First, a classical description of three time-series components is offered. Then the moving average and seasonally adjusted time-series are explored. Time trend regression, exponential smoothing and forecasting, and the Holt–Winters forecasting model for non-seasonal series are investigated in detail. Finally, the autoregressive forecasting model is discussed in some detail. Appendix 25.A addresses the Holt–Winters forecasting model for seasonal series.

25.2. The Classical Time-Series Component Model

Several factors result in the interdependence of time-series data over time; these factors are trend, seasonal, and business cycle factors. For example, the current earnings of a growing company tend to be greater than its earnings in the period just ended, and, of course, the expected earnings in the next period will be greater than the current earnings. Therefore, the correlation between any adjacent earnings is positive, and this is due to the trend factor. Seasonal factors also contribute to the interdependence of time-series data. Retail sales in the fourth quarter account for a major portion of total annual sales of department stores. This seasonal factor ensures that the sales volume in the fourth quarter of each year is highly correlated with the fourth-quarter sales volume of any other year. The business cycle is another cause of interdependency in a time-series model. In short, it is traditionally assumed that the total variation in a time-series is composed of four basic components: a **trend component**, a **seasonal component**, a **cyclical component**, and an **irregular component**. We will now discuss these four components in some detail.

25.2.1. *The Trend Component*

A trend is a pattern that exhibits a tendency either to grow or to decrease fairly steadily over time. For example, the earnings per share (EPS) of Johnson & Johnson exhibits two separate trends (or a quadratic trend) over time (see Table 25.1 and Fig. 25.1). One of the trends is from 2001 to 2007, the other from 2008 to 2010.

Table 25.1. EPS of Johnson & Johnson.

Year	EPS
2001	1.87
2002	2.2
2003	2.42
2004	2.87
2005	3.5
2006	3.76
2007	3.67
2008	4.62
2009	4.45
2010	4.85

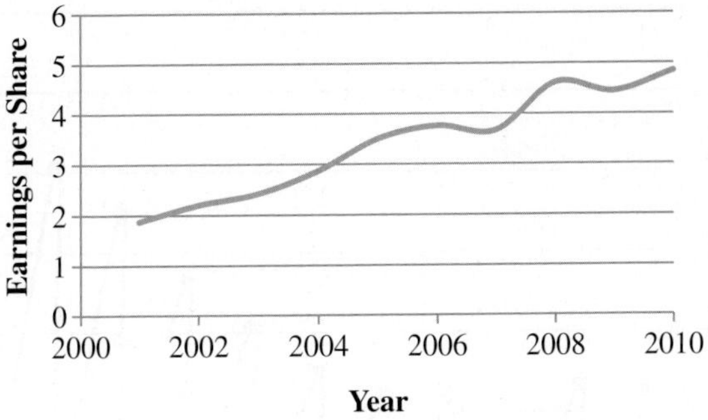

Fig. 25.1. EPS of Johnson & Johnson.

Table 25.2. Quarterly EPS of IBM corporation.

	Quarter			
Year	1	2	3	4
2000	0.85	1.95	3.06	4.58
2001	1.02	2.22	3.21	4.69
2002	0.75	1.01	2.01	3.13
2003	0.8	1.8	2.84	4.42
2004	0.81	1.84	2.77	4.48
2005	0.86	2.02	2.97	4.99
2006	1.09	2.4	3.87	6.15
2007	1.23	2.8	4.5	7.32
2008	1.67	3.67	5.79	9.07
2009	1.71	4.04	6.47	10.12
2010	2	4.64	7.49	11.69

25.2.2. *The Seasonal Component*

The phenomenon of seasonality is common in the business world. Retailers can rely on greater sales volume in December than in any other month; stock returns are typically higher in January than in most other months — the "January effect".

Table 25.2 and Fig. 25.2 show EPS of IBM Corporation over a period of 44 quarters (first quarter 2000 to fourth quarter 2010). The table offers evidence of seasonal behavior for all quarters. The fourth-quarter figures tend to be relatively high, whereas those in the first quarter are relatively low. This seasonal behavior is quite clear in Fig. 25.2, where an obvious pattern almost repeats itself each year.

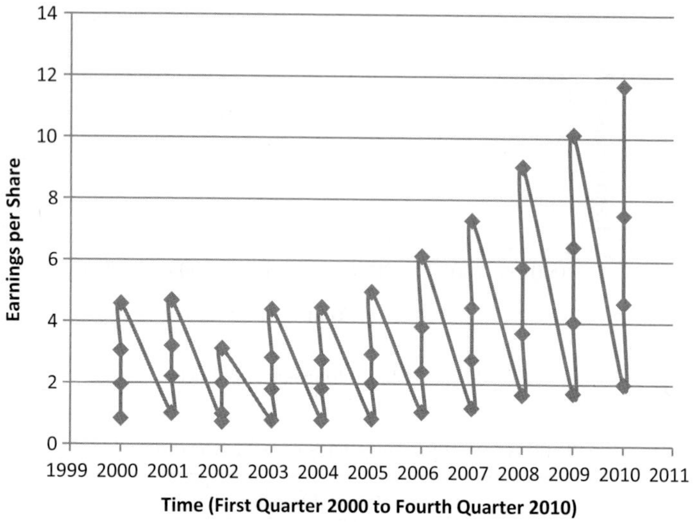

Fig. 25.2. Quarterly EPS of IBM.

25.2.3. *The Cyclical Component and Business Cycles*

Cyclical patterns are long-term oscillatory patterns that are unrelated to seasonal behavior. They are not necessarily regular but instead follow rather smooth patterns of upswings and downswings, each swing lasting more than 2 or 3 years. Figure 25.3 demonstrates the cyclical pattern of the S&P 500 Composite Index during the period of 2000–2010, which will be discussed in detail in the next chapter. Figure 25.4 shows the cyclical patterns of monthly data of 3-month interest rates-of-return on Eurodollar deposits, U.S. certificates of deposit (CDs) and Treasury bills (T-bills) during the period of 2000 to 2010.[1]

The National Bureau of Economic Research (NBER) and the U.S. Department of Commerce have specified a number of time-series as statistical business indicators of cyclical revivals and recessions. These time-series have been classified into three groups.[2] The first group is the so-called

[1]A Eurodollar is any dollar on deposit outside the United States. In the bottom portion of Fig. 25.4, "spreads" are the differences between two different kinds of interest rates. For example, the Eurodollar rate is 0.40% higher than the U.S. CD rate (0.27%) and T-Bill rate (0.14%) in November 2010.

[2]Index numbers are essential elements for these business indicators. Therefore, we discuss these business indicators after we discuss index numbers and stock market indexes in the next chapter.

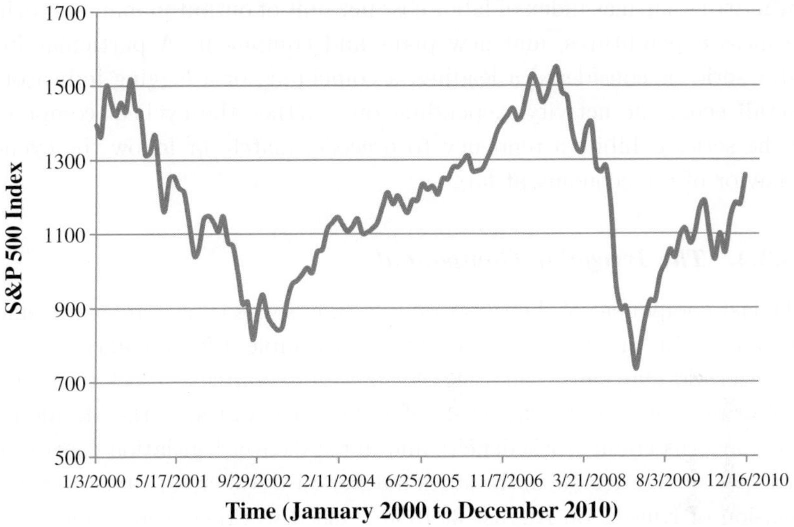

Fig. 25.3. S&P 500 composite index, January 2000 to December 2010.

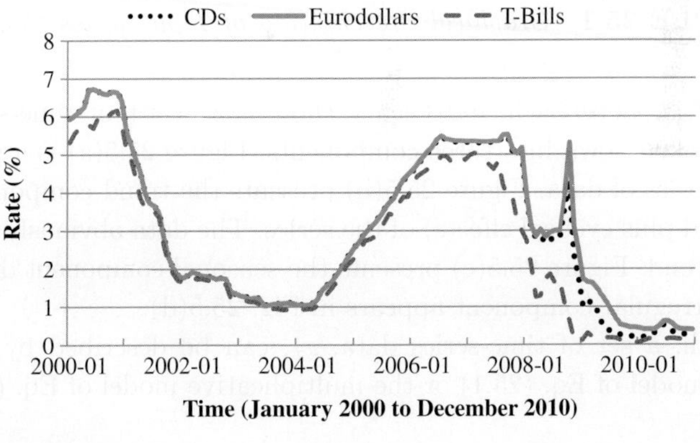

Fig. 25.4. 3-month rates on Eurodollar deposits, U.S. CDs, and U.S. T-Bills, 2000–2010 (monthly data).

leading indicators, such as the S&P index of the prices of 500 common stocks. These series have usually reached their cyclical turning points prior to the analogous turns in economic activity. The second group is the **coincident indicators,** such as unemployment rate, the index of industrial production, and GNP in current dollars. The third group is the **lagging**

indicators, such as index of labor cost per unit of output in manufacturing, business expenditures, and new plant and equipment. A particular indicator series is considered a leading, a coinciding, or a lagging indicator of overall economic activity, depending on whether the cyclical component of the series exhibits a tendency to precede, match, or follow the cyclical behavior of the economy at large.

25.2.4. *The Irregular Component*

The last component of the variation in a time-series is the irregular element introduced by the unexpected event. For example, the announcement of a takeover bid may cause the price of the target company's stock to jump up 20% or more in a single day. Fears of an outbreak of war in the Middle East and concerns about trade deficits and anti-takeover legislation contributed to a spectacular decline in the stock market on October 19, 1987. And Iraq's invasion of Kuwait on August 3, 1990, caused worldwide stock markets to drop more than 10% within a week. These irregular elements arise suddenly and have a temporary impact on time-series behavior.

EXAMPLE 25.1 *Graphical Presentation of Time-Series Components*

In Fig. 25.5, Levenbach and Cleary show how a set of time-series data can be broken down into three components. Figure 25.5(a) is a plot of the original series of data. Figure 25.5(b) presents the trend component (long-term trend plus cyclical effects) of the series. The data obviously exhibit an upward trend. Figure 25.5(c) presents the seasonal component of the data, and the irregular component appears in Fig. 25.5(d).

Overall, a set of time-series data, x_t, can be described by using the additive model of Eq. (25.1) or the multiplicative model of Eq. (25.2).

$$x_t = T_t + C_t + S_t + I_t, \tag{25.1}$$

$$x_t = T_t S_t C_t I_t, \tag{25.2}$$

where

T_t = trend component,
C_t = cyclical component,
S_t = seasonal component,
I_t = irregular component.

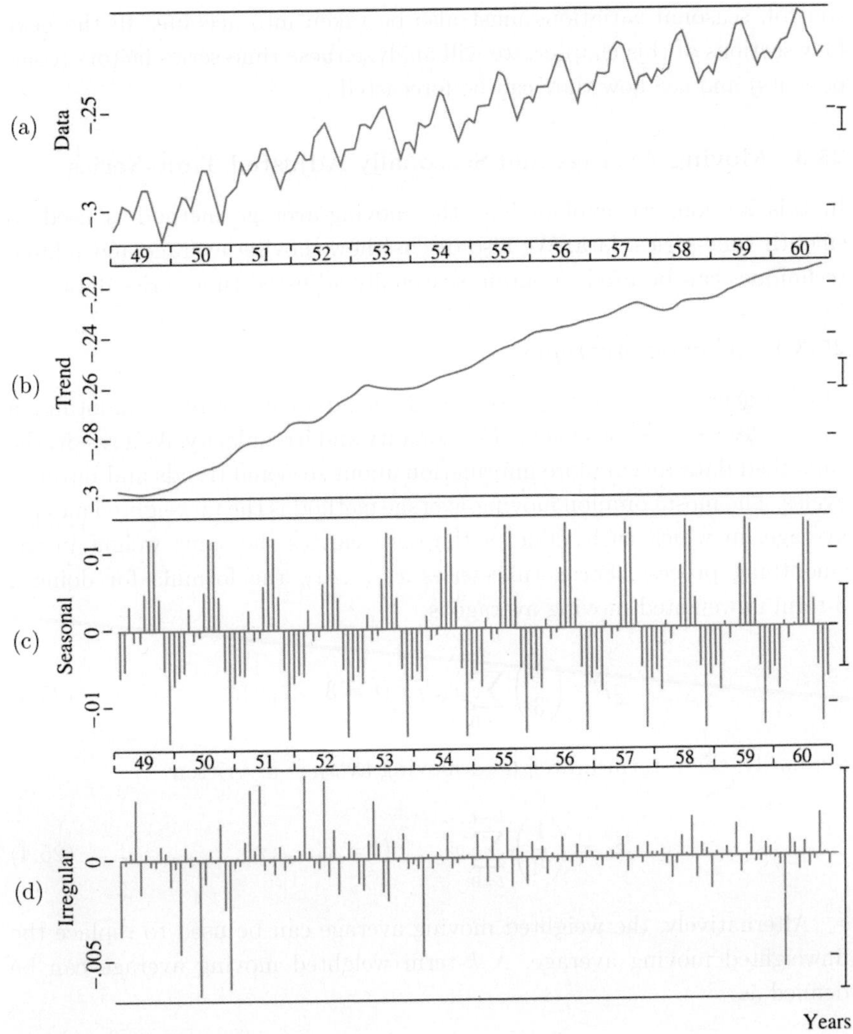

Fig. 25.5. Time-series decomposition.
Source: Levenback H and JP Cleary (1984).

For long-term planning and decision-making in terms of time-series components, business executives concentrate primarily on forecasting the trend movement. For intermediate-term planning — say, from about 2 to about 5 years — fluctuations in the business cycle are of critical importance too. For short-term planning, and for purposes of operational decisions and control, seasonal variations must also be taken into account. In the next four sections of this chapter, we will analyze these time-series factors (components) and see how they can be forecasted.

25.3. Moving Average and Seasonally Adjusted Time-Series

In this section, we explain how the moving-average method is used to smooth time-series data. We also discuss how moving average and related techniques can be used to obtain seasonally adjusted time-series data.

25.3.1. *Moving Averages*

Moving averages are usually associated with data smoothing. Smoothing a time-series reduces the effects of seasonality and irregularity. As a result, the smoothed data reveal more information about seasonal trends and business cycles. The most common moving-average method is the unweighted moving average, in which each value of the data carries the same weight in the smoothing process. For a time-series $x_1, \ldots, x_n$ the formula for doing a 3-term unweighted moving average is

$$z_t = \left(\frac{1}{3}\right)\sum_{i=0}^{2} x_{t-i} \quad (t = 3, \ldots, n). \tag{25.3}$$

Similarily, the k-term unweighted moving average is written

$$z_t = \left(\frac{1}{k}\right)\sum_{t=0}^{k-t} x_{t-i} \quad (t = k, \ldots, n). \tag{25.4}$$

Alternatively, the weighted moving average can be used to replace the unweighted moving average. A k-term weighted moving average can be defined as

$$z_t = \sum_{i=0}^{k-1} w_{t-i}x_{t-i} \quad (t = k, \ldots, n), \tag{25.5}$$

where $\sum_{i=0}^{k-1} w_{t-i} = 1$

The w_{t-i}'s are known as weights and they sum to unity. If the w_{t-i}'s do not sum to unity, they can be normalized with a new set of weights $(w*_{t-i})$ that sum to unity. The unweighted moving average is a special case of the weighted moving average with $w_i = 1/k$ for all i. An example of a weighted-average calculation appears in Table 25.3. Here, columns (1)

Table 25.3. Weighted average.

(1) Observation Value, x_{t-i}	(2) Weight, w_{t-i}	(3) $x_{t-i}w_{t-i}$
0.035	0.10	0.0035
0.002	0.30	0.0006
0.100	0.25	0.0250
0.060	0.35	0.0210
	1.00	0.0501 weighted average

and (2) represent observation value (x_{t-i}) and weight (w_i), respectively. Column (3) represents $x_{t-i}w_{t-i}$. From Table 25.3, we obtain

$$z_t = \sum_{i=0}^{3} x_{t-i}w_{t-i} = 0.0501.$$

One of the important applications of moving averages is to deseasonalize seasonal time-series data which will be discussed in the next section.

25.3.2. *Seasonal Index and Seasonally Adjusted Time-Series*

In Section 25.2, we noted that many business and economic time-series contain a strong seasonal component. This component generally needs to be removed for either monthly or quarterly data. This section demonstrates how the moving-average procedure is used to remove the seasonal component and to do related analysis.

Suppose we have a quarterly time-series, x_t, with a seasonal component. Then we can apply Eq. (25.6), which is obtained by letting $k = 4$ in Eq. (25.4), to remove the seasonal component.

$$z_i = \left(\frac{1}{4}\right)\sum_{i=0}^{3} x_{t-i} \quad (t = 4, \ldots, n). \tag{25.6}$$

EXAMPLE 25.1 *Seasonally Adjusted Quarterly EPS of Johnson & Johnson*

For the data on quarterly EPS of J&J Corporation during the period of first quarter 2000 to fourth quarter 2010 given in Table 25.4, the first number in the series of the 4-quarter moving average is

$$\frac{0.86 + 1.8 + 2.68 + 3.3}{4} = 2.16.$$

Table 25.4. Actual (x_t) and centered 4-point moving average (z_t^*) EPS of Johnson & Johnson from first quarter 2000 to fourth quarter 2010.

(1) t	(2) Earnings per Share, x_t	(3) 4-Point Moving Average, z_t	(4) Centered 4-Point, Moving Average, z_t^*
1	0.86		
2	1.8	2.16	
3	2.68	2.195	2.1775
4	3.3	1.995	2.095
5	1.0	1.7025	1.84875
6	1.0	1.345	1.52375
7	1.51	1.245	1.295
8	1.87	1.2825	1.26375
9	0.6	1.3375	1.31
10	1.15	1.42	1.37875
11	1.73	1.445	1.4325
12	2.2	1.43	1.4375
13	0.7	1.4475	1.43875
14	1.09	1.5025	1.475
15	1.8	1.5375	1.52
16	2.42	1.6825	1.61
17	0.84	1.8475	1.765
18	1.67	1.96	1.90375
19	2.46	1.99	1.975
20	2.87	2.03	2.01
21	0.96	2.085	2.0575
22	1.83	2.2125	2.14875
23	2.68	2.25	2.23125
24	3.38	2.31	2.28
25	1.11	2.3925	2.35125
26	2.07	2.4875	2.44
27	3.01	2.4325	2.46
28	3.76	2.4025	2.4175
29	0.89	2.36	2.38125
30	1.95	2.3375	2.34875
31	2.84	2.4325	2.385
32	3.67	2.5575	2.495
33	1.27	2.7575	2.6575
34	2.45	2.995	2.87625
35	3.64	2.995	2.995
36	4.62	2.99	2.9925
37	1.27	2.99	2.99
38	2.43	2.9475	2.96875
39	3.64	3.04	2.99375
40	4.45	3.155	3.0975
41	1.64	3.28	3.2175
42	2.89	3.38	3.33
43	4.14		
44	4.85		

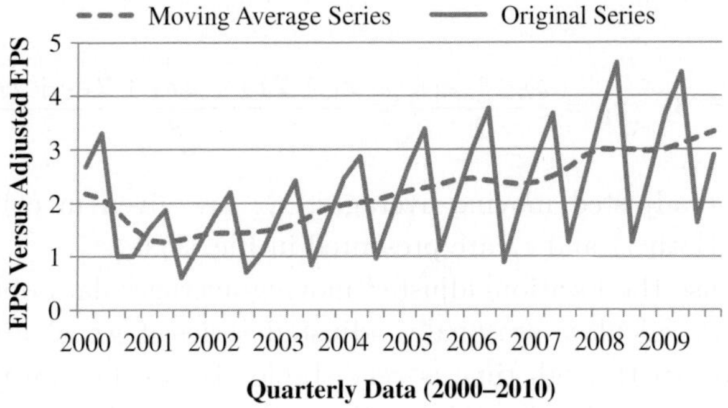

Fig. 25.6. EPS versus moving-average EPS for Johnson & Johnson.

and the second number is

$$\frac{1.8 + 2.68 + 3.3 + 1.0}{4} = 2.195.$$

The complete series appears in column (3) of Table 25.4.

This 4-quarter moving-averages time-series is free seasonally because it is always based on values such that each "season" is represented in each single observation of the new series (see Fig. 25.6). However, the location in time of the members of the series of moving averages does not correspond precisely with that of the members of the original series. Actually, the first 4-quarter moving average would be centered midway between the second-quarter and third-quarter dates. Hence, the 4-quarter moving-averages series indicated in Eq. (25.6) should be rewritten either as

$$z_{t-0.5} = \left(\frac{1}{4}\right) \sum_{i=2}^{-t} x_{t-i} \quad (t = 3, 4, \ldots, n-2) \tag{25.7}$$

or

$$z_{t+0.5} = \left(\frac{1}{4}\right) \sum_{i=-1}^{2} x_{t+i} \quad (t = 2, 3, \ldots, n-2). \tag{25.7a}$$

Then the location-adjusted (centered) moving-averages series can be written as

$$z_i^* = \frac{z_{t-0.5} + z_{t+0.5}}{2} \quad (t = 3, 4, \ldots, n-2). \tag{25.8}$$

When

$$t = 3, \quad z_3^* = \frac{z_{2.5} + z_{3.5}}{2} = \frac{x_1 + 2x_2 + 2x_3 + 2x_4 + x_5}{8}.$$

The location-adjusted moving averages, z_t^*, are given in column (4) of Table 25.4. Both x_t and z_t^* are presented in Fig. 25.6.

We can use the location-adjusted moving-averages data obtained from Eq. (25.8) to calculate seasonally adjusted series if we assume that the seasonal pattern through time is very stable. To do this, we need first to divide original data (x_t) by the location-adjusted moving averages (z_t^*) to obtain the percentage of moving average (PMA). That is,

$$\text{Percentage of moving average (PMA)} = 100\left(\frac{x_t}{z_t^*}\right). \tag{25.9}$$

The PMA of EPS for Johnson & Johnson is presented in column (4) of Table 25.5.

Table 25.5. Seasonal adjustment of EPS of Johnson & Johnson by the seasonal index method from first quarter 2000 to fourth quarter 2010.

(1) Date	(2) EPS, x_t	(3) z_t^*	(4) $100\ (x_t/z_t^*)$	(5) Seasonal Index	(6) Adjusted EPS [Col. (2)/Col. (5)] × 100
2000.1	0.86			47.1702	1.823185
2	1.8			83.71375	2.150184
3	2.68	2.1775	123.0769	120.5633	2.2229
4	3.3	2.095	157.5179	148.5528	2.221432
2001.1	1	1.84875	54.0906	47.1702	2.119983
2	1	1.52375	65.62756	83.71375	1.194547
3	1.51	1.295	116.6023	120.5633	1.252455
4	1.87	1.26375	147.9723	148.5528	1.258812
2002.1	0.6	1.31	45.80153	47.1702	1.27199
2	1.15	1.37875	83.40888	83.71375	1.373729
3	1.73	1.4325	120.7679	120.5633	1.434931
4	2.2	1.4375	153.0435	148.5528	1.480955
2003.1	0.7	1.43875	48.65334	47.1702	1.483988
2	1.09	1.475	73.89831	83.71375	1.302056
3	1.8	1.52	118.4211	120.5633	1.492992
4	2.42	1.61	150.3106	148.5528	1.62905

(*Continued*)

Table 25.5. (*Continued*)

(1) Date	(2) EPS, x_t	(3) z_t^*	(4) $100\ (x_t/z_t^*)$	(5) Seasonal Index	(6) Adjusted EPS [Col. (2) ÷ Col. (5)] × 100
2004.1	0.84	1.765	47.59207	47.1702	1.780785
2	1.67	1.90375	87.7216	83.71375	1.994893
3	2.46	1.975	124.557	120.5633	2.040423
4	2.87	2.01	142.7861	148.5528	1.931973
2005.1	0.96	2.0575	46.65857	47.1702	2.035183
2	1.83	2.14875	85.16579	83.71375	2.186021
3	2.68	2.23125	120.112	120.5633	2.2229
4	3.38	2.28	148.2456	148.5528	2.275285
2006.1	1.11	2.35125	47.20893	47.1702	2.353181
2	2.07	2.44	84.83607	83.71375	2.472712
3	3.01	2.46	122.3577	120.5633	2.496615
4	3.76	2.4175	155.5326	148.5528	2.531087
2007.1	0.89	2.38125	37.37533	47.1702	1.886785
2	1.95	2.34875	83.02288	83.71375	2.329366
3	2.84	2.385	119.0776	120.5633	2.35561
4	3.67	2.495	147.0942	148.5528	2.470502
2008.1	1.27	2.6575	47.78928	47.1702	2.692378
2	2.45	2.87625	85.18036	83.71375	2.92664
3	3.64	2.995	121.5359	120.5633	3.019162
4	4.62	2.9925	154.386	148.5528	3.110005
2009.1	1.27	2.99	42.47492	47.1702	2.692378
2	2.43	2.96875	81.85263	83.71375	2.902749
3	3.64	2.99375	121.5866	120.5633	3.019162
4	4.45	3.0975	143.6642	148.5528	2.995568
2010.1	1.64	3.2175	50.97125	47.1702	3.476772
2	2.89	3.33	86.78679	83.71375	3.45224
3	4.14			120.5633	3.433882
4	4.85			148.5528	3.264833

In our case, the first observation of PMA is

$$100\left(\frac{x_3}{z_3^*}\right) = 100\left(\frac{2.68}{2.1775}\right) = 123.0769.$$

We assume that for any given quarter, in each year, the effect of seasonality is to raise or lower the observation by a constant proportionate amount **(seasonal index)** compared with what it would have been in the absence of seasonal influences. Then we use the so-called **seasonal index method** to remove the seasonal component.

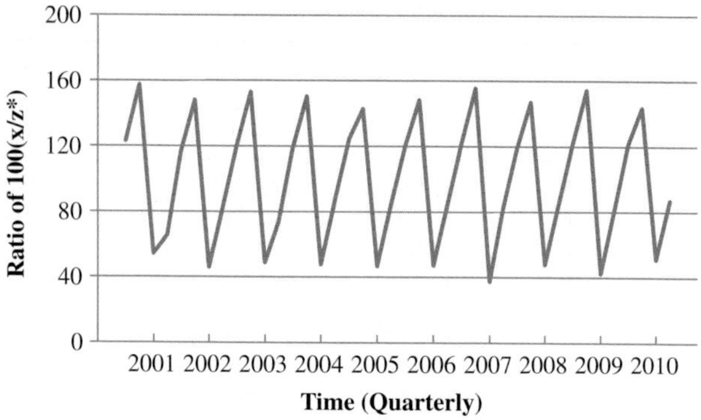

Fig. 25.7. Trend of 100 (x_t/z_t^*) for Johnson & Johnson.

Let's explore the logic of and procedure for calculating the seasonal index listed in column (5) of Table 25.5. By dividing z_t^* into x_t, we can explicitly write the PMA as

$$100\left(\frac{x_t}{z_t^*}\right) = \frac{100T_tC_tS_tI_t}{T_tC_t} = 100S_tI_t. \tag{25.10}$$

The $100S_tI_t$ series for EPS of Johnson & Johnson is presented in Fig. 25.7. This series contains both seasonal and irregular components. The next step is to remove the effect of irregular movements from 100 (x_t/z_t^*). We do this by taking the median of the percentage of moving-average figures for the same quarter as indicated in Table 25.6. The medians for the first through the fourth quarters are 47.400, 84.122, 121.152, and 149.278, respectively. The total of these medians is 401.953. It is desirable that the total of the 4 indexes be 400, in order that they average 100%, so we multiply each of them by an adjustment factor (400/401.953) to make the sum of the 4-quarter seasonal indexes equal 400. The seasonal index is presented in column (5) of Table 25.5.[3] Dividing the seasonal index into the original quarterly data and multiplying the result by 100, we obtain the adjusted series presented in column (6) of Table 25.5 and in Fig. 25.8.

This seasonal index method of seasonal adjustment shows us one possible and simple way to solve the problem of eliminating the seasonal component. In practice, however, it generally can be solved by computer. Important government monthly and quarterly economic data such

[3]The mean instead of the median can also be used to calculate the seasonal index.

Table 25.6. Calculation of seasonal indexes of EPS for Johnson & Johnson Corporation.

	Quarter				
Year	1	2	3	4	Sums
2000			123.077	157.518	
2001	54.091	65.628	116.602	147.972	
2002	45.802	83.409	120.768	153.043	
2003	48.653	73.898	118.421	150.311	
2004	47.592	87.722	124.557	142.786	
2005	46.659	85.166	120.112	148.246	
2006	47.209	84.836	122.358	155.533	
2007	37.375	83.023	119.078	147.094	
2008	47.789	85.180	121.536	154.386	
2009	42.475	81.853	121.587	143.664	
2010	50.971	86.787			
Median	47.400	84.122	121.152	149.278	401.953
Seasonal index	47.170	83.714	120.563	148.553	400.000

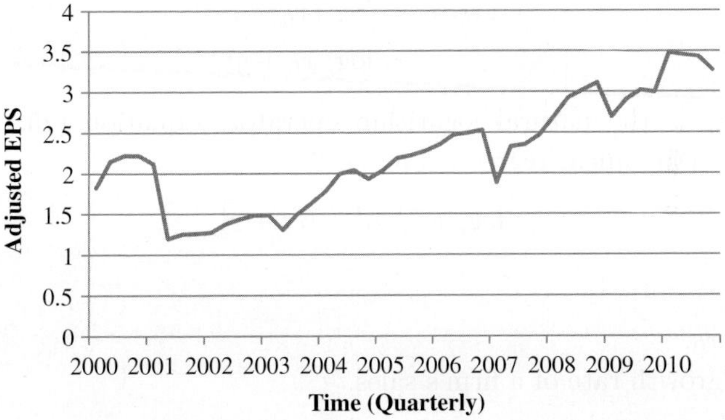

Fig. 25.8. Adjusted EPS of Johnson & Johnson.

as consumer price indexes and employment and unemployment rates have strong seasonal components, and government agencies generally publish these data in both unadjusted and adjusted forms. The seasonal adjustment procedure used in official United States government publications is the Census X-11 method which is based upon the moving-averages method.[4] In the next section, we will look at time trend regression.

[4]Lee, AC, JC Lee, and CF Lee (2009).

25.4. Linear and Log-Linear Time Trend Regressions

If a time-series is expected to change linearly overtime, the simple linear regression model defined in Eq. (25.11) can be used to relate the time-series, x_t, to time t, and the least-squares line is used to forecast future values of x_t.

$$x_t = \alpha + \beta t + \varepsilon_t, \tag{25.11}$$

If the relationship between x_t and t is multiplicative instead of additive, then transforming x_t by taking the natural logarithm enables us to make the relationship linear. For example, let x_0 and x_t be the sales of a firm in the base year and in year t, respectively. Then the underlying relationship is

$$x_t = x_0 e^{gt},$$

where x_0 is the base-year sales figure, g is the growth rate, and t is the length of time in terms of number of periods. Then, via the natural logarithm transformation, we obtain

$$\begin{aligned} \log_e x_t &= \log_e(x_0 e^{gt}) \\ &= \log_e x_0 + gt, \end{aligned} \tag{25.12}$$

where $\log_e$ is the natural logarithm operator. Equation (25.12) can be defined as a log-linear regression model,[5]

$$\log_e x_t = \alpha' + \beta' t + \varepsilon'_t, \tag{25.13}$$

where

$\alpha' = \log_e x_0$,
$\beta' = g =$ growth rate of a firm's sales.

JNJ's annual sales data (1980–2010), presented in Table 25.7, are used to show how Eq. (25.12) can be employed to forecast JNJ's future sales, and Eq. (25.13) to estimate the growth rate of JNJ's historical sales.

EXAMPLE 25.3 *Forecasting Sales and Estimating Growth Rate*

Suppose Johnson & Johnson Company is interested in forecasting its sales revenues for each of the next 6 years. The sales manager of the company would also like to estimate the historical growth rate of sales revenue.

[5]In this regression, we implicitly assume that x_t is log normally distributed and that $\log_e x_t$ is normally distributed. The relationship between the normal and lognormal distributions was discussed in Section 7.4 of Chapter 7.

Table 25.7. Johnson & Johnson's annual sales.

Year	Sales, x_t (in millions)	t
1980	$4,837.38	1
1981	$5,399.00	2
1982	$5,760.87	3
1983	$5,972.87	4
1984	$6,124.50	5
1985	$6,421.30	6
1986	$7,002.90	7
1987	$8,012.00	8
1988	$9,000.00	9
1989	$9,757.00	10
1990	$11,232.00	11
1991	$12,447.00	12
1992	$13,753.00	13
1993	$14,138.00	14
1994	$15,734.00	15
1995	$18,842.00	16
1996	$21,620.00	17
1997	$22,629.00	18
1998	$23,657.00	19
1999	$27,471.00	20
2000	$29,139.00	21
2001	$33,004.00	22
2002	$36,298.00	23
2003	$41,862.00	24
2004	$47,348.00	25
2005	$50,434.00	26
2006	$53,194.00	27
2007	$61,035.00	28
2008	$63,747.00	29
2009	$61,897.00	30
2010	$61,587.00	31

To make forecasts and assess their reliability, we must construct a time-series model for the sales revenue data listed in Table 25.7. A plot of the data (Fig. 25.9) reveals a linearly increasing trend. Therefore, the linear time trend regression defined in Eq. (25.11) can be used to do forecasting. By the method of least squares (see Section 13.3), we obtain the least-squares model in terms of sales (x_t) and time intervals (t) as

$$\hat{x}_t = \hat{\alpha} + \hat{\beta}t = -7965.026 + 2089.257t.$$

With $R^2 = 0.903$.

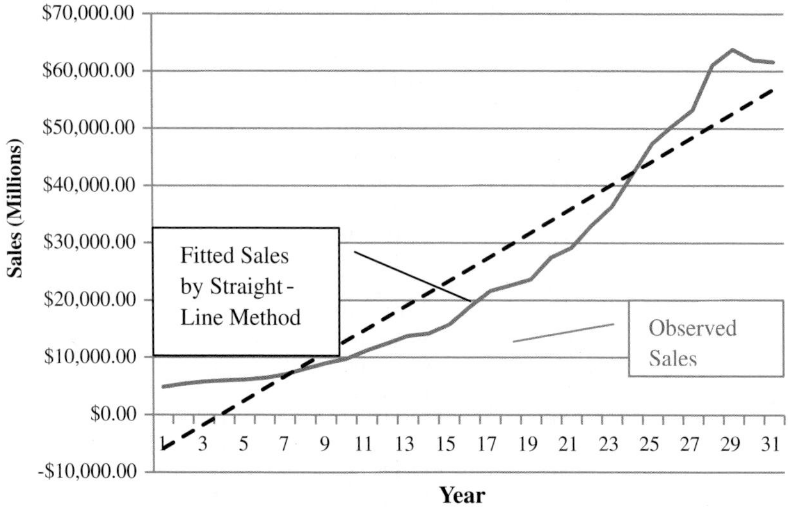

Fig. 25.9. JNJ's annual sales (1980–2010) and the linear trend regression.

SUMMARY OUTPUT

Regression Statistics	
Multiple R	0.950
R Square	0.903
Adjusted R Square	0.899
Standard Error	6346.179
Observations	31.000

ANOVA

	df	*SS*	*MS*	*F*	*Significance F*
Regression	1.000	10825189941.84	10825189941.84	268.789	0.000
Residual	29.000	1167945584.055	40273985.65		
Total	30.000	11993135525.89			

	Coefficients	*Standard Error*	*t Stat*	*P-value*	*Lower 95%*	*Upper 95%*
Intercept	-7965.026	2335.910	-3.410	0.002	-12742.498	-3187.553
t	2089.257	127.434	16.395	0.000	1828.625	2349.890

Fig. 25.10. Least-squares fit (straight-line method) to x_t = sales.

This least-squares line is shown in Fig. 25.9, and the result of straight-line model is given in Fig. 25.10. We can now forecast sales for years 2011–2016 by log-linear regression model defined in Eq. (25.13). The forecasts of sales by log-linear regression model and the corresponding 95% prediction

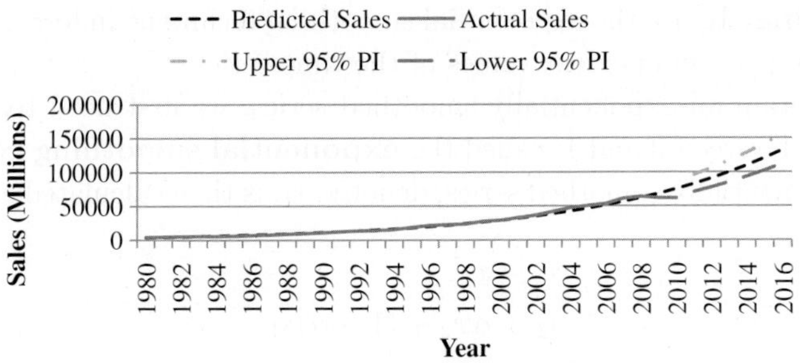

Fig. 25.11. Observed (years 1980–2010) and forecast (years 2011–2016) sales using log-linear regression model.

intervals are shown in Fig. 25.11. Although it is not easily perceptible in the figure, the prediction interval widens as we attempt to forecast further into the future. This agrees with the intuitive notion that short-term forecasts should be more reliable than long-term forecasts.

To estimate the growth rate for JNJ's sales during the period 1980–2010, we use data listed in Table 25.7 to fit the log-linear regression of Eq. (25.13) and obtain

$$\log_e \hat{x}_t = \hat{\alpha}' + \hat{\beta}' t = 8.3005 + 0.0944t$$
$$(0.027) \quad (0.001) \qquad R^2 = 0.993.$$

Figures in parentheses are standard errors. This result implies that the estimated growth rate $g = \hat{\beta}' = 9.44\%$. In other words, the annual growth rate of JNJ's sales was 9.44% during the period 1980–2010.

25.5. Exponential Smoothing and Forecasting

25.5.1. *Simple Exponential Smoothing and Forecasting*

Smoothing techniques are often used to forecast future values of a time-series. One problem that arises in using a moving average to forecast time-series is that values at the ends of the series are lost, as shown in Section 25.3. Therefore, we must subjectively extend the graph of the moving average into the future. No exact calculation of a forecast is available, because generating the moving average at a future time period t requires that we know one or more future values of the series. A technique that leads to forecasts that can be explicitly calculated is called **exponential**

smoothing. To use the exponential smoothing technique in forecasting, we need only past and current values of the time-series.

To obtain an exponentially smoothed series, we first need to choose a weight α between 0 and 1, called the **exponential smoothing constant.** The exponentially smoothed series, denoted s_t, is then calculated as follows:

$$\begin{aligned} s_1 &= x_1 \\ s_2 &= \alpha x_2 + (1-\alpha)s_1 \\ s_3 &= \alpha x_3 + (1-\alpha)s_2 \\ &\vdots \\ s_i &= \alpha x_t + (1-\alpha)s_{t-1}. \end{aligned} \tag{25.14}$$

We can see that the exponentially smoothed value at time t is simply a weighted average of the current time-series value x_t and the exponentially smoothed value at the previous time period, S_{t-1}. Then we can use s_t to do forecasting as follows:

$$\hat{x}_{t+1} = s_t = \alpha x_t + (1-\alpha)s_{t-1}, \tag{25.15}$$

where $\hat{x}_{t+1}$ is the next period's forecast value. In other words, $\hat{x}_{t+1}$ is expressed in terms of the smoothing constant times x_t plus $(1-\alpha)$ times s_{t-1}.

If the manager of a company in 1990 ($t = 1$) knows only that current sales of his or her company equal $x_1 = 5{,}000$ units and that current sales have been forecasted as $s_0 = 5{,}100$ units, then he or she can use Eq. (25.15) to forecast 1991 sales. If we choose $\alpha = 0.30$ as a smoothing constant, then the sales for 1991 are forecasted in terms of Eq. (25.15) as

$$\hat{x}_2 = s_1 = (0.30)(5,000) + (1-0.30)(5,100) = 5,070 \text{ units.}$$

Rewriting Eq. (25.15) as

$$\hat{x}_{t+1} = s_t = s_{t-1} + \alpha(x_t - s_{t-1}), \tag{25.16}$$

implies that simple exponential smoothing is the weighted average of s_{t-1} and the forecast error $(x_t - s_{t-1})$ with weights of 1 and α, respectively. The term **exponential smoothing** refers to the fact that s_t can be expressed as a weighted average with exponentially decreasing weights, as we now illustrate.

We substitute the expressions for s_{t-1} and s_{t-2} into the expression for s_t as denned in Eq. (25.15) and obtain

$$\begin{aligned} s_{t-1} &= \alpha x_{t-1} + (1-\alpha)s_{t-2} \\ s_{t-2} &= \alpha x_{t-2} + (1-\alpha)s_{t-3} \end{aligned}.$$

Repeatedly substituting s_{t-2} and s_{t-1} into Eq. (25.15) reveals that

$$\begin{aligned} s_t &= \alpha x_t + (1-\alpha)s_{t-1} \\ &= \alpha x_t + \alpha(1-\alpha)x_{t-1} + (1+\alpha)^2 s_{t-2} \\ &= \alpha x_t + \alpha(1-\alpha)x_{t-1} + \alpha(1-\alpha)^2 x_{t-2} + (1-\alpha)^3 s_{t-3}. \end{aligned}$$

Continuous substitution for s_{t-k}, where $k = 2, 3, \ldots, t$, yields

$$s_t = \left[\alpha \sum_{k=0}^{t-1} (1-\alpha)^k x_{t-k}\right] + (1-\alpha)^t s_0 \quad (0 < \alpha < 1), \tag{25.17}$$

where s_0 is an initial estimate of the smoothed value.

The sum of weights approaches unity as t approaches infinity; hence we use the term *average*.[6] The weights decrease geometrically with increasing k, so the most recent values of x_t are assigned the greatest weight. All the previous values of x_t are included in the expression for s_t. Because α is less than unity, the most remote values *of* x_t are associated with the smallest weights. The selection of α depends on the sensitivity of the response required by the model. For example, a small α is used to represent the small sensitivity of the response, and it implies that a single change won't affect the moving average much. The smaller the value of α, the slower the response. Note that the method discussed in this section is good only for short-term forecasting.

In the next example, we draw on annual EPS data for both Johnson & Johnson (J&J) and International Business Machines (IBM) to show how the simple exponential smoothing method defined in Eq. (25.15) can be used to do data analysis.

---

[6]Let $0 < \alpha = 1$, as $t \geq \infty$, $(1-\alpha)t \geq 0$. Let

$$y = \alpha + \alpha(1-\alpha) + \alpha(1-\alpha)^2 + \cdots + \alpha(1-\alpha)^{t-1} \tag{A}$$

$$(1-\alpha)y = \alpha(1-\alpha) + \alpha(1-\alpha)^2 + \cdots + \alpha(1-\alpha)^t + \cdots. \tag{B}$$

Subtracting Eq. (B) from Eq. (A) yields $y = 1 - (1-\alpha)^t$. Because $\alpha < 1$, y approaches 1 if t approaches infinity. This implies that $\alpha + \alpha(1-\alpha) + \alpha(1-\alpha)^2 + \cdots = 1$.

Table 25.8. Simple exponential smoothing. ($\alpha = 0.3$) of EPS for J&J and IBM.

t	x_t	s_t
	IBM	
2000	4.58	4.58
2001	4.45	4.541
2002	2.1	3.8087
2003	4.4	3.98609
2004	5.03	4.299263
2005	4.96	4.497484
2006	6.2	5.008239
2007	7.32	5.701767
2008	9.07	6.712237
2009	10.12	7.734566
2010	11.69	8.921196
	J&J	
2000	3.45	3.45
2001	1.87	2.976
2002	2.2	2.7432
2003	2.42	2.64624
2004	2.87	2.713368
2005	3.5	2.949358
2006	3.76	3.19255
2007	3.67	3.335785
2008	4.62	3.72105
2009	4.45	3.939735
2010	4.85	4.212814

EXAMPLE 25.4 *Simple Exponential Smoothing of EPS for Both J&J and IBM*

Consider the EPS for both J&J and IBM from 2000 to 2010 as shown in the second column of Table 25.8. Using $\alpha = 0.3$, we calculate the exponentially smoothed series presented in the third column of Table 25.8 as follows:

IBM

$$\begin{aligned} s_{00} &= x_{00} = 4.58 \\ s_{01} &= 0.3(4.45) + 0.7(4.58) = 4.541 \\ &\vdots \\ s_{10} &= 0.3(11.69) + 0.7(7.734566) \\ &= 8.921196 \end{aligned}$$

JNJ

$$\begin{aligned} s_{00} &= x_{00} = 3.45 \\ s_{01} &= 0.3(1.87) + 0.7(3.45) = 2.976 \\ &\vdots \\ s_{10} &= 0.3(4.85) + 0.7(3.939735) \\ &= 4.212814. \end{aligned}$$

We see from the table that the most recent estimates of smoothed EPS for J&J and IBM are

$$s_n = s_{10} = 8.921196 \quad \text{(IBM)}$$
$$s_n = s_{10} = 4.212814 \quad \text{(J\&J)}.$$

These values are then used as the forecast of EPS for both J&J and IBM for future years. The observed series and these forecasts for J&J and IBM are graphed in Figs. 25.12 and 25.13, respectively.

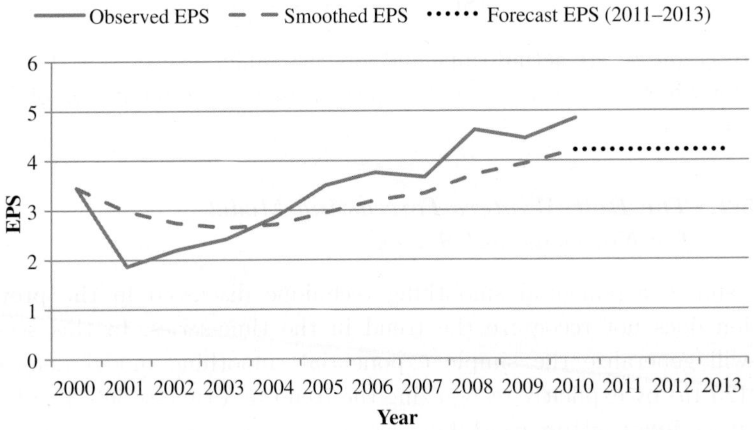

Fig. 25.12. Annual EPS of J&J (simple exponential smoothing).

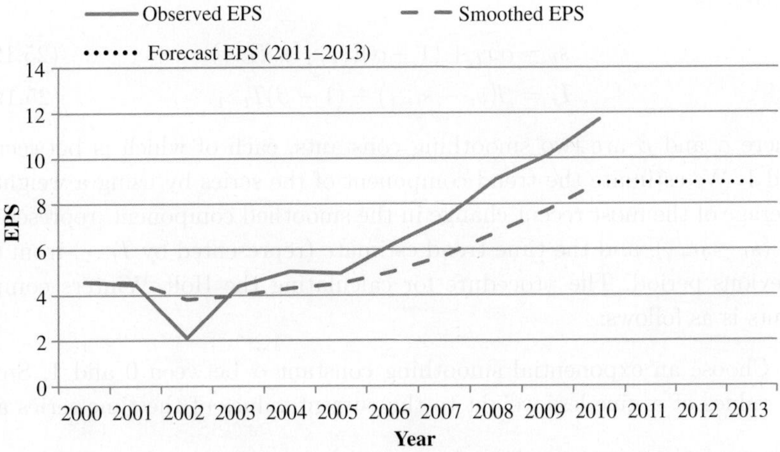

Fig. 25.13. Annual EPS of IBM (simple exponential smoothing).

Finally, note that the choice of the smoothing constant (α) affects the precision of the forecast. In practice, we can try several different values to see which would have been most successful in predicting historical movement in the time-series. For example, we might compute the smoothed series for values of α of 0.3, 0.4, 0.5, and 0.7 and calculate the forecast **mean squared error** (**MSE**) for these four different α-values.

$$\text{MSE} = \frac{\sum_{t=1}^{n} (x_t - \hat{x}_t)^2}{n}, \tag{25.18}$$

where x_t and $\hat{x}_t$ are actual value and forecast value, respectively. The value of α for which this MSE is smallest is then used in the prediction of future values.

25.5.2. *The Holt–Winters Forecasting Model for Non-seasonal Series*[7]

The simple exponential smoothing technique discussed in the previous section does not recognize the trend in the time-series. In this section, we will generalize the simple exponential smoothing model defined in Eq. (25.15) by explicitly recognizing the trend in a time-series. The **Holt–Winters forecasting model** consists of both an exponentially smoothed component (s_t) and a trend component (T_t). The trend component is used in calculating the exponentially smoothed value. Here s_t and T_t can be written as

$$s_t = \alpha x_t + (1 - \alpha)(s_{t-1} + T_{t-1}), \tag{25.19a}$$

$$T_t = \beta(s_t - s_{t-1}) + (1 - \beta)T_{t-1}, \tag{25.19b}$$

where α and β are two smoothing constants, each of which is between 0 and 1. We estimate the trend component of the series by using a weighted average of the most recent change in the smoothed component [represented by $(s_t - s_{t-1})$] and the time trend estimate (represented by T_{t-1}) from the previous period. The procedure for calculating the Holt–Winters components is as follows:

1. Choose an exponential smoothing constant α between 0 and 1. Small values of α give less weight to the current values of the time-series and

[7]The Holt–Winters forecasting model for seasonal series will be discussed in Appendix 25.B.

more weight to the past. Large values of α give more weight to the current values of the series.

2. Choose a trend smoothing constant β between 0 and 1. Small values of β give less weight to the current changes in the level of the series and more weight to the past trend. Larger choices assign more weight to the most recent trend of the series.
3. Estimate the first observation of trend T_1 by one of the following two alternative methods.

   ***Method* 1:**

   Let $T_1 = 0$. If there are a large number of observations in the time-series, this method provides an adequate initial estimate for the trend.

   ***Method* 2:**

   Use the first 5 (or so) observations to estimate the initial trend by following the linear time trend regression line

$$x_t = a + bt + e_t.$$

   Then use the estimated slope $\hat{b}$ as the first trend observation; that is, $T_1 = \hat{b}$.
4. Calculate the components s_t and T_1 from the time-series as follows:

$$\begin{aligned}
s_1 &= x_1\\
T_1 &= 0 \quad \text{or} \quad \hat{b}\\
s_2 &= \alpha x_2 + (1-\alpha)(s_1 + T_1)\\
T_2 &= \beta(s_2 - s_1) + (1-\beta)T_t\\
&\vdots\\
s_t &= \alpha x_t + (1-\alpha)(s_{t-1} + T_{t-1})\\
T_t &= \beta(s_t - s_{t-1}) + (1-\beta)T_{t-1}.
\end{aligned}$$

The data on EPS of J&J and IBM listed in Table 25.8 show how the forecasting model defined in Eqs. (25.19a) and (25.19b) can be used to do data analysis.

EXAMPLE 25.5 *Using the Holt–Winters Model to Estimate the EPS of J&J and IBM*

Now let's use the Holt–Winters model to do the exponential smoothing for the EPS data for both J&J and IBM listed in Table 25.9. We begin

Table 25.9. EPS for IBM and J&J and their smoothed series in terms of the Holt–Winters forecasting model.

t	x_t	s_t	T_t
		IBM	
2000	4.58	4.58	0.085
2001	4.45	4.6005	0.0721
2002	2.1	3.90082	−0.08226
2003	4.4	3.992995	−0.04737
2004	5.03	4.270937	0.017693
2005	4.96	4.490041	0.057975
2006	6.2	5.043611	0.157094
2007	7.32	5.836494	0.284252
2008	9.07	7.005522	0.461207
2009	10.12	8.26271	0.620403
2010	11.69	9.725179	0.788816
		J&J	
2000	3.45	3.45	0
2001	1.87	2.976	−0.0948
2002	2.2	2.67684	−0.13567
2003	2.42	2.504818	−0.14294
2004	2.87	2.514313	−0.11245
2005	3.5	2.731301	−0.04657
2006	3.76	3.007314	0.01795
2007	3.67	3.218685	0.056634
2008	4.62	3.678723	0.137315
2009	4.45	4.006227	0.175353
2010	4.85	4.382105	0.215458

by using the first 5 observations to estimate the first term of the trend component. The estimated slopes for the EPS of J&J and IBM are 0 and 1.275, respectively. Let $\alpha = 0.3$ and $\beta = 0.2$. Following the formula for the Holt–Winters components listed in step 4, we calculate

J&J

$$\begin{aligned} s_1 &= x_1 = 3.45 \\ T_1 &= 0 \\ s_2 &= 0.3(1.87) + 0.7(3.45 + 0) \\ &= 2.976 \\ T_2 &= 0.2(2.976 - 3.45) + 0.8(0) \\ &= -0.0948 \\ &\vdots \end{aligned}$$

IBM

$$\begin{aligned} s_1 &= x_1 = 4.58 \\ T_1 &= 0.085 \\ s_2 &= 0.3(4.45) + 0.7(4.58 + 0.085) \\ &= 4.6005 \\ T_2 &= 0.2(4.6005 - 4.58) + 0.8(0.085) \\ &= 0.0721 \\ &\vdots \end{aligned}$$

The remaining calculations are carried out in precisely the same way. All s_t- and T_1-values for both J&J and IBM are given in Table 25.9.

How are these estimates of EPS level and trend used to forecast future observations? Given a series $x_1, x_2, \ldots, x_n$, the most recent EPS level and trend estimates are s_n and T_n, respectively. To do forecasting, we assume that the latest trend will continue from the most recent level. In general, standing at time n and looking m time periods into the future, we define the prediction for the m period ahead as

$$\hat{x}_{t+m} = s_t + mT_t. \tag{25.20}$$

If $T_t = 0$, then this prediction reduces to the simple exponential smoothing prediction discussed in Example 25.3. On the basis of this formula and the information given in Table 25.9, we calculate the future predictions for both J&J and IBM as

J&J

$$\begin{aligned} s_{2011} &= 4.382105 + 0.215458 \\ &= 4.597563 \\ s_{2012} &= 4.382105 + (2)(0.215458) \\ &= 4.813021 \\ s_{2013} &= 4.382105 + (3)(0.215458) \\ &= 5.028479 \end{aligned}$$

IBM

$$\begin{aligned} s_{2011} &= 9.725179 + 0.788816 \\ &= 10.514 \\ s_{2012} &= 9.725179 + (2)(0.788816) \\ &= 11.30281 \\ s_{2013} &= 9.725179 + (3)(0.788816) \\ &= 12.09163 \end{aligned}$$

Figures 25.14 and 25.15 show the data series and three forecasts for J&J and IBM, respectively.

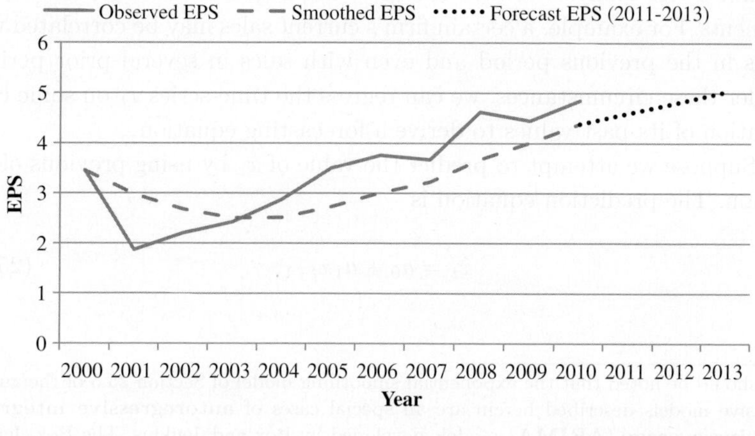

Fig. 25.14. Annual EPS of J&J with forecasts based on the Holt–Winters model.

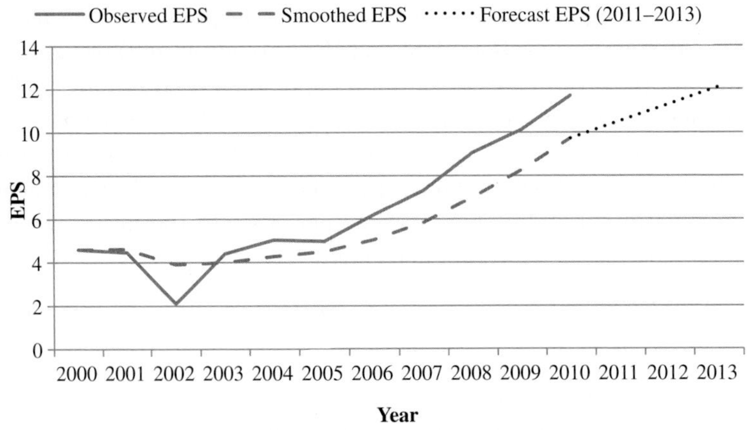

Fig. 25.15. Annual EPS of IBM with forecasts based on the Holt–Winters model.

Finally, note that the choice of smoothing constants (α and β) affects the precision of a forecast. In practice, we can try several different values of α and β to see which would have been most successful in predicting historical movement in the time-series. Again, the forecast MSE as defined in Eq. (25.18) can be used as a benchmark in deciding what values of α and β are appropriate for forecasting future observations.

25.6. Autoregressive Forecasting Model[8]

A time-series analysis always reveals some degree of correlation between elements. For example, a certain firm's current sales may be correlated with sales in the previous period and even with sales in several prior periods. Under these circumstances, we can regress the time-series x_t on some combination of its past values to derive a forecasting equation.

Suppose we attempt to predict the value of x_t by using previous observation. The prediction equation is

$$\hat{x}_t = a_0 + a_1 x_{t-1}, \tag{25.21}$$

[8]It should be noted that the exponential smoothing model of Section 25.5 of the autoregressive models described herein are all special cases of **autoregressive integrated moving average (ARIMA)** models developed by Box and Jenkins. The Box–Jenkins approach, however, is beyond the scope of this text.

where α_0, and α_1, are the least-squares regression estimates. This is called a first-order **autoregressive forecasting model,** AR (1). If the current value of a time-series depends on the two most recent observations, we can use the model

$$\hat{x}_t = a_0 + a_1 x_{t-1} + a_2 x_{t-2}, \tag{25.22}$$

where a_0, a_1, and a_2 are least-squares regression estimates. This is called a second-order autoregressive model, AR (2). Generally, the autoregressive model of order p, AR (P), can be expressed as

$$\hat{x}_t = a_0 + a_1 x_{t-1} + a_2 x_{t-2} + \cdots + a_p x_{t-p}, \tag{25.23}$$

where $a_0, a_1, a_2, \ldots, a_p$, are least-squares regression estimates.

In the next example, quarterly data on Johnson & Johnson's sales are employed to show how the autoregressive model can be used in forecasting.

EXAMPLE 25.6 *Sales Forecast for Johnson & Johnson*

Quarterly sales data for Johnson & Johnson from first quarter 2000 through fourth quarter 2010 are presented in Table 25.10 and Fig. 25.16.

Using the data in Table 25.10, we run the AR (1), AR (2), and AR (3) models.

$$\text{AR(1): Sales}_t = \underset{}{552.7913} + \underset{(0.026)}{0.9703}\ \text{sales}_{t-1} \qquad R^2 = 0.9719 \tag{25.24}$$

$$\text{AR(2): Sales}_t = 586.6586 + \underset{(0.1623)}{0.9106}\ \text{sales}_{t-1} + \underset{(0.1590)}{0.0580}\ \text{sales}_{t-2} \qquad R^2 = 0.9702 \tag{25.25}$$

$$\text{AR(3): Sales}_t = 737.5405 + \underset{(0.1616)}{0.8987}\ \text{sales}_{t-1} - \underset{(0.2220)}{0.1082}\ \text{sales}_{t-2} + \underset{(0.1603)}{0.1697}\ \text{sales}_{t-3} \qquad R^2 = 0.9698. \tag{25.26}$$

In Eqs. (22.24), (22.25), and (25.26), figures in parentheses under the coefficients are standard errors.

Table 25.10. Quarterly sales data for Johnson & Johnson (first quarter 2000 to fourth quarter 2010).

Quarter	S_t	S_{t-1}	S_{t-2}	S_{t-3}
2000Q1	7440			
2000Q2	7670	7440		
2000Q3	7438	7670	7440	
2000Q4	7298	7438	7670	7440
2001Q1	7855	7298	7438	7670
2001Q2	8179	7855	7298	7438
2001Q3	8058	8179	7855	7298
2001Q4	8225	8058	8179	7855
2002Q1	8743	8225	8058	8179
2002Q2	9073	8743	8225	8058
2002Q3	9079	9073	8743	8225
2002Q4	9403	9079	9073	8743
2003Q1	9821	9403	9079	9073
2003Q2	10333	9821	9403	9079
2003Q3	10454	10333	9821	9403
2003Q4	11254	10454	10333	9821
2004Q1	11559	11254	10454	10333
2004Q2	11484	11559	11254	10454
2004Q3	11553	11484	11559	11254
2004Q4	12752	11553	11484	11559
2005Q1	12832	12752	11553	11484
2005Q2	12762	12832	12752	11553
2005Q3	12230	12762	12832	12752
2005Q4	12610	12230	12762	12832
2006Q1	12992	12610	12230	12762
2006Q2	13363	12992	12610	12230
2006Q3	13157	13363	12992	12610
2006Q4	13682	13157	13363	12992
2007Q1	15037	13682	13157	13363
2007Q2	15131	15037	13682	13157
2007Q3	14910	15131	15037	13682
2007Q4	15957	14910	15131	15037
2008Q1	16194	15957	14910	15131
2008Q2	16450	16194	15957	14910
2008Q3	15921	16450	16194	15957
2008Q4	15182	15921	16450	16194
2009Q1	15026	15182	15921	16450
2009Q2	15239	15026	15182	15921
2009Q3	15081	15239	15026	15182
2009Q4	16551	15081	15239	15026
2010Q1	15631	16551	15081	15239
2010Q2	15330	15631	16551	15081
2010Q3	14982	15330	15631	16551
2010Q4	15644	14982	15330	15631

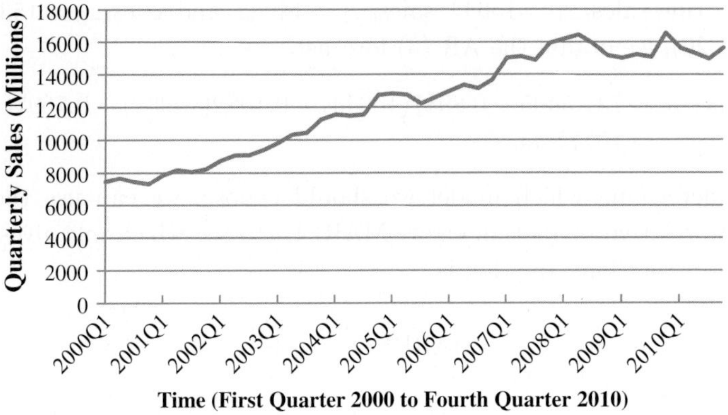

Fig. 25.16. Quarterly sales data for Johnson & Johnson.

Table 25.10 makes it clear that the observations used to run AR (1), AR (2), and AR (3) are 43, 42, and 41 respectively. Therefore, by the central limit theorem, the parameter estimators divided by their standard errors approximate standard normal distributions.

From the standard error indicated in the parentheses and the parameter estimator, we can calculate the Z statistic for each regression slope. Looking up these Z statistics in Table 25.A.3 of Appendix 25.A reveals that coefficients of sales_{t-1} in the AR (1), AR (2), and AR (3) model are significantly different from zero at the significance level of $\alpha = 0.05$. Hence we conclude that the autoregressive processes can be used to forecast quarterly sales of Johnson & Johnson.

Substituting related quarterly sales data into the AR (1), AR (2), and AR (3) models, we obtain the following three alternative forecasted sales for the first quarter of 2011. Substituting $\text{sales}_{t-1} = 15644$ into Eq. (25.24), we obtain the AR (1) forecast.

$$\begin{aligned}\text{Sales}_{2011Q1} &= 552.7913 + 0.9703(15644)\\ &= 15732.\end{aligned}$$

Substituting $\text{sales}_{t-1} = 15644$ and $\text{sales}_{t-2} = 14982$ into Eq. (25.25), we obtain the AR (2) forecast.

$$\begin{aligned}\text{Sales}_{2011Q1} &= 586.6586 + 0.9106(15644) + 0.0580(14982)\\ &= 15700.72.\end{aligned}$$

Substituting $\text{sales}_{t-1} = 15644$, $\text{sales}_{t-2} = 14982$, and $\text{sales}_{t-3} = 15330$ into Eq. (25.26), we obtain the AR (3) forecast.

$$\begin{aligned}\text{Sales}_{2011Q1} &= 737.5405 + 0.8987(15644) - 0.1082(14982) + 0.1697(15330)\\ &= 15777.44.\end{aligned}$$

To determine which model we should choose, we can use the mean absolute relative prediction error (MARPE) to see which one gives us the smallest error. The equation is

$$\text{MARPE}=\frac{|\hat{S}_t - S_t|}{S_t}, \quad (25.27)$$

where $\hat{S}_t$ represents the sales forecast for time period t and S_t represents actual reported sales for time period t.

25.7. Summary

In this chapter, we examined time-series component analysis and several methods of forecasting. The major components of a time-series are the trend, cyclical, seasonal, and irregular components. To analyze these time-series components, we used the moving-average method to obtain seasonally adjusted time-series. After investigating the analysis of time-series components, we discussed several forecasting models in detail. These forecasting models are linear time trend regression, simple exponential smoothing, the Holt–Winters forecasting model without seasonality, the Holt–Winters forecasting model with seasonality, and autoregressive forecasting.

Many factors determine the power of any forecasting model. They include the time horizon of the forecast, the stability of variance of data, and the presence of a trend, seasonal, or cyclical component.

Problem Set

1. Consider a time-series whose first value was recorded in December 1945. The last period for which there are records is June 1984.
   - **a.** How many full months of data are available?
   - **b.** How many full quarters of data are available?
   - **c.** How many full years of data are available?
2. Give an example of a time-series you think may have
   - **a.** A moderately increasing linear trend.
   - **b.** A decreasing linear trend.
   - **c.** A curvilinear trend.

3. The accompanying data indicate the number of mergers (x_t) that took place in a certain industry over a 15-year period.

Year	x_t	Year	x_t	Year	x_t
1970	15	1975	41	1980	148
1971	17	1976	85	1981	203
1972	24	1977	90	1982	249
1973	26	1978	110	1983	280
1974	30	1979	125	1984	307

a. Plot these data on a frequency polygon.
b. What type of trend (linear or non-linear) might best be fitted to this time-series?
c. Is there evidence of seasonal variation in this series?

4. When a 5-month moving average is found for a time-series, how many months do not have averages associated with them (a) at the beginning of the time-series and (b) at the end of the time-series?
5. Find the 3-year moving-average values for the merger time-series described in question 3.
6. Find a 4-year moving-average series for the merger data given in question 3. Center the average on the years.
7. Use MINITAB to fit a least-squares trend line to the merger data given in question 3. Let $t = 1$ for 1970.
8. The following quarterly data show the number of cameras (in hundreds) returned to a particular manufacturer for warranty service over the past 5 years.

	Quarter			
Year	I	II	III	IV
5	0.6	0.4	0.3	0.6
4	0.9	0.6	0.5	0.8
3	1.6	1.8	1.8	1.6
2	1.3	1.1	1.0	1.3
1	1.5	1.3	1.1	1.5

Use MINITAB to answer the following questions.

a. Plot this time-series with time on the horizontal axis. Let $t = 1$ be the first quarter 5 years ago.

b. Find the equation of the least-squares linear trend line that fits this time-series. Let $t = 1$ be the first quarter 5 years ago.

c. What would be the trend line for the second quarter of the current year — that is, 2 periods beyond the end of the actual date?

9. Determine the quarterly seasonal indexes for the warranty service time-series described in question 8.

10. A cab company has supplied the accompanying data, which show the number of accidents involving its cabs over the past 5 years.

Year	Winter	Spring	Summer	Fall
5 years ago	7	5	4	6
4 years ago	7	7	5	7
3 years ago	11	10	6	9
2 years ago	22	11	7	10
Last year	16	12	9	12

Find the four seasonal indexes for accidents.

11. Actual billings for the Weygant Corporation were $135,478 in March, and the March seasonal index for this corporation's billings is 104. What is the seasonally adjusted March billing figure? What would be the expected annual billings based on the March figure?

12. The accompanying time-series represents the number of patients received in a clinic emergency room. The seasonal indexes for each quarter are also given. Find the seasonally adjusted figures for the time-series. Do these seasonal indexes tell the emergency room manager how many staff members to have on hand and what supplies to order for each quarter?

	Quarter			
	I	II	III	IV
Patient Visits	8,220	6,150	5,316	6,834
Seasonal index	115	73	85	110

13. What are time-series data? Why would we ever be interested in looking at time-series data? Give some examples of time-series data.

14. What is a seasonal factor? Why is seasonality sometimes a problem in modeling time-series data? Give some examples of seasonal effects.

15. Why do we sometimes need special techniques to analyze time-series data?

16. What is a business cycle? Why must businesses be able to forecast business cycles?

17. Define the four components of a time-series.

18. Explain why it is easier to forecast when the time-series contains seasonal effects rather than a cyclical effect?

19. Which of the components would you expect to exist in each of the following time-series?

a. The quarterly earnings of Ford for the years 1981 through 1990.
b. The monthly sales of Sears for 1990.
c. The U.S. unemployment rate for each year from 1981 through 1990.
d. The U.S. unemployment rate for each month in 1990.

20. What are the advantages and disadvantages of using a simple moving-average technique for forecasting?

21. What are the advantages and disadvantages of using a linear trend for forecasting?

22. What are the advantages and disadvantages of using a non-linear trend for forecasting?

23. What is exponential smoothing? What are the advantages and disadvantages of using exponential smoothing for forecasting?

24. What is an autoregressive process? What are the advantages and disadvantages of using an autoregressive process for forecasting?

25. What is the X-11 model? What is it used for? Briefly explain how the X-11 model is used in forecasting.

26. If you were asked to forecast the population of your town over the next 5 years, how would you do it? What information would you ask for?

27. Three time-series graphs follow. Try to identify the components of each time-series.

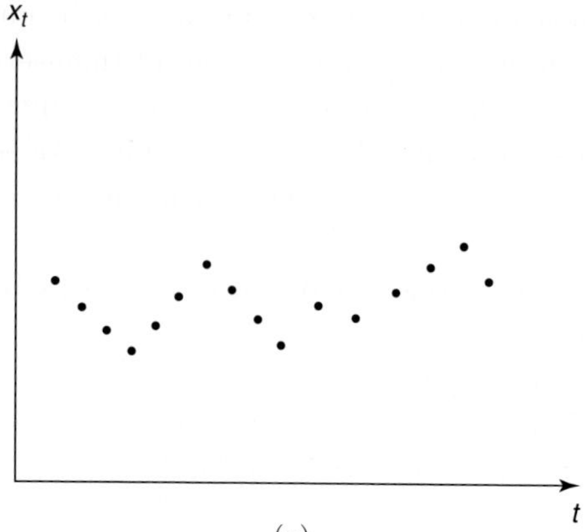

(a)

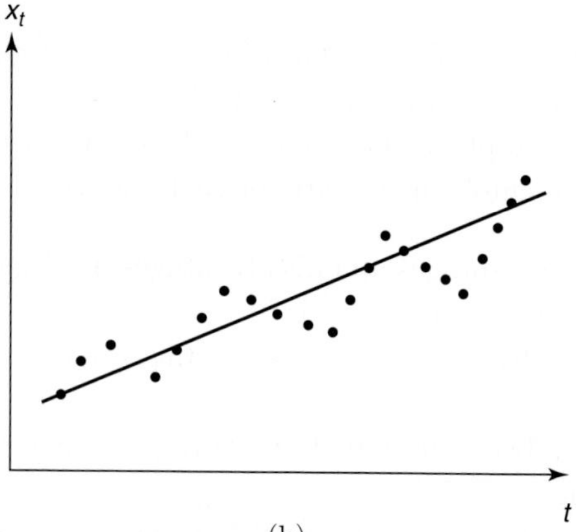

(b)

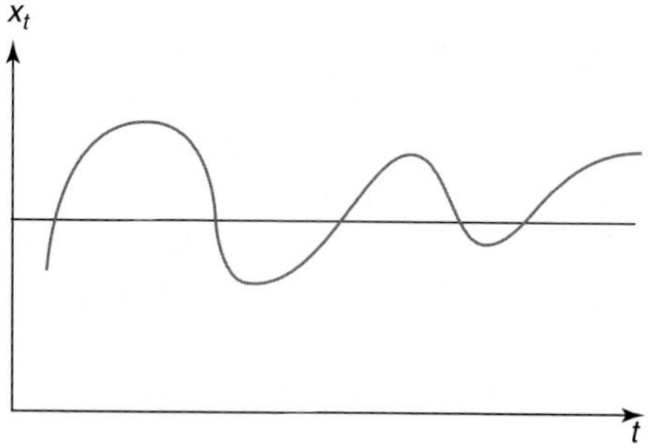

(c)

28. Look at Fig. 25.1. What are the components of this time-series? If you were asked to forecast this time-series, what method would you use?

29. Look at Fig. 25.2. What are the components of this time-series? If you were asked to forecast this time-series, what method would you use?

30. Look at Fig. 25.3. What are the components of this time-series? If you were asked to forecast the S&P 500 index, what method would you use?

31. If you were asked to forecast the size of the entering class at a college, how would you do this? What information would be useful in conducting your forecast?

32. You are told that the number of sales per month for a store follows an AR (1) process of the form

$$x_t = 125 + 0.6x_{t-1} + e_t,$$

where e_t is normally distributed with zero mean and constant variance. Say $x_{30} = 1,000$, $x_{31} = 1,125$, and $x_{32} = 1,227$. Forecast sales for the following time periods.

a. x_{33}, x_{34}, and x_{35} at $t = 31$,

b. x_{34} and x_{35} at $t = 30$.

33. You are told that the number of sales per month for a store follows an AR (2) process of the form

$$x_t = 15 + 0.6x_{t-1} - 0.2x_{t-2} + e_t,$$

where e_t has a mean of zero and $E[e_t e_{t'}] = 0$ when $t \neq t'$. The values for the last 3 periods are $x_{101} = 823$, $x_{102} = 927$, and $x_{103} = 992$. Forecast sales for the next three periods $t = 104$, 105, and 106.

Use the following information to answer questions 34–42. You are given the following return information for 3-month T-bills, the NYSE Index, Chrysler, Ford, and GM for the 3-year period from January 1985 through December 1987.

Month	T-Bill R_f	NYSE Index R_m	Chrysler R_t
85.01	0.006280	0.07950	0.03906
85.02	0.006687	0.01661	0.00376
85.03	0.006886	−0.00037	0.05243

(*Continued*)

(*Continued*)

Month	T-Bill R_f	NYSE Index R_m	Chrysler R_t
85.04	0.006432	−0.00277	−0.00358
85.05	0.006057	0.05872	0.02518
85.06	0.005634	0.01719	0.03158
85.07	0.005737	−0.00351	−0.00685
85.08	0.005785	−0.00463	0.02414
85.09	0.005753	−0.03667	−0.03030
85.10	0.005801	0.04462	0.11189
85.11	0.005865	0.06884	0.07233
85.12	0.005753	0.04554	0.09971
86.01	0.005729	0.00737	−0.01072
86.02	0.005721	0.07375	0.23035
86.03	0.005321	0.05560	0.19273
86.04	0.004920	−0.01322	−0.19220
86.05	0.004993	0.05147	0.02759
86.06	0.005041	0.01509	0.03020
86.07	0.004736	−0.05480	−0.06229
86.08	0.004495	0.07312	0.08392
86.09	0.004237	−0.07957	−0.06193
86.10	0.004213	0.05402	0.06944
86.11	0.004350	0.01857	0.02273
86.12	0.004495	−0.02677	−0.05143
87.01	0.004414	0.12823	0.29054
87.02	0.004543	0.04100	−0.01309
87.03	0.004543	0.02469	0.18037
87.04	0.004583	−0.01483	0.03846
87.05	0.004599	0.00644	−0.11111
87.06	0.004607	0.04797	0.01103
87.07	0.004623	0.04682	0.19414
87.08	0.004904	0.03688	0.09816
87.09	0.005193	−0.02085	−0.06983
87.10	0.004977	−0.21643	−0.35649
87.11	0.004623	−0.07547	−0.23944
87.12	0.004688	0.06851	0.10494

(*Continued*)

(*Continued*)

Month	Ford R_2	GM R_3
85.01	0.07945	0.06061
85.02	−0.08461	−0.02857
85.03	−0.05042	−0.08176
85.04	−0.02124	−0.07363
85.05	0.06422	0.07763
85.06	0.03736	0.00524
85.07	0.00222	−0.01736
85.08	−0.01401	−0.03003
85.09	0.00568	−0.00557
85.10	0.06667	−0.00373
85.11	0.16129	0.06929
85.12	0.07407	0.03084
86.01	0.09181	0.05151
86.02	0.14571	0.06757
86.03	0.14111	0.10932
86.04	−0.06626	−0.07246
86.05	0.06446	0.01250
86.06	0.02717	−0.02665
86.07	−0.01950	−0.12238
86.08	0.11682	0.07523
86.09	−0.11297	−0.05903
86.10	0.09481	0.04981
86.11	0.01961	0.04218
86.12	−0.03846	−0.09434
87.01	0.33378	0.14015
87.02	0.02689	0.00831
87.03	0.10475	0.04690
87.04	0.08741	0.15200
87.05	−0.00137	−0.03889
87.06	0.08941	−0.03079
87.07	0.03409	0.07564
87.08	0.06273	0.04923
87.09	−0.09259	−0.09783
87.10	−0.21939	−0.29518
87.11	−0.05795	−0.01496
87.12	0.05975	0.08869

34. Use MINITAB to plot the return data for T-bills against time. (Let $t = 1$ be the first month). Can you identify any of the components of the time-series?

35. Compute a simple 3-period moving average for the return on T-bills. Forecast the value for January 1988, using this method.

36. With the MINITAB program, use an AR (1) model to describe the time-series behavior of T-bills. Forecast the value for January 1988, using the AR (1) procedure.

37. Using only data from January 1985 through November 1987, forecast the value for December 1987, using both the 3-period moving average and the AR (1) model. Compare your results. Which model forecasts better?

38. Repeat question 37, using the data for the NYSE index.

39. Repeat question 37, using the data for Chrysler.

40. Repeat question 37, using the data for Ford.

41. Repeat question 37, using the data for GM.

42. Compare the two methods you used for forecasting in questions 34–41. Is one method superior to the other in all cases?

43. Suppose you are an investment analyst and are interested in estimating the future dividend for Hamby Corp. You know that Hamby's dividends grow at an exponential rate — that is,

$$D_t = D_0(1 + g)^t,$$

where D_t is the dividend in year t, D_0 is the dividend this year, and g is the growth rate of dividends (assumed to be constant). Is there any way to transform this model into a linear regression?

44. Suppose you are given the following dividend information for Hamby Corp. Forecast the dividend for years 6, 7, 8, 9, and 10, using the method you proposed in question 43.

Year	D
0	1.25
1	1.32
2	1.37
3	1.45
4	1.53
5	1.60

45. Again use the data given in question 44, but this time apply a linear time trend. Plot the estimates from this regression and from your results in question 44.

46. Suppose you have the following information about a company's EPS. What would be the best method for modeling this company's EPS? Forecast the EPS for years 6, 7, 8, 9, and 10.

Year	EPS
0	\$3.25
1	3.65
2	4.03
3	4.45
4	4.87
5	5.09

47. Explain why we use t as an explanatory variable in a linear time trend model when it is not time that causes the dependent variable to change.

48. Suppose you are given the following sales information for Julian Corp. Estimate the growth rate of sales for Julian Crop. Use this information to forecast the company's sales for year 10.

Year	Sales
0	1,250,625
1	1,321,001
2	1,372,435
3	1,458,020
4	1,531,035
5	1,600,995

49. Evaluate the following statement: "Because sales have increased at a steady rate over the last 10 years, the best way to forecast future sales is to use a linear time trend".

50. Go to the library and obtain the EPS for General Motors for the years 1979 through 1988. Use the data for earnings in 1979 through 1988 to obtain a forecasting equation.

51. Indicate which component of a time-series will be affected by each of the following events.

a. A hurricane that results in the postponement of consumer purchases
b. A downturn in business activity
c. The annual Columbus Day sale at a department store
d. A flood at a wholesale warehouse that results in a delay in the shipment of clothing to a local department store
e. A general increase in the demand for video cameras

52. You are given the following sales information (in millions of dollars) on Acme Widget Company:

Year	Sales ($)	Year	Sales ($)
1985	3.2	1989	4.8
1986	4.5	1990	5.1
1987	3.9	1991	5.6
1988	4.2		

a. Use a line chart to graph sales.
b. Estimate the relationship between sales and time, using a time trend regression.

Use the following information on total non-farm payrolls in New Jersey from 1965 to 1989, which is taken from *New Jersey Economic Indicators*, March 1990, to answer questions 53–57.

Total Non-farm		Total Non-farm	
Year	Payrolls	Year	Payrolls
1965	2,257.8	1978	2,961.9
1966	2,359.1	1979	3,027.2
1967	2,421.5	1980	3,060.4

(*Continued*)

(Continued)

	Total Non-farm		Total Non-farm
Year	Payrolls	Year	Payrolls
1968	2,485.2	1980	3,060.4
1969	2,569.6	1981	3,089.9
1970	2,606.2	1982	3,092.7
1971	2,607.6	1983	3,165.1
1972	2,674.4	1984	3,329.3
1973	2,760.8	1985	3,414.1
1974	2,783.4	1986	3,489.9
1975	2,699.9	1987	3,581.6
1976	2,753.7	1988	3,659.5
1977	2,836.9	1989	3,709.8

53. Use the MINITAB program to plot the data for non-farm income, and identify the components of the time-series.

54. Compute the 3-year moving average for non-farm income. Use this information to forecast non-farm income in 1990 and in 1991.

55. Use the MINITAB program to do a time trend regression to forecast non-farm income in 1990 and in 1991.

56. Use a first-order autoregressive process to forecast non-farm income in 1990 and in 1991.

57. Compare the different forecasts of non-farm income that you made in questions 54–56.

Use the following employment data (in thousands) for the United States and for New Jersey to answer questions 58–65.

	Employment	
Year	United States	New Jersey
1970	78,678	2,859
1971	79,367	2,840
1972	82,153	2,935

(Continued)

(*Continued*)

	Employment	
Year	United States	New Jersey
1973	85,064	3,011
1974	86,794	3,023
1975	85,846	2,929
1976	88,752	2,973
1977	92,017	3,065
1978	96,048	3,209
1979	98,824	3,323
1980	99,303	3,334
1981	100,397	3,330
1982	99,526	3,306
1983	100,834	3,385
1984	105,005	3,589
1985	107,150	3,621
1986	109,597	3,712
1987	112,440	3,806
1988	114,968	3,824
1989	117,342	3,826

58. Graph the employment for the United States, and try to identify the components of the time-series.

59. Compute the 4-year moving average for employment in the United States. Use this information to forecast employment in the United States in 1990.

60. Use a time trend regression to forecast employment in the United States in 1990, 1991, and 1992.

61. Use a first-order autoregressive model to forecast employment in the United States in 1990, 1991, and 1992.

62. Do you think the first-order AR (1) is a good model to use to explain the data?

63. Compare the different forecasts generated for 1990 by the methods you used in questions 59–62. Which method do you think is best? Why?

64. Plot the New Jersey employment data. Do you think the linear trend model provides a good approximation of the data? Use the data to forecast the employment in 1990.

65. Compare your forecasts for New Jersey with your forecasts for the United States. Which set of data is harder to forecast? Why?

Use the following data on the labor force in thousands of people in the United States and in New Jersey to answer questions 66–70.

	Labor Force	
Year	United States	New Jersey
1970	82,771	2,996
1971	84,382	3,012
1972	87,034	3,117
1973	89,429	3,190
1974	91,949	3,226
1975	93,775	3,264
1976	96,158	3,318
1977	99,009	3,383
1978	102,251	3,457
1979	104,962	3,570
1980	106,940	3,594
1981	108,670	3,593
1982	110,204	3,632
1983	111,550	3,673
1984	113,544	3,825
1985	115,461	3,839
1986	117,834	3,908
1987	119,865	3,966
1988	121,669	3,975
1989	123,869	3,989

66. Plot the labor force in the United States and in New Jersey, and try to identify the components of the time-series. Which labor force data appear to be more stable?

67. Compute the 5-year moving averages for the labor force in the United States and in New Jersey.

68. Use a linear time trend regression to estimate the labor force in the United States and in New Jersey in 1990, 1991, and 1992.

69. Use an exponential trend model to forecast the labor force in the United States and in New Jersey for 1990–1993.

70. What are the growth rates of the United States and New Jersey labor forces? Does the linear model or the exponential trend model give a faster growth estimate?

71. Suppose you generate the following data by tossing a coin 50 times. Let the initial value be $50. If you toss a head, increase the value by $0.50. If you toss a tail, decrease the value by $0.50. Graph the data. Does this series of data exhibit any time-series pattern? What time-series pattern would you expect it to exhibit?

72. Can you use any regression or time-series method to forecast the values in periods 50, 51, and 52 in question 71?

73. What is the best forecast for the value at period 51?

74. Suppose you adjusted the data generated in question 71 by adding $0.25 to every fourth coin toss. Graph these data. Does this new series exhibit any time-series pattern? What time-series pattern would you expect it to exhibit?

75. What is the best forecast for the time-series generated in question 74?

76. Johnson & Johnson's quarterly sales, in millions of dollars, from first quarter 1990 to first quarter 1991 are

First quarter 1990	2,809
Second quarter 1990	2,825
Third quarter 1990	2,775
Fourth quarter 1990	2,794
First quarter 1991	3,149

Use this set of data and the data in Table 25.10 to run an autoregression model with 1, 2, and 3 lags from first quarter 1980 to fourth quarter 1990. Use MINITAB. Then use actual sales data for first quarter 1991 to calculate the prediction error as defined in Eq. (25.13).

Appendix 25.A. The X-11 Model for Decomposing Time-Series Components[9]

The classical method of analyzing the relative contribution of each trend-cycle, seasonal, and irregular component to changes in an original set of time-series data can be improved by using the **X-11 model.**

The X-11 model has a long history of application by government and business forecasters. The U.S. Bureau of the Census designed it to analyze historical time-series and to determine seasonal adjustments and growth trends.[10] It first decomposes the time-series data into trend-cycle (C), seasonal (S), trading-day (TD), and irregular (I) components and then uses the recategorized data to construct a seasonally adjusted series (Section 25.3 in the text). The X-11 program is based on the premise that seasonal fluctuations can be measured in an original series of economic data and separated from trend, cyclical, trading-day, and irregular fluctuations. The seasonal component (S) reflects an intra-year pattern of variation — one that is repeated from year to year or one that evolves. The **trend-cycle component** (C) includes the long-term trend and the business cycle. The **trading-day component** (TD) consists of variations that are attributed to the composition of the calendar. The **irregular component** (I) is composed of residual variations that reflect the effect of random or unexplained events in the time-series. Shiskin (1967) has shown that the relationship among these six variables can be defined as follows:

$$\overline{O_t^2} = \bar{I}_t^2 + \bar{C}_t^2 + \bar{S}_t^2 + \bar{P}_t^2 + \overline{TD}_t^2, \tag{25.A.1}$$

where the bar over each variable represents the mean of the absolute changes. For example, $\bar{O}_t$ represents the average of $|O_2 - O_1|$, $|O_3 - O_2| \ldots |O_t - O_{t-1}|$. O_t = original series; I_t = final irregular series; C_t = final trend-cycle; S_t = final seasonal factors; P_t = prior monthly adjustment factors (not applicable to the quarterly model); and TD_t = final trading-day adjustment factors (not applicable to the quarterly model). In general, the sum of squares of the means of the absolute changes does not exactly equal $\bar{O}_t^2$, and $(\bar{O}_t')^2$ is substituted, where $(\bar{O}_t')^2 = \bar{I}_t^2 + \bar{C}_t^2 + \bar{S}_t^2$. In addition, the relative contribution of the changes in each component for each time span is given by the ratio $\bar{I}_t^2/(\bar{O}_t')^2, \bar{C}_t^2/(\bar{O}_t')^2$, or $\bar{S}_t^2/(\bar{O}_t')^2$.

[9]This appendix is essentially drawn from Gentry JA and CF Lee (1983).
[10]Shiskin J *et al.* (1967).

EXAMPLE 25.A.1 *Using the X-11 Model to Analyze Caterpillar's Quarterly Sales Data*

Let's look more closely at the statistical computation of the relative contributions of the C, S, and I components to the percentage change in the original time-series. The quarterly sales of Caterpillar Tractor Company from first quarter 1969 to the fourth quarter 1980 are the data used in this example. These original sales data are given in Table 25.A.1 and are graphically presented in the upper portion of Fig. 25.A.1.

The first step in calculating the relative contribution of each component for a 1-quarter time span is to determine the absolute change in the original sales series (O_t) that took place during that quarter — that is, $|O_1 - O_2|$. Sales in the first and second quarters of 1969 (O_1 and O_2) were \$500.4 million and \$558.9 million, respectively, so the absolute change in sales between the first and second quarters was \$58.4 million. The absolute difference in sales between the third and fourth quarters, $|O_3 - O_4|$, was \$23.1 million, $|\$432.7 - \$459.6|$. Thus for the original sales series (O_t), the X-11 routine is used to calculate the absolute change in sales for each of the 36 pairs of successive quarters: $|O_1 - O_2|$, $O_2 - O_3|$, $|O_3 - O_4| \ldots |O_{34} - O_{35}|$, $|O_{35} - O_{36}|$. The mean of the changes in the original sales series $\bar{O}_t$, was \$109.12 million; this is shown in Table 25.A.2.

The X-11 routine also involves calculating the absolute change in the original sales for a time span of 2, 3, and 4 quarters. Because the procedure

Table 25.A.1. Original quarterly sales data for caterpillar tractor, first quarter 1969 to fourth quarter 1980 (in millions of dollars).

Original	Quarterly Sales Data				
Series Year	1st Quarter	2nd Quarter	3rd Quarter	4th Quarter	Total
1969	500.4	558.9	482.7	459.6	2001.6
1970	524.6	537.0	579.1	487.1	2127.8
1971	564.4	585.1	522.3	503.4	2175.2
1972	620.8	653.6	678.5	649.3	2602.2
1973	751.8	800.2	823.4	807.0	3182.4
1974	822.4	956.8	1081.7	1221.2	4082.1
1975	1125.8	1328.7	1293.0	1216.2	4963.7
1976	1199.8	1266.6	1312.9	1263.0	5042.3
1977	1363.5	1454.6	1513.2	1517.6	5848.9
1978	1630.1	1843.7	1816.8	1928.6	7219.2
1979	1923.7	2136.7	2232.2	1320.6	7613.2
1980	2100.4	2316.3	2085.7	2095.4	8597.8

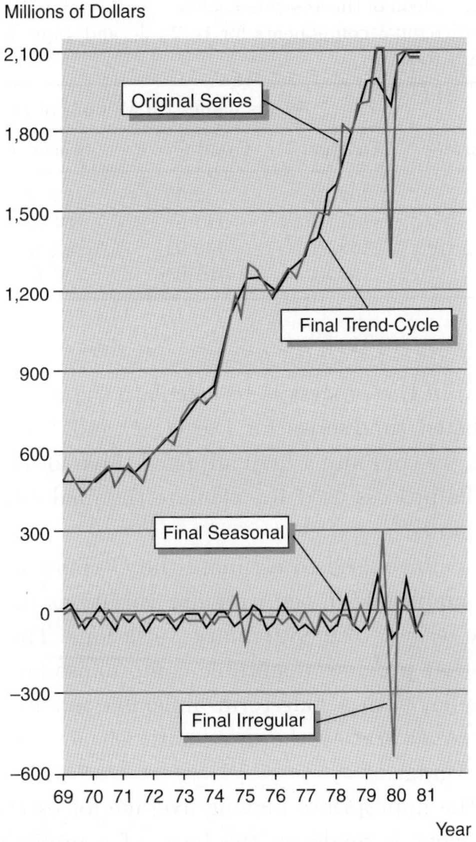

Fig. 25.A.1. Original sales and the X-11 final component series of caterpillar, 1969–1980.

Source: Gentry JA and CF Lee (1983).

is similar for each time span, we will use the 4-quarter time span to illustrate it. The absolute change in sales every 4 quarters is calculated with this model. All possible 4-quarter combinations of changes in sales are computed: $|O_1 - O_5|$, $|O_5 - O_9|$, $|O_9 - O_{13}|, \ldots, |O_{29} - O_{33}|$, $|O_2 - O_6|$, $|O_6 - O_{10}|, \ldots, |O_{30} - O_{34}|$, $|O_3 - O_7|, \ldots, |O_{31} - O_{35}|$, $|O_4 - O_8|, \ldots, |O_{32} - O_{36}|$. The same procedure is utilized to calculate a 2- and a 3-quarter time span. The means of the changes in the original series (O_t) or a 2-, a 3-, and a 4-quarter time span were \$141.93 million, \$153.38 million, and \$190.84 million. These values are also presented in Table 25.A.2.

Table 25.A.2. Mean of the absolute changes in sales related to trend-cycle, seasonal, and irregular components for 1-, 2-, 3-, and 4-quarter time spans without regard to sign.

	Mean Values (in Millions of Dollars)			
Span in Quarters	Original	Trend-Cycle	Seasonal	Irregular
1	109.12	42.05	53.83	72.36
2	141.93	114.51	64.72	60.22
3	153.38	146.92	52.22	61.98
4	190.84	191.05	6.49	69.67

The next step in the process is to calculate the mean absolute change in the final adjusted time-series for the C, I, and S components. Using the X-11 method, we compute a final adjusted table for each component. A brief review of the process used to calculate the final estimated C, I, and S components follows.

The moving average used to estimate the C component is selected on the basis of the amplitude of the irregular variations in the data relative to the amplitude of long-term systematic variations. The routine selects a moving average that provides a suitable compromise between the need to smooth the irregular with a long-term, inflexible moving average and the need to reproduce accurately the systematic element with a short-term, flexible moving average.[11]

Selection of the appropriate moving average for estimating the trend-cycle (C) component is made on the basis of a preliminary estimate of the $\bar{I}/\bar{C}$ rate (the ratio of the mean absolute quarter-to-quarter change in the irregular component to that in the trend-cycle component). A 13-term Henderson average (given in the form of Eq. (25.5)) of the preliminary seasonally adjusted series is used as the preliminary estimate of C, and the ratio of the preliminary seasonally adjusted series to the 13-term average is used as the estimate of the I component (Shiskin, p. 3). The extreme values of the series are replaced through a smoothing routine. Finally, a 5-term Henderson curve given in the form of Eq. (25.5) is used to modify the seasonally adjusted series to obtain the final trend-cycle (C) and irregular (I) series (Shiskin, pp. 3, 4). The final trend-cycle, 5-term Henderson curve is presented graphically in Fig. 25.A.1. Figure 25.A.1

[11]Shiskin J *et al.* (1967).

shows that the C component tracks the original time-series reasonably closely.

The S/I ratios for each quarter are smoothed by a 3×5-term moving average (a 3-term average of a 5-term average) to estimate final seasonal factors. Because the statistical calculations of the final C, S, and I components are lengthy and complex, the numerous tables generated by the model are not presented. The final S and I series appear in Fig. 25.A.1. The irregular component is substantially more volatile than the seasonal component for Caterpillar sales. A strike in fourth quarter 1979 caused a substantial deviation from the original series and had a profound effect on the I component. A summary of the mean absolute changes in sales in the C, S, and I series for 1-, 2-, 3-, and 4-quarter time-series is presented in Table 25.A.2. The calculation of these mean absolute changes follows the same procedure used in computing the change in the original sales series. These mean values in Table 25.A.2 provide the base for computing the relative contribution of each component to changes in the original series. A revision to Eq. (25.A.1) is shown in Eq. (25.A.2), which specifies the relationships we use in calculating the relative contributions of the C, S, and I components.

$$(\bar{O}')^2 = \bar{I}^2 + \bar{C}^2 + \bar{S}^2. \tag{25.A.2}$$

The calculations utilize the data in Table 25.A.2.

The following example illustrates computation of the relative contribution of each component to changes in the original Caterpillar sales series for a 1-quarter time span. Substituting the values of $\bar{I}$, $\bar{C}$, and $\bar{S}$ from Table 25.A.2 into Eq. (25.A.2) produces

$$(72.358)^2 + (42.051)^2 + (53.831)^2 = 9901.842064 = (99.508)^2.$$

For a 1-quarter time span, the relative contributions of the three components are

$$I \text{ component} = \frac{\bar{I}^2}{(\bar{O}')^2} = \frac{(72.358)^2}{(99.508)^2} = 52.88\%,$$

$$C \text{ component} = \frac{\bar{C}^2}{(\bar{O}')^2} = \frac{(42.051)^2}{(99.508)^2} = 17.86\%,$$

$$S \text{ component} = \frac{\bar{S}^2}{(\bar{O}')^2} = \frac{(53.831)^2}{(99.508)^2} = \frac{29.27\%}{100.00\%}.$$

Table 25.A.3. Relative contributions of components to changes in caterpillar sales for 1-, 2-, 3-, and 4-quarter time spans.

	Relative Contribution (in Percent)			
Span in Quarters	Trend-Cycle	Seasonal	Irregular	Total
1	17.86	29.27	52.88	100.00
2	46.94	28.44	24.62	100.00
3	68.50	13.08	18.42	100.00
4	82.58	0.15	17.27	100.00

These data indicate that the irregular component contributed 52.88% of the change in the original sales series for Caterpillar Tractor Company. Another 17.86% of the change in the original sales series was related to the trend-cycle component, and the seasonal component was responsible for 29.27% of the change. In summary, permanent information signals contributed 47% of the change in past quarterly sales of Caterpillar, and random events accounted for 53%.

The relative contribution of each component to changes in Caterpillar's original sales series for 1-, 2-, 3-, and 4-quarter time spans are shown in Table 25.A.3. For the 2-, 3-, and 4-quarter time spans, the irregular component composes approximately 25%, 18%, and 17%, respectively, of the change in sales. The trend-cycle component increased as the length of the time span increased. The seasonal component declined as the time span increased. It ended at almost zero for a 4-quarter time span. This change over time in the relative contribution of each S, C, and I component is referred to as the time effect. For further information related to the X-11 model, see Makridakis *et al.* Levenback and Cleary also cite reasons for using the X-11 model.[12]

Appendix 25.B. The Holt–Winters Forecasting Model for Seasonal Series

In this appendix, we will generalize the Holt–Winters forecasting model discussed in Section 25.5 to take into account the existence of seasonality. As in the non-seasonal case, we will use x_t, s_t and T_t to denote, respectively, the observed value and the level and trend estimates at time t. F_t is used to

[12]Makridakis SG, SC Wheelwright and VE McGee (1983).

denote the seasonal factor, so if the time-series contains L periods per year, the seasonal factor for the corresponding period in the previous period will be F_{t-L}. The Holt–Winters method for seasonal series can be expressed by the following three equations:

$$s_t = \alpha\left(\frac{x_t}{F_{t-L}}\right) + (1-\alpha)(s_{t-1} + T_{t-1}), \tag{25.B.1}$$

$$T_t = \beta(s_t - s_{t-1}) + (1-\beta)T_{t-1}, \tag{25.B.2}$$

$$F_t = \gamma\left(\frac{x_t}{s_t}\right) + (1-\gamma)F_{t-L}. \tag{25.B.3}$$

where α, β, and γ are smoothing constants whose values are set between 0 and 1.

In Eq. (25.B.1), the term $s_{t-1} + T_{t-1}$ represents an estimate of the level at time t, formed 1 time period earlier. This estimate is updated when the new observation x_t becomes available. However, here it is necessary to remove the influence of seasonality from that observation by deflating it by the latest available estimate, F_{t-L}, of the seasonal factor for that period. The updating equation for trend, Eq. (25.B.2), is identical to that used previously, Eq. (25.19b) in the text.

Finally, the seasonal factor is estimated by Eq. (25.B.3). The most recent estimate of the factor, available from the previous year, is F_{t-L}. However, dividing the new observation x_t by the level estimate s_t suggests a seasonal factor x_t/s_t. The new estimate of the seasonal factor is then a weighted average of these two quantities.

The procedure for forecasting via the Holt–Winters forecasting model for seasonal series is similar to that for non-seasonal series. Here the forecast for a particular month includes the effect of all three smoothing equations. The forecast for m periods ahead is

$$\hat{x}_{t+m} = (s_t + mT_t)(F_{t+m-L}). \tag{25.B.4}$$

If no seasonality exists — that is, if $F_{t+m-L} = 1$, then this equation reduces to Eq. (25.20) in the text.

We will use quarterly data listed in Table 25.4 in the text for Johnson & Johnson (J&J) during the period first quarter 1980 through second quarter 1990 to demonstrate how Eqs. (25.B.1), (25.B.2), (25.B.3), and (25.B.4) are used to do exponential smoothing and forecasting.

EXAMPLE 25.B.1 *The Holt–Winters Forecasting Model for J&J's Quarterly EPS*

Table 25.4 and Fig. 25.6 in the text make it clear that Johnson & Johnson's quarterly EPS in the period 2000–2010 exhibited significant seasonality. The fourth-quarter EPS especially appeared to be considerably higher than those for the other three quarters.

The Holt–Winters forecasting model with seasonality is used to determine the smoothed value, s_t, and the predicted value, $\hat{x}$, for each time period. The smoothing constants are $\alpha = 0.2$, $\beta = 0.3$, and $\gamma = 0.3$.

First, we use the first 3 years of data to determine the seasonal indexes. Working with Eq. (25.B.9), we present the PMA in terms of the first 3 years' data in column (4) of Table 25.B.1. Table 25.B.2 shows the procedure

Table 25.B.1. Seasonal index and seasonally adjusted EPS for J&J in terms of the first 12 quarters' data.

(1) Date	(2) x_t	(3) z_t^*	(4) x_t/z_t^*	(5) Seasonal Index	(6) Seasonally Adjusted EPS, d_t
2000.1	0.86			0.503173	1.709154
2	1.8			0.750721	2.397696
3	2.68	2.1775	1.230769	1.207303	2.219824
4	3.3	2.095	1.575179	1.538804	2.144523
2001.1	1	1.84875	0.540906	0.503173	1.987389
2	1	1.52375	0.656276	0.750721	1.332053
3	1.51	1.295	1.166023	1.207303	1.250722
4	1.87	1.26375	1.479723	1.538804	1.21523
2002.1	0.6	1.31	0.458015	0.503173	1.192433
2	1.15	1.37875	0.834089	0.750721	1.531861
3	1.73			1.207303	1.432946
4	2.2			1.538804	1.429682

Table 25.B.2. Calculation of seasonal indexes of EPS for J&J.

Year	Quarter 1	2	3	4	Sums
2000			1.231	1.575	
2001	0.541	0.656	1.166	1.480	
2002	0.458	0.834			
Median	0.499	0.745	1.198	1.527	3.970
Seasonal Index	0.503	0.751	1.207	1.539	4.000

for calculating the seasonal index in terms of the first 3 years' data. These indexes are

$$\text{Quarter 1} = 0.503 \quad \text{Quarter 2} = 0.751$$
$$\text{Quarter 3} = 1.207 \quad \text{Quarter 4} = 1.539$$

and these are the four values of F_t in 1999.

The data from the first 3 years were seasonally adjusted to obtain d_t; see column (6) of Table 25.B.1. Drawing a least-squares line through these 12 values by means of simple time trend linear regression produces

$$\hat{d}_t = 2.192966 - 0.08298t.$$

The value $\hat{b} = 0.08298$ becomes the initial trend estimate of T_0. Finally, the initial smoothed value for fourth quarter 1999 is

$$\begin{aligned} s_0 &= [a + b(0)](\text{initial seasonal index for fourth quarter}) \\ &= (2.192996)(1.539) = 3.374543 \end{aligned}$$

This estimate of $s_0$becomes the forecast value for each of the quarters in 2000, as indicated in column (6) of Table 25.B.3.

Table 25.B.3. Solution using Holt–Winters model with seasonality ($\alpha = 0.2$, $\beta = 0.3$, $\gamma = 0.3$).

t	x_t	T_t	F_t	s_t	$\hat{x}_t$	$x_t - \hat{x}_t$
			0.503173			
			0.750721			
			1.207303			
		−0.08298	1.538804	3.374543		
1	0.86	−0.17792	0.438941	2.975085	1.656227	−0.79623
2	1.8	−0.20189	0.724233	2.717271	2.09989	−0.29989
3	2.68	−0.21962	1.172438	2.456271	3.03683	−0.35683
4	3.3	−0.22515	1.523465	2.218224	3.441764	−0.14176
5	1	−0.20804	0.453593	2.050102	0.874843	0.125157
6	1	−0.23572	0.678411	1.749802	1.334081	−0.33408
7	1.51	−0.24929	1.129111	1.46885	1.775169	−0.26517
8	1.87	−0.24881	1.525832	1.221142	1.857959	0.012041
9	0.6	−0.22779	0.490191	1.042416	0.441041	0.158959
10	1.15	−0.17496	0.823116	0.99073	0.552653	0.597347
11	1.73	−0.13197	1.331536	0.959054	0.921098	0.808902
12	2.2	−0.09509	1.762796	0.950032	1.261986	0.938014
13	0.7	−0.0607	0.559727	0.969558	0.419086	0.280914
14	1.09	−0.03578	0.905841	0.991931	0.748093	0.341907
15	1.8	−0.01204	1.453671	1.035285	1.273149	0.526851
16	2.42	0.008934	1.898087	1.09316	1.803772	0.616228
17	0.84	0.032852	0.605039	1.181821	0.616872	0.223128

(*Continued*)

Table 25.B.3. (*Continued*)

t	x_t	T_t	F_t	s_t	$\hat{x}_t$	$x_t - \hat{x}_t$
18	1.67	0.070587	1.007842	1.340457	1.100301	0.569699
19	2.46	0.087461	1.520538	1.467289	2.051194	0.408806
20	2.87	0.084899	1.885506	1.54621	2.951051	−0.08105
21	0.96	0.082233	0.601062	1.622222	0.986885	−0.02688
22	1.83	0.088911	1.023434	1.726716	1.717821	0.112179
23	2.68	0.085726	1.509804	1.805008	2.760729	−0.08073
24	3.38	0.079839	1.861778	1.871112	3.564991	−0.18499
25	1.11	0.073586	0.593272	1.930107	1.172642	−0.06264
26	2.07	0.07472	1.025748	2.007475	2.050647	0.019353
27	3.01	0.069407	1.49426	2.064483	3.143705	−0.13371
28	3.76	0.062548	1.837582	2.111027	3.97283	−0.21283
29	0.89	0.022143	0.546244	2.038891	1.289522	−0.39952
30	1.95	0.012544	1.006337	2.029037	2.1141	−0.1641
31	2.84	0.004085	1.46915	2.013386	3.050653	−0.21065
32	3.67	0.002868	1.833139	2.013415	3.707269	−0.03727
33	1.27	0.021389	0.565719	2.07802	1.101383	0.168617
34	2.45	0.041499	1.043702	2.166442	2.112714	0.337286
35	3.64	0.05768	1.51119	2.261878	3.243796	0.396204
36	4.62	0.069723	1.870561	2.359699	4.252072	0.367928
37	1.27	0.058653	0.555249	2.392524	1.374369	−0.10437
38	2.43	0.051278	1.031013	2.426592	2.558299	−0.1283
39	3.64	0.047127	1.501008	2.464035	3.744531	−0.10453
40	4.45	0.039196	1.846676	2.484723	4.697282	−0.24728
41	1.64	0.064978	0.57719	2.609861	1.401404	0.238596
42	2.89	0.072672	1.042762	2.700485	2.757794	0.132206
43	4.14	0.071771	1.499056	2.770155	4.162532	−0.02253
44	4.85	0.058836	1.812537	2.798809	5.248116	−0.39812

The calculation of Table 25.B.3 in terms of $t = 10$ is shown as follows:

1. $x_{10} = 1.15$

2. Substituting related information into Eq. (25.B.1) yields

$$\begin{aligned} s_{10} &= 0.2\left(\frac{x_{10}}{F_{10-4}}\right) + 0.8(s_9 + T_9) \\ &= 0.2\left(\frac{x_{10}}{F_6}\right) + 0.8(s_9 + T_9) \\ &= 0.2\left(\frac{1.15}{0.678411}\right) + 0.8(1.042416 - 0.22779) \\ &= 0.99073. \end{aligned}$$

3. Substituting related information into Eq. (25.B.2) yields

$$\begin{aligned} T_{10} &= 0.3(s_{10} - s_9) + 0.7T_9 \\ &= 0.3(0.99073 - 1.042416) + 0.7(-0.22779) \\ &= -0.17496. \end{aligned}$$

4. Substituting related information into Eq. (25.B.3) yields

$$\begin{aligned} F_{10} &= 0.3\left(\frac{x_{10}}{s_{10}}\right) + 0.7F_6 \\ &= 0.3\left(\frac{1.15}{0.99073}\right) + 0.7(0.678411) \\ &= 0.823116. \end{aligned}$$

Similarly, we can calculate all other values of s_t, T_t, and F_t, which are listed in columns (5), (3), and (4), respectively. Figure 25.B.1 presents actual data and smoothed data s_t.

Using Eq. (25.B.4), we estimate $\hat{x}_{t+1}$ ($t = 5, 6, \ldots, 44$); it is shown in column (6) of Table 25.B.3. For example,

$$\begin{aligned} \hat{x}_{11} &= (s_{10} + T_{10})(F_7) = (0.99073 - 0.17496)(0.678411) \\ &= 0.921098. \end{aligned}$$

Figure 25.B.2 presents actual data and forecasted data ($\hat{x}_t$). If we let $m \geq 1$, then we can forecast future observations. For example, to forecast the EPS of J&J in the third quarter of 2002, we let $m = 1$. Finally, in the last column of Table 25.B.3, we present the residual in period t, $(x_t - \hat{x}_t)$.

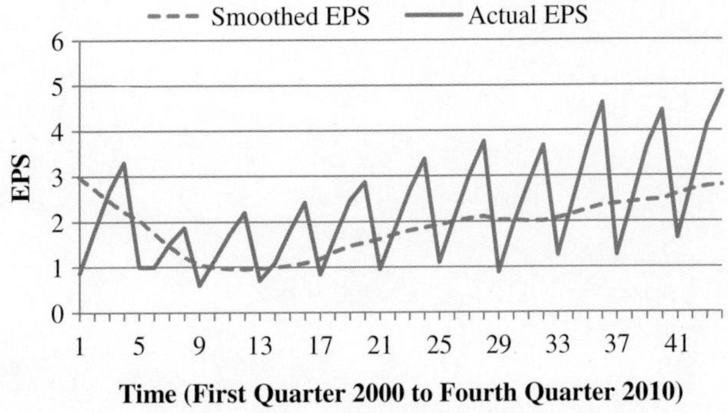

Fig. 25.B.1. Quarterly EPS of J&J (actual and smoothed EPS).

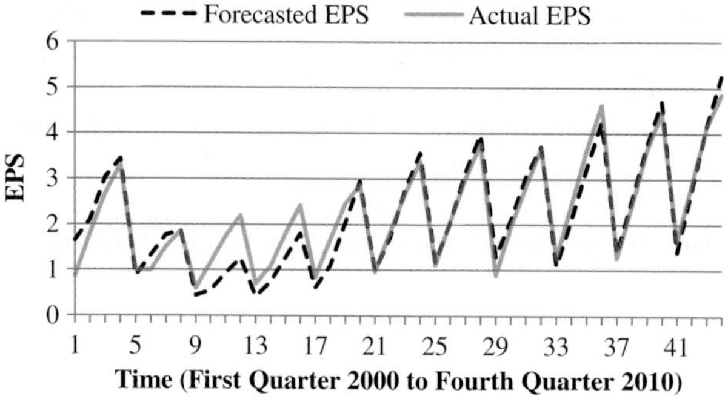

Fig. 25.B.2. Quarterly EPS of J&J (actual and forecasted EPS).

References for Chapter 25

Gentry, JA and CF Lee (1983). Measuring and interpreting time, firm and ledger effect. In *Financial Analysis and Planning: Theory and Application, A Book of Readings*, CF Lee (ed.).

Lee, AC, JC Lee, and CF Lee (2009). *Financial Analysis, Planning and Forecasting: Theory and Application*, 2nd ed. Singapore: World Scientific Publishing Company.

Levenback, H and JP Cleary (1984). *The Modem Forecaster*, New York: Lifetime Learning Publications, 50.

Makridakis, SG, SC Wheelwright, and VE McGee (1983). *Forecasting Methods and Applications*, New York: Wiley.

Shiskin, J, AH Young, and JC Musgrave (February 1967). *The X-11 Variant of the Census Method II Seasonal Adjustment Program.* Technical paper No. 15, U.S. Department of Commerce.

Chapter 26

Econometric Approach to Financial Analysis, Planning, and Forecasting

26.1. Introduction

In the last three chapters, we considered linear programming and simultaneous-equation approaches to financial analysis, planning, and forecasting. In this chapter, we will discuss how econometric techniques can be used as an important alternative for financial analysis, planning, and forecasting. The econometric approach can be classified as both a single-equation and a simultaneous-equation approach. The simultaneous-equation approach can either explicitly or implicitly consider the interrelationships among financial variables. The implicit approach uses an estimation technique to take into account interrelationships for a set of equations; this set of equations does not explicitly specify their structural relationship. The explicit approach uses the econometric simultaneous-equation concept, and explicitly defines the structural relationships for one set of equations. Then this set of structural econometric relationships can be either separately or jointly estimated.

The basic concepts needed to understand this chapter will be discussed in Section 26.2. In Section 26.3, the issue of simultaneity and the dynamics of corporate-budgeting decisions will be explored by using the finance theory. Spies' empirical results will be used to show how the theoretical model can be empirically implemented. Section 26.4 discusses how Zellner's (1962) seemingly uncorrelated regression (SUR) technique can be used in financial analysis and planning. Notably, the role of firm-related variables in capital-asset pricing and the role of capital structure in the financing decision are discussed in some detail. Section 26.5 explores applications of a structural simultaneous-equation model for financial planning and forecasting. In Section 26.6, the interrelationships among the programming, the simultaneous equations, and the econometrics approaches are briefly discussed. In Section 26.7, possible applications of financial-planning models to strategic business decisions are reviewed and discussed. Finally, the results of this chapter are summarized.

26.2. Simultaneous Nature of Financial Analysis, Planning, and Forecasting

26.2.1. *Basic Concepts of Simultaneous Econometric Models*

There are two alternative approaches, the implicit and the explicit, to deal with the interrelationships between accounting information and financial decision policies. The implicit approach uses the estimation technique of simultaneously estimating a set of regression equations; the explicit approach uses specification technique to derive a set of structural equations. The structural simultaneous-equation system can be either separately or simultaneously estimated.

In the structural simultaneous-equation system, the variables can be classified into endogenous and exogenous variables. Exogenous variables are inputs to the system and they are determined outside the equation system. The endogenous variables are derived inside the model, and are to be estimated by using the information about the exogenous variables. Before the structural simultaneous-equation system is set up, the identification condition should be examined. Following Theil (1971) and Johnston (1972), an equation should be either just-identified or over identified to be meaningfully used in the empirical analysis.

26.2.2. *Interrelationship of Accounting Information*

Accounting information provides the major inputs for both the programming approach and the simultaneous-equation approach to financial planning and forecasting. The simultaneous nature of accounting data lies in the requirement that sources of funds should be equal to the uses of funds in the accounting system.

26.2.3. *Interrelationship of Financial Policies*

The interaction of investment policy, financing policy, and dividend policy has been theoretically investigated in an earlier chapter. The interrelationship of these three policies is the basic assumption for specifying the simultaneous-equation financial-planning and forecasting model. Similarly, the interrelationship between financial policies is also the main theoretical justification for using either implicit or explicit simultaneous-equation econometric techniques for financial planning and forecasting. In the econometric type of financial planning and forecasting models, however, the interrelationships among alternative financial policies are assumed to be stochastic instead of deterministic.

26.3. The Simultaneity and Dynamics of Corporate-Budgeting Decisions

26.3.1. *Definitions of Endogenous and Exogenous Variables*

To investigate the interrelationship among investment, financing, and dividends decisions, Spies (1974) developed five multiple regressions to describe the behavior of five alternative financial-management decisions. The stacking technique, a variant of the ordinary least-squares (OLS), is used by Spies to estimate all the equations at once.[1] Then he used this model to demonstrate that investment, financing, and dividend policies generally are jointly determined within an individual industry or in the aggregated manufacture sector.

Through the partial adjustment model, the five endogenous variables (shown in Table 26.1) are determined simultaneously through the use of the sources-equals-uses accounting identity. This identity ensures that the adjustment of each component of the budgeting process (the endogenous variables) depends not only on the distance by which the component misses its target, but also on the simultaneous adjustment of the other four components.

[1] The stacking technique, which was first suggested by de Leeuw (1965), can be replaced by either the SUR or the constrained SUR technique. (See the next section and Appendix B for detail.) It should be noted that these techniques themselves can be omitted from the lecture without affecting the substance of the econometric approach to financial analysis and planning.

Table 26.1. Endogenous and exogenous variables.

1. The endogenous variables are:
   - (a) $X_{1,t} = \text{DIV}_t$ = Cash dividends paid in period t;
   - (b) $X_{2,t} = \text{IST}_t$ = Net investment in short-term assets during period t;
   - (c) $X_{3,t} = \text{ILT}_t$ = Gross investment in long-term assets during period t;
   - (d) $X_{4,t} = -\text{DF}_t$ = Minus the net proceeds from the new debt issues during period t;
   - (e) $X_{5,t} = -\text{EQF}_t$ = Minus the net proceeds from new equity issues during period t.
2. The exogenous variables are:
   - (a) $Y_t = \sum_{i=1}^{5} X_{i,t} = \sum_{i=1}^{5} X^*_{i,t}$, where Y = net profits + depreciation allowance; a reformulation of the sources = uses identity.
   - (b) RCB = Corporate Bond Rate (which corresponds to the weighted-average cost of long-term debt in the FR Model [Eqs. (23.20), (23.23), and (23.24) in Table 23.10], and the parameter for average interest rate in the WS Model [Eq. (23.7) in Table 23.1].
   - (c) RDP_t = Average Dividend–Price Ratio (or dividend yield, related to the P/E ratio used by WS as well as the Gordon cost-of-capital model, discussed in Chapter 8).
     The dividend–price ratio represents the yield expected by investors in a no-growth, no-dividend firm.
   - (d) DEL_t = Debt–Equity Ratio (parameter used by WS in Eq. (23.18) of Table 23.1).
   - (e) R_t = The rates-of-return the corporation could expect to earn on its future long-term investment (or the internal rate-of-return discussed in Chapter 12).
   - (f) CU_t = Rates of Capacity Utilization (used by FR to lag capital requirements behind changes in percent sales; used here to define the R_t expected).

26.3.2. *Model Specification and Applications*[2]

(a) An Adjustment Model of Capital Budgeting

The problem of capital budgeting is one that affects the entire structure of the modern corporation; its solution determine the very nature of that corporation. Therefore, the capital budget has been treated at great length in the literature of finance. In most of this work, it has been explicitly recognized that the components of the capital budget are jointly determined. The investment, dividend, and financing decisions are tied together by the

[2]This section is essentially drawn from Spies' (1974) paper. Reprinted with permission of the *Journal of Finance* and the author. Basic concepts of matrix algebra used in this section can be found in Chapter 3. The simultaneous equation used in this section can be found in Appendix 2.B in Chapter 2 of this book. In addition, the autoregressive model used in this chapter can be found in Section 24.6 in Chapter 24.

"uses-equals-sources" identity, a simple accounting identity which requires that all capital invested or distributed to stockholders be accounted for. Despite the obviousness of this relationship, however, very few attempts have been made to incorporate it into an econometric model. Instead, most of the empirical work in this area has concentrated on the components of the capital budget separately. It is the purpose of this section to describe Spies' (1974) econometric capital budgeting model that explicitly recognizes the "uses-equals-sources" identity.

In his empirical work, Spies broke the capital budget into its five basic components: dividends, short-term investment, gross long-term investment, debt financing, and new equity financing. The first three are uses of funds, while the latter two are sources. The dividends component includes all cash payments to stockholders and must be non-negative. Short-term investment is the net change in the corporation's holdings of short-term assets during the period. These assets include both inventories and short-term financial assets, such as cash, government securities, and trade credits. This component of the capital budget can be either positive or negative. Long-term investment is defined as the change in gross long-term assets during the period. Thus, the replacement of worn-out equipment is considered to be positive investment. Long-term investment can be negative but only if the sale of long-term assets exceeds this replacement investment.

The debt finance component is simply the net change in the corporation's liabilities. These liabilities include corporate bonds, bank loans, taxes owed, and other accounts payable. Since a corporation can either increase its liabilities or retire those already existing, this variable can be either positive or negative. Finally, new equity financing is the change in stockholder's equity minus the amount due to retained earnings. This should represent the capital raised by the sale of new shares of common stock. Although individual corporations frequently repurchase stock already sold, this variable is almost always positive when aggregated.

The first step is to develop a theoretical model that describes the optimal capital budget as a set of predetermined economic variables.[3] The first of these variables is a measure of cash flow, net profits plus depreciation allowances. This variable, denoted by Y, is exogenous as long as the policies determining production, pricing, advertising, taxes, and the like cannot be changed quickly enough to affect the present period's earnings. Since the

[3]Theoretical development of this optimal model can be found in Spies' (1971) dissertation.

data used in this work are quarterly, this does not seem to be an unreasonable assumption. It should also be noted that the "uses-equals-sources" identity ensures that:

$$\sum_{i=1}^{5} X_{i,t} = \sum_{i=1}^{5} X_{i,1}^{*} = Y_t, \tag{26.1}$$

where $X_{1,t}, X_{2,t}, X_{3,t}, X_{4,t}, X_{5,t}, X_{1,t}^{*}$ and Y_t are identical to those defined in Table 26.1.

Expanding Eq. (26.1) we obtain

$$\begin{aligned} X_{1,t} &+ X_{2,t} + X_{3,t} + X_{4,t} + X_{5,t} \\ &= X_{1,t}^{*} + X_{2,t}^{*} + X_{3,t}^{*} + X_{4,t}^{*} + X_{5,t}^{*} = Y_t. \end{aligned} \tag{26.1$'$}$$

The second exogenous variable in the model is the corporate bond rate, RCB_t. This was used as a measure of the borrowing rate faced by the corporation. In addition, the debt–equity ratio at the start of the period, DEL_t, was included to allow for the increase in the cost of financing due to leverage. The average dividend–price ratio for all stocks, RDP_t, was used as a measure of the rate-of-return demanded by investors in a no-growth, unlevered corporation for the average risk class. The last two exogenous variables, R_t and CU_t, describe the rate-of-return the corporation could expect to earn on its future long-term investment. The ratio of the change in earnings to investment in the previous quarter should provide a rough measure of the rate-of-return to that investment. A four-quarter average of that ratio, R_t, was used by Spies to smooth out the normal fluctuations in earnings. The rate of capacity utilization, CU_t, was also included in an attempt to improve this measure of expected rate-of-return. Finally, a constant and three seasonal dummies were included. The exogenous variables are summarized in the lower portion of Table 26.1. The matrix for this model is:

$$X_t^{*} = AZ_t, \tag{26.2}$$

where

$$\begin{aligned} X^{*'} &= (\text{DIV}^{*}\text{IST}^{*}\text{ILT}^{*} - \text{DF}^{*} - \text{EQF}^{*}), \\ Z' &= (1\, Q1\, Q2\, Q3\, \text{Y}\, \text{RCB}\, \text{RDP}\, \text{DEL}\, R\, \text{CU}), \\ A &= \begin{bmatrix} a_{10} & a_{11} & \cdots & a_{19} \\ \vdots & & & \vdots \\ a_{50} & a_{51} & \cdots & a_{59} \end{bmatrix}. \end{aligned}$$

In order to better comprehend this model, let us look at the expanded version of Eq. (26.2):

$$\begin{aligned}
\mathrm{DIV}_t^* &= a_{10} + a_{11}Q_1 + a_{12}Q_2 + a_{13}Q_3 + a_{14}Y_t + a_5\mathrm{RCB}_t + a_{16}\mathrm{RDP}_t \\
&\quad + a_{17}\mathrm{DEL}_t + a_{18}R_t + a_{19}\mathrm{CU}_t, \\
\mathrm{IST}_t^* &= a_{20} + a_{21}Q_1 + a_{22}Q_2 + a_{23}Q_3 + a_{24}Y_t + a_{25}\mathrm{RCB}_t + a_{26}\mathrm{RDP}_t \\
&\quad + a_{27}\mathrm{DEL}_t + a_{28}R_t + a_{29}\mathrm{CU}_t, \\
\mathrm{ILT}_t^* &= a_{30} + a_{31}Q_1 + a_{32}Q_2 + a_{33}Q_3 + a_{34}Y_t + a_{35}\mathrm{RCB}_t + a_{36}\mathrm{RDP}_t \\
&\quad + a_{37}\mathrm{DEL}_t + a_{38}R_t + a_{39}\mathrm{CU}_t, \\
-\mathrm{DF}_t^* &= a_{40} + a_{41}Q_1 + a_{42}Q_2 + a_{43}Q_3 + a_{44}Y_t + a_{45}\mathrm{RCB}_t + a_{46}\mathrm{RDP}_t \\
&\quad + a_{47}\mathrm{DEL}_t + a_{48}R_t + a_{49}\mathrm{CU}_t, \\
-\mathrm{EQF}_t^* &= a_{50} + a_{51}Q_1 + a_{52}Q_2 + a_{53}Q_3 + a_{54}Y_t + a_{55}\mathrm{RCB}_t + a_{56}\mathrm{RDP}_t \\
&\quad + a_{57}\mathrm{DEL}_t + a_{58}R_t + a_{59}\mathrm{CU}_t.
\end{aligned}$$

Although this model itself is not a good description of actual capital-budgeting practices, it can be integrated with a partial adjustment model to derive a more realistic model.

The typical corporation is not flexible enough to achieve this optimal capital budget every quarter. Corporate planners are normally reluctant to deviate very much from their past levels of dividends, investment, and financing.[4,5] This kind of behavior can best be described by a

---

[4]Bower (1970) provides an interesting discussion of corporate decision-making and its ability to adapt to a changing environment.

[5]The constraint on the values of δ_{ij} is a result of the "uses-equals-sources" identity. Summing Eq. (18.4) over **i** gives

$$\sum_{i=1}^{5} X_{i,t} = \sum_{i=1}^{5} X_{i,t-1} + \sum_{i=1}^{5}\sum_{i=1}^{5} \delta_{ij}(X_{j,t-1}^*),$$

This can be rewritten as

$$\sum_i (X_{i,t} - X_{i,t-1}) = \sum_j (X_{j,t}^* - X_{j,t-1}) \sum_i \delta_{ij}.$$

The identity ensures that $\sum_j X_{j,t} = \sum_j X_{j,t}^*$, and therefore,

$$\sum_i (X_{i,t} - X_{i,t-1}) = \sum_j (X_{j,t} - X_{j,t-1}) \sum_i \delta_{ij}.$$

partial adjustment model. In such a model, the capital budget depends on both the optimal budget and the actual budgets of the past. In its simplest form, the partial adjustment model makes the change in the level of X_i from period $(t - 1)$ to period t a function of the difference between its desired level for period t and its actual level for period $(t - 1)$. Using a linear relationship, this becomes

$$X_{i,t} = X_{i,t-1} + \delta_i(X^*_{i,t} - X_{i,t-1}) \tag{26.3}$$

or

(a) $X_{1,t} = X_{1,t-1} + \delta_1(X^*_{1,t} - X_{1,t-1})$,
(b) $X_{2,t} = X_{2,t-1} + \delta_2(X^*_{2,t} - X_{2,t-1})$,
(c) $X_{3,t} = X_{3,t-1} + \delta_3(X^*_{3,t} - X_{3,t-1})$,
(d) $X_{4,t} = X_{4,t-1} + \delta(X^*_{4,t} - X_{4,t-1})$,
(e) $X_{5,t} = X_{5,t-1} + \delta_5(X^*_{5,t} - X_{5,t-1})$.

This assumes that the corporation adjusts the level of X_i, a flow variable, in the direction of its optimal level. The speed of this adjustment is measured by the parameter δ_1. However, Eq. (26.3) does not incorporate the "uses-equals-sources" identity. Suppose $X^*_{1,t} > X_{i,t-1}$ for all $i \neq 1$. If $\delta_1 < 1$, then X_1 will not completely adjust in period t and will remain below its optimal level. But the "uses-equals-sources" identity ensures that

$$\sum_{i=1}^{5} X^*_{i,t} = \sum_{i=1}^{5} X_{i,t} = Y_t.$$

Therefore, the fact that X_1 is less than desired implies that at least one other X_i is above its desired level. Suppose it is X_2 that alone compensates for the slow adjustment of X_1. Then, even though $X^*_{2,t} = X_{2,t-1}$, we will have $X_{2,t} > X_{2,t-1}$. In fact,

$$X_{2,t} = X_{2,t-1} + (1 - \delta_1)(X^*_{1,t} - X_{1,t-1}).$$

Changing the notation slightly, this becomes

$$\sum_j (X_{j,t} - X_{j,t-1}) = \sum_j (X_{j,t} - X_{j,t-1}) \sum_i \delta_{ij}$$

or

$$1 = \sum_i \delta_{ij}.$$

The result of the "uses-equals-sources" identity is that the adjustment of each X_i may depend on the distance of every X_i from its optimal level, not just its own level. Equation (26.3) should be rewritten as:

$$X_{i,t} = X_{i,t-1} + \sum_{j=1}^{5} \delta_{ij}(X^*_{j,t} - X_{j,t-1}) \quad (i = 1, 2, 3, 4, 5), \tag{26.4}$$

where

$$\sum_{i=1}^{5} \delta_{ij} = 1.$$

Putting Eq. (26.4) into matrix form and combining it with Eq. (26.2), we get

$$\begin{aligned} X_t &= X_{t-1} + D(X^*_t - X_{t-1}) \\ &= X_{t-1} + D(AZ_t - X_{t-1}) \\ &= X_{t-1} + DAZ_t - DX_{t-1} \\ &= (I - D)X_{t-1} + DAZ_t, \end{aligned} \tag{26.5}$$

where I is the 5×5 identity matrix and

$$\begin{bmatrix} \delta_{11} & \delta_{12} & \ldots & \delta_{15} \\ \vdots & & & \vdots \\ \delta_{51} & \delta_{52} & \ldots & \delta_{55} \end{bmatrix}.$$

Equation (26.5) is an implicit, simultaneous, dynamic capital-budgeting model. The expansion is in Table 26.2.

It was argued above that the adjustment of each component of the capital budget depends not only on its own distance from the optimal level, but also on the distances of the other components. This would imply that at least some of the off-diagonal elements of D are non-zero. The fact that the X_i are competing uses of the available funds would generally lead one to believe that they should be negative. If dividends were below their optimal level, for example, we might expect dividends to rise and investment to fall. At the same time, however, the normal assumption with models of this type is that $0 < \delta_{11} < 1$. But we have already seen that $\sum_{i=1}^{5} \delta_{ij} = 1$ for all j. Therefore, it is not possible for all of the off-diagonal elements to be negative unless the δ_{ij} are greater than one. This means that the signs of the δ_{ij}

Table 26.2. An expanded version of Eq. (26.5).

$$X_1 = DIV_t = DIV_{t-1} + \delta_{11}(DIV_t^* - DIV_{t-1}) + \delta_{12}(IST_t^* - IST_{t-1})$$
$$+ \delta_{13}(ILT_t^* - ILT_{t-1}) + \delta_{14}(-DF_t^* + DF_{t-1}) + \delta_{15}(EQF_t^* + EQF_{t-1})$$
$$X_2 = IST_t = IDT_{t-1} + \delta_{21}(DIV_t^* - DIV_{t-1}) + \delta_{22}(IST_t^* - IST_{t-1})$$
$$+ \delta_{23}(ILT_t^* - ILT_{t-1}) + \delta_{24}(-DF_t^* + DF_{t-1}) + \delta_{25}(EQF_t^* + EQF_{t-1})$$
$$X_3 = ILT_t = ILT_{t-1} + \delta_{31}(DIV_t^* - DIV_{t-1}) + \delta_{312}(IST_t^* - IST_{t-1})$$
$$+ \delta_{33}(ILT_t^* - ILT_{t-1}) + \delta_{34}(-DF_t^* + DF_{t-1}) + \delta_{35}(EQF_t^* + EQF_{t-1})$$
$$X_4 = -DF_t = -DF_{t-1} + \delta_{41}(DIV_t^* - DIV_{t-1}) + \delta_{52}(IST_t^* - IST_{t-1})$$
$$+ \delta_{43}(ILT_t^* - ILT_{t-1}) + \delta_{44}(-DF_t^* + DF_{t-1}) + \delta_{45}(EQF_t^* + EQF_{t-1})$$
$$X_5 = -EQF_t = -EQF_{t-1} + \delta_{51}(DIV_t^* - DIV_{t-1}) + \delta_{52}(IST_t^* - IST_{t-1})$$
$$+ \delta_{53}(ILT_t^* - ILT_{t-1}) + \delta_{54}(-DF_t^* + DF_{t-1}) + \delta_{515}(EQF_t^* + EQF_{t-1})$$

coefficients cannot be predicted with absolute certainty. However, it should be noted that the primary reason most corporations hold liquid assets is to facilitate this type of adjustment process; the role of liquid assets is to give flexibility to the capital budget. Therefore, it is reasonable to expect short-term investment to take up the slack caused by the adjustments of the other components. Going back to the dividend example, we would expect short-term investment to rise to ensure that $\sum_{i=1}^{5} \delta_{i1} = 1$. It is then possible that $0 < \delta < 1$, and $\delta_{31}, \delta_{41}, \delta_{51} < 0$. Although this is not the only adjustment process a corporation can choose, it appears to be the most likely one.

(b) Some Empirical Results

For the purposes of estimation, Eq. (26.5) can be rewritten as

$$X = BX_{t-1} + CZ_t + U_t, \tag{26.6}$$

where B is a 5×5 matrix and C a 5×10 matrix of coefficients. The components of D and A can then be estimated by the following equations:

$$D = 1 - B, \tag{26.7}$$

$$A = D^{-1}C. \tag{26.8}$$

[An expanded form of Eq. (26.6) can be found in Table 26.3.] The estimation procedure used was the stacking technique that was first suggested

Table 26.3. An expanded form of Eq. (26.6).

$$\begin{bmatrix} DIV_t \\ IST_t \\ ILT_t \\ -DF_t \\ -EQF_t \end{bmatrix} = \begin{bmatrix} b_{11} b_{12} b_{13} b_{14} b_{15} c_{10} c_{11} c_{12} c_{13} c_{14} c_{15} c_{16} c_{17} c_{18} c_{19} \\ b_{21} b_{22} b_{23} b_{24} b_{25} c_{20} c_{21} c_{22} c_{23} c_{24} c_{25} c_{26} c_{27} c_{28} c_{29} \\ b_{31} b_{32} b_{33} b_{34} b_{35} c_{30} c_{31} c_{32} c_{33} c_{34} c_{35} c_{36} c_{37} c_{38} c_{39} \\ b_{41} b_{42} b_{43} b_{44} b_{45} c_{40} c_{41} c_{42} c_{43} c_{44} c_{45} c_{46} c_{47} c_{48} c_{49} \\ b_{51} b_{52} b_{53} b_{54} b_{55} c_{50} c_{51} c_{52} c_{53} c_{54} c_{55} c_{56} c_{57} c_{58} c_{59} \end{bmatrix} \begin{bmatrix} DIV_{t-1} \\ STI_{t-1} \\ LTI_{t-1} \\ DF_{t-1} \\ EQF_{t-1} \\ I \\ Q_1 \\ Q_2 \\ Q_3 \\ Y \\ RCB \\ RDP \\ DEL \\ R \\ CU \end{bmatrix}$$

by de Leeuw (1965). We have already seen that the "uses-equals-sources" identity implies that

$$\sum_{i=1}^{5} X_{it} = Y_t \quad \text{for every period } t.$$

In order to incorporate this into the estimation procedure, the estimators must be restricted in such a way that, across equations, the coefficients of Y add up to one, while the coefficients of the other predetermined variables add up to zero. In other words, we must ensure that

$$\sum_{i=1}^{5} b_{ij} = \sum_{i=1}^{5} \hat{c}_{ik} = 0 \quad \text{for all } j \text{ and all } k \neq 4,$$

and that

$$\sum_{i=1}^{5} \hat{c} = 1.$$

This is a simple adding-up constraint.[6]

[6]This constraint ensures that the "uses-equals-sources" identity will hold for the estimated equations. First of all, we know that $\sum_i {}_{ij} = 1$, since

$$ij = \begin{cases} 1 - b_{ij} & \text{for } i = j, \\ -b_{ij} & \text{for } i \neq . \end{cases}$$

Now that we have completed our discussion of the nature of this model, we will consider some empirical results from using the model. While the purpose of the model is to plan capital budgeting for a single firm, Spies' empirical results presented here used industry data instead of that of the individual firms. We will consider the application of the model to a single firm in Appendix 26.B.

The data used by Spies were taken mainly from the FTC-SEC Quarterly Financial Report for Manufacturing Corporations and covered the year 1969. Regression results are reported for the aggregated manufacturing

---

Therefore,

$$\sum_i ij = 1 - \sum_i b_{ij} = 1 - 0 = 1.$$

In addition, it can be shown that $X^*_{i,t} = Y_t$. To show this, it is necessary only to show that

$$\sum_j a_{jk} = \begin{cases} 0 & \text{for all } k \neq 4, \\ 1 & \text{for all } k = 4. \end{cases}$$

Note that $_{ik} = \sum_{jijajk}$. Since we have constrained

$$\sum_i c_{ik} = \begin{cases} 0 & \text{for all } k \neq 4, \\ 1 & \text{for all } k = 4. \end{cases}$$

we can see that

$$\begin{aligned} \sum_i C_{ik} &= \sum_{ij} \sum_{ijajk} \\ &= \sum \left(\sum_{ij} \right) a_{jk} \\ &= \sum_j (1) a_{jk} \\ &= \sum_j a_{jk}. \end{aligned}$$

Therefore,

$$\sum_j a_{jk} = \begin{cases} 1 & \text{for all } k \neq 4, \\ 1 & \text{for all } k = 4. \end{cases}$$

From all of this, it is clear that

$$\widehat{\sum_i} X_{i,t} = \widehat{\sum_i} X^*_{i,t} = Y_t.$$

sector and 10 industry subsectors. Those industries and their SIC classification numbers are:

1. Food and Kindred Products (20)
2. Textile Mill Products (22)
3. Furniture and Fixtures (25)
4. Paper and Allied Products (26)
5. Chemicals and Allied Products (28)
6. Leather and Leather Products (31)
7. Stone, Clay, and Glass Products (32)
8. Other Machinery (35)
9. Electric Machinery, Equipment, and Supplies (36)
10. Motor Vehicles and Equipment (37)

This model is supposed to provide a realistic picture of the capital-budgeting practices of individual corporations, but Spies used aggregated data to test it. He indicated that there is no reason to expect the parameters of the model to be the same for all manufacturing corporations, or even for all corporations within a particular industry. There is no way to refute this argument on theoretical grounds. It is probably true, in theory at least, that individual-firm data would have provided a better test of the model. However, such data might present serious problems for an empirical study of this kind. The capital-budgeting decisions of actual corporations are often dictated by outside influences and considerations that cannot be explained in a very general model of this kind. For example, a single large investment project could dominate a corporation's entire capital budget for several periods. Such things as labor negotiations and antitrust actions could also affect capital-budgeting decisions. It would be very difficult to incorporate all these factors into our general model. As a result, the capital budget of an individual corporation will often be very different from that predicted by our model. This could happen even if the model is an accurate description of the normal behavior of that corporation. Spies argued that aggregated data instead of individual firms' data have smoothed out the effects of these outside influences.

The estimates of the δ_{ij} coefficients are reported in Spies' (1974) Tables 26.1–26.5. In the estimation procedure employed here, we had to use the negative of the values of debt and equity financing in order to preserve the adding-up constraint. However, in reporting the results, we have adjusted the signs of these coefficients to eliminate this convention. In other words, the X_t and X_{t-1} vectors of Eq. (26.5) have been adjusted to make $X' =$ (DIV IST ILT DF EQF). This transformed system of equations is equivalent to the old one and is much easier to interpret.

Spies used five tables to show the adjustment coefficients δ_{ij} for the aggregated manufacturing sector and the 10 industry subsectors. Each table contains the estimates of δ_{ij} for $i = 1, 2, 3, 4, 5$, and a given value of j. For example, Table 19.4 shows that if the optimal level of dividends in the aggregated manufacturing sector exceeds last period's actual level by \$1.00 (that is, $\text{DIV}_t^* = \text{DIV}_{t-1} = 1$), then dividends will be raised \$0.83. In addition, short-term investment will rise by \$3.23, debt financing by \$2.09, and equity financing by \$0.97.

Table 26.4 contains the estimates of the coefficients of $\text{DIV}_t^* - \text{DIV}_{t-1}$. The own-adjustment coefficients of dividends are given in the first column.

Table 26.4. Adjustment coefficients of $DIV_t - DIV_{t-1}$.

	ΔDIV_t	ΔIST_t	ΔILT_t	ΔDF_t	ΔEQF_t
Food	1	2.8688	−2.8688	0	0
		(4.14)*	(4.14)		
Textile	1.1156	1.6469	01.9930	1.0763	−1.3041
	(8.97)	(2.19)	(2.29)	(1.38)	(2.20)
Furniture	0.9194	2.9337	0	0	2.8531
	(12.09)	(2.34)			(3.58)
Paper	0.2475	0	6.1983	1.8321	3.6137
	(0.37)		(5.30)	(1.76)	(2.96)
Chemical	0.1894	0.8106	0	0	0
	(0.64)	(2.74)			
Leather	0.6412	1.6059	1.5603	5.4753	−2.6679
	(1.68)	(0.90)	(1.03)	(3.05)	(2.12)
Stone, clay and glass	0.7037	1.5594	−1.2631	0	0
	(3.32)	(2.14)	(3.09)		
Other machinery	1.2340	3.7843	0	4.0183	0
	(5.22)	(5.37)		(5.23)	
Electrical machinery	0.8355	0	0	−1.3451	1.1806
	(4.16)			(1.06)	(0.87)
Motor vehicle	1.0158	0.9799	−0.6723	0	0.3234
	(16.72)	(4.15)	(2.63)		(1.33)
Aggregated	0.8328	3.2308	0	2.0902	0.9734
	(6.67)	(6.59)		(7.64)	(1.96)

*The numbers in parentheses are t-statistics. The 95% significance level is $t = 1.96$. the entries without t-statistics listed represent the coefficients of variables that were left out of the regression. These coefficients are equal to one for the own-adjustment coefficients and zero for all the others. From Spies (1974). Reprinted by permission.

They range from a low of 0.1894 for the chemical industry to a high of 1.2340 for "other machinery." Three of the industries have coefficients greater than one, but none of them is significantly different from one. Except for the chemical and paper industries, all the estimates are quite close to one. This would indicate that most corporations adjust dividends quite rapidly to their optimal level.

The other components of the capital budget also adjust to a non-optimality in dividends. The second column of Table 26.4 illustrates the reaction of short-term investment to such a non-optimality. Except for the two zero values, all the estimates are positive and relatively large. There is a strong support for the argument that corporations build up their supplies of liquid assets because of a planned increase in dividends. Long-term investment, on the other hand, seems to adjust downward. Eight of the 10 industry coefficients are negative or zero, and one of the positive coefficients is insignificant. Thus the evidence suggests that long-term investment might fall in the face of a planned increase in dividends. Since investment has to compete with dividends for funds, this result is not altogether surprising. Only the very large positive coefficient for the paper industry provides conflicting evidence.

By the same type of argument, it is clear that both debt and equity financing should rise in response to an expected increase in dividends. Nine of the 10 industry adjustment coefficients for debt financing are positive or zero, and the other is not significant. In the equity finance equation, eight of the 10 coefficients are positive or zero. In other words, both sources of funds are increased to meet the financing requirements of the new, liberalized dividend policy.

Results of the other four sets of partial-adjustment coefficients can be interpreted in a similar manner. Spies' summarized empirical results are indicated in Table 26.5, which indicates that adjustment coefficients are remarkably consistent from industry to industry (at least in terms of signs). Of course, none of the industries nor the aggregated manufacturing sector looks exactly like Table 26.5, but they all follow the general pattern to some degree. Hence, this general pattern has shed some light for financial managers on the various financial interrelationships.

Using Eq. (26.6), Spies performed a simple simulation to investigate the dynamic nature of simultaneous capital-budgeting decisions. Graphically, the simulation results are indicated in Fig. 26.1.

Figure 26.1 describes the changes in the capital budget that would result from a unit increase in gross earnings for the aggregated manufacturing

Table 26.5. Summary of results.

	$DIV_t^* - DIV_{t-1}$	$IST_t^* - IST_{t-1}$	$ILT_t^* - ILT_{t-1}$	$DF_t^* - DF_{t-1}$	$EQF_t^* - EQF_{t-1}$
ΔDIV	Close to 1	Negative (but not significant)	Negative (but not significant)	Positive (but not significant)	Positive (but not significant)
ΔIST	Positive and large	Greater than 1	Positive and large	Negative and large	Negative and large
ΔILT	Negative	Negative*	Between 0 and 1	Positive	Positive
ΔDF	Positive*	Positive*	Positive*	Close to 1	Negative
ΔEQF	Positive	Positive*	Positive*	Negative*	Close to 1

*The items marked with an asterisk are those where at least five industries had estimated coefficients set equal to zero. Because of this large number of insignificant estimates, our conclusions about the signs of these coefficients must be viewed with caution.
From Spies (1974). Reprinted with permission).

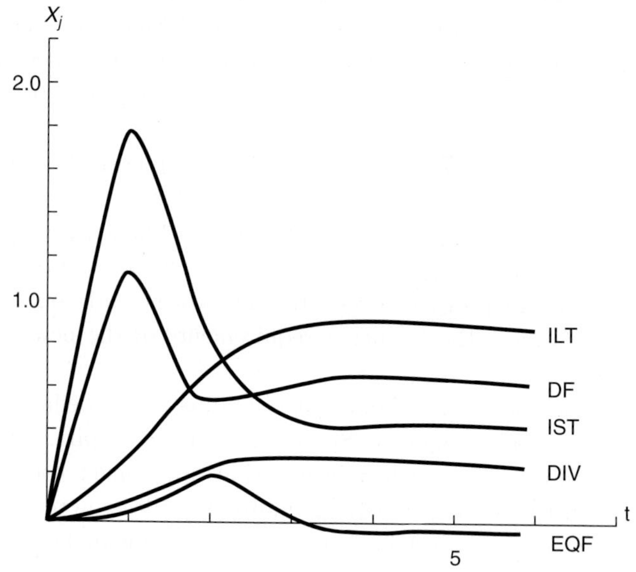

Fig. 26.1.
Source: Spies (1974). Reprinted with permission.

sector. The difference between each component and its initial level is plotted against time. All the other exogenous variables are assumed to remain constant. The adjustment process seems quite clear. Dividends and long-term investment rise slowly but steadily to their new optimal levels. In the first few quarters, short-term investment takes up the slack caused by this slow adjustment. It rises sharply in the first quarter and remains well above its optimal level in the second. This means merely that the corporations are stockpiling liquid assets in preparation for the higher dividend and long-term investment levels. Debt financing rises sharply in the first quarter before falling to its new optimum. To a lesser degree, equity finance does the same thing. By the fourth quarter, all the components of the capital budget have just about reached their optimal levels. This is a much more rapid adjustment than those implied by most single-equation models. This is one of the most interesting results of the complete partial-adjustment model.

(c) Concluding Remarks

In general, the model developed by Spies performs quite well. The evidence strongly supports a complete partial adjustment model. The individual adjustment coefficients are reasonable for most industries, and the systems are all stable. If the capital budget is out of equilibrium, dividends and long-term investment move steadily toward their equilibrium values. Debt and equity financing change quickly to help finance the other adjustments before moving to their own equilibrium levels. Finally, short-term investment takes up the slack. It adjusts rapidly to compensate for the slower adjustment of the other components and preserve the "uses-equals-sources" identity. Such behavior is generally consistent with actual capital-budgeting practices.

There are a number of interesting conclusions that can be drawn from Spies' empirical results. The first concerns the place of dividends in corporate planning. Apparently dividends adjust to a new optimum almost immediately. It should be pointed out that the actual dividend policies of most corporations are asymmetric. Dividends are virtually rigid downward, while they are much more flexible upward. The preponderance of periods of rapid growth in earnings and dividends in our sample could very well affect the estimates of this speed of adjustment. In any event, dividends do not react significantly to a non-optimality in any other component of the capital budget. It seems clear that the dividend level is of paramount importance to corporate planners. The evidence strongly supports the hypothesis that dividend policy is determined almost independently of the rest of the capital budget.

26.4. Applications of SUR Estimation Method in Financial Analysis and Planning

The SUR technique developed by Zellner (1962) has recently been extensively used in financial analysis and planning (Peterson, 1980). Frecka and Lee (1983) used the SUR method to improve the estimation efficiency of determining the dynamic financial-ratio adjustment process. The main justification of this application is that the changes for the liquidity, leverage, activity, and profitability ratios are generally interrelated. Lee and Vinso (1980) used the SUR to examine the role of firm-related variables in capital-asset pricing. Taggart (1977) used the SUR approach to study the role of capital structure in financing decisions. In this section, the last two studies are used to show how the SUR method can be used to improve the empirical results of financial analysis and planning.

26.4.1. *The Role of Firm-Related Variables in Capital-Asset Pricing*[7]

Lee and Vinso (1980) and Lee and Zumwalt (1981) used the SUR method to investigate the role of firm-related variables in capital-asset pricing. Following Lee and Vinso, the simultaneous market model is defined as:

$$\begin{aligned} R_{1t} &= \alpha_1 + \beta_1 R_{mt} + \gamma_{11} X_{11} + \gamma_{12} X_{12} + \gamma_{13} X_{13} + E_{1t}, \\ R_{2t} &= \alpha_2 + \beta_2 R_{mt} + \gamma_{21} X_{21} + \gamma_{22} X_{22} + \gamma_{23} X_{23} + E_{2t}, \\ &\vdots \\ R_{nt} &= \alpha_n + \beta_n R_{mt} + \gamma_{n1} X_{n1} + \gamma_{n2} X_{n2} + \gamma_{n3} X_{n3} + E_{nt}, \end{aligned}$$

where

R_{jt} = Return on the jth security over time interval t $(j = 1, 2, \ldots, n)$,
R_{mt} = Return on a market index over time interval t,
X_{j1t} = Profitability index of jth firm over time interval t $(j = 1, 2, \ldots, n)$,
X_{j2t} = Leverage index of jth firm over time period t $(j = 1, 2, \ldots, n)$,
X_{j3t} = Dividend policy index of jth firm over time period t $(j = 1, 2, \ldots, n)$,

[7]Major portion of this section was drawn from Lee and Vinso (1980). Reprinted with permission of *Journal of Business Research*.

γ_{jk} = Coefficient of the kth firm-related variable in the jth equation ($k = 1, 2, 3$),

β_j = Coefficient of market rate-of-return in the jth equation

E_{jt} = Disturbance term for the jth equation, and a_j's are intercepts ($j = 1, 2, \ldots, n$).

If the estimated coefficients of γ_{jk} are trivial and the variance–covariance matrix of Eq. (26.9) is a diagonal matrix, then we obtain Sharpe's (1963) diagonal model, which is:

$$R_{jt} = \alpha' + \beta' + E_{jt}. \tag{26.10}$$

To investigate the SUR returns-generating process presented here, relative to the usual market model, annual data of stock price and firm-related variables (the profitability index, the leverage index, and the dividend policy index) from the period 1945–1973 for seven oil companies are used to calculate the related rates-of-return. The profitability index is defined as annual retained profit (retained earnings plus interest and preferred dividends) divided by total assets; the leverage index is defined as annual change of long-term debt plus annual change of outstanding preferred stock divided by total assets; and the dividend policy index is defined as annual change of total dividends divided by the book value of equity. Other firm-related variables can be added or substituted for those used here. The appropriate rates-of-return for each company are adjusted for dividends and stock splits. The annual Standard and Poor index (SPI) with dividends is used to calculate the annual rate-of-return on the market.

To test the validity of the SUR market model specified in Eq. (26.9), OLS is first used to estimate the necessary parameters of seven oil companies (see Table 26.6). It can be seen that five of the seven R^2 associated with OLS estimates of the SUR market model are higher than those of the Sharpe model shown in Table 26.7. These results indicate that the firm-related variables increase the explanatory power of the market model. The residual correlation coefficient matrix for these seven companies (shown in Table 26.8) indicates these firms are highly interrelated in that 10 residual correlation coefficients involving all seven firms are significantly different from zero at the 0.05 level. The SUR estimation method can improve the efficiency of some estimators.

Parameter estimates utilizing the SUR method are also provided in Table 26.6. When the SUR estimation method is applied to the market

Table 26.6. OLS and SUR estimates of oil industry.

		α_j	β_j	γ_{j1}	γ_{j2}	γ_{j3}	$\bar{R}^2$
R_1	OLS	−0.44	0.76	6.04	0.45	−2.08	0.22
		(1.64)	(2.47)‡	(1.72)	(0.29)	(−0.17)	
	SUR	−0.28	0.76	4.20	0.86	−6.97	
		(1.18)	(2.55)‡	(1.36)	(0.62)	(−0.66)	
R_2	OLS	−0.82	0.54	1.06	−1.21	5.29	0.02
		(−0.26)	(1.31)	(0.23)	(−1.21)	(0.27)	
	SUR	−0.16	0.58	2.45	−0.81	−8.50	
		(−0.80)	(1.43)	(0.85)	(−1.27)	(0.67)	
R_3	OLS	−0.22	1.12	2.05	2.51	−0.51	0.45
		(−1.72)	(3.98)‡	(1.42)	(2.15)‡	(−0.06)	
	SUR	−0.30	1.08	2.91	2.66	−2.53	
		(2.63)‡	(3.88)‡	(2.39)‡	(2.81)‡	(−0.41)	
R_4	OLS	−0.15	0.72	2.10	−0.23	25.29	0.30
		(−0.86)	(3.05)‡	(0.78)	(−0.27)	(1.81)†	
	SUR	−0.05	0.64	−0.98	0.42	26.35	
		(−0.35)	(2.75)‡	(−0.43)	(0.58)	(2.337)‡	
R_5	OLS	−0.00	1.16	−0.75	1.83	15.60	0.05
		(−0.01)	(2.08)‡	(−0.22)	(1.34)	(0.89)	
	SUR	−0.00	1.16	−0.86	1.88	0.91	
		(−0.02)	(2.30)‡	(−0.41)	(2.49)‡	(0.95)	
R_6	OLS	−0.14	0.70	0.68	0.91	62.20	0.27
		(1.43)	(3.09)‡	(0.55)	(1.30)	(1.71)	
	SUR	−0.15	0.70	0.85	0.90	54.11	
		(1.99)†	(3.17)‡	(1.01)	(2.02)‡	(2.40)‡	
R_7	OLS	−0.11	1.01	1.34	0.64	4.53	0.46
		(−0.91)	(4.75)‡	(0.78)	(1.24)	(0.75)	
	SUR	−0.06	1.01	0.65	0.96	3.96	
		(−0.58)	(4.68)‡	(0.42)	(2.08)‡	(0.74)	

*t-values appear in parentheses beneath the corresponding coefficients.
†Denotes significant at 0.10 level of significant or better for two-tailed test.
‡Denotes significant at 0.05 level of significant or better for two-tailed test.
From Lee and Vinso (1980). Copyright 1980 by Elsevier Science Publishing Co., Inc. Reprinted by permission of the publisher.

model, in most cases the efficiency of the estimators appears to be increased. The gain associated with the SUR estimation method is measured using the t-statistic of the regression coefficient as the coefficient of determination for the SUR estimation method is not provided by the SUR computer program. The efficiency of SUR is greater than with OLS. Thus, the SUR market model developed here can result in more efficient estimators while also increasing the explanatory power of the market model.

Results of the SUR market model have a great deal of intuitive appeal. For example, Imperial Oil, which is a Canadian firm, shows the lowest

Table 26.7. OLS parameter estimates of oil industry-Sharpe Model.*

		α'	β'	$\bar{R}^2$
R_1	Imperial Oil	0.04	0.74 (2.66)	0.18
R_2	Philips Petroleum	−0.01	0.65 (1.67)	0.06
R_3	Shell Oil	−0.01	1.23 (4.24)	0.38
R_4	S.O. of IN	0.04	0.68 (2.86)	0.20
R_5	S.O. of OH	−0.02	0.87 (1.81)	0.07
R_6	Sun Oil	0.01	0.62 (2.71)	0.19
R_7	Union Oil of CA	0.01	1.02 (4.67)	0.43

*t-values appear in parenthesis beneath the corresponding coefficients.
From Lee, and Vinso (1980). Copyright 1980 by Elsevier Science Publishing Co., Inc. Reprinted with permission of the publisher.

Table 26.8. Residual correlation coefficient matrix after OLS estimate.

	R_1	R_2	R_3	R_4	R_5	R_6	R_7
R_1	1.00	0.17	0.16	0.44*	0.55	0.11	0.14
R_2		1.00	0.20	0.23	0.74*	0.44*	−0.07
R_3			1.00	0.16	0.35*	0.57*	0.21
R_4				1.00	0.17	0.36*	0.33*
R_5					1.00	0.66*	0.62*
R_6						1.00	0.31*
R_7							1.00

*Denotes significantly different from zero at 0.05 level of significance.
From Lee and Vinso (1980). Copyright 1980 by Elsevier Science Publishing Co., Inc. Reprinted with permission of the publisher.

correlation with other firms, as might be expected. In Table 26.7, the residuals of Phillips Petroleum is highly correlated with those of Standard Oil of Ohio and Sun Oil, but the SUR estimation does not improve the efficiency of estimators for Phillips Petroleum. One possible reason is that the financial-management policies of this company may be highly correlated with those of other companies in the oil industry. When the explanatory variables of a regression become more similar to those of other regressions in the same industry, the gain from the SUR estimation method will be smaller. While these results are interesting, they can be viewed with confidence only if the assumptions of the regression model are fulfilled. Tests of residuals show that the regression requirements are indeed met. Hence, the SUR market model can be used to determine the role of firm-related variables.

Now that the validity of the SUR market model has been shown, the three firm-related variables used by Simkowitz and Logue (1973) in capital-asset pricing are of interest. The roles played by three firm-related variables are to identify the simultaneous-equation system of the security market and to improve the explanatory power of the diagonal security-market model. These same firm-related variables also are explicitly included in the SUR market model indicated in Eq. (26.9). Using the SUR estimates of the market model, the importance of these firm-related variables in the returns-generation process can be analyzed. The profitability index is significant in explaining the rate-of-return of Shell Oil; the dividend-policy index is significant in explaining the rates-of-return of Shell Oil, Standard Oil of Ohio, Sun Oil, and Union Oil of California. These results imply that both leverage and dividend policies can be addition factors important in capital-asset pricing. Both leverage and dividend policies are unique factors of an industry from a financial-management viewpoint. The market index itself cannot be used to accommodate the change of these two policies associated with a particular industry.

Thus, the SUR market model is formulated by introducing such accounting information as indices of profitability, leverage, and dividend policy into Sharpe's model. It explicitly takes into account the possible impact of accounting information on the behavior of security prices. This multi-index model differs from other multi-index models in several aspects. First, the additional indices employed in the SUR market model are the accounting information of an individual firm rather than general economic-activity indicators. Secondly, the indices of accounting information are relatively orthogonal to the market rate-of-return and the multicollinearity problem is much less essential relative to that of other multi-index models. Finally, the SUR estimation method can be used to take care of the interdependent relationship among securities of a particular industry. As quarterly data instead of annual data are employed to estimate the parameters for a particular industry, the gain associated with the SUR estimation method will become much more important [see Zellner (1962) for details]. Since Lee and Vinso (1980) have shown that the SUR model is consistent with the multi-beta interpretations of Sharpe (1977) and others, the results obtained here should be consistent with empirical tests of those models.

26.4.2. *The Role of Capital Structure in Corporate-Financing Decisions*

Taggart (1977) indicated that all empirical studies but Spies' (1974) model, in investigating the change of various balance-sheet items, takes the size of the external financing deficit as exogenous. In addition, he argued that there are two possible weaknesses existing in Spies' model. Firs, Spies' model does not make systematic use of the theory of optimal capital structure. Secondly, Spies did not allow for the possibility that balance sheet interrelationships may enter through the error terms. To deal with these estimation weaknesses, Taggart showed that Zellner's SUR method can be used to improve the efficiency of estimation.

Taggart uses five equations to describe the behavior of (a) the change of long-term debt (ΔLDBT), (b) the change of gross stock issues (ΔGSTK), (c) stock retirements (SRET), (d) the change of liquid assets (ΔLIQ), and (e) the change in short-term debt (ΔSDBT). These equations can be defined as:

$$\Delta\text{LDBT} = \alpha_1(\text{LDBT}^* - \text{LDBT}_{t-1}) + \alpha_2(\text{PCB}^* - \text{PCB}_{t-1} - \text{RE}) + \alpha_3\text{STOCKT} + \alpha_4\text{RT} + \varepsilon_1, \quad (26.11)$$

$$\Delta\text{GSTK} = \beta_1(\text{LDBT}^* - \text{LDBT}_{t-1}) + \beta_2(\text{PCB}^* - \text{PCB}_{t-1} - \text{RE}) + \beta_3\text{STOCKT} + \beta_4\text{RT} + \varepsilon_2, \quad (26.12)$$

$$\text{STRET} = \eta_1(\text{LDBT}^* - \text{LDBT}_{t-1}) + \eta_2(\text{PCB}^* - \text{PCB}_{t-1} - \text{RE}) + \eta_4\text{RT} + \varepsilon_3, \quad (26.13)$$

$$\Delta\text{LIQ} = \text{LIQ}^* + \gamma_2(\text{TC}^* - \text{TC}_{t-1}) + \gamma_3(\Delta\text{A} - \text{RE}) + \gamma_4\text{RT} + \varepsilon_4, \quad (26.14)$$

$$\Delta\text{SDBT} = \Delta\text{LIQ}^* + \lambda_2(\text{TC}^* - \text{TC}_{t-1}) + \lambda_3(\Delta\text{A} - \text{RE}) + \lambda_4\text{RT} + \varepsilon_5, \quad (26.15)$$

where

$\text{LDBT}^* = \text{bSTOCK}(i/i)$ = A target for the book value of long-term debt,

STOCK = Market value of equity,

b = LDM/STOCK = Desired debt–equity ratio,
LDM = Market value of debt = (LDBT)(i/i),
i/i = Ratio between the average contractual interest rate on long-term debt outstanding and the current new-issue rate on long-term debt,
LDBT_{t-1} = Book value of long-term debt in previous period,
PCB^* = Permanent capital (book value) = net capital stock (NK) + the permanent portion of working assets (NWA),
PCB_{t-1} = Permanent capital in the previous period,
RE = Stock retirements,
STOCKT = Stock-market timing variable = average short-term market value of equity divided by average long-term market value of equity,
RT = Interest timing variable, weighted average (with weight 0.67 and 0.33) of two most recent quarters' changes in the commercial paper rate,
TC^* = Target short-term capital = short-term asset-liquid assets,
TC_{t-1} = Short-term debt in the previous period,
ΔA = Changes in total assets,
ΔLIQ^* = Change of target liquidity assets.

Both OLS and Zellner's SUR method (1962) are used to estimate these behavioral equations in terms of quarterly aggregated data. To resolve the singular covariance problem caused by the balance-sheet constraint, Taggart omitted the stock-retirement equation when using the SUR method. To deal with the seasonal fluctuation problem associated with quarterly data, Taggart also introduced seasonal dummy variables into each equation.

Overall, Taggart's study contributes to the understanding of corporate-financing patterns by including a market value debt–equity ratio as a determinant of long-term debt capacity and using the SUR method, which explicitly accounts for balance-sheet interrelationships. Taggart infers from his estimates that firms base their stock- and bond-issue decisions on the need for permanent capital, and on their long-term debt capacity. He has also found that retained earnings is the primary source of funds used by firms to increase the permanent capital. Both new bond and new stock issues are the supporting sources of funds in increasing the permanent capital. In addition, Taggart also found that liquid assets and short-term debt play an important role in absorbing short-run fluctuations in the external financing deficit.

26.5. Applications of Structural Econometric Models in Financial Analysis and Planning

26.5.1. *A Brief Review*

Modigliani and Miller (2009) [M&M] and Lee and Wu (2009) used the simultaneous-equation approach to improve the precision of the cost-of-capital estimate. Simkowitz and Logue (1973) and Lee (1974) used simultaneous-equation specifications to investigate the interdependent structure of security returns. Oudet (1973) used a two-equation, simultaneous-equation system to show that inflation had a negative effect on stock returns. Elliott (1972) used a simultaneous econometric model to evaluate the corporate financial performance of a firm. Davis *et al.* (1973) developed an econometric planning model for American Telephone and Telegraph (AT&T) Company.

26.5.2. *AT&T's Econometric Planning Model*

Following Davis *et al.* (1973) [DCC], the econometric model of the Bell system has been developed as a planning tool to assist in evaluating the impact of general changes in the economy and other environmental changes for alternative Bell system policy. These policies are concerned with long-range planning. The model is called FORECYT, an acronym for Econometric *FORE*casting Model for Corporate Poli*CY* Analysis for *T* (the ticker symbol for AT&T). The overall modeling approach is based upon the premise that the state of the economy determines an individual firm's demand, making it externally derived rather than created by the firm's supply capacity. With this model, Bell system demand is assumed dependent upon economic factors external to the corporation and supply is a reaction, via corporate policy actions, to the demand.

FORECYT has a tripartite structure (see Fig. 26.2) consisting of three submodels, which are further divided into modules to facilitate

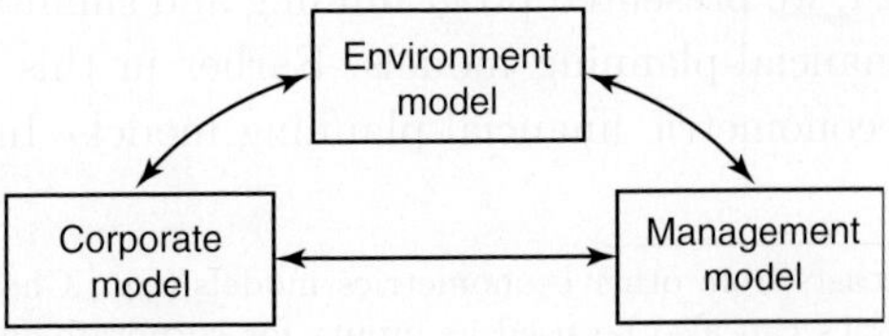

Fig. 26.2. Tripartite structure of FORECYT.

disaggregation as interest dictates and data allow. The flowchart of three submodels and their related modules are indicated in Fig. 26.3.

From the flowchart indicated in Fig. 26.3, the three submodels can be discussed in some detail as:

(i) The environment model is a construct of the "world" or "environment" with which the corporation interacts. This model contains (a) the National Economy Module, (b) the Regulatory Module, and (c) the Price-wage Review Module.
(ii) The corporate model is an econometric construct of the Bell system. This model contains (a) the demand module, (b) the price module, (c) the capital market module, (d) the financial module, (e) the revenue module, and (f) the production (or supply) module.
(iii) The management model is a logical construct providing policy variables for control (in the input module) and displaying corporate indicators of performance (in the output module). Policy variables include finance mix and factor mix; corporate indicators of performance include earnings per share and realized rates-of-return.

To specify this FORECYT, finance theories are directly needed to determine the capital-market module and input module. Needless to say, economic indicators and AT&T's market and accounting information are definitely needed to use this kind of corporate-decision model.

Using Data Resources, Incorporated's (1972) economic forecasts and other related data as inputs, DCC obtained some interesting and useful financial planning and forecasting results for AT&T.[8] Other updated concepts and corporate planning, using aggregated economic forecasting results, can be found in Eckstein's (1981) speech on decision-support systems for corporate planning.

26.6. Programming versus Simultaneous versus Econometric Financial Models

In Chapters 22–24, we presented programming and simultaneous-equations approaches to financial-planning models. Earlier in this chapter we have discussed some econometric financial-planning models. In this section, we

[8]The economic forecasts from other econometrics models (e.g., Chase Econometric and Wharton Econometrics can also be used as inputs for corporate-analysis planning and forecasting.

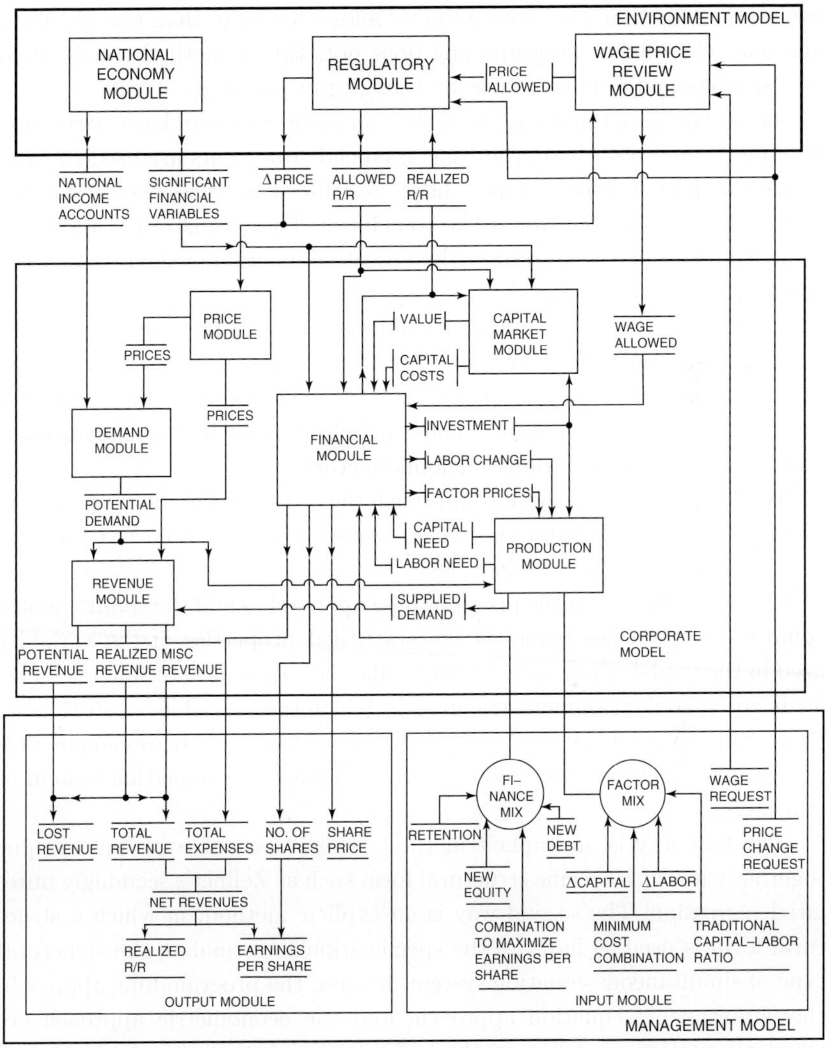

Fig. 26.3. Flowchart of FORECYT.

Source: From Davis *et al.* (1973). Copyright © 1973, The American Telephone and Telegraph Company. Reprinted with permission.

will attempt to compare these models, looking at their strengths and weaknesses.

Two types of programming were examined in Chapters 22 and 23: linear- and goal-programming. One of the major differences between these two methods is that goal programming allows for more than one objective function while linear programming does not. Either method can be used for working-capital management and long-term planning.

These two programming methods also have a similar basic structure. Starting from a data base, the basic financial statements are used to categorize the data and then finance theory is utilized to set up the constraints and goals that the firm would like to achieve. These constraints and goals come from two major sources — the objective function of the firm and the overall policies of the firm.

Usually the objective function is concerned with the valuation of the firm; that is, usually the overall goal for a firm is the maximization of shareholder wealth. As for major policies, they are the investment, financing, dividend, and production policies. These policies are set by top management and are influenced by various economic factors.

While under a programming approach the objective function is explicitly identified, under the simultaneous-equations method the objective function is implicit from the set of equations.

One thing that both the programming approaches and the simultaneous-equations approaches ignore is the statistical properties of the variables used in the model. These two methods take the values as deterministic. This leads one to look at econometric models, which take variables as stochastic. Econometric models attempt to integrate single-equation regression models and simultaneous-equation models into a simultaneous-equation system in two ways.

The first way is an implicit method, where a set of equations are put together without a specific structural form such as Zellner's seemingly unrelated regression. The second way is an explicit method, in which a structural form is used to improve the specification to formulate the structural type of simultaneous-equation system. In sum, the programming approach, the simultaneous-equation approach, and the econometric approach are three alternative modeling methods for financial analysis, planning, and forecasting. The relative empirical performance between these models in financial planning and forecasting is still to be investigated.

26.7. Financial Analysis and Business Policy Decisions

Traditionally, business policy has been approached with a case method that uses qualitative analysis. However, in the last decade or so, the use of quantitative analysis in business policy analysis has gained acceptance through the increased use of industry and national econometric planning models. The question is, how should a firm utilize financial planning models in setting its business policy? Hopefully, we will be able to show that financial training is important for a solid understanding of business policy.

In their paper, Duhaime and Thomas (1983) address the issue of the role of financial analysis in strategic management. The authors evaluate financial management for a corporate viewpoint that is not just in financial terms, but rather, looks at the contribution of financial management to overall corporate goals such as innovation and growth, business efficiency, maintenance, operations and profitability control, and flexibility to changes in strategy.

Duhaime and Thomas define strategic management as encompassing "the firm's activities of determining, enacting, and maintaining an appropriate and desirable match between the firm's resources and skills and the opportunities and threats posed by its continually changing environment." The process of strategic management involves the steps of: (1) identification of problems and resources, (ii) formulation of alternative strategies, (iii) evaluating and choosing from these alternatives, (iv) implementing the chosen strategy, and (v) monitoring and evaluating the performance of the adopted strategy.

There are three areas of strategic management in which financial planning can be utilized: planning phases, organization level, and corporate strategic type.

The planning phase encompasses basic financial planning, forecast-based planning, externally oriented planning, and corporate planning.

As for the organizational level, the increased use of diversification and divisional organizational structures makes the use of financial-planning models more important when examining alternative diversification strategies or organizational structures.

Finally, the corporate strategic type is involved with the question of what businesses the firm should be involved in and how the firm should compete in those businesses.

Having set the picture of strategic management, let us look at the application of financial approaches to strategic management. In the context of strategic management, financial managers should match strategic objectives with corporate long-term resources since financial resources are often vital for achieving these objectives.

One problem with the use of financial approaches is that they may become too rigid in their criteria and limit proper options that a firm might take. Normative finance theory needs to include behavioral and political variables as well.

Many financial models take a deterministic approach, which is "bottom-up" in nature, in that they use accounting data and are decision-support rather than optimizing models. These models are very complex.

Another set of models that are very helpful to the manager of a firm comprises sensitivity analysis and risk-analysis models that allow the manager to look at the different effects of different strategies and different inputs. Risk analysis can be used in the corporate development process of analyzing existing activities of the firm, choosing new activities, portfolios of new activities, and combined portfolios of new and existing activities.

What strategic risk analysis should do for the managers of a firm is highlight what alternatives should be considered, and look at the effects of uncertainty on contingency planning. Managers hope that the initial analysis will stimulate further investigation into the assumptions, values, and uncertainties, in order to come up with a better problem solution.

Another use of financial approaches is in strategic portfolio planning. A popular model in this area is the growth-per-share matrix developed by the Boston Consulting Group (see Zakon (1968, 1976) and Hedley (1977)). In this model, the markets where the firm operates are defined by two parameters: market growth rate and relative market share. Market growth rate is a proxy for cash use, such that the investment needed to maintain market share is a function of that market's growth rate. Relative market share is a proxy for cash generation, such that profitability of competing products is a function of their market share.

Planning models can also be used to analyze major decisions such as acquisitions, divestments, and expansions. These potential changes can be analyzed in terms of their expected financial and synergistic effects.

Duhaime and Thomas come to several conclusions in their paper of note. First, they indicated that there is a need for integrating various models of investment and financing in order to come up with an overall financial strategy. Financial management should be judged not only in terms of profitability, efficiency, and control, but also in terms of organizational adaptability and flexibility criteria.

Lastly, Duhaime and Thomas point out that strategic management includes more than strategic financial management; it also includes structural uncertainty and behavioral and political dimensions.

26.8. Summary

Based upon the information, theory, and methods discussed in previous chapters, we discussed how the econometrics approach can be used as alternative to both the programming approach and simultaneous-equation approach to financial planning and forecasting. Both the SUR method and the structural simultaneous-equation method were used to show how the interrelationships among different financial-policy variables can be more effectively taken into account. In addition, it is also shown that financial planning and forecasting models can also be incorporated with the environment model and the management model to perform business-policy decisions.

Problem Set

1. Discuss the basic concepts of simultaneous econometric models. Also how can accounting information be used in the econometric approach to do financial planning and forecasting?
2. Briefly discuss the use of econometric models to deal with dynamic capital-budgeting decisions. How can these kinds of capital-budgeting decisions be useful to the financial manager?
3. Why is the SUR Estimation Method needed in some financial analysis and planning decisions?
4. Briefly compare programming versus simultaneous versus econometric financial models. Which seems better for use in financial planning?
5. How should a firm utilize financial-planning models in setting its business policies?
6. Use the Johnson & Johnson financial data, as listed in Table 26.B.6.A and 26.B.6.B in the Appendix of this chapter to verify, step-by-step, the OLS estimated empirical results of Table 26.B.7A.

Appendix 26.A. Instrumental Variables and Two-Stages Least Squares

Let us assume that each of the independent variables in the linear regression model was uncorrelated with the true error term. If this assumption does not hold, then the estimated slope will not necessarily be unbiased. If the sample slope estimator is equal to the population slope estimator, then this sample slope estimate is an unbiased estimator. There are three instances when independent variables may be correlated with the associated error term:

1. One or more of the independent variables is measured with error.
2. One or more of the independent variables is determined in part (through one or more separate equations) by the dependent variable.
3. One or more of the independent variables is a lagged dependent in a model which the error term is serially correlated.

All three of these cases appear in empirical finance research.

There exist error-in-variable problems in the estimation of systematic risk and in the estimation of the relative effect of dividends and retained earnings on the price of common stocks. There are simultaneous equation problems in estimating the joint determination of financial ratios and in estimating the cost of capital. There exist serial correlation problems in estimating the dynamic ratio-adjustment process, and in estimating partial adjustment coefficients in the dividend decision model. All these problems can be resolved by the instrumental variable, two-stage least squares, or modified instrumental variable technique of estimation.

26.A.1. *Errors-In-Variable Problem*

In Chapter 7, we used the market model to estimate systematic risk. The market model is defined as:

$$R_{j,t} = A_j + B_j R_{m,t} + \varepsilon_t, \tag{26.A.1}$$

where $R_{j,t}$ and $R_{m,t}$ are the rates-of-return for the jth security in period t and the market rate-of-return in period t, respectively. As true market rate-of-return, $R_{m,t}$ is not directly observable, the equity market rate-of-return, $R^*_{m,t}$ is used as a proxy. Hence, there are proxies errors that result form the use of $R^*_{m,t}$ to replace $R_{m,t}$. The relationship between $R_{m,t}$ and $R_{m,t}$ can be defined as:

$$R^*_{m,t} = R_{m,t} + V_t, \tag{26.A.2}$$

where V_t is the proxy error (or measurement error), and

$$\text{Var}(R^*_{m,t}) = \text{Var}(R_{m,t} + V_t) = \sigma^2_m + \sigma^2_V. \tag{26.A.3}$$

Substituting Eq. (25.A.2) into Eq. (25.A.1) yields the actual empirical regression model shown in Eq. (25.A.4):

$$R_{j,t} = A_j + B_j R^*_{m,t} + \varepsilon^*_t, \tag{26.A.4}$$

where $\varepsilon^* = \varepsilon - B_j V_j$.

In Eq. (26.A.4), $\text{Cov}[R^*_{m,t}, \varepsilon^*_t] = -B_j\sigma^2_V$; that is, the independent variable $R^*_{m,t}$ is correlated with the error terms. Therefore, the least-squares estimates of regression parameters will be biased. In addition, this implies that the standard least-squares slope estimates are not reliable systematic risk measures for investment analysis and financial management.

Based upon the OLS estimate for $B1/2j$ derived in Appendix 2.A of Chapter 2, we have

$$\begin{aligned}\hat{B}_j &= \frac{\text{Cov}(R^*_{m,t}, R_{jt})}{\text{Var}(R^*_{m,t})} = \frac{\text{Cov}(R_{m,t} + V_t, \alpha_j + B_j R_{m,t} + \varepsilon_t)}{\text{Var}(R_{m,t}) + \text{Var}(V_t)} \\ &= \frac{B_j \text{Cov}(R_{m,t}, R_{m,t}) + \text{Cov}(V_t, \varepsilon_t)}{\text{Var}(R_{m,t}) + \text{Var}(V_t)} = \frac{B_j}{1 + \dfrac{\sigma^2_V}{\sigma^2_M}} \end{aligned} \tag{26.A.5}$$

if $\text{Cov}(V_{t1}, \varepsilon_t) = 0$.

Equation (26.A.5) shows that even if measurement errors are assumed to be independent of $R_{m,t}$ and ε_t, the estimated slope, b, will be biased downward; σ^2_V/σ^2_M is generally used to measure the quality of the data.

There are two generally accepted techniques for overcoming the problems of errors in variables: (1) grouping, and (2) instrumental variables. Black *et al.* (1972) and Lee (1976) use the grouping method to estimate beta coefficients. The grouping method can reduce measurement errors because the errors of individual observations tend to be cancelled out by their mutual independence. Hence, there is less measurement error in a group average than there would be if sample data were not grouped. In addition, Lee also suggests an instrumental variable method to estimate the beta coefficients.

26.A.2. *Instrumental Variables*

Instrumental variables can be defined from both the error-in-variable and the two-stage, least-squares estimation viewpoints. In classical error-in-variable problems, an instrumental variable is one that is highly correlated with the independent variable, but independent of the measurement error associated with independent variable, V_t, and the true regression error, ε_t. If Z_t is the instrumental variable to be used to reduce the measurement error associated with $R^*_{m,t}$ in estimated beta, as discussed in Section 26.A.1, then Z_t should be independent of both Z_t and ε_t. Lee (1976) uses the rank order (i.e., with values $1, 2, 3, \ldots, N$) as the variable Z for estimating

Beta coefficients. Taking the covariance of Z with respect to all variables in Eq. (26.A.1) yields:

$$\mathrm{Cov}(R_j, Z) = B_j \mathrm{Cov}(R_m, Z) + \mathrm{Cov}(Z, \varepsilon). \tag{26.A.6}$$

If $\mathrm{Cov}[Z, V] = \mathrm{Cov}[Z, \varepsilon]$, then:

$$\hat{B}_j = \frac{\mathrm{Cov}(R_j, Z)}{\mathrm{Cov}(R_m^*, Z)} = \frac{\mathrm{Cov}(R_j, Z)}{\mathrm{Cov}(R_m, Z)}. \tag{26.A.7}$$

Here $\hat{B}_j$ is a consistent estimator of B_j. Note that this method is sometimes called the "covariance" method of estimating beta.

In estimating the parameters of simultaneous equation system, a two-stage, least-squares estimator is generally an instrumental variable estimably more than a single equation regression can capture. Specifically, seldom is a variable determined by a single relationship (equation). Normally, a variable determined simultaneously with many other variables in a whole system of simultaneous equations. For example, the current ratio is determined simultaneously with the leverage ratio, the activity ratio, and the profitability ratio, as discussed earlier.

Using a two-equation system to serve as an example to discuss identification problems, we have

$$Y_1 = A_0 + A_1 Y_2 + E_1, \tag{26.A.8a}$$

$$Y_2 = B_0 + B_1 Y_1 + B_2 Z_1 + E_2; \tag{26.A.8b}$$

$$Y_1 = A_0 + A_1 Y_2 + A_2 Z_2 + E_1, \tag{26.A.9a}$$

$$Y_2 = B_0 + B_1 Y_1 + B_2 Z_1 + E_2; \tag{26.A.9b}$$

$$Y_1 = A_0 + A_1 Y_2 + A_2 Z_2 + A_3 Z_3 + E_1 Y, \tag{26.A.10a}$$

$$Y_2 = B_0 + B_1 Y_1 + B_2 Z_1 + E_2. \tag{26.A.10b}$$

Equations (26.A.8), (26.A.9), and (26.A.10) are three different simultaneous equation systems. Y_1 and Y_2 are endogenous variables determined within the system of equations, while $Z_1 Z_2$, and Z_3 are exogenous variables and E_1 and E_2 are residual terms. There are two methods to distinguish between the endogenous and exogenous variables. Conceptually, the exogenous variables, $Z_1 Z_2$, and Z_3, are determined outside this system of equations. They can also be referred to as predetermined variables. The essential point is that their values are determined elsewhere and are not influenced by Y_1, Y_2, E_1 or E_2. On the other hand, Y_1 and Y_2 are jointly dependent, or endogenous, variables: their values are determined within the model, and thus they are influenced $Z_1 Z_2, Z_3, E_1$ and E_2 Statistically, Y_2 and E_1 and Y_1 and E_2 are dependent. Therefore, they face the error-in-variable problem (or simultaneous equation bias) when the ordinary least-squares (OLS) method is used to estimate the parameters of the model. The exogenous variables, $Z_1 Z_2$, and Z_3, and the error terms, E_1 and E_2, are statistically independent.

A requirement for identifying an equation is that the number of exogenous variables that are excluded from the equation (K) must be at least equal to the number of endogenous variables that are included on the right-hand side of that equation (H). The equations above are defined as follows:

1. In Eqs. (26.A.8a), (26.A.9a), (26.A.9b), and (26.A.10a), $K = H$. These are "exactly identified" equations.
2. In Eq. (26.A.8b), $K < H$. Equation (26.A.8b) is an "under identified" equation.
3. In Eq. (26.A.10b), $K > H$. Equation (26.A.10b) is an "over identified" equation.

In an under identified equation, the related regression parameters cannot be statistically estimated. If an equation is either exactly identified or over identified, the instrumental variable and the two-stage, least-squares (2SLS) technique can be used to statistically estimate the related regression parameters. Johnston and Dinardo (1996) has shown that 2SLS and instrumental-variable techniques are equivalent procedures, on the condition that the first stage system and on the condition that the instrument used in the instrumental-variable procedure is the fitted value of the first-stage regression.

26.A.3. *Two-Stage, Least-Square*

Equations (26.A.10a) and (26.A.10b) will serve as an example in the discussion of the 2SLS estimation procedure.

Stage 1: Use OLS to estimate the following two reduced-form equations:

$$Y_1 = C_0 + C_1 Z_1 + C_2 Z_2 + C_3 Z_3 + E_1, \tag{26.A.11a}$$

$$Y_2 = D_0 + D_1 Z_1 + D_2 Z_2 + D_3 Z_3 + E_2. \tag{26.A.11b}$$

Stage 2: Use OLS to estimate the following structural equations:

$$Y_1 = A_0 + A_1\hat{Y}_2 + A_2Z_2 + A_3Z_3 + E_1, \qquad (26.A.10'a)$$

$$Y_2 = B_0 + B_1\hat{Y}_1 + B_2Z_1 + E_2, \qquad (26.A.10'b)$$

where $\hat{Y}_1$ and $\hat{Y}_2$ are the estimates of Y_1 and Y_2.

The stochastic components associated with the error terms E_1 and E_2 have been purged in Stage 1. The estimated parameters, $\hat{C}_0, \hat{C}_1, \hat{C}_2, \hat{C}_3$, $\hat{D}_0, \hat{D}_1, \hat{D}_2$ and $\hat{D}_3$, are reduced-form parameters, while the estimated parameters, $\hat{A}_0, \hat{A}_1, \hat{A}_2, \hat{A}_3, \hat{B}_0, \hat{B}_1$ and $\hat{B}_2$ are structural parameters. Johnston and Dinardo (1996) has used the relationship between the structural parameters and reduced-form parameters to discuss the identification problem. An equation is unidentified if there is no way of estimating all the structural parameters from the reduced-form parameters. Furthermore, an equation is exactly identified if a unique value is obtainable for some parameters.

The 2SLS estimating method is used by Modigliani and Miller (1966) to reduce the measurement errors of accounting earnings, in estimating the cost of capital for the electric utility industry. The simultaneous current ratio and leverage ratio determination process was defined in Chapter 2 Eq. (2.9), and was estimated by using Johnson & Johnson's ratio data. The first-stage regression results associated with Eqs. (26.A.11a) and (26.A.11b), in terms of Johnson & Johnson's current ratio and leverage ratio, are:

$$\begin{aligned} Y_1 &= -0.2399 + 0.8198Z_1 - 1.9004Z_1, \quad R^2 = 0.3449, \\ &\quad (0.1012) \quad (0.2802) \qquad (1.245) \end{aligned} \qquad (26.A.12a)$$

$$\begin{aligned} Y_2 &= 0.0746 - 0.1133Z_1 + 0.7849Z_2, \quad R^2 = 0.4240, \\ &\quad (0.0195)\ (0.0541) \qquad (0.2405) \end{aligned} \qquad (26.A.12b)$$

where the digits below the regression coefficients are standard errors of estimates, and Z_1 and Z_2 represent the firm's current-ratio and leverage-ratio deviations from the related industry average in previous period.

Based upon Eqs. (26.A.12a) and (26.A.12b), the estimated current ratio and leverage ratio for Johnson & Johnson Corporation can be estimated. These estimated endogenous variables are then used in the structural equations, as indicated in Eqs. (26.A.10′a) and (26.A.10′b) to obtain the results of second-stage regressions. The second-stage regression results associated with Johnson & Johnson's current and leverage ratios are listed in Table 2.10 in Chapter 2.

Reference for Appendix 26.A

Black, F, MC Jensen, and M Scholes (1972). The capital asset pricing model: Some empirical tests. In *Studies in the Theory of Capital Markets*, MC Jensen (ed.) pp. 79–121. New York: Praeger.

Greene, WH (2011). *Econometric Analysis*, 7th ed. Englewood Cliffs, NJ: Prentice Hall Inc.

Hamilton, JD (1994). *Time Series Analysis*, Princeton, NJ: Princeton University Press.

Johnston, J and J Dinardo (1996). *Econometrics Methods*, 4th ed. New York: McGraw-Hill.

Lee, CF (1976). Performance measure, systematic risk, and errors-in-variable estimation method. *Journal of Economics and Business*, 122–127.

Miller, MH and F Modigliani (1966). Some estimates of the cost of capital for the electric utility industry, 1954–57. *American Economic Review*, 333–391.

Appendix 26.B. Johnson & Johnson as A Case Study

26.B.1. *Introduction*

The purpose of this appendix is to use Johnson & Johnson's (J&J) annual data as an example to show how Spies' model can be use to analyze an individual firm's dynamic capital-budget decisions. First, J&J operations are briefly reviewed. Secondly, both the balance sheet and the income statement for J&J during the period of 1997–2006 are used to evaluate its financial performance. Thirdly, both the endogenous and the exogenous variables needed to estimate the equation system. Implications of these regression results are also briefly analyzed.

26.B.2. *Study of the Company'S Operations*

Johnson & Johnson was incorporated in New Jersey on November 10, 1887. The company is engaged in the manufacture and sale of a broad range of products in the health care and other fields in many countries of the world. J&J's worldwide operations are divided into three industry segments: Consumer, Pharmaceutical, and Medical Devices and Diagnostics.

- **Consumer**

  Consumer products encompass baby and child care items, skin care products, oral care products, wound care products, women's health care products.

- **Pharmaceuticals**

  The pharmaceutical sector includes products in the following areas: anti-fungal, anti-infective, cardiovascular, contraceptive, dermatology, gastrointestinal, hematology, immunology, neurology, oncology, virology, pain management, psychotropic, and urology fields.

- **Medical Devices and Diagnostics**

  The Medical Devices and Diagnostics segment includes suture and mechanical wound closure products, surgical equipment and devices, wound management and infection prevention products, interventional and diagnostic cardiology products, diagnostic equipment and supplies, joint replacements and disposable contact lenses.

Table 26.B.1 shows that all three divisions of the company are quite profitable and its product lines well diversified. One should also note that the international division contributes as mush as the domestic division, making the company less susceptible to the ups and downs of the U.S. economy.

Research activities are important to J&J's business and account for about 14% of sales. The company employs about 122,000 persons worldwide engaged in the research and development, manufacture and sale of a broad range of products in the health care field.

26.B.3. *Analysis of the Company'S Financial Performance*

Tables 26.B.2, 26.B.3(A), and 26.B.3(B) show J&J's balance sheet and common-size income statements for the period 1997 to 2006. Tables 26.B.4

Table 26.B.1. Sales in Different Segment.

	2003		2004		2005		2006	
	Sales	Profits	Sales	Profits	Sales	Profits	Sales	Profits
Division	(%)		(%)		(%)		(%)	
Consumer	18	13	18	11	18	12	18	10
Pharmaceuticals	47	56	47	58	44	48	44	48
Medical Devices and Diagnostics	36	31	36	31	38	40	38	43
Total	100	100	100	100	100	100	100	100
Domestic	60		59		56		56	
International	40		41		44		44	
Total	100		100		100		100	

Table 26.B.2. Balance Sheet.

	1997	1998	1999	2000	2001	2002	2003	2004	2005	2006
Asset	(Figures in Million $)									
1 Account receivables	3,329	3,661	4,233	4,464	4,630	5,399	6,574	6,831	7,010	8,712
2 Inventories	2,516	2,853	3,095	2,842	2,992	3,303	3,588	3,744	3,959	4,889
3 Other Current Assets	1,819	2,040	1,993	2,400	2,879	3,089	3,310	3,861	4,287	5,290
4 Total Current Assets $(1+2+3)$	10,563	11,132	13,200	15,450	18,473	19,266	22,995	27,320	31,394	22,975
5 Gross Fixed Assets	9,444	10,024	11,046	11,248	12,458	14,314	17,052	18,664	19,716	24,028
6 Less: Depreciation	3,634	3,784	4,327	4,277	4,739	5,604	7,206	8,228	8,886	10,984
7 Net Fixed Assets $(5-6)$	5,810	6,240	6,719	6,971	7,719	8,710	9,846	10,436	10,830	13,044
8 Other Assets	5,080	8,839	9,244	8,900	12,296	12,580	15,422	15,561	15,801	34,537
9 TOTAL ASSETS $(4+7+8)$	21,453	26,211	29,163	31,321	38,488	40,556	48,263	53,317	58,025	70,556
Liabilities										
10 Common equity	12,359	13,590	16,213	18,808	24,233	22,697	26,869	31,813	37,871	39,318
11 Preferred stock	0	0	0	0	0	0	0	0	0	0
12 Shareholder's Equity $(10+11)$	12,359	13,590	16,213	18,808	24,233	22,697	26,869	31,813	37,871	39,318
13 Current Liabilities	5,283	8,162	7,454	7,140	8,044	11,449	13,448	13,927	12,635	19,161
14 Long-Term Liabilities	1,126	1,269	2,450	2,037	2,217	2,022	2,955	2,565	2,017	2,014
15 Other Liabilities	2,685	3,190	3,046	3,336	3,994	4,388	4,991	5,012	5,502	10,063
16 TOTAL LIABILITIES	9,094	12,621	12,950	12,513	14,255	17,859	21,394	21,504	20,154	31,238
17 WORKING-CAPITAL $(4-13)$	5,280	2,970	5,746	8,310	10,429	7,817	9,547	13,393	18,759	3,814

Table 26.B.3(A). Common-size income statement ($ in millions).

	1997		1998		1999		2000		2001	
	$	%	$	%	$	%	$	%	$	%
1 Total Sales	22629	100	23657	100	27471	100	29139	100	33004	100
2 Cost of Goods Sold	6085	26.89	6190	26.17	6998	25.47	7346	25.21	7931	24.03
3 Gross Profit (1 − 2)	16544	73.11	17467	73.83	20473	74.53	21793	74.79	25073	75.97
Less: Expenses:										
4 Operating Expenses	10855	47.97	11176	47.24	13103	47.70	13801	47.36	15583	47.22
5 Interest Expenses	160	0.71	181	0.77	278	1.01	242	0.83	248	0.75
6 Total Expenses (4 + 5)	11015	48.68	11357	48.01	13381	48.71	14043	48.19	15831	47.97
7 Operating Profit (3 − 6)	5529	24.43	6110	25.83	7092	25.82	7750	26.60	9242	28.00
8 Depreciation	1067	4.72	1246	5.27	1444	5.26	1515	5.20	1605	4.86
9 Other Income	114	0.50	−595	−2.52	105	0.38	387	1.33	261	0.79
10 Profit before tax (7 − 8 + 9)	4576	20.22	4269	18.05	5753	20.94	6622	22.73	7898	23.93
11 Tax	1273	5.63	1210	5.11	1586	5.77	1822	6.25	2230	6.76
12 Net Profit (10 − 11)	3303	14.60	3059	12.93	4167	15.17	4800	16.47	5668	17.17
13 Tax Rate (11/10)	28%		28%		28%		28%		28%	
14 Dividend	1137	5.02	1305	5.52	1479	5.38	1724	5.92	2047	6.20
15 Retained Earnings (12 − 14)	2166	9.57	1754	7.41	2688	9.78	3076	10.56	3621	10.97
16 Payout Ratio (14/12)	34%		43%		35%		36%		36%	

Table 26.B.3(B). Common-size income statement ($ in millions).

	2002		2003		2004		2005		2006	
	$	%	$	%	$	%	$	%	$	%
1 Total Sales	36298	160	41862	177	47348	172	50434	173	53194	161
2 Cost of Goods Sold	8785	38.82	10307	43.57	11298	41.13	11861	40.70	12880	39.03
3 Gross Profit (1 − 2)	27513	121.58	31555	133.39	36050	131.23	38573	132.38	40314	122.15
Less: Expenses:										
4 Operating Expenses	16173	71.47	18815	79.53	21063	76.67	23189	79.58	24558	74.41
5 Interest Expenses	258	1.14	315	1.33	323	1.18	165	0.57	181	0.55
6 Total Expenses (4 + 5)	16431	72.61	19130	80.86	21386	77.85	23354	80.15	24739	74.96
7 Operating Profit (3 − 6)	11082	48.97	12425	52.52	14664	53.38	15219	52.23	15575	47.19
8 Depreciation	1662	7.34	1869	7.90	2124	7.73	2093	7.18	2177	6.60
9 Other Income	−129	−0.57	−248	−1.05	298	1.08	530	1.82	1189	3.60
10 Profit before tax (7 − 8 + 9)	9291	41.06	10308	43.57	12838	46.73	13656	46.87	14587	44.20
11 Tax	2694	11.91	3111	13.15	4329	15.76	3245	11.14	3534	10.71
12 Net Profit (10 − 11)	6597	29.15	7197	30.42	8509	30.97	10411	35.73	11053	33.49
13 Tax Rate (11/10)	29%		30%		34%		24%		24%	
14 Dividend	2381	10.52	2746	11.61	3251	11.83	3793	13.02	4267	12.93
15 Retained Earnings (12 − 14)	4216	18.63	4451	18.81	5258	19.14	6618	22.71	6786	20.56
16 Payout Ratio (14/12)	36%		38%		38%		36%		39%	

Table 26.B.4. Ratio analysis.

	1997	1998	1999	2000	2001	2002	2003	2004	2005	2006
Current Ratio	2.00	1.36	1.77	2.16	2.30	1.68	1.71	1.96	2.48	1.20
Quick Ratio	1.52	1.01	1.36	1.77	1.92	1.39	1.44	1.69	2.17	0.94
Sales/Receivables	6.80	6.46	6.49	6.53	7.13	6.72	6.37	6.93	7.19	6.11
Sales/Inventories	8.99	8.29	8.88	10.25	11.03	10.99	11.67	12.65	12.74	10.88
Debt/Equity %	9.11	9.34	15.11	10.83	9.15	8.91	11.00	8.06	5.33	5.12
TREND ANALYSIS (1997=100)										
Sales Trend	100.0	104.5	121.4	128.8	145.8	160.4	185.0	209.2	222.9	235.1
Net Profit Trend	100.0	92.6	126.2	145.3	171.6	199.7	217.9	257.6	315.2	334.6
Working-Capital Trend	100.0	56.3	108.8	157.4	197.5	148.0	180.8	253.7	355.3	72.2
Gross Fixed Assets Trend	100.0	106.1	117.0	119.1	131.9	151.6	180.6	197.6	208.8	254.4
Net Worth Trend	100.0	110.0	131.2	152.2	196.1	183.6	217.4	257.4	306.4	318.1
Total Assets Trend	100.0	122.2	135.9	146.0	179.4	189.0	225.0	248.5	270.5	328.9
Dividends Trend	100.0	114.8	130.1	151.6	180.0	209.4	241.5	285.9	333.6	375.3
Price/Earnings Multiple										
Average for the year	24.15	27.48	31.03	25.65	37.63	24.95	19.48	18.03	18.38	16.72
At year-end	26.67	30.72	30.78	30.19	30.31	23.25	19.13	20.46	17.07	17.75
Price Range										
High	66.94	89.00	106.13	105.06	103.10	65.49	58.67	63.76	69.40	69.10
Low	49.75	64.00	78.06	67.38	50.00	41.85	48.73	49.50	60.04	56.80

Table 26.B.5. Dupont analysis.

	1997	1998	1999	2000	2001	2002	2003	2004	2005
Sales/Total Assets	1.05	0.90	0.94	0.93	0.86	0.90	0.87	0.89	0.87
Gross Profit/Sales %	0.73	0.74	0.75	0.75	0.76	0.76	0.75	0.76	0.76
EBIT/Gross Profit %	0.28	0.29	0.29	0.30	0.31	0.35	0.34	0.36	0.34
EBIT/Total Assets %	0.22	0.19	0.20	0.21	0.20	0.24	0.23	0.24	0.23
Net Profit/EBIT %	0.71	0.61	0.70	0.74	0.72	0.68	0.66	0.66	0.78
Total Assets/Shareholders' Equity	1.74	1.93	1.80	1.67	1.59	1.79	1.80	1.68	1.53
Net Profit/Shareholders' Equity	0.27	0.23	0.26	0.26	0.23	0.29	0.27	0.27	0.27
Retained Earnings/Net Profit %	0.66	0.57	0.65	0.64	0.64	0.64	0.62	0.62	0.64
Retained Earnings/Shareholders' Equity %	0.18	0.13	0.17	0.16	0.15	0.19	0.17	0.17	0.17

Formulas used:
(Sales/Total Assets)×(Gross Profit/Sales)% × (EBIT/Gross Profit) = (EBIT/Total Assets)% (EBIT/Total Assets)% × (Net Profit/EBIT) × (total Assets/Shareholders' Equity) = (Net Profit/Shareholders' Equity) (Net Profit/Shareholders' Equity)% × (Retained Earnings/Net Profit) = (Retained Earnings/Shareholders' Equity)%.

and 26.B.5 analyze the company's performance as reflected in key ratios, trends, and the Dupont Analysis.

As can be seen from Table 26.B.4, the company has a fairly comfortable current ratio and quick ratio. However, since 2006 the ratios have been declining slightly. On examining the receivables and inventory-turnover ratios, one notes that the receivables turnover ratio has been increasing over the same period, implying that J&J is shortening the periods of credit to generate sales. Inventory-turnover has fluctuated between 8.3 times and 12.7 times over the 10-year period. In other words, the average raw-materials and finished-goods inventory ranged between one to one-half months' sales, which shows that the firm does not carry a high inventory of slow-moving stocks; it also holds sufficient inventory to avoid stock-outs. On the overall, J&J seems to have a fairly comfortable working-capital and short-term liquidity position

The long-term leverage position can be analyzed by examining the debt-equity ratio. From Table 26.A.4, one can see that, while this ratio has been rising since 1999, it is trying to lower its financial leverage which is around 5% in 2006. While this shows very low financial risk, it could also mean that the company is not taking advantage of financial leverage, especially since the company does not have much business risk, as will be seen in the Dupont analysis.

An analysis of the various trends show that sales have grown over twice and the growth has been very steady over the period. In fact, sales have been growing ever since 1950. Profits have kept pace with the sales growth, which is a healthy sign. Sales have grown faster than gross investment and working-capital, implying that J&J is utilizing its capacity and working-capital funds better. A cursory glance of the balance sheet shows that the lower working-capital growth is due to the increase in current liabilities, which grew 4 times since 1997. Since the company has the funds to repay its account payables if necessary, this shows that J&J's creditors are granting it longer periods of credit, showing increasing faith in the company's stability.

Net worth (shareholders' equity), sales and profits have grown similarly, and this is because the company has been paying stable rate of dividends as reflected in the payout ratio in Table 26.B.3 and the dividend trend in Table 26.B.4. The formulas at the end of Table 26.B.5 show that the Dupont analysis is divided into three sections:

1. Operating performance as reflected in the asset turnover, gross profit margin, and operating leverage,
2. Financial efficiency as reflected in the financial leverage and assets/equity ratios,
3. Growth as shown in the retention ratio.

Asset turnover has been decreasing during 1997–2006. Gross profit margin has been fairly steady. However, the operating leverage as reflected in the EBIT/Gross profit ratio has been increasing since 1973. This has been offset by the decrease in asset turnover, resulting in a steady return on investment (EBIT/Total assets).

The company's Net Profit/EBIT ratio has been improving and this is because of decreasing debt leverage as described earlier. The assets/equity ratio has fluctuated slightly over the period. The combined impact of both these ratios resulted in J&J's return on equity (net profit/shareholders' equity) does not change too much in the last 10 years. The company's retention ratio has also been fairly stable, as was also seen earlier. The overall effect is that the ratio of retained earnings to equity has been fairly steady over the last 10 years, with a slight fall in 1998 and 2001.

The combined impact of all three aspects shows that the company has a very steady operating performance with improving financial efficiency.

The final aspect of the analysis of the company's financial performance is a comparison with the industry and the stock market as a whole. Value Line's comparison of J&J's rankings with the market as a whole is given in the following table:

Category	Rank
Timeliness	3
Safety	1
Financial Strength	A++
Stock-Price Stability	95
Earnings Predictability	100
Beta	0.60

Note: Based upon Value Line report on November 30th, 2007.

From the above study of J&J's operations and performance, one can see that the company has an excellent track record, especially as evidenced by the industry and overall rankings shown above. Further, the hospital-supplies industry to which J&J belongs is a very steady industry and not affected by cyclical influences and other factors like changes in consumer's tastes and preferences. While research and development is an important area in this industry, the technological developments are not so rapid to make this industry as volatile as some others, like the electronics industry.

This historical study has been restricted mainly to the last 10 years because the observations made in this section will be used to supplement the analysis made using Spies' model. One should also note that many of the comments made on J&J's performance in the 2000's were also applicable to earlier time periods.

26.B.4. *Variables and Time Horizon*

The variables used in the empirical testing of the model were exactly the same as those used in Spies' model. The following section explains the methodology followed in computing the various variables used in the model.

Dividends (DIV). Only equity dividend was considered in the computation of this variable. Preferred dividend was paid only up to 1955, and therefore, for consistency's sake, preferred dividend was deducted from cash flow for the period and not added to equity dividends. Also, stock dividends were not considered in the computation.

Short-Term Investment (IST). Short-term investment is the net change in the corporation's holdings of current and other short-term assets.

Long-Term Investments (ILT). Long-term investments is defined as the change in gross long-term fixed assets and non-current marketable securities.

Debt Financing (DF). This component is simply the net change in the corporation's liabilities, both long-term and current.

Equity Financing (EQF). The change in stockholders' equity, minus the amount due to retained earnings, was used 'as the definition of equity financing, Though no new shares were issued to the public over the period studied, adjustments were made for stock splits, changes in common stock in treasury, and stock issued to employees under options exercised and stock compensation agreements.

Cash Flow (*Y*). This variable was calculated by adding depreciation to net profit for the period and adjusting for other non-cash entries in the retained-earnings statement as well as for preferred dividends paid.

Corporate Bond Rate (RCB). This variable was not included in the model, since the corporate bond rate is not available in Compustat.

Debt–Equity Leverage (DEL). The debt–equity ratio at the beginning of each period was computed for this variable.

Dividend–Price Ratio (RDP). For this variable, the average dividend–price ratio for the period was used.

Rate-of-Return (*R*). The ratio of the change in earnings to long-term investment in the previous period was taken as a measure of the rate-of-return on investments.

Capacity Utilized (CU). Since J&J is a multi-product company, the ratio of sales to gross fixed assets was taken as a proxy for the capacity utilized.

Time Horizon. Annual data was used in the empirical study and the time period covered was 1950–1979.

Tables 26.B.6(A) and 26.B.6(B) list the data collected for the variables above. The data for 1969 has been omitted from the study because J&J consolidated its accounts that year, to include its foreign subsidiaries and this distorted the sources and uses of funds for that year.

Table 26.B.6(A). Input data.

Year	DIV	IST	ILT	DF	EQF	Year	DIV	IST	ILT	DF	EQF
1949	2.52	−8.96	2.24	−7.97	−5.49	1978	100.72	221.70	140.88	140.82	23.41
1950	3.98	7360.00	13.40	12.96	−4.79	1979	122.20	216.69	274.90	205.77	55.96
1951	2.31	3.20	1.50	−0.84	−0.28	1980	136.90	252.83	215.72	186.09	18.66
1952	2.09	5.70	−0.80	1.78	−2.96	1981	158.60	231.20	246.70	219.10	−50.20
1953	3.45	2.90	−0.50	−3.20	0.14	1982	182.40	50.90	338.27	117.60	−19.43
1954	3.46	2.40	2.60	0.10	−1.10	1983	204.60	204.00	47.93	24.90	−57.37
1955	3.47	6.50	1.08	1.60	−1.74	1984	219.90	56.60	23.28	174.40	−389.13
1956	3.47	−2.00	14.48	1.90	1.12	1985	233.20	382.80	98.66	134.80	38.42
1957	3.81	7.80	0.61	−1.62	0.66	1986	244.70	305.10	160.27	1308.30	−611.53
1958	3.61	6.40	2.84	−0.32	0.62	1987	278.00	70.40	370.04	8.50	105.84
1959	4.74	9.00	8.71	2.08	4.92	1988	327.00	231.00	355.00	555.00	−629.00
1960	5.93	4.70	8.68	2.89	0.64	1989	373.00	273.00	432.00	155.00	−64.00
1961	5.95	4.90	12.62	2.30	4.86	1990	436.00	888.00	697.00	835.00	45.00
1962	5.98	4.60	6.30	−0.88	−0.22	1991	513.00	269.00	706.00	281.00	−222.00
1963	6.63	11.00	5.78	2.54	0.20	1992	587.00	490.00	903.00	1826.00	−898.00
1964	7.19	8.40	8.00	3.92	−5.11	1993	659.00	−206.00	355.00	−39.00	−731.00
1965	8.71	27.30	22.30	23.80	3.45	1994	727.00	1463.00	485.00	1872.00	275.00
1966	9.85	3.60	19.90	5.29	−8.16	1995	827.00	1258.00	400.00	282.00	347.00
1967	11.11	28.70	14.60	6.53	6.71	1996	974.00	1432.00	548.00	346.00	−122.00
1968	11.79	43.30	10.60	10.79	5.25	1997	1137.00	1193.00	96.00	−80.00	−643.00
1969	15.52	26.78	21.68	1.67	11.00	1998	1305.00	569.00	241.00	3527.00	−523.00
1970	18.89	174.78	50.98	82.80	77.38	1999	1479.00	2068.00	522.00	329.00	−65.00
1971	24.02	88.73	35.47	34.94	10.70	2000	1724.00	2250.00	223.00	−437.00	−481.00
1972	25.14	114.70	37.28	40.89	14.98	2001	2047.00	3023.00	2323.00	1742.00	1804.00
1973	29.88	77.46	131.12	72.13	16.99	2002	2381.00	793.00	1106.00	3604.00	−5752.0
1974	41.79	110.86	105.40	85.59	11.17	2003	2746.00	3729.00	1685.00	3535.00	−279.00
1975	49.18	111.48	34.35	−5.65	16.84	2004	3251.00	4325.00	426.00	110.00	−314.00
1976	61.01	120.36	58.86	28.11	6.73	2005	3793.00	4074.00	301.00	−1350.0	−560.00
1977	81.77	212.45	76.63	111.94	11.59	2006	4267.00	−8419.0	4437.00	11084.0	−5339.0

Table 26.B.6(B). Input data.

Year	Y	DEL	RDP	R	CU	Year	Y	DEL	RDP	R	CU
1950	163562	8.05	1.63	30.87	2.778	1979	230.843	44.6637	2.52366	40.1784	4.4436
1951	3.23	34.2649	1.61798	18.3521	4.7892	1980	262	47.3051	2.23058	34.8091	4.16334
1952	2.94	35.0809	1.70213	17.8384	5.04737	1981	67.9	51.1294	2.29414	34.2099	4.04238
1953	3.7	29.5074	2.249	19.8	5.33244	1982	−61.5	50.3702	1.95466	29.339	3.65097
1954	3.99	28.1263	2.12903	21.2584	5.13165	1983	61	47.4146	2.62997	25.0535	3.58043
1955	5.34	28.0099	2.10191	24.0127	5.55309	1984	16	54.8914	3.2526	25.7282	3.55951
1956	5.92	27.0749	2.20736	26.8784	4.59888	1985	293.098	52.0519	2.4228	30.3358	3.49003
1957	4.88	23.5878	2.0059	21.0175	4.74863	1986	216.9	108.085	2.09524	15.5301	3.65439
1958	3.52	21.6554	1.22371	19.9298	4.7102	1987	−58	87.8336	2.15025	36.5037	3.56089
1959	5.75	20.7863	1.32231	23.3557	4.9703	1988	−93	103.226	2.25551	36.727	3.61011
1960	5.11	21.2534	1.33779	20.8498	4.55423	1989	−77	90.9113	1.88632	35.9827	3.42832
1961	5.19	20.6873	1.03627	19.8683	4.59637	1990	374	94	1.82578	33.2364	3.45919
1962	5.77	18.9179	1.36519	18.7054	4.63494	1991	−237	86.8646	1.34498	35.324	3.39433
1963	7.08	18.8653	1.07843	19.9074	4.38462	1992	156	129.82	1.76238	21.2722	3.34216
1964	10.99	19.5993	1.07383	22.902	4.459	1993	−373	119.864	2.2507	31.1053	3.20881
1965	16.34	27.4276	0.8418	26.7298	4.47358	1994	264	119.994	2.06393	32.8852	3.20448
1966	20.84	27.5443	0.96491	26.1516	4.42311	1995	565	97.6009	1.49708	36.492	3.62625
1967	23.793	26.3234	0.67215	25.9867	4.13365	1996	810	84.6622	1.47739	41.3314	3.82587
1968	30.63	26.1589	0.61033	28.6994	4.33723	1997	742	73.582	1.29032	43.8471	3.89484
1969	37.023	22.9665	0.47222	31.9695	4.25344	1998	−826	92.8698	1.15648	40.097	3.79119
1970	50.964	32.3613	0.59649	40.7517	4.18981	1999	369	79.8742	1.1689	52.9479	4.08855
1971	65.113	33.3743	0.43655	39.7339	4.23275	2000	1048	66.5302	1.18025	57.1973	4.18003
1972	78.222	33.9194	0.34268	41.3766	4.37299	2001	−520	58.8247	1.18443	65.7922	4.27568
1973	97.229	36.9335	0.46563	45.0989	4.41428	2002	−864	78.6844	1.48017	60.3127	4.16739
1974	100.586	40.657	0.89645	35.1249	4.14812	2003	2483	79.6234	1.79055	59.7559	4.25168
1975	115.213	34.8153	0.94708	32.5037	4.2114	2004	3826	67.595	1.72658	61.9783	4.53699
1976	127.834	32.934	1.34615	34.2361	4.43747	2005	6852	53.2175	2.12146	73.55	4.65688
1977	160.822	36.5578	1.8241	37.5442	4.46691	2006	−11972	79.4496	2.20388	76.4596	4.07804
1978	195.918	40.0712	2.30508	40.6681	4.43689						

26.B.5. *Model and Empirical Results*[2]

The model used in the empirical study was the regression model developed by Spies (1974). Following Eq. (26.B.6) of the text, the model is defined as

$$X_t = BX_{t-1} + CZ + U_t, \tag{26.B.1}$$

where

X_t is a 5×1 matrix with the following variables:

$X_t' = (\text{DIV}_t\ \text{IST}_t\ \text{ILT}_t\!-\text{DF}_t\!-\text{EQF}_t)$';

Z_t is a 6×1 matrix, which includes a constant (I) where

$Z_t' = (1\ \text{Y}_t\ \text{RDP}_t\ \text{DEL}_t\ \text{R}_t\ \text{CU}_t)$';

B is a $5\times$ matrix of coefficients and C is a 5×6 matrix of coefficients;

U_t is a 5×1 matrix which represents error terms.

Since annual data have been used, no dummy variables are used to remove seasonality.

The "sources-equals-uses" identity implies that $\Sigma_i X_{i,t} = Y_t$ must be true for every period t; here $X_{i,t}$ is defined as the ith variable in the X-matrix at period t. In order to incorporate this into the estimation procedure, the estimators must be restricted in such a way that, across equations, the coefficients of Y add up to 1, while the coefficients of the other exogenous variables add up to zero. Algebraically, these constraints can be stated as:

$$\sum_{i=1}^{5} \hat{c}_{i2} = 1 \quad \text{and} \quad \sum_{i=1}^{5} \hat{b}_{ij} = \sum_{i=1}^{5} \hat{c}_{ik} = 0 \text{ for all } j \text{ and all } k \neq 2,$$

where b_{ij} is a coefficient in the B-matrix corresponding to the ith row and jth column and c_{ik} corresponds to the ith row and kth column in the C-matrix, and c_{i2} refers to the column for the variable Y_t as discussed in Section 25.3 of the text.

Equation (26.B.1) defines five multiple regressions, which are used to describe the behavior of five endogenous variables, DIV, IST, ILT, DF, and EQF. Exogenous variables for these multiple regressions are Y, DEL, RDP, R, and CU.

Based upon data listed in Tables 26.B.6(A) and 26.B.6(B), both OLS and constrained SUR methods are used to estimate the coefficients of five multiple regressions. OLS regression results are listed in Table 26.B.7(A) and the SUR results are listed in Table 26.B.7(B). There are 10 OLS

Table 26.B.7(A). OLS estimates for the period 1950–2006.

X	Intercept	$X_{1,t-1}$	$X_{2,t-1}$	$X_{3,t-1}$	$X_{4,t-1}$	$X_{5,t-1}$	Y	DEL	RDP	R	CU
$X_{1,t}$	−84.810	1.134*	0.002	0.027*	0.003	0.001	0.000	−0.033	−1.897	0.805*	14.757
	(−1.77)	(131.34)	(0.83)	(2.35)	(0.65)	(0.31)	(1.17)	(−0.18)	(−0.41)	(2.00)	(1.67)
$X_{2,t}$	−4229.844	−0.883	0.081	0.416	0.780*	−0.175	0.057*	10.515	−131.906	33.828	726.736
	(−1.35)	(−1.57)	(0.45)	(0.55)	(2.55)	(−0.63)	(5.22)	(0.90)	(−0.43)	(1.29)	(1.26)
$X_{3,t}$	313.367	0.520*	−0.021	0.132	−0.325*	−0.182	−0.002	2.256	−5.631	5.398	−110.324
	(0.30)	(2.74)	(−0.34)	(0.52)	(−3.15)	(−1.94)	(−0.61)	(0.57)	(−0.05)	(0.61)	(−0.57)
$X_{4,t}$	1646.386	1.663*	−0.140	0.691	−0.992*	−0.439	−0.004	7.099	−193.664	−27.856	−191.113
	(0.56)	(3.13)	(−0.82)	(0.97)	(−3.44)	(−1.67)	(−0.36)	(0.65)	(−0.67)	(−1.13)	(−0.35)
$X_{5,t}$	−1273.649	−0.908*	0.081	−1.610*	0.468*	−0.251	0.003	5.010	−28.205	21.725	147.348
	(−0.69)	(−2.74)	(0.76)	(−3.62)	(2.61)	(−1.54)	(0.47)	(0.73)	(−0.16)	(1.41)	(0.43)
Total	−602.846	0.382	−0.040	−0.074	−0.043	−0.193	0.040	4.821	−74.769	6.325	94.281

Table 26.B.7(B). Constrained SUR estimates for the period 1950–2006.

X	Intercept	$X_{1,t-1}$	$X_{2,t-1}$	$X_{3,t-1}$	$X_{4,t-1}$	$X_{5,t-1}$	Y	DEL	RDP	R	CU
$X_{1,t}$	−84.810	1.134*	0.002	0.027*	0.003	0.001	0.000	−0.033	−1.897	0.805*	14.757
	(−1.97)	(146.20)	(0.93)	(2.62)	(0.73)	(0.34)	(1.30)	(−0.20)	(−0.45)	(2.23)	(1.86)
$X_{2,t}$	−4229.844	−0.883	0.081	0.416	0.780*	−0.175	0.057*	10.515	−131.906	33.828	726.736
	(−1.50)	(−1.74)	(0.50)	(0.61)	(2.84)	(−0.70)	(5.81)	(1.00)	(−0.48)	(1.44)	(1.40)
$X_{3,t}$	313.367	0.520*	−0.021	0.132	−0.325*	−0.182*	−0.002	2.256	−5.631	5.398	−110.324
	(0.33)	(3.05)	(−0.38)	(0.57)	(−3.51)	(−2.16)	(−0.68)	(0.64)	(−0.06)	(0.68)	(−0.63)
$X_{4,t}$	1646.386	1.663*	−0.140	0.691	−0.992*	−0.439	−0.004	7.099	−193.664	−27.856	−191.113
	(0.62)	(3.48)	(−0.91)	(1.08)	(−3.83)	(−1.86)	(−0.40)	(0.72)	(−0.75)	(−1.25)	(−0.39)
$X_{5,t}$	−1273.649	−0.908*	0.081	−1.610*	0.468*	−0.251	0.003	5.010	−28.205	21.725	147.348
	(−0.77)	(−3.05)	(0.84)	(−4.03)	(2.90)	(−1.71)	(0.52)	(0.81)	(−0.17)	(1.57)	(0.48)
Total	−725.710	0.305	0.001	−0.069	−0.013	−0.209	0.011	4.969	−72.261	6.780	117.481

Table 26.B.7(C). Two Stage Least Square estimates for the period 1951–2006.

X	Intercept	$X_{1,t-1}$	$X_{2,t-1}$	$X_{3,t-1}$	$X_{4,t-1}$	$X_{5,t-1}$	Y	DEL	RDP	R	Intercept
$X_{1,t}$	−50.178	1.115	0.025	0.022	−0.004	−0.007	0.007	−0.010	−2.519	$X_{1,t}$	−50.178
	(−1.84)	(105.54)	(3.16)	(3.35)	(−1.46)	(−1.79)	(7.62)	(−0.10)	(−0.96)		(−1.84)
$X2t$	−1423.4	0.207	−0.279	0.233	0.119	−0.011	0.705	8.318	−189.484	$X2t$	−1423.4
	(−1.09)	(0.41)	(−0.75)	(0.74)	(0.88)	(−0.06)	(15.11)	(1.71)	(−1.50)		(−1.09)
$X3t$	−553.258	0.227	0.056	0.191	−0.123	−0.220	−0.200	2.890	11.709	$X3t$	−553.258
	(−0.93)	(0.98)	(0.33)	(1.33)	(−1.99)	(−2.68)	(−9.38)	(1.30)	(0.20)		(−0.93)
$X4t$	−902.203	1.838	−0.794	0.971	−0.424	−0.221	−0.568	7.221	−169.025	$X4t$	−902.203
	(−0.80)	(4.18)	(−2.45)	(3.55)	(−3.62)	(−1.42)	(−14.04)	(1.71)	(−1.31)		(−0.80)
$X5t$	−85.188	−1.476	0.790	−1.786	0.219	−0.505	0.253	5.688	−49.962	$X5t$	−85.188
	(−0.07)	(−2.99)	(2.17)	(−5.83)	(1.67)	(−2.89)	(5.58)	(1.20)	(−0.41)		(−0.07)
Total	−602.845	0.382	−0.040	−0.074	−0.043	−0.193	0.040	4.821	−79.856	Total	−602.845

*significant at the 10% level (cut-off point = 1.96).

regression-coefficient estimates that are significantly different from zero under 10% significance. However, there are 14 constrained SUR coefficient-estimates that are significantly different from zero under the same significance level. This implies that the efficiency of the constrained SUR method is higher than that of the OLS method. In addition, the results in Table 26.B.7(B) indicate that the empirical results for DIV_t, DF_t, and EQF_t are more significant than those for IST_t and ILT_t. If quarterly instead of annual data are used to estimate these five equations, we would expect that the performance of empirical results would improve substantially. Considering that OLS and SUR methods neglect information contained in the other equations, we use two-stage least squares method to estimate the coefficients of five multiple regressions. Similar to SUR method, Table 26.B.7(C) shows that the 2SLS results for DIV_t, DF_t, and EQF_t are more significant than the 2SLS results for IST_t and ILT_t.

Finally, Spies (1974) indicated that Eq. (26.B.1) can be used to predict X_t given Z_t, and Z_{t-1}. The model used to do one-period forecasting can be easily derived from Eq. (26.B.1) as

$$\begin{aligned} X_{t-1} &= BX_t + CZ_{t+1} + U_t \\ &= B^2X_{t-1} + BCZ_t + CZ_{t+1} + BU_t + U_{t-1}. \end{aligned} \tag{26.B.2}$$

The applications of Eq. (26.B.2) to forecast are left to students themselves by using the data in Tables 26.B.6(A) and 26.B.6(B).

Notes

1. Taggart (1977) argued that the stacking technique cannot allow for the possibility that balance-sheet interrelationship may enter through the error terms. Hsieh and Lee (1984) show that the constrained SUR method is the generalized case of the stacking technique. Conceptually, the constrained SUR can be obtained by imposing constraints on regression coefficients of the SUR model. Hence, the constrained SUR replaces the stacking technique used by Spies (1974). Note that the estimation procedure of both the SUR and the constrained SUR are not required for understanding Spies' dynamic capital-budgeting model.
2. All formulas and definitions of variables used in this section are identical to those defined in Section 26.3 of the text.

Reference for Appendix 26.B

Annual Report of Johnson & Johnson (1950–2006).

Black, F, MC Jensen, and M Scholes (1972). The capital asset pricing model: Some empirical tests. In *Studies in the Theory of Capital Markets*, MC Jensen (ed.), New York: Praeger, pp. 79–121.

Greene, WH (2002). *Econometric Analysis*, 5th ed. New Jersey: Prentice Hall.

Hendenshatt, PH (1979). *Understand Capital Markets*. Lexington, MA: Lexington Books.

Hsieh, CC and CF Lee (1984). *Constrained SUR Approach to Dynamic Capital-Budgeting Decision*. Mimeo.

Johnston, J and J Dinardo (1996). *Econometrics Methods*, 4th ed. New York: McGraw-Hill.

Lee, CF (1976). Performance measure, systematic risk, and errors-in-variable estimation method. *Journal of Economics and Business*, 122–127.

Spies, RR (1974). The dynamics of corporate capital budgeting. *Journal of Finance*, 29, 29–45.

Standard & Poors Compustat, a Division of The McGraw-Hill Companies, Inc.

Taggart, RA, Jr (1977). A model of corporate financing decisions. *Journal of Finance*, 32, 478–484.

The Center for Research in Security Prices (CRSP) (2007). A Research Center at Chicago GSB Value line investment survey, November 16.

References for Chapter 26

Anderson, WHL (1964). *Corporate Finance and Fixed Investment: An Econometric*, Study. Boston: Harvard Business School.

Baumol, WJ (1959). *Economic Dynamics: An Introduction*, 2nd ed., New York: Macmillan Company.

Bower, JL (1970). Planning within the firm. *American Economic Review*, 60, 186–194.

Brainard, WC and J Tobin (1968). Pitfall in financial-model building. *American Economic Review*, 58, 99–122.

Data Resources, Incorporated. "The Data Resources Review" (December 20, 1971).

——— "Ten-year Projections of the U.S. Economy." The Data Resources Review, No. 7 (July 14, 1972).

Davis, BE, GC Caccappolo, and MA Chaudry (1973). An econometric planning model for American Telephone and Telegraph Company. *The Bell Journal of Economics and Management Science*, 4, 29–56.

de Leeuw, F (1965). A model of financial behavior. In *The Brookings Inst. Quarterly Econometric Model of the United States*, JS Duesenberry, G Fromm, LR Klein, and E Kuh (eds.). Chicago: Rand-McNally Company.

Dhrymes, PJ and M Kurz (1967). Investment, dividend, and external finance behavior of firms. In *Determinants of Investment Behavior: A Conference of the Universities*, National Bureau Committee for Economic Research, R Ferber (ed.). New York: Columbia University Press.

Duhaime, IM and H Thomas (1983). Financial analysis and strategic management. *Journal of Economics and Business*, 35, 413–440.

Eckstein, O (1983). Decision-support systems for corporate planning. *Data Resources*, U.S. Review, February, 1.9–1.23. Also in Lee, CF (ed.) (1983). *Financial Analysis and Planning, Theory and Application — A Book of Readings*. Reading, MA: Addison-Wesley Publishing Company.

Elliott, JW (1972). Forecasting and analysis of corporate financial performance with an econometric model of the firm. *Journal of Financial and Quantitative Analysis*, 7, 1499–1526.

Frecke, T and CF Lee (1983). A SUR approach to analyzing and forecasting financial ratios. *Journal of Economics and Business* in press.

Gordon, MJ (1962). *The Investment, Financing, and Valuation of the Corporation*, Homewood, IL: Richard D. Irwin, Inc.

Hedley, B (1977). Strategy and business portfolio. *Long Range Planning*, 9–15.

Johnston, J (1972) *Econometric Methods*, 2nd ed., New York: McGraw-Hill.

Lee, CF (1974). A note on the interdependent structure of security returns. *Journal of Financial and Quantitative Analysis*, 9, 73–86.

Lee, CF and JD Vinso (1980). Single vs. simultaneous-equation models in capital-asset pricing: The role of firm-related variables. *Journal of Business Research*, 65–80.

Lee, CF and ALC Wu (2009). *Handbook of Quantitative Finance and Risk Management*. New York: Springer.

Lee, CF and JK Zumwalt (1981). Associations between alternative accounting profitability measures and security returns. *Journal of Financial and Quantitative Analysis*, 16, 71–93.

Miller, MH and F Modigliani (1966). Some estimates of the cost of capital for the electric utility industry, 1954–57. *American Economic Review*, 333–391.

Naylor, TH (ed.) (1979). *Simulation Models in Corporate Planning*. New York: Praeger Publishing Company.

Oudet, BA (1973). The variation of the return on stocks in a period of inflation. *Journal of Financial and Quantitative Analysis*, 8, 247–258.

Peterson, PP (1980). A re-examination of seemingly unrelated regressions methodology applied to estimation of financial relationship. *Journal of Financial Research*, 3, 297–308.

Sharpe, William (1963). A simplified model for portfolio analysis. *Management Science*, 9, 277–293.

Sharpe, William (1977). The capital asset pricing model: A multi-beta interpretation. In *Financial Decision Making Under Uncertainty*, eds. H. Levy and M. Samat. New York: Academic Press.

Spies, RR (1971). Corporate investment, dividends, and finance: A simultaneous approach. unpublished Ph.D. dissertation, Princeton University.

Spies, RR (1974). The dynamics of corporate capital budgeting. *Journal of Finance*, 29, 829–845.

Simkowitz, MA and DE Logue (1973). The interdependent structure of security returns. *Journal of Financial and Quantitative Analysis*, 8, 259–272.

Taggart Jr, RA (1977). A model of corporate financing decisions. *Journal of Finance*, 32, 1467–1484.

Theil, H (1971). *Principles of Econometrics*. New York: John Wiley & Sons, Inc.

Zakon, A (1971). *Growth and Financial Strategies*. Boston, MA: Boston Consulting Group.

Zakon, AJ (1976). *Capital-Structure Optimization*. Boston, MA: Boston Consulting Group.

Zellner, A (1962). An efficient method of estimating seemingly unrelated regression and tests for aggregation bias. *Journal of American Statistical Association*, 57, 348–368.

Zellner, A (1968). *Growth and Financial Strategies*, Boston: Boston Consulting Group.

Project V

Financial Planning and Forecasting

Author Index

D

E

F

G

H

R

S

Y

Z

Subject Index

A

J

K

L

M

N

O

P

Q

R

S